ELEMENTS OF Writing

REVISED EDITION

Fourth Course

James L. Kinneavy
John E. Warriner

HOLT, RINEHART AND WINSTON

Harcourt Brace & Company

Austin • New York • Orlando • Atlanta • San Francisco
Boston • Dallas • Toronto • London

Critical Readers

T2

James L. Kinneavy, the Jane and Roland Blumberg Centennial Professor of English at The University of Texas at Austin, directed the development and writing of the composition strand in the program. He is the author of *A Theory of Discourse* and coauthor of *Writing in the Liberal Arts Tradition.* Professor Kinneavy is a leader in the field of rhetoric and composition and a respected educator whose teaching experience spans all levels—elementary, secondary, and college. He has continually been concerned with teaching writing to high school students.

John E. Warriner developed the organizational structure for the Handbook of Grammar, Usage, and Mechanics in the book. He coauthored the *English Workshop* series, was general editor of the *Composition: Models and Exercises* series, and editor of *Short Stories: Characters in Conflict.* He taught English for thirty-two years in junior and senior high school and college.

Writers and Editors

H. Edward Deluzain has a Ph.D. in English Education from Florida State University. He teaches at A. Crawford Mosley High School in Panama City, Florida. He is a writer of educational material in literature and composition.

Patti Day-Miller has an M.A. with a Reading Endorsement from Indiana University. She has been the reading consultant for the Bartholomew Consolidated School Corporation of Columbus, Indiana, and has written educational material for composition and literature textbooks.

Peter Harris has a Ph.D. in English literature from Texas Tech University. He is an Associate Professor of English at West Virginia Institute of Technology in Montgomery, West Virginia.

Mary Elizabeth Podhaizer has an M. Ed. from The University of Vermont. She has been a writer of educational material in literature and composition for fifteen years. She is currently engaged in research on secondary students' responses to literature.

Jim Skelton has an Ed.D. in Teaching Composition and Rhetoric from East Texas State University. He has been a newspaper reporter, a teacher of secondary English, and a writer of educational materials in composition and literature. He currently teaches English and Developmental Writing at Kingwood College near Houston, Texas.

Glenda A. Zumwalt has an Ed.D. in Teaching Composition and Rhetoric from East Texas State University. She teaches composition at Southeastern Oklahoma State University. She is a writer of educational material in composition and literature.

Staff Credits

Associate Director: Mescal K. Evler

Managing Editor: Steve Welch

Senior Editors: Lynda Abbott, Richard Blake, Suzanne Thompson

Editorial Staff: *Editors:* Cheryl Christian, Adrienne Greer, Scott Hall, Colleen Hobbs, Eileen Joyce, Ginny Power, Laura Cottam Sajbel, Elizabeth Smith, Stephen Wesson; *Copyeditors:* Joel Bourgeois, Roger Boylan, Mary Malone, Michael Neibergall, Copyediting Supervisor; *Editorial Coordinators:* Susan Grafton Alexander, Amanda F. Beard, Rebecca Bennett, Wendy Langabeer, Marie Hoffman Price; *Support:* Ruth A. Hooker, Senior Word Processor; Christina Barnes, Kelly Keeley, Margaret Sanchez, Raquel Sosa, Pat Stover

Editorial Permissions: Catherine J. Paré, Janet Harrington

Production: *Pre-press:* Beth Prevelige, Simira Davis, Sergio Durante

Manufacturing: Mike Roche

Media: Belinda Barbosa

Page Production: Preface, Inc.

Design: Richard Metzger, *Art Director;* Lori Male, *Designer*

Photo Research: Peggy Cooper, *Photo Research Manager;* Mavournea Hay, Mike Gobbi, Victoria Smith, *Photo Research Team*

Acknowledgments

We wish to thank the following teachers who participated in field testing of pre-publication materials for this series:

Susan Almand-Myers
Meadow Park Intermediate School
Beaverton, Oregon

Theresa L. Bagwell
Naylor Middle School
Tucson, Arizona

Ruth Bird
Freeport High School
Sarver, Pennsylvania

Joan M. Brooks
Central Junior High School
Guymon, Oklahoma

Candice C. Bush
J. D. Smith Junior High School
N. Las Vegas, Nevada

Mary Jane Childs
Moore West Junior High School
Oklahoma City, Oklahoma

Brian Christensen
Valley High School
West Des Moines, Iowa

Lenise Christopher
Western High School
Las Vegas, Nevada

Mary Ann Crawford
Ruskin Senior High School
Kansas City, Missouri

Linda Dancy
Greenwood Lakes Middle School
Lake Mary, Florida

Elaine A. Espindle
Peabody Veterans Memorial High School
Peabody, Massachusetts

Joan Justice
North Middle School
O'Fallon, Missouri

Beverly Kahwaty
Pueblo High School
Tucson, Arizona

Lamont Leon
Van Buren Junior High School
Tampa, Florida

Susan Lusch
Fort Zumwalt South High School
St. Peters, Missouri

Michele K. Lyall
Rhodes Junior High School
Mesa, Arizona

Belinda Manard
McKinley Senior High School
Canton, Ohio

Nathan Masterson
Peabody Veterans Memorial High School
Peabody, Massachusetts

Marianne Mayer
Swope Middle School
Reno, Nevada

Penne Parker
Greenwood Lakes Middle School
Lake Mary, Florida

Amy Ribble
Gretna Junior-Senior High School
Gretna, Nebraska

Kathleen R. St. Clair
Western High School
Las Vegas, Nevada

Carla Sankovich
Billinghurst Middle School
Reno, Nevada

Sheila Shaffer
Cholla Middle School
Phoenix, Arizona

Joann Smith
Lehman Junior High School
Canton, Ohio

Margie Stevens
Raytown Middle School
Raytown, Missouri

Mary Webster
Central Junior High School
Guymon, Oklahoma

Susan M. Yentz
Oviedo High School
Oviedo, Florida

Contents in Brief

Table of Contents

CHAPTER 2 UNDERSTANDING PARAGRAPH STRUCTURE

▶ CHAPTER 3 UNDERSTANDING COMPOSITION STRUCTURE

CHAPTER 4 EXPRESSIVE WRITING: NARRATION

CHAPTER 5 USING DESCRIPTION

CHAPTER 7 WRITING TO INFORM: EXPOSITION

CHAPTER 8 WRITING TO EXPLAIN: EXPOSITION

► CHAPTER 9 WRITING TO PERSUADE

CHAPTER 11 WRITING A RESEARCH PAPER: EXPOSITION

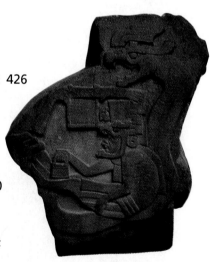

The Granger Collection, New York.

▶ CHAPTER *14* ENGLISH: ORIGINS AND USES

CHAPTER 14 PLANNING GUIDE **483A–483D**

► CHAPTER **15** THE PARTS OF SPEECH

Their Identification and Function

▶ CHAPTER *19* AGREEMENT   616

Subject and Verb, Pronoun and Antecedent

▶ CHAPTER 22 USING MODIFIERS CORRECTLY 712

Forms, Comparison, and Placement

The Granger Collection, New York.

▶CHAPTER 37 READING, STUDYING, AND TEST TAKING 983

Fiction

Italo Calvino, "Mushrooms in the city," *Marcovaldo, or The Seasons in the City*

Harold Courlander with Ezekiel A. Eshugbayi, "Why No One Lends His Beauty," *Lode the Hunter and Other Tales from Nigeria*

Umberto Eco, *The Name of the Rose*

Edith Hamilton, *Mythology*

David Low, "Winterblossom Garden," *Ploughshares*

Lucy Maud Montgomery, *Anne of Green Gables*

R. K. Narayan, "An Astrologer's Day"

Tim O'Brien, "Where Have You Gone, Charming Billy?" *Going After Cacciato*

Ann Petry, *The Street*

Marta Salinas, "The Scholarship Jacket"

Ntozake Shange, *Sassafras, Cypress, and Indigo*

John Steinbeck, *The Pearl*

Carl Stephenson, "Leiningen Versus the Ants"

Nonfiction

Emily R. Alling, "Letter to the Editor," *Newsweek*

Sandra R. Arbetter, "Introverts and Extroverts," *Current Health*

Sherry Baker, "Pioneers Underfoot," *Omni*

Robert D. Ballard, *Exploring the Titanic*

Stanley Bing, "The Most Beautiful Girl in the World," *Esquire*

Jane Bosveld, "Can Bicycles Save the World?" *Omni*

Albert Britt, *Great Indian Chiefs*

Christy Brown, *My Left Foot*

Malcolm W. Browne, "3 Scientists Say Travel in Time Isn't So Far Out," *The New York Times*

Robert B. Carlson, "America's Ancient Skywatchers," *National Geographic*

"CD & Videodisc Players," *Consumer Digest*

James R. Chiles, "To break the unbreakable codes," *Smithsonian*

Susan Chollar, "The Psychological Benefits of Exercise," *American Health*

John Ciardi, "bits," *A Browser's Dictionary*

Michael D. Coe, "Olmec and Maya: A Study in Relationships," *The Origins of Maya Civilization*

Mason Crum, *Gullah*

Leonardo da Vinci, "Leonardo da Vinci to the Duke of Milan: 'certain of my secrets,'" *A Treasury of the World's Great Letters*

R. A. Deckert, "Quasi-Humans," *Omni*

Annie Dillard, *An American Childhood*

Roger Ebert, *The Chicago Sun-Times*

Timothy Egan, "School for Homeless Children: A Rare Experience," *The New York Times*

John Elkington, et al., *Going Green: A Kid's Handbook to Saving the Planet*

Betty Lou English, *Behind the Headlines at a Big City Paper*

Laurence M. Fisher, "A Thirsty California Is Trying Desalination," *The New York Times*

Lisa W. Foderaro, "At Rye High, Students Not Only Must Do Well, They Must Do Good," *The New York Times*

Billie Follensbee, "Olmec Heads: A Product of the Americas"

Roy A. Gallant, *Private Lives of the Stars*

Ellen Goodman, *On Being a Writer*, ed. Bill Strickland

John Steele Gordon, "Financial Folklore," *American Heritage*

Evan and Janet Hadingham, *Garbage! Where It Comes From, Where It Goes*

Helen Hayes, "Hayes: There Is So Much To Do"

Jesse L. Jackson, "We Need Power, Program, and Progress," *The Progressive*

Suzanne Jurmain, *Once Upon a Horse*

Pauline Kael, review—"Driving Miss Daisy," *The New Yorker*

Coretta Scott King, *My Life with Martin Luther King, Jr.*

Maxine Hong Kingston, "White Tigers," *The Woman Warrior*

Doris G. Kinney, "Reopening the Gateway to America," *Life*

Kwei-li, *Golden Lilies*

William Least Heat-Moon, *Blue Highways*

Aldo Leopold, "Sky Dance," *A Sand County Almanac*

Charles Mann and Gwenda Blair, "Juan's Place," *Geo*

Milton Meltzer, ed., *Voices from the Civil War*

Sidney Moncrief, *Moncrief: My Journey to the NBA*

Darrell Moore, "Frankenstein," *The Best, Worst, and Most Unusual: Horror Films*

Daniel D. Morrison, "Date with Dracula," *American Way*

"Mourning Dove (Hum-ishu-ma)," *The Norton Anthology of Literature by Women*

John G. Neihardt, "Black Elk Speaks," *Black Elk Speaks: Being the Life Story of a Holy Man of the Oglala Sioux*

George Plimpton, "Neil Armstrong's Famous First Words," *Esquire*

Joyce Pope, *Do Animals Dream?*

"A Progress Report from the NAEP 1994 Geography Report Card," *NAEP 1994 Geography Report Card*

Ernie Pyle, "North Africa: November 1942–June 1943," *Ernie's War: The Best of Ernie Pyle's World War II Dispatches*

Bob Secter, "Time out! Is baseball Finnished?" *Miami Herald*

Ellen Ruppel Shell, "Seeds in the bank could stave off disaster on the farm," *Smithsonian*

Monica Sone, *Nisei Daughter*

Gary Soto, "Foreword," *A Fire in My Hands*

Shannon Stocker, "Stretchbreak: Good Morning Wake-Up Stretch," *Prevention*

Kathleen Teltsch, "For Young and Old, A Pocket Paradise," *The New York Times*

Paul Theroux, *Riding the Iron Rooster*

Susan Allen Toth, "Nothing Happened," *Blooming: A Small Town Girlhood*

Mark Twain, "A Genuine Mexican Plug"

"Two tornadoes damage airport, Miami school," *The Ledger*

Ed Ward, et al., *Rock of Ages: The "Rolling Stone" History of Rock & Roll*

Geoffrey C. Ward and Ken Burns, *Baseball: An Illustrated History*

H. G. Wells, *A Modern Utopia*

Tom Wolfe, "Clean Fun at Riverhead"

Rick Wolff, "A Yen for Baseball Cards," *Sports Illustrated*

Arthur Zich, "Japanese Americans: Home at Last," *National Geographic*

Poetry

Gwendolyn Brooks, "The Bean Eaters," *Blacks*

Geoffrey Chaucer, *The Canterbury Tales*

N. Scott Momaday, "The Eagle-Feather Fan," *The Gourd Dancer*

David Wagoner, "Tumbleweed," *Collected Poems 1945–1976*

A Teacher's Guide to

ELEMENTS OF WRITING

CONTENTS

DONALD MURRAY

KAREN GREENBERG

LEE ODELL

BARBARA
SHADE

MAXINE
HAIRSTON

NORBERT
ELLIOT

WANDA
SCHINDLEY

HOW DARE THEY?

. . . IN THE SPIRIT OF MAINTAINING THE LASTING VALUES AND STANDARDS OF THE SERIES . . .

Certainly when teachers saw a new name listed on *Elements of Writing* as a coauthor with John E. Warriner, some must have said, "How can the editors dare do this?" Warriner has been a legendary name in high school English composition and grammar books since 1941, the year of the first edition of his series. His high school textbooks have changed somewhat through the decades, but they have stood the test of half a century—despite many educational trends and fashions—because they have incorporated important values and standards. Warriner's texts have assumed an almost biblical authority.

But even the Bible is translated anew for different generations. So it is in the spirit of maintaining the lasting values and standards of the series that this new edition of the series is published with a new coauthor. I was properly flattered when Holt, Rinehart and Winston asked me to be the consultant for the composition sections of the books in the new series. But I was also in awe of this long tradition of excellence and can only hope that this tradition can be upheld.

Like John E. Warriner, I have a long and varied experience as a teacher. He taught in junior high, high school, and college. I have taught in elementary school, high school, and college. He taught for many years; I have been teaching since 1941 and continue to teach today. For the past twenty-five years I have given workshops to high school students involved in state-wide competition in extemporaneous writing. Like Warriner, I have attempted to keep up with the profession and to reflect in my writings what we have learned and continue to learn about teaching the language arts. I have trained students to teach at all grade levels from elementary school through graduate school. I have also observed student teachers for years at the high school and college levels.

You will find in this series, therefore, an attempt to maintain the best values of the Warriner series and to add to it a few new features that teachers, administrators, and scholars think will make it an even better set of books.

THE TEACHER'S EDITION IS A *GREAT* HELP

I know that teaching school is incredibly time consuming: You're there at 8:00 and leave at 4:00; then you take on extra professional chores in the evening, and spend weekends correcting papers, read to keep up professionally, work on extra-curricular activities, and attend conventions. Clearly you need all of the timesavers you can find.

You will find help in this series. On each page you will find that your objectives, your lesson plan, and your resources are involved with the student text. Questions for the students are provided with answers. Vocabulary items are defined. Adaptations for more-advanced students, less-advanced students, and ESL students are suggested. Opportunities for critical thinking and for cooperative learning are continually provided.

So, before spending hours looking up supplementary materials for a class, look in your teacher's edition. Someone else may have done your work already and saved you hours

Also, beginning teachers should exploit these thorough materials to avoid some all-too-common problems in the classroom.

RELATIONSHIP BETWEEN COMPOSITION AND GRAMMAR

Elements of Writing demonstrates the same close relationship between composition and grammar that has characterized the Warriner's series since its inception. You can see this by simply looking at the table of contents, which makes quite clear that primary attention is given to writing, and that grammar is a support to writing. Yet both are covered extensively.

Given the increasing importance of rhetoric in public schools and in college, you will find more depth in the composition section of this textbook. Lesson plans add more discernible structure to the chapters on writing. The chapters cover the kinds of writing students need to succeed in school and in life. Thus, there is a chapter devoted to each of the major purposes of writing—to inform or explain, to persuade, to entertain, and to express oneself. Strategies or modes of writing, such as narration, description, classification, and evaluation, are also discussed at each grade level.

In each chapter, the close relationship between composition and grammar is maintained. A relevant grammatical issue is covered in each writing chapter. Thus, a chapter on persuasion may consider fragments and a chapter on description may consider adjectives and adverbs. Finally, the composition chapters refer to the grammar chapters for coverage of issues that relate to the kind of writing under consideration.

Studies at all levels, from elementary school through college, confirm that grammar is learned best when taught in conjunction with composition, as well as with speaking and listening and literature. For instance, consistent fragments in a student's paper suggest a need for a lesson in the parts of the sentence. A mini-lesson about fragments should increase students' awareness of sentence structure. The mini-lesson would be followed with an activity in which students read peers' papers,

WHAT THIS TEXTBOOK DOES NOT WANT TO DO IS TO ENCOURAGE THE ISOLATED TEACHING OF GRAMMATICAL SKILLS IN A ROTE MANNER.

identify fragments, and resolve them with the writer. You will have reinforced a grammatical point and, more importantly, integrated grammar and composition. This textbook does not want to encourage the isolated teaching of grammatical skills in a rote manner. Most of the time, the grammar is linked to a writing assignment and even motivated by it.

THE PROCESSES OF COMPOSING

Elements of Writing consistently focuses on the processes of writing in every writing chapter. The stress on process is evident in the structuring of the chapters by the stages of the writing process— prewriting, writing, evaluating, revising, publishing, and finally reflecting.

A COOPERATIVE ATMOSPHERE

The idea that writing is a solitary, sedentary process, as a poet once said, is not at all adhered to in this textbook. Rather writing is viewed as a collaborative and cooperative action. Working cooperatively enables students to receive support from one another and from the teacher.

The students who work in *peer groups* of three or four help each other turn out better work. The members plan the papers, critique drafts, and provide a real audience for the final paper. The members of the group are like a team working toward a common goal.

The *teacher* moves from group to group, helping in the planning and discussing problems. Like the members of the peer groups, the teacher fulfills different functions:

at times the teacher is a motivator, a problem solver, a careful listener, a constructive critic, a sympathetic reader, and above all, a fellow writer.

With this view of the writing process, the teacher with a *heavy paper load* can be assisted by students. The teacher now is not the only person who reads and evaluates a student's paper. The support group also provides useful feedback to the author about mechanics, word choice, organization, ideas, and style. If the teacher trains peer groups to be constructively critical, a good deal of the drudgery of grading papers can be avoided.

The writing process often results in some kind of *publication*, such as a public speech, a performance, a class newspaper, or placement in a permanent portfolio that the student keeps of his or her progress as a writer.

The general structure of *Elements of Writing* places the composition chapters before grammar, usage, and mechanics chapters, thus mirroring the process in which students write rapidly and enthusiastically in their first plans, sketches, and drafts, without stopping to check spelling, word choice, or grammatical purity. The idea is to support the writing process as a creative surge in the beginning. The mechanical and stylistic matters are better addressed in revision with peers.

THE AIMS OR PURPOSES OF WRITING AND DIFFERENT LANGUAGE STYLES

Different levels of formality are suggested with the different pur-

poses of writing presented in *Elements of Writing*. In the chapters on expressive writing, a casual, personal, and familiar style is suggested. At the other extreme, in the chapters on information and proof, a more formal sense of grammar and word choice is expected. This is true in real life and in the classroom. In between self-expression and these types of expository writing, there are various shades of formality in persuasive, creative, and exploratory writing.

The model adopted here is that of Martin Joos, whose book *The Five Clocks* distinguishes five different levels of formality that nearly all of us use, depending on the circumstances. Joos calls these the intimate, the colloquial, the consultative, the formal, and the ritual levels. We speak to our family members in a familiar language. We speak to our friends in an ordinary conversation on the colloquial level. We adopt the consultative tone usually when we are teaching class. We use a formal level when we are giving speeches at a convention. And we use the ritual level of formality when we are at church or are graduating or are being initiated into a society.

But teachers are not the only people who have their five levels of formality. Teenagers also have their own colloquial, consultative, formal, and ritual levels as do middle-aged adults and older people.

WRITING AND LITERATURE

This series is permeated with reading and literature. Each writing chapter includes models of the type of writing that is being studied. Many samples are drawn from

the literary canon. In one grade level, for instance, an excellent poem by William Stafford illustrates the aims of writing. Nearly every writing chapter in the student's edition contains similar material. Of course, all of these selections used as writing models are annotated. Further, in the teacher's edition, are **Literature Links,** which take common literary selections and relate them to the material being studied.

Some writing chapters are almost completely devoted to literary writing, especially the chapters on creative writing, narration, and description. Thus writing and literature are highly integrated by a common underlying philosophy of language.

WRITING AND THE OTHER LANGUAGE ARTS

In addition to being highly integrated with literature, *Elements of Writing* is also integrated with reading, speaking and listening, and viewing.

Each chapter contains several reading samples of the type of writing being studied. These are carefully analyzed by the students by means of questions after each selection. These questions may be answered orally. The oral emphasis continues throughout the chapter as each stage of the writing process is carried out by means of peer discussion groups. Frequently, the publication of the paper takes an oral form as persuasive speeches are delivered to the class.

The peer group is also clearly a speaking and listening group. Students must learn to listen care-

fully to each other in order to make constructive suggestions for improvement.

Thus the four language arts are carefully interwoven into the structure of each chapter at each stage of the writing process.

WRITING AND NEW TECHNOLOGIES

Whenever possible, teachers should take advantage of the new technologies that are increasingly becoming available at the high school level. Consequently, throughout this edition there are continual reminders of these possibilities.

Networking with Computers

Many schools have computers available for use in teaching writing. Some are even networked to allow student interactions with each other, either with the entire class or with selected groups. The simultaneous writing reactions of all members of the class to a common reading assignment is one of the most effective methods to ensure one hundred percent participation in group discussions, especially if the right questions are asked. And the use of computers to set up small support groups for the different stages of the writing process is also an exceptionally efficient technique of using small groups in teaching writing.

Revising and Computers

Even without networking, however, the use of computers is to be commended whenever possible, particularly because of the manner in which revising is accomplished on computers. Students who formerly hated to revise now see revision as an easy and enjoyable manner to improve their work, not just at the level of vocabulary or mechanics, but even at the level of full discourse changes.

Computers also bring substantial help to the poor speller and to the student having trouble finding the right word. Nearly all word-processing programs have some type of spell-check feature that shows students which words are incorrectly spelled. Thus each student can keep a list of his or her own problem words. This is acknowledged by nearly all spelling research as the single best way to improve spelling. Most spell-check programs are accompanied by programs that properly hyphenate words at the end of a line. This is an additional bonus for students who use computers.

In addition, most word-processing programs now come with a thesaurus and grammar program. The first enables students to look for options in vocabulary, even while working at the computer.

The grammar programs can check tense, case, subject-verb agreement, fragments, and so forth.

Publishing and Word Processors

It is possible to use a computer as a desktop publisher to enable students to see some of their writings in elegant print and format. These can be put into portfolios for permanent records. Throughout the annotated teacher's edition there are reminders of this option of publishing.

A FINAL WORD

Possibly after reading this essay, which brings together many of the rather complex tasks of the writing teacher, you may be worried about the size of the task. But luckily you don't have to solve all of these problems overnight. The teaching of writing is a slow and cumulative process. Each chapter of this textbook focuses on a very specific issue and tries to address just that particular skill. Subsequent chapters build on the skill just learned. The students then slowly build up a range of abilities.

Just remember that your predecessors have worked with the students whom you now face, just as your colleagues will pick up where you leave off. And you are not alone at the present time: Your current colleagues are working with the same students in other classes.

In other words, just as writing is a cooperative endeavor for your students, so also is it a cooperative endeavor for you with the teachers from year to year and among a group of teachers one year at a time.

No One Does A More Important Job

Finally, you should be assured that your task is at the top of educational priorities. No one does a more important job than the teacher of writing. Such a person is also teaching students how to read, think, listen, and speak in ways that will enable them to contribute to a complex modern society as educated communicators.

By Donald M. Murray, Professor Emeritus of English, The University of New Hampshire

Use Genre as Lens

We write about what we don't know about what we know.

Students are usually introduced to each genre—essay, narrative, poem—in isolated units, as if one form of writing would contaminate another. But each genre is a lens, a way to observe, record, and examine the world. Students should be encouraged to use each genre to explore a single important experience.

Student writers and their teachers should begin the exploration with a personal experience—an event, a person, a place—that holds a significant mystery for them. Mystery is the starting place for most writing, what Grace Paley described when she said, "We write about what we don't know about what we know." Invite your students to explore a moment in their lives to which they keep returning in memory, the way the tongue seeks the missing tooth.

Encourage your students to play with the fragments of language connected with that experience in their minds and on paper to discover a line, a phrase, or a word that contains a tension or conflict within the experience. The "line" might be a word—*Christmas*—that might have special implications for a student with a Catholic mother and a Jewish father. It might be a phrase—*the debts of Christmas*—to a person whose family spends too much money to make up for their true family feelings. The "line" could be a sentence—"Each Christmas I remember my sister who will never grow old."—for someone who lost a sister years before. Each "line" has a tension and mystery the writer needs to understand by writing.

Before your students begin, it is important to remind them that all writing is experimental, that experimentation implies failure, and that failure is instructive. It is not possible they will fail; it is imperative that they fail. We do not improve our writing by avoiding failure, but by making use of it.

To guarantee failure, urge students to write the first draft fast. Velocity is as important in writing as it is in bicycle racing. Speed will produce the accidents of language, connection, and insight that will propel the draft forward towards meaning. And velocity allows students to escape, for the moment, the censor that demands premature correctness.

They should allow their drafts to instruct them. The evolving text will take its own course, exploring the experience as it is relived. If they are patient, receptive, and open to surprise, the text will tell them what they have to say. You may want to write two statements by E. M. Forster on the chalkboard:

Think before you speak is criticism's motto; speak before you think creation's.

and

How do I know what I think until I see what I say?

Students should write out loud, hearing the text as they write it. They may actually do this—it is your classroom—or read silently but *listen* to the text. As they tune their voices to the story being told, the voice—angry, nostalgic, humorous, sad, analytical, instructive, argumentative, poetic, even narrative—will reveal the meaning of the draft to the writer.

I invite you to stand beside me at my workbench and to observe me

as I use genre to explore an experience of mine.

THE ESSAY

I prefer the term *reflective essay* to *personal essay* because the writer reflects on personal experience, or on a topic of personal interest. The essay is neither a simple narrative of experience nor of thought unanchored by experience, but a combination of thought and experience, an effort to discover and share meaning in experience. The essay is a demonstration of critical thinking.

Some notes on the craft of the essay.

• Narrow the territory to be explored so you can achieve depth.

• Be specific. The specific will instruct. The more specific you are, the more universal your audience will be.

• Work locally; the paragraph you have just written contains the seed of the next paragraph. For example, if you have said the experience was important, show how it was important in the next paragraph.

• Answer the reader's questions. Writing is a conversation between reader and writer.

• When the draft surprises you, pay attention. Develop the surprise to discover its meaning.

On April 21, while visiting a daughter and her husband in their new home, I got up early without the alarm, as is my habit, and ended up sitting at the top of the stairs waiting for my family to wake, and I found mystery in the experience. It was a moment full of emotion, and I needed—not wanted, but needed—to explore that moment through writing.

I made a few notes in my daybook:

I can remember myself as a small boy in Doctor Denton's trying to be quiet sitting at the head of the stairs (night) waiting for the family to get up

I can remember my own daughter's impatient waiting

Sunday morning I sit at the head of the stairs a good place to read, a good place legs waiting, wife, behind me in the room, my wife

The next day I wrote the column that was published in *The Boston Globe*, April 30, 1991:

I am, once again a small boy in Dr. Denton's sitting at the top of the stairs waiting for the snoring to stop and another day to begin.

I am, at the same time, an old man sitting at the top of the stairs in the new home of a daughter and her husband, waiting once more for the snoring to stop and a new day to begin.

Minnie Mae and I, on our first visit, have taken their bed, and they sleep on the hide-a-bed in the living room. They work in the theatre and have agreed to get up early—at 9 o'clock on Sunday morning—because the old folks are here.

But I followed the custom of many old men and was up at 5:33 A.M. I tiptoed downstairs, went out to the car, explored Mount Kisco, sipped a cup of coffee at Dunkin Donuts—yes, and had a doughnut, and yes, juice to get down my six pills I take because of previous doughnuts—bought the Sunday *New York Times*, sat in the car reading it, and now, at 8 A.M. sit at the head of the stairs where I can stretch my legs, flex my football knee, and read my book and wait.

It has been a good morning, and I feel little guilt that I have not been able to sleep in. They will laugh at my compulsion to be up and doing, and I will tease them for their laziness, but they will not understand the joy I, like many over sixties, experience when I am up in the lonely hours of dawn.

I ruminate—early morning is ideal for rumination—on the fact that as a child I was always up early when I could lose myself in a book—no TV then—explore the backyard or the vacant lot where the morning glories grew.

Awake before the grown-ups, I could be what I needed to be: Lindbergh crossing the Atlantic

WE DO NOT IMPROVE OUR WRITING BY AVOIDING FAILURE, BUT BY MAKING USE OF IT.

alone, Admiral Byrd isolated in his tiny room under the Antarctic ice, the unnamed Indian scout watching the palefaces land on the Maine coast

As a teenager I bicycled my route for Gallagher's News Agency in Quincy finishing before the sun was up, drove Miller's grocery truck to market in Boston or cleaned the vegetables and laid them out in rows on the boxes balanced in front of the small store on Beach Street.

Only now I confess that when I nicked myself trimming the lettuce that was packed in ice, my hands numb and clumsy, I would turn that lettuce head so the blood did not show. I was apprentice to Miller's game: profit through deceit.

I still remember playing grown-up early in the morning, the grocer's apron twice tucked so it did not sweep the sawdust strewn floor. The profit would be Miller's not mine, but I anticipated the

customers who might, this Depression Saturday, pay cash. That anticipation would last until midnight when Mr. Miller would go out and scan the street right and left and reluctantly, when no one was on the street, give the command to close.

In combat I preferred the early morning patrols, guard duty when I was alone to watch the theatre of morning's change from dark to light, the promise of a new day even when the landscape was littered with last night's dead.

After college I worked for a morning newspaper and liked the mystery and companionship of the night worker, enjoyed the coming home at dawn. Eventually I returned to days, and morning became my best writing time as it is for most writers.

Goethe advised, "Use the day before the day. Early morning hours have gold in their mouth." John Hersey testified that "To be a writer is to sit down at one's desk in the chill portion of every day, and to write." A few years ago poet Donald Hall said, "In summer I'll be up at 4:30, make coffee, let out the dog, go pick up *The Boston Globe*. Then I write."

In retirement I, like so many other over sixties, still get up early when there are no cows to milk, no

commuter train to meet, no factory shift to join. It is habit, but for me a habit built not from compulsion but delight.

Sitting at the top of the stairs waiting for the young—and the not-so-young Minnie Mae—to wake, I try to define the strange emotion I feel. At last it comes to me. I am, after a lifetime of chasing the carrot, content.

I have another day to celebrate. Sitting here alone, I can enjoy the feeling of this house that is turning so quickly into a home. I am comfortable in this home and know that soon my wife will wake with a groan and a smile, and downstairs I will hear conversation and music, smell coffee and we will all make plans for the day not too far off when a grandchild will sit where I sit, perhaps beside me, waiting for another day to begin.

The grandchild has arrived. His name is Joshua. I have not yet sat beside him at the top of the stairs but I will.

THE NARRATIVE

There are many wonderful ways to tell stories, but I suggest student fiction writers begin with the scene. Conrad is supposed to have said that a novel is a series of scenes of confrontation. The writer experienced in nonfiction tells *about* the story; the fiction writer *reveals* the story. That is an enormous difference, and the writing of a scene is the best way to cross the divide. Students can draw on their experiences with TV and film. The reader observes a room with the fourth wall removed; the action within the room tells the story and the reader discovers its meaning. As the short-story writer Becky Rule points out, students think that fiction has no rules, but the rules come from the story, and they are established early; if Hamlet is an indecisive prince he can suddenly become a king but not a decisive one.

Some notes on the craft of narrative.
• Start with character, not theme. The story and its meaning are revealed through the interaction of the characters.
• Write in the third person. It gives you more room and detachment.
• Dialogue is action, what the characters do to each other. Joan Didion says, "I don't have a very clear idea of who the characters are until they start talking."
• Point of view is where the camera is positioned to record the scene. In the beginning, stick with one point of view, perhaps entering into one head but not jumping in and out of every head. If you are in one sister's head, you don't know Frank is in the freezer; in the other sister's head, you do.
• Kurt Vonnegut counsels, "Don't put anything in a story that does not reveal character or advance the action."

In writing a draft of my novel, I found myself stealing the experience from my own essay and began a scene:

Melissa found Iain sitting in the shadows at the top of the stairs, "It's 5:30 in the morning."
He nodded.
"On guard duty?"
"In a way. I often sit here in winter, watch the light just before dawn, the woods, the field that goes down to the lake."

She thought for a moment of what it would be like to be a spy to your life, always on guard and asked, "You said last night that wherever you are, you see a field of fire, are aware of where to dig in, put the machine guns, even after all these years?"
"I'm not proud of it, Melissa. It's just my geography, an infantryman's geography."
"Do you always see a geography of war?"
"Always first, then I can make it go away, Most times.

It's natural, just the way I see things. The doctor sees you as kidney or a colon; I'm an old soldier, I see a field of fire, where the attack would come from."
"That's sad."
"Tedd's a soldier too, Melissa."
They hear the key probe for the lock, at last find it, and hurried down the stairs....

That is just a small fragment of narrative, and yet you can see

how the story is revealing itself dramatically to the writer and the reader.

THE POEM

Poetry is the most disciplined and difficult form of writing. It is also the most fun. Experience is distilled by the writing of poetry. Poetry is always play—play with image and language so that meaning is revealed directly without rhetoric getting between the writer and reader or between experience and reader. Inexperienced poets often write with adjectives and adverbs, trying to describe their own feelings. The experienced poet writes with information, revealing specifics, provocative details, and compelling images that make the reader feel and think. The meaning is rarely stated but always there. In the poem, even more than fiction, the meaning is implied. The poem is the stimulus to the reader's thinking.

Some notes on the craft of poetry.
• Forget, for the moment, rhyme, meter, and traditional verse forms.
• Brainstorm images and other specifics, creating a list that may become a poem.
• Draft lines—not sentences but fragments of language—that capture an event, person, or place.
• Rearrange the lines until they reveal a meaningful pattern.
• Pay attention to the line breaks, trying to end on a strong word that causes the reader to read on.

The morning I wrote the column, I also wrote, on the computer, what might become a poem for my poetry group that was meeting that Thursday evening. I pasted this in my daybook:

Sitting at the top of the stairs
I listen to the silences
to understand Grandma's war with Mother

Sitting at the top of the stairs
I tune
train myself to 1 elinesss

Later that day I made a handwritten note I also cut out and pasted in the daybook:

I lived at the top of the stairs, behind the living room couch, under the dining room table, the tent of tablecloth—in the apple tree, under the porch,

And still later I drafted a poem that went through one radical and three or four extensive revisions (periods of word play) until it became the following completed poem:

Childhood Espionage

Spy to my life, I lived at the top of the stairs, recorded silence, mapped how hurt was done. Under the porch, at the bedroom door, behind living room

sofa, I filled notebooks with what was not said, not done, escaped to the sidewalk, tried to read the shades drawn against my life. It must be Mother's shadow

sitting on the edge of the double bed, must be father's kneeling to pray. I cannot be sure, circle the block, listen to the neighbor's opera of argument, stand under

an open window where conversation will pour over me Once I saw my friend's older sister. She never pulled the shade. The dogs learned my smell

and let me patrol back yard, alley, vacant lot, in silence. I found the room where the Beckers kept the boy with the enormous head, watched comfort flow

from a priest's dancing hands as he gave the last rites to Vinnie's grandma, swayed to the rhythm of the Mitchells' bedroom dancing, lying down. Late, I returned to the home

of closed doors where we passed each other without touching. We never raised our voices, never stood between light and shade, never let a secret fall out a window.

Students should be encouraged to take central experiences from their lives—Willa Cather said, "Most of the basic material a writer works with is acquired before the age of fifteen"—and explore them with an array of genre, using each lens—essay, narrative, poem—and then examining the subject through other genre, perhaps argument, report, screenplay, or news story, to discover the many meanings in their lives. ❧

*P*OETRY IS THE MOST DISCIPLINED AND DIFFICULT FORM OF WRITING. IT IS ALSO THE MOST FUN.

Sources quoted include Grace Paley, Joan Didion, and Kurt Vonnegut cited in the following work: Donald M. Murray, *Shoptalk: Learning to Write with Writers*, Boynton/Cook Publishers, Inc., 1990.

By James L. Kinneavy

Meet the Aims and Modes of Writing

THE PLACE TO START (AND END) THE TEACHING OF WRITING IS TO HAVE STUDENTS SEE WHAT WRITTEN LANGUAGE CAN DO FOR THEM.

WHY WRITE? WHERE DO I BEGIN?

Writing is a very complex activity, and so is the teaching of writing. I admit these facts, and I have been teaching writing for fifty years. You may be teaching your first class this year, and you probably have the same problem: In the face of this complex process, where do you start?

Some teachers recommend what may seem to be a very simple and logical approach: Start with the simple building blocks of writing and gradually work up to more complex blocks. In other words, teach students some elementary things about words, then move up to phrases, afterwards teach sentences, eventually work up to paragraphs, and finally, have students write full themes. Some say this is how children learn to use language orally. At first blush this theory has a kind of plausible simplicity to it. Years of research, however, have shown that it doesn't work and that it isn't the way children learn language.

LANGUAGE GETS THINGS DONE

Babies see the family members around them accomplish things by using language, and they quickly learn to use it themselves to get food, drink, or attention. This is the motivation behind all language acquisition and usage, from cradle to grave—language gets things done.

Consequently, if we can keep this elementary driving force behind our attempts to teach writing (or any language art for that matter), we can draw on a basic incentive that even babies understand. But when language teaching is divorced from getting things done, students rightly find it boring and uninteresting.

For this reason, the place to start (and end) the teaching of writing is to have students see what written language can do for them. What can writing do? In one introductory chapter, we attempt to get students to look around and see what language is getting done. We call language-users the hidden agents behind many of the mir-

acles of our age, we say that language is where the action is, and we call language-users the movers and shakers of the world.

Using very concrete examples, we focus the student's attention on the different kinds of things that language accomplishes. But the principle is the same at every grade-level and on into the college educations, careers, and adult lives of our graduates: The central concept in the teaching of writing at every level is an awareness of the aims or purposes of writing.

THE FOUR MAJOR AIMS OR PURPOSES OF WRITING

Luckily for you as well as for the students, these aims are not infinite, unpredictable, and unmanageable. They can be reduced to a few basic categories, and both you and the students have a good deal of practical experience with the categories in general. For example, one kind of language experience with which you are very familiar has to do with attempts to explain to or inform an audience about something of which it is partially or totally ignorant. You do this daily in the classroom and the students are the targets of this use of language. Other examples of this kind of writing are news stories in newspapers and magazines, encyclopedia articles, reports, textbooks, discussions, proposed solutions to problems, and research studies. *The emphasis is always on the subject matter, considered more or less objectively.* This kind of writing is generically referred to as **expository writing.**

As a teacher, you are only too aware of a second kind of writing that places more emphasis on the writer. In this case, the writing reveals the feelings of the writer, allows the writer to voice his or her aspirations or reactions to something in a quite personal way, or gives the writer a chance to articulate important beliefs. Examples of this kind of writing are journals, diaries, myths, prayers, credos, and protests. Of course, some of this writing may also overlap with other kinds. *The major emphasis in this kind of writing is on the writer.* This kind of writing is often called **expressive writing.**

As a teacher, you often try to convince your students of the importance of an education and of their duties as citizens. As a matter of fact, in our culture we are bombarded with attempts to get readers

to vote a certain way, to change attitudes or beliefs, to buy certain products, to switch allegiances, etc. Examples of such writing are advertising, political speeches, legal oratory, editorials, and religious sermons. In all of these cases, *the focus of the use of language is on the receiver of the message.* Usually, this kind of writing is called rhetorical or **persuasive writing.**

A fourth kind of writing, probably your favorite, is literature. This type of writing is given an honored place in English classes. We read selections of literature. They are intended to delight us and sometimes to teach us lessons. Examples of literature range from simple jokes, funny stories, ballads, small poems, and TV sitcoms to serious dramas, movies, novels, and epics. We try to get students to write this way when we teach creative writing. *Although all writing involves originality, we usually reserve the term* **creative writing** *for this kind of writing.*

THE COMMUNICATION BASIS OF THE AIMS OF WRITING

As a perceptive reader, you may have noticed as we went through the four major aims of writing that each one emphasized a different element of the communication process. It is not accidental that the

major purposes of writing generally can be reduced to four. The structure of the written communication process is based on a writer, a reader, a language, and the subject matter.

To assist you to get students to see the different roles of each aim, the relationship between the elements of the communication process and those of the aims of discourse is expressed graphically below. (The major aims of writing and the main parts of the communication process).

Self-Expression (Writer)   Persuasion (Reader)

Literature (Language)

Expository (Subject Matter)

The major parts of the communication process and the aims of writing.

Consequently, from aim to aim, there is a continual shifting of roles in the communication process. The lead role determines the major purpose of the writing and the other roles become subordinate. Many teachers have found this simple diagram enables students to grasp the changing dynamics of language use.

DOMINANT AIMS AND OVERLAP

As a teacher, you have probably written one or two of these different kinds of writing, but you may not have written all of them. In your own writing you are certainly aware that most writing does not

attempt to achieve all of these aims at the same time. A specific piece of writing usually has a single dominant aim, subordinating the others to avoid conflicts and confusion. Though subordinate, the other aims are still present. Thus, movie ads in the newspaper contain important information about actors, actresses, directors, titles, and show times, but the information is there to persuade people to come to the movies.

Indeed, all the aims overlap each other.

WHY ARE THE BASIC AIMS IMPORTANT?

Despite overlaps, however, it is quite important to distinguish the various aims. As a teacher, you are very aware that the criteria by which one kind of discourse is judged are different from the criteria by which another kind of discourse is judged. You try to impress upon your students that expository writing is judged on the basis of objective evidence; the appeal of the writer as such is not relevant to the final proof or explanation, nor is the use of emotion or humor. For this reason, you know that when you teach expository writing, it is important to discourage the use of these other kinds of appeal—they are, in fact, considered inappropriate in news stories, scientific reports, or textbooks. Thus the pedagogy of expository writing follows from the nature of this kind of writing.

But when you teach other kinds of writing, these other appeals are important. In persuasion, for example, the emphasis is on the appeal of the writer and the appeal to the interests of the audience. **The differences among exposi-**

AS A TEACHER YOU OFTEN TRY TO CONVINCE YOUR STUDENTS OF THE IMPORTANCE OF AN EDUCATION . . .

tion, persuasion, literature, and self-expression force you to emphasize different criteria when teaching these different kinds of writing. There is no single criterion of aim which makes all writing good. That is why the different aims are taught separately.

THE MODES OF WRITING

After all this talk about the aims of writing, you, as a teacher, might ask, "Are you maintaining that if I get students to pay attention to the aims of their writing, all other problems will disappear? There are many other facets of the process of writing to which we teachers have to pay attention. Grammar is clearly a persistent concern, as are spelling, vocabulary, sentence structure, paragraphing, genres of writing (letter, report, story, poem, speech, ad, etc.), subject matter, and last but not least, the modes. What do you propose to do with all of these issues?"

I recognize all of these concerns and reply that they will be given close and continuous attention throughout the entire course, but I would like to stress the last dimension, that of the modes of writing.

JAMES L. KINNEAVY
AUTHOR OF
ELEMENTS OF WRITING

This dimension bridges the two mentioned just before it—genre and subject matter, and it implicates a major concern of all writing teachers—organization. More than any other aspect of writing, modes determine overall organization. This particular essay, for example, is a series of classifications and definitions.

At times in the history of writing, modes have been given almost as much attention as the aims, but most of the time they have been a serious second candidate. The modes are listed differently in various books. In this textbook we call narration, description, classification, and evaluation the modes. They could be called the genres of writing, and they could be called ways of looking at subject matter.

When I want to introduce students to the modes, I use a newspaper. I ask students to find examples of news stories (narratives). I ask them to find classifications, especially in the classifieds, as they are called. I ask the students to examine individual items within each section of the classifieds and to tell me what the details are. It becomes clear to them that there are specific descriptions of cars, houses, lost dogs, or jobs in the classifieds. Finally, I have students check reviews of books, movies, television programs, or concerts. These are all evaluations.

Like the aims, the modes have to be taught separately. **What makes a good narrative is not what makes a good evaluation or a good description or a good classification.** Consequently, the modes are given careful consideration in this textbook. 🍃

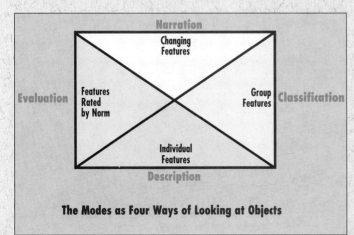

The Modes as Four Ways of Looking at Objects

BY DR. LEE ODELL, RENSSELAER POLYTECHNIC INSTITUTE

MODELING

MAKE US SEE WHAT YOU'RE TALKING ABOUT.

For some time now, teachers of writing have made a point of exhorting students to make their writing "show, not tell." Don't just tell us your reactions or opinions, we say to them. Make us see what you're talking about. If you're trying to describe a person, let us see facial expressions, details of clothing, mannerisms, actions; let us hear exactly what the person says. Or, if students are trying to write persuasively, we insist: Don't just give us your generalized conclusions. Give us some specific information that lets us see what you base your judgment on and that lets us decide for ourselves whether your judgement makes sense.

This advice is not an infallible, inflexible rule. Writers can't elaborate on everything. Furthermore, readers sometimes let a generali-zation pass unchallenged because it seems to ring true or because writers have sufficient authority for us simply to take their word on the matter. But if we are judicious in asking students to "show, not tell," the phrase constitutes good advice for writers and excellent advice for teachers. If we want students to make significant progress as writers, we will have to show them—not just tell them, *show*

LEE ODELL OPENS HIS CLASSROOM DOOR AT RENSSELAER POLYTECHNIC INSTITUTE.

them—what we mean. In effect, we need to make sure they have models, not just of the kinds of writing they will do but of the writing processes.

There is, of course, a long history to the practice of working with models. For centuries, teachers of rhetoric and writing have required students to study the works of great writers, sometimes having students copy model texts word for word or asking students to imitate the sentence structures they found in these works. Indeed, a version of this practice persisted through the middle 1980's in the form of sentence combining. This system did not ask students to emulate one specific writer, but it did show them frequently used sentence patterns in the works of highly admired professional writers so students could construct their own sentences based on a wide variety of these patterns.

Traditional approaches to using models have their uses, but these approaches are not what I'm talking about here. I'm suggesting that we depart from traditional practice in several ways. For one thing, the model should come not solely from famous authors but rather from books and magazines students read willingly and have readily accessible. Also, teachers don't have to provide all the models; students should be asked to bring in articles or excerpts from books that they personally find engaging and effective. Finally, these models should not be treated as though they are sacred; they are, instead, objects for analysis—for criticism as well as for praise. We and our students need to examine entire models where writers have used successful strategies that students might incorporate into their own writing, as the occasion warrants. But we and our students also need to identify things that don't work and maybe even to collaborate on devising ways to improve the model.

There are several ways we might use models, but my favorite is to use them to help students solve their own writing difficulties. For example, a number of my students can't figure out how to begin a piece of writing, what Donald Murray would refer to as a "lead." When this is a problem, I ask students to bring in copies of the first pages of articles that they somehow found themselves reading, even though the topics might not normally have concerned them.

For example, one student brought in an article entitled "Hell on Wheels," which began this way:

Almost from the time the downtown No. 4 subway train began its 21-mile run below New York City at 11:38 p.m. on the night of Tuesday, Aug. 27, something seemed amiss. Heading from the Bronx to Manhattan, the train overshot the platform at a couple of stations. At times it slowed to a crawl and then accelerated to breakneck speeds. The conductor contacted the motorman, Robert Ray, 38, several times on the intercom to find out if everything was all right. Ray replied that he was fine. But that was clearly not the case....

This article begins of course, with a claim about a specific event ("something seemed amiss") and then illustrates this claim with a series of incidents. It mentions specific, troubling things that happened (for example, the train "slowed to a crawl and then accelerated to breakneck speeds"); it reports what people said to each other; and then it challenges what one of the people said ("But that clearly was not the case...."). In this last sentence, the author creates a conflict that engages the reader and lets the reader know

I DON'T WANT STUDENTS TO THINK THERE IS JUST ONE WAY TO BEGIN A PIECE OF WRITING.

what the rest of the article will be about (i.e., it will show how the driver's claim was "not the case").

Other articles brought in by the students began quite differently—by citing troubling statistics, for example, or by describing general trends in society that a reader was almost certain to know and be concerned about. These differences are important. I don't want students to think there is just one way to begin a piece of writing. Consequently, I photocopied a variety of examples and asked students to talk them through to identify the strategies writers had used to engage readers. My goal was to help students recognize some of the options that are open to them in doing their own writing.

In addition to bringing in models written by professionals, it can be extremely useful for us to bring in copies of our own efforts to do the same kind of writing students are working on. And once we have developed an atmosphere of trust, it can be useful to bring in effective examples of student work, continually asking such questions as these: What did the writer do here? How did he or she go about capturing our interest and letting us know what to expect in the rest of the text? Is there anything that this writer is doing that you might profitably do? Again, the goal is not to provide recipes or rules chiseled on tablets of stone but to get students to see what is possible.

MODELING THE COMPOSING PROCESS

Thus far, I have been describing ways we might use written products as models. In addition, we also need models of the composing processes of writers. This modeling can be as sophisticated or as rudimentary as our students need. It can focus on the work of an individual writer as Donald Murray shows in his "Use Genre as Lens" essay or on the efforts of peers as they revise their initial drafts. That is, we need to let students see the processes professional writers and students go through in doing their own writing and even in responding to classmates' writing.

There are several activities teachers can use that allow students to observe their peers' writing processes. For example, a colleague was concerned that her tenth-graders would have difficulty passing the state basic competency test that is required for high school graduation. Knowing that one of the questions on that test was likely to require students to report information in a well-organized form, she could have concentrated on paragraph form and the proper use of transitions. But suspecting that her students' difficulties were more profound than that, she decided that her students weren't paragraphing because they did not understand that certain kinds of expository paragraphs require writers to group facts by setting up categories that the paragraphs would be about.

Consequently, she asked students to watch a videotape of a movie that she was fairly certain they would find moving, an account of the difficulties encountered by a child who had been classified as mentally retarded but who had, nonetheless, a number of good traits and who was personally likable. After students had watched the videotape, she asked them to write down every fact they could remember from the movie and to collaborate as a class to make the list as complete as possible. That night she typed a complete list of facts, made an overhead transparency of them, and then cut the transparency into strips, each strip containing one fact.

The next day, she asked students to collaborate on ways to group these facts. For instance, students noticed that many of the facts pertained to ways people reacted to the young boy, while others could be grouped under such headings

as the boy's reactions to other people or his abilities. As students discussed ways of grouping facts, the teacher reflected what they were saying by moving the transparency strips around on the overhead projector. She was showing, not telling, her students about the basic process they needed to create one type of organized paragraph.

Another approach to modeling the composing process comes from a ninth-grade teacher concerned that her students' descriptive writing was bland. She believed their real problem was not a lack of descriptive adjectives and adverbs but that students weren't really looking closely at the people or objects they were describing.

She also knew that television programs routinely provide excellent examples of the process of observing. That is, as a rule, television cameras do not stay in one

spot to observe everything from the same angle and distance. Instead, the cameras change position to vary the angles and the distances from which they view things. For example, one detective program began with a close-up shot of a ringing phone. Then the camera moved back so that the viewers could see a well-dressed man hurrying across an elegant apartment toward the phone. Next the camera moved in to focus on the man's trembling hands as he nervously dried his sweaty palms on his handkerchief before picking up the phone. Finally, the camera shifted focus again, to show the head and shoulders of a burly, unshaven man speaking into a pay phone. These shifts in focus set the scene for the entire episode.

To help students understand this process of observing by shifting focus, the teacher asked students,

as part of their homework, to watch one of their favorite TV programs and to count the number of times the camera shifted its focus in a two-minute period. She also asked them to make notes about the different things they saw every time the camera shifted focus. The next day they discussed these episodes and concluded that a program in which the camera did not shift focus would almost certainly be dull.

To help students see how this process applied to writing, the teacher gave students the following description:

She probably has false teeth and wears glasses. She wears her hair up in a bun and wears dresses from the 1930's. She has a habit of tapping her pencil on her desk.

Students readily agreed that this passage was uninteresting. To help them see why, the teacher asked students to think of the grammatical subject of each sentence as the visual focus of the sentence. (In response to the predictable question, the teacher told students that, for this passage, they could think of the grammatical subject as "how the writer begins each sentence.") Students saw readily that this writer's "camera" was standing in one place, not shifting at all. So the teacher asked students to work in groups to revise the passage so that the grammatical focus reflected changes in visual focus.

As one group collaborated on revising the passage, the following discussion took place:

"OK. Let's start with her false teeth—yeah—write that down."
She has false teeth.
"No, dummy. We gotta start the sentence with 'her false teeth'."
Her false teeth
"OK, now what?"
"Oh, no. If we start with that we gotta add stuff. Like.... 'Her false teeth look funny'."
"Yeah, put that down."
"No, you gotta tell what 'funny' means. She'll [the teacher] only ask 'What's funny mean?'"
"I got it." Her false teeth look yellow. *"My grandma's are."*
"Yeah, 'cause they're old, like her."
"Hey. Who's writing?"
"I am." Her false teeth are yellow because they're old.
"That's good."
"OK, now the stuff on glasses. Oh, gosh. We're gonna have to add stuff to everything!"

Indeed, they would. And that was just the point. Their teacher wanted them to see that as they shifted visual focus, they would have to explore their subject further. Not only was their teacher showing these students a fundamental process of observing, but also she was showing them how the process of observing translated into the process of writing.

In addition to modeling the writing process, we also need to model the process of responding to writing. It is true that students can learn to make very helpful comments about their peers' writing. But the important phrase here is *learn to*. As Karen Spear has pointed out in her excellent book *Sharing Writing*, working in response groups is a complex process. It requires that students be able to go beyond uninformative, global comments ("Yeah, it's pretty good." "I guess it's OK.") and do two things: pay attention to specific words, phrases, or ideas and explain why and how they personally react to those things. The ninth-grade class I've just described illustrates one way to model the process of responding. When the teacher asked students to revise the bland description, she was showing them a process they could use in responding to each other's drafts. That is, she was helping them see that when they responded to a classmate's descriptive writing, they might consider whether the student had shifted focus and whether the shifts in focus helped give the reader a clearer visual picture of the person, object, or place being described. Indeed, the teacher made sure students worked as a class to give this sort

of response to one or two students' subsequent drafts.

But modeling the response process may not be enough. It may also be necessary to model the processes of listening to and using those responses. Listening can be especially difficult when the response implies that a writer's work is unclear or in need of further effort. In such cases, any writer—and students are no exception—may well become defensive, more eager to prove that responses are invalid or irrelevant than to listen to those responses and consider the uses they might have. In other words, students may need to learn how to respond to responses.

If so, teachers may need to model the way we want student writers to react to their classmates' comments. Specifically, we should bring in our own efforts to do some of the same writing students are doing and ask students to respond to it. Where is it clear or unclear? What sort of personality or attitude is our writ-

ing conveying? At what points have we said things that seem appropriate or inappropriate for the audience we are addressing? My experience in doing this sort of work with students is that if they trust us, they can be very perceptive and painfully direct. If they don't get it, they can tell us so in no uncertain terms. In doing so, they give us a chance to show how a writer listens to readers, not by arguing but by attempting to find out why readers react as they do and then using that information to revise a subsequent draft.

❦

The process of modeling is, like everything else about teaching writing, a slow business. One example rarely does the trick. But if we are persistent in showing students what is involved in producing good writing through the writing process, we can usually count on results. But if we don't model, we should expect our distinction between *showing* and *telling* to fall on deaf ears. If we don't follow our own advice, why should they? ❦

*I*N ADDITION TO MODELING THE WRITING PROCESS, WE ALSO NEED TO MODEL THE PROCESS OF RESPONDING TO WRITING.

❦❦❦❦❦

BY DR. MAXINE HAIRSTON, FORMER DIRECTOR OF FRESHMAN ENGLISH, THE UNIVERSITY OF TEXAS

THE JOY OF WRITING

STUDENTS NEED TO GET SOME FUN OUT OF WHAT THEY'RE DOING.

MAXINE HAIRSTON TAKES A BREAK FROM CLASSES.

In recent years I have come to believe that the most important job I can do as a writing teacher is to help my students enjoy writing. I say this because I am convinced that unless students find some pleasure in their writing classes, most of them will not be willing to invest the time and energy required to turn out work that they—and we, as their teachers—can be proud of. Few adults are disciplined and determined enough to drudge away at some project—whether it's exercising or learning Spanish verbs—simply because someone else tells us that it will be good for us in the long run. We just won't stay with some projects unless there's some satisfaction in the process itself. How much harder it is, then, for youngsters to whom college or even next fall seems light years away to subject themselves to the hard work of learning to write if they get no pleasure from it at the time. Deficit motivation, working to avoid penalties or simply for a passing grade, isn't enough; students need to get some fun out of what they're doing. Fortunately, given what we now know about teaching the writing process, it's quite possible to create a writing classroom in which many students work from growth motivation; that is, they work at their writing because they enjoy doing it for its own sake.

Cognitive studies, ethnographic studies about writing, and the national projects argue that four characteristics define the congenial writing classroom, the kind in which students are likely to enjoy writing and to flourish as writers.

First, teachers provide a low-risk environment that encourages students to write without fear. Second, teachers have students develop their papers through a series of drafts and revisions. Third, teachers honor the students' right to their own writing, allowing students to choose their own topics and encouraging them to write about their interests. Fourth, teachers create and support a collaborative learning environment.

ESTABLISHING A LOW-RISK CLASSROOM

Creating a low-risk environment in the writing classroom may seem like a formidable challenge, and indeed it can be at the beginning of a new term when many students are as wary as stray cats. They're nervous for fear someone is going to try to trap them. In the first week of a writing class sometimes I feel as if I want to wear a banner across my chest, emblazoned with "Trust me! It's going to be all right!" But I can understand students' anxiety. Students who have come from writing courses with a heavy emphasis on rules and form, courses in which they did badly, have good reason to see a composition course as a high-risk situation. No wonder they start out by trying to stay in the safety zone of rules and formulas.

The humanistic psychologist Abraham Maslow theorizes that all people have two sets of forces operating within them: a need for safety and a fear of risk on one hand and an urge toward growth and autonomy on the other hand. Maslow also believes that every individual has an innate urge to create, to grow, to discover new abilities and talents. I agree; I think all children want to communicate, to write something that catches the interest and attention of others, but most will hesitate if they think they will be punished for breaking rules. As Maslow points out, "Safety needs are prepotent over growth needs.... [and] in general, only a child who feels safe dares to grow forward healthily" (49). He adds, "Only the [teacher] who respects fear and defense can teach; ..." (53).

The writing teacher's challenge is to foster the low-risk environment that will encourage creativity and expression but at the same time to work toward helping students master the writing conventions that they must know to be accepted as writers. There are several ways teachers can do this. First, of course, is to emphasize that we write in stages; we plan, we draft, we read and reread, and we revise. Final details matter when a writer gets ready to publish, but the most-productive writers learn how to suspend their error monitors in the early stages.

*I*N THE FIRST WEEK OF A WRITING CLASS SOMETIMES I FEEL AS IF I WANT TO WEAR A BANNER ACROSS MY CHEST, EMBLAZONED WITH "TRUST ME! IT'S GOING TO BE ALL RIGHT!"

I have found it helps me to suspend my own error monitor when reading early drafts if I can put down my pencil and force myself to read strictly for content, good practice for trying to become a courteous reader. I ask myself, what is this writer trying to express? Why? How? Then I make only a large-scale response, focusing on being positive and on asking questions that could help the next draft. I emphasize that I hope to see substantial change and development in that draft. It would waste time even to mention error at this stage. When students realize that I really am not looking for mistakes in their drafts, they begin to relax and become more venturesome.

On second drafts, I still try to avoid writing on the paper, but focus on more specific suggestions for improvement. I also make checks in the margins to indicate potential trouble spots that the writers need to be aware of when they begin to polish their papers, sometimes adding a comment that the writer should be alert for problems with commas, subject-verb agreement, or whatever area seems most troublesome. This gives the writer specific areas to concentrate on at proofreading/editing time.

Probably one of the best ways to reduce risk in the writing classroom is to set up a portfolio system that allows students to draft a variety of papers over a period of time and then to choose a limited number to develop fully and submit for final evaluation. This method has become increasingly popular for a number of reasons. For one, student writers can work more as adult working writers do. They can attempt different kinds of writing, can stay with those projects that go well and, putting the others aside, they can invest as much as they like in them. It also gives students more control over the evaluation process. They decide which pieces they want evaluated; the teacher doesn't even have to see the others. There is considerable literature on the portfolio system if you find it an attractive option. (See also Elliot and Greenberg's essay "The Direct Assessment of Writing: Notes for Teachers.")

A final specific suggestion for reducing your students' anxieties is to establish a hierarchy of errors. We know from research that not all errors are created equal. Some are truly damaging: for instance, wrong verb forms, egregious sentence fragments, double negatives and faulty parallelism. Errors like these set off alarms for most readers. Others, such as split infinitives, comparison of absolutes, or misusing *lie* and *lay* cause scarcely a riffle with most audiences. We should be lenient about such lapses and reduce the number of things our students have to worry about.

We should also remember that the more a writer attempts, the more mistakes he or she is likely to make. But if we are encouraging growth, we need to let student writers know that we regard such mistakes as the natural accompaniment of growth and as less important than the students' fresh ideas.

TEACHING THE WRITING PROCESS THROUGH A SYSTEM OF DRAFTS

Because this textbook so strongly emphasizes that drafting, evaluating, and revising are essential parts of the writing process, I don't feel I need to build an elaborate case for having students develop their papers in drafts. Fortunately, with most writing teachers and curriculum supervisors embracing the concept of writing as a process, students accept drafting as a routine practice. I hope so, because students write more freely and more confidently when they know that their readers view their drafts as "work in progress," not as finished products to be critiqued and judged. Under such a system, knowing they're not irrevocably committed to what they've written, writers can afford experiments. Writing tentatively, they can count on getting help from their readers to help them work out their ideas. That's very reassuring, particularly to students who haven't written much and aren't sure they have anything to say.

The less articulate, inexperienced writers are probably those who get the most out of numerous drafts because they have the opportunity to improve first attempts

WRITING CAN BECOME A GENUINE JOY FOR GOOD WRITERS WORKING AT THEIR PEAK.

substantially before they must submit the papers for evaluation. They also have the chance to get feedback *during* the writing process, feedback that is far more valuable than comments on a paper that has already been graded. We know that many students, perhaps even most, pay scant attention to comments written on graded papers, especially negative comments. But when they get comments—both written and oral—on drafts, they are likely to pay attention because they use them to real advantage.

Good students also benefit from drafts, although sometimes they may resist doing them because the system requires more work than they've usually had to do in order to get good grades. But for some good writers, developing a paper through drafts can be a heady experience as they tap into talent they didn't know they had and then earn new recognition from their peers. Writing can become a genuine joy for good writers working at their peak.

In my opinion the worst possible system for having students write papers is to give a fresh assignment each week, have everyone write the paper only once and turn it in for a grade, and then return the graded papers and repeat the process. Under such circumstances the anxiety level skyrockets for all but the most able

students, writers get no help during the process (when they need it most), and teachers never learn what most students can really do. Even when students write in class, those papers should be drafts that they can work on again during the next class periods. Only then are students likely to develop their potential.

LETTING STUDENTS CHOOSE THEIR OWN TOPICS FOR WRITING

After several years of having students choose their own writing topics, I am committed to the practice because it has several invaluable benefits. First, most students have never had an opportunity to write about matters they're genuinely interested in and can write about with authority. Too often they see traditional assignments that ask everyone to write on the same topic as meaningless exercises in which the teacher seems to be forgetting that students are individuals.

Second, students are more likely to put time and energy into their writing when they can explore topics that interest them. When students are writing on their own topics, they may also discover a potent truth: Writing is a powerful tool for learning, one that will serve them well.

Third, when students choose their own topics, a rich diversity

can develop as they write about their own special interests. Some students may write about family rituals that come from their ethnic heritages or about unusual people in their families; others may write about living in another country or on a military base; others may write about hobbies—bicycling or scuba diving or canoeing. The possibilities are almost endless. In many schools, a rich multicultural tapestry can emerge as students from diverse backgrounds and cultures read each other's work and share stories.

Fourth, students will become more confident as writers because they have more control over their writing. As they develop their expertise in some area, they begin to realize how much they know about something, whether it's car stereos or cooking hamburgers. They can take on a new identity in the class and find that people pay attention to what they have to say. That's good for all of us.

Finally when students choose their own writing topics, the class simply becomes more interesting for everyone. Students may cover a remarkable range of subjects, and even those writing on similar topics bring different perspectives to them. Boredom drops quickly because everyone is constantly learning directly from other people's experiences. Perhaps the greatest bonus is to teachers, who not only garner a wealth of information about their students, but also over a period of years become mini-experts on numerous topics. Furthermore, they are spared trying to think up a good writing topic and then having to read fifty papers on that topic.

I BELIEVE STRONGLY IN PEER GROUPS AND COLLABORATIVE LEARNING IN WRITING CLASSES.

It does take considerable class time to help select topics, since many students will protest that they have nothing to write about, but such obstacles can be overcome in a few days of brainstorming and group work in class. As teacher, you can come in with a list of possible topics and then work with the class to generate subtopics. Or ask everyone to bring in a list of fifteen things to write about, encouraging the concrete and specific rather than large, abstract categories.

I have had good success with asking students to choose a general topic to write on for the whole term and then to pick subtopics for individual papers. That way they get into their topics in some depth and eliminate the process of having to work through choosing a fresh topic for each paper. You may want to specify the kinds of papers students write within their topics—informative, expressive, persuasive, and so on—to focus the class within the formats they're learning from the textbook.

ESTABLISHING A COLLABORATIVE-LEARNING CLASSROOM

I believe strongly in peer groups and collaborative learning in writing classes. Perhaps their greatest advantage is that they give students an immediate sense of audience, something that's hard to achieve when the teacher is the only reader for the drafts. Usually they respect each other's opinions; in fact, they may take their peers' responses more seriously than they do the teacher's because they feel closer to peers and they genuinely want to communicate.

Students also begin to see how useful collaboration can be for generating ideas. Most students in writing groups readily admit how much their classmates have contributed to the final versions of their papers. Each class period when I hand back graded papers, I pick two or three of the best ones to read aloud and then ask the writer and the writer's group to comment on how the paper developed through drafts. Their accounts are revealing, and the investment they feel in each other's work is truly gratifying.

I favor randomly chosen groups of at least four students so if someone is absent, the discussion doesn't break down. I reorganize groups to allow working with as many writers as possible. This arrangement also enhances every student's exposure to diverse cultural experiences as they get to know other students more closely. Managing groups in the classroom may not be easy, although I suspect trained secondary teachers know considerably more about it than most college teachers do. For the teacher who doesn't feel comfortable with groups, there is considerable literature on the concept.

Ultimately, groups help to establish the whole class as a community of writers who work together, feel a common sense of purpose, and see writing as a shared enterprise that's important to everyone. We all know intuitively that the most important element for achieving a congenial writing classroom is the teacher's attitude, and for that reason it's important for the teacher to be a part of that community, not to be an outside authority and a judge. Teachers need to write with students during writing workshops and share writing with them—its joys and frustrations. With luck and time, I am convinced that both teachers and students will enjoy being in a writing classroom more than they might have thought possible. ☙

References

Maslow, Abraham. Toward a Psychology of Being, 2nd ed. New York: D. Van Nostrand Company. 1968.

TEACHERS NEED TO WRITE WITH STUDENTS DURING WRITING WORKSHOPS AND SHARE WRITING WITH THEM —ITS JOYS AND FRUSTRATIONS.

BY DR. BARBARA J. SHADE, PROFESSOR AND DEAN,
SCHOOL OF EDUCATION, THE UNIVERSITY OF WISCONSIN–PARKSIDE

TEACHING FOR LEARNING'S SAKE

THIS APPROACH TO TEACHING WILL EMPOWER STUDENTS AS LEARNERS.

Helping students incorporate ideas, skills, and concepts that will improve their ability to perform tasks and to solve problems is the ultimate goal of teaching. Teachers who achieve this goal effectively find ways to accommodate students' different learning styles so that the teaching-learning process works more efficiently.

What do we mean by *learning styles?* Over the years, researchers have identified three dimensions in which students have specific learning preferences: (1) their preferences for various environmental factors that influence the learning climate; (2) their preferences about the ways they choose to engage in the learning process (motivational style); and (3) their preferences for the various ways in which they process information (cognitive style).

ENVIRONMENTAL PREFERENCES

Individual environmental preferences focus on the lighting, temperature, and furniture used in the learning process. For example, some individuals might prefer bright light while others prefer it muted; some might prefer a warm room while others like it cool. A variation in studying postures has also been noted, with some individuals preferring to sit in a traditional classroom desk while others prefer to stand or recline when engaged in a learning task.[1]

MOTIVATIONAL STYLE

The second dimension of learning style focuses upon the extent to which students take responsibility for their own learning. Teachers often incorrectly assume that students' desire to engage in work is inherent. As with other aspects of learning, the extent to which individuals become involved in work depends upon how they have been socialized to respond to work. Some students, for example, have been taught to rely on others for assistance, to follow directions as given, and to perform the task as modeled. Others have been made more independent of others and have been taught to work alone, to find their own solutions, and to decide whether or not they can complete the work before asking for assistance. Corno and Mandinach refer to this stylistic dimension as a preference for resource management, and students tend to use the approach that makes them feel the most comfortable and the most competent.

The teaching-learning process involves human interaction, and students prefer different levels of involvement with others, depending upon the social and personality development that emanates from their families and communities. Families stressing prosocial behavior encourage children to help, to share, and to work toward benefiting others.

These students are more likely to give and receive assistance in the learning process and to like cooperative-learning ventures. Children trained to be highly individualistic and self-oriented are less likely to cooperate

[1] For a more detailed description of the social and physical environment preferences of students, the reader should examine the writings of Kenneth and Rita Dunn.

and offer help. Learners with this orientation function well in a competitive setting because they prefer to work alone and are less likely to enjoy cooperative-learning activities unless there is a reward or a method of accommodating their need for individuality.

COGNITIVE STYLE

The least discussed dimension of learning style—that of cognitive style—represents individually preferred ways of perceiving, organizing, and evaluating information so that it can be learned.

Three cognitive processes influence the way individuals acquire and produce knowledge. These are the perceptual, the conceptual, and the evaluative processes.

1. Perceptual Processes: The most recognized area in learning-style literature, this area focuses on the sensory modalities. Through cultural socialization, learners develop a preference for either the visual modality (photographs, graphs, art, texts); the aural modality (records, tapes, lectures); the haptic/kinesthetic modality (group discussions, interactive debates, drama); or some combination of these. Instruction delivered through the preferred modality establishes an instant rapport that allows students to process information more easily.

Different cultures socialize their children to attend to different cues in the environment; therefore, students have selective attention. Some students focus their attention on the task or idea being presented. For others, the people, their peers, their self-evaluation, or even the teacher's reaction to them are the most important

elements on which to focus. How children choose to attend to cues is an important dimension of learning, and teachers who wish to ensure cognitive engagement find ways to influence the perceptive focus of the students.

2. Conceptual Processes: Having focused on an idea that must be learned, students must then classify it based upon prior experiences. The techniques involved include assessing similarities and differences to prior knowledge, as well as determining how best to define or describe the concepts. Again, the extent to which students can manipulate various concepts depends upon whether or not the ideas can be communi-

cated to them using a common language with commonly accepted images.

Some students prefer to have ideas presented in a hierarchical manner, beginning with the big picture followed by the details involved (whole to part). Other

students prefer to have the information presented in a more sequential approach, beginning with the minute details and building toward the larger concept (part to whole). Regardless of the technique used, teachers must include methods of helping learners make connections with prior knowledge.

3. Evaluative Processes: The third aspect of cognitive style focuses on the processes of thinking about the information. *Thinking* is difficult to define, but many researchers define it as "comprehension monitoring." The major focus of thinking centers on the individual's ability to plan, monitor, and evaluate his or her learning and understanding about the information he or she is seeking to learn.

Again, teachers should look for variations in the way individuals approach thinking. On one hand, individuals may spend time using their imaginations to create ideas based upon personal views or

*T*HE KEY TO A GOOD GROUP DISCUSSION IS A TEACHER WHO IS AN EXCELLENT QUESTIONER, WHO IS REFLECTIVE, WHO CAN LEAD STUDENTS TO REFLECT AND INQUIRE . . .

beliefs. On the other hand, some individuals will engage in a more formal logic, which requires familiarity with the rules in order to select the correct problem-solving strategies. In the first type of information processing, individuals seem to arrive at their decisions rather intuitively, using a process that seems to be generated from an internalized logic. In the second type, the one most influenced by instruction, students learn to organize and review their approach to information or problems through an analytical process.

ACCOMMODATING VARIATIONS IN LEARNING STYLES

When teachers are first introduced to the concept of learning styles, they immediately conjure up visions of having to construct thirty different learning plans to accommodate their students. *Learning styles* is not another euphemism for individually guided education. Instead, it is an entreaty to teachers to provide different approaches and strategies that individuals can use as they work at learning.

In today's classrooms, there are basically *two distinct modes of learning:* the *traditional orientation,* the one to which most instruction is geared; and the *community orientation,* the one more likely to be displayed by African American, Hispanic American, Native American and immigrant Asian students who identify closely with the culture of their ethnic communities.

Particular suggestions to enhance the instructional process for the community-oriented students who are often ignored in instructional delivery system include the following ones:

Environment Style Accommodation: For the community-oriented students, the classroom should become inviting and supportive as an experiential setting in which students can use various media to explore concepts that may be foreign to them because they are not prevalent in their communities or because their economic situation does not permit the type of travel or involvement in enrichment activities that is true of the more successful, economically affluent students. Being able to see an enlarged picture of the Eiffel Tower in the classroom can provide an important conceptual image that might be needed to foster comprehension. Because learning centers permit self-exploration, they should also become important aspects of the classroom design for all levels of students in all types of classes.

Motivational Style Accommodation: Having the opportunity to participate in a good class discussion on lesson content motivates community-oriented students, satisfying their needs to share information with others and to obtain feedback. Moreover, it provides them an opportunity to listen to different perspectives. Teachers should note, however, that group discussion is not the same as class recitation in which students are asked to recite facts and information to the teacher from a textbook. For example, it is not enough to discuss nouns as a part of speech without leading students through the concept of a complete sentence and the purpose of using nouns within sentences and paragraphs. Moreover, students need to be able to identify nouns within the framework of their own speech and written narratives as well as to determine how and why they have used a particular word as a noun.

The key to a good group discussion is a teacher who is an excellent questioner, who is reflective, who can lead students to reflect and inquire, and who has an excellent understanding of the broad structure and relationships within the lesson content.

Information Processing Style Accommodation: Teachers can facilitate the processing of information by students through the use of some of the following techniques:

1. Present concepts with multimedia using a variety of modalities.

2. Assist the students in identifying the relationships of concepts through cognitive mapping, brainstorming, or reciprocal teaching.

3. Take time to ensure there is a common understanding of words, concepts, or ideas. Bilingual students should be encouraged to interpret the words in their languages. Students should also be encouraged to develop art projects and to use new words orally.

4. Model the thinking processes needed to complete tasks successfully. Provide students time to think about a problem or to complete an assignment. Students learn best when they can perform when the teacher is available for feedback.

Teachers must remember that students have different perceptions of the world and teach to these perceptions. Assisting students in learning requires lots of talking—talking between students and teachers and between students.

When considering the use of learning styles, teachers must confront three important perceptions. First, teachers should understand that the identified style preference should not and cannot be used as evidence of deficiencies. Second, teachers should not think that the community-oriented style reflects all members of a group. It is merely behavior that is most likely to be found within the community. Third, teachers who use the concept of learning styles should do so as indicators of approaches to lesson design and to the selection of methods of instruction, not as the basis for judging intellectual potential.

A FINAL CAVEAT

Developing a successful learner is the ultimate goal of a successful teacher, and ensuring that children become successful learners requires that teachers see themselves not as the ultimate purveyors of knowledge, but as guides through the learning process. This approach to teaching will empower students as learners and will permit them to approach the learning process in their own words. When learners grasp the ideas, their sense of self-worth and confidence and their intellectual strength improve tremendously. It is at this point teachers know they, too, have been successful. What a great sense of accomplishment! ❧

MULTIPLE INTELLIGENCES AND THE WRITING CLASSROOM

The theory of multiple intelligences was developed by Harvard psychologist Howard Gardner, who, in researching the function of the human brain in trauma, discovered that damage to one area of the brain, such as the speech center, does not necessarily incapacitate other areas of intelligence, such as appreciation of music or artistic ability. This discovery led to the proposal that the human brain does not operate with one single intelligence, but with seven.

Gardner labeled the seven intelligences logical-mathematical, linguistic, musical, bodily-kinesthetic, interpersonal, intrapersonal, and spatial.

Each intelligence operates both independently and cooperatively with the others in every human brain. Gardner contends that even though a certain intelligence may not be fully developed or even apparent in every person, the potential for that development exists and its expansion depends in large part on the environment in which the person lives or works.

IDENTIFYING STUDENTS' MULTIPLE INTELLIGENCES

The most immediate challenge for teachers is to identify students' intelligences and then to apply strategies and to create opportunities for students that will allow them to use and develop all their intelligences in the classroom. Discovering students' intelligences should

An overview of the seven intelligences		
Intelligence	Characteristics	Possible vocation using this intelligence
Linguistic	Uses language effectively, orally or in writing	Writer, storyteller, editor
Logical-Mathematical	Uses numbers and figures effectively, reasons, identifies patterns, has organizing skills	Accountant, lawyer, journalist
Spatial	Observes or perceives relationships between real or imaginary objects	Artist, architect, nature guide
Bodily-Kinesthetic	Has sense of ease in movement of one's body to express ideas or to create or transform something	Dancer, mechanic, surgeon
Musical	Perceives and/or creates music, rhythm, pitch, or harmony	Musician, composer, disc jockey
Interpersonal	Interacts with the outside world, is sensitive to the feelings, actions and motivations of others	Social worker, politician, parent
Intrapersonal	Is sensitive to one's own thoughts, feelings, ideas, and place in the world	Poet, artist, singer

not be a time-consuming process. But it does require that teachers become better acquainted with their students so that they can learn **how students perform, what students prefer to do,** and **how students perceive themselves.**

Thomas Armstrong, the author of *Multiple Intelligences in the Classroom,* suggests several approaches.

• Consider preparing a questionnaire or checklist of the characteristics of the multiple intelligences for students and ask them to choose the items that apply to them.

• Give students an informal, oral survey that, with general questions about their likes and dislikes and talents, identifies which intelligences dominate the class.

• Use journal entries or personal narratives as an opportunity to evaluate the intelligences of students.

Keep in mind, though, that students usually have strengths in several areas. Armstrong also suggests that teachers identify their own intelligences and mention them to students as a way to explain their approaches to the subject matter so that students can see how their intelligences are compatible with their teachers'.

INSTRUCTIONAL STRATEGIES THAT TARGET THE MULTIPLE INTELLIGENCES

The next step for teachers is to target the kinds of strategies that facilitate students' multiple intelligences and to include those in their instruction. The following list gives samples of some strategies for each learning style. However, you should try to develop some of your own adaptations to address the needs of your classroom.

Stage of the Writing Process	Activities and Multiple Intelligences
Prewriting	**Brainstorming:** Linguistic, Interpersonal **Cluster/Diagramming:** Spatial, Intrapersonal, Interpersonal **Freewriting/Journaling:** Intrapersonal **Researching/Asking questions:** Logical-Mathematical **Observing/Imagining:** Spatial, Musical, Bodily-Kinesthetic **Reading with a Focus:** Linguistic, Logical-Mathematical, Intrapersonal **Listening with a Focus:** Musical, Interpersonal, Logical-Mathematical
Drafting	**Expressive/Creative Writing:** Interpersonal, Musical, Linguistic, Bodily-Kinesthetic **Informative Writing:** Logical-Mathematical **Writing to Explain:** Spatial, Logical-Mathematical, Interpersonal **Writing to Explore:** Logical-Mathematical **Writing about Literature:** Musical, Bodily-Kinesthetic, Spatial **Writing a Research paper:** Logical-Mathematical (depends also on the subject researched)
Evaluating and Revising	**Peer revision:** Interpersonal **Attention to details and organization:** Logical-Mathematical **Organization of text:** Bodily-Kinesthetic **Attention to images:** Spatial
Proofreading and Publishing	**Peer revision, public reading, performance:** Interpersonal **Polishing manuscript:** Intrapersonal **Reflecting:** Interpersonal, Linguistic

• **Spatial learners** benefit from watching videotapes or from drawing on overhead transparencies, a chalkboard, or a computer screen.

• **Interpersonal learners** thrive in discussion groups, especially if given opportunities to act as the group leader.

• **Intrapersonal learners** need individual goal-setting sessions and time for reflection in personal journals or portfolios.

• **Bodily-Kinesthetic learners** benefit from acting out concepts alone or in front of the class and from being able to physically manipulate things, such as a puzzle pieces, flashcards, index cards, or sections of a written draft.

• **Musical learners** are more productive if music is played during discussion sessions or while reading or writing, particularly if the music reflects the emotional content of the work.

• **Logical-mathematical learners** need a set of direct questions to work on and independent time to explore and research answers.

• **Linguistic learners** do well using tape recorders to record oral brainstorming sessions and having opportunities to discuss their ideas with their teacher or their peers.

It is important to remember that the activities mentioned here engage more than one intelligence at a time. Consider experimenting with different activities, and ask for student feedback.

APPLYING MULTIPLE INTELLIGENCES TO THE WRITING PROCESS

Being flexible and recursive, the writing process allows student writers to use their multiple intelligences at each of the four stages—prewriting; drafting; evaluating and revising; and proofreading, publishing, and reflecting.

Writing projects draw heavily on linguistic and intrapersonal intelligences, but consider the chart above for other possible intelligences that can be addressed at each stage in the writing process.

References

Armstrong, Thomas. *Multiple Intelligences in the Classroom.* Alexandria, VA: Association for Supervision and Curriculum Development. 1994.
Gardner, Howard. *Frames of Mind: The Theory of Multiple Intelligences.* 1983. NY: Basic Books. 1985.
Grow, Gerald. "Writing and Multiple Intelligences." June 1996. Online. Internet. 18 July 1996. Available HTTP://www.famu.edu/sjmga/ggrow/7In/7IntelIndex.html

DR. WANDA B. SCHINDLEY, NORTHEAST TEXAS COMMUNITY COLLEGE

INTEGRATING THE LANGUAGE ARTS

INTEGRATING THE TEACHING OF THE LANGUAGE ARTS CREATES THE MAGIC THAT HELPS STUDENTS LEARN.

Thirty-five years ago in a rural classroom, a creative woman integrated the teaching of reading, writing, speaking, listening, and even math. Her second-graders built a playhouse-size cardboard post office, made block-letter signs, wrote and read letters, counted tokens to buy and sell stamps, and spoke and listened as postmaster and customer. That teacher had not read research on the integration of skills or on using whole-language methodologies, but she knew intuitively what worked. I don't remember much about my experiences in kindergarten, first grade, third grade, or even fourth grade, but I remember well that second-grade classroom; I remember the magic of learning.

Integrating the teaching of the language arts creates the magic that helps students learn. It creates a context for developing language proficiency and relevancy for reading, writing, speaking, and listening activities. Students grow through active participation in language activities. Although categorizing the language arts may be necessary for describing curricula, in the classroom language skills are best learned through doing—through seeking meaning from texts, through writing and revising, and through sharing ideas and opinions.

WANDA SCHINDLEY IS A SPECIALIST FOR THE WORKPLACE PARTNERSHIP.

SUGGESTIONS FOR INTEGRATING THE LANGUAGE ARTS

• Involve students in prereading activities such as discussion, writing, research, and sometimes, vocabulary development. Creating a context for reading involves discussing themes and related issues, making predictions, recalling prior knowledge and related experiences, and searching out related information.

• Involve students in prewriting activities such as discussion of possible topics and details, reading model essays, searching out and reading informative pieces, reading literary writing, interviewing others, and sentence-combining or sentence-revision activities. Like the writing process itself, development of language proficiency involves a recursive practice in reading, writing, thinking, speaking, and listening.

• Make writing assignments relevant by having students write for and share with real audiences for meaningful purposes. Have students share their writing with peers.

• Relate correctness—development of conventional usage, spelling, grammar, and punctuation—to the revising and proofreading stages of the writing process. Correctness becomes important to students when it helps them communicate their ideas clearly. Class review of grammar, usage, and mechanics can be done with sentences from student papers and with sentence-combining, sentence manipulation, and vocabulary activities.

• Approach standard usage in speech as appropriate for use in business and academic situations, not as a replacement for all vernacular expression.

• Encourage student involvement in class discussion, team study groups, cooperative research projects and presentations, group creative writing, and role playing.

• Foster an atmosphere in which students feel free to respond to, to evaluate, and to critique literature.

• Act as facilitator in students' discovery processes through activities that encourage creative and critical thinking—decision making and problem solving—and allow students to take more responsibility for their own learning.

Create an atmosphere of cooperation, caring, and high expectations.

*L*IKE THE WRITING PROCESS ITSELF, DEVELOPMENT OF LANGUAGE PROFICIENCY INVOLVES A RECURSIVE PRACTICE IN READING, WRITING, THINKING, SPEAKING, AND LISTENING.

USING THE TEXTBOOK IN AN INTEGRATED APPROACH

Literature selections are provided in each chapter to give students opportunities to read before writing. However, this book can be used in a literature-driven approach as the springboard to writing by incorporating into the study of each chapter ample readings from literature anthologies, magazines, and student papers. The features in each chapter of the *Teacher's Edition* contain suggestions for integrating additional literature selections (**Integrating the Language Arts: Literature Link**), using a variety of group activities (**Cooperative Learning**), and encouraging students to use higher-level thinking skills to contribute to class discussion (**Critical Thinking**).

The **Common Error** and **Integrating the Language Arts** features in each chapter of the *Teacher's Edition* contain suggestions for integrating the teaching of grammar, usage, and mechanics into the stages of the writing process, as do the suggestions for integrating the language arts in the introduction of each composition chapter.

Sample Integrated Lesson Plan

A lesson on creative writing might begin with a class discussion about stories and poems.

Guiding questions encourage students to share attitudes: What kinds of stories/poems do you like?

—to recall prior knowledge about the structure of stories: What happened toward the end of a favorite story? How did you feel as you read? What name do we use for the most exciting or scary part of the story?

—to synthesize knowledge about fiction: What characteristics do stories and poems have in common? What other forms might a writer use to tell about an event or to express an idea?

Teachers can use group stories and poems as guided practice and as a non-threatening introduction to creative writing. A group activity in which students write noun poems might begin informal grammar instruction. Small groups can then choose from the list of topics for noun-metaphor poems.

Example: Dreams are
    Envelopes of hope,
    Fluffy clouds that
      disappear in daylight,
    Stars to reach for.

As groups begin to revise and proofread their poems for class presentation, teachers might focus on the use of commas and end marks.

When students begin the creative writing assignments, they are again given opportunities to write, discuss, read, think, talk, revise, and so on. Instruction in usage and mechanics can be provided to the class as the need arises, to partners as they debate an issue of correctness, and to individuals in one-on-one conferences.

Finally, students share their work with the class—perhaps anonymously at first, but eventually as accomplished and proud authors who share a firsthand knowledge of the creation of literature and a greater understanding of language. ❧

DR. JUDITH IRVIN, FLORIDA STATE UNIVERSITY

BECOMING A STRATEGIC READER

BECOMING A PROFICIENT READER AND WRITER IS A LIFE-LONG PROCESS.

In the past, reading was viewed as a simple task of decoding words. Educators generally emphasized the strategies of sounding out words, recognizing words out of context by sight, and reproducing content by answering comprehension questions. Research has led to a new conceptualization of the reading process—that, as writing is, reading is a complex learning process. In this new view, readers construct meaning from a text, not simply by decoding words, but by using reading strategies that incorporate and expand their prior knowledge. Prior knowledge includes not only readers' knowledge of the definition of a word, but also their responses to the context of the word—the entire text. Careful reading of a text using strategies like those explained in the following pages will allow readers to use their prior knowledge to create meaning and to extend their understanding of a text. As students become more involved in developing and reflecting on their reading and learning processes, meaning may now be defined as "something that is actively created rather than passively received" (Buehl, 1995, p. 8).

As will be explained, the process of constructing meaning both in writing and in reading is not linear, but recursive and interactive and helps to create a richer, more productive experience.

THE READER

Former models of reading focused on whether or not students had acquired specific skills. Recent models of reading allow that students come to learning with previous information about particular topics, with definite attitudes about reading, writing, and school in general, and with varying motivations for reading and learning. It is the interaction of what is in reader's minds with what is on the page within a particular context that helps them to comprehend what they read.

SCHEMA THEORY

It is impossible for readers to learn anything new without making connections to their prior knowledge or schemata. The schemata are like the components of an elaborate filing system inside every reader's head. If the reader's mind is the filing system, the schemata, then, are the ideas contained in the file folders within the system. For example, you probably have a schema for a computer, a mental picture of what a computer is and what it does. You probably also bring to that basic picture many other associations, ideas, and feelings. If you use computers regularly, your schema may include positive feelings about their limitless applications. If the computer revolution has left you yearning for the days of yellow note pads and typewriters, then you may have feelings of anxiety as you approach a computer manual. For teachers, it is important to remember that readers encountering new ideas must often be shown how the new material fits into their existing filing system.

THE TEXT

The content, format, and organization of a text are factors that make a text easy or difficult for students to understand. If students' schemata tell them that a particular assignment will be difficult or unrelated to their personal experiences, they will probably be reluctant to read it and will most likely not make much meaning of it. The students know with one look that they will read and respond to a poem differently than they will to a chapter in a science book. A teacher should be prepared to exercise flexibility and sensitivity in presenting the text so as to encourage students to use their schemata to enhance their reading experiences.

THE CONTEXT

Readers and writers approach texts differently, and they also vary their processes according to their purposes. If they are reading for pleasure, students may skip over a difficult word or read an exciting passage more than once. But if they are reading for class, skipping a word might mean not understanding an important concept needed in class the next day. A reader's purpose for reading also dictates how attentive he or she is to details and how much effort will be put into remembering what is read. Similarly, when and where the reading is done affects the reading process. Readers will make less meaning from texts they read on the bus or with thoughts of a sick relative in the backs of their minds than they might make if they had a quiet space and clear thoughts.

STRATEGIC LEARNING

Suppose that during a racquetball game you hit a straight shot down the right side of the court, and your opponent misses the ball. The point is yours. This well-placed shot may have been a lucky one, or it may have been the result of a strategy. Before you hit the ball, you may have noticed that your opponent was standing in the middle of the court, and you remembered that she is left-handed with a weak backhand. You hit the ball to exactly the right spot deliberately and strategically. The analogy of planning your shots in a game can be applied to learning.

Strategic learning involves analyzing the reading task, establishing a purpose for reading, and then selecting strategies for making meaning. A strategy is a conscious effort by the reader to attend to comprehension while reading. Weinstein explains that "learning strategies include any thoughts or behaviors that help us to acquire new information in such a way that the new information is integrated with our existing knowledge" (Weinstein, p. 590). Strategies occur before reading when readers activate prior knowledge by thinking and discussing the title and topic and by identifying a purpose for reading. They also occur during reading as readers use context to figure out unknown words and monitor their understanding, and beyond the reading when readers summarize or evaluate the main ideas of the text.

METACOGNITION

Reading is often referred to as a cognitive event. It is also a metacognitive event. Cognition refers to a person's using the knowledge and skills he or she possesses; metacognition refers to a person's awareness and understanding of that knowledge and conscious control over those skills. It is essentially, thinking about one's way of thinking. Metacognition, then, is knowing how and when to use strategies to solve problems in understanding. It develops as a reader matures, usually during adolescence, but it can be taught and strengthened by explicit instruction and practice.

Becoming a proficient reader and writer is a life-long process. Accepting the premise that meaning is constructed in the mind of the learner implies that metacognitive abilities must be operational for learning to occur. Adolescents are just beginning to be able to consider their own thinking in relation to the thoughts of others. The middle and high school level years are an ideal time to develop the metacognitive abilities that will serve them throughout life.

STRATEGIC READING

Good readers are strategic, and being strategic involves the metacognitive abilities to think, plan, and evaluate their understanding of a text.

Adolescence is partially characterized by a new capacity for thought. Students are moving from the concrete stage (able to think logically about real experiences) to the formal stage (able to consider "what ifs," think reflectively, and reason abstractly). This intellectual change is gradual and may occur in different contexts at different times for different students.

Formal thinking is just developing during the middle school years, so concrete examples and step-by-step modeling are necessary to move students to the more abstract metacognitive thinking. The following concepts help students to focus on their own reading strategies:

- activating schema (prior knowledge) and building background information
- predicting and confirming
- organizing information
- drawing conclusions
- making inferences
- text differences
- retelling/summarizing

As strategic readers, before they read, students use their prior knowledge by making predictions about the content of a selection, to establish a clear purpose for reading, and to think about reading strategies they might use as they read. During the reading process, students use context to connect what they are reading with what they already know and to continue to monitor and evaluate their comprehension. And after completing their reading, students review their reading through peer discussion, class discussion, preparing entries in Reader's Logs, and using graphic organizers.

New research and practice in literacy learning reflects a more holistic view of understanding text. Students need opportunities to apply reading strategies to a variety of texts in a meaningful manner. ❦

References

Buehl, D. *Classroom Strategies for Interactive Learning.*
Schofield, WI: Wisconsin State Reading Association, 1995.
Weinstein, C.E. "Fostering Learning Autonomy Through the Use of Learning Strategies." *Journal of Reading* 30 (1987): 590-595.

SHOW DON'T TELL: THE ORIGINAL VIRTUAL REALITY

GOOD WRITING

THAT SHOWS

TAKES US

THROUGH THE

EXPERIENCE . . .

Perhaps one of the oldest pieces of advice offered by master writers to neophytes is "show don't tell." Likewise, one of the most frequent pieces of advice offered by teachers to fledgling student writers is "show don't tell."

The truth is the old "show don't tell" adage lives as the original virtual reality and makes sense to students if presented that way. Think about it. Our brains receive and process sensory signals from our environment through our five senses in order to make sense of our world, our experiences. Good writing that shows takes us through the experience; it excites the brain by wrapping pictures and sounds, tastes, smells and movements around its readers and immersing their senses in such a way that the writing actually creates another world. Catherine Drinker Bowen, biographer and writer on musical subjects, puts it more poetically, "Writing, I think, is not apart from living. Writing is a kind of double living."

Phrased in the positive, this "showing," this "going through the experience" causes the reader to feel an immediacy, a vitality, and an authenticity. When we're finished reading writing that shows, we often think, "I wish this wouldn't end." Flip-flopping to the negative, writing devoid of this "showing" reads flat, seems plastic, and bores the brain. If we even finish reading writing that tells, we find ourselves yawning and asking, "What did I just read?"

But there's an irony in "show don't tell." The maxim itself tells. It's right up there with "develop your writing" and "liven those verbs." There is no doubt about it—the advice is sound—it's just too abstract. Therein lies the rub. What can we teachers do to make "show don't tell" more concrete, more understandable for students? I'd like to share five ways to involve students in learning this concept. Students

• Analyze the work of published authors

• Compare telling writing to showing writing

• Identify telling parts in their own writing

• Replace the telling parts of their writing with showing passages

• Recognize and use "show don't tell" as an elaboration technique

ANALYZING THE WORK OF PUBLISHED AUTHORS

When examining the work of published authors, I start with Mark Twain's words, "Don't say the old lady screamed. Bring her on and let her scream." It's a great quote that begs great questions, "What does Twain mean?" "How might we describe her?" "Where is she?" "What words could we use to hear her scream?" "Why is she screaming?" It's fun to divide the room—half tells about the old lady, while the other half shows. Students of all ages delight in the comparison and begin their move toward understanding.

Will Hobbs, noted YA author, says it this way, "Let's say I almost drowned last summer, when a rip tide was taking me out to sea, and I'm trying to tell a reader what it was like: 'I was drowning. It was really bad. I thought I was going to die…' Now, is my writing coming to life? Does the reader feel what it was like? Not really. Did I tell, or did I show? I told. I didn't use the five senses. Where's the taste of salt water, the powerful tug of the rip tide, the voices at the shore dimming, the squawk of a gull?" (Hobbs, 19).

Now what Hobbs suggests is pure virtual reality. No one really wants to experience drowning, but if the writer crafts the experience by showing not telling then the reader experiences the virtual reality of drowning. It works this way because of the sensory signals the words conjure; the brain makes a connection and consequently makes meaning. Since our senses are the primary information gatherers, constantly sending signals to the brain, Hobbs invites student writers to stimulate all five senses through the power of words. That way, after the brain has reconstructed and synthesized the signals, it makes an identification and the reader understands. Helping that connection equals good writing.

Once students awaken to "show don't tell" in their writing it becomes an excellent technique for literary analysis. Imagine students quibbling over colonist Edward Winslow's letter to a friend in England, pointing out how much more powerful it would have been had he taken his friend through the experience of the "harvest being gotten in" instead of just telling him. Or picture a group of students eagerly identifying examples of showing not telling in *The Red Badge of Courage*. After reading, "One of the wounded men had a shoeful of blood. He hopped like a schoolboy in a game. He was laughing hysterically…." (Crane, 44), it is unlikely they would settle for, "One man was shot in the foot. He was in pain."

COMPARE TELLING WRITING TO SHOWING WRITING

One of the attributes of showing writing is specificity and concern for detail. Using comparisons of different versions of the same story helps students see this. For example, take the passage that first describes Baba Yaba in the Russian, Romania, Yugoslavian, Polish folktale called by titles such as "The Doll," "The Doll in Her Pocket," "Vasalisa the Wise," "Vassilisa the Wise," "Vasilisa the Beautiful," "Baba Yaga and Vasilisa the Brave," or simply "Vasilisa."

Version One: "When they had entered the hut the old witch threw herself down on the stove, stretched out her bony legs and said…" (Sierra, 97).

Version Two: "When Vasilisa entered the hut, Baba Yaga was already sitting in her chair by the fire. Her black eyes sparkled as she fixed them on the girl" (Mayer).

Version Three: "Suddenly the forest was filled with a terrible noise, and Baba Yaga came flying through the trees. She was riding in a great iron mortar and driving it with a pestle, and as she rode, she swept away her trail with a kitchen broom" (Winthrop, 17).

Finally we come to Version Four. This version is embedded in the penetrating psychological study *Women Who Run With the Wolves: Myths and Stories of the Wild Woman Archetype* by Clarissa Pinkola Estes.

Now the Baba Yaga was a very fearsome creature. She traveled not in a chariot, not in a coach, but in a cauldron shaped like a mortar which flew along all by itself. She rowed this vehicle with an oar

shaped like a pestle, and all the while she swept out the tracks of where she'd been with a broom made of long-dead persons' hair.

And the cauldron flew through the sky with Baba Yaga's own greasy hair flying behind. Her long chin curved up and her long nose curved down, and they met in the middle. She had a tiny white goatee and warts on her skin from her trade in toads. Her brown-stained fingernails were thick and ridged like roofs, and so curled over she could not make a fist (Estes, 77).

Juxtaposing these versions (or versions of other literary pieces) illuminates the power of "show don't tell." While the first three versions, taken from children's literature, rely on pictures to convey most of the detail, even the slowest student will see how ably Estes crafted her showing of Baba Yaga from the opening, somewhat telling statement, through the layers of detail, calling upon each of the reader's senses to prove Baba Yaga's fearsomeness.

Again, after an exercise such as this, students no longer write, "She was ugly." They are no longer satisfied with "She was a witch." Their journey into the lushness of writing and literature is enriched.

IDENTIFYING TELLING PARTS IN THEIR OWN WRITING

Armed now with clearly concrete experiences between telling and showing in writing, the students are better able to assess their own writing with new eyes and finding parts to improve is an awesome cognitive task, especially for adolescents.

As students reread their work,

they simply highlight the telling statements, share and discuss them with peers or teacher, and ultimately decide if each is fine as it is (some telling is inevitable in any piece of writing) or if it needs reworking. This process not only invites higher-level thinking and decision-making, but it also paves the way by patterning the brain for the day-to-day coping of considerations based on importance, need, aptness, and priority.

REPLACE THE TELLING PARTS OF THEIR WRITING WITH SHOWING PASSAGES

This represents the pith of the showing/telling dichotomy. When students become facile enough to enliven their writing with powerful passages that show not tell, they have learned the concept. Following is an example from Adrian's writing. He highlighted his first three sentences:

I stayed over at Robert's house last Friday. We were going camping. That was our favorite thing to do even though we only pretended.

On his next draft he replaced those telling with this showing passage:

I was spending Friday night at Robert's house, so our camping gear was strewn across the backyard. We pretended we had pitched camp in the outback of Australia, so we called each other "mate" alot.

"Ay, mate," I'd call even though we were pretty close to each other in that backyard. "Let's take a walkabout." (I had seen a movie about that.)

"Ay, mate," he'd call back louder. "Let's throw some shrimp on the barbee." (I knew he saw that commercial on T.V.)

Finally, we went to bed. Robert had asthma and was lying in the tent on his cot wheezing like a water pump gone dry. My buddy did many things better than me, but I envied his asthmatic wheeze the most. That night he wheezed out a little tune in his sleep and I accompanied him on the drums by playing my stomach and cot.

While Adrian did some throat clearing first, the passage about Robert's asthma takes us through what Adrian went through. It shows promise and a grasp of the "show don't tell" concept.

RECOGNIZE AND USE "SHOW DON'T TELL" AS AN ELABORATION TECHNIQUE

I opened the novel in full view of the class. "Take out some paper and write down these sentences," I invited.

I remember the day Claire Louise started first grade. . . . She had on a red dress. . . . Mother made all our clothes. . . . She had a book satchel my grandmother bought for her. . . . That was a Saturday (Arnold, 7–8).

"What do you think about that writing?" I asked.

Students, who typically want to please the teacher, began by tenta-

tively, and without much enthusiasm, saying, "It's O.K." But then they quickly pulled the turn-about and asked, "Who is Claire Louise?" "Why are you reading this?"

I continued to probe. "She's a character in this novel, but I really want to know what you think of the writing."

Eventually a brave soul admitted, "It sounds dull." Another agreed and collectively they determined it was definitely telling not showing.

At this point I wrote ELABORATION on the board. I explained how showing helps the writer achieve an elaborated piece, one that reveals depth of thought. Under "elaboration" I wrote D.I.D. I told the students that although there are many ways to achieve this depth, these letters stood as a mnemonic device to remember at least three of them.

Their first response was "dialogue," which we had worked on previously and which is one way to achieve elaboration. We talked about that, but I wanted them to explore further. After some nudges and discussion, they came up with DESCRIPTION, ILLUSTRATION, DETAIL.

Together we defined DESCRIPTION by comparing it to a camera shot in movies. It's the long shot as in "the gray house sitting way up on the hill in the distance." Following that analogy, we defined DETAIL as a close-up as in "the run-down gray house squatted on a crumbling foundation. Its paint puckered and peeled as one shutter banged against the wood like some large, slow-witted woodpecker. Weeds marked flower beds and masked a stone walkway lead-

ing to the discolored, stained back door." ILLUSTRATION gave us a tussle. What finally worked was inserting the phrase "for instance" as a reminder that an illustration serves as an example, a support for a telling sentence.

Then I told them I would read the passage from the novel exactly as it was written and cautioned them to listen for D.I.D.

I remember the day Claire Louise started first grade. Everyone claims I'd have been too young to remember that, that at two years old I couldn't possibly remember Claire Louise starting school. But I do remember. She had on a red dress. Red was always my favorite color, still is for that matter. The dress was red checks and had a starched white collar and puffy white sleeves with white cuffs on them. And the belt that went with the dress my mother bought from the store to go with it, the dress she made herself. Mother made all our clothes. Mostly she made Claire Louise's clothes and I wore them four years later. And Claire Louise even had red socks to go with her dress and she wore her black and white saddle oxfords that my mother bought to be her school shoes. She had a book satchel my grandmother bought for her, and all the school supplies the drugstore had printed on the first-grade list on the lowest shelf. She had those in the book bag. She had carefully printed her name on everything

that went in her bag. We watched her do it, my mother and me. I sat in my mother's lap and watched Claire Louise get ready for her first day at school. That was a Saturday, I'm sure, because I can remember the sound of the lawn mower as Claire Louise carefully wrote her name, and my father only mowed on Saturday morning.

The students caught the big picture, the description of the narrator on her mother's lap. They reveled in all the details of color of collar, belt, and satchel. They realized the moving proved to be an illustration, a proof. (This technique can be used with any rich piece of writing.)

They were ready, once again, to reenter their writing. They added some description and lots of detail. One young man asked, "Now what's illustration again?" I told him to find a telling sentence in his writing. He offered, "My little brother loves me." I asked him to insert "for instance" and give me an example. After some thought, he said, "For instance, he runs down the sidewalk to meet me after school and gives me a high-five."

"Perfect," I said. Although none of us really saw his little brother running to meet him, hand extended, we did see it in the virtual reality of writing that shows. ❧

References

Arnold, Janis. *Daughters of Memory*. Chapel Hill, NC: Algonquin Books, 1991.

Crane, Stephen. *The Red Badge of Courage*. New York: W.W. Norton & Co., 1962.

Estes, Clarissa Pinkola. *Women Who Run With the Wolves: Myths and Stories of the Wild Woman Archetype*. New York: Ballantine Books, 1992.

Hobbs, Will. "Bringing Your Words to Life." *R & E Journal*. (Spring, 1996): 19–21.

Mayer, Marianna. *Baba Yaga and Vasilisa the Brave*. New York: Morrow Junior Books, 1994.

Sierra, Judy. *The Oryx Multicultural Folktale Series: Cinderella*. Phoenix, AZ: The Oryx Press, 1992.

Winthrop, Elizabeth. *Vasilissa the Beautiful*. New York: Harper Collins, 1991.

BLOCK SCHEDULING

A BLOCK SCHEDULE ARRANGES CLASSES INTO LONGER TIME PERIODS...

WHAT IS BLOCK SCHEDULING?

A block schedule arranges classes into longer time periods of approximately ninety minutes. Classes may meet every day for one semester—called the A/B or the rotating block. Or, they may meet every other day for a full year—called the 4 x 4 or semester block.

WHAT ARE ITS BENEFITS?

There are several advantages to implementing block scheduling, both for the teacher and for the students. Block scheduling

- Is economical, allowing teachers to teach more students and requiring fewer textbooks and other materials.
- Allows more time for instruction and for more personalized student-teacher interaction.
- Promotes teaching a concept or skill in more depth.
- Affords more time for teachers to identify and respond to student needs and performances.
- Provides the opportunity for structuring interdisciplinary coordination.

- Provides for greater opportunities for multiple and creative teaching strategies and for use of more resources during a given class period (library resources, laboratory space, computers).
- Allows for varied assessment strategies.
- Reduces the number of classes students must prepare for each day.
- Allows students to earn more credits each year.
- Decreases the number of teachers students must adjust to.

HOW DOES BLOCK SCHEDULING AFFECT TEACHING?

In preparing for a block scheduling classroom, teachers should carefully examine their curriculum and be prepared for adjustments. Consider the following guidelines:
- Pare down the curriculum rather than padding it to fill an extended teaching period. Don't try to teach twice as much. This practice will frustrate you and your students. Covering less material can actually be more effective in block scheduling classes. The key phrase has been "more is less" because teach-

ers have taught fewer concepts but have taught them in more depth.
- Concentrate on a few key skills or concepts that you want students to master at the end of the course and plan your units and lessons around these skills.
- Think about the class period in terms of smaller time segments. Most adults can maintain focus for only twenty to thirty minutes. The average students are no different, so plan to their advantage—base your lessons on shorter, attention-getting activities and allow students to work in groups on longer, more enriching assignments.
- Use authentic assessments such as portfolios; peer groups and peer evaluation; and displays of student products. Allow students to learn and demonstrate mastery of their learning in ways that are successful for them.

HOW DOES A TYPICAL BLOCK-SCHEDULE CLASS PERIOD WORK?

The following is a general format that suggests the flexibility and variety that a teacher can explore in a block scheduling classroom.

Sample format for one ninety-minute class

1. Mini lesson/introduction/warm-up (5–15 minutes)
2. Small group/Independent work or reading (20–25 minutes)
   - Student generated question and answers
   - Teacher generated work
   - Manipulative activity (sentence strips, sequencing)
   - Oral reading
3. Large group work/Independent work (20–25 minutes)
4. Review, regroup, reteach (20–25 minutes)

By varying activities, a teacher can maintain students' attention, increase students' motivation, and create an environment that encourages learning.

HOW DOES BLOCK SCHEDULING AFFECT THE LANGUAGE ARTS CLASSROOM?

Block scheduling is particularly conducive to the teaching of language arts.

• The ninety-minute class period allows for a more seamless blending of reading, writing, language, and speaking and listening.

• Because the lessons are less fragmented, the connections between the strands can be seen more readily. For example, if literature is used as a springboard for writing, there is an opportunity for a more immediate shift from literature to writing.

• Also, for teaching the writing process in a block schedule, a watchful teacher can tailor the time spent on each stage of the process to fit the needs of the students. If students need more time revising than they do brainstorming, that is figured into a schedule that allows for more flexibility. If students need periodic mini-lessons on the uses of quotation marks, the block schedule allows for that, too.

EXPECTATIONS FOR TRANSITION/ TROUBLESHOOTING

Achieving a successfully balanced learning experience in a block schedule may take some time. However, keeping careful records of planning and daily activities and a file of ideas for varying instruction can help. Consider establishing a support group with other teachers. Sharing common problems and success stories will help the transition.

In the classroom, some regularity will help students adjust to the longer time period. Consider the following ideas for instruction:

- Begin class quickly.
- Deliver short lectures only.
- Allow some student movement/ interaction.
- Monitor student responses well.
- Vary activities every 15-20 minutes on average.
- State expectations very clearly before students begin any activity.

For classroom management, try some of the following suggestions:

• Devote a portion of team meetings to discussion of the block.
• Color code class rosters, student files, gradebook by day.
• Keep a notebook to record after class the basics of each lesson.
• Fill in only the dates in your gradebook on which classes actually meet to help avoid confusion regarding dates students were in class.
• Consider allowing students a short break from time to time during a longer class period.

CONCLUSION

Although it is a fairly new concept in education, block scheduling seems to be popular with educators because it provides them with the opportunity to control the time factor in learning. In schools that have instituted block scheduling, no longer are students racing from one 50-minute class to another, attending as many as seven classes in a single day. Teachers are not having to rush to get through the period's objectives before the bell.

In general, teachers and students seem to like longer classes. According to John O'Neil in his article "Finding Time to Learn," most teachers don't want to return to traditional scheduling—not because things are easier in block scheduling, but because they think they have been more successful in working with their students. ❦

*B*LOCK SCHEDULING SEEMS TO BE POPULAR WITH EDUCATORS BECAUSE IT PROVIDES THEM WITH THE OPPORTUNITY TO CONTROL THE TIME FACTOR IN LEARNING.

❦❦❦❦❦

BY HILVE FIREK, COLLEGE OF EDUCATION AND ALLIED PROFESSIONS, UNIVERSITY OF NORTH CAROLINA AT CHARLOTTE

TECHNOLOGY IN THE LANGUAGE ARTS CLASSROOM

IF WE'VE LEARNED ONE THING FROM TECHNOLOGY, IT IS THAT WE EXIST IN A STATE OF FLUX.

If we've learned one thing from technology, it is that we exist in a state of flux. What is cutting-edge today may be obsolete tomorrow. What the following day will bring is anybody's guess. But regardless of the frenetic changes, the need to communicate effectively in writing remains constant.

So, how do we teach composition in the glare of the bright lights, pulsating sounds, and moving images that are everywhere in today's technologically-fascinated society? Simple. We use the lights, sounds, and images to build bridges between popular culture and the culture of the classroom. We use what is familiar to teach what is new. *In essence, we use technology to inspire students to want to learn to write.*

TELEVISION AND VIDEOS

Let's begin with a technology your students know extremely well— television. If you doubt the intimate relationship our young people have with TV, listen to them talk about the characters and situations on the latest sitcoms, soaps, or prime-time dramas. Or eavesdrop on a discussion of the most popular music videos on MTV or BET. Without their even knowing it, these young adults have developed for themselves a rather complex understanding of plot, characterization, symbolism, and other literary devices used by the most skilled writers. The challenge for educators is to help students span the distance between what television has already taught them and what we, as facilitators of the language arts, are attempting to teach them.

Let's examine ways we might use television to reach students in teaching the writing process. If you spend an hour or two watching the shows your students watch, chances are you will encounter any number of situations that reflect the human condition. In a single segment, a program may explore the emotions of love, hate, jealousy, and desire through the dramatic elements of conflict and complications or through such devices as irony and satire. For the most part, the plot has a discernible beginning, middle, and end. Of course, setting plays a critical role in establishing tone; for example, a love affair set against the backdrop of a hospital emergency room differs from a summer romance on the beaches of California. Further, devices common in television, such as laugh and music tracks, steer viewers to specific responses.

The problem is that adolescents process this information that they see on TV without necessarily being cognizant of how each part contributes to the whole. Using this popular medium, teachers can help students recognize the numerous means by which messages are conveyed. Once they learn the tools that are utilized on television, students can build on this learning to understand the tools writers employ in their craft. In essence, by becoming critical viewers, students may more readily learn to see themselves as critical writers. For instance, if your students decide to change the format of a popular show from a situational comedy to a dramatic miniseries, what writing devices would they utilize? How would the dialogue change? How would the setting change? Would the characters develop differently?

By envisioning what they might see on the small screen, students can envision what they must put down on paper or key into their word-processing programs.

WORD PROCESSING AND DESKTOP PUBLISHING

Though most of us tend to think of word-processing software as an elementary tool that permits us to correct typos easily, most programs now offer features that serve to engage spatial learners in the written word. Simply by changing font styles and sizes and by incorporating such options as bold, italics, and underline, students can add a visual flair to their compositions impossible with a blue ballpoint pen. Additionally, many word-processing programs interface easily with desktop publishing software, thus providing users with the means to import clip art, digitized photos, charts, and graphs into their documents. The paintbrush feature found on many programs allows students to create their own illustrations, giving spatial learners the opportunity to express their thoughts in visual terms before embarking on the writing process.

The ample features of today's desktop publishing software encourage writers to experiment with eclectic blends of text and images to create new and ever-changing forms of communication where style conveys every bit as much as content. The increasing popularity among adolescents of alternative publications, known as *zines*, reflects this interest in multi-layered combinations of words, type styles, and graphics. Armed with computers, printers, and copiers, students turned off by the rigid structure of the five paragraph essay are using zines to experiment with voice, to share ideas, and to create unique products via a medium heretofore available only to professional writers (Williamson). By utilizing software commonly loaded on computers, young adults can begin to understand the connection between how messages are presented and how they are received. We teachers of the language arts can help our students incorporate this understanding.

AUTHENTIC COLLABORATION AND PUBLICATIONS: THE INTERNET

Netzines

As more and more schools across the country obtain Internet access, teens are establishing for themselves a writing-centered subculture that revolves around electronic versions of alternative publications, or *netzines*. Traditionally a forum for free expression, the Internet provides adolescents with the opportunity to share ideas through a creative blending of words, art, animation, sound, and video with little or no interference, or criticism, from adults. Jon Katz, in his article "The Rights of Kids in the Digital Age," asserts that America's youth is finding its identity tied inextricably to the digital world and the information age (122). Netzines created by and for kids are everywhere on the World Wide Web, and their often-uncensored formats may concern some parents and teachers.

Still, Internet access has ignited in many young people a desire, even a compulsion, to write. Since they have the freedom to play with words, young adults take risks with expression, experimenting with style, spelling, diction, capitalization, and punctuation in ways that proclaim a message of artistic experimentation. For example, young women who create electronic publications often refer to their creations as *gurl-* or *grrrl-zines;* in doing so, they have used alternative spellings to define themselves in a way other teens immediately recognize.

Netzines also give adolescents a chance to explore, in writing, topics of their own choosing, topics that are rarely addressed in the language arts classroom. Of course, kids discuss among themselves the issues frequently considered taboo in schools, but they also write untiringly about topics that may be considered too frivolous for the academic classroom or too embarrassing to share with a teacher, such as friends, dating, parents, fashion, cars, skating, and music.

Traditional Writing and Netzines

The idea of students writing and publishing their own magazines via computer technology is exciting, but most language arts teachers are expected, if not required, to teach standard methods of composition using standard rules of the English language. Describing a potential date as a wAy2KoOl chick may be acceptable in the underground press, but a similar statement on a job application might give a potential employer an excuse to join the education bashing that is so popular in this country. How then, might caring educators teach the rigors of composition without crushing the fervor teens show for writing?

The answer may reside in the zines themselves. If language arts teachers use zines, either the electronic or paper variety, to introduce written communication, they offer their students a chance to begin their writing journeys by learning to express themselves honestly and for real purpose. Interestingly, at least one study suggests that the writing young people do for their peers via the Net is often actually better than the writing they produce in traditional classroom assignments. In 1989, two researchers from the University of California at San Diego compared compositions written for teachers with those addressed to peers in other countries linked by the Internet. The compositions written and transferred by way of the Internet received distinctly better grades than those written for the teachers (Leslie 20).

EDUCATIONAL MULTIMEDIA PROGRAMS

There is also a whole new world of CD-ROM programs that address a variety of needs in the language arts classroom. These multimedia products capture the imaginations of even the most reluctant learners because of their dynamic nature and visual appeal. For example, Holt, Rinehart and Winston's CD-ROM software *Writer's Workshop* uses an environmental interface to engage students who might otherwise be completely disinterested in writing. It also includes music, a media center, author interviews, video

Internet Resources (If you cannot access an Internet address, use a simple Internet search to find a similar resource.)

Netzines

Edge: A bimonthly cyberzine for high-performance students.
  http://www.jayi.com/jayi/Fishnet/Edge
Virtually React: The webzine where teens make news
  http://www.react.com
Writes of Passage: The online source for teenagers
  http://www.writes.org/index.htm
Cyberschool Mag: Teen-zine
  http://www.cyberschoolmag.com
NANDO Next: The voice of the next generation
  http://www2.nando.net/links/nandonext/next.html
Spank!: Youth culture online
  http://www.spank.com
foxy: Another net-check/gurl ezine
  http://www.tumyeto.com/tydu/foxy/foxy.htm
E-zine FAQ: Frequently asked questions on creating ezines
  http://www.well.com/conf/f5/ezines.faq
Penworld@ A club for young writers, ages 7–15
  http://members.aol.com/callista21/penworld.htm

Writing Resources

Strunk's Elements of Style Online
  http://www.cc.columbia.edu/acis/bartleby/strunk
The Writers' Homepage
  http://www.rtpnet.org/~jacobs/index.html
Writer's Resource Center
  http://www.azstarnet.com/~poewar/writer/writer.html

The Purdue Online Writing Laboratory
  http://owl.english.purdue.edu
Dakota State University's Email Writing Lab
  owl@columbia.dsu.edu
The State University of New York at Albany's Email Writing Lab
  writing@albnyvms.albany.edu
George Mason University's Email Writing Lab
  wcenter@gmu.edu
The Grammar Hotline Directory
  http://www.infi.net/tcc/tcresourc/hotline.html
The Grammar Help Page
  http://www.hut.fi/~rvilmi/help/grammar_help

Finding Projects and Keypals Online

The Encyclopedia of Women's History
  http://www.teleport.com/~megaines/women.html
KidPub
  http://en-garde.com/kidpub/intro.html
Web66: A K-12 World Wide Web Project
  http://web66.coled.umn.edu
Kidlink
  http://www.kidlink.org

Using Technology in Writing

Voice of the Shuttle: Technology and Writing Page
  http://humanitas.ucsb.edu/shuttle/techwrit.html
The Alliance for Computers and Writing
  http://english.ttu.edu/acw
RhetNet: A Cyberjournal for Rhetoric and Writing
  http://www.missouri.edu/~rhetnet/index.html

---

clips, graphic organizers, photos, and online chat features to inspire students during prewriting, writing, or revising.

To involve students when teaching grammar, usage, and mechanics, Holt, Rinehart and Winston also offers *Language Workshop.* This award-winning CD-ROM program offers interactive instruction with options for on-screen self-assessment through performance-based practice. Along with these features for the student, *Language Workshop* has monitoring and assessment features exclusively for the teacher.

ON-LINE RESOURCES

Those of us who have attempted to teach research writing know that the struggle to engage young people in a systematic process of research can be tough. The Internet not only offers students the means by which they can publish their work, but also serves as a resource tool on topics of interest and on writing itself. Students who wouldn't be caught dead with a copy of Strunk's *Elements of Style* might not think twice about accessing the online version of the book.

Also, Net aficionados form a community of people, so that there is always an expert to be found on any subject, including composition. If students have World Wide Web access from home, they can do a keyword search for grammar and find a site that lists a state-by-state Grammar Hotline Directory. Or if they are too shy to speak aloud in class, they can post questions to tutors at several writing labs available through e-mail. Teachers just need to be aware that because these resources are sometimes public forums, the content on them can be unpredictable.

The Internet also serves as a resource for those of us who teach composition. If you access any major search engine, you will find a link to education-related sites; from there you can narrow your search as needed. On the World Wide Web teachers can find lesson plans, collaborative project ideas, supplementary materials, and even a netzine or two. And since teaching is all too often an isolated activity, many educators find reward in discussing their chosen field with colleagues in chat groups or on such e-mail discussion lists as the Dead Teachers Society.

Regardless of the position we take on the humans versus machines conflict, we cannot deny that technological innovations are now a part of everyday life. What still seems magical to us is commonplace to children who grow up expecting more than a hundred channels on their television sets and instant information from their computers. As concerned teachers, we can use technology to our own advantages—to incite interest, to simulate reality, and to open the world to our students. And if one of our goals as teachers of composition is to instill a love of writing—a need to write—then we owe it to our students to foster this love using all the tools we can find. ❧

References

Katz, Jon. "The Rights of Kids in the Digital Age." *Wired* July 1996: 120+

Leslie, Jacques. "Connecting Kids: On-line Technology Can Reform Our Schools." *Wired* Nov. 1993: 20-23.

Williamson, Judith. "Engaging Resistant Writers through Zines in the Classroom." College Composition and Communication Conference. Nashville, TN. March 1994.

BY DR. NORBERT ELLIOT, WRITING PROGRAM DIRECTOR, NEW JERSEY INSTITUTE OF TECHNOLOGY &
DR. KAREN GREENBERG, ASSOCIATE PROFESSOR, HUNTER COLLEGE OF THE CITY UNIVERSITY OF NEW YORK

THE DIRECT ASSESSMENT OF WRITING:

Notes For Teachers

HOW CAN ASSESSMENT STRATEGIES BE MODIFIED TO HELP BOTH TEACHERS AND STUDENTS?

Teachers spend a great deal of time assessing students' writing: They correct errors, offer suggestions, and assign grades. This process can be exhausting to teachers and discouraging for students. How can assessment strategies be modified to help both teachers and students?

Instruction and assessment can be aligned so that the two work together. To enable instruction and assessment to complement each other, teachers have turned to two relatively new methods of direct assessment: holistic scoring and portfolio assessment.

HOLISTIC SCORING

One of the most common methods of scoring writing samples is holistic scoring, a procedure based on the responses of con-cerned readers to a meaningful whole composition. Holistic scoring involves reading a writing sample for an overall impression of the writing and assigning the sample a score based on a set of consistent scoring criteria. Most holistic scoring systems use a scoring scale, or guide, that describes papers at six or eight different levels of competence.

Holistic scoring has many advantages:

1. It communicates to students that writing is a process leading to a unified, synergistic piece of writing.

2. Writing samples that have been holistically scored provide students with clear information about the quality of their writing, but they are less intimidating than grades or written critiques.

NORBERT ELLIOT, DIRECTOR OF THE WRITING PROGRAM AT THE NEW JERSEY INSTITUTE OF TECHNOLOGY.

3. Holistic scoring is rapid. Readers spend only minutes judging the total effect of a paper.
4. The criteria on a holistic scoring scale give teachers a vocabulary to use in discussing essays with students and their parents.
5. The process of developing holistic scoring guides and scoring writing samples enables teachers to share their unique responses to writing, as well as their evaluative criteria. If an entire department uses the same scoring guide, students will realize that effective writing has definable features upon which all of their English teachers agree.

Nevertheless, there are weaknesses to this method. It alone cannot, for instance, provide diagnostic information about specific writing proficiencies and deficiencies. The score cannot substitute for a teacher's detailed responses to an essay—the provocative notes in the margin, the encouraging comments at the end, etc. This weakness, however, can be overcome if teachers review papers with their students in light of the scoring criteria.

Another weakness is more serious. Using holistic scoring, teachers often consider only one piece of writing during assessment. If only one sample of writing is evaluated, then teachers may not get a representative idea of students' writing ability, because this ability does not exist in a vacuum but varies from day to day and across the aims and modes of writing. In response to this concern, teachers have investigated a second method of direct assessment.

KAREN GREENBERG, DIRECTOR OF THE NATIONAL TESTING NETWORK IN WRITING.

PORTFOLIO ASSESSMENT

Portfolio assessment allows writing teachers to evaluate various samples of students' work, taken at various times under various conditions. Consequently, portfolio assessment can provide a fuller portrait of writing abilities.

To begin portfolio assessment, teachers develop a series of writing assignments that express the goals of a course. For instance, a group of teachers might require their students to write papers based on each of James Kinneavy's aims: expressive writing (a journal entry), informative writing (a summary of a news article), literary writing (a short story), and persuasive writing (an editorial). Over time, students work on these papers both at home and in class. Portfolios can include other forms of communication that students have produced, such as artwork, audio recordings, or videotapes.

Teachers need not assess everything that is included in a portfolio. In fact, it is often preferable not to evaluate every piece of a student's writing. This strategy allows teachers to separate instruction and response from formed evaluation. Portfolio assessment, therefore, can be based on samples that the teacher, the student, or both consider to be the student's best writing.

Clearly, there are advantages to this method:
1. Because multiple samples are assessed, portfolio assessment is a valid, authentic evaluation.
2. Because the authenticity of the assessment is increased, the curriculum becomes enriched.

As teachers plan tasks, they debate curricular values and strategies, devise workable instructional schemes for the classroom, and design thoughtful evaluative criteria for assignments.

With portfolio assessment, students gain a more positive attitude toward writing. Because they invest in their writing, students seek both teacher and peer response, create multiple drafts, and revise for their readers. Over time, a school's entire writing program can become an exciting adventure in communication and critical thinking.

CONCLUSION

There is still much to be investigated about the evaluation of writing. What kind of assessment best suits the multiple literacies on which our democratic society rests? What kind of local assessments will best supplement large-scale assessment? How can assessment reveal more about effective teaching? Answers will have to come from those who know students best: their teachers. ✾

*P*ORTFOLIO ASSESSMENT ALLOWS WRITING TEACHERS TO EVALUATE VARIOUS SAMPLES OF STUDENTS' WORK, TAKEN AT VARIOUS TIMES UNDER VARIOUS CONDITIONS.

To the Teacher

A new feature in the Annotated Teacher's Edition *for* Elements of Writing *is the Chapter Planning Guide. Located at the beginning of each of the writing chapters, this four-page guide includes the features listed below. Within each guide, we have included lesson plans for you to use in customizing your instruction. The instructional choices and lesson pacing in these plans are only suggestions. We recognize that any determination of lesson planning must be based on the needs of your individual classrooms.*

Objectives
Identifies the major objectives covered in the chapter.

Writing-in-Process Assignments
Provides an overview of the cumulative writing assignments that culminate in the main writing assignment of the chapter. Also outlines the developmental skills addressed in the chapter exercises.

Cross-Curriculum feature
Workplace Writing feature
Vary with each writing chapter in the Pupil's Edition. These features suggest ways to tailor the writing instruction addressed in the chapter to either a cross-discipline writing activity or to a form of writing used in the workplace.

Integrating the Language Arts Chart
Offers a convenient overview of the different strands of the language arts curriculum as they are incorporated in the activities provided in the Pupil's Edition.

Suggested Integrated Unit Plan
Appears only with chapters that address a particular kind of writing, such as a personal narrative or the research paper. Provides teachers with a unit plan that addresses reading; writing; listening and speaking; and language.

Chapter Planning Guide—Pupil's Edition
Suggests lesson plans and pacing for the instructional material, writing assignments, and exercises in each writing chapter in the Pupil's Edition. Outlines plans for students at three levels of learning—**developmental, core,** and **accelerated**.

Suggested pacing can be used to develop lesson plans for either a block or a traditional schedule.

Chapter Planning Guide— Program Resources
Provides an overview of the many program resources that support the instruction for each segment of the chapter.

These resources include various blackline masters for practice and assessment, transparencies for reinforcement, and writing and language CD-ROMs for instruction and practice.

Elements of Writing: Curriculum Connections
Identifies the activities at the end of each writing chapter that incorporate a cross-disciplinary approach.

Assessment Options
Identifies the assessment materials that accompany *Elements of Writing*. Addresses summative, portfolio, on-going, and self-assessment opportunities for evaluation.

THE WRITING PROCESS COMES *Alive!*

If you're going to teach writing, *Elements of Writing* is *the* program to use. With *Elements of Writing,* students explore the writing process through unique lessons that take the puzzlement and perplexity out of the experience and put the excitement of discovery back in.

A Pupil's Edition that Shows *and* Explains

This student book opens up the writing process with an easy-to-follow, interactive style that hones students' writing skills and that talks to students in a friendly, encouraging tone. The program includes

- Brief, accessible segments of instruction immediately followed by practice
- Four writing models in *every* chapter to accommodate different learning styles
- Specific revision strategies for each major chapter
- A superb grammar handbook for reference and practice
- **NEW TO THIS EDITION!** More workplace writing; more grammar, usage, and mechanics; more student models; and even more attention to the revision process.

A Teacher's Edition at Work for You

In addition to pacing charts, program managers, and ideas for integrating workplace writing and reading skills, the *Elements of Writing* Annotated *Teacher's Edition* includes

Instructional Strategies to help you meet the needs of your students in efficient, effective, and creative ways.

- *Visual Connections*
- *Meeting Individual Needs*
- *Using the Selection*
- *A Different Approach*
- *Timesaver*
- *Critical Thinking*
- *Integrating the Language Arts*
- *Cooperative Learning*

Lesson Plans that provide clear and easy suggestions for managing the program at each step in the lesson.

- *Objectives*
- *Teaching the Lesson*
- *Guided* and *Independent Practice*
- *Assessment*
- *Reteaching*
- *Closure*
- *Motivation*
- *Extension*

Elements of Writing Supplements— The *joy* of Following Through

Every teacher knows the importance of following through. With *Elements of Writing,* you get a comprehensive array of support materials to help students follow through with a piece of writing and succeed in the writing process. Practice sheets, technology, instructional transparencies, activity booklets, and a whole lot more let your class discover just how joyful and relevant the writing process can be.

Teaching Resources

Outstanding materials reinforce concepts and strategies for students and provide teachers with support for reteaching and assessment. Supplements include

Academic and Workplace Skills

Practice for Assessment in Reading, Vocabulary, and Spelling

Practicing the Writing Process

Strategies for Writing

Word Choice and Sentence Style

Language Skills Practice and Assessment

Holistic Scoring: Prompts and Models

Portfolio Assessment

Fine Art and Instructional Transparencies

Transparencies for each major writing chapter, including teacher's notes and graphic organizers, prompt students to generate and organize ideas.

Available separately are other invaluable resources that will add an extra dimension to your instruction. These include **Merriam-Webster Middle School** and **High School Dictionaries, Holt Complete School Atlas, English Workshop,** and **Vocabulary Workshop.**

Multimedia and Technology

HRW Multimedia and Technology opens doors, expands options, and turns possibilities into realities. Connections that begin in the textbook move to a new level— a level that motivates students to get involved, to look farther, deeper, and beyond the page. **HRW Multimedia and Technology** also gives you the flexibility to teach the way you want, whether you have only a few computers or a writing lab for 30 students.

TEST GENERATOR A software package that allows you to revise, edit, or re-sort existing worksheets, quizzes, or tests for each grammar, usage, and mechanics chapter in the *Pupil's Edition.*

LANGUAGE WORKSHOP CD-ROMs for Macintosh® and Windows® A software program for your students that gives additional instruction and practice with grammar, usage, and mechanics, while engaging students with lively, interactive examples, prompts, and exercises.

WRITER'S WORKSHOP 1 AND 2 CD-ROMs for Macintosh® and Windows® Writing process software that provides visual and spoken prompts to guide students through the eight most common assignments, such as writing a story, an informative report, or a persuasive essay.

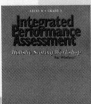

HOLISTIC SCORING WORKSHOP An effective teacher-tutorial program in integrated performance assessment that instructs you in the use of holistic scoring of student reading and writing and that gives you practice with actual student papers.

ELEMENTS OF
Writing

REVISED EDITION

Fourth Course

James L. Kinneavy

John E. Warriner

HOLT, RINEHART AND WINSTON
Harcourt Brace & Company

Austin • New York • Orlando • Atlanta • San Francisco
Boston • Dallas • Toronto • London

Critical Readers

Grateful acknowledgment is made to the following critical readers who reviewed pre-publication materials for this book:

Staff Credits

Associate Director: Mescal K. Evler
Executive Editors: Kristine E. Marshall, Robert R. Hoyt
Editorial Staff: Managing Editor, Steve Welch; *Editors,* Cheryl Christian, A. Maria Hong, Constance D. Israel, Kathryn Rogers Johnson, Karen Kolar, Christy McBride, Laura Cottam Sajbel, Patricia Saunders, Michael L. Smith, Suzanne Thompson, Katie Vignery; *Copyeditors,* Michael Neibergall, Katherine E. Hoyt, Carrie Laing Pickett, Joseph S. Schofield IV, Barbara Sutherland; *Editorial Coordinators,* Amanda F. Beard, Rebecca Bennett, Susan G. Alexander, Wendy Langabeer, Marie H. Price; *Support,* Ruth A. Hooker, Christina Barnes, Kelly Keeley, Margaret Sanchez, Raquel Sosa, Pat Stover
Permissions: Catherine J. Paré, Janet Harrington
Production: Pre-press, Beth Prevelige, Simira Davis; *Manufacturing,* Michael Roche
Design: Richard Metzger, *Art Director;* Lori Male, *Designer*
Photo Research: Peggy Cooper, *Photo Research Manager;* Tim Taylor, Sherrie Cass, *Photo Research Team*

1 2 3 4 5 6 7   040   00 99 98 97

Authors

James L. Kinneavy, the Jane and Roland Blumberg Centennial Professor of English at The University of Texas at Austin, directed the development and writing of the composition strand in the program. He is the author of *A Theory of Discourse* and coauthor of *Writing in the Liberal Arts Tradition*. Professor Kinneavy is a leader in the field of rhetoric and composition and a respected educator whose teaching experience spans all levels—elementary, secondary, and college. He has continually been concerned with teaching writing to high school students.

John E. Warriner developed the organizational structure for the Handbook of Grammar, Usage, and Mechanics in the book. He coauthored the *English Workshop* series, was general editor of the *Composition: Models and Exercises* series, and editor of *Short Stories: Characters in Conflict*. He taught English for thirty-two years in junior and senior high school and college.

Writers and Editors

Ellen Ashdown has a Ph.D. in English from the University of Florida. She has taught composition and literature at the college level. She is a professional writer of educational materials and has published articles and reviews on education and art.

Phyllis Goldenberg has an A.B. in English from the University of Chicago. She has been a writer and editor of educational materials in literature, grammar, composition, and critical thinking for over thirty-five years.

Elizabeth McCurnin majored in English at Valparaiso University. A professional writer and editor, she has over twenty-five years' experience in educational publishing.

John Roberts has an M.A. in English Education from the University of Kentucky. He has taught English in secondary school. He is an editor and a writer of educational materials in literature, grammar, and composition.

Alice M. Sohn has a Ph.D. in English Education from Florida State University. She has taught English in middle school, secondary school, and college. She has been a writer and editor of educational materials in language arts for seventeen years.

Raymond Teague has an A.B. in English and journalism from Texas Christian University. He has been children's book editor for the *Fort Worth Star-Telegram* for more than fifteen years and has been a writer and editor of educational materials for twelve years.

Carolyn Calhoun Walter has an M.A.T. in English Education from the University of Chicago. She has taught English in grades nine through twelve. She is a professional writer and editor of educational materials in composition and literature.

PART ONE

WRITING

PART ONE: WRITING
The following **Teaching Resources** booklets contain materials that may be used with this part of the Pupil's Edition.

WRITING HANDBOOK
- *Practicing the Writing Process*
- *Portfolio Assessment*
- *Practice for Assessment in Reading, Vocabulary, and Spelling* (for Ch. 3)

AIMS FOR WRITING
- *Strategies for Writing*
- *Holistic Scoring: Prompts and Models*
- *Portfolio Assessment*
- *Practice for Assessment in Reading, Vocabulary, and Spelling*

LANGUAGE AND STYLE
- *Word Choice and Sentence Style*
- *Portfolio Assessment*

SECRET FORCES *(pp. 2–15)*

OBJECTIVES

- To explore the ways that writers and writing affect the world
- To identify and analyze the aims of writing
- To compare and contrast the aims of writing

INTRODUCTION TO WRITING

SECRET FORCES

James L. Kinneavy

USING THE INTRODUCTION TO WRITING

This introduction to writing is just that—an introduction. It starts by talking briefly about the power of writing in peoples' lives, to emphasize that writing is more than just schoolwork. Next, it touches upon the two central focuses of the writing chapters in the textbook—the "how" of writing (modes) and the "why" of writing (aims).

The communication triangle graphically reflects the four major aims of James Kinneavy's theory of discourse. For more information, refer to Dr. Kinneavy's essay in the front of this book entitled "**Meet the Aims and Modes of Writing**," or to his two

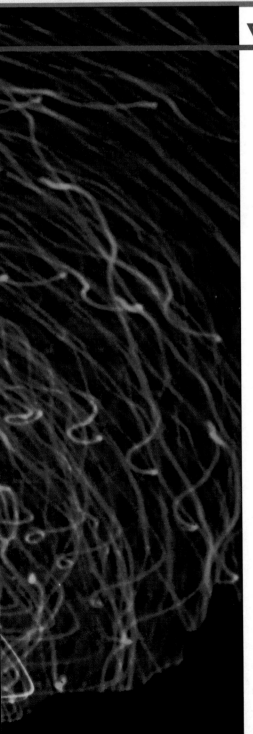

The world is not always what it seems. Even now you are surrounded by unseen forces. These powerful forces influence your life in many ways. They educate and entertain and connect. They make possible marvelous things like talking computers, telephones for people who are deaf, and manned space stations.

These forces are everywhere. You read about and see the results of them every day. In fact, you may become one of the **secret forces** yourself someday.

Have you guessed who these forces are? Do you know what gives them their power?

books, *A Theory of Discourse* and *Writing in the Liberal Arts Tradition.* ■

4

Who Are These Forces?

These forces are often unseen, but they aren't really mysterious. In fact, the secret forces are all around you. They're the writers, planners, and communicators of the world. They're hard at work in every office, factory, museum, and laboratory.

They're political leaders, scientists, environmentalists, and city planners who determine what your world will be like someday. They're advertising people, song writers, and cartoonists who affect how you look at the world today. They're Nobel and Pulitzer Prize winners, dynamic public speakers, or famous generals. They're unknown speechwriters for government figures who change the world. They're scriptwriters whose works delight you or move you or thrill you. They're newspaper or magazine writers who tell you about the world around you. The secret forces are people who see a need and set out to meet it.

Whether you see them or not, these forces are an important part of your life. They wield the power that shapes the world you live in.

What Is Their Power ?

Whether they're in the spotlight or behind the scenes, all writers and planners have in common the power of communication. *Writers* have something to say (a *subject*), someone to say it to (an *audience*), and a way to say it (a *language*). You can think of these elements as a communications triangle with language—both written and spoken—at its very center.

How Do They Communicate ?

The Writing Process

Powerful communication comes from presenting ideas effectively. Good writers use a general method for developing their ideas and communicating them clearly. The method is called the *writing process.* Different writers use the process differently—there's no right way or wrong way to go through it. But there are several steps, or stages, writers usually work through.

Prewriting	Thinking and planning; deciding what subject to write about and for what purpose and audience; gathering ideas and details; building a plan for presenting ideas
Writing	Writing a first draft; following some kind of plan to put ideas into sentences and paragraphs; including new ideas as they occur to you
Evaluating and Revising	Rereading the draft to decide about strengths and weaknesses; making changes to improve it
Proofreading and Publishing	Finding and fixing errors; making a final copy and sharing it with an audience

Why Do They Communicate ?

The Aims of Writing

Writers who are secret forces always have an *aim*—a purpose—in mind when they write. Sometimes they have more than one. But they know what they want to accomplish. There are four basic aims of writing: to inform, to persuade, to express oneself, and to create literature.

To Inform	Sometimes writers want to give information or to explain something to readers.
To Persuade	Writers may want to convince people to change their minds about something, or to stir people into action.
To Express Themselves	Sometimes writers want simply to explore their thoughts and feelings about something.
To Create Literature	Writers may use their talents to create literature—stories, poems, songs, and plays.

On the following pages, you'll read four models. They all have the same topic—home loan foreclosures—but each model exemplifies a different aim for writing. Notice how the writing changes when the aim changes.

INFORMATIVE WRITING

Mayor Asks for Federal Help

At a press conference earlier today, Mayor Jane Wing announced that she is asking for the federal government's help in dealing with the city's financial crisis.

Wing said that the closing of Resticon Corporation last fall caused the city's unemployment rate to triple. She added that sales tax revenues declined nearly fifty percent this quarter because the unemployed ex-Resticon workers had little or no money to spend. Property tax payments are late or unpaid for the same reason, adding to the city's financial crisis.

Wing said that her major concern is that many local homeowners can no longer meet their mortgage payments. She is requesting a federally backed program that will allow local banks to offer low-interest loans to people needing to refinance their homes.

"Such a loan program," she said, "will help prevent foreclosure and enable people to keep their homes while they seek other employment. By keeping our work force, we have a good chance of attracting another major employer like Resticon. The loan program will benefit the people now, and the city in the long run."

READER'S RESPONSE

1. If your family lived in Mayor Wing's city and were faced with foreclosure, would you be interested in the information in this article? What else might you want to know about the low-interest mortgage program?
2. What information does the article give about the reasons for the city's financial problems?

ANSWERS

Reader's Response

Responses will vary.

1. Many students will relate to the prospect of foreclosures in the community and will say they would be interested in the information in the article because it is presented to show the effect on the whole community. Students may want to know who would qualify for the loans, how much could be borrowed, where applications could be made, how soon the money could be loaned, and so on.

2. The economic conditions presented in the news story show the reader how one business's closing affects the entire community. The article states that the city's financial crisis began with the closing of Resticon Corporation. When this company failed, the unemployment rate tripled. Sales in the community dropped because workers couldn't afford to spend money; therefore, city sales tax revenues fell and property tax payments were uncollected. In addition, many homeowners could not meet their mortgage payments and were faced with foreclosure.

PERSUASIVE WRITING

Fellow Representatives, as you know, I represent the people of the fifth district of my state. It is an honor and a privilege. The people of the fifth district are a special group of people. Honest, hard-working, and self-reliant, they know the true value of the American life. They have dreamed the American dream and found it within their grasp. Now they are in danger of having it taken from them.

Recently, the fifth district has fallen on hard times. Resticon, the major employer, closed shop last fall, leaving more than 2,000 people unemployed. Such massive unemployment has affected the economic well-being of the entire area. Now, the people of my district are struggling to hang on. Their homes, the shining examples of their American dreams, are in danger of foreclosure.

Ladies and gentlemen, these good people are the backbone of America. Their dream is our dream. They work hard, they pay their taxes, they support their country in peace and war, they struggle to educate their children and pass on the dream to them. They need a chance to salvage that dream from the hard times surrounding them. They need our help.

Let's make it possible for them to hang on to their dreams. Please vote for this program that will allow these wonderful people to refinance their homes at low interest rates. Don't turn the best of America out into the street. I thank you, and the people of the fifth district thank you.

READER'S RESPONSE

1. If you were a member of Congress, would this speech persuade you to vote for the special legislation? Explain why or why not.
2. What ideas does this persuasive speech include that the informative article on page 8 does not?

ANSWERS
Reader's Response
Responses will vary.

1. Some students will say that this speech is persuasive because it plays on the emotions—the need for shelter and the dream of homeownership. Others will find that it is persuasive because it presents facts about the economic conditions in the fifth district—2,000 people are unemployed because the major employer closed. Encourage students to decide what is the most convincing to them.

2. This persuasive speech describes the people living in the district as honest, hard-working, and self-reliant. It compares the economic conditions of the community now with the American dream they are losing. It tells how the people in the fifth district live and explains what the speaker wants from the audience.

EXPRESSIVE WRITING

Dear Angie,

    I wanted to drop you a note to let you know I really miss you. The old neighborhood just isn't the same since you left. Since the plant closed, <u>For Sale</u> signs have gone up all over town. Dino and his family just left and let their house go back to the bank. They couldn't make their mortgage payments any more. He didn't even say good-bye, but he left a school picture and a rose from his mama's garden on our front porch. I cried for a long time.

    We don't know how long we can keep up the payments on our house. Dad says we may be able to refinance the house if the low-interest loan program goes through. He's working, and so is Mama, but they don't make near as much as they did at the plant. Our savings are almost gone. There's a rumor that a big company might start up in the old plant next spring. I'm scared that we won't be able to hang on till then.

    Write to me about life in sunny California. I can't imagine a year without winter. To tell the truth, it seems like winter all the time here since you and Dino left. Write me. Write me.

Love,
Celina

READER'S RESPONSE

1. Suppose you were Celina and watched your friends lose their homes. What would you think and feel?
2. In expressive writing, the writer explores or expresses thoughts and feelings. What thoughts and feelings does Celina express in this letter?

ANSWERS
Reader's Response

1. Students will respond in different ways to the letter. Many will say that if they were Celina, they would feel sad, dejected, lonely, or depressed. Others will say that watching friends lose their homes would make them angry, alienated, or resentful. Some may say they would be jealous of the friend who lives in a sunny community without economic problems.

2. Celina tells her friend that she really misses her and that the old neighborhood isn't the same since she left. She says she cried when Dino left, and since both friends are gone, it seems like winter all the time. She's afraid that her family won't be able to hang on financially until a new company opens up. She asks her friend to write to her about life in California.

LITERARY WRITING

LITERARY WRITING

HOME

by Gwendolyn Brooks

What had been wanted was this always, this always to last, the talking softly on this porch, with the snake plant in the jardiniere in the southwest corner, and the obstinate slip from Aunt Eppie's magnificent Michigan fern at the left side of the friendly door. Mama, Maud Martha, and Helen rocked slowly in their rocking chairs, and looked at the late afternoon light on the lawn and at the emphatic iron of the fence and at the poplar tree. These things might soon be theirs no longer. Those shafts and pools of light, the tree, the graceful iron, might soon be viewed possessively by different eyes.

Papa was to have gone that noon, during his lunch hour, to the office of the Home Owners' Loan. If he had not succeeded in getting another extension, they would be leaving this house in which they had lived for more than fourteen years. There was little hope. The Home Owners' Loan was hard. They sat, making their plans.

"We'll be moving into a nice flat somewhere," said Mama. "Somewhere on South Park, or Michigan, or in Washington Park Court." Those flats, as the girls and Mama knew well, were burdens on wages twice the size of Papa's. This was not mentioned now.

"They're much prettier than this old house," said Helen. "I have friends I'd just as soon not bring here. And I have other friends who wouldn't come down this far for anything, unless they were in a taxi."

Yesterday, Maud Martha would have attacked her. Tomorrow she might. Today she said nothing. She merely gazed at a little hopping robin in the tree, her tree, and tried to keep the fronts of her eyes dry.

"Well, I do know," said Mama, turning her hands over and over, "that I've been getting tireder and tireder of doing that firing. From October to April, there's firing to be done."

"But lately we've been helping, Harry and I," said Maud Martha. "And sometimes in March and April and in October, and even in November, we could build a little fire in the fireplace. Sometimes the weather was just right for that."

She knew, from the way they looked at her, that this had been a mistake. They did not want to cry.

But she felt that the little line of white, sometimes ridged with smoked purple, and all that cream-shot saffron would never drift across any western sky except that in back of this house. The rain would drum with as sweet a dullness nowhere but here. The birds on South Park were mechanical birds, no better than the poor caught canaries in those "rich" women's sun parlors.

"It's just going to kill Papa!" burst out Maud Martha. "He loves this house! He *lives* for this house!"

"He lives for us," said Helen. "It's us he loves. He wouldn't want this house, except for us."

"And he'll have us," added Mama, "wherever."

"You know," Helen sighed, "if you want to know the truth, this is a relief. If this hadn't come up, we would have gone on, just dragged on, hanging out here forever."

"It might," allowed Mama, "be an act of God. God may just have reached down and picked up the reins."

"Yes," Maud Martha cracked in, "that's what you always say—that God knows best."

Her mother looked at her quickly, decided that the statement was not suspect, looked away.

Helen saw Papa coming. "There's Papa," said Helen.

They could not tell a thing from the way Papa was walking. It was that same dear little staccato walk, one shoulder down, then the other, then repeat, and repeat. They watched his progress. He passed the Kennedys', he passed the vacant lot, he passed Mrs. Blakemore's. They wanted to hurl themselves over the fence, into the street, and shake the truth out of his collar. He opened his gate—the gate—and still his stride and face told them nothing.

"Hello," he said.

Mama got up and followed him through the front door. The girls knew better than to go in too.

Presently Mama's head emerged. Her eyes were lamps turned on.

"It's all right," she exclaimed. "He got it. It's all over. Everything is all right."

The door slammed shut. Mama's footsteps hurried away.

"I think," said Helen, rocking rapidly, "I think I'll give a party. I haven't given a party since I was eleven. I'd like some of my friends to just casually see that we're homeowners."

READER'S RESPONSE

1. How did you feel about the problems with home loan payments when you read the article on page 8? How are your feelings different now?
2. The basic aim of literary writing is to create a work of art. What other aims might Gwendolyn Brooks have had in writing this story? Explain.

ANSWERS
Reader's Response

Responses will vary.

1. Many students will notice that the newspaper article emphasizes how home loans will affect many people, while the short story shows the effect on just one family. Many will say that the emphasis on the feelings of one family is more powerful in influencing their views about home loans than the facts presented in the informative article.

2. In addition to the literary aim, Gwendolyn Brooks may also have intended to express her feelings about personal loss, to inform her readers how a family can persist in adversity, and to persuade her readers to empathize with her characters.

ANSWERS
Writing and Thinking Activities

1a. The representative's speech tries to persuade the audience by appealing to the listeners' emotions and by presenting facts about economic conditions.

b. The newspaper article explains the problems facing the city.

c. Responses will vary, but most students will agree that the story reveals the most about human emotions.

d. Responses will vary, but most students will find that the letter reveals the most about what the writer feels and thinks about the situation.

Questions 2 and 4 might be writing journal activities. Question 3 is a group activity. You might want to save these projects to work on at a later date.

Writing and Thinking Activities

1. Meet with two or three classmates to discuss the following questions about the four models you've read.
   a. Which model tries to convince people to do something? How?
   b. Which model explains the problems facing the city?
   c. Which model most dramatically shows the human emotions triggered by the financial crisis?
   d. Which model is mostly about what the writer feels and thinks about the situation?
2. Consider your own communication techniques. During a two-hour stretch of a typical day, make a list of all the different ways you communicate—writing, reading, speaking, and listening. Keep track of how much of your communication is informative, persuasive, self-expressive, or literary. Then, sit down with two or three classmates and discuss your communication patterns. Are they similar?

3. Notice how professional writers communicate. Bring a magazine or newspaper to class. Work with two or three classmates to find examples of these four kinds of writing: informative, persuasive, self-expressive, and creative writing. Which type of writing is used most often? Does each magazine and newspaper have about the same percentage of each type of writing?

4. When you hear the words *creative writing,* what do you think of—short stories? poems? novels? plays? What about other kinds of writing? Can letters to the editor, speeches, editorials, or journal entries also be creative? In what way? What other kinds of writing would you call original or creative?

1

WRITING AND THINKING

OBJECTIVES

- To use various prewriting techniques to develop writing ideas
- To arrange information in an order that suits intended purpose and audience
- To plan and write a first draft
- To use the techniques of peer evaluation in helping others revise writing
- To use proofreading guidelines and marks
- To create ideas for publishing written works

---

cross CURRICULUM

Approaching Essay Test Questions for Social Studies

When students face essay questions on a social studies test, they often panic and forget about the writing process. If you team teach with a social studies teacher, work with that teacher to hold a writing workshop on preparing answers to essay questions. Present the following steps to students. (The schedule is based on 30 minutes per question.)

1. Read all the essay questions on the test and determine which questions must be answered and which will take the longest to prepare. (2 minutes)

2. Choose and reread one question and underline the key *5W-How?* words that need to be addressed. (1 minute)

3. Plan an answer. (12 minutes)

Remind students that they already know three important elements of the writing process—the topic (posed in the question), the audience (the teacher), and the purpose (to demonstrate their knowledge to the teacher). The planning process is for gathering information and organizing it in a way that reveals the depth of the student's understanding. Encourage students to generate ideas by using the strategies suggested on pp. 26–29 or by turning the essay question into a statement of cause and effect (Example: The Roman empire fell *because* a) it had become overextended, b) the Goths were too powerful, and so on.)

Students should reserve two or three minutes of planning time for organizing their answers. See p. 39 for strategies.

4. Write the answer. (7–10 minutes)

Students need to stress the planning stage because, in a test situation, they cannot rewrite; their first drafts need to be their final drafts. Reassure students that getting their ideas on paper in a coherent manner, not style, is what is important.

5. Reread and proofread answer. (2–5 minutes)

Writing for a test does not leave much time for evaluating, revising, and proofreading, so students should reread their answers for sense and for errors in spelling, subject-verb agreement, tense, and punctuation.

INTEGRATING THE LANGUAGE ARTS

SELECTION	READING AND LITERATURE	WRITING AND CRITICAL THINKING	LANGUAGE AND SYNTAX	SPEAKING, LISTENING, AND OTHER EXPRESSION SKILLS
• from **A Fire in My Hands** by Gary Soto pp. 18–20 • Film review from the *Chicago Sun-Times* by Roger Ebert p. 37 • from **A Browser's Dictionary** by John Ciardi p. 40 • from **The Norton Anthology of Literature by Women: The Tradition in English** by Sandra M. Gilbert and Susan Gubar p. 41 • from **"We Need Power, Program, and Progress"** by Jesse L. Jackson p. 42 • from **The Name of the Rose** by Umberto Eco p. 42	• Responding personally to literature p. 20 • Applying interpretive and creative thinking pp. 20, 49–50, 54 • Drawing conclusions and making inferences pp. 20, 44 • Locating and interpreting information pp. 30, 41–42, 44, 46	• Recording personal observations pp. 20, 25–26, 27, 31, 33–34, 49–50 • Writing a journal entry pp. 25–26 • Using freewriting and looping p. 27 • Generating ideas by association pp. 28, 29 • Using brainstorming pp. 28, 33, 34, 59, 61 • Using clustering pp. 29, 33 • Finding information pp. 30, 31, 32–34, 41–42, 59 • Gathering sensory details p. 31 • Taking notes pp. 32–34 • Drawing conclusions and making inferences pp. 33–34, 41–42, 44 • Applying interpretive and creative thinking pp. 34, 38, 41–42, 46, 49–50, 54, 59 • Writing a persuasive piece p. 38 • Writing an informative piece pp. 38, 46 • Analyzing the arrangement of information pp. 41–42, 46, 54 • Arranging ideas pp. 44, 46 • Classifying information pp. 44, 46 • Writing a first draft p. 46 • Evaluating a paragraph pp. 49–50, 54 • Revising a paragraph p. 54 • Brainstorming with a computer p. 61	• Proofreading for errors in grammar, usage, and mechanics pp. 54, 56–57	• Brainstorming with classmates pp. 28, 34, 59 • Working in a team to find information p. 30 • Listening with a focus pp. 33–34 • Working with classmates to organize information p. 44 • Working with classmates to evaluate a paragraph pp. 49–50

CHAPTER 1: WRITING AND THINKING

Use this guide for creating an instructional plan that addresses the individual needs of your students. Assignments accompanied by the following symbol (✽) may be completed out of class. Times given for pacing lessons are estimated.

CHAPTER PLANNING GUIDE—PUPIL'S EDITION

LESSONS	LITERARY MODEL pp. 18–20 from *A Fire In My Hands* by Gary Soto	PREWRITING pp. 24–44	
		Generating Ideas	**Gathering/Organizing**
DEVELOPMENTAL PROGRAM	🕐 **30–35 minutes** • Read model aloud to class and ask students to answer questions orally on p. 20	🕐 **90 minutes** • Main Assignment: Looking Ahead p. 21 • Aim and Process pp. 22–23 • Finding Ideas for Writing pp. 24–34 • Exercises 1–6, 9 pp. 25–34 in pairs • Thinking About Purpose, Audience, Tone pp. 35–36	🕐 **45–50 minutes** • Arranging Ideas p. 39 • Critical Thinking pp. 41–43 as a class • Critical Thinking pp. 43–44
CORE PROGRAM	🕐 **25–30 minutes** • Assign student pairs to read the model and answer questions on p. 20	🕐 **55–60 minutes** • Main Assignment: Looking Ahead p. 21 • Aim and Process pp. 22–23 • Finding Ideas for Writing pp. 24–34 • Exercises 1, 4, 7, 8, 9 pp. 25–34✽ • Thinking About Purpose, Audience, and Tone pp. 35–36 • Critical Thinking pp. 36–38	🕐 **35–40 minutes** • Arranging Ideas p. 39 • Critical Thinking p. 41–43 in pairs • Critical Thinking pp. 43–44
ACCELERATED PROGRAM	🕐 **20–25 minutes** • Assign students to read the model independently and to discuss the questions on p. 20 with a partner	🕐 **30–35 minutes** • Main Assignment: Looking Ahead p. 21 • Prewriting Techniques Chart p. 24 • Exercises 1, 2, 4, 7, 8, 9 pp. 25–34✽ • Critical Thinking pp. 36–38	🕐 **20–25 minutes** • Critical Thinking pp. 41–43✽ • Critical Thinking pp. 43–44

CHAPTER PLANNING GUIDE—PROGRAM RESOURCES

	LITERARY MODEL	PREWRITING
PRINT	• Reading Master 1, *Practice for Assessment in Reading, Vocabulary, and Spelling* p. 1	• Freewriting and Brainstorming; Clustering and Asking Questions; Using Your Five Senses; Reading and Listening with a Focus; Imagining; Purpose, Audience, and Tone; Arranging Ideas; Using Charts, *Practicing the Writing Process* pp. 1–9 • The Writing Process, *English Workshop* pp. 1–14
MEDIA		• Graphic Organizer 1: The Aims of Writing, *Transparency Binder* • Graphic Organizer 2: The Writing Process, *Transparency Binder*

WRITING pp. 45–46	EVALUATING AND REVISING pp. 47–54	PROOFREADING AND PUBLISHING pp. 55–60

🕐 **35–40 minutes**
• Writing a First Draft
  pp. 45–46
• Exercise 10 p. 46 in pairs
	🕐 **50–55 minutes**
	• Evaluating pp. 47–48
	• Critical Thinking
	  pp. 49–50
	• Revising pp. 50–52
	• Guidelines Chart p. 53
	• Exercise 11 p. 54
		🕐 **45–50 minutes**
		• Proofreading pp. 55–56
		• Exercises 12, 13
		  pp. 56–57, 59 in pairs
		• Publishing pp. 57–58
		• Critical Thinking p. 58
		• Symbols Chart p. 60

🕐 **30–35 minutes**
• Writing a First Draft
  pp. 45–46
• Exercise 10 p. 46*
	🕐 **40–45 minutes**
	• Evaluating pp. 47–48
	• Critical Thinking
	  pp. 49–50
	• Revising pp. 50–52
	• Guidelines Chart p. 53
	• Exercise 11 p. 54
		🕐 **40–45 minutes**
		• Proofreading pp. 55–56
		• Exercises 12, 13*
		  pp. 56–57, 59
		• Publishing pp. 57–58
		• Critical Thinking p. 58
		• Manuscript Form Chart
		  p. 59
		• Symbols Chart p. 60

🕐 **25–30 minutes**
• Writing a First Draft
  pp. 45–46
	🕐 **35–40 minutes**
	• Evaluating Chart p. 48
	• Critical Thinking
	  pp. 49–50*
	• Revising Chart p. 51
	• Guidelines Chart p. 53
	• Exercise 11 p. 54*
		🕐 **35–40 minutes**
		• Proofreading Chart p. 56
		• Guidelines Chart p. 56
		• Exercise 12 pp. 56–57*
		• Critical Thinking p. 58
		• Manuscript Form Chart
		  p. 59
		• Symbols Chart p. 60

WRITING	EVALUATING AND REVISING	PROOFREADING AND PUBLISHING
• The First Draft, *Practicing the Writing Process* p. 10	• Peer Evaluation, Revising by Adding, Revising by Replacing, *Practicing the Writing Process* pp. 11–13	• Proofreading, Manuscript Form, *Practicing the Writing Process* pp. 14–15
	• Revision Transparencies 1–2, *Transparency Binder*	• *Language Workshop:* Lessons 5–7, 9–10, 27, 34–51

ELEMENTS OF WRITING: CURRICULUM CONNECTIONS

Making Connections
• Brainstorming with a Computer p. 61

ASSESSMENT OPTIONS

Reflection
Self-assessment Record, *Portfolio Assessment* p. 19
Portfolio forms, *Portfolio Assessment* pp. 5–25

Summative Assessment
Review: The Aim and Process of Writing, *Practicing the Writing Process* p. 16

💾 Computer disk or CD-ROM

📽 Overhead transparencies

LOOKING AT THE PROCESS

OBJECTIVES

- To write personal responses to literature
- To identify writing obstacles
- To explain the influence of poetry on a writer

TEACHING THE LESSON

As motivation, initiate a discussion by asking for students' opinions about greeting cards. Lead students to the idea that people choose cards that express what they would like to say. Ask students which they appreciate more, a card or a personal note. Ask why people send cards, as opposed to notes. Are

1 WRITING AND THINKING

people afraid they will not be able to express their feelings in writing?

Before reading the introductory paragraphs of the lesson, ask students what they would prefer—discussing or writing. Some of the answers to the questions under **Writing and You** may help you identify the kinds of difficulties students encounter when trying to write. Tell students that many writers have the same problems with writing. In this unit, students will learn ways to make writing easier.

You may want to have a volunteer read the excerpt from *a fire in my hands.* Then, guide students in finding and listing the parts of the writing process that Soto describes. Try to include discovery, getting started (his early attempts), finding

Looking at the Process

Being a good writer starts with being a good thinker and planner. The writing comes later, as part of the entire writing **process.**

Writing and You.   Is writing easy for you? Or do you often find yourself sitting and staring at a blank sheet of paper? Do you enjoy writing or is it a pain that you'd rather live without? All writers, even professional writers, get frustrated. They have trouble getting started, finding information, thinking up ideas, and then putting their ideas on paper. Which of these parts of the writing process cause you the greatest trouble?

As You Read.   As you read the following foreword from Gary Soto's book of poems, think about the difficulties he faced and how he dealt with them.

Henri Matisse, *Interior with Etruscan Vase* (1940). Oil on canvas, 29" × 39 1/2". Collection of The Cleveland Museum of Art, Gift of the Hanna Fund, 52.153. © 1993 Succession H. Matisse, Paris/ Artist Rights Society (ARS), New York.

 QUOTATION FOR THE DAY
"Reading furnishes the mind only with materials of knowledge; it is thinking makes what we read ours." (John Locke, 1632–1704, English philosopher)

 VISUAL CONNECTIONS
Interior with Etruscan Vase
About the Artist. Henri Matisse was born in France in 1869. He studied law at the University of Paris from 1887 to 1891 and then decided to paint.

During the first several years of his career, Matisse learned about composition and form by copying masterpieces from the Louvre and by doing landscapes and still-life paintings in the traditional, realistic style. By the late 1890s, Matisse had adopted Impressionist techniques. His style continued to develop, and in later works he used bold, opposing colors to capture the essence of his subjects. *Interior with Etruscan Vase,* painted in 1940, is an example of this style.

Matisse also sculpted figures in bronze and stone, and in the early 1950s, he started to cross the boundaries between sculpture and painting. Cutting forms directly out of colored paper, Matisse constructed artworks by pasting up the cutouts to form compositions. These pictures are characterized by their pure, bright colors and their abstract simplicity. Matisse died in 1954, but his artwork continues to inspire and influence artists today.

17

ideas (reading other poets and looking at his own experience), and putting ideas on paper.

If possible, select a poem by Soto that you think will appeal to the class and show it on the overhead projector. Have students list in their writing journals details from the poem about the geography and culture of the San Joaquin Valley. Then have them list analogous details from their own environments beside Soto's descriptions.

Guide students through the first and second **Reader's Response** questions. Use the third question as independent practice by having students freewrite their opinions about using everyday objects as poetic subjects.

After discussing the three maxims in the box following the **Reader's Response**

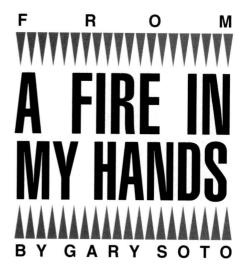

FROM

A FIRE IN MY HANDS

BY GARY SOTO

I began writing poems fifteen years ago while I was in college. One day I was in the library, working on a term paper, when by chance I came across an anthology of contemporary poetry. I don't remember the title of the book or any of the titles of the poems except one: "Frankenstein's Daughter." The poem was wild, almost rude, and nothing like the rhyme-and-meter poetry I had read in high school. I had always thought that poetry was flowery writing about sunsets and walks on the beach, but that library book contained a direct and sometimes shocking poetry about dogs, junked cars, rundown houses, and TVs. I checked the book out, curious to read more.

Soon afterward, I started filling a notebook with my own poems. At first I was scared, partly because my poetry teacher, to whom this book is dedicated, was a stern man who could see the errors in my poems. Also, I realized the seriousness of my dedication. I gave up geography to study poetry, which a good many friends said offered no future. I ignored them because I liked working with words, using them to reconstruct the past, which has always been a source of poetry for me.

When I first studied poetry, I was single-minded. I woke to poetry and went to bed with poetry. I memorized poems, read English poets because I was told they would help shape my poems, and read classical Chinese poetry because I was told that

questions, you could copy and display them in a prominent place in the classroom as a visual reminder for students.

CLOSURE
Select students to identify troubles writers have and ways Soto or they might overcome these obstacles.

"...that library book contained a direct and sometimes shocking poetry about dogs, junked cars, rundown houses, and TVs."

VISUAL CONNECTIONS
Exploring the Subject. Gary Soto, a teacher of English and Chicano Studies at the University of California at Berkeley, is considered one of the most talented contemporary American poets. His first book of poetry, *The Elements of San Joaquin* (1977), won the U.S. Award of the International Poetry Forum. Most of Soto's poems reflect his memories of an impoverished youth and his experiences as a migrant worker. His poetry has helped enlighten others about the feelings and lifestyles of many Mexican Americans.

4
Pablo Neruda (1904–1973), a Chilean writer, won the 1971 Nobel Prize for literature. His approach to poetry changed continually throughout his life. He used obscure and violent imagery to convey a sense of universal chaos.

5
How do you think Neruda's poetry influenced Soto? [Responses will vary. One possibility is that Soto's poetry also reflects personal experiences.]

it would add clarity to my work. But I was most taken by Spanish
4 and Latin American poets, particularly Pablo Neruda. My favorites of his were the <u>odes</u>—long, short-lined poems celebrating common things like tomatoes, socks, scissors, and artichokes. I
5 felt joyful when I read these odes; and when I began to write my own poems, I tried to remain faithful to the common things of my childhood—dogs, alleys, my baseball mitt, curbs, and the fruit of the valley, especially the orange. I wanted to give these things life, to write so well that my poems would express their simple beauty.

You might ask students to read and review some of Gary Soto's poetry and then to share their reactions with the class. Some of Soto's works are *The Elements of San Joaquin, The Cat's Meow,* and *Where Sparrows Work Hard.* ■

6

In 1979, Philip Levine won the National Book Critics Circle Prize in poetry for *Seven Years from Somewhere* and *Ashes: Poems New and Old.* Some critics believe that Levine influenced Soto's writing style. Soto is a former student of Levine.

7

Zen Buddhism: a religious movement introduced in Japan in the twelfth century that stresses the attainment of spiritual enlightenment through meditation

8

Sequoias: also called redwoods; giant evergreen trees of the bald-cypress family that reach a height of over 300 feet, found chiefly in California

ANSWERS

Reader's Response

Students should give complete, honest answers. They should also give reasons for their opinions. For question 3, if students have read poetry about common objects, they should give titles or brief descriptions of the poems. To encourage students to respond freely, refrain from penalizing mechanical or grammatical errors.

SELECTION AMENDMENT
Description of change: excerpted
Rationale: to focus on the concept of the writing process presented in this chapter

---

I also admired our own country's poetry. I saw that our poets often wrote about places where they grew up or places that impressed them deeply. James Wright wrote about Ohio and *6* West Virginia, Philip Levine about Detroit, Gary Snyder about the Sierra Nevadas and about Japan, where for years he studied *7* Zen Buddhism. I decided to write about the San Joaquin Valley, where my hometown, Fresno, is located. Some of my poems are stark observations of human violence—burglaries, muggings, fistfights—while others are spare images of nature—the orange *8* groves and vineyards, the Kings River, the bogs, the Sequoias. I fell in love with the valley, both its ugliness and its beauty, and quietly wrote poems about it to share with others.

READER'S RESPONSE

1. Are you, like Soto, ever scared to write because you don't want others to criticize your writing? How can you overcome this fear?
2. When Soto became interested in writing poetry, he started reading more poetry. Do you agree that reading the writing of others can help a writer? Why?
3. Soto says that he wants to write about common things like dogs, fistfights, and orange groves. Have you ever read poetry about such everyday events and objects? Do you think such things make good subjects for poetry? Why?

LOOKING AHEAD

In this chapter, you'll learn a general approach to writing that you can apply to all types of writing. You'll go through the stages of the writing process from choosing a topic to publishing. As you work through the chapter, remember that

- writing and thinking are both part of the process
- the writing process is flexible: you can adapt it to your own writing style and situation
- your topic, audience, and purpose emerge together when you write for yourself

"I start at the beginning, go on to the end, then stop."
Anthony Burgess

• • • •

"I always know the ending; that's where I start."
Toni Morrison

Discuss the meaning of the word *aim* with the class. Emphasize the importance of writers' knowing the aim of their writing. They must know the goal if they want to attain it. You may also want to explain that often the purposes for writing overlap, even though one purpose is usually primary.

The two most important aspects of teaching the writing process are that it is recursive and that each person's process is individualized. Have students read the introductory paragraphs for aim and process, and then you can discuss the pie chart. ■

22

Aim—The "Why" of Writing

Why do people write?—usually for the same reason they talk. They have something to say, someone to say it to, and some purpose for saying it. Of course, that's a general *why*. But what are a few *why's*, or basic purposes, people have for writing?

WHY PEOPLE WRITE	
To express themselves	To get to know themselves, to discover meaning in their own lives
To share information	To give other people information they want or need; to share some special knowledge they have
To persuade	To convince other people to do something or believe something
To create literature	To be creative, to say something in a unique way

Process—The "How" of Writing

Anything people say or write has one of the four basic purposes you've just read about—sometimes even has more than one purpose at a time. For example, a writer may want to persuade as well as to share information. Like all the other speakers and writers in the world, you'll be writing for one or more of these four purposes.

As Gary Soto's experience shows, writing doesn't just happen. A great deal of thought goes into writing, using a whole *process* or series of stages. The process begins with a prewriting stage that is mostly thinking. It moves through other stages that focus more on writing and then on to more thinking after the writing occurs. That's why some sections of this chapter focus more on thinking and other sections focus more on writing.

The following diagram shows the stages that usually take place during the writing process. As the diagram shows, you can go back to an earlier stage, or even start over again, at any point in the process.

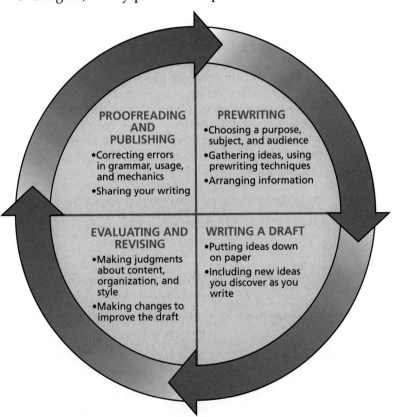

PROOFREADING AND PUBLISHING

•Correcting errors in grammar, usage, and mechanics

•Sharing your writing

PREWRITING

•Choosing a purpose, subject, and audience

•Gathering ideas, using prewriting techniques

•Arranging information

EVALUATING AND REVISING

•Making judgments about content, organization, and style

•Making changes to improve the draft

WRITING A DRAFT

•Putting ideas down on paper

•Including new ideas you discover as you write

For example, you're writing a report for art class on the life and work of artist Vincent van Gogh. You have gathered information from various books and have seen an exhibit featuring some of his works. You have your first draft almost finished. However, you read in a newspaper story that a long-lost van Gogh painting has been found, and you find another book that contains some important facts about his life that you didn't have. You go back to the prewriting stage and take more notes. Then you start writing again by adding the new information to your first draft.

A DIFFERENT APPROACH

Have students work in teams of three or four to create original artistic presentations of this diagram. First, have teams review each stage and discuss the role each plays in the writing process. Then teams can brainstorm for original artistic approaches such as clay models, jigsaw puzzles, posters, and so forth. Encourage each team to create art that is unique. Allow time for teams to present their finished projects to the class.

PREWRITING

OBJECTIVES

- To use various prewriting techniques such as freewriting, brainstorming, clustering, the *5W-How?* questions, and sensory details to find ideas for writing
- To keep a writer's journal
- To find ideas for writing by reading with a focus
- To find ideas for writing by listening for specific information
- To use "What if?" questions for prewriting

 **PROGRAM MANAGER**

PREWRITING

- **Heuristics** To help students generate ideas, see **Freewriting and Brainstorming, Clustering and Asking Questions, Using Your Five Senses, Reading and Listening with a Focus,** and **Imagining** in *Practicing the Writing Process,* pp. 1–5.

- **Analyzing** To help students analyze and organize ideas, see **Purpose, Audience, and Tone; Arranging Ideas;** and **Using Charts** in *Practicing the Writing Process,* pp. 6–9.

- **Instructional Support** See **Graphic Organizers 1** and **2.** For suggestions on how to tie the transparencies to instruction, review teacher's notes for transparencies in *Fine Art and Instructional Transparencies for Writing,* pp. 53, 55.

QUOTATION FOR THE DAY

"Writing is no trouble: you just jot down ideas as they occur to you. The jotting is simplicity itself—it is the occurring which is difficult." (Stephen Leacock, 1869–1944, English-born Canadian humorist and political scientist)

You may wish to use the quotation to initiate a discussion of where and how writers get ideas.

 *Prewriting*

Finding Ideas for Writing

"Write about anything you want" and "write about one of the assigned topics" are opposite instructions—but you may have the same reaction to both: a big blank. Where *do* professional writers get their ideas for writing? How do they get started on an assignment? Every writer might say something different (even "I don't know—I just do it"), but there are definite ways to get your brain moving when you want (or need) to write. This section will give you practical help—summarized in the following chart—for finding ideas.

PREWRITING TECHNIQUES		
Writer's Journal	Recording personal experiences and observations	Page 25
Freewriting	Writing for a few minutes about whatever comes to mind	Page 26
Brainstorming	Listing ideas as quickly as they come	Page 27
Clustering	Using circles and lines to show connections between ideas	Pages 28–29
Asking Questions	Using the reporter's *5W–How?* questions	Page 30
Using Your Five Senses	Observing details of sight, hearing, smell, taste, touch	Page 31
Reading with a Focus	Reading to find specific information	Page 32
Listening with a Focus	Listening to find specific information	Page 33
Imagining	Imagining details for creative writing	Page 34

In a discussion, ask students to identify different kinds of keys while you list the responses on the chalkboard. Note that all these keys share the same function—each opens a lock. Explain that prewriting techniques, like keys, differ from each other, but that the techniques all share the same function—unlocking the doors to writing ideas.

As you discuss the chart that summarizes the prewriting techniques, consider modeling each to help students visualize the application of the concepts. Where possible, base models on information from the excerpt from *a fire in my hands.* For example, compare Soto's notebook and his thinking about poetry each morning to keeping a writer's ☞

As the chart shows, you have many prewriting techniques to choose from and many ways to use them. You'll often use more than one technique at a time. You'll use some more than others because of your own thinking style. And you'll use different techniques for different writing situations. For example, if you're writing a personal narrative about a hiking trip, you might use all five senses to recall vivid details about the adventure. But if you're searching for details about the subject "American railroads," you might use clustering or reading with a focus.

Keeping a Writer's Journal

If you aren't already doing so, start keeping a *writer's journal.* Use it to record thoughts, feelings, opinions, and great ideas—for example, things that bug you, song lyrics, and notes about famous people you wish you knew. Your journal can be small enough to carry around or big enough for drawing and pasting in cartoons and photos. Before you know it, you'll have a surprising source book of ideas for writing.

Here are some suggestions for getting started.

1. Make a habit of writing every day, and date your entries. Some people like to set a special time for writing—others like to be spontaneous and write when the mood (or an event) hits.
2. Write for yourself—which may mean messy and misspelled. Journals don't have "mistakes."
3. Be creative (even zany). Let your imagination go in songs, drawings, movie ideas, or poems.
4. React, reflect, explore random thoughts: Record some response to anything you include (like a quotation, an ad, a newspaper editorial). Why did you choose it?

E X E R C I S E 1 ▶	Keeping a Writer's Journal

If you're not already keeping a journal, start one now. And don't worry if nothing glamorous or dramatic happened to you lately: Your personal thoughts, feelings, and

MEETING *individual* NEEDS

LEARNING STYLES

Auditory Learners. Students sometimes subvocalize when they read or write independently. Allow these students to quietly think aloud as they make entries in their writing journals.

LEP/ESL

General Strategies. Although students may feel comfortable with their oral communicative competence, some of them may be anxious and uncomfortable about their writing abilities in English. Having them work with peers in small groups may ease their transitions into this area of study. As an initial exercise, have them interview each other by asking questions such as "What makes you happy?" or "What is the funniest thing that ever happened to you?" Ask each student to write a report of his or her classmate's responses.

ANSWERS
Exercise 1

In individualized notebooks (decorated spiral binders work well), students should record events or emotions experienced recently. Mechanical and grammatical errors should not be penalized.

journal. Use his reading of other poets as an example of reading with a focus. Use his finding ideas in the culture and environment of the San Joaquin Valley to model freewriting, brainstorming, clustering, using the five senses, and imagining.

To illustrate how prewriting techniques are often used in combination, note the following examples: keeping a writer's journal may at different times include every technique except reading with a focus and listening with a focus, but these two techniques could be combined by reading along while listening to a taped recording of the work.

To help students focus their efforts as they begin keeping a writer's journal, suggest that each day they note the most

experiences are unique—and that's what makes journals fun and fascinating. To get started, try writing about one *event* or *emotion* that sticks in your mind from yesterday.

Freewriting

To *freewrite,* just let your mind go and write.

1. Use a watch or clock, set a time limit (three to five minutes is good), and keep writing until the time's up.
2. Start with a word, phrase, or topic that's important to you—like *gymnastics* or *animal rights.*
3. Write any ideas, images, or details that come to you, without stopping to think about grammar, spelling, or punctuation. Just let the words flow.
4. If the flow stops, copy the last word until something new appears, or talk to yourself: *I'm stuck—what can I say after "competition"—maybe maybe maybe "judges".* . . .
5. To vary freewriting, choose one word or phrase from your freewriting, and use it as a starting point for more writing. This process is called *focused freewriting,* or *looping,* because it allows you to make a "loop" from what you've already written and then continue writing.

Here's a sample of a few minutes of freewriting on the word *recycling.*

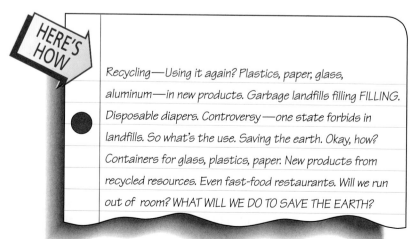

HERE'S HOW

Recycling—Using it again? Plastics, paper, glass,
aluminum—in new products. Garbage landfills filling FILLING.
Disposable diapers. Controversy—one state forbids in
landfills. So what's the use. Saving the earth. Okay, how?
Containers for glass, plastics, paper. New products from
recycled resources. Even fast-food restaurants. Will we run
out of room? WHAT WILL WE DO TO SAVE THE EARTH?

interesting things they have seen or heard in and outside class.

To help students understand freewriting, have them list in their writing journals the names of favorite books, songs, films, or television programs. Then, have them talk to partners for ten seconds about whatever comes to mind about their writer's journal entries.

To illustrate focused freewriting, display the example from the textbook on an overhead projector and discuss the similarities between focused freewriting and clustering.

You may want to use **Exercise 2** as guided practice. Begin by assessing students' knowledge of the environmental dangers cited in the textbook. Ask volunteers to ☞

EXERCISE 2 ▶ **Using Freewriting**

What's your concern about the environment? Write down a phrase that describes your thoughts and freewrite about it for three or four minutes. Then choose one phrase from your freewriting and do some focused freewriting or looping.

Brainstorming

Brainstorming generates ideas by free association. You can brainstorm alone, with a partner, or in a group.

1. Write any subject, word, or phrase at the top of a sheet of paper (or on the chalkboard).
2. Jot down *every* idea that comes to your mind. (In a group, brainstorm out loud and appoint one person to record all of the ideas.)
3. Don't stop to evaluate; just keep going until you run out of ideas.

Here are a group's brainstorming notes on electric cars. They're not all serious, but off-the-wall associations can always be cut or changed later.

HERE'S HOW

electric cars	speed? problems?
when first used?	probably dinky
need long cords	not dependent on gasoline
Who invented them?	high cost now, low later
car of the future	models: the Sparky,
no pollution	the Shocker
little pollution—	Who's building them?
what kind?	they're ready now—
how far on one charge?	just read Road and Track

ANSWERS
Exercise 2

Each student should create a phrase and use it as a starting point for freewriting. Remind students that they should write as many ideas as possible in the time allotted. Students should not be penalized for straying from the topic, as related concerns often surface during freewriting. For the second part of the assignment, students should pick their most interesting phrases, skip a few lines, and practice looping (focused freewriting) during the time you allot. Here students should stick to a subject. Mechanical and grammatical errors or incomplete sentences should not be penalized in either part of this exercise.

comment on each of these dangers. When you are satisfied that students have adequate background knowledge, tell them to free-write their thoughts on the assigned topic.

To introduce **Brainstorming**, you could have partners play an association game. Start by suggesting a broad subject such as a color, an animal, or a sport. Partners could then take five turns saying the first word that comes to mind after hearing the other prompt. Model the activity by exchanging associations with a volunteer.

Use **Exercise 3** as independent practice. Discuss the results in class as a way to assess students' comprehension. However, before class discussion, explain that as in journal entries, there are no mistakes in

ANSWERS
Exercise 3

Lists should include every idea the selected topic brings to mind, no matter how remotely related. Because the purpose here is quantity, groups might compete to see who can produce the most ideas in a given time.

A DIFFERENT APPROACH

Students might use a different-colored pen or pencil each time they divide a topic for clustering. Using colors will enable students to classify and locate topics more easily.

EXERCISE 3 ▶ Using Brainstorming

Practice brainstorming with a partner or a small group so that you'll hear ideas besides your own (which will probably spark more of your own). Together, list ideas about one of the following topics, or choose your own.

1. the funniest TV shows
2. compact discs
3. the American flag
4. slang
5. life in the year 2010
6. today's heroines

Clustering

Clustering is similar to brainstorming, but it is more visual and shows connections between ideas. Like brainstorming, clustering generally breaks a subject down into smaller parts, so it's good both for finding topics and gathering information.

1. Begin by writing a subject in the middle of your paper, and circle or box it.
2. Around the subject, write related ideas that you think of, circle them, and connect them with lines to your subject (and maybe to each other).
3. Let your new ideas lead to others. Just keep associating, circling, and connecting until you're ready to stop.

Clustering is also called *webbing*, a good name as the example shows. Even though your cluster or web may not make complete sense to someone else, you've made the connections and can follow your own thinking.

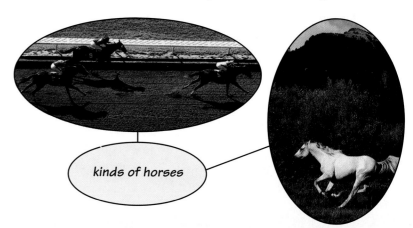

kinds of horses

brainstorming. Students should not feel inhibited while discussing their ideas by the fear that there is a pass/fail aspect to the exercise.

To explain clustering, draw an analogy to a paragraph. The cluster subject is like the main idea. The related ideas are similar to supporting information (sensory details, facts or statistics, and examples). Many of the related ideas can then be analyzed and, in turn, become the main ideas in other clusters, with their parts as related ideas.

To help students visualize the concept, note that another term for clustering is webbing. You could draw the design of a simple spider web on the chalkboard and note that the central hub, where the spider lives, is like the cluster subject. The

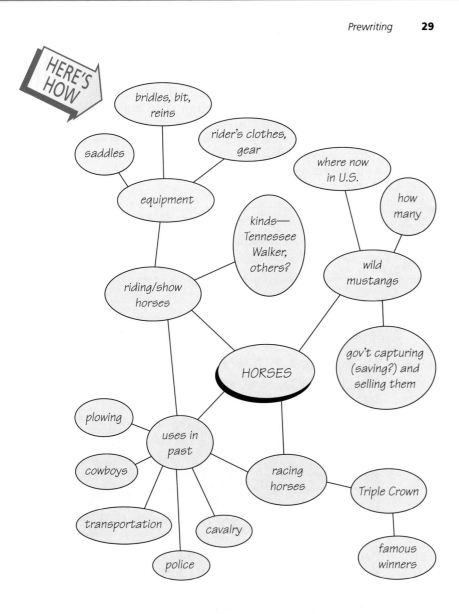

EXERCISE 4 ▶ **Using Clustering**

Create a cluster diagram using one of the topics you *didn't* use in Exercise 3 or another topic of your own choice. Use the clustering hints and Here's How diagram as guides.

INTEGRATING THE LANGUAGE ARTS

Literature Link. Have students read the poem "Richard Cory" by E. A. Robinson and use context clues to produce a cluster Robinson might have spun for the subject, "Richard Cory." Then play the song "Richard Cory" performed by Paul Simon and Art Garfunkel. Have partners produce clusters from Simon and Garfunkel's "Richard Cory" and then compare these with the clusters they created after reading the poem. Ask if Simon's details limit the reader's imagination. Note that Simon's full title is "Richard Cory, with apologies to E. A. Robinson."

ANSWERS
Exercise 4

Encourage students to use subjects that are fairly general—subjects from which a second or third level of clustering can grow. Allow students to refer to the sample cluster diagram and the clustering hints when necessary. Students will probably not develop more than three or four main subheads in their diagrams.

foundation lines that radiate outward from the hub join it to different locations on a plant or other structure. These locations support and strengthen the hub in the same way that details support the cluster subject. The foundation lines are like the relationships between the subject and the related ideas. If the relationship is strong, the line holds and the web is supported.

Prewriting webs or cluster designs vary among different writers, even changing with the same individual's writing at different times. What is important is that no matter how far from the hub or subject the web is spun, the ideas should be related. As long as the ideas are related, the foundation lines will hold, and the hub (or main idea) will be supported.

Asking Questions

One to-the-point way of investigating a topic is asking the reporter's *5W-How?* questions: *Who? What? When? Where? Why? How?* You'll find, though, that every topic doesn't equal six questions. Sometimes a question word won't apply to your topic, and often you'll think of more than one good question for a word. Here are some questions you could ask for a paper about one group of Native Americans, the Creeks.

WHO?	Who were some famous Creek leaders or chiefs?
WHAT?	What was a Creek community like?
WHERE?	Where did the Creeks live?
WHEN?	When did they first encounter white people?
WHY?	Why are they called <u>Creeks</u>—an English word?
HOW?	How did Creeks govern themselves?

Tecumseh, Opothleyahola, Jerome Tiger, Angie Debo

EXERCISE 5   **Asking the *5W-How?* Questions**

You're a reporter covering a hot story for the school paper: the school board's proposal to require students to attend school year-round. Working in teams, list as many good *5W-How?* questions for digging out information about the proposal as you can, and then compare lists.

Note that the answers to any one of the *5W-How?* questions may frame the main idea of a particular work. In storytelling, the answers to *Who?* and *What?* will often state the main idea. *Why?* explains cause and effect. *How?* explains a process. The answer to *Where?* may be the main idea in a geography report. *When?* is sometimes the main idea in a history report. It can also be the connection linking a work that has no main idea but describes a sequence of events.

Before starting **Exercise 5**, review informing and persuading as two purposes of writing. Note that the best questions for the purposes of the exercise will require informative answers. Based upon the answers to those questions, the reporter will ☞

Using Your Five Senses

Wherever you are, whatever you're doing, sensations of hearing, touch, smell, and taste are zinging into your brain right along with visual images. Pay attention to them, and you can improve your writing with vivid sensory details.

For example, here are details you could record about an experience that's probably familiar: a night football game.

TOUCH:	cold air; sharp gusts of wind; cushiony bump of padded jackets on bleacher seats
SOUND:	chants of cheerleaders and fans; deep roar and shrieks of fans; bands—sound fading in and out as they turn in formation; airplanes faint overhead
SMELL:	hot dogs and mustard; popcorn; newly cut grass; cold fall air—leaf mold?
TASTE:	greasy taste of salve on chapped lips; stale, too-salty popcorn; tangy mustard
SIGHT:	greenish-yellow of grass; funny yellowish lights and dark sky; players in maroon, orange-gold, muddy uniforms; referees in crisp black and white; fans a sea of every color, with red jumping out—blankets, hats, gloves, coats

EXERCISE 6 ▶ **Using Your Five Senses**

If you really focus on your sensations, in any situation, you'll surprise yourself with life's sensory details—and your own sensitivity to them. Choose one of the following places, if possible *go to it* (if not, imagine it), and write down the sensory details you observe. You can make a column on your paper for each sense.

1. the lobby of a movie theater
2. inside your family's or a friend's car
3. the gymnasium during any kind of game or event
4. your school lunchroom at noon on a school day
5. a yogurt shop or any store

decide whether the article should inform (appear in the news section) or inform and persuade (an editorial or opinion column).

To begin the section **Using Your Five Senses,** note that beginning writers rely mostly on the sense of sight when describing. Suggest that students occasionally close their eyes for one minute in familiar surroundings and concentrate on using one of the other senses.

When covering **Reading with a Focus,** you may want to review the requirements for citing sources when using direct quotations and paraphrasing in writing.

Note that the stories to be covered on radio or television news programs are often

MEETING *individual* NEEDS

ADVANCED STUDENTS

Students might research the history and culture of the ancient Mayas and then report their findings to the class. Have students display examples of their resources and explain the steps they followed to find information about this topic.

INTEGRATING THE LANGUAGE ARTS

Library Link. Before the groups begin **Exercise 7,** explain or review the use of the *Readers' Guide to Periodical Literature* and, if available, the library's online index for periodicals. Have groups collaborate in using these tools to discover sources. Tell students to list the sources they used to answer each question in this exercise.

Reading with a Focus

How much do you know about the ancient Mayas of Central America? If you choose a topic you haven't experienced or can't observe firsthand, you'll probably use magazines and newspapers for ideas and information. Reading for a specific purpose—to find information about your topic—is very different from reading a novel for pleasure or browsing through a magazine. When you've found a possible source of information, follow these steps.

1. "Check out" the source first; don't start reading on page 1. Look for key words in the index (*Mayas, Central America*), study the table of contents, and in the text check headings, charts, and illustrations. Be on alert for your topic.
2. Skim until you're sure you've found information on your topic, and then slow down and read every word. Take notes on both main ideas and specific details, using your own words unless the exact quotation is important. Keep track of the sources you use.

☞ REFERENCE NOTE: For more on using library resources, see pages 952–957.

EXERCISE 7 ▶ **Reading with a Focus**

In Florida, the manatee, an aquatic mammal, is in danger of extinction. In California, the condor, a large vulture, faces similar problems. What animals in your state are on the endangered species list or may soon be put there? Find some information about an endangered animal, and read to find answers to the following questions. If you work in a group, each person could find a different source and compare your answers.

identified at the start of the program in the sequence in which they will be presented. When addressing **Listening with a Focus**, students should use the program introduction as a table of contents in a book. This will help them prepare to focus if a relevant item is to be included.

Suggest that for **Exercise 8**, students prepare *5W-How?* charts to assist them in answering the main questions.

To discuss **Imagining**, note that "What if?" questions can also be asked in familiar surroundings. Writers such as Stephen King and filmmakers such as Alfred Hitchcock have often based their creative works on unusual "What if?" twists to everyday situations.

You could use **Exercise 9** as independent practice. If students have difficulty

1. What are the animal's habitat and feeding habits?
2. Why is the animal in danger of becoming extinct? (Look for multiple reasons.)
3. How long has the animal been in trouble?
4. What efforts to date have been made to save the animal? How successful have these efforts been?

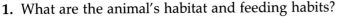

Listening with a Focus

Printed words aren't your only outside source of information. You can also listen—to radio and television programs, to video and audio tapes from the library, to people (anyone knowledgeable about your topic) in personal or telephone interviews. Good listening means focused listening, so prepare in advance.

1. Brainstorm or cluster what you already know about your topic, and reread any of your reading notes.
2. Make a list of the information you're looking for about your topic (in question form, if you want). Keep it by you as you listen.
3. Think ahead about note taking. You can't record every word, and you can't always "rewind" and rehear. Get the main points and supporting details by writing in phrases and using abbreviations.

☞ REFERENCE NOTE: For information on interviewing, see pages 943–944.

EXERCISE 8 ▶ **Listening for Specific Information**

Listen to an evening sportscast on your local television station. If there is more than one sportscast, divide the class so that some of you listen to each program. Listen for answers to the following questions.

1. What's the top sports story? Why is it ranked most important? Does it, for example, involve an outstanding sports performance, or does it involve the amount of money a player has signed for?
2. What sport is given the most time in the broadcast— football, baseball, soccer, or some other sport?

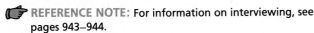

ANSWERS
Exercise 7

After locating sources, students should jot down answers as quickly as possible. The object here is for students to keep specific questions in mind as they consult no more than three sources each within a limited amount of time. At this point, no one should be penalized if sources do not provide all information. When groups compare individual answers, they can prepare a composite report with answers to all questions.

ANSWERS
Exercise 8

Although there are four main questions, this exercise calls for six answers. Be sure students have all questions in mind before they begin the listening assignment. Remind students to review questions just before the news and then to jot down notes for answers immediately after the news.

grasping the distinctions between different writing purposes, provide and discuss examples of different forms that illustrate the relationship between purpose and form. Note that in highly personal writing that others probably won't see, the purpose is often to sort out and understand feelings. Therefore, the writer is also the audience.

If you have shown examples of some literary forms listed in the textbook, you could have groups brainstorm and identify intended audience and tone in those examples. You could also have students discuss intended audience and suitable tones for the other forms of writing listed.

A DIFFERENT APPROACH

Read aloud the first chapter of H. G. Wells's *The Time Machine*. Have students take notes about the characters, plot, and unfamiliar vocabulary words. When you have finished reading, write a list of student-suggested unfamiliar words on the chalkboard. Ask individual students to find and read definitions for each. Then, initiate a discussion to lead the students in paraphrasing the plot and describing the characters.

After the discussion, tell students that they are time travelers who are about to create time machines. Explain that each student should draw or describe a design for the machine. Ask students to include brief explanations of how the machine works, where in time they will travel, and why they chose their destinations.

ANSWERS

Exercise 9

As students brainstorm, they should record ideas. Remind them to begin their questions with "What if?" When each group has ten or more ideas, students can make judgments about which idea is the best. The class might vote on the best movie idea from among group choices.

3. What's the most interesting story in the sportscast? What makes it interesting?
4. Based on the time devoted to each, whose sport seems more important—men's or women's?

Imagining

When you write creatively—stories, poems, plays, and so on—you usually write about people, places, and events that aren't real. You may begin with what you've observed, but many of the details have to come from your imagination. One way to spark your imagination for these kinds of details is to ask yourself "What if?" questions. Filmmakers and other creative people often use these kinds of questions to produce unusual ideas. The question *What if a family went on vacation and forgot to take one of the children along?* resulted in *Home Alone*—one of the biggest moneymaking movies of the early 1990s.

Here are some general questions that can help get you in a creative mode.

1. *What if I could change one thing in the past?* (What if my family had moved to a lighthouse off the coast of Maine? What if I had been born the greatest genius the world had ever seen?)
2. *What if something we take for granted were totally different?* (What if all the electricity all across the country went off at once and stayed off? What if everyone looked exactly alike?)
3. *What if I could create something new?* (What if I designed an invention that could move people through time as well as space? What if I could write music that would make everyone feel happy?)

EXERCISE 9 ▶   **Using the "What if?" Questions**

The movie moguls are in trouble. They've got to come up with a dynamite movie idea, or the studio will go broke. Working with several of your classmates, brainstorm a series of "What if?" questions that might result in a movie idea for the studio. When you've finished, choose the idea you think would make the best movie.

 *Prewriting*

Thinking About Purpose, Audience, and Tone

Purpose. Any piece of writing—even the most personal, that no one will ever see—has a *purpose*, a reason for being. You write in many different forms, but you always write for some end result: to express feelings, to be creative, to explain or inform, or to persuade. (You may even combine two or more purposes in a single piece of writing.) This chart shows the different forms you may use for each of the main purposes.

MAIN PURPOSE	FORMS OF WRITING
To express yourself	Journal, letter, personal essay
To be creative	Short story, poem, play, novel
To explain or inform	Science and history writing, newspaper and magazine articles, biography, autobiography, travel essay
To persuade	Persuasive essay, letter to editor, advertisement, political speech

Audience. It's also true that your *audience*—your readers—affect what you say and how you say it. To consider the needs of your audience, you can use these questions.

- Why am I writing for this audience? Do I want to inform or persuade them? to share a personal experience, amuse them, or stir their emotions?
- What does my audience already know about my topic? (You want to help readers, not bore them!)
- What will this particular audience be looking for or find interesting?
- What level of language is appropriate for this audience? A simple or more complex vocabulary? Short sentences, long sentences, or both?

MEETING individual NEEDS

LEP/ESL

Spanish and French. Speakers of Spanish and French have an advantage when it comes to audience analysis because these languages have a sense of audience built into their pronoun systems. In both languages, one set of second-person pronouns is used with audiences composed of family members, close friends, and children, and another set of more formal pronouns is used in all other situations. Thus, speakers of these languages intuitively learn how to adjust their speech to suit their audiences. You can take advantage of this fact by pointing out the analogy between pronoun usage in Spanish and French and the use of different tones and words with different audiences.

Tone. You can think of *tone* as the personality of your writing. You can sound outraged, sarcastic, serious, or funny. You can sound casual and personal or more distant and formal. How you sound—your tone—comes from the language you use. To create the tone you want, pay attention to

- choice of details (facts? sensory words? personal thoughts?)
- choice of words (slang? conversational style? figurative language? formal wording?)
- the rhythms and sounds of language (short, brisk sentences? long, leisurely ones?)

A word that's closely related to tone is voice. *Voice* simply means writing in a way that sounds like you. You can do this even when you're writing with a formal, serious tone by making your writing sound as natural as possible. Avoid using words or phrases just because they sound pretentious or knowledgeable. Use the precise word, but keep your writing as simple as possible. Let your own voice come through.

CRITICAL THINKING

Analyzing Purpose and Audience

You already tailor your writing to different situations even though you may not always stop and think about it. You don't write the same way in journal entries, reports, funny letters to friends, and thank-you letters to your aunt. Making that tailoring conscious simply makes your writing better.

Adjust your writing for both your purpose and your audience. To see how this works, read the following excerpt of a review of *Once Upon a Time . . . When We Were Colored*, a film by Tim Reid. The author's main purpose is to evaluate the film and thus to persuade others to see it.

TEACHING *ANALYZING PURPOSE AND AUDIENCE*

Before starting the **Critical Thinking Exercise**, review with the class the definitions of informing and persuading on p. 22.

Before reading the film reviews, point out that the term *colored* in the title of the film was considered a polite term for African Americans in the 1940s.

Before students write the informative piece, you could show photographs illustrating changes in automotive design over the last four decades. Suggest that drawing pictures of the car of the future may help students get started.

Before students write the evaluation (ad), suggest that they think in terms of a sequence of events or reasons that will lead a

It is almost impossible to express the cumulative power of *Once Upon a Time . . . When We Were Colored.* It isn't a slick, tightly packaged docudrama, but a film from the heart, a film that is not a protest against the years of segregation so much as a celebration of the human qualities that endured and overcame. Although the movie is about African Americans, its message is about the universal human spirit. I am aware of three screenings it has had at film festivals: before a largely black audience in Chicago, a largely white audience in Virginia, and a largely Asian audience in Honolulu. All three audiences gave it a standing ovation. There you have it.

Roger Ebert, *Chicago Sun-Times*

What guesses would you make about the audience for this review? Notice that, in addition to evaluating the film, the reviewer is careful to give enough information for readers who haven't seen the film. The audience consists of general readers, who may or may not have seen the film.

Now read a short passage that has a different purpose and a slightly different audience. The purpose of these paragraphs is to inform readers about the movie and about the actor Tim Reid's involvement with it.

MEETING *individual* NEEDS

ADVANCED STUDENTS

Students might enjoy researching Tim Reid's career and accomplishments and then reporting their findings to the class. Using this information, the class could discuss possible audiences that Tim Reid attempts to reach and how he achieves his purpose.

LESS-ADVANCED STUDENTS

Some students might have difficulty distinguishing informative from persuasive writing. Before beginning the **Critical Thinking Exercise**, guide students in examining and discussing automobile evaluations in magazines or newspapers. Work with them to look for examples of informative writing and car ads found in similar sources for examples of persuasive writing.

SELECTION AMENDMENT
Description of change: excerpted
Rationale: to focus on the concept of purpose and audience presented in this chapter

buyer to want or need this particular car. Remind them of the current concerns about fuel efficiency and pollution. After students have completed the exercise, have them review their ads to identify their judgments and to label their supporting reasons. To conclude, have partners exchange ads and write evaluations by responding as parents with three young children. Ask, "What reasons would lead you to want or need this car?" and "What reasons would you have for not wanting or needing this car?"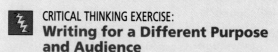

Tim Reid's *Once Upon a Time . . . When We Were Colored* has been lauded as a movie all Americans should see. Set in 1946 in the Mississippi Delta, the movie chronicles the life of Cliff, who is African American, and, likewise, the period of history and the community in which he grows up. The three actors who play Cliff at age five (Charles Earl Taylor, Jr.), age twelve (Willis Norwood, Jr.), and age sixteen (Damon Hines) are supported by strong performances from Phylicia Rashad, Richard Roundtree, Iona Morris, Nila Fontaine, Isaac Hayes, and Al Freeman, Jr.

Reid based the movie on the best-selling book by Clifton L. Taulbert; Paul W. Cooper wrote the screenplay. After reading the book, Reid, a television actor, was determined to produce the film, despite the fact that the story was not easily packaged as a box-office hit. He and the cast shot on location in North Carolina, capturing authentically—in 111 minutes of film—the feel of the era.

Notice how, in this second piece, the writer gives much more information about the film than the reviewer whose purpose is to evaluate the film.

CRITICAL THINKING EXERCISE:
Writing for a Different Purpose and Audience

What will the car of the future be like? Write a short, informative piece for readers who haven't seen the car that you plan to be driving in twenty years. Then, write an evaluation (an ad) of the same car. This time your purpose is to persuade readers to buy the car. These readers may or may not already have seen the car.

MEETING *individual* NEEDS

LEARNING STYLES

Visual Learners. Students might find inspiration for their own ideas for future cars if you display colorful pictures or posters of various antique, classic, and late-model cars.

Kinetic Learners. Students might better organize their ideas for both informing and persuading if they are permitted to draw or make clay models of their cars of the future.

ANSWERS

Critical Thinking Exercise

Responses will vary. After brainstorming for ideas about new technology and visualizing a car's appearance, students should begin a straightforward descriptive paragraph with an explanation of how the car works. The tone should be authoritative, and the point of view should be third person. ("The twin jet exhaust overdrive conserves three gallons of potato-based fuel," etc.) For the persuasive paragraph, students may find further visualization and "What if?" scenarios useful. Such a tone excites and challenges. The point of view is second person, to address readers directly.

 *Prewriting*

Arranging Ideas

By now you've gathered a ton of information. You could gather still more, but you really think you've had enough. Before writing, though, you need to think about arranging your prewriting ideas. This chart shows four common ways of ordering, or arranging, ideas.

ARRANGING IDEAS		
TYPE OF ORDER	**DEFINITION**	**EXAMPLES**
Chronological	Narration: Order that presents events as they happen in time	Story; narrative poem; explanation of a process; history
Spatial	Description: Order that describes objects according to location	Description (near to far; left to right; top to bottom; and so on)
Importance	Evaluation: Order that gives details from least to most important or the reverse	Persuasive writing; description; explanation (main idea and supporting details); evaluative writing
Logical	Classification: Order that relates items and groups	Definition; classifications; comparison and contrast

☞ REFERENCE NOTE: For more information on arranging ideas, see pages 82–85.

COOPERATIVE LEARNING
You could have the class examine the **Arranging Ideas** chart more comprehensively. Group the class into teams of three or four and assign each team one of the types of order. Explain that each team should create an original poster for its assigned order. One member should be responsible for printing the title and copying the definition. All members must collaborate to find and cut out example paragraphs from magazines and newspapers. After the paragraphs have been glued to each poster, additional artwork may be added. When all teams have finished, select one student from each team to use the poster to explain the order and to read several sample paragraphs.

TECHNOLOGY TIP
Have partners use a computer graphics program to create their organizational charts and then to type and organize their answers on the computer screen. Remind students to include their names on the printouts that they hand in for evaluation.

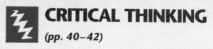
TEACHING ARRANGING INFORMATION

You may want to use the paragraph from *A Browser's Dictionary* as guided practice. Define terms with which students are not familiar. After displaying the text on an overhead projector and defining *analysis*, have students identify the main idea and bracket it in red. Then, have students identify

MEETING *individual* NEEDS

LEP/ESL

General Strategies. You may want to help students focus more clearly on the purpose of sequencing. Offer the analogy of telling a joke. Ask students, "What happens if the punchline comes before instead of after the lead-in material? Is the joke still funny?" Solicit examples from real life (such as following recipes, or starting a car) in which sequence produces desired results.

COOPERATIVE LEARNING

You could use the excerpt from *The Norton Anthology of Literature by Women* as a cooperative learning tool by having partners find details in the paragraph. After students identify each detail, suggest that they use time lines like the one following to record major events in Mourning Dove's life, from birth to the publication of her novel:

```
              Details
      1st  2nd  3rd  4th  5th
Start |----+----+----+----| End
```

SELECTION AMENDMENT
Description of change: excerpted
Rationale: to focus on the concept of arranging information presented in this chapter

---

CRITICAL THINKING
Arranging Information

When you're deciding how to arrange ideas, once again think about purpose, audience, and subject. Sometimes purpose and audience lead to a particular arrangement. If you're writing about a typical school day in a letter to a foreign exchange student who'll soon be attending your school, you'll probably describe events in the order they happened (chronological order). But if you're writing about your own day in a journal entry, you might start with the highlights and move to the more insignificant incidents (order of importance).

Often the subject itself suggests the order of ideas. For example, this paragraph contrasts how American colonists paid for large items with how they made small transactions. It's natural for this writer to use logical order.

> Colonial America, lacking an official mint, suffered a constant shortage of small coins. Large transactions could be handled with letters of credit, but how did a traveler pay for a meal or for a drink? Coins of all nations were used in making change, the commonest being the Spanish silver piece of eight, very like the later U.S. silver dollar, and so called because it was stamped with a large Arabic 8 to signify a value of eight Spanish *reals*, a *real* having a value of about 12 1/2¢. (There was a Mexican *real* of that value [later a peso], but there is no evidence that the coin had a general circulation in the early colonies.) A whole piece of eight, however, was a coin of substantial value. To provide small change, these coins were regularly cut into halves and quarters called "bits."
>
> John Ciardi, *A Browser's Dictionary*

each example of comparison/contrast. As they do, number each in blue. Ask volunteers to apply the definition of *analysis* to this activity and to explain the process in their own words.

Using the paragraph on the next page from *The Name of the Rose* as independent practice, note that in descriptive writing, some paragraphs may not have a main idea. They may simply create an overall impression by depicting a setting. If students have difficulty analyzing the order of details, draw a schematic outline of a rectangular room with an opening for a door. As students identify individual features, use letters, simple drawings, or architectural notations to locate these features on the schematic. Then, have students review order definitions. ☞

CRITICAL THINKING EXERCISE:
Analyzing the Order of Details

Using the chart on page 39, decide which type of order each of these passages uses.

1.   The first native-American woman to write and publish a novel, Mourning Dove (a translation of Hum-ishu-ma) was a member of the Okanogan tribe, whose communities were located in British Columbia and north-central Washington state. Born near Bonner's Ferry, Idaho, she was given the English name Christal Quintasket but raised in part by a grandmother who taught her to respect the rapidly vanishing traditions of her people. Although she had little formal education—three years at the Sacred Heart Convent in Ward, Washington, and brief periods at government Indian schools—Mourning Dove began early to collect and transcribe Okanogan tribal legends. In 1912, she enrolled in a business school to study English and typing so that she could improve her work on Indian tales and on the novel-in-progress which was to become her *Cogewea the Half Blood: A Depiction of the Great Montana Cattle Range* (1927).

1. chronological   Sandra M. Gilbert and Susan Gubar, *The Norton Anthology of Literature by Women: The Tradition in English*

COOPERATIVE LEARNING
Create teams of three and assign each member one paragraph of the **Critical Thinking Exercise.** Allow the students to refer to the chart on p. 39. Remind groups that team members should collaborate on answers and help each other as needed. Ask students to initial their answers before the teams hand in their assignments.

INTEGRATING THE LANGUAGE ARTS
Vocabulary Link. You may want to discuss how transitions connect ideas and how certain transitions relate to certain types of writing. Brainstorm with the class for conjunctions and prepositions that can be used as transitional words or phrases that show chronological or spatial order. List these on a chalkboard or an overhead transparency. Ask students to use the words and phrases that indicate spatial order to write five sentences describing the classroom. Then have them copy the lists in their writing journals for future reference.

SELECTION AMENDMENT
Description of change: excerpted
Rationale: to focus on the concept of analyzing the order of details presented in this chapter

2.   In the 1990s, as in the past, there will be conservatives, liberals, and progressives. Conservatives want to maintain the status quo or turn back the clock. Liberals want to change things a little, incrementally. Progressives want rapid, significant change. Too often, progressives focus almost exclusively on ends (programs) and not enough on means (power). We need power, program, and progress—in that order. Progressives need power in order to implement their program, in order to make progress.

2. logical
                     Jesse L. Jackson, "We Need Power, Program, and Progress"

3.   I said before that at this point you pushed a wooden door and found yourself in the kitchen, behind the fireplace, at the foot of the circular staircase that led to the scriptorium. And just as we were pushing that door, we heard to our left some muffled sounds within the wall. They came from the wall beside the door, where the row of niches with skulls and bones ended. Instead of a last niche, there was a stretch of blank wall of large squared blocks of stone, with an old plaque in the center that had some worn monograms carved on it. The sounds came, it seemed, from behind the plaque, or else from above the plaque, partly beyond the wall, and partly almost over our heads.

3. spatial
                     Umberto Eco, *The Name of the Rose*

⚡

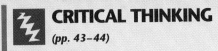
OBJECTIVE

- To make a chart classifying information according to a logical order of ideas

You may want to provide students with a model or graphic representation of the solar system to show the size and comparative distance of each planet from the sun. Tell students that an easy way to remember the planets is to organize them in order of distance from the sun (Mercury,

Using Charts

As visual organizations of information, charts are often a helpful technique for arranging your prewriting notes. They help you see "blocks" of information, and their relationships, clearly. Here's a chart about two minerals and their effects on our health. The writer organizes the information into three categories: each mineral's sources, its function, and deficiency symptoms.

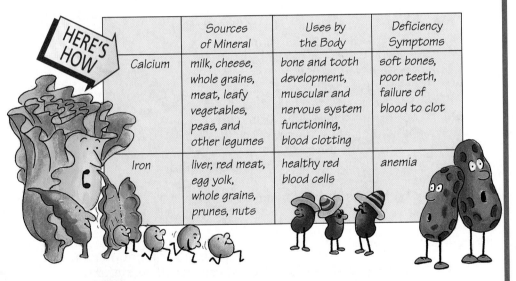

HERE'S HOW

	Sources of Mineral	Uses by the Body	Deficiency Symptoms
Calcium	milk, cheese, whole grains, meat, leafy vegetables, peas, and other legumes	bone and tooth development, muscular and nervous system functioning, blood clotting	soft bones, poor teeth, failure of blood to clot
Iron	liver, red meat, egg yolk, whole grains, prunes, nuts	healthy red blood cells	anemia

CRITICAL THINKING

Classifying Information

When you make a chart, you're *classifying*, grouping together related information. And this takes thinking—deciding on the headings, or categories, to cover your information. Here's a way to approach the task.

1. Read through your notes. When you find items that seem to go together, rewrite them in a new list.
2. Look at each list, and decide what the items have in common. Why do they belong together? Your answer is a heading or category for the list.

Venus, Earth, Mars, Jupiter, Saturn, Uranus, Neptune, Pluto).

For closure, have students refer to the charts they created for arranging ideas. Have them add a column head, "Graphics," and insert "chart" and "time line" in the appropriate places.

ANSWERS
Critical Thinking Exercise

Charts will vary. However information is arranged, charts should contain all the information in the example below.

PLANET	EARTH	SATURN
Proximity to sun	third	sixth
Characteristics	small dense warm	large not dense cold
Type	terrestrial	giant
Orbit	365 days	almost 30 years
Satellites	1	18

CRITICAL THINKING EXERCISE:
Making a Chart to Organize Information

With a small group, make a chart of the following information about the planets Saturn and Earth. Remember: first group similar information and then decide on headings. Compare your chart with another group's.

Earth—one of terrestrial planets
 (Mercury, Venus, Earth, and Mars)
Earth—third planet from sun
Earth's orbit (once around sun) 365 days
Saturn's almost 30 years
Saturn—one of giant planets
 (Jupiter, Saturn, Uranus, Neptune)
Saturn—sixth planet from sun
Giant planets—large, much less dense, and cold (because far from sun)
Terrestrial planets—small, dense, and warm
Earth—one moon
Saturn—at least 18 named satellites

A time line is a chart of chronological information. It helps you (and your readers) organize dated information by clearly showing the sequence of actions or events. Here is a time line of important events in American independence.

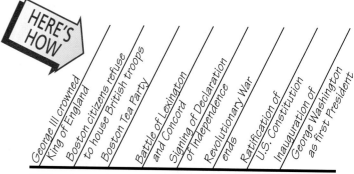

HERE'S HOW

George III crowned King of England
Boston citizens refuse to house British troops
Boston Tea Party
Battle of Lexington and Concord
Signing of Declaration of Independence
Revolutionary War ends
Ratification of U.S. Constitution
Inauguration of George Washington as first President

1760 1768 1773 1775 1776 1783 1788 1789

WRITING A FIRST DRAFT

OBJECTIVE

- To plan and develop a first draft from existing prewriting notes

TEACHING THE LESSON

Tell students to find in the dictionary the meaning of *draft* as it is used in the text. Ask volunteers to share other definitions. Note that the ways to approach writing a first draft are as varied as the dictionary definitions of the word.

You may need to distinguish between freewriting and drafting—jotting down ideas

 Writing a First Draft

It would be easy to keep prewriting . . . until your paper's due. That's not the idea. At some point, you have to dive in and start a draft.

There's no single right way to write a draft. You may feel comfortable writing a first draft based on scribbled notes only you could interpret. Or you may need a detailed outline before you begin. You may write quickly, trying just to get your ideas down on paper. Or you may shape each sentence carefully, trying to connect ideas with exactly the right word. As you write your first draft, try these suggestions.

- Use your prewriting plans to guide your draft.
- Write freely, but try to express your ideas clearly.
- Don't hesitate to add new ideas and details. Writing *is* discovery.
- Don't worry about errors in grammar, usage, and mechanics. You can find and fix them later.

COMPUTER NOTE: To avoid the urge to correct mechanical errors as you write, type with your monitor dimmed. Turn it back up to review what you've written.

Here is the first draft of a brief paper on a sport called lacrosse. Notice how the writer makes a change (a revision) even while drafting and also writes personal notes and questions that will lead back to prewriting.

 HERE'S HOW

Lacrosse is a team sport that Native Americans invented a long time ago. French explorers named it lacrosse because its long, curved playing stick looked like a bishop's staff, [what's French word?]. It's really a long-handled racket, with a mesh head like a pocket.

 **PROGRAM MANAGER**

WRITING A FIRST DRAFT

- **Instructional Support** For suggestions on developing prewriting notes into a first draft, see **The First Draft** in *Practicing the Writing Process*, p. 10.

QUOTATION FOR THE DAY

"I have never started a poem yet whose end I knew. Writing a poem is discovering." (Robert Frost, 1874–1963, American poet, winner of the Pulitzer Prize for poetry)

After writing the quotation on the chalkboard, explain to students that their starting an essay is similar to Frost's starting a poem. The writer discovers what he or she wants to say as the writing unfolds.

MEETING *individual* NEEDS

LEP/ESL

General Strategies. Because students might not have had any exposure to the two sports mentioned in the text (lacrosse and in-line skating), you may want to suggest that they write first drafts about their favorite sports.

as fast as they occur, instead of using an existing prewriting plan. Refer to the example of a first draft as illustration.

You may want to use **Exercise 10** as guided practice, suggesting clustering or another prewriting technique as an alternative.

CLOSURE

Have a volunteer explain the difference between drafting and freewriting. ■

The ball is passed and received in this stick, and players score points by kicking or throwing/hurling the ball into the goal.

Lacrosse is a rough game, but it's an ancient, formal sport. Since 18?? [check date] it's been the official national sport of Canada. Oren Lyons, on the Iroquois Nationals team [chief too—Onandagas?], has said, "We were playing team sports here when in Europe, they were still knocking people off horses, clubbing each other, fencing for keeps, all those so-called sports."

EXERCISE 10 ▶ Writing a First Draft

Here are some prewriting notes about a very modern sport, in-line skating. Work alone or with a partner to turn the notes into an interesting paragraph. You can add or drop details if you want. Then, arrange the information and start drafting.

In-line skates—roller skates similar to ice skates—four wheels in a single file down the middle of the skate

1980 first appeared—for professional ice hockey players to practice off-season

Can perform stunts—similar to skateboarding; most skaters just cruise

Expensive—$180 to $250 pair

Cheryl Rowars, Miami Beach, sells one to three pairs every day: "They sell because it's something fun to do. It's not replacing the skateboard, though."

Requires a strong sideways stroke—"A great workout" Sara Kendall, age 15

"It's a super athletic sport without contact"—Rick Carlson, South Miami

Beginning in 1981—bought by ordinary people

ANSWERS

Exercise 10

Responses will vary. Students should write a first draft using logical order. Starting with definition, they should group related ideas, add background, and include further information. Encourage students to combine related ideas into compound and complex sentences. Students may add or omit details but should include information and sources the audience needs. For example, a paragraph might begin, "In-line skates, skates with four wheels in a line, instead of a blade, first appeared in 1980. They were invented for ice hockey practice in the off-season, but by 1981 they had reached the general public."

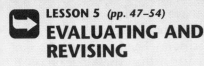
OBJECTIVE

- To evaluate and revise the first draft of a given paragraph

MOTIVATION

Have students discuss planning a picnic—choosing a date, a site, a menu, and activities. Then, have students evaluate the plan and revise it according to variables such as rain, cost, and effect of temperature on food. Afterward, relate their planning and changes to evaluating and revising.

Evaluating and Revising

Although they often occur at the same time, evaluating and revising are two separate steps in your writing.

> **Evaluating**—deciding on your paper's strengths and weaknesses
>
> **Revising**—making improvements

Evaluating

You have something to say about how good (or bad) things are every day. You evaluate your friend's new shirt and the food at a party. You evaluate your options for work: lifeguarding or tutoring. Evaluating your own writing, though, is more personal—and that means much harder.

Self-Evaluation.   Three strategies can help you evaluate your writing.

> READING CAREFULLY. Read your paper several times, concentrating each time on something different. First, read for *content* (what you say), then for *organization* (how you've arranged your ideas), and then for *style* (how you've used words and sentences).
>
> LISTENING CAREFULLY. Read your draft aloud to yourself and try to "hear" what you've written. Using a different sense—hearing instead of reading—may help you notice awkward sentences and foggy ideas.
>
> TAKING TIME. Set your first draft aside for several hours or overnight. You usually see your writing more clearly—as if it's someone else's—if you put it out of your mind for a while.

Peer Evaluation.   All professional writers expect—and even rely on—other people to read their work: friends, family, editors. Other people are simply more objective, and, after all, writers write for *readers*.

PROGRAM MANAGER

EVALUATING AND REVISING

- **Reinforcement/Reteaching** See **Revision Transparencies 1** and **2**. For suggestions on how to tie the transparencies to instruction, review teacher's notes in *Fine Art and Instructional Transparencies for Writing*, pp. 95, 97.

- **Ongoing Assessment** To help students apply peer evaluation techniques and identify four ways to revise, see **Peer Evaluation, Revising by Adding and Cutting,** and **Revising by Replacing and Reordering** in *Practicing the Writing Process*, pp. 11–13.

- **Assessment/Reflection** To assess student work and evaluate progress, see **Portfolio Forms** in *Portfolio Assessment*, pp. 5–21.

QUOTATION FOR THE DAY

"The only impeccable writers are those who never wrote." (William Hazlitt, 1778–1830, English essayist and critic)

You may wish to write the word *impeccable* on the chalkboard and ask a volunteer to define the word. Then, share the quotation with the class. As students begin evaluating and revising their first drafts, remind the class that although no writer is impeccable, it is still a goal to strive for.

Remind students that thinking and writing are part of the same process. Note that evaluating involves thinking and that revising is putting that thinking into practice through writing. Before beginning **Self-Evaluation**, p. 47, guide students toward the realization that objectivity is a critical element in personal evaluation. After reading **Self-Evaluation**, have students paraphrase the three strategies in their writing journals.

When discussing **Peer Evaluation**, p. 47, note that even the wisest person makes mistakes. Good evaluators constructively criticize the work, not the person who wrote the work.

Cont. on p. 51

MEETING *individual* NEEDS

LEP/ESL

General Strategies. Evaluating a draft could easily be one of the most critical stages for students. If at all possible, you may want to spend a short amount of time with each student, emphasizing the positive aspects of the draft and making comments that are purposefully encouraging. Your individual attention will probably prove to be the confidence-builder that each student requires.

ADVANCED STUDENTS

Have students research the lives and accomplishments of great musicians such as Mozart or Beethoven, write several paragraphs, and present their findings to the class. Tell students that you would like to use these paragraphs as examples for the evaluation process. Display one or two of these reports on an overhead projector. Using the criteria listed in the **Critical Thinking** section, guide the class in recognizing positive features as well as points for improvement.

You can have the help of outside readers by working with your classmates in peer-evaluation groups, which can be just two people or as many as four or five. Remember that in peer evaluation you have two roles: Sometimes you're the writer whose work is being evaluated, and sometimes you're the evaluator of other students' writing.

EVALUATING

Guidelines for the Writer

1. List some specific questions or concerns. What part of your paper do you think needs work?
2. Keep a positive attitude. Think of the evaluator's comments as real help for you. Don't get defensive or depressed about them.

Guidelines for the Peer Evaluator

1. Always look for strengths as well as weaknesses. Writers not only need encouragement, but they also need to know what's good in their writing and build on it.
2. Be serious and thorough about the evaluation, but also be sensitive. For example, ask the writer a question about a weakness instead of just pointing it out.
3. Make specific, positive suggestions for improvement. A criticism of a weakness without any ideas for fixing it is negative.
4. Look at content, organization, and style. Don't comment on mistakes in spelling, usage, and mechanics unless they make the meaning unclear. Proofreading comes later.

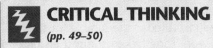

CRITICAL THINKING

(pp. 49–50)

OBJECTIVE

• To practice evaluation by applying given criteria to a model paragraph

TEACHING *EVALUATING*

Before starting the exercise, you may want to discuss the criteria by relating them to concepts that have been taught; for example, expression of a main idea through a topic sentence, kinds of supporting information, use of direct references and transitions, choosing an order of ideas, unity, and coherence.

CRITICAL THINKING

Evaluating

You know that evaluating means making a judgment about whether something is good, bad, or somewhere in between. You evaluate things all the time—movies, CDs, the latest styles of jeans. When you evaluate anything, you measure it against a set of established criteria, or standards. Here are some criteria for evaluating effective writing.

1. The writing gets and holds your attention—it's interesting.
2. The meaning is clear.
3. There is a main idea.
4. There are enough supporting details for the main idea in the piece of writing.
5. The ideas are connected smoothly—no gaps or jumps to cause confusion.
6. The ideas are arranged well; their order makes sense.
7. The writing has no clichés (trite words or phrases) or unnecessary repetition and details.

 CRITICAL THINKING EXERCISE:
Evaluating a Paragraph

Try out your peer-evaluation skills, using the seven criteria given above. With a partner or small group, discuss the following paragraph and write at least three comments about what can be improved in the paragraph. As you work, keep in mind the Guidelines for the Peer Evaluator on page 48.

> Ludwig van Beethoven lived from 1770 to 1827. He was born in Bonn, Germany. What's most amazing about Beethoven is that he composed some of his greatest music when he was totally deaf. Beethoven was from a musical family. He showed his genius early. Some of his music was published when he was twelve. When he was seventeen, he met Wolfgang Amadeus Mozart. Mozart

 TIMESAVER
Have group members initial individual comments before the group's evaluation is presented to you. You can then quickly assess student contributions and consider how well each group has collaborated.

If students appear to be having difficulty with the exercise, select volunteers to suggest a topic sentence. Ask others to find information that supports this main idea. Next, have volunteers identify persons who could be the subjects of direct references. Ask others to substitute references for their names. Then, ask volunteers to suggest transitions that could be used to connect ideas. Ask others to suggest points at which these transitions could be substituted in the sample. Last, have partners work together to suggest an order that would make the main idea clear.

ANSWERS
Critical Thinking Exercise

Groups or partners should make at least three suggestions to solve problems with appeal, clarity, focus, supporting detail, transitions, arrangement, clichés, or unnecessary repetition. Suggestions will vary. Here are some possibilities:

1. No strong topic sentence to hold two main points (early genius and later deafness) together

2. Deafness mentioned in two places, causing organizational problems

3. Many unnecessary repetitions and rough transitions because only one detail appears in each sentence

4. Unclear to reader at first that Beethoven was deaf when composing Ninth Symphony

said of Beethoven: "Keep your eyes on him. Someday, he will give the world something to talk about." Beethoven moved to Vienna. He stayed there for the rest of his life and is buried there too. He became deaf gradually but for the last nine years of his life was totally deaf. He completed his last symphony, the Ninth Symphony, in 1824. The Ninth Symphony is called the Choral Symphony because of its "Ode to Joy" chorus in the last movement. He was completely deaf then. He directed the symphony when it was first performed. He couldn't hear the music or the applause.

Peanuts reprinted by permission of United Feature Syndicate, Inc.

Revising

After your classmates evaluate your paper, you'll need some time to think about their comments and suggestions and to combine them with your own ideas of what's wrong. Which comments about problems really seem on target? Which suggested changes seem like good solutions? (Remember your purpose and audience—they'll help you make decisions.)

Once you've decided what *needs* to be done, you move on to *doing* it: revising, or making the actual changes that will fix the problems you've found. There are four basic revision techniques—adding, cutting, replacing, and reordering—that you can use to make changes. In this

Cont. from p. 48

Have students evaluate their paraphrasing of the **Self-Evaluation** strategies.
Select volunteers to read aloud what they
have written and to share their specific questions and concerns. Model peer evaluation for
the class by making comments that reflect the
Guidelines for the Peer Evaluator on p. 48.
Have partners take turns evaluating by using

the guidelines in the textbook.

Before students begin revising,
emphasize the chart of evaluating guidelines.
When discussing the **Revising Techniques**
chart, relate each technique to a concept
that the students have already learned. New
information should be added to make the
meaning clear or to provide more support
for the main idea. Cutting helps achieve

stage, look at your first draft as just what it is—a beginning—and don't be shy about marking it up. Handwrite
your corrections on the paper, using the revising and
proofreading symbols on page 60, and then make a new
copy by rewriting, retyping, or making the changes on the
computer and printing the new version.

REVISING TECHNIQUES	
TECHNIQUE	EXAMPLE
1. **Add.** Add new informa-tion and details. Add words, phrases, sen-tences, whole paragraphs.	*↑ or chain of islands↑* The Japanese archipelago is made up of four large islands and many smaller ones.
2. **Cut.** Take out informa-tion, details, examples, or words. Cut repetition, wordiness, and details unrelated to the main idea.	From 1904 to 1914 the United States built the Panama Canal, a~~canal~~ which connects ~~two bodies of water,~~ the Atlantic and Pacific oceans.
3. **Replace.** Take out weak words, clichés, awkward-sounding sentences, unnecessary information or details. Replace with more precise words, more relevant details.	Sydney, Australia, was founded in 1788 and was the *penal colony* first place for British *convicts* ~~troublemakers.~~
4. **Reorder.** Move phrases, details, examples, or paragraphs for variety and an order that makes sense.	The Galapagos Islands are in the Pacific Ocean off South America, known for their giant tortoises and other unique species.

unity and can add coherence. Replacing and reordering are directly related to coherence.

To help students visualize the relationship between the specific revisions and the concepts, have them make a chart with each of the revising techniques as a heading. Then, have partners list each revision under the appropriate heading.

Use **Exercise 11** as cooperative learning. Before students begin, you could discuss the relationship between the characteristics and the criteria for effective writing in the **Guidelines for Evaluating and Revising** on p. 53. Criteria 2, 3, 4, and 5 should be considered when evaluating content. Criteria 6 and 7 should be considered when evaluating organization. Criteria 1, 8, 9, 10, and 11

INTEGRATING THE LANGUAGE ARTS

Usage Link. Initiate a discussion about first-, second-, and third-person points of view. Brainstorm with the class to identify specific examples of magazine and newspaper articles, stories, and books that have been written from each point of view. Note that a shift in point of view may occur in dialogue or direct quotations, but that the point of view remains consistent in a narrative.

Ask each student to write two sentences from each point of view. Select students to write examples on the chalkboard and have the class evaluate and revise any point-of-view shifts found in a sentence. Remind students that they should always check for point-of-view consistency in their writing.

Here are the paragraphs on lacrosse (pages 45–46), revised by using the four revision techniques. To understand the changes, you may want to refer to the chart of symbols for revising and proofreading on page 60. Notice how the writer has answered the questions noted on the first draft.

HERE'S HOW

Lacrosse is a team sport that
Native Americans invented a long time *(more than a thousand years)*   **replace**

ago. French explorers named it lacrosse
because *(they thought)* its long, curved playing stick   **add**

looked like a bishop's staff, [what's French   *a crosier©*   **replace**

word?]. *This stick is* It's really a long-handled racket,   **cut/replace**

with a mesh head like a pocket. The ball is
passed and received *carried* in this stick, and   **add/reorder/ add**

players score points by kicking or throwing   **cut**

hurling the ball into the goal.
  Like hockey, Lacrosse is a rough game, but it's an *(with a lot of physical contact,)*   **add/cut/add**

ancient, formal sport. *(that Indian players are proud of.)* Since 18?? [check *67*   **add/replace**

date] *lacrosse has* it's been the official national sport of   **cut/replace**

Canada. Oren Lyons, *Onandaga chief and leader of* on the Iroquois   **replace**

Nationals team [chief too—Onandagas?],   **cut**

has said, "We were playing team sports

here when in Europe, they were still

knocking people off horses, clubbing each

other, fencing for keeps, all those so-called

sports."   **reorder**

When you evaluate and revise, you're focusing on three different, important aspects of your paper—content, organization, and style—so plan to read through it at least three times. Some overall guidelines for evaluating and revising follow. In later chapters, you'll find similar charts that focus on a particular type of writing.

should be considered when evaluating style.

Emphasize that there is no single correct revision. Any two good writers will produce different revisions. What matters is that the students apply the criteria in the way each thinks best. After the students complete the exercise, you could have the revising teams find and note strengths in each other's revisions.

GUIDED PRACTICE

On the overhead projector, display a paragraph that needs revision. Using the **Guidelines for Evaluating and Revising** chart on this page, guide students through revising the paragraph.

☞

GUIDELINES FOR EVALUATING AND REVISING

EVALUATION GUIDE	REVISION TECHNIQUE
CONTENT	
1 Is the writing interesting?	**Add** examples, an anecdote (brief story), dialogue, and additional details. **Cut** or **replace** repetitious or boring details.
2 Does the writing say and do what you intended it to?	**Add** details that create pictures, express feelings, persuade, or inform or explain.
3 Are there enough details?	**Add** more details, facts, examples, or quotations to support the topic.
4 Are there unrelated ideas or details that distract the reader?	**Cut** irrelevant or distracting information.
5 Are unfamiliar terms explained or defined?	**Add** definitions or other explanations of unfamiliar terms. **Replace** unfamiliar terms with familiar ones.
ORGANIZATION	
6 Are ideas and details arranged in the best possible order?	**Reorder** ideas and details to make the meaning clear.
7 Are the logical connections between ideas and sentences clear?	**Add** transitional words and phrases (*therefore, for example, because*) to link ideas.
STYLE	
8 Is the meaning clear?	**Replace** vague or unclear wording. Use precise, easy-to-understand words and phrases.
9 Does the writing contain clichés or overworked phrases?	**Cut** or **replace** with specific details and fresh comparisons.
10 Is the level of language appropriate for the audience and purpose?	**Replace** formal words with more casual, conversational ones to create an informal tone. To create a more formal tone, **replace** slang and contractions.
11 Do sentences read smoothly?	**Reorder** to vary sentence beginnings and structure.

INDEPENDENT PRACTICE

You may use **Exercise 11** as an independent assignment.

CLOSURE

Ask volunteers to help develop a profile of a good evaluator by having them suggest individual characteristics that would be a part of the profile. Some desirable characteristics might include tact, honesty, and good judgment. ■

ANSWERS
Exercise 11

Revisions may vary. Here is a possibility:

It often seems important to wear just the right outfit, yet we rarely stop to think about the origins of clothing. Originally, clothing was designed for protection from the elements and, probably, for decoration. People in different parts of the world used the materials they had to create their clothing. For example, silk was available in Japan and wool in Australia. Most people made their own clothes until the 1700s, when weaving and sewing machines were invented and started the ready-to-wear industry. In the United States, ready-to-wear has become a major industry, employing designers, weavers, models, sewing-machine operators, and advertising executives. In some places in the world, however, handmade care still goes into each garment, especially in countries that do not rely on New York's Fifth Avenue or the fashion shows in Paris for their sense of style or culture. It sometimes seems that we have lost sight of the originial purpose of clothing and how clothes used to be made.

◆ TIMESAVER

Ask students to highlight their revisions from **Exercise 11** before handing in the assignment.

EXERCISE 11 ▶ **Evaluating and Revising a Paragraph**

Work with a partner to evaluate and revise the following first draft of a paragraph. Be sure to focus on content, organization, and style for this activity, using the guidelines on page 53. (You may correct grammatical errors that you find, but that's not your main task.) Check with another revision team to see if they found similar problems and solutions.

It often seems important to wear just the right outfit. Yet we rarely stop to think about the origins of clothing. Originally, clothing was designed for protection from the elements and probably for decoration. Clothing can tell you something about the person wearing it. People in different parts of the world used the materials they had to create their clothing. For example, Japanese silk and Australian wool. Most people made their own clothes until the 1700s. When weaving and sewing machines were invented and started the ready-to-wear industry. However, in some places in the world, handmade care still goes into each garment, especially in countries that do not rely on New York's Fifth Avenue or the fashion shows in Paris for their sense of style or culture. It has become a major industry, employing designers, weavers, models, sewing-machine operators, and advertising executives. For something that is a basic need, it has gotten out of hand.

PROOFREADING AND PUBLISHING

OBJECTIVES

- To proofread a given paragraph
- To brainstorm ideas for publishing

MOTIVATION

Draw an analogy between revising a piece of writing and fine-tuning an automobile engine. Revising is making sure that all the parts of a piece of writing work together to ensure peak performance. Proofreading is like caring for the interior and exterior of a car. A person makes sure that all the details and the appearance are just right.

Proofreading and Publishing

Just as you take one final look in the mirror to fix whatever isn't "just right" before going out, you'll take a last look at your paper to be sure it's ready to face your readers. This final touching up—getting details and appearance just right—is called *proofreading*.

Proofreading

When you *proofread,* you carefully reread your revised draft to correct mistakes in grammar, usage, and mechanics (spelling, capitalization, and punctuation). Remember that your goal is to find and correct any errors. You've worked hard on your paper, and you don't want any mistakes to distract your audience from what you have to say.

To proofread, put your paper aside for a while. You've been reading it so much during revision that you're probably not noticing every word and comma. Distance can make mistakes jump out clearly.

When you proofread, slow down and read each word carefully. These techniques will make proofreading easier.

1. Focus on one line at a time. Use a sheet of paper to cover all the lines below the one you are proofreading. Some writers proofread backwards—beginning with the bottom line and moving to the top.
2. Try peer proofreading. Exchange papers with a classmate (or group of classmates) and check each other's paper for errors.
3. When in doubt, look it up. Use a college dictionary for spelling and a handbook like the one on pages 510–895 for grammar, usage, and punctuation.
4. Use the revising and proofreading symbols on page 60 to mark changes.

The following guidelines apply to almost all of the writing you'll do for school. Read them before proofreading. They'll remind you of typical errors you're looking for.

PROGRAM MANAGER

PROOFREADING AND PUBLISHING

- **Instructional Support** For help with correcting mistakes and improving a paper's appearance, see **Proofreading** and **Manuscript Form** in *Practicing the Writing Process,* pp. 14–15.
- **Review** For a review of the writing process, see **Review—The Aim and Process of Writing** in *Practicing the Writing Process,* p. 16.
- **Assessment/Reflection** To assess student work and evaluate progress, see **Portfolio Forms** in *Portfolio Assessment,* pp. 22–25.
- **Computer Guided Instruction** For additional practice with grammar, usage, and mechanics concepts as referred to in the **Guidelines for Proofreading** on p. 56, see **Lessons 5–7, 9, 10, 13–15, 27,** and **34–51** in *Language Workshop CD-ROM.*
- **Practice** To help less-advanced students with additional instruction and practice with related grammar, usage, and mechanics concepts, see **Chapters 8, 11, 14–16,** and **18–22** in *English Workshop, Fourth Course,* pp. 67–92, 129–148, 181–238, and 249–320.

Explain to students that proofreading backwards is especially helpful for checking spelling because it forces the reader to concentrate on individual words. It is less helpful for checking internal punctuation, agreement, and correct pronoun case because these sometimes require a sense of the meaning during proofreading.

To illustrate the concepts presented in the **Guidelines for Proofreading**, you could use an overhead projector to display sentences that contain examples of each problem discussed in the guidelines. Select students to identify the errors in the examples. Then, using the appropriate proofreading symbols, you can show students how to correct the errors.

QUOTATION FOR THE DAY

"Publication is a self-invasion of privacy." (Marshall McLuhan, 1911–1980, Canadian author and educator)

After students have carefully proofread their writing, you may wish to write the quotation on the chalkboard and use it to initiate a discussion of publishing. Explain that publication allows the writer to share his or her final results with an audience.

GUIDELINES FOR PROOFREADING

1. Is every sentence a complete sentence? (See pages 446–457.)
2. Does every sentence end with the appropriate punctuation mark? Are other punctuation marks correct? (See pages 787–864.)
3. Does every sentence begin with a capital letter? Are all proper nouns and appropriate proper adjectives capitalized? (See pages 762–779.)
4. Does every verb agree in number with its subject? (See pages 618–634.)
5. Are verb forms and tenses used correctly? (See pages 678–704.)
6. Are subject and object forms of personal pronouns used correctly? (See pages 649–658.)
7. Does every pronoun agree with its antecedent in number and in gender? Are pronoun references clear? (See pages 637–639.)
8. Are frequently confused words (such as *lie* and *lay, fewer* and *less*) used correctly? (See pages 661–662, 697–704, 716–717, 738–756.)
9. Are all words spelled correctly? (See pages 870–895.)
10. Is the paper neat and in correct manuscript form? (See page 59.)

ANSWERS

Exercise 12

Correction	Reason
sun's	apostrophe missing
universities	incorrect plural spelling
did	incorrect verb form used for past tense
were	incorrect subject-verb agreement
designed	misspelled "desinged"
students. They	run-on sentence
batteries	incorrect plural spelling
miles at speeds	sentence fragment
Unfortunately	misspelled "Unfortunatly"
Rains	first word of sentence should be capitalized

EXERCISE 12 ▶ **Proofreading a Paragraph**

See if you can find all ten mistakes in the following paragraph. Look for errors in grammar, usage, spelling, capitalization, and punctuation. Use the handbook at the back of the book or a dictionary to be sure you've found an error and to correct it.

How would you like to design a car that runs only on the suns power? That's what college students from universitys done in a 1,600-mile car race from Florida to Michigan. The thirty-one cars was desinged by engineering students, they had solar batterys that could be recharged only twice a day. On the first day the cars

You could also distribute copies of a paragraph that needs proofreading. First, have the students read it individually. Next, display it on the overhead one line at a time. Have students examine each line on the overhead and make the appropriate corrections on the handout.

As you discuss the **Guidelines for Manuscript Form** on p. 59, display a manuscript on the overhead projector to explain and point out an example in the model for each guideline. If other examples occur elsewhere in the manuscript, ask volunteers to find them and explain the applications of the guidelines.

Cont. on p. 59

traveled 75 miles. At speeds up to 52 miles an hour. Unfortunatly, heavy rains and cloudy skies slowed the cars. rains caused the drivers' cockpits to leak.

Publishing

Early in prewriting, your thoughts about an audience helped shape your writing. Now it's time to let some of these readers actually share the final result. Besides sharing your writing with your teacher, here are some other suggestions.

- Submit your writing for publication. Try the school newspaper or yearbook or magazine. Your local newspaper may be interested in publishing a letter to the editor or a feature article.
- Make a class anthology. Have each student contribute one piece of writing, a drawing, or a favorite cartoon. Exchange anthologies with other classes. You could donate your class anthology to a school library or children's floor in a hospital.
- Make an anthology of your best writing for your family and yourself. You can save it in a folder or notebook and add to it throughout high school.
- Enter a writing contest. Some of these have cash prizes; others award certificates. Ask your teacher or counselor for information.
- Make a video. If you can find a video camera (try your public or school library), work with a partner. While you take pictures to illustrate your writing, ask a good reader to read your writing aloud. Show your video to the class.
- Post movie and book reviews on a school bulletin board or in a library.

COOPERATIVE LEARNING

Ask students to copy the paragraph in **Exercise 12** and to use proofreading symbols on p. 60 to proofread it. Then, let them work in pairs to check each other's work and to note any errors they might have missed. Tell students that after proofreading, it is wise to have a partner double-check for possible missed errors. Students should present their proofread copies and final error-free copies for evaluation.

MEETING *individual* NEEDS

LEP/ESL

General Strategies. Although proofreading is an integral part of the writing process, you may find that placing too much emphasis on perfect spelling, mechanics, and usage can block students' creative expression and damage their self-esteem.

TECHNOLOGY TIP

Tell students that proper names and technical terminology are often not written into general spell-checker features of word-processing programs. Recommend that students consult a dictionary to verify the correct spellings of these words.

TEACHING *REFLECTING ON YOUR WRITING*

Ask students to complete the **Critical Thinking Exercise** in class. You might want to circulate among them to monitor their work and to answer questions. You might also want to allow them to write short paragraphs that address all of the questions instead of answering the questions directly.

LEP/ESL

General Strategies. Some students may have difficulty distinguishing between evaluating their writing and reflecting on it. Point out that evaluating involves making a judgment about the worth of a piece of writing, that is, answering the question "How good is it?" Reflecting, on the other hand, involves reviewing the process that resulted in the finished piece of writing and asking, "What could I have done differently?"

TEACHING NOTE

Students who consistently analyze and reflect on their writing tend to feel more ownership of their work. Many students find writing for classroom assignments to be somewhat tedious. By reflecting on their writing, students are likely to pay more attention to the writing process and to their successes or difficulties throughout the process. Having identified problem areas means that students can more readily ask for specific feedback.

GUIDELINES

Students should answer all of the questions in a thoughtful manner. They should use the terms that are employed in the textbook to describe the stages of the writing process, and their answers to the questions should be stated in complete sentences.

CRITICAL THINKING

Reflecting on Your Writing

Photograph albums and scrapbooks help people keep track of their past accomplishments. Similarly, a **portfolio,** a collection of your work, can help you to maintain a record of your writing accomplishments and measure your continuing progress. Reflecting on pieces you have written gives you a chance to improve your writing as you complete new assignments: Old topics may prompt ideas for new papers, or you may notice that a certain style is particularly effective. Keeping a portfolio may be especially helpful if college or job applications require a writing sample. Review your work to analyze what you do well and where you would like to refine your writing.

Each paper you save has something to teach you. Date each piece of writing that you include in your portfolio, and write a brief reflection about your work. Which part of the paper is your favorite? What was the most difficult part of the assignment? How did you pick a topic? What revisions made the paper better? Would the writing be clear and interesting to an audience?

 CRITICAL THINKING EXERCISE:
Reflecting on Your Writing

Reread some of your recent writing assignments. Then, using the following questions, reflect on your work. Date your written observations, and include them in your **portfolio** to keep as records to gauge your progress.

1. Which part of the writing process do you find easiest? most difficult? Why?
2. What passages of your papers would you handle differently? What passages do you like best? Why?
3. What did you learn about yourself as you wrote? What did you learn about the writing process?

Cont. from p. 57

INDEPENDENT PRACTICE

Use **Exercises 12** and **13** as independent practice. If students are having difficulty finding publishing ideas through brainstorming, suggest that they ask local businesses, civic offices, or libraries to display their works in windows or on bulletin boards.

ASSESSMENT

Use both the guided writing and publishing and the independent writing and publishing to assess comprehension.

When someone else reads your paper (your teacher, another student, or some adult outside of school), appearance is important. If you follow these guidelines for your final copy, your papers will look better.

GUIDELINES FOR MANUSCRIPT FORM

1. Use only one side of a sheet of paper.
2. Type, use a word processor, or write in blue or black ink.
3. If you type, double-space the lines. If you write, don't skip lines.
4. Leave margins of about one inch at the top, sides, and bottom of a page.
5. Indent the first line of each paragraph.
6. Number all pages (except the first page) in the upper right-hand corner.
7. All pages should be neat and clean. You may use correction fluid to make a few changes, but they should be barely noticeable.
8. Follow your teacher's instructions for placement of your name, the date, your class, and the title of your paper.

EXERCISE 13 ▶ Publishing Your Writing

Working with your classmates, brainstorm some other ideas for publishing your writing. Assign committees to follow up on all suggestions, including those listed above. Find out the specific information a writer would need to carry out each suggestion.

Frank & Ernest reprinted by permission of Newspaper Enterprise Association, Inc.

Close this lesson by discussing the following questions as a class:

1. Which proofreading guidelines were most helpful to you? Explain.
2. When you proofread, what types of errors are you mainly looking for? [errors in grammar, usage, and mechanics]
3. What types of writing do the questions under **Guidelines for Proofreading** apply to? [almost any type of writing] ■

MEETING *individual* NEEDS

LESS-ADVANCED STUDENTS

Students who are unfamiliar with proofreading symbols might be overwhelmed by the list in the textbook. For these students, you may wish to introduce the symbols a few at a time, giving students a chance to integrate a few symbols before introducing more.

A DIFFERENT APPROACH

You may want to invite local writers, newspaper reporters or editors, or television anchorpersons to speak individually or as a panel on their writing and publishing experiences. Prior to the guest experts' visit, students might collaborate in groups of three or four to brainstorm questions tailored to the visitors' occupations. The groups should take turns asking the guests questions.

The groups should also brainstorm and choose unique ways to publish what they learn. For example, one group might videotape the interview for other classes; others might write a synopsis to report to the school board or local newspaper, present a slide show at a school assembly, or take photos and write captions for a bulletin board display.

SYMBOLS FOR REVISING AND PROOFREADING

SYMBOL	EXAMPLE	MEANING OF SYMBOL
≡	Maple High school	Capitalize a lowercase letter.
/	the First person	Lowercase a capital letter.
∧	the first May	Insert a missing word, letter, or punctuation mark.
∧	seperate	Change a letter.
⌐	in the East	Replace a word.
⌐	Tell me the the plan.	Leave out a word, letter, or punctuation mark.
⌐	an unussual idea	Leave out and close up.
⌒	a water fall	Close up space.
∽	recieve	Change the order of the letters.
(tr)	the last Saturday of September in the month	Transfer the circled words. (Write (tr) in nearby margin.)
¶	¶ "Help!" someone cried.	Begin a new paragraph.
⊙	Please don't go	Add a period.
∧	Well what's new?	Add a comma.
#	birddog	Add a space.
⊙	the following ideas	Add a colon.
∧	Houston, Texas St. Louis, Missouri and Albany, New York	Add a semicolon.
=	at half mast	Add a hyphen.
∨	Sally's new job	Add an apostrophe.
(stet)	An extremely urgent	Keep the crossed-out material. (Write (stet) in nearby margin.)

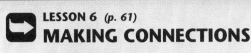

MAKING CONNECTIONS

BRAINSTORMING WITH A COMPUTER
OBJECTIVE

- To use computer software to brainstorm ideas for a composition

MAKING CONNECTIONS

BRAINSTORMING WITH A COMPUTER

Prewriting usually requires brainstorming and time. A partner can really help you brainstorm during prewriting, and a computer may be the next best thing. Computers let you quickly access large amounts of thought-provoking information, and some computer programs can even generate questions like the ones a partner might ask.

All of the computer software described below can help you generate ideas. Some of the programs can even make the prewriting stage a little more fun.

- **Thesaurus and Word-Association Programs.** These programs help you find synonyms and other terms or phrases related to words you type in. Some allow you to compare words and to find new ideas associated with combinations of words.
- **Text-Based Outliners and Visual Outliners.** These programs make it easy to expand and refine your ideas by helping you create and change outlines, cluster diagrams, and other visual organizers.
- **Questioning Programs.** These programs take the place of a brainstorming partner by asking you questions about your subject and by allowing you to type your responses and to save them.
- **World Wide Web Search Engines.** These Internet-based programs help you search the millions of documents on the Web for keywords related to your topic. Web searches can often reveal surprising links between your subject and other information.

If you have a computer and a brainstorming program, use them to generate a list of ideas for a paper. Show your list to a partner, and discuss how the software helped you. If you don't have brainstorming software, interview some people who do and ask how they use their programs. Write a short summary of your findings.

BRAINSTORMING WITH A COMPUTER
Teaching Strategies

If you have access to a computer in the classroom, you may want to demonstrate the use of the software that is discussed in the textbook. To make the demonstration easier for students to see, connect the computer to a television set. As you, or a student, work at the keyboard, the images on the computer monitor will appear on the TV screen. A librarian or technical support person in your school can probably help you assemble the TV hookup.

As students search the World Wide Web, encourage them to follow some of the links to other Web sites that appear on the sites they discover through their keyword searches. These links can provide additional information, and they can also open up areas related to the topic that students might not otherwise think of.

When students search the World Wide Web, have them record the results of their searches in cluster diagrams. They can start with the keyword in the center and record each site they access as a node coming off the center. They can represent the links they explore from each site as nodes coming from the main node for that site. Then, have them evaluate their diagrams, discarding any irrelevant nodes.

UNDERSTANDING PARAGRAPH STRUCTURE

OBJECTIVES

- To identify the characteristics of paragraphs, including main idea, topic sentence, and supporting sentences
- To analyze paragraphs for unity and to identify sentences that destroy the unity of a paragraph
- To analyze and revise paragraphs for coherence—order of ideas, direct references, and transitions
- To identify and use the strategies of development— description, narration, classification, and evaluation

CROSS CURRICULUM

How Paragraphs Work in Science

Remind students that the kind of writing they encounter in a science book will probably be organized differently from most reading they do in English class. For example, an article in a science journal might cover several different experiments. Paragraph structure is vital to the clear organization and presentation of ideas. Demonstrate to students the importance of paragraph structure by presenting an example of paragraph structure in a science text.

- **Analyzing Informative Paragraphs** Bring to class samples of paragraphs from a science textbook. Put one paragraph on an overhead transparency. Read the paragraph as a class and invite students to work in pairs to analyze the organizational structure of the paragraph using the following strategies.

- **Outlining** If the paragraph contains a topic sentence, supporting details, and a clincher sentence, then students may use an outline.

Topic sentence: _____

Detail 1: _____

Detail 2: _____

Detail 3: _____

Clincher sentence: _____

- **Fish Bone** A fish bone diagram can help visual learners map out the main idea and supporting details.

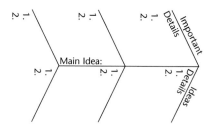

- **Sequencing chart** If the paragraph contains many details or describes events that occur in chronological or sequential order, a sequencing chart will help.

Main idea: _____.

- **Extension** Invite students to find paragraphs from their own textbooks to analyze. Have them work in pairs to create a poster or an overhead transparency of their analysis and to present it to the class. Discuss as a class which strategies were consistently helpful.

INTEGRATING THE LANGUAGE ARTS

SELECTION	READING AND LITERATURE	WRITING AND CRITICAL THINKING	LANGUAGE AND SYNTAX	SPEAKING, LISTENING, AND OTHER EXPRESSION SKILLS
FROM • *Nisei Daughter* pp. 64–65, 67 • "Japanese Americans" p. 68 • *Voices from the Civil War* p. 69 • "Reopening the Gateway to America" p. 70 • *Great Indian Chiefs* p. 70 • *Riding the Iron Rooster* p. 71 • *Going Green* p. 72 • *Garbage!* p. 73 • *Baseball* p. 74 • "A Genuine Mexican Plug" p. 76 • *Once Upon A Horse* pp. 77–78 • *Exploring the Titanic* p. 79 • "Clean Fun at Riverhead" pp. 79–80 • *The Woman Warrior* pp. 82–83 • *Anne of Green Gables* p. 83 • "Hayes: 'There Is So Much to Do'" p. 84 • *Rock of Ages* pp. 84–85 • "Leiningen Versus the Ants" p. 88 • *The Pearl* p. 90 • *Gullah* p. 94 • *Mythology* p. 95 • "Winterblossom Garden" p. 96 • "Nothing Happened" p. 96 • *Behind the Headlines* p. 98 • *Private Lives of the Stars* pp. 98–99 • *Do Animals Dream?* p. 99	• Responding personally to literature pp. 66, 69–70 • Finding main ideas pp. 66, 69–70 • Finding topic sentences pp. 69–70 • Identifying and analyzing order of ideas pp. 86–87 • Finding direct references pp. 90–91 • Finding transitional words and phrases pp. 90–91	• Writing a journal entry p. 66 • Evaluating effectiveness of paragraphs p. 66 • Comparing effectiveness of paragraphs p. 66 • Analyzing main idea pp. 66, 69–70 • Responding personally to literature pp. 66, 69–70 • Identifying main ideas and topic sentences pp. 66, 69–70 • Collecting supporting details pp. 75, 94, 101, 103–104, 104–105, 106–107 • Identifying sentences that destroy unity pp. 80–81, 103–104 • Evaluating and making judgments p. 85, 86–87, 91–92 • Synthesizing order of ideas pp. 85, 86–87, 91–92 • Identifying and analyzing order of ideas pp. 86–87, 91–92 • Rewriting a paragraph so the order of ideas makes sense pp. 86–87, 91–92 • Identifying direct references and transitions pp. 90–91 • Revising a paragraph by adding transitions pp. 91–92 • Using sensory details pp. 94, 106–107 • Applying interpretive and creative thinking pp. 96–97, 102–103, 103–105, 106–107 • Explaining a process p. 97 • Using classification p. 100 • Using evaluation p. 101 • Revising, proofreading, and publishing pp. 102–103, 104, 105, 107 • Analyzing supporting sentences pp. 103–104 • Analyzing details and topic sentences pp. 103–104, 104–105	• Identifying transitional words and phrases pp. 90–91 • Proofreading for errors in grammar, usage, and mechanics pp. 103, 104, 105, 107	• Working with a classmate to share experiences p. 66 • Explaining a process p. 97 • Publishing writing by reading aloud p. 107

CHAPTER 2: UNDERSTANDING PARAGRAPH STRUCTURE

Use this guide for creating an instructional plan that addresses the individual needs of your students. Assignments accompanied by the following symbol (∗) may be completed out of class. Times given for pacing lessons are estimated.

CHAPTER PLANNING GUIDE—PUPIL'S EDITION

LESSONS	LITERARY MODEL from *Nisei Daughter* by Monica Sone pp. 64–65	WHAT MAKES A PARAGRAPH pp. 67–76	UNITY pp. 77–81
DEVELOPMENTAL PROGRAM	⏰ **25–30 minutes** • Read model aloud in class and ask students to answer questions orally on p. 66	⏰ **40–45 minutes** • Main Assignment: Looking Ahead p. 66 • The Main Idea p. 67 • The Topic Sentence pp. 68–70 • Exercises 1, 2 pp. 69, 75 in pairs • Supporting Sentences pp. 71–75 • The Clincher Sentence p. 76	⏰ **30–35 minutes** • Unity pp. 77–81 • Exercise 3 pp. 80–81 in pairs
CORE PROGRAM	⏰ **20–25 minutes** • Assign student pairs to read the model and answer questions on p. 66	⏰ **30–35 minutes** • Main Assignment: Looking Ahead p. 66 • The Topic Sentence pp. 68–70 • Exercises 1, 2 pp. 69, 75∗ • Supporting Sentences pp. 71–75 • The Clincher Sentence p. 76	⏰ **25–30 minutes** • Unity pp. 77–81 • Exercise 3 pp. 80–81∗
ACCELERATED PROGRAM	⏰ **15–20 minutes** • Assign students to read the model independently and to answer questions 3 and 4 on p. 66	⏰ **20–35 minutes** • Main Assignment: Looking Ahead p. 66 • Supporting Sentences pp. 71–75 • Exercise 2 p. 75∗	⏰ **20–25 minutes** • Unity pp. 77–81

CHAPTER PLANNING GUIDE—PROGRAM RESOURCES

	LITERARY MODEL	WHAT MAKES A PARAGRAPH	UNITY
PRINT	• Reading Master 2, *Practice for Assessment in Reading, Vocabulary, and Spelling* p. 2	• The Main Idea, The Topic Sentence, Writing Supporting Sentences, The Clincher Sentence, *Practicing the Writing Process* pp. 21–25 • Paragraph Workshops, *English Workshop* pp. 15–26	• Achieving Unity, *Practicing the Writing Process* p. 26
MEDIA		• Graphic Organizer 3, *Transparency Binder* 🖥	

COHERENCE pp. 82–92	STRATEGIES OF DEVELOPMENT pp. 93–101
🕐 **45–50 minutes** • Coherence pp. 82–88 • Exercises 4, 5, 6 pp. 85, 86–87, 90–91 • Transitional Words and Phrases Chart p. 89	🕐 **90 minutes** • Strategies of Development pp. 93–101 • Exercises 8–12 pp. 94, 96, 97, 100, 101 in pairs
🕐 **30–35 minutes** • Coherence pp. 82–92 • Exercises 4, 5, 6, 7 pp. 85, 86–87, 90, 92* • Transitional Words and Phrases Chart p. 89	🕐 **40 minutes** • Strategies of Development pp. 93–101 • Writing Note p. 93 • Exercises 8–12 pp. 94, 96, 97, 100, 101*
🕐 **25–30 minutes** • Order of Ideas pp. 82–87 • Exercises 4, 6, 7 pp. 85, 90–92* • Transitional Words and Phrases pp. 89–92	🕐 **35–40 minutes** • Strategies Chart p. 93 • Writing Note p. 93 • Explaining Cause and Effect p. 96 • Exercises 9–12 pp. 96–97, 100–101* • Classification/Evaluation pp. 97–101

📠 Overhead transparencies

COHERENCE	STRATEGIES OF DEVELOPMENT
• Achieving Coherence, *Practicing the Writing Process* p. 27	• Developing Paragraphs, *Practicing the Writing Process* pp. 28–30
• Revision Transparency 3, 📠 *Transparency Binder*	

ELEMENTS OF WRIT
CURRICULUM
CONNECTIONS

Making Connections
• Writing Paragraphs for Different Pu pp. 102–107

ASSESSMENT OPTIONS

Summative Assessment
Review: Transitional Words and Phras *Practicing the Writing Process* p. 31

Reflection
Self-assessment Record, *Portfolio Asse* p. 19

OBJECTIVES

• To write and to share orally personal responses to literature
• To identify characteristics of paragraphs in a literary model

PROGRAM MANAGER

CHAPTER 2

■ **Practice** To help less-advanced students who need additional practice with concepts and activities related to this chapter, see **Chapter 2** in *English Workshop, Fourth Course,* pp. 15–26.

■ **Reading Support** For help with the reading selection, pp. 64–65, see **Reading Master 2** in *Practice for Assessment in Reading, Vocabulary, and Spelling,* p. 2.

 VISUAL CONNECTIONS
Relative Realities #2

About the Artwork. The artist, Mark Hartman, contrasts a flat, colorful surface with three-dimensional still-life elements. He used watercolors to paint the background before drawing the three-dimensional objects with charcoal.

Exploring the Subject. The artist includes not only a sketch of himself, but several other images as well. The calm Egyptian face in the center contrasts with the screaming face (adapted from Picasso's painting *Guernica*) in the lower left corner. The pointing fingers act as transitions by showing the relationships between objects. These images work together as sentences in a well-written paragraph would; they develop one main idea, a portrait of the artist.

2 UNDERSTANDING PARAGRAPH STRUCTURE

TEACHING THE LESSON

Before you have a volunteer read the introductory paragraphs of the chapter, point out to students that they already know a great deal about paragraphs because they have been studying them and reading them throughout their school years. You may want to have students discuss what they already know about paragraphs.

Explain that the excerpt by Monica Sone is from her autobiography. Sone grew up in a Japanese community in Seattle, Washington. Tell students to follow the instructions in **As You Read** to observe Sone's writing techniques as they read. To enrich class discussion, read the paragraphs by Sone aloud and discuss their structure.

☞

Looking at the Parts

Can you name all the parts in a computer? It has a processor, disc drives, a keyboard, and a monitor. But not all computers are alike. Some are faster or bigger or have more **parts** than others. The same is true of paragraphs. They all have certain things in common, but they are not all alike.

Writing and You. You see paragraphs all the time—in letters, books, and magazines. Some have only one word or sentence, but some go on for pages. Some paragraphs stand alone, but most of them work with others like links in a chain. What else have you noticed about paragraphs?

As You Read. As you read the following paragraphs from *Nisei Daughter*, notice how Monica Sone separates, yet links together, fond memories of her childhood.

Mark Hartman, *Relative Realities #2* (1989). Charcoal & watercolor on paper, 22" × 30". Collection of the artist.

QUOTATION FOR THE DAY

"All words are pegs to hang ideas on." (Henry Ward Beecher, 1813–1887, American clergyman)

Write the quotation on the chalkboard and ask students to freewrite for a few minutes about what the quotation means. You may wish to ask a few volunteers to read aloud their responses. Explain that words, sentences, and paragraphs are vehicles for expressing ideas.

MEETING *individual* **NEEDS**

LEP/ESL

General Strategies. Some students may be unaccustomed to the idea that a paragraph needs to have a single unifying idea. One main idea may span two or three paragraphs, or one paragraph may have two or three main ideas. To help students focus on the concept of one main idea per paragraph, you may wish to have them read a paragraph and then ask what each sentence in it is about. Show students how each sentence deals with some aspect of the paragraph's main idea.

GUIDED PRACTICE

Share with the class your response to the first **Reader's Response** question. Initiate the writing journal activity for question 2 by modeling with an experience of your own. Help students with the third question by using the annotations to analyze the first paragraph of the literary model with the class.

INDEPENDENT PRACTICE

Students can complete **Reader's Response** and **Writer's Craft** questions on their own. You may want to suggest that students include reasons for their choices of main ideas.

MEETING *individual* NEEDS

ADVANCED STUDENTS

While many writers follow the basic, standard structure of paragraphing, some writers don't. You may want to suggest that students study the paragraphing techniques of some of their favorite writers. Encourage students to share with the class examples of effective paragraphs written by their favorite authors.

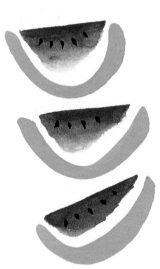

Nisei Daughter

ASSESSMENT

Have students discuss their answers to the **Reader's Response** and **Writer's Craft** questions. Based on this discussion, you can assess students' understanding of the lesson concepts.

CLOSURE

Ask the class to discuss the importance of paragraphs in writing. You may want to have students refer to Monica Sone's paragraphs for details and examples.

☛

from

1 NISEI

DAUGHTER

by

MONICA

SONE

2 $\mathcal{YES},$ life to us children was a wonderful treat—especially during hot summer nights when Father slipped out to a market stand down the block and surprised us with an enormous, ice-cold water-

3 melon. It was pure joy when we first bit into its crisp pink <u>succulence</u> and let the juice trickle and seeds fall on old newspapers spread on the round table in the parlor. Or sometimes on a wintry evening, we crowded around the kitchen table to watch Father, bath towel-apron draped around his waist, whip up a batch of raisin cookies for us. It wasn't everybody's father who could turn out thick, melting, golden cookies. We were especially proud that our father had once worked as a cook on romantic Alaska-bound freighters.

4 Life was hilarious whenever Mother played *Jan-ken-pon! Ai-kono-hoi!* with us. This was the game played by throwing out paper, scissors, and rock symbols with our hands, accompanied by the chant. The winner with the stronger symbol had the privilege of slapping the loser's wrist with two fingers. Mother pretended to cry whenever our small fingers came down on her wrist. With her oval face, lively almond-shaped eyes, and slender <u>aquiline</u> nose, Mother was a pretty, slender five feet of youth and fun.

I thought the whole world consisted of two or three old hotels on every block. And that its population consisted of families like mine who lived in a corner of the hotels. And its other inhabitants were customers—fading, balding, watery-eyed men, rough-tough bearded men, and good men like Sam, Joe, Peter, and Montana who worked for Father, all of whom lived in these hotels.

5 It was a very exciting world in which I lived.

USING THE SELECTION
from **Nisei Daughter**

1
The word *Nisei* means "second-generation." Sone's parents were referred to as *Issei* or "first generation."

2
This sentence is a generalization that all three paragraphs support.

3
Notice the sensory details Sone uses to support her idea of life as a wonderful treat.

4
This sentence serves as the topic sentence of the second paragraph.

5
How can one sentence be a paragraph? [This sentence functions as a conclusion and, set off by itself, adds emphasis to Sone's ideas.]

SELECTION AMENDMENT
Description of change: excerpted
Rationale: to focus on the concept of paragraph structure presented in this chapter

ANSWERS

Reader's Response

Answers will vary.

1. You may want to ask students to record their responses.
2. Be sure students give specific details to support their responses.

Writer's Craft

3. The main idea of the first paragraph is that life was a treat. The main idea of the second paragraph is that Sone's mother made life fun by playing a game. The main idea of the third paragraph is that as a child Sone thought the whole world was made of old hotels like hers. The last paragraph emphasizes the first sentence and acts as a conclusion.
4. The paragraphs about Sone's father and mother are longer and more effective because they have more details and contain more information than the paragraph about the hotels and the last paragraph. Length is determined by function.

READER'S RESPONSE

1. Some of Monica Sone's fondest memories are connected with eating—watermelon juice trickling onto newspapers and her father making cookies. Get together with a partner and share the eating experiences (funny or serious) that stand out in your mind.
2. As a child, Sone thought the whole world was exactly like the neighborhood she lived in. In your journal, write about some of the impressions you had of the world when you were a young child.

WRITER'S CRAFT

3. Although all of Sone's paragraphs are about her memories from childhood, each paragraph makes a slightly different point. What is the main idea of each paragraph?
4. Sone's longest paragraph has five sentences, and the shortest has only one sentence. Is one paragraph more effective than the other? What do you think determines the length of the paragraphs?

LOOKING AHEAD

In this chapter, you'll study the form and structure of paragraphs. Keep in mind that

- most paragraphs are a part of a longer piece of writing
- most paragraphs have a main idea
- a main idea may be supported or explained in several ways
- there are four basic strategies for developing paragraphs

WHAT MAKES A PARAGRAPH

OBJECTIVES

- To identify main ideas and topic sentences in paragraphs
- To develop supporting details for main ideas

MOTIVATION

You could begin this lesson by drawing a comparison with a television series. Many programs, such as *Cosby*, have features in common with paragraphs. A faithful viewer has a sense of the overall scheme of the program—the characters, the settings, and the typical problems. So, while one

What Makes a Paragraph

The Main Idea

Paragraphs, especially those that stand alone, usually are organized around one main idea. All the sentences in the paragraph make the *main idea* clear. For paragraphs that are part of longer pieces of writing, the other paragraphs help you understand the main idea.

Read the following paragraph from the selection by Monica Sone (page 65). What is its main idea?

> Life was hilarious whenever Mother played *Jan-ken-pon! Ai-kono-hoi!* with us. This was the game played by throwing out paper, scissors, and rock symbols with our hands, accompanied by the chant. The winner with the stronger symbol had the privilege of slapping the loser's wrist with two fingers. Mother pretended to cry whenever our small fingers came down on her wrist. With her oval face, lively almond-shaped eyes, and slender aquiline nose, Mother was a pretty, slender five feet of youth and fun.
>
> Monica Sone, *Nisei Daughter*

The first sentence of this paragraph states the main idea: that the author remembers her childhood as a time of great happiness. The other sentences support that idea by giving specific details about how the children played a game with their mother and how she looked and acted.

In the longer passage on page 65, you'll find that the other paragraphs help you understand this idea by giving details about other interesting experiences the author remembers from her childhood.

"IF IT SOUNDS LIKE WRITING, I REWRITE IT."

Elmore Leonard

PROGRAM MANAGER

WHAT MAKES A PARAGRAPH

- **Independent Practice/ Reteaching** For practice and reinforcement, see **The Main Idea, The Topic Sentence, Writing Supporting Sentences,** and **The Clincher Sentence** in *Practicing the Writing Process,* pp. 21–25.

- **Instructional Support** See **Graphic Organizers 3** and **4.** For suggestions on how to tie the transparencies to instruction, review teacher's notes for transparencies in *Fine Art and Instructional Transparencies for Writing,* pp. 57, 59.

QUOTATION FOR THE DAY

"A sentence should read as if its author, had he held a plough instead of a pen, could have drawn a furrow deep and straight to the end." (Henry David Thoreau, 1817–1862, American poet, essayist, and transcendentalist)

Explain that clear, straightforward sentences help create effective paragraphs. Encourage students to remember Thoreau's rule as they write topic, supporting, and clincher sentences.

SELECTION AMENDMENT
Description of change: excerpted
Rationale: to focus on the concept of main idea presented in this chapter

episode is a part of a larger whole, it usually has a main idea.

Guide students in their reading of the material about main ideas and topic sentences. Most students will already be familiar with these concepts. You may want to emphasize that paragraphs are usually part of longer pieces of writing and that there is an ongoing relationship among the parts that comprise the whole. Football players

The Topic Sentence

The main idea of a paragraph is often expressed in a single sentence, called the *topic sentence.* In writing, whether for school or for the workplace, you'll find that using a topic sentence helps the reader to identify your main idea.

Location of a Topic Sentence. The topic sentence often appears as the first or second sentence of a paragraph. You'll recall that the first sentence of Sone's paragraph on page 67—the one about playing a game with her mother—states the main idea of the paragraph.

It's easier to understand what a paragraph is about if the topic sentence appears at the beginning. However, a topic sentence can occur at any place in a paragraph. In fact, you'll sometimes find topic sentences at or near the end of a paragraph. Writers sometimes place topic sentences there to create surprise or to summarize ideas.

Here's a paragraph about the success of Japanese Americans after they were released from camps where many of them were held during World War II. As you read, notice how the writer draws all the details together and sums up the information with a topic sentence at the end.

> Twenty-five years after the camps were closed, the average personal income of Japanese Americans was 11 percent above the national average; average family income was 32 percent higher. A higher proportion of Japanese Americans were engaged in professional occupations than were whites. By 1981, an astonishing 88 percent of Sansei (third generation) children were attending college, and of these, 92 percent planned professional careers. In California, where more than a third of the nation's 720,000 Japanese Americans reside (88 percent of them U.S. born), family income remains 15 percent above the statewide average. Wrote sociologist William Petersen: "Even in a country whose patron saint is Horatio Alger, there is no parallel to this success story."
>
> Arthur Zich, "Japanese Americans: Home at Last"

MEETING individual NEEDS

LEP/ESL

General Strategies. Most students who have grown up in the United States will have already heard of the topics of the example paragraphs in this unit—Japanese internment, the American Civil War, and European immigration to the United States. However, many students—especially recent arrivals—might have studied little, if anything, about these subjects and therefore might have trouble understanding what these paragraphs are about. You could help by providing a brief historical and cultural background of each article's subject matter. For example, you could explain when, where, and why the Civil War occurred and who fought in it.

SELECTION AMENDMENT
Description of change: excerpted
Rationale: to focus on the concept of main idea presented in this chapter

Importance of a Topic Sentence. Many paragraphs don't have a topic sentence. Some paragraphs, especially those that relate a sequence of events or actions, may not even seem to have a main idea. But topic sentences are useful, both to readers and to writers. They help readers know what they might find in the rest of the paragraph. And topic sentences help you as a writer to focus your paragraphs. They keep you from wandering off the main idea.

EXERCISE 1 ▶ **Identifying Main Ideas and Topic Sentences**

Each of the following paragraphs develops a main idea. Two of the paragraphs have topic sentences, and one does not. In your own words, state the main idea of each paragraph. Then identify the topic sentences of the two paragraphs that have them.

1. Disease took more victims in the Civil War than the bullet did, and the toll from both was enormous. In the Federal forces four men died of sickness for every one killed in battle. In the early period almost one out of every four soldiers fell sick. It was just as bad or worse for the Confederates. At least half the men in a regiment could not fight for sickness, and often more. One authority on Confederate medicine estimated that on the average each Southern soldier was sick or wounded six times during the war. But five times as many fell sick as were injured.
    Milton Meltzer, *Voices from the Civil War*

MEETING *individual* NEEDS

LESS-ADVANCED STUDENTS

To help students understand the typical structure of a paragraph, show them a visual representation of the relationship between the topic sentence, the supporting sentences, the specific details, and the clincher sentence. You could use the following example:

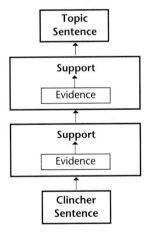

ANSWERS
Exercise 1

Statements of main ideas will vary.

1. Main Idea: In the Civil War, more people died of illness than were killed in battle.
    Topic Sentence: Disease took more victims in the Civil War than the bullet did, and the toll from both was enormous.

SELECTION AMENDMENT
Description of change: excerpted
Rationale: to focus on the concept of topic sentences presented in this chapter

It may be helpful to provide an analogy. For example, people learning a new dance step or technique focus on the structure—the way it's supposed to be done. Once they have mastered that, they add their own styles. Similarly, students need to master the basic structure of writing; then they can add their personal variations.

Guide students in their reading of **Supporting Sentences,** p. 71. After the first paragraph, remind students that the main idea of a paragraph is often expressed in a topic sentence, and even when that is not the case, the supporting sentences should always relate to a main idea.

2. Main Idea: Ellis Island, gateway for millions of Americans, has been restored, and a new museum has been opened there.

3. Main Idea: The best chiefs of American Indian groups were great because of individual differences.
Topic Sentence: These were all individual differences, basic differences in individual capacity, and it was these differences alone that set the Indian leaders off from the rest of their people.

INTEGRATING THE LANGUAGE ARTS

Test-taking Link. Suggest to students that when they answer essay questions on tests, they introduce each paragraph with a clear topic sentence. Although this format isn't always the most effective in other types of writing, beginning each paragraph of a test essay with a topic sentence identifies the main idea of the students' answers for the reader. You may also want to suggest that students prewrite before they begin their essays.

2.   The first step on American soil for 12 million immigrants was no patch of warm, welcoming earth but a wooden ramp at Ellis Island. More than 100 million living Americans trace their U.S. roots to a man, woman or child who came through Ellis Island between 1892 and 1954. America's gateway reopens this month with a new National Park Service museum commemorating four centuries of U.S. immigration. Privately funded, the $156 million restoration has been the work of the Statue of Liberty–Ellis Island Foundation, which also dressed up Miss Liberty for her 1986 birthday centennial.

Doris G. Kinney, "Reopening the Gateway to America"

3.   Pontiac had a great idea in his intertribal league against the whites. Tecumseh had a similar idea, backed by an unusual humanity toward captives and an exalted concept of a divine purpose embodied in him. Sitting Bull nourished an implacable hatred and suspicion of the whites and showed unusual power in intrigue. Chief Joseph exhibited an ability in the conduct of a losing war that Napoleon might have envied in his retreat from Moscow. . . . These were all individual differences, basic differences in individual capacity, and it was these differences alone that set the Indian leaders off from the rest of their people.

Albert Britt, *Great Indian Chiefs*

Supporting Sentences

The topic sentence of a paragraph states a general idea. To make that idea clear and interesting to the reader, you develop it with details in sentences that support the topic sentence. The kinds of details you'll use depend upon the subject. You might use *sensory details, facts or statistics, examples,* or an *anecdote.*

Sensory Details

Sensory details are details you observe through your five senses—sight, sound, smell, touch, taste. You use them to help create a picture or image in the reader's mind. If you describe the color of a snazzy new car, how the cold misty air feels, or how your favorite pizza tastes, you're using sensory details.

In this paragraph, notice how the writer uses details of sight, sound, smell, and touch to describe a train in China. In the first sentence, for example, the writer uses both sight and sound details to help you see and hear the train.

> The train pulled in, steaming and gasping, just as the sun came up. It had come from Dalian, 600 miles away, and it stopped everywhere. So it was sensationally littered with garbage—peanut shells, apple cores, chewed chicken bones, orange peels and greasy paper. It was very dirty and it was so cold inside the spit had frozen on the floor into misshapen yellow-green medallions of ice. The covering between coaches was a snow tunnel, the frost on the windows was an inch thick, the doors had no locks and so they banged and thumped as a freezing draft rushed through the carriages.
>
> Paul Theroux, *Riding the Iron Rooster*

Facts and Statistics

You can also support a main idea with facts and statistics. A *fact* is something that can be proven true by concrete information: in 1981, Sandra Day O'Connor became the first woman U.S. Supreme Court justice. A *statistic* is a fact based on numbers: according to the Motion Picture Association of America, more new films were released in

MEETING individual NEEDS

STUDENTS WITH SPECIAL NEEDS

Some students might have difficulty reading the three paragraphs in **Exercise 1** and, consequently, might have difficulty identifying the main ideas and topic sentences. Students may be able to do the critical thinking involved in this type of activity quite readily, but they may be unable to process information visually. If possible, have peers read the paragraphs aloud to each other. Once one student has identified the two topic sentences, the peer could read the sentences again slowly while the student writes the sentences on his or her paper.

AMENDMENTS TO SELECTIONS
Description of change: excerpted
Rationale: to focus on the skill of identifying main ideas, topic sentences, and supporting sentences presented in this chapter

GUIDED PRACTICE

Explain the directions for **Exercises 1** and **2** to the class and guide them through an example for each.

INDEPENDENT PRACTICE

Students can complete **Exercises 1** and **2** as homework, or you could have students practice analyzing paragraphs from their own writing.

INTEGRATING THE LANGUAGE ARTS

Literature Link. Expressive writing, such as journals or travel literature, uses many sensory details to elicit for the reader the experiences being discussed. To illustrate this concept, have students read and analyze a work such as Charles Nicholl's "A Guided Tour of the Inferno" for its use of sensory details.

Ask students to identify the descriptive details that appeal to each of the senses and to explain how these details contribute to the picture of the slaughterhouse.

Reading Link. You may want to have students find in magazines and newspapers examples of sensory details. Remind students that material must be appropriate for the classroom. Encourage them to use articles and stories, but remind them that advertising uses some of the most effective sensory language.

Have students analyze the paragraphs to determine which senses are involved and how effective the descriptions are.

SELECTION AMENDMENT
Description of change: excerpted
Rationale: to focus on the concept of supporting a main idea presented in this chapter

the United States in 1920 (796) than in 1987 (478). You can look in reference materials to check that these facts and statistics are true.

In the following paragraph, facts and statistics support and prove the main idea that the enormous amount of trash Americans throw away today is a big problem: "2,460 pounds of paper," for example, is a statistic; "that we are running out of landfill space" is a fact.

Every year, the typical American family throws out:
2,460 pounds of paper
540 pounds of metals
480 pounds of glass
480 pounds of food scraps
All told, each of us throws away more than 1,200 pounds of trash per year, far more than people in most other countries. About 80 percent of that garbage ends up in landfills—dumps, as they are more commonly known. (Of the remaining 20 percent, about half is recycled and half is incinerated.) One big problem is that we are running out of landfill space—more than half of the nation's landfills will be full within ten years.

John Elkington, Julia Hailes, Douglas Hill, and Joel Makower, *Going Green*

ASSESSMENT

You may want to have students go over their responses in class so you can evaluate their comprehension of the lesson concepts.

RETEACHING

If you find some students have not understood paragraph structure, you may want to have them work in groups on paragraphs you have highlighted from stories or essays. Highlight topic sentences in red, support sentences in green, and clinchers in blue. Then, have students identify and label eachhighlighted part. Students can ☞

Examples

Another good way for you to support a main idea is to give *examples,* which are specific instances or illustrations of a general idea. An apartment is an example of a type of housing. Getting a scholarship is an example of what can happen if your grades are good.

This paragraph uses specific examples to show the extent of Japan's longtime recycling program. As you read, look for three specific examples the writer uses to support the main idea. The first example is about containers in city parks.

> In Japan, recycling has been practiced for hundreds of years. In public places such as city parks, you'll see separate containers for paper and cans. Recycling centers are more than just the temporary storage places they are in the U.S.A. In Japan, retired or disabled people work in these centers, repairing old furniture or household appliances and then selling them again. And in Machida City, not far from Tokyo, they have a program called *chirigami kokan* ("tissue-paper exchange") in which you receive free recycled paper products, such as tissue paper, napkins, and toilet paper, in exchange for your old newspapers.
>
> Evan and Janet Hadingham, *Garbage! Where It Comes From, Where It Goes*

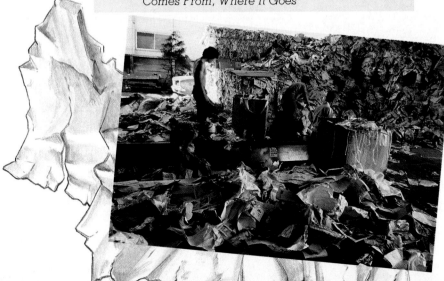

share the examples they find with other groups.

CLOSURE

To summarize the lesson, make an outline of it on the chalkboard. As you write each topic or subtopic, have students explain or define it.

What Makes a Paragraph
I. The Main Idea
II. The Topic Sentence

Anecdotes

An *anecdote* is an extended example, or story, that can be used to support a main idea. In this paragraph, for example, the main idea is stated in the first sentence. An anecdote about President William Howard Taft then supports the main idea about one of baseball's opening-day rituals.

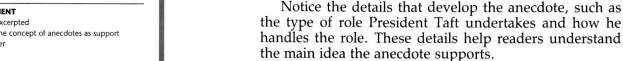

April 14, 1910, was opening day at National Park, the home of the Washington Senators and, for the first time in history, a president of the United States was on hand to throw out the first ball. That fact alone was something of a logistical triumph: President William Howard Taft weighed better than 300 pounds and, just to hold him, a specially reinforced, broad-seated chair had to be found and imported into the newly named Presidential Box next to the first-base dugout. Taft genuinely liked baseball (he had played catcher on a sandlot team in his hometown of Cincinnati). He spoke for most of the country when he said it was "a clean, straight game, [which] summons to its presence everybody who enjoys clean, straight athletics," and he wanted to identify himself with it, setting a precedent that has been followed by every subsequent president.

Geoffrey C. Ward and Ken Burns, *Baseball: An Illustrated History*

SELECTION AMENDMENT
Description of change: excerpted
Rationale: to focus on the concept of anecdotes as support presented in this chapter

Notice the details that develop the anecdote, such as the type of role President Taft undertakes and how he handles the role. These details help readers understand the main idea the anecdote supports.

A. Location
B. Importance
III. Supporting Sentences
A. Sensory Details
B. Facts and Statistics
C. Examples
D. Anecdotes
IV. The Clincher Sentence

EXTENSION

You may want to have students create collections of example paragraphs from books, magazines, newspapers, and their own writings. Students can bracket the main ideas in the paragraphs and underline in red any topic sentences. ■

EXERCISE 2 **Collecting Supporting Details**

Here's your chance to write about a monument that has meaning for every American—the Statue of Liberty. Below are four main ideas that you might use in writing a paragraph about Miss Liberty. With each idea, a type of support—sensory details, facts or statistics, examples, or an anecdote—is suggested. Think up at least two ideas to support each main idea. You may have to do a little research to find support, especially facts or statistics.

EXAMPLE **1.** The Statue of Liberty, which itself is a symbol of liberty, is adorned with symbolism. (examples)
1. *The crown on the Statue of Liberty has seven spikes, representing the world's seven seas and seven continents. A broken chain at the statue's feet and the statue's left foot thrust forward represent freedom from bondage.*

1. The dimensions of the Statue of Liberty are impressive. (facts and statistics)
2. The Statue of Liberty has special meaning for many American citizens. (examples)
3. I took a boat close to the statue one evening at sunset. (sensory details)
4. In America, we often take our liberty and the historic symbols that represent it for granted. (anecdote)

ANSWERS
Exercise 2

Responses will vary, but each paragraph should include the support that is suggested.

VISUAL CONNECTIONS
Exploring the Subject. The official name for this enormous copper statue is *Liberty Enlightening the World.* Liberty's face was modeled after the sculptor's mother, Auguste-Charlotte Bartholdi. Over one hundred years old, this statue is still a symbol of the freedom and opportunity available in the United States.

THE CLINCHER SENTENCE

You may want to explain to students that a clincher sentence is desirable in a paragraph that supports a topic sentence because it clarifies and emphasizes the main idea. A clincher gives a sense of completeness to the paragraph by restating the topic sentence. As the following diagram shows, a clincher sentence brings the discussion full circle.

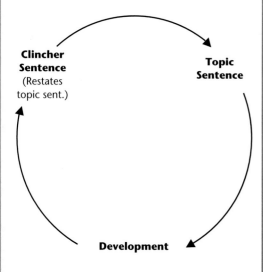

Clincher Sentence (Restates topic sent.)

Topic Sentence

Development

SELECTION AMENDMENT
Description of change: excerpted and italics added
Rationale: to focus on the concept of clincher sentences presented in this chapter

---

The Clincher Sentence

Novels and short stories have snappy endings that emphasize or summarize the authors' main ideas. You may want to add zing to the end of some of your paragraphs, especially long ones, by emphasizing or summarizing the main idea in your final sentence. This concluding sentence is called a *clincher sentence.* It pulls all your information together or emphasizes your main idea. The following paragraph uses a clincher to restate and emphasize the author's opening declaration of his determination to have a horse.

I resolved to have a horse to ride. I had never seen such wild, free, magnificent horsemanship outside of a circus as these picturesquely clad Mexicans, Californians, and Mexicanized Americans displayed in Carson streets every day. How they rode! Leaning just gently forward out of the perpendicular, easy and nonchalant, with broad slouch-hat brim blown square up in front, and long riata swinging above the head, they swept through the town like the wind! The next minute they were only a sailing puff of dust on the far desert. If they trotted, they sat up gallantly and gracefully, and seemed part of the horse; did not go jiggering up and down after the silly Miss Nancy fashion of the riding schools. I had quickly learned to tell a horse from a cow, and was full of anxiety to learn more. *I resolved to buy a horse.*

Mark Twain, "A Genuine Mexican Plug"

WRITING NOTE   Clincher sentences shouldn't be overused. Be sure your clinchers emphasize or effectively restate the main idea. Don't use weak and unnecessary clinchers such as "Those are the reasons I dislike snow."

OBJECTIVE

• To identify sentences that destroy the unity of a paragraph

You may want to read aloud the opening paragraph in the **Unity** section and to emphasize the point that a paragraph needs a main idea but doesn't always have a topic sentence. Remind students that a paragraph has unity if all the sentences relate to one main idea or to a sequence of events or actions.

Unity

A paragraph should have *unity;* that is, it should be about one main idea. Unity is created when all the sentences support the main idea, whether the main idea is stated in a topic sentence or is implied. (*Implied* means "understood but not directly stated.") In paragraphs that relate a series of actions or events, unity is achieved by the sequence of the actions or events. The unity is spoiled by any detail that doesn't relate to the main idea or to the sequence of events or actions.

All Sentences Relate to the Main Idea Stated in the Topic Sentence.   In the following paragraph, the topic sentence states the main idea—that horse-drawn chariots, though useful in battles, were a problem. As you read, notice how each of the supporting sentences includes a detail related to a problem involved in using the chariot. In the second sentence, for example, one problem is that a soldier driving alone had to wrap the reins around his waist to keep his arms free for fighting.

> By 1000 B.C. horse-drawn chariots were standard equipment in most armies, and soldiers had discovered that the world's greatest weapon was also the world's greatest nuisance. In the first place, the chariot was hard to use. A two-man chariot team could manage nicely if one man drove while the other bombarded the enemy with spears or arrows. But when a soldier

The Granger Collection, New York.

PROGRAM MANAGER

UNITY

■ **Analyzing** To help students analyze and organize ideas, see **Achieving Unity** in *Practicing the Writing Process,* p. 26.

QUOTATION FOR THE DAY

"The discipline of the writer is to learn to be still and listen to what his subject has to tell him." (Rachel Carson, 1907–1964, American marine biologist and science writer)

Write the quotation on the chalkboard, and ask students to explore the quotation in writing journal entries. Students might write about times when they learned something new from writing or reading. Explain that a paragraph that focuses on a main subject or idea is effective and unified.

GUIDED PRACTICE

Testing to see whether each sentence relates to the main idea, analyze the model paragraphs with students.

MEETING *individual* NEEDS

LEP/ESL

General Strategies. Because some students might have difficulty understanding some of the literary models in this section, they could have trouble identifying topic sentences and main ideas. Be sure that students understand the uncommon or abstract vocabulary used (such as *nuisance, spear,* or *chariot*), difficult sentence structures (such as past perfect tense and contrary-to-fact conditional clauses), and unfamiliar subject matter (such as the *Titanic's* sinking and demolition derbies).

AT-RISK STUDENTS

You may want to work with students to explain further the concept of unity. You could ask them to discuss styles of dressing. Many of them will have a distinct sense of what items go together and of what items would be out of place with a particular outfit. You can compare unity of appearance to the concept of unity in paragraphs.

ADVANCED STUDENTS

The concept of unity applies to visual arts as well as to writing. You may want to have students research the principle of unity in art. They could discuss with the class examples of paintings that do or do not have unity.

drove alone, he had to tie the reins around his waist and control the horses with his body in order to keep his hands free for fighting. Since most chariots had no seats, the passengers and driver had to stand. They struggled to keep their balance as the little cart careened across country like a crazy roller coaster car and fought to keep their tempers when the chariot came to a sudden, unexpected halt. Such stops occurred frequently because chariots had to be carried across rivers and hoisted over hedges. They fell into ruts and wouldn't roll over rocks. They were too wide to squeeze through narrow mountain passes and so fragile that they broke down regularly.

Suzanne Jurmain, *Once Upon A Horse*

All Sentences Relate to an Implied Main Idea.   The following paragraph doesn't have a topic sentence. But all the sentences work together to support an implied main idea—that the *Titanic's* two radio operators were too tired or busy to heed the last warnings before the luxury ship hit an iceberg in 1912. In the first sentence, for example, the fact that the radio operator was exhausted kept him from listening to the radio and hearing the warnings about the iceberg.

Students should be able to read the paragraphs in **Exercise 3** to find the offending sentences.

Assess students' mastery based on their performance on **Exercise 3**, or have students identify details that spoil unity in their own writing.

In the radio room, Harold Bride was exhausted. The two operators were expected to keep the radio working twenty-four hours a day, and Bride lay down to take a much-needed nap. Phillips was so busy with the passenger messages that he actually brushed off the final ice warning of the night. It was from the *Californian*. Trapped in a field of ice, she had stopped for the night about nineteen miles north of the *Titanic*. She was so close that the message literally blasted in Phillips' ears. Annoyed by the loud interruption, he cut off the *Californian*'s radio operator with the words, "Shut up, shut up. I'm busy."

Robert D. Ballard, *Exploring the Titanic*

All Sentences Relate to a Sequence of Events.
Although the following paragraph doesn't actually state a main idea, it does have purpose and unity. The purpose is to narrate a series of events that happen at a demolition derby. The paragraph's unity comes from the sequence of events described. Each action detail is part of a sequence that begins when the second driver for the finals has to be selected. This paragraph, like all other narrative paragraphs, is actually a cause-and-effect paragraph. One action in the demolition derby (cause) results in the next action (effect), and so on.

After each trial or heat at a demolition derby, two drivers go into the finals. One is the driver whose car was still going at the end. The other is the driver the crowd selects from among the 24 vanquished on the basis of his courage, showmanship, or simply the awesomeness of his crashes. The numbers of the cars are read over loudspeakers, and the crowd chooses one with its cheers. By the same token, the crowd may force a driver out of competition if he appears cowardly or merely cunning. This is the sort of driver who drifts around the edge of the battle avoiding crashes with the hope that the other cars will eliminate one another. The umpire waves a yellow flag at him and

AMENDMENT TO SELECTIONS
Description of change: excerpted
Rationale: to focus on the concept of paragraph unity presented in this chapter

RETEACHING

If students are having difficulty with paragraph unity, give them sentences on strips of paper from two different paragraphs. Then, help students to arrange the sentences in a logical order and to discard any sentences that detract from unity in either paragraph.

CLOSURE

Have students explain the meaning of *paragraph unity.* Then, have them analyze one of the paragraphs by Monica Sone in the opening literary model to determine whether it has unity.

MEETING *individual* NEEDS

LESS-ADVANCED STUDENTS

Form groups of three or four students. Have volunteers read both paragraphs of **Exercise 3.** Then, ask students to identify the main ideas of each paragraph. Have the students go through each paragraph sentence by sentence to decide whether each sentence relates to the main idea. In this way they should be able to locate the incorrect sentence in the first model.

SELECTION AMENDMENT
Description of change: excerpted
Rationale: to focus on the concept of paragraph unity presented in this chapter

---

80 WRITING HANDBOOK *Paragraphs*

he must crash into someone within 30 seconds or run the risk of being booed off the field in dishonor and disgrace.

Tom Wolfe, "Clean Fun at Riverhead"

EXERCISE 3 ▸ **Identifying Sentences That Destroy Unity**

One of the following paragraphs has unity, and the other doesn't. Try to figure out which <u>sentence destroys the unity</u> of that paragraph. Paragraph 2 has unity.

1.   A lot of wizardry went into the special effects in the 1939 MGM movie classic *The Wizard of Oz.* Perhaps the picture's most famous special effect is the tornado that carries Dorothy and her dog, Toto, to Oz. <u>Legend has it that L. Frank Baum got the idea for the name of Oz from a file cabinet drawer labeled O–Z.</u> The tornado was created by using fans, a crane, and a muslin cone rotated by a motor. Another famous special effect is the melting of the Wicked Witch. She melted away by disappearing through the floor on a hydraulic lift. Her costume was fastened to the floor, and dry ice or liquid smoke created the melting effect. The Winged Monkeys "flew" by means of support wires. The Wicked Witch's skywriting was achieved by using black liquid released from a hypodermic needle to which was fastened a small profile of the witch.

81

2.   Gloria put her head farther down and pumped harder. The three leading competitors were not as far ahead as they had been only moments ago. Perhaps they were tiring. The last section of the race was five miles of steeply rising uphill. She geared down once and pushed herself, willing herself not to waste her time by checking positions. She passed one cyclist without even glancing at him, concentrating on keeping her pace smooth and strong. She had three miles left and two riders ahead of her. "Maybe I can go faster," she thought. Gritting her teeth, she forced the pace. "I can go faster. I can. I *will*," she persuaded herself. She pushed herself harder. With less than a mile left, she passed another rider. Concentrating, willing herself to victory, she passed the last competitor and pumped victoriously across the finish line, winner of the Annual 120-Mile Bike Marathon.

OBJECTIVES

- To determine the best order of ideas for paragraphs
- To identify the order of ideas in paragraphs
- To identify and revise a paragraph that is not coherent
- To identify direct references and transitions in a paragraph
- To revise a paragraph by adding transitions

QUOTATION FOR THE DAY

"Today's poet has less trouble making himself heard than making himself plain." (Louis Untermeyer, 1885–1977, American author, poet, and editor)

Students might discuss the quotation and contribute to a list of ways writers can make their work clear. Lead the class to understand that using clearly connected ideas and arranging sentences in an order that makes sense are two ways to make paragraphs coherent.

Coherence

A paragraph has *coherence* when the ideas are clearly connected and arranged in an order that makes sense to readers. This coherence helps readers follow your ideas easily.

Order of Ideas

You can help your readers follow your ideas by the way you arrange, or order, them. Often, the subject you're writing about will suggest the order of ideas.

Chronological Order. In a story, the actions or events are usually arranged according to the order in which they occur. This is *chronological,* or time, *order.* (*Chrono-* means "time.") Chronological order works because it often shows the cause-and-effect relationship between events: one action (cause) results in another action (effect). You'll also use chronological order to explain a process, with steps in the process listed in the (time) order they are to be carried out. In the following paragraph, the writer uses chronological order to arrange the events in a story told by adults to young Chinese girls.

> When we Chinese girls listened to the adults talking-story, we learned that we failed if we grew up to be but wives or slaves. We could be heroines, swordswomen. Even if she had to rage across all China, a swordswoman got even with anybody who hurt her family. Perhaps women were once so dangerous that they had to have their feet bound. It was a woman who invented white crane boxing only two hundred years ago. She was already an expert pole fighter, daughter of a teacher trained at the Shao-lin temple, where there lived an order of fighting monks. She was combing her hair one morning when a white crane alighted outside her window. She teased it with her pole, which it pushed aside with a soft brush of its wing. Amazed, she dashed outside and tried to knock the crane off its perch. It snapped her pole in two. Recognizing the presence of great power, she asked the spirit of the white crane if it would teach her to fight. It answered with a cry that white crane

TEACHING THE LESSON

You may want to have a volunteer read the text and the model in **Chronological Order.** Help students with the unusual references in Kingston's paragraph. Tell students that *The Woman Warrior: Memoirs of a Girlhood Among Ghosts* is classified as fiction although it is largely based on experience.

Have another volunteer read the section entitled **Spatial Order,** and emphasize that spatial order is frequently used in descriptive writing.

After a volunteer reads **Order of Importance,** p. 84, have students discuss the various strengths of putting the most-important point first compared to putting it last. ☞

Coherence **83**

boxers imitate today. Later the bird returned as an old man, and he guided her boxing for many years. Thus she gave the world a new martial art.

Maxine Hong Kingston, *The Woman Warrior: Memoirs of a Girlhood Among Ghosts*

Spatial Order. When you describe something, you usually arrange the details according to their location in space. *Spatial order* allows you to show where objects are in relation to each other (such as from left to right, from near to far, from front to back). In the following paragraph, spatial order helps you picture what a girl observes, from left to right and from near to far, during a buggy ride on Canada's Prince Edward Island. In the second sentence, for example, your attention is directed to "the right hand." What other words and phrases in the paragraph help you follow the girl's observations?

The shore road was "woodsy and wild and lonesome." On the right hand, scrub firs, their spirits quite unbroken by long years of tussle with the gulf winds, grew thickly. On the left were the steep red sandstone cliffs, so near the track in places that a mare of less steadiness than the sorrel might have tried the nerves of the people behind her. Down at the base of the cliffs were heaps of surf-worn rocks or little sandy coves inlaid with pebbles as with ocean jewels; beyond lay the sea, shimmering and blue, and over it soared the gulls, their pinions flashing silvery in the sunlight.

Lucy Maud Montgomery, *Anne of Green Gables*

MEETING *individual* NEEDS

LEP/ESL

Spanish. The word *coherence* is similar to the Spanish *coherencia.* However, it's important not to assume that the concepts are familiar just because the words are cognates. Write a clear definition of *coherence* on the chalkboard. *Coherence* means "the connection of parts in a way that makes sense." When a person is incoherent, he or she is not easily understood; in fact, his or her speech doesn't make any sense to the listener.

ADVANCED STUDENTS

Some students will have mastered chronological order, so you may want to have them augment this section by doing research about the author, Maxine Hong Kingston, her book *The Woman Warrior: Memoirs of a Girlhood Among Ghosts,* or other books she has written. Students could work in pairs and report to the larger group on their findings. Or, you may wish to have students research one of the martial arts, including its history, importance, or role in society today.

AMENDMENTS TO SELECTIONS
Description of change: excerpted
Rationale: to focus on the concepts of chronological and spatial order presented in this chapter

Order of Importance. If your paragraph were to give information or persuade, you usually would arrange ideas or details in *order of importance.* You could begin with the least important idea or detail and move to the most important, or begin with the most important and move to the least important. Readers usually are more aware of what they read first or what they read last.

In this paragraph the actress Helen Hayes gives reasons why she thinks older people should write an "autobiography." She begins with the least important reason—the therapeutic value—and moves to the most important reason—the preservation of personal history.

> I also like to see older folks write an "autobiography." Writing is very therapeutic. In fact, experts say it promotes self esteem and personal integration. Personally, I think it also clears away the cobwebs and stimulates a fresh way of thinking and looking back at your life. Most important, perhaps, it leaves a private history of yourself and your family. Don't you wish your grandmother and her grandmother before her had done that?
>
> Helen Hayes, "Hayes: 'There Is So Much to Do'"

Logical Order. *Logical order* simply means the grouping of related ideas together. If your paragraph classifies, divides, defines, compares, or contrasts, you might choose logical order to arrange your ideas. The writer of the following paragraph, for example, compares selling teenagers new singing idols with selling them other fads. Notice that details about the singing idols are grouped together, followed by the details about the other fads.

> It was the industry's consensus that Tin Pan Alley had missed the boat, and that if the traditional songwriting industry was to survive, rock and roll would have to be factored in. It wasn't enough for rockers to cut the occasional standard; they would have to be given well-crafted, professionally written pop songs that had a rock-and-roll feeling. And this, it

Ask students to examine the **Transitional Words and Phrases** chart on p. 89 and to read the Steinbeck paragraph, p. 90, in its entirety to analyze its use of transitional words and phrases.

GUIDED PRACTICE

You may want to work with students to identify types of order used in sample paragraphs from a literature textbook. Possible choices for each type of ordering are "You Are Now Entering the Human Heart" by Janet Frame—chronological and logical order; "Waits" by Lewis Thomas—order of importance; and "The Mojave" by John ☞

was beginning to occur to some of the brains on Tin Pan Alley, would mean that the kids would have to be fed some new pop idols—which didn't seem that hard, really. It was already a truism that kids would buy anything, and the Wham-O company had proved it. Late in 1958 they had started a craze for a length of plastic tubing stapled into a circle, marketed under the name Hula-Hoop. Millions sold, and then Hula-Hoops vanished as quickly as they came, but Wham-O had learned a valuable lesson to be applied to its other products, Silly Putty and the redoubtable Frisbee.

Ed Ward, Geoffrey Stokes, and Ken Tucker, *Rock of Ages: The Rolling Stone History of Rock & Roll*

VISUAL CONNECTIONS

Ideas for Writing. You may want to have students write informative/descriptive paragraphs about the photograph of the Hula-Hoopers. Before students write, have them reread the types of order of ideas to decide which one would be best. Have students work with partners to discuss their descriptions and to evaluate the types of order they have chosen.

ANSWERS

Exercise 4

Answers may vary. Here are some possibilities:

1. chronological order; order of importance
2. spatial order
3. order of importance; logical order
4. chronological order
5. logical order

AMENDMENTS TO SELECTIONS
Description of change: excerpted
Rationale: to focus on the concept of paragraph ordering presented in this chapter

---

EXERCISE 4 ▶ **Choosing an Order of Ideas**

Try to figure out what order—chronological order, spatial order, order of importance, or logical order—would be best to develop each of the following topics in a paragraph. (You might use more than one type of order for some of the topics.)

1. accomplishments of Dr. Martin Luther King, Jr.
2. description of the Oval Office in the White House
3. five health reasons in favor of a vegetarian diet
4. how to make your own camera
5. comparing blues and jazz music

ANSWERS

Exercise 5

1. logical order

2. This paragraph uses chronological order, but the chronology needs revision. The sentences should be rearranged as follows:

   Sitting Bull was a mighty Sioux who distinguished himself early in life. He was born in 1834 in what is now South Dakota. At ten, he killed his first buffalo. At fourteen, he won his first honor in battle. He became known as a brave warrior and was named a chief of his nation. In 1866 he led raids against U.S. army troops moving into his people's land. The government agreed to peace talks by 1868, but Sitting Bull refused to participate. He acted as the main medicine man before the victorious Native American attack against Lieutenant Colonel George Armstrong Custer's regiment at the famous Battle of Little Bighorn on June 25, 1876.

3. spatial order

EXERCISE 5   Identifying Order of Ideas

Following are three paragraphs. Two of the paragraphs follow the types of order you've just studied, but in one paragraph the ideas have no sensible order. Identify that paragraph and rewrite it so that the flow of ideas makes sense. Then identify the type of order followed by each of the other paragraphs.

1.   W.E.B. Du Bois and Booker T. Washington were two of this century's most influential black writers. Washington wrote most of his works between 1900 and 1911. With a longer career, Du Bois wrote between 1896 and the 1960s. Their educations were not alike, although both had more education than was average for the time. Washington graduated from the Hampton Institute, a vocational school, almost twenty years before Du Bois received a Ph.D. from Harvard in 1895. Both writers were very interested in education, although they looked at it differently. Washington founded the Tuskegee Normal and Industrial Institute, which stressed vocational training as the first step in upward mobility. Du Bois believed in classical education, teaching for a time at Atlanta University. Their educational beliefs were revealed in their works, Washington's in *The Future of the American Negro* and *Up from Slavery* and Du Bois's in *The Education of Black People*.

Booker T. Washington

W.E.B. Du Bois

RETEACHING

If some students still do not understand the various types of order that make paragraphs coherent, organize students into groups of four and have them label examples from magazines and newspapers in which you have underlined and highlighted the supporting ideas and clues for each type of order. Each group should have two examples ☞

Coherence **87**

2.   Sitting Bull was a mighty Sioux who distinguished himself early in life. At fourteen, he won his first honor in battle. At ten, he killed his first buffalo. He was born in 1834 in what is now South Dakota. He became known as a brave warrior and was named a chief of his nation. He acted as the main medicine man before the victorious Native American attack against Lieutenant Colonel George Armstrong Custer's regiment at the famous Battle of Little Bighorn on June 25, 1876. In 1866 he led raids against U.S. army troops moving into his people's land. The government agreed to peace talks by 1868, but Sitting Bull refused to participate.

3.   The Sun Dance of the Plains Indians, also called the Medicine Dance or Thirst Lodge, is an annual event. This spring dance is held in a large circular open frame lodge representing the world's creation. A sacred cottonwood tree is placed in the center of the lodge. This tree acts as the focus of the dance and links sky and earth. On the tree is attached one or more sacred objects. A sacred object may be an eagle head or skull or a bison head or skull. The dancers move from the outside edge of the lodge to the tree at the center and back again. Each dancer always faces the tree. Each dancer concentrates on the tree or on one of the objects attached to the tree.

VISUAL CONNECTIONS

Exploring the Subject. In June of 1876, Sitting Bull and his followers were encamped on the Little Bighorn River searching for game. It was there later that month that Lieutenant Colonel George Armstrong Custer's regiment was defeated in a great battle. Sitting Bull was eventually killed at the age of 59 in an attempt by soldiers to arrest him on Grand River. The Sioux admired Sitting Bull for his leadership, his religious devotion, and his love for his people.

TIMESAVER

You may wish to have students work in small, mixed-ability groups to complete **Exercise 5** orally. This procedure will eliminate paper-grading time and will also allow students to learn by participating in group discussions. Each group will need to designate a member to record its revision of the second paragraph. Have one group read its corrected paragraph aloud and then lead a class discussion to analyze and possibly improve it.

of each type of order—chronological order, spatial order, order of importance, and logical order.

Have the groups exchange their labeled findings so that the class can discuss the characteristics of the types of order.

CLOSURE

Ask students to summarize the four types of order for developing topics in paragraphs, to give examples of topics that would be appropriate for each of the four types, and to explain two methods to use for coherence. ■

Connections Between Ideas

To give a paragraph coherence, you should do more than arrange the ideas in an order that makes sense; you should also show how the ideas are connected. There are two ways to show connections: (1) make *direct references* to something else in the paragraph or (2) use words that make a *transition,* or bridge, from one idea to another.

Direct References. A natural way to link ideas in a paragraph is to refer to a noun or pronoun that you've used earlier. You can make **direct references** in these three ways:

1. Use a noun or pronoun that refers to a noun or pronoun used earlier.
2. Repeat a word used earlier.
3. Use a word or phrase that means the same thing as one used earlier.

This paragraph, from a famous adventure story, has several direct references. The numbers above the references show you the type of reference.

> That same evening, however, Leiningen assembled *his*[1] workers. *He*[1] had no intention of waiting till the news reached *their*[1] ears from other sources. *Most*[1] of *them*[1] had been born in the district; the cry "The ants are coming!" was to *them*[1] an imperative signal for instant, panic-stricken flight, a spring for life itself. But so great was the *Indians'*[1] trust in *Leiningen,*[2] in *Leiningen's*[2] word, and in *Leiningen's*[2] wisdom, that *they*[1] received *his*[1] curt *tidings,*[3] and *his*[1] orders for the imminent struggle, with the calmness with which *they*[1] were given. *They*[1] waited, unafraid, alert, as if for the beginning of a new game or hunt which *he*[1] had just described to *them.*[1] The *ants*[2] were indeed mighty, but not so mighty as the *boss.*[1] Let *them*[1] come!
>
> Carl Stephenson, "Leiningen Versus the Ants"

MEETING individual NEEDS

ADVANCED STUDENTS

Students who quickly grasp the concept of transitions could evaluate the coherence achieved by a professional writer in his or her writing. A good choice for an evaluation is A. M. Rosenthal's essay "No News from Auschwitz." Students can use the following questions:

1. Does the essay have clear transitions? Give at least three examples to support your opinion.
2. Do all sentences relate to the main idea? If so, explain how. If not, give specific examples that show unrelated sentences.
3. Rate this essay on a scale from one to four. How could the writer better his score? Give at least two suggestions for improvement.

LESS-ADVANCED STUDENTS

Students can practice using transitions by filling in the blanks in a paragraph. You can provide a paragraph with blanks left where transitions had been provided and then ask students to complete the paragraph.

SELECTION AMENDMENT
Description of change: excerpted
Rationale: to focus on the concept of coherence presented in this chapter

Transitional Words and Phrases. Words and phrases that indicate the relationships between ideas are called *transitional expressions.* Prepositions that show chronological or spatial order and conjunctions are also transitions. In the chart that follows, notice the relationships shown by the different types of transitions and the types of writing to which they're related.

TRANSITIONAL WORDS AND PHRASES		
Comparing Ideas/Classification and Definition		
also	besides	similarly
and	in addition	too
another	other	
Contrasting Ideas/Classification and Definition		
although	instead	otherwise
but	nevertheless	still
however	on the other	yet
in spite of	hand	
Showing Cause and Effect/Narration		
as a result	for	therefore
because	since	thus
consequently	so	
Showing Time/Narration		
after	eventually	meanwhile
at last	finally	then
at once	first	when
before	for a time	
Showing Place/Description		
above	from	on
across	here	over
around	in	there
before	nearby	to
beyond	next	under
Showing Importance/Evaluation		
first	mainly	then
last	more important	to begin with

COMMON ERROR

Problem. Many student writers fail to have clear antecedents for pronouns they use. For example, in the sentences "Hilary brought Karima to the movie. She's the youngest girl in our class," the antecedent of *she* is not clear.

Solution. Require students to circle all the pronouns in their writing and to draw arrows back to the correct antecedents. The revision stage of the writing process would be a good place to incorporate this procedure.

In the following paragraph, transitional words, which are underlined, are used to strengthen the connections and show relationships in time and place.

> <u>Then from</u> the corner of the house came a sound so soft that it might have been simply a thought, a little furtive movement, a touch of a foot <u>on</u> earth, the almost inaudible purr of controlled breathing. Kino held his breath to listen, <u>and</u> he knew that whatever dark thing was <u>in</u> his house was holding its breath <u>too</u>, to listen. <u>For a time</u> no sound at all came <u>from</u> the corner of the brush house. <u>Then</u> Kino might have thought he had imagined the sound. <u>But</u> Juana's hand came creeping <u>over to</u> him <u>in</u> warning, <u>and then</u> the sound came again! the whisper of a foot <u>on</u> dry earth <u>and</u> the scratch of fingers <u>in</u> the soil.
>
> John Steinbeck, *The Pearl*

EXERCISE 6 ▶ **Identifying Direct References and Transitions**

The following paragraph uses both direct references and transitions to connect ideas. Label two columns "Direct References" and "Transitions." Then identify each <u>direct reference</u> and <u>transition</u> in the paragraph. Remember to refer to the chart of commonly used transitions on page 89, and to think about conjunctions and prepositions telling *when* and *where*.

EXAMPLE   Moreover, Mayor Mary Rodríguez made a promise to balance the city budget. When election day arrived, her pledge proved popular, and she won. Few people, however, realized how painful carrying out her commitment would be.

Direct References	Transitions
her	moreover
pledge	when
she	and
her	however
commitment	

SELECTION AMENDMENT
Description of change: excerpted
Rationale: to focus on the concept of transitions presented in this chapter

Although the popular cartoon *The Far Side* by Gary Larson had extraordinary success, its beginnings were modest. Larson says he always loved to draw, but he never took art lessons. Also, Larson says he always liked science. His famous panel, consequently, combined those two loves. In 1979, Larson started drawing a cartoon in the *Seattle Times* called *Nature's Way*. Before long, his drawings moved to the *San Francisco Chronicle* as *The Far Side*. Syndication began, and *The Far Side* became a household name. Larson says he frequently is asked, "Where did you get your ideas?" The artist answers that he doesn't know; most ideas came from thinking and doodling. Because people enjoyed the cartoon so much, Larson decided to write a book about his work. That volume is *The PreHistory of The Far Side*.

Courtesy of Universal Press Syndicate.

EXERCISE 7 ▶ **Using Transitions**

There's little wonder that the ideas in this paragraph are confusing—there are few transitions to make ideas clear to readers. Revise the paragraph by adding the transitions that help readers follow the order of ideas. (You may also decide to make other changes to improve the paragraph.)

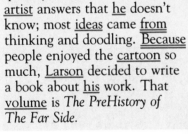

Angie was very interested in the Seven Wonders of the Ancient World. She decided to write a report on them. She went to Egypt last year. She saw the

ANSWERS
Exercise 7

Responses will vary. Here is a possibility:

Because Angie was very interested in the Seven Wonders of the Ancient World, she decided to write a report on them. Her interest began when she visited Egypt last year and saw the pyramids, the only existing wonder. To write her report, Angie first went to the library. There she checked out books on the ancient wonders and read about them in encyclopedias. Then Angie talked to her history teacher because she found conflicting information. For instance, most of the old books said that the Colossus of Rhodes stood over the harbor entrance on the Greek island of Rhodes. More modern research, however, indicates that the huge bronze statue was not at the harbor. Before she wrote her report, Angie located pictures of all the seven wonders. Since she had seen the pyramids, Angie wrote most about them.

pyramids, the only existing wonder. To write her report, Angie went to the library. She checked out books on the ancient wonders. She read about them in encyclopedias. Angie talked to her history teacher. Angie found conflicting information. Most of the old books said that the Colossus of Rhodes stood over the harbor entrance on the Greek island of Rhodes. More modern research indicates that the huge bronze statue was not at the harbor. Angie located pictures of all the seven wonders. She wrote her report. She had seen the pyramids. That's why she wrote most about them.

Zeus at Olympia

Lighthouse of Alexandria

Temple of Artemis at Ephesus

Pyramids at Giza

Colossus of Rhodes

Mausoleum at Halicarnassus

Hanging Gardens of Babylon

STRATEGIES OF DEVELOPMENT

OBJECTIVES

- To use descriptive detail as a strategy
- To use narration as a strategy for developing paragraph outlines
- To explain a process to an audience
- To use classification to develop main ideas
- To evaluate subjects and to give reasons for the evaluations

Strategies of Development

Description, narration, classification, and evaluation are four strategies for developing a main idea. The strategy, or method, you choose to develop a paragraph depends upon your specific purpose and audience for writing. The strategy determines what kind of supporting details you will use, such as facts or examples, and affects the order of your ideas. These four strategies of development are basically different ways of looking at a topic or subject.

STRATEGIES OF DEVELOPMENT	
Description	Looking at individual features of a particular subject
Narration	Looking at changes in the subject over a period of time
Classification	Looking at a subject in relation to other subjects
Evaluation	Looking at the value of the subject (judging)

Each paragraph or each piece of longer writing you create should have a purpose and a strategy that develops that purpose. You may use description to write a friend about your dream car. Or you may use narration to write in your journal about what happened during the last football game. In school you might use classification to compare and contrast the sciences of biology and zoology. And you would choose evaluation to tell your theater teacher your opinion of a play you saw.

WRITING NOTE   Frequently, paragraphs and longer pieces of writing have more than one purpose, so they use more than one strategy of development. For example, description and narration are often combined in reports, stories, and even poetry.

STRATEGIES OF DEVELOPMENT

- **Instructional Support** To help students explore several ways to develop paragraphs, see **Developing Paragraphs** in *Practicing the Writing Process,* pp. 28–30.

- **Review** For a review of transitional words and phrases, see **Review— Transitional Words and Phrases** in *Practicing the Writing Process,* p. 31.

QUOTATION FOR THE DAY

"Talent alone cannot make a writer. There must be a man behind the book." (Ralph Waldo Emerson, 1803–1882, American essayist, poet, and philosopher)

Have students freewrite responses to the quotation. Explain that a good writer usually has a definite purpose for each piece of work he or she creates and a strategy that develops that purpose.

Have a volunteer read **Strategies of Development** and the **Writing Note** on p. 93. Emphasize that writers often use a combination of strategies to achieve their purposes, especially in lengthy works.

Have a volunteer read **Description** on this page, including the model by Mason Crum. Point out that writers use description to convey a sense of people, places, and objects.

Have a volunteer read **Narration** and **Telling a Story** on p. 95, and point out that cause-and-effect relationships often make up the internal structure of a story. For example, in the model from Edith Hamilton's *Mythology*, p. 95, the Greek women elected Athena (cause), so Poseidon flooded the land (effect).

MEETING *individual* NEEDS

LEP/ESL

General Strategies. Some students might have difficulty with classification in English because the meanings of words in their native languages do not exactly match those of English words. Such small differences can lead students to feel uncertain about using English. You may wish to give some extra suggestions to English-language learners on how to define, compare, and contrast topics.

ANSWERS

Exercise 8

Be sure students appeal to all senses in their features. You may want to suggest that students use a prewriting strategy such as mapping to help them get started.

Description

What does your state flag look like? How will you recognize Gothic architecture?

To tell what something is like or what it looks like, you need to examine its particular features. Then you choose description as a strategy of development, using sensory details for support and spatial order. The following paragraph, for example, describes the brightly dressed Gullah women of the Carolina Sea Islands.

All day long they travel the highways in twos, threes, and dozens. Dressed in their best bibs and tuckers, they present a varicolored procession, moving leisurely over shell and sand roads. Every color of the rainbow is presented in their dresses, calicoes of blue, red, yellow, and green—garments simply made, and mostly homemade. They chat and laugh and enjoy the holiday spirit. Like the ancient Hebrews they have learned the happy art of combining religion and social life. A woman comes by with her large pocketbook balanced on her head—why, I do not know. A proud mother carries her baby in her arms, dressed in brilliant yellow.

Mason Crum, *Gullah*

EXERCISE 8 ▶ **Using Description as a Strategy**

"It's a really economical and smooth car," she says. "What kind is it? What does it look like?" her friend asks. Description adds information about a subject. Choose two of the following subjects and list at least five features—sensory details—to describe each one. Remember to use a technique like brainstorming or freewriting to think up sensory details (see pages 24–34).

1. a school dance
2. a favorite musician or musical group
3. your neighborhood on a winter's day
4. yourself when you have a bad cold
5. the busiest, most crowded place you've ever been

After a volunteer reads **Explaining a Process** and **Explaining Cause and Effect**, on pp. 95–96, point out that both of these types of narration almost always follow chronological order.

Read the text and models in the section **Classification** on pp. 97–99. Tell students that classification is a strategy of organization that is frequently used. Their textbooks, for example, are organized by classification. Ask students to suggest topics that would be appropriate for classification by dividing, defining, or comparing and contrasting.

Read and discuss **Evaluation**, pp. 100–101. Then, have students answer the lead-in questions about the model, ☞

Strategies of Development   **95**

Narration

What happened when young Arthur tried to pull the sword from the stone? How does a video recorder work? What economic and political events caused the Berlin Wall to come down?

To answer these questions, you use the strategy of narration, looking at events or actions in time. And to find the answers to these questions, you have to look at changes over a period of time. Since you're looking at a subject from a time perspective, you usually use chronological (or time) order. You may use narration *to tell a story or incident* (what happened when Arthur tried the sword), *to explain a process* (how a video recorder works), or *to explain cause and effect* (why the Berlin Wall came down).

Telling a Story. Storytellers use the strategy of narration to tell a story (what happened over time). The story may be either true or imaginary (fiction). In the following paragraph, the writer tells a story about a contest between the Greek gods Athena and Poseidon for the city of Athens.

> In one story of this contest between the two deities, woman's suffrage plays a part. In those early days, we are told, women voted as well as men. All the women voted for the goddess, and all the men for the god. There was one more woman than there were men, so Athena won. But the men, along with Poseidon, were greatly chagrined at this female triumph; and while Poseidon proceeded to flood the land the men decided to take the vote away from the women. Nevertheless, Athena kept Athens.
>
> Edith Hamilton, *Mythology*

Explaining a Process. Telling how something works or how to do something is *explaining a process.* You use narration to explain a process because you look at your subject as it changes over time. In the following paragraph, the writer explains how he helps his mother close the family restaurant. (The steps in the process are the changes over time.)

A DIFFERENT APPROACH

Have students explore the art of storytelling. Perhaps students have traditional stories in their families they could share. Or, you could have them research stories in the library. You may want to suggest as subjects for research particular storytellers such as Garrison Keillor, whose works they could find and listen to or read.

COOPERATIVE LEARNING

You may want to organize the class into groups of four or five students to find examples of the three types of narration. Groups can use magazines or newspapers as sources. Have each group find an example of each of the three types. Add these examples to the bulletin board and categorize them as storytelling, explaining a process, or explaining causes and effects.

AMENDMENTS TO SELECTIONS
Description of change: excerpted
Rationale: to focus on the concept of paragraph development presented in this chapter

a review of the television series *Frasier*, p. 101, as a way of discussing the use of evaluation in the paragraph.

GUIDED PRACTICE

To model the process in **Exercise 8**, list on the chalkboard sensory details for a subject you select. Model the required skills in **Exercises 9–12** by using the first part of each of the exercises.

A DIFFERENT APPROACH

Authors sometimes do not present events or steps in precisely the order in which they occurred, and they often use flashbacks. However, writers normally warn the reader of this condition by using transitional expressions such as *prior to that, in previous years,* or *we should consider.* Some students may tend to write their points as they think of them and to omit needed transitions. You could advise students to be sure that they write events or steps in the same order in which they actually occurred or to be sure to use transitions to write about the events or steps.

> At night I help my mother close the restaurant. I do what she and my father have done together for the past forty-three years. At ten o'clock I turn off the illuminated white sign above the front entrance. After all the customers leave and the last waiter says goodbye, I lock the front door and flip over the sign that says "Closed." Then I shut off the radio and the back lights.
>
> David Low, "Winterblossom Garden"

Explaining Cause and Effect. To explain what causes something or what the effects of something are, you also look at the way things have changed over the course of time. You use narration again. In this paragraph, the writer reveals the two effects of her realization that she was growing up and wouldn't always be at Ames High School. One effect is that she felt a sense of sadness. The other is that she "nestled" into familiar surroundings.

> As I grew older, I began to realize that this quiet was not going to last. Time was speeding up; at some sharply definable point I would grow up and leave Ames. At odd moments in those last years I would be surprised by sadness, a strange feeling that perhaps I had missed something, that maybe life was going to pass me by. At the same time I nestled securely in the familiar landscape of streets whose every bump and jog I knew, of people who smiled and greeted me by name wherever I went, of friends who appeared at every movie, store, or swimming pool.
>
> Susan Allen Toth, "Nothing Happened"

ANSWERS
Exercise 9

Responses will vary. You may want to have students work with partners to make their lists. Tell students each list should contain five to ten items.

AMENDMENTS TO SELECTIONS
Description of change: excerpted
Rationale: to focus on the concepts of process and cause and effect presented in this chapter

EXERCISE 9 ▶ **Using Narration as a Strategy**

You've read about the different times you can use narration to develop a paragraph—to explain causes and effects, to explain a process, and to tell a story. Now, use the following instructions for using that strategy.

INDEPENDENT PRACTICE

Have students work in small groups to complete **Exercise 8**. Students could brainstorm long lists and then choose their five favorites to record as their own work. After you have modeled the activities, assign **Exercises 9–12** as independent practice.

ASSESSMENT

Ask students to share and discuss their answers to the exercises in class.

1. List the effects of poor nutrition and lack of exercise on your health as an adult.
2. List the steps in the process for getting a learner's driving permit in your state.
3. List the actions in a story about what might happen if an alien spacecraft landed on the White House lawn.

EXERCISE 10 ▶ **Speaking and Listening: Explaining a Process**

Think about a simple process that you could explain to the class or a smaller group—perhaps how to make tortillas or how to hook up a stereo system with tape deck, CD player, receiver, and so on. Then, make a list of the major steps in the process. Using your list as an outline, explain the process to your audience. If you like, use props or visual aids to make your process clearer.

 COMPUTER NOTE: If you are writing your list on a computer, remember to save your work every ten to fifteen minutes. Use automatic Save if you have it.

Classification

What are the sizes and depths of the world's oceans? What is a laser? What are the differences between hurricanes and tornadoes?

To answer these questions, you need to *classify,* or look at a subject as it relates to other subjects in a group. There are three ways to classify: divide a subject into its

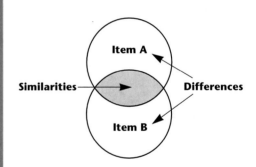

Give students several broad topics and have students suggest ways in which the topics could be approached by using each of the four writing strategies discussed here. For example, if you gave them the general topic *volleyball,* they might suggest the following approaches:

descriptive—the atmosphere in the locker room before a big game
narrative—a play-by-play report of a team winning a game
classification—how volleyball compares with other team sports
evaluation—the pros and cons of playing volleyball in high school

parts (the oceans), define it (a laser), or compare and contrast it with something else (hurricanes and tornadoes).

Dividing.   With some subjects, the best way to explain them as a whole is to look at their parts. For example, to explain what the United Nations is, you may have to divide it into the parts that make up the overall organization known as the United Nations, such as the General Assembly, the Security Council, and the International Court of Justice. This paragraph uses the strategy of dividing in order to explain the makeup of the news department at the *New York Times*.

> In the news department at *The Times* there are some 570 people who assign, gather, and edit the news. Under the executive editor, A. M. Rosenthal, are managing editor Seymour Topping and his deputy and assistants, among them the news editor. There are nine news desks, and of these, the metropolitan, national, and foreign are the best-known. Each is headed by an editor who, with a deputy and assistants, supervises a staff of reporters or correspondents and oversees the flow of news to the respective copy desk and from there to the composing room. The other news desks—business and financial, culture, family/style, science, real estate, and sports—operate in much the same way.
>
> Betty Lou English, *Behind the Headlines*

Defining.   When you *define* a subject, you first identify it as a part of a larger group or class. Then you discuss features that make the subject unique in its class. In the following paragraph, the first sentence defines "stars" and identifies the larger group to which they belong (gas). The remaining sentences give details about stars that distinguish them from other types of gases.

> Stars are hot, glowing globes of gas that emit energy. Nearly all of a star's gas is hydrogen. Because the Sun is a hot ball of hydrogen that emits huge amounts of energy, it is a star, and the star

CLOSURE

You could have volunteers summarize the four strategies for writing and give details about each.

ENRICHMENT

You may want to expand **Exercise 8** into an actual writing assignment. Allow students to choose one of the five subjects. Students must then write clear, detailed descriptive paragraphs for each of the chosen topics. ■

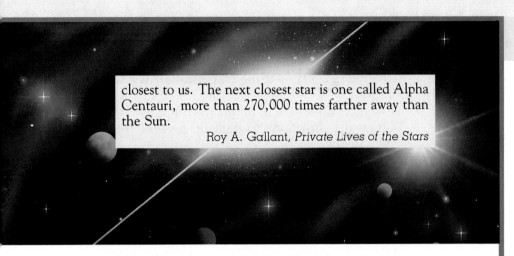

closest to us. The next closest star is one called Alpha Centauri, more than 270,000 times farther away than the Sun.

Roy A. Gallant, *Private Lives of the Stars*

VISUAL CONNECTIONS

About the Artwork. This picture of stars was generated by a computer. Computers can be used to make paintings or drawings. They can also be used to create fine art in the style of particular artists.

CRITICAL THINKING

Analysis. You might want to have students analyze the structure of Joyce Pope's paragraph to see how she contrasts subjects. You could have students use a chart like the following. After students have finished, you can have them compare their answers with the answers provided in the chart.

Feature	Spiders	Insects
wings	none	most have
bodies	2 main parts	3 main parts
legs	8 or more	6

Comparing and Contrasting. Another way to classify subjects is by comparing them (telling how they are alike), contrasting them (telling how they are different), or by both comparing and contrasting. The following paragraph contrasts the characteristics of spiders and insects.

> Spiders are not insects. Although they are often confused with them, they differ from them in many ways. Most adult insects, for example, have wings; spiders never do. All insects have bodies divided into three major parts: head, thorax and abdomen, the latter two divided into smaller segments. The thorax carries four or six legs, never more. A spider's body is in two main parts. Attached to the front one of these are eight legs, never fewer.
>
> Joyce Pope, *Do Animals Dream?*

ANSWERS
Exercise 11

Responses will vary.

1. Responses should be evaluated on whether or not the details support the particular types of individual tastes listed.

2. Responses should be evaluated on the basis of whether the features listed show schools to be different from other institutions in the larger group.

3. Responses should be evaluated on the basis of clarity and on whether or not the writer proves the main idea.

COOPERATIVE LEARNING

Organize students into groups of four or five and have them generate and discuss topics for evaluation. Write some broad topics of interest to students on the chalkboard. Possibilities include teenagers voting in elections or teenagers learning to drive. Have groups decide on a judgment for each of the topics and have them give two or three reasons to support each judgment. Be sure students can explain the criteria for their evaluations.

EXERCISE 11   **Using Classification as a Strategy**

How can you divide it, define it, compare it, or contrast it? Follow the directions to develop each of the main ideas given below.

Main Idea	Classification Strategy
1. There's a car on the market to appeal to every type of individual taste.	Examine the subject of cars by dividing them into types. List details for each type to support the main idea.
2. Take the teachers and books away, and would it still be a school?	Define the subject "school." What larger group does it belong to—political organization, an institution for learning, or some other group? Now, list some features that make it different from other groups.
3. If you're good at one computer game, will you be good at another?	Compare and contrast two computer games by listing their likenesses and differences.

Evaluation

Should our schools use suspension as a punishment for students who create discipline problems? Is Morgan Freeman's latest movie as good as his last one?

To answer such questions, you look at the value of the subject, or make a judgment about it. There are two main reasons for evaluating a subject: to inform other people or to persuade them to think or act differently. Of course, an evaluation often has both purposes at once. For example, movie reviewers tell you their opinions in order to persuade you to see or to avoid movies. When you evaluate, it's important to give some reasons to support your evaluation (that is, tell *why* you have this judgment about the subject). The following paragraph is part of a review of the television series *Frasier.* What is the reviewer's evaluation of the program? Does she make you want to see it? How does the reviewer support her evaluation?

My favorite television series this season has to be *Frasier.* It just keeps getting better and better. In only a few seasons the show has established its place among the pantheon of prime time comedies, as its writers and actors have learned how to play the quirky characters off each other to maximum comic effect. The blustery arrogance of Kelsey Grammar's Frasier is counterbalanced by both the superrefined nervousness of David Hyde Pierce's Niles and the persistent grumpiness of John Mahoney's Dad. Offsetting the quarrelsome interactions of the three male characters is Jane Leeves as the sweet-tempered, no-nonsense Daphne, the British housekeeper. Each week, the talented cast brings this mix of oddly appealing characters to life with surprising and convincing ingenuity.

EXERCISE 12 ▶ Using Evaluation as a Strategy

What's your evaluation? Why do you feel that way? Evaluate each of the following broad subjects by making a positive or negative judgment about it. Then give two or three reasons to support your judgment.

1. the latest movie you've seen
2. the latest book you've read
3. the most current fad around school (in clothes, hairstyles, or language)

MAKING CONNECTIONS

WRITING A PARAGRAPH TO EXPRESS YOURSELF OBJECTIVE

- To write an expressive paragraph

WRITING A PARAGRAPH TO EXPRESS YOURSELF

Teaching Strategies

You may want to tell students that expressive writing is personal—it explores thoughts and feelings.

Explain that expressive writing is different from other writing in that its focus is on the writer and not on the audience (with the exception of personal letters). In general, expressive writing contains the same spontaneity that talking to a friend or singing in the shower has.

GUIDELINES

Students' writing should include at least two or more of the four characteristics of expressive writing:

1. use of first-person point of view
2. feelings
3. natural language
4. strong word connotations and associations

MAKING CONNECTIONS

WRITING PARAGRAPHS FOR DIFFERENT PURPOSES

In this chapter you studied the form and structure of paragraphs. Now you can apply that knowledge by writing paragraphs for different purposes: to express yourself, to inform, to persuade, and to create.

Writing a Paragraph to Express Yourself

Do you ever find yourself thinking about things that you want to understand more? Do you have feelings that you would like to explore? Writing about your thoughts and feelings can help you learn more about yourself, whether or not you share such writing with anyone else.

A diary or a writer's notebook—or any sheet of paper—is a good place to write an expressive paragraph. Use one of the following sentences to start an expressive paragraph.

Starter Sentences for Expressive Writing

It's so great that ____.
What really frustrates me is ____.
Happiness would be understanding ____.
The person I most admire is ____.
To improve the world, each person should ____.

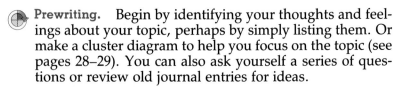 **Prewriting.** Begin by identifying your thoughts and feelings about your topic, perhaps by simply listing them. Or make a cluster diagram to help you focus on the topic (see pages 28–29). You can also ask yourself a series of questions or review old journal entries for ideas.

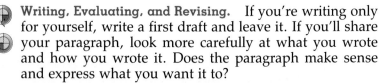 **Writing, Evaluating, and Revising.** If you're writing only for yourself, write a first draft and leave it. If you'll share your paragraph, look more carefully at what you wrote and how you wrote it. Does the paragraph make sense and express what you want it to?

• To write an informative paragraph

 Proofreading and Publishing. Review your paragraph to correct errors in usage and mechanics. You could "publish" your paragraph by reading it aloud to the class. Or you and your classmates might make a booklet of your expressive paragraphs.

Writing a Paragraph to Inform

Information is constantly available—from other people, television, radio, newspapers, books, the World Wide Web, and many other sources. People get information from you, too. When you write to inform, your purpose is to present clear, useful information.

The chart below gives some information about the impact of the Olympic Games on employment in the host city. Use the information in the chart and the following topic sentence to write an informative paragraph. If you want, research more information about the job growth in a city hosting the Olympics. Assume that your audience (classmates) knows nothing about the subject.

Topic Sentence: The Olympic Games create temporary job growth in the host city.

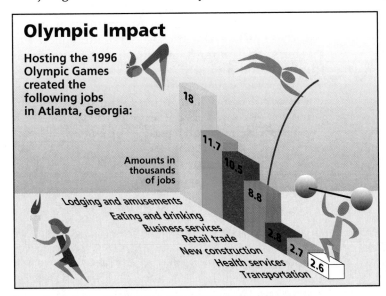

Olympic Impact

Hosting the 1996 Olympic Games created the following jobs in Atlanta, Georgia:

18
11.7
10.5
8.8
2.8
2.7
2.6

Amounts in thousands of jobs

Lodging and amusements
Eating and drinking
Business services
Retail trade
New construction
Health services
Transportation

Sources: The Atlanta Committee for the Olympic Games and the University of Georgia

WRITING A PARAGRAPH TO INFORM

Teaching Strategies

Tell students that they need to write their informative paragraphs as objectively as possible. Remind them that facts are the most important part of informative writing.

Most writing that students do in school is informative, so it is particularly important that students master this purpose. Tell the class to strive for precise, straightforward relaying of information; their language should be clear. Point out to students that in informative writing the writer removes his or her personality from the treatment of the subject.

GUIDELINES

Each paragraph should have an objective point of view and should cover the subject comprehensively. Paragraphs should contain correct grammar and precise language.

Prewriting and Writing. Study the chart carefully to understand the various new job opportunities. Next, write the topic sentence on your paper. Then, support the topic sentence with three or four sentences based on information from the chart or your own research. Be sure to arrange the information in order of importance. You may want to include a clincher sentence, too.

Evaluating and Revising. Does each supporting sentence give information (facts and statistics) about the topic sentence? If not, rewrite or cut any sentences that break the unity of your paragraph. Have you arranged the information in order of importance? If not, reorder the sentences so that you start with either your most important or least important point.

Proofreading and Publishing. Review your paragraph to correct any errors in grammar, usage, and mechanics. Share your paragraph to inform someone about the job opportunities created by the Olympics.

Writing a Paragraph to Persuade

Even though you may not realize it, people are constantly trying to persuade you. Every commercial and advertisement you see or hear tries to persuade you. Your friends, teachers, and parents frequently try to persuade you to think or act differently.

Likewise, you may find yourself in situations where you want to persuade others. Suppose you are taking sides in a controversy over whether whales should be moved from the ocean to the confinement of a local aquarium. Write a paragraph in which you try to persuade people to support or not to support having a whale tank in the local aquarium. If you want, use one of the following topic sentences.

Topic Sentences:
Whales are an ecologically delicate species and should not be moved to a small, confining aquarium.

Whales should be brought to the local aquarium so that everyone can enjoy them.

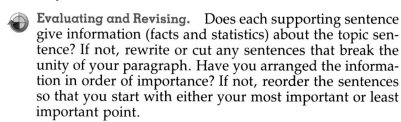

WRITING A PARAGRAPH TO PERSUADE

Teaching Strategies

Tell students that in persuasive writing they will focus on the audience—the opposite of the focus of expressive writing. Have the class discuss the reasons why the purposes have different focuses. [Persuasive writing attempts to change the reader's mind or to get the reader to act in a certain way; expressive writing is primarily intended to put into words the feelings of the writer.]

Persuasive writing appeals to the reader's sense of trust, to feelings, and to reasoning. In this particular assignment, students will want to use logical appeals and probably emotional appeals as well. Point out that persuasive writing is a vital part of political campaigns and of advertising.

GUIDELINES

Each paragraph should include three or four reasons to support the stand the writer has taken, with elaborations for each reason. Language should be appropriate to the audience—dignified and correct. Any or all of the three types of persuasive appeals can be used—personal appeal, logical appeal, or emotional appeal.

Prewriting. Which side of the controversy are you on? To decide, make two lists of reasons: one telling why you feel whales should be brought to the aquarium and another telling why they should not be brought. Suggestions: How do you feel about animals' being taken from their natural habitats? about the amount of money and resources needed to provide for them in a large aquarium? After reviewing your own beliefs, decide which side to take. (You may want to do some research to gather support for your opinion.)

Writing, Evaluating, and Revising. For your paragraph, list three or four persuasive reasons to back up your position. Be sure to state your position clearly in a topic sentence. After you write your draft, look at the reasons you have given. Do you have enough reasons? Are they persuasive? Revise your paragraph to make it more persuasive.

Proofreading and Publishing. Correct any errors in grammar, usage, and mechanics. To see if someone else would be persuaded, read your paragraph aloud to the class or to a small group.

WRITING A PARAGRAPH THAT IS CREATIVE

Teaching Strategies

Many students at this grade level read fantasy, science fiction, and other types of highly imaginative writing. You may want to have students choose especially effective paragraphs that illustrate setting and character description from their favorite books and have students read the passages aloud to the class. Discuss the ways in which the writing is effective. If necessary, review the concept of conflict.

VISUAL CONNECTIONS
High Tide: The Bathers

About the Artist. American artist Winslow Homer (1836–1910) is well known for his paintings of the sea—sailboats, sea captains, fishermen, and bathers—as well as for scenes of country and farm life. Both of his parents painted with watercolors, and he began to draw and paint as a child. During the Civil War he drew illustrations of battle scenes for *Harper's Weekly*.

High Tide: The Bathers is an oil which appeared in *Every Saturday* on August 6, 1870. A reviewer for *The Times* criticized it by saying that it was unpleasant to look at the "brick-dust" color of the young girls' legs.

Writing a Paragraph That Is Creative

Stories and poems are writers' attempts to use situations, characters, and/or language in a particular way. Look at the painting *High Tide: The Bathers*, by Winslow Homer, and write a paragraph that begins a story suggested by Homer's painting. In your paragraph, give your readers some idea about who the characters are, and describe the setting. Also, establish a conflict—a struggle of some kind—for the characters. These questions may help you imagine a scene that involves a conflict.

- Who are the bathers? What is their relationship to each other?
- Where are the bathers? What are they doing there? What do they plan to do next?
- What feelings do you get from the characters? Why do you see only one face clearly? What is the expression of the girl sitting on the beach?
- What part does the dog play in the bathers' story? Is the dog with them or with someone else?

Winslow Homer, *Eaglehead, Manchester, Massachusetts. (High Tide: The Bathers.)* Oil on canvas, 26″ × 38″. The Metropolitan Museum of Art, Gift of Mrs. William F. Milton, 1923. (23.77.2) Photograph © The Metropolitan Museum of Art 1980.

Prewriting. Study the painting to see what details you think would enrich your story. Jot down the details, along with sensory descriptions such as the color of the sky and water, the sounds, and the smells.

Writing, Evaluating, and Revising. Write a paragraph that describes the scene at the beginning of your story, introduces the characters and situation, and prepares your readers for the conflict to come. Then, exchange your paragraph with a classmate. Is the beginning of your story clear to your reader? Does your reader understand the situation and conflict? If not, add or change details.

 Proofreading and Publishing. Correct any errors in grammar, usage, and mechanics. Share your paragraph by reading it aloud to the class or to a small group. You may even want to finish writing the whole story.

Reflecting on Your Writing

If you decide to include any of your paragraphs in your **portfolio,** attach to your paper a brief reflection answering the following questions.

- How did you decide whether to state your main idea in a topic sentence?
- Was it harder to collect supporting details or to cut unrelated ideas? Why?
- Which paragraph did you most enjoy writing—expressive, informative, persuasive, or creative? Why?

> "A sentence should contain no unnecessary words, a paragraph no unnecessary sentences, for the same reason that a drawing should have no unnecessary lines and a machine no unnecessary parts."
>
> William Strunk, Jr.

GUIDELINES

Each paragraph should contain a setting, characters, and the beginning of a conflict. The emphasis of creative writing should be entertainment, so word choice is of major importance. This aspect is referred to as style, the special way a writer chooses words and phrases. Is the writing style of the paragraph unique?

TEACHING NOTE

Remind students that they can learn a lot about writing and about themselves as writers through their reflections. The first two questions in **Reflecting on Your Writing** offer students a chance to determine how they work best, which may help them with later writing assignments. Encourage students to pay special attention to these questions and to answer them as completely as possible. You can have volunteers share their reflections with the rest of the class.

UNDERSTANDING COMPOSITION STRUCTURE

OBJECTIVES

- To analyze and write thesis statements and lists of details
- To prepare a formal outline for a composition
- To analyze introductions written by professional writers
- To analyze the unity and coherence of a paragraph by identifying the main idea, supporting details, direct references, and transitional words and phrases
- To write effective conclusions

cross CURRICULUM

Writing a Summary Paper for Social Studies

One way to improve students' reading and writing skills is to have them write a summary paper of an article about a historical issue or event. A summary paper requires students to distill the main idea of the entire text, as well as the individual points of each paragraph, and to present these ideas in a composition that includes an introduction, a body, and a conclusion. Provide students with an article, such as "No News from Auschwitz" or "Lunar Landing" and have them work in pairs as they follow the steps below.

- **Steps to Summarizing**
  1. Read the article through once and write one sentence that states the point of the article as a whole.
  2. Reread the article one paragraph at a time and write a statement for each paragraph that summarizes the point of the paragraph.
  3. Reread all the statements. If the statements for each paragraph do not support the overall statement about the article, then consider revising it.

4. For the first draft of the summary paper, use the overall statement as the topic sentence for the introduction. Use the paragraph statements as the basis for the body paragraphs of the paper. The conclusion should restate and possibly extend the thesis.

- **Revising and Evaluating** Students may find that it is difficult to expand the summary sentences into a full-bodied composition. They will need to use transitions, varied sentence structure, and sentence combining strategies to craft their compositions. More importantly, students need to consider how the writer connected his or her main points in the article and be able to articulate that in their summaries. Encourage students to read and evaluate each other's papers.

- **Publishing** Post summaries around the classroom along with the articles they summarize. Ask volunteers to read their summaries aloud and have the class comment on them and on the summarizing process.

INTEGRATING THE LANGUAGE ARTS

SELECTION	READING AND LITERATURE	WRITING AND CRITICAL THINKING	LANGUAGE AND SYNTAX	SPEAKING, LISTENING, AND OTHER EXPRESSION SKILLS
FROM • "Quasi-Humans" R. A. Deckert p. 110 • "A Thirsty California Is Trying Desalination" L. M. Fisher p. 113 • "What's Your Type? Introverts and Extroverts" S. R. Arbetter p. 123 • "For Young and Old, a Pocket Paradise" K. Teltsch pp. 123, 132 • "Juan's Place" C. Mann and G. Blair p. 124 • "Financial Folklore" J. S. Gordon p. 125 • "Seeds in the bank could stave off disaster on the farm" E. R. Shell p. 125 • "Pioneers Underfoot" S. Baker p. 126 • "3 Scientists Say Travel in Time Isn't So Far Out" M. W. Browne p. 127 • "At Rye High, Students. . ." L. W. Foderaro p. 127 • "A Yen for Baseball Cards" R. Wolff p. 129 • "Stretchbreak" S. Stocker pp. 130–131 • "School for Homeless Children" T. Egan p. 131 • "Neil Armstrong's Famous First Words" G. Plimpton pp. 131–132	• Responding personally to literature pp. 111, 127 • Applying interpretive and creative thinking pp. 111, 127, 133 • Finding the main idea pp. 111, 115, 129 • Identifying supporting evidence pp. 111, 129 • Finding details pp. 115, 127, 129 • Analyzing thesis statements pp. 115, 127, 129 • Evaluating and making judgments pp. 119, 127, 129, 133 • Analyzing tone p. 127 • Analyzing techniques for writing effective introductions p. 127 • Analyzing a paragraph p. 129 • Evaluating a conclusion p. 133	• Applying interpretive and creative thinking pp. 111, 127, 133, 134, 137 • Evaluating a writer's theory p. 111 • Analyzing facts to arrive at a main idea pp. 111, 115, 127, 129 • Writing a thesis statement pp. 115–116, 137 • Constructing an early plan or an outline pp. 119, 137 • Improving a conclusion of a composition p. 133 • Writing a conclusion pp. 133, 134, 137 • Writing an informative essay pp. 135–137 • Gathering ideas for writing p. 137 • Writing an introduction to capture readers' attention p. 137 • Writing paragraphs that clearly relate to the thesis p. 137 • Writing body paragraphs that have unity and coherence p. 137 • Proofreading and publishing an essay p. 137	• Using specific, clear, lively language in thesis statements p. 115 • Identifying words that reveal tone p. 127 • Identifying direct references p. 129 • Identifying transitional words and phrases p. 129 • Proofreading for errors in grammar, usage, and mechanics p. 137	• Working with classmates to develop a thesis statement pp. 115–116 • Working with a classmate to prepare an early plan or formal outline p. 119 • Analyzing a paragraph with classmates p. 129 • Working with a classmate to improve conclusion p. 133

CHAPTER 3: UNDERSTANDING COMPOSITION STRUCTURE

Use this guide for creating an instructional plan that addresses the individual needs of your students. Assignments accompanied by the following symbol (∗) may be completed out of class. Times given for pacing lessons are estimated.

CHAPTER PLANNING GUIDE—PUPIL'S EDITION

LESSONS	LITERARY MODEL from "Quasi-Humans" by R. A. Deckert p. 110	THE THESIS STATEMENT pp. 113–116	EARLY PLANS AND FORMAL OUTLINES pp. 117–121
DEVELOPMENTAL PROGRAM	**25–30 minutes** • Have students read model aloud to partners and discuss questions on p. 111.	**30–35 minutes** • Main Assignment: Looking Ahead p. 111 • The Thesis Statement pp. 113–116 • Exercise 1 p. 115 in pairs	**35–40 minutes** • Early Plans and Formal Outlines pp. 117–121 • Exercise 3 p. 119 • Read A Writer's Model aloud pp. 120–121
CORE PROGRAM	**25–30 minutes** • Assign students to read the model and answer questions on p. 111.	**35–40 minutes** • Main Assignment: Looking Ahead p. 111 • The Thesis Statement pp. 113–116 • Writing Note p. 114 • Exercises 1, 2 pp. 115–116	**35–40 minutes** • Early Plans and Formal Outlines pp. 117–121 • Exercise 3 p. 119 • A Writer's Model pp. 120–121
ACCELERATED PROGRAM	**20–25 minutes** • Assign students to read the model independently to take notes in Reader's Logs.	**20–25 minutes** • Main Assignment: Looking Ahead p. 111 • Hints for Writing and Using a Thesis Statement pp. 113–114 • Writing Note p. 114 • Exercise 2 pp. 115–116∗	**25–30 minutes** • The Formal Outline p. 118 • Exercise 3 p. 119∗ • A Writer's Model pp. 120–121

CHAPTER PLANNING GUIDE—PROGRAM RESOURCES

	LITERARY MODEL	THE THESIS STATEMENT	EARLY PLANS AND FORMAL OUTLINES
PRINT	• Reading Master 3, *Practice for Assessment in Reading, Vocabulary, and Spelling* p. 3	• Focusing on the Thesis Statement, *Practicing the Writing Process* p. 35	• Early Plans, Formal Outlines, *Practicing the Writing Process* pp. 36–37 • Composition Workshops, *English Workshop* pp. 27–34
MEDIA			

THE INTRODUCTION pp. 122–127	THE BODY pp. 128–129	THE CONCLUSION pp. 130–134
40–45 minutes • The Introduction pp. 122–126 • Writing Note p. 126 • Exercise 4 p. 127 in pairs	**30–35 minutes** • The Body pp. 128–129 • Exercise 5 p. 129	**40–45 minutes** • The Conclusion pp. 130–134 • Exercise 6 p. 133 • Framework for a Composition Chart p. 134
30–35 minutes • The Introduction pp. 122–126 • Writing Note p. 126 • Exercise 4 p. 127	**35–40 minutes** • Unity p. 128 • Coherence pp. 128–129 • Exercise 5 p. 129	**35–40 minutes** • The Conclusion pp. 130–134 • Writing Notes pp. 133, 134 • Exercises 6, 7 pp. 133–134 • Framework for a Composition Chart p. 134
20 minutes • Techniques for Writing Introductions pp. 123–126 • Exercise 4 p. 127*	**20–25 minutes** • Coherence pp. 128–129 • Exercise 5 p. 129	**25 minutes** • Techniques for Writing Conclusions pp. 130–132 • Writing Notes pp. 133, 134 • Exercise 7 p. 134* • Framework for a Composition Chart p. 134

 Overhead transparencies

THE INTRODUCTION	THE BODY	THE CONCLUSION
• The Introduction, *Practicing the Writing Process* p. 38	• The Body, *Practicing the Writing Process* p. 39	• The Conclusion, *Practicing the Writing Process* p. 40
	• Graphic Organizer 4, *Transparency Binder*	• Revision Transparency 4, *Transparency Binder*

ELEMENTS OF WRITING: CURRICULUM CONNECTIONS

Making Connections
• Writing an Informative Composition pp. 135–137

ASSESSMENT OPTIONS

Reflection
Self-assessment Record, *Portfolio Assessment* p. 19

Summative Assessment
Review: Revising and Proofreading, *Practicing the Writing Process* p. 41

OBJECTIVES

- To respond to a composition
- To identify the thesis statement of a literary model and to analyze discussion that supports it

TEACHING THE LESSON

Ask students if they've heard the old saying, "Truth is stranger than fiction." Then introduce the article on cyborgs by stating that technology frequently and rapidly out-distances fiction. You may want to read the article aloud in class, or you could have students read the article independently. Either way, you will first want to define for students

PROGRAM MANAGER

CHAPTER 3

- **Practice** To help less-advanced students who need additional practice with concepts and activities related to this chapter, see **Chapter 3** in *English Workshop, Fourth Course,* pp. 27–34.

- **Reading Support** For help with the reading selection, p. 110, see **Reading Master 3** in *Practice for Assessment in Reading, Vocabulary, and Spelling,* p. 3.

VISUAL CONNECTIONS
Still Music

About the Artist. Ben Shahn was born in Lithuania in 1898, and his family moved to Brooklyn, New York, when he was eight. At the age of fifteen, Shahn became an apprentice at a lithography shop, where he developed techniques that he used in his later work. Shahn is known mainly for the posters and prints in which he expressed his views on social injustice. Ben Shahn died in 1969.

3 UNDERSTANDING COMPOSITION STRUCTURE

the terms *quasi* [in some degree] and *cyborg* [humans with mechanical enhancements]. The article probably will generate a lot of discussion, so allow adequate class time. The **Reader's Response** questions should help generate discussion.

Following a discussion of the article's subject, direct students' attention to the form of the article. Ask students to identify the article's introduction [first paragraph], body [rest of article until last paragraph], and conclusion [last paragraph]. When they have recognized these main parts of the composition, they should be ready for the **Writer's Craft** questions.

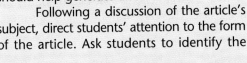

Looking at the Whole

Have you ever overheard just the punch line of a joke? Although everyone else is laughing, it doesn't seem funny to you—you didn't hear the whole joke. That's the way it is with a composition. All of the parts work together to make a **whole** composition.

Writing and You. A movie review in *Rolling Stone* . . . an article in *Life* magazine about space . . . a newspaper story about rising taxes. These are all compositions. If you look at them closely, you'll see that they have a certain form: an introduction, a body, and a conclusion. Besides magazines and newspapers, where else might you find compositions?

As You Read. As you read the following article from *Omni* magazine, notice how the writer uses composition form to tell about cyborgs.

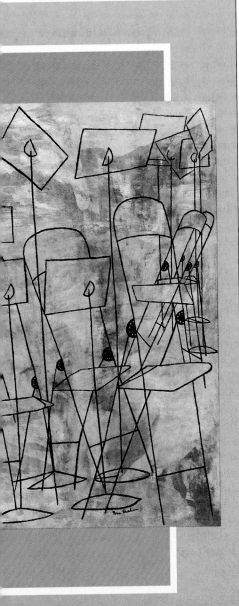

Ben Shahn, *Still Music* (1948). Casein on fabric, 48" × 83½".
Collection of The Phillips Collection, Washington, D.C. © 1993
Estate of Ben Shahn/VAGA, N.Y.

QUOTATION FOR THE DAY
"Prose is architecture, not interior decoration. . . ." (Ernest Hemingway, 1899–1961, American novelist)

Initiate a discussion by asking students what Hemingway's statement from *Death in the Afternoon* (1932) means. Lead them to understand that in building their compositions they will include introductions, body paragraphs, and conclusions that are clear and structured, rather than confusing and disorganized.

MEETING *individual* **NEEDS**

LEP/ESL

General Strategies. You may want to familiarize students with the parts of a composition [thesis statement, introduction, body, conclusion] before you go on to discuss the parts individually. This discussion should help prevent students from being confused by terminology when they should be concentrating on concepts.

GUIDED PRACTICE

To find out how well students understand the article, ask the questions from **Reader's Response**. To extend the discussion, you could ask, "What other wonders do you think are 'within the range of today's computer chips'? of tomorrow's computer chips?"

INDEPENDENT PRACTICE

After you have discussed how the cyborg article reflects the general characteristics of composition form, have students answer the **Writer's Craft** questions on their own. Remind them to cite specific information from the article when answering the last question.

USING THE SELECTION
Quasi-Humans

1

bionic: having biological performance increased by electronic devices

2

cyborgs: humans with mechanical enhancements

3

Contact lenses have been around since the late 1800s. At first they were made of glass, and later glass and plastic. A big improvement came in 1948, when they were first made with lightweight molded plastic.

4

What does the author mean by "conscious technology"? [Responses will vary, but should suggest technology that can think and perceive.]

5

Isaac Asimov pursued dual careers that give him impressive credentials for such a statement—biochemistry and science fiction writing. He started teaching biochemistry at Boston University in 1949. He is noted for his writings about both science and science fiction.

110

QUASI-HUMANS

by R. A. Deckert

1
2
The Six Million Dollar Man and the Bionic Woman were TV's first cyborgs—part human, part technowizardry. We may soon live in a world populated by these beings, futurist Jerome Glenn believes, because we are evolving into them.

Cyborgs, says Glenn, are the inevitable result of two trends about to merge into one. The first trend—the increasing use of technology to correct physical disabilities—can be seen in the **3** progression from eyeglasses to contact lenses to surgically implanted lenses. The second trend—the tendency for technology to become more humanlike—is continuing to evolve rapidly. The ability to associate ideas as well as the ability to speak and to recognize voices are all within the range of today's computer chips.

Glenn says that the two trends will usher in an age of **4** "conscious technology" in which "robots will get biochips to become more human and humans will become cyborgs" within the first half of the twenty-first century.

By then technology won't be limited to simply correcting disabilities but will increasingly be used to enhance the human body's performance. "Contact lenses with zoom vision, miniature hearing aids to hear selected sounds at greater distances, or miniature transceivers to reach out and touch someone are just some of the ways future cyborgs will go beyond our inherited biology," Glenn says.

While he is confident that he has seen the future that lies ahead for humanity, Glenn acknowledges there is a certain amount of resistance to be overcome. "As **5** [Isaac] Asimov says, 'All new technology is rejected and then accepted.' I don't see any difference with this."

ASSESSMENT

Evaluate students' answers to the **Writer's Craft** questions to assess their understanding.

CLOSURE

Ask the class to define *composition* and identify the three parts [introduction, body, and conclusion]. ■

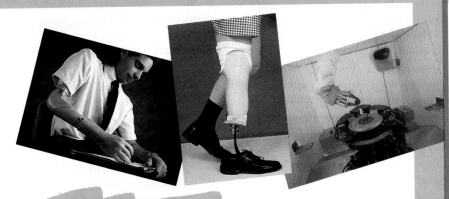

READER'S RESPONSE

1. What do you think of Jerome Glenn's theory? Do any of your own experiences and observations support his theory? Which ones?
2. Do you think it's true that people at first always reject new technology? If so, why?

WRITER'S CRAFT

3. What is the thesis statement—the sentence that tells the main idea—in this article?
4. In the body of the article, the author discusses two trends. What are they? How does this discussion reflect and support the main idea?

ANSWERS

Reader's Response

1. Answers will vary. Students should support their responses with specific personal experiences and observations.
2. Answers will vary. If students answer "yes," their explanations probably will include that people are often afraid of new things or that it is human nature to resist change.

Writer's Craft

3. The thesis statement is, "We may soon live in a world populated by these beings [cyborgs], futurist Jerome Glenn believes, because we are evolving into them."
4. The two trends are the "increasing use of technology to correct physical disabilities" and "the tendency for technology to become more humanlike." The discussion of these trends reflects and supports the main idea by giving concrete examples of how humans are evolving into cyborgs.

LOOKING AHEAD

In this chapter, you'll learn about the parts of a composition. You'll learn that

- most compositions have an introduction that attracts the reader's attention, sets the tone, and gives the thesis statement
- each body paragraph is unified and clearly connected to the surrounding paragraphs
- most compositions have a conclusion that reinforces the main idea and brings the composition to a definite close

Give students a short news story or magazine article (perhaps a three- or four-paragraph feature) that you have chosen because of its model composition form. Read the article with the students, and then ask them the following questions:

1. What is the main idea of the article?
2. What constitutes the introduction of the article, and where is the main idea stated?
3. What constitutes the body of the article?
4. What constitutes the conclusion of the article?

MEETING *individual* **NEEDS**

AT-RISK STUDENTS

Ask students to look through their favorite magazines and books to find examples of good compositions. This procedure will enable students to apply the principles of composition to topics of personal interest.

SELECTION AMENDMENT
Description of change: excerpted
Rationale: to focus on the concepts of composition structure presented in this chapter

What Makes a Composition

Not only do you read compositions for information and enjoyment—you also write them yourself for the same purposes. For instance, in school you write compositions, also called *essays*, both for assigned papers and for tests. And you'll also write compositions when you apply for college admission and scholarships and for jobs. Many colleges and businesses often ask applicants to write compositions about themselves, their interests, and their goals.

In other chapters, you'll learn how to use the composition form when writing persuasive essays and research papers, when writing about literature, or when explaining a process. In this chapter you'll concentrate on the basic principles of composition form.

"Provoke the reader.

Astonish the reader.

Writing that has no surprises is as bland as oatmeal."

Anne Bernays

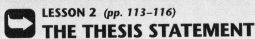

LESSON 2 *(pp. 113–116)*
THE THESIS STATEMENT

OBJECTIVES
- To analyze the purpose and characteristics of a good thesis statement
- To write thesis statements that fit particular limited topics and lists of details

TEACHING THE LESSON

Begin the lesson by drawing a clear comparison between the topic sentence of a paragraph and the thesis statement of a composition. Be sure that students understand that a thesis statement may be one or two sentences. You could use the overhead projector to display some good examples of ☞

The Thesis Statement

A *thesis statement* gives the composition's main, or unifying, idea about a topic. It's a sentence or two in the introduction that "tells your readers what you're going to tell them." It announces your limited topic and your main idea about it, just as a topic sentence does in a paragraph.

Some thesis statements simply identify the limited topic, for example: "Californians are facing a water shortage resulting from several years of drought."

But most thesis statements, including the ones you'll be asked to write, do more. They identify a main idea the writer is actually trying to prove to the reader. Here's an example of this kind of thesis statement.

> Facing a possible fifth year of sustained drought, communities along the California coast are looking to desalinated ocean or bay water as a way to quench their thirst and water their lawns.
>
> Lawrence M. Fisher, "A Thirsty California Is Trying Desalination"

Hints for Writing and Using a Thesis Statement

1. **Develop your thesis statement from information you've gathered.** Review your prewriting material—the ton of facts and details you've gathered. Ask yourself: *What main, or unifying, idea do the facts and details suggest?*
2. **Include both a limited topic and your main idea about it.** Most thesis statements answer these two questions: *What's my topic? What am I saying about my topic?* To make sure you've included both parts, underline the limited topic and circle the main idea.

   For example, notice this thesis statement: "If you're interested in bicycle touring, you need to make some specific preparations involving your bike, yourself, your clothing, and your route." It's clear that this writer is going to discuss bicycle touring (topic) and specific preparations for your bike, yourself, your clothing, and your route (main idea).

PROGRAM MANAGER

THE THESIS STATEMENT
- **Analyzing** To help students analyze and organize ideas, see **Focusing on the Thesis Statement** in *Practicing the Writing Process*, p. 35.

QUOTATION FOR THE DAY

"Only the thinking man lives his life, the thoughtless man's life passes him by." (Marie Ebner von Eschenbach, 1830–1916, German/English writer and literary figure)

Students might create writing journal entries that respond to the quotation by explaining how a thinking person might differ from a thoughtless person. Then, ask students how a paragraph without a thesis statement is like a thoughtless person.

SELECTION AMENDMENT
Description of change: excerpted
Rationale: to focus on the concept of the thesis statement presented in this chapter

topic sentences in paragraphs and thesis statements in compositions.

It also may be helpful to discuss the word *thesis* to help students understand what a thesis statement is supposed to do. Tell them that a thesis is a position or proposition that the writer is putting forth for discussion. Tell them that the statement of that position (the thesis statement) should be clear and concise, but should also adequately cover the topic.

After students have read **Hints for Writing and Using a Thesis Statement**, pp. 113–114, you may want to discuss the hints. Consider each hint individually to be sure students understand them.

Use **Exercise 1** for guided practice by reading each thesis statement aloud and

LEARNING STYLES

Visual Learners. As you go over the **Hints for Writing and Using a Thesis Statement** section with students, write the key words for each of the five hints on the chalkboard. Provide some examples of gathered information, limited topics, and clear and specific thesis statements.

3. **Be clear and specific.** Keep your language and ideas sharp and definite. Compare this vague and fuzzy thesis statement with the actual one you've just read: "So if you're interested in bicycle touring, you need to do some things before you leave."

4. **Keep your thesis statement in front of you as you plan and write.** It will help keep you on track. Every idea and detail should directly support your thesis statement, so be tough and get rid of any that don't.

WRITING NOTE Your preliminary thesis statement, the one you develop before you actually write your composition, is probably direct and straightforward. You may even think it's a little dull. Later on, you can revise it to give it more punch and zing, as professional writers do. Here's an example of how one writer revised a thesis statement.

PRELIMINARY   The opening day of the baseball season marks the beginning of a long, dramatic conflict for the pennant for both individual players and teams.

REVISED   "Play ball!" For baseball fans everywhere, the umpire's opening-day cry begins another season of high drama for individual players and teams.

asking students to identify the topic and main idea of each statement. You can also have students rewrite the statements to illustrate that there is more than one way a thesis statement can be written.

Let students work independently with partners or in small groups for **Exercise 2.** Give students adequate class time to think about the limited topics and the details.

Then, ask them to come up with their own thesis statements. You could have students read their thesis statements aloud and let them decide which ones are the best and why.

EXERCISE 1 ▶ Analyzing Thesis Statements

Do these thesis statements meet the two-part test? Does each one have a topic and a main idea? Identify the limited topic and the writer's main idea in each one.

EXAMPLE **1.** Hundreds of highly trained and motivated disabled athletes compete each year in the Paralympics, the World Championships, and Games for the Disabled.

1. *Limited topic: athletes who have disabilities*
Main idea: compete in the Paralympics, the World Championships, and Games for the Disabled

1. "No more helium-filled balloons!" Environmentalists and animal rights groups are boycotting balloons because they are concerned about wild animals that die from eating balloons.
2. If you call 911 in Darien, Connecticut, your ambulance crew will include at least one teenager, trained as a skilled volunteer emergency medical technician.
3. Mount McKinley is Denali, and Greenland has become Kalaallitt Nunaat. Dozens of geographical features and countries have had their names changed during the past decade.
4. The holiday of Kwanzaa, beginning on December 26 and lasting for seven days, is a celebration of African American history, culture, and values.

EXERCISE 2 ▶ Writing a Thesis Statement

Work with a partner or small group to develop a thesis statement for each of the sets of prewriting details on the next page. Make your thesis statement interesting, specific, clear, and lively. Also check to see that your thesis statement meets the two-part test of stating both the topic and a main idea. Your group may want to compare these thesis statements with the ones other groups write.

 COMPUTER NOTE: If you have computers at your school that are arranged in a network, you may be able to use them to do collaborative prewriting or drafting.

ANSWERS
Exercise 1

1. Limited topic: environmentalists and animal rights groups
   Main idea: are boycotting helium-filled balloons

2. Limited topic: ambulance crews in Darien, Connecticut
   Main idea: include one highly trained teenager

3. Limited topic: geographical features and countries
   Main idea: have had their names changed

4. Limited topic: the holiday of Kwanzaa
   Main idea: is a seven-day celebration of African American history, culture, and values

ANSWERS
Exercise 2

Statements will vary but should be similar to the following examples:

1. Regulating public school clothing by banning certain items and possibly requiring uniforms might create an environment more supportive of learning.

2. The world's declining whale population is a result of whales being severely overhunted by nations that kill whales for money or scientific research.

Use the answers to **Exercise 2** as your assessment of students' understanding. You also could ask students these questions:

1. What two questions do most thesis statements answer? [What's the topic? What is being said about the topic?]

2. A thesis statement should always be what and what? [clear and specific]

TIMESAVER

Depending upon how much practice you think students need, you could have each group work on only one of the two sets of prewriting details in **Exercise 2**.

CRITICAL THINKING

Synthesis. Writing a thesis statement requires students to synthesize their understanding of the topics in one or two concisely worded sentences. As you present this section, explain that a thesis statement serves both writer and audience by focusing attention on the composition's key aspects. Stress that a thesis statement can be explicitly or implicitly included in a composition's introductory paragraph.

1. Limited topic: regulating public school clothing
   Ideas and details
   - goal—create an environment supportive of learning
       uniforms as option in public schools
       students and parents in favor
       ties for boys on Fridays
       sense of unity from wearing uniforms
   - banned items
       T-shirts
       cut-off or torn jeans
       shorts
       expensive jewelry

2. Limited topic: world's declining whale population
   Ideas and details
   - whales severely overhunted
   - from the 1930s to the present, the number of blue, right, humpback, bowhead (kinds of whales) has severely declined
   - some whales, such as the northern right whale, are close to becoming extinct
   - International Whaling Commission supposed to manage whaling, but whaling nations resist controls
   - members of Greenpeace organization fight whaling—say that continued whaling threatens existence of whale
   - some countries, such as Norway, have been allowed to sell whale meat to Japan
   - nations allowed to kill whales for scientific research

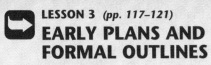
TEACHING THE LESSON

Tell students that they should be aware of the procedures and forms for preparing both early plans—you may prefer to call them rough or informal outlines—and formal outlines. In presenting this section, follow the development of the composition on bicycle touring from grouping to formal outline to composition.

Early Plans and Formal Outlines

Some people are naturally neat and tidy—but most aren't. Here's your chance to clean house. Throw out every bit of information that doesn't directly support your thesis statement, and pull together every bit that does. *Early plans* and *formal outlines* help you do this.

The Early Plan

An *early plan* is also called a rough, or informal, outline. It looks like a set of orderly notes, with each group of details arranged under a heading. The first step in making an early plan is to group your ideas and information; the next step is to order, or arrange, them.

Grouping.   Use these three questions to sort and group information: *Which details belong together? What do they have in common? Which details don't fit in any group?* (Discard these details.) Also think of a heading—a word or phrase—that identifies what the details have in common. For example, here's how one writer grouped and labeled information for a composition on bicycle touring.

---

bicycle helmet, water bottle, tire repair kit—SAFETY ITEMS

mountain bike, sport/touring bike, racing bike—TYPES OF BICYCLES

Ordering.   You have two kinds of ordering to think about: (1) order of details within each group; (2) order of groups within the composition. In both cases, arrange your information in a way that will make sense to your readers.

Sometimes your topic suggests an order. For example, if you're explaining a step-by-step process, such as how to change an automobile's flat tire, you'd use *chronological (time) order*. You'd use *spatial order* to describe the layout of your school. You may use *classification* to describe three types of school athletes, or *order of importance* (from most important reason to least important, or vice versa) to persuade eighteen-year-olds to register to vote.

PROGRAM MANAGER

EARLY PLANS AND FORMAL OUTLINES

- **Analyzing** To help students analyze and organize ideas, see **Early Plans** and **Formal Outlines** in *Practicing the Writing Process*, pp. 36–37.

QUOTATION FOR THE DAY

"If you are a writer you locate yourself behind a wall of silence and no matter what you are doing, driving a car or walking or doing housework . . . you can still be writing, because you have that space." (Joyce Carol Oates, 1938–   , American author)

Ask students to freewrite for a few minutes about one of their favorite sports or competitive activities. Have a volunteer read his or her writing aloud. Ask the class to imagine what might happen if the student never thought about the activity until the day of the competition. Explain that successful writing also demands thinking ahead, planning strategies, and practicing.

Encourage students to make rough outlines before they start writing because it's necessary to group information and to decide in what order to put it. Be sure that they understand the chapter discussions of grouping and ordering, and especially the discussion of different types of order.

Tell students that there are occasions (and assignments) when formal outlines are required, but that not all writers will make formal outlines before they start writing. Explain that some writers feel their information is sufficiently organized with a rough outline, and they work directly from that, while other writers feel they need formal outlines to help them organize and visualize their information. **Exercise 3** presents the kind of unorganized notes from which many

MEETING *individual* NEEDS

LEP/ESL

General Strategies. Some students might have problems with formal outlines and tightly structured compositions because developing discourse through digression is considered proper in some cultures. Such a technique involves circling the main idea rather than being direct. The formality of compositional structure as taught in English classes is thought of as being almost disrespectful to the reader.

To help students with English composition structure, remind them that audience is an important aspect of writing and that an English-speaking audience will not be insulted by a direct treatment of the topic and, in fact, will likely become confused by digressions in a discourse.

You may want to let students forgo formal outlines and use some other prewriting method of organization. Then, when students have written their first drafts, you can go over the drafts with the students and help them recognize and edit any digressions that pull focus away from the topic.

But sometimes none of these orders apply. Then you just have to figure out an arrangement that will let your reader follow your ideas easily. "First things first" is a good rule for organizing information. For instance, if you're writing about unrest in the former Soviet republics, you'll first need to give a paragraph of background information about what led up to the problems.

☞ REFERENCE NOTE: For more on arranging ideas, see pages 82–85.

The Formal Outline

A *formal outline* has a format that shows the order and relationship of ideas, using letters and numbers to label headings. A *sentence outline* uses complete sentences for all main headings and subheadings, while a *topic outline* uses single words or phrases.

☞ REFERENCE NOTE: For more information on formal outlines, see pages 424–425.

Here's the first part of a topic outline for the composition on pages 120–121. Notice that the outline lists the ideas in the paper's second and third paragraphs.

Title: Bicycle Touring
Thesis statement: If you're interested in bicycle touring, you need to make some specific preparations involving your bike, yourself, your clothing, and your route.

I. Your bike
  A. Type of bike
  B. Condition of bike
  C. Equipment
    1. Map
    2. Light
    3. Kits
      a. Bicycle repair kit
      b. First-aid kit
    4. Saddlebags
    5. Water container
II. Your physical condition
  A. Exercise program
    1. Muscles
    2. Endurance
  B. Goal: 10–15 miles

students might try to start writing. Organizing this information should help students see how beneficial outlines can be.

Since most students will have some experience in writing compositions for previous classes, you could ask students to discuss what methods have worked best for them and why the methods were useful.

GUIDED PRACTICE

You may want to divide **Exercise 3** into two parts. You could ask students to work with a partner in class on early plans for guided practice, and then to work independently on formal outlines. For the early plans, help students identify and name the groups they should have. Remind them to consider what

EXERCISE 3 ▶ Making an Early Plan or an Outline

Here are some notes for a composition about how to avoid getting hit by lightning. Work with a partner to organize this jumble of notes into an early plan or a formal outline for a composition. [Hint: The advice on what to do is different if you're indoors or outdoors.]

Surviving Lightning Storms

swimmers--get out of water immediately
in a small boat--get to shore
if you're inside, don't use telephone
before storm hits, unplug electric appliances
if outdoors, find shelter in a building, cave, canyon, thick growth of low trees
stay away from isolated trees, metal fences
if no shelter outdoors, keep low--away from high places, tall trees
if you're in car, stay there--a safe shelter
indoors, stay away from metal pipes, appliances, open doors, and windows
don't shower or take bath during electrical storm
number of deaths each year from lightning
people hit by lightning more frequently in summer and fall

ANSWERS
Exercise 3

Answers will vary. Here is one possibility.

Surviving Lightning Storms

I. General Information
   A. Number of deaths each year
   B. Frequency of strikes with respect to season

II. Indoors
   A. Things to do
      1. Unplug appliances
      2. Stay away from
         a. Metal pipes
         b. Appliances
         c. Open doors and windows
   B. Things not to do
      1. Use telephone
      2. Shower or bathe

III. Outdoors
   A. Safe places
      1. Building
      2. Cave
      3. Cars
      4. Canyon
      5. Thick growth of trees
      6. Low places
   B. Unsafe places
      1. In water
      2. In a boat
      3. Near isolated trees
      4. Near metal fences
      5. High places

INDEPENDENT PRACTICE

Direct the students to use their early plans to prepare formal outlines for the topic in **Exercise 3.** Give students directions on whether to use a sentence outline or a topic outline.

COOPERATIVE LEARNING

Divide the class into four groups for practice in ordering information. Assign each group one of the four kinds of order (chronological, spatial, classification, order of importance). Then, instruct each group to develop three different sets of details that would logically be arranged by the group's assigned type of order. Tell them that each set of details should consist of at least three items. To begin, students should look at the examples given in the chapter. Have the groups turn in their completed sets, and choose some to read to the class. Ask class members other than the ones in the group that originated the set to guess what kind of order is intended.

A WRITER'S MODEL

Following is the final draft of a composition based on the outline on page 118. As you read, try to think about a good title for the composition. (See the Writing Note on page 133.)

INTRODUCTION

Automobiles speed along highways about fifty-five miles an hour. Bullet trains rocket down their tracks at nearly two hundred miles an hour. And if that's not fast enough for you, the Concorde jet carries passengers faster than the speed of sound! Yet more and more people are choosing to take day trips, overnights, or extended tours the slow way--by bicycle. But don't **Thesis statement** pedal away yet. If you're interested in bicycle touring, you'll need to make some specific preparations involving your bike, yourself, your clothing, and your route.

BODY
Main topic:
Your bike

The first thing to consider is your bicycle. With so many types to choose from--road bikes, off-road bikes, mountain bikes, and all-terrain bikes--you can pick one that's appropriate for the kind of terrain you'll be traveling on. Whichever bike you choose, it should be in excellent condition. Equip it with a map, a light, a bicycle-repair kit, a first-aid kit, saddlebags for food and clothing, and a water carrier.

Main topic:
Your physical condition

Your bike may be in good shape, but what about you? Whether your trip is a few miles to the next town or across country, you need to get yourself in good physical condition. Start an exercise program and build up your muscles and endurance gradually. You should be able to easily cycle ten to fifteen miles a day.

Main topic:
Your clothing

Now think about clothing. What you pack will depend on the season, but always prepare for possible bad weather. Pack rain gear and clothing that allows freedom of movement as it protects you from strong winds, wet, and cold. In general, avoid clothing that might interfere with

ASSESSMENT

Assess students' mastery of rough outlines and formal outlines through an evaluation of their performance on **Exercise 3.**

CLOSURE

Ask students to explain the differences between an early plan and a formal outline. ■

121

CRITICAL THINKING

Analysis. After students have read the composition on bicycle touring, ask them to close their books and summarize the composition in one or two sentences. When they complete their summaries, have them open their books and compare their summaries with the thesis statement of the composition. Point out that their summaries should include information similar to that in the thesis statement because the thesis statement is, in effect, a brief summary of the composition.

your mobility or comfort, and be sure to wear a helmet. Head injuries are a cyclist's biggest worry.

Main topic: Choosing your route

Finally, talk to experienced cyclists and read books and magazines to plan your route. You may want to join the American Youth Hostels (AYH), which offers its members inexpensive lodging and group rides. Bicycling magazines appear each month with information and special features about bicycle touring. And an organization called the Adventure Cycling Association publishes guidebooks, maps of the U.S. National Bicycle Trails Network, and a list of bicycle tour operators.

CONCLUSION

If you plan your trip well, you'll discover that bicycle touring--alone or with a group--is more fun than faster ways of travel. Before you go, give yourself enough time to get your bike, your body, your clothing, and your route in top condition. Careful advance planning practically guarantees a safe trip.

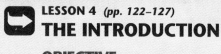
TEACHING THE LESSON

You may want to stress that two important reasons for learning how to write effective introductions are to encourage readers to read what you've written and to tell the reader what you're writing about.

Ask students why the first reason is important. Lead a discussion about the many

---

PROGRAM MANAGER

THE INTRODUCTION

■ **Analyzing** To help students analyze and organize ideas, see **The Introduction** in *Practicing the Writing Process*, p. 38.

QUOTATION FOR THE DAY

"Any writer overwhelmingly honest about pleasing himself is almost sure to please others." (Marianne Moore, 1887–1972, American poet)

Have students talk in small groups about how Moore's quotation relates to writing. You may wish to have volunteers share the results of their groups' discussions. Lead students to understand that what is entertaining to the writer is most often interesting to the reader; by composing an interesting introduction, the writer grabs the reader's attention and creates interest in the entire composition.

The Introduction

If you didn't have to, would you read a composition that begins like this: "In this composition I plan to tell you about some of the things I've learned about how scientists are studying human genes"? You probably wouldn't want to read it. It sounds too dull. An effective introduction will catch the reader's interest, set the tone of the composition, and present the thesis statement.

Catching the Reader's Interest. The introduction may be the most important paragraph in your composition. If the introduction isn't well written, your reader might not bother reading the rest of your paper. On pages 123–126 you'll find six strategies for grabbing the reader's attention.

Setting the Tone. As you introduce your topic, the words you choose and what you say set the composition's tone, the feeling you reveal about your topic. The tone of a composition may be serious, humorous, formal, informal, critical—even outraged.

For example, what can you tell about the writer's attitude from the two-sentence introduction to "Quasi-Humans" (page 110)? Its tone is definitely serious; there's nothing to indicate that this is a humorous piece. But it's also informal because a scholarly, technical discussion wouldn't refer to television shows or use the term *technowizardry*.

Presenting the Thesis Statement. You can be as clever as you want in order to catch the reader's interest, but somewhere you need to include a thesis statement that clearly summarizes the composition's main idea. Often, but not always, the thesis statement comes at the end of the introduction.

demands—including activities and reading selections—that compete for a reader's time. Introductions help readers make up their minds whether they want to take the time to read what you have written.

Be sure that students understand the three requirements of an effective introduction. They've studied the third requirement (the thesis statement) and are about to study the first (catching the reader's interest), so you may want to take a few extra minutes at this point to discuss tone. Define *tone* as an aspect of writing that shows a certain attitude on the part of the writer. Tell students that a writer's choice of words and details influences the tone of his or her writing. You may want to ask students why it's important to establish tone in the introduction. [The

Techniques for Writing Introductions

Following are six techniques for writing effective introductions. You can also try combining techniques.

1. **Begin with a question.** Some introductions begin with a question that contradicts the thesis. Others use a rhetorical question, one with no answer expected. But any question that applies to the reader can be intriguing, as in this long introduction.

> If you could design your own personality, would you rather be lively, outgoing, and the center of attention, or quiet, thoughtful, and private?
>
> It would not be surprising if you opted for the first description. You would have lots of company. According to some estimates, there are three times as many lively extroverts in the United States as reflective introverts. Our society prefers fun-loving, friendly people with "good personalities" over quiet, private types.
>
> Is one style really better than the other? Do we have a choice?
>
> Sandra R. Arbetter, "What's Your Type? Introverts and Extroverts"

2. **Begin with an anecdote or example.** An anecdote is a little story, or incident, that may be humorous or just intriguing. This introduction begins with an example.

> The rhubarb is ready for picking in Julie Kirkpatrick's garden patch on East Fourth Street and Avenue C, and Francisco Ortiz is giving away snippets of sage and tarragon. This is El Jardin del Paraiso, a lofty name for a community garden that grows upon the rubble of long-gone tenements on the Lower East Side. The fenced space where tulips and fruit trees bloom had been a dump for garbage and old bedsprings. The neighborhood is dotted with boarded-up buildings.
>
> Kathleen Teltsch, "For Young and Old, a Pocket Paradise"

SELECTION AMENDMENT
Description of change: excerpted
Rationale: to focus on the concept of introductions presented in this chapter

tone gives the reader a clearer understanding of the purpose and meaning of the work.]

Next, adapt your coverage of the techniques for writing introductions to your students' interests. They might want to discuss some of the techniques and examples more thoroughly than others. You may want to present other models at various stages of your presentation. You should help students realize the importance of introductions, but you should also help them see that deciding upon effective introductions for their writings can be fun and challenging.

Use **Exercise 4** to give students the opportunity to analyze two introductions. You may want to have students bring in more examples of introductions for additional practice.

A DIFFERENT APPROACH

Give students copies of the following introductory sentences about the growth of deserts:

1. A family gave up farming because the desert covered the garden.
2. "The sand is driving me away."
3. Deserts expand or shrink as the climate changes.
4. Did you know that some deserts are still growing?
5. Thousands of people have died and many more will die because of expanding deserts.
6. The growth of some deserts is having horrible effects on people and animals.
7. The sun was beating down on my head and the desert sand was inching its way toward my chair.

Have students identify which of the seven techniques for writing introductions is used for each one [**1.** example; **2.** quotation; **3.** background; **4.** question; **5.** startling fact; **6.** thesis statement; **7.** set scene].

3. **State a startling fact or an unusual opinion.** The article "Quasi-Humans" (page 110) uses this technique. Here's another example of an introduction designed to arouse the reader's curiosity.

> Juan de la Cruz Briceño may be the only man on earth to have an ancient Mayan city under construction in his backyard. Six days a week, a large open truck rumbles through the dawn fog behind Juan's home, scattering a flock of outraged chickens and disgorging a score of men. Behind them rise the ruins of Becan, a cluster of pyramids ringed by a destroyed canal, magnificent in their lonely desolation. The men from the truck quickly overrun the structures, swarming over rickety wooden scaffolding, working with stone and sweat to bring back the glories of this long vanished civilization. . . .
>
> Charles Mann and Gwenda Blair, "Juan's Place"

SELECTION AMENDMENT
Description of change: excerpted
Rationale: to focus on the concept of introductions presented in this chapter

4. **Begin with background information.** Facts and other specific details not only help your reader understand your main idea but may also create interest in your topic.

> Arising spontaneously from the people, folktales are little windows into the collective human psyche. Most people think of them as stories concerning the long ago and the faraway. In fact, all times and places have produced them, and modern times are no exception. Instead of dealing with dragons, wolves, and other menaces to the medieval world order, however, present-day folktales often revolve around modern technology and the attempts of human beings to come to terms with it.
>
> John Steele Gordon, "Financial Folklore"

5. **Set the scene.** Just as a short story may begin with a description of the setting (when and where the events take place), you might describe the setting of your topic. This introduction entices the reader with a vivid description of place that has little to do with the topic—storing seeds.

> It's barely 7 o'clock on a brisk spring morning, but the campus of Colorado State University in Fort Collins is already bustling with activity. On the track, joggers trot, runners sprint, while couples stroll and skateboarders glide nearby. Casting a feeble shadow over these proceedings is an undistinguished structure of tan-colored concrete and sandstone. This is the U.S. Department of Agriculture's National Seed Storage Laboratory (NSSL)—Fort Knox to our agricultural heritage. There are no bars on the windows, no security guards at the door, yet the billions of seeds stored here are beyond price—they are said to be our last line of defense against agricultural bankruptcy.
>
> Ellen Ruppel Shell, "Seeds in the bank could stave off disaster on the farm"

COOPERATIVE LEARNING

Divide the class into ten teams and assign each team one of the following tones: humorous, formal, informal, ironic, sincere, fearful, confused, philosophical, mocking, and angry. Have each team discuss the meanings of the tone assigned to it and then have the teams write sentences or short paragraphs that convey their assigned tones. You may want to remind students that writers achieve tone through word choice and details. The teams could read their examples and let the other teams guess the tones that are illustrated.

SELECTION AMENDMENT
Description of change: excerpted
Rationale: to focus on the concept of introductions presented in this chapter

ASSESSMENT

How well students analyze the introductions in **Exercise 4** will give you an indication of their understanding of attention-getting techniques and tone.

RETEACHING

Emphasize that the techniques for writing introductions are based on proven ways of getting readers' attention. Present them in their simplest forms: question, anecdote or example, fact or opinion, quotation, background, description, and thesis.

You could have each student write short examples of each of the techniques

CRITICAL THINKING

Analysis. Tell students that sometimes writers don't directly state a thesis but imply or suggest one. Readers then have to use inference—a logical or reasonable conclusion based on known facts—to construct a formal thesis statement.

Refer students to the technique used in model 3 (p. 124) which has an implied thesis statement. Ask students to write or state the main idea of the model in their own words.
[Statements will vary.

3. Workers are busily reconstructing the remains of an ancient Mayan city in a man's backyard.]

6. **Begin with a simple statement of your thesis.** You don't always have to be clever. You can be direct and straightforward and get right to your main ideas.

> Chinatown is as much a San Francisco landmark as the Golden Gate Bridge. Little is known, however, about the people who originally settled that part of the city. Now Berkeley, California, archaeologist Allen Pastron thinks his recent discovery of one of Chinatown's original buildings reveals how the unsung Chinese pioneers lived.
>
> Sherry Baker, "Pioneers Underfoot"

WRITING NOTE

Professional writers often write two- or even three-paragraph introductions. But since you're writing a brief composition, limit your introduction to a single paragraph. A long-winded introduction—even if it's funny or fascinating—can get you way off track.

SELECTION AMENDMENT
Description of change: excerpted
Rationale: to focus on the concept of introductions presented in this chapter

presented in the chapter. Tell them to concentrate only on the techniques at this point. Have them label the technique they are using for each example.

CLOSURE

Ask students to name the three requirements for an effective introduction [catches the reader's interest, sets the tone, presents the thesis], and ask them to list the seven techniques for writing effective introductions [question, anecdote or example, startling fact or opinion, quotation, background, scene, thesis]. ■

EXERCISE 4 ▶ **Analyzing Introductions**

Sharpen your skills by analyzing the introductions of professional writers. Read the two introductions below and answer the following questions about each one.

- What technique does the writer use in the introduction? (Look back over the techniques on pages 123–126.)
- How well do you think the technique works? (Would you read the article?)
- How would you describe the tone—the writer's attitude toward the topic? What words and details in the introduction reveal the tone?

1.   Could some advanced civilization devise a tunnel that would open shortcuts through space between distant regions of the universe or through time into the past?
     The traditional reaction of most scientists to such notions is to dismiss them as naïve science fiction. But three theoretical astrophysicists have published a suggestion that the laws of physics might not prohibit such "wormhole" travel through space and time.

        Malcolm W. Browne, "3 Scientists Say Travel in Time Isn't So Far Out"

2.   At Rye High School, only do-gooders get diplomas. And virtually everyone is a do-gooder. To graduate, students are required to perform 60 hours of community service over their four years.

        Lisa W. Foderaro, "At Rye High, Students Not Only Must Do Well, They Must Do Good"

ANSWERS
Exercise 4
First Introduction

- The writer begins with a question.
- Answers will vary, but most students should agree that the questions pique the reader's interest.
- Answers may vary. The writer seems to favor the theoretical astrophysicists' view over that of other scientists. The tone could be described as formal. Words that reveal tone are *traditional, dismiss,* and *naïve.*

Second Introduction

- The writer begins with what might be considered a startling fact.
- Answers will vary. Students will probably agree that the technique is effective.
- Answers may vary, but the tone seems to be positive. The term *do-gooder* helps reveal the tone.

SELECTION AMENDMENT
Description of change: excerpted
Rationale: to focus on the concept of introductions presented in this chapter

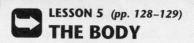

LESSON 5 (pp. 128–129)

THE BODY

OBJECTIVE

• To analyze the unity and coherence of a paragraph by identifying the main idea, supporting details, direct references, and transitional words and phrases

TEACHING THE LESSON

Give students confidence about this stage of writing by helping them to understand and use unity and coherence. Help them see that everything in a composition relating to the main idea gives the composition unity. Explain that coherence is simply having related ideas logically arranged and clearly connected.

PROGRAM MANAGER

THE BODY

■ **Instructional Support** To help students identify and use transitional expressions and direct references and reorder and delete sentences to support paragraph topics, see **The Body** in *Practicing the Writing Process*, p. 39.

■ **Instructional Support** See **Graphic Organizer 4**. For suggestions on how to tie the transparency to instruction, review teacher's notes for transparencies in *Fine Art and Instructional Transparencies for Writing*, p. 59.

QUOTATION FOR THE DAY

"Writing is the toughest thing I've ever done." (Richard Milhous Nixon, 1913–1994, 37th president of the U.S.)

MEETING *individual* **NEEDS**

STUDENTS WITH SPECIAL NEEDS

Some students might feel overwhelmed by the prospect of writing compositions. In order to overcome students' doubts, you should pair constructive criticism with much praise and positive reinforcement. Praise even such things as completion of an exercise or neat handwriting.

128

The Body

Your composition would read like a telegram if you simply stated your main ideas. And who would believe you? An effective composition consists mostly of a **body** of paragraphs. Each paragraph supports or proves a main point by developing it with supporting details.

 REFERENCE NOTE: See pages 93–101 for information on strategies of paragraph development.

Unity

It's a strain to try to follow someone whose thoughts leap illogically from topic to topic. When a composition has **unity**, the separate paragraphs work smoothly together to support a single main idea—your thesis. Drop all details and statements that detract from this sense of "oneness."

Coherence

Coherence means that ideas are woven together so they're strongly connected. In a coherent composition, the ideas are easy to follow and the writing seems to flow smoothly from beginning to end. The reader doesn't have to agonize over what something means; nothing sounds awkward or disjointed. You can make your composition coherent by arranging ideas in an order that makes sense and by using words and phrases—either direct references or transitional words and phrases—that show how ideas are connected.

Direct References. One way to connect ideas is to make direct references to something you've already mentioned. Here are three ways to use direct references.

1. Use pronouns to refer to nouns or ideas. For example, by using *she, they,* or *this,* you can avoid awkwardly repeating nouns.
2. Repeat key words or phrases. Tie paragraphs together by reminding the reader of what's important. In "Quasi-Humans" (page 110) for example, the key words *cyborgs, technology,* and *human* appear in almost every paragraph.
3. Use synonyms or slight rewordings of previous ideas and key words. Too much repetition sounds awkward.

For guided practice, review the body of **"Quasi-Humans"** with the class and discuss how the author achieves unity and coherence between paragraphs.

Assign **Exercise 5** as independent practice. Use students' responses to **Exercise 5** to determine how well they understand unity and coherence in a paragraph.

CLOSURE

Ask students to name three ways to use direct references [pronouns, repetition of key words and phrases, and synonyms or rewordings] and to tell what results from the proper use of references and transitions [unity and coherence]. ∎

Transitional Words and Phrases. *For example, therefore, of course, on the other hand*—these words and phrases connect ideas and make relationships clear.

☞ REFERENCE NOTE: See pages 88–90 for more about using direct references and transitional words and phrases.

EXERCISE 5 ▸ **Analyzing a Paragraph**

Do professional writers follow the rules? Here's a paragraph from *Sports Illustrated* magazine. With two or three classmates, look for direct references and transitional words and phrases. Find the key word(s) and pronouns, and explain what words or ideas the pronouns refer to. What's the main idea? Does every detail support it?

Japanese baseball cards were introduced in the '30s and '40s on a limited basis, and like the original U.S. cards, they continue to be used as a come-on for other products. For example, the country's leading card-maker, Calbee, attaches individually wrapped baseball cards to bags of potato chips. Because the card is on the outside of the package, someone could easily remove it without shelling out the 40 yen (31 cents) for the potato chips. "But that's not a problem in Japan," says Fuhrmann. "Kids just don't do that kind of thing."

Rick Wolff, "A Yen for Baseball Cards"

ANSWERS
Exercise 5

Answers will vary. Here are some possibilities:

Key words and pronouns and the words they refer to are *cards* and *they, Japanese baseball cards; the country's, Japan; Calbee, cardmaker; baseball cards, cards; bags of potato chips, other products; card, individually wrapped cards; package, bags of potato chips; it, card; that's, remove it; Japan, Japanese; that kind of thing, remove it.* Transitional words and phrases are *and like, For example,* and *Because.*

The paragraph's main idea is that baseball cards are used to entice people to buy other products. The initial details support this idea, but the details about the ease of removal of the cards on the bags and about Japanese children are extraneous.

SELECTION AMENDMENT
Description of change: excerpted
Rationale: to focus on the concept of the body of a composition presented in this chapter

THE CONCLUSION

OBJECTIVES

- To improve a poorly written conclusion
- To write an effective conclusion

MOTIVATION

Ask students if they know people who have a habit of not finishing their sentences or their work. Does such incompleteness bother them or others around them? Why? Most people appreciate a sense of completeness. Explain that a composition without a strong conclusion can produce an unsettling, unfinished feeling.

PROGRAM MANAGER

THE CONCLUSION

- **Instructional Support** To help students identify techniques used to write conclusions, see **The Conclusion** in *Practicing the Writing Process*, p. 40.

- **Review** For a review of revising and proofreading symbols, see **Review—Revising and Proofreading** in *Practicing the Writing Process*, p. 41.

- **Reinforcement/Reteaching** See **Revision Transparency 4.** For suggestions on how to tie the transparency to instruction, review teacher's notes in *Fine Art and Instructional Transparencies for Writing*, p. 101.

QUOTATION FOR THE DAY

"I always know the ending; that's where I start." (Toni Morrison, 1931– , American author)

You may wish to have several volunteers restate Morrison's quotation in their own words. Students might then answer the question, "What does Morrison's statement imply about the importance of endings?" Lead the class to understand that effective conclusions are essential to well-written compositions.

The Conclusion

Imagine seeing a movie that stops just before the ending or reading a novel with the last few pages missing. The conclusion of your composition is just as important as the introduction. A composition that lacks a strong conclusion leaves the reader feeling puzzled.

Techniques for Writing Conclusions

1. **Restate your main idea.** Say it again, but use different words. This is probably the easiest kind of conclusion to write. When you use this technique, it works well to put the reworded version of your thesis statement at the beginning of the last paragraph. (See the bicycle composition, pages 120–121.)

2. **Summarize the main points you've developed in the body.** Use different wording to sum up your main points. This type of conclusion emphasizes and reinforces your main points, leading right into your final words about the subject.

"When it comes to maintaining the flexibility in connective tissue like ligaments and tendons around the joints, you use it or lose it," says Dr. Findley. "If you don't take these connective tissues through their maximum range daily, eventually the range will shrink and you'll lose mobility." In addition to the long-term

The six techniques for writing conclusions are all that comprise this lesson, so you'll want to cover them thoroughly. Because examples are not provided for each technique, you may want to give some of your own, or have the students write some for practice. Make sure students understand how each technique differs from the others.

You may want to use **Exercise 6** as a vehicle for guiding the students through the six techniques for writing conclusions. After the student pairs have had a chance to discuss the conclusion, lead them in a rewriting exercise to turn that conclusion into an example of each of the six techniques.

☞

> flexibility benefits, I find that doing this stretch each morning gets my blood flowing, jumpstarts my brain and expands my chest so I can breathe deeper. Within minutes, I feel energized to greet the coming day.
>
> Sharon Stocker, "Stretchbreak: Good-Morning Wake-Up Stretch"

3. **End with a final comment or example.** Your last word may be a thoughtful observation, a personal reaction, or a look to the future or to larger issues. The writer of "Quasi-Humans" (page 110) ends by saying that a "certain amount of resistance" will have to be overcome before his vision of the future becomes a reality.

4. **End with a call to action.** Persuasive essays often end by asking the reader to take a specific action. This makes an effective ending for other kinds of compositions, too.

> Alan Tiger, director of the Y.W.C.A. here, says he would like to see the program applied on a national level. "This school came up through the grass roots," he said. "It's a simple enough idea that any city can pull it off. You need the school district to get out front on it, but don't forget community support. People want to help."
>
> Timothy Egan, "School for Homeless Children: A Rare Experience"

5. **Refer to the introduction.** Bring the reader back full circle by referring to something in your introduction. George Plimpton begins "Neil Armstrong's Famous First Words" by comparing Armstrong and Charles Lindbergh. He doesn't mention Lindbergh again until the conclusion:

> Charles Lindbergh is supposed to have said, "Well, I made it!" when he touched down at Le Bourget. What he actually said, leaning out, with the crowd surging around his plane, was: "Are there any mechanics here?" And then, "Does anyone here speak

MEETING *individual* NEEDS

LEP/ESL

General Strategies. In some cultures, bringing a discourse to an end entails a sense of finality not found in English composition. For example, such a conclusion might imply or state explicitly that there is no need for further discussion of the topic.

If your students write this type of conclusion, tell them that, in English composition, closure does not necessarily call for discontinued consideration. A conclusion that dismisses further consideration of the topic implies an arrogance that many readers might find narrow-minded.

LESS-ADVANCED STUDENTS

Some students might not grasp the differences among techniques 1, 2, and 5. Explain the difference between a restatement and a summary and compare a few examples of each. Tell students that referring to the introduction doesn't mean restating or summarizing the composition's main point. It means specifically mentioning something that was mentioned in the introduction.

SELECTION AMENDMENT
Description of change: excerpted
Rationale: to focus on the concept of conclusions presented in this chapter

As an alternate exercise, you could lead the students in rewriting the conclusion of "**Quasi-Humans**" (p. 110) to illustrate each of the six techniques. You could then use **Exercises 6** and **7** for independent practice.

INDEPENDENT PRACTICE
Students should do **Exercise 7** on their own. Remind them that the conclusions they write should not lessen the composition's unity and coherence.

VISUAL CONNECTIONS

Exploring the Subject. Charles Lindbergh and Neil Armstrong are two of the most famous Americans associated with the history of flight. Lindbergh, who was born in 1902 in Detroit, Michigan, flew the world's first solo, nonstop transatlantic flight. He left in his plane *Spirit of St. Louis* on May 20, 1927, and landed near Paris thirty-three hours and twenty-nine minutes later. Armstrong, who was born in 1930 in Wapakoneta, Ohio, was the first human to walk on the moon, which he did on July 20, 1969.

SELECTION AMENDMENT
Description of change: excerpted
Rationale: to focus on the concept of conclusions presented in this chapter

132

English?" So it is apparent that however self-deprecatory Armstrong is about his own contributions, he is certainly a giant leap ahead of Lindbergh in the immortal-words department.

George Plimpton, "Neil Armstrong's Famous First Words"

(By the way, Neil Armstrong's "famous first words"—delivered when he first stepped on the moon on July 20, 1969—were: "That's one small step for a man, one giant leap for mankind.")

6. **Use a quotation.** A quotation that's startling or moving works just as well to end a composition as it does to begin one.

The gardeners still have nagging worries they could lose El Jardin to developers. "I don't think there is another place where our neighborhood people could go," said Ms. Kirkpatrick. "You need a ray of hope and you find it seeing what can grow out of rubble."

Kathleen Teltsch, "For Young and Old, a Pocket Paradise"

ASSESSMENT

Use students' work on **Exercise 7** to evaluate their understanding of the six techniques for writing conclusions. Be sure to check the conclusions with the rest of the essay to verify that unity and coherence are maintained.

CLOSURE

Ask students to name the six techniques for writing conclusions [restate main idea, summarize main points, end with comment or example, end with call to action, refer to introduction, use a quotation]. ■

The Conclusion **133**

WRITING NOTE

You can wait until you've finished writing your composition before you worry about its title. Use your thesis statement—and your imagination—to think of a brief, catchy way to describe what your readers are about to encounter.

Try writing several titles until you find one you like. Here are some suggestions for the bicycle touring composition (pages 120–121). Which one do you like best? Can you think of others?

EXAMPLES   Seeing the Country on Two Wheels
Advice for Beginning Bicycle Trippers
Bicycle Touring: Muscle, Sweat, and Gears

EXERCISE 6   **Improving a Conclusion**

Here's the first draft of a conclusion for a composition about uniforms in public schools. Get together with a partner to answer these questions: *What's wrong with this conclusion? How can it be improved?* Then, write a better conclusion. You can change it any way you like, make up details, or even start over completely. (For some ideas, refer to the techniques on pages 130–132.)

> Someday all public school students--both boys and girls--may wear uniforms. Will uniforms make schools better or worse than the way things are today? No one knows.

ANSWERS
Exercise 6

The problem with the conclusion as written is that it raises a question that can't be answered. Revisions of the conclusion will vary. Here's an example:

> Telling students what they cannot wear to school is not far removed from dictating what they do wear. While it is true that wearing the same things can create a sense of unity among the students, whether this creates an environment supportive of learning remains to be seen. However, if current trends of regulating public school clothing continue, all public school students may someday wear uniforms.

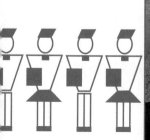

Exercise 7

Conclusions will vary. Here's an example:

> Bicycle touring can be an enjoyable and memorable experience. However, if you don't prepare for it properly, you could be in for your worst vacation ever. So choose those clothes and routes carefully and get that bike and body in shape! [call to action]

 INTEGRATING THE LANGUAGE ARTS

Literature Link. If your students' literature book contains it, have students read "No News from Auschwitz" by A.M. Rosenthal. Then, ask students to tell which of the six techniques for writing conclusions Rosenthal uses. [He ends with a final comment. Students may also note that Rosenthal's final sentence echoes his introduction.] You then could have students use other techniques to write different conclusions for the essay. Ask for volunteers to read the new conclusions.

EXERCISE 7 ▶ **Writing a Conclusion**

Use your imagination to write a different conclusion for the composition about bicycle touring (pages 120–121). Use one technique or some combination of the techniques on pages 130–132. Feel free to make up quotations and additional details. (It's a good idea to read the composition again before you begin.)

WRITING NOTE The two models of composition form you've read in this chapter are written in different points of view. The first one, "Quasi-Humans" (page 110), is written in the third-person point of view (*he, she, it, they*). Since a third-person point of view keeps the writer at a distance from the reader, it's the point of view you'll need to use when you're writing a formal composition. The second composition, the one on bicycle touring (pages 120–121), is written in the second-person point of view (*you, your*). Since the second-person point of view brings the writer closer to the reader, you may use it when your composition is more informal.

FRAMEWORK FOR A COMPOSITION

Introduction
- Arouses the reader's interest
- Sets the tone
- Presents the thesis statement

Body
- States the main points
- Provides support for the main points

Conclusion
- Reinforces the main idea
- Leaves the reader with a final impression and a sense of completeness

WRITING AN INFORMATIVE COMPOSITION OBJECTIVE

- To use the composition form studied in the chapter to write an informative essay

MAKING CONNECTIONS

WRITING AN INFORMATIVE COMPOSITION

A useful formula for writing an informative composition is *introduction + body + conclusion = composition*. Remember that to explain and inform is only one of the purposes for writing. Others are to express yourself, to be creative, and to persuade others. The composition form can also be adapted to these purposes.

In this assignment, you'll apply this three-part formula to write an informative essay about the President's Council on Physical Fitness and Sports. Since you are writing for a high school audience, your purpose will be to explain how students can qualify for awards. Imagine that the following list of facts and the following chart are the prewriting information that you've gathered so far.

Information About President's Council on Physical Fitness and Sports

1. Florence Griffith Joyner and Tom McMillen, cochairs: "Schools can nurture children's love of physical activity, laying the foundation for a healthy life."

WRITING AN INFORMATIVE COMPOSITION

Teaching Strategies

This assignment requires students to put together what they have learned in this chapter, so you will want to review what has been learned about the separate parts of a composition before students begin writing. Be sure to stress the importance of transitions when the students are ready to put the parts together into a unified whole.

Focus is another topic you will need to discuss with the students, since it determines which pieces of information are used and which are discarded. If students need more information, you may want to refer them to **Chapter 33: "The Library/Media Center"** for information on using the library.

Finally, be sure students understand each step of the writing process (prewriting, writing, evaluating and revising, and proofreading and publishing) and what each step involves.

GUIDELINES

Student essays should contain the following items:

- a one-paragraph introduction that catches the reader's interest, sets the tone, and presents the thesis statement
- a body that gives supporting details about the main idea of the composition
- a body that is coherent and makes proper use of direct references and transitional words and phrases
- a conclusion that reinforces the main idea and gives a sense of completeness to the composition

The writing process in the assignment calls for the students to

- Write a preliminary thesis statement.
- Make an early plan.
- Write an attention-getting introduction.
- Write a series of unified and coherent paragraphs.
- Write an effective conclusion.
- Submit a completed and proofread composition.

2. a nation of young couch potatoes: nearly half don't get enough exercise; only a quarter of high school students participate in physical education daily
3. Council founded in 1956: President's Challenge awards program for boys and girls 6 through 17 that recognizes achievement in physical fitness
4. more than two million students earned awards in recent years
5. students in 85th percentile in all five events get emblem and Certificate of Achievement signed by president
6. students in 50th percentile get National Physical Fitness Award emblems and certificates
7. students who have disabilities also participate
8. five events: curl-ups (sit-up with bent knees, arms crossed on chest); shuttle run (30-foot run picking up and moving blocks); 1-mile combined run and walk; pull-ups or push-ups; V-sit reach (reaching with hands through legs in sitting position)
9. free booklet *Get Fit*—from President's Council on Physical Fitness and Sports, 701 Pennsylvania Avenue, N.W., Suite 250, Washington, DC 20004

	AGE	CURL-UPS (Limited one min.)	SHUTTLE RUN (seconds)	V-SIT REACH (inches)	ONE-MILE RUN (min./sec.)	PULL-UPS
BOYS	6	33	12.1	+3.5	10:15	2
	7	36	11.5	+3.5	9:22	4
	8	40	11.1	+3.0	8:48	5
	9	41	10.9	+3.0	8:31	5
	10	45	10.3	+4.0	7:57	6
	11	47	10.0	+4.0	7:32	6
	12	50	9.8	+4.0	7:11	7
	13	53	9.5	+3.5	6:50	7
	14	56	9.1	+4.5	6:26	10
	15	57	9.0	+5.0	6:20	11
	16	56	8.7	+6.0	6:08	11
	17	55	8.7	+7.0	6:06	13
GIRLS	6	32	12.4	+5.5	11:20	2
	7	34	12.1	+5.0	10:36	2
	8	38	11.8	+4.5	10:02	2
	9	39	11.1	+5.5	9:30	2
	10	40	10.8	+6.0	9:19	3
	11	42	10.5	+6.5	9:02	3
	12	45	10.4	+7.0	8:23	2
	13	46	10.2	+7.0	8:13	2
	14	47	10.1	+8.0	7:59	2
	15	48	10.0	+8.0	8:08	2
	16	45	10.1	+9.0	8:23	1
	17	44	10.0	+8.0	8:15	1

 Prewriting. Add or subtract from the data bank given above. You don't have to use all the information given, and you can do some research to find additional facts. (Suggestions: If your school participates, what are the statistics? Interview a physical education teacher or a coach.)

Narrow your topic to one you can cover in a brief composition. Express your main idea in a preliminary thesis statement. Then, arrange the information into an early plan.

 Writing, Evaluating, and Revising. Follow your early plan as you draft your composition, and try one of the introduction techniques suggested on pages 123–126. As you draft the body, concentrate on unity and coherence. Each paragraph should develop one main point directly related to your thesis statement. When you get to the conclusion, review the techniques for writing conclusions on pages 130–132.

 Proofreading and Publishing. When you're satisfied with your revisions, change your focus, and search for errors in grammar, usage, and mechanics. Exchange papers with a partner, and proofread each other's compositions. (See the proofreading guidelines on pages 55–56.) Find a way to share your composition with an audience. If your school isn't participating in the program of the President's Council on Physical Fitness and Sports, you might use your compositions to try to get the program under way.

Reflecting on Your Writing

Date your paper, to include it in your **portfolio,** and attach a brief reflection that answers the following questions.

- What is most appealing about your introduction?
- How did you make sure that your body paragraphs maintained unity and coherence?
- Which part of the paper do you think is strongest?

EXPRESSIVE WRITING: NARRATION

OBJECTIVES

- To select an appropriate topic for a personal narrative
- To analyze purpose, audience, and tone
- To organize details and draft a personal narrative
- To evaluate and revise a personal narrative
- To proofread a personal narrative and to prepare it for publication

WRITING-IN-PROGRESS ASSIGNMENTS

Major Assignment: Writing a personal narrative
Cumulative Writing Assignments: The chart below shows the sequence of cumulative assignments that will guide students as they write a personal narrative. These writing assignments form the instructional core of Chapter 4.

PREWRITING
Writing Assignment
• Part 1: Choosing an Experience for a Personal Narrative p. 146
• Part 2: Recalling Details p. 151
• Part 3: Stating the Meaning of Your Experience p. 153
WRITING
Writing Assignment
• Part 4: Writing a Draft of Your Personal Narrative p. 162
EVALUATING AND REVISING
Writing Assignment
• Part 5: Evaluating and Revising Your Personal Narrative p. 166
PROOFREADING AND PUBLISHING
Writing Assignment
• Part 6: Proofreading and Publishing Your Personal Narrative p. 167

In addition, exercises 1–5 provide practice in tapping memory for personal experiences, creating a natural tone, analyzing a personal narrative, analyzing a writer's revisions, and evaluating a personal narrative.

Cross CURRICULUM

The Art of Self-Expression

Explain to your students that art, as well as words, is a medium for self-expression. Work with the art teacher in your school to develop a joint project—self-expression in writing and the visual arts, or use the following assignment in your own classes.

Suggest that students create self-portraits, either in addition to or in place of their personal narratives. Self-portraits need not be realistic; students may use symbols, shapes, and colors, or create collages to express their actual or desired identities. Offer examples of portraits and self-portraits, and let students share their reactions.

- **Freewriting** Encourage students to freewrite a list of objects, moods, and colors that they associate with themselves. Ask questions like the following.
  - What symbols, such as animals, emblems, or sports, might represent you?
  - What colors express your moods?
  - What impression do you want to create?
  - What emotion would you like to express?

  (Remind students to limit their expressions to material they are willing to share in class.)

- **Materials** Have students provide a list of necessary supplies. Then, arrange with an art teacher a time students could use an art room or materials. Also provide magazines and mirrors.

- **Publishing** After students have completed their portraits, ask them to write a brief statement (3–5 sentences) about their final product that will be displayed with their artwork. You might suggest one of the prompts mentioned below under "Reflecting" as a starting point. Display portraits around the classroom or exhibit them in a showcase.

- **Reflecting** For self-assessment, ask students to respond in their Reader's Logs to the following questions.
  - How does the artwork reflect my personality?
  - Is this how I want to see myself next year—or in ten years? Would I have chosen this depiction a year ago?

INTEGRATING THE LANGUAGE ARTS

SELECTION	READING AND LITERATURE	WRITING AND CRITICAL THINKING	LANGUAGE AND SYNTAX	SPEAKING, LISTENING, AND OTHER EXPRESSION SKILLS
• from **Black Elk Speaks** as told through John G. Neihardt pp. 140–142 • from **An American Childhood** by Annie Dillard pp. 156–158 • **Writers on Writing** by Ernest Hemingway p. 163 • from **A Modern Utopia** by H. G. Wells pp. 169–170 • from **A Sand County Almanac** by Aldo Leopold pp. 172–173	• Analyzing organization p. 143 • Analyzing details pp. 143, 158, 171 • Responding personally to literature pp. 143, 158, 171 • Finding details pp. 143, 158, 171 • Finding the main idea p. 158 • Understanding metaphor in a personal narrative p. 158	• Evaluating meaning pp. 143, 152, 153, 171 • Applying interpretive and creative thinking pp. 143, 152, 158, 165, 171, 172, 173 • Analyzing, organizing, and recalling details pp. 143, 146, 151, 158, 162, 165, 171, 173 • Choosing a topic p. 146 • Creating a natural tone p. 148 • Contrasting speaking and writing styles p. 148 • Analyzing a personal narrative pp. 158, 166 • Describing a personal utopia p. 171	• Identifying transitional words and phrases p. 143 • Proofreading for errors in grammar, usage, and mechanics pp. 167, 171	• Talking and listening to others p. 148 • Interpreting meaning in a group p. 152 • Working with classmates to analyze a personal narrative pp. 158, 166 • Working with classmates in evaluation and revision p. 166

SUGGESTED INTEGRATED UNIT PLAN

This plan suggests how to integrate the major strands of the language arts with this chapter. If you begin with this chapter on expressive writing or with literary selections like the following, you should focus on the common characteristics of personal narrative. You can then integrate speaking/listening and language concepts with both the writing and the literature.

Common Characteristics

- Frequent use of first person—I, me, us, we
- Figurative language that evokes a mood and appeals to the senses
- Content that is self-expressive and conveys emotion and attitudes
- Possibly rhythmic repetition of words and phrases
- Usually chronological organization
- Use of dialogue

Writing
Personal narrative

UNIT FOCUS AUTOBIOGRAPHY

Language
Grammar, style

- Action verbs
- Transitional words and phrases
- Tone

Literature
Selections such as

- "You Are Now Entering the Human Heart" Janet Frame
- *Travels With Charley* John Steinbeck
- *Silent Dancing* Judith Ortiz Cofer
- "A Child's Christmas in Wales" Dylan Thomas

Speaking/Listening

- Talking and listening to others
- Interpreting meaning in a group
- Working with classmates to analyze a personal narrative

CHAPTER 4: EXPRESSIVE WRITING: NARRATION

Use this guide for creating an instructional plan that addresses the individual needs of your students. Assignments accompanied by the following symbol (✶) may be completed out of class. Times given for pacing lessons are estimated.

CHAPTER PLANNING GUIDE—PUPIL'S EDITION

LESSONS	LITERARY MODEL pp. 140–142 from *Black Elk Speaks* as told through John G. Neihardt	PREWRITING pp. 145–154	
		Generating Ideas	**Gathering/Organizing**
DEVELOPMENTAL PROGRAM	🕐 **20–25 minutes** • Read model aloud in class and ask students to answer questions on p. 143 orally.	🕐 **50–55 minutes** • Main Assignment: Looking Ahead p. 144 • Choosing a Personal Experience pp. 145–146 • Exercise 1 p. 146 • Writing Assignment: Part 1 p. 146	🕐 **60–65 minutes** • Planning Your Personal Narrative pp. 147–151, 154 • Exercise 2 p. 148 • Writing Notes pp. 149, 154 • Writing Assignment: Parts 2, 3 pp. 151, 153
CORE PROGRAM	🕐 **20–25 minutes** • Assign student pairs to read the model and answer questions on p. 143.	🕐 **20–25 minutes** • Main Assignment: Looking Ahead p. 144 • Choosing a Personal Experience pp. 145–146 • Exercise 1 p. 146✶ • Writing Assignment: Part 1 p. 146✶	🕐 **35–40 minutes** • Planning Your Personal Narrative pp. 147–154✶ • Exercise 2 p. 148 • Writing Notes pp. 149, 154 • Reminder p. 151 • Writing Assignment: Parts 2, 3 pp. 151, 153✶ • Critical Thinking pp. 152–153
ACCELERATED PROGRAM	🕐 **20–25 minutes** • Assign students to read the model independently and to discuss the questions on p. 143 in pairs.	🕐 **10–15 minutes** • Main Assignment: Looking Ahead p. 144 • Exercise 1 p. 146✶ • Writing Assignment: Part 1 p. 146✶	🕐 **30–35 minutes** • Thinking About Purpose, Audience, and Tone p. 147 • Exercise 2 p. 148 • Writing Notes pp. 149, 154 • Chart p. 150 • Writing Assignment: Parts 2, 3 pp. 151, 153✶ • Critical Thinking pp. 152–153✶

CHAPTER PLANNING GUIDE—PROGRAM RESOURCES

	LITERARY MODEL	PREWRITING
PRINT	• Reading Master 4, *Practice for Assessment in Reading, Vocabulary, and Spelling* p. 4	• Prewriting, *Strategies for Writing* p. 2 • Expressing Yourself, *English Workshop* pp. 35–42
MEDIA	• Fine Art Transparency 1, *Transparency Binder*	• Graphic Organizers 5–6, *Transparency Binder* • *Writers Workshop 2:* Autobiographical Incident

WRITING pp. 155–162	EVALUATING AND REVISING pp. 163–166	PROOFREADING AND PUBLISHING pp. 167–168
45–50 minutes • The Structure of Your Personal Narrative p. 155 • A Writer's Model pp. 159–161 • Framework p. 162 • Writing Assignment: Part 4 p. 162*	**40–45 minutes** • Evaluating and Revising pp. 163–164 • Exercises 4, 5 pp. 165, 166* • Grammar Hint p. 166 • Writing Assignment: Part 5 p. 166	**45–50 minutes** • Proofreading and Publishing p. 167 • Writing Assignment: Part 6 p. 167 • Reflecting p. 167 • A Student Model p. 168
25–30 minutes • The Structure of Your Personal Narrative p. 155 • A Passage from an Autobiography pp. 156–158* • Exercise 3 p. 158* • Framework p. 162 • Writing Assignment: Part 4 p. 162*	**35–40 minutes** • Chart p. 164 • Reminder p. 165 • Exercise 5 p. 166* • Grammar Hint p. 166 • Writing Assignment: Part 5 p. 166	**35–40 minutes** • Writing Assignment: Part 6 p. 167 • Reflecting p. 167 • A Student Model p. 168*
20–25 minutes • The Structure of Your Personal Narrative p. 155 • A Passage from an Autobiography pp. 156–158* • Framework p. 162 • Writing Assignment: Part 4 p. 162*	**30–35 minutes** • Chart p. 164 • Reminder p. 165 • Writing Assignment: Part 5 p. 166	**30–35 minutes** • Writing Assignment: Part 6 p. 167 • Reflecting p. 167

WRITING	EVALUATING AND REVISING	PROOFREADING AND PUBLISHING
• Writing, *Strategies for Writing* p. 3	• Evaluating and Revising, *Strategies for Writing* p. 4 • *English Workshop* pp. 113–114	• Proofreading Practice, *Strategies for Writing* p. 6
	• Revision Transparencies 5–6, *Transparency Binder*	• *Language Workshop:* Lessons 2, 9–10

ELEMENTS OF WRITING: CURRICULUM CONNECTIONS

Writing Workshop
• Describing a Personal Utopia p. 171

Making Connections
• Self-Expression Across the Curriculum: Science pp. 172–173

ASSESSMENT OPTIONS

Summative Assessment
Holistic Scoring: Prompts and Models pp. 3–8

Performance Assessment
Assessment 1, *Integrated Performance Assessment, Level E* For help with evaluation, see *Holistic Scoring Workshop.*

Portfolio Assessment
Portfolio forms, *Portfolio Assessment* pp. 5–25, 44–48

Reflection
Writing Process Log, *Strategies for Writing* p. 1
Self-assessment Record, *Portfolio Assessment* p. 19

Ongoing Assessment
Proofreading, *Strategies for Writing* p. 5

Computer disk or CD-ROM

Overhead transparencies

LESSON 1 *(pp. 138–143)*

DISCOVERING YOURSELF

OBJECTIVES

- To identify and analyze the characteristics of personal expression
- To analyze the expressive qualities of a literary model

MOTIVATION

Before students open their books, put the first two lines of the literary model on the chalkboard or on a transparency. Do not identify the excerpt. After students have read the lines to themselves, begin a discussion of what concrete information students find in the lines. The discussion should evolve into an anticipation of what might follow the first

PROGRAM MANAGER

CHAPTER 4

- **Computer Guided Instruction** For a related assignment that students may use for additional instruction and practice, see **Autobiographical Incident** in *Writer's Workshop 2 CD-ROM.*

- **Practice** To help less-advanced students who need additional practice with concepts and activities related to this chapter, see **Chapter 4** in *English Workshop, Fourth Course,* pp. 35–42.

- **Summative Assessment** For a writing prompt, including grading criteria and student models, see *Holistic Scoring: Prompts and Models,* pp. 3–8.

- **Performance Assessment** Use **Assessment 1** in *Integrated Performance Assessment, Level E.* For help with evaluating student writing, see *Holistic Scoring Workshop, Level E.*

- **Extension/Enrichment** See **Fine Art Transparency 1,** *The Rehearsal of the Ballet on the Stage* by Edgar Degas. For suggestions on how to tie the transparency to instruction, review teacher's notes in *Fine Art and Instructional Transparencies for Writing,* p. 3.

- **Reading Support** For help with the reading selection, pp. 140–142, see **Reading Master 4** in *Practice for Assessment in Reading, Vocabulary, and Spelling,* p. 4.

4 EXPRESSIVE WRITING: NARRATION

two lines. What do the students predict is going to happen? What mood do they sense? Have students explain their responses. You may also want to ask students to guess what kind of writing this excerpt represents.

Discovering Yourself

What do you really know about yourself? What can you **discover** about **yourself?** One way you can find out more about your inner feelings is to write about them.

Writing and You. "I'll never forget the time when . . . " "I felt so good the day that . . . " You probably think or talk this way often. Many writers take these thoughts further by writing them down. Doing so helps us explore our deepest feelings, our fears, hopes, and dreams. You may want to write just for yourself. Or you might share your feelings with others in a personal narrative. Can you think of an emotional experience you would like to write about?

As You Read. As you read the following narrative, notice how Black Elk, an Oglala Sioux, looks inside himself to tell about the hardships of his people.

James Humetawa, *Kachina Dance* (1944). Hopi, born 1926. Watercolor. 1946.29.4. The Philbrook Museum of Art, Tulsa, Oklahoma.

139

GUIDED PRACTICE

Guide students through the **Reader's Response** questions. Have a volunteer write a list of images and a list of feelings on the chalkboard as you and the students reflect on the story.

140

MEETING *individual* NEEDS

LEP/ESL

General Strategies. Have students share any personal experiences or stories they have heard about life in their native cultures. Ask them to relate how their lives today are different from their ancestors' ways of life.

USING THE SELECTION
from Black Elk Speaks

1

What is the reader's first impression as he or she reads the first sentence?
[Answers may vary, but the reader may experience curiosity as to why the wind is mentioned first, and why they, whoever they are, can see only a little way ahead. The reader might also sense apprehension in the tone of the narrator.]

2

Lakota: Sioux

from

Black Elk Speaks

as told through

JOHN G. NEIHARDT

(Flaming Rainbow)

1 The wind came up again with the daylight, and we could see only a little way ahead when we started west in the morning. Before we came to the ridge, we saw two horses, dim in the blowing snow beside some bushes. They were huddled up with their tails to the wind and their heads hanging low. When we came closer, there was a bison robe shelter in the brush, and in it were an old man and a boy, very cold and hungry and discouraged. They were 2 Lakotas and were glad to see us, but they were feeling weak, because they had been out two days and had seen nothing but snow. We camped there with them in the brush, and then we went up on the ridge afoot. There was much timber up there. We got behind the hill in a sheltered place and waited, but we could see nothing. While we were waiting, we talked about the people starving at home, and we were all sad. Now and then the snow haze would open up for a little bit and you could see quite a distance, then it would close again. While we were talking about our hungry people, suddenly the snow haze opened a little, and we saw a shaggy bull's head coming out of the blowing snow up the <u>draw</u> that led past us below. Then seven more appeared, and the snow haze came back and shut us in there. They

INDEPENDENT PRACTICE

After students have discussed the **Reader's Response** questions, have them convey their feelings by writing in their journals. Then, they can complete the **Writer's Craft** questions on their own. Encourage students to be thorough in their answers.

ASSESSMENT

You can evaluate student understanding during the **Reader's Response** discussion through observation. Have students turn in their answers to the **Writer's Craft** questions for further assessment.

☞

could not see us, and they were drifting with the wind so that they could not smell us.

We four stood up and made vows to the four quarters of the world, saying: "Haho! haho!" Then we got our horses from the brush on the other side of the ridge and came around to the mouth of the draw where the bison would pass as they drifted with the wind.

The two old men were to shoot first and then we two boys would follow the others horseback. Soon we saw the bison coming. The old people crept up and shot, but they were so cold, and maybe excited, that they got only one bison. They cried "Hoka!" and we boys charged after the other bison. The snow was blowing hard in the wind that sucked down the draw, and when we came near them the bison were so excited that they backtracked and charged right past us bellowing. This broke

> "...when we came near them the bison were so excited that they backtracked and charged right past us bellowing."

the deep snow for our horses and it was easier to catch them. Suddenly I saw the bison I was chasing go out in a big flurry of snow, and I knew they had plunged into a snow-filled gulch, but it was too late to stop, and my

3

3
What do you suppose Black Elk means by "four quarters of the world"?
[north, south, east, and west]

4

4
Notice this is the first time the storyteller refers to himself. How old do you think Black Elk is at this time?
[He refers to himself as a boy; perhaps he is in his early teens.]

5

5
How do you feel as you read this passage?
[The word *plunged* suggests a comparison of the snow-filled gulch to a swimming pool or pond. The words *floundering and kicking* might elicit the feeling of fear or chaos.]

Ask students why they think Black Elk chose to tell about his experiences. Write their answers on the chalkboard [to entertain, to inform others]. Ask students to discuss reasons they might feel a need to publish a personal narrative. [They may be more interested in sharing what they have discovered than in merely expressing themselves.]

MEETING *individual* NEEDS

ADVANCED STUDENTS

Students might benefit from seeing how the first-person point of view is important in a personal narrative. They could form groups, choose a person other than the narrator in Black Elk's narrative, and rewrite one paragraph from that perspective. Each group could rewrite a different paragraph and then share its revision with the class. Students will observe in this activity how important the character of the narrator is in a personal narrative.

VISUAL CONNECTIONS

Exploring the Subject. Have students examine the picture of Black Elk on p. 141 and consider why his narrative is told through Neihardt. Then, have students examine the painting of the American Indians with the buffalo and discuss how this painting reflects the sensory details of the story.

SELECTION AMENDMENT
Description of change: excerpted
Rationale: to focus on the concept of expressive writing presented in this chapter

142

National Museum of American Art, Washington, D.C./Art Resource.

horse plunged right in after them. There we were all together— four bison, my horse and I all floundering and kicking, but I managed to crawl out a little way. I had a repeating rifle that they gave me back at the camp, and I killed the four bison right there, but I had thrown my mittens away and the gun froze to my hands while I was shooting, so that I had to tear the skin to get it loose.

When I went back to the others, the other boy had killed three, so we had eight bison scattered around there in the snow. It was still morning, but it took till nearly dark for my father and the other old man to do the butchering. I could not help, because my hands were frozen. We finally got the meat all piled up in one place, and then we made a camp in a fine shelter behind a big rock with brush all around it and plenty of wood. We had a big fire, and we tied our tanned robes on our horses and fed them plenty of cottonwood bark from the woods by the stream. The raw robes we used for the shelter. Then we had a big feast and we sang and were very happy.

To encourage students to be more aware of sensory details and of their thoughts and feelings, have them write journal entries for several days. They might record their observations of certain daily activities such as lunchtime in the cafeteria, a sporting event, or a particular class. Remind students to write down the sensory details they observe and to record their thoughts and feelings. Guide students to draw conclusions about the details they might have missed had they not been consciously looking for and thinking about them. ■

READER'S RESPONSE

1. What images in Black Elk's narrative are most vivid in your mind? Why do you think these details or mental pictures made a strong impression on you?
2. Black Elk's experience shows the physical hardships he faced. Can you imagine what it would be like to have to chase bison through the snow for food for your family? In your journal, write about your own life as compared with this experience of Black Elk.

WRITER'S CRAFT

3. Black Elk uses many details that help readers feel the bitter cold. How do the details about Black Elk's hands in the last two paragraphs help you feel the awful cold?
4. Black Elk uses many transitional words and phrases to help readers follow the order of events. In the first sentence, for example, he says, "The wind came up *again . . . when* we started west in the morning." What are some other transition words and phrases in the first paragraph?

"**A** people without history
is like the wind
on the buffalo grass."

Sioux Saying

ANSWERS
Reader's Response

Responses may vary.

1. Students should give specific details from the narrative and explain why the images made a strong impression.
2. Students should include specific details from their own lives and from Black Elk's narrative to support their responses. Writing journal entries should not be penalized for incomplete sentences or mechanical errors.

Writer's Craft

Responses may vary.

3. Students' answers should include specific examples from the last two paragraphs.
4. *Before, when, but, because, there, then, behind, while, now and then, again, suddenly, up, below*

INTEGRATING THE LANGUAGE ARTS

Literature Link. A good example of a personal narrative is "Hanging Fire" by Audre Lorde. Students might read this poem and list the characteristics (sensory details, thoughts and feelings of the writer, first-person point of view, organization, and transitional words) this poem shares with a personal prose narrative.

The examples in this lesson deal with four methods of development that writers use to express themselves: narration, description, classification (which includes defining and comparing/contrasting), and evaluation.

Write these terms on the chalkboard as you read and discuss the examples. Then ask students to provide additional examples of topics that could be developed by each method. Ask students to note that these methods can be used for many different written forms, from postcards to poems. ■

A DIFFERENT APPROACH

Ask students to bring their favorite magazines to class; teen magazines, sports magazines, beauty magazines, or car magazines would be appropriate. Ask them to find examples of the four different methods of development. Point out that an entire article probably won't be confined to only one of the methods because most literature employs a combination. When they think they have found at least one example of each method, ask students to share and discuss their examples.

Ways to Express Yourself

Like anyone who does expressive writing, Black Elk wants to present his own thoughts and feelings. But he's also writing to inform readers about the terrible conditions faced by the Oglala Sioux and to persuade readers that tragic changes are occurring in the lives of his people. Expressing yourself is your main reason for writing a personal narrative. Here are some examples of the ways you can develop an expressive message.

- in your journal, writing about a funny event at school
- in a letter, telling a friend about getting lost on the subway
- in a postcard, describing your fellow camp counselors
- in a poem, describing your dog's funny habits
- in a team newsletter, comparing last year's soccer team with this year's
- in a conversation with a co-worker, defining the word *enthusiasm* and explaining what it means to you
- in your school newspaper, evaluating your volunteer work at the animal shelter
- in a focus group, discussing what you think of a company's product

LOOKING AHEAD

In the main assignment in this chapter, you'll use narration to tell about an important personal experience. As you write, you'll explore and discover the meaning of your experience. Keep in mind that an effective personal narrative

- describes the important events, people, and places that were part of the experience
- includes your thoughts and feelings
- uses specific sensory details
- explains what the experience meant to you

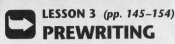

OBJECTIVES

- To select an experience as a topic for a personal narrative
- To analyze with a group the differences in speaking and writing expressively
- To recall and organize details for a personal narrative
- To state the meaning of an experience in a personal narrative

Writing a Personal Narrative

Prewriting

Choosing a Personal Experience

Some experiences stand out in your memory—and not just the "big occasions." You may never forget the first time your band played in public (absolute terror and then relief when everybody danced).

But you may also remember—vividly—your first walk on a beach, when all that happened was watching sandpipers and gathering shells, but you decided you were *determined* never to live in the city.

Your experience for a personal narrative may be simple and ordinary instead of unusual or surprising, but if it passes these three tests, it's a good topic.

1. The experience seems important to you: it has personal meaning.
2. The experience is clear in your memory: you remember details.
3. The experience is not too private: you're willing to share it with others.

Have students draw upon relatively recent memories and then work backward to earlier experiences. There are four steps in this activity: Begin by asking students to remember an incident from the day before and to record details about it, especially what they thought and how they felt. Then, have students record something they were doing on this day a week ago, and something that happened a year ago. They should concentrate on details, especially on their thoughts and feelings. Finally, ask students to record their earliest childhood memories. Have students share their responses.

MEETING *individual* NEEDS

LEP/ESL

General Strategies. When some students write about personal experiences, they often settle for general adjectives such as *happy, sad, surprised,* and *scared.* As a remedy, you can have the class brainstorm for synonyms. Start them off with *elated, disheartened, amazed,* and *petrified.* Introducing students early to a thesaurus may be a great help in expanding their vocabularies.

ANSWERS

Exercise 1

Students should freewrite in their writing journals or brainstorm in groups to find at least three important and memorable experiences that can be shared.

The first test is one to think about a bit. Unlike most other papers you write, the focus of a personal narrative is **you.** That's why the word *experience,* not *event,* is significant. You won't write about celebrations for the Chinese New Year just to describe what your neighborhood does, but because those celebrations made an impression on you. What counts is what you saw, heard, did, felt, and thought.

EXERCISE 1 ▶ **Tapping Your Memory for Personal Experiences**

How did you meet your best friend? Have you ever had to think fast in an emergency? Did your favorite aunt give you the world's ugliest sweater to wear to a party? All of these events could be topics for a personal narrative. The subjects and suggestions below can help trigger your memories. Choose two or three of the general topics below and try to remember specific, important experiences about them.

- **People:** family, coaches, friends, neighbors
- **Places:** a treehouse, the gym, a pool, a place to be alone
- **Experiences:** secrets, surprises, borrowing and lending, disappointments, graduations
- **Values:** loyalty, friendship, honesty, maturity

EXAMPLES   People: Neighbors
"I remember the time the baby in the apartment next door wandered off and I helped find her."
Places: The gym
"I remember the time when I shot the winning basket against our biggest rivals."

WRITING ASSIGNMENT

PART 1:
Choosing an Experience for a Personal Narrative

Now put the experiences you've remembered to the test. Ask yourself: Was this experience somehow significant to me? Can I recall details to bring it alive? Do I want to make it public? Choose one personal experience as a topic to write about.

Discuss the information with students. You may want to involve the memories they listed for **Motivation.** Have them consider how their memories fit the three tests. Students should be looking for one good idea that will be suitable for a personal narrative.

Model **Exercise 1** for your students by putting the first category on the chalkboard. Brainstorm aloud for experiences on one or two of the subjects.

For **Writing Assignment: Part 1,** have students choose an experience on which to focus by using the given questions. ☞

Prewriting

Planning Your Personal Narrative

The narrative you'll write is personal, but it's not a diary or journal entry meant for you alone. It's an essay written for others—a way to share your experience. This means planning and shaping your narrative for maximum effect, to communicate what you want.

Thinking About Purpose, Audience, and Tone

Purpose.   Your purpose in this paper is to express yourself. You're telling about something that happened to you and exploring your thoughts and feelings about it. In this remembering and exploring, you'll make some discovery—about yourself, others, or the world around you—and share it with an audience.

Audience.   Making your experience real and alive to an audience calls for details: Solid descriptions of both events and feelings that let your readers live through the experience with you. Think about your particular audience: teacher and classmates? family? Sometimes readers will need background to understand your topic. If you're writing for classmates about a chess competition, they'll probably want to know where and when it occurred, how it was organized, and some basic facts about the game.

Tone.   Since this is a personal expression paper, your voice should come through—as though you're talking directly to readers. You may feel happy or angry or sad about the experience, but you'll sound honest to your readers. Personal expression is informal, which means using everyday vocabulary and sentence structure. And you'll write in the first person, using *I, me, our,* and *we.*

COMPUTER NOTE: If you store your prewriting in files on a diskette, you won't have to worry about keeping track of scraps or bundles of paper.

Use your chosen topic to model the speaking and listening process outlined in **Exercise 2.**

To help students with **Writing Assignment: Part 2,** demonstrate creating a model by using a detail chart or transparency. Use the topic chosen during **Writing Assignment: Part 1.**

Demonstrate **Writing Assignment: Part 3** by using your model detail chart. Circle the key ideas as you develop your statement of meaning.

ANSWERS
Exercise 2

1. Students should write the most important, vivid parts of an experience in their sentences.

2. Narrators should tell groups the same story but with more detail.

3. Listeners should have time between speakers to note conversational words, phrases, or sentence structure.

MEETING *individual* **NEEDS**

LEP/ESL

General Strategies. Writing about themselves may be difficult for some students. Folktales and fables offer an opportunity to talk about personal experiences without direct personal disclosure. Writing a folktale or fable may be an acceptable substitute for writing a personal narrative. Students who choose such an option can still work with the concepts and techniques presented in this chapter.

EXERCISE 2 ▶ **Speaking and Listening: Creating a Natural Tone**

You have a unique style of expressing yourself—a way of talking that is only yours. If you want your writing to sound more like talking, why not try talking it out—with good listeners? To improve tone, try this method with a small group.

1. Think about your topic, write down a few sentences about it, and give them to the group to read.
2. Now *tell* your partners the same information out loud. Just talk—but don't repeat your written words.
3. Ask the listeners to pinpoint differences in your speaking and writing (words, expressions, sentence length), and discuss how to make the written sentences more natural.

Recalling Details

Have you ever had the experience of a certain smell or sound suddenly exploding a whole memory in your head? One whiff of a strong, old-fashioned soap, and you're right back in your grandfather's workshop.

In a way, that's what you need to do in your narrative: provide concrete, sensory details that will *re-create* your experience for readers.

Lively, Specific Details.   Don't just state, for example, that you stood on a diving board. Say instead that your knees had turned to mashed potatoes and that noises from the pool were a blurred roar. Readers will share in your experience if you use details that are specific, not vague, and that appeal to all the senses. See what details you can come up with now, and then add others later when you're writing your first draft.

Helps to Memory.   While some details will leap out of your memory, as fresh as when they happened, others may be cloudy or lost. If so, you can use brainstorming or freewriting to uncover them. You can also talk to other people who were involved (use *their* memories as well as your own) and even revisit places for a firsthand refresher of details.

For **Exercise 1**, give students ten minutes to freewrite or brainstorm on their chosen subjects. Have students concentrate on details and feelings rather than on the sequence of events.

Have students complete **Writing Assignment: Part 1** by applying the given questions to each of the experiences they remembered when deciding on topics for their personal narratives.

Divide the class into groups of three or four to complete **Exercise 2**.

For **Writing Assignment: Part 2**, students might find it easier to recall more specific details if the activity is assigned as homework.

Events, People, and Places. Begin with exactly what happened—first, second, third. Events are the "bones" of your narrative, its framework. First you remember main events: (1) you watched divers at a pool, (2) the lifeguard taught you some dives, and so on. Then you reach back for details about each event: You watched other kids do swan dives but you would only try plain dives from the pool's edge.

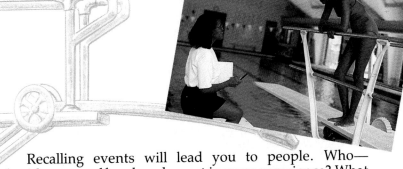

Recalling events will lead you to people. Who—besides yourself—played a part in your experience? What did they look like? What did they say? Telling that your grandfather smelled of a certain after-shave puts your readers right beside him. Use all your senses to describe yourself, another person, even crowds or animals.

Give the same all-five-senses attention to describing place details in your narrative. After all, a place can be a key part of your experience—like a white-water river on a canoe trip. But even if everything takes place somewhere ordinary—like your bedroom—put readers there. Make them *see* your posters, *smell* a candle, *feel* the cold floor.

WRITING NOTE You're telling a story, so use dialogue to add variety and bring people to life. You could write *My mother shouted at us to stop the rehearsal.* But her own words emphasize her mood: *Mother shouted, "Unplug those guitars now—or I will!"* Dialogue should fit the speaker and can be informal, including the use of slang and sentence fragments.

MEETING *individual* NEEDS

LEARNING STYLES

Auditory Learners. Students might benefit from telling their stories to one or more students who could write down the key details. These details then can be given back to the speaker for use in his or her writing. Students can help the storyteller by asking questions that will provide many and varied details for the writer to use. If possible, allow every student to serve as both a storyteller and a listener.

VISUAL CONNECTIONS

Ideas for Writing. In order to teach the importance of concrete details, ask students to consider this photograph of a diving coach and to recall a time when they were taught certain sports or skills. Ask students to gather in pairs and relate their experiences to their partners. Students should list the abstract words their partners use in one column and the concrete details in another. You may then want to challenge students to change their abstract remarks into concrete descriptions.

Have students complete **Writing Assignment: Part 3** by using the notes generated in **Writing Assignment: Part 2** as a resource in determining their statement of meaning.

ASSESSMENT

Have students turn in their charts from **Writing Assignment: Parts 2** and **3** to check for their understanding of gathering and organizing details and interpreting meaning. For **Exercises 1** and **2** and **Writing Assignment: Part 1**, you can use observation and conferencing.

COOPERATIVE LEARNING

Have students work in small groups to prepare their detail charts. Working with others on the details for their narratives might provide them with spontaneous questions and feedback for their charts.

Thoughts and Emotions.   Don't forget yourself in this living picture you're creating. What's going on *inside* you? (Look inside other people, too, if their reactions make a difference.) Use specific words to record your feelings (*furious, delighted*), and use actions, appearance, and dialogue to tell readers how you feel. ("Mashed-potato" knees show fear.) Use a chart like this one to recall and record details.

HERE'S HOW

WHO OR WHAT?	DETAILS
Events	
1. Watching divers at swim center	Kids practicing jackknives, swan dives. I dive (plain ones) from side.
2. Brian offers to help me	He says, "Why not off the board?" Try—really scared—pull it off.
3. Practice and make team	Hard work—lots of bad "landings." Water in face. Keep it a secret.
4. In first meet	Mom, Dad, Gerald, Elizabeth having picnic. My name over loudspeaker. Me on high board (shock). Picture in paper, swan dive.
People	
Me	Shy (not like G. & E.), 12—athletic, always at pool.
Brian	College student, swims like a fish, friendly smile, called me "a natural."
Gerald and Elizabeth	Older, popular, good grades, in clubs ("Oh, you're E & G's sister!")
Mom and Dad	At center a lot with us. Running (terrified I'm drowned). Amazed then proud.
Places	
Center	Pool, activity room, picnic place—really <u>hot</u>.
Pool	Diving boards, lots of kids—noisy.
Thoughts and Feelings	
Envy divers	Imagine being graceful, cutting water cleanly. Afraid to use board.
Surprise and fear!	Don't remember going up on board. Knees soft, roar in head.
Relief	Praise great!
I am a diver!	On high board, seeing family, feeling confident. No medal—but their pride.

Bring to class pictures from current magazines that depict people engaged in different activities. Distribute the pictures to the class and have students work individually or in small groups to prepare charts for the pictures, such as the **Here's How** chart on p. 150.

Ask students what insights they gained as they chose topics for personal narratives and organized their materials. Write their ideas on the chalkboard.

Prewriting   **151**

When recalling details about your experience

- look for specific details and sensory details
- use brainstorming or clustering, interviewing, and observing to help your memory
- focus on events, people, places, thoughts, and feelings

 PART 2:
Recalling Details

Sometimes relaxing is the best way to unlock memory. Make a chart like the one on page 150 to record details, and try closing your eyes and imagining yourself back in time, going through the experience again. Gather as many details as you can. "Replay" the experience in your mind as many times as you need to so you can gather the details you need.

Reflecting on the Meaning of the Experience

As you've recalled details, especially thoughts and feelings, the meaning of your experience has probably become clearer. Now is a good time to try to bring it into focus. Don't be surprised, however, if your understanding of your experience changes as you write your draft.

To reflect on (think about) why the experience was important to you, use these questions.

1. Were you somehow different at the end of the experience? If so, what were you like at the beginning? How exactly did you change?
2. Did you learn something new about yourself? What?
3. Did you learn something new about other people, human nature, or life in general? What was it?

Some unusual insight (never before thought or felt!) isn't what's necessary here. It can be as simple as "I realized that my grandfather would soon be gone. I should spend time with him *now*."

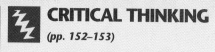
OBJECTIVE

• To interpret the meaning of an experience for a personal narrative

TEACHING *INTERPRETING MEANING*

Read the explanation of interpreting meaning to the class. Then, have students return to their groups from **Exercise 2** to work on the **Critical Thinking Exercise.** Students could use the charts they have created with their notes about main events, thoughts, and feelings for their narratives.

LEP/ESL

General Strategies. Students might benefit from a discussion about how people from other cultures feel when they first move to the United States or move to another city or state. Perhaps they can transfer their thoughts, feelings, and experiences to the story about Jae Rhee and better understand how to come up with the meaning or interpretation of a narrative.

152 *Expressive Writing*

CRITICAL THINKING

Interpreting Meaning

When you *interpret,* you bring out meaning: you explain something, make it understandable. You're used to doing this in literature. For example, a character in a story competes fiercely for a scholarship but in the end turns it down to stay at home with her mother. It's up to you to interpret her action, and you decide the girl just can't bear to leave her mother alone in her last years.

An experience may have more than one interpretation (perhaps the girl also sees that she competed mainly to beat a rival), so—whether in literature or your narrative—you aren't trying to uncover the "correct" meaning. You're trying to state a meaning that makes the facts and details understandable.

 CRITICAL THINKING EXERCISE:
Interpreting the Meaning of an Experience

The following notes give the main events of an experience, along with a person's thoughts and feelings about it. With others, read and discuss the statements, put yourself in the person's place, and suggest a possible meaning for the experience. What could be its importance? Write the meaning in one or two sentences. (You can give more than one interpretation if you want.)

- A Korean boy, Jae Rhee, and his family moved to neighborhood (last year). Not in U.S. long, but Jae's English pretty good.
- Jae and I partners for science experiments so get to know him a little. Jae's shy but tries to do his part in everything. Like him, try to be friendly.
- The Rhees open small store. I go in, Jae's unpacking fruit, says hi. When I pay for milk, Jae's mother looks away (I'm smiling at her), puts change on counter, not in my hand. Feels odd, but forget it.

Members of the groups could help one another with **Writing Assignment: Part 3** as students interpret and state the meanings of their experiences.

EXTENSION

To encourage students to stretch their imaginations, have them do some fantasy writing. Have students pretend to be in a place where they have never been. Have them freewrite their experiences as they imagine the *who, what, where, when, how,* and *why* of this fantasy place. ☞

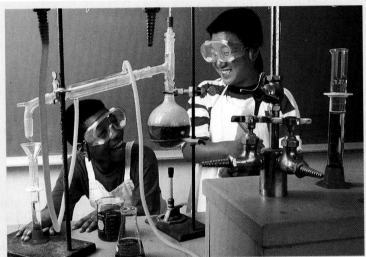

- Happens more (with Mr. Rhee too). Other people—kids *and* parents—start to talk. "Rhees unfriendly. Rude. Think they're better." Feel funny around Jae; just do experiments, don't talk.
- Rhees' store not doing well. One day Jae's not in school—they've moved, new people in store. Surprised, mixed-up feelings.
- Social studies class this year, unit on "cultural differences." Teacher talks about how gestures, feelings about personal space, and respectful behavior differ from one culture to another.

VISUAL CONNECTIONS

Ideas for Writing. Have each student write a dialogue between two students in which one student faces a problem about learning to live in a new environment. The other student should respond or react to the new student's problem. After your students have written their dialogues, they can role-play them or read them aloud.

ANSWERS
Critical Thinking Exercise

Answers may vary.

While the writer has learned something about other people from the experience (people from Asian cultures can mean something completely different by their gestures than Westerners), the writer also has experienced inner change (the writer no longer presumes an understanding of external signals, but looks for deeper communication).

PART 3:
Stating the Meaning of Your Experience

What you've just done for the experience about Jae Rhee, now do for your own experience. Look closely at your notes about main events, thoughts, and feelings, and write one statement of meaning. You can use a simple framework like "I realized that ____," or "At first, I ____, but afterward I ____."

WRITING NOTE

As students consider the possibility of using flashbacks in their narratives, it may help them to see this technique used in a literary piece. A good subject for study would be "An Occurrence at Owl Creek Bridge" by Ambrose Bierce. Have them read the story and examine its sequence of events.

VISUAL CONNECTIONS

Ideas for Writing. After discussing Gary Larson's cartoon, you may want to stress that order is important in composition; however, chronological order is not the only way to arrange narrative events. You may want to remind students that many successful writers and screenwriters use flashbacks to make their works less predictable and more interesting. Challenge students to attempt a flashback arrangement of their narrative events. Remind students to begin with the most important or striking event and then continue with the occurrences that led to the event.

154

Organizing Your Ideas

The natural order for the events of a narrative is *chronological:* what happened first, second, third, and so on. The notes you've made should already be in chronological order, but check to be sure. Do all the events follow in sequence, so that a reader can move easily from one to another?

☞ REFERENCE NOTE: For more help with chronological order, see pages 82–83.

WRITING NOTE

Are there exceptions to the rule of chronological order? Yes. You might start at the end of your experience and then "flash back" to its beginning. For example, in a narrative about losing your ring, you could first describe yourself on hands and knees, under the bleachers, searching for it. After painting that interesting scene for readers, you could explain—in chronological order—how you got there.

"And so you just threw everything together?
... Mathews, a posse is something
you have to *organize.*"

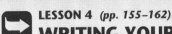
OBJECTIVES

- To analyze the details and meaning of a personal narrative
- To organize and draft a personal narrative

MOTIVATION

Begin the drafting stage of the writing process by having students consider a good personal experience story that they have heard lately. Ask students to list the elements of the story that held their interest. [They might cite the language, the events, the way the teller told the story, the subject matter, who was involved, suspense, or humor.]

Writing Your First Draft

The Structure of Your Personal Narrative

Like other essays, personal narratives have three parts: *introduction, body,* and *conclusion.* You use the introduction—one or two paragraphs—to grab your readers' attention (usually with specific details) and to supply background information: What do readers need to know about people, places, or events to understand your experience? Your introduction may also let your readers know the experience you're going to tell about has a certain importance. It's not just another story.

In the body, you present events in chronological order. To connect these events clearly for readers, you can use transitional words like *at first, then,* and *finally.*

In the conclusion (again, maybe only one paragraph), you bring your essay to a close by explaining the meaning of your experience. But that doesn't mean tacking on a moral—"I learned never to lie"—at the end. It means that the meaning should be obvious to the reader because of the way you've portrayed the experience.

 REFERENCE NOTE: For more help on writing the introduction, body, and conclusion, see pages 122–132.

As you write, remember that—to have a strong impact on readers—a personal narrative

- relates an experience that meant something to you
- describes in specific, sensory detail the events, people, and places important to the experience
- explores your thoughts and feelings
- explains the experience's meaning for you

These elements are basic, but in the hands of different writers, they still produce unique results. In the following narrative, Annie Dillard recalls a childhood incident that still moves her as an adult. As you read, remember that the writer wants you to live through the experience with her. Do you?

 **PROGRAM MANAGER**

WRITING YOUR FIRST DRAFT

- **Instructional Support** For help with writing an essay introduction, see **Writing** in *Strategies for Writing,* p. 3.

QUOTATION FOR THE DAY

"Good writing is not the perfectly tailored garment of a Personage, perfectly pressed since last he wore it; it is the rumpled suit of a living person, still relaxing from the strain of his labors, its pockets stuffed with trash and with things worth getting at." (Martin Joos, 1907–1979, American philologist)

Even though the first draft of a writing assignment needs a structure, students should know that it cannot be perfect at this stage. Ask them to discuss the importance of details as related to this quotation. They might compare "with trash and with things worth getting at" with the details that bring writing to life.

TEACHING THE LESSON

Before students read the professional model, ask a student to read aloud the introductory material on p. 155. Then, refer students to Black Elk's narrative and ask them to identify the beginning, middle, and end of that selection. Students will then need to consider their prewriting and how they might go about arranging their information

USING THE SELECTION
from An American Childhood

1

What kind of rhythmic device does Dillard use here to get our attention?
[Alliteration of the *s* sound and the repetition of the phrase "it turned."]

2

Polyphemus moth: a large, tan American silkworm moth that has an eyespot on each hind wing

3

What sensory details does Dillard use here? ["clawed"; "one leg at a time"; "the wet, mashed thing"; "green jar"]

VISUAL CONNECTIONS
Exploring the Subject. Annie Dillard, 1945– , is an American poet. She is best known for *Pilgrim at Tinker Creek,* for which she won the 1974 Pulitzer Prize in nonfiction.

156

A PASSAGE FROM AN AUTOBIOGRAPHY

from An American Childhood
by Annie Dillard

INTRODUCTION
Feelings/
Meaning of
experience

Summary of
experience

BODY
Event 1
Sensory details

Thoughts and
feelings

Sensory details

Event 2

Background
details

1 At school I saw a <u>searing</u> sight. It turned me to books; it turned me to jelly; it turned me much later, I suppose, into an early version of a runaway, a <u>scapegrace</u>. It was only 2 a freshly hatched Polyphemus moth crippled because its mason jar was too small.

The mason jar sat on the teacher's desk; the big moth emerged inside it. The moth had 3 clawed a hole in its hot cocoon and crawled out, as if agonizingly, over the course of an hour, one leg at a time; we children watched around the desk, transfixed. After it emerged, the wet, mashed thing turned around walking on the green jar's bottom, then painstakingly climbed the twig with which the jar was furnished.

There, at the twig's top, the moth shook its <u>sodden</u> clumps of wings. When it spread those wings — those beautiful wings — blood would fill their veins, and the birth fluids on the wings' frail sheets would harden to make them tough as sails. But the moth could not spread

GUIDED PRACTICE

Have students take turns reading aloud the professional model. Discuss any unfamiliar vocabulary. Prepare students for **Exercise 3** by going through the first question with them. Ask for volunteers to point out the events that occur in the narrative and write these on the chalkboard.

☞

Writing Your First Draft **157**

Detail

Sensory details

Event 3
Details

4

Sensory details

5

Details

Sensory details

its wide wings at all; the jar was too small. The wings could not fill, so they hardened while they were still crumpled from the cocoon. A smaller moth could have spread its wings to their utmost in that mason jar, but the Polyphemus moth was big. Its gold furred body was almost as big as a mouse. Its brown, yellow, pink, and blue wings would have extended six inches from tip to tip, if there had been no mason jar. It would have been big as a wren.

The teacher let the deformed creature go. We all left the classroom and paraded outside behind the teacher with pomp and circumstance. She bounced the moth from its jar and set it on the school's asphalt driveway. The moth set out walking. It could only heave the golden wrinkly clumps where its wings should have been; it could only crawl down the school driveway on its six frail legs. The moth crawled down the driveway toward the rest of Shadyside, an area of fine houses, expensive apartments, and fashionable shops. It crawled down the driveway because its shriveled wings were glued shut. It crawled down the driveway

4
pomp and circumstance: ceremonial procession; showy display

5
Why does the writer repeat the word "crawl"? [Perhaps the repetition is used to emphasize the moth's struggle to survive in the world.]

VISUAL CONNECTIONS
Exploring the Subject. The Polyphemus moth is native to North America. Although butterflies and moths are closely related (they both belong to the lepidoptera order), they differ to an extent. Butterflies usually fly by day and rest with the wings raised over the back; however, moths usually fly by night and rest with their wings wrapped over their bodies or outspread.

158   *Expressive Writing*

Background details	toward Shadyside, one of several sections of town where people like me were expected to settle after college, renting an apartment until they married one of the boys and bought a house. I watched it go.
CONCLUSION Thoughts Details Feelings Event 4 Feelings Meaning of experience	I knew that this particular moth, the big walking moth, could not travel more than a few more yards before a bird or a cat began to eat it, or a car ran over it. Nevertheless, it was crawling with what seemed wonderful vigor, as if, I thought at the time, it was still excited from being born. I watched it go till the bell rang and I had to go in. I have told this story before, and may yet tell it again, to lay the moth's ghost, for I still see it crawl down the broad black driveway, and I still see its golden wing clumps heave.

6

How does Dillard figuratively describe the moth and why? [She uses a metaphor comparing the image of the moth to a ghost, perhaps to make the reader aware of how the image keeps coming back to the author, who learned at an early age how hard it must be for frail things to survive in a world that often doesn't care.]

ANSWERS
Exercise 3

Answers may vary.

1. The moth emerges from the cocoon, walks on a twig, and tries to open its wings. The jar keeps its wings closed. The teacher takes the moth outside. Unable to fly, the moth walks off down the driveway.

2. Students should include a detail such as "gold furred body" and a feeling such as "excited from being born."

SELECTION AMENDMENT
Description of change: excerpted
Rationale: to focus on the concept of expressive writing presented in this chapter

EXERCISE 3▶   **Analyzing a Personal Narrative**

Read the essay about the crippled moth (pages 156–158), and then meet with two or three classmates to discuss these questions.

1. In this experience, the main actor is the moth, and the writer is an observer. What are the events that Annie Dillard describes?
2. Dillard is known for using precise, fresh words to describe both things and feelings. Find a sensory detail about the moth and a detail about feelings that you especially liked—or were surprised by.
3. Where does Dillard work background, or helpful explanations, into her essay? What do you learn?
4. Dillard tells us the importance of the experience in her first paragraph. What do you think the moth meant to her?
5. Dillard reveals the meaning of the experience again at the end of the narrative. How does she do that without tacking on a moral?

ASSESSMENT

Students should turn in their group answers from **Exercise 3.** Mastery of **Writing Assignment: Part 4** can be determined by observation and conferencing or by having students turn in the drafts for evaluation.

RETEACHING

To help students examine the importance of organization and details in a narrative, take a brief story and divide it into about ten or more sections, depending on the length of the story. Divide the class into small groups. Scramble the sections of the story so they are no longer in sequence, distribute the scrambled story to each group of students, and

A Basic Framework for a Personal Narrative

Annie Dillard is a professional writer, and as you saw, she's experienced enough to make her writing more than a little bit out of the ordinary. But when you're learning to write a personal narrative, a simpler model may help. The following narrative shows a good framework for your writing.

A WRITER'S MODEL

The Diving Lesson

INTRODUCTION   Without admitting it to myself, I always seemed to live in the shadows of my older brother and sister. After all, they were "A" students, popular leaders in every club. Whenever I met new people, they'd say, "Oh, you're Elizabeth and Gerald's younger sister!" I liked the attention, but it had a bad side, too. You see, I made average grades, had a few friends instead of hundreds, and was too shy even to join a club. Secretly, I always suspected people wondered how in the world we could be from the same family.

Background information

Feelings

Details

Thoughts

BODY
Event 1   But something magical happened when I turned twelve. That June, my parents began taking the family to a local community center. We could swim, play games, and visit with other families. Actually, though, I'm not sure what my brother and sister did during those hot summer days at the center, because for the first time in my life I was too busy doing my own thing.

Foreshadowing of meaning

Details

Sensory detail

Every day I watched three or four kids practice their dives: jackknives, swan dives, half gainers. I memorized all the names, studied all their moves, and imagined I was the one springing high in

Details

Thoughts

3. The explanation of the moth spreading its wings in the first part of the third paragraph and the description of the size of the jar in the latter part of that paragraph help explain what is happening physically to the moth during emergence. The moth's inability to spread its wings is compared to young people's inability to spread their wings in a stifling community.

4. The experience made Dillard a reader and a "scapegrace." Students might answer that the moth in the jar is a metaphor for how Shadyside clips its youths' wings.

5. The meaning of the experience is revealed through symbolism which catches the reader's attention because of the subtle comparison of the writer's situation and the moth's situation in the last two paragraphs. The meaning of the experience is thus as clear as a tacked-on moral could make it, and yet more subtle.

have them put the story back together. When they have done so, have each group read its story. Compare the results of each group's efforts, and then have students list the types of clues they looked for as their groups organized the stories.

CLOSURE

Allow students to discuss their concerns about this first draft. What difficulties have they encountered? What part of the writing has gone smoothly? What parts of their prewriting have they not used? Have they discovered other information they have now added? Be sure students are aware that these concerns are natural and that everyone

the air, twisting gracefully, cutting into the water without a splash. Instead I did plain dives from the pool's edge. The board was for pros.

Sensory details

Event 2   Then one day it happened. The lifeguard and diving coach, a college student who swam like he'd been born in the water, called to me just as I surfaced from a dive. "Why don't you do that off the board?" he asked. "I could teach you some others." If Brian hadn't been so friendly, I might have tried to escape. But instead I found myself on the board, knees like mashed potatoes, the pool noises just a roar in my head. There was no place to go but in--head first.

Details

Feelings
Sensory details

VISUAL CONNECTIONS
Exploring the Subject. The graceful swan dive is a dive that is made with the diver facing the water and arching her body backward when leaving the diving board. The diver leaves the board with arms and legs extended and eyes fixed on a point at the far end of the pool. As the diver's body rises, she lowers her arms at right angles to her body. As she descends, her eyes focus on a spot in the water that is 3 to 5 feet from the board. This is where the diver enters, arms overhead and body nearly vertical.

EXTENSION

To extend the idea of sensory details in expressive writing, ask students to find some details from their narratives, such as specific places, persons, or actions. Have students take these details figuratively—either through personification, metaphor, or simile—and extend the descriptions as completely as possible. Students might then ☛

Writing Your First Draft **161**

Event 3	"See?" Brian said afterward. "You're a natural." That was the right thing to say, then, because I needed praise. But this "natural" never worked so hard in her life. At first instead of perfect, splashless dives, I took a lot of water slaps in the face. Eventually, though, I was not just graceful but good enough for the center's team. Meanwhile my parents thought I was "playing at the pool."	**Thoughts** **Feelings** **Sensory details** **Thoughts**
Event 4	My mother still likes to tell the next part of this story. One Saturday, she and Dad and my brother and sister were eating lunch at the center's picnic area when they heard my name blared over a loudspeaker. Here Mother always says, "We thought you had drowned!" But by the time they ran to the pool, the announcements were about a diving and swimming meet. However, their shock wasn't over: There was their younger daughter, poised confidently on the board, waiting to execute her first competition dive.	**Details** **Sensory detail** **Feelings** **Details**
CONCLUSION **Meaning of experience**	And what a dive it was! I didn't win any medals in that meet, but I did get my picture in the newspaper (a clean swan dive from the <u>high</u> board) and had the reward of my <u>parents'</u> amazed and proud faces. Looking back, I realize now that my parents didn't need "proof" to think I was worth something. I did. I needed an accomplishment all my own, and diving was it. From then on, I felt like a person, not a shadow.	**Details** **Feelings** **Thoughts**

As you begin to write your first draft, you may find it helpful to model your essay on "The Diving Lesson." It uses the following pattern, or framework. (Notice how the framework allows you to add both events and details about these events according to what's most important in your experience.)

MEETING *individual* **NEEDS**

LEP/ESL

General Strategies. Some cultural groups engage in narration by focusing on events. Students with this orientation might produce episodic renditions of their experiences that may or may not be chronological. You may want to let students know that you encourage various organizational patterns.

create poems from their descriptions.

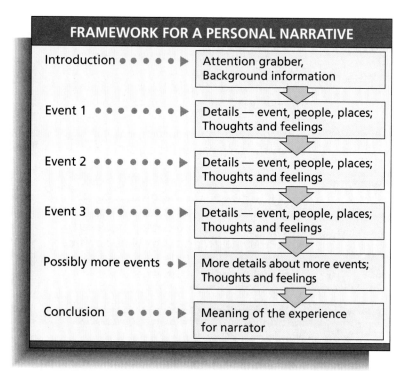

FRAMEWORK FOR A PERSONAL NARRATIVE

Introduction • • • • • ▶	Attention grabber, Background information
Event 1 • • • • • • • ▶	Details — event, people, places; Thoughts and feelings
Event 2 • • • • • • • ▶	Details — event, people, places; Thoughts and feelings
Event 3 • • • • • • • ▶	Details — event, people, places; Thoughts and feelings
Possibly more events • ▶	More details about more events; Thoughts and feelings
Conclusion • • • • • ▶	Meaning of the experience for narrator

WRITING ASSIGNMENT

PART 4:
Writing a Draft of Your Personal Narrative

You have events, you have details, you have a meaning. Now put them all together, sentence by sentence, so that readers can share your experience with you. Using your prewriting notes and following the framework above, write a rough draft.

"A writer's material is what he cares about."

John Gardner

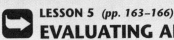

EVALUATING AND REVISING

OBJECTIVES

- To analyze the revisions of a model personal narrative

- To work collectively in evaluating and revising a personal narrative
- To evaluate and revise the content and organization of a personal narrative

Evaluating and Revising

You've just been the writer. Now you have to be a reader. A help in making this about-face is to set your draft aside for a while (to rest from your writer role). Doing this isn't so unusual. Many writers—including some famous ones—rely on reading their drafts as a start on revising them. Ernest Hemingway, for example, says this about rereading and revising (what he calls "editing") his work:

> I rise at first light and I start by rereading and editing everything I have written to the point I left off. That way I go through a book I'm writing several hundred times. Most writers slough off the toughest but most important part of their trade—editing their stuff, honing it and honing it until it gets an edge like a bullfighter's killing sword. One time my son Patrick brought me a story and asked me to edit it for him. I went over it carefully and changed one word. "But, Papa," he said, "you've only changed one word." I said: "If it's the right word, that's a lot."
>
> Ernest Hemingway, *Writers on Writing*

To evaluate and revise your own work, you can use the following chart. If you find a problem indicated in the left-hand column, use the revision technique suggested in the right-hand column.

The Granger Collection, New York.

PROGRAM MANAGER

EVALUATING AND REVISING

- **Reinforcement/Reteaching** See **Revision Transparencies 5** and **6.** For suggestions on how to tie the transparencies to instruction, review teacher's notes in *Fine Art and Instructional Transparencies for Writing,* p. 103.

- **Ongoing Assessment** For a rubric to guide assessment, see **Evaluating and Revising** in *Strategies for Writing,* p. 4.

- **Assessment/Reflection** To assess student work and evaluate progress, see **Portfolio Forms** in *Portfolio Assessment,* pp. 5–21.

- **Computer Guided Instruction** For additional instruction and practice with action verbs as noted in the **Grammar Hint** on p. 166, see **Lesson 2** in *Language Workshop CD-ROM.*

- **Practice** To help less-advanced students who need additional practice with action verbs, see **Chapter 10** in *English Workshop, Fourth Course,* pp. 113–114.

SELECTION AMENDMENT
Description of change: excerpted
Rationale: to focus on the concept of evaluating and revising presented in this chapter

MOTIVATION

Put an excerpt from a story or personal narrative on a transparency after you have deleted most of its sensory details, figurative language, and expressive elements, and added some stiff, formal wording. After students have read the story, ask them if they think the story lacks anything. List their responses on the chalkboard.

TEACHING THE LESSON

At this time, students should check the content of their drafts to make sure that they have provided enough information to interest the reader and that they have organized their stories in such a way that the events are clear.

Work through the first question of **Exercise 4** with your students.

"The joy of life is variety." (Samuel Johnson, 1709–1784, English lexicographer, critic, and writer)

Lead students in a discussion of the areas of their narratives that could be varied (for example, vocabulary, sentence type, and sentence length).

MEETING *individual* NEEDS

ADVANCED STUDENTS

Especially talented writers in a class sometimes feel they gain little from revision sessions. Point out that good writing depends on the writer's ability to make sound decisions and choices, and that good writers usually develop a sensitivity for details, word choices, and organization; therefore, they can identify and improve the weaknesses in their own work. Students also should become more adept at improving their own writing by helping to generate ideas, solutions, and possible alternatives for the problems they see in others' writing.

LEP/ESL

General Strategies. Have students verbalize their analyses of the writer's revisions in **Exercise 4** before answering the questions.

EVALUATING AND REVISING PERSONAL NARRATIVES

EVALUATION GUIDE	REVISION TECHNIQUE
1 Is the tone friendly, honest, and informal?	**Replace** stiff and formal wording with conversational language.
2 Does the writer use first-person point of view?	**Replace** third-person pronouns with first-person pronouns.
3 Is there enough background information?	**Add** details that help readers understand events, people, or feelings.
4 Do details make the events, people, and places clear and real?	**Add** details that appeal to the five senses.
5 Are thoughts and feelings described?	**Add** details about important thoughts and feelings of people in the narrative.
6 Are the events in chronological order?	**Reorder** events in the order in which they happened.
7 Has the writer revealed the meaning of the experience?	**Add** a few sentences to the conclusion showing the experience's importance to you.

Reproduce a paragraph similar to the one in **Exercise 5.** Have students point out areas that need improvement.

Have students work independently on **Exercise 4.**

You may want to have students begin **Exercise 5** independently. Have them make their evaluations and highlight the areas they feel need improvement.

For **Writing Assignment: Part 5,** have students evaluate their narratives, highlighting in different colors words that indicate a friendly and informal tone, background details, sensory details, thoughts, and feelings. Then, have them underline the sentences that express the meaning of their narratives.

When you evaluate and improve your narrative, make sure it

- begins with an attention-grabbing introduction
- includes clear transitions between events and paragraphs
- uses a variety of sentences

EXERCISE 4 ▶ **Analyzing a Writer's Revisions**

Study the writer's revision of the fifth paragraph in "The Diving Lesson" (pages 159–161). Then answer the questions that follow the paragraph.

> "See?" Brian said afterward. "You're a
> natural." That was the right thing to say,
> ~~[because I needed praise.]~~
> then, but this "natural" never worked so   **add**
>   I
> hard in her life. Eventually, though, she   **replace**
> was not just graceful but good enough for   **reorder**
>   [^ splashless]
> the center's team. At first instead of perfect   **add**
>   [took a lot of water slaps in the face.]   Meanwhile
> dives, I did pretty bad ones. My parents   **replace/add**
> thought I was "playing at the pool."

1. Why did the writer add *because I needed praise* in the third sentence? Do you think breaking this sentence into two sentences is a good idea? Why or why not?
2. Why did the writer move the sentence beginning *Eventually, though . . .*? How does this help the meaning?
3. In the same sentence, what's the reason for replacing *she* with *I*?
4. Why did the writer replace *did pretty bad ones* with *took a lot of water slaps in the face*? What's the effect of the change?
5. Why did the writer add *splashless* to the next-to-the-last sentence and *meanwhile* to the last sentence?

Have students turn in both their assignments and group notes from **Exercise 4**. For **Exercise 5**, have the groups turn in their revised paragraphs. To assess **Writing Assignment: Part 5,** have students turn in their highlighted drafts, peer evaluations, and revised drafts.

Ask students to discuss ways of evaluating and revising drafts. List their suggestions on the chalkboard and have them contemplate how they might approach evaluating and revising in the future. Would they do anything differently? ■

ANSWERS
Exercise 5

Responses may vary. Students should correlate their revisions with the **Evaluating and Revising Personal Narratives** chart. They may make revisions to create more conversational language; replace the third-person pronouns with first-person pronouns; add sensory details; reorder events; or add sentences that depict the importance of the event.

TEACHING NOTE

Evaluating Group Work. After students complete the activity in **Exercise 5,** have them briefly evaluate their group's work. Student evaluations should answer the following questions: Who participated in the group? What was the group's task? Did the group stay on task? Did every member contribute to the group? What was the group's greatest strength? Each student also should address his or her own participation and effectiveness in the group.

You may want to have students use the forms **Evaluating Group Participation** on pp. 40–41 in *Portfolio Assessment.*

GRAMMAR HINT

Students can improve their use of action verbs if they understand the difference between linking and action verbs and active and passive voice in writing. As students revise their drafts, they could circle all linking verbs and change them to more active constructions.

166

---

166   *Expressive Writing*

E X E R C I S E 5 ▶   **Evaluating a Personal Narrative**

The following paragraph ends a narrative about losing a ring—a gift from the writer's grandmother. In a small group, evaluate the paragraph and suggest changes to improve it. Use the guidelines on page 164.

> I thought seeing my grandmother's sorrowful face would be the hardest part of the whole experience. What the guilty girl learned was different. My grandmother, gentle and soft-voiced, wasn't upset about her nice ring. She got it when she was nineteen. What she said made a big impression on me. My fear was really hardest.

GRAMMAR
HINT

Using Action Verbs

Action verbs express action, both physical and mental: *She **dances** like a pro and **knows** the new styles.* Action verbs are important in a personal narrative because your whole subject is action of one kind or another: events, thoughts, and feelings. Make them as precise and vivid as possible.

EXAMPLES   I **sprang** high in the air, **twisted** gracefully, and **cut** into the water without a splash.

 REFERENCE NOTE: For more information on action verbs, see pages 524–525.

 PART 5:
WRITING ASSIGNMENT   **Evaluating and Revising Your Personal Narrative**

Now, judge and improve your own paper. Use the chart on page 164 to evaluate and revise your narrative.

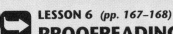
OBJECTIVE
- To proofread and publish a personal narrative

TEACHING THE LESSON

After reviewing problem areas, students can begin **Writing Assignment: Part 6.** Students should inform you of the publishing methods they have chosen and then proceed to publish their personal narratives. Ask students to compare their first and final drafts and to note changes that took place during the writing process. ■

Proofreading and Publishing

Carefully proofread your essay for mistakes in grammar, punctuation, and spelling, and publish it in some way. Here are two suggestions.

- Read your paper to the class. Practice reading out loud beforehand, so that you can read with expression and look up from the page.
- Make a performing script from your narrative for a readers' theater, a class skit, or a video.

PART 6:
Proofreading and Publishing Your Personal Narrative

Read your paper for errors, fix them, and then publish your essay, using the ideas listed above or your own.

   Reflecting on Your Writing

To include your essay in your **portfolio,** date your paper and attach a reflection answering the following questions.

- How did you decide which details to include?
- How did you make the meaning of the essay clear?
- What was the easiest part of writing this essay? Why?

"Most of the basic material a writer works with is acquired before the age of fifteen."

Willa Cather

PROGRAM MANAGER

PROOFREADING AND PUBLISHING

- **Instructional Support** For a chart students may use to evaluate their proofreading progress, see **Proofreading** in *Strategies for Writing,* p. 5.

- **Independent Practice/ Reteaching** For additional practice with language skills, see **Proofreading Practice: Using Action Verbs** in *Strategies for Writing,* p. 6.

- **Assessment/Reflection** To assess student work and evaluate progress, see **Portfolio Forms** in *Portfolio Assessment,* pp. 22–25.

TEACHING NOTE

As students answer the first question, remind them that how they decide which details to include depends on other decisions. For example, ask students to consider how changes in point of view and tone would affect their choice of details.

QUOTATION FOR THE DAY

"Watch your use of the word *because*. You don't have to link sentences up and make reasons for them. The juxtaposition speaks for itself. It is a matter of grammar. Don't get bogged down in the need to explain." (Natalie Goldberg, American writer, poet, and teacher)

A STUDENT MODEL
Evaluation

1. Hilary sets a friendly, informal tone by using first-person pronouns to relate her narrative.
2. Hilary gives enough background information to make clear why she and her brother didn't exercise caution on the water.
3. The details Hilary gives make the situation seem real, and she provides an account of her thoughts and feelings to show how the event affected her.
4. Hilary uses chronological order throughout her essay.
5. Hilary explains the meaning and significance of the experience at the end of her composition.

TECHNOLOGY TIP

To help students get started with the proofreading stage, let them try one of the computer software programs designed for that purpose. The programs highlight various errors, identify them, and offer the user various options for correction.

A STUDENT MODEL

Hilary Hutchinson, a student from Enterprise, Alabama, thought it was hard to decide what to write about in her personal narrative but says that "after I started writing, it got easier to finish the paper."

The Current
by Hilary Hutchinson

It was a beautiful day at Panama City Beach. The gulf was like a huge lake. No waves were to be seen. My brother Blair and I had our floats and were ready to relax in the calm water. My mom sat in the sand while Blair and I ran to the water.

We were floating in the sun when I noticed we were drifting out too far. I saw that I could not touch the bottom. With Blair holding on to my foot, I tried to paddle with my arms, but we were not going anywhere. A current was taking us out to sea!

My mom motioned for us to come closer, but when I was too busy paddling to wave back, she knew something was wrong. With all her clothes on, she jumped into the water to swim to us.

Finally she got there. Blair fell off his float and luckily landed on the edge of mine. His float was swept away by the strong current. With all the energy my mom and I had left, we pulled the float with Blair on it back to shore. Sitting in the sand, we looked out onto the water. Blair's float was a little dot where the sky meets the water. A chill went down me as I thought that Blair and I would have been that far out.

Blair and I are very careful now when we swim. We are also thankful. The week after our incident two men drowned in that same current. People need to learn to be careful and watch what they are doing. I just hope they do not have to learn the hard way as Blair and I did.

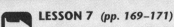
WRITING WORKSHOP

OBJECTIVES

- To analyze a description of a personal utopia
- To use the writing process to describe a personal utopia

MOTIVATION

Begin the **Writing Workshop** by asking students if there are things about the world they would like to change. Have them brainstorm what they would change and why and how they would change things. List their ideas on the chalkboard. Then, have students freewrite on one of the changes and share their responses. ☛

169

WRITING WORKSHOP

Imagining a Utopia

You've looked at the personal narrative as a form of expressive writing. Another form of expressive writing is creating a *utopia.* Long before Sir Thomas More coined the word *utopia* in 1516 (it means "no place" in Greek), people have imagined and expressed in writing their personal, perfect places or worlds. Sometimes they propose a model for the future, and sometimes their utopias are expressed in stories.

One early believer in a utopia was the writer H. G. Wells. (He also wrote *The War of the Worlds* that so terrified Americans when Orson Welles broadcast it on the radio in 1938.) In 1905, Wells described his version of utopia in the book *A Modern Utopia.* In this excerpt, Wells describes transportation in the ideal society. As you read, think about Wells's predictions of his future utopia. How right or wrong was he?

from A Modern Utopia
by H. G. Wells

1 Such great tramways as this will be used when the Utopians wish to travel fast and far; thereby you will glide all over the land surface of the planet; and feeding them and distributing from them, innumerable minor systems, clean little electric tramways I picture them, will

2 spread out over the land in finer reticulations, growing close and dense in the urban regions and thinning as the population thins. And running beside these lighter railways, and spreading beyond their range, will be the smooth minor high roads such as this one we now approach, upon which independent vehicles, motorcars, cycles, and what not, will go. I doubt if we shall see any horses upon this fine, smooth, clean road; I doubt if there will be many horses on the high

3 roads of Utopia, and, indeed, if they will use draught horses at all upon that planet. Why should they? Where the world gives turf or sand, or along special tracts, the horse will perhaps be ridden for exercise and pleasure, but that will be all the use for him; and as for

QUOTATION FOR THE DAY

"The Utopian is a poet who has gone astray." (William Ralph Inge, 1860–1954, Dean of St. Paul's Cathedral, London)

Lead students in a discussion of what "utopia" means [either an idealized place or situation or a visionary scheme for a perfect society]. Then, ask students to agree or disagree with the quotation in short writing journal entries.

USING THE SELECTION
from A Modern Utopia

1
tramway: British, a track for streetcars

2
reticulations: networks

3
draught horses: horses for pulling heavy loads

TEACHING THE LESSON

Discuss with students other ways they can express their emotions using narration [letters, conversation, journals, and diaries]. Then, you can direct students to the selection. Once students understand about utopias and how they might describe one, they can write about their own. After students read the excerpt, have them discuss how they visualize the scene Wells depicts. Then, they can discuss the questions that follow the excerpt.

Students can now proceed through the prewriting, writing, evaluating and revising, proofreading, and publishing steps on their own. They may need several days to complete their descriptions.

4

burthen: archaic for *burden*

5

What imagery do you notice in this passage? ["scented needles of the mountain pinewoods"; "rushing streams"; "wide spaces of the corn land"; "flowery garden spaces"]

MEETING individual NEEDS

LEARNING STYLES

Visual Learners. Because the **Writing Workshop** is an imaginative writing activity, a learner who relies on visual input might need to draw pictures of his or her utopia before writing about it. Or, students could look in books or magazines for pictures. Futuristic artwork might be stimulating to students as they try to visualize what they will be writing about.

SELECTION AMENDMENT
Description of change: excerpted
Rationale: to focus on the concept of expressive writing presented in this chapter

170

4 the other beasts of burthen, on the remoter mountain tracks the mule will no doubt still be a picturesque survival, in the desert men will still find a use for the camel, and the elephant may linger to play a part in the pageant of the East. But the burthen of the minor traffic, if not the whole of it, will certainly be mechanical. This is what we shall see even while the road is still remote, swift and shapely motorcars going past, cyclists, and in these agreeable mountain regions there will also be pedestrians upon their way. Cycle tracks will abound in Utopia, sometimes following beside the great high roads, but oftener taking their own more agreeable line amidst woods and crops and pastures; and there will be a rich variety of footpaths and minor ways. There will be many footpaths in Utopia. There will be pleasant ways over the **5** scented needles of the mountain pinewoods, primrose-strewn tracks amidst the budding thickets of the lower country, paths running beside rushing streams, paths across the wide spaces of the corn land, and, above all, paths through the flowery garden spaces amidst which the houses in the towns will stand. And everywhere about the world, on road and path, by sea and land, the happy holiday Utopians will go.

You may want students to turn in all steps of the writing process to check for mastery and understanding. Assess each step individually before evaluating the final product.

Ask students to summarize what they gained from creating and describing their personal utopias. Do they believe that they have the power to change the world around them for the better? If so, how do they plan to go about making those changes? ■

1. How accurate was Wells's prediction about "clean little electric tramways" that would spread out over the country?
2. In 1905, most transportation was provided by the horse. What was Wells's prediction about the horse? How accurate was he?
3. What role does Wells visualize nature playing in Utopia? Would Utopians be more or less a part of nature than people are today?

Describing a Personal Utopia

Prewriting. Think of something that really matters to you about life in your community or city, the United States, or the world. (You may want to brainstorm about education, environment, government, transportation, male/female roles, or art to find a specific focus.) Then, concentrating on your topic, imagine the utopia, or perfect world, you would want to see one hundred years from now. Use any comfortable prewriting technique to generate details. (See pages 24–34 for more information on prewriting techniques to use.)

Writing, Evaluating, and Revising. There's no set form or length for a personal expression of a utopia. But in this exercise, write informally and describe the utopia in the present tense, as if it actually exists ("No cars clog the streets as electric monorails speed by high overhead.") If possible, have someone read your draft. Can the reader picture your world? make sense of how it works or what it contains? Look for changes that will make the utopia more "real."

Proofreading and Publishing. After you check for errors and correct them, see if you and your classmates can combine your utopias into a single society. Give it a name; find or draw pictures of places, vehicles, and people; write the music that people listen to. Then, through a skit or practiced readings of your papers, present what life is like in your utopia.

Date your paper to add it to your **portfolio,** and attach a brief written reflection that summarizes how you selected appropriate details to illustrate your utopia.

ANSWERS
Writing Workshop Questions

1. Students will probably agree that Wells's prediction about electric tramways has only been fulfilled in large cities. Some might point to electric bullet trains being planned by some cities and might suggest Wells's predictions may yet come true.

2. Wells predicted horses would be used only for pleasure riding. This has proved correct. (Note: He does not mention racing because he is only discussing transportation, not sports.)

3. While this passage deals only with nature in terms of traffic in the future, students should find that Wells sees nature mostly as a decorative background. It isn't depicted as threatening danger, presenting engineering challenges, or even affording useful employment. Wells visualizes Utopians being more a part of nature than people are today as shown in the last four sentences of the excerpt.

COOPERATIVE LEARNING
Students could work in small groups to create their utopias and produce as a group descriptive writing with illustrations that could be used as a wall display.

SELF-EXPRESSION ACROSS THE CURRICULUM
OBJECTIVE

- To write a personal narrative about an encounter with a special animal

SELF-EXPRESSION ACROSS THE CURRICULUM
Teaching Strategies

The selection by Aldo Leopold should be read aloud. Students might then examine the narrative for sensory details, the author's thoughts and feelings, and the meaning of the event. As students look at the suggested activity, you may want to review the steps of the writing process.

Students can now proceed on their own to write personal narratives about their encounters with a special animal.

USING THE SELECTION
Sky Dance

1

What is the comparison here?
[The dance of the bird is metaphorically compared to a live theatrical performance.]

2

woodcock: a small game bird with short legs and a long, sensitive bill used to probe for worms; related to the snipe

---

MAKING CONNECTIONS

SELF-EXPRESSION ACROSS THE CURRICULUM

Science

Animals fascinate people. Whether the setting is a swamp where scientists observe the rare Florida crocodile, or the backyard where your sister watches a nest of wrens, human beings spend some important moments with their furred, feathered, slippery, and hard-shelled friends.

Aldo Leopold was an observer of nature. In this excerpt from *A Sand County Almanac,* he narrates the performance of a male woodcock. As you read, notice the specific details that make the bird's flight seem real.

Sky Dance
by Aldo Leopold

I owned my farm for two years before learning that the sky dance is to be seen over my woods every evening in April and May. Since we discovered it, my family and I have been reluctant to miss even a single performance.

1   The show begins on the first warm evening in April at exactly 6:50 P.M. The curtain goes up one minute later each day until 1 June, when the time is 7:50. This sliding scale is dictated by vanity, the dancer demanding a romantic light intensity of exactly 0.05 foot-candles. Do not be late, and sit quietly, lest he fly away in a huff.

The stage props, like the opening hour, reflect the temperamental demands of the performer. The stage must be an open amphitheater in woods or brush, and in its center there must be a mossy spot, a streak of sterile sand, a bare outcrop of *2* rock, or a bare roadway. Why the male woodcock should be such a stickler for a bare dance floor puzzled me at first, but I now think it is a matter of legs. The woodcock's legs are short, and his struttings cannot be executed to advantage in dense grass or weeds, nor could his lady see them there. I have more woodcocks than most farmers because I have more mossy sand, too poor to support grass.

Knowing the place and the hour, you seat yourself under a bush to the east of the dance floor and wait, watching against the sunset for the woodcock's arrival. He flies in low from some neighboring thicket, alights on the bare moss, and at once begins the overture: a series of queer throaty *peents* spaced about two seconds apart, and sounding much like the summer call of the nighthawk.

3 Suddenly the peenting ceases and the bird flutters skyward in a series of wide spirals, emitting a musical twitter. Up and up he goes, the spirals steeper and smaller, the twittering louder and louder, until the performer is only a speck in the sky. Then, without warning, he tumbles like a crippled plane, giving voice in a soft liquid warble that a March bluebird might envy. At a few feet from the ground he levels off and returns to his peenting ground, usually to the exact spot where the performance began, and there resumes his peenting.

It is soon too dark to see the bird on the ground, but you can see his flights against the sky for an hour, which is the usual duration of the show. On moonlight nights, however, it may continue, at intervals, as long as the moon continues to shine.

At daybreak the whole show is repeated. In early April the final curtain falls at 5:15 A.M.; the time advances two minutes a day until June, when the performance closes for the year at 3:15.
4 Why the disparity in sliding scale? Alas, I fear that even
5 romance tires, for it takes only a fifth as much light to stop the
6 sky dance at dawn as suffices to start it at sunset.

What animal has made a strong impression on you? Write a personal narrative about your encounter(s) with that animal. What was the importance of what happened? What can you generalize from it? Write one paragraph or more, using details to make this animal, what happened, and what you felt come alive for readers.

3
What sensory details are used here? [hearing: "musical twitter," "soft liquid warble," "peenting"; sight: "wide spirals," "tumbles like a crippled plane"]

4
disparity: difference, or lack of equality

5
What seems to be Leopold's meaning of his experience? [Perhaps he sees animals in their naturalistic setting acting out some of the very rituals that humans go through, such as wooing and courting.]

6
suffices: satisfies

GUIDELINES

Students should record specific observations about the animal by noting the time and place of their observations and details of its behavior.

SELECTION AMENDMENT
Description of change: excerpted
Rationale: to focus on the concept of expressive writing presented in this chapter

USING DESCRIPTION

OBJECTIVES

- To analyze the characteristics of descriptive writing
- To use various prewriting techniques to develop writing ideas for a description
- To organize and draft a description
- To evaluate and revise the content of a description
- To proofread and prepare a description for publication

WRITING-IN-PROGRESS ASSIGNMENTS

Major Assignment: Writing a description
Cumulative Writing Assignments: The chart below shows the sequence of cumulative assignments that will guide students as they write a description. These writing assignments form the instructional core of Chapter 5.

PREWRITING
Writing Assignment
• Part 1: Developing a Subject for Your Description p. 185
• Part 2: Collecting Details and Finding an Emphasis p. 189
• Part 3: Organizing Details p. 190

WRITING
Writing Assignment
• Part 4: Writing Your First Draft p. 199

EVALUATING AND REVISING
Writing Assignment
• Part 5: Evaluating and Revising Your Description p. 203

PROOFREADING AND PUBLISHING
Writing Assignment
• Part 6: Proofreading and Publishing p. 204

In addition, exercises 1–5 provide practice in analyzing a model, collecting details, speaking and listening, analyzing a description, and analyzing a writer's revisions.

WORKPLACE writing — Description of the Workplace

Help students acquaint themselves with the workplace by having them interview a working adult about the details of his or her job. Ask students to use the strategies presented in this chapter to write descriptions of a person at work.

- **Interviewing** Students should find someone who has a job that interests them. Guide them toward family members or people in the school community. Students will benefit from working together to create a list of items to focus on in their interviews. Consider the following items.
  - Specific tasks and responsibilities of the job
  - Skills the person uses in performing the job
  - Education/training necessary for holding the job
  - What the person likes about the job

  Students should take accurate notes during the interview so that they can accurately describe what they have seen. They may want to use a tape recorder or video camera to document the person at his or her workplace.

- **Writing, Evaluating, and Publishing** After students have gathered the details they need to write a description, give them time to work independently to organize their thoughts. Remind them that one goal of their writing is to accurately and vividly describe a person's work. (Have students review pp. 191–199 as they write.) Students may find that they need to confirm details with the subject of their interview. Publish students' work by holding a Job Fair in which students present their descriptive writing. They may include visual aids with their descriptions. Encourage students to invite the subjects of their interviews to the fair and to hold a question-and-answer period.

INTEGRATING THE LANGUAGE ARTS

SELECTION	READING AND LITERATURE	WRITING AND CRITICAL THINKING	LANGUAGE AND SYNTAX	SPEAKING, LISTENING, AND OTHER EXPRESSION SKILLS
• **"Date with Dracula"** by D. D. Morrison pp. 176–178 • **"The Most Beautiful Girl in the World"** by S. Bing pp. 184–185 • *Blue Highways* by William Least Heat-Moon p.193 • **"The Swan"** by R. Zabel p. 194 • **"The Street"** by Ann Petry pp. 196–198 • **"Tumbleweed"** D. Wagoner p. 207 • from *Ernie's War: The Best of Ernie Pyle's World War II Dispatches* by E. Pyle pp. 209–210	• Responding personally to literature pp. 178, 198, 207 • Finding details pp. 178, 198, 207, 210 • Analyzing connotation and description pp. 178, 198 • Identifying and analyzing personification pp. 178, 198 • Judging author's purpose, audience, and tone pp. 184–185 • Identifying point of view pp. 184–185 • Recognizing figurative language pp. 196–198, 210 • Recognizing free verse poetry p. 207 • Finding details in poetry p. 207	• Evaluating description and analyzing personification pp. 178, 198, 210 • Analyzing purpose, audience, point of view, and tone pp. 184–185 • Differentiating objective and subjective details pp. 185, 211 • Choosing a subject p. 185 • Collecting details using observation, recall, research, and imagination pp. 188, 189 • Listing and organizing details pp. 189–190 • Using metaphor and simile p. 195 • Evaluating descriptive writing pp. 198, 200, 202–203, 210 • Evaluating and revising p. 203 • Proofreading and publishing a descriptive essay p. 204 • Analyzing poetry p. 207 • Writing a free verse poem p. 208 • Writing an objective description p. 211	• Recognizing connotations of words p. 178 • Using metaphor and simile p. 195 • Proofreading for errors in grammar, usage, and mechanics p. 204 • Proofreading a free verse poem p. 207	• Interviewing for information p. 189 • Working with classmates to evaluate a writer's revisions pp. 202–203 • Reading poetry aloud pp. 207, 208 • Presenting an oral report p. 210

SUGGESTED INTEGRATED UNIT PLAN

This plan gives suggestions on how to integrate the major strands of the language arts with this chapter.

The suggested literary selections are nonfiction pieces that contain descriptive passages. If you begin with this chapter on using description or with the suggested selections, you should focus on the common characteristics of descriptive writing. You can then integrate speaking/listening and language concepts with both the writing and the literature.

Common Characteristics

- Content that is mainly factual but contains objective and subjective elements
- Use of evocative sensory details and figurative language
- Organization on a single, tightly focused subject
- Use of comparisons
- Clear purpose, tone, and emphasis

Writing
Descriptive writing

Language
Usage, style

- Vivid verbs and adjectives
- Parallel structure
- Comparative forms

**UNIT FOCUS
DESCRIPTIVE WRITING**

Speaking/Listening

- Conducting an interview
- Reading poetry aloud

Literature
Nonfiction such as

- from *In Search of Our Mothers' Gardens* Alice Walker
- "On Warts" Lewis Thomas
- "My Friend Moe" Marjorie Kinnan Rawlings

CHAPTER 5: USING DESCRIPTION

Use this guide for creating an instructional plan that addresses the individual needs of your students. Assignments accompanied by the following symbol (∗) may be completed out of class. Times given for pacing lessons are estimated.

CHAPTER PLANNING GUIDE—PUPIL'S EDITION

LESSONS	LITERARY MODEL pp. 176–178 From "Date with Dracula" by Daniel D. Morrison	PREWRITING pp. 181–190	
		Generating Ideas	**Gathering/Organizing**
DEVELOPMENTAL PROGRAM	🕐 **30–35 minutes** • Have pairs of students read the model aloud and answer questions orally on p. 178.	🕐 **45–50 minutes** • Main Assignment: Looking Ahead p. 180 • Focusing Your Description pp. 181–185 • Exercise 1 pp. 184–185 in pairs • Writing Assignment: Part 1 p. 185	🕐 **55–60 minutes** • Planning Your Description pp. 186–190 • Exercise 2 p. 188 in pairs • Writing Assignment: Parts 2, 3 pp. 189, 190
CORE PROGRAM	🕐 **25–30 minutes** • Assign students to read the model in pairs and answer questions together in writing on p. 178.	🕐 **35–40 minutes** • Main Assignment: Looking Ahead p. 180 • Focusing Your Description pp. 181–185 • Exercise 1 pp. 184–185∗ • Writing Assignment: Part 1 p. 185∗	🕐 **45–50 minutes** • Planning Your Description pp. 186–190 • Exercises 2, 3 pp. 188–189 • Writing Assignment: Parts 2, 3 pp. 189, 190∗
ACCELERATED PROGRAM	🕐 **20–25 minutes** • Assign students to read the model independently and to answer questions 3–4 orally with a partner on p. 178.	🕐 **20–25 minutes** • Thinking About Purpose and Audience pp. 181–182 • Deciding on Tone p. 183 • Writing Assignment: Part 1 p. 185∗	🕐 **25 minutes** • Writing Assignment: Parts 2, 3 pp. 189, 190∗ • Organizing Details pp. 189–190

CHAPTER PLANNING GUIDE—PROGRAM RESOURCES

	LITERARY MODEL	PREWRITING
PRINT	• Reading Master 5, *Practice for Assessment in Reading, Vocabulary, and Spelling* p. 5	• Prewriting, *Strategies for Writing* p. 9 • Using Description, *English Workshop* p. 21
MEDIA	• Fine Art Transparency 2, *Transparency Binder*	• Graphic Organizers 7–8, *Transparency Binder* • *Writers Workshop 2:* Observational Writing

WRITING pp. 191–199	EVALUATING AND REVISING pp. 200–203	PROOFREADING AND PUBLISHING pp. 204–206
🕐 **70–75 minutes** • Using Descriptive Language pp. 191–194 • Critical Thinking p. 195 in pairs • Writing Note p. 196 • A Writer's Model p. 199 • Writing Assignment: Part 4 p. 199	🕐 **50–55 minutes** • Evaluating/Revising p. 200 • Evaluating Chart p. 201 • Grammar Hint p. 202 • Exercise 5 p. 202 in pairs • Writing Assignment: Part 5 p. 203	🕐 **55–60 minutes** • Proofreading/Publishing p. 204 • Writing Assignment: Part 6 p. 204 • Reflecting p. 205 • A Student Model pp. 205–206
🕐 **55–60 minutes** • Using Descriptive Language pp. 191–194 • Critical Thinking p. 195 • Writing Note p. 196 • A Passage/Exercise 4 pp. 196–198 • Writing Assignment: Part 4 p. 199*	🕐 **45–50 minutes** • Evaluating/Revising p. 200 • Evaluating Chart p. 201 • Grammar Hint p. 202 • Exercise 5 p. 202 • Writing Assignment: Part 5 p. 203	🕐 **30–35 minutes** • Proofreading/Publishing p. 204 • Writing Assignment: Part 6 p. 204* • Reflecting p. 205 • A Student Model pp. 205–206*
🕐 **30 minutes** • Word Bank p. 192 • Figurative Language Chart p. 194 • Critical Thinking p. 195* • A Passage pp. 196–198 • Writing Assignment: Part 4 p. 199*	🕐 **40–45 minutes** • Evaluating Chart p. 201 • Grammar Hint p. 202 • Writing Assignment: Part 5 p. 203	🕐 **15 minutes** • Writing Assignment: Part 6 p. 204* • Reflecting p. 205

WRITING	EVALUATING AND REVISING	PROOFREADING AND PUBLISHING
• Writing, *Strategies for Writing* p. 10	• Evaluating and Revising, *Strategies for Writing* p. 11 • *English Workshop* pp. 153–154	• Proofreading Practice, *Strategies for Writing* p. 13
	• Revision Transparencies 7–8, *Transparency Binder*	• *Language Workshop:* Lesson 20

ELEMENTS OF WRITING: CURRICULUM CONNECTIONS

Writing Workshop
• A Free Verse Poem pp. 207–208

Making Connections
• Combining Description with Narration pp. 209–210
• Objective Description in Science pp. 210–211

ASSESSMENT OPTIONS

Summative Assessment
Holistic Scoring: Prompts and Models pp. 9–14

Portfolio Assessment
Portfolio forms, *Portfolio Assessment* pp. 5–25, 44–48

Reflection
Writing Process Log, *Strategies for Writing* p. 8
Self-assessment Record, *Portfolio Assessment* p. 19

Ongoing Assessment
Proofreading, *Strategies for Writing* p. 12

💾 Computer disk or CD-ROM

📽 Overhead transparencies

CREATING PICTURES AND IMAGES

OBJECTIVES

- To write personal responses to literature
- To identify and analyze the characteristics of description in writing

TEACHING THE LESSON

You may want to initiate a class discussion about description before beginning the chapter. Begin by asking a student to describe his or her favorite food. Prompt the student with questions about taste, smell, or feel. Then use the resulting description to generate responses to these questions:

PROGRAM MANAGER

CHAPTER 5

- **Computer Guided Instruction** For a related assignment that students may use for additional instruction and practice, see **Observational Writing** in *Writer's Workshop 2.*

- **Additional Instruction** To help less-advanced students who need additional practice with concepts and activities related to this chapter, see **Chapter 5** in *English Workshop, Fourth Course,* pp. 43–50.

- **Summative Assessment** For a writing prompt, including grading criteria and student models, see *Holistic Scoring: Prompts and Models,* pp. 9–14.

- **Extension/Enrichment** See **Fine Art Transparency 2,** *Four Moons* by Jerome Tiger. For suggestions on how to tie the transparencies to instruction, review teacher's notes in *Fine Art and Instructional Transparencies for Writing,* p. 9.

- **Reading Support** For help with the reading selection, pp. 176–178, see **Reading Master 5** in *Practice for Assessment in Reading, Vocabulary, and Spelling,* p. 5.

5 USING DESCRIPTION

1. What type of information helps to describe an object? [sensory details]
2. Why is detailed description necessary? [assists the reader in experiencing the picture or understanding the ideas]

Have a volunteer read the introductory paragraphs of the chapter. Pointing out the sensory details, read aloud the literary model. Explain the importance of these details when describing. The model contains vocabulary that may be unfamiliar to some students; be certain they are able to understand the content.

You may want to guide students through the **Reader's Response** questions and allow a few students to share stories of their own. If students are hesitant to share, you may want to tell a short anecdote of

Creating Pictures and Images

One way to explain what something looks like is to show a picture of it. Another way is to **create a picture or image** with words.

Writing and You. When you read a novel, you feel closer to the main character when you picture what he or she looks like. When you read about the sea, a foreign land, or a mysterious setting, images begin to form in your head. Like painters—Van Gogh, for example—writers help you form these images by appealing to your senses. They bring them to life with their words. Have you ever tried to describe your room to someone who has never seen it?

As You Read. In the following selection, Daniel D. Morrison describes a castle in Romania. As you read, notice how he uses sensory details to bring the scene to life.

Vincent van Gogh, *The Bedroom at Arles* (1888). Oil on canvas, 29 1/2" × 37". The Art Institute of Chicago, Helen Birch Bartlett Memorial Collection, 1926.417. Photograph © 1996, The Art Institute of Chicago. All rights reserved.

 VISUAL CONNECTIONS
The Bedroom at Arles

About the Artist. Vincent van Gogh was born in the Netherlands in 1853. He began painting when he was 27 years old, and moved to Paris at age 33.

In 1889 van Gogh was admitted to a hospital at Saint-Rémy for treatment of his mental illness, but he committed suicide the following year. Although van Gogh is considered an impressionist painter, his work differs from that of other impressionists, who painted realistic subjects in an expressive style. Van Gogh adapted impressionist techniques to paint what he imagined, and referred only indirectly to reality.

QUOTATION FOR THE DAY
"The artist picks, perhaps, just a tiny corner of life and shows you how life really is." (Jean Renoir, 1894–1979, French film director)

MEETING *individual* **NEEDS**

LESS-ADVANCED STUDENTS

Students might need help to understand *connotations* as discussed in **Writer's Craft.** Explain that words can have very close meanings (denotation) but have very different feelings (connotations). Give several examples to illustrate this concept, such as *curious* and *nosy* or *remind* and *nag.*

your own. Discuss the slide glosses of the model with your students to model analyzing literature.

Before asking students to answer the **Writer's Craft** questions on their own, make sure all students understand the words *personification* and *connotations*.

Ask the class to give a brief explanation of *description* and to explain the importance of sensory detail. Have students think of at least three situations in which description would be important.

from

"DATE WITH DRACULA"

by Daniel D. Morrison

USING THE SELECTION
from **Date with Dracula**

1

British author Bram Stoker's novel *Dracula* (1897) helped to popularize the legend of the vampire. In these legends that originated in Asia and Europe, the vampire is an unsettled soul, usually a criminal, who must suck human blood to survive. All of the evil-doing was done by night; the vampires must return to sleep in their coffins during daylight.

2

What kind of place is Morrison describing? How do the words he uses make you feel about the castle grounds? [It is a frightening place. The words are full of evil or danger.]

3

What does the character probably imagine is coming toward him? What do you think Morrison intends you to think is coming? [Answers may vary. A likely answer is Dracula.]

1

2 Dracula once stood on the steps where I was now standing. I backed slowly away from the castle door and sat on a large rock overlooking the castle grounds. It was nearly dark now. The trees glared silently but shook their branches with <u>malevolent</u> intent; the rocks all around me squatted like black <u>gnomes</u>. A mist began to fall down upon the valley, wrapping the mountains in a dirty gray shroud. Below me, on the hillside, the leaves rustled; someone, or something walked toward me. Then it stopped. Was it watching, waiting?

My fears now rising uncontrollably, I decided to return to the shop below to join Monique. But as I turned to walk down **3** the trail, I could hear someone coming up the trail toward me, so I called out, no more than a whisper. "Monique?" There was no answer, but the steps continued their steady advance on the gravel trail. I called again; again, no answer. I backed up to where the hilltop ended in a precipice. I could retreat no farther.

ENRICHMENT

You might want to have students read the British novel *Dracula* by Bram Stoker. Published in 1897, this novel has been the basis for several film versions, including *Nosferatu* in 1922, *Dracula* in 1931, and *Bram Stoker's Dracula* in 1992. ■

VISUAL CONNECTIONS
Exploring the Subject. The actor Bela Lugosi starred in Tod Browning's classic film *Dracula* (1931). Dozens of vampire movies followed throughout the twentieth century. Lugosi's Dracula, with his pallid face, protruding incisors, and dark hair, helped to create the vampire stereotype known today.

"There was nothing I could do, nowhere to run, no one to help me."

Whoever it was—whatever it was—continued to approach, hidden from view by the boulders strewn among the trees. I stood waiting, the sound of my heart competing with the excited voices in the forest.

4   Slowly, steadily, a low dark form rounded a boulder and crested the hill. A dog, all broad shoulders and massive muscles, walked toward me, its head hung low to the ground, its eyes staring directly at me. It had thick, black fur, with a wide muzzle, lips curled back just slightly with the hint of a snarl. It walked with purpose in its steps, the stare <u>malicious</u>. The animal blocked my only avenue of escape. There was nothing I could do, nowhere to run, no one to help me.

4

What senses does Morrison use in describing the dog? [sight, hearing, touch]

As the dog neared, I could hear its labored breath, could see the drool on its jowls, the white of its pointed canine fangs. Its eyes locked onto mine and never blinked. This, I thought, has to be a nightmare. The voices in the trees grew louder, then hushed as if in anticipation of what was about to happen. The creature walked to within a few feet of where I stood, and it seemed I could feel the heat of its moist breath on my face, on my neck. Then it stopped.

READER'S RESPONSE

1. Do Morrison's descriptions seem real and believable to you? Why? How do they make you feel?
2. Like Morrison, have you ever been frightened by your own imagination? (Why not swap stories with your classmates?)

WRITER'S CRAFT

3. What are five specific details from the description that appeal to your senses of sight or hearing?
4. Descriptive writers sometimes use personification— giving human qualities to nonhuman objects—to help tell about a scene or an incident. How does Morrison use personification to describe trees and rocks?
5. Connotations—the emotional overtones—of words are often important in descriptions. In Morrison's description of the dog, what are some words that especially make you see and feel the author's terror?

ANSWERS

Reader's Response

Answers will vary.

1. Morrison's descriptions do seem real and believable because they are so detailed and concrete and because they play on a variety of senses. They make the reader feel as if he or she were present at the scene.
2. Each student should have a different story to tell.

Writer's Craft

Answers will vary.

3. "nearly dark" (sight), "rocks . . . squatted" (sight), "mist began to fall" (sight), "leaves rustled" (hearing), someone, or something walked toward me" (hearing—he cannot see it yet)
4. Morrison writes that "the trees glared silently but shook their branches with malevolent intent," and "the rocks . . . squatted."
5. "lips curled . . . with the hint of a snarl," "the stare malicious," "drool on its jowls," "white of its pointed canine fangs," "never blinked," "creature"

SELECTION AMENDMENT
Description of change: excerpted and indention added
Rationale: to focus on the concept of descriptive writing presented in this chapter

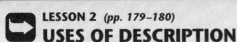
TEACHING *USES OF DESCRIPTION*

This lesson is designed to give students a simple overview of the possible uses of description. Discuss the different purposes of writing—informative, expressive, persuasive, and creative—and have students suggest additional examples for each. If possible, point out uses of description in examples you suggest. You may also want to bring newspaper articles to class and to ask students to identify the use of description in different articles, as well as the purposes behind the articles.

Another way to help students focus on descriptive writing is to have them listen

179

Uses of Description

Descriptive writing usually has a primary purpose. This is true whether the author is trying to present an accurate description of something real or a picture that reveals his or her feelings or beliefs. The author carefully chooses details that support the primary purpose. There are many uses of description. Here are some examples.

- in a newspaper article, describing the grand opening of a music store with a high-tech interior
- in a report for an archaeologist, describing the landscape and finds at a dinosaur dig in Colorado
- in your journal, writing about a school or community event that particularly affected you
- in a letter to the editor, describing the success of a fund-raising dinner
- in an article for a city magazine, describing the effects of pollution on a specific lake or river to persuade people to clean up the environment in the region
- in a letter to the city council, describing a neglected area of town to convince council members to improve conditions
- in a short story, creating the setting and describing the characters
- in a poem, re-creating the sights and sounds of a storm that caused boats to break loose from their moorings
- in a memorandum to your supervisor, describing the tasks that need to be accomplished on a new project

If you pick up a brochure at a travel agency, you'll find a description of faraway lands. If you read the sports section of your local newspaper, you'll find descriptions of specific plays made by the players of various sports. If you look for them, you'll find descriptions around you everywhere—in novels, in encyclopedias, in news stories, in poems, in biographies, even in textbooks. Descriptions, if they are effective, have one thing in common—they "paint a picture" in the mind of the reader.

COOPERATIVE LEARNING

Divide the class into groups of four or five students. Give groups several old magazines and ask students to find examples of descriptive writing in articles or advertisements. You may also want students to create collages of the descriptions and to label the different purposes for which descriptive writing is used.

Assess students' understanding of the purposes by having individual students tell which purpose a specific use of description is trying to achieve. ■

◈ INTEGRATING THE LANGUAGE ARTS

Literature Link. If the work is available in your literature textbook, ask students to analyze the use of description in Mark Twain's "A Genuine Mexican Plug." Have students label the purpose of different selections of descriptive writing from the story. For example, ask students if Twain's first-paragraph description of horse riding is mainly intended to be informative, expressive, persuasive, or creative. You may want to point out to students that although Twain's primary purpose is expressive, he also informs and entertains.

180 *Using Description*

LOOKING AHEAD

In the main part of this chapter, you'll write a description that is subjective. Your primary purpose will be expressive or creative. Keep in mind that descriptive writing

- uses precise words
- provides sensory details that re-create in the mind of your reader a person, place, thing, or event
- is organized in a manner that is easy to follow

" Don't describe it. Show it. That's what I try to teach all young writers – take it out! Don't describe a purple sunset, make me see that it is purple."

James Baldwin

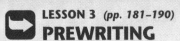
OBJECTIVES

- To analyze purpose, audience, and tone in an expressive/descriptive passage
- To develop an appropriate topic for descriptive writing
- To use observation, recall, research, and imagination to collect details
- To collect details by conducting an interview
- To choose an impression for a description
- To organize details for a description

Writing a Description

Focusing Your Description

Have you ever been in a movie audience when the picture became fuzzy, and the audience began to chant "Focus! Focus!"? Like a clear, sharp movie image, a good description also needs a focus. Before you write, bring your description into focus by thinking about your subject, your purpose and audience, and your attitude toward the subject.

Choosing a Subject

Many times outside circumstances decide the subject of your description for you. For example, if you were involved in an accident, you'd need to describe the damage for an insurance claim. Or, your history teacher might ask you to describe conditions that led up to the French Revolution.

But if the choice of a subject is yours, it's a good idea to think of a specific person, object, or place that you already know well or that you can observe directly.

Thinking About Purpose and Audience

At times, good description stands on its own. For instance, you may just want to recapture a specific moment for your journal. More often, however, good description is used for a specific *purpose*, as an important part of other types of writing. For example, if you're writing to inform your chemistry teacher about the results of your lab experiment, part of your report might be a description of the color, texture, and odor of the resulting solution. Or, if you're writing a letter to the editor urging an all-school, anti-litter campaign, your most convincing support might be a detailed description of the bleachers after last Saturday's game.

PROGRAM MANAGER

PREWRITING

- **Self-Assessment** Before beginning instruction of the writing process, see **Writing Process Log** in *Strategies for Writing*, p. 8.

- **Heuristics** To help students generate ideas, see **Prewriting** in *Strategies for Writing*, p. 9.

- **Instructional Support** See **Graphic Organizers 7** and **8**. For suggestions on how to tie the transparencies to instruction, review teacher's notes in *Fine Art and Instructional Transparencies for Writing*, pp. 65, 67.

QUOTATION FOR THE DAY
"Every novel is an attempt to capture time, to weave something solid out of air." (David Beaty, 1919–   , British novelist)

You may wish to use the quotation to help students begin thinking about the subjects, purposes, and audiences for their descriptive writing. Ask students to recall novels or short stories they have read recently and to freewrite for a few minutes about some scenes or descriptive details they remember. Lead the class to understand that details help make descriptions more memorable and more realistic.

Begin by having students brainstorm a list of possible topics. As they make suggestions, have a student list the possibilities on the chalkboard. Urge students to give as many ideas as possible to show them the diversity of subjects they might choose to describe.

As you read over the material on audience, purpose, and tone, remind students that these considerations will eliminate some of the numerous ideas presented during the **Motivation** or that they have come up with on their own.

For each stage of the prewriting material, have student volunteers read the text-

MEETING *individual* NEEDS

LEP/ESL

Asian Languages. The word *tone* has several meanings in English, such as "musical sound," "body condition," "aspect of writing," and "aspect of some languages." Chinese, Thai, Lao, and Vietnamese also have tone; in these languages the meaning of a word depends on the musical pitch at which it is spoken. For example, *bain* in Vietnamese may mean "three," "grandmother," or "cypress," depending on pitch.

LESS-ADVANCED STUDENTS

To aid students in gathering details and to help strengthen their powers of observation, have them use a cluster organizer like the following example:

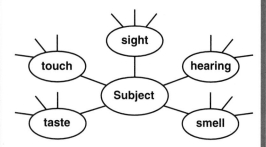

Your *audience* for a description is usually very closely tied to your purpose. As you think about why you're writing your description, consider your readers by asking:

- Who is going to read this?
- Why are they reading it?
- What do I want my audience to think, feel, do, or know after reading my description?

Once you know why you're writing a description and who your audience is, you'll also know whether your description should be *objective* or *subjective*.

Objective Description. An *objective description* creates an accurate, thorough picture without revealing a particular judgment or feeling about the subject. You write this kind of description when your purpose is to inform and sometimes to persuade. Objective description consists mostly of realistic, or factual, details, as this short description of a starfish shows.

A typical starfish has five arms, one of which is slightly bent. Its surface is etched with small nodules. Many starfishes are a uniform color, a pale mustard yellow.

Subjective Description. A *subjective description* creates a selective picture that reveals the writer's thoughts and feelings about the subject. When your purpose is to express yourself, to be creative, and sometimes to persuade, you will probably write a subjective description. Subjective description consists mostly of sensory details and figurative language (see pages 191–194), as this second starfish description on the next page shows.

book explanations and examples to aid in understanding the concepts and skills of descriptive writing. Reinforce for students that expressive writing is solely for self-expression; therefore, it is controlled only by what the writer wants, not by what another reader likes. This concept could be confusing when you address audience and point of view.

GUIDED PRACTICE

To help prepare students to answer questions about purpose, audience, and tone in **Exercise 1**, copy parts of both of the objective and subjective descriptions about the starfish (p. 182) on the chalkboard. Discuss with students possible audiences, purposes, and tones of each description. ☞

> When I look at the starfish skeleton on the table, it almost seems alive. It's like a little man, his head bent slightly as he looks at me and points with one hand back to the sea where I found him.

Deciding on Tone

You also focus your description by deciding on an appropriate tone. In an objective description, you usually use a more formal, impersonal tone. To remain more distant from your subject, you usually use the ***third-person point of view***—pronouns such as *it, she, he,* and *they.* Like the writer of the objective description about the starfish, you aren't in the picture at all—you remain separate from it, never revealing your own thoughts and feelings.

In a subjective description, you often use an informal, personal tone to bring yourself close to the subject. Like the writer of the subjective starfish description, you put yourself in the picture by including your own thoughts and feelings. In this case, you use first-person pronouns such as *I* and *we*—the ***first-person point of view.*** (In some instances, such as writing a description to persuade an audience, you may choose a third-person point of view instead.)

Charting the decisions you make now can help you focus your description as you continue developing it. For example, if your subject is the black-necked crane of Asia, you might record your decisions this way.

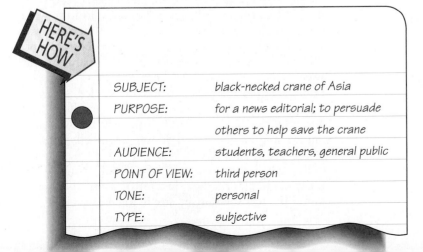

SUBJECT:	black-necked crane of Asia
PURPOSE:	for a news editorial; to persuade others to help save the crane
AUDIENCE:	students, teachers, general public
POINT OF VIEW:	third person
TONE:	personal
TYPE:	subjective

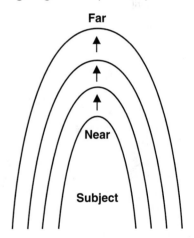

Work with students to describe another animal objectively or subjectively. Then students might speculate on the audience, purpose, and tone involved.

Use this class discussion to help guide students in their choices of a writing topic.

To help students with **Exercise 2**, practice gathering details with the class.

Divide the class into four groups and assign each group a collecting method: direct observation, recall, imagining, or researching. Have each group use one of the topics generated during **Motivation** to list all details about that topic that it can. (The research group might need some time in the library or with resource materials.) Then have each

INTEGRATING THE LANGUAGE ARTS

Reading Link. You may want to reinforce the importance of point of view in establishing the tone in writing. Present several magazine or newspaper articles with differing points of view to your students. Guide your students in a discussion of the differing effects of first-person point of view versus third-person point of view.

CRITICAL THINKING

Analysis. Have students rewrite an editorial from a current newspaper or magazine by using a point of view different from that used by the author. For instance, if the article were written in first person, it should be rewritten in third person. Divide the students into small groups to analyze the different effects of the original article and the rewrite. One student in each group should be designated as the reporter. This student will report the group's decisions to the entire class.

Saving the Black-necked Crane

E X E R C I S E 1   **Analyzing Purpose, Audience, and Tone**

Read this description about an unusual dog named Elizabeth. Then answer the questions that follow.

I named the dog Elizabeth. Height: about thirty inches. Weight: thirty-five pounds. Eyes: brown. Tongue: red. Tail: rich and plumy. A coat of pure china white, so thick and lustrous and profuse that people would later suggest that I shear her and turn the output into a serape. In the summer she shed badly. In the winter, worse. All my clothes and furniture were coated with a fine layer of white flax. When she was young, her tummy was as pink as a baby's bottom, and she had a marvelous, doggy smell, clean, pungent, yet sweet. Her personality? All I can say is that when the Lord made her, he forgot to add any malice, guile, or aggressiveness. Didn't chase squirrels, even. If another dog attacked her, she would roll over on her back immediately and expose her soft underbelly, clearly conveying the message: "Go ahead and kill me. I don't mind, but I think it would be a totally unnecessary waste of energy. But hey, just my opinion." Not once in her life was she hurt by any living creature.

group list its details on the chalkboard. Emphasize the large number and variety of details generated by these collection methods.

Before assigning **Exercise 3,** discuss possible interview questions with your class. Have students make lists of questions from the suggestions of other students.

Between assigning **Writing Assignments: Part 2** and **3,** discuss with students possible organizational methods. Remember that some students will need extra time for research and for arranging interviews before completing these writing assignments.

☞

Illustration by
Blair Dawson.

Elizabeth was not smart, but she made the most of it. "She's the sweetest dog in the world," said a friend about her. "But she's got an IQ somewhere between a brick and a houseplant." . . . For all intents and purposes, she was mute: Not a bark, yelp, nor whimper escaped her. In fourteen years, I heard her voice maybe three times. It was always a shock.
Stanley Bing, "The Most Beautiful Girl in the World"

1. What is the author's purpose: to express himself, to inform, or to persuade the reader to do or believe something? How can you tell?
2. Who do you think is the writer's audience? Why would they be reading this description?
3. What is the writer's tone? How does he feel about his subject?
4. What point of view does the writer use?
5. Is the description objective or subjective? How can you tell?

PART 1:
Developing a Subject for Your Description

The writer of the description you've just read wrote about his dog. Now, choose a specific person, place, or object as the subject for your own subjective description. Then, fill out a chart like the one on page 183, recording your ideas about your subject, purpose, audience, point of view, tone, and type.

ANSWERS
Exercise 1

1. The writer is primarily expressing his own experience. It is written as a personal reminiscence. He is also informing and entertaining the reader.

2. The audience is probably other dog owners/lovers who are reading for pleasure.

3. The tone is informal and humorous. The writer is close to and fond of his subject.

4. The writer uses first-person point of view.

5. The description is subjective. It uses informal, conversational style and tone (for example, sentence fragments, imaginary speeches from the dog, and slang words like *tummy*) and first-person point of view to reveal the writer's feelings about the dog. Words and phrases such as "marvelous," "sweetest dog in the world," and the statement about Elizabeth's IQ clearly convey personal impressions.

SELECTION AMENDMENT
Description of change: excerpted
Rationale: to focus on the concept of purpose, audience, and tone presented in this chapter

Prewriting

Planning Your Description

Have you ever arrived at the library without your library card or shown up for a test without a pencil? Anyone making an extra trip to retrieve the library card or to find a pencil probably has vowed to plan ahead next time. In writing a description, planning ahead means collecting details, determining an emphasis for your description, and organizing details. It will be time well spent.

Collecting Details

An effective description is made up of specific details. You can collect these details in several ways.

Observing Directly. If you're writing about something you can observe firsthand, go directly to the source and study your subject carefully. For example, if you're describing your bicycle for a newspaper classified ad, look at the bike carefully. What is the exact color? Is the seat leather or vinyl—smooth or textured? How tall is it?

Recalling. Sometimes your description may be about a subject you've seen before but can't observe directly now. Then, you have to tap into all the little details stored in your memory. Imagine yourself back in the time when

you were actually observing your subject. For example, you might describe your experience last year at the Indianapolis 500 auto race. To re-create the scene, you would try to remember the sights (mobs of people), the sounds (loud roar of engines), and the smells (oil and grease).

Researching.   Sometimes you may have to describe a subject you haven't experienced directly. In this case, you can gather details from other sources: books, magazines, pictures, audiovisual materials, or interviews. For example, you might collect details about undersea sights and sounds by watching a Jacques Cousteau film. You might collect details on George Washington's life and appearance by reading an encyclopedia article, biography, or collection of letters and by observing his portraits.

Imagining.   Description can move beyond the boundaries of reality. To create a description of an imaginary person, place, or object, begin with what you know. For example, you know the features you'd identify in describing a real person. To create an imaginary one, just create the details in your mind—for a man, you'd decide on the color of his hair, the shape of his nose, the way he walks, stands, sits, talks, and so on.

Identifying an Emphasis

At times you may want to describe all parts of your subject. At other times you may want to create a special *emphasis,* or impression. For example, if you're trying to persuade your classmates to save the sandhill crane, you may want to emphasize its beauty. In this case, you would probably gather details about how the sandhill crane looks in majestic flight. However, you'd probably omit the loud penetrating noise that the crane makes. Or, in describing your dog, you may want to emphasize its friendliness. Details such as "sparkling eyes" and "thumping tail" would support this impression, but "muddy paws" or "matted fur" would not.

Decide whether you want your description to convey a particular impression, and, if so, what it will be. Then evaluate the details you've gathered to decide which ones support that impression.

Write a brief description of a room on the chalkboard. Do not put the details in any specific order; rather, make the description convoluted and confusing. Work with students to rewrite the sentences in a new order that helps in understanding what the room really looks like.

Ask students to discuss the successes and difficulties they had while gathering details. Students should describe which collecting methods they found most helpful. Remind them that their descriptions are not written yet, and they may find more details to add in later.

188   *Using Description*

ANSWERS

Exercise 2

Details will vary, but students should include details for senses other than just sight. For instance, the shoes might "click" or "whisper" as the wearer walks.

1. Each student should look carefully at the shoe and note its texture, color, shape, and odor. The student may also want to think about the way the shoe now feels on the foot. Observations should involve a variety of senses.

2. The student should at the same time compare the shoe with the way it once looked.

3. Each student should choose a specific kind of shoe for research.

4. It is very important that the student have a specific purpose in mind. Are the shoes for dress? For class? For running? For basketball? For hiking? Each purpose involves a different kind of shoe.

EXERCISE 2 ▶	**Collecting Details**

Using the following steps, exercise your collecting skills on the subject of shoes.

1. Observe one of the shoes you're wearing now.
2. Recall how your shoe looked when it was new.
3. Research a shoe. Read up on high-button shoes or the latest trends in athletic shoes.
4. Imagine the "perfect" shoe: design and describe the "perfect" shoe for a specific purpose or for a special outfit.

On your paper, make a copy of the following chart. Use it as a guide for collecting as many kinds of details about shoes as you can. You probably won't fill in all the spaces.

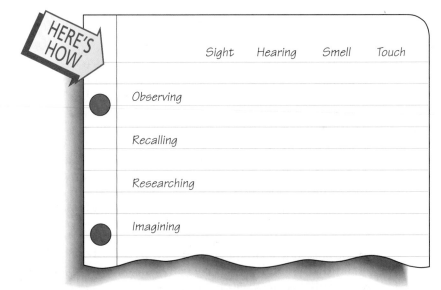

HERE'S HOW

	Sight	Hearing	Smell	Touch
Observing				
Recalling				
Researching				
Imagining				

EXTENSION

Have students extend their observational skills to write informative paragraphs using the narrative and descriptive modes. First, each student should choose a person to observe and then watch and record every detail of the person, the actions, and the setting. Then the writer will make a conclusion about the subject based on his or her observations and use this judgment as the topic sentence. Support should include sensory details and narrative details (actions). An example of a topic sentence might be, "It was obvious that the teacher wanted the day to end." ■

EXERCISE 3 ▶ **Speaking and Listening: Collecting Details**

Another way to gather details when you can't observe directly is to interview someone who has. To gather details about shoes teenagers once wore, interview a parent or an older friend or relative about their shoes when they were your age. Ask questions about style and appearance, but also ask for details related to other senses as well. For example, how did the shoes sound when the person walked down the sidewalk?

WRITING ASSIGNMENT

PART 2:
Collecting Details and Finding an Emphasis

Now that you're experienced in collecting details, concentrate on details for the subject you selected in Writing Assignment, Part 1 (page 185). List as many details about your subject as you can, using any of the techniques for gathering details: observing, recalling, researching, and imagining. If you feel it's appropriate, decide on an emphasis or impression you'd like to convey, too.

Organizing Details

You can create a vivid picture and highlight your emphasis by presenting details in a clear order. Spatial order, order of importance, and chronological order are three possibilities for doing this. The order that you actually use will depend on your purpose for writing and how you want your readers to feel or think.

TYPE OF ORDER	WHEN TO USE	EXAMPLE
spatial (from top to bottom, from side to side, from near to far)	primarily for sight details; to show how details are located in space	describe how a building looks from top to bottom or from left to right
importance (from least to most important, from most to least important)	for all types of details; to identify emphasis or to convey an idea or impression	describe sounds in the woods on a dark night, loudest to softest
chronological (time order)	for all types of details; to show the order in which events or actions occur	describe a crying child as she begins to cry and then gets louder and louder

☞ **REFERENCE NOTE:** For more information on the types of order, see pages 82–85.

To plan your description

- observe, recall, research, or imagine your subject
- identify an emphasis or impression you want to convey
- arrange your details in a clear order

PART 3:
Organizing Details

Look carefully at the list of details you gathered in Writing Assignment, Part 2 (page 189). Thinking about your purpose, audience, and emphasis, decide on the best way to present your details. Add, subtract, or change any details that don't fit your plan. When you've finished, number the details in the order you think you'll be using them in your description.

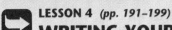
WRITING YOUR FIRST DRAFT

OBJECTIVES

- To analyze a description
- To write a first draft of a description

MOTIVATION

Give students one minute to look intently at a large poster or picture at the front of the room. Then have them freewrite a detailed description of the picture or poster. Allow students to share their descriptions with the class. Students who caught details not mentioned by others may want to point out these details. Bring the class to a

Writing Your First Draft

Now that you've collected and organized details for your description, it's time to write your first draft.

To create a clear image of your subject, you need to select specific words. For example, when the writer William Least Heat-Moon describes a room lighted by "three fifty-watt bulbs," you know exactly how much and what kind of light there was. When you describe how the sun reflects off a new car, *glinted* gives your readers a more specific picture than *shone*.

Good descriptions include specific adjectives, adverbs, nouns, and verbs that appeal to your senses. They may also include comparisons that help you understand the subject and give you new insights. When Virginia Wolfe describes sea anemones "stuck like lumps of jelly to the side of the rock," you understand how a sea anemone looks even if you haven't seen one firsthand.

Using Descriptive Language

Sensory Words. When you write, words and phrases that appeal to the senses make your observations come alive for your readers. Whenever possible, use the precise sound—*roared,* or *twittered,* or *cawed;* or touch—*icy* or *slimy;* or taste—*bitter* or *sour;* or smell—*rotten* or *sweet.* If you don't have a name for a smell, or a taste, or a touch, just name the source of the observation—"the scent of freshly baked bread."

PROGRAM MANAGER

WRITING YOUR FIRST DRAFT

- **Instructional Support** For help with writing a descriptive paragraph, see **Writing** in *Strategies for Writing,* p. 10.

QUOTATION FOR THE DAY

"You can get help from teachers, but you are going to have to learn a lot by yourself, sitting alone in a room." (Theodor Seuss Geisel, "Dr. Seuss," 1904–1991, American children's author and cartoonist)

As students begin writing their first drafts, share the quotation with the class. Explain that creating the first draft of a description is a part of the process that writers most often do by themselves. Tell students that they alone have access to the mental pictures they want to recreate on paper by using sensory words and figurative language.

VISUAL CONNECTIONS

Ideas for Writing. You may want students to locate pictures of various types of sea anemones in encyclopedias or other books and to write sensory descriptions of each type found. This collection of descriptive phrases and colorful pictures might make a pleasant display.

consensus on the prominent details. Explain to students that this vivid description is what they want to capture in their own writing.

TEACHING THE LESSON

Have student volunteers read the opening paragraphs on p. 191. Be sure to discuss the importance of word choice with your students. Before reading **Using Descriptive Language** (pp. 191–194), you may want to have students offer suggestions about ways they might improve the descriptiveness of words in their own writing.

Using a Word Bank. Sometimes writers keep lists of words, or word banks, to refer to when they're looking for just the right word. It's a little like having their own specialized thesaurus. Here's a word bank of sensory words you might refer to when you're writing descriptions.

A SENSORY WORD BANK		
SIGHT WORDS		
Appearance		
frail	glossy	flushed
sturdy	slender	muscular
pale	portly	angular
tapered	swollen	shapely
Color		
ivory	ebony	crimson
rose	hazel	canary
bronze	raven	pearl
milky	bleached	azure
SOUND WORDS		
boom	roar	rasp
whine	shriek	screech
hum	mutter	sigh
growl	snort	whimper
SMELL WORDS		
fragrant	earthy	spoiled
stench	piney	musty
flowery	stale	fresh
TOUCH WORDS		
cool	icy	fuzzy
oily	silky	velvety
gritty	sandy	slippery
TASTE WORDS		
sweet	tart	salty
tangy	sour	bittersweet
spicy	bitter	mellow

MEETING *individual* NEEDS

LEP/ESL

General Strategies. You may find that some of your students try to develop figurative language by first thinking of the appropriate words in their native languages and then looking the words up in bilingual dictionaries to find English equivalents. Often, something is lost in the translation. For example, instead of "The fist of loud music pounded all thought from my mind," a student might write "The hand of loud music pushed all thinking from my spirit." Some English-language learners might need some extra time with you to work with additional examples of figurative speech.

ADVANCED STUDENTS

Ask students to try to include onomatopoetic words in their descriptions. You may need to remind your students that these are words whose sounds imitate the sounds they name, as in *sigh* or *murmur*.

Have students attempt to add words to **A Sensory Word Bank** on p. 192. Also, some students may need to see or hear other examples of figurative language.

When reading the **Model for Description** (p. 196), occasionally point out the sensory details, similes, metaphors, and other devices used.

Stress that **A Writer's Model** on p. 199 is a model for students' own writing. Once again, you may want to pause while reading to have students point out especially descriptive details.

William Least Heat-Moon wrote a book about his travels on America's side roads. As you read this paragraph, notice how he re-creates what he observed through his senses.

> The old store, lighted only by three fifty-watt bulbs, smelled of coal oil and baking bread. In the middle of the rectangular room, where the oak floor sagged a little, stood an iron stove. To the right was a wooden table with an unfinished game of checkers and a stool made from an apple-tree stump. On shelves around the walls sat earthen jugs with corncob stoppers, a few canned goods, and some of the two thousand old clocks and clockworks Thurmond Watts owned. Only one was ticking; the others he just looked at.
>
> William Least Heat-Moon, *Blue Highways*

Although William Least Heat-Moon's description appeals most to his readers' sense of sight, it also includes details of sound ("ticking") and smell ("coal oil" and "baking bread"). The sensory words you use will vary depending upon your subject and emphasis. But remember that for both you and your readers, your five senses usually work together in creating an impression.

Figurative Language.   To describe a person or object, you often make a comparison: "He acts just like his older brother." When you use *figurative language* (sometimes called figures of speech), you are also comparing. But, instead of comparing similar things, you're comparing

MEETING *individual* NEEDS

STUDENTS WITH SPECIAL NEEDS

Some students will probably have difficulty sitting still to write for long periods. You may want to provide opportunities for students to break up their writing periods. If you provide a peer-conference area or a teacher-student conference area, students will be able to get up and move around.

INTEGRATING THE LANGUAGE ARTS

Library Link. When trying to think of vividly descriptive words or phrases, students might need to use a thesaurus. For practice in using a thesaurus, have students look up words to add to the sensory word bank.

SELECTION AMENDMENT
Description of change: excerpted
Rationale: to focus on the concept of sensory description presented in this chapter

GUIDED PRACTICE

Sometimes students have difficulty expanding details to make them more descriptive. You may want to give a list of descriptive words such as *red, loud, fast,* or *smooth* and work with students to develop vivid phrases.

Have students answer the questions in **Exercise 4** as a class activity to reinforce the reasons one answer is correct or better than another.

Cont. on p. 196

COOPERATIVE LEARNING

As students add to the word bank, have five groups of students create a bulletin-board size chart to use as a reference throughout the unit. Each group of students could be given a different section to fill—sight words, sound words, smell words, touch words, or taste words. Students could have a week of competition to place as many words as they can on their section of the board.

INTEGRATING THE LANGUAGE ARTS

Literature Link. Anne Tyler, in her short story "With All Flags Flying," describes characters in many different ways, the least of which is a physical description of their looks. If your literature textbook contains it, have students read this short story. Have them pay close attention to the character description. How is the old man described? What descriptions of other objects or places help the reader to see him clearly? What about Clara? Francie? Lead students in an analysis of the descriptions used. What was most effective? Least effective?

194

---

unlike things that share one basic feature. Because the comparison is so unusual, it catches your audience's attention. Here's an example:

> A tightly smoothed *quilt* of brown, green, and gold blanketed *South Dakota*.

The basic feature South Dakota and a quilt have in common is that they are flat and have alternating colors. Otherwise, they are very unlike things and make for an unusual comparison.

Used wisely, figurative language can help your readers' understanding by linking a familiar image with an unfamiliar one: *"Looking like a harmless drifting log, a crocodile can float unnoticed toward its prey."* As the following chart shows, figurative language may express comparisons in several ways.

TYPE OF FIGURATIVE LANGUAGE	EXAMPLE
A **simile** uses the words *like* or *as* to make the comparison.	The loud music shielded me like a crash helmet.
A **metaphor** makes a direct comparison.	The loud music was my crash helmet, protecting me from outside forces.
Personification gives human characteristics to things.	The fist of loud music pounded all thought from my mind.

TEACHING *MAKING COMPARISONS*

After reading the explanations and examples given in the textbook, work with students to use descriptions of classroom objects to create similes and metaphors. To assess students' understanding of these devices, evaluate students' performance on the **Critical Thinking Exercise.**

CRITICAL THINKING

Making Comparisons

If you're lucky, a fresh, creative comparison may occur to you as a sudden inspiration. Usually, though, you have to devote some effort to looking at reality in a new way.

To create a unique figure of speech, analyze the parts of your subject carefully. If you're describing a melting icicle, the drip may remind you of tears: *The dripping icicles were crying over their own departure.* Or, the icicle's shape may remind you of a sword: *The icicle is winter's sword.*

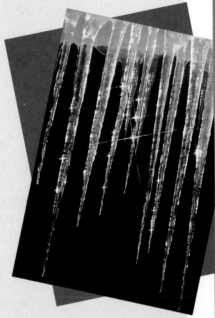

CRITICAL THINKING EXERCISE:
Making Comparisons

Stretch your imagination. Create at least three original metaphors or similes by comparing an item from Column A with an item from Column B. Write a sentence expressing your comparison, adding descriptive words or phrases as you wish.

EXAMPLE   *The frightened child clung like a stamp to its mother.*

Column A	Column B
fog	sand
puppy	stamp
sailboat	leaf
bicycle	ball
child	tablecloth

MEETING
individual
NEEDS

LEP/ESL

General Strategies. Being able to detect nuance of meaning is a skill that requires a broad and continuous exposure to English. You may want to present the **Critical Thinking Exercise** as a whole-class activity to offer support for English-language learners. Ask the class to suggest sentences using the words in the columns, and write the suggestions on the chalkboard.

ANSWERS
Critical Thinking Exercise

Answers will vary. Possible comparisons include "The ball fled over the fence like an escaping puppy" and "The fog was a tablecloth completely covering the city." Additional possibilities include "The sailboat sailed over the water like a leaf on the wind," "The sleeping puppy was a ball that had rolled under the table," "The fog was thick as sand on a beach," "The bicycle coasted as effortlessly as a leaf falling from a tree," and "The tumbling child was a ball bouncing down the lawn."

Cont. from p. 194
INDEPENDENT PRACTICE

Keep in mind that the first sentences are often the most difficult for the students to write. You may want to tell students they can worry about the best way to introduce their descriptions after most of the body has been written.

Students will need to write their first drafts independently. Student-teacher conferences during this stage of the writing process will help you to assess the students' progress while also allowing you to help students stay on task.

WRITING NOTE

With overuse, figurative language loses all its freshness and originality and becomes stale and worn out. These worn-out expressions (for example, "cool as a cucumber" or "busy as a bee") are called *clichés.* Try to avoid them in your writing.

A Model for Description

Ann Petry created the following description for the opening of a novel. As you read, notice the specific words that appeal to various senses and emphasize a harsh, desolate feeling. Look for the writer's use of figurative language as she makes the wind seem human.

A PASSAGE FROM A NOVEL

from **The Street**
by Ann Petry

Personification

There was a cold November wind blowing through 116th Street. It rattled the tops of garbage cans, sucked window shades out through the top of opened windows and set them flapping back against the windows; and it drove most of the people off the street in the block between Seventh and Eighth Avenues except for a few hurried pedestrians who bent double in an effort to offer the least possible exposed surface to its violent assault.

Sight detail

Specific details

It found every scrap of paper along the street—theater throwaways, announcements of dances and lodge meetings, the heavy waxed paper that loaves of bread had been wrapped in, the thinner waxed paper that had enclosed sandwiches, old envelopes, newspapers. Fingering its way along the curb, the wind set the bits of paper

---

USING THE SELECTION
from **The Street**

1

Ann Petry (1908–   ) is a graduate of the University of Connecticut. During her life she has been a pharmacist, salesperson, reporter, novelist, short-story writer, and biographer. Two of her better known novels include *The Narrows* (1953), about racial conflict in a New England town, and *The Street* (1946), which concerns poor people in a ghetto.

2

How does the description in the first paragraph of the selection make you feel? What kind of response do you think Petry wants to elicit from her readers? [The reader feels cold; she probably wants the reader to sense the harshness of the street.]

ASSESSMENT

To assess students' mastery of the use of figurative language, evaluate their performance on **Exercise 4.** Student-teacher conferences during the writing stages will help you to evaluate the progress of students' writing.

RETEACHING

Provide eight to ten relatively unfamiliar images (such as that of a woolly mammoth) and have students compare the unfamiliar image to a familiar one: for example, "A woolly mammoth lumbered across the horizon like a giant, slow army tank."

Writing Your First Draft   **197**

3 | to dancing high in the air, so that a barrage of paper swirled into the faces of the people on the street. It even took time to rush into doorways and areaways and find chicken bones and pork-chop bones and pushed them along the curb.

It did everything it could to discourage the people walking along the street. It found all the dirt and dust and grime on the sidewalk and lifted it up so that the dirt got into their noses, making it difficult to breathe; the dust got into their eyes and blinded them; and the grit stung their skins. It wrapped newspaper around their feet entangling them until the people cursed deep in their throats, stamped their feet, kicked at the paper. The wind blew it back again and again until they were forced to stoop and dislodge the paper with their hands. And then the wind grabbed their hats, pried their scarves from around their necks, stuck its fingers inside their coat collars, blew their coats away from their bodies.

Touch detail

Sound details

3

barrage: a continuous attack of questions; a continuous firing of guns

NEEDS

LEP/ESL

General Strategies. A Writer's Model includes words not used with their usual meanings, such as "cloud of pizza odors," in which *cloud* names something olfactory rather than visual; or "head for" in which *head* means "go." Such word uses, as well as some words such as *saucers* or *flickers,* may be unfamiliar to English-language learners and may hinder their understanding of the passage. It is a good idea to check to see that students understand uncommon words and meanings.

The wind lifted Lutie Johnson's hair away from the back of her neck so that she felt suddenly naked and bald, for her hair had been resting softly and warmly against her skin. She shivered as the cold fingers of the wind touched the back of her neck, explored the sides of her head. It even blew her eyelashes away from her eyes so that her eyeballs were bathed in a rush of coldness and she had to blink in order to read the words on the sign swaying back and forth over her head.

ANSWERS

Exercise 4

Answers for all except number 1 will vary. Here are some possibilities:

1. Petry announces her subject in her first sentence.

2. She writes of the wind's sucking window shades out of windows, driving people from the street, and of the wind's "violent assault"; she writes of it sending a "barrage" of paper into people's faces; it blinds people, stings them, and entangles them with paper.

3. The wind "sucked," "drove"; Petry's writing of the wind's "assault," its finding scraps of paper, "fingering" its way, taking time to rush into doorways and areaways, finding bones and pushing them, trying to discourage people.

4. Sound: the wind rattles tops of garbage cans; window shades flap; people curse and stamp their feet
Touch: cold November wind; dust got in eyes; grit stung skins; the wind's cold fingers went inside collars, touched the back of Lutie Johnson's neck

5. Some students might think Petry exaggerates. Others might suggest eliminating the material about the window shades.

| EXERCISE 4 ▶ | **Analyzing a Description** |

1. Where does Petry announce the subject of her description?
2. Petry uses many details that emphasize the wind's violent nature. What are some of these details?
3. From the second sentence on, Petry *personifies* the wind—making it seem human—when she says that "it rattled the tops of garbage cans." What are other examples where the writer personifies the wind?
4. Petry uses many sight details in this description. What are three or four sound details that she uses? Touch details?
5. Have you ever been in a heavy, violent wind like the one Petry describes? Do you think her description is accurate? Would you add or change anything in her description?

A Writer's Model for You

Ann Petry is a professional writer who imagines specific details right down to two different types of wax paper— "heavy" and "thinner." Most of the time you'll be observing or recalling details from experience. But like Ann Petry, you can also create a specific word picture by using figurative language and sensory details. As you write your own description, you might follow this shorter model—it describes a place like one you might know.

SELECTION AMENDMENT
Description of change: excerpted
Rationale: to focus on the concept of specific description presented in this chapter

A WRITER'S MODEL

Subject
Emphasis

Sound detail
Sight detail

Simile

Touch detail

Smell details

Sight details

Writer's
feeling

Whenever I'm hungry for a snack, I head for Angela's Pizza Place, just around the corner from school. Angela's is quite a place. It looks as though it's been there forever. On the outside, there's an ancient neon sign that buzzes and flickers against the peeling white paint on the red brick wall. Inside, an antique espresso machine sits like a brass robot guarding the front door. And on the shiny dining room walls, bright colors reflect off the fake Tiffany lamps hanging over every booth.

Each time I turn the greasy doorknob to open Angela's front door, the first thing that greets me is a wonderful warm cloud of pizza odors. My mouth starts to water as the cheese and garlic aromas embrace me. While I wait for my order, I usually watch the chef in the kitchen, tossing dough, pouring sauces, putting pies in the oven, and cutting slices. As entertaining as the airborne saucers of dough are, though, no one comes to Angela's for the sights alone. My first bite of hot melted cheese always reminds me of exactly why I come here.

PART 4:
Writing Your First Draft

Remember that the two models above have been revised and proofread. No one expects your first draft to be perfect. Write a paragraph or two on the subject you've been developing. Include details you've gathered, but don't hesitate to include details that occur to you as you write.

COMPUTER NOTE: If you're writing on a computer, use boldface, italics, or underlining to mark words you plan to revise.

CRITICAL THINKING

Analysis. Ask students to analyze the order in which details are arranged in **A Writer's Model** [spatial order]. Why is this order appropriate? [When you come upon any structure, you must start with the outside before moving inside; therefore, the outside is a natural starting place for arranging the details in this case.]

COMPUTER NOTE

Remind students that they can change ordinary text to boldface or italic in most word-processing programs by highlighting the text and selecting the appropriate type style from the menu. There may also be shortcut keys they can use for this purpose. Thus, students do not have to decide before they write a sentence that it will need to be set in bold or italic typeface. Also remind students that they should print a copy of their drafts to work with during evaluation and revision.

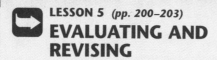

EVALUATING AND REVISING

OBJECTIVES

- To analyze a description's strengths and weaknesses
- To evaluate and revise a descriptive paragraph to eliminate weaknesses

TEACHING THE LESSON

You may want to begin by passing around an extremely out-of-focus picture and asking students to identify the content. Students will likely have difficulty identifying it or will make quite different guesses. Point out the importance of clear focus and details in their descriptive writing.

PROGRAM MANAGER

EVALUATING AND REVISING

■ **Reinforcement/Reteaching** See **Revision Transparencies 7** and **8**. For suggestions on how to tie the transparencies to instruction, review teacher's notes in *Fine Art and Instructional Transparencies for Writing*, p. 107.

■ **Ongoing Assessment** For a rubric to guide assessment, see **Evaluating and Revising** in *Strategies for Writing*, p. 11.

■ **Assessment/Reflection** To assess student work and evaluate progress, see **Portfolio Forms** in *Portfolio Assessment*, pp. 5–21.

■ **Computer Guided Instruction** For additional instruction and practice with participles as noted in the **Grammar Hint** on p. 202, see **Lesson 20** in *Language Workshop CD-ROM*.

■ **Practice** To help less-advanced students who need additional practice with participles, see **Chapter 12** in *English Workshop, Fourth Course*, pp. 153–154.

QUOTATION FOR THE DAY

"In all pointed sentences, some degree of accuracy must be sacrificed to conciseness." (Samuel Johnson, 1709–1784, English writer)

continued on next page

200

Evaluating and Revising

Evaluating. Now that you've drafted your description, it's time to evaluate it—to judge it for both strengths and weaknesses, to see what works and what doesn't.

Revising. If you identify any problems, revise by making the changes that will improve your paper. To do so, ask yourself the questions in the left-hand column in the chart on the next page. Then, if you identify a particular problem, use the suggestions in the right-hand column as a guide for revising.

The **Evaluating and Revising Description** chart is designed to help students identify strengths and rectify weaknesses in their papers. You may find it helpful to provide a few examples to help students use the chart effectively. Remind students that they are revising content, not proofreading for grammatical or mechanical errors. Their papers are still first drafts that may not be ready to turn in. Use the **Grammar Hint** on p. 202 as a tool to improve the style of students' papers.

Exercise 5 provides an opportunity to model the skills required for revision. It especially focuses on improving clarity and detail.

Writing Assignment: Part 5 provides students the opportunity to evaluate

EVALUATING AND REVISING DESCRIPTION

EVALUATION GUIDE	REVISION TECHNIQUE
1 Does the description identify what or who is being described?	**Add** a sentence or a phrase that clearly identifies your subject.
2 Is the tone of the description consistent?	**Cut** or **replace** any words or remarks that don't accurately convey your attitude toward your subject.
3 Are the details of the description arranged in an order that makes sense to readers?	**Reorder** the details so that they support your purpose and emphasis.
4 Does the description contain realistic sensory details?	**Add** precise details about the person, place, or thing that appeal to the reader's senses.
5 Does the description present a clear emphasis or a main impression?	**Add** details that support the emphasis you want to present. **Cut** details that do not contribute to your intended main impression.
6 Are specific words and figurative language used effectively?	**Replace** general words with specific and vivid nouns, verbs, adjectives, and adverbs; **cut** any clichés; **add** fresh comparisons.

Explain that writers often describe scenes, people, or objects that are much too complex to be completely and accurately described in a brief paper. Instead, they may include only those details that give the reader some insight into the real essence or character of whatever is being described. Encourage students to evaluate the quality of the details they have selected for their papers.

MEETING *individual* **NEEDS**

LEP/ESL

Asian Languages. Many languages (such as Chinese, Lao, Vietnamese, Malay, Tagalog, and Japanese) do not have participles. Therefore, some students might avoid using participles and use the present tense instead. Explain participles. Then give the infinitive form, such as *see,* and have the students form the participles [*seeing* and *seen*] and make phrases and sentences using these participles ["seeing-eye dog" and "The article seen by me was on page 4 of the paper"].

ADVANCED STUDENTS

Because of the continual push for adequate detail in descriptive writing, some students may tend to over-describe. Work with these students on analyzing the necessity of individual details and on evaluating the importance of specific details. For example, tell students to use vivid nouns instead of an abundance of adjectives.

and revise their own work independently. You may want to have students who have not yet read each other's work exchange papers so that objective evaluations may be made.

Have students fill in a chart like that on p. 201 when they are first evaluating their papers for **Writing Assignment: Part 5** and when they complete the assignment for another student. This way you will be better able to assess students' development in evaluation and revision.

GRAMMAR HINT

You may want students to check their drafts for the correct use of participles. Explain that writers sometimes create dangling modifiers or misplaced modifiers that obscure the meaning of their writing. To be sure that students have logical, clear references for all participles, have them circle any participles in their papers and draw arrows to the word or words modified.

LEARNING STYLES

Visual Learners. Students might benefit from the opportunity to illustrate their descriptions. This activity will help them see the objects they are describing and lead them to notice details that are missing in the writing. The pictures might also make a nice display for the completed descriptive paragraphs.

202

GRAMMAR HINT

Using Participles

As an observer, you can take in a variety of sensory details at once. Good description offers readers the same opportunity. Look over your sentences. You can combine actions and concentrate images by using participles, verb forms that can act as adjectives. (In the combined sentences below, the participles are shown in italic type.)

EXAMPLES		
	Two Sentences	The rain was pouring. It ran in rivulets down the gutter.
	Combined	The *pouring* rain ran in rivulets down the gutter.
	Two Sentences	The nervous coach watched the clock. She paced the sidelines.
	Combined	*Watching* the clock, the nervous coach paced the sidelines.
	Two Sentences	The clerk was startled. He was called by the customer.
	Combined	*Called* by the customer, the clerk was startled.

☞ REFERENCE NOTE: For more help with participles, see pages 579–580.

EXERCISE 5 ▶   **Analyzing a Writer's Revisions**

Following is the first draft of a paragraph taken from the writer's model on page 199. Working with one or two classmates, try to decide why you think the writer made the changes that are shown in the revision. Use the evaluating and revising chart on page 201 to help you answer the questions that follow the paragraph. Discuss your responses with your classmates.

Ask students the following questions:

1. Were you able to identify strengths in your writing?
2. What are some of the strengths?
3. Were you able to discover weaknesses in your writing?
4. What are some of the weaknesses?
5. How were you able to correct the weaknesses? ■

Whenever I'm hungry for a snack, I head for Angela's Pizza Place, just around the corner. *(from school. Angela's is quite a place.)* It looks as though it's been **add**

there forever. Inside, an antique espresso machine sits like a brass robot guarding the front door. On the outside, there's an ancient neon sign *that buzzes and flickers* against the peeling **reorder**

white paint on the red brick wall. And on the shiny dining room walls, bright colors reflect off the ~~lights~~ *fake Tiffany lamps* hanging over every **add**

booth. ~~I've seen the place when it was dirty inside though, and it's not as appealing.~~ **replace**

cut

1. Why did the writer add the words *from school* to the first sentence?
2. Why did the writer rearrange the order of the third and fourth sentences? What type of order does the paragraph now have?
3. Why did the writer add the words *that buzzes and flickers* to the description of the neon sign?
4. Why did the writer replace the word *lights* with *fake Tiffany lamps* in the next-to-last sentence?
5. Why did the writer cut the last sentence? [Hint: Review page 187].

WRITING ASSIGNMENT

PART 5:
Evaluating and Revising Your Description

Now try evaluating and revising your own description. Exchange descriptions with a classmate and evaluate each other's work. Next, go over your own paper, using the chart on page 201 as a guide. Think carefully about your classmate's suggestions and your own evaluation. Then, make any changes that will improve your description.

ANSWERS
Exercise 5

Answers will vary. Here are some possibilities:

1. It gives a clearer identification of the subject and locates it more precisely.
2. Rearranging enhances spatial order: outside to inside. It shows things in the order in which one would see them.
3. The addition gives a specific sound detail and makes it easier for the reader to perceive the scene.
4. It adds fresh figurative language and is more concrete and thus easier to visualize.
5. Cutting makes the paragraph support the purpose: describing Angela's as a good place to go for a snack.

TIMESAVER

If you are planning to read the drafts as well as the final versions of the papers, you may want to have students underline or highlight sections in the drafts that were changed for the final copy. Not only will this help you to identify revisions quickly, but it will also help students see what improvements they have made in their writing.

LESSON 6 (pp. 204–206)
PROOFREADING AND PUBLISHING

OBJECTIVE
- To proofread an essay for publication

TEACHING THE LESSON

To demonstrate the importance of proper grammar and mechanics, have students attempt to correct the following sentence without changing the given order of the words:

pete said sarah may call tom.

PROGRAM MANAGER

PROOFREADING AND PUBLISHING

- **Instructional Support** For a chart students may use to evaluate their proofreading progress, see **Proofreading** in *Strategies for Writing*, p. 12.

- **Independent Practice/ Reteaching** For additional practice with language skills, see **Proofreading Practice: Using Participles** in *Strategies for Writing*, p. 13.

- **Assessment/Reflection** To assess student work and evaluate progress, see **Portfolio Forms in Portfolio Assessment**, pp. 22–25.

QUOTATION FOR THE DAY

"We want the creative faculty to imagine that which we know." (Percy Bysshe Shelley, 1792–1822, British poet)

Write the quotation on the chalkboard and ask students in small groups to discuss the quotation and how it might relate to descriptive writing. Have a representative from each group share thoughts and ideas about the quotation with the class before students begin proofreading and publishing their descriptions.

204

---

204   *Using Description*

Proofreading and Publishing

Proofreading.   Polish your description by proofreading carefully so that your readers "see" your subject rather than any distracting errors.

Publishing.   When your polished description is ready for a wider audience, try these two suggestions to reach some readers.

- If your classmates are familiar with your subject, read your description aloud to them without naming your subject. Then ask classmates to identify your subject. If they guess correctly, ask them which details were most helpful in uncovering its identify.
- Submit your description to the school newspaper or literary magazine.

WRITING ASSIGNMENT

PART 6:
Proofreading and Publishing

Let your readers "see" your subject by proofreading your description carefully, one line at a time, and correcting any errors. Then use one of the suggestions you've just read or one of your own to share your work with an audience.

You may want to lead students in discussion of the links between punctuation, capitalization, and meaning.

After reading **A Student Model**, discuss the strengths and weaknesses of this essay. Next, assign **Writing Assignment: Part 6.** Remind students that careful proofreading takes time and concentration, but leads to a much-improved essay.

After students have carefully proofread their essays, you may want to discuss various methods of publication before students write their final versions. They will need to keep their audience in mind as they neatly rewrite the essays.

 ## Reflecting on Your Writing

To add your description to your **portfolio,** date your paper, and attach a brief written reflection prompted by these questions:

- What method helped you collect descriptive details for this assignment?
- Which part of the essay do you think is most vivid, and why?
- What main impression does your description make? Is that impression the one you intended to convey?

A STUDENT MODEL

In talking about her description, Alissa Bird says what she found hardest to do was "to get all the grammar correct" and "to write in a certain form." Nevertheless, Alissa—a student at Crestwood High School in Roswell, Georgia—vividly describes a person and a place important to her.

The Wise Lady
by Alissa Bird

I saw my great-grandmother for the first time when I was about seven years old. She was sitting in her blue quilted armchair with a copy of <u>Reader's Digest</u> in her small, soft, wrinkly hands. Blue veins protruded from her transparent skin. When she heard the banging of the screen door, she got up and scooped me up into her arms and planted a big kiss on my cheek.

The one thing that sticks out in my mind is her pink bathroom where everything was always spotless. The entire bathroom was pink: the towels, the carpet, the walls, the bathtub, and even the bottle of bubble bath on the rim. I also

TEACHING NOTE

Remind students that the purpose of writing reflections on their work is to give them a chance to think about how they work and to learn from experience how to work better in the future. The first question is well suited to helping students learn from their experience of writing description. Point out that careful thought now may well save them a great deal of time and effort in the future.

A STUDENT MODEL
Evaluation

1. In the first paragraph, Alissa clearly identifies her great-grandmother as the subject of her description.
2. Alissa's very positive attitude toward her great-grandmother is reflected with words such as "small," "soft," "delicious aroma," and "inspiration."
3. The details of this description are ordered to emphasize the importance of the lessons Alissa obtained from her great-grandmother.
4. Alissa includes numerous details to present a clear impression: for example, "scooped me up" and "mysterious winding stairs."
5. Specific color and concrete images are used effectively in sentences such as "The entire bathroom was pink" and "The stairs creaked like a haunted house."

Discuss the importance of publishing. Why do teachers insist on published work? How do students feel about sharing their work? What types of sharing make students feel most comfortable? Most uncomfortable? ■

INTEGRATING THE LANGUAGE ARTS

Mechanics Link. When students are checking the spelling in their papers, it helps if they read the paper from back to front. If they read the essay correctly, it is easy to get caught up in the content and to forget to check the spelling. By reading one word at a time backwards, they must concentrate on the words themselves.

CRITICAL THINKING

Evaluation. Often, it helps students better understand the grades they receive on papers if they have completed the grading process themselves. You may want to provide students with the grading scale or methods you will be using to evaluate their writing. Students should then evaluate "**The Wise Lady**" on p. 205. Discuss with students the results of their evaluations. Did results differ? What were similarities in the evaluations?

remember the mysterious winding stairs that went up to the unknown rooms. When I got the chance to explore the upstairs, I remember how the stairs creaked like a haunted house.

I can still hear the chirp of the birds in the backyard by the huge vegetable garden she always kept weedless. The sound of an oven buzzer reminds me of the times when I was at her house and her buzzer would go off. When she opened the oven door, the delicious aroma of chocolate chip cookies would fill the air.

I will forever remember the long summers I spent with that wise old lady. I will always remember how we took walks around the town and to the grocery store just about every day I was there. My great-grandmother taught me about real life and that life is what you make it. She has been a real inspiration to me, and I hope that when I have grandchildren of my own I can inspire them just as much.

WRITING WORKSHOP

OBJECTIVES

- To analyze free verse
- To identify an appropriate topic for poetry
- To use the writing process to create free verse

TEACHING THE LESSON

You may want to begin by sharing several examples of free verse with your students. Initiate a discussion of the characteristics of free verse. The explanation at the beginning of this lesson explains these characteristics well. After reading Wagoner's poem, ask students to respond orally to the questions. You may want to use these ☞

WRITING WORKSHOP

207

A Free Verse Poem

A good description captures and expresses an image, feeling, or idea by using specific sensory detail. Free verse poetry also does this—but in a condensed way. When you write free verse poetry, you usually don't have a regular pattern of rhythm and rhyme. Instead, you arrange words in each line according to your natural speech patterns. And, as in a good subjective description, you use sensory details and figurative language.

The following free verse poem is about a plant that grows in the American West. Its name comes from the way the plant breaks off near the ground and tumbles over and over as the wind blows it.

Tumbleweed
by David Wagoner

Here comes another, bumping over the sage
Among the greasewood, wobbling diagonally
Downhill, then skimming a moment on its edge,
Tilting lopsided, bouncing end over end
And springing from the puffs of its own dust
To catch at the barbed wire
And hang there, shaking, like a riddled prisoner.

Half the sharp seeds have fallen from this tumbler,
Knocked out for good by head-stands and pratfalls
Between here and wherever it grew up.
I carry it in the wind across the road
To the other fence. It jerks in my hands,
Butts backwards, corkscrews, lunges and swivels,
Then yaws away as soon as it's let go,
Hopping the scrub uphill like a kicked maverick.
The air goes hard and straight through the wires and weeds.
Here comes another, flopping among the sage.

QUOTATION FOR THE DAY

 "Great poetry is always written by somebody straining to go beyond what he can do." (Stephen Spender, 1909–1995, British poet)

Share the quotation with the class and ask students to respond by writing journal entries about personal accomplishments or goals they have reached.

MEETING *individual* NEEDS

ADVANCED STUDENTS

Allow each student to write one poem based on the model and one following a different format. Let students read their poems to the class and have them discuss the power of the images created.

LEARNING STYLES

Auditory Learners. Arrange for students to talk-write their rough drafts to partners. One person could describe his or her subject aloud while the other person could write down words and phrases. Students can then trade roles.

responses to assess students' understanding of the poetry.

To help students develop their own topics for free verse, have them spend a few minutes brainstorming possibilities as a class activity.

Have students complete the requisite writing steps as indicated. You may wish to complete the assignment over several days.

Ask students to explain the importance of descriptive writing in poetry. How does it differ from description in prose? ■

ANSWERS
Writing Workshop Questions

Answers will vary. Here are some possibilities:

1. He uses, among others, "bumping," "wobbling," "skimming," "Tilting," "lopsided," "shaking," and "riddled."

2. The two similes are "like a riddled prisoner" and "like a kicked maverick." They encourage sympathy for the tumbleweed.

3. The poem has more of a sense of movement or flowing when it is read without the breaks.

4. It could represent people who are bounced around by life's circumstances.

TECHNOLOGY TIP

You may want to have students type their poetry for display. If students are using computers, they could attempt to print their poems in the shape of the animal or plant being written about. They might also be able to use the computers to generate illustrations for their poems.

1. What sensory words does the poet use to show the actions or behaviors of the tumbleweeds?
2. What two similes does the poet use? How do they affect your feelings about the tumbleweeds?
3. Read the poem once as it is written, recognizing the line breaks. Then, read it again as though it were a paragraph, pausing for punctuation but ignoring the line breaks. What is the effect of the change?
4. If you read this poem on a symbolic level, what kinds of people might the tumbleweed represent?

Writing a Free Verse Poem

Prewriting. Many plants and animals have characteristics that remind us of people in general or of particular people. Brainstorm or freewrite to think of a plant or animal that has some interesting similarities to human beings. Then, use these questions to gather details for your poem:

- What are the most obvious characteristics, behaviors, or actions of the plant or animal you have identified?
- What features of the plant or animal could be compared to someone you know or to people in general?
- What sensory details could you include to highlight those features? visual details? details of sound?
- What similes would give your subject human qualities?

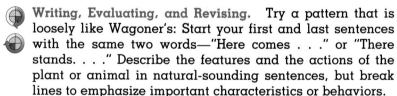

Writing, Evaluating, and Revising. Try a pattern that is loosely like Wagoner's: Start your first and last sentences with the same two words—"Here comes . . ." or "There stands. . . ." Describe the features and the actions of the plant or animal in natural-sounding sentences, but break lines to emphasize important characteristics or behaviors.

Read your poem aloud and see if your ideas are clear. Then, ask someone else to read your poem. Use your evaluation and your reader's feedback to revise your poem.

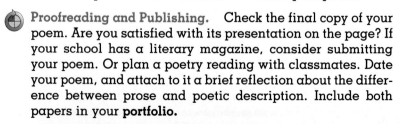

Proofreading and Publishing. Check the final copy of your poem. Are you satisfied with its presentation on the page? If your school has a literary magazine, consider submitting your poem. Or plan a poetry reading with classmates. Date your poem, and attach to it a brief reflection about the difference between prose and poetic description. Include both papers in your **portfolio.**

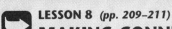
MAKING CONNECTIONS

COMBINING DESCRIPTION WITH NARRATION

OBJECTIVE

- To read and report orally on an informative passage that combines description and narration

MAKING CONNECTIONS

COMBINING DESCRIPTION WITH NARRATION

Description is narrative's comfortable companion. In a narrative, the story's actions come alive through the descriptions of the people, places, objects, and feelings they involve.

Many people think Ernie Pyle was America's best war correspondent during World War II. Notice how he combines narration with description in the following dispatch from the front lines of Africa in 1943.

from Ernie's War: The Best of Ernie Pyle's World War II Dispatches
by Ernie Pyle

1   "A narrow path comes like a ribbon over a hill miles away, down a long slope, across a creek, up a slope and over another hill.

"All along the length of this ribbon there is now a thin line of men. For four days and nights they have fought hard, eaten little, washed none, and slept hardly at all. Their nights have been violent with attack, fright, butchery, and their days sleepless and miserable with the crash of artillery.

2   "The men are walking. They are 50 feet apart, for dispersal. Their walk is slow, for they are dead weary, as you can tell even when looking at them from behind. Every line and sag of their bodies speaks their inhuman exhaustion.

COMBINING DESCRIPTION WITH NARRATION

Teaching Strategies

You may want to have students write narratives of their own. Have each student choose an event such as a family gathering, a vacation, or a performance. Students should attempt to narrate the happenings as Ernie Pyle does. The narration is written in the present tense; he is describing something that is happening as he speaks. Students should duplicate this method to make their readers feel that the events are occurring as they read. Remind students to use plentiful, accurate, picture-forming details.

USING THE SELECTION

from **Ernie's War: The Best of Ernie Pyle's World War II Dispatches**

1

Why is this selection written in quotation marks? [It is quoted from Ernie Pyle; he is speaking the words that are written down.]

2

dispersal: distribution

DESCRIPTION ACROSS THE CURRICULUM

OBJECTIVES

- To analyze a scientific description
- To reword a subjective description into an objective description

3

Notice the metaphorical description of the men's movements.

GUIDELINES

If you have students present oral reports from their own reading, you may want to have peers evaluate the presentations. Reports will vary depending on the time given for preparation and the subject chosen.

"On their shoulders and backs they carry heavy steel tripods, machine-gun barrels, leaden boxes of ammunition. Their feet seem to sink into the ground from the overload they are bearing.

"They don't slouch. It is the terrible deliberation of each step that spells out their appalling tiredness. Their faces are black and unshaven. They are young men, but the grime and whiskers and exhaustion make them look middle-aged.

"In their eyes as they pass is not hatred, not excitement, not despair, not the tonic of their victory—there is just the simple expression of being here as though they had been here doing this forever, and nothing else.

3 "The line moves on, but it never ends. All afternoon men keep coming round the hill and vanishing eventually over the horizon. It is one long tired line of antlike men."

Pyle reported events as he saw them, but his descriptive details help you to "see" them too. What figure of speech does Pyle use when he describes the line of moving men? What is Pyle's overall emphasis in his description of the soldiers? What details in his writing support this impression?

Until he was killed by a sniper's bullet in 1945, Pyle filed six newspaper columns a week for his thirteen million readers. He rarely reported the war's events on a "grand scale." Instead, Pyle's subjects were usually individual soldiers and their stories. Some of his best columns are collected in books, including *Ernie's War: The Best of Ernie Pyle's World War II Dispatches.* You might like to find one of these books and read about the very human face of war. Then share your reading in an oral report to your classmates.

DESCRIPTION ACROSS THE CURRICULUM

Objective Description in Science

Description in the sciences informs its readers about exact observations. Notice the realistic, factual details and specific words in the following description of a crocodile.

A crocodile is an aquatic, meat-eating reptile that has lived in the warmer parts of this earth for about 135 million years. It is often called a "living fossil" because scientists believe that it looks pretty much the same now as it originally did. It has thick, tough, dark green skin stretched over an armor of bony plates. A crocodile's long triangular snout contains forty to sixty razor-sharp teeth set in sockets in each jawbone. When the snout is closed, these teeth interlock, with two very large ones sticking out from the lower jaw. With eyes and nostrils on top of its head, the crocodile can see, breathe, and smell, while hiding most of its body under the often cloudy swamp water.

Is this an objective or subjective description? How can you tell? Reread the subjective description of the dog described on pages 184–185. Keeping the same subject, write a paragraph of objective description, as though you were describing the dog for a science report. (Remember that scientists take pride in using accurate, realistic details.)

DESCRIPTION ACROSS THE CURRICULUM
Teaching Strategies

You may want to have students bring other examples of objective and subjective description they find in magazines, science books, or encyclopedias.

Rather than have all students rewrite the collie description, you may want to have some students rewrite articles that they bring to class.

GUIDELINES

The description of the crocodile is objective. The details do not convey emotions. The description is straightforward and precise. The only opinion (as opposed to what seems to be fact) is presented in quotation marks and explained.

The paragraph written about the dog by the students would have to be unlike the one about Elizabeth in several ways: It could use no slang (*tummy*); it would have to be in third person (no use of *I*); it would use complete sentences; it would include no personal anecdotes; and it would not make jokes about the dog's IQ.

Chapter 6

CREATIVE WRITING: NARRATION

OBJECTIVES

- To determine a story's purpose, audience, and tone
- To develop a story by selecting an idea, as well as point of view, characters, setting, and plot
- To write a draft of a story using selected story elements
- To evaluate and revise, proofread and publish a story

WRITING-IN-PROGRESS ASSIGNMENTS

Major Assignment: Writing a story

Cumulative Writing Assignments: The chart below shows the sequence of cumulative assignments that will guide students as they write a story. These writing assignments form the instructional core of Chapter 6.

PREWRITING

Writing Assignment
- Part 1: Developing a Story Idea p. 222
- Part 2: Describing Your Characters and Setting p. 226
- Part 3: Gathering Plot Details p. 227
- Part 4: Developing a Story Map p. 228

WRITING

Writing Assignment
- Part 5: Writing a Draft of Your Story p. 238

EVALUATING AND REVISING

Writing Assignment
- Part 6: Evaluating and Revising Your Story p. 240

PROOFREADING AND PUBLISHING

Writing Assignment
- Part 7: Proofreading and Publishing Your Story p. 241

In addition, exercises 1–3 provide practice in evaluating dialogue, analyzing the organization of a short story, and analyzing a writer's revisions.

CROSS CURRICULUM

Narratives of Discovery in Biology

Remind students that stories are not the only opportunity for narratives. True stories, such as news events, biographies, historical accounts, and accounts of scientific discovery, can also be told in a narrative form. Have students research and write a narrative of a scientific discovery. For example, students may write the story of the discoveries Charles Darwin made on his voyage on the *Beagle*.

- **Research** Encourage students interested in similar topics to work together as they research. Research sources include science textbooks, histories of science, biographies and autobiographies of the people involved in the discoveries, and the Internet.

- **Planning** Students should consider how the elements of a short story may be adapted to their narratives. Offer them a chart like the one below.

Character: Treat the scientist who made the discovery as a character; research details about his or her life, such as appearance and habits; invent dialogue.

Chronology of events: Focus on only a few events that directly tie to or lead into the discovery; use a storyboard format to map out the first draft.

Setting: Research the setting of the discovery; it might be a laboratory, a study, or a ship.

Conflict: This makes any narrative interesting; look for conflicts or problems the scientist faced, either internally or externally.

Narrator: Use the third person, or have the scientist narrate his or her own discovery in the first person.

- **Reflecting** Ask students to respond in journals to the following questions. 1) What was the most challenging part of creating the narrative? 2) What about your narrative pleases you most? 3) What insight into writing did you gain?

INTEGRATING THE LANGUAGE ARTS

SELECTION	READING AND LITERATURE	WRITING AND CRITICAL THINKING	LANGUAGE AND SYNTAX	SPEAKING, LISTENING, AND OTHER EXPRESSION SKILLS
• "The Scholarship Jacket" by Marta Salinas pp. 214–219 • from "Where Have You Gone, Charming Billy?" by Tim O'Brien p. 224 • "Mushrooms in the city" by Italo Calvino pp. 231–235 • "Memoirs of an Adolescent" by Noah Kramer-Dover, p. 243 • "Tornadoes Damage School" from *The Ledger*, Lakeland, Florida pp. 244–245	• Making and supporting inferences about characters pp. 219, 236 • Identifying conflict pp. 219, 236 • Analyzing characters pp. 219, 236 • Applying interpretive and creative thinking pp. 219, 236, 245 • Identifying facts and details in a news story p. 245 • Comparing informative and literary paragraphs p. 245	• Writing from a character's point of view pp. 219, 224 • Rewriting a passage from third to first person p. 224 • Finding the main idea pp. 224, 236 • Developing characters and setting pp. 226, 238 • Creating a chain-of-events outline p. 227 • Organizing a story map p. 228 • Writing and evaluating dialogue p. 230 • Analyzing suspense, mood, setting, and characterization in a short story p. 236 • Using the *5W-How?* questions pp. 245–246 • Writing a news story or fable pp. 245–246, 247 • Researching and writing a historical narrative p. 247	• Using pronouns consistent with the first person point of view p. 224 • Proofreading for errors in grammar, usage, and mechanics pp. 242, 246	• Discussing and rewriting a passage's point of view p. 224 • Discussing character and setting descriptions pp. 226, 236 • Writing dialogue in a small group p. 230 • Answering questions in a small group about a literary model p. 236 • Working in a group to revise story drafts p. 240 • Sharing stories with classmates p. 247

SUGGESTED INTEGRATED UNIT PLAN

This plan suggests how to integrate the major strands of the language arts with this chapter.

If you begin with this chapter on creative writing or with the suggested short stories, you should focus on the common characteristics of creative writing. You can then integrate speaking/listening and language concepts with both the writing and the literature.

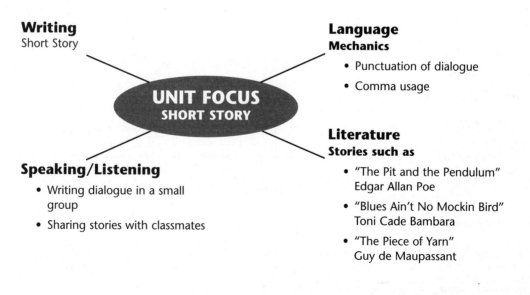

Common Characteristics

- Content choices that are consistent with choice of form and style and that involve presentation, climax, and resolution of a conflict
- Chronological organization, basic units are sentences and paragraphs
- Content and language entertain readers
- Effective choice and use of point of view

Writing
Short Story

Speaking/Listening

- Writing dialogue in a small group
- Sharing stories with classmates

UNIT FOCUS
SHORT STORY

Language
Mechanics

- Punctuation of dialogue
- Comma usage

Literature
Stories such as

- "The Pit and the Pendulum" Edgar Allan Poe
- "Blues Ain't No Mockin Bird" Toni Cade Bambara
- "The Piece of Yarn" Guy de Maupassant

CHAPTER 6: CREATIVE WRITING: NARRATION

Use this guide for creating an instructional plan that addresses the individual needs of your students. Assignments accompanied by the following symbol (✱) may be completed out of class. Times given for pacing lessons are estimated.

CHAPTER PLANNING GUIDE—PUPIL'S EDITION

LESSONS	LITERARY MODEL pp. 214–219 "The Scholarship Jacket" by Marta Salinas	PREWRITING pp. 221–228	
		Generating Ideas	Gathering/Organizing
DEVELOPMENTAL PROGRAM	🕐 **20–25 minutes** • Read model aloud in class and ask students to answer questions on p. 219 orally.	🕐 **25–30 minutes** • Main Assignment: Looking Ahead p. 220 • Exploring Story Ideas p. 221 • Writing Assignment: Part 1 p. 222	🕐 **60–65 minutes** • Planning Your Story pp. 223–227 • Writing Assignments: Parts 2, 3, 4 pp. 226, 227, 228
CORE PROGRAM	🕐 **20–25 minutes** • Assign student pairs to read the model and answer questions on p. 219.	🕐 **20–25 minutes** • Main Assignment: Looking Ahead p. 220 • Exploring Story Ideas p. 221 • Writing Assignment: Part 1 p. 222✱	🕐 **40–45 minutes** • Critical Thinking pp. 223–224 • Reminder p. 226 • Charts p. 227, 228 • Writing Assignments: Parts 2, 3, 4 pp. 226, 227, 228✱
ACCELERATED PROGRAM	🕐 **20–25 minutes** • Assign students to read the model independently and to discuss the questions on p. 219 with partners.	🕐 **15–20 minutes** • Main Assignment: Looking Ahead p. 220 • Reminder p. 222 • Writing Assignment: Part 1 p. 222✱	🕐 **25–30 minutes** • Critical Thinking pp. 223–224✱ • Reminder p. 226 • Charts p. 227, 228 • Writing Assignments: Parts 2, 3, 4 pp. 226, 227, 228✱

CHAPTER PLANNING GUIDE—PROGRAM RESOURCES

	LITERARY MODEL	PREWRITING
PRINT	• Reading Master 6, *Practice for Assessment in Reading, Vocabulary, and Spelling* p. 6	• Prewriting, *Strategies for Writing* pp. 16–19 • Creative Writing, *English Workshop* pp. 43–50
MEDIA	• Fine Art Transparency 3, *Transparency Binder*	• Graphic Organizers 9–10, *Transparency Binder*

WRITING pp. 229–238	EVALUATING AND REVISING pp. 239–240	PROOFREADING AND PUBLISHING pp. 241–243

⏱ **90 minutes**
• Basic Elements
  pp. 229–230
• Exercise 1 p. 230
• A Writer's Model
  pp. 236–238
• Writing Assignment:
  Part 5 p. 238
	⏱ **40–45 minutes**
	• Evaluating and Revising
	  p. 239
	• Exercise 3 p. 240
	• Writing Assignment:
	  Part 6 p. 240
		⏱ **45–50 minutes**
		• Proofreading and
		  Publishing p. 241
		• Mechanics Hint p. 241
		• Writing Assignment:
		  Part 7 p. 241
		• Reflecting p. 242
		• A Student Model p. 243

⏱ **50–55 minutes**
• Basic Elements
  pp. 229–230
• Looking at a Short Story
  pp. 230–235
• Writing Note p. 235
• Exercise 2 p. 236
• Writing Assignment:
  Part 5 p. 238*
	⏱ **30–35 minutes**
	• Evaluating and Revising
	  Short Stories Chart
	  p. 239
	• Exercise 3 p. 240*
	• Writing Assignment:
	  Part 6 p. 240
		⏱ **35–40 minutes**
		• Mechanics Hint p. 241
		• Writing Assignment:
		  Part 7 p. 241
		• Reflecting p. 242
		• A Student Model p. 243*

⏱ **25–30 minutes**
• Basic Elements
  pp. 229–230
• Looking at a Short Story
  pp. 230–235*
• Writing Note p. 235
• Writing Assignment:
  Part 5 p. 238*
	⏱ **30–35 minutes**
	• Evaluating and Revising
	  Short Stories Chart
	  p. 239
	• Writing Assignment:
	  Part 6 p. 240
		⏱ **20–25 minutes**
		• Writing Assignment:
		  Part 7 p. 241
		• Reflecting p. 242

WRITING	EVALUATING AND REVISING	PROOFREADING AND PUBLISHING

• Writing, *Strategies for
  Writing* p. 20
	• Evaluating and Revising,
	  Strategies for Writing
	  p. 21
		• Proofreading Practice,
		  Strategies for Writing
		  p. 23
		• *English Workshop*
		  pp. 297–299

	• Revision Transparencies
	  9–10, *Transparency
	  Binder*
		• *Language Workshop,*
		  Lesson 42

ELEMENTS OF WRITING: CURRICULUM CONNECTIONS

Writing Workshop
• A News Story p. 244–246

Making Connections
• Speaking and Listening: Creating a Fable p. 247
• Short Story Writing Across the Curriculum: History p. 247

ASSESSMENT OPTIONS

Summative Assessment
Holistic Scoring: Prompts and Models pp. 15–20

Portfolio Assessment
Portfolio forms, *Portfolio Assessment* pp. 5–25, 44–48

Reflection
Writing Process Log, *Strategies for Writing* p. 15
Self-assessment Record, *Portfolio Assessment* p. 19

Ongoing Assessment
Proofreading, *Strategies for Writing* p. 22

💾 Computer disk or CD-ROM

📽 Overhead transparencies

LESSON 1 *(pp. 212–219)*
IMAGINING OTHER WORLDS

OBJECTIVES

- To evaluate a short story by analyzing its plot, conflict, and characters
- To write a new ending for a story

PROGRAM MANAGER

CHAPTER 6

- **Practice** To help less-advanced students who need additional practice with concepts and activities related to this chapter, see **Chapter 5** in *English Workshop, Fourth Course,* pp. 43–50.

- **Summative Assessment** For a writing prompt, including grading criteria and student models, see *Holistic Scoring: Prompts and Models,* pp. 15–20.

- **Extension/Enrichment** See **Fine Art Transparency 3,** *Great Wave off Kanagawa* by Katsushika Hokusai. For suggestions on how to tie the transparency to instruction, review teacher's notes in *Fine Art and Instructional Transparencies for Writing,* p. 15.

- **Reading Support** For help with the reading selection, pp. 214–219, see **Reading Master 6** in *Practice for Assessment in Reading, Vocabulary, and Spelling,* p. 6.

VISUAL CONNECTIONS
Ships of the Long Range Pioneer Fleet

About the Artist. As a child, Julian Baum found the wonders of the night sky inspiring, and he later attended the Cheshire School of Art and Design to learn techniques for producing science

6 CREATIVE WRITING: NARRATION

MOTIVATION

Have students name short stories they have read and reasons why they liked these stories. Then, ask further questions about these stories. Lead students to realize that the primary purpose of most stories is to entertain.

TEACHING THE LESSON

Before students begin reading the story, review the concept of conflict as an element of the plot of a literary work. Write *internal conflict* and *external conflict* on the chalkboard, and have volunteers explain the meaning of each term.

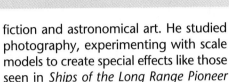

Imagining Other Worlds

Think about what life would be like without **imagination**—how boring it would be. Imagination takes us where we can never go in real life. It propels us into **other worlds** where things are whatever we want them to be.

Writing and You. Using their imaginations, writers write stories we never tire of reading and hearing—novels, mysteries, science fiction, children's stories. Some writers write about things that never were and never will be, yet they seem real because they play on our imaginations. Other writers start with real events and use their imaginations—and ours—to make them into something entirely new. How much do you use your imagination?

As You Read. In the following story, Marta Salinas writes about an event that seems believable to anyone who has faced unfairness. How is her story real? How is it fiction?

Julian Baum, *Ships of the Long Range Pioneer Fleet* (1985). Mixed media, 12" × 16". Science Photo Library/ Photo Researchers, Inc.

fiction and astronomical art. He studied photography, experimenting with scale models to create special effects like those seen in *Ships of the Long Range Pioneer Fleet.*

Ideas for Writing. Ask students to discuss the picture and its title, and then have each student write an introduction for a short story about the voyage of the ships. Suggest to students that they write from the point of view of a character in the story.

QUOTATION FOR THE DAY

"Imagination, n. A warehouse of facts, with poet and liar in joint ownership." (Ambrose Bierce, 1842–c.1914, American journalist, short-story writer, and poet)

Ask students to apply this quotation to pieces of literature they have read. Have volunteers discuss what elements of the poet and the liar they find in the piece.

MEETING *individual* NEEDS

LEP/ESL

General Strategies. This is an opportunity for students to create daily writing journals. Keeping writing journals will allow students to practice expressing themselves by recording dreams, family stories, and experiences. They can also use their writing journals to ask questions and to try out ideas for short stories.

Explain that authors of fiction frequently have multiple purposes for their writing, and ask students if they find in the story any deeper meanings or purposes beyond entertainment. [Students might say the author wishes to express a feeling or to describe a situation.]

GUIDED PRACTICE

The **Reader's Response** and **Writer's Craft** questions provide an opportunity for guided practice. Before discussing the questions, answer the first question for the students to help stimulate class discussion. Then, have volunteers discuss their answers to this question. You can continue with questions 3 and 4 in the same manner.

USING THE SELECTION
The Scholarship Jacket

1

Why does the narrator want the jacket so badly? [Answers will vary. Students might think she wants it for the prestige and honor it represents.]

2

The narrator's unhappiness with her appearance is the internal conflict that receiving the jacket will help resolve. The jacket will give her the status and self-esteem that she thinks her physical appearance robs her of.

3

What attitude does the narrator seem to have toward being on the team? [She seems to like the idea.] Is this attitude consistent with her feelings about her appearance? [Answers may vary. Some students may think the two things aren't related. Others may think this attitude is inconsistent because she's worried about appearing in class in shorts, but she would have to appear in a uniform before a large audience if she were on the team.]

214

THE
SCHOLARSHIP JACKET

by Marta Salinas

The small Texas school that I attended carried out a tradition every year during the eighth-grade graduation; a beautiful gold and green jacket, the school colors, was awarded to the class valedictorian, the student who had maintained the highest grades for eight years. The scholarship jacket had a big gold S on the left front side, and the winner's name was written in gold letters on the pocket.

My oldest sister Rosie had won the jacket a few years back and I fully expected to win also. I was fourteen and in the eighth grade. I had been a straight-A student since the first grade, and the last year I had looked forward to owning that jacket. My father was a farm laborer who couldn't earn enough money to feed eight children, so when I was six I was given to my grandparents to raise. We couldn't participate in sports at school because there were registration fees, uniform costs, and trips out of town; so even though we were quite agile and athletic, there would never be a sports school jacket for us. This one, the scholarship jacket, was our only chance.

In May, close to graduation, spring fever struck, and no one paid any attention in class; instead we stared out the windows and at each other, wanting to speed up the last few weeks of school. I despaired every time I looked in the mirror. Pencil thin, not a curve anywhere, I was called "Beanpole" and "String Bean" and I knew that's what I looked like. A flat chest, no hips, and a brain, that's what I had. That really isn't much for a fourteen-year-old to work with, I thought, as I absent-mindedly wandered from my history class to the gym. Another hour of sweating in basketball and displaying my toothpick legs was coming up. Then I remembered my P.E. shorts were still in a bag under my desk where I'd forgotten them. I had to walk all the way back and get them. Coach Thompson was a real bear if anyone wasn't dressed for P.E. She had said I was a good forward and once she even tried to talk Grandma into letting me join the team. Grandma, of course, said no.

1

2

3

INDEPENDENT PRACTICE

Have students write their answers to the second question in **Reader's Response.** Working in groups of four, students can exchange papers and read one another's paragraphs. Then, have each group pick one paragraph to read aloud to the class.

ASSESSMENT

If you choose to grade the paragraph written for the **Reader's Response** question, you may want to check to see that students maintain the style and the first-person point of view established in the story.

4   I was almost back at my classroom's door when I heard angry voices and arguing. I stopped. I didn't mean to eavesdrop; I just hesitated, not knowing what to do. I needed those shorts and I was going to be late, but I didn't want to interrupt an argument between my teachers. I recognized the voices: Mr. Schmidt, my history teacher, and Mr. Boone, my math teacher. They seemed to be arguing about me. I couldn't believe it. I still remember the shock that rooted me flat against the wall as if I were trying to blend in with the graffiti written there.

"I refuse to do it! I don't care who her father is, her grades don't even begin to compare to Martha's. I won't lie or falsify records. Martha has a straight-A-plus average and you know it." That was Mr. Schmidt and he sounded very angry. Mr. Boone's voice sounded calm and quiet.

5   "Look, Joann's father is not only on the Board, he owns the only store in town; we could say it was a close tie and—"

The pounding in my ears drowned out the rest of the words;
6   only a word here and there filtered through. ". . . Martha is
7   Mexican. . . . resign. . . . won't do it. . . ." Mr. Schmidt came rushing out, and luckily for me went down the opposite way toward the auditorium, so he didn't see me. Shaking, I waited

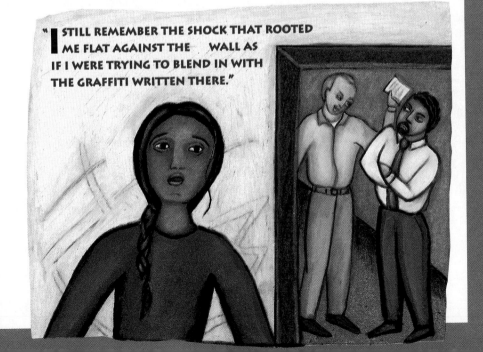

"I STILL REMEMBER THE SHOCK THAT ROOTED ME FLAT AGAINST THE WALL AS IF I WERE TRYING TO BLEND IN WITH THE GRAFFITI WRITTEN THERE."

4
This scene introduces the major conflict of the story: Martha versus Mr. Boone and his supporters. This external conflict is made more severe by Martha's internal conflict about her appearance.

5
Why is Mr. Boone concerned about Joann's father? [Answers may vary. Joann's father may be a friend of Mr. Boone, or Mr. Boone may want to please her father because he is a prominent person in the town. Mr. Boone may think Joann's father will help him out in return for his arguing in favor of Joann's receiving the jacket.]

6
Based on these words that Martha overhears, ask students how they think the rest of the conversation between the two teachers may have gone. [Responses may vary. Here is one possibility: Boone: "Besides, Martha is Mexican." Schmidt: "If she doesn't receive the jacket because she is Mexican, I will resign." Boone: "Come on, Schmidt. Play along on this one. Change Martha's grades." Schmidt: "No! I won't do it."]

7
Why doesn't Martha want Mr. Schmidt to see her? [Perhaps she is embarrassed over what she just overheard. Perhaps she doesn't want Mr. Schmidt to think she was eavesdropping.]

CLOSURE

Conclude the lesson by asking students to summarize the story, paying particular attention to the conflicts that the story contains. You can make the point that there is often a cause-and-effect relationship among internal and external conflicts. ■

8

Why does the principal look uncomfortable and unhappy? [He doesn't like having to tell Martha she isn't going to receive the jacket. This is his internal conflict.]

9

What effect on the symbolic significance of the jacket does this decision have? [The decision destroys the symbolic significance. It turns the jacket into a symbol of having done well in school and of being able to pay for the jacket, not of academic achievement alone.]

a few minutes and then went in and grabbed my bag and fled from the room. Mr. Boone looked up when I came in but didn't say anything. To this day I don't remember if I got in trouble in P.E. for being late or how I made it through the rest of the afternoon. I went home very sad and cried into my pillow that night so Grandmother wouldn't hear me. It seemed a cruel coincidence that I had overheard that conversation.

The next day when the principal called me into his office, I knew what it would be about. He looked uncomfortable and **8** unhappy. I decided I wasn't going to make it any easier for him, so I looked him straight in the eye. He looked away and fidgeted with the papers on his desk.

"Martha," he said, "there's been a change in policy this year regarding the scholarship jacket. As you know, it has always been free." He cleared his throat and continued. "This year **9** the Board decided to charge fifteen dollars—which still won't cover the complete cost of the jacket."

"...IF YOU PAY FOR IT, MARTA, IT'S NOT A SCHOLARSHIP JACKET...."

I stared at him in shock and a small sound of dismay escaped my throat. I hadn't expected this. He still avoided looking in my eyes.

"So if you are unable to pay the fifteen dollars for the jacket, it will be given to the next one in line."

Standing with all the dignity I could muster, I said, "I'll speak to my grandfather about it, sir, and let you know tomorrow." I cried on the walk home from the bus stop. The dirt road was a quarter of a mile from the highway, so by the time I got home, my eyes were red and puffy.

"Where's Grandpa?" I asked Grandma, looking down at the floor so she wouldn't ask me why I'd been crying. She was sewing on a quilt and didn't look up.

"I think he's out back working in the bean field."

I went outside and looked out at the fields. There he was. I could see him walking between the rows, his body bent over the little plants, hoe in hand. I walked slowly out to him, trying to think how I could best ask him for the money. There was a cool breeze blowing and a sweet smell of mesquite in the air, but I didn't appreciate it. I kicked at a dirt clod. I wanted that jacket so much. It was more than just being a valedictorian and giving a little thank-you speech for the jacket on graduation night. It represented eight years of hard work and expectation. I knew I had to be honest with Grandpa; it was my only chance. He saw me and looked up.

He waited for me to speak. I cleared my throat nervously and clasped my hands behind my back so he wouldn't see them shaking. "Grandpa, I have a big favor to ask you," I said in Spanish, the only language he knew. He still waited silently.

10   I tried again. "Grandpa, this year the principal said the scholarship jacket is not going to be free. It's going to cost fifteen dollars and I have to take the money in tomorrow, otherwise it'll be given to someone else." The last words came out in an eager rush. Grandpa straightened up tiredly and leaned his chin on the hoe handle. He looked out over the field that was filled with the tiny green bean plants. I waited, desperately hoping he'd say I could have the money.

He turned to me and asked quietly, "What does a scholarship jacket mean?"

I answered quickly; maybe there was a chance. "It means you've earned it by having the highest grades for eight years and that's why they're giving it to you." Too late I realized the

11   significance of my words. Grandpa knew that I understood it was not a matter of money. It wasn't that. He went back to hoeing the weeds that sprang up between the delicate little bean plants. It was a time-consuming job; sometimes the small shoots were right next to each other. Finally he spoke again.

"Then if you pay for it, Marta, it's not a scholarship jacket,

12   is it? Tell your principal I will not pay the fifteen dollars."

I walked back to the house and locked myself in the bathroom for a long time. I was angry with Grandfather even though I knew he was right, and I was angry with the Board, whoever they were. Why did they have to change the rules just when it was my turn to win the jacket?

It was a very sad and withdrawn girl who dragged into the principal's office the next day. This time he did look me in the eyes.

"What did your grandfather say?"

10
Why doesn't Martha tell Grandpa about the conversation she overheard between Mr. Schmidt and Mr. Boone? [Answers will vary. Perhaps she thinks it will make Grandpa angry to learn that Joann is going to receive the jacket based on who her father is, rather than on merit.]

11
If it isn't a matter of money, what is it a matter of? [Answers will vary. Students might think it is a matter of pride or principle.]

12
What do the words "will not pay," rather than "cannot pay," suggest about Grandpa's feelings toward the matter? [Answers will vary. Some students might think the words suggest that Grandpa suspects the new rule is a sham to keep Martha from receiving the jacket. By saying "will not," he implies that he will not be a party to anything that is underhanded.]

I sat very straight in my chair.

"He said to tell you he won't pay the fifteen dollars."

The principal muttered something I couldn't understand **13** under his breath, and walked over to the window. He stood looking at something outside. He looked bigger than usual when he stood up; he was a tall, gaunt man with gray hair, and I watched the back of his head while I waited for him to speak.

"Why?" he finally asked. "Your grandfather has the money. Doesn't he own a small bean farm?"

I looked at him, forcing my eyes to stay dry. "He said if I had to pay for it, then it wouldn't be a scholarship jacket," I said and stood up to leave. "I guess you'll just have to give it to Joann." I hadn't meant to say that; it had just slipped out. I was almost to the door when he stopped me.

"Martha—wait."

I turned and looked at him, waiting. What did he want now? I could feel my heart pounding. Something bitter and vile tasting was coming up in my mouth; I was afraid I was going to be sick. I didn't need any sympathy speeches. He sighed loudly and went back to his big desk. He looked at me, biting his lip, as if thinking.

"Okay, damn it. We'll make an exception in your case. I'll **14** tell the Board; you'll get your jacket."

I could hardly believe it. I spoke in a trembling rush. "Oh, thank you, sir!" Suddenly I felt great. I didn't know about adrenaline in those days, but I knew something was pumping through me, making me feel as tall as the sky. I wanted to yell, jump, run the mile, do something. I ran out so I could cry in the hall where there was no one to see me. At the end of the day, Mr. Schmidt winked at me and said, "I hear you're getting a scholarship jacket this year."

His face looked as happy and innocent as a baby's, but I **15** knew better. Without answering, I gave him a quick hug and ran to the bus. I cried on the walk home again, but this time because I was so happy. I couldn't wait to tell Grandpa and ran straight to the field. I joined him in the row where he was working and without saying anything I crouched down and started pulling up the weeds with my hands. Grandpa worked alongside me for a few minutes, but he didn't ask what had happened. After I had a little pile of weeds between the rows, I stood up and faced him.

13

What does the principal's behavior suggest about his attitude toward the issue of the jacket and Martha's receiving it? [That he is uncomfortable with the decision to require Martha's family to pay the fifteen dollars.]

14

The principal's strong expression here has been retained in printing to convey his exasperation.

15

Why does Martha imply that Mr. Schmidt isn't "innocent"? [She knows he has been fighting for her and that she knows all about the decision to make her pay fifteen dollars to receive the jacket.]

"The principal said he's making an exception for me, Grandpa, and I'm getting the jacket after all. That's after I told him what you said."

Grandpa didn't say anything, he just gave me a pat on the shoulder and a smile. He pulled out the crumpled red handkerchief that he always carried in his back pocket and wiped the sweat off his forehead.

"Better go see if your grandmother needs any help with supper."

16 I gave him a big grin. He didn't fool me. I skipped and ran back to the house whistling some silly tune.

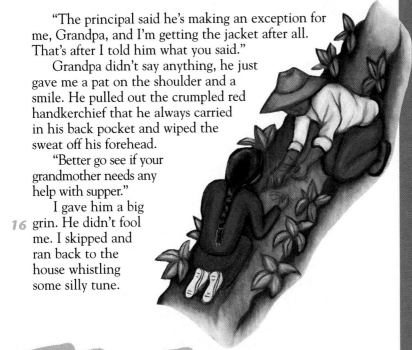

READER'S RESPONSE

1. A good fiction story, though not true or factual, seems real. Does this story seem real to you? Is it easy to believe that the events in the story actually happened to a young girl? Explain.
2. Is there another way this story could have ended? Might the principal have been more honest? Could the girl have reacted differently to him? Use your imagination and write a new ending for the story.

WRITER'S CRAFT

3. The author uses dialogue and the narrator's thoughts to bring her characters to life. What do you know about the narrator? What do you know about the principal?
4. Every story has some kind of conflict or problem. What is the conflict in this story?

16

What doesn't Grandpa fool Martha about?
[Responses will vary. Students might think that Grandpa knew that the issue would be resolved in Martha's favor. Students might also think that Grandpa is happy for Martha, even though he doesn't show it.]

ANSWERS
Reader's Response

Responses will vary.

1. Students might say the story seems real because of Martha's descriptions of her feelings. Students might say it is believable, since there is a hint that the decision not to give Martha the jacket might have been based on favoritism.

2. Possible endings are that Martha refused the jacket because of the policy or that she complained publicly and garnered public opinion to her side.

Writer's Craft

Answers may vary.

3. Readers know that Martha is sensitive about her appearance, that the jacket is important to her, and that her family is poor. Readers know that the principal is troubled about the decision to charge for the jacket and that he does not follow the decision when Martha confronts him.

4. Martha and the principal have internal conflicts (Martha about her appearance and the principal about the decision). There is an external conflict between Mr. Schmidt and Mr. Boone about who should receive the jacket and between Martha and a system that is willing to reward Joann because of who her father is.

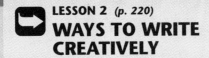
TEACHING *WAYS TO WRITE CREATIVELY*

The examples in this lesson illustrate each of the four basic methods of development of creative writing: narration, description, classification (comparison/contrast), and evaluation. Write these four terms on the chalkboard, and ask students to brainstorm definitions for each method as they would be applied to a short story. You could also ask students to bring to class a literary work that makes obvious use of one of the methods other than narration. ■

CRITICAL THINKING

Synthesis. The basic methods of development rarely occur alone in writing, and you may want to stress that any piece of literature might contain examples of all four methods, even if one method, such as narration, predominates. Therefore, for students to synthesize the lesson, have them work in groups of four; ask each group to find a piece of literature embodying more than one method. Then, have each group prepare a short oral report on the use of the methods found in the chosen literary work.

Ways to Write Creatively

A story, like the one you just read and the one you'll write in this chapter, is one way to write creatively. When people write creatively, they produce literature—stories, poems, songs and ballads, plays, and movie and television scripts. The key elements of creative writing are the use of imagination and the use of language in special and unique ways. Here are some ways in which writers develop creative writing.

- in a story, telling about a girl who witnesses events of the American Revolution
- in a movie script, telling the story of a Texas Ranger's life in a frontier settlement
- in a science fiction story, describing the interior of a space station
- in a poem about a festival, describing the smells of the food and the sounds of the games and music
- in a novel that takes place in London and Paris, comparing and contrasting the two cities
- in a poem about a fish, comparing its glistening scales to a kaleidoscope of silver, pink, and green
- in a play, showing how power can corrupt a person who becomes king
- in a story, creating a parody (an amusing imitation) of the fairly tale "Little Red Riding Hood"

LOOKING AHEAD

In the main assignment in this chapter, you'll use narration to write a story. As you work through the chapter, keep in mind that a short story

- has a plot involving a problem or conflict
- may contain characters, settings, plots, and details based on real life
- is developed mostly through the author's own imagination

OBJECTIVES
- To discover an idea to develop into a short story
- To develop character and setting for a story
- To create a plot outline listing the story's main conflict and events
- To develop a story map detailing point of view, characters, setting, and plot

Writing a Short Story

Exploring Story Ideas

Ideas for stories are everywhere. One way to find an idea is to ask yourself "What if?" questions, much as these writers may have.

- What if a ferocious shark terrorized a beach in the summer?
- What if a selfish Southern belle had to struggle through the Civil War and Reconstruction?
- What if a French nobleman escaped an unjust imprisonment, discovered a fabulous treasure, and sought revenge against his accusers?

Each of these questions inspired a book and then a movie. That's all you need to get started—a spark of an idea that your imagination can nurture and transform into a story.

Where can you find ideas? First, look around you. Notice people, events, places that intrigue you. Recall vivid experiences, crazy dreams, interesting conversations. Anything that interests, horrifies, tickles, or angers you might be an idea just waiting to become a story.

PROGRAM MANAGER

PREWRITING

- **Self-Assessment** Before beginning instruction of the writing process, see **Writing Process Log** in *Strategies for Writing*, p. 15.
- **Heuristics** To help students generate ideas, see **Prewriting** in *Strategies for Writing*, pp. 16–19.
- **Instructional Support** See **Graphic Organizers 9** and **10**. For suggestions on how to tie the transparencies to instruction, review teacher's notes in *Fine Art and Instructional Transparencies for Writing*, pp. 69, 71.

QUOTATION FOR THE DAY

"He is so stupid you can't trust him with an idea./He is so clever he will catch you in the least error./He will not buy short books./He will not buy long books./He is part moron, part genius and part ogre./There is some doubt as to whether he can read." (John Steinbeck, 1902–1968, American novelist and winner of the 1962 Nobel Prize for literature)

Steinbeck half-seriously describes his reader, someone he obviously considers during his writing process. Have students write detailed descriptions of their readers.

MOTIVATION

Have students recall the plot, setting, and characters in the last story that the class read. Explain to students that their stories will also contain these elements.

Cont. on p. 224

222   *Creative Writing*

Reminder

To find story ideas, think about

- a journal entry about your first date, touchdown, or A+
- an early memory about a special family holiday
- a picture of your favorite place
- a top-ten list of your worst fears, biggest pet peeves, most embarrassing moments

---

PART 1:
Developing a Story Idea

Ignite your imagination to find a story idea. You might mull over your experiences, flip through photo albums, watch people, or talk to friends. "What if?" questions can jump-start your imagination if you're having a hard time getting started. Keep at it until you find an idea you'd like to develop into a story.

"What I am trying to achieve is a voice sitting by a fireplace telling you a story on a winter's evening."

Truman Capote

TEACHING *ANALYZING POINT OF VIEW*

Use the four questions on p. 224 as the basis for a class discussion of point of view, and present an example from your literature textbook of each point of view. Ask students to analyze these examples. Then, have students recall the favorite stories they described before reading the chapter's

Prewriting

Planning Your Story

With just the spark of an idea, you're ready to start planning your story. Planning involves thinking about purpose, audience, and tone. You'll also be looking at point of view, characters, setting, and plot.

Thinking About Purpose, Audience, and Tone

Your main *purpose* in story writing is to be creative. And since you're the author, you have many opportunities to do so. Your characters, settings, and problems can be whatever you alone decide they should be. But another purpose in story writing is to entertain your *audience*—your readers. So you'll want to keep their interests and knowledge in mind as you plan. What will keep them entertained? Classmates, for example, might enjoy a detailed description of a teenage character's dress. Still another purpose might be to share an idea—about friendship or love, for example. Such an underlying idea is called a *theme.*

Writing stories also gives you flexibility in your tone. *Tone* is the attitude you take towards your characters and the events in your story. And you communicate that tone through the details and words you choose. The tone in your story can be serious, humorous, mysterious, or sarcastic. There are many other tones you can adopt as well.

CRITICAL THINKING

Analyzing Point of View

Point of view means who's telling the story. A story is always told by a narrator (who is not the author). Sometimes the narrator is a character in the story, and sometimes the narrator remains outside the story. You can use the following questions to analyze the point of view.

ADVANCED STUDENTS

To challenge advanced students to explore their interests, have them take a cross-curricular approach in developing their story ideas, characters, settings, and plots. For example, encourage students interested in computers to set their stories in a computer lab, computer class, or computer business and then to incorporate their knowledge of computers into the stories.

TEACHING THE LESSON

This lesson covers plot, setting, and characters. First, you may want to check to see that students understand what the textbook means by a "What if?" question. You can have students brainstorm "What if?" questions and write the best ones on the chalkboard. In addition, discuss the other ways

MEETING *individual* NEEDS

LEP/ESL

General Strategies. When discussing point of view, it is helpful first to review pronoun forms. Explain that the first-person point of view uses *I, me,* and *my,* while third person uses the pronouns *he, she,* and *it.* As practice for the **Critical Thinking Exercise**, have students change a model sentence from third- to first-person point of view.

⚡ TIMESAVER

After groups have rewritten O'Brien's passage, ask them to highlight all indicators of the first person, such as personal pronouns. These marks will help them check their work, and it will also make your grading easier.

ANSWERS

Critical Thinking Exercise

Revisions will vary. The following paragraph is an example:

Ahead of me other soldiers are flopped down in weeds beside the road. But I can't look. I can't feel another thing. Just gritty pebbles on the road shoulder where I lie and the smooth plastic of the rifle stock against my forehead.

SELECTION AMENDMENT
Description of change: excerpted
Rationale: to focus on the concept of point of view as presented in this chapter

1. Is the narrator a character in the story? Does the narrator use first-person pronouns like *I* and *me*? Does the narrator express his or her own thoughts and feelings, but not those of other characters? If so, the story has a *first-person point of view.*
2. Is the narrator outside the story and not a character in the story? Does the narrator use third-person pronouns like *he* and *she*? If so, the story has a *third-person narrator.*
3. Does the third-person narrator look at the story through the eyes of *one character only*? This type of narrator can't tell what other characters are thinking or feeling. This is called a *limited narrator.*
4. Can the third-person narrator tell what *everyone* is thinking and feeling? This is called an *omniscient (all-knowing) narrator.*

⚡ CRITICAL THINKING EXERCISE: Analyzing Point of View

What goes through a soldier's mind as he's facing battle? In this excerpt, the narrator describes the feelings of one soldier. The passage is written in the third-person point of view. You're Private Berlin. Working with some classmates, rewrite the passage from the first-person point of view. Use the pronouns *I* and *me*. Make up details if you wish. You might imagine, for example, what it is that Private Berlin is pretending about his camping trip.

At the rear of the column, Private First Class Paul Berlin lay quietly with his forehead resting on the black plastic stock of his rifle, his eyes closed. He was pretending he was not in the war, pretending he had not watched Billy Boy Watkins die of a heart attack that afternoon. He was pretending he was a boy again, camping with his father in the midnight summer along the Des Moines River. In the dark, with his eyes pinched shut, he pretended.

Tim O'Brien, "Where Have You Gone, Charming Billy?"

to brainstorm main ideas such as recalling experiences, dreams, and conversations.

You may want to suggest to students that finding one creative idea is analogous to formulating a thesis statement for an expository essay.

Review with students the material devoted to purpose, audience, and tone, and cite examples from familiar literature. Next, introduce one or two examples of character and setting from favorite stories of yours and discuss their strengths. You could give students copies of the descriptions to use as models.

You may also want to review the **Types of Conflict** chart on p. 227 with students. Ask volunteers to offer specific examples of other types of external and internal conflicts.

MEETING *individual* **NEEDS**

LESS-ADVANCED STUDENTS

You might suggest that students create character and setting collages from magazine pictures. These collages can be used as visual writing prompts. For example, instead of writing ideas about different characters and settings, suggest that students first create two collages, one containing ten pictures of characters and one containing ten pictures of settings.

Thinking About Characters and Setting

Characters.   Who will be the people in your story? And what will they be like? You can create a completely made-up character, maybe using traits from all different kinds of people. Perhaps you'll create a character who has the humor of Bill Cosby, the looks of Kevin Costner, and the brains of Albert Einstein. Or you might take a person you know and change a few details to fit the character your story needs. Just keep developing details about your characters until you feel you know them well.

Setting.   Stories are always set in a particular time and place. The time and place might be as unusual as nine hundred years ago in a medieval castle in Scotland. Or they can be as ordinary as your back yard last week. When the time and place aren't central to the story, the details of setting may not be very important. But if you want to create a mood—or feeling, such as mystery or suspense—setting can be very important. That's why a ghost story set in an overgrown graveyard on a dark and stormy night is scary. The setting helps the reader feel the mood of mystery and heightens the suspense.

In **Writing Assignment: Part 1,** you could help students by first choosing a familiar character, perhaps from a popular TV show. Create a "What If?" situation for this character. Then, for **Writing Assignments: Parts 2** and **3,** answer the review questions about this character and create a setting. Finally, to model **Writing Assignment: Part 4,** create a sample story map on the chalkboard.

INTEGRATING THE LANGUAGE ARTS

Literature Link. Available in some literature textbooks, "Mr. Parker" by Laurie Colwin is a model of character and setting (as well as of plot conflict and development). Ask students to read the story and to mark all passages of particularly vivid character and setting descriptions. In a class discussion, have students explain why the passages are successful descriptions.

Point out the contrasts in the descriptions of the two piano teachers and what the differences indicate about their characters.

COOPERATIVE LEARNING

Ask students to choose partners to help them brainstorm for story details. Students could first brainstorm ideas separately on paper and then discuss their ideas. Encourage students to finish the exercise by recording five details they might use for a story.

Reminder

Ask yourself the following questions to get ideas for your characters and setting.

Characters:
- How do the characters look, walk, and talk?
- How do they dress?
- How do they stand, move, and sit?
- What do they think about?
- What kind of personality do they have? Are they absent-minded? shy? anxious? bubbly?
- What do other characters in the story think about them?

Setting:
- What's the time and place of the story?
- What kind of houses do people live in at this time?
- What kind of work do they do?
- How important is the time and place to the story?
- Do I want the setting to create a mood, or feeling? What sights, sounds, and smells should I describe?

WRITING ASSIGNMENT

PART 2:
Developing Your Characters and Setting

Can you see your characters in your mind? Do you feel the setting? Write a short paragraph describing your main character with as much detail as you can. Then write another paragraph about your setting. Share your paragraphs with a couple of classmates. Ask them if your character seems real. Can they imagine your setting? What mood does it suggest?

Developing the Plot

What will happen in your story? Does boy meet girl? Does boy lose girl? What happens in a story is called the *plot.* Most plots open with a *conflict,* or problem, that can be either *external* or *internal.*

Students should now be prepared to complete all of the **Writing Assignments** independently. You may want to have them work in pairs or in groups of three to complete one or more of the parts.

You may want to try a credit/no credit system of evaluation for the **Writing Assignments**. Because students are only formulating ideas, they will benefit most from supportive comments.

TYPES OF CONFLICT	
EXTERNAL CONFLICT	**EXAMPLES**
A character faces a conflict with another character or group.	John argues with his father over his curfew.
A character faces a conflict with nature.	As he is on his way home to make his curfew, a heavy rain causes Julio's car motor to die.
INTERNAL CONFLICT	**EXAMPLE**
A character struggles with opposite thoughts and feelings within himself or herself.	Sue wants to stay longer at the party—but she knows she'll be grounded if she breaks her curfew.

TIMESAVER

Let peer-editing groups review several of the prewriting exercises, such as the character and setting descriptions and the story map. Have them underline the best sentence and the one which needs the most work. You can then focus on the remaining sentences.

After the opening conflict, the plot unfolds in a series of events that build on and cause each other. Will Sally's speeding ticket cause her parents to take away the car? Will she lose her part-time job if she can't drive? *Suspense* builds when readers wonder about what will happen next. Event builds upon event until the main conflict is resolved at the end.

As you develop your plot, think about the order of events. Listing events in the order they happen (chronological order) can help you develop a quick plot outline. You'll also be able to see if the events lead logically to the ending. Maybe your ending is a surprise, but it should still flow naturally from the story's events and characters.

WRITING ASSIGNMENT

PART 3:
Gathering Plot Details

What will happen in your story? What conflict will set the chain of events in motion? What will be the order of events? How will the story end? Jot down your ideas, creating a chain of events that outlines your plot.

Write the following sentence on the chalkboard:

Zuni Littlefoot trudged beneath the broiling Arizona sun.

Ask students what information they have learned from this sentence [setting— Arizona; character—American Indian]. Next, ask students what they don't know [details about plot, character, and conflict]. Explain to students that they determine basic elements during prewriting. ■

A DIFFERENT APPROACH

To help students generate story ideas, you could choose a large photo from a popular magazine and work with the class to create a story map based on this photo. The person pictured could be famous or totally unknown, or you could even choose a setting to work from.

Begin by showing the picture to the class and then asking questions such as "Who is this and what is he or she going to do next?" Then, build on students' answers until you have a completed story map.

Making a Story Map. As you plot your story's course, you may find it helpful to create a story map. Then you can see how all your story elements fit together. Here's how one writer developed a story map.

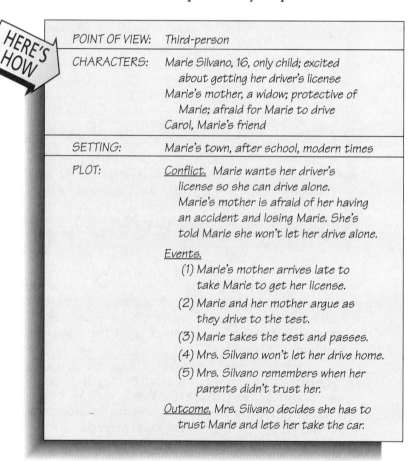

POINT OF VIEW:	*Third-person*
CHARACTERS:	*Marie Silvano, 16, only child; excited about getting her driver's license*
	Marie's mother, a widow; protective of Marie; afraid for Marie to drive
	Carol, Marie's friend
SETTING:	*Marie's town, after school, modern times*
PLOT:	<u>*Conflict.*</u> *Marie wants her driver's license so she can drive alone. Marie's mother is afraid of her having an accident and losing Marie. She's told Marie she won't let her drive alone.*
	<u>*Events.*</u>
	(1) Marie's mother arrives late to take Marie to get her license.
	(2) Marie and her mother argue as they drive to the test.
	(3) Marie takes the test and passes.
	(4) Mrs. Silvano won't let her drive home.
	(5) Mrs. Silvano remembers when her parents didn't trust her.
	<u>*Outcome.*</u> *Mrs. Silvano decides she has to trust Marie and lets her take the car.*

WRITING ASSIGNMENT

PART 4:
Developing a Story Map

With the main landmarks for your story almost in place, you're ready to develop a story map. Using all the ideas you've developed so far, create a map for your story. Keep your plan handy as you write your story.

WRITING YOUR FIRST DRAFT

OBJECTIVES

- To work with others to add dialogue to a story paragraph
- To analyze a short story's character, setting, conflict, and ending
- To write a rough draft of a short story

MOTIVATION

Ask students to think about all the times they tell stories informally, such as recounting incidents to friends or explaining their behavior to parents. Tell students that writing a rough draft is very similar to telling someone a story.

☞

Writing Your First Draft

The Basic Elements of Stories

If you've read many stories, you know they vary widely. Most stories, however, center on effective characters—people who seem so real they almost leap off the pages—and their dialogue.

Writing stories gives you total creative control. You create characters, choose their hair color, decide their fate. While you're being creative, just remember that your readers want a good, suspenseful story. Effective characters and dialogue are sure to keep them reading.

Characters.   Think of the people in your story as real. How can your readers get to know them? The answer is simple: the same way they get to know people in real life! Writers can reveal characters by

- telling readers directly what the character is like
- describing how the character looks and dresses
- having the character speak
- revealing the character's thoughts and feelings
- showing how others respond to the character
- showing the character's actions

Dialogue.   The dialogue, or talk, of the characters does two important things. First, it shows what kind of people the characters are. Second, it moves the plot along in a natural, interesting way. Following are some questions to ask yourself as you write dialogue.

- Do the words and sentences fit the characters? Do the children talk like children and the adults talk like adults?
- Do the characters sound natural? Do they use phrases, contractions, and slang?
- Does the dialogue show what characters are like and/or move the story along?
- Do the dialogue tags—phrases like "they said," "he groaned," or "she screamed"—identify the speaker and add interest?

PROGRAM MANAGER

WRITING YOUR FIRST DRAFT

- **Instructional Support** For help with creating dialogue, see **Writing** in *Strategies for Writing*, p. 20.

QUOTATION FOR THE DAY

"For me Calvino is one of the most wonderful writers, and the magic in his work is something that has been an influence. . . ." (Louise Erdrich, 1954–   , American Indian poet, novelist, and short-story writer)

You may want to save this quotation to use after students have read the story **"Mushrooms in the city"** by Italo Calvino. Ask students to make a conjecture about the meaning of *magic* as Erdrich uses it and to decide whether they see magic in the Calvino story.

To introduce and discuss the ways to reveal characters, ask students to reexamine their character descriptions, and look for examples of each strategy. Then, ask volunteers to read aloud examples illustrating all of the strategies.

Read aloud the four questions in the text that concern dialogue. Then, show students models of dialogue that might help them answer those questions. See if students can find examples of dialogue from other stories they have read in the textbook.

As an introduction to **A Writer's Model** on pp. 236–238, discuss what "Mushrooms in the city" says about human nature, emotions, and interactions, and how the conflict, plot, characters, and

ANSWERS
Exercise 1

Responses will vary. In recording and reading dialogue to the class, students should include opening and closing sentences, and they should also include dialogue tags.

TEACHING NOTE

Evaluating Group Work. After students complete the activity in **Exercise 1,** have them briefly evaluate their group's work. Student evaluations should answer the following questions: Who participated in the group? What was the group's task? Did the group stay on task? Did every member contribute to the group? What was the group's greatest strength? Each student should also address his or her own participation and effectiveness in the group.

The forms **Evaluating Group Participation** on pp. 40–41 in *Portfolio Assessment* may encourage students to answer these questions fully.

---

230   *Creative Writing*

COMPUTER NOTE: Some computer programs help you format screenplays and keep track of characters in a story.

EXERCISE 1 ▶ **Speaking and Listening: Evaluating Dialogue**

Here's part of a story about two brothers who manage to argue about everything. The writer hasn't used much dialogue. Get together with three or four of your classmates. See if you can liven up the paragraph by writing convincing dialogue for the characters. Then take turns letting each group read its dialogue aloud. Listen to the different versions, and evaluate the dialogue. Make specific suggestions for improving the dialogue, using the questions on the previous page and above as a guide.

> World War III was just erupting when I walked into the kitchen. Jesse asked Tom if Tom was planning to ignore the full trash can. Tom said it wasn't his turn. After a few heated exchanges, Mom intervened. Then they tried to blame her for the argument. She silenced them both by banishing them to their rooms and taking away their car keys. Mom always was the world's greatest peacemaker.

Looking at a Short Story

The following excerpt is from the story "Spring," by professional writer Italo Calvino. It has a simple plot about a worker who discovers wild mushrooms growing in the city. The main conflict is not directly presented. To discover it, think about what the mushrooms represent to Marcovaldo. [Hint: Remember that one type of conflict can be nature versus man or woman.]

setting convey these meanings. Ask students to keep these ideas in mind and then read **A Writer's Model** aloud. Point out the dialogue tags in the story and ask the class to suggest more descriptive verbs.

After examining these two models, students should be ready to write the first rough drafts of their stories. Remind them to review their prewriting notes and story maps and to refer to this material while writing.

☞

A SHORT STORY

Mushrooms in the city
by Italo Calvino

BEGINNING
Attention grabber

The wind, coming to the city from far away, brings it unusual gifts, noticed by only a few sensitive souls, such as hay-fever victims, who sneeze at the pollen from flowers of other lands.

Setting

One day, to the narrow strip of ground flanking a city avenue came a gust of spores from God knows where; and some mushrooms germinated. Nobody noticed them except Marcovaldo, the worker who caught his <u>tram</u> just there every morning.

Introduction of main character
1
2

This Marcovaldo possessed an eye ill-suited to city life: billboards, traffic-lights, shop-windows, neon signs, posters, no matter how carefully devised to catch the attention, never arrested his gaze, which might have been running over the desert sands. Instead, he would never miss a leaf yellowing on a branch, a feather trapped by a roof-tile; there was no horsefly on a horse's back, no worm-hole in a plank, or fig-peel squashed on the sidewalk that Marcovaldo didn't remark and ponder over, discovering the changes of season, the yearnings of his heart, and the woes of his existence.

Character development

MIDDLE

Thus, one morning, as he was waiting for the tram that would take him to Sbav and Co., where he was employed as an unskilled laborer, he noticed something unusual near the stop, in the sterile, encrusted strip of earth beneath the avenue's line of trees; at certain points, near the tree trunks, some bumps seemed to rise and, here and there, they had opened, allowing roundish <u>subterranean</u> bodies to peep out.

USING THE SELECTION
Mushrooms in the city

1

You could point out that in short stories, the main character may be introduced very early in the text. As an example, tell students to notice that Marcovaldo is first mentioned at the end of the second paragraph.

2

Ask students to list three things they are told about Marcovaldo. [Students might say that Marcovaldo is an observant person, an unhappy city dweller, and an unskilled laborer.]

You can first model **Exercise 1** by either providing an example of good dialogue from a literary selection or by creating some sample dialogue on the chalkboard. To illustrate the analysis of a short story required in **Exercise 2,** try choosing a familiar selection from your literature textbook.

Then, identify this story's conflict, setting, and other features for students.

232   *Creative Writing*

Character development/ thoughts

Bending to tie his shoes, he took a better look: they were mushrooms, real mushrooms, sprouting right in the heart of the city! To Marcovaldo the gray and wretched world surrounding him seemed suddenly generous with hidden riches; something could still be expected of life, beyond the hourly wage of his <u>stipulated</u> salary, with inflation index, family grant, and cost-of-living allowance.

3

On the job he was more absent-minded than usual; he kept thinking that while he was there unloading cases and boxes, in the darkness of the earth the slow, silent mushrooms, known only to him, were ripening their <u>porous</u> flesh, were <u>assimilating</u> underground <u>humors</u>, breaking the crust of clods. "One night's rain would be enough," he said to himself, "then they would be ready to pick." And he couldn't wait to share his discovery with his wife and his six children.

Suspense

Character development/ dialogue

"I'm telling you!" he announced during their <u>scant</u> supper. "In a week's time we'll be eating mushrooms! A great fry! That's a promise!"

And to the smaller children, who did not know what mushrooms were, he explained ecstatically the beauty of the numerous species, the delicacy of their flavor, the way they should be cooked; and so he also drew

3

Why might the author choose to use the description of Marcovaldo as "absent-minded"? [Calvino may be trying to indicate that the character is prone to make mistakes. This would serve as foreshadowing for future action.]

VISUAL CONNECTIONS

Exploring the Subject. The mushroom is actually a fungus that is producing fruit. *Mushroom* is the word used generally to identify the edible species, while *toadstool* is reserved for the poisonous species.

Mushrooms have been an important part of the folklore of many countries. The ancient Greeks and Romans considered them to be one of the foods of the gods. Because they appear unexpectedly and disappear quickly, mushrooms have inspired much speculation.

into the discussion his wife, Domitilla, who until then had appeared rather <u>incredulous</u> and <u>abstracted</u>.

"Where are these mushrooms?" the children asked. "Tell us where they grow!"

Conflict

At this question Marcovaldo's enthusiasm was <u>curbed</u> by a suspicious thought: Now if I tell them the place, they'll go and hunt for them with the usual gang of kids, word will spread through the neighborhood, and the mushrooms will end up in somebody else's pan! And so that discovery, which had promptly filled his heart with universal love,

Character development/ thoughts

now made him wildly possessive, surrounded him with jealous and distrusting fear.

Dialogue— suspense 4

"I know where the mushrooms are, and I'm the only one who knows," he said to his children, "and God help you if you breathe a word to anybody."

Suspense

The next morning, as he approached the tram stop, Marcovaldo was filled with apprehension. He bent to look at the ground and, to his relief, saw that the mushrooms had grown a little, but not much, and were still almost completely hidden by the earth.

He was bent in this position when he realized there was someone behind him. He straightened up at once and tried to act <u>indifferent</u>. It was the street-cleaner, leaning on his broom and looking at him.

Character 5 **development/ description**

This street-cleaner, whose jurisdiction included the place where the mushrooms grew, was a lanky youth with eyeglasses. His name was Amadigi, and Marcovaldo had long <u>harbored</u> a dislike of him, perhaps because of those eyeglasses that examined the pavement of the streets, seeking any trace of nature, to be <u>eradicated</u> by his broom.

Conflict

It was Saturday; and Marcovaldo spent his free half-day circling the bed of dirt with an absent air, keeping an eye on the street-cleaner in the distance and on the mushrooms,

4
What does the dialogue reveal about Marcovaldo's character? [Students might say that he is not a character who trusts others.]

5
How does Calvino develop the character of Amadigi? [He gives a brief physical description and he gives another character's opinion of Amadigi.]

ASSESSMENT

When examining rough drafts, provide suggestions about the stories' strengths and weaknesses. Point out any weaknesses that may affect the final story, such as a lack of conflict or an illogical chain of events.

RETEACHING

If students still have trouble creating interesting dialogue, have them work in pairs to use magazine or newspaper photos as prompts for their dialogue.

234   *Creative Writing*

Suspense

and calculating how much time they needed to ripen.

That night it rained: like peasants who, after months of drought, wake up and leap with joy at the sound of the first drops, so Marcovaldo, alone in all the city, sat up in bed and called to his family: "It's raining! It's raining!" and breathed in the smell of moistened dust and fresh mold that came from outside.

At dawn—it was Sunday—with the children and a borrowed basket, he ran immediately to the patch. There were the mushrooms, erect on their stems, their caps high over the still-soaked earth. "Hurrah!"—and they fell to gathering them.

Conflict

"Papà! Look how many that man over there has found," Michelino said, and his father, raising his eyes, saw Amadigi standing beside them, also with a basket full of mushrooms under his arm.

Dialogue—suspense

"Ah, you're gathering them, too?" the street-cleaner said. "Then they're edible? I picked a few, but I wasn't sure . . . Farther down the avenue some others have sprouted, even bigger ones . . . Well, now that I know, I'll tell my relatives; they're down there arguing whether it's a good idea to pick them or not . . ." And he walked off in a hurry.

Character development   6

Marcovaldo was speechless: even bigger mushrooms, which he hadn't noticed, an unhoped-for harvest, being taken from him like this, before his very eyes. For a moment he was almost frozen with anger, fury, then— as sometimes happens—the collapse of individual passion led to a generous impulse. At that hour, many people were waiting for the tram, umbrellas over their arms, because the weather was still damp and uncertain. "Hey, you! Do you want to eat fried mushrooms tonight?" Marcovaldo shouted to the crowd of people at the stop. "Mushrooms are growing here by the street! Come along! There's

Dialogue—suspense

6

What emotions do the story's conflicts generate in Marcovaldo? [His conflict with himself about revealing the mushroom's location to his children causes him to feel first "universal love" and then "wildly possessive, surrounded . . . with jealous and distrusting fear." His conflict with Amadigi makes him feel "frozen with anger, fury" and then "a generous impulse."]

CLOSURE

Ask students to discuss what they found easiest about writing their drafts and what they found most difficult. List responses in two columns on the chalkboard.

EXTENSION

Bring in a short example of dialogue written in formal English. Ask students to work in small groups to rewrite the dialogue using informal English. Then, ask a volunteer from each group to read aloud his or her group's revised dialogue.

Writing Your First Draft **235**

plenty for all!" And he walked off after Amadigi, with a string of people behind him.

They all found plenty of mushrooms, and lacking baskets, they used their open umbrellas. Somebody said: "It would be nice to have a big feast, all of us together!" But, instead, each took his own share and went home.

OUTCOME

They saw one another again soon, however; that very evening, in fact, in the same ward of the hospital, after the stomach-pump had saved them all from poisoning. It was not serious, because the number of mushrooms eaten by each person was quite small.

Marcovaldo and Amadigi had <u>adjacent</u> beds; they glared at each other.

translated by William Weaver

WRITING NOTE

In this story, the writer doesn't present the conflict immediately. Instead, he begins with descriptions of the setting and of the main character, Marcovaldo. As you read the story, you realized that these descriptions are important to understanding the main conflict. It arises both from the city setting, where mushrooms are seldom found, and Marcovaldo's love of nature.

MEETING *individual* NEEDS

LEARNING STYLES

Auditory Learners. To help students assess the completeness of their character descriptions, organize the class into pairs and ask each pair to introduce their fictional characters to one another. Use the following questions:

1. Who is the character?
2. Where does he or she live?
3. What does he or she do?
4. In what is he or she most interested?

Visual Learners. You may want to show a filmed version of a short story, preferably one students have read in class. Discuss how the film handles description of character and setting. You could also discuss the dialogue, character motivation, and the plot's conflict and resolution.

ADVANCED STUDENTS

Ask advanced students as a group to find stories that contain interesting openings or closings, fully described characters, realistic conflicts and plots, and creative dialogue. Ask the group to present some of the stories as dramatic readings.

ANSWERS

Exercise 2

Answers will vary. The following answers are possibilities:

1. The main conflict is that Marcovaldo is trying to get the mushrooms (humanity vs. nature). A minor conflict is that Marcovaldo feels he must protect the mushrooms from destruction by others.

2. Calvino shows Marcovaldo's feelings (in thoughts and words) as hope, fear, greed, possessiveness, generosity, and excitement. Two examples are his absent-mindedness on the job as he thinks of growing mushrooms and his switch from expansive descriptions to guardedness when older children ask about where the mushrooms grow.

3. The setting is very important to the story. This story needed to be set in the city to make the conflicts plausible.

4. Students probably will have been surprised by the ending. One clue is Amadigi and the relatives' hesitation about whether mushrooms are safe.

COOPERATIVE LEARNING

Explain that although **A Writer's Model** is written in the third person, the narrator enters the mind of only one character—Marie. Ask students to think about how different the story would be if it were told from Mrs. Silvano's point of view. Then, have students work in groups of three to rewrite the story from Mrs. Silvano's viewpoint.

236

EXERCISE 2 ▶ **Analyzing the Organization of a Short Story**

Meet with a small group of classmates to discuss the answers to the following questions about "Mushrooms in the City."

1. What is the main conflict in the story? What are some minor conflicts?
2. Marcovaldo might seem a little odd to you. How does Calvino make him seem real, despite his quirks? Point to specific examples in the story to explain your answer.
3. How important is the setting? Could the story have happened anywhere else?
4. Were you surprised by the ending? What clues in the story prepare you for the surprise ending?

A Basic Framework for a Story

"Mushrooms in the City" shows how a master of storytelling combines plot, characters, and setting to create several levels of meaning. The following story, which you might want to use as a model for your own, gives you a less complicated model to follow. The conflict in this story is revealed more through events and dialogue.

A WRITER'S MODEL

Licensed to Drive

BEGINNING **Event 1** **Character development and conflict**	"Where is she?" Marie sighed, checking her watch again. "It'd be just like her to forget--on purpose. You know she doesn't want me to do this."
	"Calm down," Carol said. "Isn't that your mother's car?" She pointed to the old, blue car making a wide turn into the school parking lot, slowly heading toward the girls.
Dialogue	"Finally. Let me drive," Marie said as her mother pulled up. Marie drove slowly out of the parking lot as Carol gave her the thumbs up sign.

Event 2

Character development/ dialogue Conflict

Background

Event 3

Event 4 Suspense MIDDLE

Character development/ thoughts

Dialogue

Event 5 Character development/ dialogue

"You're fifteen minutes late, Mom," complained Marie.

"I couldn't get out of work earlier," Mrs. Silvano said. "This is too early, if you ask me. You just turned 16! I hope you don't pass. And even if you do, I'm not sure I'll let you drive alone."

Marie shook her head and bit her tongue to keep from speaking back to her mother. She knew this speech; she'd heard it a million times. Her father had been killed by a reckless teenage driver just three years before. Her mother couldn't stand the thought of Marie driving alone and had made that clear.

"I'd be more careful," Marie promised, as she turned into the test site. "You know you can trust me."

Marie was excited when she passed the test so easily, but her mother didn't say a word. When Marie asked to drive home, Mrs. Silvano snapped, "No, it's almost dark."

The ride home was silent and tense. Marie wanted desperately to take the car out, to show Carol, to drive with the windows down and the radio tuned to her favorite rock station. But she knew better than to push her mother now. Mrs. Silvano would only dig her heels in. She tried to think of something to say.

"Carol's brother's getting married."

"Who, Paul?" Mrs. Silvano asked, perking up just a bit.

"Yeah, and Carol's parents are furious. Said he's too young, it won't last, he should wait." Marie sighed, thinking of parents who don't understand their kids.

"Well, he's 20, isn't he? And he finished school? I was young when I married your papa." She smiled, thinking of the memory. "My parents didn't like it one bit, not one bit. But I knew better and I was right, too. He was such a good man, always thoughtful to me, and a wonderful father. We were married and happy for a long time. Marriage lasted 22 years. We'd still be married if he was alive."

INTEGRATING THE LANGUAGE ARTS

Literature Link. If this story is available in your literature textbook, ask students to trace the plot structure in Isaac Bashevis Singer's "The Fatalist." Students should identify the two narrative voices [first person for both the frame and inner stories]. You could also have them note any interesting character and setting descriptions as well as words indicating tone and mood.

Vocabulary Link. Students might need help including interesting word choices in their drafts. To focus on vocabulary, hand out a sheet listing descriptive and dynamic words. Or, list rather plain and simple words on the chalkboard and ask students to suggest more descriptive alternatives. Use a model paragraph which contains spaces for deleted words. Have students add descriptive words to this model.

CRITICAL THINKING

Analysis. Explain to students that what a character says and does should be clearly motivated. Ask students to use the following questions to analyze character motivation in **"Mushrooms in the city"**:

1. Why does the world suddenly seem "generous with hidden riches" to Marcovaldo when he discovers the mushrooms? [Marcovaldo is a "sensitive" soul who possesses "an eye ill-suited to city life." Thus, the mushrooms help him to connect with nature and to escape temporarily from his daily life.]

2. Why does Marcovaldo's enthusiasm turn to suspicion and "jealous and distrusting fear" when his children ask the location of the mushrooms? [He is afraid the children will tell their friends, who will harvest the mushroom crop. Thus, his fear makes him overly possessive of his find.]

TIMESAVER

Before turning in their rough drafts, ask students to color-code character and setting descriptions with highlighters. Also, ask them to underline all dialogue and dialogue tags. These marks will help you focus more quickly on these aspects of the drafts.

238

Dialogue

Suspense

OUTCOME

Dialogue

She choked up and fell silent. Even after three years she couldn't talk about her husband without crying.

"I know, Mom," Marie said. "But not all kids are bad drivers."

"Maybe," grunted Mrs. Silvano, clenching the steering wheel tighter.

Marie sighed and closed her eyes. It's hopeless. I'll be the only kid in school with a license who can't drive, she thought.

They arrived home and got out. As Mrs. Silvano unlocked the front door, she paused as if she had something to say. Then she suddenly jabbed the keys into Marie's hand.

"Don't you want to drive over to Carol's?" she said roughly.

"You mean it, Mom? Really?"

"Well, I guess I have to trust you sometime. Might as well be now. Hearing about Paul made me remember when my parents didn't trust me. But I want you to be careful. Night driving can be tricky. And be back in thirty minutes or no more driving."

Marie gave her a quick hug and jumped in the car. The headlights of the old car shone through the darkness as she drove away.

WRITING ASSIGNMENT

PART 5:
Writing a Draft of Your Story

By now you should have a good idea of how your story will develop. Use your prewriting ideas and story map to make your characters, setting, and plot come to life.

EVALUATING AND REVISING

OBJECTIVES

- To analyze a writer's revisions
- To use peer feedback and an evaluating and revising chart to revise a rough draft of a story

TEACHING THE LESSON

Discuss and clarify each strategy in the **Evaluating and Revising Short Stories** chart. Then, provide a copy of a poorly written short story and revise the story by using the chart's criteria as guided practice. Next, read **Exercise 3** in class and discuss the revisions by answering the questions.

Evaluating and Revising

You may want to read your story to others in a small group and then listen to their feedback. You can also use the chart below to help you analyze and improve each other's stories. Ask yourself each question in the left-hand column. If your answer is no, use the revision technique suggested in the right-hand column.

EVALUATING AND REVISING SHORT STORIES

EVALUATION GUIDE	REVISION TECHNIQUE
1 Does a conflict set a chain of events in motion? Is the order of events clear?	**Add** a conflict between characters or within a character. **Reorder** events in the order they happen.
2 Do the events create suspense? Do the actions lead to a logical ending?	**Cut** events that slow the story down. **Add** details that build suspense. **Add** details that prepare for the ending.
3 Are the characters interesting and real?	**Add** details about what the characters do, feel, say, and think. **Add** realistic dialogue.
4 Is the point of view consistent? Is it either first-person or third-person?	**Cut** details that make the point of view inconsistent. **Add** first-person or third-person details as necessary.
5 Does the setting help readers picture the action or establish a mood?	**Add** specific sensory details. **Cut** details that detract from the mood.

PROGRAM MANAGER

EVALUATING AND REVISING

- **Reinforcement/Reteaching** See **Revision Transparencies 9** and **10.** For suggestions on how to tie the transparencies to instruction, review teacher's notes in *Fine Art and Instructional Transparencies for Writing,* p. 111.

- **Ongoing Assessment** For a rubric to guide assessment, see **Evaluating and Revising** in *Strategies for Writing,* p. 21.

- **Assessment/Reflection** To assess student work and evaluate progress, see **Portfolio Forms** in *Portfolio Assessment,* pp. 5–21.

QUOTATION FOR THE DAY

"Listen!/All of you beauty-makers,/Give up beauty for a moment./Look at harshness, look at pain,/Look at life again . . ." (Langston Hughes, 1902–1967, African American poet)

Ask each student to choose a well-written sentence or paragraph in his or her story and to apply this quotation to that sentence or paragraph. Volunteers might then share their observations of whether this exercise led them to reevaluate or change their writing.

Have students work with partners to read each other's stories and discuss changes, using the **Evaluating and Revising Short Stories** chart as a guide. After students have finished the work with partners, they should be ready to evaluate and revise their own stories.

CLOSURE

Ask students to describe what they learned about writing, evaluating, and revising as a result of working on their stories. ■

ANSWERS
Exercise 3

1. The question creates suspense. Although Marie's dialogue would have been realistic either way, this new order establishes conflict first, then explains it, thus creating a more logical explanation.
2. The new dialogue tag adds detail about how Marie feels.
3. Specific sensory details of the car provide more information.
4. The writer needed to correct an inconsistent point of view. The rest of the story is written in third person.
5. The specific sensory detail adds a note of spirit and hope to the teenage side of the conflict (to change the mood of frustration at the mother's frightened protectiveness). Also, this change lets readers see Carol more clearly.

TIMESAVER

If you plan to read students' drafts before evaluating the final stories, you may find it helpful to attach an evaluation sheet to each draft. You could use the **Evaluating and Revising Short Stories** chart or construct your own. Then, read the drafts quickly, commenting by responding *yes* or *no* to the chart questions.

EXERCISE 3 ▶ **Analyzing a Writer's Revisions**

Study the writer's revision of the first three paragraphs of the story on pages 236–238. Then, answer the questions that follow the paragraph.

> "It'd be just like her to forget--on purpose. You know she doesn't want me to do this." "Where is she?" Marie ~~said~~, *sighed*   **replace/** checking her watch again.   **reorder**
>
> "Calm down," Carol said. "Isn't that your mother's car?" She pointed to the *old, blue* car   **add** making a wide turn into the school parking lot, slowly heading toward the girls.
>
> "Finally. Let me drive," ~~I~~ *Marie* said as ~~my~~ *her*   **replace** mother pulled up. Marie drove slowly out of the parking lot as Carol gave her an *the thumbs*   **replace** ~~up sign~~ ~~encouraging look.~~

1. Why did the writer move the third sentence to the beginning of the paragraph?
2. In the third sentence, why did the writer replace *Marie said* with *Marie sighed*?
3. In the second paragraph, why did the writer add the words *old, blue* before the word *car*?
4. In the last paragraph, why did the writer change the word *I* to *Marie* and the word *my* to *her*?
5. In the last sentence, why did the writer replace *an encouraging look* with *the thumbs up sign*?

WRITING ASSIGNMENT

PART 6:
Evaluating and Revising Your Story

Use feedback from your classmates and the chart on page 239 to revise your story. Like a professional writer, make changes that will make readers want to keep reading.

PROOFREADING AND PUBLISHING

OBJECTIVES

- To proofread a short story
- To share a short story with an audience

TEACHING THE LESSON

Compose a proofreading checklist with students. Next, identify and correct the errors in a writing sample for the class. Then, have each student proofread a partner's paper. Ask students to describe the errors they found in their papers. Continue with

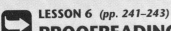

Proofreading and Publishing

Your story is almost ready, but don't forget to proofread. Once your story is ready, use these ideas for sharing it.

- Publish your stories in a literary magazine.
- If the story involves friends or family members, consider giving or mailing it with a brief note.

MECHANICS HINT

Punctuating Dialogue

Remember these points when proofreading dialogue.

1. Begin a new paragraph when the speaker changes.
2. Use quotation marks around the speaker's words.
3. Separate dialogue tags from the rest of the sentence with a comma, a question mark, or an exclamation point. Begin a new sentence with a capital letter.
4. Do not capitalize the second half of a sentence that is separated by the dialogue tag.

EXAMPLES   "Watch out!" he screamed. "There's a car coming!"
"I'm trying to get out of the way," she shouted, "as safely as I can."

 REFERENCE NOTE: For more information on punctuating dialogue, see pages 834–838.

 PART 7:
Proofreading and Publishing Your Story

You've worked hard on your story, so proofread it carefully. Then publish or share your story with others.

PROGRAM MANAGER

PROOFREADING AND PUBLISHING

- **Instructional Support** For a chart students may use to evaluate their proofreading progress, see **Proofreading** in *Strategies for Writing,* p. 22.

- **Independent Practice/ Reteaching** For additional practice with language skills, see **Proofreading Practice: Punctuating Dialogue** in *Strategies for Writing,* p. 23.

- **Computer Guided Instruction** For additional instruction and practice with punctuating dialogue as noted in the **Mechanics Hint,** see **Lesson 42** in *Language Workshop CD-ROM.*

- **Practice** To help less-advanced students who need additional practice with punctuating dialogue, see **Chapter 21** in *English Workshop, Fourth Course,* pp. 297–299.

- **Assessment/Reflection** To assess student work and evaluate progress, see **Portfolio Forms** in *Portfolio Assessment,* pp. 22–25.

You may want to require students to read **A Student Model** on p. 243 for another example of a polished paper.

QUOTATION FOR THE DAY

"One has to dismount from an idea, and get into the saddle again, at every parenthesis." (Oliver Wendell Holmes, 1809–1894, American physician, professor, and man of letters).

Lead students in a discussion of their writing styles. Do they revise, rewrite, and proofread as they go along, or do they write rapidly and make changes later?

TEACHING NOTE

Point out to students that by reflecting on their writing, they are learning more about the process of analyzing a literary work. In the second question, for example, students should look carefully at the details they used in their stories to pick out the ones that help build suspense. Encourage students to be especially thoughtful when they answer the third question and to look for those aspects of their stories that might affect readers.

Reflecting on Your Writing

To include it in your **portfolio,** date your story, and attach a short reflection answering the following questions.

- How did you make your characters seem real?
- What details help build suspense in your story?
- How do you think your story will affect readers?

Peanuts reprinted by permission of United Feature Syndicate, Inc.

Have students share ideas for publishing their stories. ■

A STUDENT MODEL

This excerpt of a story about a boy at basketball camp was written by Noah Kramer-Dover, a student in Alexandria, Virginia. Notice how Noah builds event upon event to create suspense.

from Memoirs of an Adolescent
by Noah Kramer-Dover

It was my turn. My stomach sank to the floor. I walked all the way to the other side of the gym, so as to get a long runway. I turned around to face the basket, my team, and the cheerleaders. Everyone was staring at me. I had never felt so small in my whole life. The court had never looked longer. I then stretched my arms and legs, blew into the palms of my hands, wiped the bottom of my shoes, and proceeded to waste as much time as I possibly could.

I was then interrupted by the laughter of my teammates. I looked over and saw they were all doing their own imitations of me. The cheerleaders smirked.

I guessed it was now or never. I started running. When I got to the foul line, I slowed down. I looked at the rim. My left foot hit the floor and I pushed away from the ground. I rose. I was higher than I had ever been before. I was above the rim. I knew I could do it. I cocked my arm back. I slammed the ball through the hoop. My hand grasped the rim and the basket shook. When I came down to the floor, the basket still shook.

I looked around to make sure the ball hadn't flown off the rim. I was on the ground, so my hand had not gotten stuck in the net. I heard some applause. I had dunked it.

The temperature in the gym became quite pleasant to me. The sun seemed to shine a little brighter. I looked to my teammates, who were at half-court. I walked back to them with a little bit of a strut. I then approached one of our guards, Jerome, and said, "I believe it's your turn."

First appeared in *Merlyn's Pen: The National Magazines of Student Writing.*

A STUDENT MODEL
Evaluation

1. Noah introduces the conflict in the first sentence of the story, and the other details in the first paragraph build suspense.
2. Although the event only lasted a few minutes, Noah relates the story in strict chronological order.
3. Noah's character is interesting, and he seems very real.
4. Noah is consistent in his use of the first-person point of view, and the setting establishes the mood for the story.

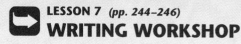

LESSON 7 *(pp. 244–246)*
WRITING WORKSHOP
OBJECTIVES

- To analyze the structure and techniques used in a news story
- To use the writing process to compose and publish a news story

TEACHING THE LESSON

Read the commentary on a news story to the class and then ask a student to read aloud **"Tornadoes Damage School."** Have volunteers provide answers for the four study questions.

Bring in copies of two well-written news stories, one from the local newspaper and one from the school paper. Identify how

QUOTATION FOR THE DAY

"A well-written lead makes commitments to the reader, and they have to be fulfilled. The lead makes a point, or perhaps several. The story proves them. Look at it that way, and the lead will provide a road map for the story that follows." (John Chancellor, 1927–1996, and Walter R. Mears, 1935–   , American journalists)

As Chancellor and Mears explain in their book, *The News Business* (1983), a lead introduces the story, sets the tone of the piece, and summarizes its most important points. Have students spend time creating interesting, well-written leads.

244

WRITING WORKSHOP

A News Story

Did you notice the headline in today's newspaper? Maybe it said "Firefighter Rescues Baby" or "Jury Finds Defendant Not Guilty." These headlines summarize real-life stories that unfold every day. A news story is similar to a fictional story in that it usually tells about a conflict or problem. But it's different because it must rely only on facts, not on a writer's imagination, to tell its story.

News stories are usually short and follow a very tight structure. The opening paragraph is called the **lead.** It summarizes the important facts of the story by answering the *5W-How?* questions—*Who? What? When? Where? Why?* and *How?* The rest of the story then fills in the details, with the most important details first. See how the news story below follows this format.

Tornadoes Damage School

MIAMI—Tornadoes smashed windows and doors in an elementary school, injuring a teacher, and ripped through a small airport, damaged homes and tore off a warehouse roof Tuesday.

The first twister touched down near Sylvania Heights Elementary School in West Miami, injuring a teacher caught outside.

"It was a miracle only one person got hurt," Principal Lucy Williams said.

About 30 children under the supervision of the physical education teacher were outside waiting for parents to pick them up at dismissal time when the instructor spotted the oncoming tornado, she said.

the *5W-How?* questions are answered in one story. Then, have students find these elements in the other story.

Next, discuss any questions students might have about the writing process and assignment.

In a class discussion, ask students to compare and contrast the writing process for a creative short story and a news story. Which process did they enjoy more? Why? ■

Teachers and administrators rushed the children into a corridor moments before the storm hit, but a teacher was caught outside.

"It picked her up and dropped her down, and when she came in she was all covered in mud and had a cut on her forehead," said Williams.

The storm broke out the school's front doors and smashed windows, she said, and tore the tin covering off the roof.

A second tornado ripped through the Pembroke Pines area. Planes at North Perry Airport were overturned and torn apart.

The Ledger, Lakeland, Florida

1. Which *5W-How?* questions does the writer answer in the lead paragraph?
2. What facts do the other paragraphs give you about the tornadoes?
3. Why does the writer quote the principal?
4. Compare the average length of paragraphs in "Mushrooms in the City" (pages 231–235) to the average length of paragraphs in this news story. What is the difference?

Writing a News Story

Prewriting.   To start your news story, look for a story that's important to your school or local community. Dig out all the facts of your story by asking *Who? What? When? Where? Why?* and *How?* Keep digging for facts and interviewing people until you know everything you possibly can about your story.

ANSWERS
Writing Workshop Questions

1. Where—Miami; Why—tornadoes; What—elementary school, airport, homes, warehouse; Who—teacher; When—Tuesday; How—injured one and smashed windows and doors at school, ripped up airport, damaged homes, tore off roof of warehouse

2. One tornado hit the school at dismissal time (with children outside), picked up and dropped a teacher, and removed part of the roof. The second tornado hit a subdivision and an airport.

3. The principal's words are the eyewitness report of an authority—a spokesperson who knows what happened at the school.

4. The paragraphs are much longer in the short story.

SELECTION AMENDMENT
Description of change: excerpted
Rationale: to focus on the concept of writing a news story as presented in this chapter

MEETING *individual* NEEDS

LEP/ESL

General Strategies. The format of a news story is very unlike that of a short story. You may find that your students need to look at one or two more news stories to get a better idea of how these two types of writing differ. They might bring in news items of interest to them (which will help them get started on getting ideas for their own stories) and identify the lead paragraphs and the *5W-How?* questions answered in the leads. Have students examine the paragraphs in the news stories and identify how the format differs from that of short stories.

INTEGRATING THE LANGUAGE ARTS

Usage Link. This activity provides an opportunity to discuss or review the difference between active and passive voice, since students will need to use the active voice in their news stories. Ask students to create sentences in the passive voice and then to revise the sentences so that they are in the active voice. Then, have volunteers put their examples on the chalkboard.

 Writing, Evaluating, and Revising. Start your news story with a vivid lead that summarizes the story's important facts. Notice how the story about the tornado uses active verbs like *smashed* and *ripped* in its lead to catch the reader's interest. Then, use short, concise paragraphs to report the story's main facts. Be sure your story portrays the events and people accurately. Whenever possible, use quotes from the people involved. When you evaluate and revise, check the accuracy of your facts and quotes.

Proofreading and Publishing. Proofread your news story carefully for mistakes in grammar and usage. To publish it, consider submitting it to your school or local newspaper. A local radio or TV station might also like the angle a student reporter can give. Date your news story, and attach a reflection to include in your **portfolio:** Is reporting still creative writing? How?

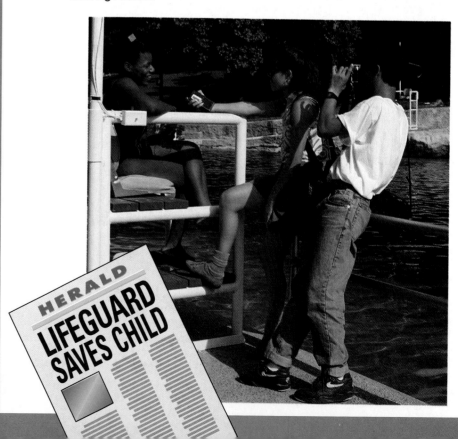

MAKING CONNECTIONS

SPEAKING AND LISTENING OBJECTIVE

• To write a fable

SHORT-STORY WRITING ACROSS THE CURRICULUM OBJECTIVE

• To write a short story for children that explains an important historical event or an event in the life of a historical figure

MAKING CONNECTIONS

SPEAKING AND LISTENING

Creating a Fable

Do you ever hear sayings like "A bird in the hand is worth two in the bush"? Many sayings started as the moral from a fable. A fable is a very short story that teaches a lesson about life. The characters in a fable are usually animals that speak and behave like humans.

To create your own fable, think of a proverb, motto, or saying that sums up an important truth about life. Then, make up a simple plot that contains just one or two incidents. Remember, the outcome of the conflict must teach the moral you've chosen. Think of animal characters and the human quality connected with each one. For example, foxes are often considered sly and crafty, while dogs are portrayed as loyal and friendly.

Read your first draft to a small group of your classmates. Ask them to guess the moral of your fable. Then, repeat the process as classmates read their fables to you.

SHORT-STORY WRITING ACROSS THE CURRICULUM

History

You're writing a biography or history book for young children. Choose an important event in history or in the life of a hero whose life you can research in an encyclopedia. Maybe you want to explain how Ponce de León arrived in what is now Florida or why Betsy Ross made a flag for the new nation. What will catch and keep your young readers' interest? Before you write, make a story map. Be sure that all the historical details are factual. Then, write a short story—geared toward small children—that explains this event.

GUIDELINES

Fables must include morals, of course, and you may want students to underline the moral to make assessment easier. Students also should include two plot incidents, although you may want to specify more. You could have peer-editing groups evaluate different aspects of the fable.

SHORT-STORY WRITING ACROSS THE CURRICULUM

Teaching Strategies

You may want to coordinate the lesson with students' history classes.

Ask students for examples of historical narratives they have enjoyed. Ask them to specify, with examples and details, why they enjoyed the narratives.

Bring to class an example of a historical narrative. The example could even be a literary one such as the *Iliad,* the *Odyssey,* "Paul Revere's Ride," or an excerpt from a literary piece such as one of Shakespeare's histories. Ask students to read the selection, or, if it is short, you may want to read it aloud. Then, discuss its structure, characterizations, and setting. You may also want to discuss the author's use of language, details, examples, and historical facts.

GUIDELINES

Students will have to use proper language for a young audience. You may want to have them turn in their story maps. Assessment can also be limited to one feature such as character development or plot organization.

7 WRITING TO INFORM: EXPOSITION

OBJECTIVES

- To analyze the characteristics of a comparison/contrast informative essay
- To use various prewriting techniques to develop writing ideas for a comparison/contrast essay
- To organize and draft a comparison/contrast essay
- To evaluate and revise the content of a comparison/contrast essay
- To proofread and prepare a comparison/contrast essay for publication

WRITING-IN-PROGRESS ASSIGNMENTS

Major Assignment: Writing a comparison/contrast essay
Cumulative Writing Assignments: The chart below shows the sequence of cumulative assignments that will guide students as they write a comparison/contrast essay. These writing assignments form the instructional core of Chapter 7.

PREWRITING

Writing Assignment
- Part 1: Choosing Subjects for Comparison/Contrast p. 259
- Part 2: Gathering Information pp. 261–262
- Part 3: Arranging Information p. 264
- Part 4: Developing a Thesis Statement p. 265

WRITING

Writing Assignment
- Part 5: Writing a First Draft p. 273

EVALUATING AND REVISING

Writing Assignment
- Part 6: Evaluating and Revising Your Comparison/Contrast Paper p. 277

PROOFREADING AND PUBLISHING

Writing Assignment
- Part 7: Proofreading and Publishing Your Essay p. 279

In addition, exercises 1–2 provide practice in analyzing a model and analyzing a writer's revisions.

WORKPLACE writing — Competitive Analyses

Explain to students that one way companies evaluate their products or services is to compare them to the competition. A competitive analysis describes common characteristics as well as important differences between similar products. Also, the analysis may include a recommendation of possible product improvements.

- **Assignment** Have students compare two similar products in a competitive analysis. Students may work in pairs to brainstorm the products and to complete research of the products.

- **Prewriting** Bring in copies of consumer magazines to show students examples of product comparisons. Research of products may be done by comparison shopping, scanning advertisements, talking to people familiar with the products, and researching consumer periodicals and the Internet. Work as a class to create a format and a general set of criteria to follow. Consider the following:
  - Products to be analyzed: Car X and Car Y
  - Purpose of these products: Family transportation

Comparison Chart

	Car X	Car Y
Maker	Acme Car Co.	Emca Car Co.
Price	$4,000	$3,200
Size	Compact	Mid-size
Mileage	300 m.p.g.	100 m.p.g.
Warranty	Repairs for 7 years	Repairs for 3 years

Students will need to analyze data and draw conclusions. Based on the above data, Car X is probably more economical in the long run.

- **Writing** Have students review the instructional material on pp. 262–267 on arranging and presenting data. Remind them to include a thesis statement, to present their points of comparison, and to develop a logical conclusion in their analyses.

INTEGRATING THE LANGUAGE ARTS

SELECTION	READING AND LITERATURE	WRITING AND CRITICAL THINKING	LANGUAGE AND SYNTAX	SPEAKING, LISTENING, AND OTHER EXPRESSION SKILLS
• from **Moncrief: My Journey to the NBA** by Sidney Moncrief with Myra McLarey pp. 250–253 • **"Time out! Is baseball Finnished?"** from *The Miami Herald* by Bob Secter pp. 267–270 • **"The Eagle-Feather Fan"** by N. Scott Momaday p. 287	• Responding personally to literature pp. 254, 270–271 • Analyzing organization pp. 254, 270, 271 • Understanding comparison/contrast pp. 254, 257, 286–287 • Finding main idea pp. 257, 282–283 • Locating and interpreting information pp. 261, 270–271, 276–277, 283, 286–287 • Finding details pp. 270–271, 276–277, 282–283, 285–287 • Identifying metaphor pp. 286–287 • Recognizing elements of style pp. 286–287	• Responding personally to literature p. 254 • Analyzing structure pp. 254, 276–277 • Classifying objects and ideas p. 257 • Determining purpose and audience pp. 259, 270–271, 284 • Choosing a subject p. 259 • Gathering and arranging information pp. 261–262, 264, 284 • Developing thesis statement p. 265 • Evaluating and revising p. 277 • Proofreading and publishing a revised draft p. 279 • Using research to support a thesis p. 284 • Writing an extended definition p. 284 • Writing for an essay test pp. 285–286 • Writing comparison/contrast poem p. 287	• Proofreading for errors in grammar, usage, and mechanics pp. 279, 284 • Using reference materials pp. 282–283	• Working with a classmate to classify objects and ideas p. 257 • Making a chart to arrange information p. 264 • Reading a poem aloud pp. 268–287 • Working with a classmate to analyze organization pp. 270–271 • Evaluating a classmate's revisions p. 277

SUGGESTED INTEGRATED UNIT PLAN

This plan gives suggestions on how to integrate the major strands of the language arts with this chapter.

If you begin with this chapter on writing to inform or with the suggested selections in which two or more people or things are compared and contrasted, you should focus on the common characteristics of informative writing. You can then integrate speaking/listening and language concepts with both the writing and the literature.

Common Characteristics

- Content that is factual and comprehensive
- Precise language that is neutral and unbiased documentation of facts
- Comparison and contrast of specific features of items discussed; inclusion of a thesis statement
- Block method or point-by-point method of organization

Writing
Informative writing

Language
Usage, style
- Degrees of comparison
- Subject/verb agreement
- Metaphors and similes

UNIT FOCUS
INFORMATIVE NONFICTION

Speaking/Listening
- Working with a classmate to analyze organization and evaluate revisions
- Reading poetry aloud

Literature
Selections such as
- "Day Work" James P. Comer
- from *Out of Africa* Isak Dinesen
- "Shall I Compare Thee to a Summer's Day?" William Shakespeare

CHAPTER 7: WRITING TO INFORM: EXPOSITION

Use this guide for creating an instructional plan that addresses the individual needs of your students. Assignments accompanied by the following symbol (∗) may be completed out of class. Times given for pacing lessons are estimated.

CHAPTER PLANNING GUIDE—PUPIL'S EDITION

LESSONS	LITERARY MODEL pp. 250–253: From *Moncrief: My Journey to the NBA* by Sidney Moncrief with Myra McLarey	PREWRITING pp. 256–265	
		Generating Ideas	Gathering/Organizing
DEVELOPMENTAL PROGRAM	🕐 **30–35 minutes** • Read the model aloud and have pairs of students answer questions orally on p. 254	🕐 **50–55 minutes** • Main Assignment: Looking Ahead p. 255 • Choosing Subjects p. 256 • Critical Thinking p. 257 • Thinking About Purpose and Audience p. 258 • Writing Note p. 259 • Writing Assignment: Part 1 p. 259	🕐 **90 minutes** • Gathering and Arranging Information pp. 260–264 • Writing Assignment: Parts 2, 3, 4 pp. 261–262, 264, 265 • Developing a Thesis Statement p. 265 • Writing Note p. 265
CORE PROGRAM	🕐 **25–30 minutes** • Have students read the model individually and answer questions on p. 254 with a partner	🕐 **30–35 minutes** • Main Assignment: Looking Ahead p. 255 • Choosing Subjects p. 256 • Critical Thinking p. 257 • Thinking About Purpose and Audience p. 258 • Writing Note p. 259 • Writing Assignment: Part 1 p. 259∗	🕐 **40–45 minutes** • Gathering and Arranging Information pp. 260–264 • Writing Assignment: Parts 2, 3, 4 pp. 261–262, 264, 265∗ • Developing a Thesis Statement p. 265 • Writing Note p. 265
ACCELERATED PROGRAM	🕐 **20–25 minutes** • Assign students to read the model independently and to discuss the questions on p. 254 with a partner	🕐 **20–25 minutes** • Main Assignment: Looking Ahead p. 255 • Critical Thinking p. 257∗ • Writing Assignment: Part 1 p. 259∗	🕐 **30–35 minutes** • Gathering Information pp. 260–264 • Writing Assignment: Parts 2, 3, 4 pp. 261–262, 264, 265∗ • Writing Note p. 265

CHAPTER PLANNING GUIDE—PROGRAM RESOURCES

	LITERARY MODEL	PREWRITING
PRINT	• Reading Master 7, *Practice for Assessment in Reading, Vocabulary, and Spelling* p. 7	• Prewriting, *Strategies for Writing* p. 26 • Informing Others, *English Workshop* pp. 51–58
MEDIA	• Fine Art Transparency 4, *Transparency Binder* 🖥️	• Graphic Organizers 11–12, *Transparency Binder* 🖥️ • *Writers Workshop 2:* Informative Report 💾💿🖥️

WRITING pp. 266–273	EVALUATING AND REVISING pp. 274–277	PROOFREADING AND PUBLISHING pp. 278–281
45–50 minutes • The Elements of a Comparison/Contrast Essay pp. 266–267 • A Basic Framework/ A Writer's Model pp. 271–273 • Writing Assignment: Part 5 p. 273	**35–40 minutes** • Evaluating and Revising Chart p. 275 • Exercise 2 pp. 276–277 in pairs • Writing Assignment: Part 6 p. 277	**45–50 minutes** • Proofreading/Publishing p. 278 • Grammar Hint p. 279 • Writing Assignment: Part 7 p. 279 • Reflecting p. 280 • A Student Model pp. 280–281
45–50 minutes • The Elements of a Comparison/Contrast Essay pp. 266–267 • Looking at a Comparison/ Contrast Essay/An Article/ Exercise 1 pp. 267–271 • Writing Assignment: Part 5 p. 273*	**40–45 minutes** • Evaluating/Revising Chart p. 275 • Exercise 2 pp. 276–277* • Writing Assignment: Part 6 p. 277	**30–35 minutes** • Proofreading/Publishing p. 278 • Grammar Hint p. 279 • Writing Assignment: Part 7 p. 279 • Reflecting p. 280 • A Student Model pp. 280–281*
25–30 minutes • Looking at a Comparison/Contrast Essay p. 267 • A Newspaper Article pp. 267–270* • Writing Assignment: Part 5 p. 273*	**20–25 minutes** • Evaluating/Revising Chart p. 275 • Writing Assignment: Part 6 p. 277	**25 minutes** • Grammar Hint p. 279 • Writing Assignment: Part 7 p. 279 • Reflecting p. 280

WRITING	EVALUATING AND REVISING	PROOFREADING AND PUBLISHING
• Writing, *Strategies for Writing* p. 27	• Evaluating and Revising, *Strategies for Writing* p. 28	• Proofreading Practice, *Strategies for Writing* p. 30 • *English Workshop,* pp. 239–242
	• Revision Transparencies 11–12, *Transparency Binder*	• *Language Workshop:* Lessons 16–17

ELEMENTS OF WRITING: CURRICULUM CONNECTIONS

Writing Workshop
• An Extended Definition pp. 282–284

Making Connections
• Test Taking pp. 285–286
• Comparison Across the Curriculum pp. 286–287

ASSESSMENT OPTIONS

Summative Assessment
Holistic Scoring: Prompts and Models pp. 21–26

Portfolio Assessment
Portfolio forms, *Portfolio Assessment* pp. 5–25, 44–48

Reflection
Writing Process Log, *Strategies for Writing* p. 25
Self-assessment Record, *Portfolio Assessment* p. 19

Ongoing Assessment
Proofreading, *Strategies for Writing* p. 29

Performance Assessment
Assessment 4, *Integrated Performance Assessment, Level E* For help with evaluation, see *Holistic Scoring Workshop.*

Computer disk or CD-ROM

Overhead transparencies

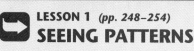
OBJECTIVES

- To analyze the construction of a comparison/contrast essay
- To write personal responses to a literary model

MOTIVATION

Letting students find comparisons and contrasts, discuss the opening picture of the lesson.

PROGRAM MANAGER

CHAPTER 7

- **Computer Guided Instruction** For a related assignment that students may use for additional instruction and practice, see **Informative Report** in *Writer's Workshop 2 CD-ROM.*

- **Summative Assessment** For a writing prompt, including grading criteria and student models, see *Holistic Scoring: Prompts and Models*, pp. 21–26.

- **Extension/Enrichment** See **Fine Art Transparency 4,** *Still Life Supreme* by Martha Mayer Erlebacher. For suggestions on how to tie the transparency to instruction, review teacher's notes in *Fine Art and Instructional Transparencies for Writing*, p. 21.

- **Reading Support** For help with the reading selection, pp. 250–253, see **Reading Master 7** in *Practice for Assessment in Reading, Vocabulary, and Spelling*, p. 7.

VISUAL CONNECTIONS
Still Life with Telephone and Flowers

About the Artist. Leigh Behnke is noted for her paintings of New York City, in which she often contrasts different views of the same image. Behnke

continued on next page

7 WRITING TO INFORM: EXPOSITION

TEACHING THE LESSON

Begin by having a student read the introductory paragraphs aloud. Then discuss how the the artwork is pertinent to the lesson.

Have a volunteer read the essay and note the structure of the introduction [a dynamic and intriguing opening sentence followed by a series of parallel examples of the players who will be compared and contrasted, and the thesis statement].

After reading the entire essay, discuss the essay's structure. [The paragraphs are ordered by the three players who are being compared and contrasted. Most of the paragraphs compare and contrast within

Seeing Patterns

Would you accept these challenges? Define *poetry* without saying the words *creative writing* or *literature*. Tell someone what the movie *Toy Story* is like without mentioning computer animation. Write a report on the Vietnam War without referring to any other U.S. war. No? No wonder. In life, nothing stands totally alone. **Seeing patterns and relationships** is one of the most natural ways to understand our world and to give information about it.

Writing and You. You use this strategy in different ways. You define *poetry* by how it's like and unlike other literature. You discuss *Toy Story* within the category of animated film. You understand the Vietnam War by contrasting it with World War II. Look at whatever interests you: Are there patterns or relationships to explore?

As You Read. In the following selection, Sidney Moncrief looks at patterns among three great basketball players. What does he see?

Leigh Behnke, *Still Life with Telephone and Flowers* (1983). Watercolor on paper, 40 1/2" × 52 1/4". Collection of Glenn C. Janss. Courtesy of Fischbach Gallery, N.Y.

focuses mainly on architectural subjects, and many of her paintings show how changing light affects a scene.

QUOTATION FOR THE DAY

"So before writing, learn to think." (Nicolas Boileau-Despréaux, 1636–1711, French critic and poet)

Ask students to list five important experiences they remember. Then, with the help of a small group, have them look for patterns, similarities, and differences among the events. Finally, have each group write a brief statement about how the quotation relates to writing comparison and contrast papers.

MEETING individual NEEDS

LEP/ESL

General Strategies. One technique to introduce classification to your English-language learners would be through a clustering or webbing activity. This organizer helps students see how items or ideas are classified into categories. It can be further expanded to a comparison and contrast activity. For instance, students can compare the schools in their native countries to schools in the United States.

GUIDED PRACTICE

After reviewing the essay, work with students to draw a line chart that analyzes the essay. The lines should be as follows: top line—the title; second line—the exciting opening sentence, beginning paragraph, and thesis statement; third line—paragraphs 3, 4, and 5, where Moncrief compares and contrasts himself with Larry Bird; fourth

250

from Moncrief: My Journey to the NBA

by Sidney Moncrief with Myra McLarey

USING THE SELECTION
My Journey to the NBA

1
Notice that the author uses first-person point of view.

2
Paragraph 2 is a transition paragraph between the introduction and the first body paragraph.

1 My fear of being in the pros soon dissipated. It helped that I was never in awe of the talent of the big-name players—such as Larry Bird, Michael Jordan and Dr. J. I respected the stars and their talent, but I also knew I could compete.

2 Playing the best challenged me to be my best—to test my limits. It was also just plain fun to play against players with such skill. I found I could be playing very hard against a guy on another team and still be impressed with his play. If an opponent made a good shot or a great move or an impressive pass, in my mind I'd say, *What a play!* Sometimes I even complimented the player if I got the chance. I think you can play better if you allow yourself to respect your opponent.

I played against so many good players that it's impossible, really, to single out the best. Of course, Larry Bird would have to be high on anybody's list. He's intense, he works hard, he's versatile, and he's a real team player. With our difference in size I didn't guard Larry that much in the pros. I did go one-on-one with him the last game of my college career.

line—paragraphs 6 and 7, which compare Magic Johnson with Bird and Moncrief; and fifth line—the last two paragraphs that compare Dr. J and Moncrief.

Also, share your personal responses to **Reader's Response.**

INDEPENDENT PRACTICE

You can use both **Reader's Response** and **Writer's Craft** questions as independent practice.

☞

"Larry Bird [is]... intense, he works hard, he's versatile, and he's a real team player."

VISUAL CONNECTIONS

Exploring the Subject. Larry Bird, born in 1956 in French Lick, Indiana, was a forward for the Boston Celtics. He played college basketball at Indiana State University before joining the Celtics in 1979. For 1979–1980 he was named the NBA Rookie of the Year. He played with the Celtics for thirteen seasons, helping them win three NBA championships. Larry Bird wrote his autobiography, *Drive,* in 1989.

No matter how great a college coach is, he doesn't have the time or the <u>expertise</u> to fully analyze an opponent. So when I played Bird in college, we didn't have any detailed <u>tendency</u> reports on him. When I guarded him the second half of the game, I had no idea of his specific moves. I had not seen him play before, and I was too busy the first half guarding someone else to watch him. I was simply playing defense the way I had always played it. His offensive skills were not nearly as refined as they are now, and he didn't have teammates who could get the ball to him like he does now, so my athletic ability allowed me to do a pretty good job on him. Sometimes I guarded Larry in the pros, but it was a different story then. I couldn't really play him in the pros—I'm too small.

3   If I were bigger and could play him, though, I'd push him to his right, because he likes to move to his left to shoot. I'd push him to his right, play him tight to force him to drive, and then I'd try to block him out on any shots. On post, I'd try to front him and not let him get the basketball.

3

Although this paragraph is still about Larry Bird, the author paragraphs for cosmetic purposes, to break the look of too much solid text.

CLOSURE

Ask students to discuss how this line-by-line layout of the essay can serve as an example for their essays.

EXTENSION

As with all essays, comparison/contrast essays rely on sentence structure to be effective. Take students back through this essay and discuss where the long sentences and short sentences occur and why. Longer sentences give information and carry a reader along with them. Short sentences, on

252

4

Moncrief achieves interest in the opening sentence by asking a rhetorical question.

4 **What** can I say about Magic Johnson except that he deserves his name? He controls the tempo of the game. He gets all the players involved and, like Bird, he plays an unselfish ball game. He's very right-handed, so he has a strong tendency to move to his right. Even though he's good enough to go left or right, you play him to go right. His outside shot is pretty good too, so you have to play him tight. If he's on the post, he's very difficult to guard because he's so big—he's 6'8"—and agile. You can't play behind him; if he gets the ball with his back to the basket, he's just going to hook it. You can't front him; he'll be able to catch a lob.

What you do with Magic is pick him up in the back court and make him turn. You don't want him coming at you face forward; you want him to come at you with his back turned and back you down the court. That way you can get help from your defense. Magic is not as difficult to keep from scoring as Jordan or Bird. But he's such a great all-around player, and like Bird, he can beat you so many different ways. If he can't beat you scoring, he'll beat you with his passing, and his play-making—he'll beat you by making things happen on the court.

**"... he'll beat you
by making things
happen on
the court."**

the other hand, are meant for emphasis, and they usually stop a reader to make a point.

ENRICHMENT

Students might be interested in reading the rest of Sidney Moncrief's book *Moncrief—My Journey to the NBA*. It was published by August House Publishers, Inc. in 1990. ■

253

"**Mostly, though, with Dr. J, you just had to yell for help.**"

5 **D**r. J was extremely difficult to guard. He is big. And he is good. Doc is right-handed and he likes his right. But if he wanted to shoot a jump shot, he liked to move to his left, take one dribble, then pull up and bank it off the glass. With Doc, I tried to take away his right hand and force him to take the jumper. On the post, you couldn't front him, you couldn't play behind him—you had to play him in-between. I used a move Eddie Sutton had taught me in college (we called it half-mooning): face him from the side and get a hand in front of his face. You also had to try to keep Doc out of the open court—he was one of the best open-court players in the history of the sport—by picking him up early and not letting him get the basketball.

Mostly, though, with Dr. J, you just had to yell for help.

5
Moncrief orders his paragraphs not only by the three players, but also by the expertise of each one; the abilities get stronger with each player discussed.

"Playing the best
challenged me to
be my best—to
test my limits."

READER'S RESPONSE

1. Do you know anything about the three basketball players Moncrief is giving information about? Do you think it is interesting to see what one great athlete thinks about the skills of other great athletes? Why?
2. What sport or entertainment medium are you interested in—football? auto racing? rock music? movies? In your journal write about two or three of the big names in that field. How are they alike? How are they different?

WRITER'S CRAFT

3. Moncrief lets readers know all three athletes better by *comparing* and *contrasting* them. He starts out with the obvious similarities among the men; they are all great basketball players. How does he contrast them?
4. How is the information about the three players organized? How could Moncrief have organized the information to make the differences among the men more obvious? What is the advantage of the organization he used?

ANSWERS

Reader's Response

1. Each student should include a rationale for his or her opinions.
2. Be sure students give specific details.

Writer's Craft

3. He explains each man's best skills and the strategies needed to defend each.
4. The essay organizes the information by the difficulty level involved in guarding each man. Perhaps the author could have used the skills of each player as the categories of comparison and contrast. The organization makes it easy to follow.

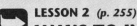
255

Ways to Inform

A quick glance at one general-interest magazine or a list of nonfiction best-sellers will show you that informative writing can be developed in many ways. Examining patterns and relationships is just one way to inform. Here are a few examples of ways to inform:

- in a travel essay, writing about your visit to the Taos Pueblo
- in a press release, writing a biographical sketch of a Nobel Prize winner
- in a paper for science class, describing the surface of Mars
- in an article for your school newspaper, describing the features of the new gymnasium
- in an essay for literature class, contrasting the hero and the villain of a short story
- in a presentation to new students, defining *advanced placement*
- on a World Wide Web page, listing nonprofit organizations that welcome teenage volunteers
- in a recipe, describing how to make tamales
- in a music review for the local paper, evaluating a new CD you think people would enjoy
- in a conversation with your supervisor, explaining why you think the store's merchandise should be rearranged

LOOKING AHEAD

In the main assignment in this chapter, you'll use comparison and contrast in an informative essay. You'll be using classification. As you work, keep in mind that a comparison/contrast essay

- looks at relationships or patterns
- focuses on two or more subjects
- discusses similarities, differences, or both

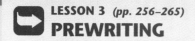

LESSON 3 *(pp. 256–265)*
PREWRITING

OBJECTIVES

- To choose subjects for a comparison/contrast essay
- To gather and arrange information for a comparison/contrast essay

- To develop a thesis statement for a comparison/contrast essay

Cont. on p. 258

PROGRAM MANAGER

PREWRITING

■ **Self-Assessment** Before beginning instruction of the writing process, see **Writing Process Log** in *Strategies for Writing,* p. 25.

■ **Heuristics** To help students generate ideas, see **Prewriting** in *Strategies for Writing,* p. 26.

■ **Instructional Support** See **Graphic Organizers 11** and **12.** For suggestions on how to tie the transparencies to instruction, review teacher's notes in *Fine Art and Instructional Transparencies for Writing,* pp. 73, 75.

LEP/ESL

General Strategies. If there are significant numbers of English-language learners with similar language and cultural backgrounds, allow the students to work together to come up with new sets of subjects. When subject matter is relevant to personal interests and experiences, and when students are given the autonomy to explore information that has immediate application to their daily lives, they are more likely to perform successfully.

256

Writing a Comparison/Contrast Essay

 Prewriting

Choosing Subjects

Sometimes a writing situation leads naturally to comparison/contrast subjects. For example, if you were interested in a new Civil War movie, you might naturally compare and contrast it with the classic film *Gone with the Wind.* In a newspaper article about a candidate for class president, you'd probably compare and contrast that candidate with others running for the same office.

When you write comparison/contrast essays, you have three choices:

1. You can write about the similarities only.
2. You can write about the differences only.
3. You can write about both similarities and differences.

If your teacher assigns a comparison/contrast essay, be sure to understand the assignment. Sometimes, *compare* is used as an "umbrella" term that means analyze *both* similarities and differences.

In choosing subjects for comparison and contrast, be sure of two things:

■ the subjects have some basic similarities
■ the subjects are different enough to be interesting

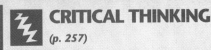

CRITICAL THINKING
(p. 257)

OBJECTIVE

• To classify objects and ideas

TEACHING CLASSIFYING OBJECTS AND IDEAS

The way the TV show *Jeopardy* sets up its categories is a perfect example of a way to classify objects and ideas. Another example is the binomial nomenclature used in biological sciences. For explanation, discuss the reasons that the mosquito is classified

Prewriting   **257**

CRITICAL THINKING

Classifying Objects and Ideas

When you choose subjects to compare and contrast, you must understand (1) *if* they have anything in common, and (2) *what* it is they have in common. You're actually using the critical thinking skill of classifying: grouping objects or ideas into categories that show their similarities.

If you were playing a game that required you to identify categories, the questioner might ask you, "What is the category for algebra, history, physics?" One good answer, of course, would be "school courses"! After identifying the categories for "cars, buses, trains" (types of land transportation) and for "moon, sun, comet" (celestial bodies), you win!

 CRITICAL THINKING EXERCISE:
Classifying Objects and Ideas

Now make your own game. Work with a partner to figure out the category that tells what each of the following groups has in common. Be as specific as you can in stating the category. [Hint: One group can't be classified because the items have nothing in common.]

EXAMPLE   **1.** honesty, kindness, courage, dependability
          1. *Category: desirable character traits*

1. Classical period, Middle Ages, Renaissance
2. lions, tigers, elephants, gorillas
3. mumps, chickenpox, German measles
4. football, baseball, soccer
5. oxygen, television, spaghetti
6. Washington, D.C.; Paris, France; Tokyo, Japan; London, England
7. Himalayas, Alps, Rockies
8. a poem, a painting, an opera
9. democracy, monarchy, dictatorship
10. a sunset, a ballgame, a movie

ANSWERS
Critical Thinking Exercise

1. historical eras
2. wild animals
3. childhood diseases
4. team sports
5. no commonality
6. capitals of countries
7. mountain ranges
8. types of artistic works
9. types of governments
10. things to watch

differently than the spider. To assess, ask a volunteer to define the word *classify*. ⚡

Cont. from p. 256
MOTIVATION

Discuss other movies that might be compared to *Gone with the Wind*. When students give their opinions about movies they like, use this interest to talk about the differences between the persuasive and informative aims.

 *Prewriting*

Thinking About Purpose and Audience

Purpose. Your *purpose* in exploring subjects with comparison/contrast may be any one of the four basic purposes for writing: to inform, to persuade, to express yourself, or to be creative. In this chapter, however, you'll focus on informing. And within that basic purpose, you'll have a more narrow one. You may

- Show similarities between subjects

    EXAMPLE   Show how competitive in-line skating and ice skating are alike

- Show differences between subjects

    EXAMPLE   Show how factories in the United States and Japan are different

- Show both similarities and differences between the subjects

    EXAMPLE   Show how two types of weight-training equipment available for home use have both similar and different features

Audience.   When you inform, you have to think about what your *audience* knows and doesn't know so that you can define unfamiliar terms and give background information. It's also important to think about what will interest your readers—remember that you want to hold your readers' attention while you inform them! This can mean a subject that will be new to many of them, as high-tech Japanese factories might be. But it can also mean your approach to your subject. Perhaps your audience knows something about weight-training equipment but would really like to know how two systems compare for developing certain muscles. Perhaps your readers would like to know how two systems compare in possible modifications as the user's ability increases. Try to make your comparison/contrast one that will bring a new subject to light or shed new light on a familiar one.

QUOTATION FOR THE DAY
"He who does not expect a million readers should not write a line." (J. W. Goethe, 1794–1832, German poet, dramatist, and thinker)

Write the quotation on the chalkboard and ask students to freewrite about the importance of audience when choosing a subject for a paper.

A DIFFERENT APPROACH

Ask students to find and analyze examples of classification in the letters to the editor of the local newspaper. Explain that most of these letters will have a persuasive aim.

Students should mount the letters on paper and analyze them for purpose, point of view, and points of comparison.

Have a student read the information under **Purpose.** Explain that classifying information allows a person to understand a subject better. In fact, many school assignments require students to make comparisons and contrasts.

Next, have another student read about audience. Then expand on the material in the textbook by discussing how important it is to have an audience other than just the teacher. The purpose of this paper is to inform someone besides the teacher about whatever subject the student chooses.

For **Gathering Information** (pp. 260–261), discuss who Michelangelo and Leonardo da Vinci were. Carefully discuss the six features listed in the chart and tell ☞

WRITING NOTE

As with other types of writing, remember to narrow your subjects. It's hard to write an interesting, detailed essay comparing the Middle Ages with today or even comparing New York with Miami. However, you could compare and contrast transportation in the Middle Ages with transportation today, or the architecture of New York and Miami.

MEETING *individual* NEEDS

LEARNING STYLES

Visual Learners. Students will benefit from seeing a Venn diagram that shows the relevant features and specifics for the comparison of *Home Improvement* and *The Cosby Show* given on p. 260. Have the class discuss possible details while you write them down.

WRITING ASSIGNMENT

PART 1:
Choosing Subjects for Comparison/Contrast

After digging around in your mind, select two subjects that interest you for your comparison/contrast essay. Test your subjects to make sure that they meet these two requirements: (1) they have some basic similarities, and (2) they have enough differences to make the comparison/contrast significant. Remember to consider the purpose and audience for your essay.

students that to collect this information one would have had to do some research. Then you can explain that to write good, informative, comparison/contrast essays, students might need to do some research. You should then call on students and have them explain why, for instance, the information under feature 2 is not under feature 5.

Arranging Information on p. 262 can be read silently by students in class. Then you can go back to the organization chart and discuss why the features about Michelangelo and Leonardo were ordered as they were. Ask students if the order could have been different. Then read the paragraphs at the bottom of p. 262 about the block and point-by-point methods.

Prewriting

Gathering and Arranging Information

After you've chosen subjects and thought about your purpose and audience, you need to figure out the *relevant features* you'll compare and contrast. Then you can gather and organize information about these relevant features.

Gathering Information

On TV courtroom dramas, you'll hear lawyers saying things like, "That's not relevant, your honor." *Relevant* means "related to the main point." When you're exploring a subject by comparison/contrast, you look at the ***relevant features*** of both items. These are the features that will inform readers about your main idea.

Suppose your purpose is to inform readers about the TV programs *Home Improvement* and *The Cosby Show*. You think that both programs show families as they are in real life. That's the basic thing they have in common, and it's also your main idea. How can you inform readers of this main idea? What details will you use to support it? You might compare and contrast the settings (time and place), the ages of the main characters, and typical situations in the shows. These would be the relevant features, about which you'd gather information for your paper. What is relevant may differ depending on your audience, however. For example, a teenage audience might be interested in the typical situations, while another audience might be more interested in the settings.

If you're familiar with your subjects (two television programs, for example), you can probably recall or observe all of the information you'll need for your paper. But if your subjects are unfamiliar (two historical periods or two places you've never been), you'll need to do some research to gather information.

The following chart shows how you could gather information about two famous artists: Michelangelo and Leonardo da Vinci. Notice that most of the relevant features are similarities.

MEETING individual NEEDS

LESS-ADVANCED STUDENTS

If students seem to be having trouble with this writing assignment, you may want to allow them to use the information on Michelangelo and Leonardo da Vinci as the basis of their papers. Tell students they can add or subtract details as needed.

INTEGRATING THE LANGUAGE ARTS

Library Link. Because the third paragraph under **Gathering Information** indicates that students might need to do research first, be sure to take them to the library or allow for some library time.

Continue by reading and discussing the method chart on p. 263 carefully.

Finally, have a volunteer read aloud the material about developing a thesis statement. Draw students' attention to the **Reference Note** on p. 265 for more help.

GUIDED PRACTICE

Before having students do **Writing Assignment: Part 1,** brainstorm for topic ideas and talk about similarities and differences. A suggestion might be two types of bicycles—touring bikes and dirt bikes. To make sure students understand the informative aim, emphasize that many comparisons do not end in making a choice. If students

HERE'S HOW

Relevant Features		
	Subject 1: Michelangelo	*Subject 2:* Leonardo da Vinci
Feature 1: accomplishments	sculptor, painter, architect, writer of sonnets	painter, sculptor, architect, engineer, scientist
Feature 2: commitment	dedicated to art; often went days without sleeping or eating	dedicated to art; often went days without sleeping or eating
Feature 3: innovations	master of perspective; pioneered unpainted statuary	master of perspective; inventor of classic style of painting during Renaissance
Feature 4: most famous work	murals of Sistine Chapel	*The Last Supper* and *Mona Lisa*
Feature 5: new information	restoration of Sistine Chapel shows use of brilliant, not dark, colors	restoration of *The Last Supper* shows use of brilliant, not dark, colors
Feature 6: fame	famous in his lifetime and throughout history	famous in his lifetime and throughout history

INTEGRATING THE LANGUAGE ARTS

Literature Link. If available, have students read parts of Plutarch's *Life of Caesar* and Shakespeare's *Tragedy of Julius Caesar.* Then have each student write a comparison/contrast essay about the comparable details in each. Students should organize their data in charts before they begin writing.

WRITING ASSIGNMENT

PART 2:
Gathering Information

Now it's your turn to gather information for your essay. As an aid in gathering information, make a chart like the one above for the two subjects you have chosen to compare and contrast. Decide what relevant features you will use, and write them in the chart. Don't forget your audi-

state that touring bikes are more fun than dirt bikes, explain that writers are entitled to opinions, but that in this discussion, students need to state only the facts, not make choices.

Have the class take a few moments to compare the two television shows discussed on p. 260 or two other shows with which the entire class is familiar. Have students write these similarities or differences in columns on the chalkboard.

ence. What features do they care about? (You may need to do some research first.) As you gather information, you may need to revise the chart.

© Grimmy Inc. Reprinted by permission.

Arranging Information

You need to make an important decision before you begin writing: how to organize your paper. There are two helpful ways to organize comparison/contrast writing: the *block method* and the *point-by-point method*.

With the ***block method,*** you discuss all the features of one subject and then all the features of the second subject. When you use this method, you discuss the same features for the second subject as you do for the first. With the ***point-by-point method,*** you discuss one feature of the first subject and the same feature of the second subject. Then you move to the second feature, and so on.

For example, in an essay about Leonardo da Vinci and Michelangelo, you might group information by discussing Leonardo first (his achievements, innovations, and major works.) Then you might discuss Michelangelo (his achievements, innovations, and major works). That's the block method.

INDEPENDENT PRACTICE

After a short discussion, read the directions for **Writing Assignment: Part 1** aloud and give students time to think about their subjects independently.

Allow students to work in groups to help each other make charts for **Writing Assignment: Part 2.** Students could work independently to complete **Writing Assign-** ment: **Parts 3** and **4.** Students could then meet with their groups to check each other's organizational charts and thesis statements.

Or you might start with the idea that both Michelangelo and Leonardo were geniuses in many fields. Then you could go on to the next features: their dedication, new contributions, most famous works, and fame in their lifetimes. This is the point-by-point method.

Remember to treat the relevant features in the same order for both subjects. The order of the relevant features is often most to least or least to most important.

The following chart on two African American writers from the colonial period to the Civil War illustrates the two methods of arranging information in a comparison/contrast essay.

HERE'S HOW

BLOCK METHOD	POINT-BY-POINT METHOD

Subject 1: Phillis Wheatley (1753?–1784)
    Feature 1: born a slave
    Feature 2: 1st black woman to publish volume of poetry in U.S.
    Feature 3: well read in the Bible and Latin classics
    Feature 4: dedicated her life to poetry
	Feature 1: status at birth
	    Subject 1: Phillis Wheatley born a slave
	    Subject 2: Jarena Lee born a free woman
	
	Feature 2: accomplishment in writing
	    Subject 1: Phillis Wheatley 1st black woman to publish volume of poetry in U.S.
	    Subject 2: Jarena Lee 1st black woman to write autobiography in U.S.

Subject 2: Jarena Lee (1783–?)
    Feature 1: born a free woman
    Feature 2: 1st black woman to write her autobiography in U.S.
    Feature 3: well read in the Bible; wanted to become female preacher
    Feature 4: dedicated her life to evangelizing
	Feature 3: knowledge
	    Subject 1: Phillis Wheatley well read in the Bible and Latin classics
	    Subject 2: Jarena Lee well read in Bible; wanted to become a female preacher
	
	Feature 4: purpose in life
	    Subject 1: Phillis Wheatley dedicated her life to poetry
	    Subject 2: Jarena Lee dedicated her life to evangelizing

MEETING *individual* NEEDS

LEARNING STYLES

Visual and Kinetic Learners. Make copies of a blank chart for your class like this one with the **Block Method** and **Point-by-Point Method** columns. Students can manipulate the information to see which is the better format for their essay subjects.

As students finish and share their organizational charts with teammates, you can move from student to student to make sure all charts are workable. Charts that are not workable can be referred back to the groups.

Have students review the steps involved in the prewriting stage: choosing topics, gathering information, arranging information, and developing a thesis statement.

![Visual Connections icon] **VISUAL CONNECTIONS**

Exploring the Subject. Phillis Wheatley was born in what is now Senegal, West Africa in about 1753. Brought to Boston on a slave ship in 1761, she was sold to the family of John Wheatley, a merchant. Recognizing her talents, the family allowed Wheatley to learn to read and write. Her first poem to be published was "An Elegiac Poem on the Death of the Celebrated Divine . . . George Whitefield" (1770). This work praises the life of the famous English minister, George Whitefield. Subsequent publication of other poems brought Wheatley acclaim in Europe.

264   *Writing to Inform*

Jarena Lee

Phillis Wheatley

The Granger Collection, New York.

To gather and arrange information

- decide on the relevant features of the subjects
- make a chart showing similarities and/or differences
- choose the point-by-point method or the block method

WRITING ASSIGNMENT

PART 3:
Arranging Information

You've done most of the hard work by gathering information. Now you need to decide on how to arrange that information. It's your decision. Choose the organization that you think you'll be more comfortable with. Using the block method or the point-by-point method, make a chart like the one shown on page 263.

Have each student write an informative paper comparing a common idea in two or more pieces of literature. Explain to students that they can use another prewriting method for gathering their information—reading and taking notes. Good choices to use as the basis of this paper are the poems "The Courage That My Mother Had" by Edna St. Vincent Millay and "Mother to Son" by Langston Hughes. ■

Prewriting

Developing a Thesis Statement

The thesis statement of a comparison/contrast paper should state your subjects and your approach. It must

- identify what people, things, or ideas you are comparing or contrasting
- identify whether you will emphasize comparisons, emphasize contrasts, or balance the two

Here is a thesis statement that will emphasize contrasts. First the writer identifies the two things she's going to write about—the American and the French revolutions. Then she shows that she'll concentrate on contrasts by saying that the two events had only one similarity.

> The American Revolution and the French Revolution both started out to give power to the common people, but the similarities stopped there.

 REFERENCE NOTE: For more information on writing thesis statements, see pages 113–114.

WRITING NOTE Very often in an essay that explores differences, you begin with the one or two similarities the subjects have in common and then explore the differences. In the same way, to explore similarities, you may begin with the one or two differences between the subjects and then devote most of your paper to exploring similarities.

WRITING ASSIGNMENT
PART 4:
Developing a Thesis Statement

Are you going to compare your subjects? Contrast them? Or compare and contrast them? Write a thesis statement that announces to your reader what you plan to do in your paper. Use your prewriting chart from page 261 for ideas.

DEVELOPING A THESIS STATEMENT

Be sure to remind students that when using the point-by-point method, the order in which they discuss the categories in the bodies of their papers should follow the order that categories are listed in their thesis statements. For example, if a thesis statement comparing Michelangelo and Leonardo da Vinci is "Michelangelo and Leonardo da Vinci share many similarities in their achievements, innovations, and major works," the three body paragraphs will be about achievements, innovations, and major works, in that order.

TIMESAVER
Because the thesis statement controls the paper, writing it is a crucial step. Conduct individual conferences with students to be sure they have strong thesis statements. Spending an extra amount of time early will save time later when the essays are to be graded.

WRITING YOUR FIRST DRAFT

OBJECTIVES

- To analyze the organization of a comparison/contrast informative essay
- To write the first draft of a comparison/contrast informative essay

MOTIVATION

Ask students what the next step for builders is after they get all their materials gathered and organized. [Students will probably say that the next step is to start building the structure.] Explain that students are also in the building stage. They have gathered and organized their information and are now ready to write their drafts.

PROGRAM MANAGER

WRITING YOUR FIRST DRAFT

- Instructional Support For help with writing a paragraph, see **Writing** in *Strategies for Writing*, p. 27.

QUOTATION FOR THE DAY

"How many good books suffer neglect through the inefficiency of their beginnings!" (Edgar Allan Poe, 1809–1849, American story writer and poet)

Use the quotation to emphasize the importance of creating interesting introductory paragraphs. Ask students to write journal entries about times when they have made judgments about people or places based on first impressions. Explain that readers also make judgments based on first impressions, so good writers attempt to pique the readers' interests with their introductions.

Writing Your First Draft

You've completed much of the important work on your paper. All that's left to do is to put the information in your prewriting chart into sentences and paragraphs. You'll also have to think about an introduction, body, and conclusion.

The Elements of a Comparison/Contrast Essay

Introduction. As in any essay, the introductory paragraph should capture your reader's attention. You might begin the introduction of a paper about two Renaissance artists by saying "Leonardo and Michelangelo are not just names for Ninja Turtles; they were real people with real gifts." The introduction should also include the thesis statement, usually placed at the end.

Body. The body is the place to use the block method or the point-by-point method to present details about your subjects. Use transitions to connect and clarify ideas. Words and phrases like *also, similarly, both, in the same way,* and *just as* signal a comparison. *By contrast, however, unlike,* and *on the other hand* signal a contrast.

☞ REFERENCE NOTE: For more information about transitions, see pages 89–90.

In the body, you develop ideas with specific details, facts and examples, and quotations. In the paper about the two Renaissance artists, for example, you might discuss details about the artists' paintings: "Both Michelangelo and Leonardo recorded their ties to the church. Michelangelo painted the ceiling of the Sistine Chapel, and Leonardo painted a religious scene in *The Last Supper* on the wall of a monastery dining hall."

Conclusion. The ending of any essay must make the reader feel satisfied. A good, safe way to end is to summarize the information in the body and show how it sup-

Ask a volunteer to read aloud the information about the structure of the essay (introduction, body, and conclusion) and have the class discuss it. You may want to use a graphic organizer as a visual reinforcement of the structure; for example, an inverted triangle for the introduction, boxes for the body paragraphs, and a triangle for the conclusion.

The newspaper article about baseball can be introduced by talking about the origin of baseball, some great names associated with the game, and so forth. Discuss the vocabulary words before beginning. Then focus on why this is an informative essay [facts and information, not opinion] ☞

ports the thesis. Another way to end your essay is with an evaluation, a final comment that judges the relative worth of the two subjects. To end an essay comparing two sports cars, for example, you might say, "The Hawk and the Tornado are fairly evenly matched in terms of quality; but if you want to have fun, drive a Hawk."

Looking at a Comparison/Contrast Essay

The article that follows explains the similarities and differences (mostly the differences) between baseball in the United States and a Finnish sport called *pesapallo.* Notice how the writer inserts a reference to the comedy routine of Abbott and Costello, as well as background information on the game of *pesapallo,* to keep the reader interested.

A NEWSPAPER ARTICLE

1 | **Time out! Is baseball Finnished?**
by Bob Secter

INTRODUCTION

Attention grabber

HANCOCK, Mich.—There were lots of reasons why Jimmy Piersall was known as a flake back when he played major league baseball; but one of the best came the day he hit a home run as a New York Met and ran the bases backward.

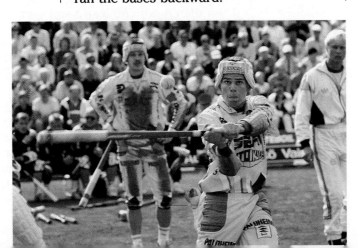

MEETING *individual* NEEDS

LESS-ADVANCED STUDENTS
Some students will shy away from choosing essay topics that require research simply because their research skills are poorly developed. Planning a field trip to the library and pairing students with peer tutors may be an effective strategy for helping them to use the card catalog system, to access magazine and newspaper articles, and to learn how to find their way through the stacks.

USING THE SELECTION
Time out! Is baseball Finnished?

1
Finnished: a play on words using the name of the country Finland

GUIDED PRACTICE

Have students read and analyze the essay on snorkeling for its organizational methods and structural elements. Ask students for examples of these elements from the essay, and write these elements on a transparency. Follow with a short discussion of diction and placement of facts in an essay.

268   *Writing to Inform*

2

chauvinist: having an unreasoning devotion to one's country

3

An allusion to Abbott and Costello's comedy routine.

4

guarantor: one who is responsible for something

5

eked out: barely managed to make

Background

Difference— Factual support

Difference— Factual support

Background

Background

All of which has little to do with the subject of this story, except to illustrate the <u>maxim</u> that what may seem like <u>buffoonery</u> in one setting could make perfect sense in another. Had Piersall been playing in, say, Helsinki rather than New York, he might have fit right in.

Yes. Baseball has been Finlandized.

2 The Finns call the game *pesapallo* and are so crazy about it that it is considered their national pastime. Of course they do it a little differently. They don't actually backpedal their way from base to base a la Piersall, but, looking at it from a <u>chauvinist</u> American perspective, they do take a backward route around the base paths.

First base is where third base ought to be, second is sort of around where first should be and third is somewhere out in left field.

3 That's right, Abbott. Who isn't on first. I Don't Know is. Sort of.

Anyway, Finnish <u>emigres</u> have spread the game to Scandinavia, Canada and even Australia. And over the weekend, they took their first crack at the toughest market of **4** all—the United States, the guarantor of all that is pure and noble about baseball.

Here in Michigan's rugged upper peninsula, the heart of Finnish America, two Canadian *pesapallo* teams squared off Saturday in a demonstration game before thousands of slightly <u>befuddled</u> spectators at an ethnic festival. In a real slugfest, the Toronto Sisu **5** eked out a 16–15 win over the archrival Thunder Bay Repais.

Organizers of the annual FinnFest say that they hope to field enough domestic talent to stage home-grown *pesapallo* matches at future gatherings. Already, the Hancock High School baseball coach is talking about teaching the Finnish version to his team.

Have students work in groups of three to complete **Exercise 1.** Each group should choose a reporter to speak for the group during the next class discussion, a recorder to take notes, and a chairman to coordinate the group's activities. Groups should work jointly on the answers to the three exercise questions. Students should then be ready to work on their first drafts for **Writing Assignment: Part 5.**

Difference—
Factual support

The main selling point of *pesapallo,* devotees say, is action. There are no long pauses between pitches, the ball is almost constantly in play and both fielders and runners are forever scampering all over the place.

Difference—
Quotation

"In American baseball, a runner on second is in scoring position but in our game, he's just tired," winked Jari Lemonen, who plays for the Repais. "Usually when we get out there, we pack a lunch."

Background—
History

6 The Abner Doubleday of Finland was Lauri Pihkala, a professor who apparently was <u>mesmerized</u> by baseball during early 20th century study tours in the United States. He combined the American game with some native ball-playing sports and *pesapallo* was born.

Similarities—
Factual support/
Statistics

Both baseball and *pesapallo* feature four bases, three outs an inning, nine innings, nine players on a side, a hard ball, mitts and a bat—although the Louisville Slugger of Finland is called a "Jarvinen Kanuuna."

Difference—
Factual support

That's where the similarities end. The *pesapallo* pitcher, for instance, stands next to the plate and tosses the ball up in the air, varying his delivery not with curves or sliders but by the height the ball goes.

6
Abner Doubleday: a United States Army officer who is noted as the traditional inventor of baseball

ASSESSMENT

From the group reports for **Exercise 1**, you can assess whether students can analyze a comparison/contrast essay. Use student-teacher conferences to evaluate students' first drafts. Be positive and reassuring in this early stage of the writing process.

RETEACHING

Color-code and discuss with the class another sample comparison/contrast essay. Highlight the introduction and conclusion in one color, the features for one of the subjects in another, and the features for the other subject in a third. This color-coding should make the organization more obvious.

MEETING individual NEEDS

LESS-ADVANCED STUDENTS

If students are having trouble organizing their essays, you may want to offer them an alternative graphic organizer. The following example is one possibility:

Title:	Intro. Para.
	Thesis
Topic Sent.: (Feature 1) 1. Subject 1 2. Subject 2	**Topic Sent.:** (Feature 2) 1. Subject 1 2. Subject 2
Topic Sent.: (Feature 3) 1. Subject 1 2. Subject 2	**Concl. Para.**

Difference— Factual support

Instead of waiting in a dugout, teammates of the batter stand around what is roughly equivalent to the batter's box and scream out advice whether to swing or not at a pitch. The batter can hit as many as three fair balls before he has to run. And the route around the basepaths sort of zigzags first to the left, then the right, then the left again.

Difference— Factual support/ Statistics

Confused? Try this. A three-base hit is a *kunnari,* or home run. The batter scores, even though he is allowed to stay on third and score again if somebody knocks him in. But getting a *kunnari* is not easy because a ball that's knocked out of the park—about 300 feet from home to the farthest point of the *pesapallo* outfield—is considered a *laiton* (foul).

Difference

When an outfielder catches a fly ball, that doesn't necessarily mean the batter is out. He might just be *haava* (wounded), a sort of purgatory state for sluggers that requires them to forfeit the turn at bat but doesn't exactly count toward ending the inning. And when someone does make an out, he's not just out, he's *pallo* (killed). This is no game for wimps, that's for sure.

CONCLUSION Difference— Quotation

There's one other important difference. At the end of the game, American ballplayers hit the showers. "When we're done," said Thunder Bay shortstop Pavli Kaki, "we go off to the sauna."

The Miami Herald

EXERCISE 1 ▶ **Analyzing the Organization of a Comparison/Contrast Article**

Now it's your turn to analyze the professional's work. Meet with two or three classmates to answer the following questions about the *pesapallo* article.

CLOSURE

Ask students to explain the elements of a comparison/contrast essay. Students should mention the introductory paragraph with the thesis statement, the block and point-by-point methods of comparison and contrast, and the concluding paragraph.

ENRICHMENT

You could have students research two other comparable sports to write informative comparison/contrast essays similar to the comparison/contrast of *pesapallo* and baseball in **"Time out! Is baseball Finnished?"** Possible subjects are rugby and football, squash and racketball, and lacrosse and hockey. ■

1. Why do you think the writer doesn't give equal space to discussing the rules and history of baseball?
2. Besides discussing *pesapallo* rules, what background information does the article provide?
3. At the midpoint of the article (paragraph 13), the writer summarizes several similarities between baseball and *pesapallo*. Then he goes on to discuss another five features that apply only to *pesapallo*. Why is he able to do this without explaining each contrasting feature in baseball? [Hint: What does the audience know?]

A Basic Framework for a Comparison/Contrast Essay

The professional model on *pesapallo* does not use a simple block or point-by-point method of organization—it doesn't give the two subjects equal time. (It's also written by a professional who earns his living by writing.) But using a simple block or point-by-point method may help you write and organize your essay more effectively. The following writer's model illustrates the block method of organization. Notice that the writer discusses all of the features (equipment, training, and dangers) for snorkeling, and then deals with all the same features for scuba diving.

A WRITER'S MODEL

Snorkeling and Scuba Diving

INTRODUCTION   If you're out on the water and see a red and white flag on a boat or pole, beware of creatures beneath the sea. The flag signals that human beings are underwater. They may be snorkeling or scuba diving. Both sports let people glimpse the amazing underwater plants and animals, but snorkeling and scuba diving are worlds apart.

Attention grabber

Thesis statement

ANSWERS

Exercise 1

1. The basics of baseball are probably already known by most readers.
2. The article tells how the game was started and by whom, the equipment used, the advantages of the sport, and its introduction to the United States.
3. He doesn't need to give information already known by most readers.

MEETING *individual* **NEEDS**

ADVANCED STUDENTS

After students have read **A Writer's Model,** challenge them to find more information about *pesapallo* and its introduction into the United States. Ask students to present the information to the class.

**BODY
Subject 1:
Snorkeling**

Snorkeling is easy. It doesn't take any special training and requires minimum equipment. You need a mask to keep the water out of your eyes and nose, and a snorkel, a short breathing tube that fits in your mouth and has an opening at the surface. The snorkel lets you keep your head underwater and breathe air at the same time. Many snorkelers use fins, but they're optional. Snorkelers can dive below the surface of the water for as long as they can hold their breath--probably about ten feet. The only real danger that snorkelers face is being run over by a boat; that's the point of the diving flag.

**Feature 1:
Training**

**Feature 2:
Equipment**

**Feature 3:
Time
underwater**

**Feature 4:
Dangers**

**Subject 2:
Scuba diving**

Scuba diving is a much more elaborate sport with far greater rewards. If snorkelers get a peek at underwater life, scuba divers get a long and leisurely look. You must take classes (three to five weeks' worth in a classroom, pool, and natural body of water) to become a certified diver. Besides the mask and fins that snorkelers wear, scuba divers also need a tank of air, a weight belt, a regulator, a buoyancy compensator, and a watch. The air that you carry lets you stay under for forty-five minutes or an hour at a depth of thirty feet. Scuba divers also need one other

**Feature 1:
Training**

**Feature 2:
Equipment**

**Feature 3:
Time
underwater**

essential thing: a buddy. Scuba diving can be dangerous; divers are told not to dive alone. The dangers that scuba divers face include overexpansion of the lungs, air embolism to the brain, the bends, running out of air, disorientation, and nitrogen narcosis. You should be in good physical condition. But it's a safe sport if you know what you're doing. According to scuba divers, what you experience near a reef is like nothing else.

Feature 4: Dangers

CONCLUSION So if you're willing to spend more money (you need access to a boat) and get special training, scuba diving lets you get a better, close-up, longer look at underwater life. But snorkeling is an inexpensive substitute, and it still gives you a breathtaking view of life in another medium. It's like visiting another planet.

Evaluation

Final comment

PART 5:
Writing a First Draft

Now is the time to use the information you developed in previous parts of your writing assignment to write a rough draft of your paper. Try to state your ideas as clearly as possible. Remember to give evidence in the form of facts, examples, and quotations to support each feature.

A DIFFERENT APPROACH

Ask students to form two panels of two students each. One panel will tell about a sport or product, and another will tell about a sport or product to which the first will be compared. An example is football and soccer or classical music and country and western music. Be sure that the pairs maintain an informative dialogue, rather than argue about which is best. A panel monitor might set up a point-by-point method of delivering the information. First one side and then the other will cite a parallel fact. Or a block method could be used, in which the two students on one side could list all their facts first, followed by the other side.

INTEGRATING THE LANGUAGE ARTS

Usage Link. Using transitions correctly is often very difficult for students. Be sure to refer to the **Reference Note** on p. 266 if students need more help with transitions. Ask each student to create a list of transitions that can be referred to in the writing process. Words students might include are *alike, also, both, similarly, in contrast, however,* and *yet.*

EVALUATING AND REVISING

OBJECTIVES

- To analyze a writer's revisions of a comparison/contrast informative essay
- To revise a comparison/contrast informative essay

TEACHING THE LESSON

You may want to put the history of the word *revise* on the chalkboard and ask students how its original meaning ties in with its meaning within the writing process. [*re*, "again" + *vis*, "look"]

Have a volunteer read the six evaluation questions and discuss each one with the class. To provide practice, read through

PROGRAM MANAGER

EVALUATING AND REVISING

- **Reinforcement/Reteaching** See **Revision Transparencies 11** and **12.** For suggestions on how to tie the transparencies to instruction, review teacher's notes in *Fine Art and Instructional Transparencies for Writing,* p. 115.

- **Ongoing Assessment** For a rubric to guide assessment, see **Evaluating and Revising** in *Strategies for Writing,* p. 28.

- **Assessment/Reflection** To assess student work and evaluate progress, see *Portfolio Forms* in *Portfolio Assessment,* pp. 5–21.

TECHNOLOGY TIP

Even if your school computers aren't arranged in a network, students can still use highlighting techniques and type comments next to the highlighted text. Students can save their work on disks, and other students can work with the disks. Also, students can attach their essays to e-mail messages and mail them to other students in the same building. They can then edit each other's work and mail it back.

SELECTION AMENDMENT
Description of change: excerpted
Rationale: to focus on the concept of evaluation and revision presented in this chapter

---

274 *Writing to Inform*

Evaluating and Revising

Cast a cold eye over your first draft as you look for ways to improve it. Use the following guidelines for both self-evaluation and peer evaluation (see pages 47–48). First, ask yourself the questions in the left-hand column of the chart on the next page. If you identify a weakness, use the revision technique suggested in the right-hand column.

COMPUTER NOTE: If the computers at your school are arranged in a network, you may be able to use them to do collaborative evaluation of writing assignments. Peer editors can use highlighting techniques such as italics or color-coding to mark words or phrases; then, they may type comments in brackets next to the highlighted text.

"In baseball you only get three strikes and you're out. In rewriting, you get almost as many swings as you want and you know, sooner or later, you'll hit the ball."

Neil Simon

Exercise 2 with the class and have volunteers answer questions 1–4. To provide independent practice, ask students to complete **Writing Assignment: Part 6.**

ASSESSMENT

You can have your students write their revisions on their first drafts in a different color ink than they used originally. You can also use the questions in the **Evaluating and Revising Comparison/Contrast Essays** chart to guide your assessment of students' revisions.

☞

EVALUATING AND REVISING COMPARISON/CONTRAST ESSAYS

EVALUATION GUIDE	REVISION TECHNIQUE
1 Do the first one or two sentences grab the audience's attention?	**Add** an interesting statement or example, or **replace** existing sentences with one.
2 Are the subjects similar enough to compare and different enough to be interesting?	**Cut** subjects that aren't similar or different enough, and **replace** with new subjects.
3 Does the thesis statement clearly identify the subjects and main idea of the essay?	**Add** a sentence (or **replace** an existing one) that clearly identifies the subjects and main idea of the essay.
4 Is the essay body organized by the block method or the point-by-point method?	**Reorder** the organization by moving sentences to create the block method or the point-by-point method.
5 Are each of the features of the two subjects handled in the same order?	**Reorder** the arrangement of sentences so the features of the two subjects are handled in the same order.
6 Is the conclusion effective?	**Cut** the ineffective sentences, and **add** effective statements that summarize or evaluate.

QUOTATION FOR THE DAY

"Boredom, after all, is a form of criticism." (William Phillips, 1906–   , American writer and editor)

As students begin evaluating and revising their first drafts, share the quotation with the class. Encourage students to revise any sentences that might bore or confuse their readers.

MEETING *individual* **NEEDS**

LEP/ESL

General Strategies. Many students will need individual attention at this stage of writing. If feasible, meet with students privately and have them read their essays aloud. Your immediate feedback will build confidence and give them information necessary to make effective revisions. Refrain from correction, but do note problem areas.

COOPERATIVE LEARNING

Put students in groups of four and assign each student a specific evaluation task. One student could evaluate all the opening sentences for effectiveness. Another student could evaluate to see if the thesis statement is supported. A third student could evaluate transitions, while a fourth could examine the concluding paragraph.

EXTENSION

Besides evaluating and revising the content of their essays, students might also evaluate and revise the stylistic aspects of their papers. You could have students employ the following revision strategies to guide them as they assess their writing:

COOPERATIVE LEARNING

Have students meet in groups of three or four to complete peer evaluations. Use the following instructions to guide students as they evaluate:

1. Underline or highlight what you think is the thesis statement.
2. Share your essay with the group by passing it to each member to read.
3. Have the group suggest needed changes on the essay in pencil.
4. Each student should indicate one strong sentence or word choice the author has made.
5. Have students initial the top of the first page of the essay to indicate that they have read it.

276   *Writing to Inform*

EXERCISE 2 ▶ Analyzing a Writer's Revisions

Here's a revision of the first two paragraphs of the writer's model on pages 271–273. See if you can figure out why these changes are improvements. Then answer the questions that follow.

> If you're out on the water and see a red and white flag on a boat or pole, beware of creatures beneath the sea. The flag signals that human beings are underwater. They may be snorkeling or scuba diving. Both sports let people glimpse the amazing underwater plants and animals, ⌃ *but snorkeling and scuba diving are worlds apart.*   **add**
>
> Snorkeling is easy, ⌃ ~~but scuba diving is harder.~~ It doesn't take any special training   **cut**
> and requires minimum equipment. The snorkel lets you keep your head underwater and breathe air at the same time. You need a mask to keep the water out of your eyes and nose, and a snorkel, a short breathing tube that fits in your mouth and has an opening at the surface. Many   **reorder**
> ~~people~~ use fins, *snorkelers* ⌃ *but they're optional.* Snorkelers can dive below   **replace/add**
> the surface of the water for as long as they can hold their breath--probably about ten feet. The only real danger that snorkelers face is being run over by a boat; that's the point of the diving flag.

1. Bracket the first words of all sentences to check for sentence variety.

2. Highlight all verbs to check for active voice and vivid verbs. (not in quotations)

3. Circle all *who, which,* and *that* constructions to check for possible subordinations. ∎

1. Why did the writer add the clause *but snorkeling and scuba diving are worlds apart* to the end of the first paragraph? [Hint: What is the thesis statement? Does the paper compare or contrast the two sports?]

2. In the first sentence of the second paragraph, why did the writer cut the clause *but scuba diving is harder*? [Hint: Is this paper developed by the block method or the point-by-point method?]

3. Why did the writer move the fourth sentence of the second paragraph?

4. In the fifth sentence of the second paragraph, why did the writer replace the word *people* with *snorkelers* and add the clause *but they're optional*?

WRITING ASSIGNMENT

PART 6:
Evaluating and Revising Your Comparison/Contrast Paper

It's hard to evaluate objectively the way your own hair looks before you leave for school in the morning. It's even harder to cast a cold, objective eye on your own writing. Use the questions from the chart on page 275 to evaluate your paper. Then exchange papers with a partner, and use the questions to evaluate each other's papers. Use your partner's comments and your own evaluations to revise your essay. Remember to be helpful in giving specific suggestions to your partner for improvements.

ANSWERS
Exercise 2

1. The words are added to make the thesis reflect the fact that the essay both compares and contrasts the subjects.

2. Because the writer uses the block method, scuba diving shouldn't be discussed until later in the essay.

3. The fourth sentence is a specific detail that is introduced by the second sentence.

4. These changes make the sentence more specific and more factual.

ONE'S FIRM, SLICK... / ONE'S SOFTER... KIND OF OILY FEELING / WHAT ARE YOU DOING? / COMPARING APPLES AND ORANGES

JOHNSON   2/2

Arlo and Janis reprinted by permission of Newspaper Enterprise Association, Inc.

PROOFREADING AND PUBLISHING

OBJECTIVES

- To proofread a comparison/contrast essay
- To publish a comparison/contrast essay

MOTIVATION

Ask students why people dress differently for different occasions. Elicit the idea that there are times when a person's appearance is very important in making a good impression. Tell students that proofreading helps writers find errors that would detract from the ideas they want to publish.

Proofreading and Publishing

Proofreading.   Put the finishing touches on your paper by checking the revised draft for mistakes in spelling, capitalization, punctuation, and usage. (See page 56 for Guidelines for Proofreading.) Try peer proofreading, too. Your classmates may be able to spot mistakes you've missed.

Publishing.   Then try these ideas for publishing your finished paper.

- Your comparison/contrast paper may be of interest to the teacher and students in another course in your school. For example, a physical education teacher might distribute your comparisons of two sports. A history teacher might share your paper on two American presidents.
- Post your opinions. You can post papers that compare/contrast subjects of interest (books, movies, TV shows, restaurants, cars) on a bulletin board where everyone in the class can read them.

TEACHING THE LESSON

You may want to focus on two or three specific problems in the proofreading stage. For example, you may find students are having trouble with capitalization or pronoun usage. Remind students that because it is often difficult to see errors in one's own writing, they should each have at least one other person read their essays.

Tell students to use the **Guidelines for Proofreading** to guide them as they look for problems in their papers.

Use a sample paragraph you have created to model proofreading. Then have students complete **Writing Assignment: Part 7.**

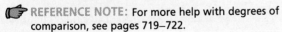

GRAMMAR HINT

Using the Degrees of Comparison

What's wrong with these statements?
a. *Pesapallo* is most exciting than baseball.
b. Of all the kinds of swimming, I like scuba diving better.

When you use adjectives and adverbs in a comparison/contrast paper, you need to be aware of the degrees of comparison. Most adjectives and adverbs have three degrees of comparison:

POSITIVE	COMPARATIVE	SUPERLATIVE
cold	colder	coldest
bad	worse	worst
ridiculous	more ridiculous	most ridiculous

1. When comparing two items, use the comparative degree.

   Pesapallo is **more exciting** than baseball.

2. When comparing three or more items, use the superlative degree.

   Many people consider *pesapallo*, soccer, and lacrosse the **most exciting** sports of all.

☞ REFERENCE NOTE: For more help with degrees of comparison, see pages 719–722.

WRITING ASSIGNMENT

PART 7:
Proofreading and Publishing Your Essay

It's time to be picky. Proofread your essay carefully to correct all errors. Write your final version, and proofread it. Then decide how you will publish your essay or share it with others.

QUOTATION FOR THE DAY

"Sloppily prepared pieces, peppered with mechanical glitches that could easily have been caught and corrected by the writer, are rarely going to sell—and the few that do are bound to be heavily edited." (David Petersen, 1946–   , American author and editor)

Copy this quotation on the chalkboard and ask students to discuss why they think writing with good content but with poor grammatical form might not sell.

MEETING individual NEEDS

LEP/ESL

General Strategies. English-language learners may have problems with prepositions. Even when the students go to a dictionary, the multiple definitions for such words tend to be confusing. Therefore, you may want to scan students' essays to see that prepositions are used correctly. You may need to offer extra practice in this area.

A DIFFERENT APPROACH

Students can make suggestions for ways to share their essays. One way is to display the essays in the school hallway, perhaps with hand-drawn illustrations, magazine photos, cartoons, or computer-generated graphics or pictures.

CLOSURE

For closure, have a volunteer give a quick definition of proofreading.

EXTENSION

The model essay can be used as the springboard for a review of all the essays presented in the chapter. Discuss the audience and purpose of "Football and Cyberball," the essay's structure, and where it could be published. Next, ask students about the audience, purpose, and structure of the other essays: "Time out! Is baseball Finnished?"

280   *Writing to Inform*

 Reflecting on Your Writing

Date your paper, and attach a brief reflection answering the following questions. Include both in your **portfolio.**

- What was the hardest part of selecting your topic?
- How did you decide on the order of your points?
- Which of your revisions were most effective? Why?

A STUDENT MODEL

Things to compare and contrast are all around you, as Chris Chavis shows in the following essay. Chris, a student at Central Mid High School in Norman, Oklahoma, effectively compares two all-American pastimes—playing football and playing a video game. As you read, see if you agree with his ideas.

Football and Cyberball
by Chris Chavis

The smell of hot popcorn and hot dogs drifts through the stadium. On the field, the home team scores a touchdown and the crowd ignites into a wild cheer. This is another typical afternoon watching one of America's favorite pastimes, but now, thanks to modern technology, you can play football in the comfort of your own home, or anywhere else for that matter. Today, instead of sitting in the hot sun watching football, you can actually participate in electronic Cyberball, one of the best arcade football games ever made. Football and Cyberball have many similarities, but, as usual, the shift from old technology to new creates many changes--some better and some worse.

TEACHING NOTE

After students have written their reflections, you might consider allowing a panel of students to share their reflections with the rest of the class. In this discussion, students should focus on sharing what they learned about themselves as writers and about the writing process that might be of some use to others. You can videotape or audiotape the discussion and include it in the participants' portfolios as well.

A STUDENT MODEL
Evaluation

1. To grab the audience's attention, Chris uses sensory details—"smell of hot popcorn and hot dogs"—in his description of a football game.
2. Cyberball and football are similar enough to compare but different enough to be interesting.
3. The thesis statement (the last sentence of the introduction) clearly identifies the topics and purposes of the essay.
4. Chris uses a modified block method to organize his essay.
5. He handles each of the features of cyberball and football in the same order.

Cyberball is easier to play than football. Cyberball requires the machine, the program, and, if you're playing at the arcade, several quarters. Cyberball also requires a significant amount of physical coordination. Manual dexterity is not necessarily a must, but if you expect to do well, you'll have to possess some hand-eye coordination.

Football requires a considerable amount of equipment. In order to play, you have to have enough people to form two teams, protective gear for each team--padding and helmets, and a football. Generally, football is played in a field or a vacant lot outdoors somewhere. And, in order for your team to be successful, you need to have several players with extraordinary physical skill.

Cyberball develops several important, fundamental skills. By having to control your futuristic, robotic players by manipulating a joystick, you develop extraordinary hand-eye coordination. The computer's quick moves when it is on offense also demand that you develop even faster reflexes in order to dominate. You must learn problem-solving skills and develop your intellect.

Football also develops many important, though more physical, skills. Football builds many muscles and can greatly enhance your physical fitness. You can also develop stamina and quicker reflexes by running and dodging the opposing team. However, one of the greatest skills developed from football is strong leadership, which many football players keep the rest of their lives.

Football and Cyberball have several obvious similarities, and, in fact, Cyberball is strongly based on football. They are different in many ways, however. I believe that Cyberball has many advantages over football and is what I prefer to play.

◈ INTEGRATING THE LANGUAGE ARTS

Vocabulary Link. A discussion of strong verbs works well in exploring the opening sentences of **A Student Model.** The author uses such vivid verbs as *drifts, scores,* and *ignites.* These verbs entice the reader to continue. Take a few minutes to discuss other strong verbs such as *demand, control,* and *whisper.* Talk about why *whisper* is a strong verb even though the meaning of the word "is to speak quietly." Next, let students brainstorm strong verbs they like to use in their own vocabulary. Discuss the appropriateness or inappropriateness of slang words.

and "Snorkeling and Scuba Diving." Discuss with students the importance of having a specific audience, purpose, and structure in mind when writing. ■

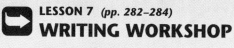
TEACHING THE LESSON

Read the explanation and example of extended definition in class and answer any questions students have. After discussing the answers to questions 1 and 2 on p. 283, divide the class into cooperative-learning groups of three or four.

Allow groups to brainstorm for a list of possible topics. Then students can use this

QUOTATION FOR THE DAY

"From time to time I find myself terribly limited by the dictionary." (Marcel Aymé, 1902–1967, French author)

Allow students in small groups to discuss the quotation and to write statements about what the quotation means. Ask a representative from each group to share the results with the class. Then tell students that extended definitions give more information than dictionary definitions, which present only the category and distinguishing characteristics of a word.

282

WRITING WORKSHOP

An Extended Definition

Comparison/contrast is one way to use the strategy of *classification*. Definition is another. When you define, you reverse the process you use to compare and contrast. To compare and contrast, you start with a large group or class (artists or sports) and pull out individual members to examine. To **define,** you group individual things together in a common group or class. A **dictionary definition** is a brief explanation of a word's meaning. When the word being defined is a noun (an object, place, person, or idea), the definition does two things:

- names the general class or category to which the word belongs
- gives the characteristics that distinguish the word from all other words in its general class

In the following dictionary definition, the general class is underlined. The rest of the definition tells how the word differs from other members of its class.

> *Pesapallo* is a <u>sport</u> resembling baseball, generally played in Finland, having bases run in an order backward to U.S. baseball.

You can also write an extended definition that is anywhere from one paragraph to several pages long. Here are some ways to extend a definition.

- Give an example.
- Tell how it works.
- Describe its properties.
- Tell other facts about it.
- Use a quotation from an authority.

The following model gives an extended definition of an Athabascan Indian concept. As you read, think how the writer extends the definition.

prewriting to create their first drafts independently. Suggest to students that they follow the instructions in the textbook for each stage of the process.

Encourage students to write reflections on their essays. Remind them that their reflections involve thinking about themselves as writers in order to improve their writing processes.

ASSESSMENT

Ask students to volunteer to read their definitions. Pay attention to not only the definitions, but also to the sentence transitions that create coherence. Call on all students so that assessment can be total.

☞

Instead of "goodbye," Athabascans say "Tlaa" when they leave each other. Tlaa means something like "See you" or "Until we meet again." An Athabascan would be puzzled by our idea of "goodbye." To say goodbye is so final. An Athabascan would say that people cannot really leave each other because they are always in each other's mind and heart. People cannot really be away from each other when each one is a part of the other. If the daughter goes away to school, the mother says "Tlaa." The mother thinks the daughter is coming back home. And, if she doesn't come home, then they will see each other at another place. The Athabascan language has no word for goodbye.

1. What is the word being defined? What is its simple, dictionary definition?
2. What examples or concepts does the author use to extend the definition?

MEETING *individual* NEEDS

LEP/ESL

General Strategies. If there are several language groups represented in your classroom, use the definition model as a springboard to discuss how other languages and cultures say "good-bye." Be aware of vocabulary words in this lesson (such as *properties, authority, concept,* and *philosophy*) with which your English-language learners might be unfamiliar.

ANSWERS
Writing Workshop Questions

1. *Tlaa* is being defined. Its simple definition is "see you" or "until we meet again."

2. The author talks about how people can't really leave each other and gives an example of how this can be true.

284

Writing an Extended Definition

 Prewriting. Choose as your subject an object or idea that interests you. Make sure that your subject is complex enough so that there's more to say about it than one sentence.

EXAMPLES		
	School:	a slang term, summer vacation, a hard class
	Sports:	an athlete, a coach, a free agent
	Society:	a shopping mall, a great car, a strict parent
	Philosophy:	duty, freedom, wisdom

Think of examples, descriptive details, or facts, or find appropriate quotations to extend the definition. To get some ideas, consult several dictionaries or encyclopedias. Who is your audience? Make sure you include any necessary background information.

Writing, Evaluating, and Revising. To write a one- or two-paragraph definition, begin with a one-sentence definition similar to what a dictionary might give. (Don't copy a dictionary's definition. Reword it so that it is distinctly your own.) Then, extend your definition by adding an example, descriptive details, facts, or quotations. Use peer editing for suggestions on improving your definition. Consider these questions: Does the paragraph begin with a precisely worded one-sentence definition? Does the extended definition include an attention-getting example, descriptive details, or a quotation from an author?

 Proofreading and Publishing. Proofread your definition to be sure it's free of careless errors before you give it to someone else to read. You could read your definition to a small group of classmates or to the whole class (withhold the word you are defining), and see if they can guess the subject.

Don't forget to date your paper. If you choose to include your definition in your **portfolio,** attach a brief written reflection to answer these questions: How did you decide on the best method for extending your definition? Which phrases help most to define the word?

285

MAKING CONNECTIONS

TEST TAKING

Writing for an Essay Test Question

In school, especially in civics and history classes, you'll often be faced with test questions that require comparison/contrast answers. You need to look carefully at each comparison/contrast question to decide whether to balance comparison and contrast, to emphasize comparison, or to emphasize contrast.

Here's some information on two women rulers you might study in a world history class. If your teacher gave you a test with an essay question asking you to compare and/or contrast them, what would you do? Do the two monarchs have more similarities or more differences? Would you base your paragraph on comparison or contrast? Write a paragraph about the two women in which you emphasize either their similarities or their differences.

WOMEN MONARCHS		
	ELIZABETH I	CATHERINE II
Position	absolute monarch	absolute monarch
Power	absolute	absolute
Title	Queen of England and Ireland	Empress of Russia
Birth-Death	1533–1603	1729–1796
Time of reign	1558–1603	1762–1796
Marital status	single	widow
Nickname	Good Queen Bess	Catherine the Great

(continued)

- To analyze a poem for metaphors

WOMEN MONARCHS (continued)		
	ELIZABETH I	CATHERINE II
Occurrences during reign	encouraged trade and commerce court as artistic center influenced by Renaissance encouraged rise of serious drama (Shakespeare) commissioned portraits by famous painters established large naval force, defeated Spanish Armada planned governmental reforms established Church of England	encouraged trade and commerce court as artistic center influenced by Enlightenment permitted private printing presses and relaxed the censorship of literature commissioned portraits by famous painters established large naval force increased landowners' control of serfs and stifled peasant rebellion granted freedom of worship

ELIZABETH I

CATHERINE II

Portraits courtesy of The Granger Collection, New York.

COMPARISON ACROSS THE CURRICULUM

Literature

A *metaphor* is a figure of speech that makes a direct comparison between two basically unlike things without using the words *like* or *as*. The poet Anne Sexton, for example, creates a metaphor when she says "each spring will be a sword you'll sharpen. . . ." What is compared in the following poem about a fan? Can you find the metaphors?

COMPARISON ACROSS THE CURRICULUM

Teaching Strategies

Have students meet in groups to discuss metaphors and to read their poems to each other. Each group should choose one poem to share with the entire class. Add at least one metaphor from each student's poem to a metaphor bulletin board. Include on the board the name of the poet, the poem, and the student.

GUIDELINES

You may want to have each student write down the metaphors and an analysis of the two things compared.

The Granger Collection, New York.

The Eagle-Feather Fan

by N. Scott Momaday

The eagle is my power,

And my fan is an eagle.

1   It is strong and beautiful

In my hand. And it is real.

My fingers hold upon it

As if the beaded handle

2   Were the twist of bristlecone.

The bones of my hand are fine

And hollow; the fan bears them.

3   My hand veers in the thin air

Of the summits. All morning

4   It scuds on the cold currents;

All afternoon it circles

To the singing, to the drums.

Bring a poem (you may write your own) to class that has a metaphor comparing two unlike things. Read the poem aloud, and ask everyone to listen carefully to find the metaphor. Have them tell what two things are being compared and how they are alike.

If you write your own poem, think about comparing two things that are not generally considered alike. Remember that a poem is not always rhymed and that it can be about many subjects—baseball, concrete mixers, and even giraffes. (See pages 207–208 on writing poems.)

USING THE SELECTION
The Eagle-Feather Fan

1

This metaphor compares a fan to an eagle. The feather fan gives the narrator power to fly as an eagle and to feel the eagle's strength.

2

bristlecone: the cone from the bristlecone pine tree, the needles of which grow in clusters of five

3

veers: changes direction

4

scuds: glides or skims along easily

INTEGRATING THE LANGUAGE ARTS

Vocabulary Link. Riddles, extremely popular in Anglo-Saxon England, often had kennings in them. A kenning is a two-word metaphor, such as "battle-flasher" for *sword*.

Discuss with the students riddles they know. Reinforce how words are used to describe something without saying the name of the object or concept itself.

Have students create their own riddles and tell each student to incorporate at least one kenning. Then ask students to read their riddles aloud to see if the class can guess the answers.

WRITING TO EXPLAIN: EXPOSITION

OBJECTIVES

- To use various prewriting techniques
- To organize and draft a progress report
- To evaluate and revise the content of a progress report
- To proofread and prepare a progress report for publication

WRITING-IN-PROGRESS ASSIGNMENTS

Major Assignment: Writing a progress report
Cumulative Writing Assignments: The chart below shows the sequence of cumulative assignments that will guide students as they write a progress report. These writing assignments form the instructional core of Chapter 8.

PREWRITING

Writing Assignment
- Part 1: Choosing a Subject p. 296
- Part 2: Gathering Information p. 301
- Part 3: Organizing Information p. 302

WRITING

Writing Assignment
- Part 4: Writing a First Draft p. 309

EVALUATING AND REVISING

Writing Assignment
- Part 5: Evaluating and Revising Your First Draft p. 312

PROOFREADING AND PUBLISHING

Writing Assignment
- Part 6: Proofreading and Publishing Your Paper p. 314

In addition, exercises 1–3 provide practice in exploring possible topics, analyzing a progress report, and analyzing a writer's revisions.

CROSS CURRICULUM

Goal!: Progress Reports and Physical Education

So that your students can practice using progress reports in another class, work with physical education teachers in your school to create a project in which students set goals for completing a physical fitness regimen and then document the process of meeting those goals. Encourage students in the same physical education classes to work together to create their fitness goals, to plan a regimen, and to document their progress. Before students begin the project, you and they should agree at what points in the semester they will document their progress.

- **Note taking** Students may find it helpful to keep track of their progress on a chart like the following.

	Day 1	Day 2	Day 3	Goal (Day 28)
Sit-ups	15/minute			45 per minute
Pull-ups	8/minute			20 per minute
40 m. run	40 seconds			18 seconds

Students should also take notes on their routines in their logs, including any changes and improvements.

Day 2: • Stretched to warm up • Started with sit-ups, then ran the 40 meters, and did pull-ups • Did weights for strength; **Day 6:** • Stretched • Did weights before doing pull-ups; improved by three seconds. (Did new routine help?)

- **Reflection** Suggest that students add a statement to the final reports in which they answer these questions: 1) Overall, how did you progress toward your goal? Be specific. 2) At any point, did you doubt that you would meet your goal? If so, how did you handle your feelings? 3) How does writing about your progress help you reach goals?

- **Assessment** Work with physical education teachers to share assessment responsibilities. You should assess the written report, and the physical education teachers should assess students' progress in their fitness level.

INTEGRATING THE LANGUAGE ARTS

SELECTION	READING AND LITERATURE	WRITING AND CRITICAL THINKING	LANGUAGE AND SYNTAX	SPEAKING, LISTENING, AND OTHER EXPRESSION SKILLS
• from **My Left Foot** by Christy Brown pp. 290–292 • from the **NAEP 1994 Geography Report Card** pp. 304–306 • from "**The Psychological Benefits of Exercise**" by Susan Chollar pp. 316–317 • "**Why No One Lends His Beauty**" by Harold Courlander with Ezekiel A. Eshugbayi pp. 321–322	• Analyzing the author's purpose pp. 292, 306, 317 • Responding personally to literature pp. 292, 306, 318 • Applying interpretive and creative thinking pp. 292, 306, 323 • Summarizing main ideas p. 306 • Analyzing a progress report p. 306 • Identifying sequence of events pp. 306, 318 • Reading for details p. 317 • Listing steps in a process p. 318 • Discussing a folk tale pp. 322–323	• Responding personally to literature pp. 292, 306, 318 • Brainstorming p. 296 • Choosing a topic pp. 296, 321 • Gathering and organizing information for writing pp. 301, 321 • Evaluating a progress report for content and structure pp. 306, 312 • Analyzing a progress report pp. 306, 312 • Writing, evaluating and revising a draft pp. 309–310 • Writing a cause-and-effect essay p. 318 • Evaluating a cause-and-effect essay p. 318 • Analyzing a visual aid p. 320 • Writing a folk tale or myth p. 323	• Proofreading for errors in grammar, usage, and mechanics pp. 314, 318	• Working with classmates to brainstorm topics p. 296 • Creating visuals to organize information p. 301 • Giving an oral presentation pp. 300, 320 • Working with classmates to analyze a progress report pp. 306, 312 • Sharing an essay with an audience p. 314 • Creating a visual to explain a process p. 320 • Working with classmates to analyze, research, and write folk tales pp. 322–323

SUGGESTED INTEGRATED UNIT PLAN

This plan gives suggestions on how to integrate the major strands of the language arts with this chapter.

The selections listed below are narratives that document the progression of an event. If you begin with this chapter on writing a progress report or with the suggested selections, you should focus on the common characteristics of writing to explain. You can then integrate speaking/listening and language concepts with both the writing and the literature.

Common Characteristics

- Content that is mainly factual and comprehensive
- Precise language that is neutral and unbiased documentation of facts
- Technical terms with definitions
- Usually chronological organization

Writing
Progress Report

UNIT FOCUS
NONFICTION: EXPOSITION

Speaking/Listening

- Working with classmates to brainstorm for topics
- Presenting an oral report

Language
Usage, style

- Active voice
- Verb tense
- Sentence fragments

Literature
Nonfiction such as

- *Survive the Savage Sea* Dougal Robertson
- "R.M.S. Titanic" Hanson W. Baldwin
- "A Presentation of Whales" Barry Lopez

CHAPTER 8: WRITING TO EXPLAIN: EXPOSITION

Use this guide for creating an instructional plan that addresses the individual needs of your students. Assignments followed by the following symbol (∗) may be completed out of class. Times given for pacing lessons are estimated.

CHAPTER PLANNING GUIDE—PUPIL'S EDITION

LESSONS	LITERARY MODEL pp. 290–292 From *My Left Foot* by Christy Brown	PREWRITING pp. 294–302	
		Generating Ideas	Gathering/Organizing
DEVELOPMENTAL PROGRAM	🕐 **30–35 minutes** • Read the model aloud and ask students to answer questions 1–2 on p. 292 orally.	🕐 **55–60 minutes** • Main Assignment: Looking Ahead p. 293 • Showing Progress pp. 294–296 • Exercise 1 p. 296 • Writing Assignment: Part 1 p. 296	🕐 **90 minutes** • Gathering and Organizing Information pp. 297–302 • Critical Thinking pp. 299–300 in pairs • Writing Assignment: Parts 2, 3 pp. 301–302
CORE PROGRAM	🕐 **25–30 minutes** Assign students to read the model aloud in pairs and to discuss the questions on p. 292.	🕐 **40–45 minutes** • Main Assignment: Looking Ahead p. 293 • Showing Progress pp. 294–296 • Exercise 1 p. 296 • Writing Assignment: Part 1 p. 296∗	🕐 **55–60 minutes** • Gathering and Organizing Information pp. 297–302 • Critical Thinking pp. 299–300 • Writing Assignment: Parts 2, 3 pp. 301–302∗
ACCELERATED PROGRAM	🕐 **20–25 minutes** • Assign students to read the model independently and to take notes in their Reader's Logs.	🕐 **30–35 minutes** • Main Assignment: Looking Ahead p. 293 • Thinking About Purpose, Audience, and Tone pp. 295–296 • Writing Assignment: Part 1 p. 296∗	🕐 **30–35 minutes** • Critical Thinking pp. 299–300 • Writing Assignment: Parts 2, 3 pp. 301–302∗

CHAPTER PLANNING GUIDE—PROGRAM RESOURCES

	LITERARY MODEL	PREWRITING
PRINT	• Reading Master 8, *Practice for Assessment in Reading, Vocabulary, and Spelling* p. 8	• Prewriting, *Strategies for Writing* p. 33
MEDIA	• Fine Art Transparency 5, *Transparency Binder*	• Graphic Organizers 13–14, *Transparency Binder*

WRITING pp. 303–309	EVALUATING AND REVISING pp. 310–312	PROOFREADING AND PUBLISHING p. 313–315
🕐 **70–75 minutes** • Writing Your First Draft pp. 303–309 • Writing Note p. 303 • A Writer's Model pp. 307–308 • Writing Assignment: Part 4 p. 309	🕐 **60 minutes** • Evaluating/Revising Chart p. 311 • Exercise 3 p. 312 • Writing Assignment: Part 5 p. 312	🕐 **60 minutes** • Proofreading/Publishing p. 313 • Usage Hint p. 313 • Writing Assignment: Part 6 p. 314 • Reflecting p. 314 • A Student Model pp. 314–315
🕐 **55–60 minutes** • Writing Your First Draft pp. 303–309 • Looking at a Progress Report pp. 304–306 • Exercise 2 p. 306 • Writing Assignment: Part 4 p. 309*	🕐 **55–60 minutes** • Evaluating/Revising Chart p. 311 • Exercise 3 p. 312 • Writing Assignment: Part 5 p. 312	🕐 **40–45 minutes** • Proofreading/Publishing p. 313 • Usage Hint p. 313 • Writing Assignment: Part 6 p. 314* • Reflecting p. 314 • A Student Model pp. 314–315*
🕐 **30–35 minutes** • Looking at a Progress Report pp. 304–306 • Writing Assignment: Part 4 p. 309*	🕐 **30 minutes** • Evaluating/Revising Chart p. 311 • Writing Assignment: Part 5 p. 312	🕐 **20 minutes** • Writing Assignment: Part 6 p. 314* • Reflecting p. 314

 Computer disk or CD-ROM   Overhead transparencies

WRITING	EVALUATING AND REVISING	PROOFREADING AND PUBLISHING
• Writing, *Strategies for Writing,* p. 34	• Evaluating and Revising, *Strategies for Writing,* p. 35	• Proofreading Practice, *Strategies for Writing* p. 37 • *English Workshop* pp. 225–228
	• Revision Transparencies 13–14, *Transparency* *Binder*	• *Language Workshop:* Lesson 10

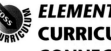

ELEMENTS OF WRITING: CURRICULUM CONNECTIONS

Writing Workshop
• Writing a Cause-and-Effect Essay
pp. 316–318

Making Connections
• Process Explanations pp. 319–320
• Cause and Effect in Literature pp. 320–323

ASSESSMENT OPTIONS

Summative Assessment
Holistic Scoring: Prompts and Models
pp. 27–32

Portfolio Assessment
Portfolio forms, *Portfolio Assessment*
pp. 5–25, 44–48

Reflection
Writing Process Log, *Strategies for Writing*
p. 32
Self-assessment Record, *Portfolio Assessment,*
p. 19

Ongoing Assessment
Proofreading, *Strategies for Writing* p. 36

LESSON 1 *(pp. 288–292)*
MAKING THINGS CLEAR
OBJECTIVES
- To write personal responses to literature
- To analyze parts of a progress report

TEACHING THE LESSON

To motivate students for this lesson, ask students to role-play a situation between a parent and a teenager. The parent has told the teenager to do a household chore, such as cleaning a room. In the role-playing, ask two characters, a parent and a teenager, to act out a conversation in which the teenager reports on progress in completing the chore.

PROGRAM MANAGER

CHAPTER 8

- **Computer Guided Instruction** For a related assignment that students may use for additional instruction and practice, see **Cause and Effect** in *Writer's Workshop 2 CD-ROM.*

- **Summative Assessment** For a writing prompt, including grading criteria and student models, see *Holistic Scoring: Prompts and Models*, pp. 27–32.

- **Performance Assessment** Use **Assessment 3** in *Integrated Performance Assessment, Level E.* For help with evaluating student writing, see *Holistic Scoring Workshop, Level E.*

- **Extension/Enrichment** See **Fine Art Transparency 5**, *The Golden Thread* by Will Barnet. For suggestions on how to tie the transparency to instruction, review teacher's notes in *Fine Art and Instructional Transparencies for Writing*, p. 27.

- **Reading Support** For help with the reading selection, pp. 290–292, see **Reading Master 8** in *Practice for Assessment in Reading, Vocabulary, and Spelling*, p. 8.

WRITING TO EXPLAIN: EXPOSITION

8

WORKPLACE writing

As members of the class watch the role-playing, ask them to notice the kinds of information the teenager reports and the order in which he or she reports it.

Point out to students that they will learn how to write progress reports in this chapter, but also point out that they already know something about reporting progress, as the role-playing indicated. Have a volunteer read the selection from *My Left Foot* aloud for the class.

☞

Making Things Clear

"How's it going?" your friends ask when you're looking for a part-time job. Your younger brother asks the same question when you're fixing his bike. And your track coach asks it when you're training for a meet. People are naturally curious about other people's activities, and looking for explanations that **make things clear** is something we all do.

Writing and You. You look for explanations, too. You look to a newspaper's weather page for the status of a hurricane, to a magazine for in-depth coverage of a space shuttle mission, to a technical manual for information about your CD player. What activities of your own would you like to make clear to others?

As You Read. The following excerpt describes the moment when the narrator, Christy Brown, first tries to write. Brown was born with cerebral palsy, a disorder of the nervous system that results in lack of muscle control.

Mark Hayden, *The Master of Lowell's* (1991). Pastel, 20 × 24".
Courtesy of the artist.

QUOTATION FOR THE DAY
"When you're writing, you're trying to find out something which you don't know." (James Baldwin, 1924–1987, American novelist, essayist, and playwright)

Share the quotation with your class and discuss how writing can be a tool to help people understand the progress of a project. Ask students how it might be possible for a writer to find out something as a result of writing.

VISUAL CONNECTIONS
The Master of Lowell's
About the Artwork. Mark Hayden says that he used to have trouble with color, but that working in pastels helped him learn about color and reflected light. Artists cannot mix pastels as they can oils, acrylics, or watercolors; instead, artists take up a pastel and apply its color directly to the painting surface. While artists have hundreds of pastel colors at their disposal, they must choose just the right colors for a particular painting to keep the painting fresh.

USING THE SELECTION
from My Left Foot

1

What does the vividness of the author's memory suggest about the significance of what he is about to recall? [That the event was of great importance in his life.]

2

Why does the author use italics for the phrase "with my left foot"? [To emphasize that this was something extraordinary.]

3

Why hadn't the author noticed before what change had come over the others in the room? [Answers may vary. Some students might say he was too busy concentrating on writing with the chalk to notice what the other people in the room were doing.]

4

Why does the author break out in a sweat? [Answers may vary. Some students might say it is from the physical effort it took for him to write with his foot. Others might say it is because of the emotional stress involved in writing with his foot for the first time.]

290

290

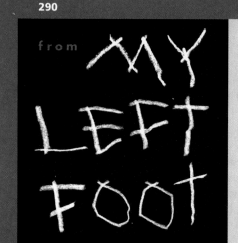

from **MY LEFT FOOT**

by Christy Brown

It happened so quickly, 1 so simply after all the years of waiting and uncertainty that I can see and feel the whole scene as if it had happened last week. . . .

In a corner Mona and Paddy were sitting huddled together, a few torn school primers before them. They were writing down little sums on to an old chipped slate, using a bright piece of yellow chalk. I was close to them, propped up by a few pillows against the wall, watching.

It was the chalk that attracted me so much. It was a long, slender stick of vivid yellow. I had never seen anything like it before, and it showed up so well against the black surface of the slate that I was fascinated by it as much as if it had been a stick of gold.

Suddenly I wanted desperately to do what my sister was doing. Then—without thinking or knowing exactly what I was doing, I reached out and took the stick of chalk out of my sister's hand—*with my left foot.*

I do not know why I used my left foot to do this. It is a puzzle to many people as well as to myself, for, although I had displayed a curious interest in my toes at an early age, I had never attempted before this to use either of my feet in any way. They could have been as useless to me as were my hands. That day, however, my left foot, apparently on its own <u>volition</u>, reached out and very impolitely took the chalk out of my sister's hand.

I held it tightly between my toes, and, acting on an impulse, made a wild sort of scribble with it on the slate. Next moment I stopped, a bit dazed, surprised, looking down at the stick of yellow chalk stuck between my toes, not knowing what to do with it next, hardly knowing how it got there. Then I 3 looked up and became aware that everyone had stopped talking and were staring at me silently. Nobody stirred. Mona, her black curls framing her chubby little face, stared at me with great big eyes and open mouth. Across the open hearth, his face lit by flames, sat my father, leaning forward, hands outspread on his knees, his shoulders tense. I felt the sweat break 4 out on my forehead.

ASSESSMENT

Your evaluation of students' answers to both the **Reader's Response** and the **Writer's Craft** questions should help you assess your students' comprehension at this point.

RETEACHING

If students are having difficulty understanding how the passage from *My Left Foot* is a progress report, ask them to think of it as a description of a phase in a long and difficult process. This critical incident is the beginning of a journey that will lead to greater accomplishments.

291

My mother came in from the pantry with a steaming pot in
5 her hand. She stopped midway between the table and the fire, feeling the tension flowing through the room. She followed their stare and saw me, in the corner. Her eyes looked from my face down to my foot, with the chalk gripped between my toes. She put down the pot.

6   Then she crossed over to me and knelt down beside me, as she had done so many times before.

"I'll show you what to do with it, Chris," she said, very slowly and in a queer, jerky way, her face flushed as if with some inner excitement.

Taking another piece of chalk from Mona, she hesitated, then very deliberately drew, on the floor in front of me, *the single letter 'A.'*

"Copy that," she said, looking steadily at me. "Copy it, Christy."

I couldn't.

I looked about me, looked around at the faces that were turned towards me, tense, excited faces that were at that moment frozen, immobile, eager, waiting for a miracle in their midst. . . .

I tried again. I put out my foot and made a wild jerking stab with the chalk which produced a very crooked line and nothing more. Mother held the slate steady for me.

"Try again, Chris," she whispered in my ear. "Again."

Christy (Hugh O'Conor) makes his first successful attempt to communicate in the movie version of *My Left Foot* (1989).

"Try again, Chris. . . . Again."

5

Why is there tension in the room? [Answers may vary. Some students might say that the people in the room know that if Brown succeeds in writing with his foot, then maybe he will be able to communicate effectively and do other things, as well.]

6

What might Brown's mother be thinking as she kneels to help her son? [Answers will vary. Some students might say she is imagining what being able to write will mean for her son in the future.]

Ask students to explain in a few sentences how the events in a progress report are organized. Have students show how the selection from *My Left Foot* is an example of this type of organization. ■

292

I did. I stiffened my body and put my left foot out again, for the third time. I drew one side of the letter. I drew half the other side. Then the stick of chalk broke and I was left with a stump. I wanted to fling it away and give up. Then I felt my mother's hand on my shoulder. I tried once more. Out went my foot. I shook, I sweated and strained every muscle. My hands were so tightly clenched that my fingernails bit into the flesh. I set my teeth so hard that I nearly pierced my lower lip. Everything in the room swam till the faces around me were mere patches of white. But—I drew it— *the letter 'A.'* There it was on the floor before me. Shaky, with awkward, wobbly sides and a very uneven center line. But it *was* the letter 'A.' I looked up. I saw my mother's face for a moment, tears on her cheeks. Then my father stooped down and hoisted me on to his shoulder.

7

"I had done it! It had started...."

I had done it! It had started—the thing that was to give my mind its chance of expressing itself. True, I couldn't speak with my lips, but now I would speak through something more lasting than spoken words—written words.

READER'S RESPONSE

1. Christy Brown mentions the tension in the room as he makes his first attempt to write. What was your response as you read?
2. Can you think of a moment when you or someone you know took a huge step forward or experienced a breakthrough? What were your feelings at the time?

WRITER'S CRAFT

3. Brown describes in great detail the few moments in which he struggles to write a letter. What is the sequence of events?
4. What, according to the narrator, is the significance of his accomplishment?

7

What emotions might be expressed in Mr. Brown's action? [Answers will vary. Students may say that the father is joyful at his son's accomplishment and lifts him onto his shoulder as one would the victor of a contest. He wants his son to feel good about his accomplishment and wants to encourage him to continue.]

ANSWERS

Reader's Response

1. Answers will vary. Be sure students give reasons to support their opinions.

2. You may want students to list each step taken that led to the huge step forward in the experiences they choose.

Writer's Craft

3. The first time he tries to draw the letter, he fails. The second time, he puts out his foot, makes a stabbing motion with the chalk, and writes a crooked line. On the third try, he draws one side of the letter. The chalk breaks after he draws half of the other side, but he strains every muscle and completes the letter.

4. Learning how to write would give him the opportunity to express himself.

SELECTION AMENDMENT
Description of change: excerpted
Rationale: to focus on writing a progress report as presented in this chapter

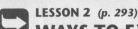
Emphasize to students that there are four basic methods of development that they can use to explain information. These four are narration, description, classification (which includes both definition and comparison/contrast), and evaluation. Ask students to give further examples, similar to the ones given below, of how each method might be used in developing a composition that explains progress. ■

293

Ways to Explain

Christy Brown explains his breakthrough using *narration*. Narration presents events that happen over time; it shows change. Narration is just one of several ways you can write when your purpose is to explain. Here are some other examples.

- in an essay for history class, narrating the events leading to U.S. involvement in World War I
- in a letter to your cousin, telling about the effects of baking soda on electrical fires
- in a progress report, relating what tasks have been accomplished in a house-painting project
- in a field observation report for science class, explaining the environmental importance of wetlands
- in a student council report to the school board, proposing and giving evidence that a dance class should be classified as a physical education course
- in a business report, evaluating a computer printer by pointing out its various typefaces, its speed, and its controls
- on a Web site, reviewing the lyrics, melodies, and musical performances on a new CD

LOOKING AHEAD

In the main assignment in this chapter, you'll use narration to write a progress report. Your purpose in writing will be to explain. As you work through each writing assignment in this chapter, keep in mind that a progress report

- focuses on a particular project or activity
- explains the writer's accomplishments, findings, or results, and includes appropriate supporting information
- describes any unexpected problems the writer has encountered
- provides an overall view of the project's current standing

COOPERATIVE LEARNING

Divide the class into groups of four, with one person in each group representing one of the four strategies. Instruct each group to work together to select topics that could be developed in compositions using the strategies. Then, tell group members to work together to come up with at least five details that could be included in compositions on the chosen topics. Each group could share its work with the rest of the class. Finally, involve students in a discussion about the appropriateness and workability of the topics and details they have developed.

INTEGRATING THE LANGUAGE ARTS

Literature Link. Ask students to examine their favorite short stories and to analyze them to determine which methods of development they contain. If several students like the same story, you can let them work in a group on this activity, or you can assign stories for groups of students to use. In either case, have students report to the class on their findings. Be sure to have them cite examples of each method of development when they give their reports.

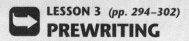
OBJECTIVES

- To arrange information for a progress report in chronological or logical order
- To brainstorm and choose an appropriate topic for a progress report
- To create a list or chart itemizing accomplishments, describing problems, and listing supporting details

Writing a Progress Report

Showing Progress

When we want to demonstrate to someone—including ourselves—that we're making progress on a project, we can write a progress report. A progress report gives an account of the work done on an ongoing project over a specific time period. "Work done" can refer either to tasks accomplished on a project or to the results or findings of that project. In the workplace, progress reports are written for people who need to be kept informed about a project. They enable decision makers to decide whether the project should be continued as is, modified, or ended. Since progress reports are generally written at fixed intervals—every week, month, or few months—they also serve as a record of the project after it is completed.

Choosing a Subject

Progress reports written in the workplace have a set subject: the project or projects the employee is working on. Even as a student, your subject for a progress report may be decided for you. For example, your chemistry teacher may ask you to submit regular reports explaining the results of a series of lab experiments. The teacher may even give you forms to fill out, or describe the precise format you're expected to follow.

When you're free to choose your own subject, ideas can come from almost any area of your life. For school, you may be preparing a display for the history fair, learning to play the trombone, or designing sets for a play. At home, you may be working on a merit badge in photography for the Scouts, tutoring a neighbor's sixth-grader in math, or saving money to buy a used car. In the community, you may be circulating a petition for a new teen center, spearheading a neighborhood cleanup project, or training to become a tour guide at the zoo. Any of these activities—in fact, any ongoing activity (one you've begun but haven't completed yet)—is a suitable subject for a progress report, as long as it's one that leads toward a goal.

WRITING NOTE

Remember that you're writing a short report, not a book. Choose a limited topic that you can explain clearly in a brief report.

TOO BROAD	Birdwatching
LIMITED	Creating a backyard habitat for birds

Thinking About Purpose, Audience, and Tone

Remember that the *purpose* of your progress report is to explain. You want to communicate to your readers what you've accomplished and the nature of any problems that have arisen.

Since you want your report to be useful, you'll want to ask yourself several questions about your readers. First, who is your *audience,* and what do they already know about your project? For example, your audience might be your teacher or your classmates; or it might be your supervisor, or colleagues working on different parts of the same project. It could even be people who don't know anything about your project. In each case, you'll want to adjust the information you provide to suit your audience. Second, what do your readers *need* to know—either as background

MEETING *individual* NEEDS

LESS-ADVANCED STUDENTS

Some students may need help in identifying a project they are involved in that would be a suitable topic for a progress report. Work with students individually or in small groups. Ask them to consider any projects they may be working on at home, at a part-time job, in a school club or extracurricular activity, at church, or in sports. Suggest that they make a list of all the projects they identify and analyze this list to see if any of these projects could serve as the basis of a progress report.

by the students in the **Motivation** activity by asking "Is it an ongoing project?" and "Does it accomplish a long-term task?" Next, determine whether the topic is focused enough. Finally, decide who the audience will be and whether the topic will be interesting. Suggest to students that they choose topics that interest them.

Ask student volunteers to read the rest of the **Prewriting** lesson aloud to the class. Stress the importance of supporting information in an informative essay.

Help students choose topics for their essays by dividing the class into small groups and having the groups do **Exercise 1.** Circulate from group to group to answer questions and to check students' progress.

A DIFFERENT APPROACH

Newspapers often run articles about ongoing civic projects. Ask students to search daily newspapers to find articles that deal with the progress being made in a particular project. Ask students to determine the method of organization used in the articles, the accomplishments that have been achieved, whether the people conducting the project are facing any problems, and the project's current standing.

ANSWERS
Exercise 1

Each small group should have generated at least five topics. Check topics to make sure they are ongoing projects.

---

or in order to carry on with or adjust their own activities? Finally, how much and what kind of information will make your readers confident that your report is sound and reliable?

Unless you haven't made any progress at all, aim for a *tone* that's confident and optimistic. You don't want to promise more than you can deliver, but you do want to reassure your readers that you're on top of the situation. If you've run into problems, explain them in a straightforward way. You can put a positive spin on setbacks by telling how you plan to overcome them.

Notice the difference in tone between these two approaches:

NEGATIVE   The plastic gauze I need for my 3-D sculpture is out of stock at the art-supply store.

POSITIVE   I ordered the plastic gauze I need from a mail-order house, which has promised delivery in five days.

You'll be discussing your own efforts, so plan to use the *first-person point of view:* Use pronouns such as *I, me,* and *my.*

EXERCISE 1 ▶ **Exploring Possible Subjects**

What are you trying to accomplish? Think of some ongoing projects or activities that you could explain in a progress report. Working with a small group, brainstorm several suitable subjects, including some about home and community projects as well as ones that focus on school activities.

PART 1:
WRITING ASSIGNMENT
Choosing a Subject

One benefit of writing a progress report is gaining an overall perspective on your project. In fact, charting your progress by writing about it may help you work through any difficulties you're having on your project. Consider these advantages as you choose a subject to write about—either one your group identified in Exercise 1 above or another ongoing project or activity.

To model organizing information for students, go through **Writing Assignment: Parts 2** and **3** on the chalkboard with a sample topic. Try different methods of organizing a progress report (chronological order or logical order), and ask students which method would be appropriate for different topics.

Your students should be ready to do **Writing Assignment: Parts 2** and **3** independently. Students might need time for research, either to review the status of the project or to interview others who work with them on the project.

Prewriting

Gathering and Organizing Information

Your goal is to give readers an overview of your project. In order to do so, you will need to provide relevant information that is organized so that readers can easily identify your accomplishments.

Gathering Information

What information—and how much of it—should you include in a progress report? Certainly, vague statements such as "Everything's coming along fine" aren't convincing, yet too much detail can make your report hard to read.

In most cases, you can gather information by mentally reviewing your activities since your last report. Take notes as you review your accomplishments. If you develop a habit of jotting down notes as you work on your project, you'll find them a useful tool when drafting your report.

Now that you have notes describing what you've done on your project, how do you select what information to include in your report? Remember that your primary purpose is to present a clear picture of your progress. You also want to convince readers that your report accurately reflects reality. With these goals in mind, you can use the following two rules of thumb in choosing information to include in your report.

First, select information that will be useful to your reader. For typical progress reports, useful information includes

- identification of the project and its purpose
- time period covered by the report, and a list of specific tasks accomplished in that period
- data, results, or findings that would be of immediate interest to your readers
- any unforeseen problems that have arisen and how you are dealing with them
- what the plans are for the immediate future
- any additional resources needed
- any changes to the project schedule

ASSESSMENT

Use **Writing Assignment: Part 2** as a means of assessing students' understanding. Be sure that students have chosen suitable topics, have identified accomplishments and problems, and have gathered supporting information.

CLOSURE

Write on the chalkboard a topic that would not work for a progress report, such as a report on the profits from a car wash. Ask your class whether it is a good topic and then have them explain why it is not a good topic. ■

A DIFFERENT APPROACH

The annual State of the Union message by the President of the United States is essentially a progress report on how the country is faring. Have students watch a portion of a videotape of a recent State of the Union address and analyze it to determine its organization, the accomplishments the president claims, the problems the president lists, and the overall status of the country. If a videotape of a State of the Union address isn't available, find a printed copy of the text and have students work with it. You might want to have students work in groups of three or four on this activity.

Avoid the temptation to talk about every detail that you've learned or every small obstacle you encountered: Readers of progress reports appreciate a narrative that sticks to essential information.

As a second guideline in selecting information to include, bear in mind that too little information is as ineffective as too much. Generalizations in progress reports are neither informative nor confidence-inspiring. For example, if your project is creating a video of your school, you can't simply state that things are going well and expect readers to take your word for it. They'll want evidence—perhaps details about what you've videotaped, how much of the soundtrack you've recorded, and whether you're on schedule to meet your original deadline. In other words, be as specific as you can when you list your accomplishments, without overwhelming your reader with details. Where appropriate, include "hard" evidence such as facts, statistics, or examples. In the case of the videotaping project, hard evidence could be a proposed title and the amount of footage (in minutes or hours) that has been videotaped or recorded.

CRITICAL THINKING

Analyzing Accomplishments

Sometimes your accomplishments on a project are obvious, especially when they're tangible ones—ones you can see or touch. For example, it's easy to see your progress when you're building a model of Shakespeare's Globe Theater— you can identify the parts you've constructed and explain the order in which you assembled them. But sometimes accomplishments are not so apparent; perhaps your project is still in the planning stage, or maybe you've spent a lot of time solving a problem. In cases like this, you'll need to analyze the specific tasks you've completed so that in your report you can point to concrete accomplishments.

For example, suppose you are working on an antilittering campaign for your school. If you haven't yet established a campaign, you may think there's nothing to report. But you may actually have done a great deal of work. To show your progress, you could break down the work you've done into the specific tasks involved.

Topic: Organizing a schoolwide antilittering campaign

Accomplishment: Established need for campaign

Task 1. Walked around school grounds every day for two weeks to monitor amount of litter on ground; on average, filled one 5-gallon garbage bag per day

Task 2. Counted number of trash cans on school grounds, calculated percentage overflowing by noon, and determined number of times they're emptied each day

Task 3. Conducted opinion poll among students and teachers about the problem: results overwhelmingly support need for a campaign

students what steps they would follow in finding a used car to buy. Some steps would include deciding on a price range, checking classified ads, visiting used-car lots, and doing research on the safety and performance of cars they like.

To close the lesson, have students share their analyses with the class.

ANSWERS
Critical Thinking Exercise

Task analyses may vary. Here are some possibilities.

Mixed-media collage: listed all of the possible topics students could brainstorm; investigated resources available for each topic; assessed the cost in both time and money

Used car: decided on price range; checked classified ads in newspaper; visited used-car lots to see the cars that were available; called private sellers for an inspection; researched safety and performance information

Spanish Club: surveyed student interest; compiled survey results; solicited potential faculty sponsors; wrote the proposal; submitted the proposal

Car wash: selected date and times; secured a facility; recruited volunteers; advertised car wash; sold advance tickets; trained volunteers

Part-time job: determined time available for work; secured transportation; checked want ads in newspaper; submitted applications; participated in interviews

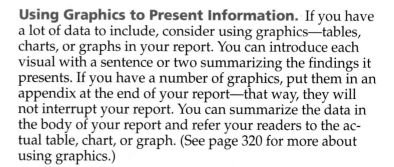

CRITICAL THINKING EXERCISE:
Analyzing Accomplishments

You've made progress—but how did you do it? With a partner, choose one of the following accomplishments, and break it down into each of the smaller tasks that had to be completed first.

- settled on a subject for a mixed-media collage for an art exhibit
- found a used car to buy
- submitted a proposal for starting a Spanish Club at school
- held a car wash to raise money for a local theater group
- was hired for a part-time job

Using Graphics to Present Information. If you have a lot of data to include, consider using graphics—tables, charts, or graphs in your report. You can introduce each visual with a sentence or two summarizing the findings it presents. If you have a number of graphics, put them in an appendix at the end of your report—that way, they will not interrupt your report. You can summarize the data in the body of your report and refer your readers to the actual table, chart, or graph. (See page 320 for more about using graphics.)

Addressing Problems. If you've run into problems with your project—or if you foresee problems in the time remaining—your best course is to bring them to your readers' attention and explain the causes. (Doing so helps inspire your readers' confidence in what you're reporting.) Then, you can either explain how you plan to resolve the problems or, if necessary, ask for help. For example, if a scheduled interview fell through because the person had to be out of town that day, you can explain that you've rescheduled (or plan to reschedule) the meeting. If the person has moved away, though, you might need to ask for help in identifying someone else to interview.

WRITING ASSIGNMENT

PART 2:
Gathering Information

Begin pulling your material together by making a list or chart itemizing your accomplishments; also, include any problems you've encountered. For each accomplishment or result, jot down at least one supporting fact, statistic, or example; for each problem, see if you can list one step you've taken to resolve it. Then, cross out details that would not be useful to your readers. If you have useful information that could be presented visually, decide what kind of graphic (chart, table, graph, and so on) would be most appropriate.

Organizing Information

Now that you've gathered information for your progress report, you need to decide how to organize it. Usually, writers of progress reports use *chronological* (time) *order:* They explain the tasks they've accomplished since the project began

"Hey! Where's my science project?"

© 1996; reprinted courtesy of Bunny Hoest and *Parade Magazine.*

(or since the last report) in the order in which they performed them. But some projects require you to carry out several different tasks at the same time. In such cases, using *logical order*—organizing the material by tasks or findings instead of by time—would be much clearer.

The chart on page 302 shows how a writer arranged information about two different projects. For her first project—a plant biology experiment—the writer chose to organize topically because she was working with several groups of plants, each at a different stage of development. For her second project—a course in learning how to swim—she chose to organize her information chronologically because she learned a skill each week.

TIMESAVER
Before students complete **Writing Assignment: Parts 2** and **3,** you may want to make sure they have chosen appropriate topics. Do this by passing around a sheet of paper so students can write their names and the topics they have chosen. This procedure should provide a quick and easy way for you to detect inappropriate topics.

INTEGRATING THE LANGUAGE ARTS

Speaking and Listening. Progress reports are often given orally in meetings of clubs or other groups that students belong to. Ask students to prepare speaking notes based on their topics and to deliver their reports to a small group.

HERE'S HOW

LOGICAL ORDER	CHRONOLOGICAL ORDER
Plant biology experiment	Swimming lessons
Task 1: Germinating (sprouting) seeds. Germinated three dozen bean plants and two dozen corn plants	Week 1: practiced survival bobbing
	Week 2: learned flutter and breaststroke kicks
Task 2: Planting seeds. Planted twenty bean seedlings one week after germination; watered them every second day	Week 3: learned crawl and backstroke arm techniques
	Week 4: learned breaststroke arm technique
Task 3: Monitoring seed growth. Took daily measurements of corn seedlings after they'd been planted six weeks; noted an average weekly growth of 1 1/2 inches	Week 5: practiced synchronizing flutter kick and crawl arm technique
	Week 6: practiced flutter kick with backstroke arm technique
	Week 7: practiced breaststroke arm technique with breaststroke kick

COMPUTER NOTE: Create tables within your word-processing program, and use them to record tasks as you accomplish them. That way, you will have notes to work from when you draft your progress report.

WRITING ASSIGNMENT

PART 3:
Organizing Information

Now's the time to decide whether you'll use chronological or logical order in your progress report. Arrange the information you selected in Writing Assignment, Part 2 (page 301) by numbering your accomplishments, and any problems, in the order you'll present them.

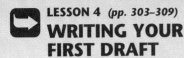
MOTIVATION

You may want to stress to your class that a first draft is like a base coat of paint—it should cover the subject, but it does not have to be perfect. Tell them that the most important thing will be just to start writing.

Writing Your First Draft

As you draft your report, try to make it as complete as possible without burdening it with excessive detail. Also, strive for accuracy and clarity; use the simplest terminology you can, and opt for concrete language whenever possible.

Writing the Introduction. Establish a context for your readers by identifying the project or activity you're reporting on and the time period covered. If necessary, refresh their memory by briefly stating the purpose of the report— exactly what it is you're trying to accomplish. For an example of an effective introduction, study the first paragraph of the Writer's Model on pages 307–308.

Writing the Body. Recall what your audience knows and what they need to know. Include any necessary background information, and define unfamiliar terms at the beginning of the body. Then, draft a separate paragraph for each significant accomplishment, finding, or result, using your information list or chart as a guide. Be sure to back up your statements with specific information from your list or chart (facts, examples, statistics). Depending on your situation, you may either explain any problems as you go along or deal with the problems in a separate section, as the Writer's Model on pages 307–308 does.

Writing the Conclusion. Use the conclusion of your report to give readers an overall view of your progress. You may also want to confirm—or revise—the time you originally estimated it would take to complete the project.

WRITING NOTE Progress reports may be written as memos, as letters, or as formal reports with title pages, summaries, tables of contents, and appendixes. For the assignment in this chapter, you may simply write your report as a narrative (see the Writer's Model on pages 307–308 for an example).

PROGRAM MANAGER

WRITING YOUR FIRST DRAFT

- **Instructional Support** For help with writing an introductory paragraph, see **Writing** in *Strategies for Writing*, p. 34.

QUOTATION FOR THE DAY

"That writer does the most, who gives his reader the *most* knowledge, and takes from him the *least* time." (C. C. Colton, c. 1780–1832, American author and clergyman)

Write the quotation on the chalkboard and ask small groups of students to discuss some reasons why the quotation might be especially true for writers of progress reports.

MEETING *individual* NEEDS

LEP/ESL

General Strategies. Encourage students to write their initial drafts without being overly concerned about making mistakes in grammar, usage, and punctuation. If students use computers to draft their papers, you can have them try dimming the screens or turning the monitors off to encourage them to write freely.

As a student volunteer reads the introductory paragraphs on p. 303, make an outline like the following on the chalkboard.

I. Introduction
A. Establish context
1. identify project or activity
2. identify time period covered by the report

You can leave the outline on the chalkboard, or transfer it to a sheet of poster paper, while students work on their drafts in class. You can also have students copy the outline into their notebooks so they can refer to it as they work on their drafts at home.

You may then want to apply the **Framework for a Progress Report**, p. 308, to **A Writer's Model**, pp. 307–308. When

---

USING THE SELECTION
A Progress Report from the *NAEP 1994 Geography Report Card*

1

What assumption does this statement rest on? [It rests on the assumption that people know what skills and knowledge are necessary to participate in today's economic and political worlds.]

2

What might some of the subgroups of the general population be? [Answers will vary. They could include groups determined by sex, race, region of the country, and household income.]

---

304 *Writing to Explain*

Looking at a Progress Report

The following report discusses a geography test administered by the National Assessment of Educational Progress (NAEP) and taken by students throughout the nation.

A PROGRESS REPORT

from the *NAEP 1994 Geography Report Card*

INTRODUCTION
Background information/ Purpose of overall project

1

For more than 25 years, the National Assessment of Educational Progress (NAEP) has probed students' abilities in a variety of subject areas, reporting both on what students know and can do and on the relationships between instructional, institutional, and background variables and differing levels of educational achievement. As the nation's foremost ongoing education survey, the national assessment data track trends in student performance and allow concerned readers to evaluate whether America's students have the skills and knowledge necessary to participate in today's economic and political worlds.

Project being reported on; time period

2

In 1994, NAEP conducted national assessments in reading, geography, and United States history at grades 4, 8, and 12. The geography results included in this *Report Card* describe students' achievement at each grade and within subgroups of the general population. This information will give educators a context for evaluating the geography achievement of students and data that may be used to guide reform efforts.

BODY

Student performance on the NAEP 1994 geography assessment is summarized on the NAEP geography scale, which ranges from 0 to 500. The geography scale allows

they write their first drafts for **Writing Assignment: Part 4,** students can use this framework in conjunction with the organizational patterns they worked out in **Writing Assignment: Part 3.**

GUIDED PRACTICE

Guide your students through **Exercise 3** by initiating a class discussion of the questions. To model the skills required for **Writing Assignment: Part 4,** begin a progress report of your own by writing it on a transparency while your class helps you. ☞

for the discussion of what students *know and can do* in terms of the geography content covered by the assessment.

Graphic

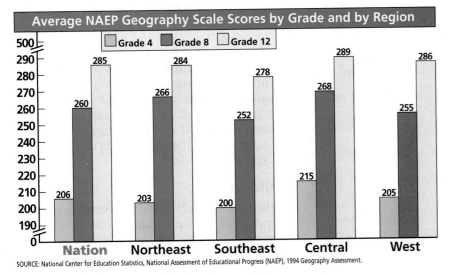

Average NAEP Geography Scale Scores by Grade and by Region

Grade 4 | Grade 8 | Grade 12

Region	Grade 4	Grade 8	Grade 12
Nation	206	260	285
Northeast	203	266	284
Southeast	200	252	278
Central	215	268	289
West	205	255	286

SOURCE: National Center for Education Statistics, National Assessment of Educational Progress (NAEP), 1994 Geography Assessment.

For each grade, three levels were set— *Basic, Proficient,* and *Advanced.* These are based on judgments, made by broadly representative panels, about what students *should know and should be able to do* in geography.

The *Proficient* achievement level represents solid academic performance that demonstrates competency over challenging subject matter for each grade assessed. The *Basic* achievement level denotes partial mastery of <u>prerequisite</u> knowledge and skills that are fundamental for proficient work. The *Advanced* achievement level signifies superior performance.

Major Findings for the Nation

■ The *Proficient* achievement level was reached by 22 percent of fourth-graders, 28 percent of eighth-graders, and 27 percent of twelfth-graders.

3
Italics are used to highlight terms and what they designate.

4
Why are panels needed to make judgments about what students should know and should be able to do in geography? [Answers may vary. Some students might say there is no uniform definition of what constitutes basic, proficient, and advanced knowledge of geography.]

3
4

Finding 1

Students should be ready to do **Writing Assignment: Part 4** independently. Use student-teacher conferences to help students who are having problems. At this point, focus on what students are doing well, rather than on what they are doing poorly.

ASSESSMENT

You can probably get a good idea of how students are doing on their drafts from your student-teacher conferences.

5

What does the expression "background data" mean? [Information about individual students who participated in the study, such as sex, age, race, location, etc.]

◆ TIMESAVER

Rather than evaluating students' answers to the questions in **Exercise 2**, you may want just to discuss students' responses in class.

ANSWERS
Exercise 2

1. The purpose is to report what students know and can do in a variety of subject areas. This particular report focuses on students' performance in geography. The project has spanned more than twenty-five years.

2. The writers organize information topically, because the assessment and the results all occur at the same time.

3. Students' answers will vary, but they should accurately reflect the information in the four findings in the report.

4. Students' responses will vary. Here are some possibilities: Study the students who scored at the advanced level to find out more about them and the kind of education they received; study the students who scored below the basic level to see if geography was part of their schooling and, if so, how it was instructed.

SELECTION AMENDMENT
Description of change: excerpted
Rationale: to focus on the concept of drafting a progress report presented in this chapter

---

306   *Writing to Explain*

Finding 2

Finding 3

Finding 4

- At each grade, roughly 70 percent of students were at or above the *Basic* level.
- As students' geography scores increased, the complexity and sophistication of the geographic knowledge and skills they exhibited increased.
- Generally, students across grades in the higher percentiles exhibited greater abilities to work with a range of geographic tools, create maps based on <u>tabular</u> or narrative data, grasp processes and relationships, bring outside knowledge to bear on answering questions, and analyze data.

Summary

CONCLUSION
Summary and future prospects

While the NAEP results presented in this report cannot be used to draw causal <u>inferences</u>, they do point out interesting characteristics and patterns of student performance. Future research and other projects and analyses can use NAEP data to shed more light on relationships between performance and background data, which in turn can be used by policymakers, educators, and citizens to bring change to the United States educational system.

5

EXERCISE 2 ▶ **Analyzing a Progress Report**

After reading the NAEP report, meet with two or three classmates to discuss the following questions.

1. What is the purpose of the project, and over what time period was it conducted?
2. How do the writers organize this information, topically or chronologically? Why do you think they chose this method of organization?
3. In your own words, summarize the NAEP findings.
4. If you were a consultant to the NAEP, what follow-up projects would you recommend the organization pursue?

A Writer's Model for You

Because the NAEP report describes a completed project, you could think of it as a final progress report. Your own progress report, however, will cover an ongoing project, like the one discussed in the report below. Notice what kinds of evidence the writer uses to support her statements.

A WRITER'S MODEL

INTRODUCTION
Project, purpose, and time period

This is a report on the progress I have made on my history fair project during the last two weeks. My project is a display illustrating the major events in the life of Elizabeth Blackwell, the first woman in the United States to receive a medical degree.

BODY
Accomplishment 1
Evidence

During this period, I completed a diorama of Blackwell's office at the New York Infirmary for Women and Children. The diorama includes miniatures of many of the items pictured in a photograph that I found in a biography of the doctor. I included an examining table, a doctor's scale, and a stethoscope.

Accomplishment 2
Evidence

I also completed a combination map/time line showing the sequence of important events in Blackwell's life. For this section of the display, I used different-colored pushpins to show the location of the events, and I color-coded the time line to match.

Problem—
Discussion

The only item I'm still waiting for is a copy of Blackwell's diploma from the Geneva (N.Y.) Medical College. I called the New York State Historical Society yesterday and spoke with Mr. Roy Lassiter, who explained that he was on vacation when my letter of request arrived. He assured me that he will ship the copy by the end of this week. Since I've already purchased a frame for it, once it arrives I can simply mount it.

Ask students the following question: "If friends came to you asking for advice on how to write a progress report, what would you tell them?" List appropriate responses on the chalkboard.

To have students practice skills developed in this lesson, ask students to find interesting magazine or newspaper articles that report progress. Have students analyze and label the articles in the same way that the model reports in the lesson are labeled.

COOPERATIVE LEARNING

Divide the class into groups of three. Have the groups each conduct a search of the World Wide Web for sites that provide progress reports on a subject they're interested in. Possible subjects include cancer research, environmental cleanup, art restorations, and highway construction. Ask the groups to read the information at one of the sites they find and to report on whether the progress report they read conforms to the guidelines in this chapter.

308 *Writing to Explain*

CONCLUSION
Overall standing
of project

Although I'm a few days behind the schedule I originally set for myself, overall the project is going well. I'm confident that I will have the finished display ready for judging by the deadline, February 22.

THE NEW YORK INFIRMARY FOR WOMEN AND CHILDREN.

If you organize your report by tasks, you can follow the pattern of the Writer's Model, illustrated in the following chart.

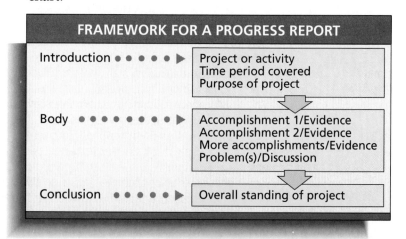

FRAMEWORK FOR A PROGRESS REPORT	
Introduction ● ● ● ● ● ▶	Project or activity Time period covered Purpose of project
Body ● ● ● ● ● ● ● ● ▶	Accomplishment 1/Evidence Accomplishment 2/Evidence More accomplishments/Evidence Problem(s)/Discussion
Conclusion ● ● ● ● ● ▶	Overall standing of project

Ask students to consider a personal improvement project, such as preparing to run a marathon or learning to use new computer software. Then, have students work in groups of three or four to prepare and deliver a dramatization of a conversation about their individual progress among friends working on the same goal. Encour-

age creativity and the use of humor. You can have students present their skits to the class and videotape their performances for inclusion in their portfolios. ■

A progress report organized chronologically will follow a slightly different pattern: It would list accomplishments in the order they were completed. Other differences may grow out of the needs of your readers or out of the topic itself. If you haven't encountered any problems, for example, you won't need to devote a section to explaining and proposing solutions to them.

As you draft your paper, remember that a progress report should

- clearly answer these questions: *What have you accomplished so far? What problems have you encountered?*
- include evidence to support findings or results
- present information in an effective order
- have a confident, optimistic tone

 PART 4:
Writing a First Draft

Your notes from Writing Assignment, Part 3, page 302, are all you need to write your first draft. These reminders will help you get started:

1. Write a sentence or two identifying your project, the time period your report covers, and the purpose of the project.
2. Write the body—limiting one accomplishment (or finding or result) to a paragraph. Be sure to develop each paragraph with facts, examples, and so on. Discuss any problems—their causes and what you've done (or plan to do) to resolve them—as you go along or in a separate section.
3. Write a conclusion that explains the overall standing of the project.
4. As you write your report, keep in mind your purpose and audience. Remember to keep your tone confident and optimistic.

Tell students that all writers need to use transitions that point clearly to the order of events in a progress report developed chronologically. It might be helpful to give students a list of the most commonly used terms so that they can use the terms as they write. You could put the following words on the chalkboard and ask students to copy them:

1. first, second, third, etc.
2. next
3. subsequently
4. finally
5. initially

EVALUATING AND REVISING

OBJECTIVES

- To analyze a writer's revisions
- To evaluate a classmate's first draft
- To use a classmate's evaluation to improve one's essay

TEACHING THE LESSON

You may want to analyze and discuss the **Evaluating and Revising Progress Reports** chart with your class. Ask students to provide examples of each criterion from their drafts. For instance, ask students to read aloud their introductions that identify the project and the reporting period or to explain how they have organized their accomplishments.

 PROGRAM MANAGER

EVALUATING AND REVISING

- **Reinforcement/Reteaching** See **Revision Transparencies 13** and **14.** For suggestions on how to tie the transparencies to instruction, review teacher's notes in *Fine Art and Instructional Transparencies for Writing,* p. 119.

- **Ongoing Assessment** For a rubric to guide assessment, see **Evaluating and Revising** in *Strategies for Writing,* p. 35.

- **Assessment/Reflection** To assess student work and evaluate progress, see **Portfolio Forms** in *Portfolio Assessment,* pp. 5–21.

QUOTATION FOR THE DAY

"Blot out, correct, insert, refine,/ Enlarge, diminish, interline;/Be mindful, when invention fails,/To scratch your head, and bite your nails." (Jonathan Swift, 1667–1745, Irish satirist)

Ask students to brainstorm in small groups lists of actions associated with revision. Then, share the quotation with the class and encourage students to remember the actions listed as they begin evaluating and revising their work.

 ## *Evaluating and Revising*

With a first draft in hand, you're ready to evaluate and revise your description. Remember that the goal of progress reports is to inform other people of the work you've accomplished on a project. It's important to make sure that your report includes all the information your readers need. One way to do this is to put your draft aside for a day or two; then read it carefully to make sure it presents a clear record of your progress. Are there any accomplishments or findings you neglected to include? If so, add them along with supporting details.

To evaluate other aspects of your draft, use the chart on page 311 to help you make changes. Begin by asking yourself a question in the left-hand column of the chart. If you identify a particular weakness, use the revision technique suggested in the right-hand column.

Drawing by Booth; © 1974 The New Yorker Magazine, Inc.

BOOTH

"It seems some days like I make a little progress, then other days it seems like I'm not getting anywhere at all."

You may also want to remind students that at this stage they will probably be making substantial changes—reorganizing, adding to, or deleting from their first drafts. The fact that they are making big changes now probably means that they are doing a good job of evaluating and revising.

Go through **Exercise 3** orally with the class by asking for and discussing students' responses to each question.

Writing Assignment: Part 5 combines cooperative learning with independent practice. Ultimately, however, the changes students decide to make in their papers are up to them.

EVALUATING AND REVISING PROGRESS REPORTS

EVALUATION GUIDE	REVISION TECHNIQUE
1 Does the introduction identify the project and the reporting period?	**Add** a sentence that clearly identifies the project and the time covered by the report.
2 Does the introduction state the purpose of the project?	**Add** a sentence (or **replace** an existing sentence) to identify the purpose of the project.
3 Are accomplishments or findings adequately developed and supported? Does the narrative stick to essential information?	**Add** facts, statistics, or examples that support the findings or results. **Cut** excessive or irrelevant information.
4 Is the information presented in an effective order?	**Reorder** results and/or problems in either logical or chronological order.
5 Is the information clear and accurate? Is language concrete and as simple as possible?	**Replace** vague or unclear descriptions with ones that use concrete, straightforward language.
6 Does the conclusion present an overall view of your progress?	**Add** a concluding paragraph that tells how the project is going overall.

MEETING *individual* NEEDS

ADVANCED STUDENTS

Students might be interested in learning how professional writers have revised their works. Many libraries carry famous authors' biographies that show writers' works in various stages. Ask students to report to the class on their findings.

ASSESSMENT

Observing students' papers while the class is working on **Writing Assignment: Part 5** should give you an idea of how students are doing at evaluating and revising their progress reports.

CLOSURE

After students have finished evaluating and revising their drafts, lead the class in a discussion of the most common kinds of revisions made. ■

ANSWERS
Exercise 3

1. The new phrase is more concise and avoids repetition. The use of "her" without an antecedent is vague.

2. The deletion makes the phrases parallel.

3. The writer moved the sentence to reflect the logical order of the items described. Moving this sentence allows the reader to go from a general description of the item to specific details about it.

4. The addition of these words makes the sentence more accurate and specific.

5. The last sentence is evaluative and doesn't belong in a progress report.

MEETING individual NEEDS

LEARNING STYLES

Visual Learners. Have students use graphic organizers to check that they have included all the necessary supporting information in their drafts. After putting the following chart on the chalkboard, ask students to copy it and to fill it in with the information in their drafts.

Accomplishment	Support
Body Paragraph 1	
2	
3	

312

EXERCISE 3 ▶ **Analyzing a Writer's Revisions**

Here is the writer's revision of the second paragraph of the paper on pages 307–308. With some classmates, discuss the writer's revisions. Then, answer the questions that follow.

> (this period ∧)
> During the past two weeks I completed   **replace**
> Blackwell's
> a diorama of her office at the New York   **replace**
> Infirmary for Women and Children. I
> (n)
> included a rectangular white metal (tr)   **add/cut**
> examining table, a doctor's scale, and a
> miniatures of
> stethoscope. The diorama includes many   **reorder/add**
> of the items pictured in a photograph of
> the office that I found in a biography of   **cut**
> the doctor. It really turned out neat.   **cut**

1. In the first sentence, why did the writer replace *the past two weeks* with *this period* and *her* with *Blackwell's*?
2. In the second sentence, why did the writer cut *rectangular white metal*?
3. Why did the writer move the third sentence?
4. In the same sentence, why did the writer add the words *miniatures of* before *many of the items*?
5. Why did the writer cut the last sentence of this paragraph? (Hint: What is the purpose of a progress report?)

WRITING ASSIGNMENT

PART 5:
Evaluating and Revising Your First Draft

It's usually much easier to spot weaknesses in someone else's writing than in your own. Exchange papers with another student, and apply the questions from the chart on page 311. Discuss your evaluations with your partner, and make changes to improve your paper.

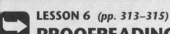
• To write a reflection on writing a progress
report

OBJECTIVES

• To proofread and correct a progress report
• To share a progress report with an
audience

Proofreading and Publishing

Proofreading. You've worked hard on your progress
report. Now, give it the final touches. If you have even the
slightest doubt about the spelling of a word, the placement
of a comma, or the form of a verb, consult a dictionary or
the Handbook that begins on page 510.

USAGE HINT

Verb Tenses

When you're explaining change over time, you may
need to use different tenses to show the sequence of
events. When you do so, make sure you've used verb
tenses correctly so that your readers understand the
relationship between the events.

CONFUSING   After I finished the frame, I **have cut** out the
plywood for the side walls.

CLEAR   After I finished the frame, I **cut** out the plywood for the side walls.

 REFERENCE NOTE: For more information about clear tense
sequence, see pages 684–692.

Publishing. Remember that the purpose of your report
is to explain your progress to one or more readers. Here
are some suggestions for sharing your progress report:

■ Give a copy to the person who assigned the project or to
someone who has encouraged your efforts.
■ With a group of classmates, prepare a panel presentation
of your progress reports.
■ Working with classmates whose reports fall into the
same general category as yours (for example, art projects),
compile your reports into a "progress anthology."

TEACHING THE LESSON

You may want to give several more examples of correct and incorrect use of verb tenses on the chalkboard. (See **Usage Hint** on p. 313.) Then, remind your students of all the other things they could be looking for as they proofread their papers: spelling and capitalization errors, comma errors, and subject-verb agreement errors.

After students have proofread their papers, conduct a brainstorming session to come up with additional ideas for publishing students' essays. Finally, you could read **A Student Model** aloud as an example of a student essay that did get published.

MEETING individual NEEDS

LESS-ADVANCED STUDENTS

Students might need to be reminded that content is not usually changed during the proofreading process. Virtually all content should be in place by now. The objective of proofreading is to check for other problems: misspelled words, improper use of apostrophes and commas, lack of subject-verb agreement, run-on sentences, and overuse of the passive voice. As a note of encouragement, emphasize that professional writers often have several people check their final drafts.

 PART 6:
Proofreading and Publishing Your Paper

Proofread your progress report carefully, and correct all errors. When you've made your corrections, share your essay with an audience.

 Reflecting on Your Writing

To add your progress report to your **portfolio,** date it and answer these questions in a brief reflection:

- How did you decide on a subject for your report?
- Did writing the report help you gain an overall perspective on your project? Did it help you work through any difficulties you faced?

A STUDENT MODEL

This final progress report was written by Chad Stoloff, a student in Carson City, Nevada. His advice about writing a progress report is to have all your facts together before you start to write. This, says Chad, will make the writing go more smoothly.

Progress Report: A Holiday Gift Drive
by Chad Stoloff

Over Christmas our English class decided to collect holiday food and other gifts for needy people because I came up with the idea from a previous project and mentioned it to my teacher. We decided to have a competition between Mrs. Anderson's English classes. Our goal was to contribute enough food for some needy families so they could have good meals over the Christmas holidays. The winning class of the competition would win a pizza party, and so both classes tried very hard to win.

A point system was set up for the food collected. We gave certain foods more points than others. For example, turkeys and hams were top on the list for points, while canned foods were at the bottom of the list with the least number of points.

Starting the competition two weeks before they let us out of school for Christmas vacation gave us a good amount of time to get our items together. Along with many kinds of food, our class contributed bikes, clothes, and toys to the families that needed them. Several class members sold suckers after school; the money from that was used to buy much needed clothes for the families.

The fund-raiser was for a good cause, and helping people out gave us a great feeling inside. Our class provided a large amount, while the other class contributed a lesser amount, but their effort was still very important to the needy. Every person in each class provided time and effort, and many also contributed money or items to help people out. The whole experience brought my classmates and me closer together.

A STUDENT MODEL
Evaluation

1. Chad identifies the project and the project's purpose in the opening sentence.
2. Chad develops and supports the accomplishments of the project and sticks to essential information.
3. Chad effectively uses logical order to organize his information.
4. Chad uses simple and concrete language to present information clearly and accurately.
5. The conclusion presents an overall view of the progress of the project.

COOPERATIVE LEARNING
You may want to group students in pairs to proofread each other's papers. You could hold each student accountable for how good a job she or he does proofreading by having students sign the papers that they proofread.

➡️ WRITING WORKSHOP

OBJECTIVES

- To analyze a cause-and-effect essay
- To write a cause-and-effect essay

TEACHING THE LESSON

Begin by having a volunteer read **Writing a Cause-and-Effect Essay.** Have students discuss the causes that lead to an effect, such as the "greenhouse effect." Tell the class that the purpose of their essays will be to explain.

You may want to define the term *fallacies* as "false beliefs." Explain false cause and effect by providing students with the

❤️ QUOTATION FOR THE DAY

"As I see it, writing is applied psychology because it is the art of creating desired effects. It follows from this that our chief need is to know *what* effects are desirable and *how* to create them." (John R. Trimble, American writer and teacher)

STUDENTS WITH SPECIAL NEEDS

Find an article or an essay that uses cause and effect and highlight causes in one color, effects in another, and supporting evidence in a third. Write the following definitions on the chalkboard:

1. cause—an event or situation that produces a result
2. effect—anything brought about by a cause
3. evidence—factual information used to back up a belief or position

Then, have students label each element as cause, effect, or evidence.

ADVANCED LEARNERS

Some students might enjoy investigating events or situations where experts disagree about causes and effects. For example, after they have read the opinions of several experts, students could report on the causes and effects of the Vietnam War. You can lead a discussion on the factors that may contribute to differences of opinion among experts.

316

316

WRITING WORKSHOP

Writing a Cause-and-Effect Essay

In the course of writing your progress report, you may have found yourself explaining the origins and results of a problem you encountered. If your aim was to help your readers understand a situation by explaining its causes, effects, or both, you were writing a *cause-and-effect explanation.*

If you can ask and answer one or both of these questions about a topic, the topic is suitable for a cause-and-effect essay:

1. *Why did it happen?* [CAUSE]
2. *What is the result?* [EFFECT]

Cause-and-effect writing has two other main characteristics.

- It focuses on a particular situation or event.
- It gives evidence that the explanation is sound.

A sound explanation avoids two common thinking errors, or *fallacies*, in cause-and-effect explanations: **false cause and effect,** in which the writer incorrectly assumes that an effect is the direct result of a cause, and **oversimplifying,** in which the writer identifies a major cause but ignores other causes.

The following excerpt is from a magazine article about the benefits of regular workouts. What does the writer say are the effects of exercise?

> Sarah Cain loves to run. Most days after work she makes her way along the trails that cut through the redwood forest near her home, leaping over roots that snake across the tree-lined path. And when winter's failing light darkens the forest, she pounds the streets of the small towns that edge California's Monterey Bay. Forty-five miles each week, more than 2,000 miles a year. Year in and year out.

following example: If you have a flat tire after oversleeping one morning, it is false reasoning to claim that oversleeping caused the flat tire.

As guided practice, go through the prewriting process with your class. Have students brainstorm together for a topic while a volunteer writes the ideas on the chalkboard. You can then choose one of the topics and demonstrate how it could be outlined.

As independent practice, students should write their own cause-and-effect essays. As this assignment might take students several class periods, you may want to assign the essay as homework.

☞

The 35-year-old agricultural research technician likes what exercise does for her body. It keeps her fit, muscular, and slim. But she *loves* what it does for her mind. "It keeps me from being depressed and calms me down," she says. "I get a warm, glowing feeling after I run. It takes the edge off."

Although many people are lured to exercise for its well-known cardiovascular benefits or because it makes them look good, a growing number are working up a sweat for the psychological benefits. Exercise can't transform an aggressive, type A personality into a calm type B, but scientists now know that even moderate activity—say, a brisk walk at lunchtime—can lift spirits or dispel tension. And therapists are increasingly prescribing exercise to help their patients cope with more long-term psychological ailments such as anxiety and clinical depression.

Susan Chollar, "The Psychological Benefits of Exercise"

1. List the benefits, or the effects, of exercise mentioned in the article.
2. What information does the writer present as evidence for the benefits of exercise?
3. Does the article present any false causes and effects, attributing benefits to exercise that may be caused by another source? Explain.
4. Consider that this article was printed in *American Health* magazine. Do you think the writer's purpose is just to explain, or is she also trying to persuade? Why?

A DIFFERENT APPROACH

The relationship between cause and effect provides the action for many cartoons and comic strips. Students will probably have seen some Roadrunner cartoons. Tell the students to think about how many of those cartoons are based on the effects of Wile E. Coyote's attempts to catch Roadrunner. You might even want to bring in a cartoon from a newspaper and ask students to identify the depicted cause and effect.

Then, have each student draw a comic strip in which the action is based on cause and effect. Students could choose well-known cartoon characters or they could create their own.

ANSWERS
Writing Workshop Questions

1. Exercise can keep a person fit, muscular, and slim. It can also produce psychological effects, such as relief of anxiety and depression.

2. She presents as evidence the personal testimony of a runner, the opinions of scientists, and the practice of therapists.

3. The article does not present any false causes and effects. In fact, the writer explains that exercise can't transform personality types.

4. The article is also trying to persuade people who are already interested in health to consider exercise as part of a healthy lifestyle.

SELECTION AMENDMENT
Description of change: excerpted
Rationale: to focus on the concept of drafting a cause-and-effect essay presented in this chapter

CLOSURE

To close this lesson, ask your class to give the two questions that signal cause-and-effect writing [Why did it happen? (cause) and What is the result? (effect)]

ENRICHMENT

Students who would like more information about the physical and mental benefits of exercise might find a book in the library that discusses this topic, or they might interview a physical education teacher or physical trainer. ■

318

INTEGRATING THE LANGUAGE ARTS

Library Link. Because many students may have chosen to write about current events, you may want to encourage them to look for magazine and newspaper articles on their subjects. Remind students that the *Readers' Guide to Periodical Literature* indexes articles alphabetically by subject and by author. You may need to go over the information in the *Readers' Guide* with your class.

Literature Link. Most people don't think of cause and effect when they think of poetry, but cause-and-effect relationships are everywhere, even in poetry. To demonstrate this concept, have your students read a poem such as Elizabeth Bishop's "The Fish." After students have read the poem, ask what they think causes the speaker of the poem to "let the fish go." You may want to let students discuss their opinions orally or to have them write informative paragraphs explaining their opinions. In either case, make sure students substantiate their opinions with specific evidence from the poem.

CRITICAL THINKING

Analysis. Ask students to speculate on the effects of an event of significant magnitude. For example, what might happen if their locale lost electric power for a week or more? Lead the class in a discussion of this topic or of another topic of interest.

Writing a Cause-and-Effect Essay

Prewriting. Choose a limited topic that you can discuss thoroughly in a brief essay. Remember: If you can answer one or both of these questions—*Why did it happen? What is the result?*—your topic is a suitable one. Also, remember to choose a topic that will interest your audience: your classmates. In your essay, you will be helping them understand a situation by explaining its causes, effects, or both. Your essay might analyze one of the following:

1. The causes of a situation or event (for example, why the African elephant is endangered)
2. The effects of a situation or event (for example, the results of a high school's change to block scheduling)
3. Both causes and effects of a situation or event (for example, why someone begins practicing vegetarianism and what happens as a result)

When you've chosen a topic, brainstorm the causes, effects, or both by asking *Why did it happen?* or *What is the result?* and listing your answers. Arrange your information in one of these ways: *order of importance, chronological order,* or *most familiar to least familiar.* Be sure you have evidence to back up your statements.

Writing, Evaluating, and Revising. First, draft an introduction that entices your reader with a question, a brief story, or a striking example. Your introduction should also include a thesis statement. For the body of your essay, draft a separate paragraph for each cause or effect, including information to back up your statements. Conclude by summarizing your main points. Ask two classmates to read your first draft and tell you if anything confuses them. Then, revise your essay for clarity and completeness.

Proofreading and Publishing. Proofread your revised version carefully (see the guidelines for proofreading on page 56). To share your writing, read your essay aloud to your class; or, if your essay covers a timely topic, convert it to a letter to the editor, and send it to your local newspaper. If you include this paper in your **portfolio,** date it and write a brief reflection explaining how you chose a topic to explore.

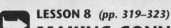

319

MAKING CONNECTIONS

PROCESS EXPLANATIONS

Cause-and-effect explanations are very closely related to another kind of explanation—the ***process explanation.*** Both explanations are narrative; they explain events over the course of time. Cause-and-effect explanations focus on *why* something happens, and process explanations focus on *how* something happens, for example: How does a forward slam-dunk a basketball? How does a compact disc player work? How does a tadpole become a frog?

There are two basic types of process explanations.

1. **How to perform a process.** In this type of essay, you explain a process you know well or one you'd like to learn, for example: how to make spinach lasagna, how to play a guitar, how to handpaint a T-shirt, or how to snorkel. By following your step-by-step directions, readers should be able to do the process.

2. **How something works or happens.** This type of essay explains a process that's more abstract or technical, one that readers can't "do" themselves. For example, you may explain how a computer files information, how an automatic teller machine works, or how fluorocarbons destroy the ozone layer of the atmosphere.

Both types of process essays have three requirements: completeness, order, and tone.

- **Completeness.** Mention every step in the process; don't leave anything out. Depending on your audience, you may need to explain necessary materials and define unfamiliar terms.
- **Order.** In process essays, order is crucial. Discuss each step in chronological order, the order in which each step must be done.
- **Tone.** Use simple, straightforward language. An ideal process essay is not only clear but also lively and interesting.

PROCESS EXPLANATIONS
Teaching Strategies

Have students take turns reading aloud the introductory material on this page. After giving students a chance to study the visual on p. 320, have them discuss how it helps to explain the process.

Demonstrate how visuals can help readers understand a process or a set of directions. First, ask the class to suggest a suitable process to explain. Then, have students discuss possible visuals that would illustrate the process.

- To analyze cause and effect in a folktale
- To write a folktale or a myth that explains the causes or effects of a human trait

CAUSE AND EFFECT IN LITERATURE

Teaching Strategies

You may want to read this folktale to your class. Involve the class by asking students to follow along in their books and to read aloud what the people said whenever they see the words *people said.* For example, in the first paragraph they would read aloud, "When before has anyone seen such beauty?" (Or you might want to ask a group of volunteers to read the people's statements.)

If you wish, ask for a volunteer to read the chief's part as well.

320

Graphics (diagrams, drawing, charts) can make a complicated process or a set of directions much easier to understand. What complicated process does the following graphic explain?

How 'greenhouse effect' works

This year has been the USA's third-warmest on record, putting new focus on the debate about the "greenhouse effect." The current amount of greenhouse warming makes the Earth livable, but more could cause trouble.

1. Sun's energy warms the Earth . . .

2. . . . but the Earth radiates away heat.

3. Molecules of carbon dioxide, some other gases, radiate some heat back, keeping earth at an average of around 59 degrees. Without them, it would cool to around zero.

5. Scientists fear added gases will reflect too much heat back, warming the Earth and changing weather patterns.

4. Human activities, such as using fossil fuels, burning tropical rain forests, add carbon dioxide, other gases to the atmosphere.

USA Today, December 4, 1990. © 1990, *USA Today.* Reprinted with permission.

Think of a process you can explain or a set of directions you can give to other students in your class. (For example, you might explain how a pearl is formed in an oyster shell or how to change the oil in a car.) Create a visual that illustrates the steps or directions you are describing. Then, prepare an oral presentation for the class.

CAUSE AND EFFECT IN LITERATURE

Folktales

Just as we do today, our ancestors wondered why the world is the way it is: why animals are the way they are and why people have certain characteristics. To make connections between the causes and effects they saw and to explain the world of human and animal behavior, our ancestors told folktales. As you read the following Nigerian folktale, ask yourself what it is trying to explain about beauty and character.

Why No One Lends His Beauty
by Harold Courlander with Ezekiel A. Eshugbayi

1   BEFORE, before, in the beginning of things, people wore their beauty as they wore clothes. It is said that there was a girl named Shoye who possessed beauty that was the pride of her village. Wherever she went, people said: "When before has anyone seen such beauty?"

There was another girl in the village named Tinuke. She did not have such beauty to wear. She envied Shoye. She went to her one day and said: "I must go on a journey for my family. I have no beauty. Lend me your good looks

2 until I return." Shoye did not hesitate. She gave her good looks to Tinuke. Tinuke took the beauty. Her face shone with it. She walked gracefully. She left the village and went on her journey.

3   People who saw her said: "Whenever has such a beautiful girl been seen?" She went to the town where a chief lived. His friends told him: "There is a girl in the town. She comes from another place. She has great beauty." The chief sent for Tinuke. He saw her beauty. He took her as a wife. She did not return to her own village.

Shoye waited. She was very ugly. When she went to the market, people said: "When before has anyone seen such ugliness?"

4   Tinuke did not return. Shoye's friends said: "Tinuke has surely stolen your beauty. You must find her." So Shoye went in search of Tinuke. She came to the town of the chief.

5   People said: "What ugliness! She has a hideous face! It will bring bad luck on us. Send her away!" But Shoye would not go away. She heard that Tinuke now lived in the house of the chief. She went there. She asked for Tinuke.

6 Tinuke would not come. She hid behind the walls of the chief's compound.

Copyright © 1968 by Harold Courlander.

USING THE SELECTION
Why No One Lends His Beauty

1
The word *before* is repeated to emphasize that this story took place a very long time ago.

2
What does this say about Shoye's character? [that she is generous and trusting]

3
Folktales are tales that are handed down orally from generation to generation. Notice how important the voice of the people is throughout this folktale.

4
Imagine beauty being a possession, like clothes. Do you think people would buy and sell it? What about plastic surgery? Can beauty be bought?

5
This is false cause and effect. Ugliness does not really cause bad luck.

6
What does this say about Tinuke's character? [Tinuke is ashamed of her behavior.]

When the chief passed through his gate, he saw Shoye there. He said: "Who is the girl with the ugly face crouching before my estate?"

His guards said: "She asks for Tinuke. Tinuke will not see her."

The chief spoke to Shoye. He said: "Why do you wait here?"

Shoye answered: "I have a friend in my village. She borrowed my beauty. She came here. She now lives in your house. She does not return to her village. She does not return what she borrowed."

The chief said: "You mean that beautiful girl that I have taken as my wife? How could such beauty not belong to the one who wears it?" He sent for Tinuke. She came. She

7 saw Shoye. She was ashamed. She gave Shoye's beauty back to her. Shoye took it. Her face shone. She walked gracefully. Tinuke was now ugly.

People said: "Whenever has a chief had so ugly a wife?"

The chief said: "Beauty and good character are not the same thing. Because a woman wears beauty does not mean that she behaves well. This girl Tinuke came to me wearing beauty, but her character was faulty. Shoye, who was ugly because someone else borrowed her beauty, her behavior was good. One may borrow beauty but not good character.

8 Thus, beauty deceives. And, therefore, I order that henceforth one may not lend his beauty to another. Each person shall wear what is his own."

9 Thereafter, it was this way. One could neither lend nor borrow beauty. Each person wore what was his own. And there came to be a saying:

10 "Beauty is only worn; it is not the same as character."

Get together with two or three classmates, and complete the following activities. You might want to divide up the questions among you and do some library research.

1. How is the problem between Tinuke and Shoye resolved? How does this folktale explain the expression "Beauty is only skin-deep"? What false cause and effect is described in this tale?

7

Can you think of other stories in which someone who seemed ugly became beautiful? ["The Ugly Duckling," "The Frog Prince"]

8

This is personification. Beauty cannot really deceive—people deceive.

9

This story tells us the cause for the fact that, today, beauty is not something one can wear like clothes.

10

Stories from many cultures communicate the same message—that good character is more essential than beauty. Do you think that people have learned this lesson? Why or why not?

ANSWERS

1. Tinuke returns Shoye's beauty. This folktale demonstrates the truth of the expression "beauty is only skin-deep" by emphasizing the importance of good character over good looks.

SELECTION AMENDMENT
Description of change: excerpted
Rationale: to focus on the concept of cause and effect in literature presented in this chapter

2. Many cultures (groups of people) have myths or folktales that attempt to explain some aspect of human behavior. Find another folktale or myth, and share it with your class. (For example, in the story of Daedalus and Icarus, the Greeks explained the dangers of being overconfident.)
3. Try writing a folktale, myth, or other narrative that explains a human trait or characteristic.

2. If students have difficulty finding appropriate folktales or myths, refer them to *World Tales,* collected by Idries Shah, published by Harcourt Brace Jovanovich, Inc.
3. Students' folktales or myths should explain the causes or the effects of some human trait.

"WHEN THE CHARACTER'S RIGHT, LOOKS ARE A GREATER DELIGHT."
OVID

WRITING TO PERSUADE

OBJECTIVES

- To choose a topic for a persuasive essay and to gather supporting details
- To write a draft of a persuasive essay
- To evaluate and revise a draft of a persuasive essay
- To proofread and publish a final draft of a persuasive essay

WRITING-IN-PROGRESS ASSIGNMENTS

Major Assignment: Writing a persuasive essay

Cumulative Writing Assignments: The chart below shows the sequence of cumulative assignments that will guide students as they write a description. These writing assignments form the instructional core of Chapter 9.

PREWRITING

Writing Assignment
- Part 1: Choosing a Topic p. 334
- Part 2: Supporting Your Opinion p. 342

WRITING

Writing Assignment
- Part 3: Writing a Draft of Your Persuasive Essay p. 350

EVALUATING AND REVISING

Writing Assignment
- Part 4: Evaluating and Revising Your Persuasive Essay p. 354

PROOFREADING AND PUBLISHING

Writing Assignment
- Part 5: Proofreading and Publishing Your Essay p. 355

In addition, exercises 1–5 provide practice in distinguishing fact from opinion, identifying opposing arguments, analyzing a persuasive essay, analyzing a writer's revisions, and evaluating a persuasive essay.

WORKPLACE writing — Persuasion and Speech

As an alternative to the persuasive essay assignment in this chapter, invite students to write and present a persuasive speech on an issue that is important in their community.

- **Prewriting** To trigger ideas for a community issue, suggest that students skim recent copies of a local or regional newspaper, especially the local news and the editorial pages. Also, students can review the guidelines on p. 332 for choosing a topic.

- **Writing** Direct students to keep their speeches brief—about two to three minutes in length. See pp. 930–933 for further instruction on writing and giving speeches.

- **Evaluating and Revising** After students have drafted their speeches, have them deliver them to a partner. Partners should take turns evaluating each other's written and oral presentations. Students should consider whether the speech presents a valid argument, sound reasoning, supporting evidence, and a strong conclusion. Students, in evaluating each other's oral presentations, should consider eye contact, confidence of tone, clear diction, and speed of delivery.

- **Publishing** Have students deliver their speeches to the class, and ask class members to respond afterward by naming the persuasive strategies used in the speech. If students also want to deliver their speeches to the city council, you will need to obtain information on the process for asking to speak at a council meeting. You might also want to arrange for a field trip to one of the council meetings or ask a member of the council to come speak to your students. Some councils have the meetings videotaped to be televised on local access channels.

INTEGRATING THE LANGUAGE ARTS

SELECTION	READING AND LITERATURE	WRITING AND CRITICAL THINKING	LANGUAGE AND SYNTAX	SPEAKING, LISTENING, AND OTHER EXPRESSION SKILLS
• "A Letter to the Duke of Milan" by Leonardo da Vinci pp. 326–329 • "Can Bicycles Save the World?" by Jane Bosveld pp. 343–346 • from *On Being a Writer* by Ellen Goodman p. 351 • A letter to the editor of *Newsweek* by Emily R. Alling p. 357 • from *My Life with Martin Luther King, Jr.* by Coretta Scott King pp. 360–361	• Finding details pp. 329, 342, 346 • Finding the main idea pp. 329, 358 • Evaluating a writer's opinion pp. 329, 346, 358 • Identifying tone p. 346 • Interpreting a title p. 346 • Analyzing a letter to the editor pp. 357–358	• Evaluating a writer's effectiveness pp. 329, 346, 353–354, 358 • Responding personally to persuasive writing pp. 329, 346, 358 • Writing an opinion statement pp. 334, 358 • Choosing a topic pp. 334, 358, 361 • Identifying opposing arguments pp. 336, 350, 358 • Analyzing illogical statements pp. 341–342 • Organizing support for an opinion pp. 342, 358 • Analyzing a persuasive essay pp. 346, 351–352, 353–354 • Evaluating and revising a draft pp. 351–352, 353–354 • Proofreading and publishing pp. 355, 358 • Identifying logical and emotional appeals p. 358 • Writing a letter to the editor p. 358 • Analyzing advertising for persuasive language p. 359 • Writing a persuasive speech p. 361	• Identifying connotations of words p. 346 • Analyzing connotation and tone pp. 346, 353 • Selecting appropriate tone p. 350 • Analyzing the effects of specific words p. 353 • Proofreading for errors pp. 355, 358 • Analyzing loaded words, snob appeal, and testimonials pp. 359–360	• Working with classmates to distinguish fact from opinion p. 334 • Identifying opposing arguments with classmates p. 336 • Working with classmates to analyze a persuasive essay pp. 346, 353–354 • Making decisions in a small discussion group pp. 353–354 • Delivering a persuasive speech p. 361

SUGGESTED INTEGRATED UNIT PLAN

This plan gives suggestions on how to integrate the major strands of the language arts with this chapter.

If you begin with this chapter on writing to persuade or with the suggested persuasive literary selections, you should focus on the common characteristics of persuasive writing. You can then integrate speaking/listening and language concepts with both the writing and the literature.

Common Characteristics

- Content that is mainly evidence and explanation mixed with emotional appeal
- A purpose that is to convince a specific audience
- Language that appeals to the intended audience
- Organization of ideas from most to least important

Writing
Persuasive Essay

UNIT FOCUS
NONFICTION: PERSUASION

Speaking/Listening

- Working with classmates to distinguish fact from opinion
- Delivering a persuasive speech

Language
Style, Usage

- Connotation and denotation
- Varied sentence beginnings
- Voice and tone

Literature

- "The Lowest Animal" Mark Twain
- "The Man in the Water" Roger Rosenblatt
- "Letter from Birmingham Jail" Martin Luther King, Jr.
- "Montgomery Boycott" Coretta Scott King

CHAPTER 9: WRITING TO PERSUADE

Use this guide for creating an instructional plan that addresses the individual needs of your students. Assignments accompanied by the following symbol (∗) may be completed out of class. Times given for pacing lessons are estimated.

CHAPTER PLANNING GUIDE—PUPIL'S EDITION

LESSONS	LITERARY MODEL pp. 326–329 "A Letter to the Duke of Milan" by Leonardo da Vinci	PREWRITING pp. 332–342	
		Generating Ideas	**Gathering/Organizing**
DEVELOPMENTAL PROGRAM	⏰ **30–35 minutes** • Have pairs of students read the model aloud to partners and discuss questions on p. 329 as a class.	⏰ **55–60 minutes** • Main Assignment: Looking Ahead p. 331 • Choosing a Topic pp. 332–334 • Exercises 1, 2 pp. 334, 336 • Writing Assignment: Part 1 p. 334 • Thinking About Purpose, Audience, and Tone p. 335	⏰ **50–55 minutes** • Supporting Your Opinion pp. 337–339 • Critical Thinking pp. 340–342 in pairs • Writing Assignment: Part 2 p. 342
CORE PROGRAM	⏰ **25–30 minutes** • Assign students to read the model in pairs and discuss questions on p. 329 in pairs.	⏰ **45–50 minutes** • Main Assignment: Looking Ahead p. 331 • Choosing a Topic pp. 332–334 • Exercises 1, 2 pp. 334, 336∗ • Writing Assignment: Part 1 p. 334∗ • Thinking About Purpose, Audience, and Tone p. 335	⏰ **45–50 minutes** • Supporting Your Opinion pp. 337–339 • Writing Note p. 339 • Critical Thinking pp. 340–342 • Writing Assignment: Part 2 p. 342∗
ACCELERATED PROGRAM	⏰ **20–25 minutes** • Assign students to read the model independently and to answer the questions on p. 329 in writing.	⏰ **35–40 minutes** • Main Assignment: Looking Ahead p. 331 • An Opinion Statement p. 333 • Writing Assignment: Part 1 p. 334∗ • Thinking About Purpose, Audience, and Tone p. 335	⏰ **35–40 minutes** • Supporting Your Opinion pp. 337–339 • Writing Note p. 339 • Critical Thinking pp. 340–342∗ • Writing Assignment: Part 2 p. 342∗

CHAPTER PLANNING GUIDE—PROGRAM RESOURCES

	LITERARY MODEL	PREWRITING
PRINT	• Reading Master 9, *Practice for Assessment in Reading, Vocabulary, and Spelling* p. 9	• Prewriting, *Strategies for Writing* p. 40 • Persuading Others, *English Workshop* pp. 59–66
MEDIA	• Fine Art Transparency 6, *Transparency Binder*	• Graphic Organizers 15–16, *Transparency Binder* • *Writer's Workshop 2:* Controversial Issue

WRITING pp. 343–350	EVALUATING AND REVISING pp. 351–354	PROOFREADING AND PUBLISHING pp. 355–356

🕐 **90 minutes**
• The Basic Elements p. 343
• Writing Note p. 347
• A Writer's Model
  pp. 347–349
• Framework Chart p. 350
• Writing Assignment:
  Part 3 p. 350
	🕐 **55–60 minutes**
	• Evaluating and Revising
	  pp. 351–352
	• Exercises 4, 5
	  pp. 353–354 in pairs
	• Grammar Hint p. 354
	• Writing Assignment:
	  Part 4 p. 354
		🕐 **45–50 minutes**
		• Proofreading and
		  Publishing p. 355
		• Writing Assignment:
		  Part 5 p. 355
		• Reflecting p. 355
		• A Student Model
		  pp. 355–356

🕐 **40–45 minutes**
• The Basic Elements p. 343
• A Magazine Editorial/
  Exercise 3 pp. 343–346
• Writing Note p. 347
• Framework Chart p. 350
• Writing Assignment:
  Part 3 p. 350*
	🕐 **40–45 minutes**
	• Evaluating and Revising
	  pp. 351–352
	• Exercises 4, 5
	  pp. 353–354*
	• Grammar Hint p. 354
	• Writing Assignment:
	  Part 4 p. 354
		🕐 **40–45 minutes**
		• Proofreading and
		  Publishing p. 355
		• Writing Assignment:
		  Part 5 p. 355*
		• Reflecting p. 355
		• A Student Model
		  pp. 355–356*

🕐 **30–35 minutes**
• A Magazine Editorial
  pp. 343–346
• Writing Note p. 347
• Framework Chart p. 350
• Writing Assignment:
  Part 3 p. 350*
	🕐 **35–40 minutes**
	• Evaluating/Revising
	  Chart p. 352
	• Grammar Hint p. 354
	• Writing Assignment:
	  Part 4 p. 354
		🕐 **20 minutes**
		• Writing Assignment:
		  Part 5 p. 355*
		• Reflecting p. 355

 Computer disk or CD-ROM   Overhead transparencies

WRITING	EVALUATING AND REVISING	PROOFREADING AND PUBLISHING

• Writing, *Strategies for
  Writing* p. 41
	• Evaluating and Revising,
	  Strategies for Writing
	  p. 42
		• Proofreading Practice,
		  Strategies for Writing,
		  p. 44
		• Sentence Workshops,
		  English Workshop
		  pp. 67–92

	• Revision Transparencies
	  15–16, *Transparency
	  Binder*
		• *Language Workshop:*
		  Lesson 32

 ELEMENTS OF WRITING:
CURRICULUM
CONNECTIONS

Writing Workshop
• A Letter to the Editor pp. 357–358

Making Connections
• Advertising and Persuasion pp. 359–360
• Public Speaking and Persuasion
  pp. 360–361

ASSESSMENT OPTIONS

Summative Assessment
Holistic Scoring: Prompts and Models
pp. 33–38

Performance Assessment
Assessment 2, *Integrated Performance
Assessment, Level E* For help with evaluation,
see *Holistic Scoring Workshop.*

Portfolio Assessment
Portfolio forms, *Portfolio Assessment*
pp. 5–25, 44–48

Reflection
Writing Process Log, *Strategies for Writing*
p. 39
Self-assessment Record, *Portfolio Assessment*
p. 19

Ongoing Assessment
Proofreading, *Strategies for Writing* p. 43

OBJECTIVES

- To write responses to literature
- To identify and analyze the characteristics of persuasion
- To evaluate the persuasive qualities of a literary model

MOTIVATION

Initiate a class discussion on persuasion by using the following question:

When do you try to persuade someone to do something or to believe something?

Encourage varied responses and list them on the chalkboard.

PROGRAM MANAGER

CHAPTER 9

- Computer Guided Instruction See **Controversial Issue** in *Writer's Workshop 2 CD-ROM.*
- Practice See **Chapter 7** in *English Workshop, Fourth Course,* pp. 59–66.
- Summative Assessment See *Holistic Scoring: Prompts and Models,* pp. 33–38.
- Extension/Enrichment See **Fine Art Transparency 6,** *Non-Violence* by Karl Fredrik Reuterswärd. For suggestions on how to tie the transparency to instruction, review teacher's notes in *Fine Art and Instructional Transparencies for Writing,* p. 33.
- Reading Support For help with the reading selection, pp. 326–329, see **Reading Master 9** in *Practice for Assessment in Reading, Vocabulary, and Spelling,* p. 9.

VISUAL CONNECTIONS
Welders

Exploring the Subject. This print by Ben Shahn (1898–1969) was intended to support racial integration. It also served, with the added caption, to persuade workers to vote. The Congress of Industrial Organizations used the poster in its 1944 voter registration campaign.

9 WRITING TO PERSUADE

for full employment after th
REGISTER

TEACHING THE LESSON

Have a volunteer read aloud the introductory paragraphs of the chapter. Point out that persuasive writing responds to the needs and values of the audience. Leonardo da Vinci's audience is a nobleman, Ludovico Sforza, for whom power and military superiority are of great importance.

The opening paragraph of the model on the next page might puzzle many of your students. Begin with a paraphrase of the paragraph to put the vocabulary difficulties aside and to prepare students for the list of reasons that Leonardo presents to the duke. You may choose to read the entire letter to your class as they follow in the textbook. ☞

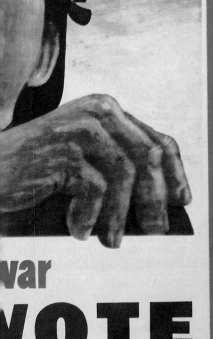

Taking a Stand

Persuasion is the world of beliefs and opinions—the world where people **take a stand** and try to convince others to join them.

Writing and You.   Like the artist whose work appears on these pages, we all take a stand at some time. Sometimes we use logical reasons to persuade others, but most of the time we use both logical reasons and emotional appeals. Politicians, for example, try to convince you to vote for them. Advertisers try to get you to buy their products. And you try to convince your parents to let you borrow the car on Saturday night. When was the last time you took a stand on something?

As You Read.   Following is a letter written by Leonardo da Vinci in the fifteenth century. As you read, notice how he tries to persuade an Italian nobleman to give him a job.

Ben Shahn, *Welders* or *For Full Employment After the War* (1944). Lithograph in colors (poster), 27 3/8" × 37 3/8". Collection of the New Jersey State Museum, Trenton, N.J. Gift of Circle F, FA1970.64.13. © 1993 Estate of Ben Shahn/VAGA, N.Y.

QUOTATION FOR THE DAY

"The best cause requires a good pleader." (Dutch proverb)

Write the quotation on the chalkboard and ask students to list in their writing journals some causes on which they would be willing to take a stand. Encouraging students to share their lists could help simplify the upcoming task of choosing topics for persuasive essays.

MEETING *individual* NEEDS

LEP/ESL

General Strategies.   You may want to allow students to work in small groups to answer the questions on p. 329 about Leonardo's letter. Cooperation in group activities helps create a more relaxed classroom atmosphere, and students will be less afraid to ask questions and take risks.

325

![eye icon] **VISUAL CONNECTIONS**
Exploring the Subject.
Leonardo da Vinci (1452–1519) was an artist, scientist, and scholar. He studied astronomy, botany, and geology and also designed machines and drew plans for hundreds of inventions. Ask students to explain the subject of each of these disciplines. Then, have them discuss how the study of these subjects could help Leonardo substantiate specific claims he makes in his letter.

USING THE SELECTION
A Letter to the Duke of Milan

1

Leonardo da Vinci is engaging in the age-old advertising trick of undercutting the competition. He implies that others only pretend to be ("pose as") masters and suggests that their inventions are ordinary.

326

326

A Letter to the
Duke of Milan
by Leonardo da Vinci

1 **H**aving, most illustrious lord, seen and considered the experiments of all those who pose as masters in the art of inventing instruments of war, and finding that their inventions differ in no way from those in common use, I am emboldened, without prejudice to anyone, to solicit an appointment of acquainting your Excellency with certain of my secrets.

Give students samples of a short news story and of an editorial, preferably on the same subject. Work with the students to analyze and contrast both selections for their aims of writing [news story—informative; editorial—persuasive]

Ask the class to give a brief definition of *persuasion.* Then, ask student volunteers each to describe a situation that might call for persuasive speaking and one that might call for persuasive writing [speaking—asking to use the car; writing—applying for a scholarship]

327

I   I can construct bridges which are very light and strong and very portable, with which to pursue and defeat the enemy; and others more solid, which resist fire or assault, yet are easily removed and placed in position; and I can also burn and destroy those of the enemy.

II   In case of a siege I can cut off water from the trenches and make <u>pontoons</u> and scaling ladders and other similar <u>contrivances</u>.

III   If by reason of the elevation or the strength of its position a place cannot be bombarded, I can demolish every fortress if its foundations have not been set on stone.

IV   I can also make a kind of cannon which is light and easy of transport, with which to hurl small stones like hail, and of which the smoke causes great terror to the enemy, so that they suffer heavy loss and confusion.

2

Why doesn't Leonardo explain his promises, such as how he would demolish fortresses? [Responses may vary. Perhaps he doesn't want to reveal his secrets; perhaps he is exaggerating.]

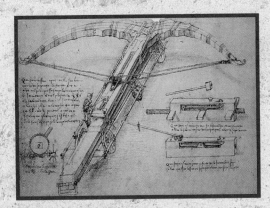

3

What would be the advantage of having Leonardo "noiselessly construct" underground passages? [Noise might give away the troops' position.]

4

What does *ornamental* mean here? [beautiful, decorative]
Why would Leonardo say this about weapons? [Perhaps he is aware that the duke wants the army to look good.]

328

V
3 I can noiselessly construct to any prescribed point subterranean passages either straight or winding, passing if necessary underneath trenches or a river.

VI I can make armored wagons carrying artillery, which shall break through the most serried ranks of the enemy, and so open a safe passage for his infantry.

VII If occasion should arise, I can construct cannon and mortars
4 and light ordnance in shape both ornamental and useful and different from those in common use.

VIII When it is impossible to use cannon I can supply in their stead catapults, mangonels, *trabocchi*, and other instruments of admirable efficiency not in general use—In short, as the occasion requires I can supply infinite means of attack and defense.

IX And if the fight should take place upon the sea I can construct many engines most suitable either for attack or defense and ships which can resist the fire of the heaviest cannon, and powders or weapons.

X In time of peace, I believe that I can give you as complete satisfaction as anyone else in the construction of buildings both public and private, and in conducting water from one place to another.

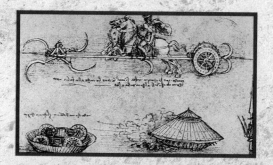

You may want your students to research Leonardo da Vinci's career to find out if the duke of Milan was persuaded to hire him. Ask students to find out what kinds of duties Leonardo performed after he was, indeed, employed by the duke. ■

329

I can further execute sculpture in marble, bronze or clay, also in painting I can do as much as anyone else, whoever he may be.

Moreover, I would undertake the commission of the bronze horse, which shall endue with immortal glory and eternal honour the auspicious memory of your father and of the illustrious house of Sforza. ——

And if any of the aforesaid things should seem to anyone impossible or impracticable, I offer myself as ready to make trial of them in your park or in whatever place shall please your Excellency, to whom I commend myself with all possible humility.

READER'S RESPONSE

1. Does this letter seem convincing to you? If you were the duke, would you hire Leonardo? Why?
2. Like Leonardo, have you ever tried to persuade someone to give you a job? What about the opposite—to persuade someone (probably a parent or a teacher) *not* to give you a job? In your journal, write a paragraph or two about your experience. Were you convincing?

WRITER'S CRAFT

3. What examples does Leonardo use to convince the duke that his inventions are different? Why does he include so many?
4. In the last paragraph, Leonardo uses a technique advertisers often use to persuade you to try something. What does he offer to do?
5. What picture of the writer comes through by the end of the letter?

5
To what emotions is Leonardo appealing? [Responses may vary. He appeals to the duke's pride in his family.]

ANSWERS
Reader's Response
Responses will vary.

1. Most students will agree that Leonardo presents a convincing case, although some might be skeptical of his claims. Students will likely say that they would hire him or at least accept his offer of a demonstration.

2. Students should provide specific details.

Writer's Craft
Responses will vary.

3a. Possible answers include his skill at building portable bridges, pontoons, ladders, light artillery, and armored weapons.

b. Leonardo wants to show the duke that he has many valuable skills. If the duke can't use one of Leonardo's talents, perhaps he can use another.

4. Leonardo makes a "free trial offer."

5. He is confident, respectful, and humble.

The examples in the textbook relate to four basic methods of development that writers use: narration, description, classification (which includes definition and comparison/ contrast), and evaluation. Review these terms with students.

Some students might not immediately understand how evaluation is related to persuasion. Ordinarily, *evaluation* refers to making value judgments about something. When using evaluation as a means of persuading, writers concentrate on the good

COOPERATIVE LEARNING

Ask students to bring to class examples of persuasive material their families have received in the mail. Let students work in groups of three or four to analyze the methods of development used in the material. Point out that some writers use a combination of methods to develop their arguments, so students shouldn't be surprised to find more than one method in a given document.

A DIFFERENT APPROACH

Show students a videotape of a commercial, and ask them to make a list of the methods of development that are used in the commercial. As you show the videotape, you may want to stop it periodically to discuss how a particular method is used.

330

Ways to Persuade

Writers trying to persuade are like Leonardo—they want to get their readers to accept their opinion or move their readers to action.

Persuasive writing appears in many different forms and places—as newspaper editorials, as magazine articles, as speeches, and even as business memos. In each case, you as a writer or speaker are trying to convince others to accept your opinion. Here are some examples of the ways you can develop a persuasive message.

- in a speech to convince people not to litter our lakes and rivers, telling a story about a duck you found with a plastic ring around its neck
- in a memorandum, explaining to your supervisor that a traffic incident caused you to be late
- in a flyer, describing your bicycle to interested potential buyers
- in a postcard, describing a beach to convince your friends to join you there next summer
- in an editorial, defining the word *freedom* to convince people that they should register to vote
- in a conversation, describing two shopping centers to convince your best friend that one is a better place to go
- in a review, explaining a book you just read and recommending it to other readers
- in a letter to the editor of the local newspaper, stating your opinion about the importance of seat belts and making a recommendation about them to readers

Council should approve environmental package

BUDGET CUTS WARRANT CLOSER LOOK

Education bill deserves speedy approval

aspects of the idea or product to persuade others to accept the idea or product.

The textbook gives examples of the kinds of writing topics that can be approached through each method. You may want to elaborate on this concept by having students work alone or in small groups to develop two or three more possible topics under each method. You can then discuss these topics in class to make sure that everyone understands the four methods and their relation to persuasive writing.

To focus students more directly on evaluation, bring to class several ads from magazines and ask students to analyze the ads by making a list of the good points about the products being emphasized. ■

LOOKING AHEAD

In the main assignment in this chapter, you'll develop a persuasive essay. As you work through the writing assignments in the chapter, keep in mind that an effective piece of persuasive writing

- states the writer's opinion, or point of view, about the topic
- provides convincing support for the writer's opinion
- may use reasons and evidence as well as emotional appeals

MEETING *individual* NEEDS

ADVANCED STUDENTS

Some students might enjoy the challenge of conducting original research to see which methods of development are used most often in editorial writing. Ask students to gather editorials from a variety of newspapers and magazines and to analyze each editorial to find the primary method and the secondary method(s) used in each.

By calculating the percentage of use for each method, students can analyze the data they collect. You may want to have students work in pairs. In any case, all of the students involved in this research can pool their information to determine overall percentages. Ask students to explain why they think the numbers turned out the way they did.

This is Earth.

This is Earth without the ozone layer.

Don Wright reprinted by permission: Tribune Media Services.

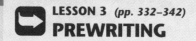
OBJECTIVES

- To distinguish statements of fact from statements of opinion
- To select a topic for a persuasive essay and to create an opinion statement
- To use speaking and listening skills to identify and create support for opposing arguments
- To find and organize reasons and evidence to support an opinion

---

PROGRAM MANAGER

PREWRITING

- **Self-Assessment** Before beginning instruction of the writing process, see **Writing Process Log** in *Strategies for Writing*, p. 39.

- **Heuristics** To help students generate ideas, see **Prewriting** in *Strategies for Writing*, p. 40.

- **Instructional Support** See **Graphic Organizers 15** and **16.** For suggestions on how to tie the transparencies to instruction, review teacher's notes in *Fine Art and Instructional Transparencies for Writing*, pp. 81, 83.

QUOTATION FOR THE DAY

"All men have a reason, but not all men can give a reason." (John Henry Cardinal Newman, 1801–1890, English theologian and writer)

Use the quotation as a springboard for discussion about using reasons to support a belief. Ask students if they can think of times when this quotation applied to them.

Writing a Persuasive Essay

Prewriting

Choosing a Topic

You have opinions on many different questions. For example, do you believe it's right or wrong to kill animals so that people can wear fur? Do you think that the government should ban the use of chemicals that may be changing the earth's climate? Or should the government wait for more evidence to come in?

Those particular questions may not matter much to you, but you may feel strongly about other issues that would be good topics for a persuasive essay. Before you choose a topic, think about these questions.

1. Is the topic important to you?
2. Do you have an opinion on the topic?
3. Do people have different opinions about the topic?
4. Is there an audience for you to convince?

An Important Topic. You may write about a topic of local interest, such as the need for a traffic signal at an intersection in your town. Or you may choose a topic of national interest, such as whether U.S. companies should sell advanced weapon systems to other countries.

Whatever topic you choose should matter to you, and it should be important enough to argue about. You won't change your readers' minds about a question of personal taste. For example, you can't persuade a cat owner that dogs are better pets than cats. Don't even try. But you

Lead students in a discussion of how they think advertisement writers prewrite. [They should mention very careful audience analysis, the product image the writers want to project, and the reasons that will be most convincing to the audience.] You may want to mention that the careers of many business people stand or fall on how persuasive their writing is. You could even invite a business professional, especially one in sales, to talk to the class about the role of persuasion in his or her career.

☛

might want to argue for or against clearing the streets of all stray dogs and cats.

An Opinion, Not a Fact.   Remember the difference between an opinion and a fact. An *opinion* is a belief or a point of view. People can have different opinions about the same subject. For example, some people think that all teenagers are excellent drivers, but others believe that all teenagers are terrible drivers. You can't prove that either opinion is true—or untrue.

A *fact*, on the other hand, is a statement that can be checked—in reference works, for example. It's a fact, for instance, that insurance companies charge teenagers a higher premium than older drivers.

Opposing Opinions.   The saying "There are two sides to every question" applies especially to choosing a topic for a persuasive essay. A good topic has at least two conflicting sides. For instance, some people believe that students in public high schools should be required to wear uniforms. Others believe that such uniforms violate students' freedoms. And both sides offer sound arguments to support their opinion.

Finding Your Audience.   As you consider different topics, you need to think about who your audience will be. What group of people will most strongly object to what you have to say? And what are their reasons? As part of your essay, you'll have to refute (argue against) their reasons.

An Opinion Statement

Stating your opinion on the topic in one clear sentence will help you focus your thinking. Because this statement tells where you stand (your "position" on the topic), it's also called a position statement or proposition. Here are some examples.

Our school should offer courses in an Asian language.
Baseball stars deserve the high salaries they receive.
Two years of community or military service should be
    required after graduation from high school.

VISUAL CONNECTIONS
Exploring the Subject. The baby seal in the photograph on p. 332 is a harp seal. At one time, this species was widely hunted—sought after for its soft, white fur, which the seals shed within a month after birth. Because many people opposed the harvest of newborn harp seals, the sale of pelts was banned in several European countries. The large-scale harvest of baby seals off the coast of Newfoundland ended by 1985.

This lesson is divided into three very closely related concerns that a writer must address before beginning a persuasive essay. You may want to approach the lesson with the idea that all three areas affect one another in a circular fashion. For example, the topic will appeal to a particular audience, but the audience will also affect how the writer's position is stated. The topic and audience will affect the reasons and evidence used in the essay, and the availability of reasons and evidence will in part determine how the topic is stated.

Have students survey the lesson by skimming the pages and reading the bold-face titles. List on the chalkboard the sections in the lesson and explain how they are

CRITICAL THINKING

Evaluation. It isn't always easy to judge whether a statement is fact or opinion because some statements are based on different interpretations of data. For example, the assertion by some scientists that global warming is taking place is based on one set of figures, but other scientists dispute that conclusion and say that those who believe in global warming aren't looking at the right set of numbers.

You can point out this problem to your students and discuss with them strategies for distinguishing fact from opinion. [Some methods of analysis students might mention are investigating the credentials and possible self-interest of experts, learning about both sides of an issue before making a judgment, and maintaining a healthy skepticism.]

Reminder

When choosing a topic for a persuasive essay

- find a topic that's important to you by looking through magazines and newspapers, listening to television and radio, and brainstorming (see pages 27 and 32–33)
- know the opinions that conflict with yours on the issue
- identify the part of your audience that disagrees with you, the people that you want to convince
- write an opinion statement, a sentence that clearly states the topic and your opinion on it

EXERCISE 1   **Distinguishing Fact from Opinion**

In an argument, you can't let anyone pass off an opinion as if it were a fact. How good are you at telling them apart? Work with a partner or small group to decide whether each of the following statements is an *opinion* or a *fact*. Remember that an opinion is a point of view or a belief. A fact is a statement that can be checked or proved.

1. Earth is the most important planet in the solar system.
2. In 1609 Galileo aimed a telescope at the stars and discovered four of Jupiter's moons.   **1.** opinion   **2.** fact
3. When it re-enters the earth's atmosphere, the space shuttle orbiter is traveling more than 16,000 miles per hour.   **3.** fact
4. We know that there must be other intelligent beings in the universe.   **4.** opinion   **5.** fact
5. The Hubble space telescope cost 1.5 billion dollars.

WRITING ASSIGNMENT

PART 1:
Choosing a Topic

Now you're ready to decide on a topic for your persuasive essay. Choose a topic that's important to you. For example, if you think that your community needs a youth center, who do you think should pay for it? When you have your topic clearly in mind, write an opinion statement.

interrelated. You may want to ask volunteers to read the material aloud so you can stop and comment on important areas of the lesson to make sure students understand the relevant concepts.

Some students might have trouble finding meaningful topics that are truly persuasive. You can help with this problem by encouraging students to review their writing journals and to think about events or situations at home or at school that they'd like to see changed. Review students' topics carefully to make sure they're appropriate for the assignment.

 Prewriting

Thinking About Purpose, Audience, and Tone

Your *purpose* in writing persuasion is to convince your readers (1) to follow the course of action you suggest or (2) to think differently about an issue.

To win your *audience* to your point of view, you must find out as much as you can about them. What do they already know about the issue? What concerns do they share with you? Why is their opinion different from yours? What's the strongest argument that they can come up with? For example, if you think that the food in the high school cafeteria should be improved, you may have to persuade several different groups. To analyze their concerns, you might make a chart like this one.

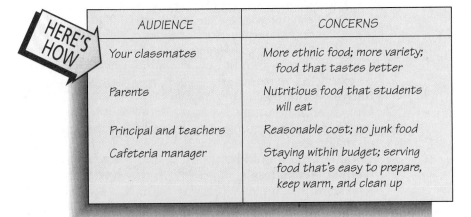

HERE'S HOW

AUDIENCE	CONCERNS
Your classmates	More ethnic food; more variety; food that tastes better
Parents	Nutritious food that students will eat
Principal and teachers	Reasonable cost; no junk food
Cafeteria manager	Staying within budget; serving food that's easy to prepare, keep warm, and clean up

The *tone* of your essay is important because it reveals your attitude toward both your topic and your audience. (Remember that your attitude is conveyed by the language you use to write about your topic.) Describing the cafeteria food in a sarcastic tone may entertain your classmates, but it might turn off the people you most need to convince. A little humor might be effective, but your overall tone should be serious and formal.

COOPERATIVE LEARNING
The directions for **Exercise 1** ask students to work with a partner or small groups. When they've finished the items in the exercise, ask each group or pair to analyze an editorial from a newspaper or magazine and to identify the statements of fact and opinion they find.

A DIFFERENT APPROACH
One way to help students understand the idea of audience for their essays is to have each student come up with a mental picture of his or her ideal reader.

You can use the first two items in **Exercise 1** for guided practice. Work students through the items by talking about why the first item is an opinion and the second is a fact. You can do the same thing with **Exercise 2**.

You can provide guided practice for **Writing Assignment: Parts 1** and **2** in a class discussion. Ask a student to suggest a topic. Write it on the chalkboard and lead the class in an analysis of why the topic is good or not good for the assignment. Handle the reasons to support the topic in the same way.

ANSWERS

Exercise 2

Responses will vary.

Every item should include a specific audience that is likely to object and logical objections the audience might raise. Here are some possibilities:

1. Some taxpayers might disagree, claiming that year-round school would increase taxes to pay for additional teachers, supplies, and so forth.

2. Some taxpayers might disagree because building the extra lanes would cost money that would have to come from higher taxes.

3. Toy manufacturers might disagree because it would cut back on the sale of their products and limit their right to free speech.

4. Physical education teachers might disagree because many students don't have time for physical exercise except during physical education classes.

5. High school athletes might disagree because this restriction isn't placed on any other school activity.

336

---

336   *Writing to Persuade*

> EXERCISE **2** ▶ **Speaking and Listening: Identifying Opposing Arguments**

A good debater can argue either side of an issue. This exercise gives you practice in looking at issues from opposing points of view. Work in a small group to focus on these two questions:

   a. *What group might strongly disagree with this opinion?*
   b. *What might their reasons be for disagreeing?*

For each opinion statement, let one person identify an audience that might strongly disagree. Then have other group members pretend to be that opposing audience, thinking of their reasons for disagreeing with the opinion statement.

> EXAMPLE OPINION: Motorcyclists should be required to wear safety helmets.
>
> *What group might strongly disagree?* some motorcyclists
> *What reasons might they give for disagreeing?*
> 1. A helmet takes away much of the pleasure we get from riding a motorcycle. We like to feel the wind in our hair.
> 2. It's our right to make decisions about our own safety.

1. The school year should be extended year-round to twelve months.
2. Our community must create bicycle lanes on all major roads.
3. Commercials should be banned on children's television programs.
4. Physical education classes are unnecessary for high school students.
5. High school athletes should be required to have a 3.0 grade-point average to participate in school sports.

Bad Debater!
Wow. You gotta point there.

hickerson

The Quigmans, copyright, 1990. Distributed by Los Angeles Times Syndicate. Reprinted with permission.

Let students work on the exercises and the writing assignments independently. If you have students generate topics as homework, you may want to spend some time the next day in class putting some of the topics on the chalkboard and talking about their strengths and weaknesses. You can do the same thing with students' reasons and evidence. After you've discussed several topics, give students an opportunity to rethink some of their topics before you collect assignments.

Prewriting

Supporting Your Opinion

Experience may have already taught you that most people won't change just because you tell them they should change. To persuade others, you have to present your reasons logically and back up each reason with evidence. Sometimes it helps to appeal to their emotions, too.

No matter what you write, you may be unable to persuade people who strongly oppose your opinion. But your essay will be successful if you can at least make them understand and respect your point of view.

Logical Appeals

Two kinds of logical appeals—*reasons* and *evidence*—are aimed at your audience's ability to think.

Reasons. *Reasons* tell why readers should accept an opinion. For example:

Opinion: A drivers' training course should be a requirement for high school graduation.

Reasons: 1. Teenagers who take drivers' training courses are better drivers.
2. Good driving is an essential skill for nearly every adult.

But reasons alone will persuade few readers. Most readers want proof that your reasons make sense.

Evidence. *Evidence* supplies proof for your reasons. There are two kinds of evidence:

■ *facts*—statements that can be checked by testing, personal observation, or reading a reliable reference source.

a. Of the students who took drivers' training at our school last year, 93 percent passed the state licensing examination on the first try.
b. Because teenagers who take drivers' training have fewer accidents, insurance companies charge them lower rates.

You can use performance on the exercises to assess students' understanding of the concepts. The topics should be statements of opinion on subjects that students are likely to know something about (or be able to find information about), and they should also be specific enough to be handled in essays of three to four body paragraphs. Reasons and evidence should be factual and should appeal to the audiences the students intend to persuade. Reasons should be organized in a logical pattern, probably least-to-most important, although other patterns are possible.

CRITICAL THINKING
Evaluation. Rarely are all the facts given in support of an opinion equally relevant. Lead your students in a discussion of the criteria they should use in judging whether a fact is useful or not. Some useful criteria include how old the fact or statistic is, how large a group the fact or statistic represents, and the relevance of the fact to the situation under discussion.

INTEGRATING THE LANGUAGE ARTS

Library Link. The school library can be a valuable resource for students who are writing persuasive essays. Ask your librarian to give an orientation talk to your class, with special emphasis on the library's vertical file and periodicals collection.

- *expert opinion*—statements by a recognized authority on the subject.

  Alida Shumway, state highway commissioner, has said, "Teenagers who have completed a driver training course are safe drivers. There's no substitute for quality instruction from professionals in a school setting."

Finding Reasons and Evidence.   For some opinions, you'll be able to use reasons and evidence that come from common knowledge and your own observations. For other issues, such as those having to do with national policy or science, for example, you may depend heavily on expert opinions and current information from reliable sources. You may also want to use nonprint sources—such as documentary and instructional videotapes and audiotapes—to gather support for your opinion. As you collect ideas and information, be sure to take notes. Don't try to sort out the stronger reasons and pieces of evidence from the weak ones until you've finished your research.

To find reasons and evidence to support your opinion

- brainstorm, cluster, or freewrite to find out what you already know (see pages 26–29)
- read books, magazine articles, or newspapers for information on your topic
- talk with experts and others interested in the topic

RETEACHING

If students need help distinguishing between fact and opinion, give them index cards on which you have written facts and opinions. Have students work in groups, with each student taking a turn reading a card aloud to identify the statement as fact or opinion.

CLOSURE

Lead students in a discussion of the most important pieces of persuasive writing they've ever seen. These could include TV commercials, printed ads, editorials, or any other type of persuasion. Ask students to identify the one feature of the writing that they found most effective.

Cont. on p. 342

Prewriting   **339**

Emotional Appeals

Which do you think are more powerful—appeals to logic or appeals to emotion (feelings)? Don't underestimate emotions. Advertisers rely almost entirely on emotional appeals to persuade you to buy their products. Emotional appeals can be convincing in a persuasive essay, too.

Think about how you want your audience to feel about your topic. Then tell about a personal experience or include an example that appeals to that emotion. For example, if you want to convince your audience to volunteer to read at a nursing home, you might use examples that awaken feelings of compassion. You could describe your visit with a stroke patient, a former teacher who helped many children learn to read, but can no longer read on her own.

Emotional appeals alone won't persuade people who strongly disagree with you. In fact, they are likely to become angry at this tactic. Use emotional appeals only when you think they might convince the audience.

WRITING NOTE   As you know, words have both denotative and connotative meanings. The ***denotative*** meaning is the dictionary definition. ***Connotative*** meanings are the feelings or attitudes that a word suggests. Words like *predator, slaughter, victim, home, family*, and *freedom* are just a few of the many words that are loaded with emotional meanings. Recognize the power of emotional words, and choose them carefully in an essay that emphasizes logical reasons and evidence.

CRITICAL THINKING

Analysis. Ask students to work in pairs to analyze ads from magazines for emotional appeal. Students might focus on identifying the aspects of the ads that have emotional appeal and on recognizing the emotions to which they appeal. Is the emotional appeal justified? Does the emotional appeal divert readers from more serious questions about the product? Does the emotional appeal distort the truth about the product?

Peanuts reprinted by permission of United Feature Syndicate, Inc.

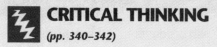

TEACHING *EVALUATING YOUR REASONING*

Begin the lesson by asking students how they react when they hear or read something that is obviously illogical. You can point out that sometimes people make illogical statements on purpose.

Ask students to read the first item, **Attacking the Person**, and to comment on

ADVANCED STUDENTS

Have students use the following questions to evaluate and analyze four television commercials:

1. What is the product's name?
2. What sales techniques are used?
3. What connotative language is used?
4. How would you evaluate the persuasive appeal of each commercial?

LESS-ADVANCED STUDENTS

You may want to rearrange the order of the **Critical Thinking** lesson slightly in working with students. Start with the second example of illogical reasoning, **False Cause and Effect**, because it is clearer than some of the others. After your students understand the concept of illogical reasoning, you can work with them on the other examples.

CRITICAL THINKING

Evaluating Your Reasoning

Your persuasive essay should be based on sound reasons and factual evidence. Here are five kinds of statements that look like reasons but really aren't because they're not logical. Study these five kinds of tricky statements carefully. When you're the person who's being persuaded, you should read and listen critically and be able to say, "Hey, wait a minute. *That's* not logical at all."

Statements Disguised as Reasons

1. **Attacking the Person.** Called "negative campaigning" in politics, this technique is also known as "name-calling." It weakens an argument because it doesn't deal with the real issues.

Attacking the Person	People who vote "no" on the school referendum don't care about children.
Facing the Issue	We need to hire more teachers. If we don't pass the school referendum, classes will have 35–40 students next year.

2. **False Cause and Effect.** Don't assume that one event caused the event that happened next. One event can follow another without having anything to do with the first event. What's wrong with the reasoning in this example?

First Event	A pharmaceutical company built a plant near the river this spring.
Second Event	Tests this summer show that the river is polluted.
False Cause-Effect	This plant is causing the river's pollution.

3. **Hasty Generalization.** Don't base a conclusion on inadequate evidence.

Inadequate Evidence	The first time I played baseball, I hit a home run.
Hasty Generalization	Baseball is an easy game that I can play well without having to practice.

why this reasoning is illogical. [It draws attention away from the main argument and is therefore also misleading; in the example, for instance, the technique denies the fact that people who care about children may have good reasons for voting against the referendum.] Then, ask students to give other examples of this kind of illogical reasoning.

Handle each of the five types of illogical reasoning in this manner.

You can check students' understanding of illogical reasoning by examining how well they do on the **Critical Thinking Exercise** or how well they are able to eliminate illogical reasoning from their writing. ⚡

4. **Circular Reasoning.** When you restate your opinion in different words, don't try to pass off the restatement as a reason. In this example, both sentences say the same thing.

Statement of Opinion   Anna is the best choice for tenth-grade student council representative.

Circular Reasoning   She's the person who can do the finest job as tenth-grade student council representative.

5. **Either-Or.** The either-or thinker describes a situation in terms of two extreme alternatives and suggests that there is only one correct choice. Usually there are several choices between the two extremes.

Either-Or Reasoning   If you don't call me every night, you don't love me.

There may be several other reasons why someone doesn't call every night.

⚡ CRITICAL THINKING EXERCISE:
Evaluating Reasons

Can you detect illogical statements disguised as reasons? Read the opinion and the statements that support it. Tell whether each statement is (a) attacking the person, (b) false cause and effect, (c) hasty generalization, (d) circular reasoning, or (e) either-or reasoning.

Opinion: Offering advanced placement (AP) classes is a waste of school time and money.

Supporting Statements:
1. Some AP students score poorly on the AP exam, which proves that AP classes don't get results.
2. Anyone who thinks that AP classes should be kept must be completely out of touch with reality.
3. We must cut the AP classes, or we won't be able to give an adequate education to our average students.

COOPERATIVE LEARNING

You may want to let your students work in groups of three or four to examine letters to the editor of a local newspaper to identify examples of faulty reasoning. You can also have them analyze newspaper and magazine headlines for examples of **False Cause and Effect.**

ANSWERS
Critical Thinking Exercise

1. hasty generalization
2. attacking the person
3. either-or reasoning

Cont. from p. 339
ENRICHMENT

Consumer Reports magazine regularly publishes a feature in which readers write in to point out misleading and false claims in advertising. Ask your school librarian for back issues to share with the class. Then, ask students to give examples of their experiences with products or services they feel were misrepresented in advertising. Ask students what consumers can do to protect themselves from false advertising claims. [Suggestions might include researching publications like *Consumer Reports,* checking with friends who have tried the products, and reading disclaimers carefully.] ■

4. circular reasoning
5. false cause and effect

COOPERATIVE LEARNING

Students can work on **Writing Assignment: Part 2** in groups of three or four. The groups can brainstorm to find ideas for each group member, and then the members can help each other to evaluate the usefulness of each reason or piece of evidence.

---

4. AP classes are the courses that are most easily dispensed with. Therefore, these are the courses that should be cut from the curriculum.
5. Before we had AP classes, our overall dropout rate at the high school was 10 percent. Now our overall dropout rate is 18 percent. It's obvious that our concentration of time and money on AP classes has increased the number of dropouts.

WRITING ASSIGNMENT

PART 2:
Supporting Your Opinion

Build your argument on a solid foundation of reasons and evidence to support your opinion. To organize your ideas, you can use a chart like the following one. As you list your reasons and evidence, decide what order you'll put them in. If you need more reasons, facts, and expert opinions, find them by reading and talking about your topic. Try to include an emotional appeal unless your teacher asks you to use only logical appeals.

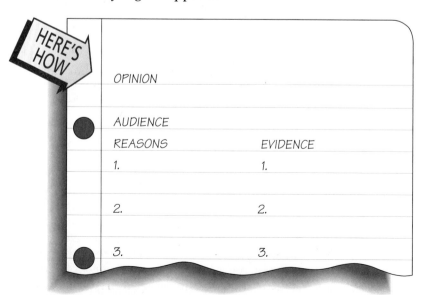

HERE'S HOW

OPINION	
AUDIENCE	
REASONS	EVIDENCE
1.	1.
2.	2.
3.	3.

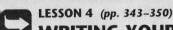

WRITING YOUR FIRST DRAFT

OBJECTIVES

- To analyze a persuasive essay
- To write the first draft of a persuasive essay

MOTIVATION

Have students draw upon their experiences of watching television programs about lawyers and court trials. Ask what kinds of things lawyers say in their summation speeches to persuade the jury. Lead students to the realization that lawyers use the same techniques writers use to persuade— ☞

Writing Your First Draft

The Basic Elements of Persuasive Essays

You've gathered your ideas for a persuasive essay. Now it's time to organize them into a composition that will convince your audience.

Keep in mind that a persuasive essay

- takes a stand on a topic that people disagree on
- tries to persuade an audience to think and perhaps act as the writer suggests
- uses reasons and evidence
- sometimes appeals to the audience's emotions

Professional writers combine these basic elements in different ways. As you read the following editorial, notice how the writer uses these basic elements to convince you.

A MAGAZINE EDITORIAL

Opinion	
Attention grabber	
Background	
Emotional appeal	
Opposing opinion	
Emotional appeal	
Opinion	

Can Bicycles Save the World?
by Jane Bosveld

"**G**reat Britain isn't as advanced as we are," wrote an American student in 1967. "Probably half the people still ride bicycles." The student was wrong about bicycle ridership in Britain—only about one in four Brits owns a bike, and most ride for leisure, not as alternative transport. But the American student's observation reflects the prevailing attitude in industrial nations that bicycles are somehow second-class vehicles, dwarfed by the power and convenience of automobiles. A bike, of course, won't win any contests of speed or long-distance commuting, but in an age when the <u>implications</u> of pollution threaten the health of the world, human power is looking better and better.

PROGRAM MANAGER

WRITING YOUR FIRST DRAFT

- **Instructional Support** To help students write effective body paragraphs, see **Writing** in *Strategies for Writing*, p. 41.

QUOTATION FOR THE DAY

"There is no rule on how it is to write. Sometimes it comes easily and perfectly. Sometimes it is like drilling rock and then blasting it out with charges." (Ernest Hemingway, 1899–1961, American writer)

As students begin writing their first drafts, share the quotation with the class. You may wish to have students write journal entries telling whether or not they agree with Hemingway's comments about writing.

USING THE SELECTION
Can Bicycles Save the World?

1

Why does Bosveld use this slang term for the British? [It helps create an informal tone.] Would British people find this offensive? [They probably are not any more offended by this than Americans are offended by being called Yanks by the British.]

TEACHING THE LESSON

You may want to consider having student volunteers read this lesson orally. The model essay on bicycles contains several vocabulary words and figures of speech that may be unfamiliar to students, and you can help them derive the meanings from context.

One of the questions in **Exercise 3** asks that students identify the tone of the

2

Why does Bosveld use the expression "horseless carriages" instead of "automobiles" or "cars"? [This suggests that it's been a long time since bicycles had much prestige as a means of transportation. It also supports the informal tone.]

Emotional appeals

2 Bicycle lovers have longed for the day when their machines would regain the respectability lost after horseless carriages took over the streets. They have <u>proselytized</u> about the joys of bike riding: the closeness one feels to nature when pedaling through the countryside; the <u>exhilaration</u> one feels at making it up a long hill or skillfully maneuvering through a busy intersection. Biking, they contend, is the one exercise suitable for just about everyone. When you ride a bike, the bike bears the weight of your body, allowing you to exercise your muscles without taxing your joints. Many an individual suffering from arthritis or knee trouble has turned to the bicycle for relief.

Opinion

Reasons

3

lobbying: attempting to influence, usually referring to pressure put on lawmakers to adopt, modify, or stop a particular bill

Background

Emotional appeal

3 Bicycle activists have mobilized in most North American and European cities, lobbying transportation departments for bike lanes and trying to rustle up support from nonbicycle riders. Despite these efforts, however, transportation planners have remained <u>notoriously</u> unsympathetic to the needs of bikers. It is a stance we may all come to regret. Consider these facts published in a recent article by the Worldwatch **4** Institute, a major think tank for environmental conservation:

4

think tank: an informal name for an institution devoted to research and analysis of data

model. Because tone is a concept that students often have difficulty with, you can help by suggesting that they imagine how the tone of voice of the writer, Jane Bosveld, would sound if she were reading the essay aloud. Then, explain and illustrate how the connotations of words help create tone so that students will be attentive to informal words and expressions that denote tone.

You can model analyzing an essay for **Exercise 3** by discussing the first item in the exercise with the class. You can point out that a good title often deals with the implied theme or main idea of a piece of writing.

You can use the framework in the chart on p. 350 for guided practice in writing a first draft. Ask students to write the opening paragraphs of their drafts and then to

Evidence/Facts   5
   6

• Gasoline and diesel fuel emissions are major contributors to acid rain and the depletion of the ozone layer. They are also linked to about 30,000 deaths each year in the United States alone. Interestingly, the worst pollution comes from short car trips, because a cold engine is particularly inefficient, releasing a high percentage of un-burned <u>hydrocarbons</u> into the atmosphere. Many of these short trips could easily be done on a bike.

Evidence/Facts

• If just 10 percent of the Americans who commute to work by car rode their bikes to work or to a train or bus that would take them to work, more than $1.3 billion could be cut from the U.S. oil import bill. Oil imports account for nearly a quarter of the country's $171 billion trade deficit. . . .

Expert opinion   7

"In their enthusiasm for engine power," writes Marcia D. Lowe, author of the World-watch article, "transit planners have over-looked the value of human power. With congestion, pollution, and debt threatening both the industrial and developing worlds, the vehicle of the future clearly rides on two wheels. . . ."

Call to action

But what would happen if we began to use bicycles more frequently? If, say, we hopped on a bike to go get a gallon of milk or to visit friends on the other side of town? What if we saved the car for big hauls and long trips? Before this can happen, of course, much must be done to make bicycle riding safe and pleasurable. Biking may be wonderful exercise and environmentally sound, but few individuals will be willing to pedal down roads where cars and trucks zoom past them with inches to spare, leaving the biker to wobble in a blast of air. Until roads are built with bike lanes or at least wide shoulders, few people are likely to get in the habit of biking. Even with those improvements, it will

Summary of reasons

Emotional appeal

Call to action   8

5
Notice how Bosveld persuades through evaluation. Here she points out the disadvantages of the types of vehicles that have replaced the bicycle.

6
Acid rain contains particles of toxic pollution that turn the rain from a neutral liquid into an acid that makes the water deadly to animals and kills vegetation.

7
In trade deficit, more money is spent buying imported goods than is earned selling exported goods. When this happens, interest rates (the cost of borrowing money) rise and business growth slows down.

8
Notice that Bosveld states another opinion as though it were a fact. How are her arguments about transportation planning related to the bicycle? [Bike lanes must exist before people will start taking advantage of the bicycle for transportation.] Is this reason logically sound? [Bosveld comes close to committing the fallacy of false cause and effect.]

share these with the class. By discussing some of the better opening paragraphs with the whole group, you can guide students' work in this phase of their writing.

INDEPENDENT PRACTICE

Even if you work through one or two of the items in **Exercise 3** with the whole class, the other items in the exercise should provide students with ample practice in analyzing persuasive writing. You can let students work on their drafts independently either in class or at home.

Emotional appeal

Call to action

Emotional appeal

take a shifting of attitudes to get most people to take up two-wheel travel. People will need to believe that even one less trip in the car adds up to something, that riding a bicycle is, like recycling paper or conserving electricity, an endeavor worth pursuing. Deciding to ride a bike is taking on responsibility. Not everyone will choose to do so, but for everyone who does, the world, rest assured, will be at least a little better off.

Omni

ANSWERS
Exercise 3

Responses will vary.

1. Bosveld's opinion statement seems to be "People can help save the environment by riding bicycles." Some students might be unconvinced, but most will probably be persuaded by Bosveld's arguments.

2. The essay's title is a statement of the main idea of the essay. Students' opinions of the title will vary.

3. Bosveld's main reason is that by cutting down the number of motorized vehicles people use, bicycle riding will help preserve the environment. She probably provides so much evidence to support this point because she knows that riding bicycles represents a radical departure from the lifestyles most Americans are used to. Her other reasons include the closeness to nature a person feels on a bike, the exhilaration that comes from a bike ride, and the exercise that bike riding provides.

4. Some strong connotative meanings are found in the words *Brits, dwarfed, horseless carriages, proselytized, countryside, maneuvering, rustle up, notoriously,* and *hopped.* The tone is informal and hopeful.

EXERCISE 3 ▶ **Analyzing a Persuasive Essay**

Meet with two or three classmates to discuss the following questions.

1. What opinion statement do you think Jane Bosveld might have started with? Does she convince you?
2. What does the essay's title have to do with the writer's opinion? How do you like her title?
3. Which reason for her opinion does Bosveld emphasize? Why do you think she supplies so much evidence for this reason? What other reason(s) does she give?
4. Find some words that have strong connotative meanings. What would you say is the tone of this essay?

WRITING NOTE

Professional writers' persuasive essays aren't all alike. For instance, the statement of opinion may come right at the beginning of the essay, or it may appear much later. It may be stated directly in a sentence or two, or indirectly in a question or title. The number of reasons varies, and so does the order in which they're given. (The most important reason can be first or saved for last.) Some writers stick to logical appeals alone, but most include emotional appeals. A call to action—telling readers what action to take—may be present or left out entirely.

A Simple Framework for a Persuasive Essay

The essay "Can Bicycles Save the World?" shows you how one professional writer put together a persuasive essay. The following essay illustrates a framework or basic structure that you can use for your own essay.

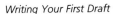

A WRITER'S MODEL

Something Good for the Earth

INTRODUCTION   Garbage! It smells bad and looks disgusting. Most people prefer not to think about trash more than once a day when they "take it out." We in the United States get rid of a great deal of garbage. In fact, we throw away 40 percent of all the garbage in the world.

Attention grabber

Background

BODY   What's in that garbage that we toss out? Of the 200 million tons of garbage that U.S. citizens produce yearly, approximately 42 percent is paper (made from trees), 8 percent is glass, 9 percent is metal (from ore, a natural resource), 7 percent is plastic (from petroleum, a natural resource), 8 percent is rubber (from rain forests), 8 percent is food waste, and 18 percent is yard waste.

Facts and statistics

Try using **A Writer's Model** for reteaching. Work with students to answer the following questions:

1. Why does the writer give statistics in the second paragraph? [They help to establish the extent of the problem.]

2. How does the title reflect the writer's opinion? [The title is a restatement of the writer's feelings on the value of recycling.]

3. Has the writer chosen the best order in which to present reasons? [Yes, the statement of opinion follows an attention grabber and is supported by reasons and evidence.]

INTEGRATING THE LANGUAGE ARTS

Literature Link. If the work is available in your literature textbook, have students read "The Legend of Paper Plates" by John Haines before they read **A Writer's Model.** After students read the poem, ask them to address the following questions:

1. What words or literary elements does the writer use to enhance the emotional appeal of the poem? [Haines uses words such as *family, proud, strong, young people, manhood,* and *womanhood* to humanize the trees. This personification enhances the destructive power of the action verbs *cut, sold, crushed,* and *bleached.*]

2. How can this poem be considered a piece of persuasive writing in favor of conservation? [The poet indirectly persuades readers to conserve natural resources by sharply contrasting the trees—distinct living entities—with the inanimate, expendable paper plates.]

Government officials estimate that 60 percent of our nation's trash could be recycled. Environmentalists suggest a much higher figure—as much as 70 to 90 percent.

Statistics

You can help do something good for the earth by recycling. Perhaps the most important reason for recycling is that it saves precious natural resources. Every week, for example, 50,000 trees are sacrificed to produce Sunday newspapers in the United States. Just by recycling newspapers, you can help to save a forest.

Statement of opinion

Reason

In addition to the direct savings of natural resources, recycling saves water and energy. Recycling paper instead of making paper from trees reduces water use by 60 percent and energy use by 70 percent. Aluminum cans show the biggest saving from recycling. It takes 95 percent less energy to produce a can from recycled aluminum than from ore.

Reason

Explanation

Evidence/ Facts

The third reason for recycling is that it reduces the mountains of garbage we produce. Garbage, unfortunately, doesn't disappear like magic after it's hauled away. For many years garbage was dumped into landfills, which also created

Reason

Explanation

CLOSURE

Ask for a volunteer to give the basic elements of a persuasive essay [takes a stand on an arguable topic, persuades reader to act or think as the writer, uses reasons and evidence, sometimes uses emotional appeals]

☛

Writing Your First Draft **349**

monumental pollution problems. In older landfills, toxins leached into the soil and ground water, finding their way eventually into the food chain. And now we're running out of places that will accept garbage for landfill. The Environmental Protection Agency estimates that in the next ten years 10 percent of our cities will run out of landfill space.

Evidence/ Facts

Evidence/ Expert opinion

People object to recycling projects for two reasons. Recycling costs too much, they complain, adding to already over-burdened budgets. But most taxpayers also approve recycling fees, and recycling actually saves money because there's less solid waste disposal. Their second objection is that people are too lazy to separate trash and wash out cans and bottles. But that's not true. Across the nation, officials have been amazed at how willing residents pitch in and recycle.

Opposing argument

Facts against

Opposing argument

Facts against

CONCLUSION Recycling is something each of us can do to help the earth. Trash makes our home, this planet, less livable for the children of today and tomorrow. We caused the problem, and we can solve it. Will you help?

Restatement of opinion

Emotional appeal

Call to action

⟲ A DIFFERENT APPROACH

Some students who are familiar with outlining might find it a convenient way to organize their essays. You can refer students to the material on outlining in **Chapter 3: "Understanding Composition Structure."**

◈ INTEGRATING THE LANGUAGE ARTS

Literature Link. Have your students evaluate Mark Antony's funeral speech in Shakespeare's *Tragedy of Julius Caesar* for its persuasive devices. Students can use the following chart to gather support in prewriting:

Devices	Examples
Logical Appeals (evidence)	
Personal Appeals (gaining audience's trust)	
Emotional Appeals (wants and needs of the audience)	

You may find it helpful to model your own persuasive essay after the one on recycling. It follows the framework given below. The number of reasons and amount of evidence you use will depend on your topic and your audience.

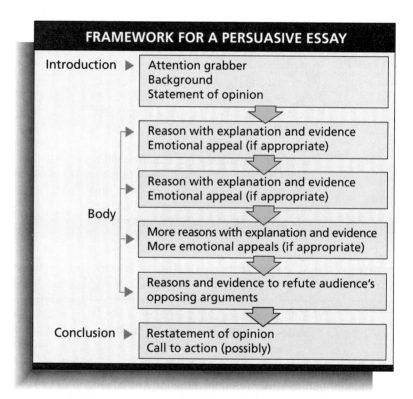

FRAMEWORK FOR A PERSUASIVE ESSAY

Introduction ▶	Attention grabber Background Statement of opinion
Body	Reason with explanation and evidence Emotional appeal (if appropriate)
	Reason with explanation and evidence Emotional appeal (if appropriate)
	More reasons with explanation and evidence More emotional appeals (if appropriate)
	Reasons and evidence to refute audience's opposing arguments
Conclusion ▶	Restatement of opinion Call to action (possibly)

A DIFFERENT APPROACH

Another more complex structure for a persuasive essay is a framework called "straw man." In it the writer systematically presents and then refutes the arguments that would oppose his or her thesis. The following diagram shows the structure:

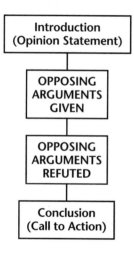

```
      Introduction
   (Opinion Statement)
           |
       OPPOSING
       ARGUMENTS
         GIVEN
           |
       OPPOSING
       ARGUMENTS
        REFUTED
           |
       Conclusion
    (Call to Action)
```

WRITING ASSIGNMENT

PART 3:
Writing a Draft of Your Persuasive Essay

You have everything you need to start writing. Using the basic framework as a model, write a first draft of your persuasive essay. Keep your audience in mind as you write. Think of the strongest objection opponents might have to your opinion. What reasons and evidence can you use to convince them to change their thinking?

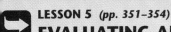
EVALUATING AND REVISING

OBJECTIVES

- To analyze a writer's revisions
- To evaluate and revise a persuasive essay

TEACHING THE LESSON

The central focus of this lesson is the chart on p. 352. You may want to read and analyze it with your students. After students have had a chance to ask questions, you can let them work on **Exercises 4** and **5** before they attempt to evaluate and revise their drafts.

Evaluating and Revising

You have what looks like a whole essay, but you're not really finished yet. Now you need to decide what changes would make it better. Most professional writers treat evaluating and revising as essential parts of the writing process. Ellen Goodman is a Pulitzer Prize winner and a nationally syndicated columnist—and here's what she has to say about making that extra effort in her writing.

© 1998, The Boston Globe Newspaper Co./Washington Post Writers Group. Reprinted with permission.

> What makes me happy is rewriting. In the first draft, you get your ideas and your theme clear. If you're using some kind of metaphor you get that established, and certainly you have to know where you're coming out. But the next time through, it's like cleaning house, getting rid of all the junk, getting things in the right order, tightening things up. I like the process of making writing neat. When I read my column in the paper and I find I've used the same word twice close together or if I've got something dangling, I can't stand it.
>
> Ellen Goodman, from *On Being a Writer*

COMPUTER NOTE: Your word-processing program's Find command can help you look for overused words. Use the online thesaurus to replace them with synonyms.

Use the chart on the next page to improve your first draft. Ask yourself each of the questions in the left-hand column. When you discover a weakness in your essay, use the revision technique suggested in the right-hand column.

PROGRAM MANAGER

EVALUATING AND REVISING

- **Reinforcement/Reteaching** See **Revision Transparencies 15** and **16.** For suggestions on how to tie the transparencies to instruction, review teacher's notes in *Fine Art and Instructional Transparencies for Writing*, p. 123.

- **Ongoing Assessment** For a rubric to guide assessment, see **Evaluating and Revising** in *Strategies for Writing*, p. 42.

- **Assessment/Reflection** To assess student work and evaluate progress, see **Portfolio Forms** in *Portfolio Assessment*, pp. 5–21.

COMPUTER NOTE

You might want to caution students that thesauruses can sometimes cause problems if they aren't used correctly. Students should use the thesaurus to be reminded of synonyms they already know for a word they want to replace. Using a word a student isn't familiar with might result in the use of a "near synonym" that doesn't fit the context of the sentence.

SELECTION AMENDMENT
Description of change: excerpted
Rationale: to focus on the concept of evaluating and revising presented in this chapter

If you collect the drafts and comment on the revisions they require, you can probably let your students work independently. You may want to provide some time in class for students to start the evaluation and revision process so that they can ask questions and seek help from you or from peers.

You may also want to try using peer evaluation. After the class has been divided into peer evaluation groups, refer the groups to the lesson in **Chapter 1: "Writing and Thinking"** that discusses peer evaluation. At this grade level, evaluation and revision are still difficult for many students, so many of them will need your help.

QUOTATION FOR THE DAY

"Genius not only diagnoses the situation but supplies the answer." (Robert Graves, 1895–1985, British writer and poet)

Write the quotation on the chalkboard and explain that being a good writer also involves diagnosing the situation and providing an answer; writers must evaluate their work and make revisions to improve their finished products.

A DIFFERENT APPROACH

Students often need very specific directions when they are evaluating writing. It's a difficult task to respond to every element of an essay. To help students overcome this problem, ask them for specific examples of the strengths and weaknesses in the writing. You can use the following questions as a guide:

1. Which sentence states the opinion?
2. How many reasons has the writer given to support the opinion? What are they?
3. What words or phrases are the specific evidence?
4. What words or phrases are for emotional appeal?

EVALUATING AND REVISING PERSUASIVE ESSAYS

EVALUATION GUIDE	REVISION TECHNIQUE
1 Do the first one or two sentences grab the reader's attention?	**Add** an interesting example, fact, or observation, or **replace** existing sentences with one.
2 Does a clear statement of the writer's opinion appear early in the essay?	**Add** a sentence (or **replace** one) that clearly states the topic and your opinion.
3 Is background information given to help explain the topic?	**Add** examples or facts that will help your audience understand the topic.
4 Are there enough reasons and evidence to convince readers?	Research and **add** more reasons, facts, or expert opinions to your essay.
5 Are all of the reasons strong?	**Cut** statements that aren't real reasons at all (see pages 340–341). **Add** sound reasons that will make sense to your readers.
6 Does the essay respond to opposing arguments?	**Add** (or **replace**) reasons, explanations, and evidence to refute your opponents' strongest arguments.
7 If appropriate, does the essay contain emotional appeals?	**Add** sentences (or **replace** existing sentences) that clearly appeal to the emotions of your audience.
8 Is the conclusion effective?	Rewrite the conclusion. **Add** a sentence that uses different words but restates your opinion. **Add** a call to action.

GUIDED PRACTICE

You can provide guided practice on **Exercise 4** by conducting a class discussion on the first item in the exercise or by letting students work on the exercise in class while you circulate to offer help. You can give guided practice on **Exercise 5** by spending time working with each group.

INDEPENDENT PRACTICE

The exercises and the writing assignment should provide sufficient independent practice if you allow students to work on their own. You can assign both exercises for homework and then go over them in class the next day to answer any questions or to clear up any confusion students have.

Evaluating and Revising   **353**

E X E R C I S E 4 ▶   Analyzing a Writer's Revisions

Study the changes the writer made in her first draft of the second paragraph on page 348. Figure out why each change is an improvement by answering the questions.

> *do something good for the earth*
> You can help by recycling. Perhaps   **add**
>
> the most important reason for recycling is
>
> that it saves precious natural resources.
>
> ~~And the earth's natural resources are~~   **cut**
>
> ~~too precious to waste.~~ Every week, for
> *50,000*   *sacrificed*
> example, ~~many~~ trees are ~~used~~ to produce   **replace**
>
> Sunday newspapers in the United States.
>   *(newspapers)*
> Just by recycling you can help *to save a forest.*   **add**

1. Why did the writer change the first sentence? (Hint: Do the changes appeal to logic or feelings?)
2. Why did the writer cut the third sentence?
3. Which is more persuasive: *many trees* or *50,000 trees*? Why?
4. In the fourth sentence, what kind of appeal did the writer add by changing the word *used* to *sacrificed*?
5. Why did the writer add the word *newspapers* in the last sentence? What kind of appeal does the phrase "to save a forest" have?

E X E R C I S E 5 ▶   Evaluating a Persuasive Essay

Following is the first part of a brief essay. Work with others in a small group to decide what changes might improve this first draft. Be sure to refer to the evaluating and revising chart on page 352.

ANSWERS
Exercise 4

Answers may vary. Here are some possibilities:

1. The addition changes the appeal from logic to emotion.
2. The third sentence repeats the idea that natural resources are precious.
3. The exact figure of "50,000 trees" is more persuasive because it is more specific.
4. The writer added emotional appeal.
5. The word "newspapers" makes it clear that individuals can make a major contribution to the environmental effort by doing something as easy as recycling newspapers. The phrase has emotional appeal because it makes individuals feel responsible for something important.

ANSWERS
Exercise 5

Answers may vary. Here is a possible revision:

Nobody in this town should pay for swimming lessons because swimming is a skill that everybody needs. There are some poor families here who can't afford even a small fee. If kids from these families drown, we'll have nobody to blame but ourselves for being stingy.

353

ASSESSMENT

Evaluate students' performance on **Exercise 5** and **Writing Assignment: Part 4** to assess their understanding. To see if they can implement the guidelines in the chart on p. 352, collect the revised drafts that students worked on in the writing assignment.

CLOSURE

Bring to class the first and final drafts of a paragraph you've written so students can see your revisions. Let them analyze your paragraph in the same way they analyzed the paragraph in **Exercise 5.** ■

A DIFFERENT APPROACH

If you have students conduct peer evaluations, make sure they understand that they need to be sensitive to the feelings of their classmates. They should be encouraged to point out strengths as well as weaknesses in the papers of the other members of the group.

You could use the following questions to guide students' responses:

1. What support is the strongest in the paper?
2. Which word choice is the best in the paper?
3. Which words grab your attention in the introduction?
4. What is the best part of the paper?
5. Would the paper persuade you? Why?

I guess pretty much everyone already has an opinion on this issue, but I want to tell you how I feel. First of all I think that nobody in this town should pay for swimming lessons. Swimming is a skill that everybody needs because it's important to everyone. There are some poor families here who can't afford even a small fee. If kids from these families drown, we'll have nobody to blame but ourselves for being stingy.

GRAMMAR HINT

Changing Sentence Length for Emphasis

To persuade others to your point of view, you need to be forceful. A short sentence gains force or emphasis if it's a change of pace from mostly longer sentences.

EXAMPLES *Not emphatic* There's a great deal of disunity on this issue, but we must work together.

Emphatic There's a great deal of disunity on this issue. We must work together.

☞ REFERENCE NOTE: For more information on sentence variety, see page 481.

WRITING ASSIGNMENT

PART 4:
Evaluating and Revising Your Persuasive Essay

Two heads are better than one, the saying goes. Borrow another head by exchanging essays with a classmate. Evaluate each other's essay by using the questions on page 352. After reading your partner's comments, evaluate your own essay, and revise any weaknesses you find.

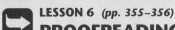

OBJECTIVE

- To proofread and publish a persuasive
  essay

TEACHING THE LESSON

You may want to focus your students'
proofreading on a few common errors, especially if you've spent time reviewing material
on these errors.

It isn't always easy to find realistic
ways of publishing student work for a general audience, but you can encourage

Proofreading and Publishing

Proofreading and Publishing.   Proofread to correct
errors in punctuation, spelling, usage, and capitalization.
Then, think about publishing your essay.

- Send your essay to the school board or to a local or national official. Be sure you include your name and address.
- With your classmates, choose the strongest essays in
  the class to send to your newspaper and to radio or
  television stations.

PART 5:
**Proofreading and Publishing
Your Essay**

Proofread your essay carefully, and correct any errors you
find. To find spelling errors, try reading one line at a time.
Recopy your essay and share it with others.

 Reflecting on Your Writing

To include it in your **portfolio,** date your paper and attach
a brief reflection addressing the following questions.

- How did you grab the reader's attention?
- How did you make the paper convincing?
- Which reasons do you think were strongest? Why?

A STUDENT MODEL

*Controversial issues touch everyone's life. Katie
Baker, who attends Holmes High School in
Covington, Kentucky, supports the opinion that
public school students should wear uniforms. Does
Katie's essay convince you to make the switch to a
school uniform?*

QUOTATION FOR THE DAY
"Words are but the signs of ideas."
(Samuel Johnson, 1709–1784, English
writer, lexicographer, and essayist)

**REFLECTING ON YOUR
WRITING**

Teaching Note. Point out to students
that much of the writing they will do in
the workplace will be persuasive. By
reflecting carefully on their writing now,
they might well learn something that
will enable them to write better persuasive compositions in the world of work.
The first two questions are likely to yield
information that students will find useful
later on.

students to submit their papers to the school newspaper.

You can use the framework on p. 350 and the questions for evaluation in the chart on p. 352 to direct your own evaluation of students' persuasive writing.

Conclude this phase of the chapter with a general discussion of what students have learned about persuasive writing. Are they better persuaders? Are they more alert to how others try to persuade them? Are they better able to evaluate persuasive arguments? ■

A STUDENT MODEL
Evaluation

1. Katie gives her opinion early in the essay: "Students enrolled in a public high school should be required to wear a school uniform."
2. Katie's second sentence gives background information to help explain her topic.
3. To support her opinion, Katie presents an expert's opinion (Mrs. Chung) and two strong reasons (lowering clothing expenses and reducing competition among students).
4. The essay addresses an opposing argument (loss of individual freedom).
5. Katie includes an emotional appeal with her choice of words such as *embarrassed* and *threat*.
6. Katie's conclusion restates in different words the statement of opinion.

TECHNOLOGY TIP

Students who use computers or word-processing programs with spell-checking features might need to be reminded to proofread their papers carefully themselves. The spell-checker can't tell, for example, when *than* should be *then*.

Uniforms Reduce Problems
by Katie Baker

Students enrolled in a public high school should be required to wear a school uniform. Many studies show improvement in both attitude and school work. Wearing uniforms would also reduce clothing costs and many problems related to competition in dress.

Mrs. Chung, a principal at a high school, conducted research on the results of wearing uniforms. She said, "In the past two or three years, several schools in the nation have begun to require a school uniform. All of these schools are reporting improved student grades and improved student behavior."

Uniforms are also less expensive than regular clothing. An outfit for a student can easily cost sixty dollars. A uniform would cost fifty-four dollars or less and would save money. This would be especially helpful to families on a low budget.

Last, uniforms would reduce the competition in dress among students. Students who don't have as much money as others wouldn't have to be embarrassed about their parents' income.

Uniforms wouldn't cause a threat to a student's individual freedom because there are lots of other things that make you "you" besides clothing. Wearing uniforms would reduce many problems and would improve grades and behavior. Therefore, students enrolled in a public high school should be required to wear a school uniform.

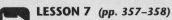

WRITING WORKSHOP

OBJECTIVES

- To analyze a letter to the editor
- To write a letter to the editor on a topic of personal interest

TEACHING THE LESSON

You can use this lesson as a follow-up to the persuasive essay—a way of linking classwork to the real world. If students aren't able to arrive at an appropriate topic for a local newspaper or a national magazine, encourage them to write for the school newspaper.

☞

WRITING WORKSHOP

A Letter to the Editor

Like a persuasive essay, a persuasive letter states an opinion, supports the opinion with reasons and evidence, and suggests a course of action. When you write a letter to persuade a friend to stay with your family during the summer, you expect an answer.

One way to get people to respond to your ideas is to write a letter to the editor of a magazine or newspaper. Such letters reach not only the editor, but also a specific audience of readers concerned about the topic.

The following letter to the editor responds to an article in a previous issue of the magazine. As you read, decide whether you agree or disagree with the writer's opinion.

> To the Editor,
>
> Your attempt to help the "older generation" understand adolescents by packaging them into neat little bundles like "Malljammers" or "House Hoppers". . . unwittingly touched upon what is perhaps the greatest problem in high schools today: stereotyping. Rather than letting their own identities come out, many teens are assigning themselves to one of these groups and adopting a prescribed personality. Your promotion of these cliques as a means of expression for teens who need to feel accepted does nothing to encourage them to seek their own selves. I am about to enter my senior year in high school, and it appalls me to see people erect invisible barriers between themselves and other groups. In the future, please try to remind us all of the merits of individualism.
>
> Emily R. Alling
> Ledyard, Conn.
> *Newsweek*

1. What caused Emily Alling to write this letter?
2. What topic concerns the writer? What is her opinion?

QUOTATION FOR THE DAY

"By persuading others, we convince ourselves." (Junius, pseudonym of the author of a series of letters, The Letters of Junius, that were printed in the London *Public Advertiser* during the years 1769–1771)

Have students discuss what this quotation means. Also, have them consider whether this would apply to someone writing a letter to the editor. [Students might say that a person would probably have to feel strongly about an issue to write a letter to the editor, so they would already have been convinced.]

ANSWERS

Writing Workshop Questions

Answers may vary.

1. *Newsweek* apparently published an article about adolescents that categorized adolescents into "neat little bundles."

2. Alling's topic is stereotyping. Her opinion is that stereotypes isolate people and squelch individualism.

Remind students that each letter should state an opinion early, use logical reasons and evidence, and include a call to action, if appropriate. Each letter should also address opposing viewpoints.

The reflection should be based on an analysis of techniques of persuasion used in the letter.

CLOSURE

Ask a student to share his or her letter with the class. Let the class analyze it for the required elements. ■

3. In addition to the editor, Alling may be trying to address adults who foster stereotyping and adolescents who give in to the urge to stereotype themselves. Her opposing argument is that joining groups on the basis of stereotypes is a way for some people to feel accepted. She refutes this position by citing her personal experience that this type of grouping is harmful.

4. Alling's logical appeal is that adopting a "prescribed personality" discourages people from finding their true identities. Her emotional appeal is in favor of the American virtue of individualism. Many students will probably agree with Alling, but others will probably argue in favor of the comfort of their groups.

◈ INTEGRATING THE LANGUAGE ARTS

Letter-writing Link. Students might need to review the accepted form of a business letter and the proper way to address an envelope. You can refer them to **Chapter 36: "Letters and Forms"** if they need to review these matters.

3. In addition to the editor, what audience might the writer be trying to reach? What strong opposing argument does she mention? How does she try to refute it?
4. What logical and emotional appeals does the writer use to persuade her readers? Does she convince you?

Writing a Letter to the Editor

Prewriting. Think of a current topic you really care about. Have you heard some name-calling at school that makes you angry? Do you feel strongly that no child in the United States should go to bed hungry? Look through your favorite magazine or newspaper for topic ideas. Once you've found a topic, write a sentence that states your opinion. Then, list the reasons and evidence you'll use to support your opinion. If you need more support, do some reading or talk to someone who knows something about your topic.

"Letters are expectation packaged in an envelope."
Shana Alexander

Writing, Evaluating, and Revising. Before you begin writing, read some published letters to the editor. Notice that these letters are short and to the point. They immediately catch the reader's attention, often by stating the writer's opinion in an interesting way. After you've written a rough draft of your letter, ask a friend to read and evaluate it. Then, revise your draft to make it more convincing.

Proofreading and Publishing. Proofread your letter carefully, and then send it to a newspaper or magazine whose readers will be interested in the topic. For example, if you're writing about teenagers and dating, you might send your letter to *Seventeen* magazine. Remember: Editors receive many more letters than they can print, so they choose only those that make the best impression.

When you are ready to put your paper in your **portfolio,** attach a short, written reflection explaining why your letter should effectively persuade your readers.

LESSON 8 *(pp. 359–361)*
MAKING CONNECTIONS

PERSUASION ACROSS THE CURRICULUM OBJECTIVES

- To analyze a 1931 advertisement for an automobile

- To compare a 1931 advertisement for a Pierce-Arrow car to a contemporary advertisement for a car
- To write and design an advertisement for a car of the future

☞

359

MAKING CONNECTIONS

PERSUASION ACROSS THE CURRICULUM

Advertising and Persuasion

Advertisers use a wide array of techniques to persuade people to buy products. In addition to logical reasoning, they rely heavily on these emotional appeals:

- *Loaded words* are words that carry strongly positive or negative connotations. (See page 505.) Advertisers appeal to your emotions by using words that suggest positive feelings. Who can resist a breakfast food, for instance, that's *delicious* and *crunchy*?
- *Snob appeal* uses words and pictures that appeal to your dreams of being rich and carefree. Ads that sell perfume and watches, for example, may show a woman driving an expensive car.
- *Testimonials* bring praise for the product from famous or wealthy people (not experts). Advertisers hope you'll transfer your admiration for the movie star to the cat food she recommends.

Study the following 1931 advertisement (page 360) for a Pierce-Arrow car. Analyze the ad to see what kinds of appeals it uses. Then find and bring to school a full-page car ad from a recent newspaper or magazine. Compare the modern ad to the 1931 ad. What similar and different techniques can you find? What emotional appeals do you notice? Are they convincing? You and your classmates might enjoy sharing your observations.

After you analyze the Pierce-Arrow ad, try this activity by yourself or with a partner. Write and design an ad for the car of the future, perhaps the year 2500. Be sure that the words and the picture work together to sell the product. Use emotional appeals to help convince your audience.

PERSUASION ACROSS THE CURRICULUM

Teaching Strategies

Ask the school librarian to lend you back issues of magazines for your students to use in class. You can let students work in groups of three or four to look through the magazines for examples of loaded words, snob appeal, and testimonials. They can share what they find with the rest of the class.

When students analyze the Pierce-Arrow ad and compare it with a current ad, make sure they can give evidence for each of the techniques they find.

GUIDELINES

The ads students write and design should be creative, and they should use at least one of the three techniques discussed in this lesson.

360

Convertible Coupe of the Salon Group . . . $1275 at Buffalo

Against a background of tradition and quality singular to Pierce-Arrow alone among fine cars, Pierce-Arrow presents today's concept of all that can create distinguished motoring . . . Styled and engineered for those influential groups who have approved Pierce-Arrow for 30 years, and whose preference stamps any-thing as the finest of its kind, the new Pierce-Arrows are done with characteristic finish and finesse . . . Pierce-Arrow confidently looks to these, the finest cars it has ever produced . . . the very pinnacle of fine car values . . . to extend still further the high position with which it has been honored by two generations.

Twenty-nine New Models . . with Free Wheeling . . from $2685 to $6400 at Buffalo

PIERCE-ARROW

(Custom-built Models up to $10,000)

SPEAKING AND LISTENING

Public Speaking and Persuasion

Dr. Martin Luther King, Jr., one of the great speakers of the twentieth century, was awarded the Nobel Peace Prize in 1964. The following excerpt is from a persuasive speech given by Dr. King's wife, Coretta Scott King, on April 8, 1968, shortly after Dr. King was killed. This excerpt does not include Mrs. King's opinion statement for the whole speech. What do you think her opinion statement might be? Notice how Mrs. King skillfully combines logical and emotional appeals.

from My Life with Martin Luther King, Jr.
by Coretta Scott King

We must carry on because this is the way he would have wanted it to have been. We are not going to get bogged down.

I hope in this moment we are going to go forward; we are going to continue his work to make all people truly free and to make every person feel that he is a human being. His campaign for the poor must go on. . . .

We are concerned about not only the Negro poor, but the poor all over America and all over the world. Every man deserves a right to a job or an income so that he can pursue liberty, life, and happiness. Our great nation, as he often said, has the resources, but his question was: Do we have the will? Somehow I hope . . . the will will be created within the hearts, and minds, and the souls, and the spirits of those who have the power to make these changes come about. . . .

1   He often said, unearned suffering is redemptive, and if you give your life to a cause in which you believe, and which is right and just — and it is — and if your life comes to an end as a result of this, then your life could not have been lived in a more redemptive way. And I think that this is what my husband has done.

But then I ask the question: How many men must die before we can really have a free and true and peaceful society? How long will it take? If we can catch the spirit, and the true meaning of this experience, I believe that this nation can be transformed into a society of love, of justice, peace, and brotherhood where all men can really be brothers.

Think of someone whose actions you admire. Your hero may be an important historical figure such as Abraham Lincoln or Joan of Arc. Or it may be someone you know personally. Write and present a brief speech that you might give in tribute to this person. Try to persuade your audience to admire your hero.

USING THE SELECTION
from **My Life with Martin Luther King, Jr.**

1

redemptive: capable of saving people from some evil or harm

VISUAL CONNECTIONS
Exploring the Subject. Coretta Scott King, born in Marion, Alabama, on April 27, 1927, is the widow of the Rev. Dr. Martin Luther King, Jr. On April 4, 1968, Dr. King was assassinated in Memphis, Tennessee, while he was in that city to organize a strike by municipal sanitation workers. Dr. King, also an Alabamian, led the civil rights movement through his work with the Southern Christian Leadership Conference from the mid–1950s until his death. His work was at least partly responsible for passage of the 1964 Civil Rights Act and the 1965 Voting Rights Act. He won the Nobel Peace Prize in 1964. After he was assassinated, Mrs. King took over many of her husband's public responsibilities.

Chapter 10
WRITING ABOUT LITERATURE: EXPOSITION

OBJECTIVES

- To choose a story and use suggested questions to analyze its elements
- To use various prewriting techniques to develop writing ideas for a critical analysis
- To organize and draft a critical analysis
- To evaluate and revise the content of a critical analysis
- To proofread and prepare a critical analysis for publication

WRITING-IN-PROGRESS ASSIGNMENTS

Major Assignment: Writing a critical analysis

Cumulative Writing Assignments: The chart below shows the sequence of cumulative assignments that will guide students as they write a critical analysis. These writing assignments form the instructional core of Chapter 10.

PREWRITING

Writing Assignment
- Part 1: Choosing a Story and Analyzing Its Elements p. 380
- Part 2: Writing a Thesis Statement p. 382
- Part 3: Collecting Support and Organizing Your Ideas p. 383

WRITING

Writing Assignment
- Part 4: Writing a First Draft of Your Critical Analysis p. 386

EVALUATING AND REVISING

Writing Assignment
- Part 5: Evaluating and Revising Your Critical Analysis p. 389

PROOFREADING AND PUBLISHING

Writing Assignment
- Part 6: Proofreading and Publishing Your Critical Analysis p. 391

In addition, exercises 1–3 provide practice in responding and reading actively, exploring stories and literary elements, and analyzing a writer's revisions.

WORKPLACE writing — Critical Analysis of Advertising

Advertisers create images that will persuade people to buy certain products or to live a certain way. Advertising analysts look critically at the effects advertising has on readers and viewers. Help students develop similarly critical stances toward advertising by having them apply the critical reading strategies in Chapter 10 to an advertisement and then write a critical analysis. You may want to choose the advertisement or allow students to choose their own.

- **Active Reading** Allow groups of students to work on the same advertisement, which can be in print or video format. First, they should discuss for ten minutes their immediate reactions to the ad. Then, for fifteen minutes, they should answer these questions.
  - Did the advertiser get your attention or persuade you? How?
  - What response do you think the advertiser wanted to provoke?
  - Why would an advertiser want you to respond a certain way?
  Remind students that advertisements usually contain elements similar to those in a short story; they may have a specific setting, characters who reveal themselves through actions or words, a plot, and a distinct point of view.

- **Writing and Publishing** Direct students to focus on the effectiveness of the advertisement. (They should review pp. 384–386 before they begin.) Remind them, too, that a critical analysis should include a thesis statement, a description of the ad, supporting evidence, and a conclusion. Publish the analyses by displaying them with copies of the ads. If the ads are on video, have students show the videos and then read aloud their analyses.

INTEGRATING THE LANGUAGE ARTS

SELECTION	READING AND LITERATURE	WRITING AND CRITICAL THINKING	LANGUAGE AND SYNTAX	SPEAKING, LISTENING, AND OTHER EXPRESSION SKILLS
• from **The Best, Worst, and Most Unusual: Horror Films** by Darrell Moore pp. 364–367 • **"An Astrologer's Day"** by R. K. Narayan pp. 370–375 • Movie review by Pauline Kael from *The New Yorker* pp. 393–394 • **"The Bean Eaters"** by Gwendolyn Brooks p. 396 • from **CD and Videodisc Players** from *Consumers Digest* p. 398	• Identifying supporting evidence p. 367 • Finding details pp. 367, 379 • Responding personally to literature pp. 367, 375, 379, 380, 393–394, 396–397 • Applying interpretive and creative thinking pp. 367, 375, 396–397 • Identifying criteria used by professional critics pp. 367, 393–394 • Evaluating and making judgments pp. 367, 375, 379, 380, 393–394, 396–397 • Identifying and discussing elements of fiction pp. 379, 380	• Writing a personal response to literature pp. 367, 375, 379, 380, 397 • Thinking about literature from an author's or a character's point of view p. 375 • Writing a critical analysis of a short story pp. 379, 380 • Writing a thesis statement p. 382 • Gathering ideas for writing pp. 383, 395 • Using descriptive details to support the main idea pp. 385–386, 395 • Revising for main idea, support, organization, coherence, audience, and form p. 389 • Writing a review p. 395 • Responding personally to poetry pp. 396–397 • Writing an analysis for a magazine p. 399	• Using quotation marks correctly pp. 390, 391 • Proofreading for errors in grammar, usage, and mechanics pp. 390–391, 395	• Responding actively and imaginatively to literature pp. 375, 380 • Identifying and discussing elements of fiction p. 379, 380 • Participating in peer evaluation pp. 389, 395 • Giving an informal explanation p. 399

SUGGESTED INTEGRATED UNIT PLAN

This plan gives suggestions on how to integrate the major strands of the language arts with this chapter. The literature selections listed below are reviews of film and theater and an excerpt from a longer critical analysis. If you begin with this chapter on writing a critical analysis or with the suggested selections, you should focus on the common characteristics of writing about literature. You can then integrate speaking/listening and language concepts with both the writing and the selections.

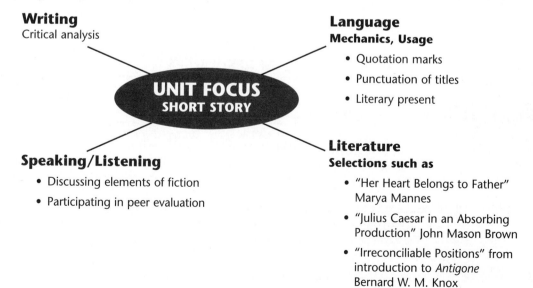

Common Characteristics

- Content that is mainly factual and contains evidence
- Focus on a specific work
- Combination of personal response and an objective viewpoint
- Use of a set of critical criteria
- Evaluative purpose, with a conclusion

Writing
Critical analysis

UNIT FOCUS
SHORT STORY

Speaking/Listening

- Discussing elements of fiction
- Participating in peer evaluation

Language
Mechanics, Usage

- Quotation marks
- Punctuation of titles
- Literary present

Literature
Selections such as

- "Her Heart Belongs to Father" Marya Mannes
- "Julius Caesar in an Absorbing Production" John Mason Brown
- "Irreconcilable Positions" from introduction to *Antigone* Bernard W. M. Knox

CHAPTER 10: WRITING ABOUT LITERATURE: EXPOSITION

Use this guide for creating an instructional plan that addresses the individual needs of your students. Assignments accompanied by the following symbol (✱) may be completed out of class. Times given for pacing lessons are estimated.

CHAPTER PLANNING GUIDE—PUPIL'S EDITION

LESSONS	LITERARY MODEL pp. 364–367: From *The Best, Worst, and Most Unusual: Horror Films* by Darrell Moore	PREWRITING pp. 369–383	
		Generating Ideas	Gathering/Organizing
DEVELOPMENTAL PROGRAM	🕐 **30–35 minutes** • Have students read the model aloud in small groups and discuss questions 1–2 on p. 367	🕐 **90 minutes** • Main Assignment: Looking Ahead p. 368 • Reading and Responding to Stories/ Read aloud A Short Story to class pp. 369–375 • Exercises 1, 2 pp. 375, 379 • Critical Thinking pp. 379–380 • Writing Assignment: Part 1 p. 380	🕐 **55–60 minutes** • Planning a Critical Analysis pp. 381–382 • Writing Assignment: Parts 2, 3 pp. 382, 383
CORE PROGRAM	🕐 **25–30 minutes** • Assign students to read the model and answer questions on p. 367 in writing with a partner	🕐 **65–70 minutes** • Main Assignment: Looking Ahead p. 368 • Reading and Responding to Stories/A Short Story pp. 369–375 • Exercise 1 p. 375 • Critical Thinking pp. 379–380 • Writing Assignment: Part 1 p. 380✱	🕐 **30–35 minutes** • Planning a Critical Analysis pp. 381–382 • Writing Assignment: Parts 2, 3 pp. 382, 383✱
ACCELERATED PROGRAM	🕐 **20–25 minutes** • Assign students to read the model independently and to take notes in Reader's Logs for questions 3–5	🕐 **45–50 minutes** • Main Assignment: Looking Ahead p. 368 • A Short Story p. 370–375✱ • Exercise 2 p. 379✱ • Critical Thinking pp. 379–380 • Writing Assignment: Part 1 p. 380✱	🕐 **20–25 minutes** • Finding a Focus pp. 381–382 • Writing Assignment: Parts 2, 3 pp. 382, 383✱

CHAPTER PLANNING GUIDE—PROGRAM RESOURCES

	LITERARY MODEL	PREWRITING
PRINT	• Reading Master 10, *Practice for Assessment in Reading, Vocabulary, and Spelling* p. 10	• Prewriting, *Strategies for Writing* pp. 47–48
MEDIA	• Fine Art Transparency 7, *Transparency Binder* 📀	• Graphic Organizers 17–18, *Transparency Binder* 📀 • *Writer's Workshop 2:* Interpretation 💾 📀

WRITING pp. 384–386	EVALUATING AND REVISING pp. 387–389	PROOFREADING AND PUBLISHING pp. 390–392
60 minutes • Writing Your First Draft p. 384 • A Writer's Model pp. 385–386 • Writing Assignment: Part 4 p. 386	**50–55 minutes** • Evaluating/Revising Chart p. 387 • Exercise 3 pp. 388–389 in pairs • Writing Assignment: Part 5 p. 389	**50–55 minutes** • Proofreading/Publishing pp. 390–391 • Mechanics Hint p. 390 • Writing Assignment: Part 6 p. 391 • Reflecting p. 391 • A Student Model pp. 391–392
35–40 minutes • Writing Your First Draft p. 384 • A Writer's Model pp. 385–386 • Writing Assignment: Part 4 p. 386*	**40–45 minutes** • Evaluating/Revising Chart p. 387 • Exercise 3 pp. 388–389* • Writing Note p. 389 • Writing Assignment: Part 5 p. 389	**25–30 minutes** • Proofreading/Publishing pp. 390–391 • Writing Assignment: Part 6 p. 391 • Reflecting p. 391 • A Student Model pp. 391–392*
30–35 minutes • A Writer's Model pp. 385–386 • Writing Assignment: Part 4 p. 386*	**35–40 minutes** • Evaluating/Revising Chart p. 387 • Writing Note p. 389 • Writing Assignment: Part 5 p. 389	**20 minutes** • Writing Assignment: Part 6 p. 391* • Reflecting p. 391

 Computer disk or CD-ROM Overhead transparencies

WRITING	EVALUATING AND REVISING	PROOFREADING AND PUBLISHING
• Writing, *Strategies for Writing*, p. 49	• Evaluating and Revising, *Strategies for Writing*, p. 50	• Proofreading Practice, *Strategies for Writing*, p. 52 • *English Workshop* pp. 295–299
	• Revision Transparencies 17–18, *Transparency Binder*	• *Language Workshop:* Lesson 41

ELEMENTS OF WRITING: CURRICULUM CONNECTIONS

Writing Workshop
• A Critical Review pp. 393–395

Making Connections
• Responding to Literature pp. 396–397
• Critical Analysis Across the Curriculum pp. 398–399

ASSESSMENT OPTIONS

Summative Assessment
Holistic Scoring: Prompts and Models pp. 39–44

Portfolio Assessment
Portfolio forms, *Portfolio Assessment* pp. 5–25, 44–48

Reflection
Writing Process Log, *Strategies for Writing* p. 46
Self-assessment Record, *Portfolio Assessment* p. 19

Ongoing Assessment
Proofreading, *Strategies for Writing* p. 51

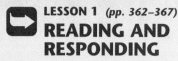
TEACHING THE LESSON

Ask a volunteer to read aloud the opening paragraphs of the chapter. To familiarize students with establishing criteria, have them state the qualities of a great pizza. Then, list on the chalkboard the criteria they think make a great movie. [Students might list action, interesting characters and plot, good acting, directing, special effects, and so forth.]

PROGRAM MANAGER

CHAPTER 10

- **Computer Guided Instruction** See **Evaluation** in *Writer's Workshop 2 CD-ROM.*

- **Summative Assessment** See *Holistic Scoring: Prompts and Models,* pp. 45–51.

- **Performance Assessment** Use **Assessment 4** in *Integrated Performance Assessment, Level E.* Also see *Holistic Scoring Workshop, Level E.*

- **Extension/Enrichment** See **Fine Art Transparency 7,** *Mother Courage II* by Charles White. Review teacher's notes in *Fine Art and Instructional Transparencies for Writing,* p. 39.

- **Reading Support** See **Reading Master 10** in *Practice for Assessment in Reading, Vocabulary, and Spelling,* p. 10.

VISUAL CONNECTIONS
Books on a Table

About the Artist. For years, John Peto's paintings were attributed to William Harnett, an acquaintance of Peto's who painted in a similar style. Both men are recognized as masters of the *trompe l'oeil* (fool the eye) style, in which objects are painted so realistically that they appear to be three-dimensional.

10 WRITING ABOUT LITERATURE: EXPOSITION

As a volunteer reads the analysis, have students identify each reference to the criteria on your list. Add any new ideas to the list.

Have students write replies to **Reader's Response/Writer's Craft** before sharing them in small groups or with the entire class. Assure students that any response is acceptable if supported by references from the model analysis.

Reading and Responding

We're all critics at heart. We **read** a book or see a movie, then **respond** by saying, "That was great!" or "That was awful!" Responding to what we read, see, or hear is a big part of our everyday lives.

Writing and You. Writers also respond to what they read, see, and hear. Professional critics write about the latest books or movies. In literature class, you write about the story you've just read. These written responses are more than casual reactions. The writer looks closely at plot and characters to see what makes a book or movie work. Do you ever read a review before you see a movie?

As You Read. Following is a review of the movie *Frankenstein*. As you read it, notice how the writer responds to all the various elements of the movie.

John Frederick Peto, *Books on a Table* (1900). Oil on canvas. The Nelson-Atkins Museum of Art, Kansas City, Missouri. (Purchase: Nelson Trust through the exchange of a Gift of the Friends of Art.)

Lead students in a discussion of what they expect from book and movie reviews. Ask whether they prefer to read a review before or after they read the book or see the movie, and why.

MEETING individual NEEDS

LEP/ESL

General Strategies. Try to give students one question at a time from **Reader's Response/Writer's Craft** and allow ample response time. Avoid questions that allow a yes or no answer, as students may not expand on the question. You might start with the more concrete questions. If possible, expose students to a question both before and after they read the text.

ASSESSMENT

Class discussion of responses to **Reader's Response/Writer's Craft** will help you assess students' understanding of analysis. Close checking of answers to questions 1 and 3 will show if students understand plot, theme, criteria, and evidence.

CLOSURE

Ask students to list the elements of a great movie that are cited in the model critical analysis [great direction, great acting, great theme]. Also, have students recall why the review does or does not convince them that *Frankenstein* is a great film. [Answers may vary. Make sure students back up their opinions with examples.] ∎

364

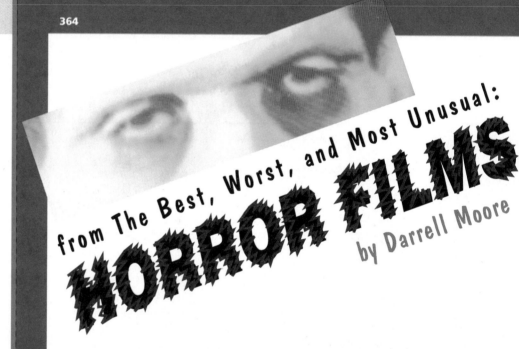

from The Best, Worst, and Most Unusual:

HORROR FILMS

by Darrell Moore

USING THE SELECTION
from **The Best, Worst, and Most Unusual: Horror Films**

1

phenomenon: a highly unusual or significant occurrence

2

Whale also directed *Bride of Frankenstein* (1935) and *The Invisible Man* (1933).

3

In *Frankenstein—1970* (1958), Karloff plays Dr. Frankenstein, the creator of the monster.

4

What element of the movie is Moore analyzing in this paragraph? [the story or plot]

5

tragedy: a noble character engages in a moral struggle that leads to his or her downfall

1
2
3   FRANKENSTEIN (1931) is a cultural phenomenon, the most famous horror film of all time. It was made by a great director, James Whale, and it featured a great actor, Boris Karloff. But there's more working here than the proper combination of great cinematic talents. The idea of the film, the portrayal of the film, the image and look of the film—even the timing of its release—are inseparable from its success.

4   This is, of course, the story of the scientist who created a monster from graverobbed parts. It is significant that Dr. Frankenstein is not mad. He is merely a brilliant scientist who wants to develop and test some equally brilliant theories. The basic plot is structured around the creation of the monster and the impact that creation has on a parochial and superstitious

5   society. And while the story plays out as tragedy—with the monster trapped and burned by the townspeople at the end—the film encourages the viewer to speculate: What would have happened if Dr. Frankenstein's assistant Fritz had procured a healthy, instead of a criminal, brain? Is the film tragic because the doctor dared too much, or simply because his experiment failed?

364

"The horror of the creature is matched only by our desire that such a creature exist."

6 The movie takes a stand on the question: The doctor dared too much. That stand is made evident once the creature breathes life and the doctor must <u>imbue</u> that life with meaning. The doctor—or any mortal man—is fundamentally unable to give meaning to the creature's existence. Man is an insufficient God. This is the real tragedy of the film, and what sets it apart from an inspired mad-scientist film like *The Island of Lost Souls.*

This theme is sounded without being spoken. But great films are not sermons; *Frankenstein* is exciting and physical. Through a scientific magic show (that we don't believe for a minute) of scrap iron and pure energy, Dr. Frankenstein (Colin Clive) gives life to a body made up of dead

6
What aspect of the movie is Moore analyzing in this paragraph?
[theme]

VISUAL CONNECTIONS

Exploring the Subject. The world of makeup man Jack Pierce was filled with creepy characters, but that was fine with him. His research into surgical techniques for *Frankenstein* provided realistic details that helped audiences accept the fantasy that a doctor gives life to an assortment of body parts. Pierce also created the creepy looks of three of the most famous monsters in movie history—Dracula, the Wolfman, and the Mummy.

A MONSTER SCIENCE CREATED But Could Not Destroy!

FRANKENSTEIN

THE WALKING NIGHTMARE THAT FRIGHTENED THE WORLD!

BORIS KARLOFF as The MONSTER

7

The record for the longest time spent applying makeup reportedly is 20 hours. Nine people applied tattoos to actor Rod Steiger for *The Illustrated Man* (1969). Such sacrifices are common in horror films. In *Bride of Frankenstein,* actress Elsa Lanchester kept her monster makeup intact by eating food through a tube.

graverobbed parts. Suddenly, there is a living creature on the slab. The horror of the creature is matched only by our desire that such a creature exist. Fifty years of familiarity take away the shock—but not the marvel—of the creature's appearance.

7   The credit for the creature's enduring look goes to Universal make-up man Jack Pierce—who took five hours a day to build up Karloff's face. It was an image so striking that Universal was able to copyright it. But it was not created on a whim. Pierce had discovered—after research in several areas, including surgery, criminology, and <u>electrodynamics</u>—that there are "six ways a surgeon can cut the skull." Pierce went on to say that: "I figured Dr. Frankenstein, who was not a practicing surgeon, would take the easiest. That is, he would cut the top of the skull off, straight across like a pot lid, hinge it, pop the brain in, and clamp it tight. That's the reason I decided to make the Monster's

head square and flat like a box, and dig that big scar across his forehead, and have metal clamps hold it together."

Karloff was further fitted with a five-pound steel spine, eighteen-pound asphalt spreader's boots, and steel <u>struts</u> on his legs. The make-up of the monster was so critical to the success of the horror film that Karloff was led to and from the set with his head under a cloth (much like the Elephant Man in the steamboat scene) to conceal his appearance during production. He ate alone, and was totally isolated from everyone not connected with the film.

Ironically, Bela Lugosi was originally offered the role of the creature in Universal's *Frankenstein*. He refused the role, apparently because of the lack of a speaking part. The role went, of course, to Boris Karloff, who became more of a cultural <u>icon</u> as Frankenstein's monster than Lugosi did as Dracula.

READER'S RESPONSE

1. Does the author convince you that *Frankenstein* is a great film? Why or why not?
2. How would your feelings about the film have been different if Dr. Frankenstein had succeeded in his experiment?

WRITER'S CRAFT

3. In this review of *Frankenstein,* the writer focuses attention on plot and make up. What might a music review stress? a review of a novel?
4. Why do you think the author gives such a thorough description of Boris Karloff's makeup and costume?
5. The author's evaluation—judgment—of *Frankenstein* is that it is "exciting and physical." What evidence does he give to support this evaluation?

ANSWERS

Reader's Response

Responses will vary.

1. Proponents may stress acting, directing, makeup, or tragic theme. Opponents may mention lack of evidence for "great" acting and directing and claim that too much emphasis is put on makeup.

2. Most students will probably say they would feel less intrigued by the story if Frankenstein had succeeded.

Writer's Craft

Responses will vary.

3. A music review might stress lyrics and bass playing. A review of a novel might stress plot and character.

4. The makeup and costume descriptions show the attention to detail and commitment to excellence that went into the film.

5. The author's evidence includes mentions of "graverobbed parts," being "trapped and burned," using a criminal's brain, the "magic show" of the creation, the horror of the creature, and the weight of the costume.

SELECTION AMENDMENT
Description of change: excerpted
Rationale: to focus on the concept of writing about literature presented in this chapter

LESSON 2 *(p. 368)*

PURPOSES FOR WRITING ABOUT LITERATURE

TEACHING *PURPOSES FOR WRITING ABOUT LITERATURE*

To help students understand the basic purposes writers have for writing about literature, write *self-expression, persuasion,* *information,* and *creative writing* on the chalkboard in a random order. Then, go through the examples in the textbook and ask students to decide under which heading each example fits. [Examples 1 and 2: self-expression; 3 and 4: persuasion; 5 and 6: information; 7 and 8: creative writing.] Ask students to give additional examples for each purpose. ■

INTEGRATING THE LANGUAGE ARTS

Literature Link. If the selection is available in your literature textbook, have students outline the plot of Bernard Malamud's "The First Seven Years" and show how actions reveal character. They also could contrast how the sisters feel about school in "By Any Other Name" by Santha Rama Rau or could evaluate the ending of Gabriel García Márquez's "A Very Old Man with Enormous Wings."

Purposes for Writing About Literature

The writer of the *Frankenstein* review had a specific purpose: to evaluate the movie and make a recommendation to readers. You might write about literature for the same reason, in book reviews and in some book reports. But there are other reasons to write about literature. Your purpose may be just to jot down a few notes that only you will ever see. Or your purpose may be to analyze the work in great detail and to share what you've learned with your readers. Here are some specific examples of the many purposes for writing about literature.

- in a journal, writing about a book you read that made you feel especially good about yourself
- in a letter to a friend, saying that you think Tolkien's hobbits are the greatest characters ever created
- in a book review, urging your readers to borrow or buy a book you think is worthwhile
- in a letter to the editor, asking parents to read a particular story to their children
- in a critical analysis for a literature course, explaining the similarities between the characters in two novels
- in a presentation for a book club, giving a summary of the novel that members will be discussing
- in an original poem, imitating the style of another poem
- in a short story, creating a sequel to a story you've read

LOOKING AHEAD

In the main assignment in this chapter, you'll write a critical analysis. Your basic purpose will be to inform your readers of the results of your analysis. Keep in mind that an effective literary analysis

- has a thesis statement that presents at least one literary element and a main idea about it
- includes details from the work being analyzed
- is organized so it makes sense to the reader

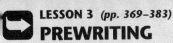

PREWRITING

OBJECTIVES

- To freewrite a response to a story and to answer questions about the story while posing as the author or a character
- To write responses to stories by focusing specifically on their literary elements
- To analyze a story using a set of questions
- To write a one-sentence thesis statement for an analysis of a short story
- To collect support, to arrange ideas and details, and to create a rough outline

Writing a Critical Analysis

 *Prewriting*

Reading and Responding to Stories

When you read a story, all sorts of thoughts and feelings buzz around in your head, thoughts like *Don't trust her—she's lying!* or *Boy, all this talking is boring.* Shouldn't serious readers shut off this mental activity? Absolutely not!

Responding to Stories as an Active Reader

The thoughts and feelings you have while you're reading mean you're reading actively—just like a lively conversation between you and the story. And the more you put into it, the more you'll get out of it. So tune in your inner thoughts, and use the following tips to expand them. (In parentheses you'll see active-reading thoughts about "An Astrologer's Day," a story you'll read on pages 370–375.)

- **Always respond personally** to what you read. (*I sort of like this phony stargazer and his funny sales lines.*)
- **Use your own experience and knowledge** to understand a character, action, or situation. (*This Town Hall Park sounds more like our flea market.*)
- **Question** anything that confuses, puzzles, or provokes you. (*"Honest" work? Should I buy this?*)
- **Predict** what will happen. If you're wrong (which is okay), figure out why you are. (*Something shadowy in this guy's past is going to haunt him.*)
- **React to the whole story,** and be definite about what you do and don't like. (*Sorry, you'll have to supply your own example for that last hint.*)

Looking at a Story

Following is a story about appearances. As you read, try to decide what kind of man the astrologer is. As always, "listen" to yourself read—pay attention to your own response.

PROGRAM MANAGER

PREWRITING

- **Self-Assessment** Before beginning instruction of the writing process, see **Writing Process Log** in *Strategies for Writing*, p. 46.
- **Analyzing** To help students analyze and organize ideas, see **Prewriting** in *Strategies for Writing*, pp. 47–48.
- **Instructional Support** See **Graphic Organizers 17** and **18.** For suggestions on how to tie the transparencies to instruction, review teacher's notes in *Fine Art and Instructional Transparencies for Writing*, pp. 85, 87.

QUOTATION FOR THE DAY

"The good critic is one who tells of his mind's adventures among masterpieces." (Anatole France, 1844–1924, French novelist and winner of the 1921 Nobel Prize in literature)

Ask each student to name a favorite story and to tell briefly why he or she likes it.

MOTIVATION

Write the following movie situation on the chalkboard and ask students how they might respond to such a scene:

The protagonist, alone in a dark house, decides to investigate a noise in the attic. [Students might respond, "Don't open that door!"]

Tell students that this chapter will help them respond to stories the same way.

TEACHING THE LESSON

After a volunteer reads the tips preceding the story, you may want to model active reading using the first few lines of **"An Astrologer's Day."** (Example: "What are 'cowrie shells'? 'Obscure mystic charts' makes him sound like a fortuneteller. His 'abnormal gleam' probably means he'll do

370   *Writing About Literature*

A SHORT STORY

An Astrologer's Day
by R. K. Narayan

Punctually at midday he opened his bag and spread out his professional equipment, which consisted of a dozen <u>cowrie shells</u>, a square piece of cloth with obscure mystic charts on it, a notebook, and a bundle of <u>palmyra writing</u>. His forehead was resplendent with sacred ash and <u>vermilion</u>, and his eyes sparkled with a sharp abnormal gleam which was really an outcome of a continual searching look for customers, but which his simple clients took to be a prophetic light and felt comforted. The power of his eyes was considerably enhanced by their position— placed as they were between the painted forehead and the dark whiskers which streamed down his cheeks: even a half-wit's eyes would sparkle in such a setting. To crown the effect he wound a <u>saffron</u>-colored turban around his head. This color scheme never failed. People were attracted to him as bees are attracted to cosmos or dahlia stalks. He sat under the boughs of a spreading tamarind tree which flanked a path running through the Town Hall Park. It was a remarkable place in many ways: a surging crowd was always moving up and down this narrow road morning till night. A variety of trades and occupations was represented all along its way: medicine sellers, sellers of stolen hardware and junk, magicians, and, above all, an auctioneer of cheap cloth, who created enough <u>din</u> all day to attract the whole town. Next to him in <u>vociferousness</u> came a vendor of fried groundnut, who gave his ware a fancy name each day, calling it "Bombay Ice Cream" one day, and on the next "Delhi Almond," and on the third "Raja's Delicacy," and so on and so forth, and people flocked to him. A considerable portion of this crowd dallied before the astrologer too. The astrologer transacted his business by the light of a flare which crackled and smoked up above the groundnut heap nearby. Half the enchantment of the place was due to the fact that it did not have the benefit of municipal lighting. The place was lit up by shop lights. One or two had hissing gaslights, some had naked flares stuck on poles, some were lit up by old cycle lamps, and one or two, like the astrologer's, managed without lights of their own. It was a bewil-

USING THE SELECTION
An Astrologer's Day

1
sacred ash and vermilion: ash and red-orange coloring imitate markings once used by Brahmans, the highest caste in Hindu society

2
How does the author use physical description to reveal character? [The narrator reveals that the sparkle in the man's eyes results not from knowing the future but from continually searching for customers.]

3
cosmos or dahlia stalks: brightly colored tropical American plants

4
What mood is created by the description of the gaslights, flares, cycle lamps, and moving shadows? [a dark, mysterious, enchanted mood]

370

dering crisscross of light rays and moving shadows. This suited the astrologer very well, for the simple reason that he had not in the least intended to be an astrologer when he began life; and he knew no more of what was going to happen to others than he knew what was going to happen to himself next minute. He was as much a stranger to the stars as were his innocent customers. Yet he said things which pleased and astonished everyone: that was more a matter of study, practice, and shrewd guesswork. All 5 the same, it was as much an honest man's labor as any other, and he deserved the wages he carried home at the end of a day.

5

Is there anything ironic about claiming the astrologer's work is "as much an honest man's labor as any other"? [The astrologer is a fake; his work is dishonest.]

VISUAL CONNECTIONS

Exploring the Subject. Indian street markets provide an array of sounds, sights, and smells. Peddlers loudly advertise their wares and bargain with customers over the price of fire-wood, jewelry, or ornamental boxes. Bright, hand-woven carpets and silk saris (traditional garments for women) catch the eye. The aroma of vegetables, fruits, Indian tea, and spices fills the air.

He had left his village without any previous thought or plan. If he had continued there he would have carried on the work of his forefathers—namely, tilling the land, living, marrying, and ripening in his cornfield and ancestral home. But that was not to be. He had to leave home without telling anyone, and he could not rest till he left it behind a couple of hundred miles. To a villager it is a great deal, as if an ocean flowed between.

He had a working analysis of mankind's troubles: marriage, money, and the tangles of human ties. Long practice had sharpened his perception. Within five minutes he understood what was wrong. He charged three <u>pies</u> per question, never opened his mouth till the other had spoken for at least ten minutes, which provided him enough stuff for a dozen answers and advices.

Emphasize that although terms such as *foreshadowing* and *irony* may be new, they have used these elements, perhaps without knowing what they were called, for most of their lives. Ask students for examples of each element from their favorite stories, movies, or TV shows.

GUIDED PRACTICE

Before students work on **Exercise 1**, you may want to guide them through the process. Ask the class to suggest responses and to choose one they want to tell the author or a character. Then, have them create replies. (Example: "I find it hard to believe that Guru Nayak does not recognize a man who stabbed him." Reply: "Many years have

6
The astrologer may be a fake, but he understands human nature.

6 When he told the person before him, gazing at his palm, "In many ways you are not getting the fullest results for your efforts," nine out of ten were disposed to agree with him. Or he questioned: "Is there any woman in your family, maybe even a distant relative, who is not well disposed toward you?" Or he gave an analysis of character: "Most of your troubles are due to your nature. How can you be otherwise with Saturn where he is? You have an <u>impetuous</u> nature and a rough exterior." This endeared him to their hearts immediately, for even the mildest of us loves to think that he has a forbidding exterior.

The nuts vendor blew out his flare and rose to go home. This was a signal for the astrologer to bundle up too, since it left him in darkness except for a little shaft of green light which strayed in from somewhere and touched the ground before him. He picked up his cowrie shells and <u>paraphernalia</u> and was putting

7
What mood is created by having the stranger blot out "the green shaft of light"? [an ominous, foreboding mood; the astrologer is placed in total darkness]

7 them back into his bag when the green shaft of light was blotted out; he looked up and saw a man standing before him. He sensed a possible client and said: "You look so <u>careworn</u>. It will do you good to sit down for a while and chat with me." The other grumbled some reply vaguely. The astrologer pressed his invitation; whereupon the other thrust his palm under his nose, saying: "You call yourself an astrologer?" The astrologer felt challenged and said, tilting the other's palm toward the green shaft of light: "Yours is a nature . . ." "Oh, stop that," the other said. "Tell me something worthwhile. . . ."

8
pies (pīs): The rupee (roo′pē) is the monetary unit of India, and a pie is a coin of slight value.

8 Our friend felt <u>piqued</u>. "I charge only three pies per question, and what you get ought to be good enough for your money. . . ."

INDEPENDENT PRACTICE

Exercises 1 and **2** provide practice in active reading and responding and in discussing literary elements. As students work, circulate through the room, answering questions and offering suggestions.

For **Exercise 1**, stress sincerity to your students. Their purpose is not to impress or trick their partners but to try to understand ☞

Prewriting   **373**

At this the other withdrew his arm, took out an anna, and flung it out to him, saying: "I have some questions to ask. If I prove you are bluffing, you must return that anna to me with interest."

9   "If you find my answers satisfactory, will you give me five rupees?"

"No."

"Or will you give me eight annas?"

"All right, provided you give me twice as much if you are wrong," said the stranger. This pact was accepted after a little further argument. The astrologer sent up a prayer to heaven as the other lit a cheroot. The astrologer caught a glimpse of his face by the matchlight. There was a pause as cars hooted on the

10   road, *jutka* drivers swore at their horses, and the babble of the crowd agitated the semidarkness of the park. The other sat down, sucking his cheroot, puffing out, sat there ruthlessly. The astrologer felt very uncomfortable. "Here, take your anna back. I am not used to such challenges. It is late for me today. . . ." He

11   made preparations to bundle up. The other held his wrist and said: "You can't get out of it now. You dragged me in while I was passing." The astrologer shivered in his grip; and his voice shook and became faint. "Leave me today. I will speak to you tomorrow." The other thrust his palm in his face and said: "Challenge is challenge. Go on." The astrologer proceeded with his throat drying up: "There is a woman . . ."

"Stop," said the other. "I don't want all that. Shall I succeed in my present search or not? Answer this and go. Otherwise I will not let you go till you disgorge all your coins." The astrologer muttered a few incantations and replied: "All right. I will speak. But will you give me a rupee if what I say is convincing? Otherwise I will not open my mouth, and you may do what you like." After a good deal of haggling the other agreed. The astrologer said: "You were left for dead. Am I right?"

"Ah, tell me more."

12   "A knife has passed through you once?" said the astrologer.

"Good fellow!" He bared his chest to show the scar. "What else?"

"And then you were pushed into a well nearby in the field. You were left for dead."

"I should have been dead if some passerby had not chanced to peep into the well," exclaimed the other, overwhelmed by enthusiasm.

9
How does negotiating the cost contribute realism to the story? [Bargaining over price would be expected at such a bazaar.]

10
jutka: horse-drawn taxi

11
What do the stranger's actions suggest about his character? [He will use physical violence to get his way.]

12
Since the astrologer is a fake, what is the only way he could know all this? [He was the man with the knife.]

ASSESSMENT

You can assess whether students understand active reading and responding by watching them act out their freewriting responses as called for in **Exercise 1**. After two or three minutes, you could have the partners switch roles.

To see if students understand literary elements, grade their written comments in

374

13

Why might this be the story climax, the scene that determines how things turn out? [If Guru Nayak is not convinced the astrologer is genuine, he may realize the astrologer's true identity.]

14

The astrologer wants to make sure Guru Nayak will not continue to search.

15

What is humorous (ironic) about the astrologer's claim? [He cannot know the future. Also, if Guru Nayak stays home, the astrologer has a chance to live to be a hundred.]

16

Guru Nayak, reflective and regretful, believes his enemy is dead. The astrologer is safe.

17

Why does the astrologer choose this death? [He knows that hearing an old enemy has been crushed by a wagon will gratify Guru Nayak and help him accept the story.]

"When shall I get at him?" he asked, clenching his fist.

"In the next world," answered the astrologer. "He died four months ago in a far-off town. You will never see any more of him." The other groaned on hearing it. The astrologer proceeded:

"Guru Nayak—"

13 "You know my name!" the other said, taken aback.

"As I know all other things. Guru Nayak, listen carefully to what I have to say. Your village is two days' journey due north of
14 this town. Take the next train and be gone. I see once again great danger to your life if you go from home." He took out a pinch of sacred ash and held it to him. "Rub it on your forehead
15 and go home. Never travel southward again, and you will live to be a hundred."

16 "Why should I leave home again?" the other said reflectively. "I was only going away now and then to look for him and to choke out his life if I met him." He shook his head regretfully. "He has escaped my hands. I hope at least he died as he
17 deserved." "Yes," said the astrologer. "He was crushed under a lorry." The other looked gratified to hear it.

The place was deserted by the time the astrologer picked up his articles and put them into his bag. The green shaft was also gone, leaving the place in darkness and silence. The stranger had gone off into the night, after giving the astrologer a handful of coins.

It was nearly midnight when the astrologer reached home. His wife was waiting for him at the door and demanded an

Exercise 2 or evaluate content and performance when they share their comments with
classmates.

RETEACHING

People usually remember the out-
landish and unusual. If students need a different approach to understand literary
elements, divide the class into small groups
to act out any elements that need reinforcing. One group might present skits that
show each way to characterize—by speech,
actions, appearance, or thoughts. Another ☛

Prewriting   **375**

explanation. He flung the coins at her and said: "Count them.
One man gave all that."

"Twelve and a half annas," she said, counting. She was over-
joyed. "I can buy some jaggery and coconut tomorrow. The child
has been asking for sweets for so many days now. I will prepare
some nice stuff for her."

"The swine has cheated me! He promised me a rupee," said
the astrologer. She looked up at him. "You look worried. What
is wrong?"

"Nothing."

After dinner, sitting on the *pyol*, he told her: "Do you know
a great load is gone from me today? I thought I had the blood of
a man on my hands all these years. That was the reason why I
ran away from home, settled here, and married you. He is alive."

She gasped. "You tried to kill!"

"Yes, in our village, when I was a silly youngster. We drank,
gambled, and quarreled badly one day—why think of it now?
18 Time to sleep," he said, yawning, and stretched himself on
the *pyol*.

| **EXERCISE 1** ▶ | **Speaking and Listening: Responding and Reading Actively** |

Did you ever wish you could talk to an author or a character? After reading "An Astrologer's Day," freewrite a
response for one minute, *as if you're speaking directly to the
writer or a character.* Here are some questions to get you
started: Did you like the way the story ended? Or did you
feel tricked? How do you feel about the astrologer? Then
act out your freewriting response with a partner, following these pointers:

1. Look your partner in the eye; then read your
   response.
2. Your partner—taking the place of author or
   character—will listen carefully and "answer" you.
3. Keep the back-and-forth active responses going as
   long as you can.
4. Change places. Become the author or character, and
   answer your partner's freewriting response.

18
Will the astrologer sleep well? [He may
sleep better than before, knowing he is
not a killer and that Guru Nayak will not
seek him.]

ANSWERS
Exercise 1

Questions and answers will vary. Students
might enjoy the irony of the ending, or
they might feel tricked by a plot based on
a coincidental meeting and on Guru
Nayak's not recognizing his assailant.
Some students will probably feel the
astrologer is smart and resourceful; others
might find him unethical and shallow.

You may want to model the freewriting
and dialogue with a volunteer. Students
who like to perform might want to share
their dialogues with the entire class.

group might act out external or internal conflicts. A third group might enact scenes with verbal, dramatic, or situational irony. Each skit should be followed by a brief summary of the lesson to be learned.

CLOSURE

Ask students to name the hints for active reading and responding. Then, ask volunteers to briefly summarize the seven literary elements.

Understanding and Using Literary Elements

Already you've been responding to some basic elements of a short story, perhaps the main character or the plot of "An Astrologer's Day." To write about a story, you need a good understanding—a working knowledge—of literary elements, and you need to keep them clearly in mind as you read.

You'll find that the elements below make your reading and writing more specific and sharp. They let you look *inside* a story—at its parts and the writer's techniques—and talk about it in clear, precise terms.

Plot. *Plot* is the story's "action," or series of events. Look closely, and you'll see that *conflict*—the problems the characters face—keeps the plot moving. Conflicts can be external (struggles with people, nature, or society) or internal (struggles with the character's own feelings or beliefs). The *climax* of a plot is the tense or exciting scene that settles the story's main conflict—that determines how things turn out.

Setting. *Setting* is the story's time and place; it may include weather, clothes, landscape, buildings, cars, rickshaws—many physical and social details. Setting provides important background for understanding people and events, and it may also create conflict (imagine a

MEETING *individual* NEEDS

AT-RISK STUDENTS

Students might write an "after" story to become familiar with plot, conflict, and climax. Beginning where **"An Astrologer's Day"** leaves off, ask students to imagine a scenario in which Guru Nayak guesses who the astrologer might be. What would Nayak do? How would the astrologer react? [conflict] What scene would settle it all? [climax]

Students who are inexperienced with dialogue, speaker tags, and so forth might summarize the ending.

To show how literary elements are related, let students place the titles of favorite movies in a container and the names of the main characters of favorite movies in another container. Have each student pick a slip from each container and discuss changes that would occur from the new combination. If a student happens to draw two slips that actu- ally match, have the student trade one slip with another student. How would plot, theme, irony, and setting be affected, for example, if Arnold Schwarzenegger in *Terminator 2* were replaced by Winnie the Pooh? What if Dorothy from *The Wizard of Oz* took the place of Indiana Jones? ∎

destructive avalanche, for example) or set an emotional mood, or atmosphere (imagine a festive carnival).

Character.   Characters are the individuals in a story (animals or aliens, as well as people), and *characterization* is the way the writer reveals their qualities and traits. Writers can describe personality directly, but they can also show it indirectly through the characters' speech, appearance, thoughts, actions, and effects on others (what people say and feel about them). To understand a character, you may need to consider the motivation for actions and decide whether the character changes in the story.

Point of View.   *Point of view* is the angle from which a story is told: who tells it, how close this narrator is to the action, what *is* told, and what *isn't*.

In *first-person point of view,* the narrator is a character in the story and speaks as *I*. This narrator can only tell us what he or she sees and hears, is told, or *believes*. Maybe the character is reliable, but maybe not: Readers must decide.

In *third-person point of view,* the narrator is outside the story—not a character—and doesn't use the words *I, me,* and *mine,* but does use *he, her,* and *them* (third-person pronouns). A *third-person omniscient* narrator can tell the thoughts of any character (*omniscient* means "all-knowing"), relate any event, and even speak right to the reader or skip around in time.

In *third-person limited point of view,* the outside narrator reveals the thoughts of just one character. The story's events are filtered through the mind of one person.

Foreshadowing.   *Foreshadowing* is a hint or suggestion of coming events—a clue, in a way, that heightens our interest or prepares us for significant actions. Sometimes we recognize foreshadowing immediately: A jeweled bracelet shines "coldly" in its "padded coffin of a case," and we're instantly on alert for danger. But sometimes foreshadowing is less obvious: A character sees two dogs fight to exhaustion over a bone, but we don't learn

INTEGRATING THE LANGUAGE ARTS

Literature Link. Students might analyze literary elements in a story such as Juanita Platero and Siyowin Miller's "Chee's Daughter."

1. Plot: Chee argues with his in-laws over his daughter's return.
2. Setting: Chee's home (family compound blends into landscape of canyons and desert) contrasts with the trading post (barren land with ugly buildings along a highway).
3. Character: Love motivates Chee; greed motivates Old Man Fat.
4. Point of view: Third-person limited helps readers identify with Chee.
5. Foreshadowing: The cold wind suggests the winter that helps Chee.
6. Irony: The young man, not his elders, follows Navajo tradition.
7. Theme: A traditional lifestyle is superior to a modern lifestyle.

TIMESAVER

If lack of time is a problem, you may choose to modify **Exercise 2.** Have each student choose one story instead of two. The drawback is that one story is unlikely to include as many diverse elements. Also, a student might choose a story he or she has read before, and familiarity might diminish reactions to some elements in the story. You may have to encourage the students to admit to negative reactions to favorite stories.

until later that he will battle his brother—for a girl who loves neither one.

Irony.   *Irony* is basically a contrast between appearance or expectation and reality. Writers use surprising, ironic twists to make us laugh but also to make us thoughtful or sad: Life and people don't always behave as we want. Writers use three kinds of irony. (All three examples come from a famous ironic story, Edgar Allan Poe's "The Cask of Amontillado." Read it if you haven't!)

- *verbal irony:* one thing is said but another is meant: A man who plans to kill his unsuspecting friend offers the toast "To your health!"
- *situational irony:* what is expected is not what happens: The friend attends a carnival expecting fun but instead meets his death.
- *dramatic irony:* the reader (or playgoer or moviegoer) knows something that a character does not: Readers know the man plans murder, but his friend does not.

Theme.   *Theme* is an important idea about life or human nature revealed in a story. It isn't just a subject (like "war"), but an insight ("War wounds are not just physical; they are carried inside forever"). Writers often don't state their themes directly, and you have to draw your own conclusions from characters, events, description, and dialogue. (Sometimes the title or the conflict may be clues.) You may find more than one theme in a story.

When you read a short story (or any other literary work)

- respond freely, by letting your thoughts and feelings flow naturally
- read actively, by responding personally, applying your own experience, questioning, predicting, and reacting to the whole
- think about the work's literary elements and how the writer uses them to get you to respond as you do

CRITICAL THINKING

OBJECTIVE

- To analyze the literary elements of a short story by using a set of suggested questions

TEACHING *ANALYZING A SHORT STORY*

Read and discuss the questions to be sure students understand them. Emphasize that the questions address the literary elements students have already studied. You may want to model the **Critical Thinking Exercise** by answering question 4 (about setting) with specific details from the story. Stress that

EXERCISE 2 ▶ **Exploring Stories and Literary Elements**

What hooks you in a story? A shocking twist (heavy on the irony)? Weird settings in the future? Believable characters? Find out for yourself. Choose two stories (favorite or unknown ones), and respond to them actively, in writing, as you did in Exercise 1. This time, though, focus specifically on literary elements, using what you've just learned. Write out your comments to share with your classmates: "What I Like or Don't Like in Stories—and Why."

CRITICAL THINKING

Analyzing a Short Story

Analyzing means examining in detail: looking closely at the parts of a whole and their relationships. You're doing this naturally whenever you respond to different parts of stories—funny dialogue, a tragic ending—and you simply do it in a deeper, systematic way when you write a critical analysis.

Here are some questions that can help you analyze any short story. But remember: Literature is not a statement of scientific fact, but a creation in words of experience. Its readers vary, and so will its interpretations. In discussions, you'll naturally compare your answers with those of your classmates, but don't look for right or wrong answers.

1. What important conflicts or problems, external and internal, does the main character(s) face?
2. What is the story's climax, the outcome of the central conflict?
3. Where and when does the story take place?
4. Does the setting help explain characters and events, cause a conflict, or set a mood? (More than one may apply.) Explain.
5. What is the story's main character(s) like? (Use appearance, speech, thoughts, actions, and reactions of others.)

ANSWERS
Exercise 2

As students prepare to read two stories, suggest that they list the literary elements at the top of a sheet of paper to serve as reminders. As something in the stories affects them positively or negatively, they might put a plus (+) or minus sign (–) on their papers and freewrite their reactions. This can provide insight into what they like or do not like about the stories.

ANSWERS
Critical Thinking Exercise

Responses may vary. Here are some possibilities:

1. Guru Nayak: find and punish his attacker (external); Astrologer: trick Guru Nayak into leaving (external) and control his own emotions and fears (internal)
2. The astrologer reveals information about Guru Nayak's past; his tale reveals that he may be caught up in Guru Nayak's story. The conflict is resolved when Guru Nayak accepts the astrologer's explanation, and the astrologer is spared retribution.
3. The setting is an Indian market in Town Hall Park, from midday until after midnight.
4. The market, lively and filled with hucksters, suggests the unexpected. It sets a mood of enchantment, with strange lighting that makes people appear shadowy.

each question should involve both an answer and a reference to details from the story.

5. Appearance: dark whiskers, turban, sacred ash on his forehead, abnormal gleam of eyes.
Speech: He first speaks clichés, but later skillfully convinces Guru Nayak his enemy is dead.
Thoughts: He senses a client, feels piqued when challenged, and feels uncomfortable at recognizing his foe.
Actions: He presses Guru Nayak to have his fortune told; tricks him.
Others' reactions: Guru Nayak shows the astrologer little respect until the story rings true.

6. The astrologer wants to hide, make money, and survive. Guru Nayak is motivated by hate. The astrologer feels relieved; Guru Nayak, disappointed, will no longer seek his attacker.

7. The point of view is third-person limited. The narrator does not reveal the astrologer's thoughts at the moment of recognition.

8. The setting foreshadows the strange events. "People were attracted to him . . ." suggests that someone will arrive. That "nine out of ten" usually agree with him implies a tenth who will not.

9. Dramatic irony occurs as the reader becomes aware that the astrologer is Guru Nayak's attacker. Verbal irony occurs when the astrologer says he can make Guru Nayak feel better. There is situational irony because the attacker becomes an astrologer to escape his past, which attracts his victim.

10. Good, bad, guilt, and punishment often are not clearly defined.

6. What motivates the main character(s) to act? Does the character(s) change in the story? If so, how?

7. Is the point of view first-person, omniscient, or third-person limited? Does the point of view affect what *you* know and feel? How?

8. Does foreshadowing help prepare for later events or situations? If so, give examples that you found effective.

9. Is irony—verbal, situational, or dramatic—at work in this story? Give examples, and discuss its effect.

10. What important idea about life or people do you find in this story?

CRITICAL THINKING EXERCISE:
Analyzing a Short Story

Working with a partner or a small group, analyze "An Astrologer's Day" by asking the questions above and on page 379. Your group might enjoy exchanging interpretations with another group—and remember that it's okay for your viewpoints to differ. (In fact, discussing with your group *why* your individual interpretations are different can also be interesting.)

| WRITING ASSIGNMENT | PART 1: **Choosing a Story and Analyzing Its Elements** |

It's time to settle on a story that you'd like to think more about, feel and understand better, analyze closely, and tell others about in writing. Choose a story from your literature textbook or a favorite story of your own. Then use the questions above and on page 379 to analyze it.

 *Prewriting*

Planning a Critical Analysis

Now it's time to turn your ideas about your short story into the raw material you'll use to write your essay.

Thinking About Purpose and Audience

You can write about literature for many purposes, but this chapter focuses on *critical analysis*. In your essay, you're taking on the role of "literary investigator": a close reader who knows, and can tell an audience, something about the literary elements in a short story.

For a critical analysis, you assume that your audience has read the story, which means that you don't need to retell the plot. Think of your audience as interested readers who want to know more.

Finding a Focus and Developing a Main Idea

In a short essay, you'll usually write about one story element or two or three that fit together somehow. Your choice depends on two things: (1) your interest (What drew you to the story? A crazy character? A great historical setting?) and (2) the story itself (What did your analysis uncover? For what parts or aspects of the story do you have many notes or probing questions?). Write about something that attracts you and seems important in the story.

With a topic (element) in mind, your next step is to develop a main idea. What do you want to say *about* the element and the story? Write a sentence—a thesis statement—that connects your topic and main idea.

Following are some thesis statements you might write about "An Astrologer's Day":

Nayak's violent character is shown through his actions and speech.

The setting of "An Astrologer's Day" gives us a good picture of what life is like for the city's people.

A DIFFERENT APPROACH

In the **Evaluating and Revising** lesson, students will see exactly how to cut from their analysis sections unnecessary restatement of the plot. However, a more effective time to emphasize this type of revision might be during prewriting. You may want to highlight some of the phrasing used in the *Frankenstein* critique in which the author showcases events in the movie without actually restating the plot.

> The setting of "An Astrologer's Day" creates a "bewildering" mood and also brings about the plot's main conflict.

> In "An Astrologer's Day," verbal, dramatic, and situational irony are used to make us doubt the astrologer, to build suspense, and to develop theme.

Notice that the examples show you basic *kinds* of ideas used in literary analysis. You can write about an element's

- function (how it works in the story)
- effect (what you feel or understand because of it)
- development (how the writer builds or creates it)

The sample thesis statements also show how much flexibility you have in writing about elements. For example, you can write about one function of setting or two; you can write about one type of irony or about all three types plus theme. As long as you match the topic to the length of the assignment, the focus is yours.

WRITING ASSIGNMENT

PART 2:
Writing a Thesis Statement

You may already have a writing focus in mind once you've analyzed your story. What made you choose this story? What did you discover about it? Pinpoint your focus and the main idea you want to convey. Write your thesis statement in one sentence.

Collecting Support and Organizing Your Ideas

Collecting Support. A critical analysis of literature, like persuasive writing, requires evidence to support your ideas. The "evidence" in this case, though, comes from the literature. In other words, you don't just tell readers that Nayak has a violent character; you *show* them. Evidence may take the form of quotations, paraphrases, summaries, or specific details.

REFERENCE NOTE: For more information on using sources to support your ideas, see pages 414–415.

Organizing Your Ideas. With your main points listed and supporting details recorded, you can produce an early plan by arranging the information. Often your topic and ideas will suggest a natural way to do this.

For example, if you're analyzing a character and showing how he or she changes, chronological order (the plot order) makes sense. If a setting both sets a mood and causes a major plot problem, you'll probably want to begin with mood (which is background) and end with conflict. And you can also order ideas and supporting details by importance (most-to-least, least-to-most). Look for an arrangement that readers can easily follow.

"*Once upon a time, they lived happily ever after.*"

Drawing by H. Martin, © 1991 by the New Yorker Magazine, Inc.

WRITING ASSIGNMENT	PART 3: **Collecting Support and Organizing Your Ideas**

Remember: You want to *show* your readers, not just *tell* them. Now is the time to make notes of story details that led you to your ideas in the first place. (And you may also discover new evidence.) After collecting support, arrange both ideas and details, and create either a rough or a formal outline.

 COMPUTER NOTE: Use the multiple-window feature of your word-processing program to view your prewriting notes and your outline at the same time.

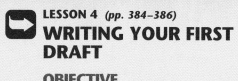
TEACHING THE LESSON

As students read the model, point out labeled parts of the essay. Have students find topic sentences for the paragraphs and remind them that the topic sentence is followed by evidence that proves or illustrates it.

You may want to use the chalkboard to paraphrase, quote, and summarize passages as models for your students. Point out

PROGRAM MANAGER

WRITING YOUR FIRST DRAFT

■ **Instructional Support** For help with writing a body paragraph, see **Writing** in *Strategies for Writing*, p. 49.

 QUOTATION FOR THE DAY

"Nothing is ended with honour which does not conclude better than it began." (Samuel Johnson, 1709–1784, English lexicographer, essayist, and poet)

MEETING *individual* NEEDS

LEP/ESL

General Strategies. Whereas active reading requires personal reactions to the literature, writing conventions for critical analysis require avoiding the words *I, me, my,* or *mine* when putting reactions on paper. Two techniques students can use to avoid these terms are rewording and the using of the pronoun *one.*

1. I questioned the motives of Dr. Frankenstein. [The motives of Dr. Frankenstein seemed questionable.]
2. I expected the ending to be happier. [One might have expected the ending to be happier.]

384

Writing Your First Draft

Now that you've collected support and organized your ideas, you're ready to write your first draft. The *introduction* to your critical essay must include (1) the title and author of the short story and (2) your thesis statement. It can be simple, but it has the goal of all introductions: to interest readers. Why were you attracted to the story? Set down your own interest, and you'll catch the reader's.

The essay's *body* develops your main points, using the support you've gathered. Incorporating this support smoothly into your sentences is a special element of critical writing. You can paraphrase, quote, or summarize, but all references to the story must fit grammatically into your writing, as the following examples show.

 HERE'S HOW

Because the narrator tells us that the astrologer doesn't know the future, calling his work "an honest man's labor" is irony with a sharp bite.	paraphrase / quotation
Just as ironically, Nayak might have passed on by, but the astrologer was insistent.	summary

The *conclusion* of an analysis is often a restatement of the thesis or summary of points. Other essay techniques are possible, such as echoing the introduction's ideas and details or ending with a larger observation about the story. Remember that the conclusion shouldn't be mechanical: "Now I will summarize my main points. . . ." It should be a satisfying finish for your readers.

The following Writer's Model shows you these basic essay parts for a critical analysis.

that the model has only a few words of direct quotation.

Help students get started by allowing them to write any paragraph they choose, regardless of its place in the final essay. Offer assistance as needed. If they can draft one paragraph, they can draft others step by step.

You also may want students to write their drafts in class so that you can give counsel as needed.

☞

A WRITER'S MODEL

An Analysis of Irony in
"An Astrologer's Day"

INTRODUCTION
Title and author

Thesis statement

"An Astrologer's Day," by R. K. Narayan, is ironic through and through. Almost nothing is what it seems to be, and one unexpected event follows another--for both readers and characters. This is a comic but thought-provoking story in which irony is used for several purposes: to make us doubt the astrologer, to build suspense, and to develop theme.

BODY
Support:
Quotation and details

Paraphrase and quotation

From the first sentence, Narayan uses irony to make us doubt the astrologer. His "professional" equipment (the shells, the cloth with mysterious writing, and so on) is only for show. Ordinary listening skills, not the stars, help him astonish his "simple clients" with "shrewd guesswork." Because the narrator tells us that the astrologer doesn't know the future, calling his work "an honest man's labor" is irony with a sharp bite. The narrator's comments expose the astrologer as a greedy fake.

Support:
Summary/
Details

The narrator also uses irony to build suspense during the fortunetelling scene. From previous clues, we realize that the astrologer is the one who knifed and left Nayak--but Nayak doesn't know it. Will the astrologer pull off his risky trick? What will happen if he doesn't? The irony of knowing something Nayak doesn't makes the scene fascinating and tense.

Support:
Summary/
Details and quotation

The story's strongest irony, however, runs all through the plot and helps create theme. One important irony is that the astrologer has tried to escape his past but ends up, in a way, bringing it to himself. He's become an astrologer to get away from his crime, but his victim is attracted to an astrologer. As Nayak says, " 'I have some questions to ask.' " Just as ironically, Nayak might have passed on by, but the astrologer was insistent.

385

CRITICAL THINKING

Classification. To help students understand irony, have small groups locate some examples in "**An Astrologer's Day**" and classify each as verbal, dramatic, or situational. Tell them to include one example of each. Answers may vary. Here are some possibilities:

1. verbal irony: "professional equipment" and "an honest man's labor"
2. dramatic irony: "knowing something Nayak doesn't"
3. situational irony: hiding as astrologer attracts Nayak, "insistent" that Nayak stop

386   *Writing About Literature*

Summary/
Details

Support:
Interpretation
of theme

Quotation

Quotations
Summary/
Details

CONCLUSION

Return to
introduction

But the story gets still more ironic: When the astrologer recognizes Nayak, he uses the truth to deceive him! For once, the astrologer really does know facts about a customer, and he uses them to save his own life. In the end, posing as an astrologer is an advantage.

Every situation in this story takes an unexpected twist, and we are left with the message that life never turns out as expected and that even good and bad aren't what they seem. For example, it is awful that the astrologer can say " 'why think of it now?' " about leaving a man for dead, but we certainly didn't want Nayak to shed more blood to punish him. It is dishonest to take money for fake prophecies, but the astrologer's customers are "comforted" and "pleased." It is the astrologer who is guilty of a violent crime, but Nayak was probably violent too--and still is.

The irony is so strong in "An Astrologer's Day" that good, bad, guilt, and punishment aren't clear-cut. What should we think? Obviously, R. K. Narayan doesn't want us to take this tale too seriously. Because no real harm is done, we can laugh at this upside-down world, not be shocked by it. We can simply enjoy all of the author's ironies.

WRITING
ASSIGNMENT

PART 4:
Writing a First Draft of Your Critical Analysis

The writer's model you just read was a final draft. Don't panic: A polished, finished paper isn't expected of you now. Just let the model rest in your mind as you use your rough outline to get a first draft on paper. (But if the model gave you concrete ideas for your essay, use them!) Remember: Your goal is to support your thesis with evidence from the story so that your readers will understand your interpretation.

EVALUATING AND REVISING

OBJECTIVES

- To analyze and answer questions about a writer's revisions of a critical analysis
- To evaluate and revise a critical analysis

TEACHING THE LESSON

After discussing the evaluation and revision checklist, you may want to guide students through the answering of question 2 in **Exercise 3**. If students have trouble with the exercise, provide additional practice by having them use the checklist to evaluate paragraphs from the analysis of *Frankenstein* (pp. 364–367).

 # *Evaluating and Revising*

The following checklist will help you to correct your paper's weaknesses. Ask yourself each question in the left-hand column. Then use the technique in the right-hand column to correct any problems.

EVALUATING AND REVISING A LITERARY ANALYSIS

EVALUATION GUIDE	REVISION TECHNIQUE
1 Does the introduction include the title and the author?	**Add** the missing title or author.
2 Does the introduction identify the thesis, or focus, of the analysis?	**Add** a sentence or two (or replace an existing one) identifying a literary element and your main idea about it.
3 Is there enough support from the story for your ideas?	**Add** quotations, plot events, or other details.
4 Is support smoothly incorporated into the sentences?	**Add** or **replace** words and punctuation so that quotations and paraphrases are grammatically complete.
5 Have purpose and audience been considered in writing the critical analysis?	**Cut** informal expressions. **Cut** plot details that the audience may know or that are not related to your purpose.
6 Does the conclusion bring the essay to a definite close?	**Add** a sentence or two (or **replace** existing ones) that restate your main idea or summarize existing points.

PROGRAM MANAGER

EVALUATING AND REVISING

- **Reinforcement/Reteaching** See **Revision Transparencies 17** and **18.** For suggestions on how to tie the transparencies to instruction, review teacher's notes in *Fine Art and Instructional Transparencies for Writing,* p. 127.

- **Ongoing Assessment** See **Evaluating and Revising** in *Strategies for Writing,* p. 50.

- **Assessment/Reflection** See **Portfolio Forms** in *Portfolio Assessment,* pp. 5–21.

QUOTATION FOR THE DAY

"True ease in writing comes from art, not chance, / As those move easiest who have learn'd to dance." (Alexander Pope, 1688–1744, English poet)

Encourage students to make both positive and negative comments on each of the questions from the evaluation checklist. Also, remind them they must decide whether to accept or to ignore suggestions for revisions.

CLOSURE

Ask students to recall the questions used to help them evaluate and revise their critical analyses. Also, ask them to list possible revision techniques. ∎

TIMESAVER

You may want to assign **Exercise 3** as homework. Have students briefly compare responses and discuss differences in small groups before discussing responses as a class.

Students might also make copies of their papers so that peer evaluation can also be assigned as homework.

CRITICAL THINKING

Synthesis. Revision may seem complicated to students. Emphasize that revising consists of only four techniques: replacing, cutting, reordering, or adding. These techniques can be used for evaluating and revising almost anything. Ask students to think of ways to redesign their school using the four revision choices. [They might replace buildings, cut unused lockers, reorder (rearrange) classrooms, or add parking space.]

ANSWERS
Exercise 3

1. Listing the author and title reveals quickly what story is being analyzed.
2. The original sentence states the plot. The writer changed it to a thesis statement that gives, in the order they will be discussed, three specific ways that the author uses irony in the story.

EXERCISE 3 **Analyzing a Writer's Revisions**

Study the writer's revisions of the first two paragraphs of the model analysis on page 385. Then answer the questions that follow the paragraphs.

("An Astrologer's Day," by R. K. Narayan)

~~This~~ story is ironic through and through. Almost nothing is what it seems to be, and one unexpected event follows another--for both readers and characters.   **replace**

This is a comic but thought-provoking story, *in which irony is used for several purposes:* ~~In it, an astrologer meets the man~~ *to make us doubt the astrologer, to build suspense,* ~~he once wounded with a knife, pushed in~~ *and to develop theme.* ~~a well, and left for dead.~~   **replace**

Because the narrator tells us that the astrologer doesn't know the future, calling his work *("an honest man's labor")* ~~honest~~ is irony with a sharp bite.   **replace**

From the first sentence, Narayan uses irony to make us doubt the astrologer. His "professional" equipment (the shells, the cloth with mysterious writing, and so on) is only for show. Ordinary listening skills, not the stars, help him astonish his "simple clients" with "shrewd guesswork."   **reorder**

The narrator's comments expose the astrologer *as a greedy fake.*   **add**

1. Why did the writer add the title and author of the story to the first line?
2. Why did the writer make such extensive changes in the last sentence of the first paragraph? [Hint: What is the thesis statement of the critical analysis?]

3. In the first sentence of the second paragraph, why did the writer replace the word *honest* with the quote *"an honest man's labor"*?
4. Why did the writer move the second, third, and fourth sentences of the second paragraph?
5. Why did the writer add the words *as a greedy fake* to the last sentence of the second paragraph?

WRITING NOTE   As you evaluate and revise your paper, remember that not all your support should be direct quotations. Too many quotations can have a choppy, unoriginal, and even irritating effect (do *you* like to read strung-together quotations?). Use quotations when the author's exact wording is especially striking, important to your point, or more precise than a paraphrase. The rest of the time you can paraphrase or summarize ideas and details from the literary work.

WRITING ASSIGNMENT   PART 5:
Evaluating and Revising Your Critical Analysis

Exchange papers with another student, and use the questions from the evaluating and revising chart on page 387 to evaluate each other's papers. Be prepared to explain to your partner where changes are needed to improve his or her essay. Then use your partner's comments and your own evaluation to revise your critical analysis.

"The answers you get from literature depend upon the questions you pose."

Margaret Atwood

3. The exact quote is striking. The writer probably felt the verbal irony should be shown word for word.
4. The writer wanted the original first sentence to be a conclusion drawn from the three sentences that follow it; therefore, the three sentences were moved to precede it.
5. Many readers might wonder what he was exposed as.

MEETING individual NEEDS

LEP/ESL

General Strategies.   Exchanging papers for evaluation can provide an opportunity for students to develop the awareness that criticism can give constructive feedback. You may want to offer the following examples when students make suggestions to their classmates:

1. You might want to . . .
2. I wonder if this is the best way to put this. . . .

PROOFREADING AND PUBLISHING

OBJECTIVE

- To proofread and publish a critical analysis

TEACHING THE LESSON

Ask students to share any proofreading methods they use. Stress multiple proofreadings with a different goal each time—to check quotation marks, correct spelling, and so forth.

Carefully review rules for using underlining. You may choose sentences from a

---

PROGRAM MANAGER

PROOFREADING AND PUBLISHING

- **Instructional Support** For a chart students may use to evaluate their proofreading progress, see **Proofreading** in *Strategies for Writing*, p. 51.

- **Independent Practice/ Reteaching** For additional practice with language skills, see **Proofreading Practice: Using Underlining** in *Strategies for Writing*, p. 52.

- **Assessment/Reflection** To assess student work and evaluate progress, see **Portfolio Forms** in *Portfolio Assessment*, pp. 22–25.

- **Computer Guided Instruction** For additional instruction and practice with underlining, as noted in the **Mechanics Hint**, see **Lesson 41** in *Language Workshop CD-ROM*.

- **Practice** To help less-advanced students who need additional practice with underlining, see **Chapter 21** in *English Workshop, Fourth Course*, pp. 295–296.

QUOTATION FOR THE DAY

"Patience is not only a virtue, but it pays." (B. C. Forbes, 1880–1954, U.S. businessman and editor of *Forbes Magazine* from 1917 to 1954)

Proofreading and Publishing

Proofreading. Use your usual method of proofreading, but then proofread again another way (perhaps backward). For this essay, also pay special attention to

- quotation marks (Do you have opening *and* closing marks?)
- punctuation used with quotation marks (See pages 834–836.)
- the story title (Is it enclosed in quotation marks?)

MECHANICS HINT

Denoting Titles

When you write about literature or other art forms, you need to know how to indicate the title of the work. Sometimes you use quotation marks, and sometimes you use underlining. (The italic type produced on a computer serves the same purpose as underlining.)

1. Use quotation marks to enclose the titles of stories, poems, songs, book chapters, and articles.

    One of Elizabeth Bishop's poems is called "The Fish."
    Alice Walker's short story "Everyday Use" is told in the first-person point of view.

2. Underline the titles of books, paintings, television programs, plays, and movies.

    The setting of Stephen Crane's novel *The Red Badge of Courage* is a battlefield during the Civil War.
    The movie *Sense and Sensibility* won an Oscar.

☞ REFERENCE NOTE: See pages 831–840 for more information about quotation marks and underlining.

Publishing. With your teacher's help, you might use the following ideas to share your paper with others.

story and use them to model correct and incorrect use of underlining.

Suggest publication possibilities and ask students to add to your suggestions. Ask students for publication possibilities such as presenting on videotape, circulating writing in an exchange group, or adapting stories in the form of plays. Emphasize to students that writing is meant to be read. This last step reinforces the connection between reading and writing. You may want to reward students with praise or points for sharing their work.

- Get together with other students who wrote on the same general topic: character, conflict, point of view, and so on. Read each other's papers, and talk about what attracted you to the story and literary element you wrote about.
- Make a class file of essays as a reference tool for future assignments. Make an index that will let students look up essays by topic, story title, or story author.

PART 6:
Proofreading and Publishing Your Critical Analysis

Proofread your paper (remember to try a new method as a double-check). Then, use the suggestions above, take your essay home to your family, or surprise a former teacher by offering it (name removed, if you like) for his or her files.

Reflecting on Your Writing

Write a brief reflection answering the following questions. Date it, and include it with your paper in your **portfolio.**

- How did you choose support for your thesis?
- What was hardest about writing this paper? Why?
- What skills did you learn from this assignment?

A STUDENT MODEL

Matt Sanders, a student at East Mecklenburg High School in Charlotte, North Carolina, discusses Thomas Mann's "The Infant Prodigy." Matt has this advice for you: "It is very important to know the work of literature thoroughly and to understand it. Prewriting and planning are very important in getting your thoughts analyzed and your ideas organized. Once a suitable thesis is concocted, the paper should write itself."

INTEGRATING THE LANGUAGE ARTS

Mechanics Link. Students sometimes have trouble distinguishing ellipses and periods. You could use the chalkboard to emphasize the difference visually. For several days, place a period in the upper right corner of the chalkboard and place three ellipsis marks in the upper left corner. Remind students that four marks are used together only when ellipsis marks are followed by a period.

COOPERATIVE LEARNING

Some students might combine their critical analyses and create casebooks with artfully designed construction paper or cardboard covers. These might be kept on file for future students.

Casebooks might focus on a particular story or on a literary element such as plot or theme. Students might collaborate on a brief introduction that introduces the story or literary element and that gives a brief synopsis of each analysis in the collection.

REFLECTING ON YOUR WRITING

Teaching Note. Encourage students to jot down ideas before they begin writing their reflections. In response to the third question, you can suggest that students start a list of skills they learn or improve in writing this assignment and subsequent ones. In this and subsequent assignments, they can refer to this list to observe their progress as writers.

CLOSURE

Ask students to describe the proof-reading methods they used with their critical analyses. Also, have volunteers explain the proper use of ellipses and quotation marks. ■

The Big Picture
by Matt Sanders

A full portrait of a character cannot be created by revealing just his or her thoughts. The thoughts of others about that character play a crucial role in telling the complete story. By using the omniscient point of view, Thomas Mann creates a full portrait of Bibi, the main character in "The Infant Prodigy."

Many different pictures of Bibi are painted. One picture shows Bibi as an innocent, prodigious child who is full of talent. One character, the old man, sees Bibi's talent as being a gift from God. The businessman, while analyzing the monetary aspects of the performance, says " 'Really he does not play so badly.' " The young girl sees Bibi as an innocent child with a talent of expressing passion. The critic also sees the innocence and talent in Bibi. " 'As an individual he still has to develop, but as a type he is already quite complete, the artist par excellence.' "

Another picture created by the omniscient narrator shows Bibi and his performance as a hoax used to play up to the audience. It sees through Bibi's dazzling performance. The piano teacher criticizes his performance as being unoriginal. Of his form she thinks, " 'And his hand position is entirely amateur. One must be able to lay a coin on the back of his hand--I would use a ruler on him.' " The critic also sees through Bibi's performance. He sees every move as a publicity stunt. The impresario's kiss is a " 'good old gag.' "

The third and final picture painted by the omniscient narrator is painted by Bibi himself. This is a picture of contempt for the audience. Bibi, on the outside, is a talented performer who loves pleasing the audience. However, through his thoughts, the true Bibi is seen. He thinks that the audience is unaware of true musical talent: "Now I will play the fantasy, it is a lot better than Le Hibou, of course, especially the C-sharp passage. But you idiots dote on the Hibou, though it is the first and silliest thing I wrote." When the princess talks to him about his music, he thinks, " 'Oh, what a stupid old princess!' "

By using the omniscient point of view, the author can tell the complete story. By combining the thoughts of Bibi and the other characters in the story, Thomas Mann paints a full portrait of Bibi.

A STUDENT MODEL
Evaluation

1. Matt includes the title and author in the first paragraph.
2. Matt identifies the thesis of the analysis in the last sentence of the first paragraph.
3. Purpose and audience are considered in this critical analysis because it does not contain informal expressions and does not contain details of the plot that are unrelated to the purpose.
4. The conclusion brings the essay to a definite close by restating the main idea.

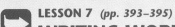

LESSON 7 *(pp. 393–395)*
WRITING WORKSHOP

OBJECTIVE

• To plan, write, evaluate, revise, proofread, and publish a critical review of a movie or television program

TEACHING THE LESSON

Students probably understand the main literary elements by now, but you may need to review direction, acting, and other elements of film.

Students might analyze other brief reviews in magazines or in local newspapers. For practice, you could guide the class through planning and writing a short review ☞

393

WRITING WORKSHOP

A Critical Review

Everyone is a movie and television reviewer once in a while. "Don't bother spending money on *Killer Cows III,*" you tell a friend. "Even the cows are bored, not scary." Your reviews for friends are casual, but they have the same final purpose as published reviews: to judge whether the movie or program is worth watching.

Reviews (whether for films, television, or books) combine critical analysis of a work's elements with evaluation, or judgment. How good or effective is the movie—in its elements and as a whole? Judgments like this are opinions, but they're opinions based on standards (for example, the standard that a horror movie like *Killer Cows* should be scary). A reviewer who conveys only the message that "This was the stupidest excuse for a movie I've ever seen" without telling *why* won't convince anyone (or keep many readers).

Of course, reviews must tell you something of the work's subject, plot, or theme. Yet they have to strike a careful balance: enough information for understanding but not enough to spoil enjoyment. A special kind of review is the mini-review that newspapers and magazines often publish of movies they have reviewed at greater length in previous issues. The mini-review must combine information about the film for the reader who hasn't yet seen it and the reviewer's evaluation of it—the acting, directing, production values, and so on in a very short space. Following is a mini-review of the film *Driving Miss Daisy*. What do you learn about the content of the film itself? What is the reviewer's opinion of the film?

> Alfred Uhry's adaptation of his much honored play is still full of manipulative bits—it's virtually all manipulative bits—but the director, Bruce Beresford, understands how to work them while cutting down on their obviousness. Set in Atlanta, starting in 1948,

of a movie or television program you have shown in class. Stress taking a stand by pointing out the many judgmental terms in Kael's review: "manipulative," "suspicious," "fine," and so forth.

As students work in groups to plan, write, and revise their reviews, you could circulate to answer questions. Remind students of their purpose: A positive review should make readers want to see the program; a negative review should make readers want to avoid it.

Remind students that their reflections should be based on serious thought about the questions raised by the programs they viewed.

COOPERATIVE LEARNING

Put students in small groups to identify characteristics of television shows or movies they have seen. After students have listed and shared positive and negative aspects of their movies or television programs, others who saw the production might add their own reactions for consideration.

VISUAL CONNECTIONS

Exploring the Subject. Until *Driving Miss Daisy,* Alfred Uhry had written no plays except musicals. Based on real persons and originally scheduled to run only five weeks in a nonprofit theater with 74 seats, the play won the 1988 Pulitzer Prize.

The movie, adapted by Uhry, won the Academy Award for Best Picture of 1989.

the movie is the story of the companionship that develops between stubborn, suspicious Miss Daisy (Jessica Tandy), a wealthy Jewish widow of seventy-two, and her resilient chauffeur, Hoke (Morgan Freeman), a widower about a decade younger than she is. Essentially, it's about how he changes her. He's made upright, considerate, humane—he's made perfect—so that nothing will disturb our appreciation of the gentle, bittersweet reverie we're watching. But it's acted (and directed) eloquently. Tandy and Freeman achieve a beautiful equilibrium. And Dan Aykroyd comes through with a fine performance as Miss Daisy's good-old-boy son.

Pauline Kael, *The New Yorker*

SELECTION AMENDMENT
Description of change: excerpted
Rationale: to focus on the concept of critical reviews presented in this chapter

A checklist may help you quickly assess students' critical reviews:

1. title and overall evaluation
2. concise plot statement
3. judgments and examples of important elements

CLOSURE

Ask students to list the purpose and the major features of a critical review. Have them recall criteria for evaluating plot, direction, acting, and other specific elements. ■

Writing a Mini-Review of a Movie or Television Program

Prewriting. Choose a movie or television show to review. Before anything else, think clearly about your standards: the elements, and qualities you'll be looking for. If possible, work with a group to identify the most important story elements, like characterization and plot, acting, and photography. Remember that a mini-review is condensed; you won't have much space.

As you watch the movie or program, make notes of specific details and your reactions. Then, review your notes to focus your ideas. You can use a simple focusing tool like *The good things about the movie (program) are* ___. *The things that don't work well are* ___.

Writing, Evaluating, and Revising. Remember that the reader is looking to you for basic information in a very short space: title, director and writer (if possible), actors, and a one- or two-sentence plot summary. In the body of your short review, use as many details as possible so readers can picture what you mean. When you have a draft, ask a partner to answer these questions: Is there enough plot information for people who haven't seen the movie? Are specific elements of the movie praised or criticized? Does the review bring the movie or show to life? Use your partner's evaluation as you revise. Try to keep your review as short as Pauline Kael's review of *Driving Miss Daisy*.

Proofreading and Publishing. Proofread your revised review, ask your partner to check it, and correct all errors. (Titles of films and television programs are underlined or italicized.) Then, go on the air with your review: Stage it for your classmates in pairs as though you were Roger Ebert and Gene Siskel (above), or another pair of film reviewers.

Include your review in your **portfolio** with a reflection: How did this paper affect the way you look at movies? Why?

VISUAL CONNECTIONS

Exploring the Subject. Gene Siskel and Roger Ebert are movie critics for the *Chicago Tribune* and *Chicago Sun-Times,* respectively. They are also co-hosts of a movie review show where they show approval or disapproval of a film with a thumbs-up or a thumbs-down gesture.

INTEGRATING THE LANGUAGE ARTS

Speaking Link. Students might co-operate for paired film reviews. Assign one student the main review of the film that he or she will give first. The other student should develop ideas to present but also must respond spontaneously to the partner's main review.

If possible, videotape the reviews. If students write about current movies or recent additions to video rental stores, they might submit their reviews to the school newspaper.

MAKING CONNECTIONS

RESPONDING TO LITERATURE
OBJECTIVE

- To write a personal response that relates thoughts and feelings about a poem, a story, or a play

RESPONDING TO LITERATURE

Teaching Strategies

Point out that most people do not read literature or see films to marvel at the writer's craft or to closely analyze elements. They simply hope the story will make them laugh or cry or give some insight into their lives. Tell students that this lesson will let them respond more personally, emotionally, and informally to a poem, a story, or a play.

USING THE SELECTION
The Bean Eaters

1

Details of food and tableware suggest age and poverty.

2

Brooks knows that readers will identify with people who are "Mostly Good" and not seemingly perfect.

3

What might be suggested by associating "remembering" with "twinklings and twinges"? ["Twinklings" might suggest bright and shiny memories; "twinges" could suggest pain or regret.]

MAKING CONNECTIONS

RESPONDING TO LITERATURE

Many times in life, "Don't take it personally" is good advice—but not when you're reading literature. As you saw in this chapter, even for a formal critical essay the starting point is your individual reaction. Personal involvement is one of the pleasures and powers of art in any form: to feel that what you're reading, seeing, or hearing makes a direct connection.

Here's a poem you may have read and then one reader's response to it. As you read, think of your own thoughts and feelings about the poem. Does it remind you of anyone? What does it make you think of? What do you think of the poem?

The Bean Eaters
by Gwendolyn Brooks

They eat beans mostly, this old yellow pair.
Dinner is a casual affair.
1 Plain chipware on a plain and creaking wood,
Tin flatware.

2 Two who are Mostly Good.
Two who have lived their day,
But keep on putting on their clothes
and putting things away.

And remembering . . .
3 Remembering, with twinklings and twinges,
As they lean over the beans in their rented back room that
   is full of beads and receipts and dolls and cloths,
      tobacco crumbs, vases and fringes.

Related Expression Skills. Illustrations or photographs often accompany literary works. Guide students in a discussion of how the photograph of this elderly couple influences their response to the poem or how the poem influences their response to the photograph.

You may want to remind students to respond to the **"The Bean Eaters"** as active readers. Give them a few minutes to list their thoughts and feelings by clustering or freewriting. Ask for volunteers to share some of these responses with the class before reading the response in their textbooks.

To emphasize the informal and subjective nature of personal responses, have students read the textbook response and count the number of times the textbook uses *I* [11], *I thought* [4], and variations of *I felt* [4].

HERE'S HOW

Response

I guess at first I just felt sort of sorry for these older people. What I thought was really sad was that they seemed to be good people, but they just didn't have anything—they must be very lonely. Then I thought about this "remembering" and the things their room seems to be full of. And I thought about all the times I felt down and would get out my old scrapbook full of stupid, little things like drawings and postcards from friends and ribbons I won six years ago. And I would feel sad that those times were past, but glad that I had them to remember. And then I thought these people still have their memories—their "twinklings." And I didn't feel so sad about them anymore.

Now write your own response to the poem—or to any poem, story, or play that you want to choose. Write it as if you're talking to someone you feel comfortable with— perhaps your best friend.

GUIDELINES

Responses will vary. Since the audience is supposed to be a friend, you may want to evaluate responses at the student's option, perhaps as extra credit.

• To write or deliver a speech that is a
critical analysis

CRITICAL ANALYSIS ACROSS THE CURRICULUM

Teaching Strategies

One purpose of a critical analysis is to provide information about how something works. Stress that students can be confident that subjects they find interesting and enjoyable will be interesting and enjoyable to someone else (school, hobbies, new products, and so forth).

Each student should list a subject, its purpose or value, its parts and features, and how it works before beginning a rough draft. Ask students to find or invent a magazine or a club that would be interested in their topics. Encourage them to publish or present their work in class or in a real magazine or club.

Give students an opportunity to react to each other's work before they finish their final drafts. A good approach is to have students read in small groups and have listeners ask questions at any point where they feel confused. They can stop at that point and discuss the problem.

CRITICAL ANALYSIS ACROSS THE CURRICULUM

In critical analysis, you use a knowledge of elements (component parts) to analyze something in detail. You can apply this skill not only to short stories but also to cars, snow skis, scientific equipment—to anything whose parts and features you know well. Following is an analysis of CD changers.

from CD & VIDEODISC PLAYERS

Remember jukeboxes? Today's CD equivalents can hold and play as many as 100 discs at a time . . . and sell for as little as $400. Here you select which discs you want to play by flipping through a three-ring binder that holds the small booklets that come with the CDs, and you enter the numbers of the desired discs via a remote control.

The more-common and less-costly three- to six-disc changers generally come in two varieties: the carousel, which rotates discs on a round platter, and changers that store discs in a small cartridge called a "magazine" and slide them out one at a time for playback. Our tests indicate that the carousel-type CD changers tend to be more reliable than those that use magazine cartridges to hold the discs.

Note that not all carousel players are created equal; some, for example, allow changing one or more CDs while another is playing. The 100-disc megachangers are a little slow and clunky in operation, but they make up for it with convenience and capacity.

. . . Most experts agree that the audible differences between players of any kind are actually quite small, though not all CD players perform equally well in all areas. It's generally believed that dual D/A (digital-to-analog) converters offer the best design, at least from a theoretical point of view . . . , but experts advise that the type of D/A converter often isn't as important as how well the CD player is designed in the first place.

Consumers Digest

What are you interested in and fairly expert in (if you do say so yourself): maps? athletic equipment? telescopes? clarinets? Choose something that you would enjoy explaining clearly—either in writing or in an informal talk.

You can analyze, as in the example above, a certain *type* or *category* of your subject area. For example, if your subject area is "bicycles," you could analyze the recent "hybrid bikes." Or you can analyze a *particular example*, such as a specific new model of hybrid bicycle, whose features you'd like to scrutinize.

If you're writing your analysis, imagine that it's going to be published in a magazine specifically for lovers of your subject (and give the magazine a name: *Map Maniacs*, say, or *Clarinet Freaks*). If you're outlining and delivering a talk, imagine that it's for a club (like the Grand Order of Off-road Vehicle Owners).

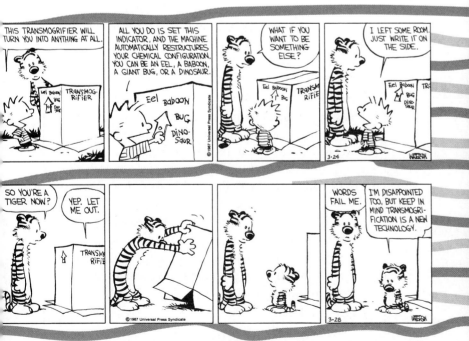

Calvin & Hobbes copyright 1987 Watterson. Distributed by Universal Press Syndicate. Reprinted with permission. All rights reserved.

GUIDELINES

Analyses will vary but should contain the topic's purpose or value, how it works, and its features or parts.

VISUAL CONNECTIONS

About the Artist. *Calvin and Hobbes,* a comic strip about a young boy and his stuffed tiger, was created by Bill Watterson in 1985. Watterson, born in 1958, worked briefly as a political cartoonist before developing *Calvin and Hobbes.* The cartoon first appeared in 1985 and became one of the most popular cartoons in syndication before Watterson retired in 1996 .

WRITING A RESEARCH PAPER: EXPOSITION

OBJECTIVES

- To select an appropriate topic for a research paper and to use various prewriting techniques to prepare an outline for a research paper
- To write a draft of a research paper and prepare a Works Cited list
- To evaluate and revise the content and organization of a research paper
- To proofread a research paper and prepare it for publication

WRITING-IN-PROGRESS ASSIGNMENTS

Major Assignment: Writing a research paper
Cumulative Writing Assignments: The chart below shows the sequence of cumulative assignments that will guide students as they write a research paper. These writing assignments form the instructional core of Chapter 11.

PREWRITING

Writing Assignment
- Part 1: Developing a Specific Topic p. 409
- Part 2: Beginning Your Research p. 413
- Part 3: Collecting and Evaluating Sources p. 419
- Part 4: Preparing Source Cards p. 419
- Part 5: Planning and Note Taking p. 423
- Part 6: Preparing an Outline p. 425

WRITING

Writing Assignment
- Part 7: Writing Your First Draft p. 435

EVALUATING AND REVISING

Writing Assignment
- Part 8: Evaluating and Revising Your Report p. 437

PROOFREADING AND PUBLISHING

Writing Assignment
- Part 9: Proofreading and Publishing Your Report p. 439

In addition, exercises 1–5 provide practice in evaluating topics for research; analyzing purpose, audience, and tone; analyzing audience for your report; using library and community resources; and analyzing a writer's revisions.

cross CURRICULUM

Documenting History on Video

Consider asking students to use the research skills presented in Chapter 11 to investigate some event in history as it affected people in students' families or communities. And, rather than producing a traditional research paper, ask students to create instead a script and a video that document their research. To help students prepare to make a video, show them segments of any of Ken Burns's documentaries on baseball, the Civil War, or the American West and have them discuss the elements of the video format.

- **Research** Students should begin their research by asking family members or neighbors about their experiences or about changes they witnessed in the community during a particular historic event. Students might suggest events such as the assassination of John F. Kennedy, the first lunar landing, or the release of U.S. hostages from Iran. Once an event is decided on, students need to complete more research to obtain necessary background. (Have students review pp. 412–419.) Students should use their research to form the questions they will ask their interview subjects. They should also research with an eye toward visual images that can help them tell the story on video. Students may find photographs, film clips, and maps or posters useful.

- **Interviewing** Have students review pp. 943–944 for ideas on conducting an interview. Students should interview in pairs, so that one student may ask questions while the partner runs the camera. Ask your school librarian or multimedia expert to demonstrate how to edit videotape. Give students time in class to work on scripts for their videos.

- **Works Cited** Finally, ask that students include with their videos a Works Cited page that documents their research. Ask students to follow the MLA format and to work again in pairs to proofread and revise each other's documentation.

INTEGRATING THE LANGUAGE ARTS

SELECTION	READING AND LITERATURE	WRITING AND CRITICAL THINKING	LANGUAGE AND SYNTAX	SPEAKING, LISTENING, AND OTHER EXPRESSION SKILLS
• from *"America's Ancient Sky-watchers"* by Robert B. Carlson pp. 402–404 • from *"To Break the Unbreakable Codes"* by James R. Chiles p. 411	• Identifying facts and theories p. 405 • Identifying supporting details pp. 405, 441–442 • Identifying sources of information p. 405 • Reading for purpose, audience, and tone pp. 411–412	• Writing about personal experiences p. 405 • Formulating an opinion p. 405 • Identifying information sources p. 405 • Evaluating topics for research pp. 409, 424 • Thinking about purpose and audience pp. 411–413, 444–445 • Collecting and evaluating sources and preparing source cards p. 419 • Taking notes pp. 423, 442 • Writing thesis statements pp. 424, 442 • Preparing an outline and a *Works Cited* list pp. 425, 435 • Evaluating and revising a report p. 437 • Analyzing and writing a book report pp. 441–442 • Writing objective questions pp. 444–445	• Punctuating titles correctly pp. 419, 423, 435 • Proofreading for errors in grammar, usage, and mechanics pp. 439, 442	• Discussing questions about purpose, audience, and tone pp. 411–412 • Interviewing classmates about a topic p. 412 • Brainstorming with classmates about library and community resources p. 419 • Evaluating and revising a classmate's report p. 437 • Using visuals in an oral presentation pp. 443–444 • Conducting a public opinion poll pp. 444–445 • Sharing results of a public opinion poll pp. 444–445

SUGGESTED INTEGRATED UNIT PLAN

This plan gives suggestions on how to integrate the major strands of the language arts with this chapter.

You may begin with this chapter on writing a research paper, or you may use the suggested examples of writings that required research. You can then integrate speaking/listening and language concepts with both the writing and the literature.

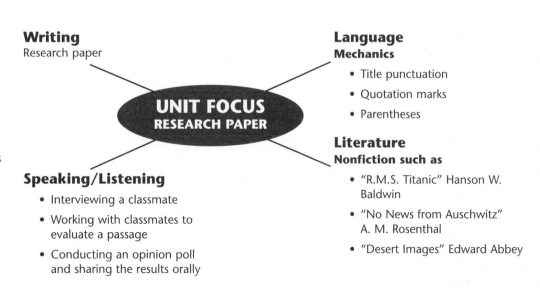

Common Characteristics

- Content that is mainly factual and comprehensive
- Precise language that is neutral and unbiased
- Documentation of facts
- Technical terms with definitions
- Avoidance of first person point of view
- Organization of ideas usually from least to most important

Writing
Research paper

UNIT FOCUS
RESEARCH PAPER

Speaking/Listening

- Interviewing a classmate
- Working with classmates to evaluate a passage
- Conducting an opinion poll and sharing the results orally

Language
Mechanics

- Title punctuation
- Quotation marks
- Parentheses

Literature
Nonfiction such as

- "R.M.S. Titanic" Hanson W. Baldwin
- "No News from Auschwitz" A. M. Rosenthal
- "Desert Images" Edward Abbey

CHAPTER 11: WRITING A RESEARCH PAPER: EXPOSITION

Use this guide for creating an instructional plan that addresses the individual needs of your students. Assignments followed by the following symbol (∗) may be completed out of class. Times given for pacing lessons are estimated.

CHAPTER PLANNING GUIDE—PUPIL'S EDITION

LESSONS	LITERARY MODEL pp. 402–404 From "America's Ancient Skywatchers" by Robert B. Carlson	PREWRITING pp. 407–425	
		Generating Ideas	**Gathering/Organizing**
DEVELOPMENTAL PROGRAM	🕐 **30–35 minutes** • Read the model aloud and have students answer questions on p. 405 orally.	🕐 **90 minutes** • Main Assignment: Looking Ahead p. 406 • Finding and Limiting a Subject pp. 407–413 • Exercises 1, 2 pp. 409, 411 • Writing Assignment: Parts 1, 2 pp. 409, 413	🕐 **90 minutes** • Finding and Evaluating Sources pp. 414–419 • Writing Notes pp. 419, 422 • Exercise 4 p. 419 • Writing Assignment: Parts 3, 4, 5, 6 pp. 419, 423, 425 • Planning, Recording and Organizing Information pp. 420–422
CORE PROGRAM	🕐 **30–35 minutes** • Assign students pairs to read the model and to answers questions on p. 405 orally.	🕐 **40–45 minutes** • Main Assignment: Looking Ahead p. 406 • Finding and Limiting a Subject pp. 407–413 • Exercises 2, 3 pp. 411–412 • Writing Assignment: Parts 1, 2 pp. 409, 413∗	🕐 **70-75 minutes** • Finding and Evaluating Sources pp. 414–419 • Writing Notes pp. 419, 422 • Exercise 4 p. 419 • Writing Assignment: Parts 3, 4, 5, 6 pp. 419, 423, 425∗ • Planning, Recording, and Organizing pp. 420–422 • Critical Thinking pp. 423–424
ACCELERATED PROGRAM	🕐 **30–35 minutes** • Assign students to read the model independently and to answer the questions on p. 405	🕐 **25–30 minutes** • Main Assignment: Looking Ahead p. 406 • Thinking About Purpose, Audience, and Tone pp. 410–413 • Exercise 3 p. 412 • Writing Assignment: Parts 1, 2 pp. 409, 413∗	🕐 **45–50 minutes** • Resources Charts pp. 414–415 • Guidelines Chart pp. 416–418 • Writing Assignment: Parts 3, 4, 5, 6 pp. 419, 423, 425∗ • Writing Notes pp. 419, 422 • Critical Thinking pp. 423–424∗

CHAPTER PLANNING GUIDE—PROGRAM RESOURCES

	LITERARY MODEL	PREWRITING
PRINT	• Reading Master 11, *Practice for Assessment in Reading, Vocabulary, and Spelling,* p. 11	• Prewriting, *Strategies for Writing,* pp. 55–56 • Informing Others, *English Workshop,* pp. 51–58
MEDIA	• Fine Art Transparency 8, *Transparency Binder*	• Graphic Organizers 19–20, *Transparency Binder* • *Writer's Workshop 2:* Informative Report

WRITING pp. 426–435	EVALUATING AND REVISING pp. 436–438	PROOFREADING AND PUBLISHING pp. 439–440

🕐 **70–75 minutes**
• Writing Your First Draft
  pp. 426–430
• Mechanics Hint p. 427
• A Writer's Model
  pp. 430–435
• Writing Assignment:
  Part 7 p. 435
	🕐 **50–55 minutes**
	• Exercise 5 pp. 436–437
	  in pairs
	• Writing Assignment:
	  Part 8 p. 437
	• Evaluating and Revising
	  Chart p. 438
		🕐 **30–35 minutes**
		• Proofreading and
		  Publishing p. 439
		• Writing Assignment:
		  Part 9 p. 439
		• Reflecting p. 439
		• A Student Model
		  p. 440

🕐 **30–35 minutes**
• Writing Your First Draft
  pp. 426–430
• Mechanics Hint p. 427
• A Writer's Model
  pp. 430–435*
• Writing Assignment:
  Part 7 p. 435*
	🕐 **40–45 minutes**
	• Exercise 5 pp. 436–437*
	• Writing Assignment:
	  Part 8 p. 437
	• Evaluating and Revising
	  Chart p. 438
		🕐 **20–25 minutes**
		• Writing Assignment:
		  Part 9 p. 439
		• Reflecting p. 439
		• A Student Model
		  p. 440*

🕐 **25–30 minutes**
• Mechanics Hint p. 427
• Guidelines Charts
  pp. 428–429
• A Writer's Model
  pp. 430–435*
• Writing Assignment:
  Part 7 p. 435*
	🕐 **40–45 minutes**
	• Writing Assignment:
	  Part 8 p. 437
	• Evaluating and Revising
	  Chart p. 438
		🕐 **20–25 minutes**
		• Writing Assignment:
		  Part 9 p. 439
		• Reflecting p. 439

 Computer disk or CD-ROM   Overhead transparencies

WRITING	EVALUATING AND REVISING	PROOFREADING AND PUBLISHING
• Writing, *Strategies for Writing*, p. 57 • Quotation Marks, *English Workshop*, pp. 297–299	• Evaluating and Revising, *Strategies for Writing*, p. 58	• Proofreading Practice, *Strategies for Writing*, p. 60
• *Language Workshop:* Lesson 42	• Revision Trans- parencies 19–20, *Transparency Binder*	

 ELEMENTS OF WRITING: CURRICULUM CONNECTIONS

Writing Workshop
• A Book Report That Evaluates pp. 441–442

Making Connections
• The Visual Arts pp. 443–444
• Creating Research Sources: Public Opinion Polls pp. 444–445

ASSESSMENT OPTIONS

Summative Assessment
Holistic Scoring: Prompts and Models pp. 45–51

Portfolio Assessment
Portfolio forms, *Portfolio Assessment* pp. 5–25, 44–48

Reflection
Writing Process Log, *Strategies for Writing* p. 54
Self-assessment Record, *Portfolio Assessment* p. 19

Ongoing Assessment
Proofreading, *Strategies for Writing* p. 59

LESSON 1 *(pp. 400–405)*
EXPLORING YOUR WORLD

OBJECTIVES

- To respond to a sample research report
- To analyze the structure and content of a sample research report

MOTIVATION

Bring an assortment of high-interest, research-based articles to class for students to read.

PROGRAM MANAGER

CHAPTER 11

- **Computer Guided Instruction** For a related assignment that students may use for additional instruction and practice, see **Informative Report** in *Writer's Workshop 2 CD-ROM.*

- **Summative Assessment** For a writing prompt, including grading criteria and student models, see *Holistic Scoring: Prompts and Models*, pp. 45–51.

- **Extension/Enrichment** See **Fine Art Transparency 8,** *Joan of Arc* by Jules Bastien-Lepage. For suggestions on how to tie the transparency to instruction, review teacher's notes in *Fine Art and Instructional Transparencies for Writing*, p. 45.

- **Reading Support** For help with the reading selection, pp. 402–404, see **Reading Master 11** in *Practice for Assessment in Reading, Vocabulary, and Spelling*, p. 11.

VISUAL CONNECTIONS
Detail from *Cosmic Blink*

Exploring the Subject. This detail from the mural *Cosmic Blink* illustrates some of the achievements of science and commemorates the people who expanded our understanding of the universe. The three large figures are, from left to right, Kepler, Einstein, and Newton.

11 WRITING A RESEARCH PAPER: EXPOSITION

You may want to read the excerpt from the article **"America's Ancient Skywatchers"** aloud. Then you might invite students to discuss the article and the second **Reader's Response** question that follows it.

Next, guide students through an analysis of the article and lead a discussion of possible sources of information for such a report.

After you and your students have discussed the article and various research sources, students can answer the **Writer's Craft** questions independently. Suggest that students re-read the article before answering the questions.

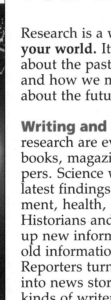

Exploring Your World

Research is a way of **exploring your world.** It's how we learn about the past and the present, and how we make decisions about the future.

Writing and You. Reports of research are everywhere—in books, magazines, and newspapers. Science writers report the latest findings on the environment, health, and astronomy. Historians and biographers dig up new information or give old information a new twist. Reporters turn their research into news stories. What other kinds of writers write research reports?

As You Read. Researchers have discovered that the ancient Incan and Mayan people knew a great deal about astronomy. As you read the following report, see if you can tell which information is factual and which is yet to be proved.

Billy Morrow Jackson, detail of *Cosmic Blink* (1988–89). Oil on panel. Entire painting is 48 × 96". Collection of Parkland College, Champaign, Ill.

QUOTATION FOR THE DAY
"We shall not cease from exploration and the end of all our exploring will be to arrive where we started and know the place for the first time." (T. S. Eliot, 1888–1965, poet and dramatist)

You may wish to ask students to freewrite for a few minutes about what this quotation means to them. Then, several volunteers might read their responses to the class. Lead students to understand that exploration plays an important part in researching and writing reports. Just as travelers explore new lands or astronauts explore space, writers explore by finding and considering information.

MEETING individual NEEDS

LEP/ESL

General Strategies. One way to assist students in expanding their vocabularies is to offer practice in determining the meanings of words from their contexts. The excerpt from **"America's Ancient Skywatchers"** provides fertile ground for this activity. For example, point out that the statement "astronomy was not a science as we who are schooled in the Western tradition tend to think of it" reveals that astronomy is considered a science.

Have students use context clues to define *tapestry, discern, shamans, illuminate, celestial,* and *fanciful.*

RETEACHING

Give students copies of daily newspapers and let each student choose an article of interest. Ask students if they can tell from the articles what sources of information the writers used. Did the writers use interviews, print sources, or other media sources?

402

FROM

AMERICA'S ANCIENT SKYWATCHERS

by Robert B. Carlson

1 For many pre-Columbian Americans, whether Inca, Maya, Anasazi—or indeed many among their living descendants— astronomy was not a science as we who are schooled in the Western tradition

2 tend to think of it. Rather, the movements of sun and moon were the journeys of gods personified. In Mesoamerica the stars and the bright planets in their intricate wanderings were often conceived of as gods moving through the night sky en route to rebirth each

3 sunup. They wove an enormous celestial <u>tapestry</u> mirrored in the warp and weft of the lives of the people themselves.

USING THE SELECTION
from America's Ancient Skywatchers

1

The Incas established a great empire centered in Peru that lasted until the Spanish arrived in the 1500s. The Maya lived in Central America and flourished before the Spanish conquest. The Anasazi were cliff dwellers who lived before A.D. 1300 in the area where New Mexico, Arizona, Utah, and Colorado meet.

2

Why do you think people have often thought of celestial bodies as gods? [Responses will vary. One possibility is that celestial bodies are very impressive, and people tend to deify what impresses them.]

3

In weaving, the *warp* are the threads that run lengthwise in the loom, and the *weft* are the threads that go back and forth across the warp. In this metaphor, Carlson is relating weaving to the movements of the stars and planets and to the events in people's lives.

CLOSURE

Ask the class to give a brief definition of *research*. Then, ask students to name three places where they encounter writing that has research.

ENRICHMENT

Ask students to find examples of well-researched articles in textbooks for other courses, such as social studies or science. Have them analyze why the articles are interesting and what sources the writers may have used. ■

To observe and predict the recurrent paths of divine lights was to know the fates of kings and empires, to discern the proper day for rituals, to forecast animal migrations, the season of the life-giving rain, and the time for planting. The power to foretell required that observers, probably spe-

4 cially trained shamans or priests, make accurate records and preserve them. The information must have been accumulated over generations and generations, the observers

5 using naked-eye sighting techniques to discover the patterns of movement in the

6 universe. Their knowledge reached a level comparable to that of ancient cultures of the Old World.

"...the movements of sun and moon were the journeys of gods personified."

Their records were preserved in calendars made of wood, string, and stone or, in Mesoamerica, written in accordion-fold books of animal hide or plaster-coated bark paper. Heavenly comings and goings were also recorded in the alignment of buildings and in city plans. These provided sight lines to mark significant risings and settings of celestial bodies. Such constructions often approached our own scientific astronomy in accuracy, but they had a sacred purpose.

7 We might compare this combination of technical knowledge and religious motive to a church window so placed that sunlight passing through it will illuminate a saint's statue on the saint's day.

Stone Calendar

4
In gathering research for this article, why would books or articles on shamans be useful? [Stories of their experiences and observations might provide important and interesting details.]

5
The refracting telescope was invented in the early 1600s.

6
England's Stonehenge is a familiar example of an ancient alignment that may have traced the movements of celestial bodies.

7
Does the author's analogy help you understand the ancient architects' purpose? [Responses will vary.]

8

invested: endowed, thought of as having a quality of

9

Note the transitional expressions that the author uses in this paragraph to lend clarity and coherence: *too* in the first sentence and *just as* and *so* in the last sentence.

10

The Nazca were among the earliest settlers in Peru, arriving there in the first centuries A.D. They made colorful pottery, some of which was shaped like animals and vegetables.

11

Students might know another explanation sometimes offered for the Nazca Lines— that they were made by extraterrestrials as landing sites for spaceships. Are such explanations reasonable? [Responses will vary and could produce a lively discussion. Interested students might research this idea.]

12

mutually exclusive: incompatible

---

8   Earth too was invested with divinity. Many
9 pre-Columbian American groups believed that their ancestors emerged from the underworld by way of a cave—the mouth of the earth. The earth's surface they divided into four quarters, often endowed

Nazca Lines (Hummingbird)

with distinctive trees, animals, deities, periods of time, and colors. Just as they marked the sky, so they set down paths of pilgrimage on the sacred landscape.

    The most notable—and controversial—of these routes may be the ground drawings made on the bone-dry desert of southern Peru. The geometric figures of animals and plants; the spirals, zigzags, trapezoids, triangles; and the straight lines that stretch as far
10 as the eye can see—all these are called Nazca Lines for the culture that established itself in that forbidding terrain 2,000 years ago.

11   **M**any speculations, some reasonable, some fanciful, have been made about the significance of the lines. One explanation suggests that the straight lines were aligned to astronomical risings and settings. Another that at least some of the effigy figures represented constellations. Still another idea, recently investigated in depth by astronomer-anthropologist Anthony Aveni and anthropologists Gary Urton and Persis Clarkson, maintains that the long, straight

Nazca Lines (Bird)

lines connected sacred sites and marked ritual pathways walked by celebrants to make offerings at
12 the far ends. These hypotheses are not mutually exclusive; all may have an element of truth.

Nazca Lines (Spider)

READER'S RESPONSE

1. When the ancient Americans looked up at the night sky, they saw more than just stars and planets—they saw stories in the sky. As a child (or even now), you may have done the same thing, perhaps at a summer camp-out. In a brief journal entry, tell about your own skywatching stories or experiences.
2. Like the ancient skywatchers, people who believe in astrology depend on the stars to plan their daily lives. What's your opinion of astrology?

WRITER'S CRAFT

3. What's the difference between a *fact* and a *theory*? Give two examples of facts in this report. Where does Carlson give some theories?
4. Writers of research reports must support their main ideas with specific examples and details. Give three details that Carlson uses to support his idea that Mesoamericans believed the movements of the sun and moon were related to the activities of their gods.
5. Carlson identifies some sources for some of the information he is sharing. What are those sources?

VISUAL CONNECTIONS
Exploring the Subject. The Nazca Lines are huge geometric forms and animal shapes scratched into the desert in southern Peru. Among the shapes are flowers, a monkey, a spider, and a bird. Some of the shapes are hundreds of feet in length.

ANSWERS
Reader's Response

Responses will vary.

1. Some students may not have had skywatching experiences. Allow such students to write fictional accounts.
2. Students should give reasons for their opinions.

Writer's Craft

Answers may vary.

3. A fact can be proven to be true; a theory is an assumption or set of assumptions. Examples of facts include the location of Nazca Lines and their shapes. Examples of theories include ideas about the role of shamans and speculation about the significance of Nazca Lines.
4. Details include the fact that observers recorded the movements of celestial bodies in calendars and in the alignments of buildings, and that they used these movements to decide days for rituals.
5. Carlson mentions astronomer-anthropologist Anthony Aveni and anthropologists Gary Urton and Persis Clarkson as sources.

LESSON 2 *(p. 406)*
WAYS TO DEVELOP RESEARCH

The examples in the textbook relate to four basic methods of development that can be used for research writing. These include narration (examples 1 and 2), description (3 and 4), classification (5), and evaluation (6 and 7). Review these terms with students and ask them to supply additional examples like the ones in the textbook. ■

INTEGRATING THE LANGUAGE ARTS

Literature Link. To make the point that authors often do research for various types of writing, have students read a short story such as "Trap of Gold" by Louis L'Amour or "Leiningen Versus the Ants" by Carl Stephenson. Tell students that although the purpose in a short story is primarily literary rather than informative, research is often involved in writing a short story. After each student has read a short story, ask him or her to determine what information the author might have researched and what sources the author might have used.

Ways to Develop Research

You live at a time when you can find out more than you want to know about almost anything. Newspapers, magazines, and journals give the latest information about research results. Universities, libraries, businesses, and others post regularly updated information on the Internet.

Some of these research papers are informal, and some are formal. Robert Carlson's paper on ancient skywatchers is *informal* because it doesn't give a detailed list of sources. A *formal* report, on the other hand, like the ones in journals (periodicals that publish scientific reports) and the ones you write for school, always has a detailed list of sources. Readers of formal reports demand to know, "Where does this information come from?" Reports can be developed in various ways. Here are some examples:

- in a biographical report, describing the role your favorite athlete played in an important game
- in a world history report, recounting political changes in Africa during the twentieth century
- in an art report, describing a Navajo sand painting
- in a science report, describing a space-shuttle liftoff
- in a report for a biology class, classifying the functions of different parts of the human brain
- in a workplace report, evaluating your job duties and describing your short- and long-term career goals
- in a report for a chemistry class, evaluating the claims made in TV commercials for beauty products

LOOKING AHEAD

In the main assignment in this chapter, you'll write a formal research paper. Before you write the actual report, you'll need to collect and organize information on your topic. Keep in mind that a research paper

- presents factual information about the topic
- presents information from several sources
- tells readers the source of the information

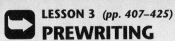
OBJECTIVES

- To evaluate topics for research
- To choose a subject and limit it to a specific topic
- To analyze the purpose, audience, and tone of a paragraph from a report
- To analyze, through discussion, the audience of a report
- To develop research questions
- To identify and evaluate resources
- To prepare source cards for a report
- To record and organize information for a report
- To prepare a final outline for a report

Writing a Research Paper

Finding and Limiting a Subject

You've probably heard the expression "starting off on the right foot." In writing a research paper, the "right foot" is an interesting subject that you can develop into a suitable topic.

Choosing a Subject

A good research subject is one that's interesting to both you and your readers. To be interesting, however, your subject does not have to be exotic or far away. In looking for a subject, don't neglect what's available right in "your own back yard." After all, you may not be able to travel to the ruins in Peru, but you can discover the origins of your town or village just by visiting your library or historical society. Remember that some research captures our attention and imagination merely by shedding new light on familiar subjects.

To find possible research subjects, you can

- browse the World Wide Web using a directory that organizes Web sites into subject categories
- look through the materials in your library's vertical file
- browse through the nonfiction shelves in the library or along the documentary shelves in a videotape store
- skim articles of local and national interest in current newspapers and magazines
- watch television programs, such as *NOVA*, on scientific or historical topics
- talk with adult relatives or friends who have unusual or interesting jobs or backgrounds
- visit local museums and historical societies

PROGRAM MANAGER

PREWRITING

- **Self-Assessment** Before beginning instruction of the writing process, see **Writing Process Log** in *Strategies for Writing*, p. 54.
- **Heuristics** To help students generate ideas, see **Prewriting** in *Strategies for Writing*, pp. 55–56.
- **Instructional Support** See **Graphic Organizers 19** and **20.** For suggestions on how to tie the transparencies to instruction, review teacher's notes in *Fine Art and Instructional Transparencies for Writing*, pp. 89, 91.

QUOTATION FOR THE DAY

"Penetrating so many secrets, we cease to believe in the unknowable. But there it sits nevertheless, calmly licking its chops." (H. L. Mencken, 1880–1956, American journalist, editor, and critic)

Lead students in a discussion of the seemingly infinite amount of information available today. Tell students that during their research they will probably discover that they are unable to include in their reports everything there is to know about their topics.

Ask students to talk about tasks that they've found overwhelming. Perhaps they've had to mow, rake, trim, and weed a whole yard. Maybe they've washed dishes at a busy restaurant. Point out that they probably made it through the tasks by taking one step at a time. And they probably were proud of their accomplishments afterward.

Tell students that writing a research report is similar. The task may seem overwhelming, but when taken one step at a time, it's not.

MEETING *individual* **NEEDS**

LEP/ESL

General Strategies. You may want to encourage English-language learners who were born outside the United States to write reports dealing with current events in their native countries. This strategy reinforces the links between students and their native cultures and offers them topics that are probably of personal interest to them.

AT-RISK STUDENTS

While most of the exercises call for a partner or for group participation, you may want to plan even more cooperative work. At-risk students can benefit greatly from discussing progress on their reports with their classmates. In fact, you may want to pair each student with a research partner or to have students work in small groups throughout the study of this chapter.

408 *Writing a Research Paper*

Limiting Your Subject to a Specific Topic

You may already know that the key to good writing is using specific details. Even if your research paper were twenty pages long, you still wouldn't have space to discuss a broad subject in any detail. Suppose, for example, you chose the subject "the civil rights movement." You'd be faced with the impossible task of trying to cover dozens of subtopics, including "voting rights," "sit-ins," and "Montgomery bus boycott."

Maybe you chose the subject "the civil rights movement" because you vaguely remember an interesting magazine article about it. But at this point you have no specific information. Start by getting some general knowledge, an overview, of your subject. That will help you identify some smaller parts of the broad subject. Here are some ways to go about getting an overview.

- Read two or three general articles in reference books like encyclopedias. Notice headings and subheadings in the articles.
- Search the World Wide Web for pages or sites containing keywords related to your subject.
- Look up your subject in the *Readers' Guide to Periodical Literature* or in the library's card catalog or online catalog. Note the topics that are listed under the subject headings.
- Discuss your subject with someone (a teacher, neighbor, parent, and so on) who has expert knowledge about it.

Selecting a Suitable Topic

After getting an overview of your subject, you will probably have several possible topics in mind. But they may not all work well as topics for a research paper. To choose the best possible topic, ask yourself the following questions:

1. *Are there a variety of sources for this topic?* A highly personal topic such as "my experience on opening night of the class play" would not be a good choice because it has only one source: *you*. On the other hand, "favorite opening night experiences of three leading ladies" might have real possibilities. You

This lesson provides information about the first stage of the writing process and starts students on writing assignments that lead to students' finished research reports. The prewriting stage of the writing process is divided into several steps, so it's natural to break your teaching into those steps. Allow plenty of time to discuss each

step and focus on students' comprehension. Be sure that students understand how to apply each step to the preparation of their research reports before proceeding. Here are five divisions with textbook headings to use when teaching this lesson:

Finding and Limiting a Subject. Have students generate suitable subjects, and write them on the chalkboard. Then, for each

could read the autobiographies of several famous stage actresses and perhaps interview the "star" of a local theater group.

2. *Are sources of information readily available?* You may have trouble finding the information you need if a topic is too recent or too technical, or if the source material isn't available locally. For example, information about "legal precedents for *Brown v. Board of Education of Topeka*" would be too technical to appear in most popular publications.

EXERCISE 1 **Evaluating Topics for Research**

Which of the following topics could you use for a five-page research report? Some topics are too personal or technical, and some would be difficult to find information about. Which topics are too general to be covered in detail in a short paper? For each topic that seems unsuitable, first identify the problem, and then suggest a more limited or workable topic.

1. Chinese immigration to America
2. two successful experiments in a recent U.S. space mission
3. detailed analysis of evidence of microbial life in a Mars meteorite
4. ancient art of Egyptian hieroglyphics
5. my favorite grade-B horror movies

PART 1:
Developing a Specific Topic

Get off on the right foot by thinking about your own choice of a subject. Choose one subject that interests you, and use the techniques listed on page 408 to get an overview. Next, identify three or four possible topics related to your subject. After making certain that there are sources of information available, choose one of these topics for your report.

INTEGRATING THE LANGUAGE ARTS

Speaking Link. Stress that getting a good overview of a subject is very important when limiting the subject to a specific topic. To ensure that students take this step seriously, have them make short oral reports on the information they have learned in their overviews.

ANSWERS
Exercise 1

Suggestions for workable topics will vary.

1. too general; possible limited topic: Chinese immigration to America in the 1980s

2. appropriate

3. too technical; possible workable topic: two recent scientific experiments conducted in space or two discoveries made as a result of space exploration

4. appropriate

5. too personal; possible workable topic: recent trends in grade-B horror movies

subject, model the process of limiting the subject to a specific topic. You'll probably want to discuss the two questions in **Selecting a Suitable Topic** before assigning **Exercise 1**.

Thinking About Purpose, Audience, and Tone and **Developing Research Questions.** Give students copies of a short report or show them a short documentary film or video, and lead a discussion about the purpose, intended audience, and tone of the report or documentary. Then, guide students through the process of developing research questions by formulating, with students' help, research questions that might have been used to develop the report or documentary.

WRITING NOTE

Stress to students that although the writing process is presented here in a linear fashion, it is actually a cyclical process. Point out that even as students work through the prewriting stages of their reports, they will be evaluating and revising their ideas constantly, and that after they have written their first drafts, they may need to use prewriting strategies to research additional information.

TIMESAVER

If your students have studied purpose, audience, and tone in connection with other compositions, have students read the information in **Thinking About Purpose, Audience, and Tone** at home and skip the two exercises pertaining to those concepts.

A DIFFERENT APPROACH

To give students practice analyzing purpose, audience, and tone, have some students bring articles from popular magazines, such as *People,* whose primary purpose is to entertain and whose tone is usually informal. Have other students bring articles from such magazines as *Smithsonian, National Geographic,* or *Psychology Today,* whose primary purpose is to inform and whose tone tends to be formal. Have students read paragraphs from the articles aloud as other students listen for items that illustrate the purpose, audience, and tone of each article.

WRITING NOTE   This chapter takes you step-by-step through the process of writing a research paper, but you'll find that you often move through the steps differently from your classmates. For example, if you are already very familiar with your subject, you may jump ahead to limiting your topic right away. Or, you may move "backward" if you realize that your topic isn't a good choice. If you do repeat a step, don't get discouraged. You'll make up for lost time and produce a much better report by changing direction when you need to.

Thinking About Purpose, Audience, and Tone

Purpose.   The basic purpose of a research paper is to inform. As you conduct your research, you will gather information and develop your own ideas about your topic. When you write your report, you'll inform readers about what you've learned.

Audience.   People who read a research report are looking for information. They want to come away from the report with a better understanding of the topic. As you explore your topic and write your report, consider your audience's interest level and information level.

- *Interest level.* Look for an unusual approach to the topic or surprising details about it.
- *Information level.* Take your readers beyond what they already know. But don't get so technical or complex that your readers will have difficulty understanding your report.

Tone.   TV documentaries, such as the Public Broadcasting System's *NOVA* or the National Geographic specials, often have a narrator who explains the images that you see on the screen. The narrator's tone of voice—usually calm, serious, and formal—lends authority to the information you're getting. If you use a serious, relatively formal tone in your report, your readers will be more likely to take it seriously.

Finding and Evaluating Sources of Information and **Preparing Source Cards.** You may first want to lead a discussion of why it's important to evaluate sources of information. Bring to class several potential sources for a report, and model the process of evaluating sources. Then, using the sources that were evaluated favorably, show students how to prepare source cards. You could draw large rectangles on the chalkboard to represent index cards and solicit students' help in filling them out.

Planning, Recording, and Organizing Information. Show students how to draft an early plan by reconstructing on the chalkboard a possible early plan for the excerpt from **"America's Ancient Skywatchers."**

EXERCISE 2 ▶ **Analyzing Purpose, Audience, and Tone**

What do you know about how secret codes work? Read the following paragraph from a report on secret codes. Then get together with a small group of classmates to discuss the questions that follow on page 412.

> A typical code takes ideas in the message—words or even whole phrases—and changes them into something else, usually groups of numbers taken out of a codebook resembling a small dictionary. To compose a coded message, the sender first writes what he intends to say ("Attack is imminent") and then looks up the words in his codebook. "Attack" is 1140, and "imminent" is 4539. And that's his message: 1140 4539. To further confound the enemy, the sender might scramble the signal by using a special key to encipher those numbers, by switching around the order, or both. The receiver must have an identical codebook and know anything extra the sender has done to scramble the number groups.
>
> James R. Chiles, "To Break the Unbreakable Codes"

INTEGRATING THE LANGUAGE ARTS

Literature Link. Remind students that tone is determined by the attitude a writer takes toward his or her subject or readers. Tell students that a writer's choice of words and details helps determine tone. To give students a vivid example of tone, have them read, if available, the autobiographical essay "A Child's Christmas in Wales" by Dylan Thomas. Ask them to find specific words and details that contribute to the essay's nostalgic and whimsical tone. [A nostalgic tone is created by the use of phrases and sentences such as *All the Christmases, in my memory, years and years and years ago, when I was a boy,* and *Always on Christmas there was music.* A whimsical tone is created, in part, by the use of unexpected combinations of words such as *headlong moon, fish-freezing sea, ice-cream hills,* and *tea-tray-slithered run.*]

Calvin & Hobbes copyright 1986 Watterson. Distributed by Universal Press Syndicate. Reprinted with permission. All rights reserved.

Then, if students have not had extensive note-taking experience, model various note-taking methods on the chalkboard.

Developing a Thesis Statement and **Preparing an Outline.** You can use the **Critical Thinking Exercise** to show students how to form thesis statements. Do either all or part of the exercise as a class.

After you've discussed the various steps of the prewriting stage and let students work through the exercises in class, assign **Writing Assignment: Parts 1–6** as independent practice.

1. The writer's purpose is to inform readers about secret codes. How might the paragraph have been different if the subject stayed the same but the writer's purpose were to entertain readers?
2. How can you tell the writer assumed that most readers had never seen a codebook? What does the writer do to make the explanation of how a secret code works clear to readers?
3. How would you describe the tone of this paragraph?

ANSWERS

Exercise 2

Responses will vary. Here are some possibilities:

1. The writer might have told an exciting story about secret agents and secret codes.
2. The writer describes the codebooks. The writer gives a specific example and explains it in simple, clear language.
3. The tone is formal.

ANSWERS

Exercise 3

Encourage students to give direct, helpful answers to their classmates' questions.

EXERCISE 3 ▶ **Speaking and Listening: Analyzing the Audience for Your Report**

To help you get a better feeling for your audience, interview one or more of the classmates who will be the readers of your report. Start by telling your classmate briefly what you've learned about your topic and what you plan to find out. Then ask your classmate these questions.

1. How much do you already know about the topic? Have you ever read any articles or books about it? Do any television shows or tapes discuss it?
2. What seems interesting to you about the topic? What would you like to know about it?
3. Is anything about the topic confusing to you? What would help you understand the topic better?

Developing Research Questions

Your research will be much easier if you're searching for the answers to specific questions. Rely on your natural curiosity. Think about what you want to know about your topic, and jot down some questions to research. Here are some general questions that will help you think of specific questions about your topic.

- What is the topic? How can you define it?
- What groups, or classes, make up the topic?
- What are the topic's parts, and how do they work together?
- How has the topic changed over time?
- How is the topic similar to or different from related topics?
- What are the topic's advantages or disadvantages?

ASSESSMENT

The six parts of the writing assignment in this lesson provide a good opportunity to measure students' prewriting skills.

RETEACHING

Display on an overhead transparency a short article that includes research, perhaps an article from a magazine. Give students time to read the article. Then, trace the author's logical prewriting steps with your students. Have students consider these questions:

1. What is the subject of the article?

Prewriting **413**

To find a topic and begin your research

- use resource materials to find a general subject
- limit the general subject to a suitable topic
- stop to think about your purpose, audience, and tone
- develop a list of research questions about your topic

 PART 2:
Beginning Your Research

Use your natural curiosity and what you already know about the topic to begin your research. Start by thinking about your purpose and audience. Then make a list of three or four research questions about your topic.

INTEGRATING THE LANGUAGE ARTS

Listening Link. Have several representatives from the community speak about the information available at their businesses or offices. If possible, have these speakers bring samples of the information they have available. For example, a representative from a local environmental agency could bring copies of the results of studies the agency has done recently.

413

2. What is the specific topic?
3. What is the purpose of the article?
4. Who is the audience?
5. What is the tone of the article?
6. What are three research questions that the author might have asked about the topic?

7. What sources might the author have used?
8. What is the article's thesis statement?
9. What are three details that support that thesis statement?

INTEGRATING THE LANGUAGE ARTS

Library Link. You may want to have students review **Chapter 33: "The Library/Media Center."** You may also want to work with your school librarian to arrange an orientation session in your school library.

Give students a short list of topics and have them work in groups to locate information about one of the topics in at least three of the following library resources: card catalog or online catalog, *Readers' Guide to Periodical Literature,* microfilm or microfiche, general reference sources, specialized reference sources, videotapes and audiotapes, and vertical file.

 *Prewriting*

Finding and Evaluating Sources of Information

We're bombarded daily with so much information that this has been called "the age of information." You may not even realize how many sources of information surround you. Here are some library and community sources you can use for your research.

LIBRARY RESOURCES	
RESOURCE	**SOURCE OR INFORMATION**
Card catalog or online catalog	Books listed by title, author, and subject (most libraries also list audiovisual materials)
Readers' Guide to Periodical Literature or *National Newspaper Index*	Subject and author index to magazine and journal articles, index to major newspapers
Microfilm or microfiche	Indexes to major newspapers such as *The New York Times* and *The Washington Post,* back issues of newspapers and magazines
General reference books or CD-ROMs	Encyclopedias, encyclopedia yearbooks, dictionaries
Specialized reference books or CD-ROMs	Biographical reference sources, encyclopedias of special subjects (sports, art, etc.), atlases, almanacs (See pages 955–957 for more about reference sources.)
Videotapes and audiotapes	Movies, documentaries, filmstrips, videotapes, audiotapes of books
Vertical file	Pamphlets listed by subject, clippings
The librarian	Help in finding and using sources

 REFERENCE NOTE: For more information on using the library, including online catalogs, online databases, and the Internet, see pages 952–957.

CLOSURE

Ask students to summarize briefly the steps in the prewriting stage of the writing process.

EXTENSION

If students have problems limiting subjects, they might need instruction in moving from the general to the specific. To help students master this skill, put the following ladder of abstraction on the chalkboard:

I found an animal in the kitchen.
I found a reptile in the kitchen.

Prewriting **415**

COMMUNITY RESOURCES	
RESOURCE	**SOURCE OR INFORMATION**
World Wide Web and online services	Articles, interviews, bibliographies, pictures, videos, sound recordings
Local government offices	Facts and statistics, information on local government policies, experts on local government
Local offices of state and federal officials	Voting records of government officials, recent or pending legislation, experts on state and federal government
Museums and historical societies	Special exhibits, libraries and bookstores, experts on various subjects
Schools and colleges	Libraries, experts on various subjects
Local newspaper offices	Clippings, files on local events and history

Evaluating Sources of Information

Some sources are more useful than others. Before you use a source, make sure that the 4 *R*'s apply.

1. *Relevant.* Does the source have information directly related to your topic? For a book, check the table of contents and the index. For a nonprint source, read a review or summary of the work.
2. *Reliable.* Can you trust your source to be accurate and objective? Well-respected magazines and newspapers such as *Smithsonian* or the *Christian Science Monitor* are usually reliable sources.
3. *Recent.* How up-to-date is the information? What is the copyright date? Even a historical topic, such as "women artists in the Middle Ages," should have some recent sources. New information is continually being researched and published.
4. *Representative.* If your topic is controversial, you need to find sources with opinions and information on both sides of the issue. For example, if some scientists say exercise adds to life span and others say it doesn't, you must report both theories.

MEETING individual NEEDS

ADVANCED STUDENTS

In addition to having students use both print and nonprint sources, you may also want to distinguish between primary and secondary sources and have students use both for their reports. Examples of primary sources include interviews, journals, letters, books of fiction, and works of art.

LEARNING STYLES

Kinetic Learners. Some students might especially benefit from a trip to the library to let them have hands-on experience with the online catalog, the *Readers' Guide to Periodical Literature*, microfilm or microfiche, videotapes and audiotapes, the vertical file, and other library resources.

I found a snake in the kitchen.
I found a python in the kitchen.
I found Peter, my pet python, in the kitchen.

Discuss the fact that an animal could be any of millions of creatures. As students move down the ladder, the possibilities become more limited until the reference is to one specific animal. Have students construct

ladders of abstraction for their subjects. They should place the general subject at the top as in the example.

Preparing Source Cards

You have this great quotation you want to use in your report, but you can't remember where you found it. If you've ever had anything like that happen, you know it's important to keep a record of your sources. That's where source cards come into the picture.

For each of your sources, record the author, title, and publication information on an index card or sheet of notebook paper, or in a computer file. (Source cards are sometimes called *bibliography cards*.) Give each source a number. With good source information, you won't need to run back again and again to the card catalog or *Readers' Guide*. These source cards will also make it easier to prepare the final list of sources, or *Works Cited*, that accompanies your report.

The following guidelines tell you how to record the necessary information for different types of sources. As you fill out your cards, refer to these guidelines, and note the special uses of punctuation.

GUIDELINES FOR RECORDING SOURCE INFORMATION

1. **Book with One Author.** Write the author's or editor's name, last name first (follow the names of editors with a comma and the abbreviation *ed.*); the title of the book; the place of publication; the publishing company's name; and the year of publication. (To make it easier to locate a book later, put its call number in the upper right-hand part of the index card, paper, or computer file.)

   EXAMPLE   Piña Chan, Román. The Olmec: Mother Culture of Mesoamerica. New York: Rizzoli, 1989.

2. **Source with More Than One Author.** For the first listed author, write the last name first. For all other authors, write the first name first.

   EXAMPLE   Rust, William F., and Robert J. Sharer. . . .

(continued)

MEETING *individual* NEEDS

LEARNING STYLES

Visual and Kinetic Learners. Most tenth-graders have not had extensive experience with the research report format, so the mechanics of filling out source cards may pose some problems. Before students fill out their cards, try some whole-class practice. Have students bring information on their sources to class. They should include a mixture of books, articles, and nonprint sources. Then, have kinetic learners write examples of source cards on the chalkboard. Visual learners can watch for errors as the other students work.

TECHNOLOGY TIP

The *Writer's Workshop CD-ROM* composition program provides a **Bibliography Maker** that will automatically arrange the student's bibliographical source information into a standard bibliography format. If students input their source information early on in their research, the form on the computer screen will serve as a reminder should they forget to note important data. Students will still have time, then, to collect the missing information and complete their final lists of sources.

Prewriting **417**

GUIDELINES FOR RECORDING SOURCE INFORMATION *(continued)*

3. **Magazine or Newspaper Article.** Write the author's name (if given), last name first; the title of the article; the name of the magazine or newspaper; the day (if given), month, and year of publication; and page numbers on which the article begins and ends. For an article in a newspaper that has different editions or multiple sections, specify the edition (use *ed.*) and/or section before the page number.

EXAMPLE   Stuart, George E. "New Light on the Olmec." National Geographic Nov. 1993: 88-114.

EXAMPLE   Mack, Tara. "The 9 1/2-ton Head of State." Washington Post 6 June 1996, early ed.: C1.

4. **Encyclopedia Article.** Write the author's name (if given), last name first; the title of the article; the name of the encyclopedia; the edition (if given); and the year of publication. (Use the abbreviation *ed.* for *edition.*)

EXAMPLE   "Pre-Columbian Civilizations." The New Encyclopaedia Britannica: Macropaedia. 15th ed. 1988.

5. **Radio or Television Program.** Write the program title; the name of the network; the call letters and city of the local station (if any); and the broadcast date.

EXAMPLE   NBC Nightly News. NBC. WNBC, New York. 8 July 1997.

6. **Movie or Video Recording.** Write the title of the work and the director or producer's name; for movies, write the original distributor's name (for movies not available on video) and year of release; for video recordings, write the word *Videocassette* or *Videodisc*, the distributor's name, and the year the video recording was released. (Use *Dir.* for *Director* and *Prod.* for *Producer.*)

EXAMPLE   Maya: Lords of the Jungle. Dir. John Angier. Videocassette. PBS Home Video, 1981.

(continued)

COOPERATIVE LEARNING

You could let students work in groups of three or four to write bogus source cards that break all the rules in the guidelines. For example, the cards could lack punctuation marks or list information in the wrong order. When each group has finished its bogus cards, ask groups to exchange cards. Groups should then correct or redo the cards they receive in the exchange.

RADIO OR TELEVISION PROGRAM

If the network is not identified in the program title, students should list it before the affiliate call letters. A period should be placed after the network. If pertinent, students should list the narrator (Narr. Hugh Downs), producer (Prod. Tony Burden), or director (Dir. Sarah Marino) between the title and network. A period should follow each of these entries.

INTEGRATING THE LANGUAGE ARTS

Mechanics Link. To give students practice using quotation marks to enclose a person's exact words, have students interview each other about the topics of their research reports and use quotation marks as they record responses. For example, a student might ask a classmate why she chose a particular topic. The student might then record the classmate's response: Margaret said, "I chose to research the history of comic books because I have always loved them."

TEACHING NOTE

Although MLA style requires listing a city of publication for CD-ROM databases, you may want to allow students to omit the city when the information is not readily available. For example, the city name may be printed on the box that the CD-ROM came in, but the city name and other copyright information may not be available from within the database itself.

Students may be confused when a sentence ends with an Internet address and a period follows the address. Remind students that the final period in such a listing is punctuation for the sentence; the period is not part of the Internet address. Although the mark for a period looks the same as the mark used to separate parts of an Internet address, that mark is called a *dot* when it appears in an Internet address.

418

GUIDELINES FOR RECORDING SOURCE INFORMATION *(continued)*

7. **Interview.** Write the interviewee's name, last name first; the type of interview (Personal or Telephone); and the day, month, and year of the interview.

   EXAMPLE   Sutphin, Andrea. Telephone interview. 17 Apr. 1997.

8. **Electronic Materials.** Write the author's name (if given), last name first; title (include print publisher, date, and page numbers if material was first in a print source); posting date (online); title of CD-ROM or database (if any, for online sources); type of source (*CD-ROM* or *Online*); location of source (*Internet,* online service, or city, if given, for CD-ROMs); distributor (CD-ROMs); date of publication (CD-ROMs) or date of access; and Internet address (if any), preceded by the word *Available.*

   EXAMPLE   Follensbee, Billie. Olmec Heads: A Product of the Americas. 30 Apr. 1996. Online. Internet. 12 Dec. 1997. Available http://copan.bioz .unibas.ch/meso/olmec.html.

☞ **REFERENCE NOTE:** For help with capitalizing and punctuating titles, see pages 777–778, 831–832, and 840.

Reminder

As you prepare your source cards, be sure to

- follow a specific format for recording source information
- record all information accurately, double-checking authors' names, titles, and page numbers
- use quotation marks to indicate when you are quoting an author's exact words
- follow the rules for punctuating and capitalizing titles (pages 777–778, 831–832, and 840) and for using quotation marks to give an author's exact words (pages 834–836)

WRITING NOTE The format for identifying sources in this chapter is that of the Modern Language Association of America (MLA). You'll use it for preparing source cards, taking notes, and preparing your final list of sources. Your teacher may instead ask you to use a different format, such as that of the American Psychological Association (APA).

EXERCISE 4 **Using Library and Community Resources**

With a small group, brainstorm some sources for answering the two practical, everyday questions that follow. For each question, try to think of two library sources and two community sources. Check the 4 *R*'s: Are your sources relevant, reliable, recent, and representative?

1. What percentage of eligible people voted in the last election? are registered? How can we get more 18-year-olds to register and vote?
2. What approaches are your community and the nation taking to decrease the dropout rate?

WRITING ASSIGNMENT

PART 3:
Collecting and Evaluating Sources

Explore your library and community sources to see what you can find out about your topic. (Find five or six sources of information.) Then evaluate each source by checking its 4 *R*'s (see page 415). You and a classmate might exchange your lists and evaluate each other's sources.

WRITING ASSIGNMENT

PART 4:
Preparing Source Cards

Prepare a source card for each source you've decided to use. Use the guidelines and examples on pages 416–418.

A DIFFERENT APPROACH

Ask someone who has written and published research articles to speak to the class. Ask the writer to offer personal hints and suggestions to help students with their research and their writing.

Prewriting

Planning, Recording, and Organizing Information

You've identified some sources that look promising. Now you need to collect information and find some way of organizing it.

Drafting an Early Plan

Faced with a stack of books or an interview date, you may be uncertain about where to begin. After all, you can't take notes or ask questions about *everything* concerning your topic. One way to get some idea about where to start is to make an **early plan**—a list of points that you plan to research. For example, suppose you read some new information about the Olmecs' form of government and learned that the Olmecs developed a calendar and a form of writing. Here's the way you could use this information in an early plan.

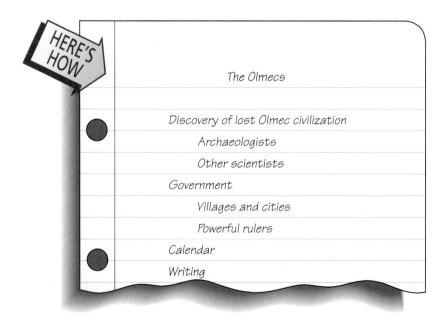

HERE'S HOW

The Olmecs

Discovery of lost Olmec civilization
Archaeologists
Other scientists
Government
Villages and cities
Powerful rulers
Calendar
Writing

Refer to your early plan as you take notes, and use its headings in deciding what information to record. But remember that your early plan can be changed. If you discover new information related to your topic, add a heading to your early plan. Or, if you decide not to develop a point in your early plan, delete the heading.

Taking Notes

As you take notes from a source, you can either quote, summarize, or paraphrase the material. Notice how these three techniques are used to take notes on Billie Follensbee's *Olmec Heads: A Product of the Americas*.

TECHNIQUE	EXAMPLE
Quote only when the author's exact words, as well as ideas, are important. To quote, copy the source material word for word, and put quotation marks around it.	"There is . . . overwhelming archaeological evidence that the Olmec Colossal Heads were made by and for Native Americans." "In short, those who have claimed the Olmec Colossal Heads to be of foreign origin have only noticed some superficial physical similarities with groups of people on the other side of the ocean, and without any concrete evidence for support, they have given credit for these works to far-away foreign cultures."
Summarize when you need to remember only the main idea. Read or listen to the material first. Then, write your notes in your own words.	Follensbee says that the Olmec colossal heads were created by Native Americans. She says that others have claimed, without support, that they were created by people from a foreign culture.
Paraphrase when you need to remember more detailed information. Restate the material by using your own vocabulary and sentence structure.	Follensbee says that the creators of the Olmec great stone heads clearly were Native Americans. Though people see a likeness between the physical features of the statues and those of other groups, Follensbee says there is no clear evidence to suggest that the creators came from a culture in a distant part of the world.

Whichever method you use, always check your notes against the original to be certain that you have quoted, summarized, or paraphrased accurately.

Unless you attack note taking in an orderly way, you'll be faced with trying to untangle a jumble of notes. Experienced note-takers give this advice:

- If you take notes on 4″ × 6″ note cards, use a separate card for each item of information and each source. If you use paper or computer files, use a separate sheet or file for each source.
- In the upper left corner, write a keyword or key phrase (perhaps a heading from your early plan) so you can tell at a glance what the note is about.
- In the upper right-hand corner, write the source card number (see page 416). End each note with the page number where you found the information.

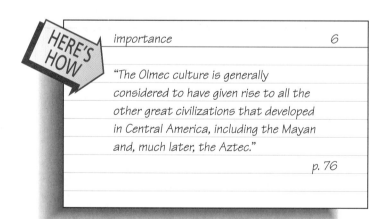

HERE'S HOW

importance	6

"The Olmec culture is generally considered to have given rise to all the other great civilizations that developed in Central America, including the Mayan and, much later, the Aztec."

p. 76

WRITING NOTE

Unless you're quoting a source directly, *always* take notes in your own words. Change the sentence structure, too. When you use someone else's words or ideas without giving proper credit, you're *plagiarizing*. No matter how you ultimately use your source (direct quotation, paraphrase, or summary), you must give credit for other people's ideas as well as their words.

WRITING NOTE

To emphasize the inappropriateness of plagiarism, liken it to literary theft. Explain that it's stealing to claim someone else's words or ideas.

Discuss with students each of the four possible approaches to a topic and the accompanying sample thesis statements. Then, work with students to use the four approaches to generate thesis statements for another topic.

 PART 5:
Planning and Note Taking

Use what you've already learned about your topic to identify points you'd like to explore further. Make these the headings as you draft your early plan. Then, start taking notes from your sources. You can't, of course, take notes about *everything*. Use the headings in your early plan to decide what information to record.

Developing a Thesis Statement

Your *thesis statement* is a signpost to guide both you and your reader. It expresses the main idea of your report and indicates what you plan to cover. Think about the ideas and conclusions you've drawn from your research so far, and write a preliminary thesis statement. (You can always revise it later.) Right now it will help focus your note taking, and later it will help you organize your report.

 REFERENCE NOTE: See pages 113–114 for more help with writing thesis statements.

 CRITICAL THINKING

Analyzing Your Topic

When you *analyze* a topic, you break it down into its smaller parts and think about how the parts are related. For any topic it's possible to take several different approaches. Analyzing the possible approaches is an important first step in writing your thesis statement.

For example, following are four possible approaches and sample thesis statements for the topic "the role of women in the American military services." Notice that each approach emphasizes a different aspect of this topic.

■ **Exploring new information**

EXAMPLE In the 1990s, women in the American military services have many varied roles.

A DIFFERENT APPROACH

Select an article from a newspaper or a magazine about a topic of interest to students. Read the article aloud or have a student read it aloud. Then, ask students to tell you the main idea of the article. Lead a class discussion of the writer's approach to the topic. Ask students to tell you some details that are indicative of that approach. You could write the details on the chalkboard. Then, ask students what other approaches the author might have taken with the same topic.

ANSWERS

Critical Thinking Exercise

Responses will vary. Here are some guidelines for evaluation:

1. This thesis statement should clearly reflect the fact that the report will give new information or new ideas about the topic.

2. References to time and change should be central to this thesis statement.

3. Be sure that this thesis statement mentions both cause and effect.

4. This thesis statement should clearly state what is being compared or contrasted.

■ **Examining how the topic has changed over time**

EXAMPLE   Women's roles in the American military services have changed drastically since women were first admitted to the armed services.

■ **Demonstrating a cause-and-effect relationship**

EXAMPLE   Past successes of American women in the military have resulted in their broader roles in the 1990s.

■ **Demonstrating a comparison/contrast relationship**

EXAMPLE   Roles for American women in the military services are much more limited than those for women in the armed services of many other countries.

CRITICAL THINKING EXERCISE: Analyzing a Topic

Suppose you're planning to write a research report about some aspect of space exploration. You've done some research, and you're ready to develop a preliminary thesis statement. How will you approach your topic? Write four thesis statements to illustrate these different approaches: (1) exploring new information, (2) examining how the topic has changed over time, (3) demonstrating a cause/effect relationship, and (4) demonstrating a comparison/contrast relationship. To get some ideas, look back at the example thesis statements on women in the armed forces. Make up whatever details you need for your thesis statements.

Preparing an Outline

Your early plan helped you organize your research. Now that you've found information, you'll need to do more organizing. You may not know exactly how you will organize your report until you have written and revised your first draft, but it helps to make a plan before you start writing. One good way to do this is to create an outline.

To create an outline, group your note cards into sets, using the headings in your early plan. Then, create subheadings and divide your sets into smaller sets, or group several small, related sets together under a single heading.

COMPUTER NOTE: Use a stand-alone outlining program or your word-processing program's outline feature to organize your prewriting notes into an outline for your first draft.

Here's an outline a writer created after doing research on the Olmecs. A *formal* outline like this, with Roman numerals and capital letters, can also be made after a report is written. It then serves as a table of contents for the report.

 REFERENCE NOTE: For help with writing a formal outline, see page 118.

The Olmecs: New Light on a Dark Past

I. Early research on the Olmecs
  A. Work of archaeologist Melgar
  B. Theory about relics and unknown culture
  C. Excavations and scientific study
II. Olmec society and government
  A. Villages and cities
  B. Powerful rulers
    1. Colossal heads
    2. Stones moved by sledge, raft
    3. Earthen mounds
III. Olmecs as advanced civilization
  A. Sophisticated calendar
  B. Hieroglyphic writing
IV. Speculation about Olmec origins
V. Importance of Olmecs

WRITING ASSIGNMENT

PART 6:
Preparing an Outline

Organize your notes and create an outline. Use it as a guide as you write, but feel free to revise it as needed.

MOTIVATION

Tell students that the hardest stages of the writing process for a research report—the research and planning stages—are behind them. If they have laid good foundations in prewriting, actually writing their reports should not be too difficult.

MEETING *individual* NEEDS

LEARNING STYLES

Visual Learners. You may want to make a chart on poster board of the basic elements of a research report and display it in a prominent place in the classroom so that students can refer to it as needed.

SELECTION AMENDMENT
Description of change: excerpted
Rationale: to focus on the concept of writing presented in this chapter

426

Writing Your First Draft

All your careful preparations will finally pay off. Now that you've collected and organized your information, the actual writing will be easy.

Combining the Basic Elements of a Research Report

Keep these two goals in mind as you begin writing. You want to interest your readers and help them understand your topic. You also need to pull together, or synthesize, ideas and information from a variety of sources and state them in your own words. Like any informative composition, your research report should include all of these elements:

- an interesting opening that captures your reader's attention
- a thesis statement that presents your main idea
- a series of body paragraphs that develop and support the thesis statement
- a clear order for your ideas and information
- a conclusion that restates your main points

☞ **REFERENCE NOTE:** To review the basic elements of a composition, see pages 122–134.

As you write the first draft of your body paragraphs, be guided by your final outline. You'll develop each main heading into one or two paragraphs.

> *" I believe more in the scissors than I do in the pencil."*
>
> *Truman Capote*

TEACHING THE LESSON

Begin this section by leading a class review of the basic elements of a research report. Tell your students that a research paper includes the same basic elements as any informative composition.

Next, go over the material on incorporating quotations and documenting sources. Stress that guidelines for documenting sources are to be understood and referred to rather than memorized. Before students begin their drafts, have them read **A Writer's Model.**

After students have read the model, you could use the side-margin annotations to focus a discussion on its organization and form. Be sure that students understand the basic elements of an informative composition

MECHANICS HINT

Using Quotations

To give your paper credibility, sprinkle it lightly with direct quotations, following these guidelines:

1. Place a directly quoted phrase or clause into your own sentence, and enclose it in quotation marks.

   Researcher Michael D. Coe says experts are almost unanimous in their belief that "the Olmec civilization is older than any other in Mesoamerica" (183).

2. Run a short quotation (four lines or fewer) into your text. Introduce it in your own words, and enclose it in quotation marks.

   According to Coe, "There is now little or no dissent from the proposition that the Olmec civilization is older than any other in Mesoamerica, including the Classic Maya" (183).

3. Set off a longer quotation by indenting each line ten spaces from the left margin. Introduce the quotation in your own words, usually followed by a colon, but do not use quotation marks.

   Archaeologists have solved the mystery of when the Olmecs flourished:

   > There is now little or no dissent from the proposition that the Olmec civilization is older than any other in Mesoamerica, including the Classic Maya. Recent excavations in both lowland and highland Mexico have proved this beyond all doubt (Coe 183).

   (**Source:** Coe, Michael D. "Olmec and Maya: A Study in Relationships." The Origins of Maya Civilization. Ed. Richard E. W. Adams. Albuquerque: U of New Mexico P, 1977. 183-195.)

QUOTATION FOR THE DAY

"According to [some] scholars, the Olmecs believed they were descended from a race of were-jaguars—the offspring of a male jaguar and a human female . . ." (Richard A. Diehl, professor of anthropology, University of Alabama)

You could use this quotation to spark students' interest in **A Writer's Model,** which is about the Olmecs. Ask students to speculate why a group of people might have believed they were descended from jaguars.

MECHANICS HINT

Have each student find three examples from printed sources (newspapers, magazines, books) that illustrate the three guidelines for using and punctuating direct quotations. Have students underline the examples. Then, have students exchange examples and identify each as representing guideline 1, 2, or 3.

TIMESAVER

Instead of discussing individually the basic elements of a research paper, the use of quotations, and the documentation of sources, you may want to proceed straight to **A Writer's Model** and teach these items as you read through the report. You may find this an especially good alternative method if your class is advanced.

before they start writing their first drafts. Depending on the nature and capabilities of your class, you may want to give students a definite length requirement for their first drafts.

GUIDED PRACTICE

You could give students time in class to begin their first drafts (**Writing Assignment: Part 7**) so that you can assist them with any initial problems. Be sure that students have written clear thesis statements and that they are properly citing their sources and correctly using quotation marks.

Giving Credit to Your Sources

In your report you'll document your sources throughout the paper itself and in a separate list at the end, labeled *Works Cited.*

Giving Credit Within the Body of Your Report. Every researcher-writer faces two problems: (1) when to give credit, and (2) how to give credit.

1. *How do you decide when to give credit?* As a rule, it's not necessary to acknowledge general information you already know or can easily find in general reference sources. (*In Chinatown in San Francisco, signs are written in both Chinese and English.*) You also don't have to acknowledge general information from public sources like newspapers or TV. (*Smoking may cause cancer and heart disease.*)

2. *How do you show the credit?* There are several styles for giving credit. In this chapter, documentation follows the format recommended by the Modern Language Association of America (MLA), which uses parenthetical citations. Some teachers prefer footnotes, placed at the bottom of the page and corresponding to numbers in the text. Here's one example; but if you need to use footnotes, you'll have to follow another style guide.

[1] Román Piña Chan, The Olmec: Mother Culture of Mesoamerica (New York: Rizzoli, 1989) 25.

MEETING *individual* NEEDS

LEP/ESL

General Strategies. The guidelines for giving credit to sources may contain too much information for students to assimilate on their own. Before preparing a Works Cited page, students might need extra practice with the bibliographical form. Pair English-language learners with English-proficient speakers and give the pairs several incorrect versions of the Olmec report's Works Cited page. Have students correct the incorrect versions by comparing them to the original on p. 435.

LESS-ADVANCED STUDENTS

Deciding when to give credit to a source may be difficult for some students. To help them see the difference between general information that doesn't need to be credited and information that should be credited, locate ten bits of information that would need to be credited in a research report and mix them up with ten bits of information that can be found in general reference sources.

Read the mixed-up list to your class. As you read each fact, ask the class if it should be credited or not and have students support their answers.

GUIDELINES FOR GIVING CREDIT WITHIN THE REPORT

Place the information in parentheses at the end of the sentence in which you've used someone else's words or ideas.

1. **Source with One Author.** Author's last name followed by the page number(s). (Piña Chan 83)

2. **Sources by Authors with the Same Last Name.** First and last names of each author followed by the page number(s). (Mary Smith 21) (John Smith 102)

3. **Source with More Than One Author.** All authors' last names, followed by the page number(s). (Rust and Sharer 102)

After you think students have a good understanding of the basic elements of an informative composition and know how to document sources correctly, have them write the remainders of their first drafts on their own.

ASSESSMENT

Use students' first drafts to assess their mastery of the skills involved in writing research reports, including the documentation of sources and the incorporation of direct quotations.

☞

GUIDELINES FOR GIVING CREDIT WITHIN THE REPORT (continued)

4. **Source with No Author Given.** Title, or a shortened form, and the page number(s). ("New Information" 34)

5. **One-page Source, Unpaginated Source, CD-ROM or Online Source, or Article from an Encyclopedia or Other Work Arranged Alphabetically.** Author's name only. If no author's name is given, title only. (Follensbee)

6. **More Than One Source by the Same Author.** Author's last name and the title or a shortened form of it, followed by the page number(s). (Nissen, "Olmec Legacy" 21) (Nissen, "New Discoveries" 45)

7. **Author's Name Given in Paragraph.** Page number only. (76)

Preparing the List of Sources. The citations in the body of your report refer to a detailed list, the **Works Cited** page at the end of your report. (If you've used print sources only, you can call this a *Bibliography*.) Readers who want to know complete publication information can refer to this page as they read your paper.

GUIDELINES FOR PREPARING THE LIST OF WORKS CITED

1. On a separate sheet, center the words *Works Cited* (or the word *Bibliography*) one inch from the top.
2. For each entry on the list, follow the format you used for your source cards (pages 416–419).
3. List your sources by the author's last name. If no author is given, alphabetize by the first important word in the title. If you use two or more sources by the same author, write the author's name in the first entry only. For all other entries, write three hyphens where the author's name should be, followed by a period. Then give the title, publication information, and page number(s).
4. Begin each listing at the left margin. If a listing is longer than one line, indent all the following lines five spaces.

MEETING *individual* NEEDS

ADVANCED STUDENTS

Most students probably won't want to hear about any style for giving credit other than the one you want them to follow. However, you may want to introduce students to a few other crediting styles. You may also want to point out the footnoting capabilities of current word-processing programs, which can save time and reduce frustration.

◈ INTEGRATING THE LANGUAGE ARTS

Vocabulary Link. Previously, what is called the Works Cited page today was referred to as the bibliography. You may want to explain to students why this shift occurred. The base word in *bibliography* is the Greek word for book, *biblion*. Hence, a bibliography has been associated with the citing of books and other printed publications. However, nonprint sources are often used today. *Works Cited* has developed as a general heading that more adequately covers all sources, print and nonprint.

If some students are still having difficulty mastering the basics of writing a research report, show your class a short, informative documentary film or video. Tell them to listen for an interesting opening, a thesis statement, supporting details, the organization of ideas, and a conclusion. Students should also listen for direct quotations and citations of sources. If you are using a VCR, you may want to pause during the videotape to discuss the various elements as they occur.

INTEGRATING THE LANGUAGE ARTS

Library Link. Remind students that one method of writing an effective introduction is to use a pertinent quotation. For example, a report might begin, "Shakespeare said that '. . . ,' but unfortunately that's not true today." To help students find quotations, identify the books of quotations frequently available in libraries. Bartlett's *Familiar Quotations* is one of the most widely known of these books.

MEETING individual NEEDS

LEARNING STYLES

Auditory Learners. You may want to read aloud **A Writer's Model** and discuss its content and form as you go along.

430　*Writing a Research Paper*

Now, read the following research report about the Olmecs. Notice how the report combines basic composition form with documentation of sources.

A WRITER'S MODEL

The Olmecs: New Light on a Dark Past

INTRODUCTION
Interest grabber

In an old movie, a dashing adventurer hacks his way through tangled jungle vines, searching for a lost civilization. Suddenly he stumbles upon a dark pit hidden by the dense undergrowth. At the bottom, he finds a huge stone monument covered with strange carvings. He smiles because he realizes right away that he has chanced upon the remains of an unknown civilization that existed thousands of years ago.

Background information

More than three thousand years ago, in the jungles near the Gulf of Mexico, the people now known as the Olmecs developed a complex civilization that lasted for at least eight hundred years before mysteriously disappearing (Autry). Today, thanks to the work of many scholars and

CLOSURE

Ask students to list the basic elements of a research report.

EXTENSION

Encourage students to provide visuals for their research reports. Students could create original visuals or find appropriate existing ones. ■

Writing Your First Draft **431**

Thesis statement

archaeologists, people from around the world can learn about the Olmecs and see the artifacts they left behind. There was no solo adventurer who, after stumbling upon Olmec monuments, immediately realized their significance. Instead, researchers have gradually pieced together the story of the Olmecs after years of puzzling finds, careful excavation, and cooperative research.

BODY
Rediscovery of Olmecs

Source with one author

Summary

Field research related to the Olmecs began around 1860 in Tres Zapotes, Mexico. Villagers there unearthed a five-foot-high stone head in a field a workman had been clearing (Stuart 95). In 1862, the scholar José Melgar saw the head and went on to publish an article about it in 1869 (Piña Chan 25). Over the years, other archaeologists wrote about discoveries of similar stone heads, old monuments, and smaller relics which did not seem to have been created by any of the early cultures that were already documented. Archaeologists gradually started to theorize that the objects must have come from a previously unknown ancient culture, one they began to call "Olmec," because it seemed to have been centered in Olman, the ancient Aztec "Rubber Country" (Fagan 97).

Topic sentence—introduces paragraph

Since full-scale excavations of the Olmec areas began in 1938, archaeologists have used many scientific methods to locate the Olmec ruins and learn about Olmec culture. Some of

MEETING *individual* NEEDS

LESS-ADVANCED STUDENTS

To help students visualize the organization of the report, you may want to write an outline of **A Writer's Model** on the chalkboard.

ADVANCED STUDENTS

You may want to have students write alternative introductions and conclusions for **A Writer's Model.** Students could review the six techniques for writing effective introductions and the six techniques for writing conclusions in **Chapter 3: "Understanding Composition Structure."** You could ask volunteers to read their alternatives to the rest of the class.

A DIFFERENT APPROACH

Refer students to the section in **Chapter 2: "Understanding Para-graph Structure"** on connecting ideas within and between sentences in a para-graph. Explain that direct references and transitional expressions are also used to connect ideas between paragraphs in a longer composition. Work with students to find the direct references and transi-tional expressions that help link ideas between paragraphs in **A Writer's Model.**

Specific examples

Olmec society

One-page source

Olmec rulers

Two different sources

Two pages from the same source

the ruins, for example, were discovered or mapped by aerial photography or, more recently, by satellites. Scientists used radioactive carbon dating to establish the age of bones and relics found at the sites. Specialists studied the fossil remains of plants and animals (Grove 27).

Using these methods, researchers have learned much about how the Olmecs lived. From the excavations, experts learned that the Olmec society consisted of farming villages grouped around large centers or "cities." At first scholars believed that the Olmecs used these centers only for religious ceremonies (Piña Chan 83). However, excavations in 1986 convinced many archaeolo-gists that the Olmecs also lived in the centers, not just in the outlying villages (Bower).

Early Olmecs probably struggled to grow enough food to eat. Gradually, though, as they developed irrigation and improved farming methods, they were able to grow a surplus of food. This surplus probably became controlled by a class of strong leaders, allowing some Olmecs to become specialized artisans instead of farmers. The leaders built the centers discovered during excavations and commissioned artisans to create monuments to their power (Piña Chan 83).

Fifteen more heads like the one Melgar wrote about have been found over the years. These stone heads, which may preserve the features of actual Olmec rulers, are from five to eleven feet high, and weigh as much as thirty-six thousand pounds (Stuart 104; Autry). The stone used to create them is not native to many of the areas where they have been found; it came from mountains nearby. Experts believe the Olmecs may have moved the huge stones first on sledges or rolling logs, and then down rivers on large rafts (Stuart 95, 102). Along with the heads, the Olmecs built large earthen mounds. Scholars surmise that only powerful rulers would have had the means to plan such colossal projects and to command the many people needed to create them (Stuart 104).

Advanced civilization

Calendar

Evidence indicates that the Olmec civilization was highly advanced. Dates carved on some Olmec artifacts suggest that the Olmecs may have used one of the world's first carefully constructed calendars, even before the Mayas. It was a ritual calendar, based on a 260-day cycle. Since the average term of a human pregnancy is about 266 days, and the planting-and-harvesting cycle in the Olmec area lasts about the same number of days, some writers have suggested that the Olmecs might have associated the calendar with fertility (Fagan 120).

Writing

Background information/ definition

Many archaeologists also believe that the Olmecs were the first to use hieroglyphic writing within Mesoamerica. (In hieroglyphic writing, a picture represents a word, syllable, or sound.) Evidence for this includes an Olmec sculpture carved with the figure of a man who seems to be walking. Behind him is a carving of a human foot, which experts believe is the hieroglyphic symbol for "walking" or "marching." Other sculptures have carvings of stars and clouds which appear to be hieroglyphic symbols (Piña Chan 184). Olmec hieroglyphics, along with the quality of Olmec art, hint at the sophistication and learning of the culture that produced them.

VISUAL CONNECTIONS

Related Expression Skills. A **Writer's Model** cites expert opinion that the stone heads were probably made to represent Olmec rulers. Have interested students create heads to represent past leaders that they admire. Students could model heads of papier mâché or clay or they could draw or paint heads. Display students' artwork along with a picture of one of the Olmecs' stone heads.

Students who are intrigued by the Olmec calendar or the Olmec hieroglyphs might want to prepare brief oral reports about these subjects. They also might want to compare Olmec calendars or hieroglyphs with those of other ancient civilizations. Other students might want to research and use maps to trace possible routes between Africa and Mexico.

CRITICAL THINKING

Analysis. Remind students that informative writing should be as objective as possible. Point out how the author of **A Writer's Model** introduces various opinions about the Olmecs without seeming to show a bias toward one opinion. Because students might have difficulty identifying bias, bring some examples of biased writing to class to show them. Discuss how each example is biased and how the bias is evident. Discuss how tone and the connotations of words can contribute to biased writing.

Tell students that if they are writing about topics that are controversial and that they have strong opinions about, they might want to reveal their biases to readers at the beginnings of their reports.

TECHNOLOGY TIP

Students can use the *Writer's Workshop CD-ROM* composition program, which has a **Bibliography Maker** feature that will automatically format the student's source information into MLA or APA bibliography style. This bibliography-making feature can be very helpful to students who become easily frustrated by the attention to detail that correctly writing a bibliography often requires.

434

Speculation

Olmec art has also inspired speculation about Olmec origins. To some writers, the features of the stone heads and other artifacts suggest that the Olmecs had contact with people from Africa and Europe, and that the Olmec rulers originally came from distant lands. Olmec archaeology specialist Billie Follensbee responds:

Longer direct quotation

> Those who have claimed the Olmec Colossal Heads to be of foreign origin have only noticed some superficial physical similarities with groups of people on the other side of the ocean, and without any concrete evidence for support, they have given the credit for these works to far-away foreign cultures. This is both academically irresponsible and unfair to the cultures that truly produced them.

Online source— author's name mentioned in paragraph

Follensbee, along with many others, concludes that there is "overwhelming archaeological evidence that the Olmec Colossal Heads were made by and for Native Americans."

Encyclopedia article

About twenty-four hundred years ago, the last great Olmec cultural center was violently destroyed ("Pre-Columbian Civilizations"). Archaeologists disagree about the cause. Some believe the Olmec peasants revolted against their rulers, bringing down the civilization in the process. Others believe that invaders from nearby may have been responsible (Piña Chan 208).

Importance

Most archaeologists, however, agree that the Olmecs played an important and influential role in the early history of the region. One writer summarizes the opinion of many scholars in the field when he writes that the Olmecs "created Mesoamerica's first civilization 3,000 years ago-- and left a rich cultural heritage to later groups, from the Maya to the Aztec" (Stuart 88). For many years, not much was known about this important civilization. Today, however, thanks to years of research and analysis, scientists are bringing light to a dark past.

Direct quotation

CONCLUSION
Summary statement

Works Cited

Autry, William O. "Olmec Indians." <u>World Book</u>
<u>Multimedia Encyclopedia</u>. 1995 ed.
CD-ROM. World Book, 1995.

Bower, B. "Domesticating an Ancient 'Temple
Town.'" <u>Science News</u> 15 Oct. 1988: 246.

Fagan, Brian M. <u>Kingdoms of Gold, Kingdoms of</u>
<u>Jade</u>. London: Thames and Hudson, 1991.

Follensbee, Billie. <u>Olmec Heads: A Product of the</u>
<u>Americas</u>. 30 Apr. 1996. Online. Internet.
12 Dec. 1997. Available http://copan.bioz
.unibas.ch/meso/olmec.html.

Grove, David C. <u>Chalcatzingo: Excavations on the</u>
<u>Olmec Frontier</u>. New York: Thames and
Hudson, 1984.

Piña Chan, Román. <u>The Olmec: Mother Culture</u>
<u>of Mesoamerica</u>. New York: Rizzoli, 1989.

"Pre-Columbian Civilizations." <u>The New</u>
<u>Encyclopaedia Britannica: Macropaedia</u>.
15th ed. 1988.

Stuart, George E. "New Light on the Olmec."
<u>National Geographic</u> Nov. 1993: 88-114.

WRITING ASSIGNMENT

PART 7:
Writing Your First Draft

Now you're ready to write! Using your final outline and note cards as a guide, write the first draft of your report. Give credit to your sources by using parenthetical citations following the MLA format in this chapter. Then prepare your Works Cited list. Be sure to list only the sources you actually used in your report.

WORKS CITED

The MLA format calls for a 5-space indent. For the typeface used in this book, the 5-space indent translates into a printer's measure that is slightly different.

TIMESAVER

You may want to appoint a team of students to be in charge of checking the forms for the Works Cited pages for students' reports. This team could also help other students with problems in preparing their Works Cited pages. Such a technical task might appeal to some students, and their assistance will help other students and save you time.

MEETING *individual* NEEDS

AT-RISK STUDENTS

If your schedule allows, set up meetings to discuss first drafts with students one-on-one. Also, encourage students to discuss their reports with one another.

435

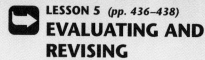
TEACHING THE LESSON

Be sure that students understand how to use the chart, **Evaluating and Revising Research Reports.** You may want to call attention to the three verbs most often emphasized under **Revision Technique** [*add, replace, cut*]. As guided practice, go over **Exercise 5** with students in class. Then, as independent practice, have students work

QUOTATION FOR THE DAY

"The only sure weapon against bad ideas is better ideas." (Whitney Griswold, 1909–1963, American educator)

This quotation could serve as a reminder to students that the ideas in their writing must be logical and based on facts. Tell students to keep the quotation in mind as they evaluate the ideas in their reports.

436

---

436   *Writing a Research Paper*

Evaluating and Revising

Use the chart on page 438 to evaluate and revise your report. Ask yourself the questions on the left. Then, use the revision techniques on the right to fix any problems.

EXERCISE 5   **Analyzing a Writer's Revisions**

Below are the revisions that were made to a first draft of the ninth paragraph of the Writer's Model (page 433). Study the revisions, and answer the questions that follow.

> Olmec hieroglyphics, along with the   **reorder**
> quality of Olmec art, hint at the sophisti-
> cation and learning of the culture that
> produced them. Many archaeologists also
>   *the Olmecs*
> believe that ~~these people~~ were the first to   **replace**
> use hieroglyphic writing within Meso-
> *(In hieroglyphic writing, a picture represents a word, syllable, or sound.)*
> america. Evidence for this includes an   **add**
> Olmec sculpture carved with the figure of
> a man who seems to be walking. Behind
> him is a carving of a human foot, which
> experts believe is the hieroglyphic symbol
> for "walking" or "marching." Other sculp-
> tures have carvings of stars and clouds
> which appear to be hieroglyphic symbols
> (Piña Chan, 184). ~~Of course, the Egyptians~~   **cut/cut**
> ~~also had a calendar and used hieroglyphic~~
> ~~symbols for similar purposes, but the Egyp-~~
> ~~tian hieroglyphics were very different from~~
> ~~the ones that the Olmecs and Mayans used.~~

RETEACHING

Write three headings on the chalkboard: *Add, Replace,* and *Cut.* Then, give examples from graded student papers of sentences that need something added, replaced, and cut.

☛

1. Notice that the writer moved the first sentence from the beginning to the end of the paragraph. Why do you think this change was made?
2. Why did the writer replace the phrase *these people* with the phrase *the Olmecs*?
3. Why was a new sentence added after the second sentence of the paragraph?
4. For what reason did the writer delete the sentence that begins *Of course, the Egyptians . . .*?
5. Why did the writer delete the comma from the citation in the fifth sentence of the paragraph?

WRITING ASSIGNMENT

PART 8:
Evaluating and Revising Your Report

Get some help by exchanging your report with a classmate. Use the evaluating and revising guidelines in the chart on page 438 to give each other friendly advice. Apply the guidelines to your own report also, and make changes to improve your first draft.

Calvin & Hobbes copyright 1989 Watterson.
Distributed by Universal Press Syndicate.
Reprinted with permission. All rights reserved.

ANSWERS
Exercise 5

1. The first sentence is a conclusion about the culture based on the information presented throughout the paragraph. As a concluding sentence, it brings closure to the paragraph.

2. The phrase *the Olmecs* is more specific than *these people*. Also, once the first sentence is moved, it is necessary to identify by name which people the writer is talking about.

3. The new sentence defines hieroglyphic writing.

4. This sentence is irrelevant to the subject of Olmec hieroglyphics. Consequently, it breaks the unity of the paragraph.

5. According to MLA format, no comma separates an author's name and the page number(s).

INTEGRATING THE LANGUAGE ARTS

Grammar Link. You might need to remind your students to use a variety of compound, complex, and compound-complex sentences in their writing. Using a variety of sentence structures will improve students' writing style and will help their readers see the connections between ideas and pieces of information. Review the sentence structures with students, and then have students read through their reports specifically for sentence structures. Tell students to revise and combine sentences if they have too many sentences with the same type of sentence structure in their reports.

Refer students to the cartoon on p. 437 and ask them what advice they would give Calvin to help him revise his essay. [Possible answers include reminding Calvin that something "made up" is not a fact and telling him that he should probably include several facts in his essay.] ■

MEETING individual NEEDS

LEP/ESL

General Strategies. If possible, guide each student individually through the **Evaluating and Revising Research Reports** chart. You may need to clarify guidelines such as "Is the report suitable for its audience?" and "Is the tone of the report appropriate?" Try using specific examples from their reports to help students understand whether or not they are meeting the necessary criteria.

EVALUATING AND REVISING RESEARCH REPORTS

EVALUATION GUIDE	REVISION TECHNIQUE
1 Does a thesis statement appear early in the report?	**Add** a thesis statement to the first or second paragraph of your report.
2 Is the report suitable for its audience? Is it interesting, informative, and clear?	**Add** interesting, unusual, or surprising details. **Add** necessary definitions, background information, and explanations.
3 Is the tone of the report appropriate?	**Replace** words or phrases that give your report a casual or informal tone.
4 Are sources relevant, reliable, recent, and representative?	**Cut** information that is irrelevant or out-of-date. **Replace** with information from better sources.
5 Are ideas and information pulled together (synthesized) and stated in the writer's own words?	Check that each topic sentence expresses your ideas in your own words. **Add** or **replace** topic sentences as necessary.
6 Are ideas developed and supported with adequate information? Will readers find the information complete?	**Add** facts and figures, theories, and expert opinions about your topic where necessary.
7 Does all the information relate directly to the topic and approach?	**Cut** unnecessary information.
8 Is proper credit given for each source of information?	**Add** documentation for any information that isn't common knowledge. Check format guidelines.
9 Does documentation follow the format recommended by your teacher?	**Replace** as necessary to follow the MLA format or other format recommended by your teacher.

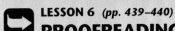

PROOFREADING AND PUBLISHING

OBJECTIVE

- To proofread and share a research report

TEACHING THE LESSON

Ask students what they will be checking for as they proofread their reports. Write appropriate responses on the chalkboard. Afterward, write on the chalkboard anything that students failed to mention. ■

Proofreading and Publishing

So far, you've focused on the content of your paper. Now it's time to work on its appearance. Take another look at your report, and clean up all grammar, mechanics, and usage errors. Make a final check of your documentation as well. To share what you've learned, try one of the ideas below, or come up with a publishing idea of your own.

- If you're applying for a part-time job or for a special award or honor, submit your report as an example of your ability to plan and carry out a long-term project.
- Plan a bulletin board that features research as a theme. Select one in a location where all students can stop and look—maybe the front hall of your school. Post examples of research reports from your English class as well as from history and science classes.

WRITING ASSIGNMENT

PART 9:
Proofreading and Publishing Your Report

Proofread your report carefully and correct any errors. Be extra careful to get your documentation (citations and *Works Cited* page) just right. Publish or share your report with others.

 Reflecting on Your Writing

If you plan to add your report to your **portfolio,** make sure to date the report and to include written responses to each of the following questions.

- How did you narrow your subject down to a topic?
- What kinds of research materials did you find most useful? Which were not so useful? Explain.
- How did your notes or outline help you when you began to write your report?

PROGRAM MANAGER

PROOFREADING AND PUBLISHING

- **Instructional Support** For a chart students may use to evaluate their proofreading progress, see **Proofreading** in *Strategies for Writing*, p. 59.
- **Independent Practice/ Reteaching** For additional practice with language skills, see **Proofreading Practice: Using Quotations** in *Strategies for Writing*, p. 60.
- **Assessment/Reflection** To assess student work and evaluate progress, see **Portfolio Forms** in *Portfolio Assessment*, pp. 22–25.

TEACHING NOTE

Once the research paper assignment is completed, some students may be reluctant to revisit it to write a reflection. Remind them that they will write research reports in the future and that putting down on paper what they learned from their experience this year will help them in the years to come. Ask students to pay particular attention to their responses to the second question and to keep their reflections in their portfolios to refer to in the future.

QUOTATION FOR THE DAY

"Good swimmers are oftenest drowned." (Thomas Fuller, M.D., 1654–1734, English physician, writer, and compiler)

Lead students in a discussion of the relationship of this quotation to the proofreading part of the writing process. Suggest that those most confident about their spelling and usage may not be as careful as they should be in proofreading their reports.

A STUDENT MODEL
Evaluation

1. Lam states the report's thesis at the very beginning.
2. Lam's report is appropriate for a general audience, and it is interesting, informative, and clear. The neutral tone is appropriate for the subject, the audience, and the type of writing.
3. The sources are relevant and reliable, and most of the information is stated in Lam's own words rather than in direct quotations.
4. The information in the report is complete and well explained, and all of the information relates directly to the topic.
5. All of the information is credited to sources.

A STUDENT MODEL

The following paragraphs were excerpted from a report by Lam Votran, a student in Walnut Creek, California. Lam advises other student writers to "always make an outline" before starting a draft of a report.

A Moving Tune
by Lam Votran

Music has extraordinary power. It can inspire, it can irritate, and it can provide deep states of mental relaxation. Sometimes you can't say what it is about a particular piece of music that touches you, but the attraction is so strong that you can't resist it.

Therapists have found that music and singing can be effective in the treatment of children with emotional and mental problems. In their book *Music Therapy in Special Education*, Paul Nordoff and Clive Robbins write about their experiences of using songs to educate children about their emotions. They say that every song has "an emotional content that it can impart to the children who sing it. . . . Songs can arouse children to excitement, gladden them with pleasure, calm them to thoughtfulness" (32).

Even violent criminals can be touched by certain kinds of music. In a letter published in the *Canadian Medical Association Journal*, the medical director of a psychiatric prison hospital in British Columbia writes that classical music seemed to have a calming effect on the inmates he worked with-- men who had been convicted of violent offenses like murder and assault.

The inmates were given a chance to voluntarily take part in music-listening sessions. They chose the music selections themselves, and they were asked to participate in discussions afterward. Although the inmates sometimes became disruptive while listening to rock music, the medical director says that they listened to classical music "intently," without any disruptions. Tchaikovsky and Debussy, he says, were the two most popular listening choices (Roy 1170).

WRITING WORKSHOP

OBJECTIVES

- To analyze a book report on an autobiography
- To write a book report on an autobiography

TEACHING THE LESSON

Start by tying the **Writing Workshop** in with writing research reports. Point out the similarities and differences between book reports and research reports. Then, read or have a student volunteer read the excerpt of the sample book report. You may want to lead a class discussion that applies the **Guidelines for Evaluating Autobiography**

WRITING WORKSHOP

A Book Report That Evaluates

You evaluate movies by judging them against criteria, or guidelines. For example, you may like movies that are filled with action. You can also use criteria to evaluate a book. Below are guidelines for evaluating an autobiography.

GUIDELINES FOR EVALUATING AUTOBIOGRAPHY

1. Is the author honest? Does he or she write about details that make the author's life seem less than perfect?
2. Does the author present details of places, people, and events that we otherwise wouldn't have known about?
3. Does the author use fresh and natural-sounding language?
4. Does the author write about his or her thoughts and feelings, as well as events?

Here is the opening of a report on an autobiography. See if you think the writer evaluates it using the criteria above.

Golden Lilies by Kwei-li is a series of letters by a Chinese woman who was born in 1867. In the first half of the book, eighteen-year-old Kwei-li writes letters to her husband. He has been appointed to a distant political post, and has left his young wife in the home of her mother-in-law. Twenty-five years later, in the book's second half, Kwei-li writes letters to her mother-in-law. She now lives in Kiang-su with her politically powerful husband. Throughout this superior autobiography, the voice of a real woman shines through.

In her letters Kwei-li writes of both her joys and her sorrows. Early in the book she speaks of her love for her husband: "Few women have the joy I feel when I look into my loved one's face and know that I am his and he is mine, and that our lives are twined together for all the days to come" (34-35). She writes also of her great joy at the birth of her

QUOTATION FOR THE DAY

"How many good books suffer neglect through the inefficiency of their beginnings!" (Edgar Allan Poe, 1809–1849, American author and poet)

Ask students if they have ever stopped reading a book because they didn't like the beginning. Then, ask students to share what qualities they think a good book, particularly a good autobiography, should have.

CRITICAL THINKING

Evaluation. The third guideline for evaluating autobiographies calls for a sophisticated evaluation of diction. Work with students to develop criteria by which to evaluate diction. Criteria might include avoidance of clichés and tired adjectives and adverbs and avoidance of stilted or pompous-sounding language. You may want to bring to class examples of boring, contrived writing and examples of fresh and natural-sounding language.

MEETING individual NEEDS

LEP/ESL

General Strategies. Because this assignment requires a very thorough understanding of a book, you may want to allow English-language learners to read autobiographies written in their native languages. Then, have students write their book reports in English.

to the sample book report.

Discuss with students the answers to the four questions that follow the sample book report. Then, instruct students to follow the stages of the writing process to write book reports on autobiographies independently.

If students use additional criteria in their reports, you can ask them to specify these in their reflections.

CLOSURE

Ask students to repeat the four items from **Guidelines for Evaluating Autobiography** and to tell why each of these guidelines is important to consider when writing a book report. ■

ANSWERS
Writing Workshop Questions

Responses may vary. Here are some possibilities:

1. The information helps the reader understand the people involved and the basic situations of their lives.

2. The writer uses a quotation from the book to better show Kwei-li's personality and the strength of her feelings. The quotation also shows her natural-sounding language.

3. The writer clearly states that the details help the reader's understanding.

4. The evaluation is positive. In the first paragraph, the writer states that the work is a "superior autobiography" and that Kwei-li's voice "shines through." In the second paragraph, the writer seems pleased that Kwei-li writes of both her joys and sorrows. In the third paragraph, the writer states that the author provides helpful details and uses words to paint China's beauty.

TEACHING NOTE

Student Self-evaluation. After students deliver their oral presentations, have them write brief self-evaluations. Each student should rate his or her preparation based on the following items: topic and purpose, introduction, development, conclusion, verbal delivery, nonverbal delivery, and language.

Students may find the checklist format of **Evaluating a Speech** on p. 38 of *Portfolio Assessment* helpful in completing their self-evaluations.

first son and her almost unbearable sorrow at his death even before his father has seen him. In the second half, she mourns the passing of the old Chinese ways: Her daughter wants to be a doctor; and her son is accused of treason.

Kwei-li's details help the reader to understand the old and new China. We see the endless labor of peasants doomed to spend the rest of their lives grinding herbs. They are "harnessed to great stones" and go "round and round all day, like buffalo at the waterwheel" (40). Throughout the book, Kwei-li paints in words China's great beauty. She watches "the mists cling lovingly to the hilltops, while leaves from giant banyan trees sway idly in the morning wind . . ." (171).

1. In the first paragraph, the writer provides some background information. Why is this information important?
2. In the second paragraph, why do you think the writer quoted some of Kwei-li's words from the book?
3. The third paragraph evaluates Kwei-li's use of details. What do you think is the writer's evaluation on this point?
4. Based on this portion of the book report, do you think the writer's evaluation is positive or negative? Why?

Writing a Book Report

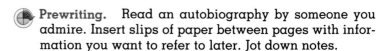 **Prewriting.** Read an autobiography by someone you admire. Insert slips of paper between pages with information you want to refer to later. Jot down notes.

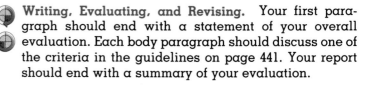 **Writing, Evaluating, and Revising.** Your first paragraph should end with a statement of your overall evaluation. Each body paragraph should discuss one of the criteria in the guidelines on page 441. Your report should end with a summary of your evaluation.

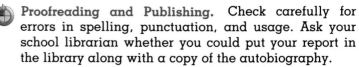 **Proofreading and Publishing.** Check carefully for errors in spelling, punctuation, and usage. Ask your school librarian whether you could put your report in the library along with a copy of the autobiography.

If you decide to include your book report in your **portfolio,** date the report and attach a note responding to these questions: How did the guidelines on page 441 help you to write your report? What other criteria did you consider?

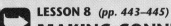
RESEARCH ACROSS THE CURRICULUM

OBJECTIVE

- To analyze ways that research has played a role in the restoration of two masterpieces

☞

443

MAKING CONNECTIONS

RESEARCH ACROSS THE CURRICULUM

The Visual Arts

Research is playing an important role in the preservation of two of the world's greatest art masterpieces which might otherwise be someday lost forever. Leonardo da Vinci's *Last Supper*, painted on a wall of a monastery in Milan, Italy, and Michelangelo's frescoes, painted on the ceiling of the Sistine Chapel in Rome, are about five hundred years old. Over the years, heat, humidity, dirt, pollution, and wars have badly damaged both works. Previous attempts at restoration damaged them even further when layers of paint, glue, and varnish were added to the originals.

During the 1970s restorers began extensive projects to clean, preserve, and restore both works as nearly as possible to their original condition. Research has been an important part of both projects. Restorers need to know as much as possible about how da Vinci and Michelangelo actually painted—what kinds of brush strokes they used and how they mixed their colors, for example. In earlier restorations, painters often added new layers of colors

RESEARCH ACROSS THE CURRICULUM

Teaching Strategies

If possible, show students a videotape of the *NOVA* episode that documents the restoration of the Sistine Chapel. Afterward, discuss how research was used in the restoration project. Challenge students to find more information about this or other restoration projects.

👁 VISUAL CONNECTIONS

Exploring the Subject. Six major restorations since 1726 may have done more harm than good to Leonardo da Vinci's *The Last Supper* by darkening it with oil- and dirt-collecting glue and wax and by destroying the original paint with harsh solvents. Some restorers changed lines on the Apostles' faces and obliterated considerable detail.

GUIDELINES

Each student should be able to tell you at least one way that research played a role in the restorations.

SPEAKING AND LISTENING

Teaching Strategies

If your class is very big, individual pollsters might wear out their welcome fast. Have the class conduct one public opinion poll, or divide the class into four or five groups and have each group conduct a different poll. You could invite students to suggest some other topics about which they would like to conduct polls. Write appropriate ideas on the chalkboard and let the class or groups vote on the ideas for their polls.

Students might need some help in formulating questions that are objective and neutral. Tell students to avoid loaded words, words with connotations that might affect answers.

and even beards or clothes to the figures. Understanding the techniques of da Vinci and Michelangelo helps restorers decide what is original and what was added later.

A *NOVA* episode, available on videotape, documents the restoration of the Sistine Chapel. Popular magazines, such as *Time, Newsweek,* and *National Geographic,* gave the restorations extensive coverage including photographs. You might want to view the videotape (it's available at many video stores). Or use the *Readers' Guide* to find articles about both restoration projects. Bring the articles to class to share with your classmates. As you view the videotape or read the articles, look for ways that research has played a role in the restorations.

SPEAKING AND LISTENING

Creating Research Sources: Public Opinion Polls

You've probably been met in shopping malls by people conducting public opinion polls about your shopping habits and product preferences. The results of these polls are used to help businesses increase their sales.

Consider taking some public opinion polls in your own school. If you want the poll to represent the opinions of all students, you need to poll students from all grade levels. Or, you might restrict the poll to your own grade level. Try to poll ten percent of the population. If there are three hundred students in your grade, for instance, talk to thirty of them. Also try to select students who represent the entire group. You might, for example, select every tenth person from an alphabetical listing of the class.

Write some objective questions with answers that you can easily tally. For example, if you want to find out about favorite and least favorite lunchroom foods, have students rank five foods from 1 to 5 (with 5 being the favorite). To find out students' opinions on an issue, give them a neutral statement and then ask whether they agree or disagree. Such a statement might be "A constitutional amendment should be passed prohibiting the burning of the American flag."

GUIDELINES

Presentations will vary. Ensure that poll questions are objective and neutral.

Try one of the ideas on the following list, and conduct a public opinion poll in your school. (You may also have ideas about different topics.)

- Favorite/least favorite foods served in the lunchroom
- Favorite/least favorite musicians, actors, television shows, movies, and so on
- Ideas to improve education in your community
- Opinions on national/foreign policy issues

When you finish your poll, tally your findings and present the results to your class. Consider using the results in an article for your school newspaper or a letter to the editor of your local newspaper.

12 WRITING COMPLETE SENTENCES

OBJECTIVES

- To identify and correct sentence fragments and run-on sentences
- To create complete sentences from phrases and clauses

cross CURRICULUM

Science in Complete Sentences

Discuss with students the usefulness of sentence fragments in the process of taking notes. Students will probably observe that using fragments helps them keep pace with a lecture or with their reading. However, students should also realize that translating their notes into complete sentences is an excellent study skill. If you team teach with a science teacher, consider collaborating on the following activity to practice translating fragments into complete sentences.

- **Assignment** Have students observe or participate in a science experiment or lab session. Students should take accurate notes at each step of the procedure. Again, these notes will most likely be in fragment form. Then, when students are in your class, have them work with partners to translate orally the fragments in their notes into complete sentences. They may do this by reviewing their notes and then telling each other in complete sentences what took place during the experiment or lab. The listening partner should pay careful attention to any sentence fragments and work to correct them. If possible, have students record their discussions and replay them to identify any incomplete sentences and to revise them. After both partners translate their notes and listen to their partners, have them work together to write a one- or two-paragraph summary of the lab or experiment. Have pairs present their summaries and compare them to others in the class.

- **Reflection** After students present their summaries, give them time to write in their journals responses to the following questions:
  - What was the hardest part of the activity? What was the easiest?
  - What did you learn about how you take notes?
  - What differences did you notice between note taking, speaking, and writing a summary?

INTEGRATING THE LANGUAGE ARTS

SELECTION	READING AND LITERATURE	WRITING AND CRITICAL THINKING	LANGUAGE AND SYNTAX	SPEAKING, LISTENING, AND OTHER EXPRESSION SKILLS
• from *I Know Why the Caged Bird Sings* by Maya Angelou p. 448	• Contrasting sentence fragments and complete sentences pp. 448–449 • Identifying the missing parts of incomplete sentences pp. 448–449 • Identifying subordinate clause fragments p. 453 • Identifying sentence fragments in a paragraph pp. 453, 455, 459, 460 • Identifying and revising sentence fragments and run-on sentences pp. 453, 455, 459, 460	• Analyzing sentence fragments pp. 448–449 • Applying interpretive and creative thinking pp. 451, 454 • Creating complete sentences from phrase fragments p. 451 • Combining subordinate clauses with independent clauses to form complete sentences p. 453 • Evaluating and revising sentence fragments in a paragraph pp. 453, 455, 459, 460 • Creating complete sentences form subordinate clauses p. 454 • Evaluating and revising fragments and run-on sentences pp. 458–459 • Creating a paragraph with complete sentences p. 460 • Evaluating and revising a paragraph with phrase and clause fragments p. 460	• Proofreading for errors in grammar, usage, and mechanics pp. 451, 454, 460 • Correcting fragments and run-on sentences by changing punctuation and capitalization pp. 453, 455, 458, 459, 460	• Working with classmates to write and analyze paragraphs p. 460

CHAPTER 12: WRITING COMPLETE SENTENCES

Use this guide for creating an instructional plan that addresses the individual needs of your students. Assignments accompanied by the following symbol (∗) may be completed out of class. Times given for pacing lessons are estimated.

CHAPTER PLANNING GUIDE—PUPIL'S EDITION

LESSONS	SENTENCE FRAGMENTS pp. 446–455	RUN-ON SENTENCES pp. 456–459
DEVELOPMENTAL PROGRAM	🕐 **65–70 minutes** • Main Assignment: Looking Ahead p. 446 • Sentence Fragments pp. 446–455 • Style Note p. 448 • Exercises 1–5 pp. 448–449, 451, 453, 454, 455 in pairs • Writing Notes pp. 450, 452, 454	🕐 **35–40 minutes** • Run-on Sentences pp. 456–459 • Writing Note p. 456 • Exercise 6 #1–5 p. 458 in pairs
CORE PROGRAM	🕐 **35–40 minutes** • Main Assignment: Looking Ahead p. 446 • Sentence Fragments pp. 446–455 • Style Note p. 448 • Exercises 1–5 pp. 448–449, 451, 453, 454, 455∗ • Writing Notes pp. 450, 452, 454	🕐 **25–30 minutes** • Run-on Sentences pp. 456–459 • Writing Note p. 456 • Exercise 6 p. 458∗
ACCELERATED PROGRAM	🕐 **30–35 minutes** • Main Assignment: Looking Ahead p. 446 • Style Note p. 448 • Phrase Fragments/Exercise 2 pp. 449–451∗ • Subordinate Clause Fragments/Exercise 5 pp. 451–455∗ • Writing Notes pp. 450, 452, 454	🕐 **25–30 minutes** • Revising Run-on Sentences pp. 456–459 • Exercise 6 p. 458∗

CHAPTER PLANNING GUIDE—PROGRAM RESOURCES

	SENTENCE FRAGMENTS pp. 446–455	RUN-ON SENTENCES pp. 456–459
PRINT	• Types of Sentence Fragments A and B, *Word Choice and Sentence Style* pp. 1–2 • Sentence Fragments, *English Workshop* pp. 67–72, 77–92	• Identifying Run-on Sentences, *Word Choice and Sentence Style* p. 3 • Run-on Sentences, *English Workshop* pp. 73–74, 91–92
MEDIA	• *Language Workshop:* Lessons 24, 27, 30–33	• *Language Workshop:* Lessons 28, 30–33

 Computer disk or CD–ROM

ASSESSMENT OPTIONS

Reflection
Self-assessment Record, *Portfolio Assessment* p. 19

Summative Assessment
Review, *Elements of Writing,* Pupil's Edition, p. 459
Reviews A and B: Writing Complete Sentences, *Word Choice and Sentence Style* pp. 4–7

ELEMENTS OF WRITING: CURRICULUM CONNECTIONS

Making Connections
• Fill in the Missing Pieces p. 460

SENTENCE FRAGMENTS

OBJECTIVES

- To use the three-part test to identify the sentence parts missing in fragments
- To create complete sentences from phrase fragments
- To identify and correct subordinate clause fragments in a paragraph
- To create complete sentences from subordinate clause fragments
- To identify and correct fragments in a paragraph

12 WRITING COMPLETE SENTENCES

LOOKING AHEAD

Sentences are the building blocks of your writing. That's why it's important to check your sentences for clarity and completeness. As you work through this chapter, you will learn how to

- identify and correct sentence fragments
- identify and correct run-on sentences

Sentence Fragments

A *sentence fragment* is a group of words that is only a part of a sentence. Since a fragment of something is not the whole thing, it won't be as useful to you as it could be. Just as a fragment of a bowl can't hold much food, a fragment of a sentence may not communicate what you want to say. To communicate clearly, whether at school or in the workplace, you must write complete sentences.

To be complete, a sentence must (1) have a subject, (2) have a verb, and (3) express a complete thought. If any of these pieces are missing, the group of words is a fragment rather than a complete sentence.

You may want to introduce this section by writing *Before we begin class* and *Your writing assignment* on the chalkboard. This should get the students' attention and cause some consternation among them. If you then act as if the students are supposed to do something, their nervousness might increase until one of them asks for more instructions. You could then act surprised and ask, "What's wrong with my instructions? Aren't they clear?" The ensuing discussion should provide adequate opportunity for you to begin the lesson on fragments.

Sentence Fragments **447**

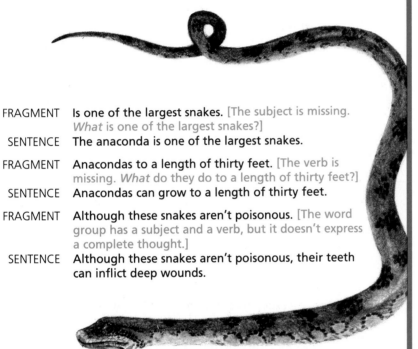

FRAGMENT   Is one of the largest snakes. [The subject is missing. *What* is one of the largest snakes?]

SENTENCE   The anaconda is one of the largest snakes.

FRAGMENT   Anacondas to a length of thirty feet. [The verb is missing. *What* do they do to a length of thirty feet?]

SENTENCE   Anacondas can grow to a length of thirty feet.

FRAGMENT   Although these snakes aren't poisonous. [The word group has a subject and a verb, but it doesn't express a complete thought.]

SENTENCE   Although these snakes aren't poisonous, their teeth can inflict deep wounds.

Fragments usually occur when you're writing in a hurry or are a little careless. For example, you might create a fragment by leaving out an important word or two. Or you might chop off part of a sentence by putting in a period too soon.

To find out if what you've written is a fragment, you can use this simple three-part test:

1. Does the group of words have a subject?
2. Does it have a verb?
3. Does it express a complete thought?

If even one of your answers is "no," then you have a fragment.

COMPUTER NOTE: Some word-processing programs have a tool to check grammatical construction. This tool can find sentence fragments and run-on sentences for you to revise.

MEETING *individual* NEEDS

LEP/ESL

General Strategies. To help English-language learners become familiar with the parts of a complete sentence, write the following lists on the chalkboard and have students match words and phrases to form complete sentences:

Subjects: The birds, Felix, They, A rock, The band

Verbs: sat, flew, left, played, broke

Objects/complements/modifiers: the window, quickly, on the fence, a song, by the tree

LEARNING STYLES

Kinetic Learners. You may want to put the items in the lists above on separate cards and let students arrange them to form sentences.

TECHNOLOGY TIP

Grammar-checking programs sometimes allow students to set the style of writing they want the program to check for. In other words, for a research report, they may want to set the program to look for possible errors related to all rules, whereas for an informal letter, they may wish to use a more casual style. Encourage students to adapt the style of the grammar check to suit the subject, purpose, and audience of their compositions.

The **Motivation** activity will help get students involved in this lesson by illustrating how sentence fragments represent incomplete thoughts and how this problem in communication can affect the students. The discussion that follows the activity should center on how sentence fragments are confusing because they lack important information. Try to lead students to discover how the missing information in sentence fragments can be supplied by asking and then answering the appropriate questions. For example, if the fragment *Before we begin class* is to be made into a complete sentence, the questions "What will happen?" or "What are we supposed to do?" would help students supply the missing information.

INTEGRATING THE LANGUAGE ARTS

Literature Link. If your students' literature book has Sandra Cisneros' short story "Geraldo No Last Name," have the students read and discuss the story. Then, ask them to identify the sentence fragments. (There are at least thirteen.) Ask the students to identify the types of fragments used and to tell why they think Cisneros used fragments at all. [Basically, the fragments give the impression that the story is being told in an informal, conversational tone.]

STYLE NOTE

By itself, a sentence fragment doesn't express a complete thought. But a fragment can make sense in writing if it is clearly related to a sentence that comes before or after it.

Read the following groups of words from Maya Angelou's autobiography *I Know Why the Caged Bird Sings:*

> The birthday girl. The center.

By themselves, these fragments don't make sense because we don't know what they relate to. But now read them along with the sentence that the writer placed before them:

> In the Store I was the person of the moment.
> The birthday girl. The center.

As you can see, the sentence gives the fragments meaning. It fills in the missing parts.

Experienced writers like Maya Angelou sometimes use sentence fragments for effect. As a beginning writer, however, you should avoid using fragments. Eventually you'll feel comfortable enough to experiment, but it's important to master the basics first.

EXERCISE 1   **Identifying Sentence Fragments**

Try the three-part test on each of the following groups of words. In each case, identify what, if anything, is missing. If the group of words is missing a subject, write <u>S</u>. If it is missing a verb, write <u>V</u>. If the group of words has both a subject and a verb but doesn't express a complete thought, write <u>I</u>. Write <u>C</u> if the words form a complete sentence.

1. Vampire bats only in the tropics of Central and South America.   **1.** V
2. Most horror tales about vampire bats aren't true. **2.** C
3. Vampire bats very small mammals. **3.** V
4. Although they do bite other animals. **4.** I
5. Don't drain their victims of blood. **5.** S

One way to help students learn about fragments and how to correct them would be to have each student write a verbal phrase, an appositive phrase, a prepositional phrase, and a subordinate clause. Then, one at a time, have the students copy their fragments on the chalkboard so that you can determine whether they understand the differences between the types of fragments.

Next, ask volunteers to form complete sentences using the fragments. Occasionally, you may want to suggest alternative structures so the class can see the variety of ways fragments can be made into complete sentences.

Because this activity could take lots of time, you may want to spread it out over a few days, or you could choose a few volunteers and use their fragments for examples.

6. Their small teeth are as sharp as needles. **6.** C
7. While animals are sleeping. **7.** I
8. But can be dangerous. **8.** S
9. The greatest danger to victims is infection. **9.** C
10. Vampire bats carriers of rabies. **10.** V

"What was it like back in the days when people talked and wrote in complete sentences?"

Berry's World reprinted by permission of Newspaper Enterprise Association, Inc.

Phrase Fragments

A *phrase* is a group of words that does not contain a subject and a verb. Because it doesn't have all the basic parts of a sentence, a phrase by itself is a fragment. Three kinds of phrases are often mistaken for sentences: *verbal phrases, appositive phrases,* and *prepositional phrases.*

Verbal Phrases

A *verbal* is a word that is formed from a verb but is used as another part of speech. Because verbs and verbals are look-alikes, it is sometimes hard to tell the difference between them. That's why *verbal phrases*—phrases that contain verbals—are easily mistaken for sentences. They can appear to have verbs in them when they really don't.

Watch for verbals in phrases. Some verbals have endings such as *–ing, –d,* or *–ed* and may have helping verbs (like *is, were,* or *have*). Another kind of verbal has the word *to* in front of it (*to run, to look*). A verbal phrase alone doesn't express a complete thought.

Another possibility is to divide the class into groups once the students have written their fragments. Let the groups form sample sentences and check each other's work while you monitor the groups. This activity can also be used in simplified form for each type of phrase and clause.

Exercise 1 can be used to assess students' ability to recognize fragments and can be covered orally as guided practice or used as a diagnostic test. You may want to have students identify the missing information as you suggest questions that would lead them to supply that information. Conversely, leading students to discover what kind of

COOPERATIVE LEARNING

Divide the class into groups of three students each and have them write paragraphs composed of fragments—two fragments from each student in the group. Then, have the groups trade paragraphs to revise the fragments into complete sentences. Finally, have one representative from each group read the revised paragraphs to the class.

You may want to allow discussions between the groups that wrote the paragraphs and the groups that revised them. How were the fragments revised and why were they revised in that manner? What other revisions are possible? How might other revisions change the effect or focus of the sentences?

---

450 *Writing Complete Sentences*

FRAGMENT | To see Devils Tower National Monument.
SENTENCE | We stopped in northeastern Wyoming to see Devils Tower National Monument.

FRAGMENT | Established in 1906.
SENTENCE | Established in 1906, Devils Tower was the first national monument in the United States.

FRAGMENT | Seeing the movie *Close Encounters of the Third Kind.*
SENTENCE | Seeing the movie *Close Encounters of the Third Kind* made me interested in Devils Tower.

Appositive Phrases

An *appositive* is a word that identifies or explains a nearby word in the sentence. An *appositive phrase* is an appositive and its modifiers. Because an appositive phrase does not have a verb and does not express a complete thought, it cannot stand alone as a complete sentence.

FRAGMENT | A strange rock formation.
SENTENCE | Devils Tower, a strange rock formation, has special significance in the movie.

Prepositional Phrases

A *prepositional phrase* is a group of words that begins with a preposition and ends with a noun or pronoun.

FRAGMENT | Of volcanic rock.
SENTENCE | Devils Tower is an 865-foot-tall tower of volcanic rock.

WRITING NOTE When a verbal phrase modifies, or describes, another word in the sentence, it's usually best to place the phrase as close as possible to the word it modifies. For instance, in the example at the top of this page, the verbal phrase *established in 1906* needs to stay close to *Devils Tower*. But some verbal phrases, such as the phrase *to see Devils Tower National Monument*, make sense either at the beginning or at the end of the sentence.

 REFERENCE NOTE: For more help with phrase placement in sentences, see pages 465–466 and 728–730.

INDEPENDENT PRACTICE

Exercises **2**, **3**, **4**, and **5** can be used as independent practice, although you may also use some of them as guided practice. If, for example, students don't do well on **Exercise 2**, you may want to work with them on **Exercise 4**. The same principle applies with **Exercises 3** and **5**.

☞

Sentence Fragments **451**

EXERCISE 2 ▶ **Revising Phrase Fragments**

Using the photograph to help spark your imagination, create a sentence from each of the following phrase fragments. You may (1) add the fragment to a complete sentence or (2) develop the fragment into a complete sentence by adding a subject, a verb, or both.

EXAMPLE **1.** climbing up the cliff
 1. *Climbing up the cliff, I tried not to look down.*
 or
 I was climbing up the cliff.

1. in the jungle
2. watching for wild animals
3. to swing on huge vines
4. on the way
5. scratched and bruised
6. the fearless explorer
7. led by experienced guides
8. at the top of the cliff
9. surprised by a loud noise
10. to write about the experience

Subordinate Clause Fragments

A *clause* is a group of words that has a subject and a verb. One kind of clause, an *independent clause*, expresses a complete thought and can stand alone as a sentence. For example, the independent clause *I missed the bus* is a com-

ANSWERS
Exercise 2

Sentences will vary. Here are some possibilities:

1. The photographers were hired to take pictures in the jungle.
2. They spent many hours watching for wild animals.
3. Chimpanzees like to swing on huge vines.
4. On the way to the water hole, the photographers saw an elephant.
5. The photographers were scratched and bruised when they fell off the cliff.
6. The fearless explorer saved them from the hungry lion.
7. They were led by experienced guides to the elephant graveyard.
8. At the top of the cliff, the photographers admired the view.
9. They were suddenly surprised by a loud noise.
10. After they returned, the photographers decided to write about the experience.

TIMESAVER
To save yourself some time, tell students to underline the fragments they use to make sentences in **Exercises 2** and **4** and to circle the places in **Exercises 3** and **5** where fragments have been joined to each other or to independent clauses. This procedure will allow you to check the students' work quickly and accurately.

ASSESSMENT

To determine how well students have mastered the material on sentence fragments, carefully check students' answers to **Exercises 2–5. Exercises 2** and **4** should show how well the students have learned to revise fragments, while **Exercises 3** and **5** should reveal how good students are at recognizing and revising fragments.

CLOSURE

Ask the class to recite the questions that make up the three-part test for sentence fragments. [Does the group of words have a subject? Does it have a verb? Does it express a complete thought?] ■

452   *Writing Complete Sentences*

plete sentence. But another kind of clause, a *subordinate clause,* doesn't express a complete thought and can't stand alone as a sentence. A subordinate clause fragment is easy to identify because it suggests a question that it doesn't answer.

FRAGMENT   **Because the weather often changed several times a day.** [*What* was the result of the weather changing?]

SENTENCE   **Because the weather often changed several times a day, filming *White Fang* in Alaska was very difficult.**

FRAGMENT   **Who directed *White Fang.*** [Note that this group of words would be a complete sentence if it ended with a question mark. But as a statement, it doesn't express a complete thought. It doesn't tell *who* directed the movie.]

SENTENCE   **Randal Kleiser, who directed *White Fang,* thought it was worth the trouble to film the movie in Alaska.**

FRAGMENT   **That needed constant care.** [*What* needed constant care?]

SENTENCE   **The cast of *White Fang* included many animals that needed constant care.**

☞ **REFERENCE NOTE:** For more about independent and subordinate clauses, see pages 597–611.

WRITING NOTE

A subordinate clause telling *why, where, when,* or *how* (an adverb clause) may be placed before or after the independent clause. When you combine sentences by inserting an adverb clause, try the clause in both positions to see which sounds best to you.

EXAMPLES   **Because the setting added to the beauty of the film, everyone was glad *White Fang* had been filmed in Alaska.**

or

Everyone was glad *White Fang* had been filmed in Alaska because the setting added to the beauty of the film.

When the subordinate clause comes first, remember to separate it from the independent clause with a comma.

EXERCISE 3 ▶ **Revising Subordinate Clause Fragments**

Use what you've learned about subordinate clause fragments to correct the following paragraph. First, find the clause fragments. Then, revise the paragraph, combining the subordinate clauses with independent clauses. (There may be more than one way to do this.) Change the punctuation and capitalization as necessary.

Before and during the Civil War, the Underground Railroad helped hundreds of slaves to escape to the North. The Underground Railroad was a system of travel. That moved the slaves from one house to another. Until they reached the North and freedom. "Conductors" on the Underground Railroad would plan the slaves' journey to the next "station." One conductor on the Underground Railroad was Harriet Tubman. Who was born a slave in 1821. She escaped from the South in 1849. Which was a very dangerous thing for a female slave to do alone. Because of Harriet Tubman. More than three hundred people were able to reach freedom.

The Granger Collection, New York.

ANSWERS
Exercise 4

Sentences will vary. Here are some possibilities:

1. I am going to see Mariah Carey, who is a popular singer.
2. I first heard her when you played your new record album.
3. Because the concert is next Friday, I'm going to buy tickets today.
4. I'll get you one if the tickets aren't sold out.
5. I hope she sings "Hero," which is my favorite song.

EXERCISE 4 ▶ **Using Subordinate Clauses in Sentences**

You've had some practice at revising subordinate clause fragments. Now use your skills and your imagination to make a complete sentence from each of the following subordinate clauses. To make a complete sentence, add an independent clause at the beginning or at the end of the subordinate clause. Add capitalization and punctuation wherever you need to.

EXAMPLE   1. because her family came from Mexico
           1. *Because her family came from Mexico, Linda Ronstadt heard many Mexican folk songs while she was growing up.*

1. who is a popular singer
2. when you played your new record album
3. because the concert is next Friday
4. if the tickets aren't sold out
5. which is my favorite song

WRITING NOTE   You've seen that it's easy to mistake phrases and subordinate clauses for complete sentences. It's also easy to mistake a series of items for a complete sentence. In the following example, the series of items in dark type is a fragment. It may make sense along with the sentence that comes before it, but it can't stand on its own because it doesn't express a complete thought.

FRAGMENT   I tried out for different positions on the team. **Pitcher, shortstop, and catcher.**

To correct the series fragment, you can
- make it into a complete sentence
- link it to the previous sentence with a colon

SENTENCE   I tried out for different positions on the team. **I tried out for** pitcher, shortstop, and catcher.

or

I tried out for different positions on the team: pitcher, shortstop, and catcher.

E X E R C I S E 5   **Identifying and Revising Fragments**

The writer of the following paragraph wants to describe the high point of her summer—a white-water rafting trip. But the sentence fragments in the paragraph make the meaning unclear. Help make the paragraph clearer by finding and revising the fragments. To correct each fragment, you can (1) link it to an independent clause or (2) develop it into a complete sentence.

Whenever I look at photographs of white-water rafting, I remember what a great time I had on my first raft trip. The first mile or so of the raft trip was easy. As we paddled slowly in the moving current. The guide pointed out the strange rock formations along the banks of the river. Once we got used to paddling, we were ready for adventure. Wanted to experience the thrill of the white water. The guide helped us navigate "the eye of the needle." Which was a difficult stretch of the rapids. Paddling through the rapids, I almost hit a rock. Lost my balance and almost fell overboard. The white water was scary. But was exhilarating too. I hope I can take another raft trip next summer!

ANSWERS
Exercise 5

Revisions will vary. Here is an example:

Whenever I look at photographs of white-water rafting, I remember what a great time I had on my first raft trip. The first mile or so of the raft trip was easy. As we paddled slowly in the moving current, the guide pointed out the strange rock formations along the banks of the river. Once we got used to paddling, we were ready for adventure. We wanted to experience the thrill of the white water, so the guide helped us navigate "the eye of the needle," which was a difficult stretch of the rapids. Paddling through the rapids, I almost hit a rock. As a result, I lost my balance and almost fell overboard. The white water was scary but was exhilarating too. I hope I can take another raft trip next summer!

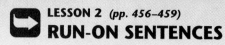
OBJECTIVES

- To identify and revise run-on sentences
- To identify sentence fragments and run-on sentences in a paragraph

MOTIVATION

Write the following passage on the chalkboard and invite students to decipher it: that that is is that that is not is not.

Without proper punctuation, this sentence will probably seem to be nothing more than a list of repeated words. When supplied with punctuation, it becomes "That that is, is. That that is not, is not." Use this example as a

---

RUN-ON SENTENCES

- **Independent Practice/Reteaching** For practice and reinforcement, see **Identifying Run-on Sentences** in *Word Choice and Sentence Style*, p. 3.
- **Computer Guided Instruction** For additional instruction and practice with run-on sentences, see **Lesson 28** in *Language Workshop CD-ROM*.

QUOTATION FOR THE DAY

"Talking and eloquence are not the same: to speak, and to speak well, are two things. A fool may talk, but a wise man speaks." (Ben Jonson, 1572–1637, English dramatist and poet)

If talking and eloquence are not the same, neither then are writing and writing eloquently. The run-on sentence is one type of mistake that keeps writing from becoming eloquent. Remind students that in the real world, as well as in school, people are often judged by their ability (or inability) to write well. In school, grades depend on this ability. After graduation, being successful in a chosen career field may depend upon being able to write well. Lead students in a discussion of how writing well is important to different careers.

Run-on Sentences

A *run-on sentence* is two or more complete sentences that are written as one sentence. Because run-on sentences don't show where one idea ends and another begins, they are confusing to the reader. There are two kinds of run-on sentences: the *fused sentence* and the *comma splice*.

In a *fused sentence*, the writer has joined two or more sentences with no punctuation between them.

RUN-ON	Measurements originally were related to the sizes of people's hands, arms, and feet an inch was the width of a thumb.
CORRECT	Measurements originally were related to the sizes of people's hands, arms, and feet. An inch was the width of a thumb.

In a *comma splice*, the writer has joined two or more sentences with only a comma to separate them.

RUN-ON	A foot was the length of a person's foot, a yard was the distance from a man's nose to the end of his thumb when his arm was outstretched.
CORRECT	A foot was the length of a person's foot. A yard was the distance from a man's nose to the end of his thumb when his arm was outstretched.

WRITING NOTE To identify run-on sentences, try reading your writing aloud. A natural, distinct pause in your voice usually means that you've come to the end of a thought. If your voice pauses but your sentence keeps going, you may have a run-on.

Another way to spot run-ons is to look for subjects and verbs. This will help you see where one complete thought ends and another one begins.

Revising Run-on Sentences

There are several ways to revise a run-on sentence. As shown in the examples on this page, you can always make

MAKING CONNECTIONS

FILL IN THE MISSING PIECES
OBJECTIVES

- To write a paragraph by using correct sentences
- To revise sentence fragments in a paragraph

FILL IN THE MISSING PIECES

Teaching Strategies

Although this activity is designed to get students to revise paragraphs to their original forms, it is more important for students to be able to recognize and correct fragments and run-ons. Reassure the students that if their revisions do not match the original paragraphs this does not mean they have failed. There are many ways to revise fragments and run-ons, any of which can be as valid as the original sentences.

When the students are through revising and begin comparing the revisions to the originals, any differences can be used as prompts for discussion of the revision process. However, evaluations of which versions are better should be kept to a minimum as long as the revisions are appropriate. The main point of concern is whether the revisions are grammatically correct.

GUIDELINES

You may want to caution students not to take out too much from their paragraphs. It should not be impossible for the students revising the paragraphs to come close to the originals.

460

MAKING CONNECTIONS

Fill in the Missing Pieces

You've learned that sentence fragments are confusing because they are missing some important parts. Here's a chance to see just how confusing fragments can be.

First, team up with one of your classmates. Working together, write a paragraph in response to the photograph that follows. Use complete sentences, and make your paragraph as clear as possible.

Next, write a second version of the paragraph, leaving out several subjects and verbs and creating phrase and clause fragments. Then, trade your second version with that of another team. Try to fill in the missing pieces of each other's paragraphs to reconstruct the original, complete sentences.

Compare your final versions to the original paragraphs. How well did you do in supplying the missing parts? How has the meaning of each paragraph changed?

ASSESSMENT

To evaluate students' understanding of the methods to correct run-on sentences, check students' responses to **Exercise 6** and the **Review**. Make sure that the methods the students used for correcting each sentence in **Exercise 6** is the one called for in the directions.

CLOSURE

Ask the class to recite the methods of correcting run-ons. [(**1**) making two sentences (**2**) separating independent clauses with a semicolon (**3**) separating independent clauses with a comma and a coordinating conjunction (**4**) separating independent clauses with a semicolon and a conjunctive adverb followed by a comma] ■

Run-on Sentences **459**

| R E V I E W ▶ | **Revising Fragments and Run-on Sentences** |

When you read the following paragraphs, you'll notice several sentence fragments and run-on sentences. First identify each fragment and run-on. Then rewrite the passage correctly. Change the punctuation and capitalization wherever necessary. **Revisions may vary.**

  Today, the pyramids of Egypt are fascinating to
F tourists, archaeologists, and historians, Who travel to
  Africa to see them. The pyramids symbolize a great
R/F ancient civilization, Egypt was a powerful influence, for
  thousands of years in the ancient world.
F The main purpose of the pyramids, Was to entomb the
  pharaohs. Sometimes a pharaoh's wife was buried with
F him in the pyramid. All his worldly possessions, also **were**
R buried, food, clothing, and water were provided for the
F journey, To the other world.
  Although many pyramids have been emptied of their
F treasures, The pyramids themselves continue to interest
R people, they are the only one of the Seven Wonders of the
F Ancient World, That is still standing.

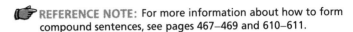 **REFERENCE NOTE:** For more information about how to form compound sentences, see pages 467–469 and 610–611.

INTEGRATING THE LANGUAGE ARTS

Mechanics Link. To show students that correcting run-on sentences includes adding the proper punctuation, write the following sentence on the chalkboard:

I went to the grocery store the jars on the shelves were empty.

Read the sentence aloud to the class and emphasize the lack of pauses by reading at a steady pace. Ask the students to tell what is wrong with the sentence. [It contains two separate ideas but is punctuated as a single sentence.] Then, ask them what is confusing about the sentence. [The word *store* can be both a noun and a verb, and it is unclear exactly how the word is to be used.] Now correct the sentence for the students. Use each of the four methods for correcting run-ons. [**(1)** I went to the grocery store. The jars on the shelves were empty. **(2)** I went to the grocery store, but the jars on the shelves were empty. **(3)** I went to the grocery store; the jars on the shelves were empty. **(4)** I went to the grocery store; however, the jars on the shelves were empty.]

EXERCISE 6 ▶   **Revising by Correcting Run-ons**

The following items are confusing because they're run-on sentences. Clear up the confusion by correcting them. To correct each run-on, use the method of revision that is given in parentheses.

1. Knights in the Middle Ages were bound by a code of honor it was called the code of chivalry. (two sentences)
2. Knights were supposed to be brave and loyal they were supposed to protect defenseless people. (comma and coordinating conjunction) **2. , and**
3. Some knights were true to the code of chivalry many fell short of the ideal. (semicolon and conjunctive adverb) **3. ; however,**
4. A knight could be punished for showing cowardice; his sword would be broken in half to show his disgrace. (semicolon)
5. A knight depended on his horse for transportation and in battle his horse was very valuable to him. (semicolon and conjunctive adverb) **5. ; therefore,**
6. Many knights belonged to strict religious orders they were monks who fought as soldiers. (two sentences)
7. Originally, knighthood wasn't a mark of distinction; the first knights were ordinary mounted soldiers. (semicolon)
8. Eventually knighthood became a sign of nobility the knights were considered part of the upper class. (comma and coordinating conjunction) **8. , and**
9. Orders of knighthood still exist in Great Britain knighthood doesn't have the same meaning that it did in the Middle Ages. (comma and coordinating conjunction) **9. , but**
10. Knighthood is now an honorary order it is bestowed on people to recognize great achievements. (semicolon)

TEACHING THE LESSON

The problem with run-on sentences is primarily one of punctuation, so you may want to review the appropriate rules in **Chapters 25** and **26** with your students. The gist of this lesson will be the four ways to correctly punctuate connected independent clauses as discussed under **Revising Run-on Sentences. Exercise 6** provides practice in ☛

two separate sentences. But you can also make a compound sentence if the independent clauses in the run-on are closely related.

1. You can make a compound sentence by adding a comma and a coordinating conjunction (*and, but, or, yet,* or *nor*).

RUN-ON   Spanish is the official language of Guatemala many Guatemalans speak Maya Indian languages.

REVISED   Spanish is the official language of Guatemala, **but** many Guatemalans speak Maya Indian languages.

2. You can make a compound sentence by adding a semicolon.

RUN-ON   About half the people in Guatemala are descended from Maya Indians about half have mixed Spanish and Indian ancestry.

REVISED   About half the people in Guatemala are descended from Maya Indians; about half have mixed Spanish and Indian ancestry.

3. You can make a compound sentence by adding a semicolon and a *conjunctive adverb*—a word such as *therefore, instead, meanwhile, still, also, nevertheless,* or *however*. A conjunctive adverb needs to be followed by a comma.

RUN-ON   Guatemala's rich soil is its greatest natural resource, agriculture is one of the country's main industries.

REVISED   Guatemala's rich soil is its greatest natural resource; **therefore,** agriculture is one of the country's main industries.

OBJECTIVES

- To use several strategies to combine sentences into compound and complex sentences
- To use various strategies to revise stringy and wordy sentences
- To revise a paragraph by using a variety of sentence structures

cross CURRICULUM

Does the News Have Sentence Style?

You might want to work with the journalism teacher in your school to create a writing workshop session on sentence style. The focus of the workshop should be on the contrast between sentence style for newswriting and sentence style for academic writing.

- **Procedure** Ask your journalism teacher to address the sentence-style requirements newswriters have. Then, review the points of sentence style discussed in this chapter, such as sentence combining and varying sentence beginnings.

  Specific points for journalism sentence style should include the following:

  - To communicate with a mass audience, newspapers must present information in a simple manner—this includes sentence length and structure—so that almost everyone will be able to read and to understand. Sentence length affects readability.
  - Rewrite and divide long sentences into shorter units. The longer a sentence is, the more difficult it is to understand.

- Do not put too many ideas in one sentence. Even some short sentences can be overloaded.
- Vary sentence length so that sentences do not become choppy and repetitive. However, even a long sentence should not be complicated. It is better to make a sentence too short than too long.
- Vary your sentence beginnings so that the same words do not begin each sentence. However, remember the rule about putting no more than one to two ideas in a sentence.
- Try to use the normal word order in your sentences: subject, verb, and direct object. This produces much clearer and more concise writing.

- **Activity** Have students work in groups to write a short report evaluating copies of news stories you provide them. Students should use the points discussed by the journalism teacher as the criteria for their evaluations.

CHAPTER 13: WRITING EFFECTIVE SENTENCES

Use this guide for creating an instructional plan that addresses the individual needs of your students. Assignments accompanied by the following symbol (∗) may be completed out of class. Times given for pacing lessons are estimated.

CHAPTER PLANNING GUIDE—PUPIL'S EDITION

LESSONS	COMBINING SENTENCES pp. 461–473	IMPROVING SENTENCE STYLE pp. 474–482
DEVELOPMENTAL PROGRAM	🕐 **90–95 minutes** • Main Assignment: Looking Ahead p. 461 • Combining Sentences pp. 461–473 • Writing Note p. 463 • Exercises 1, 3–6 pp. 463–464, 466–467, 468, 469–470, 472–473 in pairs • Grammar Hint p. 468 • Mechanics Hint p. 471	🕐 **90 minutes** • Improving Sentence Style pp. 474–482 • Exercises 7–11 pp. 474–475, 476–477, 478, 479–480, 482 in pairs
CORE PROGRAM	🕐 **60 minutes** • Main Assignment: Looking Ahead p. 461 • Combining Sentences pp. 461–473 • Exercises 2–6 pp. 464, 466–467, 468, 469–470, 472–473 • Grammar Hint p. 468 • Mechanics Hint p. 471	🕐 **60 minutes** • Improving Sentence Style pp. 474–482 • Exercises 7–11 pp. 474–475, 476–477, 478, 479–480, 482
ACCELERATED PROGRAM	🕐 **40–45 minutes** • Main Assignment: Looking Ahead p. 461 • Combining Sentences pp. 461–473 • Exercises 3–6 pp. 466–467, 468, 469–470, 472–473∗	🕐 **40–45 minutes** • Improving Sentence Style pp. 474–482 • Exercises 7–11 pp. 474–475, 476–477, 478, 479–480, 482∗

CHAPTER PLANNING GUIDE—PROGRAM RESOURCES

	COMBINING SENTENCES pp. 461–473	IMPROVING SENTENCE STYLE pp. 474–482
PRINT	• Inserting Words and Phrases, Using Compound Subjects and Verbs, Creating a Compound Sentence, Creating a Complex Sentence, *Word Choice and Sentence Style* pp. 11–14 • Sentence Workshops, *English Workshop* pp. 77–84 • The Adjective Clause, *English Workshop* pp. 171–172	• Using Parallel Structure, Stringy and Wordy Sentences, Varying Your Sentences, *Word Choice and Sentence Style* pp. 15–17 • Sentence Workshops, *English Workshop* pp. 85–90
MEDIA	• *Language Workshop:* Lessons 5–7, 23, 30–31, 34–37	• *Language Workshop:* Lessons 29, 32–33

 Computer disk or CD–ROM

ASSESSMENT OPTIONS

Reflection

Self-assessment Record, *Portfolio Assessment* p. 19

Summative Assessment

Reviews A and B, *Elements of Writing,* Pupil's Edition, pp. 473, 482

Reviews A and B: Writing Effective Sentences, *Word Choice and Sentence Style* pp. 18–21

Chapter Review, *English Workshop* pp. 91–92

ELEMENTS OF WRITING: CURRICULUM CONNECTIONS

Making Connections

• Enter a Contest p. 483

INTEGRATING THE LANGUAGE ARTS

READING AND LITERATURE	WRITING AND CRITICAL THINKING	LANGUAGE AND SYNTAX	SPEAKING, LISTENING, AND OTHER EXPRESSION SKILLS
• Recognizing sentences that need revisions in a paragraph pp. 473, 482 • Identifying faulty parallelism in sentences pp. 474–475 • Reading and evaluating sentences for wordiness p. 478	• Combining sentences by inserting words pp. 463–464 • Combining sentences by inserting phrases pp. 466–467 • Combining sentences by using compound subjects and verbs p. 468 • Combining sentences into compound sentences pp. 469–470 • Combining sentences into complex sentences pp. 472–473 • Revising a paragraph by combining sentences p. 473 • Revising sentences to create parallelism pp. 474–475 • Revising stringy sentences pp. 476–477 • Revising wordy sentences p. 478 • Revising sentences to vary sentence beginnings pp. 479–480 • Revising a paragraph to create a variety of sentence structures p. 482 • Writing a composition using a variety of sentence structures p. 482 • Writing and revising awkward and confusing sentences p. 483	• Using commas to separate nonessential phrases and clauses p. 466 • Using commas after introductory words, phrases, or clauses pp. 466, 472–473 • Using commas and coordinating conjunctions, semicolons, or semicolons and conjunctive adverbs to form compound sentences pp. 469–470	• Choosing a creative name for a class contest p. 483 • Voting for winning contest entries p. 483

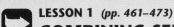

LESSON 1 *(pp. 461–473)*
COMBINING SENTENCES

OBJECTIVES

- To combine sentences by inserting words and phrases
- To combine sentences by using compound subjects and compound verbs

- To combine pairs of sentences into compound sentences
- To combine pairs of sentences into complex sentences

13 WRITING EFFECTIVE SENTENCES

LOOKING AHEAD

You've heard that "variety is the spice of life." In this chapter, you will learn how to add spice, or variety, to your sentences by

- using sentence-combining techniques
- improving your sentence style

Combining Sentences

Whether you are writing a school or workplace assignment or a personal letter, your goal is to communicate your ideas. Therefore, you want your writing to be clear, effective, and interesting. Short sentences can be effective, but too many of them make writing sound choppy. For example, notice how the many short sentences in the following paragraph make it boring to read.

PROGRAM MANAGER

FOR THE WHOLE CHAPTER

- **Review** For exercises on chapter concepts, see **Review Form A** and **Review Form B** in *Word Choice and Sentence Style,* pp. 18–21.

PROGRAM MANAGER

COMBINING SENTENCES

- **Independent Practice/ Reteaching** For practice and reinforcement, see **Inserting Words and Phrases, Using Compound Subjects and Verbs, Creating a Compound Sentence,** and **Creating a Complex Sentence** in *Word Choice and Sentence Style,* pp. 11–14.

- **Computer Guided Instruction** See **Lessons 30** and **31** in *Language Workshop CD-ROM.* To practice checking for subject-verb agreement as noted in the **Grammar Hint** on p. 468, see **Lessons 5–7.** To practice punctuating adjective clauses as noted in the **Mechanics Hint** on p. 471, see **Lesson 23.**

- **Practice** See **Chapter 14** in *English Workshop, Fourth Course,* pp. 183–184. To practice punctuating adjective clauses as noted in the **Mechanics Hint** on p. 471, see **Chapter 13,** pp. 171–172.

Have students recall the sentences they read in their first-grade primers. Students might recall having read simple sentences with subject-verb-object constructions. Ask students if such sentences would hold their attention today. Tell students that in this lesson they will learn how to combine short, choppy sentences into longer, more interesting sentences.

QUOTATION FOR THE DAY

"You never want to bore your readers. It's the biggest sin, next to misleading them and lying. One way to stay interesting is to change the length of your sentences, so that the rhythm is interesting." (Ethel Grodzins Romm, American writer)

Ask students if they've ever felt sleepy when listening to a repetitive sound such as the lapping of waves or the tick of a clock. Point out that just as certain repetitive sounds often lull people to sleep, repetitive sentences often bore readers.

VISUAL CONNECTIONS

Ideas for Writing. Protective coloration is common among animals. Many animals have coloring that helps them to blend in with their habitats, thus concealing them from predators. Some are even capable of changing color dramatically as they move from place to place.

Have interested students write informative paragraphs about the protective coloring of one or more animals. Remind students to avoid using too many short, choppy sentences in their paragraphs.

462   *Writing Effective Sentences*

Penguins have black backs. Penguins have white fronts. These colors act as camouflage. Some of a penguin's enemies fly. Some of a penguin's enemies swim. From above, a penguin's black back doesn't show in the water. From below, its white front just looks like sunlight on the water.

Sentence combining is a way to improve choppy writing. See how the paragraph about penguins can be improved by combining the short sentences into longer, smoother sentences.

Notice that even though the sentences are longer, the revised paragraph is shorter and more precise. That's because sentence combining has helped to eliminate repeated words and ideas.

Penguins have black backs and white fronts that act as camouflage. Some of a penguin's enemies fly and some swim. From above, a penguin's black back doesn't show in the water, and from below, its white front just looks like sunlight on the water.

Inserting Words

You can combine short sentences by taking a key word from one sentence and inserting it into another sentence. When you do this, you may need to delete one or more words. You may also need to change the form of the word you insert.

TEACHING THE LESSON

As you lead students through the various methods for combining sentences, ask for volunteers to read aloud the original sample sentences and then to read the revised ones. Discuss with students how each revision was achieved. You may also want to give students additional examples of each technique for combining sentences.

As you teach each of the sentence-combining techniques in this lesson, you may want to integrate some grammar review from **Chapters 15–19** to help students understand the terminology used. You may also want to review some of the rules of punctuation presented in **Chapters 25** and **26.**

Combining Sentences   **463**

USING THE SAME FORM	
ORIGINAL	James Thurber wrote many short stories. His stories are amusing.
COMBINED	James Thurber wrote many **amusing** short stories.
CHANGING THE FORM	
ORIGINAL	Thurber's illustrated stories are especially fun to read. The illustrations are humorous.
REVISED	Thurber's **humorously** illustrated stories are especially fun to read.

WRITING NOTE   When you change the form of a word before inserting it into a sentence, you often add an ending that makes the word an adjective or an adverb. The endings you'll use most frequently are *–ed, –ful, –ing,* and *–ly.*

EXERCISE 1 ▶ **Combining Sentences by Inserting Words**

Here are five sets of sentences about the many uses of common plants. Combine each set into one sentence by inserting the italicized word(s) into the first sentence. The directions in parentheses will tell you how to change the form of a word if it is necessary to do so.   **Answers may vary.**

EXAMPLE **1.** You can find books that describe the uses of herbs. These books describe the *many* uses that herbs have.
  1. *You can find books that describe the many uses of herbs.*

1. Plants have always been valued for their˄properties. ~~These properties are *medicinal.*~~ **1. medicinal**
2. Digitalis,˄a medicine for heart failure, is extracted from the foxglove plant. ~~Digitalis is an *effective* medicine.~~ **2. an effective**
3. ˄~~T~~he recipes for many old-fashioned herbal remedies have been lost. ~~The loss of these recipes is *unfortunate.*~~ (Add an *–ly.*) **3. Unfortunately,**

CRITICAL THINKING

Analysis. Direct students' attention to the example of sentence combining given under **Changing the Form** in the chart on this page. Ask students whether or not the sentences could have been combined to read "Thurber's humorous, illustrated stories are especially fun to read." [No.] Why not? [The meaning of the sentences is changed. In the original pair of sentences, the word *humorous* describes *illustrations.* In this combination, *humorous* describes *stories.*]

GUIDED PRACTICE

On the chalkboard, model the first sentence combination from each exercise in this lesson. Enlist students' participation and guide them through the sentence-combining process dictated by each exercise.

INDEPENDENT PRACTICE

Exercises 1–6 and **Review A** can provide students with independent practice in combining sentences. You may also want to ask students to write original paragraphs on topics of their choice. In their paragraphs, students should use the sentence-combining techniques presented in this lesson.

INTEGRATING THE LANGUAGE ARTS

Literature Link. Sometimes writers use short, choppy sentences to create certain effects. If the story is available have students read "The Pit and the Pendulum," by Edgar Allan Poe. When they have finished, direct their attention to the story's last paragraph and have a volunteer read the paragraph aloud. Ask students what impression its short, choppy sentences convey. [Responses will vary. The succession of short sentences conveys the rapidity of the sequence of events described and helps to create a breathless quality. The narrator of the story seems unable to breathe due to extreme excitement.]

464   *Writing Effective Sentences*

4. Some⌃herbal remedies have been passed down through many generations of families. ~~The families~~ *trust* ~~these remedies.~~ (Add an *–ed*.)   **4. trusted**
5. Plants are still used to make⌃products such as shampoos and hair dyes. ~~These products are *beauty* products.~~   **5. beauty**

EXERCISE 2 ▸   **Combining Sentences by Inserting Words**

In Exercise 1, the key words were italicized for you. Now it's up to you to decide which words to insert. There may be more than one way to combine each set of sentences; choose the combination you think is best. Change the forms of words wherever you need to.   **Revisions will vary.**

1. Isak Dinesen's book *Out of Africa* tells about her experiences on a⌃plantation in Africa. ~~It was a coffee plantation.~~   **1. coffee**
2. Dinesen⌃managed the plantation for ten years. ~~She managed it single-handedly.~~   **2. single-handedly**
3. One year, a⌃swarm of grasshoppers descended on her farm. ~~The swarm was huge.~~   **3. huge**   **4. detailed**
4. Dinesen's⌃descriptions paint a vivid picture of her life in Africa. ~~Her descriptions have a lot of detail.~~
5. *Out of Africa* was made into a⌃movie. ~~The movie was a success.~~   **5. successful**

ASSESSMENT

You could use **Review A** in conjunction with samples of students' writing to evaluate students' mastery of the variety of sentence-combining techniques discussed in this lesson.

RETEACHING

Provide copies of a paragraph consisting of short, choppy sentences and have students use the sentence-combining techniques described in this lesson to revise the paragraph. You could use an old student paper or create an appropriate paragraph.

Or provide copies of well-written paragraphs and have students revise the

Combining Sentences   **465**

Inserting Phrases

You also can combine closely related sentences by reducing one sentence to a phrase and inserting it into the other sentence. When it is inserted, the phrase gives additional information about an idea expressed in the sentence.

Prepositional Phrases

A *prepositional phrase* contains a preposition and its object. Usually, you can insert a prepositional phrase into another sentence without changing it in any way.

ORIGINAL   My sister loaned me a copy of *The Martian Chronicles.* It is by Ray Bradbury.

REVISED   My sister loaned me a copy of *The Martian Chronicles* **by Ray Bradbury.**

Participial Phrases

A *participle* is a word that is formed from a verb but is used as an adjective. A participle usually ends in *–ing* or *–ed*. A *participial phrase* contains a participle and words related to it. The whole participial phrase acts as an adjective in a sentence.

Sometimes you can combine sentences by reducing one sentence to a participial phrase. When you insert the participial phrase into the other sentence, place it close to the noun or pronoun it modifies. Otherwise you may confuse your reader.

ORIGINAL   Juanita Platero describes the conflict between old and new ideas. She does this as she writes about Navajo culture.

REVISED   **Writing about Navajo culture,** Juanita Platero describes the conflict between old and new ideas.

Appositive Phrases

An *appositive phrase* is made up of an appositive and its modifiers. It identifies or explains a noun or pronoun in a sentence. Sometimes you can change one sentence into an appositive phrase and insert it into another sentence. Like a participial phrase, an appositive phrase needs to be placed directly before or after the noun or pronoun it modifies. The phrase should be separated from the rest of

465

paragraphs so that they include only short choppy sentences. You could then discuss with students which versions of the paragraphs are more effective and why.

CLOSURE
Ask students to identify the different methods for combining sentences.

466   *Writing Effective Sentences*

the sentence by a comma (or two commas if you place the phrase in the middle of the sentence).

ORIGINAL   Ray Bradbury is best known for his science fiction stories. Ray Bradbury is an American writer.

REVISED   Ray Bradbury**, an American writer,** is best known for his science fiction stories.

☞ **REFERENCE NOTE:** For more information about the different kinds of phrases, see pages 573–591.

EXERCISE 3 ▶ **Combining Sentences by Inserting Phrases**

Insert phrases to combine each of the following sets of sentences into one sentence. (There may be more than one way to combine each set.) For each sentence set, the hints in parentheses will tell you when to change the forms of words and when to add commas. To help you get started, the words you need to insert are italicized in the first five sentence sets.

EXAMPLE   **1.** Migrant farm workers move from region to region. They follow the seasonal crop harvests. (Change *follow* to *following*.)

1. *Following the seasonal crop harvests, migrant farm workers move from region to region.*

1. Migrant laborers move constantly. They *search for work.* (Change *search* to *searching,* and add a comma.)
2. Many live in extreme poverty. They live *without adequate food, shelter, and medical care.*

VISUAL CONNECTIONS
Ideas for Writing. Interested students could research and write informative paragraphs describing the living and working conditions of migrant workers. Remind students to use varied sentence lengths in their paragraphs.

ANSWERS
Exercise 3

Revisions will vary. Here are some possibilities:

1. Migrant laborers move constantly, searching for work.

2. Many live in extreme poverty, without adequate food, shelter, and medical care.

466

1. Is the revision more interesting than the original paragraph?
2. Does the revision retain the meaning of the original paragraph?
3. Are several of the sentence-combining techniques used in the revision? ■

3. Many migrant laborers are unable to find other kinds of work. They *lack education*. (Change *lack* to *lacking*, and add a comma.)
4. César Chávez championed the rights of migrant farm workers. He was *a labor union organizer*. (Add two commas.)
5. Chávez was born in Arizona. He was born *on a farm*.
6. His family became migrant workers. They became migrant workers after losing their farm.
7. Chávez helped make the voices of farm workers heard. He organized grape pickers in the 1960s. (Change *organized* to *organizing*, and add a comma.)
8. He established a union. It was called the National Farm Workers Association. (Add a comma.)
9. Chávez organized strikes and boycotts. He was committed to nonviolent protest. (Add a comma.)
10. He helped to improve working conditions for migrant laborers. He did this through his organizing efforts.

3. Lacking education, many migrant laborers are unable to find other kinds of work.
4. César Chávez, a labor union organizer, championed the rights of migrant farm workers.
5. Chávez was born on a farm in Arizona.
6. His family became migrant workers after losing their farm.
7. Organizing grape pickers in the 1960s, Chávez helped make the voices of farm workers heard.
8. He established a union, the National Farm Workers Association.
9. Committed to nonviolent protest, Chávez organized strikes and boycotts.
10. Through his organizing efforts, he helped to improve working conditions for migrant laborers.

Using Compound Subjects and Verbs

You can also combine sentences by using compound subjects and verbs. Just look for sentences that have the same subject or the same verb. Then use coordinating conjunctions (such as *and, but, or, nor, for,* and *yet*) to make a compound subject, a compound verb, or both.

ORIGINAL	Jaguars are large, spotted cats. Leopards are large, spotted cats.
REVISED	**Jaguars and leopards** are large, spotted cats. [compound subject with the same verb]

ORIGINAL	Jaguars live in the Americas. Jaguars hunt in the Americas.
REVISED	Jaguars **live and hunt** in the Americas. [compound verb with same subject]

ORIGINAL	Jaguars hunt and attack other animals. Leopards hunt and attack other animals. These cats rarely attack humans.
REVISED	**Jaguars and leopards hunt and attack** other animals **but rarely attack** humans. [compound subject and compound verb]

GRAMMAR HINT

Point out to students that when a compound subject is joined by *or* or *nor*, the verb should agree in number with the part of the subject that is closest to the verb. For example, in the sentence "Neither the casserole nor the corn muffins are done," the verb (*are*) agrees with the closest half of the compound subject (*corn muffins*).

Checking for Subject–Verb Agreement

When you combine sentences by using compound subjects and compound verbs, check to make sure your subjects and verbs agree in number.

ORIGINAL Asia is home to the leopard. Africa is home to the leopard.
REVISED Asia and Africa **are** home to the leopard.

☞ REFERENCE NOTE: For more information on agreement of subjects and verbs, see pages 619–634.

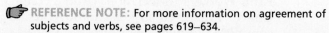

EXERCISE 4 ▶ **Combining Sentences by Using Compound Subjects and Verbs**

Here are five sets of short, choppy sentences. Combine each set into one sentence by using a compound subject, a compound verb, or both. Answers may vary.

1. Glaciers shape landforms. ~~Volcanoes also shape landforms.~~ **1.** and volcanoes
2. Antarctica is mostly covered by glaciers. ~~Greenland is mostly covered by glaciers.~~ **2.** and Greenland are
3. ~~Glaciers move slowly.~~ Glaciers shape the land as they flow across it. **3.** move slowly and
4. A volcano begins as molten rock beneath the earth's surface. ~~It~~ gradually rises upward. **4.** and
5. Volcanoes can create land area. ~~Glaciers can also create land area. They both can destroy land area.~~ **5.** and glaciers/and destroy

Creating a Compound Sentence

If the thoughts in two sentences are related to one another and are equal in importance, you can combine the sentences to form a *compound sentence.* A compound sentence is two or more simple sentences joined by

- a comma and a coordinating conjunction
  or
- a semicolon
  or
- a semicolon and a conjunctive adverb

ORIGINAL   Lions and tigers are the largest cats.
            Cheetahs are the fastest.

REVISED   Lions and tigers are the largest cats**, but**
            cheetahs are the fastest. [comma and
            coordinating conjunction]
                          or
            Lions and tigers are the largest cats**;**
            cheetahs are the fastest. [semicolon]
                          or
            Lions and tigers are the largest cats**;**
            however, cheetahs are the fastest.
            [semicolon and conjunctive adverb]

👉 REFERENCE NOTE: For more information about how to create
compound sentences, see pages 610–611.

WRITING NOTE   You can use the coordinating conjunctions *and,*
but, or, nor, for, so, and *yet* to form compound
sentences. However, because *so* is often
overworked in writing, you should think twice before using it.

EXERCISE 5 ▶   **Combining Sentences into
                    Compound Sentences**

The following sentences are fine by themselves, but
together they would make a choppy paragraph. Using
the three methods you've learned, combine each pair of
sentences into a compound sentence. Try to use each
method at least once. Add commas as necessary.
                                    Revisions will vary.

1. Amy Tan grew up in the United States⌃ Her parents
   were born in China.   **1. , but**

2. She began her writing career as a business writer⌃ She
   eventually turned to fiction.   **2. ; however,**

3. Her first novel⌃was published in 1989⌃ It became a
   best-seller almost immediately.

4. Tan's Chinese heritage is important to her. Much of her writing focuses on relationships in Chinese American families. **4.** , and

5. Her fiction often explores the positive aspects of being a second-generation American. It also explores the difficulties. **5.** , but

Creating a Complex Sentence

If two sentences are unequal in importance, you can combine them by forming a *complex sentence.* Just turn the less-important idea into a subordinate clause and attach it to the other sentence (the independent clause).

☞ REFERENCE NOTE: For information about independent and subordinate clauses, see pages 597–606.

Adjective Clauses

You can make a sentence into an adjective clause by replacing its subject with *who, which,* or *that.* Then you can use the adjective clause to give information about a noun or pronoun in another sentence.

ORIGINAL   The Sargasso Sea is a strange, still area. It is part of the Atlantic Ocean.

REVISED   The Sargasso Sea is a strange, still area **that is part of the Atlantic Ocean.**

ORIGINAL   Christopher Columbus noted the unusual quantity of floating seaweed. He crossed the Sargasso Sea.

REVISED   Christopher Columbus, **who crossed the Sargasso Sea,** noted the unusual quantity of floating seaweed.

MECHANICS HINT

Punctuating Adjective Clauses

If an adjective clause is not essential to the meaning of the sentence, set it off with commas. If it is essential to the meaning, no commas are necessary.

NONESSENTIAL That poster**,** **which was a birthday present,** is one of my favorites.

ESSENTIAL The poster **that I got for my birthday** is hanging on the wall.

☞ REFERENCE NOTE: For more about essential and nonessential clauses, see pages 797–799.

Adverb Clauses

You can also combine sentences by turning one sentence into an adverb clause. The adverb clause modifies a verb, an adjective, or another adverb in the sentence you attach it to.

To make a sentence into an adverb clause, add a subordinating conjunction (*although, after, because, if, when, while*) at the beginning. The conjunction shows the relationship between the ideas in the adverb clause and the independent clause. If the adverb clause comes first, set it off from the independent clause with a comma.

☞ REFERENCE NOTE: For a complete list of subordinating conjunctions, see page 604.

ORIGINAL Sailing ships were sometimes trapped in the Sargasso Sea. There wasn't enough current to sail by.

REVISED Sailing ships were sometimes trapped in the Sargasso Sea **when there wasn't enough current to sail by.**

ORIGINAL Sailors used to fear the Sargasso Sea. They heard strange tales about it.

REVISED **Because they heard strange tales about it,** sailors used to fear the Sargasso Sea.

Noun Clauses

You can make a sentence into a noun clause by adding a word like *that, how, what, whatever, who,* or *whoever.* Then you can insert it into another sentence just like an ordinary noun. When you combine the sentences, you may need to change or delete some words.

ORIGINAL Someone ate my lunch. That person had better confess.
REVISED **Whoever ate my lunch** had better confess.

ORIGINAL Jerome hasn't heard. Hockey practice is canceled.
REVISED Jerome hasn't heard **that hockey practice is canceled.**

E X E R C I S E 6 ▶ **Combining Sentences into a Complex Sentence**

Here are ten pairs of sentences about Greek mythology. Combine each pair by turning the second sentence into a subordinate clause and inserting it into the first sentence. For the first six pairs, you are given hints about how to create the subordinate clauses. For the last four, you'll need to use your own judgment. You may have to add or delete some words in the sentences. Add commas where necessary. [Hint: Before you begin, review the words that can be used to introduce subordinate clauses. These words are included in the explanations on pages 600–604.]

All images courtesy of The Granger Collection, New York.

REVIEW A
OBJECTIVE
• To revise a paragraph by combining
sentences in a variety of ways

1. Hercules was a brave hero of Greek mythology. He was given twelve difficult tasks. (Use *who*.)
2. The Parthenon was once a temple for the goddess Athena. The Parthenon is located in Athens. (Use *which*.)
3. Perseus was able to kill the Gorgon Medusa. The god Hermes and the goddess Athena helped him. (Use *because*.)
4. Cassandra had the power to predict the future. No one believed her prophecies, though. (Use *although*.)
5. Helios lived on the Greek island of Rhodes. Helios was the sun god of the Greeks. (Use *who*.)
6. The Greeks believed something about Hestia. Hestia protected the homes of faithful worshipers. (Use *that*.)
7. Hercules accidentally killed Linus. At the time, Linus was trying to teach him how to play the lyre.
8. Scylla was a dangerous sea monster. She lived in a cave.
9. Odysseus had many adventures. He was trying to get home to his wife and son.
10. King Midas wanted everything he touched to turn to gold. He was greedy.

R E V I E W **A** ▶ **Revising a Paragraph by Combining Sentences**

Using all the sentence-combining skills you have learned, revise and rewrite the following paragraph. Use your judgment about which sentences to combine and how to combine them. Try for smooth, varied sentences that are easy to understand, but don't change the original meaning of the paragraph.   **Revisions will vary.**

People have always been fascinated by dreams. No one knows for certain why we dream. Scientists have   , but
found out something about when we dream. Scientists try
to find out about dreaming. Scientists do this by studying
people as they sleep. They've learned that dreaming takes
place during a particular phase of sleep. The phase is
called REM sleep. REM stands for something. It stands for   , or
"rapid eye movement." REM sleep occurs each night. It
lasts for about ninety minutes.   sleep.
                                                            and

LESSON 2 (pp. 474–482)

IMPROVING SENTENCE STYLE

- To revise sentences to vary sentence beginnings
- To revise a paragraph to create a variety of sentence structures

OBJECTIVES

- To revise sentences to create parallelism
- To revise stringy and wordy sentences

474   *Writing Effective Sentences*

Improving Sentence Style

In the first part of this chapter, you learned how to reduce choppiness in your writing by combining sentences. Now you'll learn several more ways to polish your sentence style and make your writing more effective.

Using Parallel Structure

When you join several equal or related ideas in a sentence, it's important that you express these ideas in a similar way. You do this by balancing the structure of your sentence parts. For example, you balance an adjective with an adjective, a phrase with a phrase, and a clause with a clause. This kind of balance in writing is called *parallel structure.* Begin to look for parallel structure in sentences when you combine words, phrases, and clauses by using the coordinating conjunction *and*.

NOT PARALLEL	A successful athlete is three things: healthy, alert, and showing consideration. [two adjectives and a phrase]
PARALLEL	A successful athlete is three things: **healthy, alert, and considerate.** [three adjectives]
NOT PARALLEL	It takes a careful use of time to play a sport, to keep up with schoolwork, and social life. [two phrases and a noun]
PARALLEL	It takes a careful use of time **to play a sport, to keep up with schoolwork,** and **to have a social life.** [three phrases]
NOT PARALLEL	I promised that I would spend more time studying and to help out more around the house. [a clause and a phrase]
PARALLEL	I promised **that I would spend more time studying** and **that I would help out more around the house.** [two clauses]

EXERCISE 7 ▶ **Revising Sentences to Create Parallelism**

Some of the following sentences are out of balance. Bring balance to them by putting the ideas in parallel form. You

MOTIVATION

To introduce students to this lesson, write the words *parallel, stringy,* and *wordy* on the chalkboard. Ask students to define the words and to guess how they are related to writing.

TEACHING THE LESSON

As you teach the lesson, work with students to generate additional examples of each type of weak sentence discussed—unparallel, stringy, and wordy. Write examples on the chalkboard and then work with students to revise the weak sentences. For **Varying Sentence Beginnings** on p. 478, work with students to write several sentences ☞

Improving Sentence Style **475**

may need to delete or add some words. If a sentence is already correct, write C. **Revisions will vary.**

1. Athens, the capital of Greece, is known for its ancient ruins, busy lifestyle, and ~~enjoying~~ fine Greek food.
2. Because it is nearly three thousand years old and ~~having~~ a rich history, Athens attracts many visitors. **2. has**
3. Athens attracts artists,~~and~~ historians,~~and is attractive to~~ tourists.
4. People drive very fast in Athens and scare the pedestrians. **4. C**
5. Athens is fun to visit if you watch out for traffic and ~~to~~ learn to jump out of the way of cars.

Revising Stringy Sentences

What's a *stringy sentence*? Read this one.

> I woke up early so that I could get ready to catch the school bus, and I was going to the state band championships, and I hoped I would play well, and I pretended I wasn't excited, but I could barely eat my breakfast.

You've learned to combine sentences, but someone overdid this one! A ***stringy sentence*** has too many independent clauses strung together with coordinating conjunctions like *and* or *but*. Because the ideas are all treated equally, it's difficult to see how they are related to one another.

MEETING *individual* NEEDS

ADVANCED STUDENTS

Choose well-written sentences from literary selections, and have students write sentences that imitate the structural elements used in these sentences. You could also make it a practice to call attention to matters of style in the literature the class is reading and to read aloud well-written passages.

◈ INTEGRATING THE LANGUAGE ARTS

Speaking and Listening. A good example of parallel sentence structure can be provided by Martin Luther King, Jr.'s speech "I Have a Dream." Ask a student volunteer to prepare and read aloud all or part of this speech. Afterward, discuss with students where King uses parallel structure and how it contributes to the power of his speech.

475

To fix a stringy sentence, you can

- break the sentence into two or more shorter sentences
- turn some of the independent clauses into subordinate clauses or phrases

Now read the following sentences aloud and hear the difference. Notice how the writer has broken up the stringy sentence into three shorter sentences and turned an independent clause into a subordinate clause.

> I woke up early so that I could get ready to catch the school bus. I was going to the state band championships, and I hoped I would play well. Although I pretended I wasn't excited, I could barely eat my breakfast.

There are usually several ways to revise a stringy sentence. The important thing is to make the meaning clear for your reader.

EXERCISE 8 ▶ Revising Stringy Sentences

Revise each of the following stringy sentences to make the meaning clear. For some items, you can just break the stringy sentence into two or more shorter sentences. For others, you'll need to turn an independent clause into a subordinate clause or a phrase to show the relationship between the ideas. Change the punctuation wherever necessary.

1. Music is used for entertainment, relaxation, and self-expression, and it is used in every culture, and it is an important part of our lives.
2. Music is an ancient art, and people learned to make flutes around 10,000 B.C., and they began to write music around 2500 B.C.
3. Today, much popular music is electronically produced, and many musicians play electric guitars and synthesizers, and some even play electric violins.
4. Different countries have different kinds of music, but some kinds of music are internationally popular, and those kinds include rock music.

ANSWERS

Exercise 8

Revisions will vary. Here are some possibilities:

1. In every culture, people use music for entertainment, relaxation, and self-expression. It is an important part of our lives.

2. Music is an ancient art. People learned to make flutes around 10,000 B.C., and they began to write music around 2500 B.C.

3. Today, much popular music is electronically produced. Many musicians play electric guitars and synthesizers, and some even play electric violins.

4. Different countries have different kinds of music, but some kinds of music, such as rock music, are internationally popular.

Improving Sentence Style   **477**

5. Rock music first became popular in the 1950s, and it was inspired by blues and jazz music, but its sound was different from anything people had heard.

Revising Wordy Sentences

When you read sentences like the following one, you probably wonder what language the writer is using: "Anticipating that tomorrow's forthcoming examination may be perplexing, I have made the astute conclusion that we should diligently scrutinize our scholarly tomes at the decline of day." How much easier and clearer to say "The test tomorrow may be hard, so let's study tonight."

Bloom County © 1984 Berkeley Breathed. Used by permission.

Here are three tips for creating sentences that aren't too wordy.

- Don't use more words than you need to.
- Don't use fancy, difficult words where plain, simple ones will do.
- Don't repeat words or ideas unless it's absolutely necessary.

WORDY My brother's room has a lot of mess in it.
IMPROVED My brother's room is messy.

WORDY The reason I am undertaking the pursuit of ballet study is that I want to be a professional dancer someday.
IMPROVED I am taking ballet lessons because I want to be a professional dancer someday.

WORDY Makana has trained as a singer for years and is a well-trained, talented singer.
IMPROVED Makana is a well-trained, talented singer.

5. Rock music first became popular in the 1950s. Although it was inspired by blues and jazz music, its sound was different from anything people had heard.

A DIFFERENT APPROACH

Let students use thesauruses to rewrite maxims in a difficult, wordy style. For example, "Everything that coruscates is not necessarily synonymous with or in anyway identical to bullion" is a possible rephrasing of "All that glitters is not gold." Students might want to challenge their classmates to guess the original maxims.

ASSESSMENT

Assess students' grasp of the concepts in this lesson by their responses in **Review B.** Use students' performances on **Exercises 7–11** to determine whether or not they need more work on specific techniques.

RETEACHING

You could supply your class with photocopies of compositions that include unparallel, stringy, and wordy sentences. Work with students to revise the compositions to eliminate weak sentences and to include a variety of sentence structures.

INTEGRATING THE LANGUAGE ARTS

Literature Link. Have students look at the first sentences of stories in the short-story section of their literature textbooks. Students will probably discover that many short stories begin with short, simple sentences. Stories that begin with short, simple sentences include "The Cold Equations" by Tom Godwin, "The Man to Send Rain Clouds" by Leslie Marmon Silko, "Mr. Parker" by Laurie Colwin, "With All Flags Flying" by Anne Tyler, and "Boys and Girls" by Alice Munro. Ask students why authors might choose to begin stories with short, simple sentences. [Short, simple sentences serve to capture the reader's attention. First sentences often give just enough information to intrigue readers and engage their interest.]

| EXERCISE 9 ▶ | Revising Wordy Sentences |

Some of the following sentences are wordy and need improving. For each sentence, ask: Does it have any unnecessary words? Does it have any fancy words that can be replaced with simple ones? Does it repeat any ideas? If you answer "yes" to any of these questions, revise the sentence to reduce the wordiness. If a sentence doesn't need improving, write C.   Revisions will vary.

1. Caves are dark, damp areas~~that don't have any light.~~
2. Many caves have beautiful, icicle-like mineral formations called speleothems.   **2.** C
3. Luray Caverns, ~~which is~~ a cave system, ~~situated in the area of~~ northern Virginia, is famous for its colorful speleothems.   **3.** in
4. Lascaux Cave, a famous cave in southwestern France, has many ~~ancient,~~ prehistoric wall paintings.
5. Cavefish are small, cave-dwelling fish that ~~are not equipped with optical organs.~~   **5.** don't have eyes.

Varying Sentence Beginnings

You would probably get bored if you ate the same food at every meal. Variety is as important in your writing as it is in your diet. The basic subject-verb sentence pattern is fine sometimes, but if it's all you ever use, your writing will be monotonous.

Read the following paragraph. Notice that, while the paragraph is correct, it is boring because every sentence follows the same subject-verb pattern.

> The pool was nearly empty on an early weekend morning. Dedicated swimmers swam multiple laps. A few sunbathers and parents with small children sat on the grass at the edge of the pool and watched. The day grew hotter, and the sun rose higher. The pool became more crowded. The pool was soon filled with young people. They laughed as they played games and splashed each other.

Now read a revised version of the paragraph. Notice how the varied sentence beginnings break the monotony of the subject-verb pattern.

CLOSURE

Ask a volunteer to describe the methods of improving sentence style discussed in this lesson. [Answers should include using parallelism, revising stringy and wordy sentences, and varying sentence beginnings and structures.]

ENRICHMENT

An effective method of teaching sentence style is to use example sentences from past students' papers to demonstrate different kinds of weak sentences. Write sentences on the chalkboard and have the class discuss needed revisions. You may also want to give examples of good sentences from students' papers. ■

On an early weekend morning, the pool was nearly empty. Dedicated swimmers swam multiple laps. A few sunbathers and parents with small children sat on the grass at the edge of the pool and watched. As the day grew hotter and the sun rose higher, the pool became more crowded. Soon the pool was filled with young people. Laughing, they played games and splashed each other.

Instead of starting all your sentences with subjects, try opening sentences in a variety of ways. Begin with single-word modifiers, with phrases, and with subordinate clauses. Remember to add commas as necessary after introductory words, phrases, or clauses.

VARYING SENTENCE BEGINNINGS
SINGLE-WORD MODIFIERS
Grotesquely, Dr. Frankenstein's monster began to rise from the table. [adverb] **Frightened,** Dr. Frankenstein jumped back. [participle] **Cackling,** Igor ran from the room. [participle]
PHRASES
With little hope Sam entered the writing contest. [prepositional phrase] **Excited that he won,** Sam accepted the award. [participial phrase]
SUBORDINATE CLAUSES
Because Manuel was tall, people expected him to play basketball. **Although Manuel wasn't interested in playing basketball,** he always went to the games.

EXERCISE 10 ▶ **Varying Sentence Beginnings**

Using what you've learned about varying sentence beginnings, revise each of the following sentences. The hint in parentheses will tell you whether to begin with a phrase, a clause, or a single-word modifier.

INTEGRATING THE LANGUAGE ARTS

Grammar Link. Have students work in pairs to write sentences that begin with each of the following grammatical forms:

1. adverb clause [When Sam arrived at the park, he was ready to play.]
2. noun clause [How he could catch the big fish puzzled Sean.]
3. participial phrase [Pleased by the present, the child grinned broadly.]
4. prepositional phrase [In the morning we will start our journey.]
5. single-word modifier [First, we must read the instructions.]

ANSWERS
Exercise 10

Revisions will vary. Here are some possibilities:

1. Established in 1945, the United Nations was designed to promote world peace and human rights.

2. When the organization was founded, fifty nations joined the United Nations.

3. Today, over 150 nations belong to the United Nations.

4. After World War II, the United Nations tried to keep peace by getting countries to discuss their problems.

5. Although the United Nations is not always successful in its efforts, it has helped many nations to resolve their conflicts peacefully.

6. Located in New York City, the headquarters of the United Nations include several large buildings.

7. By providing food, shelter, and legal protection, the United Nations helps many refugees.

8. Because it supplies food to famine-stricken countries, the World Food Council is an important part of the United Nations' relief efforts.

9. Initially, the United Nations Children's Fund (UNICEF) provided aid for children who were victims of World War II.

10. In 1965, UNICEF was awarded the Nobel Peace Prize.

EXAMPLE   **1.** The United Nations is a worldwide organization, and it includes delegates from many nations. (phrase)
 1. *Including delegates from many nations, the United Nations is a worldwide organization.*

1. The United Nations was established in 1945, and it was designed to promote world peace and human rights. (phrase)

2. Fifty nations joined the United Nations when the organization was founded. (clause)

3. Over 150 nations belong to the United Nations today. (single-word modifier)

4. The United Nations tried to keep peace after World War II by getting countries to discuss their problems. (phrase)

5. The United Nations is not always successful in its efforts, but it has helped many nations to resolve their conflicts peacefully. (clause)

6. The headquarters of the United Nations are located in New York City and include several large buildings. (phrase)

7. The United Nations helps many refugees by providing food, shelter, and legal protection. (phrase)

8. The World Food Council is an important part of the United Nations' relief efforts because it supplies food to famine-stricken countries. (clause)

9. The United Nations Children's Fund (UNICEF) initially provided aid for children who were victims of World War II. (single-word modifier)

10. UNICEF was awarded the Nobel Peace Prize in 1965. (phrase)

Varying Sentence Structure

You've learned to create different kinds of sentences by combining and rearranging ideas. Now you can use this skill to create a better writing style. For varied, interesting paragraphs, it sometimes isn't enough just to create sentences of different lengths. You also need to use a variety of sentence structures. That means using a mix of simple, compound, complex (and sometimes even compound-complex) sentences in your writing.

☞ REFERENCE NOTE: For a discussion of how simple, compound, complex, and compound-complex sentences differ, see pages 610–611.

Read the following short paragraph, which is made up of only simple sentences.

> I visited a friend on her grandparents' farm. I was about ten years old at the time. There wasn't much room in the farmhouse. My friend and I begged hard. We got to sleep in the hayloft in the barn. It was wonderful. We lay awake at night. We counted shooting stars. We told each other our dreams and our hopes for the future.

Now read the revised version of the paragraph. The writer has included a variety of sentence structures to break the monotony of the first version.

> When I was about ten years old, I visited a friend on her grandparents' farm. Because there wasn't much room in the farmhouse and because we begged hard, my friend and I got to sleep in the hayloft in the barn. It was wonderful. We counted shooting stars as we lay awake at night, and we told each other our dreams and our hopes for the future.

In particular, notice how the use of subordinate clauses improved some sentences and made the paragraph clearer. Besides adding variety to your sentences, subordinate clauses help show how the ideas in a sentence are related.

☞ REFERENCE NOTE: For more information about using subordinate clauses in sentences, see pages 470 and 598–611.

CRITICAL THINKING

Analysis. Tell students to look through their favorite magazines for well-written articles. Then have them analyze the sentences in at least three paragraphs of the articles to determine the sentences' structures. Have students answer the following questions about the paragraphs that they analyzed:

1. Do all the sentences have the same structure?
2. Is one sentence structure predominant?
3. Can you detect any patterns in the structures of the sentences? For example, do all the paragraphs begin or end with the same types of sentences?
4. Do the structures of the sentences seem to correspond with their contents? For example, if the sentences are describing an exciting rock concert, do their structures convey a sense of excitement?

ANSWERS
Exercise 11

Paragraphs will vary. Here is a possibility:

My friends and I had lunch at the food court on the second floor of the mall. About twenty restaurants there serve food from different countries. Lin had soup and salad, I had a delicious burrito, and Joe and Debbie split a pizza. Then we walked around and looked at the people, who we all thought looked pretty funny. There was a fashion show on the main floor. Debbie and I admired the clothes, but Lin and Joe liked watching the models. Then we looked at a display of new cars and talked about the kinds of cars we'd like to have.

REVIEW B

Teaching Note. Review B calls on students to write persuasively. For an example of persuasive writing, refer students to **A Student Model** on p. 356.

ANSWERS
Review B

Paragraphs should include a variety of sentence structures and should avoid unparallel, wordy, and stringy sentences.

E X E R C I S E 11 ▶ **Revising a Paragraph to Create a Variety of Sentence Structures**

Using what you've learned about combining sentences and varying structure, revise the following paragraph to make it smoother and more varied. A combination of different kinds of sentences will make the paragraph much more fun to read.

My friends and I had lunch. We ate at a food court on the second floor of a mall. The food court has food from different countries. About twenty restaurants are there. Lin had soup and salad. I had a burrito. It was delicious. Joe and Debbie split a pizza. Then we walked around and looked at the people. We all thought they looked pretty funny. There was a fashion show on the main floor. Debbie and I admired the clothes. Lin and Joe liked watching the models. We looked at a display of new cars. We talked about the kinds of cars we'd like to have.

R E V I E W B ▶ **Writing a Composition Using a Variety of Sentence Structures**

It's Academy Award time, and your school newspaper is publishing students' nominations for the awards. Write a paragraph nominating your favorite movie, actor, or actress. If you want your reader to be convinced that your choice is the best one, you'll need to make your paragraph lively and clear. Capture your reader's attention by using a variety of interesting sentence structures. Avoid wordy and stringy sentences, and be sure to check for parallel structure as you revise.

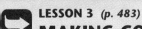

• To revise a poorly written sentence into an effective sentence

**ENTER A CONTEST
OBJECTIVES**

• To write a very awkward, poorly constructed sentence and to enter the sentence in a bad-sentence contest

---

483

MAKING CONNECTIONS

Enter a Contest

You know there are many contests that give awards for good writing. But did you know that there are also contests for *bad* writing? The most famous of these is the Bulwer-Lytton Contest, which awards prizes for the worst first sentence of an imaginary novel. The first year the contest was held, over 10,000 people entered their worst sentences.

Have your own classwide sentence contest. The rules are given here. Be creative and think of a good name for the contest.

Part I

1. Each contestant submits the most awkward, boring, and confusing sentence he or she can develop. (Reviewing the examples of stringy and wordy sentences on pages 475–477 will help you get started.)
2. After all entries are submitted, the class votes on which entry should be awarded the prize for worst sentence.

Part II

1. Each contestant now revises the winning worst sentence, making it clear, straightforward, and interesting.
2. The class votes on the second set of entries, selecting the entry that has turned the worst sentence into the best sentence.

COMPUTER NOTE: Use your word-processing program's Cut and Paste commands to move words, phrases, paragraphs, or blocks of text within a document. If you change your mind, you can always move the text again.

**ENTER A CONTEST
Teaching Strategies**

You may want to schedule the first part of this activity for the last ten or fifteen minutes of a class period and schedule the voting and revising for the following day. Such a schedule will give you a chance to type students' sentences on a ballot.

GUIDELINES

Sentences will vary. Have students identify their bad sentences as wordy, stringy, unparallel, short and choppy, or a combination of these. Then have them describe how they revised the poorly written sentence into an effective sentence.

TECHNOLOGY TIP

The Cut and Paste commands are usually found in the Edit menu. This menu often contains other useful features, including the Copy command. The Copy command copies highlighted text to a clipboard without removing it from its original location. It's useful when the same text has to be used in several places.

Chapter 14
ENGLISH: ORIGINS AND USES

OBJECTIVES

- To trace the development of the English language
- To use a dictionary to discover word origins and meanings
- To identify informal and formal English, dialects, colloquialisms, slang, idiom, and jargon
- To use precise word choice in writing
- To recognize misleading, weak, and stale language
- To evaluate the language of a piece of writing for clarity, word choice, and intended audience

Saying What You Mean in Biology

The more students know about language, the better writers they will be because their word choices will be more precise and effective. This concept proves especially true when students are writing for other disciplines. In writing papers for biology, for example, students will need to know how to explain technical terminology so that even a nonspecialist audience can understand.

- **Assignment** Have students choose three words from the list of specialized vocabulary terms below and compose a short expository essay defining the words' significance in the field of biology.

host	symbiosis
mutualism	commensalism
carcinogen	succession
ecosystem	biome

- **Audience** The audience for this paper should be an average high-school educated person who wants to know what the words mean in order to broaden his or her knowledge of biology.

- **Writing** The focus of this essay is "translating" biology terms so that the audience can understand them. The essay should have concrete details and examples that will illustrate the meaning of the terms.

A possible framework for this essay is as follows.

Introduction
Body Paragraph 1: explain first word
Body Paragraph 2: explain second word
Body Paragraph 3: explain third word
Conclusion

- **Publishing** Besides sharing one of the terms and its explanation in an oral presentation to the class, have students offer copies of their essays to their biology teacher.

INTEGRATING THE LANGUAGE ARTS

SELECTION	READING AND LITERATURE	WRITING AND CRITICAL THINKING	LANGUAGE AND SYNTAX	SPEAKING, LISTENING, AND OTHER EXPRESSION SKILLS
• from **Sassafrass, Cypress & Indigo** by Ntozake Shange p. 498	• Using reference materials p. 489 • Applying interpretive and creative thinking pp. 489, 506–507 • Responding personally to literature p. 498	• Making inferences and drawing conclusions pp. 489, 506–507 • Identifying and revising nonstandard English p. 499 • Analyzing loaded words and euphemisms p. 506 • Revising jargon pp. 506–507 • Writing and advertisement p. 509	• Understanding the development and history of English pp. 486, 491, 495 • Identifying word origins p. 493 • Identifying features of dialect p. 498 • Explaining the meanings of colloquialisms p. 502 • Identifying slang words p. 502 • Choosing appropriate synonyms pp. 503–504 • Responding to the connotations of words p. 504 • Revising sentences by replacing clichés p. 508	• Finding new words in non-print sources p. 495 • Discussing connotations with classmates p. 504

CHAPTER 14: ENGLISH: ORIGINS AND USES

Use this guide for creating an instructional plan that addresses the individual needs of your students. Assignments accompanied by the following symbol (∗) may be completed out of class. Times given for pacing lessons are estimated.

CHAPTER PLANNING GUIDE—PUPIL'S EDITION

LESSONS	WHERE ENGLISH COMES FROM pp. 484–495	HOW ENGLISH IS USED pp. 496–502	HOW TO SAY WHAT YOU MEAN pp. 503–508
DEVELOPMENTAL PROGRAM	**90 minutes** • Main Assignment: Looking Ahead p. 484 • Where English Comes From pp. 484–495 • Exercises 1, 3–5 pp. 486, 491, 493, 495 in pairs • Looking at Language pp. 488, 490, 492	**60 minutes** • How English Is Used pp. 496–502 • Exercises 6–9 pp. 498, 499, 502 in pairs	**60 minutes** • How to Say What You Mean pp. 503–508 • Exercises 10–14 pp. 503, 504, 506–507, 508 in pairs • Style Note p. 505
CORE PROGRAM	**60 minutes** • Main Assignment: Looking Ahead p. 484 • Where English Comes From pp. 484–495 • Exercises 1–5 pp. 486, 489, 491, 493, 495∗ • Looking at Language pp. 488, 490, 492	**25–30 minutes** • How English Is Used pp. 496–502 • Exercises 6–9 pp. 498, 499, 502∗	**45–50 minutes** • How to Say What You Mean pp. 503–508 • Exercises 10–14 pp. 503, 504, 506–507, 508∗ • Style Note p. 505
ACCELERATED PROGRAM	**40–45 minutes** • Main Assignment: Looking Ahead p. 484 • Where English Comes From pp. 484–495 • Exercises 2, 3, 5 pp. 489, 491, 495∗	**20–25 minutes** • How English Is Used pp. 496–502 • Exercises 7, 9 pp. 498, 502∗	**25–30 minutes** • How to Say What You Mean pp. 503–508 • Exercises 11, 13, 14 pp. 504, 506–507, 508∗

CHAPTER PLANNING GUIDE—PROGRAM RESOURCES

	WHERE ENGLISH COMES FROM pp. 484–495	HOW ENGLISH IS USED pp. 496–502	HOW TO SAY WHAT YOU MEAN pp. 503–508
PRINT	• The Tree of Language, The History of English, Modern English, *Word Choice and Sentence Style* pp. 25–27	• Formal and Informal English, *Word Choice and Sentence Style* p. 28 • Language Workshops, *English Workshop* pp. 93–96	• Choosing the Right Synonym, Denotation and Connotation, Jargon and Gobbledygook, Mixed Figures of Speech and Clichés, *Word Choice and Sentence Style* pp. 29–32 • Language Workshops, *English Workshop* pp. 97–98
MEDIA		• *Language Workshop:* Lessons 50–51	

 Computer disk or CD-ROM

ASSESSMENT OPTIONS

Reflection
Self-assessment Record, *Portfolio Assessment* p. 19

Summative Assessment
Reviews A and B: English: Origins and Uses, *Word Choice and Sentence Style* pp. 33–34
Chapter Review, *English Workshop* pp. 99–100

ELEMENTS OF WRITING: CURRICULUM CONNECTIONS

Making Connections
• Writing a Travel Ad p. 509

LESSON 1 *(pp. 484–495)*

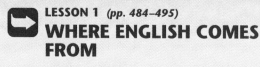

WHERE ENGLISH COMES FROM

OBJECTIVES

• To match Old English and present-day English words

• To research the Hundred Years' War

• To evaluate contributions to early Modern English

• To research the origins of loanwords

• To record new English words

PROGRAM MANAGER

FOR THE WHOLE CHAPTER

■ **Review** For exercises on chapter concepts, see **Review Form A** and **Review Form B** in *Word Choice and Sentence Style,* pp. 33–34.

PROGRAM MANAGER

WHERE ENGLISH COMES FROM

■ **Independent Practice/ Reteaching** For practice and reinforcement, see **The Tree of Language, The History of Language,** and **Modern English** in *Word Choice and Sentence Style,* pp. 25–27.

QUOTATION FOR THE DAY

"Remember that you are a human being with the divine gift of articulate speech; that your native language is the language of Shakespeare and Milton . . ." (Bernard Shaw, 1856–1950, British playwright)

Share the quotation with students and remind them that they can learn about a language by studying its history.

14 ENGLISH: ORIGINS AND USES

LOOKING AHEAD

In this chapter, you will take a close look at the English language. You will learn

■ where English comes from

■ how English continues to grow and change

■ how to choose among the many varieties of English when you speak and write

Where English Comes From

Have you ever wanted to trace your ancestry through the centuries—to discover your roots? You would find that your family tree goes back farther than recorded history. Its roots may even be in a land you never heard of.

MOTIVATION

To interest students in tracing the evolution of Modern American English, draw this diagram on either the chalkboard or the overhead transparency. The nationalities follow roughly the developmental stages of the blending process that produced Modern American English.

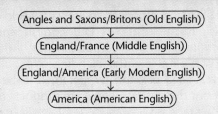

Lead a discussion of the diagram to show that American English is the result ☛

Where English Comes From **485**

The English language also has a family tree. It is one of dozens of languages that branched off from a single source, an original parent language. We call this original language ***Proto-Indo-European.*** Proto-Indo-European was spoken so long ago that we have no records of its beginnings. But we do know that it was being spoken in Eastern Europe about five thousand years ago.

The people who spoke Proto-Indo-European were wanderers. Gradually, they split up into tribes and migrated all across Europe and as far east as India. As the tribes branched off in different directions, so did their language. Each tribe developed its own *dialect*, or separate version, of Proto-Indo-European. Soon the dialects developed into distinct languages.

English, French, German, Spanish, and Italian are just a few of the languages that began as offshoots of Proto-Indo-European. These languages still bear a family resemblance. For example, notice how similar the words for *north* are in several Indo-European languages.

ENGLISH	FRENCH	GERMAN	SPANISH	ITALIAN
north	nord	norden	norte	nord

485

of English and American influences; Middle English is the result of Old English and French influences. Ask students what traits might be a result of this blending of people [physical build, coloring, temperament]. Then point out that just as people are products of their heritage, so are languages. Explain that this lesson will help students to understand how American English evolved.

TEACHING THE LESSON

Divide the class into groups of four. Have the groups outline the influences that produced Old English, Middle English, Modern English, and American English. Each student will be responsible for one of the four phases. After reading the textbook carefully and making notes, he or she will then teach the other students in the group about

MEETING *individual* NEEDS

LEARNING STYLES

Visual and Kinetic Learners. You can encourage visual and kinetic learners by asking them to create posters illustrating the development of English.

LESS-ADVANCED STUDENTS

To help students succeed as cooperative learners in the activity discussed in **Teaching the Lesson,** have all the students preparing the same notes (on Old English, for example) meet to prepare their teaching notes. Advanced students can help others with note preparation.

A DIFFERENT APPROACH

Ask students to create quizzes on the development of Modern English. Students could work in groups and then exchange quizzes. This activity could be either review, reinforcement, or assessment.

English: Origins and Uses

Old English (450–1100)

The first speakers of English were tribes known as the Angles and Saxons. In about A.D. 450, the Angles and Saxons migrated to the pleasant, fertile island of Britain, which was already inhabited by a Celtic tribe known as the Britons. The island looked like a good place to call home, and the Anglo-Saxons settled down—after killing or driving off many of the Britons. The Anglo-Saxons named their new home "land of the Angles," or *Englalond*—which eventually became *England*. We call their language **Old English.**

Old English was similar to Modern English in many ways. In fact, the Anglo-Saxons used many of the same words we do, in somewhat different forms.

OLD ENGLISH	etan	drincan	dæg	niht
MODERN ENGLISH	eat	drink	day	night

However, Old English had a very different structure from Modern English. While Modern English mostly uses word order to show the roles of words in a sentence, Old English used many different word endings to show gender, number, case, and person. For example, the noun *hund* (*hound*) had to be written *hund, hundes, hunde, hundas, hunda,* or *hundum* depending on its use in a sentence.

EXERCISE 1 ▶ **Matching Old English and Present-Day English Words**

See if you can match each present-day English word in the first column with its Old English ancestor in the second column. [Hint: Use the process of elimination.]

1. calf	**1.** c	**a.** fot
2. cow	**2.** j	**b.** eage
3. foot	**3.** a	**c.** cealf
4. snow	**4.** e	**d.** geong
5. nose	**5.** i	**e.** snaw
6. eye	**6.** b	**f.** sealt
7. heart	**7.** g	**g.** heorte
8. young	**8.** d	**h.** niwe
9. new	**9.** h	**i.** nosu
10. salt	**10.** f	**j.** cu

that phase of the development of English. You may want to add structure to the task by providing students with a list of the kinds of information that should be included in each student's report: the sources of new words, examples of new words, and the historical context.

After the peer teaching is completed, each student should have a complete set of notes on the development of English.

Old English Gains New Words

In about A.D. 600, missionaries began a vigorous conversion of the English to Christianity. The missionaries introduced a new language as well as a new religion. Educated English people began to learn Latin, the language of the Church. They borrowed many Latin words and made them part of English. For example, the words *school, altar, candle,* and *paper* are all **loanwords,** or borrowed words, from Latin.

The English also learned new words from another—at first unwelcome—source. Around 790, Vikings from Scandinavia began to raid Britain, launching savage attacks over the next several centuries. Many Vikings ended up settling in England. Eventually, about nine hundred loanwords from their language, Old Norse, entered Old English. Many of the English words that come from Old Norse begin with *sc* or *sk*.

OLD NORSE	skalpr	skrap	skith	sky
MODERN ENGLISH	scalp	scrap	ski	sky

"Egad! Vikings! And they mean business!"

Middle English (1100–1500)

In 1066, England was attacked again—this time by the Normans from France. The army led by William of Normandy defeated the English at the Battle of Hastings and took control of the country. For the next 150 years, a few

ADVANCED STUDENTS

Select a passage in Middle English from Chaucer's *Canterbury Tales,* perhaps the first few lines of the "Prologue" or the first part of one of the tales. Ask students to write paraphrases of the passage. Allow them to use the *Oxford English Dictionary* to look up meanings of words. Then have students compare their paraphrases with a Modern English translation and write informative paragraphs comparing Modern English and Middle English.

GUIDED PRACTICE

Go over **Exercises 1, 3,** and **4** as a class. (Each student will need a dictionary for **Exercise 4.**) Ask for a volunteer to report on the Hundred Years' War. Then the class can discuss **Exercise 2.**

INDEPENDENT PRACTICE

Assign **Exercise 5** to be done independently either in class or at home.

A DIFFERENT APPROACH

Show the class how language grows by asking each student to choose two words and to make a small poster illustrating the different meanings the words have had, the dates the meanings changed, and, if available, the circumstances that produced the changes in the words. You could display these posters to reinforce the point that English is a growing language.

thousand French-speaking people governed English life. French became the language of government, law, business, and literature. Latin remained the language of religion. The few English people who received schooling were educated in these languages. Not surprisingly, many English words that are linked to wealth and power were borrowed from French after the Norman Conquest.

| OLD FRENCH | jurer | leisir | taxer |
| MODERN ENGLISH | jury | leisure | tax |

LOOKING AT

A Feast of Loanwords

Some of our everyday words give clues to what English life was like after the Norman Conquest. For example, the words *hog, calf,* and *sheep* came to us from Old English; but the words *bacon, veal,* and *mutton* were borrowed from French before the fifteenth century. These word origins reflect the social structure of the times. The English peasants raised the livestock, while the French nobles got to *feast* (another French word!) on the meats.

French, the language of the educated, was used for almost all written communication. But English didn't die. It was still the spoken language of the common people—the farmers, herders, servants, and craftspeople. As these

ASSESSMENT

For a written assessment, you may want to give the class a list of the key words from this lesson and to ask students to write about the development of English by using these key words: Proto-Indo-European, Angles, Saxons, Jutes, Old English, missionaries, Latin, Vikings, Norman Conquest, French, loanwords, Middle English, Chaucer, the Hundred Years' War, the Great Vowel Shift, Modern English, Shakespeare, London dialect, William Caxton, Renaissance, travels, etymologies, and American English. You might also include major dates (all A.D.) in the list: 450–1100, 600, 790, 1066, 1100–1500, 1400s, 1476, 1500–present, 1776, 1990. This assignment could be an open-book test, an overnight test, or a

people spoke it, however, the language changed into a form we call *Middle English.* English grammar became more regular. For example, as shown on page 486, the Old English word *hund* originally had six different forms. Speakers of Middle English kept only two forms—*hund* and *hundes.*

English Triumphs

For a few hundred years, it seemed that French might prevail as the national language of England. But several factors weighed in favor of English. For one thing, the English-speaking people outnumbered the French rulers. For another, the Normans in England gradually lost contact with France.

By the mid-1300s, educated people were again using English for writing as well as for speaking. As you can see from the following passage by the fourteenth-century poet Geoffrey Chaucer, Middle English wasn't far removed from the English we use.

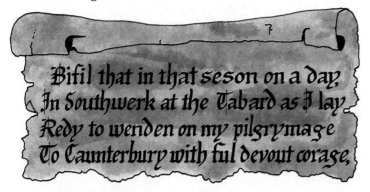

Bifil that in that seson on a day,
In Southwerk at the Tabard as I lay
Redy to wenden on my pilgrymage
To Caunterbury with ful devout corage,

EXERCISE 2 ▶ Researching the Hundred Years' War

The fate of English hung in the balance after the French conquered England. However, several factors, including the Hundred Years' War, helped English survive. Read about the Hundred Years' War in an encyclopedia or another reference source. How did the war affect English people's attitude toward the French? Why do you think the French language lost popularity in England as a result of the war?

INTEGRATING THE LANGUAGE ARTS

Vocabulary Link. Begin a vocabulary-building activity by asking students to name new terms in English as a result of the widespread use of computers. Continue to brainstorm with the class to list new words from several fields, such as science, technology, medicine, and warfare.

ANSWERS
Exercise 2

Answers may vary. Here are some possibilities:

Protracted fighting between the English and the French during the Hundred Years' War (1337–1453) began a lasting enmity between the people. English victories at Crécy (1346) and Agincourt (1415) fueled English nationalism and made French the language of a conquered enemy. Students might also find that although the war was begun by the English to protest French seizure of ancestral Anglo-Norman lands in France, the English nobility was decisively separated from France, and their grip on the French language began to slip. Their children became native English speakers.

RETEACHING

You may want to ask groups to make posters showing the family tree of the English language. Ask the students to include developmental influences on the language and changes that each influence caused. Encourage students to include as much information as possible on the posters.

A DIFFERENT APPROACH

Help students realize how quickly language changes by asking them to create a dictionary for an exchange student who has studied English from textbooks written ten to fifteen years ago. Ask the class to think of words the student would need in order to understand everyday conversation. Students might want to illustrate some words. This activity is suited to group work.

MEETING *individual* **NEEDS**

AT-RISK STUDENTS

You may want to concentrate on the backgrounds of Modern American English with students. Have them look up words they use every day to find the origins of those words. They can use any dictionary with etymological information, but if they use the *Oxford English Dictionary* they will likely need your help.

LEARNING STYLES

Visual and Auditory Learners. To teach the effects of the Great Vowel Shift, ask one or two students to create a chart or poster showing the sound changes the shift caused. After reading aloud an excerpt from Chaucer, use the chart to show how the Great Vowel Shift changed the pronunciation of the words in the excerpt.

490   *English: Origins and Uses*

Major Sources of Loan Words through 1500

Modern English (1500–Present)

Several different things happened to English as it moved into the modern period. It underwent changes in pronunciation, grammar, and spelling; it became standardized; and it expanded into an international language.

The Great Vowel Shift

Middle English sounded very different from the English we speak. For example, in Chaucer's time, *care* would have sounded like *car*, *meek* like *make*, and *bite* like *beet*. The changes in pronunciation happened gradually. By the late 1400s, they were just about complete. We call this shift in pronunciation the *Great Vowel Shift.*

LOOKING AT *Language*

Is't Modern English?

If you've ever read *Romeo and Juliet* or another of Shakespeare's plays, you know that you have to get used to Shakespeare's English. For example, he used words like *sooth* ("truth") and *thence* ("from there") that we hardly ever hear in present-day English. He also used unfamiliar contractions such as *ne'er* ("never") and *is't* ("is it").

However, Shakespeare's writing looks much more familiar to us than Chaucer's does. That's because Shakespeare used an early form of Modern English.

Ask students questions about the development of the English language and let students find the answers on their posters. To help any confused students, try using another image, such as a recipe, to explain how different events led to changes in the language.

CLOSURE

Ask a volunteer to list the four developmental stages that have produced Modern American English.

☞

EXERCISE 3 ▶ **Evaluating Contributions to Early Modern English**

Listed below are five very ordinary words in our language. These words—along with many others—were added to the language during early Modern English times. Try to write the thought expressed by the word without using the word. How important to the language are these contributions to the Modern English vocabulary?

1. leapfrog
2. lonely
3. dislocate

4. laughable
5. critical

Per6
Per2

London Sets the Standard

By 1500, almost everyone in England spoke English. But for a long time there was no standard version of the language, and different regions used completely different dialects. Scribes wrote in the dialects of their areas and spelled words whatever way they chose. However, the dialect of London eventually became the most widely used dialect, since London was the center of English culture, business, and trade.

When William Caxton brought the first printing press to England around 1475, he set up his print shop in London and began printing books in the London dialect. Printed books—which could be made faster and more cheaply than hand-copied ones—began to spread across England. As the spellings of many words were "fixed" in print, the London dialect became a national standard.

ANSWERS

Exercise 3

Answers may vary. Here are some possibilities:

1. We played one-hop-over-the-other. (*Leapfrog* is shorter.)

2. She was feeling lonesome. (Interchangeable, though we use *lonely* more today.)

3. She put her shoulder out of joint. (*Dislocated* is shorter and more specific.)

4. The dance was funny (or *risible*). (*Laughable,* or less commonly *risible,* is more derisive than *funny*—an important connotative distinction.)

5. Her father had a negative attitude toward her hairstyle. (*Critical* is shorter, more specific, and implies change could improve the situation.)

👁 VISUAL CONNECTIONS

Exploring the Subject. William Caxton set up his printing business in Westminster in London. He was born in the Weald of Kent and lived abroad for thirty years. Ironically, the first book to be printed in English, *The Recuyell of the Historyes of Troye,* was produced in Flanders.

Soon handbooks of "proper" English usage, spelling, and pronunciation appeared on the market. People also compiled lists of "hard words" and their definitions. Some of the lists grew long enough to be called dictionaries.

English had become standardized, but it didn't stop changing. Even as the first printers were setting up shop, the Renaissance was sweeping England, sparking a renewed interest in the classical languages. As a result, thousands of Greek and Latin loanwords entered English.

English Travels Abroad

In about 1600, English merchants and adventurers began to seek out riches in foreign lands across the sea. As they explored, traded with, and colonized other places, they helped to make English an international language. They also enriched English with a rich crop of loanwords from other languages. Here are just a few examples.

NATIVE AMERICAN	moccasin, raccoon
AFRICAN	chigger, marimba
HINDI	jungle, bandanna

LOOKING AT Language

Loanwords from English

Words are like people: when they move to a foreign country, they often take on the accent of the native speakers. For example, Japanese speakers adopted the English term *personal computer* but shortened it to *paso-kon*. The Polish word *ajskrym* is a respelling of *ice cream*. And the Italian word *schiacchenze* is actually *shake hands* spelled as Italian speakers pronounce it.

Sometimes English loanwords become the basis for new words. For instance, after borrowing the English word *teens*, people in Germany went a step further and coined the word *twens*. German people also use the term *steadyseller* for a book that isn't quite a "best-seller."

Every time someone uses English in a new way, the language becomes richer and more complex. How do you think English loanwords will affect the growth of other languages?

EXERCISE 4 ▶   Identifying the Origins of Loanwords

Each of the following English words was borrowed from another language. Look up each word in a dictionary that gives etymologies (word histories). What language was it borrowed from? What word was it derived from?

1. geology
2. geyser
3. cigar
4. studio
5. psychology

6. violin
7. complex
8. desperado
9. boom
10. machine

American English

American English was born when English colonists brought the English language to the Western Hemisphere. They borrowed words from Native American languages, invented new words of their own, and changed the pronunciations and uses of some old words. At the same time, they kept some older pronunciations and grammatical uses that the British back in England began to change. By 1776, the American dialect was distinct enough to be called American English.

ANSWERS
Exercise 4

Answers may vary according to the dictionary used.

1. Greek: *gaia/gē*—earth + *logos*—study, thought, reason

2. Icelandic: *Geysir*—hot spring, *gjosa*—gush

3. Spanish: *cigarro,* from Mayan: *sicar*—to smoke rolled tobacco leaves

4. Italian: *studio*—room for study, from Latin: *studium*—enthusiasm, study, literary work

5. Greek: *psychē*—soul, breath + *logos*—study, thought, reason

6. Italian: *violina*—little *viola*

7. Latin: *complexio*—dilemma, from *cum*—together + *plectere*—to braid

8. Spanish, from Latin: *de*—without + *sperare spero*—to hope

9. Middle English: *bummen*—to hum, like Dutch: *bommen*—echoic (imitative of a booming sound)

10. French, from Latin: *machina* — machine

INTEGRATING THE LANGUAGE ARTS

Library Link. To give students an idea of the diversity within the Indo-European family of languages and to introduce them to some other language families, have them consult an encyclopedia to determine which language family each of the following languages is part of:

Arabic	Hawaiian	Russian
Arapaho	Hebrew	Sanskrit
Zulu	Hopi	Spanish
Chinese	Hungarian	Tibetan

[Answers may vary slightly according to how recently the reference work was published, but possible answers are Hebrew and Arabic—Afroasiatic; Zulu—Niger-Congo; Hungarian—Ural-Altaic; Chinese and Tibetan—Sino-Tibetan; Hawaiian—Austronesian; Arapaho—Algonquian; Hopi—Uto-Aztecan; Russian, Sanskrit, and Spanish—Indo-European.]

Native Americans, Africans who came as slaves, and immigrants from most countries around the world have left their mark on American English. Following are just a few of the loanwords that took an American route into English.

NATIVE AMERICAN	coyote, toboggan
GERMAN	kindergarten, frankfurter
AFRICAN	gumbo, okra
CHINESE	yen, chop suey
SPANISH	canyon, patio

Just as America has emerged as a world power, American English has quickly become the standard for English in the twentieth century. American television, radio, movies, books, and newspapers have spread American English to even the most remote corners of the globe.

English Around the World

English has come a long way from its humble beginnings. From a dialect spoken by a few Anglo-Saxons, it has become the most widely used language in the world. About one third of the world's population speaks English, and as of 1995 it was an official language in eighty-seven nations and territories. This graph shows how the number of speakers of English has grown since the beginning of the Modern English period.

Speakers of English (in millions)

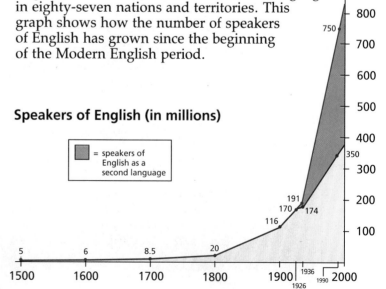

In many fields, English is the common language that allows people from different cultures to communicate. It is the world language of

- commerce
- science
- teaching
- computers
- air traffic control

A Changing Language

The history of English is a history of growth and change. Today, English is growing and changing at an even faster rate than ever.

One source of growth is English-speaking people's constant interaction with the world's many cultures and languages. This interaction brings a steady flow of new words—and new uses of old words—into the language.

Another major source of growth is the vocabulary of science and technology. At last count, over 500,000 scientific and technical terms had become part of the English language. That's about equal to the number of words in our general vocabulary!

Will English ever stop changing? The answer is probably not. Four hundred years from now, English may have changed so much that our descendants will need a translator to decode our language. Twentieth-century English will probably look as strange to them as Old English looks to us.

EXERCISE 5 ▶   Identifying New Words in English

Spend a week watching and listening for words that you think are new to English (invented within the past year). Pay attention to new slang words and technical terms that you read in magazines, that you hear on television, and that you and your friends invent. Jot down any that you find. Then look up each in a current dictionary to see if it is a new word or an old word that has been given a new meaning.

ANSWERS
Exercise 5

The purpose of the exercise is to encourage students to listen to the language around them. They should each pick a minimum of five words to look up and should record alternative meanings they find. You may remind them that not finding a word can mean several things: It was invented after the date the dictionary was published; it is so old-fashioned that it was left out; or it is slang. Encourage students to look for the word in a dictionary of slang. You may also remind the class that some new-sounding words are loanwords (like *ninja*—Japanese hired warrior), combinations from Greek or Latin (as with most new drugs), or acronyms (like HUD for *Housing and Urban Development* Office).

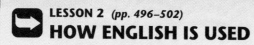
OBJECTIVES

- To write features of a dialect
- To revise nonstandard English in a paragraph
- To explain the meanings of colloquialisms
- To list and evaluate slang words

TEACHING THE LESSON

Try asking students about the English they have heard spoken by people from other places. What was different about the English? Lead students to understand that they have been describing dialects.

Because, whether they are aware of it or not, all of your students constantly adjust to different dialects, you may want to teach

QUOTATION FOR THE DAY

"I hate false words, and seek with care, difficulty, and moroseness, those that fit the thing." (Walter Savage Landor, 1775–1864, English writer)

Using the quotation as the basis for discussion, explain to the class that there are many ways to express an idea. Encourage students to select appropriate words, to be aware of words' denotations and connotations, and to avoid tired words and mixed figures of speech.

496   *English: Origins and Uses*

How English Is Used

How many ways can you think of to say "hello" to some-one? If you made a list of these words, you would have just a glimpse of the choices you make when you use English. There are many different ways of saying the same thing, and each word or expression has its appropriate use.

The words you use fall into two basic categories. They depend on

- background—where you come from and what your cultural heritage is
- circumstances—the person to whom you are talking or writing, your purpose, and the situation

Becoming familiar with the different forms, uses, and meanings of English will help you become a better writer. The more you know about your language, the more precise and effective your word choices will be.

Dialects of American English

English is spoken in many different places by many different groups of people. Because each group of English-speakers is unique, it's natural that each would develop its own special form of the language. These special forms are called *dialects.*

the lesson to make them aware of the dialects they hear. Help them identify different regional dialects they have heard and list examples of each. Then let students rewrite **Exercise 6** in groups, and have them read the results to the class.

Follow a similar procedure to teach standard and nonstandard English by having students give examples of frequently heard nonstandard English. Then rephrase each example in standard English.

To teach formal and informal English, list all of the kinds of writing students write or read, from shopping lists to research papers. Have students classify each piece of writing as formal or informal. Then introduce colloquialisms and slang to students as two forms of informal English.

☞

It's important to know that the words "right" and "wrong" don't apply to varieties of English. Different varieties can be correct for different groups of people. For people in Great Britain, British English is the correct form of English; for people in the United States, American English is the accepted form. They are simply different versions of the language.

Regional Dialects

If you live in Texas, you may think people from New York talk "funny." They may think you talk "funny" as well. Your English sounds different from theirs because you and they speak different *regional dialects.*

There are four major regional dialects in the United States: *New England, Northern, Midland,* and *Southern.* People in one region often pronounce words differently from people in another region. Some Northerners tend to drop the *r* from a word, so that *barn* sounds like "bahn." Some Midlanders and Southerners tend to add an *r* sound, so that *wash* sounds like "warsh."

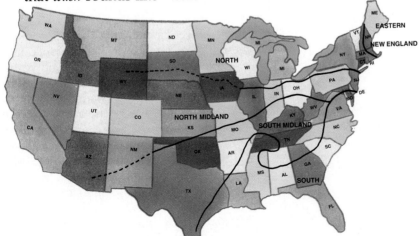

Regional dialects also differ from one another in vocabulary and grammar. For example, someone from New England might call a soft drink *tonic,* while people in other parts of the country might call it *soda* or *pop.* Someone from the South might say "sick *at* my stomach," while someone from the North might say "sick *to* my stomach."

These activities and discussions should serve to introduce to students the terms and concepts in this chapter.

You may want to use the first one or two words or sentences from **Exercises 6–9** for guided practice. Working with the whole class, go over these items to see whether students understand the new concepts. Because answers may vary, allow as many students as possible to give their solutions.

TIMESAVER

Most of the exercises in this lesson require revision of sentences or paragraphs. To help you see changes more readily, have students label the revisions they have made.

ANSWERS

Exercise 6

Most important in this exercise are students' attempts to describe the way they—not others—really talk. They should retain in their revisions the dialectical features that they actually use orally.

SELECTION AMENDMENT
Description of change: excerpted
Rationale: to focus on the concept of dialect presented in this chapter

498

Ethnic Dialects

An *ethnic dialect* is a dialect used by people who share the same cultural heritage. Because the United States is made up of many cultures, American English is also made up of many ethnic dialects. These dialects include the Irish English brought by Irish immigrants, the Yiddish English spoken by many Jews, and the Spanish-influenced English of people from Cuba, Mexico, and Puerto Rico. Black English, one of the largest ethnic dialects, has elements of African languages as well as of Southern dialect.

EXERCISE 6▶   **Identifying Features of a Dialect**

The following passage is told from the point of view of a young African American girl. The writer has written the narrative in a special way to capture the sounds of the narrator's language. Is the narrator's way of talking different from yours? How would you express the same thoughts in your own words?

> "Well. No. I love dancin', that's all. If somebody knows somethin' that's gonna make me dance more and better, I wanna know what that is. And yeah, I guess I do wanna be as close to perfect as I can be, but I want as many people to dance as want to. I want the whole world to dance, but dancers are a strange breed, Cypress—don'tchu know that. We are compulsive-obsessive, I think that's the phrase. We dance all day, move round dancers, in our spare time go see other dancers and for fun we go dancin'. There's no way to make us less intense, unless we fall in love . . . but not with another dancer."
>
> Ntozake Shange, *Sassafrass, Cypress & Indigo*

Standard American English

Every variety of English has its own set of rules and guidelines. No variety is the best or the most correct. However, one kind of English is more widely used and

Students could work alone or in pairs to complete **Exercises 6–9**.

When independent practice has been completed, have students hand in papers for evaluation. You can use students' writing to evaluate the appropriateness of their use of the different forms and varieties of English.

☞

accepted than others in the United States. This variety is called *standard American English.*

Standard American English is the one variety that belongs to all of us. Because it's commonly understood, it allows people from many different regions and cultures to communicate with one another clearly. It is the variety of English you read and hear most often in books and magazines, on radio and television. It is the kind of English that people are expected to use in most school and business situations.

The **Handbook** in this textbook gives you some of the rules and guidelines for using standard American English. To identify the differences between standard American English and other varieties of English, the **Handbook** uses the labels *standard* and *nonstandard*. *Nonstandard* doesn't mean wrong language. It means language that is inappropriate in situations where standard English is expected.

☞ REFERENCE NOTE: For more about standard English, see page 738.

EXERCISE 7   **Revising Nonstandard English**

The following paragraph is a speech that the writer plans to give to the members of a drama club. The writer has a worthwhile message, but the inappropriate use of nonstandard English is likely to distract his audience. First, identify the nonstandard features in the paragraph. Then, revise the paragraph to make it standard throughout.

> This here club isn't going to get nowhere unless we members cooperate. For one thing, we gotta start getting more enthusiastic about coming to the meetings. There's been too many absences, with too many excuses like "I would of come, but I had to feed my dog." Everybody knows about the meetings ahead of time, so you don't have no excuse for not showing up. Another thing is that the members should all take equal responsibility for the club. The same people hadn't ought to always take care of refreshments, plan the program, and books the meeting room. I'm not saying that you're all lazy, but we got a long way to go toward getting this club organized good.

ANSWERS
Exercise 7

This here club/This club
nowhere/anywhere
gotta/must
There's/There have
would of/would have
don't have no/there *is* no
Another thing is that/Also,
hadn't ought to/shouldn't
books/book
we got/we have
organized good/organized well

RETEACHING

For students who haven't mastered the lesson's concepts through the various kinds of practice already completed, you may want to try activities that are more visual and kinesthetic. Work with students to plan posters illustrating different uses of English, including terms, definitions, and examples.

CLOSURE

Ask students to list the characteristics of each type of English—informal, dialect, and formal—and to give one example of each.

MEETING *individual* NEEDS

ADVANCED STUDENTS

Ask students to select passages in informal English from their writing (about one hundred words long) and to rewrite the passages twice: first in their local dialect, and then in standard formal English. Then students should underline and identify colloquialisms and slang in the passages written in informal English and in dialect.

---

500 *English: Origins and Uses*

Standard English—Formal to Informal

The flexibility of English lets you adapt your language to almost any situation. The kinds of language that you use in different situations are called *levels of usage.* The levels of usage in standard English reach from the very formal to the very informal, with a wide range in between. No level of usage is "higher" or better than another; each has its appropriate use.

The following chart lists some of the uses of formal and informal English.

USES OF FORMAL AND INFORMAL ENGLISH		
	FORMAL	INFORMAL
SPEAKING	formal, dignified occasions, such as banquets and dedication ceremonies	everyday conversation at home, school, work, and recreation
WRITING	serious papers and reports	personal letters, journal entries, and many newspaper and magazine articles

Formal and informal English differ from one another in several ways. The main differences between them are in sentence structure, word choice, and tone.

FEATURES OF FORMAL AND INFORMAL ENGLISH		
	FORMAL	INFORMAL
SENTENCE STRUCTURE	long and complex	short and simple
WORD CHOICE	precise; often technical or scientific	simple and ordinary; often including contractions, colloquialisms, and slang
TONE	serious and dignified	conversational

ENRICHMENT

Have students find examples of dialect in literature that reinforce characterization or theme. A good source is Bernard Malamud's short story "The First Seven Years" or Langston Hughes's poem "Mother to Son."

EXTENSION

You may want to ask students to create new colloquialisms or slang words for common situations. Have students work in groups to create between three and five new terms. Ask each group to present its terms to the class. Let the class guess what the terms mean. ■

How English Is Used   **501**

Uses of Informal English

In using language, people constantly make up new words and attach new meanings to old ones. Some of the most colorful and inventive uses of English occur in informal speaking and writing. The informal words and expressions that we use fall into two categories: *colloquialisms* and *slang*.

Colloquialisms

The word *colloquial* comes from a Latin word that means "conversation." **Colloquialisms** are the colorful expressions of conversational language. They add a friendly, informal tone to speaking and writing.

EXAMPLES   Carlota was **on top of the world** after she **aced** her history exam.

The teacher knew you were trying to **put one over on** her when you said the dog ate your homework.

What's the matter? You look **down in the mouth.**

Many colloquialisms are also idioms. An **idiom** is a word or phrase that means something different from the literal meanings of the words. For example, *to put one over on* somebody has the colloquial meaning "to deceive or trick" somebody. But the literal meaning of the phrase is something quite different.

INTEGRATING THE LANGUAGE ARTS

Literature Link. Ask students to analyze the use of colloquial language in poetry. Have students read a poem such as John Updike's "Ex-Basketball Player" for examples of colloquialisms. Then ask students to write an informative paragraph explaining how these colloquialisms (*hanging loose, hang back, hang together*) make Updike's portrait of the basketball player seem more real.

ANSWERS
Exercise 8

1. explain it to me
2. I don't understand
3. don't give up
4. improvise
5. take advantage of someone

ANSWERS
Exercise 9

Students might brainstorm in groups to generate at least five words for *disgusting* and five for *amazing,* with extra points given for additional examples. Class discussion about which terms will last and which will be out of fashion next year can be based on comparison or on other good reasoning. For example, a student might reason, "*Gross* is going to last. People have been using it for years." For extra credit, students might look up their expressions in a slang dictionary to see where the phrases came from and what they meant originally. For example, *cute* originally meant *curvy,* sometimes even *bowlegged.*

502

EXERCISE 8 ▶ **Explaining the Meanings of Colloquialisms**

A pen pal from another country wants to learn some American colloquialisms. She has asked you to explain the following expressions, which are confusing to her because they can't be taken literally. Explain the meaning of each expression in simple, straightforward language. Use a dictionary to find the meanings of any expressions you can't explain.

1. clue me in
2. (I don't) get it
3. hang in there
4. play it by ear
5. slip one over on (someone)

Slang

Slang is highly informal English. It consists of made-up words or of old words used in new ways. Slang is usually clever and colorful, and it can make the user seem up-to-date. The following words are all considered slang when used with the given meanings.

> *bad:* good, excellent
> *dude:* man or boy
> *humongous:* huge, enormous
> *make like:* imitate
> *scarf down:* eat greedily

Slang words are often a special vocabulary for close-knit groups, such as students, musicians, sailors, and surfers. For example, in the 1980s the word *tubular* was surfers' slang for "pleasing, fine." Like *tubular,* most slang words live a short life.

EXERCISE 9 ▶ **Identifying Slang Words**

What slang words do you and your classmates use to mean "disgusting" and "amazing"? List as many as you can think of. Which ones do you think will become a lasting part of the language? Which will likely live a short life?

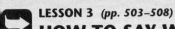

HOW TO SAY WHAT YOU MEAN

OBJECTIVES

- To choose appropriate synonyms
- To analyze responses to the connotations of words
- To analyze loaded words and euphemisms used in a magazine
- To revise jargon in a given passage
- To revise sentences by replacing clichés

How to Say What You Mean

A word can have many layers of meaning. It can also have different meanings depending on where and how it is used. To use words well, you need to understand some of the meanings and associations they may have. You want to be sure that your words will say what you want them to say.

© 1991 Jim Unger/Distributed by Universal Press Syndicate

"It states quite clearly . . . 'evening dress.'"

Synonyms

Using *synonyms*—different words that have similar meanings—is a way to bring variety to your writing. But it's important to remember that no two words are exactly alike. Each word has its own shade of meaning, and some words have more precise meanings than others. For example, read the following sentences:

> The child on the bus **looked** at me.
> The child on the bus **stared** at me.

Look and *stare* are synonyms, but they can suggest quite different things. *Look* is a very general word; *stare* is a specific word that describes a particular way of looking at something. Since the first synonym that occurs to you might not be the best one, use a thesaurus (a book of synonyms) along with a dictionary to find just the right word.

EXERCISE 10 ▶ **Choosing Appropriate Synonyms**

For each sentence, decide which of the words in parentheses is <u>the better replacement for the italicized word</u>. Keep in mind the overall meaning of the sentence. Use a dictionary to check any words you're not sure about.

1. She wrinkled her nose slightly at the *unpleasant* smell of burned oatmeal. (*revolting*, <u>*distasteful*</u>)

PROGRAM MANAGER

HOW TO SAY WHAT YOU MEAN

■ **Independent Practice/ Reteaching** For practice and reinforcement, see **Choosing the Right Synonym, Denotation and Connotation, Jargon and Gobbledygook,** and **Mixed Figures of Speech and Clichés** in *Word Choice and Sentence Style,* pp. 29–32.

QUOTATION FOR THE DAY

"Men ever had, and ever will have, leave/To coin new words well suited to the age./Words are like leaves, some wither ev'ry year,/And ev'ry year a younger race succeeds." (Horace, Quintus Horatius Flaccus, 65–8 B.C., Roman poet and satirist)

After writing the quotation on the chalkboard, ask students to restate it in their own words. Explain that the English language changes and grows over time.

To demonstrate to students that word choice is important in writing and speaking, pose a problem for them at the beginning of the lesson:

"Suppose you have been working at a local fast-food place. You have been working about forty hours a week in addition to going to school. How can you make it clear to us that you are working too hard? Tell me without using the word *work.*"

A student might use the word *labor* to mean "working very hard," or *toil* to mean "working overly hard." Make the point that revisions in word choice can make fuzzy writing clearer.

504   *English: Origins and Uses*

2. Marcia was furious at Carl for *telling* her most guarded secret. (*uttering,* <u>*divulging*</u>)
3. *Laughing* happily, the two children showered each other with crisp fall leaves. (<u>*giggling*</u>, *snickering*)
4. Each *symmetrical* snowflake glistened as it melted. (<u>*equal-sided*</u>, *well-balanced*)
5. Emphasizing the importance of the upcoming election, the senator *urged* everyone to vote. (*nagged,* <u>*pressed*</u>)

Denotation and Connotation

Compare the meanings of the following sentences:

Nan's persistence surprised everyone.
Nan's stubbornness surprised everyone.

The two sentences mean basically the same thing. *Stubbornness* is another word for *persistence,* "the quality of not giving up easily." This is the **denotation** of the words. But the effect of the words on the reader or listener can be quite different. *Stubbornness* suggests that Nan is unreasonable, narrow-minded, and unwilling to listen to others. This is the **connotation** of the word *stubborn.*

It is especially important to consider the connotations of words when you are choosing synonyms. Otherwise, you may replace a word with one that has an unintended effect on your reader.

EXERCISE 11 ▶ **Responding to the Connotations of Words**

Which of the following words have favorable connotations for you? Which have unpleasant connotations? Which don't stir any feeling at all? Compare your reactions with those of your classmates. Note which words have the same effect on everyone and which bring different responses from different people.

1. duty
2. propaganda
3. proud
4. fake
5. puppy
6. creeping
7. smile
8. serious
9. laughter
10. rain

ANSWERS
Exercise 11

Group discussion can establish whether student reactions result from personal associations or generally accepted differences. Generally accepted connotations are noted here. Any answer that may vary is indicated by an asterisk (*).

1. duty * (honor, drudgery)
2. propaganda (negative)
3. proud * (noble, haughty)
4. fake (negative)
5. puppy * (cute, not housebroken)
6. creeping (negative)
7. smile (favorable)
8. serious* (resolute, dangerous)
9. laughter * (with one, at one)
10. rain * (to cool a hot day, to spoil a picnic)

The word choices dealt with in this lesson require students to have an awareness of the exact meaning of words. Encourage students to use a dictionary when they are unsure about the full meaning of a word.

To teach the lesson on precise selection of synonyms, you can use the example given in the text on p. 503 to show why some words may be almost the same in meaning and still have quite different connotations.

Follow the same procedure to teach denotation and connotation, loaded words, jargon, euphemisms, mixed figures of speech, tired words, and clichés.

☞

Loaded Words

A word that has very strong connotations, either positive or negative, is said to be *loaded.* Loaded words appeal to our emotions. They can bias us for or against something because of the feelings they arouse.

EXAMPLES　The local diner serves cheap, greasy chicken.
　　　　　　The local diner serves inexpensive, home-fried food.

　　　　　　The mob of protesters shouted their demands.
　　　　　　The group of protesters made their voices heard.

A writer or speaker who wants to influence your opinion may use loaded words. For example, politicians, advertisers, and writers of editorials tend to use loaded language.

Euphemisms

Sometimes a word or phrase may be considered offensive because it is too direct. You may choose to replace it with a *euphemism*—an agreeable term that stands for a more direct, less pleasing one.

EUPHEMISM	MORE DIRECT TERM
dentures	false teeth
memorial park	cemetery
substandard housing	slum
washroom	toilet

Sometimes euphemisms are used to misrepresent facts or to cover up the truth. For example, a salesperson may tell you a car is "experienced" when it is actually used. And a politician may say he "misspoke" when he actually lied.

STYLE NOTE　Keep in mind the emotional effect your words are likely to have. Loaded words and euphemisms can be effective in writing, but you need to choose them carefully. Avoid words that may mislead your readers.

INTEGRATING THE LANGUAGE ARTS

Literature Link. You may want to tie this lesson in with a nonfiction literature unit. If the selection is available, have students read "R.M.S. Titanic" by Hanson W. Baldwin and ask them to list examples of nautical jargon. Using their lists, students can discuss how this language creates a feeling of authenticity.

A DIFFERENT APPROACH

Another misuse of language students could research and report on is *doublespeak.* Coined by George Orwell in his novel *1984,* this term refers to ambiguous language that is purposefully deceptive. In other words, doublespeak is more negative than jargon or gobbledygook because it attempts to use nonfactual, evasive, or self-contradictory language to hide the truth.

You could show students the following examples to explain what to look for:

DOUBLESPEAK	TRANSLATION
1. nervous wetness	sweat
2. encore telecast	rerun
3. terminal living	dying
4. discomfort	pain
5. civil disorder	riot
6. dehired	fired

Sources students might use to find more examples are *Doublespeak Dictionary* by William Lambdin and *The Language of Oppression* by Haig Bosmajian.

506

---

506   *English: Origins and Uses*

EXERCISE 12 ▶ **Analyzing Loaded Words and Euphemisms**

Look through a popular magazine, and pick an ad or an article that you find especially convincing. What makes the writing effective? What loaded words or euphemisms does the advertiser use, and how do the words influence your emotions?   Responses will vary. You may want students to include copies of their ads or articles with their answers.

Jargon

Jargon can refer to language that has a special meaning for a particular group of people, such as people who share the same profession, occupation, or hobby. For example, publishers and printers use the word *bleed* as jargon for "run an illustration off the edge of a page." This kind of jargon can be practical because it reduces many words to just one or two.

The second kind of jargon, also called *gobbledygook,* is wordy, puffed-up language. Users of gobbledygook choose big words over short ones, difficult words over simple ones. They confuse their readers with vague, pretentious language. For example, in the following cartoon, the senator uses puffed-up language to make his statement sound impressive. See how his "translator" sums up the unimpressive truth.

EXERCISE 13 ▶ **Revising Jargon**

The following passage is confusing because it is written in jargon. First, figure out what the writer was trying to say. Then, rewrite the passage in clear language, using only as many words as you need.

ASSESSMENT

You can assess students' understanding of the lesson's concepts through their answers to **Exercises 10–14**.

RETEACHING

You may want to have students look in newspapers or magazines for examples of exact synonyms, words with connotative meanings, loaded words, euphemisms, jargon, and clichés. You could pair each student who needs help with a student who has already mastered the concept. Ask the pairs of

In spite of the fact that government aviation agencies were not in agreement with respect to the question of the cause of the accident at Hartsfield Airport, the court has decided that one of the factors contributing to the crash was a motor mount that had been structurally weakened.

Handle with Care

Some words can get in the way of your meaning. They can confuse your audience or make your topic seem dull. There are three kinds of expressions you should handle with care: *mixed figures of speech, tired words,* and *clichés.*

Mixed Figures of Speech

A *figure of speech* describes one thing by comparing it to another thing. A figure of speech is not meant to be taken literally. For example, if your sister calls your room a *pigpen,* she doesn't mean that you keep pigs there. She means that your room looks rather dirty, like a pigpen.

It's important to use figures of speech in a consistent way. If you begin with one comparison and switch to another, you create a *mixed figure of speech.*

MIXED   Great waves of embarrassment broke over her, all but drying up the little confidence she had. [*Great waves* suggest water, which would hardly *dry up* anything.]

BETTER   Great waves of embarrassment broke over her, all but **washing away** the little confidence she had.

Tired Words

A *tired word* is a word that was once clear and forceful. But it has been used so often and so carelessly that it has become vague and weak. For example, overuse has watered down the original, clear meaning of *wonderful,* "causing wonder and amazement." Similar tired words are *good, nice, fine,* and *great.* These words may be acceptable in conversation, but they are too vague to be effective in writing.

students to discuss each example. Either student should be able to explain the examples.

CLOSURE

Ask students to volunteer examples of the terms in this lesson as you call them out one at a time. ■

Clichés

A tired expression is called a *cliché.* Like tired words, many clichés were once fresh and original. For example, *butterflies in my stomach* was probably a striking turn of phrase the first time it was used to describe stage fright. But it has become stale through constant use. Some clichés are overused figures of speech: *blanket of snow, busy as a bee, white as a sheet.* Others are overused phrases such as *easier said than done, fair and square, last but not least.*

E X E R C I S E **14** ▶   **Revising Sentences by Replacing Clichés**

The clichés in each of the following sentences are italicized. Rewrite each sentence, substituting simple, straightforward language for the clichés.

1. After *a meal fit for a king,* we agreed that *a good time had been had by all.*
2. *In this day and age,* political figures who remain *on the fence* when *burning questions* are argued will be *doomed to disappointment* when election day comes.
3. Although warned not to *bite off more than I could chew,* I signed up for six courses.
4. *To make a long story short,* I failed two courses, and *to add insult to injury,* I had to go to summer school.
5. The novel's main character wandered from *the straight and narrow path* and was eventually *embraced by the long arm of the law.*

COMPUTER NOTE: When you revise the drafts of your papers, use bold, italic, or underline formatting to highlight words or phrases you plan to change. The thesaurus tool can help you find substitutes for jargon, tired words, or clichés.

ANSWERS
Exercise 14

Responses will vary. Here are some possibilities:

1. After a fine meal, we agreed that we had all had a good time.
2. Today, political figures who avoid giving their opinions on important issues will lose on election day.
3. Although warned not to attempt too much, I signed up for six courses.
4. In fact, I failed two courses, and I had to go to summer school.
5. The novel's main character became a criminal and was eventually arrested.

COOPERATIVE LEARNING

Have groups of three students create mixed metaphors. After students have read the examples in the lesson, ask them to write some of their own, to put them on pieces of paper, and to draw illustrations of exactly what they have written. The pictures will be strange but will reinforce the fact that mixed metaphors are strange, too.

COMPUTER NOTE

Some students may have difficulty recognizing clichés. Encourage these students to use the grammar-checker on their word-processing program. They can set the grammar-checker to the style that calls clichés to their attention.

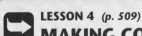
509

MAKING CONNECTIONS

Writing a Travel Ad

A beach resort has decided to advertise in a travel magazine to attract more customers. You've been hired to create their new ad. As the ad writer, your job is to convince people that the resort is a beautiful, fun, exciting place to spend their vacation. You've decided to use this collage of photographs to catch your reader's eye, but you also need to write some convincing copy.

Write an ad that will convince readers to send off for more information about the resort. Remember that ad writers don't have much space to work with. You'll need to make every word count.

WRITING A TRAVEL AD
Teaching Strategies

To get students started, brainstorm about what will best attract tourists. Then ask each student to write at least one line that might appear in the advertisement. After each student has written an idea, expand this lesson into a group activity with three or four students in each group. Ask students to share their ideas with the group and then to agree on the best ideas for the ad. Give groups sheets of typing paper and ask them to sketch their proposed ads, including a simple drawing of the beach scenes and the advertising copy lettered in the desired size. Display finished ads in front of the room and allow a representative from each group to explain the reasoning behind that group's advertisement. Ask for responses from the rest of the class about the persuasiveness of the ads.

GUIDELINES

The travel ads should be succinct and should include persuasive language. You may want to refer to **Chapter 9: "Writing to Persuade"** for help with persuasion.

PART TWO

HANDBOOK

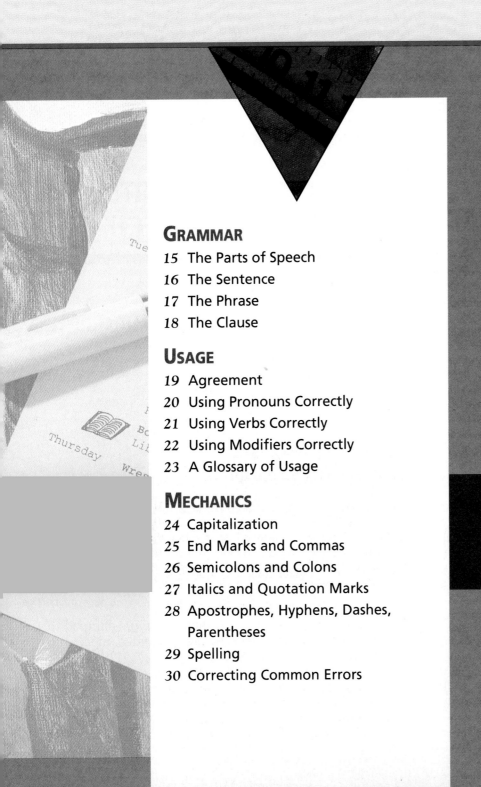

GRAMMAR

USAGE

MECHANICS

PART TWO: HANDBOOK

The following **Teaching Resources** booklets contain materials that may be used with this part of the Pupil's Edition.

- *Language Skills Practice and Assessment*
- *Practice for Assessment in Reading, Vocabulary, and Spelling* (for Ch. 29)

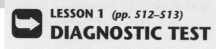
OBJECTIVE

• To identify the parts of speech of words in sentences and in a paragraph

GRAMMAR

CHAPTER OVERVIEW

This chapter discusses the eight parts of speech and how they are used. A **Writing Application** feature has each student use adjectives to describe an imagined self. A **Picture This** feature asks students to use adverbs in stage directions for a scene from *Romeo and Juliet.* A section on determining parts of speech is included before **Review: Post-tests 1** and **2.**

GRAMMAR

15 THE PARTS OF SPEECH

Their Identification and Function

Diagnostic Test

A. Identifying the Parts of Speech in Sentences

Identify the part of speech of each <u>italicized word</u> in the following sentences.

n. = noun   adj. = adjective   prep. = preposition
v. = verb   adv. = adverb   pro. = pronoun

EXAMPLE   **1.** In the nineteenth century, many men *worked* as cowboys on *cattle* drives.
1. *worked—verb; cattle—adjective*

conj. = conjunction
itj. = interjection

1. When the drive was <u>over</u>, the cattle were shipped to northern cities to meet the <u>need</u> for hides, meat, and tallow.   **1.** adj./n.
2. There <u>were</u> <u>few</u> comforts on the trail.   **2.** v./adj.
3. Some <u>improvement</u> came after <u>Charles Goodnight</u> put together the first chuck wagon.   **3.** n./n.
4. A hinged lid swung <u>down</u> from the wagon to reveal a simple <u>but</u> complete kitchen.   **4.** adv./conj.

5. The *first* chuck wagons were pulled *by* oxen. **5.** adj./prep.
6. *These* were later replaced by mules *or* horses. **6.** pro./conj.
7. *Most* of the cowhands who took part in the historic cattle drives remain *nameless*. **7.** pro./adj.
8. Cowboys were *instrumental* in opening trails used by the men and women who *settled* the frontier. **8.** adj./v.
9. *Railroads* *soon* began to crisscross the country; the cowboy was no longer needed to drive cattle. **9.** n./adv.
10. *Hey!* Did you know that ranchers still hire *cowboys* to brand and herd cattle, repair fences, and do many other jobs? **10.** itj./n.

B. Identifying the Parts of Speech in a Paragraph

Identify the part of speech of the <u>italicized word or words</u> in each sentence in the following paragraph.
For abbreviation key, see Diagnostic Test: Part A.
EXAMPLE   **[1]** *Neither* the cowboys *nor* the cattle had an *easy* life on the trail.
   1. *Neither-nor—conjunction; easy—adjective*

[11] In the *thirty* years following the Civil War, millions of longhorn cattle were driven *over* long trails from ranches in Texas to railroads in Kansas. **[12]** During this *period*, the cowboy *became* an American hero. **[13]** Novels *and* magazine articles *glorified* life on the range. **[14]** The men *who* rode this rugged land, however, had to endure *many* hardships. **[15]** Cowboys spent most of their *time* in the saddle, rounding up strays and moving the herd *along*. **[16]** Caring for sick animals, repairing fences, and, *well*, doing what needed to be done were <u>all</u> part of a normal working day. **[17]** At the end of such a day, each cowboy *not only* had to look after his horse *but also* had to cook dinner for *himself* and do a host of other chores. **[18]** The quiet *evenings* gave cowboys a chance to relax by telling stories and singing *campfire* songs. **[19]** Such details of trail life are *realistically* portrayed in the *popular* paintings of Charles M. Russell. **[20]** *Because of* these images and our need for a *truly* American hero, cowboys have become a colorful part of our history.

11. adj./prep.
12. n./v.
13. conj./v.
14. pro./adj.
15. n./adv.
16. itj./adj.
17. conj./conj./pro.
18. n./adj.
19. adv./adj.
20. prep./adv.

GRAMMAR

GRAMMAR

USING THE DIAGNOSTIC TEST

The first section of the **Diagnostic Test** asks students to identify the parts of speech of twenty italicized words in ten sentences.

Part B of the **Diagnostic Test** gives an additional twenty italicized words to classify in sentences appearing in a paragraph. Together, the two parts of the test make a good indicator of how much instruction will be needed on parts of speech. For most students, **Part A** will be easier than **Part B**.

If only a few students are unable to demonstrate mastery, you might have them work independently to review definitions and do exercises.

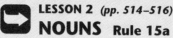
OBJECTIVES

- To identify nouns in sentences
- To replace common nouns with proper nouns

QUICK REMINDER

Write the following incomplete sentence on the chalkboard:

My favorite ____ of all time is ____.

Ask students to fill in the first blank with a common noun and the second blank with a proper noun. You might prompt students to think first of a category, such as a person, place, thing, or idea, and then to think of a particular member of that category. [Examples: My favorite <u>hero</u> of all time is <u>Amelia Earhart</u>. My favorite <u>book</u> of all time is *Watership Down.*]

---

514   *The Parts of Speech*

THE EIGHT PARTS OF SPEECH		
noun	pronoun	adjective
verb	adverb	preposition
conjunction	interjection	

Nouns

15a. A *noun* is a word used to name a person, place, thing, or idea.

Your name is a noun, and so is the name of your state. *Tree* is a noun. The names of things that you cannot see or touch are nouns: *sympathy, fairness, generosity, truth.* These words name qualities or ideas.

EXERCISE 1   **Identifying Nouns in Sentences**

Identify the twenty-five <u>nouns</u> that appear in the following paragraph. Treat as single nouns all capitalized names containing more than one word. Do not include years, such as *1815.*

EXAMPLE   [1] Elizabeth Cady Stanton was born in Johnstown, New York, in 1815.
   1. *Elizabeth Cady Stanton, Johnstown, New York*

[1] As a young <u>woman</u>, <u>Elizabeth Cady Stanton</u> studied the <u>classics</u> and <u>mathematics</u> both at <u>home</u> and at <u>Troy Female Seminary</u>, from which she graduated in 1832. [2] Beginning at an early <u>age</u>, she recognized the <u>injustices</u> suffered by <u>women</u>, especially in <u>education</u> and <u>politics</u>. [3] In 1840 she married <u>Henry Stanton</u>, a prominent <u>abolitionist</u>. [4] At an antislavery <u>convention</u> in <u>London</u>, <u>Mrs. Stanton</u> was outraged at the <u>treatment</u> of the female <u>delegates</u>. [5] She later helped to organize the first <u>meeting</u> addressed to women's <u>rights</u>. [6] At that <u>convention</u>, she read her "<u>Declaration of Sentiments</u>," outlining the inferior <u>status</u> of <u>women</u> and calling for <u>reforms</u>.

15a

Proper Nouns and Common Nouns

A *proper noun* names a *particular* person, place, thing, or idea. A *common noun* names a *class* of persons, places, things, or ideas.

PROPER NOUNS	COMMON NOUNS
Atlanta, Nantucket, Mount McKinley	city, island, mountain
Louisa May Alcott, General Powell	novelist, general
Museum of Fine Arts, World Trade Center	museum, building
Queen Elizabeth 2, Spirit of St. Louis	ship, airplane

NOTE: Compound nouns are two or more words put together to form a single noun. Some compound nouns are written as one word, some as two or more words, and some with hyphens.

ONE WORD	TWO OR MORE WORDS	HYPHENATED WORD
basketball newspaper	car pool Arts and Crafts Club	passer-by sister-in-law

EXERCISE 2 **Replacing Common Nouns with Proper Nouns**

For each of the following common nouns, give a proper noun.

EXAMPLE **1.** river
1. *Mississippi River*

1. play	**3.** street	**5.** president	**7.** ocean	**9.** poem
2. state	**4.** song	**6.** newspaper	**8.** writer	**10.** car

Concrete Nouns and Abstract Nouns

Concrete nouns name objects that can be perceived by the senses. *Abstract nouns* name a quality or an idea.

CONCRETE NOUNS   dog, sunset, thunder, silk, apple
ABSTRACT NOUNS   liberty, beauty, kindness, success

MEETING *individual* NEEDS

LEP/ESL

General Strategies. To illustrate the concept of nouns, have students develop charts in which they list persons, places, things, and ideas that are familiar to them. Then, have students classify the items in their charts as common or proper nouns.

ANSWERS
Exercise 2

Answers will vary. Here are some possibilities:

1. *A Raisin in the Sun, A Doll's House, Romeo and Juliet*
2. California, Ohio, Hawaii
3. Rodeo Drive, Main Street, Pennsylvania Avenue
4. "Home on the Range," "The Star-Spangled Banner," "Yesterday"
5. George Bush, George Washington, Abraham Lincoln
6. *The New York Times, USA Today, Washington Post*
7. Atlantic Ocean, Pacific Ocean, Indian Ocean
8. Sylvia Sanchez, Charles Dickens, S.E. Hinton
9. "The Raven," "Stopping by Woods on a Snowy Evening," "Jabberwocky"
10. Ford Mustang, Toyota Celica, Pontiac Firebird

GRAMMAR

REVIEW A

OBJECTIVE

• To identify common and proper nouns, abstract and concrete nouns, and compound nouns

516   *The Parts of Speech*

 REVIEW A   **Classifying Nouns**

Identify each of the italicized nouns in the following paragraph as *proper* or *common*, and *concrete* or *abstract*. Also, tell if a noun is c<u>ompound</u>.

1. con.

[1] *Cajuns* are descended from French settlers who were expelled from Acadia (Nova Scotia) by the British in 1755.

2. con.— cd.

When some of these displaced people settled in the [2] *Atchafalaya Basin* in southeastern Louisiana, they had to

3. abs.

invent [3] *ways* to use local foods in their traditional French

4. con.— cd.

recipes. If you've never tried Cajun food, the [4] *crawfish* and gumbo in these pictures may be unfamiliar to you. In

5. con.— cd.

addition to the plentiful crawfish, shrimp, oysters, and other [5] *seafood*, freshwater fish, alligator meat, rice, and

6. con.

many [6] *spices* find their way into Cajun cooking. Gum-

7. con.

bos, like this one, are soups flavored with [7] *filé*, which is

8. con.

powdered sassafras leaves. [8] *Gumbos* often contain okra and a meat such as sausage, chicken, or seafood. The

9. abs.

[9] *popularity* of these and other Cajun dishes has spread

10. con.— cd.

throughout the [10] *United States* in recent years.

Pronouns

15b.   A *pronoun* is a word used in place of one or more nouns or pronouns.

EXAMPLE   Susan watched the monkey make faces at her little brother and sister. **She** laughed at **it** more than **they** did. [*She* is used in place of *Susan*, *it* in place of *monkey*, and *they* in place of *brother* and *sister*.]

PROGRAM MANAGER

PRONOUNS

■ **Independent Practice/ Reteaching** For instruction and exercises, see **Types of Pronouns A** and **Types of Pronouns B** in *Language Skills Practice and Assessment,* pp. 13–14.

■ **Computer Guided Instruction** For additional instruction and practice with pronouns, see **Lesson 1** in *Language Workshop CD-ROM.*

■ **Practice** To help less-advanced students with additional instruction and practice with pronouns, see **Chapter 10** in *English Workshop, Fourth Course,* pp. 105–106.

OBJECTIVE

- To identify pronouns in sentences

Personal Pronouns

	SINGULAR	PLURAL
FIRST PERSON	I, my, mine, me	we, our, ours, us
SECOND PERSON	you, your, yours	you, your, yours
THIRD PERSON	he, his, him she, her, hers it, its	they, their, theirs, them

Other Commonly Used Pronouns

RELATIVE PRONOUNS
(used to introduce adjective and noun clauses)

who	whom	whose	which	that

INTERROGATIVE PRONOUNS
(used to begin questions)

Who . . . ?   Whose . . . ?   What . . . ?
Whom . . . ?   Which . . . ?

DEMONSTRATIVE PRONOUNS
(used to point out a specific person, place, thing, or idea)

this	that	these	those

INDEFINITE PRONOUNS
(used to refer to an indefinite person, place, thing, or idea)

all	each	more	one
another	either	most	other
any	everybody	much	several
anybody	everyone	neither	some
anyone	everything	nobody	somebody
anything	few	none	someone
both	many	no one	such

REFLEXIVE AND INTENSIVE PRONOUNS
(used to refer to or to intensify a personal pronoun)

myself	ourselves
yourself	yourselves
himself, herself, itself	themselves

QUICK REMINDER

Write the following sentences on the chalkboard:

1. Tom wanted to take <u>Tom's</u> car to the carwash and clean <u>Tom's car</u>.
2. Shani tried to study for <u>Shani's</u> test, but <u>Shani</u> was constantly interrupted by <u>Shani's</u> friends.
3. <u>All the people</u> worked hard at <u>all the people's</u> company until <u>all the people</u> went home.

Have students replace the underlined words and phrases with appropriate pronouns. [**(1)** his, it; **(2)** her, she, her; **(3)** Everybody, their, they]

You may want to point out that pronouns can shorten sentences and make them more efficient.

MEETING *individual* **NEEDS**

LEP/ESL

General Strategies. Some students will have difficulty knowing when to use possessive pronouns in English. For example, because their language does not regard a body part as something to be possessed, Spanish-speakers may say, "I have broken the arm" instead of ". . . my arm."

Explain that possessive pronouns can help writing be more specific. Ask students to think of other instances in which constructions in their native languages could be made more specific in English through the use of possessive pronouns.

ADJECTIVES Rule 15c

OBJECTIVES

- To identify the words adjectives modify
- To differentiate between adjectives and pronouns

518 *The Parts of Speech*

> **NOTE:** The words *my, your, his, her, ours,* and *their* are considered possessive pronouns in this book, rather than adjectives. Follow your teacher's instructions in referring to such words.

EXERCISE 3   Identifying Pronouns in Sentences

Identify the <u>pronouns</u> in each sentence in the following paragraph. If a pronoun is used more than once, note it each time it appears. [Note: The paragraph contains a total of twenty-five pronouns.]

[1] <u>Everybody</u> in <u>my</u> family likes to go camping, but <u>few</u> enjoy the outdoors more than <u>I</u> do. [2] Last summer <u>several</u> of <u>my</u> cousins and <u>I</u> stayed at a rustic camp in the Rocky Mountains, <u>which</u> are not far from <u>our</u> hometown. [3] At camp <u>we</u> learned how to build a campfire and how to keep <u>it</u> going. [4] A group of <u>us</u> even went beyond <u>that</u>—<u>we</u> learned to cook food over an open fire. [5] <u>One</u> of <u>our</u> counselors showed <u>those</u> <u>who</u> were interested how to cook simple meals. [6] <u>Each</u> of <u>his</u> recipes was easy to follow, and <u>everyone</u> ate <u>everything</u> in sight. [7] <u>All</u> of <u>us</u> enjoy eating <u>anything</u> cooked over an open fire.

Adjectives

15c. An *adjective* is a word used to modify a noun or pronoun.

Adjectives make the meaning of a noun or a pronoun more definite. Words used in this way are called *modifiers.*

An adjective may modify a noun or pronoun by telling *what kind, which one,* or *how many (how much).*

WHAT KIND?	WHICH ONE?	HOW MANY?
blue ink	**this** park	**twenty** miles
old friends	**these** papers	**less** time
strong winds	**that** house	**several** apples
Italian food	**Monday** morning	**one-half** inch

An adjective may be separated from the word it modifies by other words.

EXAMPLES   She is **clever.**
           The sky, which had been clear all day, became **cloudy.**

Articles

The most frequently used adjectives are *a, an,* and *the.* These words are usually called *articles.*

A and *an* are *indefinite articles.* They indicate that a noun refers to one of a general group. *A* is used before words beginning with a consonant sound; *an* is used before words beginning with a vowel sound. *An* is also used before words beginning with the consonant *h* when the *h* is not pronounced.

EXAMPLES   **A** ranger helped us.
           They planted **an** acre with corn.
           We kept watch for **an** hour.

The is the *definite article.* It indicates that a noun refers to someone or something in particular.

EXAMPLES   **The** ranger helped us.
           The hour dragged by.
           They planted **the** acre with corn.

▷ EXERCISE 4   **Identifying the Words That Adjectives Modify**

For each italicized adjective in the following sentences, identify the word the adjective modifies.

[1] By the 1890s, an *extraordinary* craze for bicycling had swept the United States. [2] Though bicycles had been *available* for years, the *early* versions made for an *awkward* ride. [3] *Ungainly* cycles like the ones shown on the next page had a very *large* wheel in the front and a *small* wheel in the back. [4] In 1885, however, a more *sensible* model was introduced, one that resembled the *modern* cycle. [5] *Energetic* people everywhere took to *this* kind of bicycle. [6] Bicycling quickly became a *national* sport. [7] Cyclists joined *special* clubs, which took *vigorous* tours through the countryside. [8] A *typical* ride might cover *twenty* miles,

QUICK REMINDER

Write the following sentences on the chalkboard and ask students to make them more meaningful by adding adjectives:

1. The violinist played a piece of music.
2. The woman won the race.
3. The men watched the fires blaze.

MEETING *individual* **NEEDS**

LEP/ESL

General Strategies. In some languages, nouns are never used without articles. Therefore, some students may have difficulty learning to use articles in English.

The best way to teach article use is through sample sentences. If possible, pair students with English-proficient speakers and have the students write simple sentences with articles.

INTEGRATING THE LANGUAGE ARTS

Literature Link. If students' literature book contains "The Fish" by Elizabeth Bishop, have different students read parts of the poem aloud. Then, ask the class which adjectives best convey the personality of the fish, as Bishop depicts it. What makes those adjectives effective?

[The description of a "grunting" weight gives sound to the fish. "Battered," "venerable," and "homely" all make the fish seem less than grand. Yet the narrator speaks of "the frightening gills, fresh and crisp with blood." The poet combines adjectives and figurative language to create the picture of a noble warrior, a fish that deserves to live.]

with a *welcome* stop along the way for refreshments. [9] Races were also *popular* with *enthusiastic* spectators, who often outnumbered those at ball games. [10] The fans enjoyed watching *these* tests of endurance, which sometimes lasted *six* days.

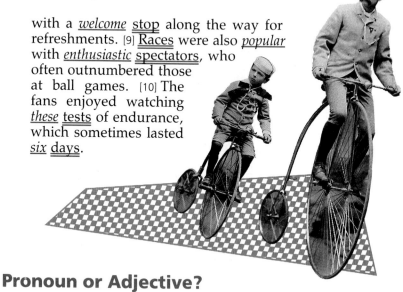

Pronoun or Adjective?

Some words may be used either as adjectives or as pronouns. To tell them apart, keep in mind what they do.

Adjectives *modify* nouns; pronouns *take the place of* nouns.

ADJECTIVE **Those** fans are excited.
PRONOUN **Those** are excited fans.

ADJECTIVE He is taller than **most** other players.
PRONOUN He is taller than **most** of the other players.

NOTE: Many pronouns, such as *my*, *your*, and *their*, may also be classified as adjectives. Follow your teacher's directions in labeling these words.

EXERCISE 5   **Identifying Words as Adjectives or Pronouns**

Identify each italicized word in the following paragraph as a *pronoun* or an *adjective*. For each adjective, give the word it modifies.

Although ants are related to wasps, [1] *these* two kinds of insects differ greatly from [2] *each* other. [3] *All* ants are social insects. They live together in colonies, [4] *each* made up of three castes: a queen, males, and workers.

Unlike ants, [5] *most* <u>wasps</u> are solitary insects. Of [6]⟨*these*⟩, [7]⟨*many*⟩ are hunting wasps [8]⟨*that*⟩ make individual nests in soil or in decaying wood. However, not all wasps are antisocial; [9]⟨*some*⟩ behave more like their cousins the ants. [10] *These* <u>wasps</u> live in permanent colonies of adults and young.

Nouns Used as Adjectives

When a noun is used as an adjective, call it an adjective.

EXAMPLES **salad** bowl   **chicken** dinner
grocery store   **gold** chain

NOTE: Sometimes pairs of nouns are used together so often that the first noun is no longer considered an adjective and the pair becomes a compound noun. When you are not sure about the form of a compound noun, look it up in a dictionary.

EXAMPLES   city hall   sun deck   Brazil nut

WRITING APPLICATION

Using Adjectives to Describe an Imagined Self

When you use adjectives to describe a person or thing, you help your readers to understand something about the nature of that person or thing. Adjectives describe by telling *what kind*, *which one*, or *how many*.

WITHOUT ADJECTIVES   I sang at the wedding.
WITH ADJECTIVES   **Happy** but **nervous**, I sang at the **large, formal** wedding.

The sentence without adjectives tells you nothing about the nature of "I" or "the wedding." Substitute different adjectives, and you'll see how the natures of both change.

WRITING ACTIVITY

Some outstanding writers have imagined themselves as an object or an animal. In the story "Metamorphosis," Franz

GRAMMAR

WRITING APPLICATION

This exercise will give students practice in choosing appropriate adjectives. These adjectives will depend to a large extent on the images the students choose to use. Tell students that adjectives that draw attention to themselves can detract from the writer's intent. Simple, specific words transmit the clearest images to the reader.

GRAMMAR

CRITICAL THINKING

Analysis. Whatever they choose as subjects, students will need to immerse themselves in their subjects, and this will require careful consideration of the proper perspective. Encourage students to recall specific incidents in their lives that might help them to see the world through their chosen perspectives. For instance, if a student chooses to take on the identity of a bird, that student might recall a time when he or she flew in an airplane, climbed a tree, or was in some other way off the ground.

EVALUATING AND REVISING

Have students look over their writing. Is it concise? Are the adjectives interesting? Is there variation? Tell students that the best time to revise a paper is after it has had a chance to sit for a while. Then the writer can look at the words more objectively. If a wait of a day or so is not possible, another person should look over the paper to decide what seems most and least effective.

REVIEW B

Teaching Note. Your instructions to students concerning the labeling of possessive pronouns will affect the answers to the first and second sentences. Students might identify *our* and *my* as adjectives rather than as pronouns.

REVIEWS B and C

OBJECTIVE

• To identify nouns, pronouns, and adjectives used in sentences and to identify the words the adjectives modify

522 *The Parts of Speech*

Kafka writes about a man who becomes an insect! Imagine that you are changed into an animal or an object. Using at least ten carefully chosen adjectives, write a paragraph or a poem describing yourself.

Prewriting Select an object or an animal that you think you would like to be. Next, freewrite descriptive words about the object or animal. You may want to consult an article in an encyclopedia for additional details or pictures of your chosen topic.

Writing As you write your first draft, concentrate on using the most vivid adjectives that you have listed.

Evaluating and Revising Read through your first draft and underline each adjective. For each one, ask yourself whether any other word more precisely describes your topic. Be sure that you have used at least ten different adjectives. Remember to count nouns used as adjectives.

Proofreading Check your paragraph or poem to be sure that all words are spelled correctly, especially any adjectives that you use infrequently in writing.

▶ REVIEW B

Identifying Nouns, Pronouns, and Adjectives

Identify the <u>nouns</u>, <u>pronouns</u>, and (adjectives) used in the following sentences. For each adjective, give the word that it modifies. (Do not include the articles *a, an,* and *the.*)

The words that adjectives modify are listed after each sentence.

1. <u>Our</u> <u>teacher</u>, <u>Mr. López</u>, identified the (various) <u>trees</u> along the (nature) <u>trail</u>. **1.** trees/trail
2. The (bird) <u>feeder</u> in the (elm) <u>tree</u> in <u>my</u> <u>yard</u> attracts <u>cardinals</u> and <u>chickadees</u>. **2.** feeder/tree
3. The <u>flag</u> over the <u>hotel</u> was a (welcome) <u>sight</u> to the (two) <u>travelers</u>. **3.** sight/travelers
4. The (antique) <u>doll</u> was dressed in a (sailor) <u>hat</u> and a (blue) <u>suit</u>. **4.** doll/hat/suit
5. A (large) <u>cake</u> sat in the <u>center</u> of the (kitchen) <u>table</u>. **5.** cake/table

6. Along <u>miles</u> of the <u>Hudson River</u>, (autumn) leaves colored the <u>highway</u> with (bright) <u>splashes</u> of <u>orange</u> and <u>red</u>. **6.** leaves/splashes

7. <u>Someone</u> has filled the (fruit) <u>bowl</u> with <u>dates</u> and <u>walnuts</u>. **7.** bowl

8. As a (young) <u>girl</u>, <u>Susan B. Anthony</u> was taught the (religious) <u>tenets</u> of the <u>Quakers</u>, <u>which</u> include the <u>belief</u> in the <u>equality</u> of (all) <u>people</u>. **8.** girl/tenets/people

9. (Many) <u>people</u> are working to clean up (polluted) <u>rivers</u> and <u>streams</u> to make <u>them</u> (livable) <u>environments</u> for <u>wildlife</u> again. **9.** people/rivers/streams/environments

10. The <u>dust jacket</u> of (that) <u>anthology</u> has certainly seen (better) <u>days</u>. **10.** anthology/days

▶ REVIEW C

Identifying Nouns, Pronouns, and Adjectives

Identify each numbered, italicized word in the following paragraph as a *noun*, a *pronoun*, or an (*adjective*).

EXAMPLE   The Spanish built the first *ranchos,* or ranches, in the
[1] *United States.*
1. *noun*

The [1] *man* in this picture is a *vaquero,* but it's okay if you call [2] *him* a cowboy—he is. *Vaqueros* got their name from the [3] *Spanish* word *vaca,* which means "cow." In fact, cowboys were at [4] *home* on the range in Mexico long

Hugo Wilhelm Arthur Nahl (1833–1889), *Californians Catching Wild Horses with Riata.* Collection of The Oakland Museum, The Oakland Museum Kahn Collection.

OBJECTIVES
- To identify verbs as transitive or intransitive
- To write sentences using linking and helping verbs properly
- To identify action verbs and linking verbs
- To identify verbs and verb phrases

PROGRAM MANAGER

VERBS

- **Independent Practice/ Reteaching** For instruction and exercises, see **Transitive and Intransitive Verbs, Action Verb or Linking Verb?,** and **Verb Phrases** in *Language Skills Practice and Assessment,* pp. 16–18.

- **Computer Guided Instruction** For additional instruction and practice with verbs, see **Lesson 2** in *Language Workshop CD-ROM.*

- **Practice** To help less-advanced students with additional instruction and practice with verbs, see **Chapter 10** in *English Workshop, Fourth Course,* pp. 113–118.

QUICK REMINDER

Write the following incomplete sentences on the chalkboard:

1. The automobile _____ the telephone pole.
2. The package _____ on time.
3. The skier _____ also a doctor.
4. He _____.
5. I _____ the door.

Ask students to fill in the blanks with appropriate verbs. Have the students indicate whether the verbs are linking or action, transitive or intransitive. [Possible answers: **(1)** hit—action, transitive; **(2)** arrived—action, intransitive; **(3)** was—linking; **(4)** yawned—action, intransitive; **(5)** opened—action, transitive]

524

---

524 *The Parts of Speech*

before they gained [5] *legendary* status in the United States. Notice that this *vaquero* wears [6] *leather* chaps (*chaparejos*) to protect his legs and uses a [7] *lariat* (*la reata*) to rope the steer. [8] *Many* other words that we associate with cowboys came into the English language from [9] *Spanish*. [10] *These* include *rodeo, stampede,* and *bronco.*

Verbs

 15d. A *verb* is a word that expresses action or a state of being.

Action Verbs

Words such as *bring, say, shout,* and *jump* are **action verbs.** Some action verbs express actions that cannot be seen— for example, *ponder, trust, evaluate,* and *review.*

Transitive Verbs

A *transitive verb* expresses an action directed toward a person or a thing named in the sentence. The action passes from the doer—the subject—to the receiver of the action, called the *object.*

EXAMPLES   **She trusts her friend.** [The action of the verb *trusts* is directed toward *friend.*]
Zora Neale Hurston wrote novels. [The action of the verb *wrote* is directed toward *novels.*]

Intransitive Verbs

An *intransitive verb* expresses action or a state of being without reference to an object.

EXAMPLES   **The audience applauded.**
The train stops here.

The same verb may be transitive in one sentence and intransitive in another. An intransitive verb is often used when the emphasis is on the action rather than on the person or thing affected by it.

EXAMPLES   Elsa **swam** the channel. [transitive]
Elsa **swam** for many hours. [intransitive]

Miss Castillo **weeds** the garden every day. [transitive]
Miss Castillo **weeds** every day. [intransitive]

"I MISS THE GOOD OLD DAYS WHEN ALL WE HAD TO WORRY ABOUT WAS NOUNS AND VERBS."

© 1984 by Sidney Harris—*Punch.*

> EXERCISE 6 **Identifying Verbs as Transitive or Intransitive**

Identify the verb in each of the following sentences, and tell whether it is *transitive* or *intransitive*.

1. The strong winds <u>died</u> down.
2. We quickly <u>packed</u> lunch for a trip to the seashore.
3. The whitecaps on the ocean <u>disappeared</u>.
4. The sunlight <u>sparkled</u> on the splashing surf.
5. At low tide, Rosita suddenly <u>spotted</u> a starfish.
6. She <u>noticed</u> its five purplish arms.
7. She <u>touched</u> a soft, brown sponge floating nearby.
8. She <u>added</u> it to her collection of seashells, dried seaweed, and driftwood.
9. Her collection <u>includes</u> several conch shells.
10. Three horseshoe crabs <u>swam</u> in the tidal pool.

Linking Verbs

Linking verbs (also called *state-of-being verbs*) help to make a statement by serving as a link between two words.

    The most commonly used linking verbs are forms of the verb *be.*

MEETING *individual* NEEDS

LEP/ESL

General Strategies. Some students may be confused by verbs that can be either transitive or intransitive. To help students understand when a verb is transitive, explain that when verbs are transitive, they connect subjects and objects through some action. This means that sentences with transitive verbs must have two nouns (or pronouns)—a subject and an object. Sentences without objects do not have transitive verbs.

LEARNING STYLES

Visual Learners. To give students extra practice with verbs, have students create comic strips that illustrate the difference between transitive and intransitive verbs.

COMMON ERROR

Problem. Students often overuse forms of the verb *be.* Instead of searching for precisely the right action verb to describe a situation, students too often settle for *is.*

Solution. Tell students to read through their papers and to look particularly for forms of the verb *be* or *have.* Can the paper be improved by replacing a verb with a more exact one? If not, can a verb phrase be made more concise?

Have student volunteers read papers aloud before and after revision.

ANSWERS

Exercise 7

Responses will vary. Examples of sentences with action (A) and linking (L) verbs are provided:

1. (L) The seagulls appear calm. (A) The seagulls appear every morning.
2. (L) The guards sound excited. (A) The guards sound the alarm.
3. (L) The rooms smell musty. (A) The girls smell smoke.
4. (L) We grow older by the minute. (A) Oranges grow in Florida.
5. (L) Trudy looks lovely today. (A) Trudy looks both ways before crossing the street.

526

Commonly Used Forms of *Be*			
be	were	shall have been	should be
being	shall be	will have been	would be
am	will be	can be	could be
is	has been	may be	should have been
are	have been	might be	would have been
was	had been	must be	could have been

Other Commonly Used Linking Verbs

appear	feel	look	seem	sound	taste
become	grow	remain	smell	stay	turn

In the following sentences, each noun or adjective that follows the linking verb refers to the subject of the verb.

> *Kelp* **is** the scientific name for seaweed. [*Kelp* = name]
> Kelp **tastes** good in a salad. [good kelp]
> As it ages, kelp **becomes** brown. [brown kelp]
> Kelp **can be** a basic source of iodine. [Kelp = source]

Many linking verbs can be used as action (nonlinking) verbs as well.

EXAMPLES   Emilia **felt** calm at the seashore. [linking verb: calm Emilia]
Emilia **felt** the waving strands of kelp. [action verb]

Some kelps **grow** long. [linking verb: long kelps]
Some kelps **grow** large bulbs. [action verb]

Even *be* is not always a linking verb. It may be followed by only an adverb. In the sentence *They are here*, the word *here* is an adverb. It does not refer to the subject, *They*. To be a linking verb, the verb must be followed by a noun, a pronoun, or an adjective that refers to the subject.

EXERCISE 7   **Writing Sentences Using Verbs as Both Linking and Action Verbs**

For each of the following verbs, write two sentences. In the first sentence, use the verb as a linking verb; in the second sentence, use it as an action verb.

1. appear   2. sound   3. smell   4. grow   5. look

The Verb Phrase

A *verb phrase* consists of the main verb and its *helping verbs* (also called *auxiliary verbs*).

Commonly Used Helping Verbs				
have	do	may	can	could
has	does	might	will	would
had	did	must	shall	should

The forms of the verb *be* are also helping verbs.

EXAMPLES   **Did** she **paint** the house?
You **might** even **have seen** this movie before.
Sally **will be launching** the canoe.
This year's budget **has** not **been approved.**

NOTE: The word *not* in a phrase such as *could not go* is not a helping verb. Both *not* and the contraction *–n't* are adverbs.

☞ REFERENCE NOTE: For more about helping verbs, see page 548.

▶ EXERCISE 8   **Identifying Verbs as Action Verbs or Linking Verbs**

Identify each italicized verb in the numbered sentences in the following paragraph as an *action verb* or a *linking verb*.

[1] Situated on the banks of the Nile River in Egypt, these ruins at Karnak *are* some of the most impressive sights in the world. [2] The largest structure there *is* the

GRAMMAR

INTEGRATING THE LANGUAGE ARTS

Literature Link. Have students read and discuss Emily Dickinson's poem "I Like to See It Lap the Miles." Have them list the verbs that describe the train's actions [*lap, lick, stop to feed, step, peer, pare, crawl, complaining, chase, neigh,* and *stop*]. What kind of verbs are these? [They are action verbs.] Is there anything strange about them? [With the exception of *stop,* they are not verbs that might typically be used to describe a train.] What effect do they give to the poem? [They give life to an inanimate object by describing its actions as though it were a living animal.]

VISUAL CONNECTIONS

Exploring the Subject. The temple of Amon-Re at Karnak is the largest of all Egyptian temples and one of the largest in the world. Its most striking feature is the vast pillared hall, with 140 pillars covering an area of 5,800 square yards.

Amon or Amon-Re was the Egyptian sun god hailed as king of the gods by his followers. He was represented in human form, sometimes with a ram's head.

INTEGRATING THE LANGUAGE ARTS

Grammar and Speaking. Divide the class into groups and have each group make a presentation on a particular verb. Each presentation should contain the verb's origin, describe the action it involves, and explain whether it is transitive or intransitive; if transitive, the presentation should list possible objects.

GRAMMAR

GRAMMAR

Great Temple of Amon-Re. [3] As you can see, its immense size *dwarfs* people who come to view this architectural marvel. [4] When visitors follow the avenue of sphinxes that leads to the entrance, they *are amazed* at the 42-meter-high gateway. [5] The ceiling of the temple *rests* more than 23 meters above the floor. [6] Of course, the central columns that support the stone roof *are* enormous. [7] The surfaces of these huge columns *are decorated* with carvings. [8] Even an amateur engineer or artist *can appreciate* the tremendous efforts that must have gone into the completion of this temple. [9] We now *know* that inclined planes, combined with levers and blocking, enabled the ancient Egyptians to raise the large stones. [10] A remarkable technical achievement, the Great Temple of Amon *remains* a monument to the ancient builders' skills.

EXERCISE 9   **Identifying Verbs and Verb Phrases**

Identify the <u>verbs and verb phrases</u> in each numbered sentence in the following paragraph. Be sure to include all helping verbs.

[1] Because of the cold weather, the members of the marching band <u>were worried</u> about their first performance. [2] Marcia and the other saxophone players <u>were clapping</u> their hands vigorously so that their fingers wouldn't <u>become</u> even number in the raw, icy air. [3] They <u>imagined</u> what <u>would happen</u> if their fingers <u>froze</u> to the keys of their instruments. [4] Instead of music, harsh noise <u>would blare</u> out and likely <u>startle</u> the spectators. [5] The other band members <u>would</u> likely <u>skip</u> a beat, and chaos <u>would</u> soon <u>spread</u> across the field. [6] Out of step, the flute players <u>might stumble</u> into the clarinet players, <u>collide</u> with the trombone players, or even <u>trip</u> over the drummers. [7] When half time <u>was called</u>, Marcia and her friends <u>rolled</u> their eyes and <u>laughed</u> about the dreadful scene they <u>had</u> just <u>pictured</u>. [8] Such a disaster <u>couldn't</u> possibly <u>happen</u>, <u>could</u> it? [9] As the band <u>marched</u> onto the field, large, white snowflakes <u>swirled</u> in the air and <u>settled</u> on the brand-new uniforms and shiny instruments. [10] People <u>were</u> already <u>leaving</u> the stands when the principal <u>announced</u> over the loudspeaker: "Ladies and gentlemen, the band <u>will</u> now <u>play</u> 'Jingle Bells.'"

OBJECTIVES

- To identify adverbs and the verbs, adjectives, and adverbs they modify in sentences
- To use adverbs correctly in sentences
- To use words as adverbs and adjectives in sentences

Adverbs **529**

15e

Adverbs

15e. An *adverb* is a word used to modify a verb, an adjective, or another adverb.

Adverbs modify by telling *how, when, where,* or *to what extent.*

Adverbs Modifying Verbs

Just as adjectives modify nouns and pronouns, adverbs modify verbs. An adverb makes the meaning of the verb clearer and more definite.

EXAMPLES   The bird was chirping **outside.** [*where*]
The bird chirped **today.** [*when*]
The bird chirped **loudly.** [*how*]
The bird chirped **constantly.** [*to what extent*]

 EXERCISE 10   **Identifying Adverbs and the Verbs They Modify**

Identify the <u>adverbs</u> in each numbered sentence in the following paragraph. For each adverb, give the <u>verb that it modifies</u>.

[1] The first balloonists <u>floated</u> <u>gently</u> above Paris in a hot-air balloon that <u>had been</u> <u>cleverly</u> <u>designed</u> by the Montgolfier brothers. [2] Although their earlier attempts

GRAMMAR

PROGRAM MANAGER

ADVERBS

- **Independent Practice/ Reteaching** For instruction and exercises, see **The Adverb** in *Language Skills Practice and Assessment,* p. 19.

- **Computer Guided Instruction** For additional instruction and practice with adverbs, see **Lesson 2** in *Language Workshop CD-ROM.*

- **Practice** To help less-advanced students with additional instruction and practice with adverbs, see **Chapter 10** in *English Workshop, Fourth Course,* pp. 119–122.

QUICK REMINDER

Write the following sentences on the chalkboard. Have students identify the adverbs and the words they modify.

1. Janet plays her silver flute beautifully.
2. Henry has become most skilled at carpentry.
3. I can type really well.
4. Kenesha's dress was too small.
5. Desperately, he ran after the train.

Remind students that adverbs can modify verbs, adjectives, or other adverbs. [Answers: **(1)** *beautifully* modifies *plays;* **(2)** *most* modifies *skilled;* **(3)** *well* modifies *can type; really* modifies *well;* **(4)** *too* modifies *small;* **(5)** *Desperately* modifies *ran.*]

GRAMMAR

LEP/ESL

General Strategies. Students may have difficulty with the placement of adverbs that tell how often something occurs. For example, they may write "Peter comes always late to breakfast," instead of "Peter always comes late to breakfast."

Tell students that most of the time, such adverbs should come before the verb.

Have students write paragraphs in which they describe activities they participate in with different frequency. Adverbs they can use to describe these activities include *always, sometimes, frequently, often, rarely,* and *never.* Let students work in pairs to help each other with revisions. Be sure to pair English-language learners with English-proficient speakers.

LEARNING STYLES

Auditory Learners. Students might benefit by hearing adverbs used in different positions in a sentence to illustrate an adverb's different uses. Read the following sentences aloud and have students discuss what each sentence means:

1. Really, I want to go.
2. I really want to go.
3. I want to really go.

[(**1**) Puts emphasis on *really,* as if to convince a disbeliever; (**2**) places emphasis on *want;* (**3**) puts emphasis on *go,* as in "to go fast in a car."]

---

530 *The Parts of Speech*

had failed, the Montgolfiers kept trying and <u>finally</u> <u>settled</u> on a balloon made of paper and linen. [3] Early balloons <u>differed</u> <u>significantly</u> from modern balloons like those on the previous page, which <u>are</u> <u>sturdily</u> <u>constructed</u> of coated nylon. [4] Despite their ingenuity, the Montgolfiers <u>originally</u> <u>thought</u> that smoke, rather than hot air, <u>would</u> <u>effectively</u> <u>push</u> a balloon <u>skyward</u>. [5] <u>Consequently</u>, in their experiments they <u>initially</u> <u>produced</u> hot smoke by burning straw and wool.

Adverbs Modifying Adjectives

EXAMPLES   It was a **fiercely** competitive game. [The adverb *fiercely* modifies the adjective *competitive.*]
The exceptionally brave police officer was given an **award.** [The adverb *exceptionally* modifies the adjective *brave.*]

NOTE: Some of the most frequently used adverbs are *too, very,* and *so.* Try to avoid these overused words in your writing. Instead, think of more precise adverbs to make your meaning clearer.

▶ EXERCISE 11   **Identifying Adverbs and the Adjectives They Modify**

In each of the following sentences, an adverb modifies an adjective. Identify the <u>adverb</u> and the <u>adjective it modifies</u>.

1. An <u>immensely</u> <u>long</u> wagon train started out from Denver, Colorado.
2. Both oxen and mules were used to pull <u>unusually large</u> wagons.
3. Even in good weather, the trail through the mountains was <u>fairly</u> <u>hazardous</u>.
4. A <u>moderately</u> <u>hard</u> rain could turn the trail into a swamp.
5. When the trail was <u>too muddy</u>, the heavier wagons became mired.
6. Wagons that were <u>extremely</u> <u>heavy</u> then had to be unloaded before they could be moved.
7. Stopping for the night along the trail was a <u>consistently</u> <u>welcome</u> experience.

8. It offered relief to <u>thoroughly</u> <u>tired</u> bones and muscles.
9. Nights in the mountains could be <u>quite</u> <u>cold</u>.
10. On <u>terribly</u> <u>cold</u> nights, the travelers would roll in blankets and sleep close to their campfires.

Adverbs Modifying Other Adverbs

EXAMPLES   The guide spoke **extremely** slowly. [The adverb *extremely* modifies the adverb *slowly*, telling *how* slowly.]

We will go **later** today. [The adverb *later* modifies the adverb *today*, telling *when* today.]

NOTE: Many adverbs end in *–ly*. However, not all words ending in *–ly* are adverbs. For instance, the following words are adjectives: *homely, kindly, lovely, deadly*. To determine a word's part of speech, look at how the word is used in the sentence. Do not rely on spelling alone.

EXERCISE 12   **Identifying Adverbs and the Words They Modify**

The following paragraphs contain twenty adverbs. Identify the adverb or adverbs in each sentence. After each adverb, give the word it modifies and the part of speech of that word.

[1] A couple of months ago, my sister Juana and I finally decided to buy a houseplant. [2] The large ones we saw were too expensive for us. [3] In addition, they are almost always raised in hothouses, and, as a result, they do not adjust easily to living in cold climates. [4] Suddenly Juana had a brainstorm. [5] "Let's buy some seeds and grow them indoors. [6] That way, the seedlings will automatically adapt themselves to the climate in our house."

[7] At the seed store, the owner, Mrs. Miller, greeted us cheerfully. [8] We explained that we wanted to grow a large plant but that our room hardly ever gets bright sunlight and in the winter it can be especially chilly and dark. [9] We also mentioned that we wanted seeds for a plant seldom sold in local shops. [10] "I know what you need," Mrs. Miller promptly replied. [11] "These are seeds of the

GRAMMAR

GRAMMAR

ANSWERS
Exercise 12

1. finally—decided, verb
2. too—expensive, adjective
3. almost—always, adverb; always—raised, verb; not—do adjust, verb; easily—do adjust, verb
4. Suddenly—had, verb
5. indoors—grow, verb
6. automatically—will adapt, verb
7. cheerfully—greeted, verb
8. hardly—ever, adverb; ever—gets, verb; especially—chilly, dark, adjectives
9. also—mentioned, verb; seldom—sold, verb
10. promptly—replied, verb
11. unusually—hardy, adjective
12. There—is, verb
13. back—got, verb
14. now—have, verb

bo tree, an unusually hardy member of the fig family native to India. [12] There this tree is sacred to Buddhists because it is said that the Buddha received enlightenment under a bo tree." [13] When we got back to our house, we planted the seeds. [14] In a short time, they sprouted, and we now have an unusual houseplant that is suited to our cold environment.

PICTURE THIS

Remind students that Romeo has just fallen in love with Juliet and now overhears her confession to the stars that she loves him, too. One way to decide on accurate stage directions is by analyzing the characters. How do they feel? What are their goals? What are their fears? What challenges do they face? What threatens them?

PICTURE THIS

You are directing this production of Shakespeare's play *Romeo and Juliet*. The actors are in position and are waiting for your instructions on how to play the famous balcony scene in which the young lovers proclaim their feelings for each other. Shakespeare provided little direction, so it's up to you. Write five sentences of stage directions that you think would be appropriate for the scene. In each sentence, use at least one adverb to tell the actors how, when, where, or to what extent to do something.

Subject: stage directions for *Romeo and Juliet*
Audience: actors playing Romeo and Juliet
Purpose: to instruct actors how to play a scene

REVIEW D

OBJECTIVE

- To identify parts of speech within a paragraph and to identify the words adjectives and adverbs modify

---

GRAMMAR

▶ EXERCISE 13 **Using Words as Adjectives and Adverbs**

Write a pair of sentences for each word. In the first sentence, use the word as an *adjective;* in the second, use it as an *adverb.*

EXAMPLE **1.** kindly
1. *She had a kindly manner—adjective.*
She spoke kindly—adverb.

1. daily **2.** fast **3.** late **4.** more **5.** far

▶ REVIEW D **Identifying Parts of Speech**   n. = noun
                                            pro. = pronoun

Identify the part of speech of each italicized word in the following paragraphs. If the word is an adjective or an adverb, be able to tell <u>what it modifies</u>.   v. = verb   adv. = adverb
                                                                         adj. = adjective

With a [1] *thunderous* <u>roar</u>, a mighty avalanche [2] *crashes*   **1.** adj.
[3] *headlong* down a mountainside. [4] *Some* of these slides   **2.** v.
travel at speeds of more than 200 miles an hour and pose   **3.** adv.
a [5] *deadly* <u>threat</u> to skiers, mountain climbers, and the   **4.** pro.
people [6] *who* live and work in the mountains.   **5.** adj.   **6.** pro.
One [7] *common* <u>suggestion</u> for surviving an avalanche   **7.** adj.
is to make swimming motions to remain on top of the   **8.** adv.
snow. However, people caught in avalanches [8] *rarely* <u>can</u>   **9.** pro.
<u>save</u> [9] *themselves.* They <u>are</u> [10] *usually* <u>immobilized</u>, and   **10.** adv.
the slide [11] *forces* snow into their nose and mouth. **11.** v.   **12.** n.
Avalanche workers in the [12] *United States* and abroad   **13.** adv.
have [13] *long* <u>realized</u> the [14] *potential* [15] *destructiveness* of   **14.** adj.
selected slide paths. They [16] *have concluded* that an   **15.** n.
avalanche <u>can be</u> [17] *greatly* <u>reduced</u> if [18] *explosives* [19] *are*   **16.** v.
used to trigger a [20] *series* of [21] *smaller* <u>slides</u> before [22] *one*   **17.** adv.
large <u>mass</u> of snow can build up. [23] *Today*, the detonation   **18.** n.
of explosives <u>has become</u> a standard [24] *practice* for con-   **19.** v.
trolling avalanches in [25] *this* <u>country</u>.   **20.** n.
   21. adj.   **22.** adj.   **23.** adv.   **24.** n.   **25.** adj.

▶ EXERCISE 14 **Using Parts of Speech to Write a Description**

In the painting on the next page, folk artist Mattie Lou O'Kelley recorded her impressions of a circus parade that came through her town when she was growing up in the early 1900s. Imagine that you were with O'Kelley, watching

---

ANSWERS
Exercise 13

Responses will vary. Here are some possibilities:

1. She has not completed her daily exercises.
His father bakes bread daily.

2. Fast cars are often not fuel efficient.
They all run fast.

3. I enjoy the late movie.
We don't like to stay up late.

4. He ate more doughnuts than you.
They work more with new tools.

5. She threw the shot put a far distance.
The spaceship flew far away.

GRAMMAR

ANSWERS
Exercise 14

One constant in the different sentences students write should be powerful action verbs. Adverbs can be used to unify the scene as the viewer looks first at one part of the parade and then at another.

533

VISUAL CONNECTIONS
The Circus Parade

About the Artist. The American folk artist Mattie Lou O'Kelley was born in Maysville, Georgia, in 1908. A self-taught artist, O'Kelley worked in both oils and watercolor. She received the Governor's Award for Outstanding Contribution to American Art from the governor of Georgia in 1976.

PROGRAM MANAGER

PREPOSITIONS

■ **Independent Practice/ Reteaching** See **The Preposition** in *Language Skills Practice and Assessment*, p. 20.

■ **Computer Guided Instruction** See **Lesson 3** in *Language Workshop CD-ROM*.

■ **Practice** See **Chapter 10** in *English Workshop, Fourth Course*, pp. 123–124.

QUICK REMINDER

Write the following sentences on the chalkboard:

1. The riders went across.
2. The riders rode across the river.

Ask students what part of speech the word *across* is used as in each sentence. [In the first sentence, it is an adverb; in the second sentence, it is a preposition.] Then, ask students why it is a different part of speech in each sentence. [In the first sentence, it tells where the riders went; in the second sentence, it shows the relationship between the verb *rode* and *river*.]

534

OBJECTIVE

• To write sentences using words as prepositions and as adverbs and to identify the prepositional phrases and the words the adverbs modify

534 *The Parts of Speech*

the parade, and write ten sentences giving your impressions of that day. Use action verbs and vivid adjectives and adverbs to capture the excitement of this spectacle. Be prepared to identify the nouns, pronouns, adjectives, verbs, and adverbs in your sentences.

EXAMPLE **1.** *The acrobat skips lightly on the elephant's back.*

Mattie Lou O'Kelley, *The Circus Parade.* Photograph courtesy of the Museum of American Folk Art, N.Y. From *The Hills of Georgia* by Mattie Lou O'Kelley. Used with permission of Atlantic Monthly Press.

Prepositions

15f. A *preposition* is a word that shows the relationship of a noun or a pronoun to some other word in the sentence.

Notice in the following examples how the prepositions show six different relationships between *village* and *rode*.

I rode **past** the village.   I rode **near** the village.
I rode **through** the village.   I rode **around** the village.
I rode **toward** the village.   I rode **beyond** the village.

A *prepositional phrase* includes a preposition, a noun or pronoun called the *object of a preposition,* and any modifiers of the object. In the examples above, the object of each preposition is *village.*

 REFERENCE NOTE: For more about prepositional phrases, see pages 574–576.

GRAMMAR

Commonly Used Prepositions

aboard	below	for	past
about	beneath	from	since
above	beside	in	through
across	besides	inside	to
after	between	into	toward
against	beyond	like	under
along	but (meaning	near	underneath
amid	except)	of	until
among	by	off	up
around	concerning	on	upon
at	down	onto	with
before	during	outside	within
behind	except	over	without

Compound Prepositions

according to	in addition to	instead of
because of	in front of	on account of
by means of	in spite of	prior to

NOTE: The same word may be either an adverb or a preposition, depending on its use in a sentence.

EXAMPLES   Marge climbed **down.** [adverb]
Marge climbed **down** the ladder. [preposition]

Above, buzzards circled lazily. [adverb]
Above the dry riverbed, buzzards circled lazily. [preposition]

▶ EXERCISE 15   **Writing Sentences Using Words as Prepositions and as Adverbs**

For each of the following words, write two sentences. In the first sentence, use the word as a preposition and underline the prepositional phrase. In the second sentence, use the word as an adverb. Be able to tell which word the adverb modifies.

EXAMPLE   **1.** In
     1. *We are going in the house now.*
     We are going in now.

1. around   **3.** inside   **5.** up
2. behind   **4.** on

MEETING *individual* NEEDS

LEP/ESL

General Strategies. Students will often have difficulty in deciding which preposition to use in certain situations, such as writing about means of transportation. Tell them that a simple rule that will help them decide between *in* and *on* is to let the number of passengers the vehicle can carry be their guide. For vehicles that carry only one person, use *on* (*get on a bicycle*); for vehicles that carry several people, use *in* (*get in the car*); for vehicles that carry about twenty or more passengers, use *on* (*get on the plane*).

ANSWERS
Exercise 15

Sentences will vary. Here are some possibilities:

1. He ran <u>around the corner.</u>
The wheel turned around.

2. The clerk stood <u>behind the counter.</u>
She put the past behind.

3. We found a cat <u>inside the box.</u>
The players ran inside.

4. Put the book <u>on the table.</u>
I turned the radio on.

5. They climbed <u>up the mountain.</u>
Don't look up.

GRAMMAR

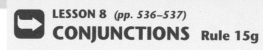

GRAMMAR

QUICK REMINDER

Write the following pairs of sentences on the chalkboard:

1. Maria likes milk. Milk is good for her.
2. Frank likes cats. Cats don't like Frank.
3. Sako will go with us to the movies. She will stay home and study.

Ask students to combine each pair of sentences with a conjunction. [Maria likes milk, and it is good for her. Frank likes cats, but they don't like Frank. Sako will go with us to the movies, or she will stay home and study.]

Remind students that conjunctions join related ideas, but the nature of the ideas' relationship dictates which conjunction is to be used.

GRAMMAR

536 *The Parts of Speech*

Conjunctions

15g. A *conjunction* is a word used to join words or groups of words.

Conjunctions join parts of a sentence that function in the same way. The parts that are joined may be words, phrases, or clauses.

☞ **REFERENCE NOTE:** For a discussion on using conjunctions in sentence combining, see pages 467–470. For the rules governing the use of punctuation with conjunctions, see pages 467–468, 794–796, and 816–819.

Coordinating Conjunctions

Conjunctions that join equal parts of a sentence are called *coordinating conjunctions.*

and	for	but	so
or	yet	nor	

EXAMPLES The orchestra played one waltz **and** two polkas.
We can walk to the mall **or** take a bus.
I looked for Hal, **but** he had already left.

Correlative Conjunctions

Conjunctions that are used in pairs are called *correlative conjunctions.* Like coordinating conjunctions, correlative conjunctions join equal parts of a sentence.

both . . . and	neither . . . nor
not only . . . but also	whether . . . or
either . . . or	

EXAMPLES **Neither** the baseball team **nor** the soccer team has practice today.
Both the track team **and** the volleyball team enjoyed a winning season.
Their victories sparked the enthusiasm **not only** of students **but also** of teachers and townspeople.

☞ **REFERENCE NOTE:** Subordinating conjunctions are discussed with subordinate clauses on pages 603–604.

INTERJECTIONS Rule 15h

OBJECTIVE

- To write sentences using interjections properly

GRAMMAR

 EXERCISE 16 **Identifying Coordinating and Correlative Conjunctions**

Identify the <u>coordinating</u> and <u>correlative</u> conjunctions in the sentences in the following paragraph.

[1] Once Nantucket <u>and</u> New Bedford, Massachusetts, were home ports of huge whaling fleets. [2] Whaling brought tremendous profits into these ports, <u>but</u> the golden days of whaling ended about the time of the American Civil War. [3] Even when it was successful, a whaling trip was no pleasure cruise for <u>either</u> the captain <u>or</u> the crew. [4] Maintaining order was no easy task on a long voyage because the food <u>and</u> living conditions were often dreadful. [5] Inevitably, the sailors had time on their hands, <u>for</u> they didn't encounter a whale every day. [6] To relieve the monotony <u>and</u> resulting boredom, whaling ships often would exchange visits. [7] <u>Not only</u> the captain <u>but also</u> the whole crew looked forward to such visits. [8] Everyone enjoyed the chance to chat <u>and</u> exchange news. [9] The decline of whaling <u>and</u> of the whaling industry was signaled by the development of a new fuel. [10] By 1860, our country no longer needed large quantities of whale oil because kerosene, a cheaper <u>and</u> better fuel, had replaced it.

Interjections

15h. An *interjection* is a word that expresses emotion and has no grammatical relation to other words in the sentence.

EXAMPLES **Ouch! Ugh! Wow! Oops! Aha!**

These words are usually followed by an exclamation mark. An interjection that shows only mild emotion is set off from the sentence by a comma or commas.

EXAMPLES **Well,** I'm just not sure.
When I'm having a bad week, **oh,** I can hardly wait for the weekend.

GRAMMAR

 PROGRAM MANAGER

INTERJECTIONS

- **Independent Practice/ Reteaching** For instruction and exercises, see **The Interjection** in *Language Skills Practice and Assessment,* p. 22.

- **Computer Guided Instruction** For additional instruction and practice with interjections, see **Lesson 3** in *Language Workshop CD-ROM.*

- **Practice** To help less-advanced students with additional instruction and practice with interjections, see **Chapter 10** in *English Workshop, Fourth Course,* pp. 125–126.

 QUICK REMINDER

Write the following sentences on the chalkboard:

1. Wow I got an A on my paper.
2. I hate worms! Ugh
3. Well I saw her last week.

Ask students to identify the interjections and to supply the missing punctuation. [(1) Wow! (2) Ugh! (3) Well,]

DETERMINING PARTS OF SPEECH Rule 15i

OBJECTIVES

- To identify parts of speech in sentences
- To use words as different parts of speech in sentences

GRAMMAR

ANSWERS

Exercise 17

Responses will vary. Here is a possibility:

Hey, I finally did it. The bus goes by the Highway Department office, and I'd told you I was thinking about taking the written test before our driver's ed course is over. Wednesday the bus stopped for the light there, and, well, I got off the bus and went and took the test.

Aw! the written test was easy! When the officer saw I'd passed it, he wanted me to take the driving test, too. Well, I didn't have a vehicle, but he said he was driving his son's car and would let me use it. It was a 1979 Chevrolet, just like my grandmother's. Cool! I passed that test, too.

PROGRAM MANAGER

DETERMINING PARTS OF SPEECH

- **Independent Practice/ Reteaching** For instruction and exercises, see **Determining Parts of Speech** in *Language Skills Practice and Assessment,* p. 23.

- **Computer Guided Instruction** For additional instruction and practice with determining parts of speech, see **Lesson 4** in *Language Workshop CD-ROM.*

- **Practice** To help less-advanced students with additional instruction and practice with determining parts of speech, see **Chapter 10** in *English Workshop, Fourth Course,* pp. 127–128.

538

---

538 *The Parts of Speech*

> **EXERCISE 17** **Using Interjections**

You just took your driver's license test. Wanting to share your feelings about the test and your results, you call your best friend. Write your conversation, using at least five interjections. You may choose interjections from the list below or use ones of your own. Be sure to use the words as interjections and not as adjectives or adverbs. Check to see that you have punctuated your interjections with exclamation points or commas as needed.

ah	cool	hey	wow	ugh
aw	great	no	yes	excellent

Determining Parts of Speech

15i. What part of speech a word is depends on how the word is used.

EXAMPLES Rich heard the **light** patter of raindrops. [adjective]
The room was filled with **light**. [noun]
Let's **light** some candles this evening. [verb]

> **EXERCISE 18** **Determining the Parts of Speech of Words**

Determine the part of speech of the <u>italicized word</u> in each of the following sentences. Be prepared to explain your answers.   n. = noun   v. = verb   adj. = adjective

1. They decided that the hedge needed a *trim*.   **1.** n.
2. Their hedges always look *trim* and neat.   **2.** adj.   **3.** v.
3. We usually *trim* the tree with homemade ornaments.
4. Mom always *shears* a couple of inches off the top of the tree.   **4.** v.
5. Later, she uses *shears* to cut straggling branches.   **5.** n.
6. My brother *spices* peach preserves with nutmeg and allspice.   **6.** v.
7. These *spices* are available in most stores.   **7.** n.
8. Sage adds a tangy *flavor* to stew.   **8.** n.
9. Many chefs also *flavor* stew with basil.   **9.** v.
10. In their family, a *cross* word is rarely spoken.   **10.** adj.

REVIEWS E and F

OBJECTIVES
- To write sentences with words used as different parts of speech
- To identify the parts of speech of various words in a paragraph

15i

GRAMMAR

 REVIEW E

Writing Sentences Using Words as Different Parts of Speech

Write three sentences for each of the following words, using the word as a different part of speech in each sentence. At the end of the sentence, write what part of speech the word is in that sentence.

1. long **2.** cut **3.** back **4.** fast **5.** iron

 REVIEW F

Determining the Parts of Speech of Words

Identify the part of speech of each italicized word or expression in the following paragraph.   n. = noun   pro. = pronoun
v. = verb   adj. = adjective   adv. = adverb   prep. = preposition   conj. = conjunction

[1] *Early* farmers on the [2] *Great Plains* eked out a rough existence, [3] *for* there were few towns, stores, or other hallmarks of civilization. [4] *Many* farm homes were constructed with sod bricks, [5] *which* were cut [6] *out of* the prairie. Trees were in short supply on these wind-swept lands, but the resourceful settler might find a few [7] *cottonwoods* growing [8] *along* a stream. [9] *These* [10] *could be used* to build a frame for the roof, which was then covered [11] *lightly* with grassy earth. Grass, both [12] *on* the roof [13] *and* in the sod, helped to hold the house together. Some of [14] *these* rugged homes had a door made of timber, but [15] *usually* a cowhide [16] *was draped* across the entrance. [17] *Inside* was a dirt floor covered with a bearskin [18] *or* a buffalo hide. As more settlers moved [19] *west* bringing furnishings and [20] *building* materials, farmers eventually abandoned these first, primitive dwellings and built more conventional homes.

1. adj.
2. n.
3. conj.
4. adj.
5. pro.
6. prep.
7. n.
8. prep.
9. pro.
10. v.
11. adv.
12. prep.
13. conj.
14. adj.
15. adv.
16. v.
17. adv.   18. conj.   19. adv.   20. adj.

 EXERCISE 19

Using Words as Different Parts of Speech

Your friend has just returned from a vacation in Europe. During her trip, she made the collage shown on the following page, picturing different types of transportation she used while traveling. After flying from the United States, she rode a bike in France, a train through the Swiss Alps, and a bus in Italy. She also went by ship to a Greek island, where she rode a donkey. Write your comments and

ANSWERS
Review E

Answers will vary. Here are some possibilities:

1. We all long for the lazy days of summer. (verb) We took the long way home. (adjective) We did not work long enough. (adverb)

2. Erris cut the cake into twenty-four neat pieces. (verb) The burglary suspect has a suspicious cut on his back. (noun) Origami is made with folded rather than with cut paper. (adjective)

3. Please back the car into the garage carefully. (verb) She turned her back and walked away. (noun) The back door slammed. (adjective)

4. Some people still fast to purify their minds and bodies. (verb) In ancient times this was the main purpose of a fast. (noun) Now, some people who go without eating are usually looking for a fast way to lose weight. (adjective)

5. Will you iron my new shirt? (verb) She had to wait until the iron was hot. (noun) Her iron will and determination will see her through the audition. (adjective)

GRAMMAR

TIMESAVER
Have students underline the words they are to use in sentences in **Exercise 19** for easy checking.

ANSWERS

Exercise 19

Answers will vary. Here are some possibilities:

1. noun: Where did you buy your bike?
verb: How far did you bike each day you were in France?

2. preposition: Aren't you glad you didn't have to pedal up the Alps on a bicycle?
adverb: Was your bicycle easy to pick up?

3. adjective: I like to ride my bicycle in the cool fall evenings.
interjection: You rode your bike all the way to the capitol? Cool!

4. conjunction: I can hardly believe you went that far, for you were only gone a month.
preposition: Were you used to riding a bicycle for exercise?

5. pronoun: That sounds like the trip of a lifetime.
adjective: That trip is something you will remember all your life.

LESSON 11 (pp. 540–542)
REVIEW: POSTTESTS 1 and 2

OBJECTIVES

- To determine the parts of speech of words
- To write sentences with words used as different parts of speech

540 *The Parts of Speech*

questions about her travels, using the following words as the parts of speech indicated. Each word will be used as two different parts of speech.

bike [noun, verb]
up [preposition, adverb]
cool [adjective, interjection]
for [conjunction, preposition]
that [pronoun, adjective]

Review: Posttest 1

Determining the Parts of Speech of Words

Identify the part of speech of each italicized word in the following paragraphs. n. = noun pro. = pronoun v. = verb
adj. = adjective adv. = adverb prep. = preposition conj. = conjunction

1. n.   Since the [1] *condition* of the roads prevented [2] *extensive*

2. adj. use of wheeled vehicles, the most reliable means of trans-

3. n.   portation in colonial times was the [3] *saddle horse*. Some

[4]*exceptionally* wealthy people kept carriages, but [5]*these* were usually heavy vehicles [6]*that* were pulled by two or more horses. Such carriages were [7]*satisfactory* for short trips, [8]*but* they were not practical for long journeys.

Stagecoaches were introduced in [9]*America* about 1750. By this time, roads ran [10]*between* such major cities as New York and Boston. Although these roads [11]*were* little more than muddy tracks, [12]*most* were wide enough for a four-wheeled coach. [13]*Three* or four pairs of horses [14]*were harnessed* to a coach. However, the vehicles were so heavy that [15]*coach* horses tired [16]*quite* [17]*rapidly* [18]*and* either had to be rested frequently [19]*or* changed at post houses along the route. The design of horse-drawn vehicles soon improved, and until the early years of the twentieth century, buggies and wagons remained a common [20]*form* of transportation.

4. adv.
5. pro.
6. pro.
7. adj.
8. conj.
9. n.
10. prep.
11. v.
12. pro.
13. adj.
14. v.
15. adj.
16. adv.
17. adv.
18. conj.
19. conj.
20. n.

GRAMMAR

Review: Posttest 2

Writing Sentences with Words Used as Different Parts of Speech

Use each of the following words or groups of words in a sentence. Then indicate what part of speech the word or word group is.

EXAMPLE   **1.** gold
    1. *Tamisha bought a gold bracelet. (adjective)*

1. novel
2. Park Avenue
3. this
4. are laughing
5. yesterday
6. tomorrow
7. or
8. but
9. both . . . and
10. silver
11. hiked
12. appeared
13. tasted
14. quietly
15. often
16. inside
17. underneath
18. oh
19. whew
20. in

ANSWERS
Posttest 2
Responses will vary.

1. Enrique checked out a novel to read this weekend. (noun) He is taking a novel approach to studying for a test. (adjective)
2. Park Avenue glittered like a jewel in the New York dusk. (noun) Linda caught the Park Avenue bus. (adjective)
3. This is the way home. (pronoun) This way is easiest. (adjective)
4. All the people in this room are laughing. (verb)
5. Yesterday seems as if it happened a hundred years ago. (noun) I can remember everything that happened yesterday. (adverb)
6. Tomorrow is a big day. (noun) Tomorrow I am flying to San Francisco. (adverb)
7. He had always kept his watch on his wrist or on the dresser. (coordinating conjunction)
8. She went to see the film but she did not stay for the ending. (coordinating conjunction) We had finished all of the problems but one. (preposition)
9. Both Juanita and Pedro read five books this month! (correlative conjunctions)
10. Iris likes to wear silver jewelry. (adjective) Tom invested his money in silver. (noun)
11. The entire biology class hiked for fifteen miles. (verb) She wore her skirt hiked up above her boots. (adjective)
12. Her face appeared in the mirror. (action verb) Her face appeared tired. (linking verb)
13. Ramiro tasted the soup carefully. (action verb) The soup tasted bland. (linking verb)

continued on next page

14. He listened quietly to the speech. (adverb)

15. She would often see the old man taking an afternoon nap on his porch. (adverb)

16. He looked inside. (adverb) He put his passport inside his jacket. (preposition) He kept valuable papers in an inside pocket. (adjective)

17. He got out of the car and looked underneath it. (preposition)

18. Oh, I forgot the ice cream. (interjection)

19. Whew! This has been a long exercise. (interjection)

20. Let me in. (adverb) The new boys arrived in town. (preposition)

SUMMARY OF PARTS OF SPEECH

Rule	Part of Speech	Use	Examples
15a	noun	names	**Larry** picks **grapefruit.**
15b	pronoun	takes the place of a noun	**Who** said **that these** are the **ones we** need?
15c	adjective	modifies a noun or a pronoun	That was a **happy** sight. They were very **noisy.**
15d	verb	shows action or a state of being	He **jumps** and **spins.** She **is** the winner.
15e	adverb	modifies a verb, an adjective, or another adverb	He learns **quickly.** She is **always** right. It flies **quite** high.
15f	preposition	relates a noun or a pronoun to another word	The cat was **by** itself **under** the oak tree **next to** the garage.
15g	conjunction	joins words or groups of words	Kyoko **and** Sheila passed the test. We can **either** go hiking **or** go swimming.
15h	interjection	expresses emotion	**My goodness!** **Hey,** stop that!

DIAGNOSTIC TEST

OBJECTIVES

- To identify subjects, verbs, predicate adjectives, predicate nominatives, direct objects, and indirect objects
- To classify sentences as declarative, interrogative, imperative, or exclamatory and to provide the correct end punctuation for each sentence

PROGRAM MANAGER

FOR THE WHOLE CHAPTER

- **Review** For exercises on chapter concepts, see **Review Form A** and **Review Form B** in *Language Skills Practice and Assessment,* pp. 41–44.

- **Assessment** For additional testing, see **Grammar Pretests** and **Grammar Mastery Tests** in *Language Skills Practice and Assessment,* pp. 1–8 and pp. 76–81.

16 THE SENTENCE

Subjects, Predicates, Complements

Diagnostic Test

A. Identifying Subjects, Verbs, and Complements

Identify the <u>italicized word or word group</u> in each of the following sentences as a *subject,* a *verb,* a *predicate adjective,* a *predicate nominative,* a *direct object,* or an *indirect object.*

1. Native *cactuses* in the Southwest are in trouble. **1.** s.
2. Some species are already *vulnerable* to extinction. **2.** p.a.
3. Cactuses *are being threatened* by landscapers, tourists, and collectors. **3.** v.
4. Many people illegally harvest these wild *plants.* **4.** d.o.
5. There are many unique *species* in Arizona. **5.** s.
6. Arizona is, therefore, an active *battlefield* in the war against the removal of endangered cactuses. **6.** p.n.
7. "Cactus cops" *patrol* the streets of Phoenix on the lookout for places with illegally acquired cactuses. **7.** v.
8. Authorized dealers must give *purchasers* permit tags as proof of legal sale. **8.** i.o.

CHAPTER OVERVIEW

This chapter discusses sentence fragments, complete and simple subjects and predicates, subject complements, and objects. The chapter also teaches students how to classify sentences by purpose as declarative, imperative, interrogative, or exclamatory. The **Writing Application** then challenges students to use appropriately varied sentences in their writing.

Knowledge of the parts of sentences will help students to write varied sentences, to revise sentences for improved style, and to proofread for subject-verb agreement.

USING THE DIAGNOSTIC TEST

You may want to use the **Diagnostic Test** in conjunction with your assessments of students' writing to evaluate their understanding of sentences.

The **Diagnostic Test** does not test students' abilities to distinguish fragments from sentences; therefore, you may wish to use **Exercise 1** to diagnose students' abilities in this area.

SENTENCES AND SENTENCE FRAGMENTS   Rule 16a

OBJECTIVE

• To identify groups of words as either sentences or fragments

9. First violations are *punishable* by a minimum fine of five hundred dollars.   **9.** p.a.
10. Illegally owned cactuses *may be confiscated* by the police.   **10.** v.
11. What a thorny problem cactus *rustling* has become!   **11.** s.   **12.** p.a.
12. Why are illegal harvesters so *hard* to keep track of?
13. Many work at night and sometimes use permit *tags* over and over.   **13.** d.o.
14. Always *examine* a large cactus for bruises.   **14.** v.
15. Legally harvested cacti *should* not *show* any damage.   **15.** v.

B.   Classifying Sentences as Declarative, Interrogative, Imperative, or Exclamatory

Classify each of the following sentences as *declarative*, *interrogative*, *imperative*, or *exclamatory*. Then give the proper end punctuation.

16. Read this article about imperiled cactuses.   **16.** imp.
17. The author describes a trip into the desert with a legal hauler.   **17.** decl.
18. Can you imagine a saguaro worth three hundred dollars?   **18.** int.
19. A crested saguaro is even rarer and can sell for thousands of dollars.   **19.** decl.
20. No wonder illegal harvesting is booming!   **20.** excl.

Sentences and Sentence Fragments

In conversation, you may leave out part of a sentence without confusing your listeners. In writing, though, it's better to use complete sentences because readers rely on them for help in understanding your meaning.

16a.   A *sentence* is a group of words that contains a subject and a verb and expresses a complete thought.

16a

To express a complete thought, a sentence must say something that makes sense by itself. A group of words that does not express a complete thought is a *fragment,* or a piece of a sentence; it is not a sentence itself.

SENTENCE	Cara won the essay contest sponsored by the magazine.
FRAGMENT	the essay contest sponsored by the magazine
SENTENCE	Her essay was chosen as the best one from over two thousand entries.
FRAGMENT	was chosen as the best one from over two thousand entries
SENTENCE	When the judges announced the winner, everyone applauded.
FRAGMENT	when the judges announced the winner

☞ REFERENCE NOTE: Fragments can be confusing when they are written as sentences, beginning with a capital letter and ending with an end mark of punctuation. See pages 446–447 for information on how to correct sentence fragments.

▶ EXERCISE 1   **Identifying Sentences and Fragments**

Identify each of the following word groups as a <u>*sentence*</u> or a *fragment*.

1. Willa Cather was born in Back Creek Valley in northern Virginia.   **1.** sent.
2. In 1883, when she was nine years old. **2.** frag.
3. Her family moved to the treeless prairie of Nebraska.   **3.** sent.
4. Fascinated by the wild and rolling plains.   **4.** frag.
5. She tracked buffalo and collected prairie flowers.   **5.** sent.
6. Listening to the stories of neighboring settlers.   **6.** frag.
7. They told memorable tales about the harsh struggles of the homesteaders.   **7.** sent.
8. After she graduated from high school in the village of Red Cloud, Nebraska.   **8.** frag.
9. The picture of Red Cloud on the next page shows shops and people that would have been familiar to Willa Cather.   **9.** sent.
10. And the Opera House at the end of the street where Cather and her class graduated in 1890.   **10.** frag.

SUBJECT AND PREDICATE Rules 16b–16g

OBJECTIVES

- To identify complete subjects and complete predicates in sentences
- To identify verbs and verb phrases in a paragraph
- To identify subjects and verbs in sentences
- To complete sentences by adding predicates

546 *The Sentence*

 EXERCISE 2   **Identifying Sentences and Fragments**

Identify each of the numbered word groups in the following paragraph as either a *sentence* or a *fragment*. Be prepared to explain your answers.

1. sent.
2. frag.
3. sent.
4. frag.
5. sent.
6. frag.
7. sent.
8. frag.
9. sent.
10. sent.

[1] In college, Willa Cather discovered her talent for writing. [2] Contributing stories and reviews to local newspapers in Lincoln, Nebraska. [3] At first, her writing failed to reach a wider audience outside her region. [4] After some years as a schoolteacher and a magazine editor in New York City. [5] She succeeded in establishing herself as a writer. [6] Although Cather enjoyed living in New York. [7] She never lost touch with the sights and sounds of her childhood. [8] In her first novel, *O Pioneers!* [9] She describes how farmers turned the unruly plains into orderly fields of wheat and corn. [10] In a later novel, *My Ántonia,* the immigrant neighbors of her childhood play prominent roles.

Subject and Predicate

16b. A sentence consists of two parts: the *subject* and the *predicate.*

The *subject* names the person, place, thing, or idea spoken about in the rest of the sentence. The *predicate* says something about the subject.

 **PROGRAM MANAGER**

SUBJECT AND PREDICATE

- **Independent Practice/Reteaching** For instruction and exercises, see **Subject and Predicate, Subjects in Unusual Positions,** and **Compound Subjects and Verbs** in *Language Skills Practice and Assessment,* pp. 34–36.

- **Computer Guided Instruction** For additional instruction and practice with the subject and the predicate, see **Lesson 24** in *Language Workshop CD-ROM.*

- **Practice** To help less-advanced students with additional instruction and practice with the subject and the predicate, see **Chapter 11** in *English Workshop, Fourth Course,* pp. 131–136.

QUICK REMINDER

Write the following sentences on the chalkboard and have students identify the simple subject and simple predicate in each.

1. My gold chain is missing!
2. Lira, my sister, remembered seeing it on my dresser.
3. We could not find it anywhere.
4. I looked in my cat's bed and found my gold chain.
5. Lira and I laughed.

16b

The subject may come at the beginning, the end, or even the middle of a sentence.

EXAMPLES

SUBJECT   PREDICATE
Some residents of the desert   can survive a long drought.

PREDICATE   SUBJECT
Noteworthy is   the Australian frog.

PREDICATE   SUBJECT   PREDICATE
For up to three years   these frogs   can live without rainfall.

PREDICATE   SUBJECT   PREDICATE
How do   animals   survive that long?

In these examples, the words labeled *subject* make up the **complete subject.** The words labeled *predicate* make up the **complete predicate.** Notice in the third and fourth examples that parts of the complete predicate can come before and after the subject.

▶ EXERCISE 3   **Identifying Subjects and Predicates**

Identify the complete subject and the complete predicate in each of the following sentences. Keep in mind that the subject may come after the predicate.

1. The discovery of platinum has been credited to people from a variety of countries.
2. Spanish explorers in search of gold supposedly discovered this precious metal in the rivers of South America.
3. However, they considered it a worthless, inferior form of silver.
4. Their name for platinum was *platina,* meaning "little silver."
5. Back into the river went the little balls of platinum!
6. The platinum might then become gold, according to one theory.
7. Europeans later mixed platinum with gold.
8. This mixture encouraged the production of counterfeit gold bars and coins.
9. Platinum commands a high price today because of its resistance to corrosion.
10. Such diverse products as jet planes and jewelry require platinum in some form.

GRAMMAR

MEETING *individual* NEEDS

LEARNING STYLES

Visual Learners. Look in books and magazines to find pictures of people performing actions, such as a baseball player hitting a ball or a parent reading to a child. Ask students to describe the subject in each picture and to tell what the subject is doing. Write on the chalkboard a complete sentence based on each description and ask the students to name the subject and the verb in each sentence.

GRAMMAR

The Simple Subject

16c. The *simple subject* is the main word or group of words in the complete subject.

EXAMPLES   **A dog with this pedigree is usually nervous.**
Complete subject   A dog with this pedigree
Simple subject   **dog**

The Taj Mahal in India is one of the most beautiful buildings in the world.
Complete subject   The Taj Mahal in India
Simple subject   **Taj Mahal**

👉 REFERENCE NOTE: Compound nouns, such as *Taj Mahal,* are considered one noun. For more about compound nouns, see page 515.

NOTE: In this book, the term *subject* refers to the simple subject unless otherwise indicated.

The Simple Predicate

16d. The *simple predicate,* or *verb,* is the main word or group of words in the complete predicate.

EXAMPLE   **Spiders snare their prey in intricate webs.**
Complete predicate   snare their prey in intricate webs
Simple predicate   **snare**

The simple predicate may be a single verb or a *verb phrase* (a verb and one or more helping verbs).

EXAMPLES   **walks   has been walking   might have walked**

When you identify the simple predicate, be sure to find all parts of a verb phrase.

EXAMPLES   **Did Rosa find you?**
Complete predicate   did find you
Simple predicate   **did find**

She has been looking for you all morning.
Complete predicate   has been looking for you
                     all morning
Simple predicate   **has been looking**

NOTE: In this book, the term *verb* refers to the simple predicate unless otherwise indicated.

GRAMMAR

EXERCISE 4 **Identifying Verbs and Verb Phrases in Sentences**

Identify the <u>verb</u> in each sentence in the following paragraph. Be sure to include all parts of a verb phrase.

[1] Scientists throughout the world <u>have expressed</u> concern about the fate of the giant panda of China. [2] In recent years, this animal's natural habitat <u>has</u> slowly <u>become</u> smaller. [3] Many forests of bamboo, the panda's favorite food, <u>have died</u>. [4] A panda like the one pictured here <u>may devour</u> as much as forty pounds of bamboo daily. [5] However, each tender green shoot of bamboo <u>contains</u> only a small amount of nutrients. [6] In addition, the large but sluggish panda <u>is</u> not <u>known</u> as a successful hunter. [7] In their concern for the panda's survival, scientists <u>are</u> now <u>studying</u> the habits of this animal. [8] A captured panda <u>is held</u> in a log trap for several hours. [9] During this time, scientists <u>attach</u> a radio to the panda's neck. [10] The radio <u>sends</u> the scientists valuable information about the freed animal's behavior.

VISUAL CONNECTIONS
Exploring the Subject. Scientists have long disagreed about whether the giant panda should be in the raccoon family, the bear family, or a family of its own. Research in the 1980s indicating that the giant panda's chromosomes are more similar to those of bears than to those of raccoons has led most zoologists now to classify the giant panda as a bear.

How to Find the Subject of a Sentence

Finding the subject of a sentence is easier if you pick out the verb first. Then ask "Who?" or "What?" followed by the verb.

GRAMMAR

EXAMPLES   **My cousin from Finland will arrive this afternoon.**
[The verb is *will arrive*. Who will arrive? *My cousin* will arrive; therefore, *cousin* is the subject.]
On the other side of the brook stands a cabin. [The verb is *stands*. What stands? *A cabin* stands; *cabin* is the subject.]

▶ EXERCISE 5   **Identifying Subjects and Verbs**

Identify the <u>subject</u> and the <u>verb</u> in each sentence in the following paragraph.

[1] Despite their fragile appearance, <u>butterflies</u> <u>have</u> a lot of stamina. [2] <u>They</u> often <u>fly</u> more than one thousand miles during migration. [3] The painted lady <u>butterfly</u>, for example, <u>has been seen</u> in the middle of the Atlantic Ocean. [4] In fact, this <u>species</u> <u>was</u> once <u>spotted</u> over the Arctic Circle. [5] During the spring, <u>millions</u> of these insects <u>flutter</u> across North America. [6] Huge <u>flocks</u> of these colorful butterflies <u>fly</u> from their winter home in New Mexico to places as far north as Newfoundland, Canada. [7] Another long-distance <u>traveler</u>, the brilliant orange-and-black monarch butterfly, <u>flies</u> south each September from Canada toward Florida, Texas, and California. [8] The migratory <u>flight</u> of the monarch <u>may cover</u> a distance of close to two thousand miles. [9] Every winter for the past several decades, <u>monarchs</u> <u>have gathered</u> in a small forest not far from San Francisco. [10] The thick <u>clusters</u> of their blazing orange wings <u>make</u> this forest very popular with tourists.

16e.   The subject is never in a prepositional phrase.

A *prepositional phrase* is a group of words that begins with a preposition and ends with a noun or pronoun.

EXAMPLES   **through the years   of mine   on the team**

☞ REFERENCE NOTE: For more about prepositional phrases, see pages 574–576.

The noun or pronoun that ends a prepositional phrase cannot be the subject of a sentence.

COMMON ERROR

Problem. Students often identify the nouns in prepositional phrases as the subjects of sentences.

Solution. Suggest that students bracket all prepositional phrases before they attempt to find the subjects in sentences.

16e

EXAMPLES   **One of my cousins has visited Ghana.** [Who has visited? *One* has visited, not *cousins,* which is part of the prepositional phrase *of my cousins.*]
On top of the building is an observatory. [What is? *Observatory* is, not *top* or *building,* which are parts of prepositional phrases.]

In many sentences you can easily isolate the subject and verb simply by crossing out all prepositional phrases.

EXAMPLE   The team ~~with the best record~~ will play ~~in the state tournament.~~
Subject   **team**
Verb   **will play**

▶ EXERCISE 6   **Identifying Subjects and Verbs**

Identify the <u>subject</u> and the <u>verb</u> of each sentence in the following paragraph. Remember that the subject won't be in a prepositional phrase.

[1] The <u>people</u> in this picture <u>are celebrating</u> an ancient Chinese tradition—heralding the arrival of the New Year. [2] These <u>festivities</u>, however, <u>are occurring</u> in the United States. [3] The Chinese New Year <u>celebration</u>, with its dragon parades and colorful decorations, <u>has added</u> another dimension to American culture. [4] In the 1850s, the earliest Chinese <u>immigrants</u> <u>came</u> to the United States for jobs in the gold mines and on the railroads. [5] At first, only <u>men</u> <u>were allowed</u> to immigrate. [6] Not until much

GRAMMAR

GRAMMAR

VISUAL CONNECTIONS
Ideas for Writing. Have students write expressive/descriptive paragraphs about this photograph. You could ask students to imagine that they are watching the parade with someone who cannot see and that they are trying to describe the scene to that person.

Tie this writing activity to the material in this chapter by having students label subjects and verbs in their completed paragraphs.

ANSWERS

Exercise 7

Predicates will vary. Here are some possibilities:

1. Last <u>month</u> <u><u>was</u></u> warm.
2. A white <u>fence</u> <u><u>surrounded</u></u> the yard.
3. The <u>surf</u> <u><u>was pounding</u></u> the shore.
4. The <u>road</u> by my house <u><u>is</u></u> bumpy.
5. The <u>students</u> in our school <u><u>held</u></u> a dance.

ANSWERS

Review A

1. complete subject: <u>Benjamin Banneker</u> (1731–1806)/ complete predicate: <u><u>was born</u></u> near Baltimore, Maryland, of a free mother and an enslaved father

2. complete subject: Considered free, <u>Banneker</u>/ complete predicate: <u><u>was</u></u> able to attend an integrated private school

3. complete subject: <u>he</u>/ complete predicate: There . . . <u><u>began</u></u> his lifelong study of science and math

4. complete subject: this young <u>man</u>/ complete predicate: Despite having only an eighth-grade education, . . . <u><u>became</u></u> a noteworthy American astronomer and mathematician

5. complete subject: His astronomical <u>research</u>/ complete predicate: <u><u>led</u></u> to his acclaimed prediction of the solar eclipse of 1789

6. complete subject: the <u>first</u> of his almanacs/ complete predicate: A few years later, . . . <u><u>was published</u></u>

7. complete subject: Banneker's <u>almanacs</u>/ complete predicate: <u><u>contained</u></u> tide tables and data on future eclipses

552

---

later <u><u>were</u></u> <u>they</u> able to send home to China for their wives and sweethearts. [7] As a result, not until the 1920s <u><u>did</u></u> the close-knit <u>society</u> of America's Chinatowns <u><u>develop</u></u>. [8] <u><u>Do</u></u> <u>you</u> <u><u>want</u></u> to know more about the Chinese experience in America? [9] <u>I</u> <u><u>recommend</u></u> the book *Longtime Californ': A Documentary Study of an American Chinatown.* [10] In this book, <u>Victor G. Nee</u> and <u>Brett de Bary Nee</u> <u><u>trace</u></u> the history of Chinese immigration to the United States and the development of the Chinese American community in San Francisco.

> EXERCISE 7 | **Completing Sentences by Supplying Predicates**

Complete each of the following sentences by adding a predicate to the complete subject. Then, underline the subject once and the verb twice.

EXAMPLE   **1.** One of the horses _____.
          1. *One of the horses <u><u>has escaped</u></u> from the corral.*

1. Last month _____.
2. A white fence _____.
3. The surf _____.
4. The road by my house _____.
5. The students in our school _____.

> REVIEW A | **Identifying Complete Subjects and Complete Predicates**

Identify the complete subject and the complete predicate in each sentence in the following paragraph. Then underline the subject once and the verb twice.

[1] Benjamin Banneker (1731–1806) was born near Baltimore, Maryland, of a free mother and an enslaved father. [2] Considered free, Banneker was able to attend an integrated private school. [3] There he began his lifelong study of science and math. [4] Despite having only an eighth-grade education, this young man became a noteworthy American astronomer and mathematician. [5] His astronomical research led to his acclaimed prediction of the solar eclipse of 1789. [6] A few years later, the first of his almanacs was published. [7] Banneker's almanacs contained tide tables and data on future eclipses. [8] Some

bits of practical advice, as well as famous sayings, were also included. [9] These popular almanacs came out every year for more than a decade. [10] In addition to his scientific discoveries, Banneker is known for his work as a surveyor during the planning of Washington, D.C.

Sentences Beginning with *There* or *Here*

The word *there* or *here* may begin a sentence, but it is usually not the subject.

EXAMPLE **There are two apples left.** [What are left? *Apples.* Therefore, *apples* is the subject.]

NOTE: In this use, *there* is an *expletive,* a word that fills out the structure of a sentence but doesn't add to the meaning.

There and *here* may be used as adverbs telling where.

EXAMPLES **There are your gloves.** [What are there? *Gloves.*]
Here is my idea. [What is here? *Idea.*]

Sentences That Ask Questions

Questions usually begin with a verb, a helping verb, or a word such as *what, when, where, how,* or *why.* In most cases, the subject follows the verb or helping verb.

EXAMPLES **Did you make the team?**
Why is he running?

In a question that begins with a helping verb, the subject always comes between the helping verb and the main verb. One way to find the subject in any question is to turn the question into a statement and find the verb. Then ask "Who?" or "What?" in front of the verb.

EXAMPLES **Were your friends early?**
becomes
Your friends were early.
[Who were early? *Friends* were.]

Where did the horses cross the river?
becomes
The horses did cross the river where.
[What did cross the river? *Horses* did.]

8. complete subject: Some <u>bits</u> of practical advice, as well as famous <u>sayings,</u>/ complete predicate: <u>were</u> also <u>included</u>

9. complete subject: These popular <u>almanacs</u>/ complete predicate: <u>came out</u> every year for more than a decade

10. complete subject: <u>Banneker</u>/ complete predicate: In addition to his scientific discoveries, . . . <u>is known</u> for his work as a surveyor during the planning of Washington, D.C.

MEETING *individual* **NEEDS**

AT-RISK STUDENTS

To engage students' interest in identifying parts of sentences, try incorporating a topic that interests many students—movies. First, have students help you to generate movie titles that are complete sentences. Write the titles on the chalkboard. [Possible titles include *The Empire Strikes Back, Heaven Can Wait, Guess Who's Coming to Dinner,* and *Diamonds Are Forever.*] Then, work with students to identify the subjects and verbs in the titles. After the class has studied **Sentences Classified by Purpose** (p. 565) you may also want to have students classify each title as declarative, imperative, exclamatory, or interrogative.

A DIFFERENT APPROACH

Students could play a game with commonly used pairs of subjects and verbs. Write sets of nouns and verbs on index cards. Here are some sets you could use:

Subject sets—Jack and Jill, salt and pepper, meat and potatoes, shoes and socks, cat and mouse

Verb sets—give and take, eat and run, touch and go, twist and shout

Group students in pairs, ask one pair to come to the front of the class, and give an index card to one of the students in the pair. Tell the student with the index card to give the first half of the set as a clue; then, the second student should supply the word that completes the set. Have each player who completes a set make up a sentence that includes the set as a compound subject or verb.

 EXERCISE 8   **Identifying Subjects and Verbs**

Identify the <u>verb</u> and the <u>subject</u> in each of the following sentences. Select the verb first.

1. There <u>were</u> three <u>questions</u> on the final exam.
2. Here <u>is</u> my <u>topic</u> for the term paper.
3. What <u>did</u> <u>you</u> <u>choose</u> for a topic?
4. <u>Will</u> <u>everyone</u> <u>be</u> ready on time?
5. There <u>will be</u> a study-group <u>meeting</u> tomorrow.
6. When <u>should</u> <u>we</u> <u>go</u> to the library?
7. There <u>were</u> very few <u>books</u> on the subject.
8. <u>Are</u> there many magazine <u>articles</u> about Nelson Mandela?
9. Where <u>will</u> our <u>conference</u> <u>be held</u>?
10. <u>Have</u> <u>you</u> <u>begun</u> the next chapter?

The Understood Subject

In requests and commands, the subject is usually not stated. In such sentences, *you* is the understood subject.

REQUEST   **(You) Please rake the yard.**
COMMAND   **(You) Pick up the fallen branches.**

When a request or command includes a person's name, the name is not the subject. The name is called a *noun of direct address. You* is still the understood subject.

EXAMPLE   **(You) Wash the dishes, Jason.**

Compound Subjects and Verbs

16f.   A *compound subject* consists of two or more subjects that are joined by a conjunction and have the same verb. The conjunctions most often used to link the parts of a compound subject are *and* and *or*.

EXAMPLES   **Mr. Olivero** and his **daughter** planted the garden.
[Who planted the garden? *Mr. Olivero, daughter.*]
Either **Mr. Olivero** or his **daughter** planted the garden. [Again, the two parts of the compound subject are *Mr. Olivero* and *daughter*.]

16g. A *compound verb* consists of two or more verbs that are joined by a conjunction and have the same subject.

EXAMPLES   At the street festival, **we danced** the rumba and **sampled** the meat pies.
I **have written** the letter but **have** not **addressed** the envelope.

NOTE: If the helping verb is the same for the two verbs in a compound verb, it may or may not be repeated. Both the subject and the verb may be compound.

EXAMPLE   My **aunt** and her **children will arrive** tomorrow and **stay** with us for the holidays.

▶ EXERCISE 9   **Identifying Subjects and Verbs**

Identify the <u>subject</u> and the <u>verb</u> in each of the following sentences. If the subject is understood, write *(You).*

1. <u>Jackets</u> and <u>ties</u> <u>are required</u> in that restaurant.
2. <u>Are</u> there any <u>bears</u> or <u>wildcats</u> <u>living</u> in these woods?
3. On our math test, <u>Ann</u> and <u>Mark</u> <u>scored</u> the highest.
4. _∧<u>Bring</u> both a pencil and a pen to the history exam.   **4. (You)**
5. <u>Miguel</u> neither <u>sings</u> nor <u>plays</u> an instrument.
6. Where <u>do</u> <u>you</u> and <u>Liz</u> <u>buy</u> your cassettes?
7. The front and back <u>tires</u> <u>are</u> low and <u>need</u> air.
8. _∧<u>Play</u> ball!   **8. (You)**
9. <u>Humor</u> and <u>wisdom</u> <u>are</u> often <u>used</u> in folk sayings.
10. Either <u>Bill</u> or <u>Jan</u> <u>may stay</u> and <u>help</u> us.

▶ EXERCISE 10   **Using Subjects and Verbs**

In preparing a report on the history of the typewriter, you've gathered the following notes and the pictures shown on the next page. Using information from these sources, write a paragraph about the development of typewriters. Underline the subject of each sentence once and the verb twice.

First typewriter designed by C. L. Sholes, 1867.
Had only capital letters—keys hard to press down.
Typed onto underside of paper, so typist couldn't see what was being typed.

ANSWERS
Exercise 10

Paragraphs will vary. Here is a possibility:

The first <u>typewriter</u> <u>was designed</u> by C. L. Sholes in 1867. <u>It</u> <u>had</u> only capital letters. The <u>keys</u> <u>were</u> difficult to press. This <u>typewriter</u> <u>typed</u> onto the underside of a piece of paper. Consequently, the <u>typist</u> <u>couldn't</u> <u>see</u> what was being typed. The odd <u>arrangement</u> of the letters on the first typewriter <u>is</u> still <u>used</u> on today's keyboards. In 1878, the <u>typewriter</u> <u>had</u> a shift key and lowercase letters. Then, in 1904, <u>Royal</u> <u>introduced</u> the first modern typewriter. Its <u>keys</u> <u>were</u> easier to press. In the early 1900s, the first portable <u>typewriter</u> <u>was</u> <u>marketed</u>. Electric <u>typewriters</u> <u>came</u> into use in the 1920s. Modern <u>typewriters</u> with computer features eventually <u>replaced</u> older models.

556 *The Sentence*

Odd arrangement of letters on first typewriter still used today.
1878—typewriter had shift key and lowercase letters.
1904—Royal was first modern typewriter, keys easier to press.
First portable typewriter—early 1900s.
Electric typewriters come into use—1920s.
Modern typewriters have computer features.

Beautiful Work in 1799.

THE YOST
TYPEWRITER
is noted not alone for its Beautiful Work, but for the way it continues to produce it during years of constant use.
Send for Art Catalogue.
YOST WRITING MACHINE C
New York London

REVIEW B   **Identifying Subjects and Verbs**

Identify the <u>subject</u> and the <u>verb</u> in each of the following sentences. If the subject is understood, write *(You)*. Then underline the subject once and the verb twice.

1. <u>Bats</u>, most <u>birds</u>, and many <u>insects</u> <u>can fly</u>.
2. Other <u>animals</u> <u>can move</u> through the air without flying.
3. The <u>flying fish</u> <u>swims</u> fast and then <u>leaps</u> out of the water.
4. How <u>does</u> the <u>flying squirrel</u> <u>glide</u> from tree to tree?
5. There <u>are</u> <u>flaps</u> of skin between its legs.
6. How <u>do</u> <u>birds</u> <u>fly</u>?
7. Their <u>wings</u> <u>lift</u> and <u>push</u> them through the air.
8. ∧<u>Look</u> carefully at an insect's wings. **8.** <u>(You)</u>
9. <u>Most</u> <u>have</u> two sets of wings.
10. The <u>pair</u> in front <u>covers</u> the pair in back.

556

LESSON 4 *(pp. 557–565)*

COMPLEMENTS Rules 16h–16k

OBJECTIVES

- To construct sentences from subjects, verbs, and complements
- To identify subjects, verbs, and complements
- To identify predicate nominatives and predicate adjectives

Complements **557**

16h

GRAMMAR

PICTURE THIS

While on a tour at the Delphi Museum in Greece, you enter a large room and see this life-size bronze statue of a young charioteer. A museum guide tells you that this statue, created in about 475 B.C., was originally part of a larger work that included a bronze chariot and four bronze horses. Write a postcard to a friend back home telling him or her about this statue and your reactions to it. Begin one sentence with *there* or *here,* include one question, and have at least one sentence in which the subject is understood.

Subject: *The Charioteer of Delphi,* a famous Greek statue
Audience: a friend
Purpose: to comment on a work of art

Complements

16h.   A *complement* is a word or group of words that completes the meaning of a predicate.

A group of words may have a subject and a verb and still not express a complete thought. Notice how the boldfaced words complete the meanings of the following sentences.

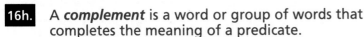

      S   V   C
That book is an **autobiography.**

PICTURE THIS

Let students work in pairs during the evaluation and revision stage of this writing assignment, using the following criteria for peer evaluation:

1. Did the writer use a warm, friendly tone?
2. Did the writer include his or her reactions to the statue?
3. Did the writer include a sentence beginning with *there* or *here?*
4. Did the writer ask one question?
5. Did the writer include a sentence with an understood subject?

Remind students to offer positive suggestions to one another.

VISUAL CONNECTIONS

Exploring the Subject. This bronze life-size statue, discovered in the excavations of Delphi, was once part of a larger work featuring the victor of a chariot race as he stood in his four-horse chariot. It is thought that the statue may date back to 477 B.C.

PROGRAM MANAGER

COMPLEMENTS

- **Independent Practice/ Reteaching** See **Subject Complements, Direct Objects,** and **Indirect Objects** in *Language Skills Practice and Assessment,* pp. 37–39.
- **Computer Guided Instruction** See **Lesson 25** in *Language Workshop CD-ROM.*
- **Practice** See **Chapter 11** in *English Workshop, Fourth Course,* pp. 139–144.

GRAMMAR

557

QUICK REMINDER

Write the following sentences on the chalkboard. Then, ask students to identify the complement in each sentence.

1. Mary Ellen is a veterinarian.
2. She is ambitious.
3. She opened a clinic for small animals.
4. She gave us a tour of her animal hospital.

INTEGRATING THE LANGUAGE ARTS

Literature Link. Poets sometimes invert the usual subject-verb-complement order to maintain a poem's rhyme scheme or to emphasize a particular word by placing it at the end of a line. Have students read a poem that includes at least one such inversion. Possible poems include "The Forester" by Wilfrid Wilson Gibson, "I Wandered Lonely as a Cloud" by William Wordsworth, and "Ozymandias" by Percy Bysshe Shelley.

After students have read the poem, have them find any inversions of the usual subject-verb-complement order and discuss as a class what effect the poet achieves by inverting the word order.

```
         S         S   V      C
Both Eric and Bob felt confident.
```

```
     S             V    C       C
Sandra Cisneros writes poetry and fiction.
```

As you can see in the last example above, a complement may be a compound.

NOTE: Every sentence has a basic framework called a *base.* In a sentence with no complement, the base is simply the subject and verb. In a sentence with a complement, the base includes the complement.

Complements can be found in both independent clauses and dependent clauses.

```
                 S    V        C
EXAMPLES  Although he appeared sluggish at the start,
```
```
          S      V    C
          Ricardo won the race.
```
```
          S  V   C        S    V
          Josie is an engineer who designs computer
```
```
          C
          hardware.
```

☞ **REFERENCE NOTE:** For a discussion of independent and dependent clauses, see Chapter 18.

NOTE: Complements are never in prepositional phrases.

EXAMPLES   Li Hua quoted the **poem.** [*Poem* is the complement.]
Li Hua quoted from the **poem.** [*Poem* is part of the prepositional phrase *from the poem.*]

An adverb modifying a verb is not a complement. Only nouns, pronouns, and adjectives serve as complements.

EXAMPLES   Lucy plays **hard.** [*Hard* is an adverb, not a complement.]
These pears are **hard.** [*Hard,* an adjective, is a complement.]

☐► EXERCISE 11   **Writing Sentences with Subjects, Verbs, and Complements**

Construct five sentences from the following sentence parts. Try to add more than only a word or two.

SUBJECT	VERB	COMPLEMENT
cyclists	planned	trip
musicians	performed	duet
speaker	looked	enthusiastic
dancer	tapped	rhythm
novel	is	suspenseful

EXERCISE 12 Identifying Subjects, Verbs, and Complements

Identify the subject(s) and the verb(s) in each sentence in the following paragraph. Then identify the complement if there is one.

[1] A hurricane is a powerful storm that can measure two or three hundred miles in diameter. [2] Such storms are notorious for causing death and destruction. [3] To be classified as a hurricane, a storm must have winds of at least seventy-four miles per hour. [4] These winds swirl around the *eye,* an area of calm in the center of the storm. [5] *Wall clouds* surround the eye of a hurricane. [6] Within these clouds the strongest winds and heaviest rain of the storm occur. [7] The winds and rain, along with the force of the sea, often produce enormous waves called a *storm surge.* [8] In a surge, tides rise several feet above normal. [9] Huge waves produce floods that destroy life and property [10] In fact, 90 percent of hurricane-related deaths result from drowning in floods.

United States of America

Gulf of Mexico

Cuba

Yucatan Peninsula

Hispaniola

Puerto Rico

ANSWERS
Exercise 11

Sentences will vary. Here are some possibilities:

1. The cyclists carefully planned the twenty-mile trip.

2. Famous musicians from Africa performed the duet.

3. The speaker looked enthusiastic when the crowd applauded.

4. The dancer tapped the complex rhythm of the song with her feet.

5. The novel is even more suspenseful than the movie.

VISUAL CONNECTIONS
Ideas for Writing. Ask students to write poems or prose paragraphs that use extended metaphors to compare a storm to something else. Students' first sentences or lines should use the linking verb *be* and a predicate nominative to make a comparison. Examples are "A storm is a child" or "The storm was an angry animal." Encourage students to include vivid, unexpected, and expressive verbs, nouns, and adjectives to strengthen their comparisons.

The Subject Complement

16i. A *subject complement* is a noun, a pronoun, or an adjective that follows a linking verb. A subject complement identifies or describes the subject.

EXAMPLES   Lani is a soccer **player.** [*Player* identifies *Lani.*]
This could be **it.** [*It* identifies *This.*]
Roscoe seems **worried.** [*Worried* describes *Roscoe.*]

☞ REFERENCE NOTE: For more information about linking verbs, see pages 525–526.

Remember that subject complements can appear in dependent clauses.

EXAMPLES   Although the watch is an **antique,** my aunt says that it is always **accurate.** [*Antique* identifies *watch* in the introductory adverb clause. *Accurate* describes *it* in the noun clause beginning with *that.*]

(1) A *predicate nominative* is a noun or a pronoun in the predicate that identifies or renames the subject of a sentence or a clause.

EXAMPLES   Some caterpillars become **butterflies.**
The winners should have been **they.**

(2) A *predicate adjective* is an adjective in the predicate that describes the subject of a sentence or a clause.

EXAMPLES   You look **happy.**
Norma appeared **calm.**

Subject complements may be compound.

EXAMPLES   Our cats' names are **Wimpy** and **Henry.** [compound predicate nominative]
The yogurt tasted **sweet** and **creamy.** [compound predicate adjective]

NOTE: The subject complement may come before the subject of a sentence or a clause.

EXAMPLES   How **silly** that commercial is! [*Silly* is a predicate adjective describing *commercial.*]
Now we know what a fine **speaker** you are. [*Speaker* is a predicate nominative identifying *you.*]

GRAMMAR

▶ EXERCISE 13   **Identifying Predicate Nominatives and Predicate Adjectives**

Identify the subject complements in the following sentences. Then, tell whether the complement is a predicate nominative or a predicate adjective. [Note: A sentence may have more than one subject complement.]

1. The last scene of the play is very intense.
2. Those two small birds are finches.
3. The music sounded lively.
4. It is difficult to choose a winner when each contestant's costume looks so elegant.
5. My goldfish Alonzo grows larger every day.
6. Andrea's report on digital recording is a highly detailed and technical one.
7. The setting of the story is a Spanish castle that looks old and deserted.
8. Your solution to this algebra problem is clever.
9. We felt full after we had eaten Thanksgiving dinner.
10. When did Uncas become a chief of the Mohegans?

▶ EXERCISE 14   **Identifying Subjects, Verbs, and Subject Complements**

Each sentence in the following paragraph contains at least one subject complement. Identify each subject, verb, and subject complement. Make a chart like the following one, and fill in the correct words.

EXAMPLE   [1] Although jazz is now popular all over the world, it was originally the music of African Americans.

SUBJECT	VERB	SUBJECT COMPLEMENT
1. *jazz*	*is*	*popular*
it	*was*	*music*

[1] A typically American musical form, jazz was the sound of Louis Armstrong, "Count" Basie, Scott Joplin, and Ella Fitzgerald. [2] Created in the early twentieth century, jazz is a blend of elements from African and European music, but its irregular, or syncopated, rhythms are strictly African. [3] Early jazz was a combination of the cakewalk, a dance that was popular with many African Americans in the 1800s, and ragtime, which was mainly

ANSWERS
Exercise 14

SUBJECT	VERB	SUBJECT COMPLEMENT
1. jazz	was	sound
2. jazz	is	blend
rhythms	are	African
3. jazz	was	combination
that	was	popular
which	was	music
4. future	appeared	bright
records	became	popular
5. People	remain	fascinated
it	sounds	new

GRAMMAR

GRAMMAR

instrumental music. [4] After 1917, the future of jazz appeared bright when jazz phonograph records became popular. [5] People remain fascinated by jazz, perhaps because it sounds new each time it's played.

Objects

Objects are complements that do not refer to the subject. They follow action verbs rather than linking verbs.

EXAMPLES   The cat was chasing a **moth.**
            Jeff's mother gave **him** some **grapes.**

☞ REFERENCE NOTE: For more information about action verbs, see pages 524–525.

Like subject complements, objects can be found in dependent clauses.

EXAMPLE   After we read the **story,** the teacher said that she would give **us** a **quiz** on it.

16j.   A **direct object** is a noun or pronoun that directly receives the action of a verb or shows the result of the action. A direct object answers the question "What?" or "Whom?" after an action verb.

EXAMPLES   The mechanic fixed their **car.** [Fixed what? *Car.*]
            She asked **them** to wait in the lobby. [Asked whom? *Them.*]

Verbs that express mental action, such as *study, dream,* and *understand,* are just as much action verbs as are verbs that express physical action, such as *push, leap,* and *stumble.*

EXAMPLE   Paco still **remembers** his first day of school. [Remembers what? *Day.*]

NOTE: Direct objects are never found in prepositional phrases.

EXAMPLES   Mom and I painted the **porch.** [*Porch* is the direct object.]

            Mom and I painted on the **porch.** [*Porch* is part of the prepositional phrase *on the porch.*]

▶ EXERCISE 15   **Identifying Verbs and Their Direct Objects**

Identify the <u>verbs</u> and the <u>direct objects</u> in the following sentences.

1. I <u>borrowed</u> my parents' new <u>camera</u> recently.
2. First I <u>loaded</u> the <u>film</u> into the camera.
3. Then I <u>set</u> the shutter <u>speed</u>.
4. I <u>focused</u> the <u>camera</u> on a distant object.
5. I <u>could read</u> the shutter <u>speed</u> in the viewfinder.
6. A flashing red light <u>signals</u> an incorrect <u>setting</u>.
7. Slowly and carefully, I <u>pressed</u> the <u>button</u>.
8. I then <u>moved</u> the <u>film</u> forward for the next shot.
9. By the end of the day, I <u>had snapped</u> more than thirty-six <u>pictures</u>.
10. Unfortunately, the film processor <u>lost</u> my <u>roll</u> of film.

16k. An ***indirect object*** is a noun or pronoun that precedes the direct object and tells *to whom* or *for whom* (or *to what* or *for what*) the action of the verb is done.

DIRECT OBJECT   Meli read her **report.** [Read what? *Report.*]
INDIRECT OBJECT   Meli read **us** her report. [Read to whom? *Us.*]

If the word *to* or *for* is used in the sentence, the noun or pronoun following it is part of a prepositional phrase, not an indirect object.

EXAMPLES   Jeff wrote **me** a note. [*Me* is the indirect object.]
Jeff wrote a note to **me.** [*Me* is part of the prepositional phrase *to me.*]

Both direct and indirect objects may be compound.

EXAMPLES   Our family recycles **glass** and **aluminum.** [compound direct object]
The ski trip had given **Lucia** and **me** a wonderful vacation. [compound indirect object]

NOTE: Don't confuse adverbs in the predicate with complements.

EXAMPLES   They turned **right.** [*Right* is an adverb telling where.]
You have the **right** to remain silent. [*Right* is a noun used as a direct object.]

MEETING *individual* **NEEDS**

LESS-ADVANCED STUDENTS

Write the following incomplete sentences on the chalkboard:

1. Baseball players throw _____.
2. The young artist painted a _____ on a building downtown.
3. Mario gives his _____ gifts on their birthdays.
4. A runner passes a _____ to another runner during a relay race.
5. Kim wrote the _____ to complain about air pollution in her city.

Have students fill in each blank. Point out that the words they supply will serve as objects in the sentences. When students have filled in the blanks, you may also want to have them identify each object as either direct or indirect.

REVIEW C

OBJECTIVE

- To distinguish fragments from sentences and to identify the subjects, verbs, and complements of sentences

564 *The Sentence*

EXERCISE 16 **Identifying Direct and Indirect Objects**

Identify the <u>direct objects</u> and <u>indirect objects</u> in the sentences in the following paragraph. Not all sentences contain both kinds of objects.

[1] Last summer, Leroy told <u>us</u> his <u>plans</u> for the future. [2] He wants a <u>place</u> on the U.S. swim team in the next Olympic Games. [3] Of course, this goal demands <u>hours</u> of hard practice. [4] Every day, Leroy swims one hundred <u>laps</u> in the college pool and works out with weights for an hour. [5] Such intense training could have cost <u>him</u> his social <u>life</u>. [6] With his rigorous schedule, Leroy doesn't have much <u>time</u> to spend with friends. [7] However, all of us understand and give <u>him</u> <u>encouragement</u> and <u>support</u>. [8] But we can't teach <u>him</u> the fine <u>points</u> of competitive swimming. [9] His coach does <u>that</u>. [10] Working together, they've already improved Leroy's best <u>time</u>.

EXERCISE 17 **Using Direct and Indirect Objects**

It's your first day working at a restaurant, and you've just taken this family's order. Because you want to be sure to get the order right, you take a minute in the kitchen to go over what each person wanted. Write five sentences that you might say to yourself to remember who should get what. In your sentences, use five direct objects and at least two indirect objects. For indirect objects, you could use pronouns or general terms such as *man* or *children*, or imagine that you know the people and use their names.

EXAMPLE **1.** *Give Margot the squid and spinach appetizer.*

SENTENCES CLASSIFIED BY PURPOSE
Rule 16l

OBJECTIVES

- To classify sentences as declarative, imperative, interrogative, or exclamatory

REVIEW C

Identifying Sentences and Fragments; Identifying Complements

Identify each of the following word groups as a <u>*sentence*</u> or a <u>*fragment*</u>. If a word group is a complete sentence, identify its <u>subject</u> and <u>verb</u>. If a sentence has a (complement) label it as a *predicate adjective*, a *predicate nominative*, a *direct object*, or an *indirect object*.

1. <u>Has</u> the planning <u>committee</u> <u>announced</u> the (date) of the school carnival? **1.** sent.—d.o.
2. Perhaps next week. **2.** frag.   **3.** sent.—i.o./d.o.
3. <u>Linda</u> <u>gave</u> (us) a (summary) of her science project.
4. <u>It</u> <u>was</u> (long) and (interesting) **4.** sent.—p.a./p.a.
5. Although it was well written. **5.** frag.
6. <u>Books</u> and <u>papers</u> <u>covered</u> the (desk) and <u>spilled</u> onto the floor. **6.** sent.—d.o.
7. <u>One</u> of those dogs <u>is</u> not very well (trained) **7.** sent.—p.a.
8. <u>Ming Chin</u> <u>gave</u> the (children) a (handful) of oatmeal cookies. **8.** sent.—i.o./d.o.
9. <u>Kim</u>, <u>Juan</u>, and <u>Tracey</u> <u>were</u> (winners) at the track meet <u>last Saturday</u>. **9.** sent.—p.n.
10. How (happy) <u>they</u> <u>were</u>! **10.** sent.—p.a.

Sentences Classified by Purpose

16l. Sentences may be classified as *declarative*, *imperative*, *interrogative*, or *exclamatory*.

(1) A ***declarative sentence*** makes a statement. All declarative sentences are followed by periods.

EXAMPLES   Gwendolyn Brooks is the poet laureate of Illinois.
Although we were tired after working all day, we still wanted to go dancing.

(2) An ***imperative sentence*** gives a command or makes a request. Imperative sentences usually end with periods, but strong commands may end with exclamation points

EXAMPLES   **Pass the salt, please.**
Speak softly.
Wait!

PROGRAM MANAGER

SENTENCES CLASSIFIED BY PURPOSE

- **Independent Practice/ Reteaching** For instruction and exercises, see **Classifying Sentences by Purpose** in *Language Skills Practice and Assessment,* p. 40.

- **Computer Guided Instruction** For additional instruction and practice with classifying sentences by purpose, see **Lesson 26** in *Language Workshop CD-ROM.*

- **Practice** To help less-advanced students with additional instruction and practice with classifying sentences by purpose, see **Chapter 11** in *English Workshop, Fourth Course,* pp. 145–146.

QUICK REMINDER

Write the names of the four types of sentences—*declarative, imperative, interrogative,* and *exclamatory*—on the chalkboard and have each student write one sentence of each type. You could then ask volunteers to read their sentences to the class.

GRAMMAR

MEETING *individual* NEEDS

LEP/ESL

Spanish. In written Spanish, interrogative and exclamatory sentences are introduced by inverted question marks and inverted exclamation points, respectively. You may want to remind students that in English such marks are found only at the ends of sentences.

LEARNING STYLES

Auditory and Kinetic Learners. Have students practice dramatic readings of the four types of sentences. You could have students use the sentences in **Exercise 18** for their readings, or you may want to have them work in groups to create skits that include the four types of sentences.

566   *The Sentence*

(3) An ***interrogative sentence*** asks a question. Interrogative sentences are followed by question marks.

EXAMPLES   **Can you speak Spanish?**
What did you say?

(4) An ***exclamatory sentence*** expresses strong feeling. Exclamatory sentences are followed by exclamation points.

EXAMPLES   **What a beautiful day this is!**
How I enjoy autumn!

NOTE: Any sentence may be spoken in such a way that it is exclamatory. In this case, it should be followed by an exclamation point.

EXAMPLES   **This is inexcusable!** [Declarative becomes exclamatory.]
Stop the car! [Imperative becomes exclamatory.]
How could you say that! [Interrogative becomes exclamatory.]

☞ REFERENCE NOTE: For a discussion of how sentences are classified by structure, see pages 610–611. For more on end marks of punctuation, see pages 789–792.

EXERCISE 18   **Classifying Sentences as Declarative, Imperative, Interrogative, or Exclamatory**

Classify each of the following sentences as *declarative*, *imperative*, *interrogative*, or *exclamatory*.

1.   The loudspeakers in our living room are small yet powerful.   **1.** decl.
2.   Turn down the sound!   **2.** imp. [*or* excl.]
3.   Is that music or noise, Ramona?   **3.** int.
4.   Listening to loud music every day can damage a person's hearing.   **4.** decl.   **5.** int.   **6.** decl.
5.   How many watts does your amplifier produce?
6.   Sound levels are measured in units called decibels.
7.   Do you know that an increase of ten decibels represents a doubling in the sound level?   **7.** int.
8.   Do not blast your sound system.   **8.** imp.
9.   Keep it quiet!   **9.** imp. [*or* excl.]
10.   Music played softly is relaxing.   **10.** decl.

▶ EXERCISE 19 **Using the Four Kinds of Sentences**

These colorful Tlingit totem poles stand in Saxman Indian Village in Ketchikan, Alaska. The Tlingits, who have lived in Alaska for hundreds of years, are well known for their carving skills, as well as their sense of humor. Yes, that's a short-legged Abraham Lincoln atop one of the poles! Write five sentences expressing your reactions to these poles. Use at least one of each kind of sentence: *declarative, imperative, interrogative,* and *exclamatory.*

EXAMPLE **1.** *What a surprise to see Abraham Lincoln on a totem pole!*

WRITING APPLICATION

Catching a Reader's Interest with Appropriately Varied Sentences

In fishing, you need the right bait to catch the kind of fish you want. In writing, you need the right bait to catch your reader's interest. Your opening sentence is this bait.

OPENER 1:   I think we should have a party.
OPENER 2:   Shouldn't we have a party?
OPENER 3:   Let's party!

These opening sentences contain similar information. Which of them would interest you to read further? Why?

GRAMMAR

ANSWERS
Exercise 19

Sentences will vary. Here are some sample sentences:

1. What a surprise to see Abraham Lincoln on a totem pole! (exclamatory)

2. Go to Alaska to see these fascinating totem poles. (imperative)

3. Have you ever seen this type of artwork before? (interrogative)

4. I am impressed by the craftsmanship it takes to create them. (declarative)

5. Which is your favorite? (interrogative)

WRITING APPLICATION

Ask students to brainstorm possible opening lines that will catch their readers' attention. Remind students that the flow of ideas is the most important element of brainstorming. Students should generate as many ideas as possible and wait until later to evaluate their work. For an example of persuasive writing, refer students to **A Student Model** on p. 356.

CRITICAL THINKING

Evaluation. Work with students to develop criteria for evaluating their opening lines. Then, model the process of evaluating an opening line using the criteria the class has developed. You could evaluate the opening line of **A Student Model** on p. 356.

GRAMMAR

REVIEWS D and E
OBJECTIVES
- To define the parts of a sentence and to give an example of each
- To identify subjects, verbs, predicate adjectives, predicate nominatives, direct objects, and indirect objects in a passage

▶ **WRITING ACTIVITY**

Your neighborhood Residents' Council would like to sponsor a dance for the teenagers on your block. However, the council is not sure what kind of dances teens would like. You've decided to write a short letter to the council to give your opinion. Write some different opening sentences for your letter. Select the one that is the best "bait" for your audience, and then write a short letter.

Prewriting   Decide how you feel about this issue. Then, jot down a few notes about why having the dance would or would not be a good idea. Next, write some different opening sentences. Choose the opener that you think will be the most interesting and effective.

Writing   As you write your letter, be sure to refer often to your prewriting notes.

Evaluating and Revising   Ask an adult you know to listen to your letter. Does he or she think your opening sentence is interesting? Does he or she find your letter persuasive? Revise any sentences or sections that aren't clear.

Proofreading   Imagine that you are a council member, and read through your letter. Are there any grammar, punctuation, or spelling errors? Does the letter follow the proper business letter form? (See pages 973–979 for the correct forms of business letters.) Make all needed corrections, and then write a clean, final copy of your letter.

▶ REVIEW D   **Understanding the Parts of a Sentence**

In your own words, define each of the following terms, and give an example to illustrate it.

1. a sentence
2. a complete subject
3. a verb (simple predicate)
4. a verb phrase
5. a complete predicate
6. a simple subject
7. a subject complement
8. a direct object
9. an understood subject
10. an indirect object

ANSWERS
Review D

Responses will vary. Each response should include an example and the following information:

1. A sentence is a group of words that contains a subject and a verb and expresses a complete thought.

2. A complete subject names the person or thing spoken about in the rest of a sentence.

3. A verb is the main word or group of words in a complete predicate.

4. A verb phrase consists of a verb and one or more helping verbs.

5. A complete predicate is the part of a sentence that says something about the subject.

6. A simple subject is the main word or group of words in a complete subject.

7. A subject complement is a noun, a pronoun, or an adjective that follows a linking verb. It identifies, describes, or explains the subject.

8. A direct object is a noun or pronoun that directly receives the action of a verb or shows the result of the action.

9. An understood subject is the unstated subject, *you,* of a request or command.

10. An indirect object is a noun or a pronoun that precedes the direct object and tells to whom or for whom (or to what or for what) the action of the verb is done.

REVIEW E

Identifying Subjects, Verbs, and Complements

Identify each of the italicized words in the following passage as a <u>s</u>ubject, a <u>v</u>erb, a <u>p</u>redicate <u>a</u>djective, a <u>p</u>redicate <u>n</u>ominative, a <u>d</u>irect <u>o</u>bject, or an <u>i</u>ndirect <u>o</u>bject.

The Great Pyramid of Khufu (Cheops) is [1] *one* of the wonders of the ancient world. [2] *It* was once encased with blocks of polished limestone. However, [3] *weather and thievery* [4] *have combined* to destroy the original structure. As you [5] *can see*, the pyramid [6] *looks* [7] *weather-beaten*. Still, it is an impressive [8] *sight*.

Hundreds of years ago, one invading Arab [9] *ruler* decided to rob the tomb of Khufu. With many workers at his disposal, he gave the [10] *men* his [11] *instructions*. The workers [12] *hacked* through the incredibly hard solid blocks of granite. Unexpectedly, [13] *they* broke into a tunnel. Imagine their [14] *excitement*! All too soon, however, they [15] *discovered* an enormous [16] *plug* of granite blocking their way. They cut around the plug and finally reached the inner [17] *chamber*.

Strangely enough, there was no [18] *gold*. No vast treasures [19] *sparkled* under the light of the torches. The tomb [20] *had* probably *been robbed* many centuries earlier by Egyptians familiar with its secret entrances.

1. p.n.
2. s.
3. s.
4. v.
5. v.
6. v.
7. p.a.
8. p.n.
9. s.
10. i.o.
11. d.o.
12. v.
13. s.
14. d.o.
15. v.
16. d.o.
17. d.o.
18. s.
19. v.
20. v.

VISUAL CONNECTIONS
Exploring the Subject. The Great Pyramid of Khufu is said to be the largest building ever built. It covers over thirteen acres and contains approximately 2,300,000 blocks of stone that weigh an average of two and one-half tons each. It is estimated that it would have taken 100,000 people working constantly for twenty years to build the pyramid.

569

LESSON 6 *(pp. 570–571)*
REVIEW: POSTTESTS 1 and 2
OBJECTIVES
• To identify subjects, verbs, predicate adjectives, predicate nominatives, direct objects, and indirect objects in sentences

570 *The Sentence*

Review: Posttest 1

A. Identifying Subjects, Verbs, and Complements

Identify each of the <u>italicized words</u> in the following sentences as a *subject*, a *verb*, a *predicate adjective*, a *predicate nominative*, a *direct object*, or an *indirect object*.

1. Have *you* ever met a robot?   **1.** s.
2. In the field of robotics, scientists have built vastly complex *robots*.   **2.** d.o.
3. Today these machines *are put* to work in factories, laboratories, and outer space.   **3.** v.
4. How were these complex *machines* first used?   **4.** s.
5. There are a *number* of interesting early examples of robots at work.   **5.** s.
6. One of the first robots was a mechanical *figure* in a clock tower.   **6.** p.n.
7. It raised a hammer and struck a *bell* every hour.   **7.** d.o.
8. At the 1939 New York World's Fair, Elektro and Sparko were popular *attractions*.   **8.** p.n.
9. Elektro was *tall*, more than seven feet high.   **9.** p.a.
10. Electric motors gave *Elektro* power for a variety of amazing tricks.   **10.** i.o.
11. Sparko was Elektro's *dog*.   **11.** p.n.
12. Sparko *could bark* and even *wag* his tail.   **12.** v.
13. Today, *some* of the simplest robots are drones in research laboratories.   **13.** s.
14. Basically, drones are *extensions* of the human arm.   **14.** p.n.
15. They can be *useful* in many different ways.   **15.** p.a.

B. Classifying Sentences as Declarative, Interrogative, Imperative, or Exclamatory

Classify each of the following sentences as *declarative*, *interrogative*, *imperative*, or *exclamatory*. Then give the proper end punctuation.

16. Can you picture a robot twenty-five feet tall**?**   **16.** int.
17. Step up and say hello to Beetle⊙   **17.** imp.

18. Perhaps you have already heard of CAM, an even more advanced robot⊙ **18.** decl.
19. It can travel on long legs across rough terrain as rapidly as thirty-five miles per hour⊙ **19.** decl.
20. How much it looks like a science fiction creature! **20.** excl.

GRAMMAR

Review: Posttest 2

Writing Sentences

Write sentences according to the following guidelines. Underline the subject once and the verb twice in each sentence. If the subject is understood, write *(You)*.

EXAMPLE **1.** a sentence with a direct object
1. *(You) Have another glass of milk.*

1. a declarative sentence with a verb phrase
2. a sentence beginning with *There*
3. an interrogative sentence
4. an exclamatory sentence
5. an imperative sentence
6. a sentence with a compound subject
7. a sentence with a predicate nominative
8. a sentence with a compound direct object and an indirect object
9. a sentence with a predicate adjective
10. a sentence with a compound verb

GRAMMAR

ANSWERS
Review: Posttest 2

Sentences will vary. Here are some possibilities:

1. I should have planted more trees on Earth Day.
2. There are many types of plants.
3. Have you studied about the plant life on our planet?
4. Plants are incredibly interesting!
5. (You) Go to the library and read about what types of plants grow in the world.
6. Eucalyptuses and tree ferns can be found in abundance in Australia's forests.
7. The mula mula is a plant.
8. The forest provides scientists fascinating plants and ecosystems to study.
9. The forest vegetation is lush in tropical regions.
10. The vegetation grows quickly and forms a series of distinct layers of trees of differing heights.

PROGRAM MANAGER

FOR THE WHOLE CHAPTER

- Review For exercises on chapter concepts, see **Review Form A** and **Review Form B** in *Language Skills Practice and Assessment,* pp. 56–59.

- Assessment For additional testing, see **Grammar Pretests** and **Grammar Mastery Tests** in *Language Skills Practice and Assessment,* pp. 1–8 and pp. 76–81.

CHAPTER OVERVIEW

This chapter begins with a definition of prepositional phrases and a description of how these phrases are used. Then the different verbals are presented. The final lesson concerns appositives and appositive phrases.

Including phrases to improve writing occurs most often during the revising stage of the writing process. In this chapter, students are given an opportunity to practice using prepositional phrases in the **Writing Application.**

GRAMMAR

17 THE PHRASE

Prepositional, Verbal, and Appositive Phrases

Diagnostic Test

A. Identifying Phrases in Sentences

Identify each <u>italicized phrase</u> in the following sentences as *prepositional, participial, gerund, infinitive,* or *appositive.*

1. The sundial was one of the first instruments used for *telling time*.   **1.** ger.
2. *Regarded chiefly as garden ornaments,* sundials are still used in some areas *to tell time*.   **2.** part./inf.
3. The shadow-casting object *on a sundial* is called a gnomon.   **3.** prep.
4. Forerunners of the sundial include poles or upright stones *used as gnomons by early humans*.   **4.** part.
5. *To improve the accuracy of the sundial,* the gnomon was set directly parallel to the earth's axis.   **5.** inf.
6. The development of trigonometry permitted more precise calculations *in the construction* of sundials.   **6.** prep.
7. For everyday use, *owning a watch* has obvious advantages over *using a sundial*.   **7.** ger./ger.

572

8. *In the past*, sundials were used *to set and check the accuracy of watches*. **8.** prep./inf.
9. The heliochronometer, *a sundial of great precision*, was used until 1900 *to set the watches of French railway workers*. **9.** app./inf.
10. The difference *between solar time and clock time* is correlated by the use of tables *showing daily variations in sun time*. **10.** prep./part.

B. Identifying Phrases in a Paragraph

Identify each <u>italicized phrase</u> in the following paragraph as *prepositional*, *participial*, *gerund*, *infinitive*, or *appositive*.

[11] A sundial is not difficult *to make with simple materials*. [12] First, find a stick *to use as a gnomon*. [13] At high noon, put the stick in the ground, *tilting it slightly northward*. [14] *To mark the first hour*, place a pebble at the tip of the shadow made by the stick. [15] An hour later, put another pebble at the tip *of the shadow*. [16] Continue this process *throughout the afternoon*. [17] *Starting the next morning*, repeat the hourly process. [18] Be sure *to place the last pebble at high noon*. [19] Observing the completed sundial, you will note that the hour markers, *the pebbles*, are not equidistant. [20] *The uneven spacing of the markers* demonstrates that shadows move faster in the morning and the evening than during the middle of the day.

11. inf.
12. inf.
13. part.
14. inf.
15. prep.
16. prep.
17. part.
18. inf.
19. app.
20. ger.

17a. A *phrase* is a group of related words that is used as a single part of speech and does not contain both a verb and its subject.

EXAMPLES   **should have waited** [verb phrase; no subject]
         for you and her [prepositional phrase; no subject or verb]

A group of words that has both a subject and a verb is not a phrase.

EXAMPLES   **They will be here soon.** [*They* is the subject of *will be.*]
         after she leaves [*She* is the subject of *leaves.*]

OBJECTIVES

- To identify prepositional phrases used as adjectives and the words they modify
- To identify prepositional phrases used as adverbs, the words they modify, and the parts of speech of the words modified

PROGRAM MANAGER

PREPOSITIONAL PHRASES

■ **Independent Practice/ Reteaching** For instruction and exercises, see **Prepositional Phrases, Adjective Phrases,** and **Adverb Phrases** in *Language Skills Practice and Assessment,* pp. 49–51.

■ **Computer Guided Instruction** For additional instruction and practice with prepositional phrases, see **Lesson 19** in *Language Workshop CD-ROM.*

■ **Practice** To help less-advanced students with additional instruction and practice with prepositional phrases, see **Chapter 12** in *English Workshop, Fourth Course,* pp. 149–152.

✔ QUICK REMINDER

Write the following sentences on the chalkboard. Then, have students identify the prepositional phrases and the words they modify.

1. The softball team travels by bus. [by bus—travels]
2. The boy with the football is Carlos. [with the football—boy]
3. She baby-sits for spending money. [for spending money—baby-sits]

Tell students that a prepositional phrase begins with a preposition, ends with a noun or pronoun that is the object of the preposition, modifies one or more other words in the sentence, and does not contain a verb or subject.

574

---

574 *The Phrase*

☞ **REFERENCE NOTE:** A group of words that has both a subject and a verb is called a *clause.* Clauses are discussed in Chapter 18.

Prepositional Phrases

17b. A *prepositional phrase* includes a preposition, a noun or a pronoun, and any modifiers of that noun or pronoun.

EXAMPLES The woman **with the helmet** is a motorcyclist.
The cashier gave the change **to me.**

NOTE: Don't confuse the common preposition *to* with the *to* that is the sign of the infinitive form of a verb: *to watch, to learn, to drive.* For more on infinitives, see pages 586–588.

17c. The noun or pronoun that ends a prepositional phrase is the *object of the preposition* that begins the phrase.

PREPOSITIONAL PHRASE	PREPOSITION	OBJECT
before the second stoplight	before	stoplight
along the highway	along	highway
according to him	according to	him

☞ **REFERENCE NOTE:** For a list of commonly used prepositions, see page 535.

A preposition may have a compound object.

EXAMPLES near **forests** and **rivers**
despite the **rain, snow,** and **ice**

Adjective Phrases

17d. A prepositional phrase that modifies a noun or a pronoun is an *adjective phrase.*

EXAMPLES   The cottages **by the lake** are quite picturesque. [The adjective phrase *by the lake* modifies the noun *cottages.*]

No one **in the class** has seen the movie yet. [The adjective phrase *in the class* modifies the pronoun *no one.*]

Two or more adjective phrases may modify the same noun or pronoun.

EXAMPLE   The picture **of their candidate** **in today's newspaper** is not at all flattering. [The two adjective phrases *of their candidate* and *in today's newspaper* both modify the same noun, *picture.*]

An adjective phrase may also modify the object of another prepositional phrase.

EXAMPLE   The coconut palms in the park **near the bay** were planted a long time ago. [*Near the bay* modifies *park*, the object of the preposition *in.*]

NOTE: Unlike single-word adjectives, adjective phrases always follow the noun or pronoun they modify.

EXERCISE 1   Identifying Adjective Phrases

Identify the <u>adjective phrases</u> in each of the following sentences. After each phrase, give the <u>word that the phrase modifies</u>.

EXAMPLE   1. Julius Caesar was one of the most successful generals in ancient Rome.
     1. *of the most successful generals—one*
     in ancient Rome—generals

1. Roman roads were one <u>reason</u> <u>for Caesar's military successes</u>.
2. The <u>roads</u> <u>of ancient Rome</u> linked the far <u>corners</u> <u>of the empire</u>.
3. Large <u>blocks</u> <u>of hard stone</u> provided a sound <u>foundation</u> <u>for most major routes</u>.
4. <u>Caesar's interest</u> <u>in military roads</u> showed his <u>understanding</u> <u>of the importance</u> <u>of communication</u>.
5. Close <u>communication</u> <u>among the empire's provinces</u> strengthened the <u>power</u> <u>of the Roman rulers</u>.

Adverb Phrases

17e. A prepositional phrase that modifies a verb, an adjective, or another adverb is an *adverb phrase.*

EXAMPLES   The mole burrowed **under the lawn.** [The adverb phrase *under the lawn* modifies the verb *burrowed.*]

Althea Gibson was graceful **on the tennis court.** [The adverb phrase *on the tennis court* modifies the adjective *graceful.*]

The baby speaks quite clearly **for a two-year-old.** [The adverb phrase *for a two-year-old* modifies the adverb *clearly.*]

Adverb phrases tell *when, where, why, how,* or *to what extent.*

EXAMPLES   The town grew quiet **after the storm.** [*when*]
He glanced **out the window.** [*where*]
Most street musicians play **for tips.** [*why*]
This summer we're going **by car.** [*how*]
She won the game **by two points.** [*to what extent*]

Adverb phrases may come before or after the words they modify, and more than one adverb phrase may modify the same word.

EXAMPLE   **In the first inning** she pitched **with great control.** [*In the first inning* tells *when* she pitched, and *with great control* tells *how* she pitched.]

EXERCISE 2   Identifying Adverb Phrases

Identify each adverb phrase in the following sentences. Then give the word it modifies and the part of speech of that word.

[1] On Friday, Dad and I were alarmed by eerie sounds that came from the abandoned house next door. [2] We searched inside the house from the attic to the basement. [3] In the basement we found two stray kittens. [4] They were crying for food. [5] The noises we'd heard had been made by them. [6] I found an empty box in the corner and gently placed the kittens in it. [7] They seemed happy

ANSWERS
Exercise 2

1. On Friday—were alarmed—verb; by eerie sounds—were alarmed—verb; from the abandoned house next door—came—verb

2. inside the house—searched—verb; from the attic—searched—verb; to the basement—searched—verb

3. In the basement—found—verb

4. for food—were crying—verb

5. by them—had been made—verb

6. in the corner—found—verb; in it—placed—verb

7. with their temporary home—happy—adjective

8. to our house—took—verb

9. with an old towel—lined—verb; in the kitchen—set—verb

10. from our house—come—verb; at all hours—come—verb

576

REVIEW A

OBJECTIVES

- To complete sentences by adding adverb or adjective phrases
- To classify, as adjective or adverb phrases, the prepositional phrases used to complete sentences

with their temporary home. [8] Then we took the kittens back to our house. [9] We lined the box with an old towel and set it in the kitchen. [10] Now the eerie sounds come from our house at all hours of the night and day.

REVIEW A Completing Sentences by Inserting Prepositional Phrases

Provide a prepositional phrase for the blank in each sentence. After the sentence, identify each phrase as an *adjective phrase* or an *adverb phrase*.

EXAMPLE **1.** ____ Mrs. Bowen reads the newspaper.
     1. *In the evening Mrs. Bowen reads the newspaper.—adverb phrase*

1. ____ the children played hopscotch.
2. I saw a spider ____.
3. We planned a drive ____.
4. Her team played ____.
5. The sky divers jumped fearlessly ____.
6. Hundreds ____ stared.
7. ____ the cyclists unpacked their lunch.
8. There ____ winds a narrow road.
9. This movie will be playing ____.
10. ____ the dancers swayed with the music.

EXERCISE 3 Using Prepositional Phrases

You are the guest director for an episode of *The Cosby Show*. It's your chance to tell Bill Cosby and the other

ANSWERS
Review A

Answers may vary. Here are some possibilities:

1. During recess—adverb phrase; For fun—adverb phrase
2. with yellow spots—adjective phrase; in science class—adverb phrase
3. for Saturday—adverb phrase; along the riverfront—adjective phrase
4. by the rules—adverb phrase; after school—adverb phrase
5. out of the plane—adverb phrase; toward the earth—adverb phrase
6. of people—adjective phrase; within view—adjective phrase
7. On the picnic tables—adverb phrase; Without a word—adverb phrase
8. along the lake—adverb phrase; behind the barn—adverb phrase
9. for two weeks—adverb phrase; at the Cinema 8—adverb phrase
10. Around the dance floor—adverb phrase; During the waltz—adverb phrase

ANSWERS
Exercise 3

Responses will vary, but all responses should relate to the scene shown and should include at least two adjective phrases and three adverb phrases.

577

WRITING APPLICATION

OBJECTIVE

• To write directions that use prepositional phrases

578 *The Phrase*

actors in his television family what to do. Write five sentences giving directions for what should happen next in the scene on the previous page. If you are unfamiliar with *The Cosby Show,* imagine that these actors are characters in one of your favorite TV shows. Make up names and roles for them. In your sentences, use at least two adjective phrases and three adverb phrases, and underline each of these phrases.

EXAMPLE **1.** *Theo should run into the kitchen and start stacking the dishes in the sink.*

WRITING APPLICATION

Using Prepositional Phrases to Write Clear Directions

It's useful to be able to explain how to do something. By giving readers a detailed and accurate explanation, you help them duplicate your method and results. Information given in prepositional phrases can make your instructions clearer and more helpful.

HELPFUL   To set the dye, rinse your new red shirt thoroughly.
MORE HELPFUL   To set the dye, rinse your new red shirt thoroughly in a basin of cool water with one quarter cup vinegar.

▶ **WRITING ACTIVITY**
A friend has asked you to explain how to perform a useful task that you are good at. Write a paragraph explaining exactly how to accomplish the task. Use at least five prepositional phrases in explaining the process.

⊕ **Prewriting** First, think of something that you know how to do and can explain. Examples are how to change a tire, how to make gift-wrapping paper, and how to serve a tennis ball. When you have chosen a topic, make a simple outline of the necessary steps in the process.

WRITING APPLICATION
The writing assignment offers students a chance to share their knowledge of performing a useful task while learning the importance of clear directions. It also gives practice in sequencing.

CRITICAL THINKING
Analysis. Remind students that they will have to analyze their intended audiences when writing directions. For instance, if the directions are about how to change a tire, they cannot assume that the reader is familiar with lug nuts, and they will need to define the term to help the reader understand.

PREWRITING
To help your students get started, try brainstorming topics together and write these on the chalkboard. Then, think of as many prepositional phrases as possible that relate to a chosen topic. A good subject to use is preparing a favorite food. For example, some phrases that might accompany making lasagna would be *in the water, on the noodles,* and *under the mushrooms.*

578

LESSON 3 *(pp. 579–584)*

THE PARTICIPLE AND PARTICIPIAL PHRASE Rules 17f, 17g

OBJECTIVES

- To identify present and past participles and the words they modify
- To revise sentences by adding participles
- To identify participial phrases and the words they modify

Verbals and Verbal Phrases **579**

17f

GRAMMAR

 Writing   Remember to refer frequently to your outline as you write your first draft.

 **Evaluating and Revising**   Read your directions to a classmate to find out if the information is clear and detailed enough. Revise any steps that your listener finds confusing. Be sure that you have used a combination of adverb and adjective phrases in your directions.

Proofreading and Publishing   Read your directions carefully, step by step. Pay special attention to the correct placement of prepositional phrases and to the clear use of verb tenses to show when each step should occur. Members of your class may want to share their knowledge and abilities by putting together a how-to book to share with other students in your school.

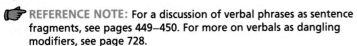

Verbals and Verbal Phrases

Verbals are forms of verbs that are used as adjectives, nouns, or adverbs. They may be modified by adverbs and adjectives and may have complements.

The three kinds of verbals are *participles*, *gerunds*, and *infinitives*.

☞ **REFERENCE NOTE:** For a discussion of verbal phrases as sentence fragments, see pages 449–450. For more on verbals as dangling modifiers, see page 728.

The Participle

17f.   A *participle* is a verb form that can be used as an adjective.

EXAMPLES   **The simmering soup smelled delicious.** [*Simmering*, formed from the verb *simmer*, modifies the noun *soup*.]

GRAMMAR

 TECHNOLOGY TIP
   If available, have students use a computer to write the paragraph. After a classmate evaluates the work, as described in the **Writing Activity,** students might identify all the prepositional phrases by making them either italic or boldfaced. This will make your assessment of the assignment less time-consuming, and it will show that students can identify prepositional phrases.

PROGRAM MANAGER

THE PARTICIPLE AND PARTICIPIAL PHRASE

- **Independent Practice/ Reteaching** For instruction and exercises, see **Participles and Participial Phrases** in *Language Skills Practice and Assessment*, p. 52.

- **Computer Guided Instruction** For additional instruction and practice with participles and participial phrases, see **Lesson 20** in *Language Workshop CD-ROM.*

- **Practice** To help less-advanced students with additional instruction and practice with participles and participial phrases, see **Chapter 12** in *English Workshop, Fourth Course,* pp. 155–156.

579

QUICK REMINDER

Write the following pair of sentences on the chalkboard:

1. The roses were blooming and looked beautiful.

2. The blooming roses looked beautiful.

Ask students how the use of *blooming* differs in the two sentences. [In the first sentence, it acts as a verb; in the second, it acts as an adjective.] Challenge the class to create another pair of sentences that illustrates this difference.

MEETING *individual* NEEDS

LEP/ESL

General Strategies. Students often have problems using participles ending in *–ing* and *–ed* as adjectives, especially those formed from the emotive verbs such as *amuse, bother, interest,* or *surprise.* This results in sentences such as "I am interesting in computers." Tell students that the *–ed* form acts as a verb, as in "I am interested in computers." The *–ing* form acts as an adjective, as in "Computers are interesting." You may want to follow up with a cloze passage where students can choose the *–ed* or the *–ing* form.

LESS-ADVANCED STUDENTS

Verbals and verbal phrases may be too difficult for some students. To give students extra practice with participles, hand out pages from a newspaper and have students circle the participles on the pages. Ask students to identify the participles and have them draw a box around the modified words.

A **chipped** fingernail can be annoying. [*Chipped,* formed from the verb *chip,* modifies the noun *fingernail.*]

There are two kinds of participles: *present participles* and *past participles.*

(1) *Present participles* end in *–ing.*

EXAMPLES   The **smiling** graduates posed for the photographer. [The present participle *smiling* modifies the noun *graduates.*]

Checking the weather forecast, the captain changed course. [The present participle *checking* modifies the noun *captain.*]

A present participle can't be used alone as a verb, but it can be combined with a helping verb to form a verb phrase.

EXAMPLES   The graduates **were smiling.**

The captain **is checking** the weather forecast.

When a present participle is used in a verb phrase, it is part of the verb and is not a verbal used as an adjective.

(2) Most *past participles* end in *–d* or *–ed.* A few are formed irregularly.

EXAMPLES   **Discovered** by the guard, the **startled** burglar was led away. [The past participles *discovered* and *startled* modify the noun *burglar.*]

Hidden under the front porch, the toy truck was safely out of the rain. [The past participle *hidden* modifies the noun *truck.*]

Like a present participle, a past participle can be part of a verb phrase. When used in a verb phrase, a past participle is part of the verb and is not a verbal used as an adjective.

EXAMPLES   The burglar **was startled** when he **was discovered** by the guard.

Why **has** Jonathan **hidden** his toy truck under the front porch?

☞ REFERENCE NOTE: For more on verb phrases, see pages 527 and 548.

> EXERCISE 4   **Identifying Participles**

Identify the <u>present participles</u> and <u>past participles</u> used as adjectives in the following sentences. (Some sentences contain more than one participle.) Give the (noun or pronoun each participle modifies.) Remember not to confuse participles used as verbals with participles used as part of a verb phrase.

EXAMPLE   **1.** We have been studying one of the most feared animals in the sea—the killer whale.
1. *feared—animals*

1. (Killer whales,) long <u>known</u> as wolves of the sea, are not nearly as vicious as many people have thought.
2. <u>Seeking</u> to test the <u>supposedly ferocious</u> nature of the killer whale, (scientists) studied the whales' behavior.
3. After extensive study, scientists discovered that there is no <u>proven</u> (case) of an attack on a human by a killer whale.
4. In fact, (scientists) <u>working</u> with killer whales have confirmed that their charges are intelligent and can be quite gentle.
5. <u>Gathered</u> together in Johnstone Strait, a narrow channel between Vancouver Island and British Columbia in Canada, (killer whales) spend the summer and fall in large family groups.
6. <u>Choosing</u> this spot to observe the mammals, (researchers) were able to identify more than one hundred whales.
7. The (team) of scientists, <u>noting</u> the unique shape of each whale's dorsal fin, named each whale in order to keep more accurate records.
8. <u>Impressed</u> by the long life span of killer whales, (scientists) have estimated that males may live fifty years and females may survive a century.
9. <u>Cruising</u> in (groups) <u>called</u> pods, (killer whales) are highly social animals.
10. During the summer and fall in Johnstone Strait, many (pods) gather, <u>splashing</u> and <u>playing</u> in "superpods."

GRAMMAR

![icon] **COMMON ERROR**
Problem. Misplaced modifiers, or dangling participles, as they are also called, often appear in writing.

Solution. Suggest that students circle the modified word and place the participial phrase next to it. They can then break down these sentences and ask questions such as "What word does this phrase describe?"

![icon] **A DIFFERENT APPROACH**
An oral game can reinforce knowledge of participles and give students practice in speaking before the class in an informal atmosphere. Divide the class into two teams and have a person on each team keep score. Name a verb and specify whether the first player should use the verb in a sentence as a participle used as an adjective or as a participle in a verb phrase. Next, continue with a player from the opposing team. Teams score one point for each correct sentence.

GRAMMAR

EXERCISE 5   **Revising Sentences by Adding Participles**

Each of the following sentences has a participle in parentheses after it. Revise each sentence by inserting the participle next to the noun it best modifies.

EXAMPLE   1. We collected funds for the restoration of the building. (*damaged*)

   1. *We collected funds for the restoration of the damaged building.*

1. The∧space shuttle was greeted with loud cheers. (*returning*)
2. The∧committee selected three television shows for their educational value. (*nominating*)
3. My sister was in the kitchen and did not hear the ∧doorbell. (*ringing*)
4. The carpenter is supposed to show us how to fix this∧chair. (*broken*)
5. In 1949, Luis Muñoz Marín became Puerto Rico's first∧governor. (*elected*)
6. The∧stream crosses the farmer's land at three places. (*winding*)
7. We handed the∧envelope to the mail carrier. (*crumpled*)
8. This∧book includes many interesting facts about dinosaurs. (*illustrated*)
9. The∧Douglas fir behind our house has become a haven for several small creatures. (*fallen*)
10. The∧plane narrowly missed a radio antenna. (*circling*)

The Participial Phrase

 17g.   A *participial phrase* consists of a participle and any complements or modifiers it may have. The entire participial phrase acts as an adjective.

In each of the following sentences, an arrow connects the participial phrase with the noun or pronoun the phrase modifies.

17g

EXAMPLES **Climbing the tree,** the monkey disappeared into the branches. [participle *climbing* with object *tree*]

I heard him **whispering to his friend.** [participle *whispering* with prepositional phrase modifier *to his friend*]

We watched the storm **blowing eastward.** [participle *blowing* with adverb modifier *eastward*]

Voted back into office, the mayor thanked her supporters. [participle *Voted* with adverb modifier *back* and prepositional phrase modifier *into office*]

The concert **scheduled for tomorrow at the park** has been postponed until next week. [participle *scheduled* with two prepositional phrase modifiers: *for tomorrow* and *at the park*]

 REFERENCE NOTE: For information on the correct placement of participial phrases near the words they modify, see pages 465 and 728–730. See pages 797–800 for the punctuation of participial phrases.

▶ EXERCISE 6 **Identifying Participial Phrases**

Identify each <u>participial phrase</u> in the following sentences. Then give the <u>noun or pronoun modified by the phrase</u>.

[1] <u>Hoping to be the first to reach the South Pole</u>, the British <u>explorer</u> Robert Scott (back row, center, in the photograph) took these four men with him on his final dash to

TIMESAVER

Try concentrating on just the second part of **Exercise 6** to make your grading simpler. Have the students list the phrases in one numbered column and the noun or pronoun in a second numbered column. You can scan the noun or pronoun list, since it is easier to check one word.

VISUAL CONNECTIONS

Exploring the Subject. Students might be interested in knowing that it was late in 1910 when Robert Scott first left New Zealand for the South Pole on the ship *Terra Nova*. The party reached Cape Evans on Ross Island, set up headquarters, and started out over the ice in October 1911.

Their bodies were found in a tent, along with all the records and diaries the men had kept. Knowing that he and his men would not survive the journey, Scott ended his journal with an appeal for help for his family and for the families of his companions.

Ideas for Writing. You may wish to use this photograph to inspire a research project, perhaps in conjunction with a social studies class, in which students research and report on famous explorers or expeditions.

OBJECTIVES
- To identify gerunds and to tell how they are used in a sentence
- To identify participles and the words they modify in a sentence

PROGRAM MANAGER

THE GERUND AND GERUND PHRASE

- **Independent Practice/Reteaching** For instruction and exercises, see **Gerunds and Gerund Phrases** in *Language Skills Practice and Assessment,* p. 53.

- **Computer Guided Instruction** For additional instruction and practice with gerunds and gerund phrases, see **Lesson 20** in *Language Workshop CD-ROM.*

- **Practice** To help less-advanced students with additional instruction and practice with gerunds and gerund phrases, see **Chapter 12** in *English Workshop, Fourth Course,* pp. 157–160.

QUICK REMINDER

Write the following sentences on the chalkboard:

1. Studying will improve your grades.
2. His favorite pastime is running.
3. I loved hearing the concert last night.
4. She relaxed by whistling songs.

Ask students what the marked words have in common. [All are verb forms ending in *–ing* and are used as nouns.] Explain that they have just described a gerund.

584

the pole in November 1911. [2] Leading Scott by sixty miles, however, a Norwegian expedition, commanded by Roald Amundsen, was moving swiftly. [3] Having learned about Amundsen, Scott realized a race to the pole was on. [4] Plagued by bad weather and bad luck, Scott fell farther behind Amundsen. [5] Reaching the pole on January 17, the British found that the Norwegians had already been there. [6] Weakened by scurvy, frostbite, and exhaustion, as is evident in the photograph, the five explorers set out on the eight-hundred-mile journey back to their base ship. [7] One member of the party, overcome by exhaustion and injuries, died before half the journey had been completed. [8] On March 15, another member, leaving the camp at night, walked deliberately to his death in a violent blizzard. [9] Eight months later, a rescue mission, sent to find out what had happened, found the bodies of Scott and his companions. [10] Today, the ill-fated Scott expedition, acclaimed for its heroism, is better known than the successful Amundsen expedition.

The Gerund

17h. A *gerund* is a verb form ending in *–ing* that is used as a noun.

Like nouns, gerunds can be subjects, predicate nominatives, direct objects, or objects of prepositions.

EXAMPLES **Reading** will increase your vocabulary. [subject]
One popular winter sport is **tobogganing.** [predicate nominative]
I enjoyed **seeing** you again. [direct object]
She cleared a path by **shoveling** the snow. [object of a preposition]

▶ EXERCISE 7 **Identifying Gerunds and Participles**

Identify the verbal in each of the following sentences and tell whether it is a gerund or a participle. If the verbal is a gerund, tell how it is used: as *subject, predicate nominative, direct object,* or *object of a preposition.* If the verbal is a participle, tell what word it modifies.

- To write a group story that uses gerund phrases
- To label the use of gerunds in a group story

EXAMPLES
1. Sleeping on the job is foolish.
   1. *Sleeping, gerund—subject*
   2. Let sleeping dogs lie.
   2. *sleeping, participle—dogs*

1. Their <u>giggling</u> annoyed the other viewers. **1.** s.
2. Virginia looks forward to <u>fishing</u>. **2.** o.p.
3. After <u>studying</u>, how do you relax? **3.** o.p.
4. I am reading a <u>fascinating</u> mystery (novel).
5. <u>Making</u> friends in a new school can be difficult. **5.** s.
6. The highlight of the season was <u>watching</u> our team win the regional tournament. **6.** p.n.
7. <u>Spinning</u> one full turn, (she) performed a pirouette.
8. Carlota makes money by <u>walking</u> dogs. **8.** o.p.
9. My grandmother and I enjoy <u>digging</u> for clams. **9.** d.o.
10. <u>Sensing</u> the danger nearby, (he) shouted for help.

The Gerund Phrase

17i. A *gerund phrase* consists of a gerund and any modifiers and complements it may have. The entire gerund phrase acts as a noun.

Because gerunds act as nouns, they may be modified by adjectives and adjective phrases.

EXAMPLE **The sudden shattering of glass** broke the silence. [The article *the*, the adjective *sudden*, and the adjective phrase *of glass* modify the gerund *shattering*. The gerund *shattering* is the subject of the sentence.]

Because gerunds are verb forms, they may also be modified by adverbs and adverb phrases.

EXAMPLE She enjoys **hiking in the mountains occasionally.** [The adverb phrase *in the mountains* and the adverb *occasionally* modify the gerund *hiking*. The gerund *hiking* is the direct object of the verb *enjoys.*]

NOTE: When a noun or pronoun comes before a gerund, it should be in the possessive form.

EXAMPLES **Eli's** dancing won him first prize in the contest.
His dancing has greatly improved since last year.

MEETING *individual* NEEDS

LESS-ADVANCED STUDENTS

You could share with students the following clue for identifying gerunds: If a pronoun can be substituted for the word or phrase in question, the word is a gerund, or the phrase is a gerund phrase.

Write the following sentences on the chalkboard and have students test the clue:

1. *Studying* often makes me hungry.
2. Ana likes *walking in the rain.*
3. *Howling loudly,* the wind frightened me.

The first two sentences contain gerunds because pronouns can be substituted: *It* often makes me hungry; Ana likes *it.* A pronoun cannot be substituted for *howling loudly,* which is a participial phrase.

ADVANCED STUDENTS

For an additional practice exercise in using gerunds, have students identify idiomatic expressions that require gerunds to complete them. Some examples are *look forward to, complain about,* and *interested in.* [One example is "I look forward to eating at the restaurant."] You may want to brainstorm with your class and make a list of the expressions on the chalkboard. Students can then write a specified number of sentences that incorporate these idioms.

Responses will vary. All responses should contain a gerund, and students should be able to tell how each gerund is used.

PROGRAM MANAGER

THE INFINITIVE AND INFINITIVE PHRASE

■ **Independent Practice/ Reteaching** For instruction and exercises, see **Infinitives and Infinitive Phrases** in *Language Skills Practice and Assessment,* p. 54.

■ **Computer Guided Instruction** For additional instruction and practice with infinitives and infinitive phrases, see **Lesson 20** in *Language Workshop CD-ROM.*

■ **Practice** To help less-advanced students with additional instruction and practice with infinitives and infinitive phrases, see **Chapter 12** in *English Workshop, Fourth Course,* pp. 161–162.

QUICK REMINDER

Write the following phrases on the chalkboard and ask the students to tell whether each is a prepositional phrase or an infinitive:

1. to me   [prepositional]
2. to walk   [infinitive]
3. to laugh   [infinitive]
4. to race   [infinitive]
5. to the race   [prepositional]

Explain that *to* followed by a noun or pronoun is a prepositional phrase, and *to* followed by a verb is an infinitive.

 LESSON 5 *(pp. 586–590)*
THE INFINITIVE AND INFINITIVE PHRASE Rules 17j, 17k

OBJECTIVE

• To identify infinitives and infinitive phrases and to classify their uses in sentences

 EXERCISE 8   **Writing Sentences with Gerund Phrases**

Have you ever played Build a Story? The first player writes the story opener, and then the next player adds another sentence. The players take turns adding sentences to make up a story. With a friend or classmate, try your hand at building a story. A special requirement for this version of the game is that each sentence must contain a gerund. Use gerunds as subjects, objects of the verb, predicate nominatives, or objects of prepositions. Be able to tell how each gerund is used. [Note: Make sure that each player goes five rounds.]

EXAMPLES   **Player 1:** *At first we enjoyed walking in the forest. (direct object)*
Player 2: *Seeing the grizzly bear, however, gave us a scare. (subject)*

The Infinitive

17j.   An *infinitive* is a verb form, usually preceded by *to*, that can be used as a noun, an adjective, or an adverb.

INFINITIVES	
USED AS	EXAMPLES
Nouns	**To err** is human. [*To err* is the subject.] His dream is **to travel.** [*To travel* is the predicate nominative.] Betty wants **to act.** [*To act* is the direct object of the verb *wants*.]
Adjectives	The candidate **to believe** is Villegas. [*To believe* modifies the noun *candidate*.] She is the one **to ask.** [*To ask* modifies the pronoun *one*.]
Adverbs	Grandmother has come **to stay.** [*To stay* modifies the verb *has come*.] The favored team was slow **to score.** [*To score* modifies the adjective *slow*.]

NOTE: The word *to* plus a noun or a pronoun (*to bed, to the movies, to her*) is a prepositional phrase, not an infinitive.

GRAMMAR

▶ EXERCISE 9   **Identifying and Classifying Infinitives**

Identify the <u>infinitives</u> in the following sentences and tell how each is used: as *<u>s</u>ubject, <u>p</u>redicate <u>n</u>ominative, <u>d</u>irect <u>o</u>bject, <u>a</u>djective,* or *<u>a</u>dverb.*

1. Do you want <u>to meet</u> at the corner?   **1.** d.o.
2. We are eager <u>to go</u>.   **2.** adv.
3. One way <u>to relax</u> is <u>to listen</u> to classical music.   **3.** adj./p.n.
4. I am ready <u>to leave</u>.   **4.** adv.
5. We are waiting <u>to talk</u> with the principal.   **5.** adv.
6. The soup is still too hot <u>to eat</u>.   **6.** adv.
7. <u>To excel</u>, one must practice.   **7.** adv.
8. This summer she hopes <u>to travel</u> in the West.   **8.** d.o.
9. <u>To hike</u> through the woods is fun.   **9.** s.
10. <u>To forgive</u> is sometimes difficult.   **10.** s.

The Infinitive Phrase

17k.   An *infinitive phrase* consists of an infinitive together with its modifiers and complements. The entire infinitive phrase can be used as a noun, an adjective, or an adverb.

EXAMPLES   **To hit a curve ball solidly** is very difficult. [The infinitive phrase, used as a noun, is the subject of the sentence. The infinitive *to hit* has an object, *ball,* and is modified by the adverb *solidly.*]

She wants **to be a truck driver.** [The infinitive phrase, used as a noun, is the direct object of the verb *wants.* The infinitive *to be* is followed by the predicate nominative *truck driver.*]

It is sometimes difficult **to listen attentively.** [The infinitive phrase, used as an adverb, modifies the adjective *difficult.* The infinitive *to listen* is modified by the adverb *attentively.*]

NOTE: An infinitive may have a subject.

EXAMPLE   I asked **him to come** to my party. [*Him* is the subject of the infinitive *to come.*]

The infinitive, together with its subject, complements, and modifiers, is sometimes called an **infinitive clause.**

GRAMMAR

MEETING *individual* NEEDS

LESS-ADVANCED STUDENTS

To give extra practice identifying how infinitives are used in sentences, give students magazines and have them find five sentences containing infinitives. One infinitive should be used as a subject, one as a predicate nominative, one as a direct object, one as an adjective, and one as an adverb.

Have students take turns putting these sentences on the chalkboard and have other students mark the infinitives and tell how they are used.

COOPERATIVE LEARNING

Have students work in pairs to write ten sentences with infinitive phrases and to identify how each infinitive phrase is used.

The Infinitive Without *to*

Sometimes the *to* that is the sign of the infinitive is omitted in a sentence.

EXAMPLES   Did you watch her (to) **play** volleyball?
He will help us (to) **paddle** the canoe.
We don't dare (to) **go** outside during the storm.

▶ EXERCISE 10   **Identifying and Classifying Infinitive Phrases**

Identify the <u>infinitive phrases</u> in the following sentences and tell how each is used: as *subject*, *predicate <u>n</u>ominative*, *direct <u>o</u>bject*, *<u>adj</u>ective*, or *<u>adv</u>erb*.

1. Our assignment was <u>to read *I Know Why the Caged Bird Sings*</u>.   **1.** p.n.
2. We were asked <u>to examine Maya Angelou's descriptions of her childhood</u>.   **2.** d.o.
3. <u>To grow up in Stamps, Arkansas, in the 1930s</u> was <u>to know great hardship</u>.   **3.** s./p.n.
4. Maya Angelou tried <u>to show the everyday lives of African Americans during the Great Depression</u>.   **4.** d.o.
5. <u>To accomplish this purpose</u> meant including many descriptions; one such passage told about the process for curing pork sausage.   **5.** s.
6. Angelou has an extraordinary ability <u>to capture vivid details in her writing</u>.   **6.** adj.
7. She helps <u>us see her grandmother's store through the eyes of a fascinated child</u>.   **7.** (to) d.o.
8. Angelou was eager <u>to experience life beyond her hometown</u>.   **8.** adv.
9. Her talents and ambition enabled <u>her to gain success as a writer, a dancer, and an actress</u>.   **9.** d.o.
10. <u>To dramatize her African American heritage</u> was a dream she realized by writing a television series.   **10.** s.

▶ REVIEW B   **Identifying Types of Verbals and Verbal Phrases**

Identify the ten <u>verbals or verbal phrases</u> in the following paragraph. Then tell whether each verbal or verbal phrase is a *participle*, a *gerund*, or an *infinitive*.

REVIEWS B and C

OBJECTIVE

• To identify and classify verbals and verbal phrases in a paragraph

EXAMPLE   [1] Looking at these control panels in the flight deck of a jumbo passenger jet, most of us feel completely lost.

1. *Looking at these control panels in the flight deck of a jumbo passenger jet—participle*

[1] Fortunately, there are <u>trained</u> people in the flight deck who know how <u>to use these controls and instruments</u>. [2] <u>Sitting in front of identical control panels</u>, both the captain and the first officer can fly the plane. [3] The captain, who uses the left-hand panel, operates a lever <u>called a yoke</u>, which controls the wing flaps and helps in <u>steering the plane</u>. [4] <u>Operating the brake panels</u> is another one of the captain's jobs. [5] To the captain's right is the first officer, whose job is <u>to help the captain</u>. [6] The throttle, which governs the engines' ability <u>to move the plane forward</u>, is located between the captain and the first officer. [7] Some of the <u>bewildering</u> instruments that you see are parts of the plane's navigation, autopilot, and communication systems. [8] At another station in the flight deck, the flight engineer monitors gauges and operates switches <u>to control the plane's generators and the pressure and temperature in the cabin</u>.

1. part./inf.
2. part.
3. part./ger.
4. ger.
5. inf.
6. inf.
7. part.
8. inf.

GRAMMAR

GRAMMAR

▶ REVIEW C   **Identifying Verbal Phrases**

Identify the twenty <u>verbal phrases</u> in the following paragraph. Then, tell what kind each phrase is: *participial, gerund,* or *infinitive.*

APPOSITIVES AND APPOSITIVE PHRASES Rules 17l, 17m

OBJECTIVES

- To identify appositives and appositive phrases and the words they identify or explain
- To write a news article, using appositives and appositive phrases

---

1. ger.
2. inf./ part.
3. ger./ ger.
4. ger./ ger./part.
5. inf./inf./ ger.
6. inf./inf./ inf./inf.
7. inf./ ger./ger.
8. ger./inf.

[1] <u>Finding a summer job</u> can be a difficult task. [2] The first step is <u>to scan the classified ads listed</u> in <u>your local newspaper</u>. [3] After <u>discovering available opportunities</u>, you can embark on the second step, which is <u>matching your skills with the requirements of a specific job</u>. [4] In most cases you can then contact a prospective employer by <u>making a phone call</u> or by <u>writing a letter</u> <u>requesting an interview</u>. [5] If you are asked <u>to interview for a job</u>, be sure <u>to take care</u> in <u>preparing for the interview</u>. [6] <u>To make a good impression</u>, be sure <u>to arrive on time</u>, <u>to dress neatly</u>, and <u>to speak courteously</u>. [7] Remember <u>to avoid such nervous habits</u> as constantly <u>checking your watch</u> or <u>shuffling your feet</u>. [8] By <u>presenting yourself as calm, confident, and courteous</u>, you may hear the magic words "We'd like you <u>to work for us</u>."

Appositives and Appositive Phrases

17l. An *appositive* is a noun or pronoun placed beside another noun or pronoun to identify or explain it.

EXAMPLES My cousin **Bryan** is my best friend. [The noun *Bryan* is an appositive that identifies the noun *cousin.*]
Soledad, an excellent **driver,** has never had an accident. [The noun *driver* is an appositive that explains the noun *Soledad.*]

17m. An *appositive phrase* is made up of an appositive and its modifiers.

EXAMPLES We saw three birds, **two robins and a cardinal.**
His grandparents, **the Vescuzos,** live on Miller Road, **a wide street lined with beech trees.**

An appositive or appositive phrase usually follows the noun or pronoun it refers to. Sometimes, though, it comes before the noun or pronoun.

EXAMPLE **A diligent and quick-witted student,** Mark always gets good grades.

PROGRAM MANAGER

APPOSITIVES AND APPOSITIVE PHRASES

- **Independent Practice/ Reteaching** For instruction and exercises, see **Appositives and Appositive Phrases** in *Language Skills Practice and Assessment,* p. 55.

- **Computer Guided Instruction** For additional instruction and practice with appositives and appositive phrases, see **Lesson 21** in *Language Workshop CD-ROM.*

- **Practice** To help less-advanced students with additional instruction and practice with appositives and appositive phrases, see **Chapter 12** in *English Workshop, Fourth Course,* pp. 165–166.

QUICK REMINDER

Write the following sentences on the chalkboard and ask students to name the noun that identifies or explains the subject:

1. My brother Ed loves track meets. [Ed]
2. Chris, a speedy runner, wins many races. [runner]
3. A dutiful and disciplined athlete, Mary trains three hours daily. [athlete]

Explain that these nouns are appositives and that an appositive usually comes after the word it modifies, but sometimes, as in the third sentence, precedes it.

Appositives and appositive phrases are usually set off by commas unless the appositive is a single word closely related to the preceding noun or pronoun. Commas are always used with appositives that refer to proper nouns.

EXAMPLES   My sister **Karen** is a tennis player.
Dr. Rosen, **our family dentist,** is a marathon runner.

EXERCISE 11   **Identifying Appositives and Appositive Phrases**

Identify the <u>appositives and appositive phrases</u> in each of the following sentences. Be prepared to tell which <u>word each one identifies or explains</u>.

1. <u>Soccer</u>, <u>my favorite sport</u>, is very popular in South America and Europe.
2. The internationally famous soccer <u>star</u> <u>Pelé</u> is from Brazil.
3. <u>Hausa</u>, <u>a Sudanese language</u>, is widely used in western Africa.
4. Have you met my <u>teacher</u> <u>Mr. Zolo</u>?
5. My youngest <u>sister</u>, <u>Susan</u>, speaks fluent Spanish.

PICTURE THIS

You are looking at some real winners. As a reporter for the local newspaper, you just saw these contestants win

MEETING *individual* NEEDS

GRAMMAR

LEP/ESL

General Strategies. Students should not have many problems with appositives, but for additional practice you may want to find a newspaper article that uses appositives. Have students identify the appositives and the words or phrases defined by them. After doing this activity, students might be more confident and better prepared to write an article on their own, as required in the **Picture This** assignment.

PICTURE THIS

Students might need to consult reference books about dogs. They might also need to read about the basic temperament of each breed, in order to discuss the dogs' personalities. You may want to write *who, what, when, where, why,* and *how* on the chalkboard and remind students that these questions are always answered in a well-written news article.

Students can read their news articles aloud to the class, and the class can listen for the appositives used.

REVIEW D

OBJECTIVE

- To identify participial, gerund, infinitive, and appositive phrases in a paragraph

at the annual dog show. Now you have to write a short news article on the show. Tell about the winners—their names, their breeds, their owners, their personalities. Describe how the winners were chosen, and tell why each winner was judged to be the best in its class. You may also want to describe other features of the show, such as the setting, the size and enthusiasm of the crowd, or the owners' preshow grooming of the contestants. In your article, use at least five appositives and appositive phrases. Newspaper articles usually present the most important information first, so be sure to include the *who, what, when,* and *where* of the dog show in the beginning of your article.

Subject: a dog show
Audience: local newspaper readers
Purpose: to inform

REVIEW D **Identifying Verbal and Appositive Phrases**

The following paragraph contains ten <u>phrases</u>. Identify each phrase as a *participial phrase*, a *gerund phrase*, an *infinitive phrase*, or an *appositive phrase*.

1. app.
2. part.
3. app.
4. inf./ app./ part.
5. ger.
6. inf.
7. ger./ ger.

[1] The Brooklyn Bridge, <u>a remarkable feat of design</u>, spans the East River in New York City. [2] <u>Linking the boroughs of Brooklyn and Manhattan</u>, it was once the longest suspension bridge in the world. [3] Most of the pedestrians who cross the bridge are impressed by the grandeur of its graceful cables—<u>a sensation the postcard on the next page cannot fully evoke</u>. [4] <u>To support the twin towers on the bridge</u>, the brilliant John A. Roebling, <u>its engineer</u>, designed airtight caissons <u>filled with concrete</u>. [5] <u>Working underwater on the caissons</u> was painstakingly slow and extremely dangerous. [6] The workers also faced great danger when they had <u>to spin the cables from one side of the river to the other</u>. [7] Because of these hazards, the bridge is remembered not only for <u>being a masterpiece of engineering</u> but also for <u>having cost the lives of many of its builders</u>.

REVIEW: POSTTESTS 1 and 2

OBJECTIVES

- To identify prepositional, participial, gerund, infinitive, and appositive phrases in a paragraph
- To write sentences, using and labeling prepositional, participial, gerund, infinitive, and appositive phrases

VISUAL CONNECTIONS

Exploring the Subject. Students might be interested in knowing that the Brooklyn Bridge, completed in 1883, is 1,595 feet long. It was under construction for fourteen years and cost fifteen million dollars.

Review: Posttest 1

Identifying Prepositional, Verbal, and Appositive Phrases

Identify each italicized phrase in the following paragraphs as a <u>prepositional phrase</u>, a <u>participial phrase</u>, a <u>gerund phrase</u>, an <u>infinitive phrase</u>, or an <u>appositive phrase</u>.

EXAMPLE   An interesting profession [1] *to consider as a career* is
[2] *practicing law.*
1. *to consider as a career—inf.*
2. *practicing law—ger.*

Susana, [1] *our next-door neighbor,* wanted [2] *to become an attorney.* After she earned a degree [3] *from a four-year college,* she took the Law School Admissions Test [4] *to gain acceptance at an approved law school.* [5] *Having completed three full years of law school,* Susana was then awarded a J.D. degree. Before [6] *practicing law,* however, she took an exam [7] *required by the state board of bar examiners.* Only after [8] *passing this exam* was she ready [9] *to be admitted to the bar* and [10] *to practice law.*

[11] *Working as an attorney,* Susana provides service and advice [12] *relating to legal rights.* Although some attorneys try hard [13] *to keep cases out of court,* Susana enjoys the challenge [14] *of presenting cases to a jury.* [15] *Representing a*

1. app.
2. inf.
3. prep.
4. inf.
5. part.
6. ger.
7. part.
8. ger.
9. inf.   10. inf.
11. part.
12. part.
13. inf.
14. prep.
15. ger.

INTEGRATING THE LANGUAGE ARTS

Grammar and Writing. To help prepare students for **Review: Posttests 1 and 2,** have them write five sentences using the following kinds of phrases:

1. prepositional phrase used as an adjective
2. prepositional phrase used as an adverb
3. participial phrase
4. gerund phrase
5. appositive phrase

Have those students who finish first write their sentences on the chalkboard while the other students are finishing. Then, have students identify and classify their phrases.

594 *The Phrase*

16. prep.

17. ger.   *client in court*, however, is only part [16] *of Susana's job.* She
18. inf.   devotes hours to [17] *gathering enough evidence* [18] *to defend a*
19. prep.   *client.* She also spends time [19] *on research* and is required
20. inf.   [20] *to write numerous reports.*

ANSWERS

Review: Posttest 2

Responses will vary. However, all responses should contain the requested prepositional or verbal phrase.

Review: Posttest 2

Writing Sentences with Phrases

Write ten sentences, following the directions below for each sentence. Underline the phrase in each sentence.

EXAMPLE   **1.** Use *to get there from here* as an infinitive phrase acting as an adjective.
            1. *What is the fastest way to get there from here?*

1. Use *in the garage* as an adjective phrase.
2. Use *for our English class* as an adverb phrase.
3. Use *from an encyclopedia* as an adverb phrase.
4. Use *by train* as an adverb phrase.
5. Use *walking by the lake* as a participial phrase.
6. Use *playing the piano* as a gerund phrase that is the subject of the sentence.
7. Use *to hit a home run* as an infinitive phrase that is the direct object of the verb.
8. Use *to find the answer to that question* as an infinitive phrase acting as an adverb.
9. Use *the new student in our class* as an appositive phrase.
10. Use *my favorite writer* as an appositive phrase.

DIAGNOSTIC TEST

OBJECTIVES

- To identify independent and subordinate clauses
- To classify sentences according to structure

PROGRAM MANAGER

FOR THE WHOLE CHAPTER

- **Review** For exercises on chapter concepts, see **Review Form A** and **Review Form B** in *Language Skills Practice and Assessment,* pp. 69–72.

- **Assessment** For additional testing, see **Grammar Pretests** and **Grammar Mastery Tests** in *Language Skills Practice and Assessment,* pp. 1–8 and pp. 76–81.

18 THE CLAUSE

Independent and Subordinate Clauses

CHAPTER OVERVIEW

Students will be better motivated to study clauses if they understand why they are studying the clauses and how the clauses relate to writing. Explain that an understanding of clauses is essential to writing complete, correctly punctuated sentences.

Instead of assigning the entire chapter, you may want to refer to specific sections in regard to problems, questions about writing, or ways of punctuating sentences or clauses. This chapter may be useful when students are revising and proofreading the writing assignments.

You may decide that some of the individualized activities will be of interest to the entire class and that your less-advanced students can learn from group participation with advanced students.

Diagnostic Test

A. Identifying and Classifying Clauses

Identify the italicized clause in each of the following sentences as an *independent clause* or a *subordinate clause*. Also, identify each subordinate clause as an *adjective clause,* an *adverb clause,* or a *noun clause.*

EXAMPLES   **1.** A soccer field measures 100–130 yards by 50–100 yards, and *the netted goals at each end of the field are 8 yards wide by 8 feet high.*
          1. *independent clause*

          2. Soccer, *which is the national sport of many European and Latin American countries,* has enjoyed only limited success in the United States.
          2. *subordinate clause—adjective clause*

595

USING THE DIAGNOSTIC TEST

The **Diagnostic Test** contains two parts: **Part A** asks students to identify clauses as independent or subordinate and then to determine how subordinate clauses are used; **Part B** requires students to classify sentences according to structure. To prevent needless reteaching, you may want to analyze the results of students' tests. For example, you may want to assign the section on adjective clauses to students who miss items 1, 3, and 6. If students miss items 4, 5, and 8, assign adverb clauses; if they miss 7 and 10, assign noun clauses.

After students have classified the sentences in **Part B**, help them to understand the importance of sentence variety by discussing whether the paragraph would have been as effective without a variety of sentence types.

596 *The Clause*

1. adj. cl.
1. During a career *that spanned twenty years*, Pelé was probably the most popular athlete in the world.
2. He was named Edson Arantes do Nascimento, but *hardly anyone recognizes that name*.

3. adj. cl.
3. Soccer fans the world over, however, knew Pelé, *who was considered the world's best soccer player*.

4. adv. cl.
4. *While he was still a teenager*, he led his Brazilian teammates to the first of their three World Cup titles.

5. adv. cl.
5. *Whenever he played*, his skill and agility awed fans.

6. adj. cl.
6. Once, he juggled the ball on his foot for fifty yards, eluding four opponents *who were trying to take the ball away from him*.

7. n. cl.
7. *That he soon became a superstar* is not surprising.

8. adv. cl.
8. *Even though soccer has never become as popular as baseball or football in the United States*, Pelé managed to spark considerable interest in the game.
9. After he signed with the New York Cosmos, *people flocked to the stands to watch him play*.

10. n. cl.
10. They soon recognized *that Pelé was an entertainer as well as an athlete*.

B. Classifying Sentences According to Structure

Classify each sentence in the following paragraph as *simple*, *compound*, *complex*, or *compound-complex*.

11. cx.
12. simp.
13. cx.
14. cd.
15. cd.-cx.
16. cx.
17. cd.

[11] Because tennis is so physically demanding, it's a sport in which strong young players can really shine. [12] Steffi Graf of Germany began playing tennis professionally at the age of thirteen. [13] Graf was still a teenager when she won the four Grand Slam tennis championships and an Olympic gold medal in 1988. [14] Another Olympic winner, Zina Garrison, began playing tennis in Houston at the age of ten, and at seventeen, she won the junior singles titles at Wimbledon and the U.S. Open. [15] The German tennis star Boris Becker won his first tournament competitions at the age of nine, but he didn't become a professional player until he graduated from high school. [16] Jennifer Capriati, who was born on Long Island, New York, won many national and international tennis competitions and had earned nearly eighty thousand dollars by the age of fourteen. [17] Another American player, Andre

OBJECTIVES

- To identify independent clauses and subordinate clauses
- To identify subjects, verbs, and complements in subordinate clauses

18. cx. **19.** cd.-cx.

Agassi, started serving on a tennis court at the age of two, and he, too, excelled at an early age. **[18]** Agassi won six major tournaments when he was only eighteen. **[19]** Tracy Austin and Chris Evert also started young; in fact, Tracy Austin was only sixteen years old when she made headlines by winning the women's title at the U.S. Open. **[20]** In tennis, young players really can become big winners.

20. simp.

Kinds of Clauses

18a. A *clause* is a group of words that contains a verb and its subject and is used as part of a sentence.

Every clause has a subject and a verb, but not all clauses express a complete thought. Those that do are called *independent clauses*. Those that do not make complete sense by themselves are called *subordinate clauses*.

Independent Clauses

18b. An *independent* (or *main*) *clause* expresses a complete thought and can stand by itself as a sentence.

EXAMPLES The outfielders were missing easy fly balls.
The infielders were throwing wildly.

Independent clauses that express related ideas can be joined together in a single sentence. Often, the clauses are linked by one of the coordinating conjunctions (*and, but, or, nor, for, so, yet*).

EXAMPLE The outfielders were missing easy fly balls, **and** the infielders were throwing wildly.

Independent clauses can also be joined by a semicolon.

EXAMPLE The outfielders were missing easy fly balls**;** the infielders were throwing wildly.

PROGRAM MANAGER

KINDS OF CLAUSES

- **Independent Practice/ Reteaching** For instruction and exercises, see **Independent and Subordinate Clauses** and **Complements and Modifiers in Clauses** in *Language Skills Practice and Assessment*, pp. 63–64.

- **Computer Guided Instruction** For additional instruction and practice with independent and subordinate clauses and complements and modifiers in clauses, see **Lesson 22** in *Language Workshop CD-ROM.*

- **Practice** To help less-advanced students with additional instruction and practice with independent and subordinate clauses, see **Chapter 13** in *English Workshop, Fourth Course*, pp. 169–170.

QUICK REMINDER

Write the following clauses on the chalkboard:

1. Alberto got an A on his examination.
2. Because he had studied carefully.

Ask students which clause makes sense by itself [the first]. Explain that this clause is independent because it does not depend on another clause to complete it. Explain also that the second clause is subordinate because it does not express a complete thought and cannot stand alone.

GRAMMAR

LEP/ESL

General Strategies. Describing a subordinate clause by using expressions such as "does not express a complete thought and cannot stand alone" will not help your English-language learners. It is better to describe this clause structurally as having a subject and a verb as well as a subordinating conjunction that links it to another clause.

LEARNING STYLES

Auditory Learners. To help auditory learners understand how independent and subordinate clauses function in writing, read aloud the paragraph from **Exercise 1.** As you read, emphasize each italicized clause. Then, ask students whether the clause could stand alone as a complete thought.

COMMON ERROR

Problem. Students often have trouble punctuating two independent clauses within the same sentence.

Solution. Ask students to study carefully the correct combinations of independent clauses shown on pp. 597–598. Summarize the three methods of linking independent clauses: a comma and a coordinating conjunction, a semicolon, or a semicolon and a conjunctive adverb.

GRAMMAR

A conjunctive adverb can be used after the semicolon to express the relationship between the independent clauses.

EXAMPLE The outfielders were missing easy fly balls; **moreover,** the infielders were throwing wildly.

☞ REFERENCE NOTE: See pages 816–819 for more information on using semicolons between independent clauses.

Subordinate Clauses

18c. A *subordinate* (or *dependent*) *clause* does not express a complete thought and cannot stand alone.

Subordinate means "less important." Words such as *who, that, because, if, when, although,* and *since* signal that the clause they introduce is subordinate and must be joined to an independent clause to make a complete sentence.

SUBORDINATE CLAUSES
who spoke to our class yesterday
that many students are eligible for scholarships
because no students have applied for them

SENTENCES
The woman **who spoke to our class yesterday** told us about sources of financial aid for college applicants.
She said **that many students are eligible for scholarships.**
Some scholarships are still available **because no students have applied for them.**

▷ EXERCISE 1 **Identifying Independent and Subordinate Clauses**

For each sentence in the following paragraph, identify the italicized clause as *independent* or *subordinate*.

[1] *Whenever I think of Barbara Jordan,* I remember her as she looks in this picture, delivering the commencement address at my sister's graduation in 1986. [2] In front of a huge audience, *Jordan spoke eloquently about the importance of values in our society*. [3] *Of course, her choice of subject matter*

surprised no one since Jordan had long been known as an important ethical force in American politics. [4] *When Jordan began her public service career in 1966,* she became the first African American woman to serve in the Texas Legislature. [5] In 1972, she won a seat in the U.S. House of Representatives, *where only one other black woman— Shirley Chisholm—had ever been a member*. [6] However, Jordan was still not widely recognized *until she gave the keynote speech at the 1976 Democratic National Convention*. [7] Seen on television by millions of people, *Jordan immediately gained national attention*. [8] Two years later, Jordan decided *that she would retire from national politics.* [9] *After she returned to Texas in 1978,* Jordan taught at the University of Texas at Austin. [10] From 1991 until her death in 1996, she served on various government committees and used *what she had learned in her many years of public service* to fight corruption in politics.

Complements and Modifiers in Subordinate Clauses

A subordinate clause may contain complements and modifiers.

EXAMPLES **Since she told us the truth** . . . [*Us* is the indirect object of *told; truth* is the direct object of *told.*]
When I am busy . . . [*Busy* is a predicate adjective modifying *I.*]
After he had cooked for us . . . [*For us* is an adverb phrase modifying *had cooked.*]
The portrait that he painted . . . [*That* is the direct object of *painted.*]
We couldn't tell who they were. [*Who* is a predicate nominative: They were *who.*]

CRITICAL THINKING

Analysis. The paragraph in **Exercise 1** presents both facts and opinions about the life of Barbara Jordan. Explain to students that a fact can be proved true or false, but an opinion cannot be proved. Then, ask students to find five facts and five opinions used in the paragraph. For example, the statement that the photograph was taken when she delivered a commencement address in 1986 is a fact because it can be tested; however, the statement that Jordan's choice of subject matter "surprised no one" is an opinion because the audience's feelings cannot be proved. When students complete their lists, have them compare and discuss their findings. You might use this exercise in conjunction with **Chapter 9.**

VISUAL CONNECTIONS

Ideas for Writing. The paragraph in **Exercise 1** records relevant and interesting facts about the life of Barbara Jordan, who is pictured in the photograph. Have each student select a photograph of a public figure from a current newspaper or magazine and have the student write a paragraph about the person's life. Ask each student to include at least five independent clauses and five subordinate clauses.

PROGRAM MANAGER

THE ADJECTIVE CLAUSE

- **Independent Practice/ Reteaching** For instruction and exercises, see **The Adjective Clause** in *Language Skills Practice and Assessment*, p. 65.

- **Computer Guided Instruction** For additional instruction and practice with the adjective clause, see **Lesson 23** in *Language Workshop CD-ROM*.

- **Practice** To help less-advanced students with additional instruction and practice with the adjective clause, see **Chapter 13** in *English Workshop, Fourth Course*, pp. 171–172.

QUICK REMINDER

Write the following sentences on the chalkboard:

1. The student <u>who wrote the best essay</u> won a $100 prize.

2. The ostrich, <u>which was seven feet tall and quite mean,</u> guarded the car lot.

Ask students whether the underlined clauses are independent or subordinate [subordinate]. Then, ask students to identify the word that each subordinate clause modifies and to explain what the clauses in these sentences have in common. [*Student* and *ostrich* are the modified words. Both clauses are adjective clauses.]

600

THE ADJECTIVE CLAUSE Rule 18d

OBJECTIVES

- To identify adjective clauses and the words they modify
- To identify relative pronouns and relative adverbs

 EXERCISE 2

Identifying Subjects, Verbs, and Complements in Subordinate Clauses

Identify the <u>subject</u> and the <u>verb</u> in each italicized subordinate clause in the following sentences. Then identify any (complements) in the clause as *direct object, predicate nominative,* or *indirect object.*

EXAMPLE **1.** *After he shows us his new boat,* we will go swimming.

1. *he—subject; shows—verb; us—indirect object; boat—direct object*

1. We couldn't see *who had won the* (race)   **1.** d.o.
2. They couldn't tell *(who) the winner was.*   **2.** p.n.   **3.** d.o.
3. She is the celebrity *(whom) we saw at the restaurant.*
4. Look for the mouse *(that) you heard last night.*   **4.** d.o.
5. He spotted a horse *that galloped away.*
6. *After we passed the* (test) we celebrated.   **6.** d.o.
7. Do you know *which country she is from?*
8. *Because you had not given* (us) *the right* (address) we missed the party.   **8.** i.o./d.o.   **9.** d.o.
9. The package will arrive on time *if you ship* (it) *today.*
10. *Until Mike lent* (me) *this* (book) I had never heard of John Steinbeck.   **10.** i.o./d.o.

The Uses of Subordinate Clauses

Subordinate clauses can be used in sentences as either adjectives, adverbs, or nouns.

The Adjective Clause

 18d. An *adjective clause* is a subordinate clause that modifies a noun or a pronoun.

An adjective clause always follows the word it modifies. If the clause is necessary, or *essential*, to the meaning of the sentence, it is not set off with commas. If the clause simply adds information and is *nonessential* to the meaning of the sentence, commas are used to set it off.

EXAMPLES   The novel **that I'm reading now** is about the Irish revolt of 1798. [The clause is necessary to identify the novel, so it is not set off by commas.]

Our town's civic center, **which was renovated last year,** has been declared a landmark. [The clause adds nonessential information, so it is set off by commas.]

☞ REFERENCE NOTE: See pages 797–799, rule 25i, for help in deciding whether a clause is essential or nonessential.

Relative Pronouns

Adjective clauses are usually introduced by *relative pronouns*.

Relative Pronouns				
who	whom	whose	which	that

These pronouns are called *relative pronouns* because they *relate* an adjective clause to the word the clause modifies—the antecedent of the relative pronoun. Each relative pronoun also has a function within the adjective clause.

EXAMPLES   Isabella Baumfree was an abolitionist **who is better known as Sojourner Truth.** [The relative pronoun *who* relates the adjective clause to *abolitionist. Who* also is the subject of the adjective clause.]

She is the person **whom I trust most.** [*Whom* relates the adjective clause to *person. Whom* is also the direct object of the verb *trust* in the adjective clause.]

The topic **about which he is writing** is controversial. [*Which* relates the adjective clause to *topic* and is the object of the preposition *about* in the adjective clause.]

Do you know the name of the group **whose recording is number one on the charts?** [*Whose* relates the adjective clause to *group. Whose* is also a possessive pronoun modifying *recording* in the adjective clause.]

Sometimes the relative pronoun is left out of a sentence. In such cases, the pronoun is understood, and it still has a function in the adjective clause.

GRAMMAR

LESS-ADVANCED STUDENTS

Provide practice for less-advanced students by asking them to fill in the missing adjective clauses in the following sentences:

1. The swimmer (*who*) ____ won the race. [who came from my high school]
2. The dog (*that*) ____ woke up the neighborhood. [that barked so loudly]
3. The singer (*whose*) ____ stayed in our hotel. [whose record was just released]

Students might work together in pairs or in small groups and then share their sentences.

🔶 **COMMON ERROR**

Problem. Students often have trouble punctuating adjective clauses.

Solution. Write the following sentences on the chalkboard:

1. The writer who won the Pulitzer Prize for fiction in 1983 is also a renowned poet.
2. Alice Walker who won the Pulitzer Prize for fiction in 1983 is also a renowned poet.

Ask students which adjective clause should be set off with commas and why. [In the first example, the clause *who won the Pulitzer Prize for fiction in 1983* is necessary to identify the writer, but this clause is simply additional information in the second example and therefore should be set off with commas.]

GRAMMAR

EXAMPLE   **Ms. Chung is the legislator** *[that* or *whom]* **we met.**
[The relative pronoun *that* or *whom* is understood. It relates the adjective clause to *legislator* and is the direct object of the verb *met* in the adjective clause.]

The relative adverbs *where* and *when* are sometimes used to introduce adjective clauses.

EXAMPLES   **Here is the spot** *where* **we will have lunch.**
This is the season *when* **it rains almost every day.**

▶ EXERCISE 3   **Identifying Adjective Clauses**

Identify each <u>adjective clause</u> in the following sentences, and underline the <u>relative pronoun or relative adverb</u> in the clause. Then, tell what word the relative pronoun or relative adverb refers to.

EXAMPLE   **1.** The topic that Melissa chose for her paper was a difficult one.
1. *that Melissa chose for her paper—topic*

1. A speech community is a group of (people) <u>who speak the same language</u>.
2. There are speech (communities) <u>that contain millions of people</u> and (some) <u>that have only a few</u>.
3. The first (language) <u>that you learn</u> is called your native language.
4. (People) <u>who master another language</u> are bilingual.
5. (People) <u>who conduct business internationally</u> often need to know more than one language.
6. (English), (French), and (Spanish), <u>which many diplomats can speak</u>, are among the six official languages of the United Nations.
7. Russian, Chinese, and Arabic are the other three (languages) <u>that are used officially at the UN</u>.
8. (People) <u>for whom language study is important</u> include telephone operators, hotel managers, and police officers.
9. Many tourists each year find themselves in parts of the (world) <u>where they would benefit from knowing the language spoken locally</u>.
10. French, for example, is a (language) <u>that is widely understood in parts of Europe, Africa, and Southeast Asia</u>.

THE ADVERB CLAUSE Rule 18e

OBJECTIVES

- To identify adverb clauses and the subordinating conjunctions that introduce them
- To write sentences with adverb clauses

18e

GRAMMAR

The Adverb Clause

18e. An *adverb clause* is a subordinate clause that modifies a verb, an adjective, or an adverb.

An adverb clause tells

how	when
where	why
to what extent	under what condition

An adverb clause may modify the action of the *main verb* (the verb in the sentence's independent clause).

EXAMPLES   Donna sounds **as if she has caught a cold.** [*As if she has caught a cold* tells how Donna sounds.]
Before we left, we turned off the lights. [*Before we left* tells when we turned off the lights.]
You will see our house **where the road turns right.** [*Where the road turns right* tells where you will see our house.]
As long as he starts early, he will arrive on time. [*As long as he starts early* tells under what condition he will arrive on time.]
Will you move over **so that I can see?** [*So that I can see* tells why I want you to move over.]

☞ REFERENCE NOTE: Introductory adverb clauses are usually set off with commas. See page 801.

An adverb clause may also modify an adjective or an adverb in the independent clause.

EXAMPLES   Your stereo is louder **than it should be.** [The adverb clause modifies the adjective *louder,* telling to what extent the stereo is louder.]
The skates cost less **because we got them on sale.** [The adverb clause modifies the adverb *less,* telling under what condition the skates cost less.]

Subordinating Conjunctions

Adverb clauses are introduced by *subordinating conjunctions.* Unlike relative pronouns, which introduce adjective clauses, subordinating conjunctions do not serve a function in the clause they introduce.

THE ADVERB CLAUSE

- **Independent Practice/ Reteaching** For instruction and exercises, see **The Adverb Clause** in *Language Skills Practice and Assessment,* p. 66.
- **Computer Guided Instruction** For additional instruction and practice with the adverb clause, see **Lesson 23** in *Language Workshop CD-ROM.*
- **Practice** To help less-advanced students with additional instruction and practice with the adverb clause, see **Chapter 13** in *English Workshop, Fourth Course,* pp. 173–174.

QUICK REMINDER

Write the following sentence fragments on the chalkboard:

1. We decided to come home early because . . .
2. Although . . ., he won the race.
3. I will prepare the salad if . . .

Ask students to complete each sentence with an adverb clause. Remind them that the subordinating conjunctions *because, although,* and *if* show relationships between the verbs and adverb clauses.

GRAMMAR

CRITICAL THINKING

Analysis. Students sometimes have trouble analyzing relationships among the ideas presented in written material. This difficulty is particularly apparent when student writers use inappropriate connecting words—*and* for *but* or *since* for *although,* for example. Provide practice with making correct word choices by asking students to insert appropriate subordinating connections in the following sentences:

1. We will not pay the repair bill _____ the television is fixed. [until, unless]
2. _____ it rained, the baseball game was postponed. [Because, Since]
3. Mother served dinner early _____ we could get to the concert on time. [so that, in order that]

ANSWERS

Exercise 5

Answers will vary, but make sure that each first line uses a different subordinating conjunction. Here are some possible answers:

1. Title: "Daniel's Song"
   First line: Until I met you, Daniel, it rained on me every day.

2. Title: "Call Me"
   First line: Unless you call me, I just can't go on.

3. Title: "Student's Song"
   First line: Before I take this little test, I'd like back all the time I killed.

Common Subordinating Conjunctions		
after	before	unless
although	even though	until
as	if	when
as if	in order that	whenever
as long as	since	where
as soon as	so that	wherever
as though	than	whether
because	though	while

NOTE: Many of the words in this list can be used as other parts of speech, such as adverbs and prepositions.

EXERCISE 4   Identifying Adverb Clauses and Subordinating Conjunctions

Identify the <u>adverb clause</u> in each sentence of the following paragraph, and circle the (subordinating conjunction).

[1] (Because) the house had been vacant for so long, we had to clean up the lawn and gardens. [2] The grass looked (as if) it hadn't been cut in months. [3] Ruth began mowing the lawn (while) Lou and I weeded the flower beds. [4] We had to borrow some tools (because) the weeds were so thick. [5] We hadn't been able to cut through the heavy undergrowth (until) we started using a machete. [6] (Before) we pulled out the weeds, we couldn't even see the roses. [7] We stacked the debris in a mound (so that) it could be hauled away later. [8] (After) Ruth had mowed the lawn, she was exhausted. [9] We all stretched out in the shade (when) we stopped for a rest. [10] Long hours in the sun had made us feel (as though) the day would never end.

EXERCISE 5   Writing Sentences with Adverb Clauses

Have you written any good songs lately? What? You say you don't write songs! Then here's your chance to give it a try. You don't have to write the whole song. Instead, think of ten song titles and a first line for each song. In each first line, use a different subordinating conjunction from the list given at the top of this page.

REVIEW A

OBJECTIVE

- To identify subordinate clauses and to classify them as adjective or adverb clauses

EXAMPLE   Title: *Baby Sitters' Blues*
First Line: *If only you'd eat your carrots, I'd let you watch TV.*

▶ REVIEW A   **Identifying Adjective and Adverb Clauses**

Identify the subordinate clauses in the following paragraph. Then, tell whether each is an *adjective clause* or an *adverb clause*.

[1] In 1978, the aeronauts Ben Abruzzo, Max Anderson, and Larry Newman, <u>whose home was Albuquerque, New Mexico</u>, became the first people to pilot a balloon across the Atlantic Ocean. [2] <u>Although Abruzzo and Anderson had been forced to land in the ocean in an earlier attempt in *Double Eagle*</u>, they didn't give up. [3] Instead, they acquired a new balloon, <u>which they named *Double Eagle II*</u>. [4] Newman joined them <u>because experience had shown the need for a third crew member</u>. [5] On its journey from Maine to France, *Double Eagle II* was airborne for 137 hours, <u>which is a little less than six days</u>. [6] The aeronauts stressed the fact <u>that *Double Eagle II* didn't just drift across the Atlantic</u>; they flew it across. [7] Abruzzo, Anderson, and Newman had to understand meteorology <u>so that they could take advantage of favorable winds</u>. [8] They also had to regulate their altitude constantly by adjusting their supply of helium and by losing ballast, <u>as the balloonists shown here are doing</u>. [9] <u>When the balloon gained too much altitude</u>, the crew lowered it by releasing some of the gas. [10] <u>If the balloon lost altitude</u>, the crew raised it by discarding ballast.

MEETING *individual* NEEDS

LEP/ESL

General Strategies. Ask students to reserve pages in their notebooks for collecting sentences that contain subordinating conjunctions ending with the word *that: now that, in view of the fact that, to the extent that, with the result that, provided that, so that,* and so forth. *That,* a word with a variety of functions in English, is often mistakenly omitted by students. Keeping a notebook of sentences, which students can review periodically, may help them master these connectors more easily.

VISUAL CONNECTIONS
Exploring the Subject. Have your students explore, in various ways, the subject of ballooning. For example, one group of students could look up ballooning in an encyclopedia, while another group could visit a local travel agent to find out about balloon outings. Give student groups additional speaking practice by asking them to report their findings to the rest of the class.

GRAMMAR

GRAMMAR

THE NOUN CLAUSE Rule 18f

OBJECTIVE

- To identify and classify noun clauses

GRAMMAR

The Noun Clause

18f. A *noun clause* is a subordinate clause used as a noun.

A noun clause may be used as a subject, a predicate nominative, a direct object, an indirect object, or the object of a preposition.

SUBJECT	**What I need** is my own room.
DIRECT OBJECT	She believes **that lost time is never found again.**
INDIRECT OBJECT	The store owner will give **whoever wins the contest** a valuable prize.
OBJECT OF PREPOSITION	She has written an article about **how she was elected to the Senate.**
PREDICATE NOMINATIVE	The happiest time in my life was **when we went to Colombia for the summer.**

Noun clauses are usually introduced by

that	where	whoever	whose
what	whether	whom	why
when	who	whomever	how

👉 **REFERENCE NOTE:** Many of these words can be used to introduce adjective clauses. See page 601.

Sometimes the introductory word has a function in the clause and sometimes it doesn't.

EXAMPLES Do you know **what the problem is?** [The introductory word *what* is a predicate nominative—*the problem is what.*]

I know **that she is worried.** [The introductory word *that* has no function in the clause.]

In some sentences, the word that introduces a noun clause can be omitted.

EXAMPLE He told us **attendance is improving.** [The introductory word *that* is understood.]
She is the judge **we interviewed.** [The introductory word *whom* is understood.]

REVIEW B

OBJECTIVE

- To identify subordinate clauses and to determine whether they are used as adjectives, adverbs, or nouns

18f

GRAMMAR

EXERCISE 6 — Identifying and Classifying Noun Clauses

Identify the noun clauses in the following sentences. Then, tell how each clause is used: as *subject*, *predicate nominative*, *direct object*, *indirect object*, or *object of a preposition*. [Note: A sentence may have more than one noun clause.]

1. Mr. Perkins, the band director, announced <u>that we would play at half time this week</u>. **1.** d.o.
2. We can never predict <u>whether he will choose a march or a show tune</u>. **2.** d.o.
3. He always gives <u>whoever will play each selection</u> a chance to express an opinion of it. **3.** i.o.
4. He is genuinely interested in <u>what we think of his choices</u>. **4.** o.p.
5. A drummer once told Mr. Perkins <u>she did not like most show tunes</u>. **5.** d.o.
6. <u>How she could say that</u> was a mystery to me. **6.** s.
7. Mr. Perkins told us <u>we would play a medley of marches</u>. **7.** d.o.
8. <u>What everyone wanted to know</u> was <u>who would play the solos</u>. **8.** p.n.   **9.** d.o.
9. He understands <u>why that was our first question</u>.
10. The crowd always applauds enthusiastically for <u>whoever plays a solo</u>. **10.** o.p.

REVIEW B — Identifying Adjective, Adverb, and Noun Clauses

Each sentence in the following paragraph has at least one subordinate clause. Identify each subordinate clause, and tell whether it is an *adjective clause*, *adverb clause*, or *noun clause*.

[1] What's so special about the Blue Grotto, or *Grotta Azzurra*, <u>as the Italians say</u>? [2] In the painting on the next page, you can see <u>that the color and the hidden location of the Blue Grotto have made it famous</u>. [3] The grotto is a cavern <u>that can be entered only from the sea</u>. [4] It is located on the west side of the Italian island of Capri, <u>which lies at the entrance to the Bay of Naples</u>. [5] <u>Since the only opening to the cavern is approximately three feet high</u>, visitors must lie down in a rowboat to enter it. [6] The

1. adv. cl.
2. n. cl.
3. adj. cl.
4. adj. cl.
5. adv. cl.

GRAMMAR

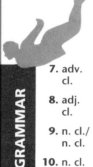

WRITING APPLICATION

OBJECTIVE

• To describe works of art in paragraphs containing details and subordinate clauses

6. adj. cl.

sapphire blue of the water inside the spacious, oval-shaped cavern is caused by light <u>that is refracted through the deep pool</u>. [7] <u>Although the calm, blue water looks inviting</u>, the grotto is no longer a swimming hole. [8] In the past, however, people <u>who lived in the area</u> greatly enjoyed swimming there. [9] Tour guides tell <u>whoever goes there</u> <u>that centuries ago Tiberius, the Roman emperor, used the Blue Grotto as his private swimming pool</u>. [10] Seeing it today, you would agree <u>that it's a pool fit for an emperor</u>.

7. adv. cl.

8. adj. cl.

9. n. cl./ n. cl.

10. n. cl.

Sandro Chia, *Grotta azzurra* (1980). Oil on canvas, 147 cm × 208 cm. Courtesy Galerie Bruno Bischofberger, Zürich, Switzerland.

VISUAL CONNECTIONS

About the Artist. Sandro Chia is one of several Italian-born artists known as postmodernists. In the 1980s, these artists rejected the modern pop style and began showing paintings that ironically combine the traditional and the modern.

As illustrated in *Grotta azzurra,* Chia's art often combines the abstract and the representational. Chia specializes in plump figures that look inflated or bloated—thus producing an ironic, barren sensuality.

WRITING APPLICATION

This assignment allows students to form opinions of visual art and to articulate those opinions in written paragraphs. The assignment further encourages students to develop maturity and variety in their writing by having each student include at least five subordinate clauses in the paragraphs.

WRITING APPLICATION

Using Subordination to Reflect Your Thoughts

When you were a child, you probably used short, choppy sentences to express your thoughts. Almost all children do. But as you got older, your thoughts became more complex, and so did your sentences.

IMMATURE   Mary Cassatt was an American painter. I enjoy her works. She was an Impressionist.

MATURE   I enjoy the works of Mary Cassatt, who was an
American impressionist painter.

How was subordination used to make the second example
sound more mature than the first?

▶ WRITING ACTIVITY

The student council has decided to decorate your school
with prints of popular artworks. To decide which prints to
get, the council has asked for recommendations, along with
brief descriptions, for artworks that students would like to
see. Write two paragraphs about two works (one paragraph
on each work) that you would like to recommend. Use
specific details and include at least five subordinate clauses.

Prewriting   Think of two paintings or prints that are your
favorites. If you do not know their titles, try looking in books
or asking a librarian or art teacher to find out what they are
titled. Think about why you particularly like these works,
and jot down your reasons.

Writing   As you write, you may think of additional details
and reasons. If you do, pause for a moment and consider
how they fit in with the rest of your notes. Add to your rough
draft any of this new information that fits in smoothly.

Evaluating and Revising   Read through your paragraphs
to be sure they each have a topic sentence supported by
your reasons for recommending a specific artwork. Check to
see that you have used a total of at least five subordinate
clauses in the two paragraphs. If you have not, try
combining sentences by creating adjective, adverb, or noun
clauses.

Proofreading   Put your paragraphs aside for a while, and
then read them again, looking for errors in grammar, punctuation, and spelling. Pay special attention to the proper
use of the relative pronouns *which, that, who,* and *whom.*
(See pages 751 and 661–662). Also, be sure that you have
punctuated all subordinate clauses correctly (see pages
797–801).

◆ CRITICAL THINKING

Analysis. Remind students that
as they select their paintings or prints
and write their paragraphs, they should
keep in mind their purpose and audience. For example, by thinking of reasons why other students would like
those paintings, they could choose
paintings that the student council would
want to use.

PREWRITING

If you choose to send students to
the school library, you may want to have
them first brainstorm what scenes or
subjects they like in art. Then, the librarian can guide them to landscapes or
seascapes, portraits, or historic genre
paintings. Having students explain why
they like the paintings they chose may
help students prepare to write.

EVALUATING AND REVISING

Have students evaluate each of
their paragraphs for unity by turning
the topic sentence into a question and
then reading each supporting sentence
in the paragraph to see if it answers the
question.

LESSON 6 *(pp. 610–613)*

SENTENCES CLASSIFIED ACCORDING TO STRUCTURE Rule 18g

OBJECTIVES

- To classify sentences as simple, compound, complex, or compound-complex
- To use the four kinds of sentences in descriptions
- To use the four kinds of sentences in a journal entry

SENTENCES CLASSIFIED ACCORDING TO STRUCTURE

- **Independent Practice/Reteaching** For instruction and exercises, see **Classifying Sentences by Structure** in *Language Skills Practice and Assessment*, p. 68.

- **Computer Guided Instruction** For additional instruction and practice with classifying sentences by structure, see **Lesson 26** in *Language Workshop CD-ROM*.

- **Practice** To help less-advanced students with additional instruction and practice with sentence structure, see **Chapter 13** in *English Workshop, Fourth Course*, pp. 177–178.

INTEGRATING THE LANGUAGE ARTS

Literature Link. James Weldon Johnson's poem "The Creation" includes a variety of sentence types. Have students read the poem carefully and ask them how Johnson uses compound and complex simple sentences effectively. [Johnson creates a powerful, rhythmic, melodic effect with the parallel structure of repeated independent clauses introduced by *And,* as in lines 10–12, and with the parallel structure of repeated adjective clauses introduced by *Who,* as in lines 81–83.]

610   *The Clause*

Sentences Classified According to Structure

The *structure* of a sentence is determined by the number and types of clauses it has.

18g. Sentences are classified according to their structure as *simple, compound, complex,* or *compound-complex.*

(1) A *simple sentence* has one independent clause and no subordinate clauses. It may have a compound subject, a compound verb, and any number of phrases.

> EXAMPLES
>
> S   S   V
> **Cora** and **Kareem bought** party supplies at the mall.
>
> S   V   V
> Later, **they drove** to school and **decorated** the cafeteria for the Latin Club's annual banquet.

(2) A *compound sentence* has two or more independent clauses but no subordinate clauses.

A compound sentence is actually two or more simple sentences joined together either by a comma and a coordinating conjunction, by a semicolon, or by a semicolon and a conjunctive adverb such as *therefore, however,* or *consequently.*

> EXAMPLES
>
> S   V
> **Cora hung** colorful streamers from the ceiling, and
>
> S   V
> **Kareem set** party favors on the tables.
>
> S   V   S
> After an hour, **they took** a short break; then **they**
>
> V
> **went** back to work.
>
> S   V
> **They agreed** not to take any more breaks; otherwise,
>
> S   V
> **they would be** late getting home.

☞ REFERENCE NOTE: See pages 796 and 816–819 for more information on punctuating compound sentences.

18g

NOTE: Don't confuse a compound predicate in a simple sentence with the two subjects and two predicates in a compound sentence.

COMPOUND
PREDICATE

To pass the time, **they talked** about school

and **told** stories about their families.

COMPOUND
SENTENCE

To pass the time, **they talked** about school,

and **they told** stories about their families.

(3) A *complex sentence* has one independent clause and *at least* one subordinate clause.

EXAMPLE When **they had finished** their work, **they**

complimented each other on the results.

(4) A *compound-complex sentence* has two or more independent clauses and *at least* one subordinate clause.

EXAMPLE **Cora waited** for just the right moment to ask

Kareem to go to the banquet with her, and **he**

promptly **accepted** her invitation, adding that

he had been planning to ask her the same thing.

☞ **REFERENCE NOTE:** For information on how sentences are classified according to purpose, see pages 565–566.

EXERCISE 7 **Classifying Sentences According to Structure**

Classify each of the sentences in the following paragraph as *simple*, *compound*, *complex*, or *compound-complex*.

[1] Our club, the Key Club, sponsored a rummage sale and requested donations from everyone at school. [2] We accepted whatever was donated, but we welcomed housewares most. [3] The principal donated a vacuum cleaner; the coach contributed a set of dishes; and several of the teachers provided towels and sheets. [4] We sold

1. simp.
2. cd.-cx.
3. cd.
4. cd.-cx.

QUICK REMINDER

Write the following sentence constructions on a transparency or on the chalkboard:

      S   V
1. The boaters rowed smoothly.
      S   V =   S
2. The swimmers swam; the boaters
   V
rowed.
      S   V
3. The boaters rowed
        S   V
while the fish watched.
      S   V =
4. The boaters rowed and the
      S   V
swimmers swam
       S   V
while the fish watched.

Ask students to identify each sentence as simple, compound, complex, or compound-complex. Explain that the clauses in a compound sentence are equal (the semicolon, comma and coordinating conjunction, or semicolon and conjunctive adverb can be visualized as an equal sign). However, the clauses in a complex sentence are not equal because one clause is subordinate to—or a part of—the other, independent clause.

LEARNING STYLES

Visual Learners. Divide your class into small groups and instruct students to read and evaluate one another's descriptions of the luau in **Exercise 8.** Have the students highlight the simple sentences in yellow, the compound sentences in blue, the complex sentences in red, and the compound-complex sentences in green. Tell them that a rainbow of colors indicates good sentence variety.

ANSWERS

Exercise 8

Answers will vary. Here are some possibilities:

1. Traditionally, roasting a pig for a luau was an event for men only, and each guest knew which piece of the pig he should be served. (compound-complex)

2. Our luau had fewer taboos. (simple)

3. The pig was cooked in an oven that was a hole in the ground. (complex)

4. The first dish was fish wrapped in ti leaves, and the second was salmon with poi, a tangy, purplish paste. (compound)

5. Hula dancers and fire jugglers performed in an atmosphere of frangipani trees and ginger blossoms. (simple)

612 *The Clause*

almost everything that had been donated, and we cele-
5. cx. brated our success with pitchers of lemonade. [5] Afterward, we gave all the profits that we had made from the
sale to the city's homeless shelter.

EXERCISE 8 **Using the Four Kinds of Sentences**

You and your family won a vacation to Hawaii. While you were there, you attended this luau. *Luau* is a Hawaiian word meaning "feast," and that's exactly what it was! There were different kinds of meats and fruits to eat, and, for entertainment, hula dancers and fire jugglers performed. Write five sentences describing the luau. If you have ever eaten any of the foods that are shown, give your impressions of them. Use at least one of each of the four kinds of sentences—simple, compound, complex, and compound-complex. Be prepared to identify the kinds of sentences that you use.

EXAMPLE **1.** *The fresh pineapple at the luau wasn't as sweet as pineapple that comes in a can. (complex)*

PICTURE THIS

You are an adventurer in a strange land and have just wandered into the mysterious place shown on the next page. Before going one step farther, you decide to make some notes about what you see. Write down your impressions of this scene. Think of reasons for the distinctive mood of the place, and theorize about who may live here.

OBJECTIVES

- To identify independent and subordinate clauses and to classify the subordinate clauses as adjective clauses, adverb clauses, or noun clauses

What should you explore first? Why? In your journal entries, include at least one simple sentence, one compound sentence, one complex sentence, and two compound-complex sentences.

Subject: thoughts at *The Rose Tower*
Audience: you and whoever may read your journal in the future
Purpose: to help you decide what to do next

Giorgio de Chirico, *The Rose Tower*. Peggy Guggenheim Collection.

PICTURE THIS

Before students begin writing their journal entries, have them discuss *The Rose Tower* in small groups. Ask them these questions: How does this painting make you feel? Does it put you in a particular kind of mood? How do the lighting and simple architecture contribute to the feeling? This group discussion should give students plenty of material for their notes.

👁 VISUAL CONNECTIONS

About the Artist. Giorgio de Chirico was born in Vólos, Greece, on July 10, 1888. His early style was influenced by the artist Arnold Böcklin, who combined the fantastic with the commonplace. Moving to Paris in 1911, de Chirico gained the admiration of Pablo Picasso by painting ominous scenes of objects overpowered by their own shadows and by severe, oppressive architecture.

Later, de Chirico adapted a more realistic style that was less widely admired.

Review: Posttest 1

A. Identifying Independent and Subordinate Clauses; Classifying Subordinate Clauses

Identify each italicized clause in the following sentences as an *independent clause* or a *subordinate clause*. Then, classify each italicized subordinate clause as an *adjective clause*, an *adverb clause*, or a *noun clause*.

- To classify sentences according to structure as simple, compound, complex, or compound-complex
- To write sentences with varied structures

EXAMPLE   **1.** The Brooklyn Bridge, *which was built in the latter half of the nineteenth century,* was the world's first steel-wire suspension bridge.
    1. *subordinate clause—adjective clause*

1. The Brooklyn Bridge, <u>*which spans the East River between Brooklyn and Manhattan in New York City*</u>, is one of the engineering wonders of the world. **1.** adj. cl.
2. Massive granite towers <u>*that are supported by concrete-filled shafts*</u> are among its remarkable features. **2.** adj. cl.
3. <u>*The bridge was designed and built by John and Washington Roebling, a father-and-son engineering team*</u> who were pioneers in the use of steel-wire cables.
4. The steel-wire cables give the bridge a graceful appearance <u>*that resembles a spider's web*</u>. **4.** adj. cl.
5. <u>*That the bridge combines strength with beauty*</u> remains a tribute to the Roebling family. **5.** n. cl.
6. The Roeblings discovered <u>*that construction work could be both slow and dangerous*</u>. **6.** n. cl.
7. <u>*Although she was not an engineer*</u>, Nora Roebling assisted in the efforts to complete the bridge. **7.** adv. cl.
8. <u>*Because they were required at times to work underwater in airtight chambers called caissons*</u>, many workers, including Washington Roebling, suffered from caisson disease, or decompression sickness. **8.** adv. cl.
9. Sailors, <u>*who were used to working at great heights*</u>, were hired to string the miles of cable. **9.** adj. cl.
10. <u>*John Roebling injured his foot at the work site*</u>, and as a result, he died of tetanus shortly after construction was begun.

B. Classifying Sentences According to Structure

Classify each of the following sentences as *simple*, *compound*, *complex*, or *compound-complex*.

11. cd.   **[11]** After succeeding his father on the project, Washington Roebling was stricken by caisson disease; there-
12. cd.-cx.   fore, he was confined to bed. **[12]** The Roeblings lived in a house that was near the construction site, and Washington supervised the work through a telescope. **[13]** He dic-
13. cd.   tated instructions to Nora, and she relayed them to the
14. cx.   work crew. **[14]** Whether the work on the bridge could

have continued without her assistance is doubtful.
[15] When the bridge was finally completed in 1883, President Chester A. Arthur attended the dedication ceremonies. **[16]** Because of his illness, Washington Roebling was unable to attend the ceremonies. **[17]** Instead, the president visited Roebling's home to honor the man who had struggled so valiantly to complete the bridge. **[18]** The bridge took fourteen years to build. **[19]** At the time of its completion, it was the world's longest suspension bridge. **[20]** The bridge is now more than a century old, and it still stands as a monument to the artistry, sacrifice, and determination of all the people who planned and built it.

15. cx.
16. simp.
17. cx.
18. simp.
19. simp.
20. cd.-cx.

GRAMMAR

Review: Posttest 2

Writing Sentences with Varied Structures

Write your own sentences according to the following guidelines.

EXAMPLE **1.** a simple sentence with a compound subject
 1. *My aunt and uncle live nearby.*

1. a simple sentence with a compound verb
2. a compound sentence with two independent clauses joined by the conjunction *but*
3. a compound sentence with two independent clauses joined by a semicolon and a conjunctive adverb
4. a complex sentence with an adjective clause
5. a complex sentence beginning with an adverb clause
6. a complex sentence ending with an adverb clause
7. a complex sentence with a noun clause used as a direct object
8. a complex sentence with a noun clause used as the subject
9. a complex sentence with a noun clause used as the object of a preposition
10. a compound-complex sentence

ANSWERS
Review: Posttest 2

Answers may vary. Here are some possibilities:

1. My sister lives and works in Brooklyn.
2. Many people came to the party, but most of them left early.
3. I missed the bus; however, I was only a few minutes late.
4. The ones whose projects are selected will attend the regional contest.
5. If I study one more hour, I should be able to finish my homework.
6. They met with the company managers as soon as they could do so.
7. The families liked what they heard about the new health plan.
8. That thousands of children die of hunger every day is becoming known.
9. It is hard to agree about what we should do.
10. We told them that their plan wouldn't work, but they wouldn't listen to us.

OBJECTIVES
- To select verbs that agree with their subjects
- To identify verbs that agree with their subjects and to identify pronouns that agree with their antecedents

PROGRAM MANAGER

FOR THE WHOLE CHAPTER

- **Review** For exercises on chapter concepts, see **Review Form A** and **Review Form B** in *Language Skills Practice and Assessment,* pp. 102–105.

- **Assessment** For additional testing, see **Usage Pretests** and **Usage Mastery Tests** in *Language Skills Practice and Assessment,* pp. 85–92 and pp. 159–166.

CHAPTER OVERVIEW

Two of the usage errors students most frequently commit are errors in subject-verb agreement and in pronoun-antecedent agreement. This chapter offers ways to help students master agreement through a number of activities. The activities involve goals well within the students' reach and lead students into learning material they might think they already know. The **Writing Application** demonstrates the importance of agreement for clarity in writing.

To reinforce learning, when students revise compositions, refer them to specific exercises that cover particularly troublesome areas.

19 AGREEMENT

Subject and Verb, Pronoun and Antecedent

Diagnostic Test

A. Selecting Verbs That Agree with Their Subjects

For each sentence, choose the <u>verb</u> in parentheses <u>that agrees with the subject</u>.

EXAMPLE **1.** Both coats *(is, are)* on sale this week.
      1. *are*

1. The jury *(has, have)* been paying close attention to the evidence in this case.
2. There *(is, are)* four herbs that almost any gardener can grow: basil, thyme, marjoram, and oregano.
3. All of these old letters *(was, were)* tied with ribbon and stored in a trunk in the attic.
4. Each of them *(is, are)* penned in bold, flowing handwriting, embellished with many flourishes.
5. Both Alicia and Isabel *(thinks, think)* that the former owner of the house put the letters in the attic.

6. Neither of them (<u>*knows*</u>, *know*) for sure who wrote that message.
7. The two songs we played in the Martin Luther King Day concert (*was*, <u>*were*</u>) written by Keneisha Watson.
8. Did you know that *archy & mehitabel* (*is*, *are*) a series of poems supposedly written by a cockroach that lives in a newspaper office with his friend, a cat?
9. Here (*is*, <u>*are*</u>) the latest scores of today's basketball games.
10. Neither potatoes nor peanuts (*is*, <u>*are*</u>) grown on this farm anymore.

B. Identifying Verbs That Agree with Their Subjects and Pronouns That Agree with Their Antecedents

In many of the following sentences, either a verb does not agree with its subject, or a pronoun does not agree with its antecedent. Identify each incorrect verb or pronoun, and give the correct form. If a sentence is correct, write *C*.

EXAMPLES   **1.** The flock of birds, almost blackening the sky, were an awe-inspiring sight.

   1. *were—was*

   2. Only a decade ago their number was declining.
   2. *C*

11. The meeting got out of hand when the discussion period began since everyone tried to express~their opinion at the same time.   **11. his or her**
12. There on the corner of your desk~is the books that I returned and that you claimed you never received.   **12. are**
13. Two students from each class~is going to the state capital to attend a special conference on education.   **13. are**
14. Each of them~are expected to bring back a report on the conference so that classmates can get firsthand information.   **14. is**
15. Since they will be on vacation next month, neither Miguel nor his sister~are going to enter the mixed-doubles tennis tournament.   **15. is**
16. The audience expressed~their admiration for the dancer's grace and skill by applauding wildly.   **16. its**

USAGE

USING THE DIAGNOSTIC TEST

The **Diagnostic Test** deals with the constructions that cause students the greatest number of problems. **Part A** tests for the ability to evaluate whether the subject of a sentence should have a singular or plural verb. The sentences in **Part A** contain collective nouns, singular and plural subjects, singular subjects that end in *–s*, and subjects separated from their verbs by phrases. **Part B** tests the same ability, but it also tests the ability to identify pronouns and their correct antecedents.

Through this test you will be able to determine where individual students need to focus their attention and where the whole class needs practice.

If only a few students miss questions involving subjects and verbs separated by phrases, you may want to have them look up the rules of subject and verb agreement. Then, you may drill them on exercises before having them write a few original sentences containing intervening phrases between subjects and verbs.

USAGE

OBJECTIVES

- To identify words as singular or plural
- To identify verbs that agree in number with their subjects

---

17. After the senator had read the proposed amendment, anyone who disagreed with the ruling was allowed to state ∧their reason.   **17.** his or her
18. This collection of old African American folk tales ∧demonstrate the wisdom, humor, and creativity of my ancestors.   **18.** demonstrates
19. She is one of those competitive people who perform best under pressure.   **19.** C
20. Since neither of you ∧have ever tasted fried plantains, my mother would like you to eat a Cuban meal at our house tonight.   **20.** has

---

Number

19a. When a word refers to one person or thing, it is *singular* in number. When a word refers to more than one, it is *plural* in number.

SINGULAR	video	child	I	thief	herself
PLURAL	videos	children	we	thieves	themselves

In general, nouns ending in –*s* are plural (*aunts, uncles, towns, crimes*); verbs ending in –*s* are singular (*gives, takes, does, has, is*).

☞ REFERENCE NOTE: For more information on the plural forms of nouns, see pages 877–880.

▶ EXERCISE 1 **Identifying Words as Singular or Plural in Number**

Identify each of the words listed below as either *plural* or *singular*.

1. stories
2. one
3. several
4. applies
5. people
6. mouse
7. genius
8. civics
9. ability
10. says
11. data
12. has
13. both
14. mumps
15. woman
16. some
17. donates
18. donation
19. mathematics
20. many

PROGRAM MANAGER

NUMBER

- **Independent Practice/ Reteaching** For instruction and exercises, see **Number: Singular or Plural?**; **Agreement of Subject and Verb**; and **Agreement and Prepositional Phrases** in *Language Skills Practice and Assessment,* pp. 95–97.

- **Computer Guided Instruction** For additional instruction and practice with subject-verb agreement, see **Lesson 5** in *Language Workshop CD-ROM.*

- **Practice** To help less-advanced students with additional instruction and practice with subject-verb agreement, see **Chapter 14** in *English Workshop, Fourth Course,* pp. 181–186.

ANSWERS
Exercise 1

1. plural		**11.** plural
2. singular		**12.** singular
3. plural		**13.** plural
4. singular		**14.** singular
5. plural		**15.** singular
6. singular		**16.** singular/plural
7. singular		**17.** singular
8. singular		**18.** singular
9. singular		**19.** singular
10. singular		**20.** plural

USAGE

Agreement of Subject and Verb

19b. A verb should agree with its subject in number.

(1) Singular subjects take singular verbs.

EXAMPLES   **Earline attends** college. [The singular verb *attends* agrees with the singular subject *Earline.*]
That boy **delivers** newspapers. [The singular verb *delivers* agrees with the singular subject *boy.*]

(2) Plural subjects take plural verbs.

EXAMPLES   **They attend** college. [The plural verb *attend* agrees with the plural subject *they.*]
Those boys **deliver** newspapers. [The plural verb *deliver* agrees with the plural subject *boys.*]

Verb phrases also agree in number with their subjects. In a verb phrase, only the first auxiliary (helping) verb changes form to agree with the subject.

EXAMPLES   Earline **is attending** college.
They **are attending** college.
A boy in my class **has been delivering** newspapers.
Two boys in my class **have been delivering** newspapers.

The form *were* is plural except when used with the singular *you* and in sentences that are contrary to fact.

EXAMPLES   **You were** right. [*You* used as subject]
If I were in charge, I would make some changes. [contrary to fact]

▶ EXERCISE 2   **Selecting Verbs That Agree with Their Subjects**

Choose the <u>verb</u> in parentheses <u>that agrees with the subject given</u>.

1. people (*walks*, <u>*walk*</u>)
2. you (*is*, <u>*are*</u>)
3. cattle (*runs*, <u>*run*</u>)
4. we (*talks*, <u>*talk*</u>)
5. Joan (<u>*was*</u>, *were*)
6. house (<u>*stands*</u>, *stand*)
7. result (<u>*is*</u>, *are*)
8. they (*believes*, <u>*believe*</u>)
9. crews (*sails*, <u>*sail*</u>)
10. women (*seems*, <u>*seem*</u>)

MEETING *individual* NEEDS

LEP/ESL

General Strategies. Textbooks give rules of standard usage. However, even well-educated English-speakers' speech varies from textbook English. This is because living languages constantly change. The first instances of change show up in spoken forms that, through common use, begin to sound correct. The textbook can be perplexing to second-language learners who put great trust in the informal speech of proficient English-speakers. You may want to discuss the fact that although a variety of forms are acceptable in casual speech, students who follow the textbook's rules will always be using standard English.

USAGE

USAGE

USAGE

Intervening Phrases

19c. The number of the subject is not changed by a phrase following the subject.

The subject is never part of a prepositional phrase.

EXAMPLES **The woman** on the stairs **is** Senator Reyes. [*woman is*]
The women in the front row **are** Cabinet officers. [*women are*]

Remember that prepositional phrases may begin with compound prepositions such as *together with, in addition to, as well as,* and *along with.* These phrases do not affect the number of the verb.

EXAMPLES **Tammy,** along with her mother and aunt, **is** going to the concert. [*Tammy is going.*]
The **wind,** together with the rain and fog, **was** making navigation difficult. [*wind was making*]
Jack's **imagination,** as well as his sense of humor, **was** delightful. [*imagination was*]

A negative construction following the subject does not change the number of the subject.

EXAMPLE **Carl,** not Juan and I, **is** doing the artwork.

▶ EXERCISE 3 **Selecting Verbs That Agree with Their Subjects**

Identify the <u>subject</u> of each of the following sentences. Then, choose the <u>verb</u> in parentheses <u>that agrees in number with the subject</u>.

EXAMPLE **1.** The price of haircuts (*has, have*) gone up.
1. *price—has*

1. A heaping <u>basket</u> of turnip greens (<u>*was*</u>, *were*) sitting on the counter.
2. <u>Displaying</u> disregard for the rights and comforts of others (<u>*is*</u>, *are*) rude.
3. The community college <u>course</u> on collecting stamps (<u>*attracts*</u>, *attract*) many people.
4. The <u>members</u> of the Pak family (*meets,* <u>*meet*</u>) for a reunion every year.

REVIEW A
OBJECTIVES

- To write sentences in which verbs agree with their subjects and pronouns agree with their antecedents
- To identify the subjects of sentences

5. The <u>carpeting</u> in the upstairs and downstairs rooms (*is*, *are*) getting worn.
6. The turquoise <u>stones</u> in this Navajo ring certainly (*is*, *are*) pretty.
7. One <u>friend</u> of my brothers (*says*, *say*) that I look like Whitney Houston.
8. The <u>package</u> of radio parts (*was*, *were*) smashed in the mail.
9. The <u>cost</u> of two new snow tires (*was*, *were*) more than I expected.
10. <u>Burt</u>, not Anne and Laura, (*has*, *have*) borrowed the bicycle pump.

> **REVIEW A**   **Completing Sentences That Demonstrate Agreement**

Anna Mary Robertson Moses (1860–1961), better known as "Grandma Moses," became famous in old age for her paintings of rural America. Add words to the word groups on the following page to complete ten sentences about this Grandma Moses painting, titled *The Barn Dance*. Make sure that all verbs agree with their subjects and all pronouns agree with their antecedents. Be prepared to identify the subject of each sentence.

EXAMPLE   **1.** barn are
　　　　　1. *The doors of the barn are wide open.*

Grandma Moses (1860–1961): *The Barn Dance*. Copyright © 1989 Grandma Moses Properties Co., New York.

USAGE

ANSWERS
Review A

Students' sentences will vary. Here are some possible sentences:

1. The <u>clouds</u> look like fluffy elephants.
2. A <u>musician</u> is playing to warm up for the dance.
3. A <u>pair</u> of horses pulls each of the wagons.
4. <u>All</u> of the people at the barn dance are enjoying the music.
5. <u>One</u> of the buildings in the distance is my house.
6. The <u>people</u> on the green wagon are waving.
7. Fiddle <u>music</u>, along with laughter and conversation, fills the air as the band begins a new dance.
8. The <u>guests</u> have noticed the cloudy sky.
9. If I <u>were</u> at this barn dance alone, I'd try to meet some new friends.
10. A <u>horse</u> is drinking from the trough.

VISUAL CONNECTIONS

About the Artist. Born Anna Mary Robertson, Grandma Moses grew up in rural New York. She began painting in 1938 at the age of seventy-eight. Her scenes of farm life in Virginia and New York were an overnight sensation, and she was famous by 1940. When she died in 1961 at the age of one hundred and one, some considered her the most famous American primitive painter.

OBJECTIVES

- To read aloud correct sentences with indefinite pronouns as subjects
- To write sentences with verbs that agree with their indefinite-pronoun subjects
- To identify subject-verb agreement in sentences
- To use given words as subjects to write a log entry

CRITICAL THINKING

Synthesis. When students have completed **Review A**, ask them to work in groups of three or four and to use the sentences they wrote to create a brief story about the picture. Ask students to evaluate their additions to the word groups and discuss particularly the groups that required additional subjects.

PROGRAM MANAGER

INDEFINITE PRONOUNS

- **Independent Practice/ Reteaching** For instruction and exercises, see **Agreement with Indefinite Pronouns** in *Language Skills Practice and Assessment,* p. 98.

- **Computer Guided Instruction** For additional instruction and practice with agreement with indefinite pronouns, see **Lesson 6** in *Language Workshop CD-ROM.*

- **Practice** To help less-advanced students with additional instruction and practice with agreement with indefinite pronouns, see **Chapter 14** in *English Workshop, Fourth Course,* pp. 187–188.

QUICK REMINDER

Write the basic definition of indefinite pronouns on the chalkboard:

indefinite pronouns—pronouns that do not refer to a specific person or thing

Ask students each to write five indefinite pronouns and to identify them as singular or plural.

622

---

622 *Agreement*

1. clouds look
2. musician is playing
3. horses pulls
4. barn dance are enjoying
5. buildings in the distance is
6. green wagon are waving
7. along with laughter and conversation, fills
8. guests have noticed the cloudy
9. I were at this barn dance
10. horse is drinking

Indefinite Pronouns

19d. The following indefinite pronouns are singular: *each, either, neither, one, everyone, everybody, no one, nobody, anyone, anybody, someone, somebody.*

Indefinite pronouns are pronouns that do not refer to a specific person or thing.

EXAMPLES **No one leaves** early.
One of the guitar strings **was** broken. [One was broken.]
Neither of them **knew** the answer.
Someone who likes apple juice **raids** the refrigerator at night.

Notice that a phrase or a clause following one of these pronouns does not affect the verb.

EXAMPLES **Everybody likes** my uncle.
Everybody in my neighborhood **likes** my uncle.
Everybody who meets my uncle **likes** him.

19e. The following indefinite pronouns are plural: *several, few, both, many.*

EXAMPLES **Several** of the women **are** pilots.
A **few** in the crowd **were** rowdy.
Have both tried harder?
Many of the students **write** and **edit** on word processors.

19f. The indefinite pronouns *some, all, any, most,* and *none* may be either singular or plural, depending on the word they refer to.

These pronouns are singular when they refer to a singular word and plural when they refer to a plural word.

SINGULAR **Most** of the day **was** gone. [*Most* refers to singular *day.*]

PLURAL **Most** of the steers **were** grazing. [*Most* refers to plural *steers.*]

SINGULAR **Has any** of the shipment arrived? [*Any* refers to singular *shipment.*]

PLURAL **Are any** of the coins new? [*Any* refers to plural *coins.*]

SINGULAR **None** of the damage **was** serious. [*None* refers to singular *damage.*]

PLURAL **None** of the students **have** finished. [*None* refers to plural *students.*]

In each of the examples above, the prepositional phrase following the subject provides a clue to the number of the pronoun. When these pronouns are used alone, their number depends on the number of the item the speaker or writer has in mind.

EXAMPLES **Most were** interesting. [a number of books, photographs, ideas, etc.]

Most was interesting. [a portion of a book, movie, conversation, etc.]

ORAL PRACTICE 1 **Using Verbs That Agree with Indefinite Pronouns**

Read the following sentences aloud, stressing the italicized words.

1. *One* of those cups *is* broken.
2. *Either* of the bikes *is* ready to go.
3. A *few* of the girls *are* experienced riders.
4. *Each* of the mariachi bands *has* performed one number.
5. *Some* of the mice *were* eating the cheese.
6. *Most* of the milk *is* gone.
7. *Neither* of the cars *has* a radio.
8. *None* of the apples *were* ripe.

USAGE

USAGE

COMMON ERROR

Problem. Students often use plural verb forms with *either* and *neither*. Because each word suggests two alternatives, students may mistake the two choices (or a plural object in a prepositional phrase) for a plural subject.

Solution. To show that a choice between two singular alternatives always takes a singular verb, ask the students to imagine two doors: one red, one blue. Behind one door is what they most want; behind the other, what they most fear. They may choose either door, or neither, but they cannot walk through both doors at once.

Remind the students that *either* means "one or the other," but that *neither* means "not one and not the other." Students have less trouble with *either*; they might remember the meaning of *neither* by thinking of it as a contraction of *not* and *either*.

USAGE

▶ EXERCISE 4 **Writing Sentences with Verbs That Agree with Their Subjects**

Rewrite each of the following sentences according to the directions in parentheses. If necessary, change the number of the verb to agree with the new subject.

1. ˄Everyone easily ~~understands~~ the rules of this game. (Change *everyone* to *most people*.) **1.** Most people/understand
2. ~~Neither~~ of the actresses˄~~was~~ nominated. (Change *neither* to *both*.) **2.** Both/were
3. ~~Has each~~ of your cousins had a turn? (Change *each* to *both*.) **3.** Have both
4. Some of the˄~~trees were~~ destroyed. (Change *trees* to *crop*.) **4.** crop was   **5.** Has/wheat
5. ˄~~Have~~ any of the˄~~apples~~ been harvested? (Change *apples* to *wheat*.)   **6.** Many of our neighbors visit
6. ˄~~Nobody visits~~ that haunted house. (Change *nobody* to *many of our neighbors*.)   **7.** Several are   **8.** All/need
7. ˄~~Each is~~ well trained. (Change *each* to *several*.)
8. ˄~~One~~ of the tires ~~needs~~ air. (Change *one* to *all*.)
9. ˄All of the˄~~fruit was~~ eaten. (Change *fruit* to *pears*.)
10. There˄is baked˄~~chicken~~ for everybody. (Change *chicken* to *potatoes*.)   **9.** pears were   **10.** are/potatoes

▶ EXERCISE 5 **Identifying Subject-Verb Agreement in Sentences**

The subjects and verbs in some of the following sentences do not agree. If a sentence is incorrect, write the correct form of the verb. If the sentence is correct, write *C*.

1. were   **2.** was

1. Several of the crew˄~~was~~ commended by the captain.
2. Neither of the coaches˄~~were~~ happy with the decision.
3. Each of us˄~~are~~ going to make a large poster for the upcoming election.   **3.** is
4. Some of the frozen yogurt has started to melt.   **4.** C
5. ˄~~Does~~ both of those games require special gear?   **5.** Do
6. ˄Either of the assistants usually gets the mail.   **6.** C
7. None of the buildings were damaged by the hail.   **7.** C
8. None of the food has been frozen.   **8.** C   **9.** was
9. Neither of the book reports˄~~were~~ finished on time.
10. Anyone who wants to can˄help me make gefilte fish for the Passover feast.   **10.** C

REVIEW B

OBJECTIVE

- To select verbs that agree with their subjects in sentences containing indefinite pronouns

▶ REVIEW B   **Selecting Verbs That Agree with Their Subjects**

For each of the following sentences, choose the <u>verb</u> in parentheses <u>that agrees with the subject</u>.

1. (*Has*, <u>*Have*</u>) any of you ever wondered how meals are served to space-shuttle astronauts?
2. Each item for the day's menu (*come*, <u>*comes*</u>) sealed in its own container.
3. To help reduce weight on the spacecraft, many of the foods (*is*, <u>*are*</u>) dehydrated.
4. At mealtime, someone in the crew (*add*, <u>*adds*</u>) water to the scrambled eggs, vegetables, and puddings.
5. All of the water mixed with these foods (<u>*is*</u>, *are*) a byproduct of the fuel cells that provide the spacecraft's electricity.
6. Of course, not one of the beverages (<u>*is*</u>, *are*) pourable because there is no gravity.
7. As you can see, uncovered liquid (*bounce*, <u>*bounces*</u>) into the air like a ball if its container is accidentally jolted.
8. Much of the food (<u>*is*</u>, *are*) covered in sauce so that surface tension will help to keep the food in dishes.
9. Amazingly, most of the foods (<u>*taste*</u>, *tastes*) delicious.
10. The menu for the astronauts even (<u>*includes*</u>, *include*) steaks and strawberries.

USAGE

USAGE

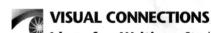

VISUAL CONNECTIONS

Ideas for Writing. Students who would enjoy imagining themselves as astronauts or in other challenging jobs might write brief narratives of their first morning in orbit or of the first day of a job. They could choose to focus on the first tasks of their morning or to describe what they see as they orbit Earth or complete an essential procedure in the space shuttle.

When students have finished their compositions, have groups of three or four identify the indefinite pronouns they used, check their use, and share the narratives and descriptions with one another.

PICTURE THIS

Before students write, lead them in a discussion of what a visitor from outer space might think about human life, beliefs, and social customs. Students may want to imagine some specific things about the planet Zan Dor and its inhabitants to help create a perspective from which to view this scene on Earth.

PICTURE THIS

You are the captain of the first spacecraft sent from the planet Zan Dor to explore Earth. As your invisible ship skims above the edge of a landmass, you look down and see this strange assembly of alien beings near a large body of water. You order your crew to cruise slowly above this scene while you try to figure out what the aliens are doing. Write a brief entry in the spacecraft's daily log, recording what you see below and speculating on what it means. As you write your log entry, use at least five of the following words as subjects: *aliens, everybody, inhabitants, we, many, most, all, none, any, some.* Be sure your subjects and verbs agree.

Subject: earthling behavior
Audience: you and future space travelers
Purpose: to inform

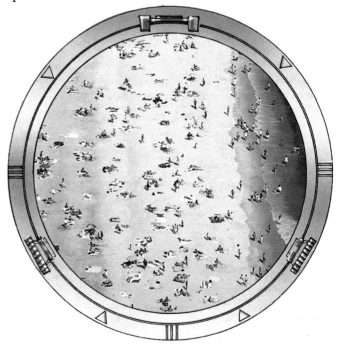

COMPOUND SUBJECTS Rules 19g–19i

OBJECTIVES

- To read aloud correct sentences with compound subjects
- To select verbs that agree with their subjects

Compound Subjects

A *compound subject* consists of two or more nouns or pronouns that are joined by a conjunction and have the same verb.

19g. Subjects joined by *and* usually take a plural verb.

EXAMPLES **Ramón** and **she like** hiking.
Her **brother,** her **uncle,** and her **cousin are** teachers.

NOTE: Subjects joined by *and* that name only one person or thing take a singular verb.

EXAMPLES Pork and beans **goes** well with barbecued chicken. [One dish goes.]
Rock-and-roll **is** here to stay. [One kind of music is.]

19h. Singular subjects joined by *or* or *nor* take a singular verb.

EXAMPLES Marcelo or Donya **knows** the address.
Does either Dad or Mom have the key?
Neither our phone nor our doorbell **was** working.

NOTE: Singular subjects that are joined by the correlative conjunction *both . . . and* take a plural verb.

EXAMPLE Both the scout and the counselor **were** helpful guides.

19i. When a singular subject and a plural subject are joined by *or* or *nor,* the verb agrees with the subject nearer the verb.

EXAMPLES Either Harry or his **aunts are** planning the activities for the beach party.
Neither the potatoes nor the **roast is** done.

You can usually avoid such awkward constructions by rewording the sentence so that each subject has its own verb.

EXAMPLES Either **Harry is** planning the activities for the beach party, or his **aunts are.**
The **potatoes are** not done, and neither **is** the **roast.**

PROGRAM MANAGER

COMPOUND SUBJECTS

- **Independent Practice/ Reteaching** For instruction and exercises, see **Agreement with Compound Subjects** in *Language Skills Practice and Assessment,*p. 99.

- **Computer Guided Instruction** For additional instruction and practice with agreement with compound subjects, see **Lesson 6** in *Language Workshop CD-ROM.*

- **Practice** To help less-advanced students with additional instruction and practice with agreement with compound subjects, see **Chapter 14** in *English Workshop, Fourth Course,* pp. 189–190.

MEETING *individual* **NEEDS**

LEP/ESL

General Strategies. Try an oral drill with the following sentences or create similar sentences by using names of students in the class.

1. Ramón and Teresa have new shoes.
2. Vanessa or Jason has braces.
3. Louis and Joanna have freckles.
4. Anil or Maria has straight A's.
5. Tanya or Tai has a job.

OTHER PROBLEMS IN AGREEMENT
Rules 19j–19r

OBJECTIVES

- To use collective nouns in sentences
- To write and revise sentences so that the verbs agree with their subjects

628 *Agreement*

 ORAL PRACTICE 2 | **Using Verbs That Agree with Compound Subjects**

Read the following sentences aloud, stressing the italicized words.

1. Every *one* of the kittens *has* been given away.
2. A *few* of us *are* going to Chicago.
3. *Each* of the photographs *was* in black and white.
4. *Neither* Sam *nor* Miguel *likes* sports.
5. *Either* Judy or Claudia *does* the dishes tonight.
6. Not *one* of the stations *is* coming in clearly.
7. *Several* of the plates *were* cracked.
8. *Both* Marilyn *and* Marge *have* summer jobs.

EXERCISE 6 | **Selecting Verbs That Agree with Their Subjects**

For each of the following sentences, choose the <u>verb</u> in parentheses <u>that agrees with the subject</u> of the sentence.

1. Neither my brother nor I (*has*, *have*) a car.
2. Marlon and she (*is*, *are*) the dance champions.
3. Our relatives and theirs (*is*, *are*) having a barbecue together.
4. Both Michael Chang and Zina Garrison-Jackson (*plays*, *play*) a good game of tennis.
5. Either the director or the actors (*is*, *are*) going to have to compromise.
6. Neither the grapes nor the cantaloupe (*was*, *were*) ripe enough to eat.
7. Both Hakeem Olajuwon and Michael Jordan (*is*, *are*) popular with fans.
8. Our class or theirs (*is*, *are*) going to sponsor the dance.
9. Either the faucet or the shower head (*leaks*, *leak*).
10. Either a transistor or a capacitor (*has*, *have*) burned out in this receiver.

Other Problems in Agreement

19j. Collective nouns may be either singular or plural.

USAGE

USAGE

- To identify sentences with correct subject-verb agreement
- To use *don't* and *doesn't* correctly in sentences
- To select verbs that agree with their subjects

A *collective noun* is singular in form, but it names a *group* of persons or things.

Collective Nouns			
army	club	group	series
assembly	committee	herd	squad
audience	crowd	jury	staff
band	faculty	majority	swarm
choir	family	number	team
class	flock	public	troop

Use a singular verb with a collective noun when you mean the group as a unit. Use a plural verb when you mean the members of the group as individuals.

EXAMPLES   The class **has met** its substitute teacher. [the class as a unit]
The class **were disagreeing** with one another about the answers. [the class as individuals]

The team **is** on the field. [the team as a unit]
The team **are working** together. [the team as individuals]

NOTE: A pronoun that refers to the collective noun should agree in number with the noun, as in the examples above.

▶ EXERCISE 7   **Using Collective Nouns in Sentences**

You are at the soccer game shown on the following page. During the game, you see many different groups of people on the field, in the bleachers, and on the bench. You notice that sometimes the members of a group act separately and sometimes a group acts together as a whole. Think of five collective nouns that name the groups you see. (See the top of this page for a list of collective nouns.) Use each noun as the subject in two sentences. After each sentence, identify the collective noun as *singular* or *plural* in that sentence.

EXAMPLE   **1.** crowd
     1. *The crowd seem to be enjoying themselves.—plural*
        The crowd has nearly filled the bleachers.—singular

USAGE

USAGE

TIMESAVER

After students have finished **Exercise 7**, ask volunteers to read their sentences aloud, to identify the collective nouns as singular or plural, and to explain the intended meaning of each sentence. Their errors will help you to determine whether reteaching is needed.

COMMON ERROR

Problem. Students sometimes use a singular verb with a collective-noun subject and then use a plural pronoun to refer to the subject.

Solution. Write the following sentence on the chalkboard and ask the class to discuss what is wrong with it:

The team was beaten badly last week; now they are out to win big. [The words *they are* should be changed to *it is*.]

After students decide what is wrong, have them think of two or three other examples of this error to write on the chalkboard. Help students through the correction process. If they can identify an error and correct it, they are less likely to commit it.

▶ EXERCISE 8   **Writing Sentences with Verbs That Agree with Their Subjects**

Rewrite the following sentences according to the instructions in parentheses, changing the number of the verb if necessary.

1. ₌Both of the records₌are in the Top Forty. (Change *both* to *neither*.)   **1.** Neither/is
2. The Boys Choir of Harlem₌has been rehearsing₌with the conductor. (Change *with the conductor* to *in small groups*.)   **2.** have/in small groups.
3. Either₌my cousins or₌Adrienne is bringing the pizza. (Reverse the order of the subjects.)   **3.** Adrienne/my cousins are
4. ₌Neither Carrie₌nor Jana₌is in the Pep Club. (Change *neither . . . nor* to *both . . . and*.)   **4.** Both/and/are
5. Gabriel García Márquez₌and Octavio Paz₌have won prizes in literature. (Change *and* to *or*.)   **5.** or/has
6. ₌All of your papers₌were graded. (Change *all* to *each*.)   **6.** each/was
7. Some of the₌wood burns. (Change *wood* to *logs*.)   **7.** logs burn
8. The delighted team₌was waving and grinning widely. (Change *waving and grinning widely* to *assembling to accept their medals*.)   **8.** were assembling to accept their medals.
9. ₌Everybody in the chorus is trying out for the play. (Change *everybody* to *no one*.)   **9.** No one
10. Macaroni₌and cheese always tastes good. (Change *and* to *or*.)   **10.** or

19k. A verb agrees with its subject, not with its predicate nominative.

EXAMPLES
S
The main **ingredient** in my hot sauce

PN
is jalapeño **peppers.**

S   PN
Jalapeño **peppers are** the main **ingredient** in my hot sauce.

When such a construction seems awkward to you, revise the sentence to avoid using a predicate nominative.

EXAMPLE   **I use** jalapeño **peppers** as the main ingredient in my hot sauce.

19l. When the subject follows the verb, make sure that the verb agrees with it.

In sentences beginning with *here* or *there* and in questions, the subject follows the verb.

EXAMPLES   Here **is** a **set** of keys.
Here **are** the **keys.**
Where **is** my **jacket**? Where **is** my **scarf**?
Where **are** my **jacket** and my **scarf**?

NOTE: Remember that contractions such as *here's, how's, what's,* and *where's* include the singular verb *is*. Use one of these contractions only if a singular subject follows it.

INCORRECT   There's several photos of the oil spill in an article in this month's *Smithsonian.*
CORRECT   There **are** several **photos** of the oil spill in an article in this month's *Smithsonian.*
CORRECT   In this month's *Smithsonian,* there**'s** an **article** with several photos of the oil spill.

▶ EXERCISE 9   **Identifying Sentences with Subject-Verb Agreement**

For each of the following sentences, if the verb agrees with the subject, write *C*. If the subject and verb do not agree, write the correct form of the verb. Be ready to explain your correction.

USAGE

◆ INTEGRATING THE LANGUAGE ARTS

Usage and Writing. Students are sometimes confused by grammatical terms that are not part of their normal vocabulary. The term *predicate nominative* is an example. Remind students that a predicate nominative is located in the predicate and that it renames the subject (the nominative).

As students write, they might check for predicate nominatives by substituting an equal sign (=) for a linking verb such as *is* or *was*. If the noun or pronoun that follows the equal sign renames the subject, it is a predicate nominative. In the example "My hobby is cars," *hobby = cars,* so *cars* is a predicate nominative. Students should make the verb agree with the subject, not with the word that renames it.

USAGE

If students make many errors in **Exercise 9,** you may wish to have them work in pairs to look up and study the rules that apply to the errors they made. Then, have each pair write two or three sentences for the rules they missed.

USAGE

USAGE

632 *Agreement*

1. Soap and water is the best cleanser for my face. **1.** C
2. ∧There's the boats I told you about. **2.** There are
3. ∧Both my father and sister∧wants to see the Dodgers game on Saturday. **3.** want   **4.** is   **5.** were
4. Either the twins or Jamie∧are playing a practical joke.
5. How∧was the swimming and sailing at the beach?
6. Each of these old photos∧show your Uncle Ahmad wearing a colorful, flowing dashiki. **6.** shows
7. Neither the windows nor the door is locked. **7.** C
8. Contemporary rock-and-roll∧are rooted in the ancient rhythms of African music. **8.** is
9. ∧There's always a number of football games on television on New Year's Day. **9.** There are
10. ∧Where's my socks? **10.** Where are

19m. Words stating an amount are usually singular.

When a weight, a measurement, or an amount of time or money is thought of as a unit, it takes a singular verb.

EXAMPLES   Two years **is** a long time.
Fifteen dollars **was** the price.
Ninety percent of the student body **is** present.

When the amount is thought of as individual pieces or parts, a plural verb is used.

EXAMPLES   **Two** of the years **were** especially rainy.
Fifteen of the dollars **were** torn.
Ninety percent of the students **are** present today.

NOTE: The expression *the number* takes a singular verb. The expression *a number* takes a plural verb.

EXAMPLES   **The number** of female athletes **is** growing.
A number of girls **like** strenuous sports.

19n. The verb in a clause following *one of those* should be plural.

EXAMPLE   Melba is one of those **students** who always **try** their best.

19o. *Every* or *many a* before a subject takes a singular verb.

632

EXAMPLES   **Every** mother, father, and grandparent **is** looking on
proudly.
Many a hopeful performer **has** gone to Broadway in
search of fame.

19p. The title of a work of art, literature, or music,
even when plural in form, takes a singular verb.

EXAMPLES   Paul Laurence Dunbar's *Majors and Minors* **is** a
collection of his poetry. [one book]
Jean-François Millet's *The Gleaners* **is** a famous
nineteenth-century painting. [one work of art]
Four Saints in Three Acts, with music by Virgil Thomson
and words by Gertrude Stein, **was** first produced in
1934, with an African American cast. [one musical
work]

19q. *Don't* and *doesn't* must agree with their
subjects.

Use *don't* (the contraction for *do not*) with the subjects *I*
and *you* and with plural subjects.

EXAMPLES   **I don't** have any paper.
You don't need special permission.
The **players don't** seem nervous.

Use *doesn't* with singular subjects.

EXAMPLES   **It [he, she] doesn't** show up in this picture.
The **tire doesn't** have enough air.

19r. Some nouns, although plural in form, take
singular verbs.

EXAMPLES   **Linguistics is** the science of language.
News of the concert's cancellation **was** disappointing
to the band members.

A few nouns ending in *–ics* may be singular or plural.

EXAMPLES   **Acoustics deals** with the transmission of sound.
The **acoustics** in the new auditorium **are** excellent.

Does politics interest you?
Your **politics are** distasteful to me.

USAGE

USAGE

 **INTEGRATING THE
LANGUAGE ARTS**

Usage and Vocabulary. Rule 19r
deals with nouns that may be singular or
plural and nouns that seem plural in
form but take singular verbs. Students
can apply a simple test to decide
whether such a noun is plural or singular. A word that ends in *–ics* is singular if
it means the science or study of something. For example, *acoustics* means
"the science that deals with the way
sound behaves in an enclosed area." The
same word is used in a plural sense to
refer to the individual kinds of sound
behavior within an area.

In the sentence "The acoustics in
the new auditorium are excellent," it is
clear that something other than a science is being described as "excellent." In
this use, *acoustics* must be plural.

> **NOTE:** Check a dictionary when you're not sure whether to use a singular verb or a plural verb with a noun that ends in *–ics.*

Some nouns that end in *–s* always take a plural verb even though they name a single item.

EXAMPLES **Are** the **scissors** sharp enough?
Your gray **slacks are** in the laundry.
The **pliers seem** to be missing.

▷ EXERCISE 10   **Using *Don't* and *Doesn't* Correctly in Sentences**

Choose the correct form (*don't* or *doesn't*) for each of the following sentences.

1. The calf ____ look very strong.   **1.** doesn't
2. It ____ matter if the weather is bad.   **2.** doesn't
3. She ____ play racquetball.   **3.** doesn't
4. ____ these piñatas look colorful?   **4.** Don't
5. I ____ mind helping out.   **5.** don't
6. You ____ have to watch the program.   **6.** don't
7. Loretta ____ enjoy cleaning house.   **7.** doesn't
8. A few of the contests ____ award cash prizes.   **8.** don't
9. ____ it arrive soon?   **9.** Doesn't
10. ____ he tinker with cars?   **10.** Doesn't

▷ EXERCISE 11   **Selecting Verbs That Agree with Their Subjects**

Choose the <u>correct form of the verb</u> given in parentheses in each of the following sentences.

1. Nguyen, along with her family, (*have,* <u>*has*</u>) invited me to the Vietnamese National Day celebration in the park.
2. They (*wasn't,* <u>*weren't*</u>) interested in learning how to play the accordion.
3. Carlos, not Martha or Jan, (<u>*was,*</u> *were*) answering all the letters.
4. Many of them (*has,* <u>*have*</u>) already read the novel.
5. *The Birds* (<u>*was,*</u> *were*) one of Alfred Hitchcock's great movies.
6. (<u>*Doesn't,*</u> *Don't*) Chuck intend to join the air force when he graduates?

CRITICAL THINKING
Evaluation. You may want to have students look carefully at **Exercises 11** and **12** to identify the intervening phrases in the sentences that contain them and to evaluate which of the phrases are important in determining the number of the verb.

USAGE

USAGE

7. Caroline, like most of her classmates, (*wishes*, *wish*) vacation could last forever.
8. There (*is*, *are*) some good programs on educational television.
9. Neither of those books by Naguib Mahfouz (*is*, *are*) on our reading list.
10. It (*doesn't*, *don't*) look good for our baseball league this season.

▶ EXERCISE 12 **Selecting Verbs That Agree with Their Subjects**

For each of the sentences following the picture below, choose the <u>correct form of the verb</u> in parentheses.

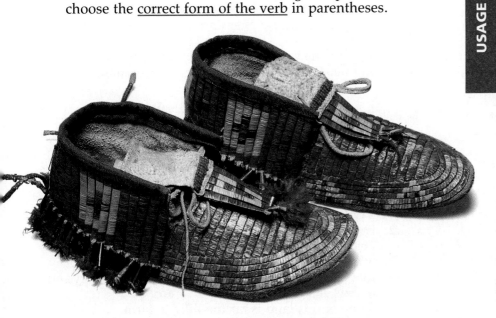

USAGE

VISUAL CONNECTIONS
Exploring the Subject. American Indians from the Great Plains developed the art of quillwork over the centuries by using their imaginations and commonly available materials. Other well-known American Indian arts are pottery, basketry, jewelry, weaving, and painting.

1. (*Doesn't*, *Don't*) these quilled moccasins look as if they are beaded?
2. Quillwork, one of the traditional Plains Indians handicrafts, (*is*, *are*) an ancient and sophisticated art form.
3. The number of quills that grow on one porcupine (*is*, *are*) higher than you might think—about thirty thousand!

USAGE

REVIEW C

OBJECTIVES

• To identify sentences in which subjects and verbs agree in number
• To identify and correctly revise sentences in which subjects and verbs do not agree in number

636 *Agreement*

4. Five inches (*is*, *are*) the maximum length of these tubular spines.
5. Before being used in quillwork, every porcupine quill (*is*, *are*) dyed a bright color, softened in water, and flattened in an unusual way.
6. The quillworker, usually a woman, (*squeezes*, *squeeze*) each quill flat by pulling it between her teeth.
7. Among the Sioux, worn teeth were considered a badge of great honor because items decorated with colorful quillwork (*was*, *were*) so important in tribal life.
8. Working the quills into complex geometric patterns (*require*, *requires*) great skill and coordination.
9. In quill weaving, each of the ribbonlike quills (*is*, *are*) passed tightly over and under threads of fiber or leather.
10. The finished quillwork (*is*, *are*) sewn onto clothing, saddlebags, or cradleboards as a decoration.

▶ REVIEW C   **Making Verbs Agree with Their Subjects**

For each of the following sentences, if the verb and subject agree, write *C*. If the verb and the subject do not agree, supply the correct form of the verb.

1. There ~~are~~ one strain of measles that lasts only three days.   **1.** is
2. Few objections, besides the one about chartering the bus, ~~was~~ raised.   **2.** were
3. *Six Characters in Search of an Author* is a modern play that raises many interesting questions about art and reality.   **3.** C   **4.** C
4. Some of this land is far too hilly to farm.   **5.** there are
5. In Maine, ~~there's~~ many miles of rocky coastline.
6. Four minutes ~~were~~ his record time in that race.   **6.** was
7. Performing in front of a thousand people ~~don't~~ seem to bother the cellist Yo-Yo Ma.   **7.** doesn't   **8.** C
8. Two thirds of a cup of milk is needed for this recipe.
9. Every three years my family ~~visit~~ Sierra Leone, the land our ancestors came from.   **9.** visits
10. Every student, teacher, and administrator ~~are~~ contributing to the fund-raising drive.   **10.** is

LESSON 6 *(pp. 637–645)*

AGREEMENT OF PRONOUN AND ANTECEDENT Rule 19s

OBJECTIVES

- To select pronouns that agree with their antecedents
- To identify and write sentences in which pronouns agree with their antecedents in gender and number

19s

EXERCISE 13

Using Subject-Verb Agreement in Sentences

Butterflies come in many shapes and sizes—and in every color of the rainbow! Make up ten sentences about the butterflies shown here. Use one of the words listed below as the subject of each sentence. Do not use the same word as the subject of more than one sentence. Be sure that each verb you use agrees with its subject.

a few	each	neither	one
all	either	none	several
both	everyone	not one	some

EXAMPLE **1.** *All of these butterflies look like flying flowers!*

Agreement of Pronoun and Antecedent

The word that a pronoun refers to is called its *antecedent*.

19s. A pronoun should agree with its antecedent in gender and number.

Most personal pronouns can refer to antecedents that are masculine or feminine or both or neither.

EXAMPLES **I** am **your** coach.
You are **my** friend.
We are with **them**.
They are **our** cousins.

USAGE

ANSWERS
Exercise 13

Sentences will vary. The singular subjects *each, either, everyone, neither, not one,* and *one* should have singular verbs. The plural subjects *a few, all, both,* and *several* should have plural verbs. *All, none,* and *some* may be either singular or plural, depending on context.

PROGRAM MANAGER

AGREEMENT OF PRONOUN AND ANTECEDENT

- **Independent Practice/ Reteaching** For instruction and exercises, see **Agreement of Pronoun and Antecedent** in *Language Skills Practice and Assessment,* p. 101.

- **Computer Guided Instruction** For additional instruction and practice with agreement of pronoun and antecedent, see **Lesson 8** in *Language Workshop CD-ROM.*

- **Practice** To help less-advanced students with additional instruction and practice with agreement of pronoun and antecedent, see **Chapter 14** in *English Workshop, Fourth Course,* pp. 197–198.

USAGE

To emphasize the importance of clear pronoun reference, read this account to students:

> When Jennifer and Ruth got there, she called home and told her mom where they'd gone after he left the mall. Her mom said they'd invite them over if he could come too.

> After reading the account, ask students to identify all the people referred to by pronouns:

1. Who had to call home?
2. Whose mom is it?
3. Who left the mall?
4. Who would be invited over?

[No certain answers are possible.]

Ask students to explain what makes the story confusing. [Some pronouns have no antecedents. Others do not have clear antecedents or do not agree with their antecedents.]

MEETING *individual* **NEEDS**

LEP/ESL

General Strategies. It generally takes an English-language learner some time to learn to use the correct gender of third-person singular pronouns in speech. Speakers might make many mistakes at first. In the meantime, it is more productive to model standard English than to correct students' speech. For example, in response to a student saying, "The boy found her wallet," you might say, "Oh, he found his wallet! That's great."

Only the third-person singular pronouns indicate the gender of their antecedents. Masculine pronouns refer to males, feminine pronouns to females, and neuter pronouns to things and, often, animals.

MASCULINE	he	him	his
FEMININE	she	her	hers
NEUTER	it	it	its

EXAMPLES   Does **Margaret** like **her** dance class?
       Arturo is doing **his** homework.
       Because the **car** wouldn't start, **it** had to be towed.

When the antecedent of a personal pronoun is another kind of pronoun, determine the gender to use by looking in a phrase following the antecedent.

EXAMPLES   **Neither** of the **girls** brought **her** own lunch.
       One of the **men** lost **his** keys.

When the antecedent could be either masculine or feminine, use both the masculine and feminine forms.

EXAMPLES   **One** of the students left **his or her** pen behind.
       Everybody in the club has paid **his or her** dues.

NOTE: You can often avoid the *his or her* construction by revising the sentence and using the plural form of the pronoun.

     EXAMPLE   **All** of the club members have paid **their** dues.

In conversation, plural personal pronouns are often used to refer to singular antecedents that could be either masculine or feminine. This form is being used more often in writing, too, and it may eventually be considered acceptable in written standard English.

EXAMPLES   **Nobody** rode **their** bikes.
       Everybody brought **their** fishing rods.

(1) Use a singular pronoun to refer to *each, either, neither, one, everyone, everybody, no one, nobody, anyone, anybody, someone,* or *somebody.* The use of a phrase or a clause after the antecedent does not change the number of the antecedent.

EXAMPLES **Each** of the teams had **its** mascot at the game.
One of the boys left **his** pen behind.
Everybody in the women's league has paid **her** dues.

NOTE: When the meaning of *everyone* or *everybody* is *clearly* plural, use the plural pronoun or, better, revise the sentence.

CONFUSING When **everybody** has arrived, explain the situation to **him.**

CLEAR When **everybody** has arrived, explain the situation to **them.**

BETTER When **all** the people have arrived, explain the situation to **them.**

(2) Use a singular pronoun to refer to two or more singular antecedents joined by *or* or *nor*.

EXAMPLE Neither Heidi nor Beth took **her** umbrella with **her.**

(3) Use a plural pronoun to refer to two or more antecedents joined by *and*.

EXAMPLE The guide and the ranger wrapped **their** rain ponchos in **their** saddle rolls.

NOTE: The number of a relative pronoun (*who, which,* and *that*) is determined by the number of the word to which it refers—its antecedent.

EXAMPLES Jessica is one **person who** has faith in **herself.** [*Who* is singular because it refers to *person.* Therefore, the singular forms *has* and *herself* are used to agree with *who.*]
All who want to volunteer should raise **their** hands. [*Who* is plural because *all* is plural. Therefore, the plural forms *want* and *their* are used to agree with *who.*]

▶ EXERCISE 14 **Selecting Pronouns That Agree with Their Antecedents**

For each blank in the following sentences, select a pronoun that will agree with its antecedent.

1. his or her

1. Each of the players had ___ own odd superstition.
2. Someone on the boy's swimming team has parked ___ car in my space. **2.** his   **3.** its
3. Neither of the sweaters had ___ price tag removed.

USAGE

COMMON ERROR

Problem. Students often do not realize that a relative pronoun takes the number of its antecedent. In a sentence such as "Books that are checked out have to be returned on Thursday," the antecedent for *that* is *books* (plural), so the verb (*have*) must be plural. A student who ignores the antecedent and thinks *that* is always singular will commit agreement errors.

Solution. Use a transparency on an overhead projector to show how the chain of reference works. Ask students to copy several sample sentences on a worksheet and to circle the antecedents and the relative pronouns. Then, have them underline the words that must have the number of the antecedent.

USAGE

4. Did everybody at the press conference change ____ mind as soon as Mayor Bradley stated the facts? **4.** his or her

5. Many of the crew got ____ first case of seasickness in the storm. **5.** their

6. One of the houses had ____ windows broken by the hail last night. **6.** its

7. All of the art students buy ____ own paper. **7.** their

8. Anyone who needs a pencil should raise ____ hand. **8.** his or her

9. Either Stu or Mike will lend me ____ fishing gear. **9.** his

10. Each of the characters in Chinese calligraphy has ____ own beauty, mystery, and grace. **10.** its

▶ EXERCISE 15 **Making Pronouns Agree with Their Antecedents**

Most of the following sentences contain pronouns that do not agree with their antecedents. If all of the pronouns in a sentence agree with their antecedents, write *C*. If any pronoun does not agree with its antecedent, supply the correct pronoun.

1. All of these students at the Royal School of Dance in College Park, Florida, are learning traditional dances that **1.** their come from ~~her~~ African heritage.

2. Some of the African and Caribbean dances have **2.** their ~~its~~ roots in African folk tales.

3. At performances, the audience are often seen **3.** their clapping ~~its~~ hands and swaying along with the music.

A DIFFERENT APPROACH

Allow students to work in groups of two or three on **Exercise 15**. Ask them to revise the sentences a second time by making the singular subjects plural and the plural subjects singular. These revisions will require changes in subjects and verbs or pronouns and antecedents.

Each student should then work alone to decide on changes and to proofread the revised sentences.

VISUAL CONNECTIONS

Related Expression Skills. Students who have taken dancing lessons or who just enjoy dancing might want to give an oral narration of an interesting or amusing experience they had while dancing, or they might describe a particular type of dance. They should make sure that their pronouns and antecedents agree.

REVIEWS D and E

OBJECTIVES

- To identify sentences in which subjects and verbs and pronouns and antecedents agree
- To identify and correctly revise sentences in which subjects and verbs or pronouns and antecedents do not agree
- To select verbs that agree with their subjects and pronouns that agree with their antecedents

Agreement of Pronoun and Antecedent **641**

4. Before the last dance recital, I noticed either Carla or Shana practicing ∧their steps. **4. her**
5. Carla is one of those students who always know their steps ahead of time. **5. C**
6. Angelique and Pamela waved ∧her arms gracefully during the first dance. **6. their**
7. Every authentic costume adds ∧their color and movement to the dramatic spectacle. **7. its**
8. Everyone in the class brings ∧their own personal style to the dances. **8. his or her**
9. Many of the dancers and singers give a great deal of credit to the traditional sources of their art form. **9. C**
10. Both their hip-hop dancing and their clothing style have ∧its origins in ancient African culture. **10. their**

> ▶ **REVIEW D**
Identifying Subject-Verb Agreement and Pronoun-Antecedent Agreement in Sentences

In some of the following sentences, either a verb does not agree with its subject or a pronoun does not agree with its antecedent. If a verb or pronoun is wrong, correct it. If the sentence is correct, write C.

1. Both Sid and Nikki like their new neighborhood and their new apartment. **1. C**
2. ∧Are either of you a member of the African American Cultural Society? **2. Is**
3. Anthony, in addition to the other contestants, ∧were ready for the competition to start. **3. was**
4. One of the local police officers was the top scorer on the rifle range. **4. C**
5. Neither Fernando nor Bruce has brought all of ∧their camping gear. **5. his**
6. *The Three Little Pigs* ∧are my young nephews' all-time favorite animated feature. **6. is**
7. Which pair of these Navajo earrings ∧were made by Narciso? **7. was**
8. Where is the Athletics Department? **8. C**
9. Just before the parade started, each of the eight men inside the gigantic dragon costume got ∧their final instructions from Mr. Yee. **9. his**

USAGE

USAGE

641

10. A few of the crowd ∧was murmuring impatiently. **10.** were

11. ∧Is there any of those peanuts left? **11.** Are

12. Either Chi Chi Rodriguez or Nancy Lopez is my golf hero. **12.** C

13. Every one of those stray cattle ∧are going to have to be rounded up. **13.** is

14. An additional feature of these models is the built-in stereo speakers. **14.** C

15. Somebody has gone off and left ∧their car running. **15.** his or her

16. If anybody calls, tell ∧them I'll be back by six o'clock this evening. **16.** him or her

17. Each team has its own colors and symbol. **17.** C

18. One of the goats ∧were nibbling on a discarded pop-corn box. **18.** was

19. Here's the pair of gloves that you forgot. **19.** C

20. ∧Are there no end to these questions? **20.** Is

REVIEW E — Selecting Verbs That Agree with Their Subjects and Pronouns That Agree with Their Antecedents

In each sentence, choose the correct one of the two forms given in parentheses.

1. Neither the manager nor the two salespeople (*was*, *were*) prepared for the number of customers.

2. Neither of the sets of barbells (*was*, *were*) easy to lift.

3. Where (*is*, *are*) the box of nails that came with this bookshelf kit?

4. A few of our classmates (*was*, *were*) invited.

5. The Harlem Globetrotters (*is*, *are*) surely one of the best-loved basketball teams in the world.

6. There (*is*, *are*) leftover macaroni and cheese in the refrigerator.

7. If anybody likes a spectacle, (*he or she*, *they*) will love seeing a drum corps competition.

8. Several of the audience (*was*, *were*) waving wildly, hoping that Martin Yan would wave back.

9. Where (*has*, *have*) the sports section of today's newspaper gone?

10. Anyone who wants to get (*his or her*, *their*) program autographed by Edward James Olmos had better hurry.

▶ EXERCISE 16   **Using Subject-Verb Agreement Correctly in Sentences**

The same thought can almost always be expressed in more than one way. Read each of the following sentences, and then express the same thought in two more sentences. For each new sentence, use one of the two subjects given in parentheses. Be sure that your subjects and verbs agree.

EXAMPLE   **1.** The boys desperately want to go to the circus. (*Both, Each*)

1. *Both of the boys desperately want to go to the circus.*
Each of the boys desperately wants to go to the circus.

1. Their father, as well as their mother, has agreed to the idea. (*Both of their parents, One of their parents*)
2. Not one of the townspeople wants to miss tonight's performance. (*Nobody, None*)
3. Each person has earned a lighthearted evening of watching clowns, horses, and elephants like those shown in these posters. (*Everybody, All*)
4. But because the Great Depression has begun, not all of the families in town have money for tickets. (*not every one, a few*)
5. Forty-nine of the fifty free tickets to the circus have been spoken for. (*All but one, Only one*)

USAGE

ANSWERS
Exercise 16

Students' sentences may vary. Here are some possibilities:

1. Both of their parents have agreed to the idea.
   Each one of their parents has agreed to the idea.

2. Nobody in town wants to miss tonight's performance.
   None of the townspeople want to miss tonight's performance.

3. Everybody has earned a lighthearted evening of watching clowns, horses, and elephants like those shown in these posters.
   All have earned a lighthearted evening of watching clowns, horses, and elephants like those shown in these posters.

4. But because the Great Depression has begun, not every one of the families in town has money for tickets.
   But because the Great Depression has begun, only a few families in town have money for tickets.

5. All but one of the fifty free tickets to the circus have been spoken for.
   Only one of the fifty free tickets to the circus has not been spoken for.

⊙ VISUAL CONNECTIONS

Ideas for Writing. Most people have had friends with whom they really enjoyed going places or doing things. Sometimes those places and activities leave vivid memories.

You may want to have each student write a character sketch of a close friend. Each student should include a brief narration of an incident that demonstrates an important point about the friend's personality. When the compositions are completed, have students work in pairs to check for agreement.

USAGE

WRITING APPLICATION

OBJECTIVE

• To write a friendly letter that includes at least five pronouns that agree with their antecedents

WRITING APPLICATION
Prewriting. As students brainstorm lists of ideas, you may wish to remind them not to decide immediately whether an idea is important. They can be selective after they have finished brainstorming. Otherwise, they might be too choosy and have little to write about.

CRITICAL THINKING
Analysis. During prewriting, students should analyze and evaluate possible subjects in relation to the interests of their audience. From among the possible subjects on their prewriting lists, students will want to select the people, places, and events that will most interest the friend. You may wish to remind them to be sure that the events they write about have occurred since the friend moved away.

USAGE

USAGE

WRITING APPLICATION

Using Agreement to Make Meaning Clear

If you want your reader to know exactly what you mean, your pronouns must clearly refer to their antecedents and agree with them. Suppose you are telling a friend about what happened at the movies last night. You say, "Melba said that Jo Ann ate all of the popcorn Bill bought for her." Whose popcorn did Jo Ann eat? The sentence should be revised to make the meaning clear.

CLEAR   Melba said that Bill bought popcorn for her, but Jo Ann ate all of it.

CLEAR   Melba said that Bill bought popcorn for Jo Ann, who ate all of it.

▶ WRITING ACTIVITY

Your best friend moved away two months ago. You have just received a postcard from him or her, asking what's been happening recently in the old neighborhood. You answer the postcard by writing a short letter that brings your friend up to date. In your letter, include at least five pronouns that agree with their antecedents.

Prewriting   Make a list of several interesting things to tell your friend. You may write about your real neighborhood or about one you have made up. Decide on the order in which you will tell about the items on your list. You may want to use time order (telling when things happened) or spatial order (telling where things happened).

Writing   As you write, think about how to make your letter interesting to your friend. Use details that will help him or her picture the neighborhood and its people.

Evaluating and Revising   Ask a classmate to read your letter. Are the events you tell about interesting? Is it absolutely clear who did what and what belongs to whom? Use your helper's suggestions to revise your letter so that nothing in it is confusing.

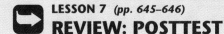
REVIEW: POSTTEST

OBJECTIVES

- To select verbs that agree with their subjects and pronouns that agree with their antecedents
- To identify and revise sentences in which pronouns do not agree with their antecedents and verbs do not agree with their subjects

 Proofreading   Check over the grammar, punctuation, and form of your letter. Use a dictionary to look up the spelling of any word you are not sure of. Be sure each pronoun agrees with its antecedent and each verb agrees with its subject.

Review: Posttest

A. Selecting Verbs That Agree with Their Subjects and Pronouns That Agree with Their Antecedents

In the following sentences, write the correct form of each incorrect verb or pronoun. If a sentence is correct, write *C*.

EXAMPLES   **1.** Each leaf, flower, and seedpod were glimmering with frost.
1. *was*

2. Were any tickets left at the box office for me?
2. *C*

1. There ~~was~~ women, as well as men, who set out on the perilous journey into new territory.   **1.** were
2. The test results showed that about 80 percent of the class was in the average group.   **2.** C
3. A hostile crowd gathered outside the courtroom to show ~~their~~ disapproval of the verdict.   **3.** its
4. *Bronzeville Boys and Girls* ~~are~~ a collection of poems by Gwendolyn Brooks.   **4.** is
5. Neither of the candidates has prepared ~~their~~ speech.   **5.** his or her
6. Mr. Ortega, along with other members of his firm, ~~have~~ established a scholarship fund for art students.   **6.** has
7. To apply for the scholarship, a student must submit at least four samples of ~~their~~ work.   **7.** his or her
8. Chester or Nina, I think, ~~have~~ the best chance of winning.   **8.** has
9. Senator Hayakawa's committee ~~was~~ preparing their speeches for the meeting.   **9.** were
10. All of the bread ~~are~~ on the table.   **10.** is

PROOFREADING

Students should check to make sure that they have incorporated the basic items for a friendly letter: a return address, the date, a salutation, and a friendly closing. The friend's first name in the salutation should be followed by a comma.

Urge students to check carefully for pronoun-antecedent agreement and to have classmates double-check their work.

USAGE

USAGE

B. Selecting Verbs That Agree with Their Subjects and Pronouns That Agree with Their Antecedents

For each sentence in the following paragraph, write the correct form of each incorrect verb or pronoun. A sentence may contain more than one error. If a sentence is correct, write C.

11. was

12. gather

13. is

14. his or her

15. leave

16. gets

17. are

18. doesn't

19. C

20. his or her/ says

[11] Neither my brothers nor my dad ~~were~~ surprised to hear that Aunt Bonnie is going to Africa next month as a Peace Corps volunteer. [12] First, she and the other members of the Kenya group ~~gathers~~ in Philadelphia for a few days of orientation. [13] Their focus at this point ~~are~~ to meet one another and get acquainted. [14] Then the whole group travels together to Nairobi, Kenya, where everyone will have ~~their~~ last chance for months to enjoy hot running water! [15] After one night in Nairobi, half of them ~~leaves~~ for the town of Naivasha for eleven weeks of cultural sensitivity training. [16] Each of the volunteers ~~get~~ to live with a Kenyan family during this period of training. [17] The close daily contact will help them learn to converse in Swahili, one of the languages that ~~is~~ spoken in Kenya. [18] Bonnie ~~don't~~ know yet where exactly in Kenya she is going to be posted. [19] She, as well as the other members of her group, expects to be assigned to the area of greatest need. [20] No one in the group has been told ~~their~~ specific job assignment, but Bonnie ~~say~~ she will probably be helping Kenyans develop small businesses.

USAGE

USAGE

646

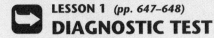
OBJECTIVES

- To identify the correct forms of pronouns in sentences
- To proofread a paragraph for correct pronoun forms

PROGRAM MANAGER

FOR THE WHOLE CHAPTER

- **Review** For exercises on chapter concepts, see **Review Form A** and **Review Form B** in *Language Skills Practice and Assessment*, pp. 115–118.
- **Assessment** For additional testing, see **Usage Pretests** and **Usage Mastery Tests** in *Language Skills Practice and Assessment*, pp. 85–92 and 159–166.

20 USING PRONOUNS CORRECTLY

Nominative and Objective Case

USAGE

CHAPTER OVERVIEW

Even accomplished writers and speakers of English have occasional difficulty with pronoun usage. In trying to be correct, speakers and writers sometimes get confused because the test of "what sounds right" won't work. Pronoun usage is a tricky instruction matter that warrants close study.

Less-advanced students and English-language learners will need to concentrate on **The Objective Case** and **The Nominative Case** lessons, while advanced students could study these as review.

Advanced students should work to master **Special Problems in Pronoun Usage** and **Pronouns in Incomplete Constructions**. Material is provided that could help these students solve all questions regarding the use of *who* and *whom*.

The **Writing Application** and **Picture This** activities lead students to focus on the correct use of pronouns. These assignments may be adapted to your students' needs and abilities.

Diagnostic Test

A. Using Pronouns Correctly in Sentences

Choose the <u>correct word</u> in parentheses in the following sentences.

EXAMPLE **1.** Was it (*he, him*) driving the car when the accident occurred?
1. *he*

1. Francis said that in a few years he would give his stamp collection to his brother and (*I, <u>me</u>*).
2. Everyone was waiting impatiently to find out (*<u>who</u>, whom*) the new cheerleader would be.
3. My little sister is a much better basketball player than (*<u>I</u>, me*).
4. Rep. Ben Nighthorse Campbell is one congressman (*<u>who</u>, whom*) thinks Native Americans should be consulted more often about legislation that concerns them.

647

USAGE

USAGE

5. We found that it was (*she*, *her*) who called twice while we were out of town.
6. The teacher said that (*whoever*, *whomever*) was ready could give a speech first.
7. Speaking of Ken Griffey, Jr., (*he*, *him*) and his dad are the first father and son ever to play professional baseball together on the same team.
8. Seeing a car with an out-of-state license plate in my driveway, I ran inside, and (*who*, *whom*) do you think was there?
9. Mrs. Martin and (*she*, *her*) have been friends since childhood.
10. As you swim, you use nearly all of your major muscles, which makes (*it*, *swimming*) one of the best forms of exercise.

B. Identifying Correct Pronoun Forms in a Paragraph

In each sentence in the following paragraph, choose the correct form from each pair of words in parentheses.

I recently read that anyone [11](*who*, *whom*) comes from a large family grows up with a desire to be surrounded by people all the time. Well, just between you and [12](*I*, *me*), that isn't always true! There aren't many teenagers who enjoy their privacy as much as [13](*I*, *me*). Because I'm the oldest child, I've spent years settling squabbles between my brothers and sisters, helping with homework, and feeding [14](*whoever*, *whomever*) was hungry. When my brothers got into trouble, I always smoothed things over between [15](*they*, *them*) and Dad. And when [16](*he*, *him*) and Mom were busy in the evening, I read to [17](*whoever*, *whomever*) had an earlier bedtime than [18](*I*, *me*). Even now that we're all older, the laughing, yelling, bickering, and commotion always let you know exactly [19](*who*, *whom*) is home at any moment. You'd better believe that [20](*this*, *this hectic upbringing*) has given me a deep craving for privacy, not for company!

CASE FORMS OF PERSONAL PRONOUNS

OBJECTIVE

- To identify and analyze personal pronouns in a paragraph

Case Forms of Personal Pronouns

Case is the form of a noun or pronoun that shows how it is used in a sentence. In English, there are three cases: *nominative, objective,* and *possessive.* Nouns have the same form in both the nominative and the objective case. They usually add an apostrophe and an *s* to form the possessive case.

☞ REFERENCE NOTE: See pages 848–849 and 851 for information on forming the possessives of nouns.

Personal pronouns change form in the different cases.

CASE FORMS OF PERSONAL PRONOUNS			
SINGULAR			
	NOMINATIVE CASE	OBJECTIVE CASE	POSSESSIVE CASE
First Person	I	me	my, mine
Second Person	you	you	your, yours
Third Person	he, she, it	him, her, it	his, her, hers, its
PLURAL			
	NOMINATIVE CASE	OBJECTIVE CASE	POSSESSIVE CASE
First Person	we	us	our, ours
Second Person	you	you	your, yours
Third Person	they	them	their, theirs

Notice that only *you* and *it* have the same form in the nominative and the objective case.

☞ REFERENCE NOTE: For more information on possessive personal pronouns, see page 850.

▶ EXERCISE 1 **Identifying Personal Pronouns in a Paragraph**

Each sentence in the following paragraph contains at least one pronoun. Identify each pronoun. Then, give its person, number, and case; also give its gender if applicable.

PROGRAM MANAGER

CASE FORMS OF PERSONAL PRONOUNS

- **Independent Practice/ Reteaching** For instruction and exercises, see **Case Forms of Personal Pronouns** in *Language Skills Practice and Assessment,* p. 109.

- **Computer Guided Instruction** For additional instruction and practice with the case forms of personal pronouns, see **Lesson 13** in *Language Workshop CD-ROM.*

- **Practice** To help less-advanced students with additional instruction and practice with the case forms of personal pronouns, see **Chapter 15** in *English Workshop, Fourth Course,* pp. 201–202.

 QUICK REMINDER

Tell students that modern English lacks a distinct second-person plural pronoun form. Ask volunteers to explain what this means. [English uses the word *you* for the second-person singular and second-person plural forms.]

Ask students to list second-person plural forms commonly used in conversation [*you guys, you all, y'all*]. You may wish to encourage students to discuss and evaluate the various substitute forms in use.

General Strategies. Some students might need a more gradual introduction to the case forms of personal pronouns than the textbook provides, so spreading practice and review over a longer period of time may help them.

ANSWERS

Exercise 1

1. your—second person singular or plural, possessive case

2. you—second person singular or plural, nominative case
   she—third person singular, nominative case, feminine

3. I—first person singular, nominative case

4. he—third person singular, nominative case, masculine
   his—third person singular, possessive case, masculine

5. he—third person singular, nominative case, masculine
   them—third person plural, objective case

6. they—third person plural, nominative case

7. I—first person singular, nominative case
   his—third person singular, possessive case, masculine
   mine—first person singular, possessive case

8. me—first person singular, objective case
   he—third person singular, nominative case, masculine

9. their—third person plural, possessive case

10. we—first person plural, nominative case

USAGE

USAGE

EXAMPLE   [1]   Jeffrey and I were chatting in front of his locker before the Art Club meeting.
           1.   *I—first person singular, nominative case; his—third person singular, possessive case, masculine*

[1] Jeffrey mentioned your interest in African art and Francine's interest in modern art. [2] Did you and she know that African tribal masks like the one below in the middle influenced the development of the Modernist movement in art? [3] I've learned that African carvings inspired such twentieth-century artists as Pablo Picasso, who created the painting on the left. [4] The year 1905 was probably when he and his friends first saw African masks exhibited in Paris. [5] Amedeo Modigliani was especially affected by the stark masks, and he and Picasso created many works based on them. [6] Notice that the eyes in Modigliani's carving on the right are very close together and that they and the lips look much like small knobs. [7] I used to think that Modigliani made his faces too long by mistake, but the error was mine. [8] Ms. Keller told me that he was copying the exaggerated shapes of Ivory Coast masks. [9] Picasso and Modigliani were only two of many European artists who got their inspiration from African art. [10] Obviously, we students weren't giving credit where credit was due!

LESSON 3 *(pp. 651–654)*

THE NOMINATIVE CASE Rules 20a, 20b

OBJECTIVES

- To read aloud sentences and stress the pronoun usage
- To complete sentences by using personal pronouns in the nominative case

The Nominative Case

20a. The subject of a verb is in the nominative case.

EXAMPLES   **I** solved the problem. [*I* is the subject of *solved.*]
Al and **she** cleaned the house. [*Al* and *she* is the compound subject of *cleaned.*]
They know that **we** are going. [*They* is the subject of *know,* and *we* is the subject of *are going.*]

When both parts of a compound subject are pronouns, you may not be sure which form to use.

EXAMPLE   (*She, Her*) and (*I, me*) studied for the test.

To choose the correct form, try each pronoun separately with the verb.

SEPARATELY   *She* studied for the test. *I* studied for the test. [*Her studied for the test* and *me studied for the test* sound strange.]
TOGETHER   **She** and **I** studied for the test.

Using *we* and *they* as the parts of a compound subject may sound awkward to you, even though doing so is correct. If so, revise the sentence.

ORIGINAL   **We** and **they** will go to the movie.
REVISED   **We** will go to the movie with **them.**

ORAL
PRACTICE 1   **Using Pronouns as Subjects**

Read each of the following sentences aloud, stressing the italicized words.

1. *She* and *I* gave the dog a bath.
2. Terry and *he* plan to try out for the soccer team.
3. *We* sophomores organized the drive.
4. James Earl Jones and *she* are excellent role models for young actors.
5. Are *you* and *he* doing the report?
6. Either *we* or *they* may go to the championship finals.
7. The drill team and *we* band members took the bus.
8. The twins and *they* go everywhere together.

USAGE

PROGRAM MANAGER

THE NOMINATIVE CASE

- **Independent Practice/ Reteaching** For instruction and exercises, see **The Nominative Case** in *Language Skills Practice and Assessment,* p. 110.
- **Computer Guided Instruction** For additional instruction and practice with the nominative case, see **Lesson 13** in *Language Workshop CD-ROM.*
- **Practice** To help less-advanced students with additional instruction and practice with the nominative case, see **Chapter 15** in *English Workshop, Fourth Course,* pp. 203–204.

QUICK REMINDER

Write on the chalkboard:
(*He, Him*) and (*I, me*) arrived early for the test Saturday morning.

Have students pair each pronoun with the verb. [He arrived. I arrived.] Tell them that when they are selecting pronoun forms for compound subjects, it is often helpful to use each form separately and to work with as few words as possible, eliminating prepositional phrases and adverbs.

LESS-ADVANCED STUDENTS

As students complete **Oral Practice 1,** you may want to have volunteers reduce the words in each sentence to make it easier to determine the correct

continued on next page

USAGE

pronoun form. For example, sentence 1 would be "She gave the dog a bath" and "I gave the dog a bath."

ANSWERS
Exercise 3

Answers may vary. Here are some possible sentences:

1. We teenagers go through many changes.

2. The other shoppers and I missed the sale.

3. He and his friends never have much money.

4. Liz, Michelle, and she are the best dancers.

5. They and their classmates have part-time jobs.

ANSWERS
Exercise 4

Answers may vary. Here are some sample sentences:

1. If my parents were in that soldier's shoes, they would worry and so would I.

2. We remember when the Iraqis invaded Kuwait and how they began a reign of terror.

3. It was even frightening secondhand, so we tuned out the newscasters, including Peter Arnett.

4. He was in Iraq, broadcasting as bombs fell on Baghdad.

5. With our Patriot missiles, we intercepted most of the Iraqi attacks on Israel.

6. Later we saw the great pain of Arab families, which they experienced in Iraq as well as in Kuwait.

- To compose sentences with pronouns in the nominative case as subjects
- To complete sentences by using pronouns as predicate nominatives

▷ EXERCISE 2 **Using Personal Pronouns in the Nominative Case to Complete Sentences**

Pronouns will vary.

Supply a personal pronoun for each blank in the following sentences. Vary your pronouns. Do not use *you* or *it*.

1. The judge and ___ studied the evidence. **1.** she
2. Ted and ___ took the wrong train. **2.** he
3. Linda and ___ are planning a party. **3.** they
4. ___ students are having a science fair. **4.** We
5. Either Julius or ___ will give you a ride. **5.** she
6. ___ and ___ have been rivals for years. **6.** We/they
7. I'm sure ___ knew about the meeting. **7.** he
8. Soon ___ and ___ will be graduating. **8.** she/I
9. Did you know that ___ and ___ saw Chita Rivera in a Broadway production of *West Side Story*? **9.** he/I
10. ___ and ___ love those little Chinese dumplings served at dim sum restaurants. **10.** She/they

▷ EXERCISE 3 **Writing Sentences with Pronouns in the Nominative Case**

Use the following subjects in sentences of your own.

1. we teenagers
2. the other shoppers and I
3. he and his friends
4. Liz, Michelle, and she
5. they and their classmates

▷ EXERCISE 4 **Writing Sentences Using Personal Pronouns**

Your cousin was too young to understand what happened during Operation Desert Storm, but now that she is older, she is curious. You show her the map and pictures appearing on the next page and explain as well as you can what happened before, during, and after the Persian Gulf Conflict. Write at least five sentences that include ten personal pronouns in the nominative case. Underline the nominative case pronouns you use.

EXAMPLE **1.** *When I saw the photos in a magazine, they made me very sad and very proud.*

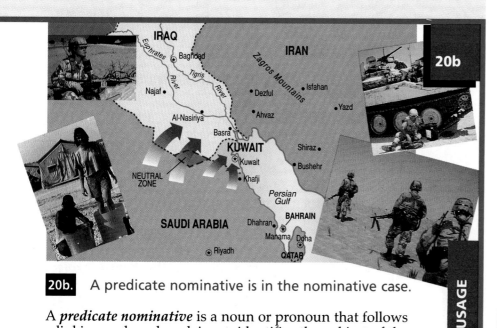

20b. A predicate nominative is in the nominative case.

A *predicate nominative* is a noun or pronoun that follows a linking verb and explains or identifies the subject of the sentence. A pronoun used as a predicate nominative always follows a form of the verb *be* or a verb phrase ending in *be* or *been*.

👉 REFERENCE NOTE: See page 560 for more information on predicate nominatives.

COMMON FORMS OF *BE*		PREDICATE NOMINATIVE
am is, are was, were may be, can be, will be, etc. has been, have been, had been, may have been, etc. should be, could be, would be	*are followed by*	I he she we you they

EXAMPLES   It was **I** who took the message.
The winner might be **he**.
Could the caller have been **she**?

NOTE: In casual conversation, expressions such as *It's me* and *That's her*, are acceptable. Avoid them in more formal speaking situations such as job interviews. In your written work, don't use them unless you're creating casual conversation in dialogue.

USAGE

⬡ **INTEGRATING THE LANGUAGE ARTS**

Literature Link. Have students read William Stafford's poem "Fifteen," and ask them to pay special attention to Stafford's use of pronouns in the nominative case. Ask the students why the narrator switches from *I* to *we* in the third stanza. [This indicates that the boy and the motorcycle have become one in the boy's fantasy.] Then ask them why they think Stafford used the first-person pronoun instead of a name. [The use of the first person creates a closer relationship between the narrator and the audience.] Explain to the students that this poem is an example of how the proper use of pronouns can relay meaning beyond that of the words themselves.

👥 **COOPERATIVE LEARNING**
As students study the material on **Rule 20b** regarding the use of the nominative case for predicate nominatives, you may want to point out that this construction is rare in casual speaking or writing. To demonstrate this, have students bring in newspaper articles or sports magazines. Have them work in groups of four or five to scan articles for the use of pronouns as predicate nominatives. They could circle each use and then trade materials with other groups to observe what they have found.

USAGE

653

REVIEWS A and B

OBJECTIVE

• To use pronouns in the nominative case correctly in sentences and paragraphs

> EXERCISE 5

Using Predicate Nominatives in Sentences

Complete each of the following sentences by supplying the personal pronoun called for in parentheses.

1. Do you think it was ____? (*third person singular, masculine*) **1.** he   **2.** she
2. It must have been ____. (*third person singular, feminine*)
3. Good friends are ____. (*third person plural*) **3.** they
4. The pranksters were ____. (*first person plural*) **4.** we
5. It was ____ at the door. (*third person plural*) **5.** they

> REVIEW A

Using Pronouns in the Nominative Case Correctly in Sentences

Supply a personal pronoun for each blank in the following sentences. Use as many different pronouns as you can. Do not use *you* or *it*. Be ready to explain the reasons for your choice.

Pronouns will vary.

1. When I saw Dame Kiri Te Kanawa in front of Lincoln Center, I couldn't believe it was ____. **1.** she
2. Everyone applauded when Patty and ____ took a bow. **2.** he
3. Where did Barry and ____ go after school? **3.** they
4. Jimmy and ____ caught the runaway piglets. **4.** I
5. It is ____ that you need to see. **5.** we
6. Skip argued that it was Lana and ____ who made the error. **6.** they
7. Was it Teresa or ____ who hit the home run? **7.** he
8. Either David or ____ might be able to do it. **8.** I
9. My sister and ____ love the South African musical group Ladysmith Black Mambazo. **9.** I   **10.** she
10. I believe that the Masked Marvel has to be ____.

> REVIEW B

Using Pronouns in the Nominative Case Correctly in a Paragraph

For each numbered blank in the following paragraph, supply an appropriate personal pronoun. Do not use *you* or *it*.

1. We

[1] ____ tenth-grade students are determined to win this year's "Save the Earth" trophy at our school. The two

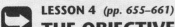
THE OBJECTIVE CASE Rules 20c, 20d

OBJECTIVES

- To use pronouns in the objective case as direct objects, indirect objects, and objects of prepositions
- To read aloud sentences and stress the pronoun usage
- To identify the correct pronoun form for objects of prepositions

---

Case Forms of Personal Pronouns **655**

20c

most enthusiastic people in our class are probably Pilar and [2] ____. I guess that's why Mrs. Nakamura asked if [3] ____ and [4] ____ would organize the paper drive by ourselves. Pilar explained to the class that if [5] ____ Americans recycled only our Sunday newspapers, half a million trees would be saved every Sunday! To illustrate her point, she showed this photo. That's [6] ____ standing next to 580 pounds of paper—the amount an average American uses in one year. [7] ____ have gathered some other facts to inspire our classmates to recycle. Our friend Ben

said that [8] ____ and his mother heard on the radio that the average American uses 1,500 aluminum drink cans every year. [9] ____ were amazed to learn that the energy saved from recycling just one aluminum can could keep a TV set running for three hours! No matter who wins the trophy, it will definitely be [10] ____ who share the prize of a cleaner, healthier planet.

2. I
3. she
4. I
5. we
6. she
7. We
8. he
9. We
10. we

USAGE

The Objective Case

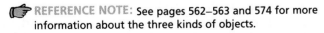

Pronouns in the objective case are used as direct objects, indirect objects, and objects of prepositions.

☞ REFERENCE NOTE: See pages 562–563 and 574 for more information about the three kinds of objects.

20c. Direct objects and indirect objects are in the objective case.

A *direct object* is a noun or pronoun that receives the action of the verb or shows the result of the action.

PROGRAM MANAGER

THE OBJECTIVE CASE

- **Independent Practice/ Reteaching** For instruction and exercises, see **The Objective Case** in *Language Skills Practice and Assessment*, p. 111.

- **Computer Guided Instruction** For additional instruction and practice with the objective case, see **Lesson 13** in *Language Workshop CD-ROM.*

- **Practice** To help less-advanced students with additional instruction and practice with the objective case, see **Chapter 15** in *English Workshop, Fourth Course,* pp. 205–208.

QUICK REMINDER

Remind students that objective-case pronouns may simply replace nouns that receive, directly or indirectly, the action of a verb. Objective-case pronouns may also be objects of prepositions.

Have students identify how the underlined pronouns are used in the following sentences:

1. Mr. Martin helped <u>me</u>.
   [direct object]

2. Liza gave <u>him</u> her car keys.
   [indirect object]

3. Wilford smiled at <u>her</u>.
   [object of the preposition]

USAGE

- To write sentences using pronouns as objects of prepositions
- To write a fable that includes ten personal pronouns

MEETING *individual* NEEDS

LEP/ESL

General Strategies. If students make errors in this section, you will need to determine whether they are confusing the case forms or need a review in identifying direct and indirect objects. Not all languages follow the subject-verb-object pattern, so you may want to give additional review in identifying objects if you suspect this is a problem.

LESS-ADVANCED STUDENTS

Rather than ask students to analyze grammatical structure by differentiating direct and indirect objects from objects of prepositions, you may want to combine the different kinds of objects. Explain that an object is generally a word that describes a person or a thing that an action is done to or for. You may want to write examples on the chalkboard.

LEARNING STYLES

Visual Learners. Familiarity with placement may help students identify correct pronouns. Have students work together as a group to design cards indicating likely placement for pronouns in the nominative and objective case. [Pronouns in the nominative case come before a verb or follow a form of the verb *be;* objective-case pronouns follow an action verb or a preposition.]

656

EXAMPLES   Coach Johnson has been training **us**.
The coach has turned **them** into the best team in the state.

An ***indirect object*** is a noun or pronoun that tells *to whom* or *for whom* the action of the verb is done.

EXAMPLES   Serena paid **him** a compliment.
Carlos saved **me** a seat in the first row.

When a direct object or an indirect object is compound, try each pronoun separately with the verb. For the sentence to be correct, all parts of the compound must be correct.

EXAMPLE: The news surprised them and we.
The news surprised them is correct.
The news surprised we is incorrect.
ANSWER: The news surprised **them** and **us**.

EXAMPLE: Bao showed her and I pictures of Vietnam.
Bao showed her pictures of Vietnam is correct.
Bao showed I pictures of Vietnam is incorrect.
ANSWER: Bao showed **her** and **me** pictures of Vietnam.

▷ EXERCISE 6   **Using Pronouns in the Objective Case to Complete Sentences**

Supply a personal pronoun for each blank in the following sentences. Use a variety of pronouns. Do not use *you* or *it*.
Pronouns will vary.

1. The old sailor warned ____ about the danger.   **1.** us
2. The city awarded ____ its highest honor for their bravery in rescuing earthquake victims.   **2.** them
3. You could ask Deborah or ____.   **3.** him
4. The crowd cheered ____ heartily.   **4.** us
5. Make sure that you ask ____ what her Social Security number is.   **5.** her
6. The shark in that movie didn't scare ____ at all.   **6.** me
7. How can I recognize ____?   **7.** him
8. We saw Norman and ____ in their horse costume at the party.   **8.** her
9. Did you give Paula and ____ their assignments?   **9.** them
10. I bought my father and ____ identical birthday presents this year.   **10.** her

▶ REVIEW C

Using Pronouns in the Nominative and Objective Cases in Sentences

The cheerleading squad is learning a new pyramid routine. To help get everyone organized, the coach has assigned each cheerleader a number. In each of the following sentences, replace the cheerleader's number with a correct personal pronoun. If *Number 1* is specified, use *I*, *we*, *me*, or *us*.

EXAMPLES
  1. Coach Welber told Cara and *Number 5* where to position themselves.
  1. *her*

  2. I asked if *Number 8 and Number 1* could be in the pyramid next time.
  2. *we*

1. The three people forming the base of the pyramid were Harley, Michael, and *Number 5*. **1.** she
2. Kimiko is the smallest, so it was *Number 6* who got to be at the top first. **2.** she
3. The coach asked *Number 8 and Number 1* to give *Number 6* a boost. **3.** us/her
4. After *Number 4* and Emilio had been in the middle row awhile, Rosie and *Number 1* asked for a turn. **4.** she/I
5. Please tell Luisa and *Number 6 and Number 3* to stop laughing and pay attention. **5.** them
6. Give Rosie or *Number 1* a signal when you want to jump down, Kimiko. **6.** me

USAGE

REVIEW C

Teaching Note. Students might not realize that when two numbers are joined by an italicized *and,* a plural pronoun should be used.

    Direct students' attention to the second example in **Review C.** Explain that when two numbers are joined by an italicized *and,* the students should use a plural pronoun to replace the two numbers.

USAGE

7. Next time, the ones in the middle row will be Harley and *Number 8*. **7.** she
8. If anyone can support the person on top well, it's *Number 3*. **8.** he
9. The winners of the next cheerleading meet will surely be *Numbers 1 through 8*. **9.** we
10. Come here and I'll tell you and *Number 4* about the next new formation. **10.** her

20d. The object of a preposition is in the objective case.

A prepositional phrase begins with a preposition and ends with a noun or pronoun called the *object of the preposition.*

EXAMPLES to **them** for **her** and **us** with **him**

When the object of a preposition is compound, try each pronoun separately in the prepositional phrase.

NONSTANDARD **Gwen wrote to her and I.** [*Gwen wrote to her* is correct. *Gwen wrote to I* is incorrect.]

STANDARD **Gwen wrote to her and me.**

NOTE: Using incorrect pronoun forms after the prepositions *between* and *for* is a common error. The pronouns should be in the objective case.

INCORRECT between *you* and *I*, for *she* and *they*
CORRECT between you and **me**, for **her** and **them**

ORAL PRACTICE 2 **Using Pronouns as Objects of Prepositions**

Read each of the following sentences aloud, stressing the italicized words.

1. There were calls *for* Walker and *us*.
2. This message is *from* Dolores and *her*.
3. We sat *with* Arnie and *them*.
4. Margo looked *toward* Francine and *me*.
5. They gave copies *to him* and *me*.
6. This drawing is *by* either Hector or *him*.
7. Don't hold this *against* Cho and *her*.
8. I walked *between* Vince and *him*.

USAGE

EXERCISE 7

Identifying the Correct Pronoun Forms for Objects of Prepositions

Identify the <u>correct pronoun</u> in parentheses in the following sentences.

1. The referee called fouls on (*he*, <u>*him*</u>) and (*I*, <u>*me*</u>).
2. Maggie is off fishing with Grandpa and (*he*, <u>*him*</u>).
3. We didn't want to leave without you and (*she*, <u>*her*</u>).
4. They assigned the same lab equipment to (*they*, <u>*them*</u>) and (*we*, <u>*us*</u>).
5. The duke directed a haughty sneer at the jester and (*he*, <u>*him*</u>).
6. After Carmen rolled the corn husks around the tamales, she handed them to Arturo and (*I*, <u>*me*</u>).
7. Everyone but Kevin and (*she*, <u>*her*</u>) thinks Ed Bradley is the best news commentator on television.
8. The player tried to dodge between Sherrie and (*I*, <u>*me*</u>).
9. The wary skunk circled around (*she*, <u>*her*</u>) and (*I*, <u>*me*</u>).
10. Uncle Vic will get the details from you and (*she*, <u>*her*</u>).

 EXERCISE 8

Writing Sentences Using Pronouns as Objects of Prepositions

Write sentences of your own, using each of the following prepositions with a compound object. Use a personal pronoun for at least one of the objects in each sentence.

1. against   2. for   3. except   4. without   5. by

PICTURE THIS

You are a helper at a day-care center. The teacher wants you to entertain the group of children shown on the next page and, at the same time, teach them something about getting along with people who look different. She asks you to write a short fable with animal characters and read it to the children. In your fable, use at least ten personal pronouns. Use some of them as compound subjects, some

TIMESAVER

To reduce paper-grading time and to increase students' exposure to correct oral usage, have students read their sentences for **Exercise 7** aloud. You will probably want to do this as a spot-check before having them exchange and grade the papers. You may want to collect the papers to check for mastery.

ANSWERS
Exercise 8

Sentences will vary. Responses should include pronouns in the objective case. Here are some sample sentences:

1. He turned Julie against John and her.
2. Mom bought new clothes for him and me.
3. Everyone's going except Colleen and him.
4. How could he do that without my parents and us?
5. The game was won by Max and me.

PICTURE THIS

You may want to further review the characteristics of fables with your students by reminding them that in most fables animals act and talk like people. Most fables also teach a lesson that is often summarized at the end.

Have students share a favorite fable with the class and encourage class discussion of the morals at the end of the stories.

as compound direct or indirect objects, and some as compound objects of prepositions. Be sure to use the correct case for your pronouns. However, in the animals' dialogue, you may include such informal expressions as "It's me."

Subject: a fable about getting along well together
Audience: a group of four- to six-year-olds
Purpose: to entertain and to teach

▶ REVIEW D   **Identifying Correct Forms of Pronouns**

Choose the <u>correct pronoun</u> in parentheses in each numbered sentence in the following paragraph.

[1] Last fall, Tina talked Susan and (*I*, <u>*me*</u>) into going on a canoe trip with the Wilderness Club. [2] She warned (*we*, <u>*us*</u>) that we might get a good dunking before we were through. [3] When we set out, Susan and (<u>*I*</u>, *me*) could barely steer our canoe. [4] We watched another canoeist and saw how (<u>*she*</u>, *her*) and her partner maneuvered their craft. [5] They and (<u>*we*</u>, *us*) both did well until we hit the rapids or, rather, the rapids hit (*we*, <u>*us*</u>). [6] Susan grabbed for our sleeping bags, and (<u>*she*</u>, *her*) and (<u>*I*</u>, *me*) both scrambled for our food cooler. [7] All of (*we*, <u>*us*</u>) would-be

Literature Link. Have students read Anne Sexton's "Courage" and have them discuss Sexton's use of pronouns.

While the referent for the pronoun *it* in the first line is not explicitly identified in the line, it is revealed by the title. A close reading of the poem will reveal eleven more occurrences of the pronoun *it* with a number of different referents. Often the pronoun is separated from its referent by many words. Tell students that such use of pronouns can be a powerful device but that if they use this strategy, they must be sure to supply the reader with enough clues to clearly identify the referent.

SPECIAL PROBLEMS IN PRONOUN USAGE Rules 20e, 20f

OBJECTIVES

- To use *who* and *whom* correctly in subordinate clauses, and to identify the use of the pronoun
- To write sentences using phrases containing pronouns and to identify how each phrase is used

20e

campers were drenched, but no quitters were (*we*, *us*). [8] Tina's warning haunted all of (*we*, *us*) as (*we*, *us*) hungry adventurers contemplated waterlogged sandwiches, soggy salads, and banana muffins with tadpoles in them. [9] Later, Susan and (*I*, *me*) discovered that our bedrolls had become portable water beds. [10] After a cold, squishy night, (*I*, *me*) concluded that wise are (*they*, *them*) who heed the voice of experience.

Special Problems in Pronoun Usage

Who and *Whom*

NOMINATIVE CASE	who, whoever
OBJECTIVE CASE	whom, whomever

NOTE: In spoken English, the use of *whom* is gradually dying out. Nowadays, it's acceptable to begin any spoken question with *who* regardless of whether the nominative or objective form is grammatically correct. In writing, though, it's still important to distinguish between *who* and *whom*.

20e. The use of *who* and *whom* in a subordinate clause depends on how the pronoun functions in the clause.

☞ **REFERENCE NOTE:** See pages 598–606 for information on subordinate clauses.

Follow these steps to decide whether to use *who* or *whom* in a subordinate clause.

STEP 1: Find the subordinate clause.
STEP 2: Decide how the pronoun is used in the clause—as subject, predicate nominative, direct object, indirect object, or object of a preposition.
STEP 3: Determine the case of the pronoun according to the rules of standard English.
STEP 4: Select the correct form of the pronoun.

PROGRAM MANAGER

SPECIAL PROBLEMS IN PRONOUN USAGE

- **Independent Practice/ Reteaching** For instruction and exercises, see *Who or Whom?* and **Pronouns Used as Appositives** in *Language Skills Practice and Assessment*, pp. 112–113.

- **Computer Guided Instruction** For additional instruction and practice with special problems in pronoun usage, see **Lesson 14** in *Language Workshop CD-ROM.*

- **Practice** To help less-advanced students with additional instruction and practice with special problems in pronoun usage, see **Chapter 15** in *English Workshop, Fourth Course*, pp. 211–212.

QUICK REMINDER

Write the following sentences on the chalkboard and have students combine them by using the pronouns in parentheses. Ask students to explain why the pronoun usage is correct.

1. Juana is the baby sitter. Juana saved the child's life. (who) [Juana is the baby sitter who saved the child's life. The pronoun referring to Juana is the subject of the subordinate clause *saved the child's life,* so it should be in the nominative case.]

2. I voted for Quay. I know Quay from the soccer team. (whom) [I voted for Quay, whom I know from the soccer team. The pronoun referring to Quay is the direct object of *I know,* so it should be in the objective case.]

LEP/ESL

General Strategies. Most languages do not have an equivalent to the *who/whom* distinction. Thus, students may not have a first-language context to which they can relate this concept. You may want to provide some additional examples. Encourage students to use the examples for oral practice.

COMMON ERROR

Problem. In an attempt to write more formally, students might use *whom* in their writing when *who* is correct.

Solution. To help students determine the correct form of the pronoun, substitute other nominative-case pronouns (such as *I, she, they*) for the word *who* or *whom*. If a nominative-case pronoun is grammatically correct, the form *who* is needed. If a nominative-case pronoun is not correct, the objective form *whom* is correct.

LESS-ADVANCED STUDENTS

The process of determining whether to use *who* or *whom* often requires more knowledge of English grammar than many students possess. However, if they frequently use *whom* incorrectly in their speech and writing, you may want to give them the rule "When in doubt, use *who*." You could also point out that *who* is acceptable in almost any informal construction.

---

662 *Using Pronouns Correctly*

EXAMPLE:	Roscoe is the only student (*who, whom*) got a perfect score.
STEP 1:	The subordinate clause is *(who, whom) got a perfect score.*
STEP 2:	In this clause, the pronoun is the subject of the verb *got*.
STEP 3:	As a subject, the pronoun should be in the nominative case.
STEP 4:	The nominative form is *who*.
ANSWER:	Roscoe is the only student **who** got a perfect score.

EXAMPLE:	Do you know (*who, whom*) she is?
STEP 1:	The subordinate clause is *(who, whom) she is.*
STEP 2:	In this clause, the pronoun (*who, whom*) is the predicate nominative: *she is (who, whom).*
STEP 3:	A pronoun used as a predicate nominative should be in the nominative case.
STEP 4:	The nominative form is *who*.
ANSWER:	Do you know **who** she is?

EXAMPLE:	I saw Sabrina, (*who, whom*) I know from school.
STEP 1:	The subordinate clause is *(who, whom) I know from school.*
STEP 2:	In this clause, the pronoun is the direct object of the verb *know: I know (who, whom).*
STEP 3:	As a direct object, the pronoun should be in the objective case.
STEP 4:	The objective form is *whom*.
ANSWER:	I saw Sabrina, **whom** I know from school.

Remember that no words outside the subordinate clause affect the case of the pronoun. In the second example above, the whole clause *who she is* is the direct object of the verb in the independent clause, *do know*. In the subordinate clause, though, *who* is used as a predicate nominative, which takes the nominative case.

NOTE: *Whom* is often left out of a subordinate clause, but its function is understood.

EXAMPLES   The actor (whom) I wrote to sent these photos. [*Whom* is understood to be the object of the preposition *to.*]
The man (whom) we saw on the elevator looked familiar. [*Whom* is understood to be the direct object of *saw.*]

Peanuts reprinted by permission of United Feature Syndicate, Inc.

▶ EXERCISE 9 **Determining the Use of *Who* and *Whom* in Subordinate Clauses**

Identify the <u>subordinate clause containing *who* or *whom*</u> in each of the following sentences. Then, tell how the relative pronoun (*who* or *whom*) is used in its own clause—as <u>s</u>ubject, <u>p</u>redicate <u>n</u>ominative, <u>d</u>irect <u>o</u>bject, or <u>o</u>bject of a preposition.

EXAMPLE **1.** She is someone whom we all admire.
1. *whom we all admire—direct object*

1. The people <u>who are born in Puerto Rico</u> live in a commonwealth, with its own Senate, Supreme Court, and governor's Cabinet. **1.** s.
2. In 1969, the governor needed a secretary of labor <u>on whom he could depend</u>. **2.** o.p.
3. The person <u>whom he appointed</u> would occupy the most difficult and sensitive position in the Cabinet. **3.** d.o.
4. Do you know <u>who the choice was</u>? **4.** p.n.
5. The choice fell to Mrs. Julia Rivera De Vincenti, <u>who became the first woman to occupy a Cabinet post in Puerto Rico</u>. **5.** s.
6. De Vincenti, <u>who had completed the requirements for a Ph.D. degree in management and collective bargaining at Cornell University</u>, was a good choice. **6.** s.
7. De Vincenti, <u>who was later appointed to the U.S. Mission to the United Nations</u>, was the first Puerto Rican to serve in that capacity. **7.** s.
8. She addressed the General Assembly and showed that she was a person <u>who knew her job well</u>. **8.** s.
9. She praised her compatriots, <u>from whom new advances in agriculture had recently come</u>. **9.** o.p.
10. And De Vincenti made history again, for she was the first woman <u>who ever wore a pantsuit to address the General Assembly</u>! **10.** s.

USAGE

USAGE

USAGE

Appositives

20f. Pronouns used as appositives should be in the same case as the word they refer to.

An *appositive* is a noun or pronoun given with another noun or pronoun to identify or explain it.

EXAMPLES   The late arrivals, **she, he,** and **I,** missed the first act. [The pronouns are in the nominative case because they are in apposition with the subject *arrivals.*]

The co-captains should be the best bowlers, **he** and **she.** [The pronouns are in the nominative case because they are in apposition with the predicate nominative *bowlers.*]

The article mentions the winners, **her** and **me.** [The pronouns are in the objective case because they are in apposition with the direct object *winners.*]

Ms. Lee gave the debaters, **them** and **us,** name tags. [The pronouns are in the objective case because they are in apposition with the indirect object *debaters.*]

The finalists were narrowed to two, **him** and **her.** [The pronouns are in the objective case because they are in apposition with the object of the preposition *two.*]

The pronouns *we* and *us* are sometimes used with noun appositives.

EXAMPLES   **We** sophomores raised the most money for charity. [The pronoun is in the nominative case because it is the subject of the sentence.]

The judges awarded **us** members of the jazz band a superior rating. [The pronoun is in the objective case because it is the indirect object of the verb *awarded.*]

To decide which form is correct for a pronoun used as an appositive or with an appositive, read the sentence with only the pronoun.

EXAMPLES   Coach Karas congratulated the two starting forwards, Angela and (*I, me*). [Omit the direct object *forwards:* Coach Karas congratulated Angela and **me.**]

(*We, Us*) girls made the playoffs! [Omit the appositive *girls:* **We** made the playoffs!]

REVIEWS E–G

OBJECTIVES

- To choose correct pronouns and describe how they are used in sentences
- To proofread a paragraph and identify correct pronoun forms
- To determine the proper case of pronouns used in sentences

20f

☞ REFERENCE NOTE: See pages 590–591 for more information on appositives.

▷ REVIEW E

Selecting Pronouns to Complete Sentences Correctly

Choose the <u>correct pronoun</u> in parentheses in each of the following sentences. Then, tell whether each is used as a <u>s</u>ubject, a <u>p</u>redicate <u>n</u>ominative, a <u>d</u>irect <u>o</u>bject, an <u>i</u>ndirect <u>o</u>bject, an <u>o</u>bject <u>o</u>f a <u>p</u>reposition, or an <u>a</u>ppositive.

1. The two winners, Sean and (*she, her*), received huge green ribbons decorated with shamrocks. **1. app.**
2. Will Meg and (*she, her*) run the concession stand? **2. s.**
3. The coach asked you and (*I, me*) for help with the equipment. **3. d.o.**
4. Becky and (*she, her*) rode their bikes to the meeting. **4. s.**
5. The lighting crew for the play was Manuel and (*I, me*). **5. p.n.**
6. They treat (*whoever, whomever*) they hire very well. **6. d.o.**
7. I think it was Denzel Washington and (*he, him*) who starred in *Glory*. **7. p.n.**
8. They met Jennie and (*she, her*) at the airport. **8. d.o.**
9. Joe Leaphorn and Jim Chee are the Navajo detectives (*who, whom*) Tony Hillerman writes about in his crime stories. **9. o.p.**
10. I think that the people who were costumed as pirates are (*they, them*). **10. p.n.**

▷ REVIEW F

Proofreading a Paragraph for Correct Pronoun Forms

Some of the sentences in the following paragraph contain one or more pronouns that are used incorrectly. If a pronoun is incorrect, write the correct form. If the sentence is correct, write *C*.

[1] ~~Us~~ cousins were getting so confused at the family reunion that Rochelle, Darla, and ~~me~~ made the Family Relationship Chart shown on the next page. [2] Before long, the busiest people at the picnic were they and ~~me~~! [3] Aunts and uncles consulted us to find out ~~who~~ they were related to and just how they were related. [4] It all started when Jules wanted to know the connection

1. We/ I
2. I
3. whom
4. C

USAGE

LESS-ADVANCED STUDENTS

As you assign **Review E,** you may wish to modify the instructions for some students. You could have them work in groups of four or five and go through the ten sentences together to determine the correct responses. Allow them to omit the analysis of how the pronouns are used in the sentence.

USAGE

A DIFFERENT APPROACH

Many television sitcoms revolve around traditional or extended families. These shows are a rich source of examples of personal pronoun usage. Have students choose one or two favorite sitcoms to view with pencil in hand. Ask them to write down phrases and sentences in which characters are using personal pronouns. Warn students not to recreate the script; they just need to capture some statements to analyze later.

Have students share their findings and categorize their examples of pronoun usage as appropriate for informal dialogue or appropriate for writing.

between him and Vicky. [5] We figured out that Vicky is the great-granddaughter of Jules's grandmother's brother, so her and Jules are second cousins once removed. [6] Looking at our chart, we could see that Vicky and Jules are in different generations, even though him and her are the same age. [7] All afternoon, curious relatives besieged Rochelle, Darla, and I with questions. [8] We helped whomever asked us. [9] Grandmother said she didn't know who to be prouder of, we or our cousins who made the refreshments. [10] Everyone learned something new about our family ties that day and gave the two other girls and I a big round of applause.

5. she

6. he/she

7. me

8. whoever

9. whom/us

10. me

Family Relationship Chart

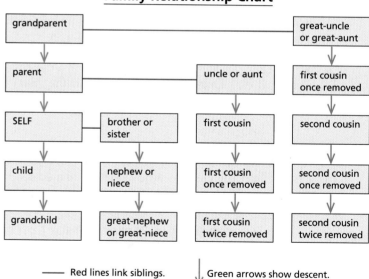

——— Red lines link siblings.   ↓ Green arrows show descent.

▶ REVIEW G

Determining the Proper Case of Pronouns in Sentences

For each of the following sentences, write *C* if the pronouns are all in the proper case. If a pronoun is incorrect, write the correct form.

1. Be careful who you tell. **1.** whom
2. May Marie and I cut a few pictures out of this old copy of *Ebony*? **2.** C

USAGE

USAGE

3. My family goes to the dentist, ~~who~~ Ms. Calhoun recommended. **3.** whom
4. Coretta said there would be other flag bearers in addition to Hugh and I. **4.** me
5. At the head of the parade were ~~us~~ Girl Scouts. **5.** we
6. The treaty gave them and the Ojibwa people the right to harvest wild rice there. **6.** C   **7.** C
7. Nobody except Josh and him finished the marathon.
8. We wish we had neighbors like Sylvia and him. **8.** C
9. Did your father and ~~them~~ reach an agreement about the boundary dispute? **9.** they
10. Joanne and ~~us~~ found a great beach. **10.** we

▶ EXERCISE 10 **Composing Sentences Using Pronouns**

Last month you joined the Climbing Club, and today you have just completed your first full day's climb. The club's advisor, Mr. Kraslow, has asked you to prepare a short report sharing your impressions of your first big climb. Use these pictures you took to help you write ten sentences for your report. Include one of the following phrases in each sentence. Be prepared to tell how each phrase is used.

1. Mr. Kraslow and us
2. Thomas and her
3. him and us
4. whoever
5. we newer climbers
6. they and Mr. Kraslow
7. he and they
8. Terri and me
9. Thomas and them
10. he and the Climbing Club

USAGE

ANSWERS
Exercise 10

Answers may vary. Here are some possibilities:

1. That's a good picture of Mr. Kraslow and us. (object of a preposition)
2. The going was hard for Thomas and her. (object of a preposition)
3. The heaviest packs were given to him and us. (object of a preposition)
4. Whoever was last had to shout to be heard by everyone. (subject)
5. We newer climbers tried too hard at first. (subject)
6. They and Mr. Kraslow paced themselves better. (subject)
7. He and they had a good time. (subject)
8. Mr. Kraslow joked with Terri and me. (object of a preposition)
9. He encouraged Thomas and them. (direct object)
10. He and the Climbing Club plan to tackle Mt. Rainier. (subject)

667

OBJECTIVES

- To identify the correct pronouns for incomplete sentence constructions and describe how the pronouns are used
- To revise sentences to correct inexact pronoun references

USAGE

668 *Using Pronouns Correctly*

Pronouns in Incomplete Constructions

20g. After *than* or *as* introducing an incomplete construction, use the pronoun form that would be used if the construction were completed.

> I know Mac better than **he** (knows Mac).
> I know Mac better than (I know) **him**.
> Do you visit Aunt Bessie as often as **we** (visit Aunt Bessie)?
> Do you visit Aunt Bessie as often as (you visit) **us**?

 EXERCISE 11   **Selecting Pronouns to Complete Incomplete Constructions in Sentences**

For each of the following sentences, choose the <u>correct form of the pronoun</u> in parentheses. Also supply in parentheses the missing part of the incomplete construction. Then, give the use of the pronoun in its clause. If a sentence may be completed in two different ways, provide both completions.

EXAMPLE   **1.** I like Arsenio Hall better than (*she, her*).
           1. *she* (*likes Arsenio Hall*)—*subject;* (*I like*) *her—direct object*

1. We played defense better than (<u>*they*</u>, *them*).
2. When Michael Chang won the men's singles title at the French Open, nobody was as pleased as (<u>*I*</u>, *me*).
3. Nobody tried harder than (<u>*she*</u>, *her*).
4. You are a month younger than (<u>*he*</u>, *him*).
5. I know Millie better than (<u>*she*</u>, <u>*her*</u>).
6. Did you get as far in that book as (<u>*I*</u>, *me*)?
7. Richard wanted more tickets than (<u>*we*</u>, *us*).
8. Bianca lives farther away than (<u>*we*</u>, *us*).
9. She visited Lisa more often than (<u>*I*</u>, <u>*me*</u>).
10. Carlos plays classical guitar in the style of Andrés Segovia but, of course, not as well as (<u>*he*</u>, *him*).

Inexact Pronoun Reference

20h. A pronoun should always refer clearly to its antecedent.

(1) Avoid an ambiguous reference.

In an *ambiguous reference,* a pronoun can refer to either of two antecedents.

AMBIGUOUS	Marissa called Yolanda while she was at the library. [Who was at the library, Marissa or Yolanda?]
CLEAR	While **Marissa** was at the library, **she** called Yolanda.
	or
CLEAR	While **Yolanda** was at the library, Marissa called **her.**
AMBIGUOUS	After viewing Roy's paintings and Elton's sculpture, the judges awarded his work the blue ribbon. [Whose work won the blue ribbon?]
CLEAR	The judges awarded **Elton** the blue ribbon after viewing **his** sculpture and Roy's paintings.
	or
CLEAR	The judges awarded **Roy** the blue ribbon after viewing **his** paintings and Elton's sculpture.

(2) Be sure that each pronoun you use has a specific, stated antecedent.

The pronouns *it, this, that, which,* and *such* are often used to refer to a general idea rather than to a specific noun. Using these pronouns in this way can lead to *general reference* errors.

GENERAL	Paul has a job interview after school today. That explains why Paul is all dressed up. [no specific antecedent for *That*]
CLEAR	Paul is all dressed up because he has a job interview after school today.
	or
CLEAR	The reason that Paul is all dressed up is that he has a job interview after school today.
GENERAL	My biology class is going on a field trip to the coast this week, which should be fun. [no specific antecedent for *which*]
CLEAR	My biology class is going on a field trip to the coast this week. The trip should be fun.
	or
CLEAR	Going on a field trip to the coast with my biology class this week should be fun.

USAGE

QUICK REMINDER

One way to determine correct pronoun usage is to finish sentences mentally. Write the following sentence on the chalkboard:

Dad loaned Tom more than me.

Ask students what the sentence means. [Students will probably say that it means the father made a larger loan to Tom than to the speaker.] Ask students how the sentence should be changed to mean that the speaker loaned less money to Tom than the father. [Dad loaned Tom more than I.] Tell students that they can check this construction by completing the sentence:

Dad loaned Tom more than I (loaned him).

MEETING *individual* NEEDS

STUDENTS WITH SPECIAL NEEDS

Some students might have a difficult time comprehending the examples of inexact pronoun references if they try to read them silently.

You may want to organize students into groups of four to read these examples aloud and to discuss what is confusing about each example. For each category—ambiguous reference, general reference, weak reference, and indefinite reference—you may wish to provide an explanation of the problem, using the first example of each category.

ADVANCED STUDENTS

You may wish to have students look for inexact pronoun references in newspapers and magazines. Ask them to share their examples with the class, and have them clarify any confusing references they find.

USAGE

COMMON ERROR

Problem. Finding inexact pronoun references is a difficult task for students during the revision process. Because students know their intended meaning, they might not recognize points at which their writing is confusing.

Solution. One approach students could take is circling each *it, this, that, which,* and *such* in their writing. They could then draw a line to the word or words the pronoun refers to. If a student runs into a problem, he or she will need to revise the sentence to provide a clear reference.

Another approach is peer evaluation. A classmate might be more apt to spot any inexact references, and the writer can revise the unclear sentences.

INTEGRATING THE LANGUAGE ARTS

Usage and Writing. You may want to assign a writing topic that lends itself to pronoun use so that students can practice what they have learned. Give them the choice of writing a sports column, a music video review, or a dance review. During prewriting, you may want to approve topics in conferences.

Tell students that their aims can be expressive, literary, informative, or persuasive, and that they should include ten to fifteen personal pronouns in their essays. As students revise, ask them to check particularly for the correct use of personal pronouns.

670

Blondie reprinted with special permission of King Features Syndicate, Inc.

Sometimes a writer will suggest a particular word or idea without stating it. A pronoun that refers to this unstated word or idea is said to have a **weak reference** to the antecedent.

WEAK When I listen in the car, I turn it up loud. [*It* may refer to a radio, tape player, or CD player. The writer suggests one of these devices but does not state which one.]

CLEAR When I listen to the **radio** in the car, I turn **it** up loud.

WEAK Royale writes stories, and she hopes to make it her career. [*It* most likely refers to the unstated noun *writing;* consequently, the writer has not made the pronoun-antecedent relationship clear.]

CLEAR Royale writes stories, and she hopes to make **writing** her career.

In conversation, people often use the pronouns *it, they,* and *you* unnecessarily. In writing, be sure to avoid such **indefinite reference** errors.

INDEFINITE In the newspaper, it reported that the robbers had been caught. [The pronoun *it* is not necessary to the meaning of the sentence. Revise the sentence to eliminate the wordiness caused by the indefinite reference.]

CLEAR **The newspaper reported that the robbers had been caught.**

INDEFINITE In the article, they include a toll-free number to call for more information. [The pronoun *they* is not necessary to the meaning of the sentence.]

CLEAR **The article includes a toll-free number to call for more information.**

NOTE: Familiar expressions such as *it is raining, it's early,* and *it seems like* are correct even though they contain inexact pronoun references. The antecedents to these pronouns are commonly understood to be the weather, time, and so forth.

WRITING APPLICATION

OBJECTIVE

• To use pronouns correctly in a letter explaining a concept

 EXERCISE 12   **Correcting Inexact Pronoun References**

Revise each sentence in the following paragraph, correcting the inexact pronoun reference. If a sentence is correct, write C.

EXAMPLE   [1] In a brochure recently published by the Environmental Protection Agency (EPA), it promotes recycling to reduce waste.

1. *A brochure recently published by the Environmental Protection Agency (EPA) promotes recycling to reduce waste.*

[1] The newest twist in recycling is *precycling*—cutting it off at its source. [2] Last month, after reading the EPA's brochure, my family decided to put its ideas into practice. [3] We now choose products that have less packaging; we carry groceries home in cloth bags instead of paper or plastic ones; and we buy containers that can be refilled, which is easy. [4] We even wrote to the Mail Preference Service, Direct Marketing Association, and asked that our names not be sold to mailing-list companies. [5] That greatly reduced the amount of junk mail we get. [6] When we do have waste products, inventing new ways to use them becomes a challenge in creative thinking; one of them was mine. [7] Now, we pack fragile objects in bits of plastic foam and other nonrecyclable materials so that they don't get broken in shipping. [8] We use plastic produce bags as sandwich wrappers or as liners for small trash cans, and it works just fine. [9] We also convert cottage cheese cartons and margarine tubs into food-storage containers, and we plan to make a habit of it. [10] In just a few short weeks, we've learned that in the 1990s, you recycle by remembering the three *r*'s: *r*educe, *r*euse, and *r*ecycle.

WRITING APPLICATION

Using Pronouns Correctly in a Letter

When you are writing about a complex event involving several people doing and saying things, your meaning can be lost if an antecedent is unclear.

USAGE

ANSWERS
Exercise 12

Answers may vary.

1. The newest twist in recycling is *precycling*—cutting waste off at its source.

2. Last month, after reading the EPA's brochure, my family decided to put the brochure's ideas into practice.

3. We now choose products that have less packaging; we carry groceries home in cloth bags instead of paper or plastic ones; and we buy containers that can be refilled easily.

4. C

5. Writing that letter greatly reduced the amount of junk mail we get.

6. When we do have waste products, inventing new ways to use them becomes a challenge in creative thinking; one of the ways was mine.

7. Now, we pack fragile objects in bits of plastic foam and other nonrecyclable material so that the fragile objects don't get broken in shipping.

8. We use plastic produce bags as sandwich wrappers or as liners for small trash cans, and the bags work just fine.

9. We also convert cottage cheese cartons and margarine tubs into food-storage containers, and we plan to make a habit of reusing items.

10. In just a few short weeks, we've learned that in the 1990s recycling involves remembering the three *r*'s: *r*educe, *r*euse, and *r*ecycle.

WRITING APPLICATION

The writing assignment provides practice in writing a letter of explanation. The assignment requires that students use pronoun references correctly. You may wish to review the proper form for letters in **Chapter 36.**

CRITICAL THINKING

Analysis. Students may create extensive, informed lists of ideas in the prewriting stage. Tell them that they must narrow their lists to fit into one video. They might need to watch several successful videos and observe how many scenes and how many performers are included in the videos. Remind students that they must keep their audience and purpose in mind when narrowing their topic.

PREWRITING

If you assign this activity as homework, you may wish to suggest that students review several music videos for ideas about scenes, performers, and action. Such a review may also help them decide on the video they want to redirect.

WRITING

Encourage students to write freely. Remind them that they need not be overly concerned with errors at this stage.

UNCLEAR   Howard slipped, and Kiley recovered the ball and made a basket. **This** caused pandemonium among the fans. [What is the *this* that caused the pandemonium?]

CLEAR   **The quick recovery** caused pandemonium among the fans.

How else could you revise the unclear sentence to make its meaning clear?

▶ WRITING ACTIVITY

Your favorite musical group isn't happy with the director of their latest video. As a result, they are sponsoring a "Be a Music Video Director" contest. To enter, you have to write a letter explaining your idea for a different video of the same song. Tell which singers, dancers, and musicians you would cast in your video. Include at least ten pronouns in your sentences. Be sure that no pronoun has an unclear antecedent.

Prewriting   Start by choosing the song you want to create a video for. Then, list some ideas for three or four scenes in your video. Next to each scene idea, list the performers you would use in that scene and describe the action. In addition to actual people, you may want to have cartoon characters or other animated figures in your video.

Writing   As you write sentences about your music video, make the sequence of events clear. Make the spatial relationships clear, too, telling where the cast members are located.

Evaluating and Revising   Check your rough draft to be sure that your explanation is clear. If you have included too many performers or too many details, eliminate the least interesting ones now. Have a classmate read your letter, looking for inexact uses of the pronouns *it, this, that,* and *which.* If he or she is confused by any sentences with inexact pronoun references, revise those sentences.

Proofreading   Carefully read your letter again to be sure that all pronouns are in the correct case.

OBJECTIVES

- To choose the correct pronouns in sentences and explain their use
- To compose sentences using pronouns and pronoun phrases correctly

Special Problems in Pronoun Usage **673**

 REVIEW H

Selecting Pronouns to Complete Sentences

Choose the <u>correct pronoun</u> in parentheses in each of the following sentences. Be prepared to give reasons for your answers.   s. = subject d.o. = direct object
p.n. = predicate nominative o.p. = object of a preposition

1. Heather and (*he, him*) live on a blueberry farm. **1.** s.
2. Did the teacher give that assignment to (*whoever, whomever*) was absent yesterday? **2.** s.
3. We wondered (*who, whom*) started the rumor. **3.** s.
4. Do you intercept passes as well as (*she, her*)? **4.** s.
5. The supporting players were Dina, Janelle, and (*she, her*). **5.** p.n.
6. I was standing in line behind Dave and (*he, him*). **6.** o.p.
7. You and (*I, me*) could write biographical sketches about General Colin L. Powell, who was chairman of the Joint Chiefs of Staff under President Bush. **7.** s.
8. The skit was written by Cy and (*he, him*). **8.** o.p.
9. The electrician warned (*he, him*) and (*I, me*) about the frayed wires. **9.** d.o./d.o.
10. Amy Tan, (*who, whom*) the critics had praised, autographed a copy of her novel *The Joy Luck Club* for me. **10.** d.o.

 REVIEW I

Using Pronouns Correctly in Original Sentences

Outdoor murals like the one on the next page give artists a chance to express themselves on a grand scale! The owners of an enormous warehouse have made one long wall available to your class. Each team of students can paint whatever they wish on a thirty-foot section. The artwork can be serious or humorous, or it can just be a colorful design. Write ten sentences about the teams and their paintings. In each sentence, use a different pronoun or phrase from the following list. Be sure all pronouns are used in the way indicated in the exercise.

Francisco and I	me and my team	he
Matthew, Talbot, and us	Trenice and she	whoever
her and them	who	them and you
they and Luann	whom	whomever

ANSWERS
Review I

Answers may vary. Here are some example sentences:

1. To whom should these brushes be offered?
2. Whoever is best in art should get one.
3. The teacher gave her and them a bucket of paint.
4. The two artists, Trenice and she, dived right in with their brushes.
5. Francisco and I had the ideas.
6. It was he who suggested painting a red tree.
7. He encouraged me and my team.
8. The teacher applauded the creative students—Matthew, Talbot, and us.
9. I liked *Red Trees* better than they and Luann.
10. She rewarded Kim more than them and you.

USAGE

USAGE

LESSON 7 *(pp. 674–675)*
REVIEW: POSTTESTS A and B

OBJECTIVES

- To determine the proper case of pronouns in sentences
- To proofread sentences and to supply correct pronoun forms

VISUAL CONNECTIONS
Related Expression Skills.
You may want to have students work in pairs to design or sketch a plan for a wall mural that reflects their interests or values. The mural sketch can be serious or funny. Have students consider what type of building they would use for a wall mural. After they have completed their sketches, you may want to have students write a paragraph describing their murals and explaining what their murals represent. Have students underline each pronoun that appears in their paragraphs.

---

674 *Using Pronouns Correctly*

EXAMPLE   **1.** predicate nominative
1. *The painters outlining the black unicorn are Trenice and she.*

1. object of a preposition
2. subject of a clause
3. indirect object
4. subject appositive
5. subject of the sentence
6. predicate nominative
7. direct object
8. object appositive
9. subject of an incomplete construction
10. direct object of an incomplete construction

Review: Posttest

A. Determining the Proper Case of Pronouns in Sentences

If a pronoun is used incorrectly in the following sentences, write the correct form of the pronoun. If a sentence is correct, write *C*.

1. Del can't do math any better than ~~her~~. **1.** she
2. There was some misunderstanding between him and his brother. **2.** C
3. To ~~who~~ was the letter addressed? **3.** whom
4. I showed the negatives to Cecilia and ~~she~~. **4.** her
5. It can't be ~~them~~; that's not their car. **5.** they

6. Ben and you can come with them and me. **6.** C
7. Leontyne Price's accomplishments were familiar to everyone in the class except him and I. **7.** me
8. Us band members have to be at school early to practice marching. **8.** We
9. He's the sportscaster who irritates me with his pretentious talk. **9.** C
10. In front of the school stood two drenched children, Charlene and he. **10.** C

B. Proofreading Sentences for the Correct Use of Pronouns

Most of the following sentences contain one or more incorrect pronouns. Identify each incorrect pronoun, and write the correct form. If all of the pronouns in a sentence are correct, write *C*.

11. There's nothing like an action-packed all-star basketball game to give Dad and I a thrill! **11.** me
12. Our team was only two points behind the opposing team when Barkley's shot bounced off the rim, and Barkley and Robinson rushed for <u>it</u>. **12.** the ball
13. As gravity pulled him and Robinson toward the floor, Barkley managed to tip the ball to Thomas. **13.** C
14. Thomas saw Stockton coming and dribbled behind his back to elude <u>he</u> and Olajuwon. **14.** him
15. When Stockton and Olajuwon collided, nobody was more surprised than <u>them</u>. **15.** they
16. "If we make <u>this</u>, the score will be tied," thought Thomas. **16.** this basket
17. Thomas looked for Jordan and realized that the blur streaking upcourt on the left was <u>him</u>. **17.** he
18. "Five seconds to go—I have to pass to <u>whomever</u> is open, and Bird's the one." **18.** whoever
19. Bird took a shot and missed; four players struggled for the ball and it went in, which meant that Thomas and his teammates had won. **19.** C
20. In the whirlwind action during the last couple of seconds, the frantic referee couldn't see <u>whom</u> had fouled <u>who</u>. **20.** who/whom

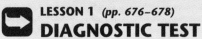

LESSON 1 *(pp. 676–678)*

DIAGNOSTIC TEST

OBJECTIVES

- To write past or past participle forms of verbs to complete sentences
- To revise verb tense and voice in a paragraph
- To identify and correct errors in the usage of *lie* and *lay, sit* and *set,* and *rise* and *raise*

PROGRAM MANAGER

FOR THE WHOLE CHAPTER

- **Review** For exercises on chapter concepts, see **Review Form A** and **Review Form B** in *Language Skills Practice and Assessment,* pp. 128–131.
- **Assessment** For additional testing, see **Usage Pretests** and **Usage Mastery Tests** in *Language Skills Practice and Assessment,* pp. 85–92 and pp. 159–166.

USAGE

CHAPTER OVERVIEW

The material in this chapter will clarify for students the sometimes confusing nature of verbs. Principal parts of regular and irregular verbs, verb tense, and active and passive voice are all thoroughly discussed. Additional explanation for troublesome verbs such as *lie* and *lay, sit* and *set,* and *rise* and *raise* is provided and is reinforced by multiple exercises.

You may want to refer to this chapter when teaching writing. A quick review of the usage of verbs before the revision stage can provide students with the help they need to make their papers clear and effective.

USAGE

21 USING VERBS CORRECTLY

Principal Parts, Tense, Voice

Diagnostic Test

A. Writing the Past or Past Participle Form of Verbs

Write the correct past or past participle form of the verb given before each of the following sentences.

EXAMPLE **1.** *do* Because he ____ his work so well, he got a raise.
1. *did*

1. *write* Although Emily Dickinson ____ poetry most of her life, very little of her work was published until after her death. **1.** wrote

2. *drink* When he saw that the animals had ____ all the water, he gave them more. **2.** drunk

3. *throw* Regarding weeds as unwanted intruders, she pulled them from the ground and ____ them over the fence. **3.** threw

4. *swim* The water was cold and daylight was fading, so he ____ only a short distance before turning back to shore. **4.** swam

5. *freeze* The dew ____ during the night, covering each twig and blade of grass with a crisp, silvery coating. **5.** froze

6. *give* After my brother had ____ his new puppy a bath, he seemed to be wetter than the dog. **6.** given

7. *speak* She ____ in such a low, hushed voice that the people in the audience had to strain to hear her remarks. **7.** spoke

8. *run* Frightened by the traffic, the deer ____ back into the forest. **8.** ran

9. *ride* Leading the parade was an officer who ____ a prancing black horse. **9.** rode

10. *ring* When the church bell ____ on Tuesday evening, the villagers became alarmed. **10.** rang

B. Revising Verb Tense or Voice

Revise the following paragraph, correcting verbs that are in the wrong tense or that use an awkward passive voice. If a sentence is correct, write *C*.

[11] Katherine Davalos Ortega is born in 1934 in Tularosa, New Mexico, and worked in her family's restaurant and other businesses since she has been a small child. [12] Early in life a teaching career was chosen by her, but she was told that being Hispanic might prevent her from getting a teaching position. [13] As a result, she decided to pursue a business career instead, and by 1975, she has become the first woman president of a California bank. [14] In recognition of her professional abilities, Ms. Ortega was nominated by President Reagan to be Treasurer of the United States and was sworn in on October 3, 1983. [15] Her signature may be familiar to you, because it is appearing on more than twenty billion dollar bills and other types of U.S. currency.

C. Determining Correct Use of *Lie* and *Lay*, *Sit* and *Set*, and *Rise* and *Raise* in Sentences

Most of the following sentences contain at least one error in the use of *lie* or *lay*, *sit* or *set*, or *rise* or *raise*. Identify each

USAGE

USING THE DIAGNOSTIC TEST

The **Diagnostic Test** can be used in conjunction with an assessment of students' writing to identify students' strengths and weaknesses. Test results may also be used to determine grouping for cooperative-learning activities, as it is often helpful to group together students with varying levels of proficiency.

ANSWERS
Diagnostic Test: Part B

Corrections are underlined.

11. Katherine Davalos Ortega <u>was</u> born in 1934 in Tularosa, New Mexico, and <u>has worked</u> in her family's restaurant <u>and other</u> businesses since she <u>was</u> a small child.

12. Early in life <u>she chose a teaching career</u>, but she was told that being Hispanic might prevent her from getting a teaching position.

13. As a result, she decided to pursue a business career instead, and by 1975, she <u>had</u> become the first woman president of a California bank.

14. C

15. Her signature may be familiar to you, because it <u>appears</u> on more than twenty billion dollar bills and other types of U.S. currency.

USAGE

incorrect verb, and give the correct verb. If a sentence is correct, write *C*.

16. sitting   **17.** laid/set

16. We left our lawn furniture~~setting~~ on the patio.
17. They~~lain~~ the bricks next to where we~~sat~~ the wood.
18. When the dough has risen for fifteen minutes, turn it out onto the floured board. **18.** C
19. When we are rising from bed in the morning, the Chinese are~~laying~~ down to sleep. **19.** lying   **20.** lay
20. The escaping slaves~~laid~~ quietly in the undergrowth.

The Principal Parts of Verbs

Every verb has four basic forms called *principal parts*. All of a verb's other forms come from its principal parts.

21a. The principal parts of a verb are the *base form*, the *present participle*, the *past*, and the *past participle*.

PRINCIPAL PARTS OF *WALK* AND *DO*			
BASE FORM	**PRESENT PARTICIPLE**	**PAST**	**PAST PARTICIPLE**
walk	(is) walking	walked	(have) walked
do	(is) doing	did	(have) done

The words *is* and *have* are included to remind you that when the present participle and past participle are used to form verb tenses, they're preceded by forms of these two helping verbs.

EXAMPLES   I **am doing** my homework now.
               I **have done** all my homework already.

☞ REFERENCE NOTE: See page 527 for more information on using helping verbs with present participles and past participles.

NOTE: Some teachers refer to the base form as the infinitive. Follow your teacher's directions in labeling these words.

REGULAR AND IRREGULAR VERBS

Rules 21a–21c

OBJECTIVES

- To read aloud sentences that include correctly used regular and irregular verbs
- To write past and past participle forms of irregular verbs to complete sentences

Regular Verbs

 21b. A *regular verb* is one that forms its past and past participle by adding *–d* or *–ed* to the base form.

BASE FORM	PRESENT PARTICIPLE	PAST	PAST PARTICIPLE
work	(is) working	worked	(have) worked
receive	(is) receiving	received	(have) received

REFERENCE NOTE: For guidelines on spelling verbs when adding *–ed* or *–ing*, see pages 874–875.

A few regular verbs have an alternate past and past participle form ending in *–t*.

BASE FORM	PRESENT PARTICIPLE	PAST	PAST PARTICIPLE
burn	(is) burning	burned *or* burnt	(have) burned *or* burnt
leap	(is) leaping	leaped *or* leapt	(have) leaped *or* leapt

NOTE: The regular verbs *deal* and *mean* always form the past and past participle by adding *–t*: *dealt, (have) dealt; meant, (have) meant.*

Irregular Verbs

 21c. An *irregular verb* is one that forms its past and past participle in some way other than by adding *–d* or *–ed* to the base form.

An irregular verb forms its past and past participle in one of the following ways:

- changing vowels *or* consonants
- changing vowels *and* consonants
- making no change

PROGRAM MANAGER

REGULAR AND IRREGULAR VERBS

- **Independent Practice/ Reteaching** For instruction and exercises, see **Principal Parts of Regular Verbs** and **Principal Parts of Irregular Verbs** in *Language Skills Practice and Assessment,* pp. 123–124.

- **Computer Guided Instruction** For additional instruction and practice with regular and irregular verbs, see **Lesson 9** in *Language Workshop CD-ROM.*

- **Practice** To help less-advanced students with additional instruction and practice with regular and irregular verbs, see **Chapter 16** in *English Workshop, Fourth Course,* pp. 219–224.

USAGE

 QUICK REMINDER

Write the following sentences on the chalkboard and ask students to identify the verb in each sentence. Then have students write the present participle, past, and past participle forms of the verbs.

1. Gina and Laurie ride their bicycles to school.
2. Jim teaches me tall tales about the Old West.
3. My cat leaps onto the table.

- To use the correct past and past participle forms of irregular verbs in a letter

680 *Using Verbs Correctly*

EXAMPLES

BASE FORM	PAST	PAST PARTICIPLE
fly	flew	(have) flown
bend	bent	(have) bent
sell	sold	(have) sold
beat	beat	(have) beaten
let	let	(have) let

NOTE: When you're not sure whether a verb is regular or irregular, check a dictionary that lists the principal parts of irregular verbs.

PRINCIPAL PARTS OF COMMON IRREGULAR VERBS			
BASE FORM	PRESENT PARTICIPLE	PAST	PAST PARTICIPLE
begin	(is) beginning	began	(have) begun
blow	(is) blowing	blew	(have) blown
break	(is) breaking	broke	(have) broken
bring	(is) bringing	brought	(have) brought
burst	(is) bursting	burst	(have) burst
choose	(is) choosing	chose	(have) chosen
come	(is) coming	came	(have) come
dive	(is) diving	dove (or dived)	(have) dived
do	(is) doing	did	(have) done
draw	(is) drawing	drew	(have) drawn
drink	(is) drinking	drank	(have) drunk
drive	(is) driving	drove	(have) driven
eat	(is) eating	ate	(have) eaten
fall	(is) falling	fell	(have) fallen
freeze	(is) freezing	froze	(have) frozen
give	(is) giving	gave	(have) given
go	(is) going	went	(have) gone
hear	(is) hearing	heard	(have) heard
know	(is) knowing	knew	(have) known
leave	(is) leaving	left	(have) left
ride	(is) riding	rode	(have) ridden
ring	(is) ringing	rang	(have) rung
run	(is) running	ran	(have) run

(continued)

USAGE

MEETING *individual* NEEDS

LEP/ESL

General Strategies. Point out to students that when they have questions about the principal parts of verbs, they can often find the answers in the dictionary. Tell them that the infinitive forms of verbs are listed as entry words and that the past, past participle, and present participle forms of irregular verbs are usually given in the entries. For example, if students look up *draw*, they will find *drew, drawn,* and *drawing.* As practice, have each student look up three irregular verbs and find the verbs' principal parts in the dictionary entry.

LESS-ADVANCED STUDENTS

Students might take one look at the **Principal Parts of Common Irregular Verbs** chart and feel overwhelmed. Ask them to choose five of these verbs and to write autobiographical sentences that incorporate the past or past participle form of each verb. For example, a student might incorporate the past participle form of *dive* into the autobiographical sentence "I have dived off the highest diving board at the public pool." Because this activity requires students to master a manageable number of verbs and to use the verbs in context, it will make the material more meaningful and less intimidating to students.

PRINCIPAL PARTS OF COMMON IRREGULAR VERBS *(continued)*			
BASE FORM	**PRESENT PARTICIPLE**	**PAST**	**PAST PARTICIPLE**
see	(is) seeing	saw	(have) seen
sing	(is) singing	sang *(or* sung*)*	(have) sung
sleep	(is) sleeping	slept	(have) slept
speak	(is) speaking	spoke	(have) spoken
steal	(is) stealing	stole	(have) stolen
swim	(is) swimming	swam	(have) swum
take	(is) taking	took	(have) taken
teach	(is) teaching	taught	(have) taught
think	(is) thinking	thought	(have) thought
throw	(is) throwing	threw	(have) thrown
write	(is) writing	wrote	(have) written

 ORAL PRACTICE 1   **Using Regular and Irregular Verbs**

Read each sentence aloud, stressing each italicized verb.

1. Keisha *is braiding* Tiffany's hair in cornrows.
2. Bob *read* the want ads today, just as he *has read* them each day this week.
3. Mom, I *am bringing* you breakfast in bed, but I *have burned* your toast!
4. Warren *designed* the posters for the fall program.
5. Paloma Picasso, the jewelry designer, *has chosen* an artistic career different from her famous father's.
6. Carrie *went* to Penn State; Hector *is going* to Boston College.
7. Someone *ate* all the leftover spaghetti, but nobody *has touched* the baked beans.
8. If you *have* never *seen* a meteor shower, *run* outside right now!

▶ EXERCISE 1   **Writing the Past or Past Participle Form of Irregular Verbs to Complete Sentences**

Give the correct past or past participle form of the verb given before each of the following sentences.

 INTEGRATING THE LANGUAGE ARTS

Usage and Vocabulary. After students have done **Oral Practice 1,** call on individual students to offer synonyms for the italicized verbs in the sentences. The synonyms should be in the same tenses and forms as the original verbs. For example, a student might substitute *is plaiting* for *is braiding* in the first sentence. Encourage students to be creative in their choices of synonyms.

1. *sing* The first drops of rain began to fall just after we had ___ the national anthem. **1.** sung
2. *begin* I had already ___ my homework. **2.** begun
3. *freeze* The sub-zero winds nearly ___ the Pawnee hunters as they tracked the herd of bison.
4. *fly* Last summer we ___ in a lighter-than-air balloon. **3.** froze **4.** flew **5.** saw
5. *see* During our visit to Hawaii, we ___ a group of performers do a traditional hula dance.
6. *take* My sister has ___ that course. **6.** taken
7. *fall* By the time Rolando finished carving the little figure of a saint, hundreds of tiny wood shavings had ___ to the floor. **7.** fallen
8. *throw* The horse had ___ its shoe. **8.** thrown **9.** broken
9. *break* We hoped we hadn't ___ the machine.
10. *speak* Harley's grandmother ___ to our class about her parents' life as sharecroppers in the early 1900s. **10.** spoke

EXERCISE 2 **Using the Correct Past or Past Participle Form of Verbs**

Give the correct form of each italicized verb in the following paragraph.

1. saw
2. chosen

We recently [1] (*see*) paintings by the African American artist Henry Ossawa Tanner. Tanner had [2] (*choose*) his lifelong career in art by the time he was thirteen years old. While walking in a park one day with his father, they had

3. come
4. wrote
5. brought
6. taught

[3] (*come*) upon a landscape artist at work. Years later, Tanner [4] (*write*), "It was this simple event that . . . set me on fire." Young Henry [5] (*bring*) such eagerness to his work that, before long, he [6] (*teach*) himself to draw well enough to be admitted to one of the finest art schools in the country. His paintings were beautiful but did not sell well, so

7. went
8. fell

Tanner [7] (*go*) abroad. He [8] (*fall*) in love with the city of Paris, and lived and worked there for the rest of his life, winning many important painting awards. Shown on the next page is his best-known work, *The Banjo Lesson*, which he painted in Paris from sketches he had [9] (*draw*) years

9. drawn
10. gave

earlier in North Carolina. In 1969, long after Tanner's death, a touring exhibit finally [10] (*give*) Americans a look at the work of this gifted artist.

Henry Ossawa Tanner, *The Banjo Lesson* (1893). Hampton University Museum, Hampton, Va.

▶ EXERCISE 3

Selecting the Past or Past Participle Form of Verbs

Choose the <u>correct form of the verb</u> in parentheses.

1. We (*did*, *done*) everything we could to help him.
2. Who has (*drank*, *drunk*) the rest of the orange juice?
3. Someone has already (*tore*, *torn*) out the coupon.
4. I wish you had (*spoke*, *spoken*) to me about it sooner.
5. I dived off the high board and (*swam*, *swum*) the length of the pool.
6. You must have (*rang*, *rung*) the doorbell while I was out.
7. Nancy had never (*ate*, *eaten*) a tamale before.
8. Lois (*blowed*, *blew*) up the balloon.
9. Suddenly the balloon (*burst*, *bursted*).
10. We were (*drove*, *driven*) to the train station in a taxi.

▶ EXERCISE 4

Using the Past and Past Participle Forms of Verbs

You have just joined a traveling circus, and you are in an acrobatic troupe with the performers shown on the next page. You work hard—not only perfecting your act but also helping with daily chores. Animals must be cared for,

OBJECTIVES

- To identify tenses of verbs in sentences and to explain the effect of different verb tenses on meanings of sentences
- To change the tenses of verbs in sentences

PROGRAM MANAGER

TENSE

- **Independent Practice/ Reteaching** For instruction and exercises, see **Verb Tense** in *Language Skills Practice and Assessment*, p. 125.

- **Computer Guided Instruction** For additional instruction and practice with verb tense, see **Lesson 10** in *Language Workshop CD-ROM*.

- **Practice** To help less-advanced students with additional instruction and practice with verb tense, see **Chapter 16** in *English Workshop, Fourth Course*, pp. 225–230.

QUICK REMINDER

Write the following sentences on the chalkboard. Have students correct the tenses of the underlined verbs.

1. I <u>talk</u> yesterday to the football coach about my position. [talked]
2. He already <u>leaves</u> when he called. [had already left]
3. Tomorrow we <u>have thought</u> about everything. [will think; will have thought]

---

684 *Using Verbs Correctly*

tents set up and taken down, and costumes made ready. You must also attend classes with a tutor! However, there's still time for fun. Write a short letter to your family, telling about your circus adventure. Use at least five past and five past participle forms of the irregular verbs listed on pages 680–681, and underline each one.

Tense

21d. Learn the names of the six tenses and how each tense is formed.

Verbs change form to show the time of the action or the idea they express. The time indicated by the form of a verb is called its *tense.* In English, every verb has six tenses:

present	present perfect
past	past perfect
future	future perfect

The following charts show all six tenses of a regular verb (*talk*) and of an irregular verb (*throw*). Listing the verb forms in this way is called *conjugating* the verb.

- To write a fictional writing journal entry that includes at least five different verb tenses
- To proofread and revise a passage for correct verb forms

21d

CONJUGATION OF THE VERB *TALK*

Present infinitive: *to talk* Perfect infinitive: *to have talked*

PRINCIPAL PARTS OF *TALK*

BASE FORM	PRESENT PARTICIPLE	PAST	PAST PARTICIPLE
talk	(is) talking	talked	(have) talked

PRESENT TENSE

SINGULAR	*PLURAL*
I talk	we talk
you talk	you talk
he, she, it talks	they talk

PAST TENSE

SINGULAR	*PLURAL*
I talked	we talked
you talked	you talked
he, she, it talked	they talked

FUTURE TENSE
(*will* or *shall* + the base form)

SINGULAR	*PLURAL*
I will (shall) talk	we will (shall) talk
you will talk	you will talk
he, she, it will talk	they will talk

PRESENT PERFECT TENSE
(*have* or *has* + the past participle)

SINGULAR	*PLURAL*
I have talked	we have talked
you have talked	you have talked
he, she, it has talked	they have talked

PAST PERFECT TENSE
(*had* + the past participle)

SINGULAR	*PLURAL*
I had talked	we had talked
you had talked	you had talked
he, she, it had talked	they had talked

(continued)

USAGE

MEETING *individual* **NEEDS**

LEP/ESL

General Strategies. You may discover that some students neither write nor pronounce the *–es* ending for present tense, third-person singular verbs, as in "She miss the bus almost every day." Similarly, they might have a tendency to omit the *–ed* ending for past tense, as in "She miss the bus yesterday." You may want to give students sentences containing these forms. Ask your students to underline all the *–es* and *–ed* endings and to read the sentences aloud. Listen carefully and model standard pronunciation when necessary.

USAGE

CONJUGATION OF THE VERB *TALK* (continued)
FUTURE PERFECT TENSE (*will have* or *shall have* + the past participle)

SINGULAR	*PLURAL*
I will (shall) have talked	we will (shall) have talked
you will have talked	you will have talked
he, she, it will have talked	they will have talked

 REFERENCE NOTE: For the conjugation of a verb in the passive voice, see pages 694–695.

In each tense another form, called the *progressive form,* may be used to show continuing action. The progressive form is made up of a form of *be* plus the verb's present participle.

Present Progressive	am, are, is talking
Past Progressive	was, were talking
Future Progressive	will (shall) be talking
Present Perfect Progressive	has, have been talking
Past Perfect Progressive	had been talking
Future Perfect Progressive	will (shall) have been talking

CONJUGATION OF THE VERB *THROW*			
Present infinitive: *to throw*		Perfect infinitive: *to have thrown*	
PRINCIPAL PARTS OF *THROW*			
BASE FORM	**PRESENT PARTICIPLE**	**PAST**	**PAST PARTICIPLE**
throw	(is) throwing	threw	(have) thrown

SINGULAR	*PLURAL*
I throw	we throw
you throw	you throw
he, she, it throws	they throw
Present progressive: *am, are, is throwing*	

(continued)

CONJUGATION OF THE VERB *THROW* (continued)

PAST TENSE

SINGULAR	PLURAL
I threw	we threw
you threw	you threw
he, she, it threw	they threw

Past progressive: *was, were throwing*

FUTURE TENSE
(*will* or *shall* + the base form)

SINGULAR	PLURAL
I will (shall) throw	we will (shall) throw
you will throw	you will throw
he, she, it will throw	they will throw

Future progressive: *will (shall) be throwing*

PRESENT PERFECT TENSE
(*has* or *have* + the past participle)

SINGULAR	PLURAL
I have thrown	we have thrown
you have thrown	you have thrown
he, she, it has thrown	they have thrown

Present perfect progressive: *has, have been throwing*

PAST PERFECT TENSE
(*had* + the past participle)

SINGULAR	PLURAL
I had thrown	we had thrown
you had thrown	you had thrown
he, she, it had thrown	they had thrown

Past perfect progressive: *had been throwing*

FUTURE PERFECT TENSE
(*will have* or *shall have* + the past participle)

SINGULAR	PLURAL
I will (shall) have thrown	we will (shall) have thrown
you will have thrown	you will have thrown
he, she, it will have thrown	they will have thrown

Future perfect progressive: *will (shall) have been throwing*

USAGE

COMMON ERROR

Problem. Students might have difficulty in distinguishing among the past perfect tense, the present perfect tense, and the future perfect tense.

Solution. Remind students to look at the tense of the verb *have. Had* is in the past tense; it is combined with the past participle of a verb to create the past perfect tense. *Have* and *has* are in the present tense. Coupling either of these verbs with a past participle will form the present perfect tense. Likewise, *will have* is in the future tense, and it is combined with the past participle of a verb to create the future perfect tense.

INTEGRATING THE LANGUAGE ARTS

Literature Link. Students are often told to stick to one verb tense in their writing and are confused when they read a short story that incorporates several tenses. Tell students to read a short story and to identify the various tenses it incorporates. "The Doll's House" by Katherine Mansfield would be a good choice. Ask students why they think short stories often include so many different verb tenses. [A short story is a fictional narrative that relates a series of events. In order to show the sequence of events, several tenses must often be used.]

21e. Learn the uses of the six tenses.

(1) The **present tense** is used to express an action or a state of being occurring now, at the present time.

EXAMPLES   Sonja **owns** a calculator.
Larry **is** in the Chess Club.
We **are rehearsing** the play. [progressive form]

The present tense may be used to indicate habitual action.

EXAMPLE   He **runs** two miles a day.

The present tense is also used to express a general truth—something that is true at all times.

EXAMPLE   Haste **makes** waste.

The present tense is often used in discussing literary works, particularly in summarizing the plot or subject of a work. This use of the present tense is called the *literary present.*

EXAMPLES   In Act III of *Julius Caesar,* the conspirators **gather** around Caesar. Casca **is** the first to stab him; then the others **plunge** their knives into Caesar.

Sometimes the present tense is used to relate past events in order to make them seem vivid. This use is called the *historical present.*

EXAMPLES   During the unstable years following the 1910 Mexican Revolution, Emiliano Zapata **commands** a large army of revolutionaries and **occupies** Mexico City three different times.

(2) The **past tense** is used to express an action or a state of being that occurred in the past but did not continue into the present.

EXAMPLES   I **ran** toward the door.
I **was running** toward the door. [progressive form]

(3) The **future tense** is used to express an action or a state of being that will occur. The future tense is formed with *will* or *shall.*

EXAMPLES   I **will leave** this week.
I **will be leaving** this week. [progressive form]

There are several other ways to indicate future time.

EXAMPLES   I **am going to leave** this week.
I **leave later** this week. [present tense with a word or phrase clearly indicating future time]

(4) The ***present perfect tense*** is used to express an action or a state of being that occurred at some indefinite time in the past. The present perfect tense is formed with *have* or *has*.

EXAMPLE   She **has visited** Chicago.

The present perfect tense is also used to express an action (or a state of being) that occurred in the past and continues into the present.

EXAMPLES   She **has worked** there several years.
I **have been playing** guitar for nearly six months. [progressive form]

(5) The ***past perfect tense*** is used to express an action or a state of being that was completed before some other past action or event took place. The past perfect tense is formed with *had.*

EXAMPLES   After she **had revised** her essay, she handed it in. [The action of revising was completed before the action of handing in.]
When he **had washed** the dishes, he sat down to rest. [The action of washing was completed before the action of resting.]

(6) The ***future perfect tense*** is used to express an action or a state of being that will be completed before some other future occurrence. The future perfect tense is formed with *shall have* or *will have.*

EXAMPLES   By the time I leave, I **will have packed** all my clothes. [The action of packing will be completed before the action of leaving.]
At the end of next year, I **will have been attending** school for eleven years. [progressive form]

USAGE

USAGE

ANSWERS
Exercise 5

1. The first sentence expresses an action that will occur in the future (future tense). The second sentence expresses an action that will be completed before some future action or event takes place (future perfect tense).

2. The first sentence expresses an action that occurred in the past but did not continue into the present (past tense). The second sentence expresses an action that occurred in the past and continues into the present (present perfect progressive tense).

3. The first sentence expresses an action that occurred in the past but did not continue into the present (past tense). The second sentence expresses an action that occurred in the past and continues into the present (present perfect tense).

4. The first sentence expresses an action that will occur in the future (future tense). The second sentence expresses an action that will be completed before some future action takes place (future perfect tense).

5. The first sentence expresses a continuing action that occurred in the past but did not continue into the present (past progressive tense). The second sentence expresses an action that occurred in the past and continues into the present (present perfect progressive tense).

 EXERCISE 5 | **Explaining the Uses of the Tenses of Verbs in Sentences**

Explain the difference in meaning between the sentences in the following pairs. Both sentences in each pair are correct. Identify the tense of the verb in each sentence.

1. I will start working by this afternoon.
   I will have started working by this afternoon.
2. What happened at the game?
   What has been happening at the game?
3. She lived in Cleveland for four years.
   She has lived in Cleveland for four years.
4. Before next year I will get a driver's license.
   Before next year I will have gotten a driver's license.
5. Some Green Berets were practicing tae kwon do during their lunch break.
   Some Green Berets have been practicing tae kwon do during their lunch break.

EXERCISE 6 | **Using the Different Tenses of Verbs in Sentences**

Change the tense of the verb in each of the following sentences, according to the directions given after the sentence.

1. Otto lived here for a year. (Change to past perfect.) **1. had**
2. When the alarm goes off, I will get up. (Change *will get* to future perfect.) **2. have gotten**
3. Have you read Thomas Sowell's excellent how-to book *Choosing a College*? (Change *have read* to present perfect progressive.) **3. been reading**
4. When I get back, will you go? (Change *will go* to future perfect.) **4. have gone**   **5. Had/been**   **6. Have/been**
5. Were they at the party? (Change to past perfect.)
6. Were you invited? (Change to present perfect.) **7. has**
7. The soloist sings well. (Change to present perfect.) **sung**
8. The bus arrives on time. (Change to future.) **8. will arrive**
9. By the time you get here, Cammi will find out. (Change *will find* to future perfect.) **9. have found**
10. At ten o'clock, the klezmer band will play for an hour without a break. (Change to future perfect progressive.) **10. have been playing**

PICTURE THIS

Recently, you visited your cousins who live on this ranch. While you were there, heavy rains caused a nearby river to flood. You and your aunt and uncle and cousins managed to save their home from the rising water by quickly building a dike. After returning home, you decide you want your future children and grandchildren to know what your experience was like. You write a short account of what you did and how you felt as the waters rose and you and your family fought to hold them back. Use at least five different verb tenses in your journal entry. Be prepared to tell the tense of each verb you use.

Subject: your experiences during a flood
Audience: your descendants
Purpose: to inform

PICTURE THIS

As prewriting, suggest that students jot down an outline of events in chronological order. What happened first, second, third, and so on? Once they have a clear idea of the sequence of events, students will be better able to use verb tenses correctly. You may want to ask students to underline the verbs in their accounts and to identify the tense of each verb.

USAGE

USAGE

USAGE

Consistency of Tense

21f. Do not change needlessly from one tense to another.

NONSTANDARD	Roy **raised** his binoculars and **sees** a large bear as it **raced** back to the woods. [All the verbs refer to actions that happened at approximately the same time. However, the verbs are a mixture of past and present tenses.]
STANDARD	Roy **raised** his binoculars and **saw** a large bear as it **raced** back to the woods. [The verbs are all in the past tense.]
STANDARD	Roy **raises** his binoculars and **sees** a large bear as it **races** back to the woods. [The verbs are all in the present tense.]

NOTE: Sometimes, to show a sequence of events, you will need to mix verb tenses.

EXAMPLE   Before we **had gone** five miles, the car **started** making funny noises, and now it **won't run** at all.

EXERCISE 7   **Proofreading Paragraphs for Correct Verb Forms**

Some of the sentences in the following passage have at least one incorrect verb form. If a verb form is incorrect, write the correct form. If a sentence is correct, write C.

[1] The painting on the next page depicts the outcome of one of the most important battles of the Revolutionary War, a battle that took place in September and October 1777 at Saratoga, New York. [2] The leader of the British troops, General John Burgoyne, had set up camp near Saratoga and is planning to march south to Albany. [3] Burgoyne's army has been weakened by a recent attack from an American militia, which had ambushed some of his troops at Bennington, Vermont. [4] Although the march to Albany is dangerous, Burgoyne decided to take the risk because he feels bound by orders from London. [5] Meanwhile, also near Saratoga, the American troops under General Horatio Gates gather reinforcements and supplies. [6] The American forces outnumbered their British enemies by a margin of nearly two to one. [7] The

USAGE

ANSWERS
Exercise 7

1. C
2. is—was
3. has—had
4. is—was; feels—felt
5. gather—had gathered (or *were gathering* or *gathered*)
6. C
7. are—were; are—were
8. launch—launched
9. withdraw—withdrew
10. have—had
11. sends—sent
12. are—were
13. C
14. leads—led
15. endure—endured; prepares—prepared
16. surround—surrounded
17. had surrendered—surrendered
18. is—was
19. becomes—became
20. C

USAGE

Americans are much better equipped than the British, whose provisions are badly depleted.

[8] In spite of these disadvantages, the British launch an attack on the Americans on September 19, 1777. [9] After four hours of fierce fighting, the Americans, led by General Gates or General Benedict Arnold (who later became an infamous traitor to the American cause), withdraw. [10] The British, however, have suffered serious losses, including many officers. [11] Burgoyne urgently sends messages to the British command in New York and asked for new orders. [12] He never received a response, possibly because the messages are intercepted. [13] Burgoyne's tactics became desperate. [14] He boldly leads a fresh attack against the Americans on October 7. [15] This time, however, his troops endure even worse casualties, and the next day Burgoyne prepares to retreat.

[16] The Americans surround Burgoyne's army before it could leave Saratoga. [17] As the painting shows, Burgoyne had surrendered to Benedict Arnold. [18] The Convention of Saratoga, by which Burgoyne gave up his entire force of six thousand troops, is signed on October 17. [19] Saratoga becomes a turning point in the Revolutionary War. [20] Six years later, in 1783, the British signed a peace treaty with the Americans, and the Revolutionary War ended.

The Granger Collection, New York.

VISUAL CONNECTIONS
The Surrender of Burgoyne

About the Artist. John Trumbull, born in 1756 in Lebanon, Connecticut, was left nearly blind in one eye by a boyhood injury. Nevertheless, Trumbull went on to become a colonel by the age of twenty-one, an amateur architect, an author, and a well-respected artist. Trumbull is best known for his paintings depicting momentous occasions in American history, his most famous painting being *The Declaration of Independence.* In 1843, John Trumbull died and, according to his wishes, was buried under the Yale Art Gallery.

USAGE

OBJECTIVES

- To identify verbs in sentences as being in the active or the passive voice
- To rewrite passive voice verbs in the active voice

PROGRAM MANAGER

ACTIVE VOICE AND PASSIVE VOICE

- **Independent Practice/ Reteaching** For instruction and exercises, see **Active and Passive Voice** in *Language Skills Practice and Assessment,* p. 126.
- **Computer Guided Instruction** For additional instruction and practice with active voice and passive voice, see **Lesson 12** in *Language Workshop CD-ROM.*
- **Practice** To help less-advanced students with additional instruction and practice with active voice and passive voice, see **Chapter 16** in *English Workshop, Fourth Course,* pp. 231–232.

QUICK REMINDER

Write the verbs *terminate, build,* and *persuade* on the chalkboard. For each verb, ask your students to compose one sentence in the active voice and one sentence in the passive voice.

ADVANCED STUDENTS

Tell students that although as a general rule they should avoid using the passive voice, there are times when it is effective. For example, the passive voice can be used to neutralize the sense of action, to create a sense of evasiveness, or to create suspense in writing. Have students look for examples of effective use of the passive voice in literature and **continued on next page**

---

694 *Using Verbs Correctly*

Active Voice and Passive Voice

21g. A verb in the *active voice* expresses an action performed *by* its subject. A verb in the *passive voice* expresses an action done *to* its subject.

ACTIVE VOICE   The blazing fire **destroyed** the outside walls. [The subject (*fire*) performs the action.]

PASSIVE VOICE   The outside walls **were destroyed** by the blazing fire. [The subject (*walls*) receives the action.]

Notice that the object of the active sentence becomes the subject of the passive sentence. The subject of the active sentence is now given in a prepositional phrase, which could even be omitted in the passive sentence.

PASSIVE VOICE   The outside walls were destroyed.

Notice, too, that the verb has been changed from *destroyed* to the verb phrase *were destroyed.* In a passive sentence, the verb phrase always includes a form of *be* (*is, was,* etc.) plus the past participle. Other helping verbs may also be included, depending on the tense.

ACTIVE VOICE   She **grows** corn on her farm.

PASSIVE VOICE   Corn **is grown** on her farm.

ACTIVE VOICE   She **will plant** the corn in two weeks.

PASSIVE VOICE   The corn **will be planted** in two weeks.

CONJUGATION OF THE VERB *PAY* IN THE PASSIVE VOICE	
PRESENT TENSE	
SINGULAR	**PLURAL**
I am paid	we are paid
you are paid	you are paid
he, she, it is paid	they are paid
Present progressive: *am, are, is being paid*	

(continued)

CONJUGATION OF THE VERB *PAY* IN THE PASSIVE VOICE (*continued*)

PAST TENSE

SINGULAR	PLURAL
I was paid	we were paid
you were paid	you were paid
he, she, it was paid	they were paid

Past progressive: *was, were being paid*

FUTURE TENSE

SINGULAR	PLURAL
I will (shall) be paid	we will (shall) be paid
you will be paid	you will be paid
he, she, it will be paid	they will be paid

Future progressive: *will (shall) be being paid*

PRESENT PERFECT TENSE

SINGULAR	PLURAL
I have been paid	we have been paid
you have been paid	you have been paid
he, she, it has been paid	they have been paid

Present perfect progressive: *has, have been being paid*

PAST PERFECT TENSE

SINGULAR	PLURAL
I had been paid	we had been paid
you had been paid	you had been paid
he, she, it had been paid	they had been paid

Past perfect progressive: *had been being paid*

FUTURE PERFECT TENSE

SINGULAR	PLURAL
I will (shall) have been paid	we will (shall) have been paid
you will have been paid	you will have been paid
he, she, it will have been paid	they will have been paid

Future perfect progressive: *will (shall) have been being paid*

NOTE: Because the use of *be* or *been* with *being* is awkward, the progressive form is usually used only in the present tense and past tense.

USAGE

in magazines and newspapers. You may want to ask students to share their examples of passive voice with the class and to explain why they are effective.

INTEGRATING THE LANGUAGE ARTS

Grammar and Writing. Ask your students to write in the passive voice brief narratives about experiences they have had. Ask volunteers to read their papers aloud. The class should listen carefully to the readers, noting examples of writing that meet the objective. Then have students change their narratives to the active voice; have volunteers read the revised narratives aloud. Discuss the differences that the use of the active voice makes.

TECHNOLOGY TIP

There are computer programs available that can check writing for overuse of passive voice. If your school's computer department has such a program, you may want to encourage students to use it.

USAGE

USAGE

CRITICAL THINKING

Analysis. The chapter gives three situations in which the passive voice is useful:

1. when the performer is difficult to specify
2. when the performer is unknown
3. when the writer or speaker doesn't want to name the performer

As a weeklong project, have students listen for and note use of the passive voice in their own speech and the speech of others. Tell students to analyze why the passive voice was used in each instance.

ANSWERS
Exercise 8

Revisions may vary.

1. passive—Many artists around the world admired the art of Lucia Wilcox.

2. active

3. passive—Raoul Dufy, Fernand Léger, Robert Motherwell, and Jackson Pollock befriended and taught her.

4. passive—Art galleries all over the world showed exhibits of her paintings.

5. active

6. passive—A tumor near the optic nerve caused it.

7. active

8. passive—She described her vision and her mind as "free of static" and "distractions."

9. passive—Because of her blindness, she altered her style from energetic silhouettes to larger canvases in lush colors.

10. passive—Many well-known artists imitated this style.

Using the Passive Voice

The passive voice emphasizes the person or thing receiving the action rather than the one performing the action. The passive voice is useful

- when the performer is difficult to specify
- when you don't know who performed an action
- when you don't want to give away the performer's identity

EXAMPLES   The mayor **was reelected** by a landslide. [performer difficult to specify]

My brother's bicycle **was stolen** yesterday. [performer unknown]

Vicious rumors **have been spread** about him. [performer deliberately concealed]

In general, though, it's a good idea to avoid the passive voice. The active voice makes your writing much more direct and forceful.

EXERCISE 8   **Identifying Sentences in the Active or Passive Voice**

Label the verb in each of the following sentences as *active* or *passive*. Then rewrite each passive voice sentence in the active voice.

1. The art of Lucia Wilcox was admired by many artists around the world.
2. Her blindness during her last years made her final works particularly interesting.
3. She was befriended and taught by Raoul Dufy, Fernand Léger, Robert Motherwell, and Jackson Pollock.
4. Exhibits of her paintings were shown in art galleries all over the world.
5. Her blindness occurred suddenly, though not unexpectedly.
6. It was caused by a tumor near the optic nerve.
7. After becoming blind, she claimed she had better sight than anyone else.
8. Her vision and her mind were described by her as "free of static" and "distractions."

SIX TROUBLESOME VERBS

OBJECTIVES

- To read aloud and to stress the correct forms of *lie* and *lay, sit* and *set,* and *rise* and *raise* in sentences
- To select the correct forms of *lie* and *lay* and *sit* and *set* to complete sentences

Six Troublesome Verbs   **697**

9. Because of her blindness, her style was altered from energetic silhouettes to larger canvases in lush colors.
10. This style was imitated by many well-known artists.

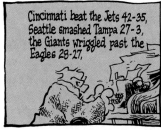

Shoe reprinted by permission: Tribune Media Services.

Six Troublesome Verbs

Lie and *Lay*

The verb *lie* means "to rest" or "to recline." It never takes an object.

The verb *lay* means "to put" or "to place" (something). It usually takes an object.

USAGE

PROGRAM MANAGER

SIX TROUBLESOME VERBS

- **Independent Practice/ Reteaching** For instruction and exercises, see **Troublesome Verbs** in *Language Skills Practice and Assessment,* p. 127.

- **Computer Guided Instruction** For additional instruction and practice with troublesome verbs, see **Lesson 11** in *Language Workshop CD-ROM.*

- **Practice** To help less-advanced students with additional instruction and practice with troublesome verbs, see **Chapter 16** in *English Workshop, Fourth Course,* pp. 233–236.

QUICK REMINDER

Write the verbs *lie, lay, sit, set, rise,* and *raise* on the chalkboard and ask students to compose one sentence for each verb. When students finish writing, give a brief definition of each word. Then ask volunteers to read their sentences aloud.

USAGE

- To proofread and revise for correct forms of *lie* and *lay* in sentences and in a passage
- To write the correct forms of *sit* and *set* to complete a paragraph
- To write the correct forms of *rise* and *raise* to complete sentences

LEARNING STYLES

Kinetic Learners. Have students use mime to illustrate the differences between the verbs in these pairs of troublesome verbs. For example, a student might mime the act of setting groceries on a counter and the act of sitting in a chair.

PRINCIPAL PARTS OF *LIE* AND *LAY*			
BASE FORM	**PRESENT PARTICIPLE**	**PAST**	**PAST PARTICIPLE**
lie (rest)	(is) lying	lay	(have) lain
lay (put)	(is) laying	laid	(have) laid

EXAMPLES   The cat often **lies** on the porch, sunning itself.
It is **lying** there now.
A thick fog **lay** over the city.
The old papers **had lain** on the desk for months.

Lay your packages here.
I am **laying** your packages here.
The mason **laid** the bricks.
He **had laid** his keys on the ledge.

To decide whether to use *lie* or *lay*, ask yourself two questions:

QUESTION 1:   What do I mean? (Is the meaning "to be in a lying position," or is it "to put something down"?)
QUESTION 2:   What time does the verb express, and which principal part accurately shows this time?

EXAMPLE: Feeling drowsy, I (lay, laid) on the couch.
QUESTION 1:   *Meaning*? Here the meaning is "to rest." Therefore, the verb should be *lie*.
QUESTION 2:   *Principal part*? The time is past. Therefore, the principal part should be *lay*.
ANSWER: Feeling drowsy, I **lay** on the couch.

EXAMPLE: The teacher (lay, laid) the cards on the desk.
QUESTION 1:   *Meaning*? Here the meaning is "to put." Therefore, the verb should be *lay*.
QUESTION 2:   *Principal part*? The time is past. Therefore, the principal part should be *laid*.
ANSWER: The teacher **laid** the cards on the desk.

 ORAL PRACTICE 2   **Stressing the Correct Forms of *Lie* and *Lay* in Sentences**

Read each of the following sentences aloud, stressing the italicized verbs.

1. The ketchup bottle should *lie* on its side.
2. A light haze *lay* over the hills.
3. The cat *laid* its toy on the doorsill.
4. Someone's books are *lying* in the hall.
5. She had *lain* down for a nap.
6. Where could I have *laid* the recipe?
7. *Lay* the material on the counter.
8. You could *lie* down and relax.

▶ EXERCISE 9 **Selecting the Correct Form of *Lie* and *Lay* to Complete Sentences**

In each of the following sentences, choose the <u>correct verb</u> in parentheses.

1. He (*lay*, <u>*laid*</u>) out the silverware.
2. Eduardo (<u>*laid*</u>, *lay*) the strips of grilled meat on the tortilla.
3. The pasture (<u>*lies*</u>, *lays*) in the valley.
4. A sheet (<u>*lay*</u>, *laid*) over the rug to catch the paint.
5. The clothing had (<u>*lain*</u>, *laid*) on the floor all week.
6. Kitty (*lay*, <u>*laid*</u>) the book down.
7. Mrs. Nakamoto was (*lying*, <u>*laying*</u>) out everything necessary for the tea ceremony.
8. The theories developed by Albert Einstein (*lay*, <u>*laid*</u>) the groundwork for many later scientific discoveries.
9. The cat has been (<u>*lying*</u>, *laying*) on my coat.
10. (*Lying*, <u>*Laying*</u>) the tip by my plate, I rose to leave the restaurant.

▶ EXERCISE 10 **Determining the Correct Use of *Lie* and *Lay* in Sentences**

For each of the following sentences, write *C* if the verb is correct. If the verb is incorrect, write the correct form.

1. The towels, ~~laying~~ in the corner all need to be washed.   **1.** lying
2. After I had tripped, I sat there feeling embarrassed, my groceries lying all around me.   **2.** C
3. Jackie Joyner-Kersee crossed the finish line and, exhausted, ~~laid~~ down in the grass.   **3.** lay
4. The fox was lying hidden in the thicket.   **4.** C

COOPERATIVE LEARNING
Working on a group project will provide an opportunity for students to clarify their confusion over the verbs *lie* and *lay*, *set* and *sit*, and *rise* and *raise*. Divide the class into groups of four or five. Assign each group the task of writing a short skit that includes the six troublesome verbs. Then have the groups perform their skits for the class.

INTEGRATING THE LANGUAGE ARTS

Literature Link. As a means of stressing to students that incorrect use of these verbs will affect the meaning of what they write, have students read a poem in which *lie, lay, sit, set, rise,* or *raise* is used correctly. Students might read "Miss Rosie" by Lucille Clifton (*sit*), or "The Road Not Taken" by Robert Frost (*lie*). After students have read the poem, have them analyze how the poem would be different if the wrong verb had been used (*set* for *sit,* or *lay* for *lie*). Would the meaning of the poem be clear to students? Would they be distracted by the incorrect usage? What might incorrect usage tell them about the speaker of the poem? Discuss these questions with your class.

700 *Using Verbs Correctly*

5. Yesterday, all we did was lie around and play CDs. **5.** C
6. He was lying under the car, tinkering with the muffler. **6.** C
7. The workers had ‸lain down their tools and gone to lunch. **7.** laid   **8.** lying   **9.** laid
8. My gym bag was ‸laying right where I had left it.
9. In his speech, César Chávez ‸lay the responsibility for social change on the shoulders of all citizens.
10. She sighed and ‸lay down the phone receiver. **10.** laid

 EXERCISE 11 **Proofreading a Paragraph for the Correct Use of *Lie* and *Lay***

In each sentence of the following paragraph, a form of *lie* or *lay* is used. If the wrong form is used, write the correct form. If a sentence is correct, write *C*.

1. C
2. laid
3. laid
4. lay
5. lying
6. lie
7. C
8. C
9. lying
10. lie

[1] Brent had planned to spend all day Saturday laying new tile in the kitchen. [2] Before he started, he ‸lay out all his materials and read the directions on the can of adhesive carefully. [3] At first, he made good progress and had ‸lain sixteen rows of tile by lunchtime. [4] Then he ate a sandwich and ‸laid down on the sofa for a few minutes. [5] When he returned to the kitchen, Brent found that his dog, Stanley, was ‸laying where the next row of tiles was supposed to go. [6] Brent had forgotten that Stanley liked to ‸lay in that particular place on the kitchen floor. [7] Unfortunately, Stanley weighed almost as much as Brent, and laying down the law to the dog had never worked. [8] Brent got a juicy meat scrap out of the refrigerator and laid it on the floor just beyond Stanley's snoring nose. [9] But the wily Stanley had been ‸laying in wait and, in a flash, grabbed the meat. [10] To Brent's dismay, Stanley resumed his nap with a satisfied sigh, and Brent learned that the worker isn't the only one who can ‸lay down on the job!

Sit and *Set*

The verb *sit* means "to rest in a seated position." It almost never takes an object.

The verb *set* means "to put," "to place" (something). It usually takes an object. Notice that *set* does not change form in the past or the past participle.

NOTE: In a few uses, *set* does not mean "to put" or "to place."

EXAMPLES the sun sets, setting hens, set your watch, set a record, set out to accomplish something

PRINCIPAL PARTS OF *SIT* AND *SET*			
BASE FORM	**PRESENT PARTICIPLE**	**PAST**	**PAST PARTICIPLE**
sit (rest)	(is) sitting	sat	(have) sat
set (put)	(is) setting	set	(have) set

EXAMPLES You may **sit.**   The car **sat** in the driveway.
　　　　　 Set your books here. We **set** the books there.

ORAL PRACTICE 3 **Stressing the Correct Forms of *Sit* and *Set* in Sentences**

Read each of the following sentences aloud, stressing the italicized verb.

1. *Set* the groceries on the counter.
2. *Sit* down anywhere you like.
3. Would you please *set* the lawn chairs under the tree in the front yard?
4. The bird *sat* on the wire.
5. During Hanukkah, we always *set* the menorah in a place of honor.
6. We had *sat* in the lobby for an hour.
7. They have been *sitting* on the porch.
8. Rosa Parks made history when she chose to *sit* rather than to give up her seat to a white passenger.

EXERCISE 12 **Selecting the Correct Form of *Sit* and *Set* to Complete Sentences**

In each of the following sentences, choose the <u>correct verb</u> in parentheses.

A DIFFERENT APPROACH
Tell students they'll be competing in a Sentence Bee in which they will be able to practice correct usage of the verbs *lie*, *lay*, *sit*, *set*, *rise*, and *raise*. Divide the class into two teams. Give a student from one team instructions such as "Compose a sentence using the past perfect tense of *lay*." The student will then compose a sentence fitting your description. If the sentence is correct, the student stays in the game. If it is incorrect, he or she is out, and the same challenge is offered to a student from the other team. Continue in this fashion until everyone has been eliminated except a winner, or until you run out of time. You may find it helpful to prepare the instructions ahead of time.

1. A few of us were (*sitting, setting*) at our desks.
2. He (*sat, set*) in the rocker, reading.
3. He (*sat, set*) the package on the doorstep.
4. Ida was (*sitting, setting*) out the chips and dip for the guests.
5. We had been (*sitting, setting*) on a freshly painted bench.
6. They (*set, sat*) the seedlings in the window boxes.
7. She (*sits, sets*) in front of me.
8. (*Set, Sit*) this Pueblo pottery in the display case.
9. I could (*sit, set*) and watch the sunset every evening.
10. Bowls of Cuban black bean soup were (*sat, set*) in front of the hungry travelers.

▶ EXERCISE 13 **Writing the Forms of *Sit* and *Set***

For each numbered blank in the following paragraph, write the correct form of *sit* or *set*.

1. sat
2. set
3. sat
4. sitting
5. sit

To gain a view of the surrounding land, Lewis and Clark's group climbed to an outcropping of gray rocks that [1] ____ atop the bluff. It was late afternoon, and the Shoshone guide Sacagawea [2] ____ her pack down beside the rocks and [3] ____ down in their shade to rest. Meriwether Lewis saw her from where he was [4] ____ nearby and approached with a friendly "May I [5] ____ here with

VISUAL CONNECTIONS
Exploring the Subject. Sacagawea, a woman of the Shoshone people, had been captured at the age of about fourteen by the Hidatsa, a Siouan tribe of North Dakota. She acted as an interpreter for Lewis and Clark on their trip west. During the trip, Sacagawea gave birth to a son. In return for her help, Sacagawea was able to return to her people in the Rocky Mountains.

The date of Sacagawea's death and her burial site are contested. According to one theory, she died in 1812 and was buried in present-day South Dakota. Another theory holds that she lived until 1884 and was buried in present-day Wyoming.

USAGE

USAGE

REVIEW A

OBJECTIVE

• To select the correct forms of *lie* and *lay* and *sit* and *set* to complete sentences

you?" Several other members of the expedition saw them
[6] ____ together and wondered what they were discussing. In fact, Lewis was asking her in what direction
she thought the party should [7] ____ out in the morning.
Gazing westward from the bluff, Sacagawea saw that she
was in familiar territory and soon [8] ____ her mind on
heading down the mountainside toward the northwest.
By the time the sun had [9] ____, Lewis agreed that the
route she had chosen would be the easiest to follow. A
wise leader, he realized that he had never [10] ____ foot in
these lands, while she had passed this way before.

6. sitting

7. set

8. set

9. set

10. set

▶ REVIEW A

Selecting the Correct Form of *Lie* and *Lay* and *Sit* and *Set* to Complete Sentences

In each of the following sentences, choose the <u>correct verb</u> in parentheses.

1. (*Sitting*, *Setting*) on the table was a pair of scissors.
2. Please (*sit*, *set*) the carton down carefully.
3. Sakura folded her kimono and (*lay*, *laid*) down on the soft, padded futon to sleep.
4. (*Sit*, *Set*) all the way back in your seat.
5. The dirty dishes had (*lain*, *laid*) in the sink for hours.
6. Yesterday Tom (*lay*, *laid*) the blame for his lateness on his alarm clock.
7. The cat always (*sits*, *sets*) on the couch.
8. If only we could have (*lain*, *laid*) our hands on that buried treasure!
9. The tickets to the Wynton Marsalis concert were (*sitting*, *setting*) right where I left them.
10. King Tut's tomb (*lay*, *laid*) undisturbed for centuries.
11. Have you ever (*sat*, *set*) around with nothing to do?
12. She (*sat*, *set*) down at her desk with her checkbook and calculator in front of her.
13. Santa Anna, (*sitting*, *setting*) on his horse, ordered his troops to attack the Alamo.
14. The beached rowboat (*lay*, *laid*) on its side.
15. She (*sat*, *set*) looking toward the horizon.
16. Laura had just (*sat*, *set*) down when the phone rang.
17. Julie (*lay*, *laid*) her handbag on the counter.

USAGE

EXERCISE 13

Teaching Note. Students might be confused by the various meanings of *set* in this exercise. In numbers seven, eight, nine, and ten, the verb *set* is not used with the meaning "to put" or "to place." Direct students to the dictionary, which gives many meanings for *set* as both a transitive and intransitive verb.

You may also want to make sure your English-language learners understand the idiomatic uses of *set* in the phrases *set out*, *set one's mind on*, and *set foot*.

LEARNING STYLES

Auditory Learners. Some students might benefit from enunciating the options in **Review A.**

USAGE

18. Pieces of the jigsaw puzzle were (*laying, lying*) on the floor.
19. Jack was (*sitting, setting*) outside on the top step.
20. Were you (*laying, lying*) down for a while before dinner?

Rise and Raise

The verb *rise* means "to go upward." It never takes an object.

The verb *raise* means "to move (something) upward" or "to bring up." It usually takes an object.

PRINCIPAL PARTS OF *RISE* AND *RAISE*			
BASE FORM	**PRESENT PARTICIPLE**	**PAST**	**PAST PARTICIPLE**
rise (go upward)	(is) rising	rose	(have) risen
raise (move [something] upward)	(is) raising	raised	(have) raised

EXAMPLES I usually **rise** at 6:00 A.M.
Prices **rose** rapidly in the early 1980s.

Raise your hand if you know the answer.
The coach **raised** the bar on the high jump.

ORAL PRACTICE 4 **Stressing the Correct Form of *Rise* and *Raise* in Sentences**

Read each of the following sentences aloud, stressing the italicized verb.

1. *Has* the moon *risen* yet?
2. The tower *rose* high into the darkening air.
3. The temperature *rose* as the sun climbed higher.
4. Listening to "I Have a Dream," a speech by Martin Luther King, Jr., always *raises* my spirits.
5. Trails of mist were *rising* from the lake.
6. How much did the river *rise* during the flood?
7. The butterfly *rose* from the leaf and flitted away.
8. The dough was *rising* in the bowl.

USAGE

USAGE

► EXERCISE 14

Writing the Correct Form of *Rise* and *Raise* to Complete Sentences

For each blank in the following sentences, write the correct form of *rise* or *raise*. The tenses of the verbs in sentences 4, 5, 6, 8, and 9 may vary.

1. ____ the flags higher, please.   **1.** Raise
2. The gigantic Kodiak bear ____ on its hind legs and looked around.   **2.** rose
3. The tide ____ and falls because of the moon.   **3.** rises
4. Carlos and Pilar ____ the piñata above the heads of the children.   **4.** raised
5. Up toward the clouds ____ the jet.   **5.** rose
6. Many Native American peoples ____ corn as a staple food crop.   **6.** raise
7. Prices have ____ in the last few years.   **7.** risen
8. The traffic officer ____ his hand to signal us.   **8.** raised
9. My sister and I ____ before the sun came up this morning.   **9.** rose
10. César Chávez ____ to fame in the 1960s.   **10.** rose

► REVIEW B

Determining Correct or Incorrect Use of *Lie* and *Lay*, *Sit* and *Set*, and *Rise* and *Raise* in Sentences

If a sentence is correct, write *C*. If it is incorrect, revise the incorrect word or words.

1. Set the eggs down carefully.   **1.** C
2. The frog was ~~setting~~ on the lily pad and croaking loudly.   **2.** sitting
3. The judge studied the papers, then ~~lay~~ them beside her gavel.   **3.** laid
4. The cattle were lying in the shade by the stream.   **4.** C
5. Do you think the temperature will ~~raise~~ much higher?   **5.** rise
6. Wanda ~~sat~~ out the equipment for the experiment.   **6.** set
7. Why don't you ~~lie~~ those things down?   **7.** lay
8. Instead of ~~laying~~ down, you should be getting some type of strenuous exercise.   **8.** lying
9. Let's sit where we can get a good view of the Juneteenth parade.   **9.** C
10. ~~Set~~ down for a while and relax.   **10.** Sit

USAGE

MEETING *individual* NEEDS

LESS-ADVANCED STUDENTS

Students might benefit from doing **Review B** in small groups. Assign the exercise to groups of two or three. You may want to group less-advanced students with those who better understand the material. Encourage students to talk about the sentences and to help one another with any problems. You may want to circulate through the room to make sure that students who need assistance are receiving the help they require.

WRITING APPLICATION

This writing assignment provides each student with the opportunity to express pride in a personal heritage. If there are students in your class who do not possess a strong sense of cultural identity, encourage them to do some research.

CRITICAL THINKING

Synthesis. This activity asks students to project, based on what they know about the present contributions of a certain cultural or ethnic group, what can be expected from that group in the future. Because this projection requires a high level of critical thinking, you may want to model this thought process for students.

For example, you might note that the Greek Americans in your community are active in city government and have organized an annual festival that showcases Greek culture. Ask students what they can predict, based on this information, about the contributions of Greek Americans in the future. [Students might say that in the future Greek Americans in the community might hold important offices in city government and that their annual festival might attract tourists from other communities, thereby bringing revenue to the city.]

USAGE

WRITING APPLICATION

OBJECTIVE

• To write an informative essay that describes the order of events by using appropriate verb tenses

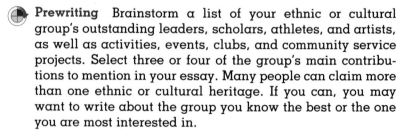

WRITING APPLICATION

Using Verb Tense to Establish Time of Action

To show the precise order of events, a writer sometimes needs to use several different tenses in a paragraph—or even in the same sentence.

EXAMPLE   The Japanese students *had planned* a tea ceremony, but because another group *was using* the activity room, they *will reschedule* the ceremony.

Each verb in the preceding sentence is in a different tense. If the verbs were all in the same tense, a reader would be confused about the order of the events.

▶ **WRITING ACTIVITY**

It's Cultural Appreciation Week at your school. Your teacher has asked you to write a short essay about your own cultural or ethnic group. In your essay, you should explore several ways in which people from your heritage have enriched life in your community. Use correct verb tenses to describe some of the contributions these people have made in the past, some activities they are currently involved in, and what you think they might offer in the future. Use at least five different verb tenses in your essay.

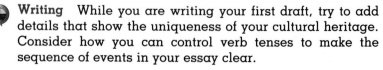 **Prewriting**   Brainstorm a list of your ethnic or cultural group's outstanding leaders, scholars, athletes, and artists, as well as activities, events, clubs, and community service projects. Select three or four of the group's main contributions to mention in your essay. Many people can claim more than one ethnic or cultural heritage. If you can, you may want to write about the group you know the best or the one you are most interested in.

Writing   While you are writing your first draft, try to add details that show the uniqueness of your cultural heritage. Consider how you can control verb tenses to make the sequence of events in your essay clear.

OBJECTIVES

- To select the correct forms of verbs to complete sentences
- To supply the correct forms of verbs to complete a paragraph

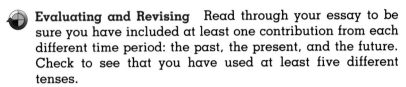 **Evaluating and Revising**   Read through your essay to be sure you have included at least one contribution from each different time period: the past, the present, and the future. Check to see that you have used at least five different tenses.

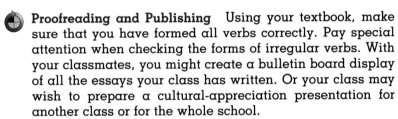 **Proofreading and Publishing**   Using your textbook, make sure that you have formed all verbs correctly. Pay special attention when checking the forms of irregular verbs. With your classmates, you might create a bulletin board display of all the essays your class has written. Or your class may wish to prepare a cultural-appreciation presentation for another class or for the whole school.

PROOFREADING AND PUBLISHING

To assist students in verifying that they have included at least five different verb tenses, ask them to label the tenses of all the verbs in their essays. This strategy will also save time for you when you are grading their papers.

USAGE

▶ REVIEW C   **Choosing the Correct Forms of Verbs to Complete Sentences**

In each of the following sentences, choose the <u>correct verb or form of the verb</u> given in parentheses.

1. Little Billy was (<u>*lying*</u>, *laying*) in wait for us.
2. He had accidentally (<u>*thrown*</u>, *throwed*) his homework away.
3. The spilled laundry (<u>*lay*</u>, *laid*) in a wet heap.
4. We ate until we almost (<u>*burst*</u>, *bursted*).
5. The kitten (*shrank*, <u>*shrunk*</u>) from the barking dog.
6. Haven't you ever (*swam*, <u>*swum*</u>) in a lake before?
7. When Chief Dan George walked to the podium, a cheer (<u>*rang*</u>, *rung*) out.
8. Have you ever (*rode*, <u>*ridden*</u>) a roller coaster?
9. I knew I should have (<u>*brought*</u>, *brung*) my camera.
10. Uh-oh, I think this phone is (*broke*, <u>*broken*</u>).

▶ REVIEW D   **Choosing the Correct Forms of Irregular Verbs**

Supply the correct form of each italicized verb in the following paragraph.

USAGE

1. seen Have you ever [1] (*see*) this fascinating picture of an impossible structure? It is called *Waterfall*, and it was **2.** drawn [2] (*draw*) by the Dutch artist M. C. Escher. He [3] (*take*) the **3.** took basic idea for this artwork from the optical illusion shown **4.** set beside it. As you can see, a two-story waterfall has [4] (*set*) a miller's wheel in motion. Then, after the water has **5.** left [5] (*leave*) the wheel, it zigzags through a channel until it **6.** comes [6] (*come*) to the top of the waterfall again. But wait—has **7.** gone the water [7] (*go*) uphill on its way back to the top of the **8.** run waterfall? No, obviously the stream has [8] (*run*) away from the fall on the same level as the bottom of the fall. But then how can the water now be back at the top where **9.** began it [9] (*begin*)? Escher never said, but he once wrote that if **10.** threw the miller simply [10] (*throw*) in a bucket of water now and then to replace water that had evaporated, he would have a "perpetual motion" machine!

1961 M. C. Escher/Cordon Art-Baarn-Holland.

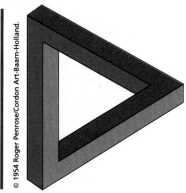

© 1954 Roger Penrose/Cordon Art-Baarn-Holland.

ANSWERS
Exercise 15

Students should produce sentences with two or more verbs, as directed. Be sure the verbs in each sentence are in different tenses and that the tenses clearly describe the sequence of events.

EXERCISE 15
Using Verbs to Express Time Relationships Clearly

The time line on the next page shows several key events from American history. Make up five sentences that establish time relationships between two or more of the events named. In each sentence, use more than one verb and make each verb a different tense. Vary your sentence structure. Be prepared to tell how the tenses you used help explain the sequence of events.

EXAMPLE *As De Soto was finishing his exploration of the Southeast, Cabrillo started to investigate the Pacific coast.*

REVIEW: POSTTEST

OBJECTIVES

- To write past or past participle forms of verbs to complete sentences
- To revise sentences to correct awkward use of voice as well as incorrect verb tenses

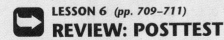

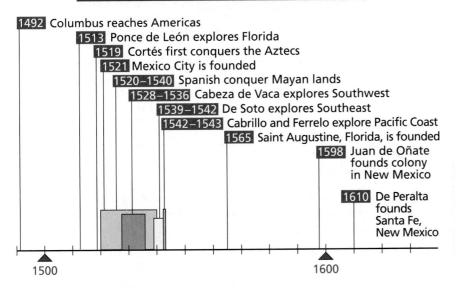

Some Important Events in American History

1492 Columbus reaches Americas
1513 Ponce de León explores Florida
1519 Cortés first conquers the Aztecs
1521 Mexico City is founded
1520–1540 Spanish conquer Mayan lands
1528–1536 Cabeza de Vaca explores Southwest
1539–1542 De Soto explores Southeast
1542–1543 Cabrillo and Ferrelo explore Pacific Coast
1565 Saint Augustine, Florida, is founded
1598 Juan de Oñate founds colony in New Mexico
1610 De Peralta founds Santa Fe, New Mexico

1500   1600

USAGE

Review: Posttest

A. Writing the Past or Past Participle Form of Verbs

For each of the following sentences, write the correct past or past participle of the verb given before the sentence.

1. *ride*   Jeffrey and Lee have ____ their bikes fifty miles today.   **1.** ridden
2. *write* I read the letters Grandpa ____ to Grandma in 1930.   **2.** wrote
3. *take*   Dad, I know that you've ____ us to two rap concerts this year, but please take us to just one more.   **3.** taken
4. *fall*   All that winter day the snow ____, blanketing everything.   **4.** fell
5. *see*   Rebecca soon ____ why the old house had sold so cheaply.   **5.** saw

6. *drink* The gerbil has ____ most of its water. **6.** drunk
7. *begin* As darkness fell and the children still did not return, I ____ to worry. **7.** began
8. *bring* Margot has ____ popcorn and apples for the party. **8.** brought
9. *speak* Police Sergeant Liakos ____ about responsible driving at the assembly yesterday. **9.** spoke
10. *give* The Nez Percé people had ____ the starving fur traders food and helped them repair their canoes. **10.** given

B. Revising Verb Tense or Voice

Rewrite the following sentences, correcting verbs that are in the wrong tense or that use an awkward voice. If a sentence is correct, write *C*.

EXAMPLES **1.** Genna gave her report on Captain James Cook and shows us some maps and pictures of the areas he explored.
  1. *Genna gave her report on Captain James Cook and showed us some maps and pictures of the areas he explored.*

  2. We were surprised to learn how many places were explored by him.
  2. *We were surprised to learn how many places he explored.*

11. Captain Cook, one of the greatest explorers of all time, sailed large areas of the Pacific Ocean and ʌmakes accurate maps of the region. **11.** made
12. Cookʌjoins the navy as a seaman in 1755, andʌmany promotions were received by him before he became the master of a ship in 1757. **12.** joined/he received
13. Because of his knowledge of geography, astronomy, and mathematics, heʌis selected to lead a scientific expedition to the Pacific. **13.** was
14. The purpose of Cook's expeditionʌis to observe the passage of Venus between Earth and the sun, a very rare occurrence. **14.** was
15. On the voyage, Cookʌwins a battle against scurvy, a serious disease caused by lack of vitamin C. **15.** won

16. ∧Raw cabbage, which∧was rich in vitamin C, ~~was eaten by the sailors~~ to prevent scurvy.   **16. The sailors ate/is**

17. By the time the voyage∧is over, the ship∧traveled around Cape Horn to Tahiti in the Pacific Ocean.   **17. was/had**

18. After∧~~he observes~~ the passage of Venus, Cook∧~~sails~~ off to explore the east coast of New Zealand, which ∧was claimed ~~by him~~ for England.   **18. observing/sailed/he**

19. ∧The Hawaiian Islands ~~were later explored by Cook~~ on his final voyage to the Pacific and ~~were~~ named∧ the Sandwich Islands~~.by him.~~   **19. Cook explored/them**

20. In a dispute over a canoe, Cook was killed by island inhabitants and in naval tradition was buried at sea in 1779.   **20. C**

C. Determining Correct Use of *Lie* and *Lay*, *Sit* and *Set*, and *Rise* and *Raise* in Sentences

If a verb in one of the following sentences is incorrect, write the correct form. If a sentence is correct, write *C*.

21. You can∧~~sit~~ the wastebasket in the corner and then set up the chairs.   **21. set**

22. Everyone rose when the judge entered the court-room and sat when she was seated.   **22. C**

23. The mysterious shape suddenly∧~~raised~~ from the shadows.   **23. rose**

24. I like to∧~~lay~~ out under the stars and just think.   **24. lie**

25. The servant had∧~~lain~~ out the emperor's silken robes of yellow, the color that only members of Chinese royalty were permitted to wear.   **25. laid**

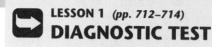
OBJECTIVES

- To correct errors in the use of comparative and superlative forms
- To revise sentences by correcting dangling and misplaced modifiers

USAGE

CHAPTER OVERVIEW

The first part of this chapter helps students to identify adjective and adverb modifiers and to correctly use the troublesome pairs *bad* and *badly, well* and *good,* and *slow* and *slowly.* The second part focuses on showing comparisons by correctly using comparative and superlative forms. The third part of the chapter shows how to recognize and correct dangling and misplaced modifiers.

USING THE DIAGNOSTIC TEST

You may want to use the **Diagnostic Test** to gauge whether students can correct errors in the use of comparative and superlative forms and whether students can revise sentences by correcting dangling and misplaced modifiers. You could supplement the test by having students write paragraphs in which they use comparative and superlative forms and correctly place phrases or clauses used as modifiers.

USAGE

22 USING MODIFIERS CORRECTLY

Forms, Comparison, and Placement

Diagnostic Test

A. Correcting Errors in the Use of the Comparative and Superlative Forms

Write the incorrect word or words from each sentence. Then write the correct form, adding or deleting words if necessary.

EXAMPLES
1. I was more hungrier than I had thought, so I ordered three sandwiches.
   1. *more hungrier—hungrier*
2. This storm was even badder than the last one.
   2. *badder—worse*

1. During the 1960s, Ralph Abernathy and Medgar Evers were among the ~~most~~ best-known civil rights activists.
2. He was the ~~more~~ able and intelligent of the three job applicants.   **2.** most
3. Is Pocahontas ~~famouser~~ than Sacagawea?   **3.** more famous

4. John, Richard's twin brother, was the ~~oldest~~ by three and a half minutes. **4.** older

5. After Diego had started lifting weights, he bragged that he was stronger than anyone in town. **5.** else

6. People who live along this road complain because it is the ~~worstest~~ in the entire township. **6.** worst

7. Floyd and his brother are landscape designers who are in demand throughout the state, but Floyd is the ~~best~~ known in this area. **7.** better

8. After the band had practiced, their music sounded ~~more~~ better.

9. When I had a choice of strawberry or vanilla, I took vanilla because I like it ~~best~~. **9.** better

10. Looking across the water at sunset, you can see the ~~beautifullest~~ view you can imagine. **10.** most beautiful

B. Revising Sentences by Correcting Dangling and Misplaced Modifiers

Each of the following sentences contains either a dangling or a misplaced modifier. Revise each sentence, arranging the words so that the meaning is logical and clear. You may have to add or delete some words. Be sure to use commas where they are needed to set off introductory and interrupting modifiers.

EXAMPLE **1.** The class sent a get-well message to their teacher on a balloon.
  1. *The class sent their teacher a get-well message on a balloon.*

11. Yipping and running in circles, they saw that the dogs could herd the sheep into the pen.

12. The winners marched off the platform carrying ribbons and trophies.

13. A police officer warned students who drive too fast about accidents during the defensive-driving class.

14. After escaping from slavery, the importance of education was often stressed by Frederick Douglass.

15. We went to visit my grandmother, who used to be a history teacher at my school yesterday.

16. Mother found a package outside our house tied with ribbons.

ANSWERS
Diagnostic Test: Part B

Answers may vary. Here are some possibilities:

11. They saw that the dogs, yipping and running in circles, could herd the sheep into the pen.

12. Carrying ribbons and trophies, the winners marched off the platform.

13. During the defensive-driving class, a police officer warned students who drive too fast about accidents.

14. Frederick Douglass, after escaping from slavery, often stressed the importance of education.

15. Yesterday, we went to visit my grandmother, who used to be a history teacher at my school.

16. Outside our house, Mother found a package tied with ribbons.

17. With a telephoto lens, Maria took a close-up photograph of a lion.

18. Sitting in a tree outside my window, a small bird is apparently building a nest on one of the limbs.

19. A young woman wearing a suit and a hat knocked on the door.

20. Walking in the sunshine, we felt warm.

PROGRAM MANAGER

ADJECTIVE AND ADVERB FORMS

■ **Independent Practice/ Reteaching** For instruction and exercises, see **Adjective and Adverb Forms** in *Language Skills Practice and Assessment*, p. 135.

■ **Computer Guided Instruction** For additional instruction and practice with adjective and adverb forms, see **Lesson 16** in *Language Workshop CD-ROM*.

QUICK REMINDER

Remind students that adverbs tell *where, when, how,* and *to what extent.* Adjectives tell *what kind, which one,* and *how many.*

Write the following sentences on the chalkboard. Have students classify each underlined word as an adjective or an adverb; then have them identify the question each word answers.

1. The storm was <u>fierce</u>. [adjective; tells what kind of storm]

2. Josh bathed his dog <u>yesterday</u>. [adverb; tells when he bathed the dog]

continued on next page

714

ADJECTIVE AND ADVERB FORMS Rule 22a

OBJECTIVES

- To identify adjectives and adverbs
- To select adjectives or adverbs to complete sentences
- To use adjective and adverb forms correctly in a paragraph

---

714 *Using Modifiers Correctly*

17. Maria took a close-up photograph of a lion with a telephoto lens.

18. Sitting in a tree outside my window, I see a small bird, apparently building a nest on one of the limbs.

19. A young woman knocked on the door wearing a suit and a hat.

20. Walking in the sunshine, it felt warm to us.

Adjective and Adverb Forms

A *modifier* is a word or a group of words that makes the meaning of another word more definite. Two parts of speech are used as modifiers: *adjectives* and *adverbs.* Adjectives modify nouns and pronouns. Adverbs modify verbs, adjectives, and other adverbs.

ADJECTIVE   Lisa does **strenuous** exercise.
ADVERB   Lisa exercises **strenuously.**

NOTE: Many adverbs end in *–ly,* but not all of them do. A few common adjectives also end in *–ly.*

EXAMPLES   **costly** repairs   **daily** schedule
lively discussion   **lonely** scene

Some words have the same form whether they're used as adjectives or as adverbs. Therefore, you can't tell whether a word is an adjective or an adverb just by looking for the *–ly* ending. Instead, you have to determine how the word is being used.

ADJECTIVES	ADVERBS
We took an **early** flight.	We left **early** this morning.
She asked a **hard** question.	She tried **hard.**
They took the **first** step.	They went **first.**

22a. If a word in the predicate modifies the subject of the verb, use the adjective form. If it modifies the verb, use the adverb form.

ADJECTIVE   The swimmer was **careful.** [careful swimmer]
   ADVERB   He swims **carefully.** [swims carefully]

In many cases, linking verbs are followed by a predicate adjective.

Common Linking Verbs		
appear	grow	smell
be (am, is, are, etc.)	look	sound
become	remain	stay
feel	seem	taste

Many linking verbs can also be used as action verbs. To tell whether a verb is a linking verb or an action verb, try a form of *seem* in its place.

LINKING   She **felt** happy. [*She seemed happy* makes sense. Therefore, *felt* is a linking verb in this sentence.]

ACTION   She **felt** the fabric. [*She seemed the fabric* doesn't make sense. Therefore, *felt* is an action verb in this sentence.]

LINKING   The old car **appeared** abandoned. [*The old car seemed abandoned* makes sense.]

ACTION   The car **appeared** suddenly. [*The car seemed suddenly* doesn't make sense.]

☞ **REFERENCE NOTE:** See pages 524–526 and 560–563 for more information on linking verbs and action verbs.

▶ EXERCISE 1   **Identifying Adjectives and Adverbs**

The following paragraph contains fifteen adjectives and ten adverbs. For each sentence, identify each adjective and adverb and give the word it modifies. [Note: Do not include the articles *a, an,* and *the.*]

EXAMPLE   [1] **First get a craft knife and some stiff black paper.**
      1. *First—adverb—get; craft—adjective—knife; some—adjective—paper; stiff—adjective—paper; black—adjective—paper*

[1] In many cultures, cutting paper to make pictures is a traditional art. [2] For example, Mexican artisans use a small, very sharp knife to cut designs in pieces of colored paper. [3] As the oddly shaped scraps fall away, an image

3. Felipe baked the <u>winning</u> dessert. [adjective; tells which dessert he baked]

4. The star appeared <u>surprisingly</u> bright in the sky. [adverb; tells to what extent it appeared bright]

MEETING *individual* **NEEDS**

USAGE

ANSWERS
Exercise 1

1. many—adjective—cultures; traditional—adjective—art

2. Mexican—adjective—artisans; small—adjective—knife; very—adverb—sharp; sharp—adjective—knife; colored—adjective—paper

3. oddly—adverb—shaped; shaped—adjective—scraps; away—adverb—fall; slowly—adverb—is revealed

4. each—adjective—part;
somehow—adverb— must connect;
another—adjective—part

5. these—adjective—designs;
sometimes—adverb—leaves;
background—adjective—pattern;
main—adjective—subject

6. not—adverb—must be;
even—adverb—slightly;
slightly—adverb—dull;
dull—adjective—knife;
accidentally—adverb—might tear;
tiny—adjective—bridges;
paper—adjective—bridges

VISUAL CONNECTIONS

Exploring the Subject. Paper-cutting, which is known as *papel picado* in Mexico, is an intricate art that is popular throughout the world. The tissue-paper cuttings shown here are reproductions from *Family Pictures* by Carmen Lomas Garza. Tissue-paper cuttings are used in Mexico to decorate Day-of-the-Dead altars and other festival sites.

COOPERATIVE LEARNING

After initial discussion of the three troublesome pairs, let students teach each other the material. Set up six-member teams. Two members will teach *bad* and *badly,* two will teach *well* and *good,* and two will teach *slow* and *slowly.* Each pair of students is also responsible for writing a six-sentence practice exercise on the material for the other members of the team.

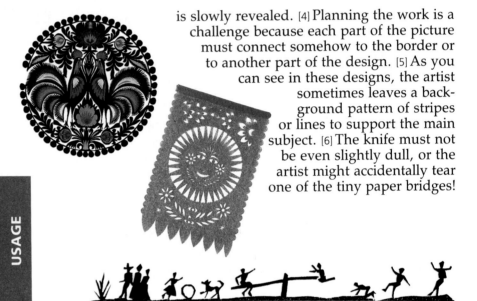

is slowly revealed. [4] Planning the work is a challenge because each part of the picture must connect somehow to the border or to another part of the design. [5] As you can see in these designs, the artist sometimes leaves a background pattern of stripes or lines to support the main subject. [6] The knife must not be even slightly dull, or the artist might accidentally tear one of the tiny paper bridges!

Three Troublesome Pairs

Bad and *Badly*

Bad is an adjective. In most uses, *badly* is an adverb.

EXAMPLES

ADJECTIVES	ADVERBS
The dog was **bad.**	The dog behaved **badly.**
The milk smelled **bad.**	The roof leaked **badly.**

Remember that a linking verb calls for an adjective form.

NONSTANDARD   The medicine tasted badly.
STANDARD   The medicine tasted **bad.**

☞ REFERENCE NOTE: See pages 498–499 for a discussion of standard and nonstandard English.

NOTE: In conversations, either *bad* or *badly* is acceptable after *feel.*

ACCEPTABLE IN   He feels **bad** about the accident.
CONVERSATION   He feels **badly** about the accident.

In writing, though, use *bad* after *feel.*

CORRECT IN WRITING   He feels **bad** about the accident.

Well and *Good*

Well may be used either as an adjective or as an adverb. As an adjective, *well* has two meanings:

(1) "in good health"

EXAMPLE   Fran is **well**.

(2) "satisfactory"

EXAMPLE   Everything is **well**.

As an adverb, *well* means "capably."

EXAMPLE   We did **well** on the test.

Good is always an adjective. It should not be used to modify a verb.

NONSTANDARD   She sings good.
STANDARD   She sings **well**.

NONSTANDARD   The car runs good.
STANDARD   The car runs **well**.

STANDARD   That color looks **good** on you. [adjective following linking verb]

NOTE: *Well* is also acceptable in sentences such as the last example above.

EXAMPLE   That color looks **well** on you.

☞ REFERENCE NOTE: For more discussion about *good* and *well*, see pages 743–744.

Slow and *Slowly*

Slow is used as both an adjective and an adverb.

EXAMPLES   We took a **slow** walk through the park. [*Slow* is an adjective modifying *walk*.]
Go **slow**. [*Slow* is an adverb modifying *go*.]

Slowly is always an adverb. In most adverb uses (other than *go slow* or *drive slow*), it is better to use *slowly*.

EXAMPLES   The tiger **slowly** crept forward.
Proceed **slowly** through each step.

USAGE

⬗ COMMON ERROR

Problem. Students often are unsure of how to choose between *good* and *well*.

Solution. Tell students that when they choose between *good* and *well*, they should always use *well* if the sentence calls for an adverb. For example, "Marta reads well." If an adjective form is needed, have students try the words *healthy* or *satisfactory* in place of *well* or *good*. If either of these replacements maintains the meaning, students should choose *well* as the adjective. If not, *good* should be the choice.

◈ INTEGRATING THE LANGUAGE ARTS

Usage and Writing. You may want to teach the troublesome pairs as students revise a writing assignment. Point out that nonstandard English is acceptable in informal conversation and in friendly letters. Standard English is generally used in formal situations. Ask students to label the following sentences as nonstandard or standard English:

1. Raphael hit the ball good in spring training. [nonstandard]
2. Edna could never eat her ice cream slow. [nonstandard]
3. Carl wanted an A very badly. [standard]

USAGE

USAGE

USAGE

EXERCISE 2 Selecting Adjectives or Adverbs to Complete Sentences

Choose the <u>correct word</u> in parentheses in each of the following sentences.

1. I can't hear you (<u>*well*</u>, *good*) when the water is running.
2. The opening paragraph is written (<u>*well*</u>, *good*).
3. The situation looks (<u>*bad*</u>, *badly*).
4. Why does ketchup come out of the bottle so (*slow*, <u>*slowly*</u>)?
5. She certainly plays the marimba (<u>*well*</u>, *good*).
6. Can you dance as (<u>*well*</u>, *good*) as you sing?
7. These shoes don't fit (*bad*, <u>*badly*</u>) at all.
8. Our coach told us to do the exercise (*slow*, <u>*slowly*</u>).
9. Did you do (<u>*well*</u>, *good*) on the last algebra test?
10. The chef at the corner cafe cooks very (*bad*, <u>*badly*</u>).

EXERCISE 3 Using Adjective and Adverb Forms Correctly in a Paragraph

Each sentence in the following paragraph contains at least one italicized adjective or adverb. If an italicized word is incorrect, give the correct form. If the sentence is correct, write *C*.

1. C

2. slowly

3. slowly

4. badly

5. C

6. well

7. C

8. well

9. bad

[1] My brother opened Skipper's Skate City last April 1, and as the graph on the next page shows, the shop did not do *well* at first. [2] Skipper wondered whether business had started *slow* because he wasn't advertising enough or because his window wasn't drawing people in. [3] He'd see people walking *slow* past the shop and pointing at the gear on display, but hardly anyone came in. [4] By the end of May, Skipper even thought about giving up, because he was doing so *bad*. [5] He would have felt really *bad* about failing, especially because my dad had loaned him money to help get started. [6] Then school let out, and within days, business was going *good*. [7] In-line skates started selling like crazy, and all summer, Skipper did so *well* that he was able to pay Dad back. [8] When school started, skateboards kept selling *good*, but total sales fell somewhat. [9] Skipper's receipts looked pretty *badly* during the fall, but thanks to Christmas and Hanukkah, all went

COMPARISON OF MODIFIERS Rule 22b

OBJECTIVE

- To write the comparative and superlative forms of modifiers

9. well **10.** good

~~good~~ in December. [10] By then, Skipper was a veteran of seasonal business cycles, so it didn't faze him a bit when January's receipts weren't as ~~well~~ as expected.

Skipper's Skate City
Cash Register Receipts, First Ten Months

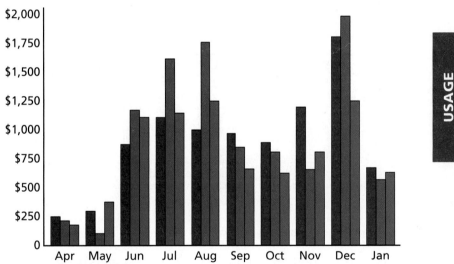

- ■ Skateboards, parts
- ■ In-line skates
- ■ Protective gear, clothes, magazines

Comparison of Modifiers

Adjectives state qualities of nouns or pronouns.

EXAMPLES   **expensive** jacket   **fluffy** clouds
           shiny metal   **original** one

You can show the degree or extent to which a noun or pronoun has a quality by comparing it with another noun or pronoun that has the same quality.

EXAMPLES   This jacket is **larger** than that jacket.
           Does it look **better** than the other one?

USAGE

USAGE

719

USAGE

MEETING *individual* NEEDS

LEP/ESL

General Strategies. Some students might need extra help in understanding the use of comparative and superlative forms. Provide students with information such as the height and age of three ficticious characters. Ask the students to write sentences that first compare two of the people and that then compare all three. Students should write as many sentences as possible, using the information.

COOPERATIVE LEARNING

Brainstorming in small groups, students might practice using positive, comparative, and superlative forms of modifiers to create witty three-line slogans such as "Going to school is smart. Staying in school is smarter. Graduating from school is smartest." Some students might make posters of the slogans or print the slogans on T-shirts.

Similarly, you can show degree or extent by using adverbs to make comparisons.

EXAMPLES   I ran well, but you ran **better.** [The adverb *better* modifies the verb *ran*.]
The other clerk will be **better** able to help you. [The adverb *better* modifies the adjective *able*.]

22b. Modifiers change form to show comparison.

The three degrees of comparison are *positive*, *comparative*, and *superlative*.

POSITIVE	COMPARATIVE	SUPERLATIVE
low	lower	lowest
fearful	more fearful	most fearful
bad	worse	worst
good	better	best
promptly	more promptly	most promptly

Regular Comparison

Most modifiers follow these regular methods of forming their comparative and superlative degrees.

(1) One-syllable modifiers form their comparative and superlative degrees by adding *—er* and *—est.*

POSITIVE	COMPARATIVE	SUPERLATIVE
thin	thinner	thinnest
safe	safer	safest
dry	drier	driest

REFERENCE NOTE: See pages 873–875 for guidelines on spelling words with suffixes.

(2) Some two-syllable modifiers form their comparative and superlative degrees by adding *—er* and *—est.* Other

two-syllable modifiers form their comparative and superlative degrees with *more* and *most.*

POSITIVE	COMPARATIVE	SUPERLATIVE
lovely	lovelier	loveliest
tricky	trickier	trickiest
awkward	more awkward	most awkward
quickly	more quickly	most quickly

NOTE: A few two-syllable modifiers may use either *—er, —est* or *more, most: able, abler, ablest,* or *able, more able, most able.*

When you're not sure about the comparative or superlative form of a two-syllable modifier, look up the positive form in an unabridged dictionary.

(3) Modifiers that have more than two syllables form their comparative and superlative degrees with *more* and *most.*

POSITIVE	COMPARATIVE	SUPERLATIVE
catastrophic	more catastrophic	most catastrophic
predictably	more predictably	most predictably

(4) Modifiers indicate less or least of a quality with the words *less* and *least.*

POSITIVE	COMPARATIVE	SUPERLATIVE
frequent	less frequent	least frequent
carefully	less carefully	least carefully

Irregular Comparison

Some adjectives and adverbs do not follow the regular methods of forming their comparative and superlative degrees.

USAGE

INTEGRATING THE LANGUAGE ARTS

Usage and Mechanics. The correct spellings of comparative and superlative forms are often arrived at by using three spelling rules for adding suffixes. As students proofread their writing, remind them of the following rules:

1. With words ending in *—y* preceded by a consonant, change *—y* to *i* before any suffix not beginning with *i.* [For example, *dry* becomes *drier* or *driest.*]

2. When an adjective ends in a single consonant following a single vowel, double the final consonant before adding the ending. [For example, *thin* becomes *thinner* or *thinnest.*]

3. Drop the final *e* before a suffix beginning with a vowel. [For example, *safe* becomes *safer* or *safest.*]

TECHNOLOGY TIP
Some word-processing programs include electronic dictionaries that students might use to check comparative and superlative forms. For example, if students are unsure whether *righter* or *more right* is the correct comparative form, they might see whether *righter* is listed in their spell-check program. If *righter* is listed, that is the correct choice. If not, *more right* is correct.

USAGE

LESSON 4 *(pp. 722–727)*

USE OF COMPARATIVE AND SUPERLATIVE FORMS Rules 22c–22f

OBJECTIVES

- To write sentences that use comparative and superlative forms of modifiers
- To identify whether modifiers are used correctly in a series of sentences and to revise modifiers that are incorrect

722 *Using Modifiers Correctly*

POSITIVE	COMPARATIVE	SUPERLATIVE
bad	worse	worst
good well	better	best
little	less	least
many much	more	most

NOTE: Do not add *–er, –est* or *more, most* to irregularly compared forms: *worse,* not *worser* or *more worse.*

ANSWERS

Exercise 4

1. littler, littlest *or* less, least
2. worse, worst
3. more humid, most humid
4. smarter, smartest
5. sillier, silliest
6. better, best
7. likelier, likeliest
8. better, best
9. more fundamental, most fundamental
10. more congenial, most congenial

 EXERCISE 4 **Writing the Comparative and Superlative Forms of Modifiers**

Write the comparative and superlative forms of the following modifiers.

1. little
2. bad
3. humid
4. smart
5. silly
6. good
7. likely
8. well
9. fundamental
10. congenial

Use of Comparative and Superlative Forms

22c. Use the comparative degree when comparing two things. Use the superlative degree when comparing more than two.

COMPARATIVE   Omaha is **larger** than Lincoln.
Roberto is a **better** student than I am.
Which of these two shirts is **less** expensive?

SUPERLATIVE   Omaha is the **largest** city in Nebraska.
Roberto is the **best** student in the class.
Which of these four shirts is **least** expensive?

NOTE: In conversation, the superlative degree is commonly used to compare two things.

EXAMPLES   May the **best** team [of two] win.
Put your **best** foot forward.

In writing, however, the comparative degree should always be used when two things are being compared.

 PROGRAM MANAGER

USE OF COMPARATIVE AND SUPERLATIVE FORMS

- **Independent Practice/ Reteaching** For instruction and exercises, see **Using Comparative and Superlative Forms** in *Language Skills Practice and Assessment,* p. 138.

- **Computer Guided Instruction** For additional instruction and practice with comparative and superlative forms, see **Lesson 16** in *Language Workshop CD-ROM.*

- **Practice** To help less-advanced students with additional instruction and practice with comparative and superlative forms, see **Chapter 17** in *English Workshop, Fourth Course,* pp. 241–242.

▶ EXERCISE 5

Writing Sentences Using the Comparative and Superlative Forms of Modifiers

At the beginning of the twentieth century, teenagers thought a ride on an elaborate, hand-carved carousel was exciting. Today, as we approach the year 2000, young people are more likely to be interested in a wild roller-coaster ride! Write five sentences using adverbs and adjectives to compare the two rides shown below. Then write five sentences comparing three rides—the carousel, the roller coaster, and a ride you imagine will be a favorite at the turn of the twenty-second century. In your sentences, use ten or more modifiers from the boxes below. After you use at least two modifiers from each box, you may use any of the others that you wish.

bright	happy		good	many	intense	colorful	exciting	stressful
simple	high							
young	pretty		little	much	expensive	thrilling		
scary	fast		bad		compelling	mature		
safe	long				enjoyable	romantic		

A HOLIDAY

ANSWERS

Exercise 5

The first five sentences should contain comparative forms of modifiers. The second five sentences should contain superlative forms of modifiers. Students should use at least ten modifiers from the boxes in their textbooks.

MEETING *individual* NEEDS

LEP/ESL

General Strategies. A double comparison occurs when *–er* or *–est* is used with *more* or *most*. To help students avoid the use of double comparisons, such as *more better* or *most smartest,* suggest that they look for the words *more* or *most* in a sentence. Then have them check for *–er* or *–est.* Remind the class that both forms of comparison should not be used in the same sentence to modify a single word.

ADVANCED STUDENTS

Ask students why the comparative degree is used in the sentence "Stan is taller than everyone else in his class." They will probably agree that *taller* sounds correct, but they might mention that Stan is being compared with more than one student.

Point out that the collective pronouns *no one, anyone, each, everybody, everyone, anybody, someone,* and *somebody* are treated as singular.

LESS-ADVANCED STUDENTS

To help students remember when to use comparative or superlative forms of modifiers, remind them that the suffix *–er* has two letters and is used to compare two things. [Basketball is rougher than baseball.] The suffix *–est* has three letters and is used to compare three or more things. [Compared with basketball and baseball, football is roughest.]

To transfer this key to comparative and superlative forms that do not use *–er* or *–est,* point out that comparisons of three or more must include a sound similar to that of the three-letter *–est,* as in *most awkward* or *least painful.*

COOPERATIVE LEARNING

Have students work in small groups. Direct each group to create three sentences in which the comparisons are unclear. Then have the groups exchange sentences for correction. With votes for their own groups not allowed, let students select the funniest entries. The following sentences are examples:

1. The cannibals enjoyed boiling lobsters even more than their neighboring tribe.
2. I would enjoy going to a movie premiere with Madonna more than Arnold Schwarzenegger.

USAGE

USAGE

22d. Include the word *other* or *else* when comparing one thing with others in the same group.

NONSTANDARD   **Stan is taller than anyone in his class.** [Stan is a member of the class, and he cannot be taller than himself. The word *else* should be added.]

STANDARD   **Stan is taller than anyone else in his class.**

NONSTANDARD   **Rhode Island is smaller than any state in the Union.** [Rhode Island is a state, and it cannot be smaller than itself. The word *other* should be added.]

STANDARD   **Rhode Island is smaller than any other state in the Union.**

22e. Avoid double comparisons.

A *double comparison* is one that uses both *–er* and *more* (or *less*) or *–est* and *most* (or *least*).

NONSTANDARD   **The second movie was more funnier than the first one.**

STANDARD   **The second movie was funnier than the first one.**

NONSTANDARD   **What is the most deadliest snake?**

STANDARD   **What is the most deadly** [or **deadliest**] **snake?**

22f. Be sure your comparisons are clear.

In making comparisons, always state clearly what things are being compared.

UNCLEAR   **The climate of Arizona is drier than South Carolina.** [The sentence incorrectly compares a climate to a state.]

CLEAR   **The climate of Arizona is drier than the climate of South Carolina.**

CLEAR   **The climate of Arizona is drier than that of South Carolina.**

UNCLEAR   **The Millers would rather grow their own vegetables than canned ones.**

CLEAR   **The Millers would rather grow their own vegetables than buy canned ones.**

Use a complete comparison if there is any chance that an incomplete one could be misunderstood.

REVIEW A

OBJECTIVE

- To identify and correct errors in the use of modifiers

UNCLEAR	We know her better than Dena.
CLEAR	We know her better than **we know** Dena.
CLEAR	We know her better than Dena **does.**

▶ EXERCISE 6   Using Modifiers Correctly in Sentences

In each of the following sentences, if a modifier is used incorrectly, write the correct form. If the sentence is correct, write C.

1. Laurie is ~~more~~ friendlier than she used to be.
2. Which of the four seasons do you like ~~better~~?   **2.** best
3. I never saw a tribal leader ~~more~~ stronger than Chief Billie of the Seminoles.
4. Margaret Mead was one of the world's most famous anthropologists.   **4.** C
5. Of the two colleges that I am considering, Spelman College in Atlanta looks more interesting.   **5.** C
6. The cheetah is the ~~most~~ fastest running animal in the world.   **7.** those in
7. Muscles in the leg are stronger than the arm.   **8.** other
8. Denver has a higher elevation than any major city in the United States.   **9.** than I wrote to Carlos. [*or* than Carlos
9. I wrote to Sally more often ~~than Carlos~~.   wrote to Sally.]
10. This year's drought was much ~~worser~~ than last year.
                                         10. worse/year's.

▶ REVIEW A   Identifying and Correcting Errors in the Use of Modifiers

The following paragraph contains ten errors in the use of adjectives and adverbs. Find each error and supply the necessary correction.
                                                   1. most famous

[1] Among Pueblo potters of the Southwest, perhaps the ~~famousest~~ are the four women who made the coiled pots shown on the next page, using techniques handed down for more than 2,000 years. [2] Lucy Lewis's Acoma pottery is more delicate than any Southwest pottery. **2.** other [3] She used the ~~most~~ whitest clay. [4] Because this clay is **4.** scarce, the walls of her pots are the ~~most thin~~. [5] Maria thinnest Martinez' San Ildefonso pottery is ~~more~~ thicker and heavier than Lewis. [6] Of all the Southwest pottery styles, **5.** 's Martinez' black-on-black pottery may be the ~~wellest~~ **6.** best known. [7] No color is used, but the background areas of

WRITING APPLICATION

OBJECTIVE

• To use comparative and superlative degrees to write a comparison paragraph

the black pot are burnished slowly with a small smooth stone until they become quite a bit ~~more~~ shinier than the main design. [8] Many of Margaret Tafoya's Santa Clara pots are also solid black, but of these two kinds of black pottery, the Santa Clara pots are the ~~heaviest~~. [9] The bold, colorful Hopi pots of Fannie Nampeyo may be the ~~more~~ impressive achievement of all, because Nampeyo's family had to re-create the technique by studying shards of ancient pots found in 1895.

8. heavier
9. most

LUCY LEWIS

MARIA MARTINEZ

MARGARET TAFOYA

FANNIE NAMPEYO

WRITING APPLICATION

Using Comparative and Superlative Degrees to Make Comparison Clear

Have you ever read a "buyer's guide" article before deciding which brand of a product to buy? People who write such articles must be especially precise in using comparatives and superlatives so that consumers can be sure which brand best suits their needs and budgets.

| COMPARING TWO | Of these models, the Matsuo 2000 is less expensive. |
| COMPARING THREE OR MORE | Of these models, the Matsuo 2000 is least expensive. |

▶ WRITING ACTIVITY

You and your sister Charlotte plan to buy a piece of audio equipment together. You have found a magazine article

---

WRITING APPLICATION

To help students write this comparison paragraph, have them refer to **Chapter 7: "Writing to Inform: Exposition"** and **Chapter 8: "Writing to Explain: Exposition."**

CRITICAL THINKING

Evaluation. Have students list the features of some imaginary equipment that would increase the listening pleasure of a person who is visually impaired. Comparing the three brands mentioned in the comparison paragraph to this equipment will help students evaluate the features of each. Students need not refer to the imaginary equipment when writing their paragraphs.

comparing several brands and showing the information in a big table. However, because Charlotte is blind, the table can't help her decide. She asks you to narrow the choices to four brands, and then to write and tape on a cassette for her a short comparison of their prices and features so that the two of you can make a decision.

Find a magazine article at home or in the library that has a table comparing different brands of a piece of audio equipment that interests you. You might choose a CD player, speakers, or a portable cassette player. Choose three products that seem acceptable. Write a clear comparison that you would tape for Charlotte, giving the most important information listed in the table about these three products. As you write, include each of the degrees of comparison: positive, comparative, and superlative.

Prewriting   Study the table. List the features that you think would be most important to you and to Charlotte. Then, write down several comparisons you want to explain in your paragraph.

Writing   As you write your first draft, carefully select comparative and superlative modifiers so that your explanation is not confusing. Tell why you would eliminate certain models from consideration. Remember, though, you are not deciding *for* Charlotte. You must present the information objectively to help her make her own decision.

Evaluating and Revising   Exchange paragraphs, along with the magazine article you used, with a classmate. Ask him or her to evaluate the information you decided to include and the clarity of your presentation. Rephrase any confusing comparisons.

Proofreading and Publishing   Using your textbook, check to be sure you have correctly used adjectives to modify nouns and pronouns and used adverbs to modify verbs, adjectives, and other adverbs. Pay special attention to the "troublesome pairs" section on pages 716–717 of this chapter. Your class may wish to collect all the paragraphs and bind them in a booklet titled *An Audio Equipment Consumer Guide.*

USAGE

PREWRITING

Remind students to consider their audience as they list important features of the equipment. Some students might enjoy numerous knobs and intricate tuning devices. Other students might prefer ease of operation over complexity.

WRITING

The following sentence shows how students might incorporate the degrees of comparison into their writing: "The maximum volume of this cassette player is dangerously loud, but the Sonic Boomer's volume is louder, and the Sound Blaster's volume is loudest of all."

EVALUATING AND REVISING

Because Charlotte would be listening to a tape of the comparison, students might read paragraphs aloud to each other to ensure that the comparisons are clear. Listeners should point out where they are confused or have questions about the comparisons.

PROOFREADING AND PUBLISHING

Listeners might also serve as additional proofreaders. A way to publish would be for students to make tapes of their paragraphs and to present them to the class.

USAGE

OBJECTIVE
- To revise sentences by correcting dangling modifiers

USAGE

QUICK REMINDER

Ask students to rewrite the following descriptions so that each modifier clearly and sensibly modifies a word in the sentence:

1. Lifting the trophy high over her head, the photographer snapped pictures of Kari. [Lifting the trophy high over her head, Kari waited as the photographer snapped pictures.]
2. Grazing peacefully, we saw a herd of buffalo in the distance. [We saw a herd of buffalo grazing peacefully in the distance.]

728

USAGE

728 *Using Modifiers Correctly*

Dangling Modifiers

22g. A modifying word, phrase, or clause that does not clearly and sensibly modify a word in the same sentence is a ***dangling modifier.***

When a sentence begins with a verbal phrase, the phrase is followed by a comma. The word that the phrase modifies should come immediately after that comma.

DANGLING Hurrying, my books slipped out of my hands and fell down the stairs. [The participle seems to modify *books*.]
CORRECT **As I was hurrying,** my books slipped out of my hands and fell down the stairs.

DANGLING Looking back over my shoulder, the team went into a huddle. [The participial phrase seems to modify *team*.]
CORRECT Looking back over my shoulder, **I** saw the team go into a huddle.

NOTE: When *you* is the understood subject of a sentence, an introductory verbal phrase is not dangling. The phrase modifies the understood subject.

EXAMPLE To get to Amy's house, (you) go south on First Street.

Correcting Dangling Modifiers

You can correct a dangling modifier by adding words that make the meaning clear and logical.

DANGLING Going to the store, my bicycle tire went flat.
CORRECT Going to the store, I got a flat tire on my bicycle.

DANGLING While filling the fuel tank, some of the gas spilled on the runway.
CORRECT While filling the fuel tank, the mechanic spilled some of the gas on the runway.
CORRECT While the mechanic was filling the fuel tank, some of the gas spilled on the runway.

DANGLING To qualify for the Olympics, many trial heats must be won.
CORRECT To qualify for the Olympics, a runner must win many trial heats.
CORRECT Before a runner may qualify for the Olympics, he or she must win many trial heats.

22g

 EXERCISE 7

Revising Sentences by Correcting Dangling Modifiers

Revise each sentence so that the modifier *clearly* and *sensibly* modifies a word in the sentence. You will have to supply some words to fill out the sentence properly.

1. Caught in the net, escape was impossible.
2. Looking through the telescope, the moon seemed enormous.
3. While out running, his mouth got dry.
4. The ocean came into view going around the bend.
5. Doing a few tap-dance steps, the floor got scratched.
6. Built on a steep hillside overlooking the ocean, we found the view breathtaking.
7. To grow plants successfully, light, temperature, and humidity must be carefully controlled.
8. After finishing the housework, the room almost sparkled.
9. To make manicotti, pasta is stuffed with ricotta cheese.
10. Exhausted, the job had finally been finished!

USAGE

Shoe reprinted by permission: Tribune Media Services

LEP/ESL

General Strategies. To reinforce the rule that the modifier has to have a logical association with a word in the sentence, provide modifiers such as *walking to school* or *to earn extra money* and have students add independent clauses. [While walking to school, I saw a beautiful rainbow. To earn extra money, Neal fixed his neighbor's car.] Have students check each other's work to see if there is a clear association between the two parts of the sentence.

ANSWERS
Exercise 7

Responses will vary, but revisions should make the sentences clearer. Here are some possibilities:

1. Caught in the net, the fish found escape impossible.
2. Looking through the telescope, I thought the moon seemed enormous.
3. While he was out running, his mouth got dry.
4. The ocean came into view as we were going around the bend.
5. While I was doing a few tap-dance steps, the floor got scratched.
6. Built on a steep hillside overlooking the ocean, the house gave us a breathtaking view.
7. To grow plants successfully, one must carefully control light, temperature, and humidity.
8. After we had finished the housework, the room almost sparkled.
9. To make manicotti, you must stuff pasta with ricotta cheese.
10. Exhausted, we had finally finished the job!

USAGE

OBJECTIVES

- To revise sentences by correcting misplaced phrase modifiers
- To revise sentences by correcting misplaced clause modifiers
- To write a descriptive paragraph

MISPLACED MODIFIERS

- **Independent Practice/ Reteaching** For instruction and exercises, see **Misplaced Modifiers** in *Language Skills Practice and Assessment,* p. 140.
- **Computer Guided Instruction** For additional instruction and practice with misplaced modifiers, see **Lesson 18** in *Language Workshop CD-ROM.*
- **Practice** To help less-advanced students with additional instruction and practice with misplaced modifiers, see **Chapter 17** in *English Workshop, Fourth Course,* pp. 245–246.

USAGE

QUICK REMINDER

Ask students to correct the misplaced modifiers in the following thesis statements:

1. I see too many fast-food restaurants driving through our city. [Driving through our city, I see too many fast-food restaurants.]

2. Athletes should go to physicians who have taken illegal steroids. [Athletes who have taken illegal steroids should go to physicians.]

ANSWERS

Exercise 8

Answers may vary. Here are some possibilities:

1. With quiet dignity, Rosa Parks calmly refused to move to the back of the bus.

2. Taking a shortcut through the woods, I found a huge boulder.

continued on next page

730

---

730 *Using Modifiers Correctly*

Misplaced Modifiers

22h. A modifying word, phrase, or clause that makes a sentence awkward or unclear because it seems to modify the wrong word or group of words is a *misplaced modifier.*

Modifying words, phrases, and clauses should be placed as near as possible to the words they modify. Notice how changing the placement of a modifier affects the meanings of the following sentences.

EXAMPLES **Only** on Saturdays, my brother and I watch cartoons on television for an hour.
On Saturdays, my **only** brother and I watch cartoons on television for an hour.
On Saturdays, my brother and I watch cartoons on television for **only** an hour.

Misplaced Phrase Modifiers

MISPLACED I'm lucky because I always feel that I can talk about my problems with my dad.
CORRECT I'm lucky because I always feel that I can talk with my dad about my problems.

MISPLACED Early Spanish explorers encountered hostile native peoples searching for gold in the Americas.
CORRECT Searching for gold in the Americas, early Spanish explorers encountered hostile native peoples.

 EXERCISE 8 **Revising Sentences by Correcting Misplaced Word and Phrase Modifiers**

In each of the following sentences, pick out the misplaced word or phrase and revise the sentence, placing the misplaced modifier near the word it should modify.

1. Rosa Parks calmly refused to move with quiet dignity to the back of the bus.
2. I found a huge boulder taking a shortcut through the woods.
3. Mr. Tate noticed some caterpillars pruning his fruit tree.

22h

4. Our ancestors hunted deer, bison, and other large animals armed with weapons made of wood and stone.
5. Missie saw a heron driving over the bridge.
6. We noticed several signs riding down the highway.
7. We could see corn growing from our car window.
8. Barking wildly and straining at the chain, the letter carrier was forced to retreat from the dog.
9. The softball team almost practices every afternoon.
10. He recounted an incident about a nuclear chain reaction during his chemistry lecture.

▶ EXERCISE 9 **Using Modifiers Correctly**

Looking through a box of old photographs, you find this photo and several others of a treehouse that you and your best friend built years ago. The pictures remind you that you have not written to your friend in a long time. Taking this photo from the box, you decide to send it along with a letter to your friend. As you write your letter, include the five phrases listed below, or use five of your own. Be sure your phrases correctly modify the words you intend.

- armed with hammers and nails
- climbing up the ladder
- from the platform
- to hold our club meetings
- resting on several branches

USAGE

3. Pruning his fruit tree, Mr. Tate noticed some caterpillars.
4. Armed with weapons made of wood and stone, our ancestors hunted deer, bison, and other large animals.
5. Driving over the bridge, Missie saw a heron.
6. Riding down the highway, we noticed several signs.
7. From our car window, we could see corn growing.
8. Barking wildly and straining at the chain, the dog forced the letter carrier to retreat.
9. The softball team practices almost every afternoon.
10. During his chemistry lecture, he recounted an incident about a nuclear chain reaction.

ANSWERS
Exercise 9

Answers will vary. Here are some possibilities.

Dear Tess,

I'm sending you this photo of our old treehouse! Do you remember how much fun we had building it? Armed with hammers and nails, we'd work on our construction project every evening until dark. Once it was built, we loved nothing more than climbing up the ladder to our "headquarters." Resting on several branches, the finished structure was awesome. From the platform, we'd survey the entire neighborhood. Eventually, we decided to hold our club meetings in our leafy retreat.

USAGE

LEP/ESL

General Strategies. Emphasize to students that a misplaced modifier can be corrected by moving the phrase or clause closer to the word it modifies. Have students work in pairs to read the following sentences and to suggest ways to correct the misplaced modifiers:

1. At the age of eight, my parents sent me to camp. [At the age of eight, I was sent to camp by my parents.]
2. There is a car in the garage that has only one door and no windshield. [In the garage, there is a car that has only one door and no windshield.]
3. I bought a seat for my bicycle that is made of vinyl. [I bought a seat that is made of vinyl for my bicycle.]

USAGE

USAGE

REVIEW B

OBJECTIVE

• To identify and correct errors in the use of modifiers

732 *Using Modifiers Correctly*

Misplaced Clause Modifiers

MISPLACED	We saw a building in the city that was being demolished.
CORRECT	In the city we saw a building that was being demolished.
MISPLACED	The bowl fell on the floor which was full of gravy and broke.
CORRECT	The bowl, which was full of gravy, fell on the floor and broke.
MISPLACED	Lynn got a package from one of the stores we had visited that she hadn't ordered.
CORRECT	From one of the stores we had visited, Lynn got a package that she hadn't ordered.

☞ **REFERENCE NOTE:** See pages 797–801 and 805–806 for information on when to use commas to set off modifying phrases and clauses.

▶ EXERCISE 10 **Revising Sentences by Correcting Misplaced Clause Modifiers**

Revise each of the following sentences by placing the misplaced clause near the word it modifies. If you find a misplaced phrase, correct it also. Answers may vary.

1. I gave four olives to my friend that I had stabbed with my fork. **1.** my friend
2. The plane landed safely on the runway that had the engine trouble. **2.** that had the engine trouble
3. The picture was hanging on the wall that we bought in Canada. **3.** that we bought in Canada
4. They took the kitten to the manager's office that appeared to be lost. **4.** that appeared to be lost
5. Jan showed the rooms to her visitors that she had painted. **5.** to her visitors.

▶ REVIEW B **Identifying and Correcting Errors in the Use of Modifiers**

Most of the sentences in the following paragraph contain at least one error in the use of modifiers. If a modifier is incorrect, write the sentence correctly. You may need to rearrange words or add words to make the meaning clear. If a sentence is correct, write *C*.

[1] Much about life in ancient Egypt before the 1800s was unknown because nobody could read Egyptian hieroglyphics. [2] Then this black stone found in the Nile delta gave Egyptology the most publicity than it had ever had before. [3] Found in 1799 near a village called Rosetta, archaeologists called the slab the Rosetta Stone. [4] The slab was inscribed with three bands across its polished surface of writing, each in a different language: hieroglyphics on the top, another unknown language in the middle, and Greek on the bottom. [5] Scholars could read the Greek writing, which stated that each of the three bands contained the same decree in honor of Ptolemy V. [6] Full of excitement, it was hoped by archaeologists that they could use the Greek part to figure out the hieroglyphics. [7] But progress in translating the individual hieroglyphics went very slow. [8] It had been thought that each of the symbols stood for a whole word until this time. [9] However, a French scholar working on the Rosetta Stone named Jean François Champollion wondered why it took more hieroglyphic symbols than Greek words to write the same message. [10] He correctly guessed that certain symbols stand for parts of words, and after working hard for twenty years, many of the signs were proved to stand for sounds.

The Granger Collection, New York.

USAGE

ANSWERS
Review B

Answers may vary.

1. Because nobody could read Egyptian hieroglyphics before the 1800s, much about life in ancient Egypt was unknown.

2. Then this black stone found in the Nile delta gave Egyptology more publicity than it had ever had before.

3. Archaeologists called the slab, found in 1799 near a village called Rosetta, the Rosetta Stone.

4. The slab was inscribed across its polished surface with three bands of writing, each in a different language: hieroglyphics on the top, another unknown language in the middle, and Greek on the bottom.

5. C

6. Full of excitement, the archaeologists hoped that they could use the Greek part to figure out the hieroglyphics.

7. But progress in translating the individual hieroglyphics went very slowly.

8. Until this time, it had been thought that each symbol stood for a whole word.

9. However, Jean François Champollion, a French scholar working on the Rosetta Stone, wondered why it took more hieroglyphic symbols than Greek words to write the same message.

10. He correctly guessed that certain symbols must stand for parts of words, and after working hard for twenty years, he proved that many of the signs stood for sounds.

USAGE

REVIEW: POSTTEST

OBJECTIVE

- To revise sentences and a paragraph by correcting errors in the use of modifiers

734 *Using Modifiers Correctly*

Review: Posttest

A. Revising Sentences by Correcting Errors in the Use of Modifiers

Answers may vary.

Most of the following sentences contain errors in the use of modifiers. Revise such sentences, correcting the faulty modifiers. If a sentence is correct, write *C.*

1. Manaba was/her

1. While ∧building a fire in front of the hogan, ∧~~Manaba's~~ dog began to tug at the hem of her doeskin dress.
2. I bought these clothes ∧with my birthday money ⊙~~that I'm wearing.~~ **2.** that I'm wearing
3. Adrianne knows more about chemistry than anybody ∧in her class. **3.** else
4. Hank worked rather ∧~~hasty~~ so he could catch up with Clay and Nina. **4.** hastily
5. Although Marian felt bad about losing the game, she knew things could be ∧~~worser.~~ **5.** worse.
6. Millie can sing as well as Scott, but of the two, he's the ∧~~best~~ dancer. **6.** better
   7. the team won
7. By playing carefully, ∧the game ⊙~~was won.~~
8. ~~Steady and confident,~~ a̲ keen sense of balance enables Mohawk ironworkers ∧to help build tall bridges and buildings. **8.** steady and confident, **9.** bad
9. Because one carton of chemicals smelled ∧~~badly~~, it was examined before being used in the laboratory.
10. Although Helen is the better actress, Wenona will probably get the leading part because she is more reliable. **10.** C

B. Revising a Paragraph by Correcting Errors in the Use of Modifiers

Some sentences in the following paragraph contain errors in the use of modifiers. If you find an error, write the sentence correctly. You may need to add or rearrange words for clarity. If a sentence is correct, write *C.*

[11] Hailed by many critics as one of today's greatest male vocalists, my Aunt Penny took me on my birthday to

see Bobby McFerrin. **[12]** Waiting for the concert to start, the auditorium was filled with eager fans. **[13]** Wondering where the band was, I kept my eyes on the empty stage. **[14]** When it was time for the show to start, a slender, barefoot man walked out from the wings, carrying a cordless microphone dressed only in blue jeans. **[15]** Assuming he was a stagehand, he began to sing, and then I realized that this was Bobby McFerrin! **[16]** Instantly, the complex rhythm of the music fascinated the audience that he made up as he went along. **[17]** I suddenly understood why one of his popularest albums is called *Spontaneous Inventions*! **[18]** Alone in the spotlight with only his voice and no band at all, two thousand people sat spellbound until he took his final bow. **[19]** All his life, Bobby McFerrin has enjoyed listening to and performing jazz, pop, rock, soul, African, and classical music. **[20]** Bobby's parents are both classical musicians, and he thanks them for giving him this rich musical environment on the back of every album he makes.

USAGE

ANSWERS
Review: Posttest Part B

Answers may vary. Here are some possibilities:

11. My Aunt Penny took me on my birthday to see Bobby McFerrin, hailed by many critics as one of today's greatest male vocalists.

12. The auditorium was filled with eager fans waiting for the concert to start.

13. C

14. When it was time for the show to start, a slender, barefoot man, dressed only in blue jeans and carrying a cordless microphone, walked out from the wings.

15. I assumed he was a stagehand until he began to sing, and then I realized that this was Bobby McFerrin!

16. Instantly the audience was fascinated by the complex rhythm of the music that he made up as he went along.

17. I suddenly understood why one of his most popular albums is called *Spontaneous Inventions*!

18. Alone in the spotlight with only his voice and no band at all, he kept two thousand people spellbound until he took his final bow.

19. C

20. Bobby's parents are both classical musicians, and on the back of every album he makes he thanks them for giving him this rich musical environment.

USAGE

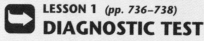

CHAPTER OVERVIEW

This chapter is designed to help students identify and correct certain usage errors. It contains an abridged alphabetical glossary of common usage problems. The chapter begins with a brief discussion of the differences between standard and nonstandard English and explains most usage problems in terms of these two types.

The contents of this chapter can be useful during the evaluation and revision stage of the writing process. It can be referred to when teaching **Chapter 1,** which covers writing and thinking, **Chapter 4,** which deals with expressive writing, and **Chapter 14,** which explores the origins and uses of English.

23 A GLOSSARY OF USAGE

Common Usage Problems

Diagnostic Test

Revising Expressions by Correcting Errors in Usage

In each of the following sets of expressions, one expression contains an error in usage. Rewrite this expression correctly, using standard formal usage.

EXAMPLE **1. a.** She taught me to sing.
   b. fewer letters in the box
   c. Set down in the shade and rest.
 1. *c. Sit down in the shade and rest.*

1. **a.** ~~anywheres~~ you travel   1. anywhere
   b. as fast as sound travels
   c. Learn French cooking from him.
2. **a.** affect the outcome
   b. candidate implied in his speech
   c. ~~among~~ his two opponents   2. between
3. **a.** made ~~illusions~~ to the Bible   3. allusions
   b. fewer participants in the contest
   c. What kind of car is that?

4. **a.** family emigrated from Germany
    b. should of gone yesterday   **4.** have
    c. discovered a new planet
5. **a.** Try and win the game.   **5.** to
    b. draw as well as her mother
    c. that kind of car
6. **a.** Let the dog out.
    b. an effect of cold weather
    c. books, pencils, papers, and etc.
7. **a.** ate everything accept the peas   **7.** except
    b. older than you
    c. Bring your records with you.
8. **a.** I heard nothing.
    b. can't hardly tell the difference   **8.** can hardly [*or* can't]
    c. Lay the book on the shelf.
9. **a.** picture fell off the wall
    b. What kind of a dog is that?
    c. larger than he
10. **a.** sitting beside the tree
    b. going a little ways   **10.** way
    c. not reality but illusion
11. **a.** coat doesn't fit well
    b. Fewer people learned how to read back then.
    c. inside of the cabinet
12. **a.** car looks like it had been wrecked   **12.** as if
    b. chair that was blue
    c. water jug that burst
13. **a.** She effected an improvement.
    b. a problem that must be resolved
    c. Less students joined the club this year.   **13.** Fewer
14. **a.** Take the package to the mailroom.
    b. Apples fell off of the tree.
    c. will scarcely be enough food for all of them
15. **a.** invented a better safety device
    b. No one beside my aunt knows.   **15.** besides
    c. played well in the tournament
16. **a.** Funds were allotted among six counties.
    b. Where is my hammer at?
    c. This is as far as the fence extends.
17. **a.** going nowhere
    b. Doesn't he know the way?
    c. She finished reading; than she wrote her essay.   **17.** then

USING THE DIAGNOSTIC TEST

The **Diagnostic Test** will help gauge students' ability to identify and correct common errors in usage. You may wish to use this test to determine whether any students rely strongly on nonstandard English in their writing. Note that some students will be able to identify errors in usage but will find it difficult to revise an expression appropriately.

A, AN–BUST, BUSTED

OBJECTIVES

- To distinguish correct expressions from errors in usage
- To correct usage errors in a paragraph

PROGRAM MANAGER

A, AN–BUST, BUSTED

- **Independent Practice/ Reteaching** For instruction and exercises, see **Common Usage Problems A** in *Language Skills Practice and Assessment,* p. 149.

- **Computer Guided Instruction** For additional instruction and practice with common usage problems, see **Lesson 50** in *Language Workshop CD-ROM.*

- **Practice** To help less-advanced students with additional instruction and practice with common usage problems, see **Chapter 18** in *English Workshop, Fourth Course,* pp. 249–252.

QUICK REMINDER

Tell students that the first step toward proper usage is to identify potential problems. Write the following sentence on the chalkboard:

He affected people anywheres he traveled, being that he was an hotel bellboy who could not accept tips.

Have students copy the sentence and correct any words or expressions that are used incorrectly [anywheres— anywhere; being that—because; an hotel—a hotel]

738

---

738   *Glossary of Usage*

18. a. We were gone for a hour.   **18.** an
     b. Try to learn this poem.
     c. Leave the green grapes on the vine.
19. a. Set the brake on the car.
     b. The fog will rise from the lake.
     c. One of them glasses broke.   **19.** those
20. a. It was an illusion caused by light on the surface.
     b. Their report implies a need for funds.
     c. That dog he limps.
21. a. no exception to this rule
     b. being that she is the oldest   **21.** because [*or* since]
     c. Bring your own tools with you.
22. a. Set that down there.
     b. looked like it had been burned   **22.** as if
     c. They ought to study before the test.
23. a. The ice busted a pipe.   **23.** burst
     b. He lay on the couch and rested.
     c. emigrate from their birthplace
24. a. Leave me have my turn.   **24.** Let
     b. the mechanic that worked on our car
     c. somewhat cold for swimming
25. a. haven't only three days of vacation   **25.** have
     b. the effect of smoking on the lungs
     c. learned that the winner had been announced

This chapter contains a short glossary of common usage problems. You will notice that some examples are labeled *standard* and *nonstandard.* **Standard English** is the most widely accepted variety of English. It's used in most books, newspapers, and magazines. **Nonstandard English** is language that doesn't follow the rules and conventions of standard English.

☞ REFERENCE NOTE: For more information on the features of standard English and nonstandard English, see pages 498–499.

a, an   These words, called *indefinite articles,* refer to one of the members of a general group.

EXAMPLES   In ancient Greece and Rome, **a** person would go to see **an** oracle to consult the gods.
The tourists searched for **a** hotel for more than **an** hour.

Use *a* before words beginning with a consonant sound; use *an* before words beginning with a vowel sound. In the second example, *a* is used before *hotel* because the *h* in *hotel* is pronounced. *An* is used before *hour* because the *h* in *hour* is not pronounced.

accept, except *Accept* is a verb that means "to receive." *Except* may be either a verb or a preposition. As a verb, it means "to leave out." As a preposition, *except* means "excluding."

> EXAMPLES   Gary could not **accept** defeat.
> Students who were absent last week will be **excepted** from today's test.
> Everybody **except** me knew the answer.

affect, effect *Affect* is usually a verb meaning "to influence." *Effect* used as a verb means "to accomplish" or "to bring about." Used as a noun, *effect* means "the result of some action."

> EXAMPLES   The heat did not seem to **affect** the team.
> Did the medicine **effect** a cure?
> The heat had no **effect** on the team.

all the farther, all the faster These expressions are used informally in some parts of the country to mean "as far as, as fast as."

> DIALECT   This is all the farther we can go.
> STANDARD   This is **as far as** we can go.

allusion, illusion An *allusion* is a reference to something. An *illusion* is a mistaken idea or a misleading appearance.

> EXAMPLES   The poem's title is an **allusion** to a Hopi folk tale.
> The documentary shattered viewers' **illusions** about migrant workers.
> The magician was a master of **illusion.**

among See **between, among.**

and etc. *Etc.* is an abbreviation of the Latin *et cetera*, which means "and other things." Thus, *etc.* already includes *and*.

> EXAMPLE   I earn money by baby-sitting, running errands, mowing lawns, **etc.** [not *and etc.*]

MEETING *individual* **NEEDS**

LEP/ESL

General Strategies. For the section on the usage of *a* and *an,* you may want to point out that not all words that start with vowels are preceded by *an.* These words begin with a *y* sound (as in *yes*) even though they are spelled with a vowel. Some examples are *European, university,* and *utility.* To show the importance of the first sound, you could say a phrase like ". . . understanding teacher" and have students decide whether to use *an* or *a.* This could be followed by a fill-in-the-blank exercise.

STUDENTS WITH SPECIAL NEEDS

This chapter may present problems for students who have trouble distinguishing between words that are similar in shape. For example, they may have trouble distinguishing between *affect* and *effect.* They may also invert or reverse letters. These characteristics also may be found in their writing.

To help with the exercises in this chapter, highlight the differences between similar words. You could also have a peer tutor read aloud while the students read along.

COOPERATIVE LEARNING
Have students select partners. Assign one student in each pair to be the "between" person and the other to be the "among" person. Then write the following sentence on the chalkboard:

The two baseball teams looked up in horror as the squadron of UFOs approached the well-lit stadium.

Have each pair compose a short narrative, using the above sentence as the opening line. Tell students that they must write the story with their partners, but that each student is responsible for properly using his or her assigned word at least three times in the story. You may want to have each pair read their story aloud.

anywheres, everywheres, nowheres, somewheres Use these words without the *s* at the end.

> EXAMPLE **Anywhere** [not *anywheres*] you travel, you see the same hotel chains.

as See **like, as.**

as if See **like, as if.**

at Do not use *at* after *where.*

> NONSTANDARD Where did you see them at?
> STANDARD Where did you see them?

being as, being that Avoid using these expressions. Use *because* or *since* instead.

> NONSTANDARD Being as her grades were so good, she got a scholarship.
> STANDARD **Because** her grades were so good, she got a scholarship.

> NONSTANDARD Being that he was late, he had to stand.
> STANDARD **Since** he was late, he had to stand.

beside, besides *Beside* means "by the side of." *Besides* as a preposition means "in addition to." As an adverb, *besides* means "moreover."

> EXAMPLES He glanced at the person **beside** him.
> Did anybody **besides** you see what happened?
> I liked the sweater, and it didn't cost much; **besides,** I needed a new one.

between, among Use *between* when you are referring to two things at a time, even if they are part of a larger group.

> EXAMPLES A strong bond exists **between** the twins.
> The survey reveals many differences **between** the New England states. [Although there are more than two New England states, each one is being compared with each of the others separately.]

Use *among* when referring to all members of a group rather than to separate individuals in the group.

> EXAMPLES We distributed the pamphlets **among** the crowd.
> There was some disagreement **among** the editorial staff about the lead story.

USAGE

USAGE

740

bring, take *Bring* means "to come carrying something." *Take* means "to go away carrying something." Think of *bring* as related to *come* and *take* as related to *go.*

EXAMPLES **Bring** your radio when you come.
Don't forget to **take** your coat when you go.

bust, busted Avoid using these words as verbs. Instead, use a form of *break* or *burst.*

EXAMPLES I **broke** [not *busted*] the switch on the stereo.
The water main **burst.** [not *busted*]

▶ EXERCISE 1 **Identifying Correct Expressions**

For each sentence, choose the <u>correct word</u> from the pair given in parentheses.

1. The tasks were divided evenly (*among,* <u>*between*</u>) the two scouts.
2. The audience was deeply (<u>*affected*</u>, *effected*) by Simon Estes' powerful baritone voice.
3. We were afraid the bull had (*busted,* <u>*broken*</u>) loose.
4. No one (*accept,* <u>*except*</u>) the sophomores is supposed to attend.
5. Please (*bring,* <u>*take*</u>) these papers when you leave.
6. Penicillin has (*affected,* <u>*effected*</u>) some remarkable recoveries.
7. I couldn't find the cat (<u>*anywhere*</u>, *anywheres*).
8. The crosslike rays radiating from the moon were an (*allusion,* <u>*illusion*</u>) caused by the screen door.
9. (*Beside,* <u>*Besides*</u>) Julie, who else has signed up for Saturday's 10K walk?
10. In his remarks about Dr. King, the speaker made an (<u>*allusion*</u>, *illusion*) to Gandhi, whose nonviolent protests paved the way for the civil rights movement in the United States.

▶ EXERCISE 2 **Proofreading a Paragraph to Correct Usage Errors**

Correct all the usage errors you find in each sentence in the following paragraph. Give the incorrect usage, followed by the correct usage. If a sentence is correct, write *C.*

CAN'T HARDLY, CAN'T SCARCELY–INVENT

OBJECTIVES

- To identify errors in usage
- To proofread a paragraph to correct errors in usage

QUICK REMINDER

Write the following sentence on the chalkboard:

My sister she lives in New York, but she don't write often.

Ask students to identify the errors in usage and to rewrite the sentence correctly. [My sister lives in New York, but she doesn't write often.]

742

---

742 *Glossary of Usage*

1. C
2. as far as
3. an/ brought
4. accepted
5. C
6. everywhere
7. C
8. Because/ among
9. C

[1] In 1903, this young Japanese artist, Frank Matsura, arrived in the backwoods settlement of Conconully, Washington. [2] This was all the farther he would go, for he lived in this rough frontier area for the remaining ten years of his life. [3] When he came to town, Matsura was wearing a elegant formal suit and was carrying bulky camera equipment he had taken with him. [4] Back in Seattle, Matsura had excepted a job in Conconully as a helper and laundryman at the Elliott Hotel. [5] Soon he was living in a tiny room behind the kitchen and bringing energy and cheer to his menial job. [6] When he was off duty, he carried his camera everywheres he went, photographing the area's people, scenery, events, and etc. [7] Later, he settled in nearby Okanogan and opened this small studio. [8] Being that Matsura was a warm, extroverted person, he made many friends between settlers and Native Americans alike. [9] Oddly, though, he never told anyone about his past. [10] To this day, nobody knows who he really was, where he was born at, or why he chose to live and die so far from his home.

can't hardly, can't scarcely See **The Double Negative** (page 756).

could of Do not use *of* with the helping verb *could*. Use *could have* instead. Also avoid *had of, ought to of, should of, would of, might of,* and *must of.*

EXAMPLE   Muriel could **have** [not *of*] gone with us.

discover, invent *Discover* means "to find, see, or learn about something that already exists." *Invent* means "to be the first to make or do something."

> EXAMPLES   Luis W. Alvarez **discovered** many subatomic particles.
> Sarah Boone **invented** the ironing board.

don't, doesn't *Don't* is the contraction of *do not*. *Doesn't* is the contraction of *does not*. Use *doesn't*, not *don't*, with *he, she, it, this, that*, and singular nouns.

> EXAMPLES   It **doesn't** [not *don't*] matter to me.
> The poem **doesn't** [not *don't*] rhyme.

effect See **affect, effect.**

emigrate, immigrate *Emigrate* means "to leave a country to settle elsewhere." *Immigrate* means "to come into a country to settle there."

> EXAMPLES   My great-grandfather **emigrated** from Mexico.
> Much of Australia's population is composed of people who **immigrated** there.

everywheres See **anywheres,** etc.

except See **accept, except.**

fewer, less *Fewer* is used with plural nouns. It tells "how many." *Less* is used with singular words. It tells "how much."

> EXAMPLES   There are **fewer** whales than there once were.
> We should have bought **less** meat [but: **fewer eggs**].

good, well *Good* is an adjective. Do not use it to modify a verb. Instead, use *well*.

> NONSTANDARD   They skate **good.**
> STANDARD   They skate **well.**

Although it is usually an adverb, *well* is used as an adjective to mean "healthy," "well dressed or well groomed," or "satisfactory."

> EXAMPLES   I didn't feel **well.**
> He looked **well** in his uniform.
> All seems **well.**

MEETING *individual* NEEDS

LEARNING STYLES

Auditory Learners. Some students might tend to confuse *of* with *have* in such expressions as *could have, should have, must have* and so on. You may want to have students work in groups to compose tongue twisters or catchy rhymes using these words. Encourage students to emphasize the pronunciation of *have* when they read their final products to the rest of the class.

COMMON ERROR

Problem. Students often confuse *immigrate* with *emigrate.*

Solution. Tell students that an easy way to remember the difference between these words is by using the initial letters to create a mnemonic device. Explain that the *e* in *emigrate* can stand for *exit* and the *i* in *immigrate* can stand for *in.*

TECHNOLOGY TIP

Have students check for proper grammar and usage within their writing by using the grammar-checking feature of a word-processing program. Grammar-checkers will readily catch a number of mistakes, including double subjects, double negatives, and nonstandard usage such as *anywheres* and *being that*. Emphasize that grammar-checkers are not foolproof. Often they will do no more than note the potential for an error and ask the user, "Is this word used correctly?" It is up to the user to understand the rules of grammar and usage.

TIMESAVER

Group students in pairs and have them complete **Exercises 3** and **4**. One student could be responsible for answering the questions in **Exercise 3**, and the other for the questions in **Exercise 4**. Have students exchange papers; correct these exercises with the class. In this way, students will be exposed to all the questions in both exercises.

744

NOTE: *Feel good* and *feel well* mean different things. *Feel good* means "to feel happy or pleased." *Feel well* means "to feel healthy."

EXAMPLES   The victory made us feel **good.**
If you don't feel **well**, lie down.

Using *good* as an adverb is acceptable in conversation but not in writing.

had of See **could of.**

had ought, hadn't ought Do not use *had* or *hadn't* with *ought*.

NONSTANDARD   You hadn't ought to say such things.
STANDARD   You **ought** not to say such things.
or
You **shouldn't** say such things.

NONSTANDARD   They had ought to have left earlier.
STANDARD   They **ought** to have left earlier.
or
They **should** have left earlier.

hardly See **The Double Negative** (page 756).

he, she, they Do not use unnecessary pronouns after nouns. This error is called the *double subject*.

NONSTANDARD   My father he works downtown.
STANDARD   My **father works** downtown.

illusion See **allusion, illusion.**

immigrate See **emigrate, immigrate.**

imply, infer *Imply* means "to suggest something." *Infer* means "to interpret" or "to get a certain meaning from a remark or an action."

EXAMPLES   In her speech, the candidate **implied** that she is for tax reform.
From the candidate's speeches, I **inferred** that she is for tax reform.

invent See **discover, invent.**

EXERCISE 3   **Identifying Correct Expressions**

For each sentence, choose the correct word from the pair given in parentheses.

1. Was it George Washington Carver or Thomas Edison who (*invented, discovered*) all those uses for peanuts?
2. From his letter I (*implied, inferred*) he would be away all summer.
3. He (*don't, doesn't*) always say what he means.
4. (*Emigration, Immigration*) to Alaska was spurred by the gold rush.
5. The heat has affected the growing season; we'll harvest (*fewer, less*) crops this year.
6. Many French Canadians (*emigrated, immigrated*) from Quebec to work in the industries of New England.
7. As beasts of burden, dogs served the Comanches (*good, well*), often pulling a travois laden with more than forty pounds of baggage.
8. Mary Beth Stearns (*discovered, invented*) a technique for studying electrons.
9. You could (*have, of*) borrowed some paper and a pencil from me.
10. Audrey must (*have, of*) taken my jacket by mistake.

▶ EXERCISE 4 **Proofreading a Paragraph to Correct Usage Errors**

Correct all the usage errors you find in each sentence in the following paragraph. Give the incorrect usage, followed by the correct usage. If a sentence is correct, write C.

[1] The scientist/philosopher/writer Douglas R. Hofstadter ~~he~~ enjoys creating perfectly symmetrical designs from written words. [2] He and a friend, ~~discovered~~ a new pastime; the resulting designs are called *ambigrams*. [3] Every word ~~don't~~ lend itself ~~good~~ to this method, but you'd be surprised how often a word can be made into an ambigram. [4] As you might ~~of~~ known already, a *palindrome* is a word or expression that has the same letters in the same sequence both forward and backward—for example, *toot* or *Madam, I'm Adam*. [5] I don't mean to ~~infer~~, though, that an ambigram has to be a palindrome— an ambigram simply has to *look* symmetrical. [6] Usually, ambigrams ~~can't~~ hardly be formed unless you tinker with the letter shapes and connect them in new ways. [7] You ~~had~~ ought to start with a word that has six letters or ~~less~~.

2. invented
3. doesn't/ well
4. have
5. imply
6. can
7. fewer

INTEGRATING THE LANGUAGE ARTS

Usage and Writing. To augment the proofreading practice provided in **Exercise 4,** have students write short paragraphs. Instruct students to choose several common errors in usage, including those highlighted in any of the exercises up to this point, and to create a paragraph with a different error in every sentence. Paragraphs should contain between five and ten sentences. Then have students exchange papers and attempt to find each other's errors.

KIND, SORT, TYPE–WOULD OF

OBJECTIVES

- To identify errors in usage
- To proofread a paragraph to correct errors in usage
- To revise expressions by correcting errors in usage

PROGRAM MANAGER

KIND, SORT, TYPE– WOULD OF

- **Independent Practice/ Reteaching** For instruction and exercises, see **Common Usage Problems C** in *Language Skills Practice and Assessment,* p. 151.

- **Computer Guided Instruction** For additional instruction and practice with common usage problems, see **Lesson 51** in *Language Workshop CD-ROM.*

- **Practice** To help less-advanced students with additional instruction and practice with common usage problems, see **Chapter 18** in *English Workshop, Fourth Course,* pp. 253–256.

QUICK REMINDER

Write the following sentence on the chalkboard and have students correct any errors:

Mark is the kind of person who believes that it takes all kind of people to make the world the kind of place in which we can kind of find our own kind of a peace.

Next, have students discuss the uses for *kind* and have them practice using the word in sentences.

746

---

746 *Glossary of Usage*

8. C

9. effects

10. have

[8] For some good ideas, look below at the ambigrams for the words *Jamal, Steve, Chris, Felix, Wendy, Mexico,* and *dance.* [9] Don't forget that you can mix cursive, printed, capital, and lowercase letters to create ~~affects~~ like the ones in these ambigrams. [10] If you become stumped, you might find that you could ˄of succeeded by adding some decorative flourishes.

Jamal

Steve

Chris

dance

Mexico

Wendy

Felix

kind, sort, type These words should always agree in number with the words *this* and *that* (singular) or *these* and *those* (plural).

> EXAMPLE I know more about **that kind** of music than about any of **those** other **kinds**.

kind of, sort of These expressions, widely used in conversation, mean "rather" or "somewhat." Avoid them in writing.

> ACCEPTABLE IN CONVERSATION
> She seemed kind of bored.
> The waves were sort of rough.

> CORRECT IN WRITING
> She seemed **rather** bored.
> The waves were **rather** [or *somewhat*] rough.

kind of a, sort of a The *a* (or *an*) is unnecessary. Omit it.

> EXAMPLE This bolt takes a special **kind of** [not *kind of a*] nut.

learn, teach *Learn* means "to acquire information." *Teach* means "to instruct" or "to show how."

> EXAMPLES She **learned** how to saddle a horse.
> The stable owner **taught** her how.

leave, let *Leave* means "to go away." *Let* means "to allow" or "to permit."

NONSTANDARD **Leave** them go first.
STANDARD **Let** them go first.
STANDARD **We let** [not *left*] the trapped bird go free.

less See **fewer, less.**

lie, lay See pages 697–698.

like, as *Like* is usually a preposition. In informal English, *like* is often used in place of the conjunction *as.* Formal English calls for *as* to introduce a subordinate clause.

EXAMPLES **The animal looked like a snake.** [The preposition *like* introduces a prepositional phrase.]
It shed its skin as a snake does. [The conjunction *as* introduces a subordinate adverb clause.]

☞ REFERENCE NOTE: Phrases are discussed in Chapter 17, and clauses are covered in Chapter 18. For more on informal and formal English, see pages 500–501.

like, as if In informal speech, *like* is often used in place of the subordinating conjunction *as if* or *as though* to introduce a subordinate clause. When writing, avoid using *like* in place of these two conjunctions.

INFORMAL **This looks like it might be the right place.**
FORMAL **This looks as if** [or *as though*] **it might be the right place.**

might of, must of See **could of.**

no, none, nothing See **The Double Negative** (page 756).

nowheres See **anywheres,** etc.

of Do not use *of* with prepositions such as *inside, off,* and *outside.*

EXAMPLES **The diver jumped off** [not *off of*] **the board.**
Outside [not *outside of*] **the building was a patio.**

☞ REFERENCE NOTE: For information on using *of* with helping verbs (*had of* and *must of*, for example), see the listing for **could of.** For information on using *of* in the expressions *kind of* and *sort of*, see the listings for **kind of, sort of** and **kind of a, sort of a.**

off of See **of.**

ought to of See **could of.**

INTEGRATING THE LANGUAGE ARTS

Literature Link. You may want to have students read a story such as Alice Walker's "Everyday Use" or any other story that includes a number of similes.

Have students discuss why they think the author sometimes chooses to use *like* and at other times chooses to use *as*. [Students might say that Walker uses *like* when making unusual comparisons such as "skin like an uncooked barley pancake" or "humor that erupted like bubbles in lye." Walker uses *as* to make less figurative comparisons such as "swept clean as a floor" and "Maggie's hand is as limp as a fish."]

INTEGRATING THE LANGUAGE ARTS

Usage and Library Skills. You may want to integrate **Exercise 5** with a study of the library. Have students use various resources in the library to find information on two subjects. Have students write paragraphs (one on each subject) using at least two of the errors identified in **Exercise 5** as potential usage problems. Next, have partners exchange paragraphs to correct each other's usage.

EXERCISE 5 **Identifying Correct Expressions**

For each sentence, choose the correct word or words from the choices given in parentheses.

1. The total length of the Great Wall of China is about 4,000 miles, if branches (*off*, *off of*) the main wall are included.
2. Carlos was (*nowhere*, *nowheres*) in sight.
3. We went to the hardware store for a special (*kind of*, *kind of a*) wrench.
4. Rachel Carson's books (*learned*, *taught*) me to care about ecology.
5. (*Leave*, *Let*) us listen without any interruptions.
6. We could (*of*, *have*) left earlier, I suppose.
7. Why did she feel (*like*, *as if*) she'd said something wrong?
8. T. J. (*ought*, *had ought*) to see this program.
9. Why didn't the U.S. government (*leave*, *let*) the Cherokee people stay in their Southeast homelands?
10. They didn't want to take the boat out because the waves looked (*kind of*, *rather*) choppy.

EXERCISE 6 **Proofreading a Paragraph to Correct Usage Errors**

Correct all the usage errors you find in each sentence in the following paragraph. Give the incorrect usage, followed by the correct usage. If a sentence is correct, write *C*.

1. C
2. rather [*or* somewhat]/ teach

4. let
5. as if
6. lie
7. C

[1] Until recent times, young girls had to master fancy needlework. [2] Beginning when a girl was kind of young, her mother or another woman would learn her many embroidery stitches. [3] Then, at the age of eight or ten, the girl would be given the task of making a sampler like the one shown on the next page, using every kind of a stitch she knew. [4] Usually, the girl's parents wouldn't leave her be idle. [5] She had to work on the sampler every day like her life depended on it! [6] When the sampler was finished, it didn't lay inside of a drawer either. [7] Instead, it was displayed to prove that the girl was industrious and well educated in the homemaking skills. [8] Many people

think that samplers must ~~of~~ ∧ been popular in America and ~~nowheres~~ else. [9] However, these ~~kind~~ ∧ of needlework exercises have been practiced in Europe, Asia, and Africa for centuries. [10] Today, girls aren't judged by their stitchery ~~like~~ they once were, and some never learn anything about needlework.

8. have/nowhere

9. kinds

10. as

Lucy Lathrop's Sampler. Cooper-Hewitt, National Museum of Design, Smithsonian Institution. Bequest of Marian Hague. Photo: Scott Hyde.

rise, raise See page 704.

scarcely See **The Double Negative** (page 756).

she See **he, she, they.**

should of See **could of.**

sit, set See pages 700–701.

some, somewhat In writing, do not use *some* as an adverb in place of *somewhat.*

> EXAMPLE This medicine should help your cough **somewhat** [not *some*].

somewheres See **anywheres,** etc.

sort See **kind, sort, type.**

sort of See **kind of, sort of.**

take, bring See **bring, take.**

USAGE

USAGE

COMMON ERROR

Problem. Students often confuse the conjunction *than* with the adverb *then.*

Solution. Explain to students that they should use *then* only when an expression answers the question *when.* Write the following reminder on the chalkboard:

then = when

At all other times, students should use *than,* which functions to compare or contrast. The following reminder can illustrate this:

than = comparison/contrast

USAGE

USAGE

teach See **learn, teach.**

than, then *Than* is a conjunction used in comparisons. *Then* is an adverb telling "when."

EXAMPLES   She is younger **than** you.
I swept the floor; **then** I emptied the trash.

that See **which, that, who.**

them Do not use *them* as an adjective. Use *those* instead.

EXAMPLE   It's one of **those** [not *them*] fancy show dogs.

they See **he, she, they.**

this here, that there *Here* and *there* are unnecessary after *this* and *that.*

EXAMPLE   Let's rent **this** [not *this here*] movie instead of **that** [not *that there*] one.

try and The correct expression is *try to.*

EXAMPLE   When you're at bat, you must **try to** [not *try and*] concentrate.

type See **kind, sort, type.**

unless See **without, unless.**

way, ways Use *way,* not *ways,* in referring to a distance.

EXAMPLE   She lives quite a **way** [not *ways*] from here.

well See **good, well.**

what Do not use *what* in place of *that* to introduce a subordinate clause.

EXAMPLE   This is the book **that** [not *what*] I told you about.

when, where Do not use *when* or *where* incorrectly in writing a definition.

NONSTANDARD   *S.R.O.* is when tickets for all the seats have been sold, leaving standing room only.
STANDARD   *S.R.O.* means that tickets for all the seats have been sold, leaving standing room only.
or
S.R.O. is the abbreviation for *standing room only,* meaning that tickets for all the seats have been sold.

where Do not use *where* for *that*.

> EXAMPLE   I read **that** [not *where*] the word *bayou* comes from the Choctaw word *bayuk,* meaning "small stream."

where . . . at See **at.**

which, that, who *Which* refers only to things. *That* refers to either people or things. *Who* refers only to people.

> EXAMPLES   These running shoes, **which** are on sale now, are the ones I want.
> This is the bulb **that** needs replacing.
> Is she the runner **that** won the medal?
> Is she the runner **who** won the medal?

who, whom See pages 661–662.

without, unless Do not use the preposition *without* in place of the conjunction *unless.*

> EXAMPLE   I can't use the car **unless** [not *without*] I ask Mom.

would of See **could of.**

EXERCISE 7   Correcting Errors in Usage

Revise each sentence, correcting errors in usage.

1. A solar eclipse is when the moon comes between the earth and the sun.
2. The workers which put up that office building were certainly fast.
3. Ronald E. McNair was the only African American astronaut aboard the space shuttle what exploded in January 1986.
4. I really like them science fiction movies.
5. A run-on sentence is where two sentences are erroneously joined as one.
6. As soon as the rain lets up some, we'll leave.
7. Them mosquitoes can drive a person nearly crazy.
8. Jerry Rice carried the ball a long ways down the field before he was tackled.
9. I read in the paper where Amy Tan has a new novel coming out soon.
10. I'm tired of trying to cut the grass with this here old lawn mower that should be in an antique exhibit.

USAGE

USAGE

ANSWERS
Exercise 7

Sentences will vary.

1. A solar eclipse occurs when the moon comes between the earth and the sun.
2. The workers who put up that office building were certainly fast.
3. Ronald E. McNair was the only African American astronaut aboard the space shuttle that exploded in January 1986.
4. I really like those science fiction movies.
5. A run-on sentence consists of two sentences erroneously joined as one.
6. As soon as the rain lets up somewhat, we'll leave.
7. Those mosquitoes can drive a person nearly crazy.
8. Jerry Rice carried the ball a long way down the field before he was tackled.
9. I read in the paper that Amy Tan has a new novel coming out soon.
10. I'm tired of trying to cut the grass with this old lawn mower, which should be in an antique exhibit. *or* I'm tired of trying to cut the grass with an old lawn mower that should be in an antique exhibit.

WRITING APPLICATION

OBJECTIVES
- To create a descriptive flier that uses standard English
- To provide and identify five examples of standard usage within a writing sample

WRITING APPLICATION
The writing assignment gives students practice in following rules of usage within a persuasive writing activity.

If there is sufficient time, have students bring in actual fliers created by an organization or have them write to request fliers. Remind students that the fliers they create for this assignment will certainly be different. Have students discuss what information the professional fliers contain that theirs should also mention.

CRITICAL THINKING
Analysis. Remind students that many people will not immediately read an unsolicited advertisement. Encourage students to examine their prewriting lists and determine which services would be most interesting and applicable to the general public.

Tell students that a flier that fully explains a few services will be more persuasive than one that says little about a lot of services.

USAGE

752 *Glossary of Usage*

WRITING APPLICATION

Using Standard English to Make a Good Impression

How you present yourself affects the way other people respond to you. When you appear to be intelligent and well-spoken, others usually have a higher regard for what you say. Like individuals, most businesses and organizations try hard to present themselves at their best. One of the ways they do so is by creating advertisements or public relations fliers. The use of correct standard English in such ads and fliers makes a good impression. Notice what different impressions you get from these two examples.

NONSTANDARD   Leave me tell you about some of the accomplishments of our association. You may of already heard about our very successful Thanksgiving food drive. Well, we also rose money for the new mobile clinic. This here clinic brings affordable, high-quality health care to people living in remote areas of our county.

STANDARD   Let me tell you about some of the accomplishments of our association. You may have already heard about our very successful Thanksgiving food drive. Well, we also raised money for the new mobile clinic. This clinic brings affordable, high-quality health care to people living in remote areas of our county.

Which of these statements would make a better impression on a potential volunteer or contributor?

▶ WRITING ACTIVITY
Create a flier for an organization that will soon be providing a public service in your community. The organization you choose might provide health, recreation, or housing services, or it might do something else. In a one-page flier, describe the organization's achievements and goals, and tell about some of the services it offers. Include at least five examples of the standard usage guidelines covered in this chapter, and underline each example.

Prewriting Begin by listing services that your community needs and noting what kinds of organizations supply these services. You may write about a real service group, such as the American Heart Association, or you may wish to write about a group that you make up. Also, list some of the positive effects the group will likely have on your community. Organize your notes so that you can present your information in several coherent paragraphs.

Writing As you write your first draft, you may think of points you'd like to add or changes you'd like to make in the presentation of your information. If so, look back over your prewriting notes, and figure out where your additions and changes will best fit.

Evaluating and Revising Exchange papers with a classmate, and as the two of you read each other's ads or fliers, ask the following questions:

- What does this group or organization do?
- Why should I trust this organization to provide the services it promises?
- How will these services benefit the people in my community?
- What other services could this organization provide that would be more useful to my community?
- What is my overall impression of this organization or group?

Use your partner's responses to these questions to help you revise your draft for clarity and audience appeal. You may also want to get pamphlets or fliers from some local public service groups to see how information is presented in these publications.

Proofreading Now that you've worked so hard on creating a good impression, don't spoil the effect with incorrect punctuation. See Chapters 25–28 for guidelines on using marks of punctuation. Read over your paper again, checking for errors in grammar, spelling, and usage. Be sure that you have included five correct expressions from this chapter.

PREWRITING

Since students are attempting to write a persuasive flier, you may want to have students also generate a list of reasons why people may not want to use the organization's services. Then they can take the list of provided services and better focus on those to be addressed in the flier.

WRITING

Encourage students to approach the flier as if it were advertising. Tell students that catchy slogans and attention-getting headlines are often the quickest way to get a flier read.

A DIFFERENT APPROACH

When students publish the fliers, have them create a drawing or provide a picture to be used on the cover.

USAGE

▶ REVIEW A   **Identifying Correct Expressions**

For each sentence, choose the <u>correct word or words</u> from the choices given in parentheses.

1. Thanks to modern medicine, there are (*fewer*, *less*) cases of tetanus and diphtheria nowadays.
2. I tried to (*learn*, *teach*) my dog to do tricks, but he just sat and stared at me.
3. I see (*where*, *that*) pandas are an endangered species.
4. Cape Porpoise is (*somewhere*, *somewheres*) near Portsmouth.
5. Priscilla wrote a longer paper (*than*, *then*) Tammy did.
6. To make Native American fry bread, you need flour, baking powder, salt, (*and etc.*, *etc.*)
7. We (*hadn't ought*, *ought not*) to decide until we know more facts.
8. It (*don't*, *doesn't*) make any difference when we finish.
9. Someone must (*of*, *have*) left the door unlocked.
10. Lewis Latimer (*discovered*, *invented*) and patented the first electric light bulb.

▶ REVIEW B   **Selecting Appropriate Expressions**

For each sentence, choose the <u>correct word or words</u> from the choices given in parentheses.

1. Stevie Wonder has written a number of hit songs since the 1960s, and it (*don't*, *doesn't*) look (*as if*, *like*) he's ever going to stop.
2. (*Inside*, *Inside of*) the box was (*a*, *an*) heap of glittering gems.
3. May I (*imply*, *infer*) from your yawns that you are bored?
4. My great-grandmother (*emigrated*, *immigrated*) from Italy when she was a young woman.
5. (*Beside*, *Besides*) speaking Spanish, Vera can speak a little Portuguese, and she reads both very (*good*, *well*).
6. Linda (*doesn't*, *don't*) enjoy doing (*them*, *those*, *that*) sort of exercise.
7. Ahead of us on the desert, a lake seemed to sparkle, but it was only an (*allusion*, *illusion*).
8. This water shortage will (*affect*, *effect*) the whole state (*accept*, *except*) for two counties.

9. I don't think my parents will (*leave, let*) me borrow the car in this kind of weather.
10. Because of the indiscriminate slaughter, each year there were (*fewer, less*) bison.

▶ REVIEW C

Proofreading a Paragraph to Correct Usage Errors

Correct each usage error you find in each sentence in the following paragraph. Give the incorrect usage, then the correct usage. If a sentence is correct, write C.

[1] Imagine single-handedly discovering a system for writing a language that had never before been written! [2] In about 1809, the Cherokee scholar Sequoyah became aware of "talking leaves," the written pages used by whites to communicate with one another. [3] Being that Sequoyah he felt that the ability to write had greatly helped whites, he decided he had ought to create a similar system for his people. [4] Instead of making up an alphabet like the one used in English, he chose to create this here *syllabary*. [5] Each character in Sequoyah's syllabary stands for one of the eighty-five syllables what are used in speaking Cherokee. [6] Sequoyah copied some letters from a English book, but in his system they have different meanings. [7] During the twelve years that it took Sequoyah to complete his writing system, he was ridiculed by many Cherokees who thought his efforts were kind of foolish. [8] But after the syllabary was finished and accepted by most Cherokees, they realized they should not of scoffed. [9] Within a few months' time, thousands learned

CHEROKEE SYLLABARY
Invented by SEQUOYAH

D a	R e	T i	Ꮼ o	Ᏻ u	i v
S ga Ꮰ ka	Ꮇ ge	Ᏼ gi	A go	J gu	E gv
Ꮂ ha	Ᏻ he	Ꮉ hi	Ᏺ ho	Ᏻ hu	Ꮧ hv
W la	Ꮯ le	Ꮲ li	Ꮐ lo	M lu	Ꮃ lv
Ꮢ ma	Ꮉ me	H mi	Ꮙ mo	Ᏻ mu	
Ꮎ na Ꮿ hna Ꮐ nah Ꮑ ne	Ꮗ nah ne	Ꮒ ni	Z no	Ꮔ nu	Ꮕ nv
Ꮖ qua	Ꮖ que	Ꮙ qui	Ꮹ quo	Ꮖ quu	Ꮛ quv
Ꮜ sa Ꭶ s	Ꮞ se	Ꮖ si	Ꮝ so	Ꮡ su	R sv
Ꮣ da W ta	Ꮞ de Ꮖ te	Ꮥ di Ꮧ ti	V do	S du	Ꮫ dv
Ꮥ dla Ꮮ tla	L tle	C tli	Ꮱ tlo	Ꮧ tlu	P tlv
Ꮳ tsa	Ꮴ tse	Ꮪ tsi	K tso	Ꮧ tsu	Ꮳ tsv
Ꮹ wa	Ꮽ we	Ꮗ wi	Ꮺ wo	Ꮹ wu	6 wv
Ꮿ ya	Ꮹ ye	Ꭵ yi	Ꮅ yo	Ꮿ yu	B yv

PRONUNCIATION GUIDE
(In words the pronunciation may be different)

a, as in ah   o, as in oh   g, as in go
e, as in they   u, as in true   ts, as j in joy
i, as in ski   v, as uh in huh

d, h, k, l, m, n, qu, s, t, w, y, as in English
NOTE: The character 'nah' is not in use.

Adapted from "Cherokee Alphabet" created by Harry A. Moneyhun, 1991.

USAGE

ANSWERS
Review C

1. discovering a system—inventing a system
2. C
3. Being that Sequoyah he felt—Because Sequoyah felt; he had ought to—he ought to
4. this here *syllabary*—this *syllabary*
5. what are used—that are used
6. a English book—an English book
7. were kind of foolish—were rather foolish
8. should not of scoffed—should not have scoffed
9. C
10. learning them—teaching them

USAGE

OBJECTIVES

- To revise sentences that contain too many negative words
- To write a descriptive paragraph that uses five expressions from the glossary of usage

THE DOUBLE NEGATIVE

- **Independent Practice/ Reteaching** For instruction and exercises, see **The Double Negative** in *Language Skills Practice and Assessment*, p. 152.

- **Computer Guided Instruction** For additional instruction and practice with the double negative, see **Lesson 51** in *Language Workshop CD-ROM.*

- **Practice** To help less-advanced students with additional instruction and practice with the double negative, see **Chapter 18** in *English Workshop, Fourth Course*, pp. 257–258.

QUICK REMINDER

Write the following sentences on the chalkboard and ask students to identify the negative words in them:

Nathaniel didn't have no shoes to wear. [didn't, no]

Layla doesn't want neither dress. [not, neither]

Explain to students that in terms of usage, only one negative word per sentence is necessary.

---

how to read and write, and soon books and newspapers were being printed in Cherokee. [10] Sequoyah was honored by his people for learning them to read and write, and his writing method is still used today.

The Double Negative

A *double negative* is the use of two negative words when one is enough. Before the 1700s, two or more negatives were often used in the same sentence for emphasis. Today this usage is no longer considered correct, and a double negative is regarded as nonstandard. Avoid using double negatives in your writing and speaking.

hardly, scarcely Do not use the words *hardly* and *scarcely* with another negative word.

> EXAMPLES You **can** [not *can't*] **hardly** see ten feet in this fog.
> We **had** [not *hadn't*] **scarcely** enough time to finish the test.

no, none, nothing Do not use any of these negative words with another negative word.

NONSTANDARD	There isn't no reason to be nervous.
STANDARD	There **is no** reason to be nervous.
STANDARD	There **isn't any** reason to be nervous.

NONSTANDARD	We searched for clues but didn't find none.
STANDARD	We searched for clues but **found none.**
STANDARD	We searched for clues but **didn't find any.**

NONSTANDARD	I didn't hear nothing.
STANDARD	I **heard nothing.**
STANDARD	I **didn't hear anything.**

REVIEW D

OBJECTIVE

- To revise expressions by correcting errors in usage

 **EXERCISE 8** | **Revising Sentences That Contain Too Many Negative Words**

Each of the following sentences contains too many negative words. Revise each sentence in two correct ways. Be careful not to change the intended meaning.

EXAMPLE | **1.** Before Sequoyah's syllabary, the Cherokee language hadn't never been written down.
| **1.** *Before Sequoyah's syllabary, the Cherokee language had never been written down.*
| *Before Sequoyah's syllabary, the Cherokee language hadn't ever been written down.*

1. As a young man, Sequoyah didn't have scarcely no contact with whites.
2. Before Sequoyah, not no person in history hadn't never single-handedly created no written language!
3. Some Cherokees didn't want no part of Sequoyah's system of writing.
4. It didn't take hardly no time at all for thousands of Cherokees to learn Sequoyah's symbols.
5. The Cherokees had a rich oral tradition, but they hadn't never been able to put none of it on paper.

 **REVIEW D** | **Revising Sentences by Correcting Errors in Usage**

Rewrite each sentence, correcting its error or errors in usage. Practice saying aloud the corrected sentences.

Revisions will vary.

1. They ~~don't~~ have hardly any chance to score before the buzzer sounds; the situation looks ~~sort of~~ hopeless to me. **1. rather**
2. You ought to have seen how beautiful Santa Fe was at Christmas, with nearly every house surrounded by flickering *farolitos*—paper-bag lanterns that have candles inside ~~of~~ them.
3. I might ~~of~~ gone to the concert if I'd ~~of~~ heard about it earlier. **3. have** | **4. can/between**
4. Pam and her sister Stacey look so much alike that you ~~can't~~ hardly see much difference ~~among~~ them.
5. My cousins ~~didn't~~ hardly ~~know~~ how to swim, but they wouldn't ~~of~~ missed going to the lake. **5. knew/have**

ANSWERS

Exercise 8

Revisions will vary. The following sentences are possibilities:

1. As a young man, Sequoyah didn't have much contact with whites.
   As a young man, Sequoyah had scarcely any contact with whites.

2. Before Sequoyah, no person in history had ever single-handedly created a written language!
   Before Sequoyah, not one person in history had ever single-handedly created a written language!

3. Some Cherokees didn't want any part of Sequoyah's system of writing.
   Some Cherokees wanted no part of Sequoyah's system of writing.

4. It didn't take much time at all for thousands of Cherokees to learn Sequoyah's symbols.
   It took hardly any time at all for thousands of Cherokees to learn Sequoyah's symbols.

5. The Cherokees had a rich oral tradition, but they had never been able to put any of it on paper.
   The Cherokees had a rich oral tradition, but they hadn't ever been able to put any of it on paper.

USAGE

6. ~~Them~~ reference books in the library are kept in some kind of ~~a~~ special section. **6. Those**
7. This ~~here~~ is the car ~~what~~ I told you about. **7. that**
8. ~~Hadn't~~ you ~~ought to~~ try ~~and~~ help them? **8. Shouldn't/to**
9. Many of the American Indian leaders ~~which~~ visited Washington, D.C., in the late 1800s proudly wore their traditional clothing rather than dress ~~like~~ their white hosts did. **9. who/as**   **10. those**
10. I wonder where ~~them~~ fishing poles are ~~at~~. **11. anymore**
11. We don't live in that ~~there~~ neighborhood ~~no more~~.
12. We might ~~of~~ gone on the tour, but we wouldn't ~~of~~ had ~~no~~ camera to take pictures. **12. have/have/a/with which**
13. A foot fault in tennis ~~is~~ when the server steps over the base line before hitting the ball. **13. occurs**
14. Since there ~~wasn't~~ scarcely any rainfall last spring, there are ~~less~~ mosquitoes this summer. **14. was/fewer**
15. When the play was over, the audience seemed ~~sort of~~ subdued. **15. somewhat**
16. Shing searched for *lomein* noodles in the grocery store, but didn't find ~~none~~. **16. any**
17. I saw on the news ~~where~~ manufacturers will start putting ~~them~~ air bags into all the new cars. **17. that/those**
18. Miss Kim ~~she~~ likes to give those ~~kind~~ of surprise quizzes. **18. kinds**
19. Let's try ~~and~~ finish early so we can relax ~~some~~. **19. to/somewhat**
20. In the early 1500s, Ponce de León searched for the Fountain of Youth ~~somewheres~~ on the island of Bimini. **20. somewhere**

PICTURE THIS

You are a professional artist looking for a fresh medium in which to work. You've just seen an unusual exhibit of painted chifforobes—pieces of furniture that combine a wardrobe with a chest of drawers. The secondhand chifforobes were decorated, inside and out, by New Orleans high school students. You admire how these young artists have presented scenes from their lives to

---

PICTURE THIS

You may want to have students form groups and discuss what they would include in their descriptions. Tell students first to use headings such as *reactions* and *ideas*. Encourage students to generate lists containing things they would like, dislike, imagine, and so on.

illustrate their dreams and fears. You have so many thoughts and impressions that you decide to write some notes to yourself to remind you of your reactions to the exhibit. Describe in detail one of the chifforobes shown here. (You can describe an imaginary one if none of these three interests you.) Tell whether you were inspired by the exhibit and how you might use the chifforobe art to enrich your own work. In your paragraph, use correctly at least five expressions covered in this chapter.

Subject: an exhibit of chifforobes painted by high
            school students
Audience: you, a professional painter
Purpose: to inform, to remind, to inspire

OBJECTIVES

- To revise expressions by correcting errors in usage
- To proofread a paragraph to correct errors in usage

USAGE

CRITICAL THINKING

Synthesis. Analyze and discuss the use of nonstandard grammar in dialogue. A good example would be either Langston Hughes's poem "Mother to Son" or Marjorie Kinnan Rawlings's short story "My Friend Moe." Emphasize that nonstandard grammar is included as a literary device to help reinforce realistic characters.

Next, tell students that they will work in groups of three to create scenes involving characters who will speak in either standard or nonstandard English.

In the groups, one student will write brief character descriptions of two different characters. The other two students then will compose dialogue for the invented characters. Students can practice speaking their dialogue and then present their scenes to the class.

USAGE

760 *Glossary of Usage*

Review: Posttest

A. Revising Expressions by Correcting Errors in Usage

In each set of expressions, one <u>expression contains an error in usage</u>. Write the expression correctly, using standard formal usage.

EXAMPLE **1. a.** Her speech implies that a change is needed.
   b. Leave me have some oranges, too.
   c. This house is somewhat larger than our old one.
  1. *b. Let me have some oranges, too.*

 1. a. ~~wasn't no~~ reason **1.** was no [*or* wasn't any]
  b. words had no effect
  c. can hardly wait

 2. a. families that ~~emigrated~~ to new lands **2.** immigrated
  b. sail as far as the channel marker
  c. made allusions to classical literature

 3. a. ~~being that~~ he was alone **3.** because [*or* since]
  b. The people accepted new ways.
  c. the woman who was elected

 4. a. what kind of gloves
  b. There is overtime besides the regular work.
  c. ~~an~~ historic moment **4.** a

 5. a. saw on TV that our team had won
  b. Lee Haney proudly ~~excepted~~ his seventh straight Mr. Olympia trophy. **5.** accepted
  c. the house beside the highway

 6. a. those lockers beside the gym
  b. ~~Leave~~ him have his own way. **6.** Let
  c. Leave the door open when you go.

 7. a. Teach your dog this trick.
  b. I'm feeling ~~kind of~~ ill. **7.** rather [*or* somewhat]
  c. might have been too late

 8. a. taller than her sister
  b. Dough will rise in a warm place.
  c. We read ~~where~~ the damage was extensive. **8.** that

 9. a. Try to be on time.
  b. They walked a long way.
  c. ~~Them~~ stairs are dangerous and need repairs. **9.** Those

10. **a.** The bag burst, spilling the rice.
     b. The Polynesian alphabet has twelve characters, fewer than half the letters in the English alphabet.
     c. <u>Take those books off ~~of~~ that shelf.</u>

B. Proofreading Paragraphs to Correct Usage Errors

Correct each usage error you find in each sentence in the following paragraphs. Give the incorrect usage, followed by the correct usage. [Note: A sentence may contain more than one error.] Revisions of double negatives will vary.

[11] After the Civil War ended, Joseph E. Clarke decided that African Americans ~~had~~ ought to start a town of their own. [12] He wanted to build such a town, but no one would sell or donate land for this kind of ~~an~~ endeavor. [13] But Joe Clarke was a man who had great determination, and he ~~wasn't~~ hardly going to give up hope. [14] Finally in 1877, with money ~~what~~ was donated by a New York philanthropist and land offered by a Floridian named Josiah Eaton, Clarke obtained the first twelve acres of what would become Eatonville, Florida.

13. was

14. that

[15] Eatonville, located just ~~besides~~ Orlando, is recognized as the oldest incorporated African American town ~~anywheres~~ in the United States. [16] This ~~here~~ community has always been populated and governed entirely by blacks. [17] The African Americans ~~which~~ flocked to Eatonville built homes, churches, and schools, and they cultivated gardens and orange groves. [18] The residents didn't lose ~~no~~ time in establishing a library, a post office, and a newspaper. [19] Today, after more than a hundred years of self-government, the citizens of Eatonville continue to feel the ~~affects~~ of Joe Clarke's courage and vision. [20] With its light industry, new businesses, and booming real estate development, Eatonville enjoys economic growth just ~~like~~ the rest of Central Florida does.

15. beside/anywhere

17. who

18. any

19. effects

20. as

USAGE

USAGE

761

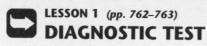

LESSON 1 *(pp. 762–763)*
DIAGNOSTIC TEST
OBJECTIVE
• To recognize and correct errors of capitalization in sentences

PROGRAM MANAGER

FOR THE WHOLE CHAPTER

■ **Review** For exercises on chapter concepts, see **Review Form A** and **Review Form B** in *Language Skills Practice and Assessment*, pp. 186–189.

■ **Assessment** For additional testing, see **Mechanics Pretests** and **Mechanics Mastery Tests** in *Language Skills Practice and Assessment*, pp. 169–177 and pp. 265–271.

CHAPTER OVERVIEW

Students can use this chapter as a reference for specific usage problems. A quick review early in the year may help your students avoid capitalization problems later.

The examples on the **Summary Style Review** chart at the end of the chapter can often teach students about correct capitalization faster than rules can. Exceptions and special problems are discussed to help students avoid confusion.

This chapter can be helpful with usage problems that may arise during the teaching of any composition chapter and **Chapter 15: "The Parts of Speech."**

MECHANICS

MECHANICS

24 CAPITALIZATION

Standard Uses of Capitalization

Diagnostic Test

Correcting Sentences by Using Capitalization Correctly

For each of the following sentences, identify the <u>word or words containing an error in capitalization</u>. If a sentence is correct, write *C*.

EXAMPLE **1.** In the Fall the trees along Main street are lovely.
            1. *fall; Street*

1. This year my easiest classes are geometry, <u>spanish</u>, and American history.
2. Mexico <u>city</u> is built on the site of <u>tenochtitlán</u>, the capital of the <u>aztec</u> empire.
3. We rent videotapes from the Grand Video <u>company</u>.
4. Colorado is located <u>West</u> of the Great Plains.
5. Lansing, Michigan, is in Ingham <u>county</u>.
6. She lives at 321 Maple <u>boulevard</u>, which is south of here.

7. My RCA <u>Stereo</u> is ten years old and still works well.
8. Carla entered her Saint Bernard in the Centerville Dog <u>club's</u> show.
9. They live half a block north of Twenty-<u>First</u> Street.
10. Our neighbors are alumni of Howard <u>university</u> in Washington, <u>d.c.</u>
11. Last <u>Spring</u> my step-sister Lisa joined the National Audubon <u>society</u>.
12. While we were in San Juan, <u>puerto rico</u>, we toured El Morro Castle.
13. The club members celebrated <u>bastille</u> <u>day</u> by having dinner at a French restaurant.
14. Has Ms. Davis written to the U.S. <u>department</u> of Agriculture for information on soybean cultivation in the Midwest?
15. Mars was the Roman <u>God</u> of war.
16. We're holding a carwash next Saturday to raise money for the <u>junior</u> Prom.
17. The <u>Islands</u> that make up the <u>west</u> <u>indies</u> separate the Atlantic <u>ocean</u> from the <u>gulf</u> of <u>mexico</u> and the Caribbean <u>sea</u>.
18. Would you like to be the first student to ride in a <u>Space</u> <u>Shuttle</u> that orbits the earth?
19. The post-Civil <u>war</u> period known as <u>reconstruction</u> officially ended in 1877, when federal troops were withdrawn from the <u>south</u>.
20. Erica wants to be <u>Secretary</u> of the Shutterbug <u>club</u>.

MECHANICS

You may want to gauge your students' general knowledge of basic capitalization rules with the **Diagnostic Test**, which consists of twenty sentences containing errors in capitalization.

With some students, the simplest approach to problem areas may be to read the rules and examples with them and assign the exercises at the end of each set. Other students might not need to spend time reviewing all of the chapter, so you can concentrate on the rules and exceptions or simply have students use this chapter as a reference tool.

MECHANICS

In your reading, you'll notice that some writers do not always follow the rules presented in this chapter. However, you will see that most writers do follow these rules most of the time. In your own writing, following these rules will help you communicate clearly with the widest possible audience.

NOTE: Some modern writers, for reasons of style, do not follow the rules governing capitalization. When you quote from a writer's work, always use capital letters exactly as the writer uses them.

☞ REFERENCE NOTE: See pages 834–835 for more about using capital letters in quotations.

OBJECTIVES

- To correct phrases and paragraphs by using capitalization correctly

PROGRAM MANAGER

FIRST WORDS, THE PRONOUN *I*, THE INTERJECTION *O*, PROPER NOUNS AND PROPER ADJECTIVES

- **Independent Practice/ Reteaching** For instruction and exercises, see **First Words, *I*, and *O*; Proper Nouns and Adjectives A; Proper Nouns and Adjectives B;** and **Proper Nouns and Adjectives C** in *Language Skills Practice and Assessment,* pp. 181–184.

- **Computer Guided Instruction** For additional instruction and practice, see **Lessons 45 and 46** in *Language Workshop CD-ROM.*

- **Practice** To help less-advanced students with additional instruction and practice, see **Chapter 19** in *English Workshop, Fourth Course,* pp. 263–264.

QUICK REMINDER

Write the following proper nouns on the chalkboard and ask students to correct capitalization errors:

1. Atlantic ocean [Ocean]
2. rotary club [Rotary Club]
3. Main street [Street]
4. Spanish armada [Armada]
5. a South Sea Island [island]
6. senator Lewis [Senator]
7. aunt Yolanda [Aunt]
8. her Aunt [aunt]
9. a committee Chairperson [chairperson]
10. congressional District [Congressional]

24a. Capitalize the first word in every sentence.

EXAMPLES
The Second Seminole War lasted nearly eight years. **A**fter the war many Seminoles remained in the Everglades and never officially made peace with the U.S. government.
After studying reports on new cars, my mom said, "**T**he models with front-wheel drive have been improved."

Traditionally, the first word in a line of poetry is capitalized.

EXAMPLES
Storm, blow me from here
With your fiercest wind
Let me float across the sky
'**T**ill I can rest again.

Maya Angelou, "Woman Work"

24b. Capitalize the pronoun *I* and the interjection *O*.

The interjection *O*, usually used only for invocations, is followed by the name of the person or thing being addressed. Don't confuse *O* with the common interjection *oh*, which is capitalized only when it begins a sentence or is part of a title.

EXAMPLES
The first line **I** read in the poem was "Hear us, **O** Zeus."
I finished the race, but **oh,** was **I** exhausted.

24c. Capitalize proper nouns and proper adjectives.

A ***common noun*** names one member of a group of people, places, or things. A ***proper noun*** names a particular person, place, or thing. ***Proper adjectives*** are formed from proper nouns.

☞ **REFERENCE NOTE:** See page 515 for more about common nouns and proper nouns.

Common nouns are not capitalized unless they

- begin a sentence
- begin a direct quotation
- are part of a title

- To proofread a paragraph to correct capitalization
- To write a paragraph using capitalization correctly

COMMON NOUNS	PROPER NOUNS	PROPER ADJECTIVES
a writer	Shakespeare	Shakespearean sonnet
a country	France	French bread
a queen	Victoria	Victorian era
a planet	Venus	Venusian terrain

In proper nouns that have more than one word, all articles and short prepositions (those with fewer than five letters) are not capitalized.

EXAMPLES   Prince **of** Wales
National Association **for** the Advancement **of** Colored People

In a compound adjective, the proper noun or proper adjective is usually the only part capitalized.

EXAMPLES   **Spanish**-speaking countries   northern **Italian** cuisine

NOTE: Proper nouns and proper adjectives may lose their capitals after long use.

EXAMPLES   **diesel   bologna   braille**

When you're not sure whether to capitalize a word, check a dictionary to see in which uses (if any) it is capitalized.

(1) Capitalize the names of persons.

GIVEN NAMES	Matthew	Jennifer	Latrice	Nguyen
SURNAMES	Bowman	Cruz	Kantor	Ryan

NOTE: Some names contain more than one capital letter. Always verify the spelling with the person, or check it in a reference source.

EXAMPLES   **De La Cruz   La Porte   McEnroe   O'Shea**
Red Cloud   Wells-Barnett   St. John   Van Gogh

The abbreviations *Jr.* (*junior*) and *Sr.* (*senior*) should always be capitalized.

EXAMPLES   **Jerome W. Wilson, Jr.   Simon L. Snyder, Sr.**

MECHANICS

You may want to read aloud the rules and examples in this lesson with a focus on special problems and exceptions to the rules. After you assess **Exercise 1**, ask students to make charts showing any specific error patterns. Students can add errors to their charts as they proceed through the chapter and can refer to the applicable rules when necessary.

◆ COMMON ERROR

Problem. Students who fail to capitalize first words might be writing run-on sentences or sentence fragments.

Solution. Have students who are having trouble with first-word capitalization review the material in **Chapter 12: "Writing Complete Sentences."** Remind students to proofread for these errors.

 EXERCISE 1   **Correcting Paragraphs by Using Capitalization**

If the capitalization of a sentence is correct, write *C*. If not, write the correct form of each incorrect word.
Words that should be capitalized or lowercased are underscored.
EXAMPLE   [1] These pictures capture only a few of the many sides of Gordon parks, renowned Photographer, film director, writer, and composer.
1. *Parks; photographer*

[1] A <u>Self</u>-taught photographer, <u>gordon</u> Parks grew up in Fort Scott, Kansas. [2] <u>after</u> winning a <u>rosenwald</u> Fellowship for a series of pictures about life in Chicago's <u>Slums, He</u> got his first full-time photography job with the Farm Security Administration in Washington, D.C. [3] In 1949, he joined the staff of *Life* <u>Magazine</u>. [4] During his nearly twenty years with *Life,* Parks covered assignments ranging from <u>Junior</u> <u>High</u> <u>School</u> science conventions to Paris <u>Fashion</u> <u>Shows</u>. [5] He also wrote many of the essays that accompanied his photographs, as well as <u>Two</u> <u>Volumes</u> of autobiography, *A Choice of Weapons* and *Voices in the Mirror.*

[6] Turning to a career in the movie industry in 1968, Parks moved to Hollywood, where his son Gordon Parks, jr., took this photograph of him preparing to direct a scene from the film version of *The Learning Tree.* [7] Parks also wrote the film's screenplay and, working at the grand piano in his Hollywood apartment, its musical score. [8] His success with the film led to other writing and directing projects, including *Shaft, Shaft's Big Score,* and *Leadbelly,* the story of blues musician Huddie <u>ledbetter</u>.

7 C

[9] In August 1988, in a White House <u>Ceremony</u>, <u>parks</u> was awarded the National Medal of Arts, and two years later he was inducted into the National Association of Black Journalists Hall of Fame. [10] His most recent projects have included an <u>Autobiographical</u> work, *Voices in <u>The</u> Mirror,* and the words and music for *Martin,* a classical <u>Ballet</u> honoring the late <u>martin luther king</u>, jr.

(2) Capitalize geographical names.

TYPE OF NAME	EXAMPLES	
Countries	Mexico Ghana	the United States of America
Towns, Cities	Chicago Berlin San Diego	Laredo Stratford-on-Avon St. Petersburg
Counties, Townships, Parishes	Orange County Franklin Township Manhattan	Caddo Parish Yorkshire Third Precinct
States	Oregon New York	Texas South Carolina
Regions	the South the West the Northeast	New England Yukon Sun Belt

NOTE: Words such as *south, east,* and *northwest* are not capitalized when they indicate direction.

EXAMPLES **west** of the bridge   heading **north**

MEETING individual NEEDS

LEP/ESL

General Strategies. You can make **Exercise 1** more manageable for English-language learners by pairing them with English-proficient speakers. The latter can act as cultural informants by telling the English-language learners exactly how many words in each sentence should be capitalized and how many should be lowercased.

Distinguishing common from proper nouns can be problematic if students don't know the meaning of a word. For example, in **Exercise 1,** the second sentence includes the phrase, ". . . life in Chicago's Slums . . ." *Slums* could sound like the name of a neighborhood to students who don't know the word's meaning. Throughout this chapter you may want to note such constructions and define for students words that may be confusing.

◆ COMMON ERROR
Problem. When the name of a particular place includes several words, students may be confused about which words to capitalize.

Solution. List on the chalkboard articles and prepositions that are likely to occur in names of particular places—*a, an, by, for, of, on,* and *the.* Remind students that an article or short preposition is capitalized only if it is the first word of a proper noun.

COOPERATIVE LEARNING

Divide the class into groups of three or four students. Ask each group to write a tourist brochure for a specific geographical region. The brochure should include information about at least one town or city and should refer to geographical features—lakes, rivers, mountains or ranges, and caves. The brochure should mention specific historical sites and figures as well as recreational and entertainment facilities. You could also have students provide directions to each attraction. Remind students to capitalize geographical names correctly. Have the groups present their brochures to the class.

TYPE OF NAME	EXAMPLES	
Continents	South America Asia	Europe Africa
Islands	Galveston Island the Lesser Antilles	the Isle of Wight Key West
Mountains	Allegheny Mountains Sierra Madre	Mount St. Helens Pikes Peak
Bodies of Water	Atlantic Ocean Red Sea Persian Gulf	Suwanee River Rio Grande Lake of the Ozarks
Parks	Redwood State Park Central Park	Stone Mountain Memorial Park
Roads, Highways, Streets	Route 41 Interstate 10 Sunshine State Parkway	Central Avenue South Fiftieth Street Pleasant Hill Road

The second word in a hyphenated number begins with a small letter: *Fifty-third Street.* Words such as *city, island, river, street,* and *park* are capitalized when they are part of a name. Otherwise, they are common nouns and are not capitalized.

PROPER NOUNS	COMMON NOUNS
traffic in **Mexico City** visiting **Captiva Island** bridging the **Ohio River** across **Delancy Street**	traffic in a large city visiting a barrier island bridging the river across a congested street

 EXERCISE 2   **Correcting Phrases by Capitalizing Words**

If a phrase is correct, write C. If a word or words should be capitalized, write the entire phrase correctly.

Words that should be capitalized are underscored.

EXAMPLE   **1.** atop granite peak
           1. *atop Granite Peak*

1. zion national park
2. gulf of tonkin
3. explored Mount ararat
4. the hiking trails in a nearby state park **4.** C
5. at moon lake
6. a house on starve island
7. beside the ohio river
8. in lancaster county
9. the illinois oil fields
10. across baffin bay
11. ventura boulevard
12. the tides in the bay **12.** C
13. new york skyline
14. forty-fifth street
15. near the isle of man
16. the west side of the river **16.** C
17. the north
18. near dundee mountain
19. coffee from brazil
20. coast of australia

▶ EXERCISE 3   **Proofreading a Paragraph to Correct Capitalization**

Capitalize the words that should begin with a capital letter in each sentence in the following paragraph. Do not include the words already capitalized. If a sentence is correct, write *C*.

EXAMPLE   [1] Until last year I'd never been farther from lawrenceburg, tennessee, than pulaski, which is only seventeen miles east.
   1. *Lawrenceburg, Tennessee, Pulaski*

[1] Naturally, I was excited when our choir decided to have an international arts and crafts fair to raise money for a trip to washington, d.c. [2] Colleen O'Roark suggested that the fair feature crafts and food from countries in europe, africa, and asia. [3] Juana Santiago, whose family is from venezuela, pointed out that we should also include items from central america and south america. [4] Julian **4.** C Moore, who recently returned from visiting his aunt in Monrovia, said he'd bring a display of Liberian baskets. [5] Karen Cohen offered items from quebec, our neighbor to the north. [6] Erin McCall, whose family moved to lexington avenue from phoenix, arizona, volunteered to bring rocks from petrified forest national park. [7] Since Maxine Hirano was born in tokyo, japan, she promised to demonstrate paper-folding. [8] Some of us met later at Paula Bowen's house, on the northeast corner of columbus street and hickory lane, to choose items to represent the united states. [9] We selected Native American artifacts

TIMESAVER
You may want to assign **Exercise 3** for homework and go over the answers with students in class. Survey the class for error patterns and review those rules that seem to be giving students problems.

INTEGRATING THE LANGUAGE ARTS

Mechanics and Writing. Have students pretend to be pioneers traveling during the 1800s to their new homes in the West. Have them write diary entries describing their trip. Students should each include at least ten proper nouns or proper adjectives.

from the <u>southwest</u>, country crafts from the <u>appalachian mountains</u>, and shell gifts from the southern states along the <u>gulf</u> of <u>mexico</u>. [10] When the fair was over, we had raised enough money to include on our trip to the nation's capital a tour of <u>mammoth</u> <u>cave</u> <u>national</u> <u>park</u> in <u>kentucky</u>.

(3) Capitalize the names of organizations, teams, business firms, institutions, buildings, and government bodies.

TYPE OF NAME	EXAMPLES	
Organizations	American Medical Association National Honor Society Organization of American States	
Teams	New York Rangers Houston Oilers Eastside Jets	Harlem Globetrotters Portsmouth Chess Masters
Business Firms	Eastern Airlines International Business Machines	Xerox Corporation National Broadcasting Company
Institutions, Buildings	Stanford University Sears Tower Fox Theater	Good Samaritan Hospital Ridgemont High School
Government Bodies	the Senate Parliament Congress Tampa City Council	Department of the Interior the Nuclear Regulatory Commission

NOTE: Do not capitalize words such as *democratic, republican,* and *socialist* when they refer to principles or forms of government. Capitalize these words only when they refer to a specific political party.

EXAMPLES Voting is part of the **d**emocratic process.
     George Bush was the **R**epublican nominee.

  The word *party* in the name of a political party may be capitalized or not; either way is correct.

EXAMPLE Republican **party**
     or
     Republican **Party**

MECHANICS

MECHANICS

770

REFERENCE NOTE: Do not capitalize words such as *building, hotel, theater, college, high school, post office,* and *courthouse* unless they are part of a proper name. For more discussion about the differences between common and proper nouns, see pages 764–765 and 515.

(4) Capitalize the names of historical events and periods, special events, and holidays and other calendar items.

TYPE OF NAME	EXAMPLES	
Historical Events and Periods	the **Dark Ages** **Great Depression** **Paleolithic Period** **Children's Crusade**	the **Battle of Gettysburg** the **Yalta Conference**
Special Events	the **Iowa State Fair** the **Boston Marathon**	the **All-Star Game** the **National Minority Job Expo**
Holidays and Other Calendar Items	**Friday** **March**	**Valentine's Day** **Earth Day**

NOTE: Do not capitalize the name of a season unless the season is being personified or is part of a proper name.

EXAMPLES We looked forward to **spring** after the long **winter**.
Are you going to the **Winter Wonderland Dance**?

"And **Winter** slumbering in the open air,
Wears on his smiling face a dream of **Spring!**"

Samuel Taylor Coleridge, "Work Without Hope"

 EXERCISE 4 **Writing a Paragraph Using Capitalization Correctly**

Your family recently inherited the abandoned town shown on the next page. Write a paragraph explaining how you would go about revitalizing the town. What would you name the town? What names would you give to streets and avenues? What organizations, business firms, institutions, government offices, and special events would you set up? Include in your paragraph a combined total of at least twenty proper nouns and proper adjectives. Use a variety of names, not just your family name.

A DIFFERENT APPROACH

Ask each student to check signs or newspaper and magazine advertisements for examples of common nouns and proper names that do not follow the accepted rules of capitalization, such as "Littering is unlAWFUL." Use these examples to lead the class into a discussion about the stylistic use of capitalization.

Ask students to give brief oral reports about the purposes of capitalization patterns in their examples. [Students might say their example used capitalization to highlight an idea or to instill an attitude in the reader's mind, to emphasize a pun, to introduce humor, or to draw attention to a serious issue.]

ANSWERS
Exercise 4

Each paragraph should include details describing the town, as well as a total of twenty capitalized proper nouns and adjectives.

VISUAL CONNECTIONS
Related Expression Skills.
Ghost town is a name for an abandoned town. To complement **Exercise 4**, ask each student to research the history of a specific ghost town in the United States and to give an oral report on the reasons for its rise and decline.

MECHANICS

EXAMPLE   *I'd name the town New Century City, and the first business I'd open would be a teenagers-only club called Syncopation.*

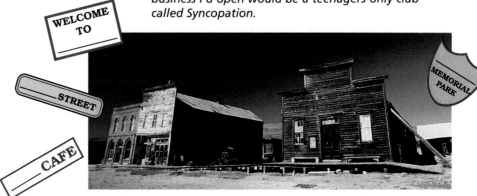

(5) Capitalize the names of nationalities, races, and peoples.

EXAMPLES   **Italian, Canadian, Caucasian, Asian, Jewish, Hispanic, Navajo, Micronesian, Indo-Iranian**

(6) Capitalize the brand names of business products.

EXAMPLES   **Sealtest frozen yogurt, Kraft cheese, Kodak camera**

Notice that the noun that often follows a brand name is not capitalized: an Apple computer.

(7) Capitalize the names of ships, monuments, awards, planets, and any other particular places, things, or events.

TYPE OF NAME	EXAMPLES	
Ships, Trains	the *Titanic*	the *Orient Express*
Aircraft, Spacecraft, Missiles	the *Spirit of St. Louis*	*Apollo* *Patriot*
Monuments, Memorials	Aztec Ruins National Monument Vietnam Veterans Memorial	
Awards	Nobel Prize Bronze Star Medal	Academy Award Stanley Cup
Planets, Stars, Constellations	Pluto Ursa Major	Betelgeuse Big Dipper

LANGUAGES, SPECIFIC COURSE NAMES, AND TITLES Rules 24d, 24e

OBJECTIVE

• To use proper nouns and proper adjectives in a descriptive letter

24d

NOTE: Do not capitalize the words *earth, moon,* and *sun* unless they are being used along with other astronomical names that are capitalized.

24d. Do *not* capitalize the names of school subjects, except for names of languages and course names followed by a number.

EXAMPLES   **E**nglish, **L**atin, **G**erman, **g**eography, **a**lgebra, **c**hemistry, **m**usic, **A**lgebra II, **C**hemistry I

NOTE: Do not capitalize the class names *senior, junior, sophomore,* and *freshman* unless they are part of a proper noun.

EXAMPLES   A number of **s**ophomores attended the **J**unior Prom.
The **S**ophomore Singers performed for the freshmen.

 REVIEW A   **Correcting Sentences by Capitalizing Words**

Identify the <u>words that should be capitalized</u> in each of the following sentences. Do not include the words already capitalized.

EXAMPLE   **1.** The spanish explorer juan ponce de león landed in florida in 1513.
1. *Spanish, Juan, Ponce de León, Florida*

1. The area now known as <u>florida</u> was originally inhabited by <u>native american</u> peoples, including the <u>apalachees</u>, the <u>creeks</u>, and the <u>seminoles</u>.
2. The state is bordered on the north by <u>alabama</u> and <u>georgia</u>, on the east by the <u>atlantic ocean</u>, on the south by the <u>straits</u> of <u>florida</u> and the <u>gulf</u> of <u>mexico</u>, and on the west by <u>alabama</u> and the <u>gulf</u> of <u>mexico</u>.
3. The <u>spanish</u> founded <u>st. augustine</u>, the state's first permanent <u>european</u> settlement, in 1565, making it the oldest colonial city in the <u>united states</u>.
4. When <u>spain</u> ceded <u>florida</u> to the <u>united states</u> in 1821, the <u>u.s.</u> government demanded that the native peoples move west.
5. The strength and dignity of the <u>seminole</u> leader <u>osceola</u>, who led his people in the fight to retain

---

PROGRAM MANAGER

LANGUAGES, SPECIFIC COURSE NAMES, AND TITLES

■ **Independent Practice/ Reteaching** For instruction and exercises, see **Titles** in *Language Skills Practice and Assessment,* p. 185.

■ **Computer Guided Instruction** For additional instruction and practice with capitalization, see **Lesson 46** in *Language Workshop CD-ROM.*

■ **Practice** To help less-advanced students with additional instruction and practice with capitalization, see **Chapter 19** in *English Workshop, Fourth Course,* pp. 269–270.

QUICK REMINDER

Write the following sentences on the chalkboard and ask volunteers to correct the capitalization errors:

1. Dr. Velez will be teaching spanish and a course in American History this year. [Spanish, history]
2. Angela is the best student in our psychology 101 class. [Psychology]
3. After struggling with algebra last year, I will take geometry 305 this year. [Geometry]
4. I saw the president addressing the press outside the white house. [President, White House]
5. My Uncle is coming for sunday dinner. [uncle, Sunday]

OBJECTIVES
- To correct sentences by capitalizing words
- To proofread paragraphs for correct capitalization

MECHANICS

VISUAL CONNECTIONS
Exploring the Subject. Osceola, the Seminole leader, became a victim of treachery when he was taken prisoner by an American general during a peace conference. He died in a prison near Charleston, South Carolina, in 1838.

COOPERATIVE LEARNING
Divide the class into groups of four or five students and have each group construct four compound-complex sentences that contain errors involving capitalization rules. Encourage students to refer to the **Notes** describing exceptions and special problems. Have students select two of their sentences for you to write on the chalkboard for the class to correct. Award five points for each sentence that stumps the class. [Here is a sample sentence with errors yet to be added: Henry David Thoreau was an advocate of civil disobedience, and his ideas in the essay "On the Duty of Civil Disobedience" (also known as "Resistance to Civil Government") have been followed by important philosophers and statesmen such as Mohandas K. Gandhi, Leo Tolstoy, and Martin Luther King, Jr.]

774

MECHANICS

774 *Capitalization*

George Catlin, *Osceola*. Courtesy of the Department of Library Services, American Museum of Natural History.

their lands, are evident in this 1838 painting by george catlin.

6. Most of the seminoles were eventually deported to present-day oklahoma, but a few hundred fled to the everglades, a huge wilderness area in south florida that now includes everglades national park.

7. Founded in 1886, eatonville, florida, is the oldest incorporated african american town in the united states.

8. After the cuban revolution in the late 1950s, and again in the early 1980s, many cubans fled to miami.

9. Miami has also served as a major point of entry for haitian refugees who've braved the atlantic ocean in search of a better life.

10. Among the asians who've settled in the state are refugees from vietnam, many of whom make their living fishing along the northern coast of florida.

▶ REVIEW B **Proofreading Paragraphs for Correct Capitalization**

Identify the words that should be capitalized in each sentence in the following paragraphs. Do not include the words already capitalized.

EXAMPLE   [1] Trivia games test your knowledge of subjects as diverse as american inventors, the korean war, and popular music.

     1. *American, Korean War*

[1] Last <u>saturday</u>, <u>may</u> 18, my brother Ted and <u>i</u> finally won our first trivia match against our parents. [2] Some of the courses Ted is taking this semester are history, political science, and <u>french</u>; mine include <u>world</u> <u>literature</u> I and <u>geography</u> II. [3] We surged into the lead when our parents couldn't remember that the first <u>u.s.</u> satellite, *<u>explorer</u>* I, followed the <u>u.s.s.r.</u>'s *<u>sputnik</u>* I into space. [4] From my geography class I remembered that <u>mount</u> McKinley is the highest point and <u>death</u> <u>valley</u> is the lowest point on the <u>north</u> <u>american</u> continent.

[5] Our parents rallied for the lead by knowing that the boy on the <u>cracker</u> <u>jack</u> box is named <u>jack</u> and that his dog's name is <u>bingo</u>. [6] Then Ted came up with the fact that the steel framework of the <u>statue</u> of <u>liberty</u> was designed by the <u>frenchman</u> <u>alexandre</u> <u>gustave</u> <u>eiffel</u>, who also designed the <u>eiffel</u> <u>tower</u> in <u>paris</u>. [7] None of us knew that <u>john</u> <u>wilkes</u> <u>booth</u> was only twenty-six years old when he shot <u>president</u> <u>lincoln</u> at <u>ford's</u> <u>theater</u> on <u>good</u> <u>friday</u> in 1865. [8] Mom, who's a loyal <u>democrat</u>, knew that *<u>engine</u> 1401*—the <u>southern</u> <u>railways</u> locomotive that carried <u>franklin</u> <u>d.</u> <u>roosevelt's</u> body from <u>warm</u> <u>springs</u>, <u>georgia</u>, to <u>washington</u>, <u>d.c.</u>—can now be seen in the <u>smithsonian</u> <u>institution</u>.

[9] Ted and I lost some points because I didn't know that <u>kleenex</u> tissues were first used as gas-mask filters during <u>world</u> <u>war</u> I. [10] But Ted won the game for us by remembering that the <u>white</u> <u>house</u> was called the <u>executive</u> <u>mansion</u> before it was burned by the <u>british</u> during the <u>war</u> of 1812.

PICTURE THIS

The year is 1850. After seeing this handbill, you and a friend decided to sign on as deckhands on the Mississippi River steamboat. Your friend, however, backed out at the

NOW HIRING
★ Deck Hands ★
★ Roustabouts ★
Wages Paid In
$ CASH $
STEAMER
ROBT E. LEE
Leave St. Louis for New Orleans
Friday, July 9th at 8:30 A.M.

MEETING *individual* **NEEDS**

LEP/ESL

General Strategies. In the **Picture This** activity, students are asked to describe a trip down the Mississippi River. Students might prefer to describe trips down rivers in their native countries. These travelogues, if read aloud, would give everyone in the class a glimpse of life in other parts of the world.

PICTURE THIS

For this assignment, students might need background material to add descriptive detail to their letters. Consider reading to the class excerpts from Mark Twain's *Life on the Mississippi*, which draws on Twain's experience as a riverboat crewman.

last minute. You've just completed your first trip down the river from St. Louis to New Orleans. Using this map, write a letter to your friend describing your experiences on the trip. Give reasons why your friend should (or should not) sign on for the next trip. In your letter, use a combined total of at least ten proper nouns and proper adjectives.

Subject: working as a deckhand on a steamboat
Audience: a friend
Purpose: to persuade

The Granger Collection, New York.

24e. Capitalize titles.

(1) Capitalize the title of a person when it comes before a name.

EXAMPLES **G**eneral Powell **D**r. Sakamoto **P**resident Kennedy

Do not capitalize a title used alone or following a name, especially if the title is preceded by *a*, *an*, or *the*.

EXAMPLES In 1987, Wilma Mankiller became the first woman elected **p**rincipal **c**hief of the Cherokee Nation of Oklahoma.
Who was **p**resident during World War II?
Ann Richards became the **g**overnor of Texas in 1991.

MEETING *individual* **NEEDS**

LEP/ESL

General Strategies. You may need to explain the term *title* to students. Students might get a clearer picture if you draw a stick figure, a book, and a painting on the chalkboard and show how each has a title. For example, you may write *Dr. Nguyen* under the stick figure, *Catcher in the Rye* under the book, and *American Gothic* under the painting.

When a title is used without a person's name in direct address, it is usually capitalized.

EXAMPLES   **Ms. M**ayor, will you please test the microphone?
Do you intend to visit the disaster area, **G**overnor?
Please be seated, **S**ir [or sir].

NOTE: For special emphasis or clarity, writers sometimes capitalize a title used alone or following a person's name.

EXAMPLES   The **G**overnor firmly stated her opinion on the issue.
According to the **P**resident, America needs to strengthen its industrial base.

(2) Capitalize words showing family relationship when used with a person's name but *not* when preceded by a possessive.

EXAMPLES   **A**unt Edith, **U**ncle Fred, **G**randmother Bechtel,
my **b**rother, your **c**ousin Louise, Maria's **n**iece

(3) Capitalize the first and last words and all important words in titles and subtitles of books, periodicals, poems, stories, plays, historical documents, movies, radio and television programs, works of art, and musical compositions.

Unimportant words in a title include

- articles: *a, an, the*
- short prepositions (fewer than five letters): *of, to, in, for, from, with*
- coordinating conjunctions: *and, but, so, nor, or, yet, for*

TYPE OF TITLE	EXAMPLES
Books	*Songs of the Tewa* *One of the Lucky Ones* *Silent Dancing: A Partial Remembrance of a Puerto Rican Childhood*
Periodicals	*U.S. News & World Report* *Chicago Sun-Times*

(continued)

MECHANICS

MECHANICS

INTEGRATING THE LANGUAGE ARTS

Literature Link. Contrast the traditional capitalization pattern of a Gwendolyn Brooks poem with that of an E. E. Cummings poem that does not conform to capitalization rules.

Ask students for ideas about the effects of capitalization patterns in poetry. [A possible response is that a humorous or whimsical tone is heightened by using lowercase letters at the beginning of lines of poetry.]

TYPE OF TITLE	EXAMPLES
Poems	"Love Without Love" "I Like to See It Lap the Miles"
Stories	"The Man to Send Rain Clouds" "The Woman Who Had No Eye for Small Details"
Plays	*A Raisin in the Sun* *Life with Father* *Sunday in the Park with George*
Historical Documents	Treaty of Versailles Emancipation Proclamation Charter of the United Nations
Movies	*Lean on Me* *North by Northwest* *The Corn Is Green*
Radio and Television Programs	*War of the Worlds* *Face the Nation* *You Can't Do That on Television*
Works of Art	*Crossing the Brook* *Two Mexican Women and Child*
Musical Compositions	"Ebony and Ivory" *Pictures at an Exhibition* *Amahl and the Night Visitors*

NOTE: The words *a, an,* and *the* written before a title are capitalized only when they are the first word of the title. They are usually not capitalized, however, at the beginning of the names of most magazines and newspapers.

EXAMPLES   Last summer, Joan read *The Outsiders* and *A Day in the Life of President Kennedy*.
Joan reads *The Atlantic Monthly* and the *Rocky Mountain News*.

 REFERENCE NOTE: For information about which titles should be italicized and which should be placed in quotation marks, see pages 831–832 and 840.

(4) Capitalize names of religions and their followers, holy days and celebrations, holy writings, and specific deities.

778

REVIEWS C and D

OBJECTIVES
- To correct sentences by capitalizing words
- To proofread paragraphs for correct capitalization

TYPE OF NAME	EXAMPLES	
Religions and Followers	Judaism Buddhism Christianity	Muslim Taoist Mormon
Holy Days and Celebrations	Ash Wednesday Ramadan Yom Kippur	Hanukkah Potlatch Pentecost
Holy Writings	the Bible the Talmud the Koran	Rig-Veda Exodus Dead Sea Scrolls
Specific Deities	Allah God	Vishnu the Holy Spirit

The words *god* and *goddess* are not capitalized when they refer to the deities of ancient mythology. The names of specific mythological deities are capitalized, however.

EXAMPLE   **Ceres was the Roman goddess of grain.**

NOTE: Some writers capitalize all pronouns that refer to the Deity. Other writers capitalize such pronouns only to prevent confusion.

EXAMPLE   Job wondered why the Lord allowed His servant to suffer.

REVIEW C   ### Correcting Sentences by Capitalizing Words

If the capitalization of a sentence is correct, write *C*. If not, write the correct form of each word that needs correcting.
Words that should be capitalized or lowercased are underscored.

1. At the <u>hirshhorn</u> <u>museum</u> in <u>washington</u>, <u>d.c.</u>, we saw one of <u>georgia</u> <u>o'keeffe's</u> finest paintings, *<u>cow's</u> <u>skull</u>: <u>red</u>, <u>white</u>, and <u>blue</u>*.
2. In *<u>people</u>* magazine, Kim read about <u>bill</u> <u>cosby's</u> previous television series *<u>the</u> <u>cosby</u> <u>show</u>* and his new one, *<u>cosby</u>*.
3. When I visited <u>grandma</u> Sánchez at <u>white</u> <u>sparrow</u> Hospital, I read to her from <u>jimmy</u> <u>santiago</u> <u>baca's</u> *<u>martín</u>* and *<u>meditations</u> on the <u>south</u> <u>valley</u>*.
4. In 1908, <u>mary</u> <u>baker</u> <u>eddy</u> founded the *<u>christian</u> <u>science</u> <u>monitor</u>*.

COOPERATIVE LEARNING
Divide the class into groups of no more than five students. Ask them to write skits with roles for mythological characters from any cultures they choose. Each student should be responsible for creating dialogue for at least one character. Ask groups to hand in copies of the skits so that you can check for understanding of the appropriate capitalization rules.

You may want to have the groups perform their skits for the class.

MECHANICS

MECHANICS

5. My cousin Judy's favorite statue is <u>*indian*</u> <u>*hunter*</u> by <u>paul</u> <u>manship</u>.
6. I enjoyed reading <u>annie</u> <u>dillard's</u> <u>*pilgrim*</u> *at* <u>*tinker*</u> <u>*creek*</u>, particularly the chapter "<u>the</u> <u>horns</u> of the <u>altar</u>."
7. Prize-winning journalist <u>carl</u> <u>t</u>. <u>rowan</u> was the first <u>african</u> <u>american</u> to serve on the National Security <u>council</u>.
8. The <u>president</u> addressed the <u>american</u> people in a television news broadcast after he had met with the president of France.
9. Last week <u>mayor</u> <u>johnson</u> and the county commissioners attended the groundbreaking ceremony for the new hospital.
10. Jane White, president of our <u>latin</u> <u>club</u>, showed us a videotape of <u>*julius*</u> <u>*caesar*</u>.

▶ REVIEW D   **Proofreading Paragraphs for Correct Capitalization**

If the capitalization in a sentence is correct, write C. If not, write the correct form of each word that needs correcting.
Words that should be capitalized or lowercased are underscored.
EXAMPLE   [1] The energetic personality of montana's former state Senator from the Fiftieth District is obvious in this painting by Christopher Magadini.
     1. *Montana's, senator*

[1] Bill Yellowtail, <u>jr</u>., the first member of the <u>crows</u> to serve in the <u>State</u> <u>Senate</u>, represented an area hit hard by drought and a decline in the demand for beef. [2] Yellowtail, a <u>democrat</u>, ran for office to help save the <u>Area's</u> remaining small family farms and ranches. [3] A <u>Rancher</u> himself, he raises cattle in the Lodge Grass <u>valley</u> in <u>Southeastern</u> Montana with his <u>Mother</u>, his brother, and his sister.

[4] Yellowtail supplements his income from ranching by guiding fly-fishing trips on the Bighorn <u>river</u>. [5] In addition, he works as a <u>Tour</u> <u>Guide</u> on the Crow reservation and at the Custer <u>battlefield</u> <u>national</u> <u>monument</u>. [6] He has also served as a consultant for the Montana-<u>wyoming</u> Agriculture-Tourism Project, as a member of the

<u>Board</u> of <u>Directors</u> of the Nature Conservancy, and as the director of the Environmental <u>protection</u> <u>agency</u>.

[7] After graduating from Lodge Grass <u>high</u> <u>school</u> at the head of his class, Yellowtail attended <u>dartmouth</u> College in <u>hanover</u>, New Hampshire. [8] Although Dartmouth was founded to educate <u>american</u> Indians, Yellowtail was the first <u>native</u> <u>american</u> to enroll there in twenty years. [9] At first he was unprepared academically, but by the time he graduated in 1971, he was on the <u>Dean's</u> list. [10] Regarding his major subject, <u>Geography</u>, Yellowtail says, "<u>the</u> relationship between humanity and the environment is little understood; it's a <u>Discipline</u> we very much need today."

VISUAL CONNECTIONS

Related Expression Skills. Ask students to create a montage or a collage of an individual they know. They should combine a photograph with other illustrations that connect the person's image to a wider environment. Then you may want students to write a paragraph that explains the collage, with details that include proper nouns and proper adjectives.

WRITING APPLICATION

OBJECTIVE

• To write an informative guidebook addressed to a specific audience

WRITING APPLICATION

Using Capital Letters Correctly

Capital letters are signals. They let your readers know that you're starting a new sentence or that you're referring to a specific person, place, or thing. Notice how the use of capital letters affects the meaning in the following examples:

> To reach the old pioneer settlement, cross the little Yellow River and turn right at the sandy road exit.
>
> To reach the Old Pioneer Settlement, cross the Little Yellow River and turn right at the Sandy Road exit.

▶ WRITING ACTIVITY

You've been asked to write a guidebook for a group of visitors from your town's sister city in Japan. Write an informative booklet that helps your visitors take a brief walking or driving tour through your town.

Prewriting List the sights you'll include in your guidebook. (If you live in a small town, you may want to include some nearby points of interest. If yours is a large city, you'll have to limit the tour to only one part of town or only main sights.) For information on the town's history, you may want to check the local library.

Writing As you write your first draft, keep in mind that this is your guests' first visit. Try to anticipate their questions without overloading them with details. If you'd like to, sketch a map of your tour with the various stops labeled.

Evaluating and Revising Take a friend on a trial run of the tour. Is the route you've chosen a sensible one? Have you included enough information about each point of interest, and is the information correct? If you made a map, be sure to check it, too. Then add, delete, change, or rearrange items to make your guide book clearer and more interesting.

Proofreading and Publishing Proofread your guidebook carefully, paying special attention to the correct use of capital letters. Remember to proofread your map if you included

---

WRITING APPLICATION

Writing guidebooks will require students to use proper nouns and adjectives as they describe features and attractions in their town. You may wish to refer your students to **Chapters 5** and **7** for information about using descriptive detail and writing to inform.

CRITICAL THINKING

Analysis. Remind students that their audience will probably not be familiar with American slang or jargon. Directions must be stated with absolute precision. Students should analyze their material to correct ambiguities.

PREWRITING

Remind students that their Japanese audience will probably be interested in aspects of American life that Americans take for granted. Tell students to check community calendars for special events and exhibits that illustrate regional American culture and history. An arts-and-crafts fair or a regional foods festival could provide a central theme for the guidebook.

EVALUATING AND REVISING

If available, word-processing programs allow students a great deal of flexibility in revising their work. However, students should be reminded that spell-checker and grammar-checker options are not foolproof. Most systems are not capable of recognizing proper nouns or capitalization errors.

REVIEW: POSTTEST

OBJECTIVES

- To capitalize sentences correctly
- To capitalize sentences in a paragraph correctly

one. Naturally, you'll also want to make sure that your grammar and usage are faultless for the visitors. After sharing your guidebook with your classmates, you could compile a larger guide to your town or city and give it to new students. You could also offer copies to the local chamber of commerce or historical society.

Review: Posttest

A. Capitalizing Sentences Correctly

For each of the following sentences, write the <u>words that should be capitalized</u>.

EXAMPLE   **1.** Renée searched everywhere in freeport, maine, until she found a gift at l. l. bean for her grandparents.
      1. *Freeport, Maine, L. L. Bean*

1. The title of her new television special, which airs next fall, is *one in a million.*
2. Both <u>ernest</u> <u>hemingway</u> and <u>walt</u> <u>disney</u> once worked for the *kansas city star.*
3. Every <u>thanksgiving</u> <u>day</u> before dinner, <u>grandma</u> <u>penny</u> sings "<u>we</u> <u>praise</u> <u>thee</u>, <u>o</u> <u>god</u>, <u>our</u> <u>redeemer</u>, <u>creator</u>," which was translated from the <u>german</u> by <u>julia</u> <u>b.</u> <u>cady</u> <u>cory</u>.
4. In 1982, <u>colombian</u> writer <u>gabriel</u> <u>garcía</u> <u>márquez</u> was awarded the <u>nobel</u> <u>prize</u> in literature.
5. The winner of the first <u>kentucky</u> <u>derby</u>, the annual race at <u>churchill</u> <u>downs</u> in <u>louisville</u>, was a horse named <u>aristides</u>.
6. In 1983, <u>sally</u> <u>ride</u> became the first <u>american</u> woman in space when the space shuttle *challenger* was launched from <u>cape</u> <u>canaveral</u>, <u>florida</u>.
7. One of the cities of the <u>incas</u>, <u>machu</u> <u>picchu</u>, lay hidden among the <u>andes</u> <u>mountains</u> in southern <u>peru</u> and was never discovered by the <u>spanish</u> conquerors.

8. Frederick <u>douglass</u> was the first <u>african american</u> member of the <u>department</u> of <u>justice's</u> <u>u.s.</u> <u>marshals service</u>.
9. If Beth passes <u>english</u> and <u>history</u> II, her parents will let her apply for a job at the 7-<u>eleven</u> store on <u>forty</u>-third <u>street</u>.
10. Our debate team argued in favor of pro-<u>american</u> economic policies as the best way to foster democracy in the developing countries of <u>africa</u>, <u>asia</u>, and <u>south america</u>.

B. Capitalizing a Paragraph Correctly

For each sentence in the following paragraph, write the <u>words that should be capitalized</u>.

EXAMPLE [1] Last summer we visited my uncle carlos, who lives in new york city.
  1. *Uncle Carlos, New York City*

[11] One of <u>new york city's</u> most popular tourist attractions is the <u>empire state building</u>. [12] The building, at <u>fifth avenue</u> and <u>thirty</u>-fourth <u>street</u>, attracts 2,500,000 visitors a year. [13] Among them are troops of <u>boy scouts</u> and <u>girl scouts</u>, who camp out on the eighty-sixth floor. [14] The building was financed by <u>john jacob raskob</u>, the founder of <u>general motors</u>. [15] It opened in 1931, during the <u>great depression</u>. [16] At the time, it was the tallest building on earth (1,250 feet), but it's since been overshadowed by the <u>world trade center</u> (1,350 feet) and by <u>chicago's sears tower</u> (1,450 feet). [17] The observatory on the one hundred and second floor accounts for much of the <u>empire state building's</u> continuing appeal; when the weather is clear, it provides a view of five states: <u>new york</u>, <u>new jersey</u>, <u>connecticut</u>, <u>pennsylvania</u>, and <u>massachusetts</u>. [18] On <u>may</u> 1, 1991, publicists threw a party to mark the building's sixtieth birthday. [19] One of those who attended was actress <u>fay wray</u>, who starred in the 1933 movie *<u>king kong</u>*, in which the building was featured. [20] Another attendee was <u>jack brod</u>, one of the original tenants, who proclaimed of the building, "<u>it's</u> got history woven into it."

SUMMARY STYLE REVIEW

Names of Persons

Mrs. Andrew D. McCall, Jr.	a family friend
Sean Jackson	the boy next door
Mr. Hank Bluehouse	a guidance counselor

Geographical Names

Kansas City	a city in Missouri
Cook County	a county in Illinois
Diego Garcia Island	an island in the Indian Ocean
Rocky Mountains	a mountain range
Arctic Ocean	on the ocean floor
Seventy-first Street	a busy street
Torreya State Park	a state park
in the West, South, Midwest	turning west, south, north

Organizations, Business Firms, Institutions, Government Bodies

Perfect Harmony Glee Club	a choral club
Head over Heels, Inc.	a gymnastics training center
Lane High School	an inner-city high school
Supreme Court	a federal court
Department of the Treasury	a department of government

Historical Events and Periods, Special Events, Calendar Items

the Vietnam War	a long war
the Ice Age	a prehistoric age
the World Series	a series of baseball games
Memorial Day	a national holiday
March, June, September, December	spring, summer, autumn, winter

Nationalities, Races, Religions

Australian	a nationality
Caucasian	a race
Christianity	a religion
God	myths about the Greek gods

(continued)

MECHANICS

MECHANICS

MECHANICS

MECHANICS

SUMMARY STYLE REVIEW *(continued)*	
Brand Names	
Chevrolet Blazer	an automobile
Amana	a refrigerator
Other Particular Places, Things, Events, Awards	
Enterprise	an aircraft carrier
Silver Streak	a train
Discovery	a spacecraft
Bancroft Prize in History	an award
the **Milky Way**	a galaxy
Earth, Mercury, Neptune	here on earth
the **Lincoln Memorial**	a memorial in Washington
Junior Prom	a junior in high school
Medal of Freedom	a cherished medal
Specific Courses, Languages	
Carpentry I	after carpentry class
Japanese	a foreign language
World History II	a history test
Titles	
Mayor Feinstein	a mayor
the **President of the United States**	the president of the club
the **Prince of Wales**	a prince's hobby
Uncle Jim	her uncle
The Color Purple	a novel
the *Sacramento Bee*	a daily newspaper
Holy Bible	a religious book

DIAGNOSTIC TEST

OBJECTIVE

- To correct sentences by adding end marks and commas

PROGRAM MANAGER

FOR THE WHOLE CHAPTER

- **Review** For exercises on chapter concepts, see **Review Form A** and **Review Form B** in *Language Skills Practice and Assessment,* pp. 201–202.

- **Assessment** For additional testing, see **Mechanics Pretests** and **Mechanics Mastery Tests** in *Language Skills Practice and Assessment,* pp. 169–177 and pp. 265–271.

25 PUNCTUATION

End Marks and Commas

MECHANICS

CHAPTER OVERVIEW

This chapter contains rules for using end marks and commas. The first section reviews the use of end marks and their role as indicators of the purpose of sentences, as well as the use of periods in abbreviations. The remainder of the chapter deals with the use of commas to set off items in a series, adjectives preceding a noun, independent clauses, certain introductory elements, non-essential phrases, clauses, and inter-rupters. Comma usage in conventional situations is also covered. The **Writing Application** challenges students to apply their knowledge of end marks to the creation of instructions for an original game. You may wish to refer to the chapter throughout the year and make individual assignments as students' writing reveals their needs.

Diagnostic Test

Correcting Sentences by Adding End Marks and Commas

Add end marks and commas where they are needed in the following sentences.   Optional commas are circled.

EXAMPLE   **1.** Well what do you want me to say
　　　　　1. *Well, what do you want me to say?*

1. Although scholars aren't certain about who was the first European printer to use movable type，Johann Gutenberg is usually credited⊙
2. The students who have signed up for the field trip may leave at noon，but all others must attend classes⊙
3. Gloria，did you notice where I left my bowling ball and bowling shoes**?**
4. Miriam Colón，who was born in Puerto Rico，founded the Puerto Rican Traveling Theatre.

MECHANICS

USING THE DIAGNOSTIC TEST

If students are having problems with using end marks or commas correctly in writing, you can use the results of this test to pinpoint error patterns and specific strengths and weaknesses. You can then assign practice accordingly.

5. The Great Pyramid in Egypt was built sometime between 2600 and 2500 B.C.

6. Vendors sold T-shirts, buttons, caps, and pennants to the sports fans outside the stadium.

7. Listening to my friend's grandfather talk about the Mexican Revolution, I realized that I'm proud to be Mexican American.

8. The hikers munched on unsalted sunflower seeds and quenched their thirst with ice-cold, refreshing spring water.

9. Their address, I think, is 1042 Cleveland Ave., Enid, OK 73703.

10. Marian Anderson, a contralto, was the first African American to become a permanent member of the Metropolitan Opera Company.

11. Rita did not call me this morning, nor did she call in the afternoon.

12. We rushed to the airport, stood in line, bought our tickets, and then heard that the flight would be delayed for three hours.

13. Norm has had an incredible run of bad luck, yet he still says that tomorrow will be a better day, for he prides himself on being an optimist.

14. The Ming vase, wrapped in cotton and packed in a crate, was delivered to the museum today.

15. If we're late for practice again, however, Ms. Stubbs will kick us off the team.

16. How lucky I was that my sister had taught me how to swim, for I could have drowned when the boat tipped over!

17. Early in the eighteenth century Chikamatsu Monzaemon wrote the first Japanese tragedies to focus on the lives of common, ordinary people.

18. Nowadays the Sioux, generally speaking, make their living as farmers and ranchers.

19. Jan Matzeliger, an inventor in Lynn, Massachusetts, revolutionized the shoe industry in 1883 with his machine that joined the top of a shoe to its sole.

20. These four students should report to the auditorium after lunch: Bob Wilcox, Amalia Gibson, Cora Mall, and Phil Assad, Jr.

MECHANICS

MECHANICS

END MARKS Rules 25a–25e

OBJECTIVE

• To correct sentences by adding appropriate end marks

In speaking, your tone of voice, your pauses, and your gestures and facial expressions help you express yourself. In writing, punctuation marks help you communicate these elements.

End Marks

End marks—periods, question marks, and exclamation points—indicate the purpose of a sentence. Periods are also used in many abbreviations.

☞ **REFERENCE NOTE:** For information on how sentences are classified according to purpose, see pages 565–566.

25a. A statement (*or* declarative sentence) is followed by a period.

EXAMPLES   Margaret Walker's poems celebrate the trials and triumphs of African Americans.
Barb asked who could give her a ride home.

As the second example above shows, a declarative sentence containing an indirect question is followed by a period.

25b. A question (*or* interrogative sentence) is followed by a question mark.

EXAMPLES   What score did you get on the road test?
Weren't you nervous?

A direct question should be followed by a question mark even if its word order is like that of a declarative sentence.

EXAMPLES   You got what score on the road test?
You weren't nervous?

NOTE: Be sure to distinguish between a declarative sentence that contains an indirect question and an interrogative sentence, which asks a direct question.

INDIRECT QUESTION   She asked me who nominated him.
[declarative]
DIRECT QUESTION   Who nominated him? [interrogative]

PROGRAM MANAGER

END MARKS

■ **Independent Practice/ Reteaching** For instruction and exercises, see **Using End Marks** in *Language Skills Practice and Assessment*, p. 193.

■ **Computer Guided Instruction** For additional instruction and practice with using end marks, see **Lesson 38** in *Language Workshop CD-ROM.*

■ **Practice** To help less-advanced students with additional instruction and practice with using end marks, see **Chapter 20** in *English Workshop, Fourth Course,* pp. 273–274.

✔ **QUICK REMINDER**

Write on the chalkboard the following sentences, omitting the end marks:

1. The parachute failed to open!
2. Please be calm.
3. Are you all right?

Ask students to identify the purposes of these sentences (to state, to question, to exclaim, or to command or request) and to suggest end marks that convey these purposes.

LEP/ESL

Spanish. Exclamation points and question marks are used somewhat differently in Spanish than they are in English. In Spanish these marks are used at the beginnings of sentences as well as at the ends and are inverted at the beginnings of sentences. Students who have been learning English for some time will probably already be familiar with the English format, but students who are beginning to learn English may need practice in making this shift in punctuation.

COOPERATIVE LEARNING

Divide the class into groups of three or four and have the members of each group collaborate to write a very short story. Students should omit end marks of any kind in their final drafts. Have groups exchange papers to supply end marks. Encourage students to try to create sentences that invite various interpretations when not punctuated.

INTEGRATING THE LANGUAGE ARTS

Punctuation and Capitalization. **Exercise 1** asks students to write the first words of the sentences that follow the end marks they add. You could take this opportunity to remind students of the punctuation rule requiring that the first words of sentences be capitalized.

25c. An exclamation is followed by an exclamation point.

EXAMPLES   Great shot**!**
Oh, no**!** Not again**!**

Declarative and interrogative sentences that express strong emotion may be followed by an exclamation point instead of a period or a question mark.

EXAMPLES   There you are**!**
Why are you always late**!**

25d. An imperative sentence is followed by either a period or an exclamation point.

EXAMPLES   Open the door, please**.**
Open the door**!**

An imperative sentence may be stated in the form of a question. However, since its purpose is to give a command or make a request, it should be followed by a period or an exclamation point.

EXAMPLES   May I have your attention, please**.**
Will you pay attention**!**

EXERCISE 1   Correcting Sentences by Adding End Marks

For each of the following paragraphs, write each <u>word that should be followed by an end mark</u>, and add the appropriate end mark. Then, if a sentence follows the end mark, write the first word of that sentence.

Triple underscores indicate capitalization.

EXAMPLE   **[1]**   What striking costumes the musicians on the next page are wearing they're members of *Campanas de América*, a mariachi group in San Antonio, Texas

    1.   *wearing! They're; Texas.*

[1] Have you ever heard mariachi <u>music</u>**?**this lively, infectious music originated in central <u>Mexico</u>**.**
[2] Before the nineteenth century, Mexican music was played by string ensembles or wind <u>bands</u>**.**around 1800 the two types of groups <u>merged</u>**.**the resulting sound came to be known as <u>mariachi</u>**.**

[3] As social gatherings became larger, brass instruments such as cornets and trumpets were added adding the brasses made the music easier to hear above the sounds of dancing usually only the lyrics of the songs were written down younger players learned the melodies by ear did you know that some schools now offer courses in Mexican folk music and award academic credit for playing in a mariachi ensemble? colleges, junior and senior high schools, and even elementary schools are incorporating mariachi music into the curriculum

[4] Now young mariachi players are studying music theory and writing their own mariachi music, sometimes adding instruments such as trombones, fluegelhorns, and accordions consequently, mariachi is changing some older players dislike the changes most people, however, applaud the music's new flexibility they ask how mariachi can grow if it doesn't change

[5] And growing is just what mariachi's doing it's becoming more popular each year in fact, the annual mariachi festival filled California's eighteen-thousand-seat Hollywood Bowl when the festival was launched in 1990 what an exciting event that must have been!

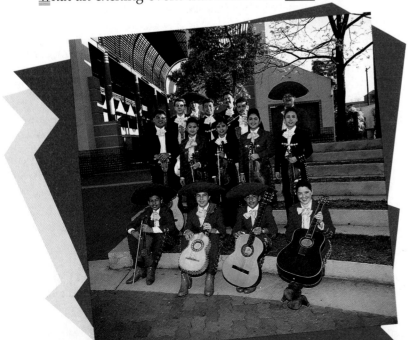

MECHANICS

VISUAL CONNECTIONS

Ideas for Writing. Mariachi music's growing popularity is just one example of new interest in the rich and varied contributions of diverse ethnic groups to United States culture.

Have students write expressive/descriptive paragraphs about their favorite contributions to culture in the United States by ethnic groups other than their own. For example, students could write about a type of food that they enjoy, such as Vietnamese food; a type of music, such as Jamaican reggae; or a holiday, such as St. Patrick's Day.

MECHANICS

OBJECTIVE

- To write original sentences that correctly use the three types of end marks

COMMON ERROR

Problem. Students might confuse abbreviations with acronyms.

Solution. Explain that while an abbreviation is usually a shortened form of one word and is followed by a period, an acronym is a shortened form of a series of words and is not followed by a period.

Examples of acronyms are *NASA* (National Aeronautics and Space Administration) and *radar* (radio detecting and ranging).

Tell students to list five acronyms each and to give the series of words represented by each acronym.

INTEGRATING THE LANGUAGE ARTS

Mechanics and Dictionary Skills. Explain to students that abbreviations like *Mr.* are alphabetized as if they were unabbreviated. For example, *Mr.* would be alphabetized with words beginning with *mi* rather than words beginning with *mr.*

25e. An abbreviation is usually followed by a period.

TYPE OF ABBREVIATION	EXAMPLES		
Personal Names	W.E.B. DuBois W. H. Auden	Susan B. Anthony N. Scott Momaday	
Organizations and Companies	Assn. Co.	Corp. Inc.	Ltd. Org.
Titles Used with Names	Mr. Ms.	Mrs. Jr.	Dr. Ph.D.
Time of Day	A.M.	P.M.	
Years	B.C. (written after the date) A.D. (written before the date)		
Addresses	Ave. Blvd.	St. Rd.	Pkwy. P.O. Box
States	Calif. Ind.	Tex. Fla.	Mass. N.Y.

NOTE: Two-letter state codes are used only when the ZIP Code is included. Two-letter state codes are not followed by periods.

EXAMPLE   Nashville, TN 37201

When an abbreviation that ends with a period comes at the end of a statement, do not add another period as an end mark. *Do* add a question mark or an exclamation point if one is needed.

EXAMPLES   The history of Egypt dates back to before 3000 B.C.
When did she move to St. Louis, Mo.?

Many common abbreviations, especially for units of measurement, are often written without periods. However, you should use a period with the abbreviation *in.* (for *inch*) to prevent confusing it with the word *in.*

EXAMPLES   TV, OK, VCR, CD, DNA, NAACP, UN, IQ, YWCA, COBOL
mph, km, cm, ml, kg, hp, lb, rpm, cc, psi

NOTE: Most abbreviations are capitalized only if the words they stand for are capitalized. If you're not sure whether to use periods with an abbreviation or whether to capitalize it, look it up in a dictionary.

OBJECTIVES

- To proofread sentences and to add commas to separate items in a series and to separate two or more adjectives preceding a noun
- To proofread sentences and to add commas to separate independent clauses joined by coordinating conjunctions

▶ REVIEW A **Using End Marks**

This chart shows the results of a 1990 *TV Guide* poll that asked people what types of TV shows they'd be willing to pay to see. Write five sentences expressing your reactions to the poll's results. Use each type of end mark—period, question mark, and exclamation point—at least once.

EXAMPLE **1.** *Why didn't the poll ask about science fiction shows?*

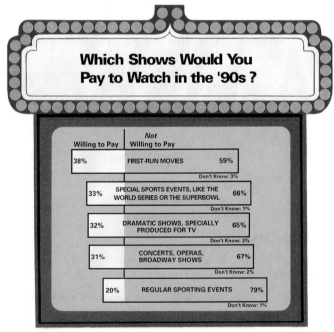

Commas

Items in a Series

25f. Use commas to separate items in a series.

EXAMPLES The camp counselor distributed baseballs, bats, volleyballs, tennis rackets, and bandages. [words]

We have a government of the people, by the people, and for the people. [phrases]

I know I will pass the test if I take good notes, if I study hard, and if I get a good night's sleep. [clauses]

ANSWERS

Review A

Students' sentences should express their reactions to the poll's results. Be sure that students have used the three types of end marks correctly.

PROGRAM MANAGER

COMMAS

- **Independent Practice/ Reteaching** For instruction and exercises, see **Commas and Items in a Series, Commas to Separate Adjectives, Commas to Join Clauses, Commas with Non-essential Elements, Commas with Introductory Elements, Commas with Elements that Interrupt,** and **Other Uses of Commas** in *Language Skills Practice and Assessment,* pp. 194–200.

- **Computer Guided Instruction** For additional instruction and practice with using commas, see **Lessons 34–36** in *Language Workshop CD-ROM.*

- **Practice** To help less-advanced students with additional instruction and practice with using commas, see **Chapter 20** in *English Workshop, Fourth Course,* pp. 277–288.

MECHANICS

- To proofread sentences and to add commas to set off nonessential phrases and clauses
- To proofread sentences and to add commas after certain introductory elements
- To proofread sentences and to add commas to set off nonrestrictive appositives and appositive phrases
- To proofread sentences and to add commas in certain conventional situations
- To write a dialogue that uses end marks and commas correctly

MECHANICS

QUICK REMINDER

Write the following sentences on the chalkboard and have students tell you where commas should be inserted:

1. I met Bette who lives next door yesterday.
2. Bette knows the names biographical dates and accomplishments of the leaders of the civil rights movement.
3. She has a photo of Martin Luther King Jr. but she also wants a poster of him.

MEETING *individual* **NEEDS**

LEP/ESL

General Strategies. English-language learners typically retain those aspects of the English language that they can use immediately, especially those aspects that best support their ability to communicate needs and desires. Knowing when and where to insert commas may not seem particularly useful or meaningful to them. When introducing students to standard punctuation, keep in mind the very different sets of learning priorities that they may bring to the classroom.

MECHANICS

794 *Punctuation*

When the last two items in a series are joined by *and*, you may omit the comma before the *and* if the comma isn't needed to make the meaning clear.

CLEAR WITHOUT COMMA   The entertainers sang, danced and juggled.

NOT CLEAR WITHOUT COMMA   John, Sue and Mary went fishing.
[Did John go fishing, or is he being addressed?]

CLEAR WITH COMMA   John, Sue, and Mary went fishing.

NOTE: Some words—such as *macaroni and cheese* and *law and order*—are paired so often that they may be considered one item in a series.

EXAMPLE   For lunch we could order a sandwich, macaroni and cheese, or soup.

(1) If all items in a series are joined by *and, or,* or *nor,* do not use commas to separate them.

EXAMPLES   We ran **and** walked **and** even limped to the finish line.
Neither poverty **nor** discrimination **nor** lack of encouragement prevented Alice Walker from becoming an accomplished writer.

(2) Independent clauses in a series are usually separated by semicolons. Short independent clauses, however, may be separated by commas.

EXAMPLES   To prepare for the race, we swam twenty-five laps in the pool; we jogged four miles around the lake; and we exercised with workout equipment.
We swam, we jogged, and we exercised.

☞ REFERENCE NOTE: Also see rule 25h on page 796.

25g. Use a comma to separate two or more adjectives preceding a noun.

EXAMPLE   I've had a long, hectic, tiring day.

When the last adjective before a noun is thought of as part of the noun, omit the comma before the adjective.

EXAMPLE   I mailed the package at the main post office.
For lunch we had smooth, creamy broccoli soup.

Compound nouns such as *post office* and *broccoli soup* are considered single units rather than two separate words.

You can use two tests to determine whether an adjective and a noun form a unit.

TEST 1: Insert the word *and* between the adjectives. If *and* fits sensibly between them, use a comma. In the first example above, *and* cannot be logically inserted: *main and post office*. In the second sentence, *and* sounds sensible between the first two adjectives (*smooth and creamy*) but not between the second and third (*creamy and broccoli*).

TEST 2: Change the order of the adjectives. If the order of the adjectives can be reversed sensibly, use a comma. *Creamy, smooth broccoli soup* makes sense, but *broccoli creamy soup* and *post main office* do not.

EXERCISE 2   Correcting Sentences by Adding Commas

Write each <u>word that should be followed by a comma</u>, and then add the comma. If a comma may or may not be used, circle the word and the comma. If a sentence is correct, write *C*.

EXAMPLE   **1.** The singer wore a red vest blue shoes and white jeans.
1. *vest, shoes,*

1. I was late because my alarm clock didn't go <u>off,</u> we were out of <u>milk,</u> and the school bus had a flat tire.
2. The river overflowed again and filled our basement and our neighbors' basements. **2.** C
3. <u>Coriander,</u> cumin, and saffron are three spices widely used in traditional Mexican cooking.
4. I took a <u>flashlight,</u> a sleeping <u>bag,</u> extra tennis <u>shoes,</u> a pocket knife, and a parka on our camping trip.
5. Magic <u>Johnson,</u> Michael <u>Jordan,</u> Larry Bird, and Julius Erving have received Most Valuable Player Awards.
6. At the gymnastics meet Les performed on the parallel <u>bars,</u> the rings, and the high bar.
7. A little blond child in faded bluejeans emerged from the shrubbery to stare at the mail carrier. **7.** C

MEETING *individual* NEEDS

STUDENTS WITH SPECIAL NEEDS

Because many students are auditory learners, read the example sentences in this lesson aloud to them so that they can hear the pauses when commas occur. Suggest that students read sentences in the exercises aloud to help themselves decide where commas should be placed.

LESS-ADVANCED STUDENTS

Since the rules in this lesson presuppose some familiarity with basic grammar terms, a quick review may be helpful. For example, you may wish to give students definitions for *independent clause, participial phrase, prepositional phrase, adverb clause,* and other terms that are found in this lesson.

8. Gwendolyn <u>Brooks</u>,Toni (Morrison)and Alice Walker have each won a Pulitzer Prize for their writing.
9. Have you read any of the novels by Jane Austen or the Brontë sisters or Virginia Woolf? **9.** C
10. With a <u>quick</u>,powerful leap, the stuntman bounded over the burning balcony.

Independent Clauses

25h. Use a comma before *and, but, or, nor, for, so,* and *yet* when they join independent clauses.

EXAMPLES   Patrick brought the sandwiches, and Cindy brought the potato salad.
We got there on time, but Jeff and María were late.

NOTE: Always use a comma before *yet, so,* or *for* joining independent clauses. The comma may be left out before *and, but, or,* and *nor* if the independent clauses are very short or if the sentence cannot be misunderstood.

EXAMPLE   I applied for the job and I got it.

Don't confuse a compound sentence with a simple sentence that has a compound verb.

SIMPLE SENTENCE   Bob brought charcoal and lighter fluid but forgot matches. [one independent clause with a compound verb]

COMPOUND SENTENCE   Bob brought charcoal and lighter fluid, but he forgot matches. [two independent clauses]

REFERENCE NOTE: For more information about simple sentences and compound sentences, see pages 610–611. For a discussion of compound subjects and compound verbs, see pages 467–468 and 554–555.

EXERCISE 3   **Correcting Compound Sentences by Adding Commas**

If a comma should be used before the conjunction, write the <u>word preceding the needed comma</u>, the comma, and the <u>conjunction</u>. If a sentence is correct, write C.

MECHANICS

MECHANICS

EXAMPLE **1.** Uncle Phil carefully steered the boat through the narrow channel and Lynn began baiting the hooks.
1. *channel, and*

1. All students must arrive on <u>time</u>͜<u>for</u> no one will be admitted late.
2. The movie review complimented all the <u>performers</u>͜ <u>but</u> the leading actress received the strongest praise.
3. A few spectators tried to climb over the <u>fence</u>͜<u>but</u> the police ordered them back.
4. The Japanese actors in Kabuki plays do not <u>speak</u>͜ <u>but</u> they pantomime lines chanted by narrators on the stage.
5. Most people today work fewer hours than their grandparents <u>did</u>͜<u>yet</u> for many there never seem to be enough hours in a day.
6. The cost of living is <u>rising</u>͜<u>for</u> consumers pay higher prices for gasoline and other products.
7. Our guide led and we followed closely. **7.** C [or <u>led</u>, <u>and</u>]
8. When two groups of Hopis disagreed about running the town of Oraibi, they settled the matter with a tug of <u>war</u>͜<u>and</u> the losers moved away and founded the town of Hotavila.
9. She said she did not like the story in the science fiction <u>magazine</u>͜<u>nor</u> did she enjoy the illustrations.
10. High school graduates may go on to college or may begin working immediately. **10.** C

Nonessential Clauses and Phrases

25i. Use commas to set off nonessential clauses and nonessential participial phrases.

A *nonessential* (or *nonrestrictive*) clause or participial phrase is one containing information that isn't needed to understand the main idea of the sentence.

NONESSENTIAL CLAUSES Emilia Ortiz**, who lives across the street from me,** won a scholarship to Stanford University.
The capital of Massachusetts is Boston**, which is sometimes called the Athens of America.**

LEARNING STYLES

Kinetic Learners. If students are having trouble deciding whether a clause or phrase is essential or nonessential, suggest that they try the following strategy:

1. Copy the sentence onto a slip of paper.
2. With scissors, cut the clause or phrase out of the sentence.
3. Piece the remaining halves of the sentence together. If the resulting sentence retains the same meaning as the original sentence, the clause or phrase is nonessential.

Visual and Auditory Learners. The activity can also be adapted for other learning styles. Visual learners could write a sentence and then bracket or mark out the clause or phrase in question. Auditory learners could read a sentence aloud, omitting the clause or phrase. In both instances, if the sentence retains its meaning without the clause or phrase, the clause or phrase is nonessential and should be set off by commas.

MECHANICS

MECHANICS

NONESSENTIAL PHRASES   Kelly**, waiting outside the stage door,** got the band leader's autograph.
Robert Hayden**, born in Detroit,** was educated at the University of Michigan and later became a distinguished professor there.

Each nonessential clause or phrase in the examples above can be left out without changing the main idea of the sentence.

EXAMPLES   Emilia Ortiz won a scholarship to Stanford University.
Boston is the capital of Massachusetts.
Kelly got the band leader's autograph.
Robert Hayden was educated at the University of Michigan and later became a distinguished professor there.

An *essential* (or *restrictive*) phrase or clause is one that can't be left out without changing the meaning of the sentence. Essential clauses and phrases are *not* set off by commas. Notice how leaving out the essential clause or phrase would change the meaning of each of the following sentences.

ESSENTIAL PHRASES   Students **planning to try out for a role in the play** should sign up no later than Friday afternoon.
Two poems **written by Lorna Dee Cervantes** are included in our literature book.

ESSENTIAL CLAUSES   The sophomores **who made the Honor Roll** were listed in the paper.
Library books **that are lost or damaged** must be paid for.

NOTE: Adjective clauses beginning with *that,* like the one in the example above, are nearly always essential.

Some clauses and participial phrases may be either essential or nonessential. The presence or absence of commas tells the reader how the clause or phrase relates to the main idea of the sentence.

NONESSENTIAL CLAUSE   Marla's sister**, who attends Stanford University,** sent her a sweatshirt. [Marla has only one sister. She sent the sweatshirt.]

ESSENTIAL CLAUSE   Marla's sister **who attends Stanford University** sent her a sweatshirt. [Marla has more than one sister. The one at Stanford sent the sweatshirt.]

NONESSENTIAL PHRASE   My former lab partner, **now living in Chicago,** visited me last week. [I have only one former lab partner. That person visited me last week.]

ESSENTIAL PHRASE   My former lab partner **now living in Chicago** visited me last week. [I have more than one former lab partner. The one from Chicago visited me last week.]

☞ REFERENCE NOTE: See Chapter 18 for more information on clauses and pages 582–583 for more on participial phrases.

▶ EXERCISE 4   **Correcting Sentences by Adding Commas**

For each of the following sentences, write each <u>word that should be followed by a comma</u>, and place a comma after it. If a sentence is correct as it is written, write C.

EXAMPLE   **1.** Gigantic supermarkets like the one on the next page which offer a stunning variety of goods and services developed from much smaller stores that first opened in the nineteenth century.
     1. *page, services,*

1. The stores that became the world's first self-serve supermarkets were designed by Clarence Saunders.   **1.** C
2. <u>Saunders,</u>who lived in Memphis, <u>Tennessee,</u>named his stores Piggly Wiggly.
3. He got the idea for the name when he saw a fat pig wiggling under a fence.   **3.** C
4. The Piggly Wiggly store that Saunders developed had only one long aisle.   **4.** C
5. Customers who shopped there saw all the products before they came to the exit.   **5.** C
6. Albert <u>Gerrard,</u>who noticed that people often had difficulty finding <u>products,</u>opened his own grocery store.
7. All of the items that were for sale were arranged alphabetically.   **7.** C

MECHANICS

INTEGRATING THE LANGUAGE ARTS

Mechanics and Writing. Tell students that they can make their writing more interesting by varying the lengths and structures of their sentences. To demonstrate the value of variation, write the following choppy paragraph on the chalkboard:

Pocahontas was an American Indian. She was the daughter of an American Indian chief. Captain John Smith said that she rescued him. He had been taken prisoner by the Indians. Later, she was taken prisoner. Colonists took her prisoner. She became a Christian. She was called Rebecca. She married a colonist. In 1616 she was taken to England. She died in England.

Have students revise the paragraph by combining some of the sentences so that sentence structures and lengths are more varied. Remind students to pay careful attention to comma usage as they combine sentences.

MECHANICS

8. The name that Gerrard selected for his store was Alpha-Beta.   **8.** C
9. George <u>Hartford</u>, who founded the Great Atlantic & Pacific Tea Company in <u>1859</u>, nicknamed his stores A & P.
10. The model for today's huge <u>supermarkets</u>, which was developed by Michael <u>Cullen</u>, opened in an abandoned garage in Queens, New York, on August 30, 1930.

Introductory Elements

25j. Use a comma after certain introductory elements.

(1) Use a comma after words such as *well, yes, no,* and *why* when they begin a sentence. Interjections such as *wow, yikes,* and *hey,* if not followed by an exclamation point, are also set off by commas.

EXAMPLES   **No,** I haven't taken the exam yet.
Sure, I'll go with you.
Wow, look at that car!

(2) Use a comma after an introductory participial phrase.

EXAMPLES   **Calling for a timeout,** the referee blew her whistle and signaled.
Exhausted after a three-mile swim, Diana emerged from the water.

A DIFFERENT APPROACH

Write the following introductory elements on the chalkboard. Have students add an independent clause and appropriate punctuation marks to each to create sentences.

1. Yikes . . .
2. Screeching harshly . . .
3. When the moon is full . . .
4. Under the magnolia tree in my yard . . .

(3) Use a comma after two or more introductory prepositional phrases.

EXAMPLE   **By the light of the harvest moon in September,** we went on an old-fashioned hayride.

A single introductory prepositional phrase does not require a comma unless the sentence could be misread or awkward to read without one.

EXAMPLES   In the book the writer develops a clever plot.
In the book, review pages 236–290.
In the book review, the critic praised the writer's clever plot.

(4) Use a comma after an introductory adverb clause.

An introductory adverb clause may appear at the beginning of a sentence or before any independent clause in the sentence.

EXAMPLES   **When you've gone to this school as long as we have,** you'll know your way around, too.
The first game of the season is Friday; **after we claim our first victory,** we'll celebrate at Darcy's Deli.

▶ EXERCISE 5   **Correcting Sentences with Introductory Elements by Adding Commas**

If a sentence lacks a comma, write the <u>word that should be followed by a comma</u>, and place a comma after it. If a sentence is correct, write *C.*

EXAMPLE   **1.** Trying to reduce the amount of fat in their diets many Americans are eating less meat.
1. *diets,*

1. For many people in the <u>world,</u>meat is not a daily food staple.
2. Serving as a main source of <u>nutrition,</u>whole grains such as corn, oats, wheat, and rice feed millions.
3. In Mexico a favorite nutritious meal is a corn tortilla and beans.   **3.** C
4. Because the soybean is high in <u>protein,</u>it has been a principal crop in Asian countries for more than five thousand years.

COOPERATIVE LEARNING
Divide the class into six groups. Have one group write at least five introductory participial phrases followed by commas; another, five interjections followed by commas; another, five adverb clauses followed by commas; and the three remaining groups, five independent clauses each—all on separate slips of paper. Mix the slips from the first three groups in one container and those from the second three groups in another. Have a student read an introductory element and then have another respond with an independent clause. You could then have students decide whether each combination expresses a complete thought.

COMMON ERROR
Problem. Students might have problems with introductory adverb clauses that are short enough to make pauses seem unnecessary, as in the sentence "When I moved here, I was very lonely."

Solution. Remind students that a dependent clause is always followed by a comma when it precedes an independent clause and have them memorize this simple formula: DC, IC.

MECHANICS

MECHANICS

802 *Punctuation*

5. If you'd like more variety in your <u>diet</u>, you may want to substitute unrefined whole grains for meat occasionally.

6. Offering healthful alternatives to <u>meat</u>, whole grains contain nutrients such as vitamins, proteins, amino acids, and starches.

7. In the process of making spoilage-resistant <u>products</u>, food manufacturers refine whole grains.

8. Refined for commercial <u>use</u>, the grains lose most of their food value because the nutritious outer hulls are stripped away.

9. If you take time in the <u>supermarket</u>, you should be able to find whole grains.

10. Since many cookbooks now include recipes for grain <u>dishes</u>, you can learn to use grains in many tasty snacks and meals.

▶ REVIEW B   **Using Commas**

For each of the following sentences, write all the <u>words that should be followed by a comma</u>. Place a comma after each one. If a comma may or may not be used after a word, circle the word and the comma.

EXAMPLE   [1]   Throughout history around the world people have used weapons for hunting for fighting and for defending themselves from wild animals.

1.   *world, hunting,* ⟨*fighting,*⟩

[1] Many weapons that were produced in early times were similar in <u>appearance</u>, ⟨function,⟩ and design. [2] The English word *weapon* is related to the Old English <u>*wæpen*</u>, the Dutch <u>*wapen*</u>, the German ⟨*Waffe*,⟩ and an earlier common root. [3] <u>Sticks</u>, ⟨stones,⟩ and natural <u>poisons</u>, such as the toxic sweat of these Central and South American <u>frogs</u>, were probably the first weapons. [4] Among those varieties of <u>weapons</u>, the stick thrown by hand became one of the most heavily specialized. [5] As you can <u>see</u>, the <u>dart</u>, the <u>arrow</u>, the <u>spear</u>, the ⟨lance,⟩ and the javelin were all developed from the stick thrown by hand. [6] Another kind of weapon, the sling, was used all over the <u>world</u>, for it was

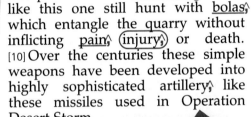

easy to make and not too difficult to master. [7] According to the Biblical account, when the Hebrew king David was just a <u>boy</u>he killed the Philistine giant Goliath with a simple handmade sling like the one shown here. [8] An unusual weapon similar to the sling is the <u>bola</u>which is a cord or thong with heavy balls of stone or wood or metal at the ends. [9] In some parts of South <u>America</u>gauchos like this one still hunt with <u>bolas</u> which entangle the quarry without inflicting <u>pain</u> injury or death. [10] Over the centuries these simple weapons have been developed into highly sophisticated artillery like these missiles used in Operation Desert Storm.

WRITING APPLICATION

Using Commas in Writing Instructions for a Game

When you talk, you punctuate your speech with pauses. When you write, you use commas to show where such pauses should occur. Commas, like pauses, indicate how parts of a sentence are related to one another. Making such relationships clear is especially important when you give directions. If commas are left out or used incorrectly, the result is an awkward or confusing sentence.

◆ WRITING APPLICATION

The **Writing Application** could be done cooperatively. Divide the class into groups of three or four. You may wish to group students according to their interests. For example, you could group students interested in science together to create a game involving science.

Each member of the group should participate in the creation of the game, and the group should submit a written version of the rules and procedures.

CRITICAL THINKING

Synthesis. This assignment requires students to synthesize previous knowledge of games with information from a subject area to create a game. To help them get started, you may want to suggest that students use the structure of a familiar game and simply change its focus. For example, the focus of a board game could be changed from acquiring money and property to saving endangered species.

WRITING

Point out to students that their knowledge of end marks and commas will be most useful in the proofreading stage. Students should not worry too much about correct punctuation during the writing stage but should focus instead on using their prior knowledge of games and their interesting facts from a subject area to produce a flow of good ideas.

AWKWARD	In the game players travel to Mars fly through the rings of Saturn and race back to Earth. [Because the sentence lacks commas, a reader may mistakenly run together *game players* or *Mars fly.*]
REVISED	In the game, players travel to Mars, fly through the rings of Saturn, and race back to Earth.
CONFUSING	The first player, who returns to Earth, wins the game. [The commas make it appear that the clause *who returns to Earth* is not essential—in other words, that the player who has the first turn always wins.]
REVISED	The first player who returns to Earth wins the game.

▶ WRITING ACTIVITY

Create an educational board game or computer game, and write instructions explaining how to play it. In your game, include information from at least one of your school subjects, such as math, science, history, or a foreign language.

Prewriting   Choose a subject area that interests you. Then decide what the object of the game will be. Jot down notes about the number of players, the kinds of supplies or equipment each player will need, and other rules of the game. Give your game a catchy title, and then arrange the instructions in an order that will be easy for players to follow.

Writing   Keep in mind that your instructions will be the players' only source of information. Try to anticipate their questions, and aim for an informal, conversational tone, as if you were explaining the game in person.

Evaluating and Revising   Ask some of your friends to play the game. As you watch them, note any problems they have with understanding the instructions. Then add, delete, change, or rearrange information to make the instructions easier to understand and the game more fun to play.

Proofreading and Publishing   Proofread your instructions carefully, paying special attention to your use of end marks and commas. Then input your instructions on a computer or photocopy them. You could offer copies of your game to your school's media center, to a local hospital, or to one of the agencies or organizations that serve your community.

25k

Interrupters

25k. Use commas to set off elements that interrupt a sentence.

(1) Appositives and appositive phrases are usually set off by commas.

An *appositive* is a noun or pronoun that follows another noun or pronoun to identify or explain it.

EXAMPLES   Nancy Landon Kassebaum, a **senator** from Kansas, was the principal speaker.
Do you know him, the **boy** wearing the blue shirt?

When you set off an appositive, be sure to include all the words that modify it.

EXAMPLES   I read *At Home in India*, a book by Cynthia Bowles.
Neil Armstrong, the first person to walk on the moon, took his historic step on July 20, 1969.

Sometimes an appositive is used to specify a particular person, place, thing, or idea. Such an appositive is called a *restrictive appositive.*

EXAMPLES   My brother **James** helped me. [The writer has more than one brother. The appositive *James* specifies which brother.]
Have you ever seen the movie *Home Alone*? [The appositive *Home Alone* specifies the particular movie.]

☞ REFERENCE NOTE: See pages 590–591 for more information on appositives and appositive phrases.

▷ EXERCISE 6

Correcting Sentences with Appositives and Appositive Phrases by Adding Commas

Correctly punctuate the appositives in the following sentences. If a sentence is correct, write *C.*

1. Leonardo da Vinci's painting *Mona Lisa* is a prized possession of the Louvre in France. **1. C**
2. The painting, a portrait of a young Florentine woman, is slightly cracked as a result of temperature changes.

MECHANICS

MEETING *individual* NEEDS

LEARNING STYLES

Auditory Learners. Have students read the following sentences aloud, first without pausing for commas, then with the appropriate pauses. Ask students to discuss the differences in meaning they perceive.

1. My sister, Susan, talks on the phone incessantly.
2. My sister Susan, who talks on the phone incessantly, is in her room.
3. My, Susan talks on the phone incessantly!

3. In 1911 an Italian house painter, Vincenzo Peruggia, stole the painting from its frame.
4. For two years the Paris police, some of the world's cleverest detectives, were baffled by the crime.
5. Since its recovery the painting, one of the most valuable portraits in the world, has been closely guarded.

(2) Words used in direct address are set off by commas.

EXAMPLES   **David,** please close the door.
Did you call me, **Mother?**
Yes, **Mr. Ramos,** I turned in my paper.

(3) Parenthetical expressions are set off by commas.

Parenthetical expressions are remarks that add incidental information or relate ideas to each other.

Commonly Used Parenthetical Expressions		
after all	however	nevertheless
at any rate	I believe	generally speaking
consequently	in fact	on the contrary
for example	that is	on the other hand
for instance	meanwhile	in the first place
of course	moreover	therefore

EXAMPLES   You are, **I hope,** planning to arrive on time.
Gwendolyn Brooks, **in fact,** is my favorite poet.

Some expressions may be used both parenthetically and not parenthetically.

EXAMPLE   Long-distance calls are a bargain, at any rate.
[parenthetical, meaning "in any case"]
Long-distance calls are a bargain at any rate.
[not parenthetical, meaning "at any cost"]

☞ REFERENCE NOTE: Parentheses and dashes are sometimes used to set off parenthetical expressions. See pages 862–864.

NOTE: A contrasting expression introduced by *not* or *yet* is parenthetical and should be set off by commas.

EXAMPLE   Emily Brontë, **not her sister Charlotte,** wrote *Wuthering Heights.*

MEETING *individual* **NEEDS**

LEP/ESL

General Strategies. The chart of Commonly Used Parenthetical Expressions can be a departure point for expanding students' vocabularies. Have students look up the single-word expressions (*consequently, however, meanwhile, moreover, nevertheless,* and *therefore*) in a bilingual dictionary and in an English dictionary. To help students understand the more idiomatic expressions, such as *at any rate, in the first place,* and *on the other hand,* pair English-language learners with classmates who can explain the expressions to them.

◆ **INTEGRATING THE LANGUAGE ARTS**

Mechanics and Writing. Find a paragraph in which parenthetical expressions are used effectively to connect ideas, and copy the paragraph onto the chalkboard. Have students read the paragraph. Then, erase the parenthetical expressions from the paragraph and have the students read it again. Initiate a discussion of whether the paragraph is more effective with parenthetical expressions or without them.

806

MECHANICS

MECHANICS

REVIEW C

OBJECTIVE

- To correct paragraphs by adding commas

 REVIEW C

Correcting Sentences by Adding Commas

For each of the following sentences, write each <u>word that should be followed by a comma</u>, and place a comma after it.

Optional commas are circled.

EXAMPLE   [1]   Artist Faith Ringgold painstakingly hand-letters her beautiful unique story quilts.

      1.   *beautiful,*

[1] Continuing the ancient tradition of <u>quilting,</u> Ringgold combines <u>printed, dyed,</u> and pieced fabric with acrylic paintings or photoetchings. [2] By placing the tradition in a new <u>context,</u> the artist gives it new meaning.

[3] <u>Ringgold,</u> whose earlier works include <u>landscapes,</u> <u>murals, masks,</u> and soft <u>sculptures,</u> began making story quilts in 1980. [4] Titled *Echoes of Harlem,* the first one was a collaboration between the artist and her <u>mother,</u> dress designer Willi <u>Posey,</u> who learned quilting from her own <u>grandmother,</u> who had learned it from her <u>mother,</u> a slave.

[5] Most of Ringgold's story quilts are designed to be viewed as parts of a <u>series,</u> not as separate <u>pieces,</u> and many include portions of a narrative linking the works in the series. [6] This <u>work,</u> *Double Dutch on the Golden Gate,* lacks an accompanying text and is from the *Woman on a Bridge* <u>series,</u> which includes five works. [7] Capturing the excitement of a childhood <u>game,</u> it depicts a pastime cherished by generations of African Americans. [8] <u>However,</u> the work speaks to more than a single culture and appeals to all people who recognize in it joyful moments from their childhood.

[9] Ringgold still lives and works in <u>Harlem,</u> the section of New York City where she was born. [10] One of her story <u>quilts,</u> which sell for <u>$40,000,</u> is in the permanent collection of the city's Guggenheim <u>Museum,</u> a major gallery of modern art.

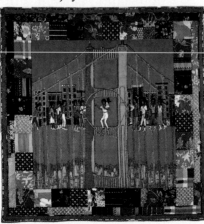

Faith Ringgold, *Double Dutch on the Golden Gate Bridge.* Acrylic, canvas, painted, dyed, pieced fabric, 68 1/2" × 68". © 1988 Faith Ringgold Inc. Private Collection.

MECHANICS

VISUAL CONNECTIONS

About the Artist. Faith Ringgold's art is boldly political, focusing on the discrimination and repression facing African Americans and women in American society. Born in Harlem in 1934, she attended City College of New York and received her Bachelor of Science degree in 1955 and her Master of Fine Arts degree in 1959.

In 1972, Ringgold helped to found the Women Students and Artists for Black Liberation, an organization that ensured that exhibitions of black artists' works gave equal space to art by both men and women. Later, she donated to the Women's House of Detention in Manhattan a large mural that depicts the roles of women in American society.

MECHANICS

AT-RISK STUDENTS

Point out to students that adherence to **Rule 25l** is very important in job applications and résumés. To help students to recognize the importance of understanding the comma usage discussed in the **Conventional Situations** section, have students write letters of application for jobs that appeal to them. Students might need to refer to **Chapter 36: "Letters and Forms"** for the correct form for a business letter. Finally, have students trade letters and evaluate each other's letters for standard punctuation.

PICTURE THIS

Before asking students to complete the **Picture This** assignment, you may want to discuss the meaning of *closed captions* and *hearing-impaired* so that students clearly understand the activity's objective.

You may wish to put students in groups or pairs for the preliminary part of this activity so that they can discuss the picture. Then, have students write their paragraphs individually. Ask them to circle each comma and end mark, citing beside it the rule that dictates its use.

MECHANICS

808

---

808 *Punctuation*

Conventional Situations

25l. Use commas in certain conventional situations.

(1) Use a comma to separate items in dates and addresses.

EXAMPLES   On Saturday, June 21, 1991, Robert moved to Miami Beach, Florida, with his parents.
His new address is 814 Georgia Avenue, Miami Beach, FL 33139.

Notice that no comma separates the month from the day, the house number from the street name, or the ZIP Code from the two-letter state code.

If the day is given before the month or if only the month and the year are given, no comma is used.

EXAMPLES   The British forces at Pensacola Bay surrendered to Bernardo de Gálvez on 10 May 1781.
The hottest month on record here was July 1962.

(2) Use a comma after the salutation of a friendly letter and after the closing of any letter.

EXAMPLES   Dear Marcus,   Dear Aunt Meg,
Affectionately yours,   Sincerely yours,

(3) Use a comma after a name followed by an abbreviation such as *Jr.*, *Sr.*, or *M.D.* and after the abbreviation when it is used in a sentence.

EXAMPLES   Elena Moreno, M.D.
Russell E. Davis, Jr., has been elected mayor.

PICTURE THIS

You're a writer for a company that prepares the closed captions that hearing-impaired viewers see on their television screens. Write a page of dialogue that might be shown with this scene from the *I Love Lucy* show, starring Lucille Ball and Desi Arnaz. Use a variety of end marks, and include commas where they are needed.

MECHANICS

Subject: a scene from *I Love Lucy*
Audience: hearing-impaired viewers
Purpose: to entertain

Unnecessary Commas

25m.   Do not use unnecessary commas.

Too many commas can be as confusing as too few. Don't use a comma unless a rule requires one or unless the meaning would be unclear without it.

CONFUSING   On Friday, after school, my friend, Rita, and I played badminton at her house until her dog, Ruffles, a frisky, golden retriever, joined us and ran off with the shuttlecock, clenched in its teeth.

CLEAR   On Friday after school, my friend Rita and I played badminton at her house until her dog Ruffles, a frisky golden retriever, joined us and ran off with the shuttlecock clenched in its teeth.

 EXERCISE 7   **Correcting Sentences by Adding Commas**

For each of the following sentences, write each <u>word that should be followed by a comma</u>, and place the comma after it.

MECHANICS

REVIEW D

OBJECTIVE

- To revise paragraphs by adding commas

EXAMPLE **1.** On our way to Birmingham Alabama we stayed overnight in Chattanooga Tennessee.
   1. *Birmingham, Alabama, Chattanooga,*

1. On August 1̲,̲1991̲,̲we moved from Eureka̲,̲California̲,̲ to 220 Tuxford Place̲,̲Thousand Oaks̲,̲California.
2. We left Tampa̲,̲Florida̲,̲on Monday̲,̲June 15̲,̲and arrived in Albuquerque̲,̲New Mexico̲,̲on June 17.
3. The hotel on Gulfport Road was destroyed by fire on Tuesday̲,̲March 13̲,̲1984.
4. My brother received a letter that started, "Dear John̲,̲ There's something I've been meaning to tell you."
5. We interviewed Franklin R. Thomas̲,̲M.D.̲,̲at his emergency clinic on Wilson Road.

▶ REVIEW D | **Revising Paragraphs by Adding Commas**

For each sentence in the following paragraphs, write each <u>word that should be followed by a comma</u>, and place the comma after it. If a sentence is correct, write C. [Note: If a comma may or may not be used, circle the word and the comma.]

Optional commas are circled.

[1] As early as the sixth century B.C.̲,̲plays were performed in this amphitheater̲,̲the Theater of Dionysus̲,̲in Athens̲,̲Greece. [2] The Theater of Dionysus is located on the south slope of the Acropolis̲,̲an elevated̲,̲fortified sec-

3. C tion of Athens. [3] The plays presented in ancient Greece marked the beginning of drama in the Western world. [4] In fact̲,̲the English word *theater* comes from the Greek word *theatron̲,̲*which means "a place for seeing."

[5] Wearing masks to show which characters they were portraying̲,̲the actors in ancient dramas often played several different roles. [6] In addition̲,̲all roles̲,̲including those of female characters̲,̲were performed by men.

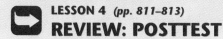

REVIEW: POSTTEST

OBJECTIVES

- To correct sentences by adding end marks and commas
- To correct paragraphs by adding end marks and commas

[7] Although records show that Greek playwrights wrote hundreds of tragedies, fewer than thirty-five of these plays survive. [8] The earliest Greek dramatist, Aeschylus, wrote the *Oresteia*, a powerful story of murder, revenge, and divine mercy. [9] Sophocles, often regarded as the greatest dramatist of all time, is credited with writing more than one hundred plays. [10] Among the surviving works of Aristophanes, whom the ancient Greeks considered the greatest comic playwright, are the three satires *The Clouds*, *The Wasps*, and *The Frogs*.

Review: Posttest

A. Correcting Sentences by Adding End Marks and Commas

Write the following sentences, adding end marks and commas where they are needed. [Note: If a comma may or may not be used, circle the comma.]

Optional commas are circled.

EXAMPLE   **1.** When is the bus coming or has it already left
    1. *When is the bus coming, or has it already left?*

1. On June 1, 1992, I wrote to the Wisconsin Department of Development at 123 Washington Ave, Madison, WI 53702.
2. Federico Peña, mayor of Denver, Colorado, from 1983 to 1991, was born in Laredo, Texas, in 1947.
3. Wow, Bill, what a great save you made in last night's game!
4. Water transports nutrients throughout the body, aids in digestion, and helps regulate body temperature.
5. I. M. Pei, who was born in China, has designed many buildings in the United States, for example, the Dallas, Texas, City Hall and the Government Center in Boston, Massachusetts.
6. The chief crops grown in Trinidad, one of the most prosperous islands in the Caribbean, are sugar, coffee, cocoa, citrus fruits, and bananas.
7. Did you know that Navajo Community College, located in Tsaile, Arizona, was founded in 1968?

8. If I finish my report, if I do the laundry, and if I promise to be home by eleven, may I go to the concert?

9. After staying up so late, I was exhausted, of course, yet I couldn't fall asleep right away.

10. In the mail last Wednesday a large, heavy package, addressed to Phyllis M. Saunders, M.D., was delivered to our house by mistake.

B. Correcting Paragraphs by Adding End Marks and Commas

For each sentence in the following paragraphs, add end marks and commas where they are needed. [Note: If a comma may or may not be used, circle the comma.]

Optional commas are circled.

EXAMPLE [1] As soon as I got home I called my best friend Stephanie to tell her about my vacation

1. *As soon as I got home, I called my best friend, Stephanie, to tell her about my vacation.*

[11] Stephanie, have you ever visited Cody, Wyoming? [12] Well, if you do, be sure to stop by the Buffalo Bill Historical Center. [13] Opened in 1927 in memory of William "Buffalo Bill" Cody, an army scout who later had his own Wild West show, the Center is actually four museums in one. [14] Under one roof are the Buffalo Bill Museum, the Whitney Gallery of Western Art, the Winchester Arms Museum, and the Plains Indian Museum.

[15] All of the museums are interesting, but the best one, I believe, is the Plains Indian Museum, which has artifacts from Native American cowhands, settlers, and roving artists. [16] Of all the treasures in the museum's collections, the highlight is an exhibit on Tatanka Yotanka, better known as Sitting Bull, the mighty Sioux warrior, holy man, chief, and statesman. [17] The exhibit includes a dozen drawings that Sitting Bull, who was born about 1831 and died in 1890, made while he was a prisoner at Fort Randall, an army post in the Dakota Territory. [18] Depicting some of his many battlefield conquests, the drawings reveal his talent for design and composition.

[19] Other displays show weapons, clothing, and accessories of the Cheyenne, Shoshone, Crow, Arapaho, Blackfeet, and Gros Ventre peoples. [20] What a journey back through time the museum offers!

MECHANICS

SUMMARY OF THE USES OF THE COMMA

25f Use commas to separate items in a series.

> (1) If all items in a series are joined by *and*, *or*, or *nor*, do not use commas to separate them.
>
> (2) Independent clauses in a series are usually separated by semicolons. Short independent clauses may be separated by commas.

25g Use commas to separate two or more adjectives preceding a noun.

25h Use a comma before *and*, *but*, *or*, *nor*, *for*, *so*, and *yet* when they join independent clauses.

25i Use commas to set off nonessential clauses and nonessential participial phrases.

25j Use commas after certain introductory elements.

> (1) Use a comma after words such as *well*, *yes*, *no*, and *why* when they begin a sentence.
>
> (2) Use a comma after an introductory participial phrase.
>
> (3) Use a comma after two or more introductory prepositional phrases.
>
> (4) Use a comma after an introductory adverb clause.

25k Use commas to set off elements that interrupt a sentence.

> (1) Appositives and appositive phrases are usually set off by commas.
>
> (2) Words used in direct address are set off by commas.
>
> (3) Parenthetical expressions are set off by commas.

25l Use commas in certain conventional situations.

> (1) Use a comma to separate items in dates and addresses.
>
> (2) Use a comma after the salutation of a friendly letter and after the closing of any letter.
>
> (3) Use a comma after a name followed by an abbreviation such as *Jr.*, *Sr.*, or *M.D.*

25m Do not use unnecessary commas.

MECHANICS

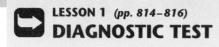

PROGRAM MANAGER

FOR THE WHOLE CHAPTER

■ **Review** For exercises on chapter concepts, see **Review Form A** and **Review Form B** in *Language Skills Practice and Assessment,* pp. 209–212.

■ **Assessment** For additional testing, see **Mechanics Pretests** and **Mechanics Mastery Tests** in *Language Skills Practice and Assessment,* pp. 169–177 and pp. 265–271.

CHAPTER OVERVIEW

This chapter stresses the idea that semicolons and colons can help writers achieve clarity when they are presenting complex ideas. It also links that complexity to maturation of the thought processes of students.

Semicolons are treated first, followed by a treatment of colons. The **Writing Activity** has each student planning an itinerary and writing a letter to procure tickets for a trip. The chapter concludes with a **Posttest** for determining students' mastery of these two punctuation marks.

USING THE DIAGNOSTIC TEST

The **Diagnostic Test** requires students to edit sentences for correct use of colons and semicolons. Most of the errors are omissions of correct punctuation. This test should indicate which students need additional help with the rules for using semicolons and colons.

MECHANICS

26 PUNCTUATION

Semicolons and Colons

Diagnostic Test

Correcting Sentences by Using Semicolons and Colons

Most of the following sentences have a comma or no punctuation mark where a semicolon or a colon should be used. Write the <u>word preceding each error</u>; then, add the needed punctuation mark. If a sentence is correct, write *C*.

EXAMPLE **1.** No, the Arthurs are not home, they've left for work.
      1. *home;*

1. Native Americans inhabited North America long before any <u>Europeans</u>⚠however, many Native Americans weren't recognized as citizens of the United States until 1924.

2. The meeting is scheduled for 3⚠30 this <u>afternoon</u>⚠ please don't be late.

3. The following committees will report at that <u>time</u>: budget, membership, awards, and programs.
4. Every morning when I get up, I read a Bible <u>verse</u>; this morning I read John <u>14:27</u>.
5. We left some food out for the stray <u>dog</u>; it looked so forlorn huddled in the doorway.
6. Our modern literature class has read these <u>poems</u>: "Incident" by Countee Cullen, "The Love Song of J. Alfred Prufrock" by T. S. Eliot, and "Ars Poetica" by Archibald MacLeish.
7. When she transferred to Barton Academy, Millie joined several clubs, helped in planning the Spring Carnival, and worked at a food bank for the <u>needy</u>; nevertheless, it took her months to make some new friends.
8. While campaigning to become mayor of San Antonio, María Antonieta Berriozábal summed up her point of view in these <u>words</u>: "Our greatest resource is our people. We have to deal with business interests and human needs simultaneously."
9. Conrad Aiken was a correspondent for *The New Yorker* and also wrote essays and short <u>stories</u>; he is best known, however, for his poetry.
10. The Bering Strait links the Arctic Ocean with the Bering <u>Sea</u>; both the strait and the sea are named for Vitus Bering, a Danish explorer.
11. S. I. Hayakawa made this <u>statement</u>: "It is not true that we have only one life to <u>live</u>; if we can read, we can live as many more lives and as many kinds of lives as we wish."
12. The winners in the Douglas Fun Run last Saturday morning were Otis Williams, a <u>sophomore</u>; Janice Hicks, a <u>senior</u>; and Rodrigo Campas, a junior.
13. They opposed every motion that came before the <u>meeting</u>; in addition, they said they would circulate petitions if any of the proposals were passed.
14. At first the children were afraid, believing that they were <u>lost</u>; only after their teacher reassured them that she knew the way did they settle down.
15. This design will be applied to the following types of <u>machines</u>: commercial, manufacturing, military, and agricultural.

OBJECTIVE

• To use semicolons and commas correctly

PROGRAM MANAGER

SEMICOLONS

■ **Independent Practice/ Reteaching** For instruction and exercises, see **Using Semicolons** in *Language Skills Practice and Assessment,* p. 207.

■ **Computer Guided Instruction** For additional instruction and practice with using semicolons, see **Lessons 37** and **43** in *Language Workshop CD-ROM.*

■ **Practice** To help less-advanced students with additional instruction and practice with using semicolons, see **Chapter 21** in *English Workshop, Fourth Course,* pp. 291–292.

QUICK REMINDER

Write the following pairs of sentences on the chalkboard and ask students to combine them by using semicolons:

1. The bell rang as I hurried toward the classroom I was tardy again. [classroom; I]

2. Mr. Scott frowned as I tried to slip into my seat he was not pleased with me. [seat; he]

3. I have no explanation in my life, lateness is a state of being. [explanation; in]

Ask the students why semicolons might be better punctuation here than periods. [Although separating the clauses with periods would make them grammatically correct sentences, the clauses are very closely related, and semicolons help indicate this close relationship.]

816

MECHANICS

---

816 *Punctuation*

16. Jennifer Lawson became programming chief of PBS in 1990; she is a former civil rights activist, film professor, and producer.

17. In addition to her coming-of-age short stories, Doris Lessing has written several novels, one of which is *African Laughter: Four Visits to Zimbabwe,* based on her life in Africa.

18. In the past twelve years, Justin has lived in Tucson, Arizona; Dallas, Texas; Shreveport, Louisiana; and Tulsa, Oklahoma.

19. For the golf tournament seasoned players were paired with players new to the game; consequently, the experienced players were frustrated and the novices were confused.

20. When Hernando Cortés invaded Mexico in 1519, he burned his ships; as a result, his troops were unable to return to Cuba.

Semicolons

26a. Use a semicolon between independent clauses in a sentence if they are not joined by *and, but, or, nor, for, so,* or *yet.*

EXAMPLE Everyone else in my family excels in a particular sport; I seem to be the only exception.

When the thoughts of two short sentences are very closely related, a semicolon can take the place of the period between them.

EXAMPLE The river is rising rapidly. It's expected to crest by noon. [two simple sentences]
The river is rising rapidly; it's expected to crest by noon.

26b. Use a semicolon between independent clauses joined by conjunctive adverbs or transitional expressions.

EXAMPLES   Leonor is planning to become an engineer**; however,** she is also interested in commercial art.

Only two people registered for the pottery lessons**; as a result,** the class was canceled.

Notice in the examples above that the conjunctive adverb and the transitional expression are followed by commas.

Commonly Used Conjunctive Adverbs

accordingly	however	moreover
besides	indeed	nevertheless
consequently	instead	otherwise
furthermore	meanwhile	therefore

Commonly Used Transitional Expressions

as a result	for example	for instance	that is
in spite of	in conclusion	in other words	in fact

NOTE: When a conjunctive adverb or a transitional expression appears *within* one of the clauses instead of *between* the clauses, it is usually set off by commas. The two clauses are still separated by a semicolon.

EXAMPLE   Ralph Ellison is best known for his 1952 novel, *Invisible Man***;** he has also**, however,** written short stories and essays.

▶ EXERCISE 1   Correcting Sentences by Adding Commas and Semicolons

For each of the following sentences, write all the <u>words that should be followed by a semicolon or a comma</u>. Place the needed punctuation mark after each one.

EXAMPLE   **1.** The clever carvings shown on the next page were handmade in southern Mexico they're sold all over the world.
1. *Mexico;*

1. The carvings come from the Oaxaca (pronounced wä hä′ kä) <u>Valley</u>;in <u>fact,</u>90 percent of the two hundred families who make them live in three villages.

MECHANICS

MECHANICS

COOPERATIVE LEARNING

Send students in groups of three to the library to find semicolons in professional writing. Assign groups to search in different types of texts: magazine articles, novels, nonfiction books, encyclopedias, dictionaries, and so on. Have the students appoint a spokesperson in each group who is to report not only the rule of use, but also what the group thinks was the writer's reason for using a semicolon instead of some other punctuation mark.

To ensure that all group members participate, make a second member responsible for turning in a written version of the report and appoint a third to write samples of the group's sentences on the chalkboard.

2. Carving has been a tradition among Oaxacans for hundreds of <u>years</u>;only <u>recently</u>,<u>however</u>,have the artists sold their work outside the valley.
3. In many families the fathers and older sons do the actual <u>carving</u>;meanwhile,the other members of the family sand and paint the figures.
4. The artists find inspiration for their creations in everyday <u>life</u>;for <u>example</u>,religion and nature are rich sources of ideas.
5. Even those carvers whose works have won world-wide acclaim have chosen to continue living in the <u>valley</u>;their ties to their families and communities are very strong.

26c. A semicolon (rather than a comma) may be needed to separate independent clauses joined by a coordinating conjunction if commas appear within the clauses.

CONFUSING   June sat with Tony, Pat, and me, and Josh sat with Flora, Zack, and Geraldo.

      CLEAR   June sat with Tony, Pat and me; and Josh sat with Flora, Zack, and Geraldo.

REVIEW A

OBJECTIVE

- To correct sentences by adding semicolons and commas

CONFUSING Searching for my house key, I found a dime, a nickel, and a penny, and, putting them into my wallet, I realized that my key had been in there all along.

      CLEAR Searching for my house key, I found a dime, a nickel, and a penny; and, putting them into my wallet, I realized that my key had been in there all along.

REFERENCE NOTE: For information on using a comma to separate independent clauses joined by a coordinating conjunction, see page 796.

26d. Use a semicolon between items in a series if the items contain commas.

EXAMPLES There are three home stations for the Goodyear blimps: Carson, California; Akron, Ohio; and Pompano Beach, Florida.

You may turn in your book reports on Thursday, September 14; Friday, September 15; Monday, September 18; or Tuesday, September 19.

REVIEW A **Correcting Sentences by Adding Commas and Semicolons**

For each of the following sentences, write all the <u>words that should be followed by a semicolon or a comma</u>. Place the needed punctuation mark after each one. If a sentence is correct, write *C*.

EXAMPLE **1.** The diagram on the next page shows the typical seating plan of a symphony orchestra the conductor occupies the podium.

      1. *orchestra;*

1. All of the instruments in a symphony orchestra are divided into classes based on how they produce <u>sound</u>many musicians can play several instruments within a class.
2. The four classes are the stringed instruments, the woodwinds, the brasses, and the percussion instruments. **2.** C
3. Woodwinds, which include the flute, the clarinet, and the saxophone, were once made solely of <u>wood</u>; but today they may be made of metal or plastic instead.

TECHNOLOGY TIP

If they have access to word-processing programs, you may want to have students correct comma splices or combine short, choppy sentences by using the insert function to add semicolons. You could enter sentences of your own for students to correct, or you might use those in **Review A.**

COMMON ERROR

Problem. After becoming acquainted with the list of commonly used conjunctive adverbs (p. 817), some students might overapply **Rule 26b** (p. 816) by using semicolons every time they encounter one of the words in the list. *Furthermore, however,* and *therefore* seem to be the words that most often get this type of treatment.

Solution. Stress that semicolons are used when these words join independent clauses, and make sure everyone understands that independent clauses have both a subject and a verb and could, in fact, be sentences by themselves. When this type of erroneous use of semicolons occurs, have the students try to find the subject and verb in each word group on either side of the semicolon. When they see that a word group is not an independent clause, they should have a better understanding of **Rule 26b** and how to apply it.

4. Some of the stringed instruments are played with a bow⌃some are plucked with the fingers or with a pick⌃and some are operated by means of a keyboard.
5. Most brass instruments, such as the trumpet, tuba, and cornet, have valves that regulate the pitch⌃but the trombone has a sliding section for this purpose.
6. Kettledrums, or timpani, are percussion instruments that can be tuned to a specific pitch⌃most other kinds of drums, the cymbals, and the triangle⌃however⌃ cannot be tuned.
7. The conductor's job is to coordinate the sounds produced by these different instruments⌃however⌃this task is only one of a conductor's responsibilities.
8. Conductors must study the history and theory of music for many years⌃furthermore⌃they must be skilled at playing at least one instrument.
9. Many people think that a conductor just establishes and maintains the tempo of the music⌃they don't realize that he or she also selects the music, interprets the composer's meaning, and brings out the best in each of the musicians.
10. The goal of every conductor is to lead a major orchestra such as one of those in London, England⌃ Mexico City, Mexico⌃Boston, Massachusetts⌃or Chicago, Illinois.

COLONS Rules 26e, 26f

OBJECTIVES

- To use at least three semicolons and two colons in a writing journal entry
- To use colons before lists and in certain other conventional situations

Colons

26e. Use a colon to mean "note what follows."

(1) Use a colon before a list of items, especially after expressions such as *as follows* **and** *the following [items]*.

EXAMPLES   In Washington, D.C., we visited four important national sites**:** the White House, the Washington Monument, the Vietnam Veterans Memorial, and the Lincoln Memorial.

The only articles allowed in the examination area **are as follows:** pencils, compasses, rulers, and protractors.

During summer vacation, Juanita read biographies of **the following people:** John Ross, Annie Wauneka, and María Martínez-Cañas.

NOTE: Do not use a colon before a list that immediately follows a verb or a preposition.

INCORRECT   At the new amusement park we rode: the roller coaster, the Ferris wheel, the bumper cars, and the water slide.

CORRECT   At the amusement park we rode the roller coaster, the Ferris wheel, the bumper cars, and the water slide.

INCORRECT   Our family has lived in: California, Arizona, North Carolina, and Texas.

CORRECT   Our family has lived in California, Arizona, North Carolina, and Texas.

(2) Use a colon before a long, formal statement or quotation.

EXAMPLE   Thomas Paine's first pamphlet in the series *The American Crisis* starts with these famous words**:**

These are the times that try men's souls. The summer soldier and the sunshine patriot will, in this crisis, shrink from the service of their country; but he that stands it *now* deserves the love and thanks of man and woman.

☞ REFERENCE NOTE: See pages 838–839 for more information on using long quotations in a composition.

MECHANICS

PICTURE THIS

Remind students that writing journal entries typically are examples of free writing and therefore don't have to be grammatically correct. However, because this exercise is designed to give students practice in the use of the colon, they should concentrate on making sure that colons appear in the correct places in their entries.

MEETING *individual* **NEEDS**

LEP/ESL

General Strategies. The **Picture This** exercise may be difficult for some students to complete. Although some students have grown up with television, movies, books, and history lessons about the western frontier, many English-language learners might not share this frame of reference.

Give students the option of writing about leaving their native countries or of writing about when their parents or ancestors left their native countries. Students' writing journal entries can tell what happened during the journey or, more specifically, what happened the day they or their families arrived. Their lists can detail what in the United States is different from their native countries.

Remind students to write about a situation they would not mind sharing with others.

PICTURE THIS

The year is 1878. Responding to this poster, your family sold its home in Tennessee, and now you're on your way to Kansas with this wagon train. The land, the people, the chores—everything is different from the life you left behind. You've decided to keep a journal so that you'll always remember this difficult but exciting journey. Write a journal entry telling what happened today on the trail. In your entry, use at least three semicolons and two colons.

Subject: traveling to Kansas with a wagon train
Audience: you some time in the future
Purpose: to record

26f. Use a colon in certain conventional situations.

(1) Use a colon between the hour and the minute.

EXAMPLES   **6:15** P.M.   **9:55 tomorrow morning**

MECHANICS

MECHANICS

(2) Use a colon between chapter and verse in biblical references and between titles and subtitles.

EXAMPLES   Psalms 8**:**9   I Corinthians 13**:** 1–13
                   Indian Oratory**:** A Collection of Famous Speeches

(3) Use a colon after the salutation of a business letter.

EXAMPLES   Dear Ms. Weinberg**:**   Dear Sales Manager**:**
              Dear Sir or Madam**:**   To Whom It May Concern**:**

NOTE: Use a comma after the salutation of a friendly letter.

       EXAMPLE   Dear Suzanne**,**

EXERCISE 2   Correcting Sentences by Adding Colons

Correct the following sentences by adding colons where they are needed. If a sentence is correct, write C.

EXAMPLE   **1.** I began my acceptance speech as follows "Fellow students, thank you for your votes!"
           1. *follows:*

1. My little sister's favorite book is *The Great Kapok Tree: A Tale of the Amazon Rain Forest* by Lynn Cherry.
2. Sometimes the paper comes at 6:15 A.M., but other times it doesn't hit the driveway until 7:00.
3. My little sister has several items embossed with Garfield's picture: a poster, a nightgown, a notebook, and a clock.
4. In William Shakespeare's play *Julius Caesar*, the general Caesar says of courage:
    Cowards die many times before their deaths,
    The valiant taste of death but once.
5. Sherry's favorite artists are Jacob Lawrence, Romare Bearden, and Margaret Burroughs. **5.** C
6. The story of Moses and Pharaoh's daughter is told in Exodus 2:5–10.
7. The directions were as follows: cover with plastic wrap, place in oven, and microwave for at least ten minutes.
8. I prefer my bicycle to a car for three reasons: I don't pay for gasoline, I don't pay for insurance, and it's all mine.

MECHANICS

MECHANICS

COOPERATIVE LEARNING
Pair students of mixed abilities for an editing exercise when they have finished the **Picture This** activity. Less-advanced students benefit doubly from the input of their partners and from seeing the exercise done well, and the better students will be required to verbalize their understanding of the writing process.

COMMON ERROR
Problem. Invariably, some students confuse the colon and the semicolon or think they are interchangeable.

Solution. Allowing a time lapse between the introduction of semicolons and that of colons is often all that is needed to prevent confusion. Explain that a colon is a kind of pointer to something that a writer wants to emphasize. A semicolon provides clarity (in setting off a list with internal commas) or accentuates a close relationship between two independent clauses.

9. In Cuba, which is a Spanish-speaking country, most of the people are of Spanish, African, or Spanish-African descent. **9.** C

10. Mr. Wise asked us to bring the following items to biology class:a deciduous leaf, a coniferous needle or branch, and wax paper.

 REVIEW B

Correcting Sentences by Adding Semicolons and Colons

For each numbered sentence in the following letter, write each <u>word that should be followed by a semicolon or a colon</u>. Place the needed punctuation mark after each word. [Note: A sentence may need more than one punctuation mark.]

EXAMPLE   [1] Hampton University was founded in 1868 it was originally named Hampton Institute.
   1. *1868;*

1238-C Landon Street
Kansas City, MO 64l05
October 17, 1993

Director
George Foster Peabody Collection
Hampton University
Hampton, VA 23668

[1] Dear Sir or <u>Madam:</u>

[2] The media coordinator at Central High School suggested that I write to <u>you;</u>she explained that Hampton has an extensive collection of materials on African American history. [3] For my history class I am preparing an oral report on the August 28, 1963, March on <u>Washington:</u>and, to make my report more interesting, I would like to display pictures of the march.

[4] I am particularly interested in pictures of the following <u>speakers:</u>Floyd <u>McKissick,</u>John <u>Lewis,</u>Roy <u>Wilkins,</u> and, of course, Martin Luther King, Jr. [5] I would also like pictures showing the size and diversity of the <u>crowd;</u>for example, a shot of the marchers filling the area around the Reflecting Pool between the Lincoln Memorial and the

WRITING APPLICATION

OBJECTIVE

- To use semicolons and colons correctly in a business letter

Washington Monument would be especially effective. [6] Either prints or slides will be <u>useful</u>;however, I would prefer slides if they are available.

[7] My grandfather, who took part in the march, remembers it <u>vividly</u>;in fact, he considers it one of the high points of his life. [8] He took several rolls of film himself that <u>day</u>;unfortunately, the pictures were lost in a fire a few years ago.

[9] Please send me information on ordering copies of suitable <u>pictures</u>;a stamped, self-addressed envelope is enclosed. [10] Thank you for your <u>help</u>;I look forward to hearing from you.

Sincerely,

Jesse Fletcher

Jesse Fletcher

WRITING APPLICATION

Using Semicolons and Colons in a Business Letter

As you grow older, your knowledge and your thoughts expand and become more complex. To express what you know and think, you begin using longer, more complex sentences. When you write, semicolons and colons can help you make these sentences easier to understand. Compare the following examples.

IMMATURE   I'd like to visit three cities. The cities are in the Southwest. One is Santa Fe, New Mexico. One is Phoenix, Arizona. One is Los Angeles, California. I can't afford to. That's unfortunate.

MATURE   I'd like to visit three cities in the Southwest: Santa Fe, New Mexico; Phoenix, Arizona; and Los Angeles, California; unfortunately, however, I can't afford to.

MECHANICS

STUDENTS WITH SPECIAL NEEDS

To help students gain a sense of the function of the colon, use scrambled sentences. Have students write sentences containing colons. Then have them cut out the words and punctuation marks with scissors. The students should then exchange work and put the words and punctuation back together.

Another activity is to choose a paragraph of high interest to the students and make incorrect changes in colon usage. Inform the students of the number of errors and have them locate and correct the errors.

WRITING APPLICATION

Writing this letter gives students an opportunity to use what they've learned about semicolons and colons. They will also gain experience in using a formal tone and in developing planning skills.

MECHANICS

CRITICAL THINKING

Analysis. Remind students that the person reading the letter is not responsible for having awarded the prize. Effusive thanks are inappropriate. The point of the letter is to establish an itinerary, not to express gratitude or to say how much the prize winner antici-pates enjoying the trip. Brevity is an asset in business correspondence.

PREWRITING

Have students make lists of the places they'd most like to visit. You may need to have maps in class to help them calculate distances and travel times between destinations.

▶ WRITING ACTIVITY

You have just won the grand prize in Blue Star Airlines' Fly-by-Night Sweepstakes. For one week, you can travel free to anywhere that Blue Star flies in the United States—just so long as your flights depart between 8 P.M. and 4 A.M. You can remain in one location for the whole week, or you can travel to as many places as you'd like. To use your prize, you must give Blue Star Airlines a detailed itinerary of your trip at least two weeks before you plan to take it. Write a letter to the airlines, giving the specific information needed to pre-pare your tickets. Use semicolons and colons to make your information easy to understand.

Prewriting First, decide where you would most like to go. (If you plan to include more than one destination, remember that the trip is to last only one week from start to finish; be as realistic as you can about the travel time required.) Then, arrange the information in an order that will be easy for the ticket agent to understand.

Writing As you write your first draft, remember that the accuracy and completeness of your letter could make the difference between an enjoyable trip and a disastrous one. Stick to the point, and try to make the information as clear as possible.

Evaluating and Revising Put yourself in the ticket agent's place as you evaluate the letter. Have you included all the necessary flight information? Have you arranged the details in an order that's easy to understand? Add, delete, change, or rearrange information to make the letter clearer and more useful. Also make sure that you use the correct form for a business letter (see pages 973–977).

Proofreading Proofread your letter carefully, paying spe-cial attention to your use of semicolons and colons. Check pages 822–823 to be sure that you have followed the rules for using colons in conventional situations. Also make sure that you have correctly spelled the names of the places you wish to visit.

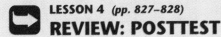

REVIEW: POSTTEST

OBJECTIVE

- To correct sentences by adding semicolons and colons

Review: Posttest

Correcting Sentences by Adding Semicolons and Colons

For each of the following sentences, write the <u>word preceding each punctuation error</u>; then write the semicolon or colon needed. If a sentence is correct, write C.

EXAMPLE   **1.** Please bring the following items books, pencils, and newspapers.
   1. *items:*

1. If you want to send fragile items through the mail, the post office recommends that you pack them in fiberboard <u>containers</u>⌃use foam, plastic, or padding to cushion <u>them</u>⌃and then seal the package carefully, reinforcing it with filament tape.
2. In 1904, Mary McLeod Bethune founded a school for girls in Daytona Beach, <u>Florida</u>⌃that school is now Bethune-Cookman College.
3. Psalms <u>23</u>⌃1–6 is one of the best-known passages in the Bible.
4. According to one of my main sources, *The Real McCoy*⌃*The Life of an African-American Inventor*, an oilcan used in railroad maintenance gave rise to the popular expression "the real McCoy."
5. If I had a million dollars, I'd visit London, <u>England</u>⌃ Cairo, <u>Egypt</u>⌃Buenos Aires, <u>Argentina</u>⌃and Tokyo, Japan.
6. We have to write reports for gym class on one of the following <u>athletes</u>⌃Jesse Owens, Sonja Henie, Jim Thorpe, Althea Gibson, or Babe Didrikson Zaharias.
7. Our neighbor's cocker spaniel barked on and off all night <u>long</u>⌃as a result, I didn't sleep well.
8. Candice will take Sandra's place in tonight's <u>performance</u>⌃unfortunately, Sandra sprained her ankle and cannot walk.
9. My aunt Pam loves to play backgammon and <u>chess</u>⌃ however, she rarely has time because she works at two jobs.

TIMESAVER
When students have completed the **Posttest,** you can save time by letting them help you grade their performances. Distribute colored pens, pencils, or fine-point markers to the class and, as you call out the answers, have the students correct their papers by writing the correct responses over any errors. The corrections in color will be more vivid to visual learners, and hearing the answers given orally will benefit auditory learners.

10. Asia has both the highest and the lowest points on earth.Mount Everest, the highest, soars 29,028 feet; the Dead Sea, a salt lake, lies 1,300 feet below sea level.

11. Instructed to be prompt, we arrived at school at 7:15, but the doors were locked;consequently, we had to wait until 7:30 to get in the building.

12. Indira Gandhi, who served for many years as the prime minister of India, grew up in the world of politics and government;for her father, Jawaharlal Nehru was the first prime minister of India, from 1947 to 1964.

13. My friends Ruth and Cindy disagree about the role of fate in life;Ruth believes that people can control their own destiny, but Cindy insists that people are simply pawns of fate.

14. I don't like to prepare outlines;nevertheless, the highest grade I ever received was for a report that I wrote from an outline.

15. Mr. Kowalski has always regretted that he didn't learn to speak Polish when he was a child;now he is taking conversational Polish.

16. The computer software industry is an enormous, growing business;for instance, people can buy software for everything from balancing budgets to plotting biorhythm charts.

17. Every morning Lonnie rises at 5:00, jogs until 5:30, showers and eats breakfast by 6:15, and catches the 6:35 bus.

18. Red Cloud, leader of the Oglala Sioux, was a military genius;he successfully defended Sioux lands against settlers who wanted to build a trail from Laramie, Wyoming, to Bozeman, Montana.

19. Gates of the Arctic National Park, which is located in northern Alaska, is known for its large populations of certain animals:caribou, grizzly bears, moose, and wolves.

20. I have ridden bicycles, horses, and motorcycles;and I have traveled in trains, buses, and planes;someday I hope to ride in a hot-air balloon.

DIAGNOSTIC TEST

OBJECTIVE

- To correct sentences by adding italics (underlining) and quotation marks where needed

PROGRAM MANAGER

FOR THE WHOLE CHAPTER

- **Review** For exercises on chapter concepts, see **Review Form A** and **Review Form B** in *Language Skills Practice and Assessment,* pp. 221–224.

- **Assessment** For additional testing, see **Mechanics Pretests** and **Mechanics Mastery Tests** in *Language Skills Practice and Assessment,* pp. 169–177 and pp. 265–271.

27 PUNCTUATION

Italics and Quotation Marks

Diagnostic Test

Correcting Sentences by Adding Italics and Quotation Marks

Write each letter, word, title, or sentence that should be in italics (underlined) or in quotation marks. Then supply the needed underlining or quotation marks.

EXAMPLES
1. Can you tell me the way to Logan Street? she asked.
1. *"Can you tell me the way to Logan Street?"*

2. Takeda Izumo, Namiki Senryo, and Miyoshi Shoraku wrote the Kabuki play cycle known in English as The Treasury of the Loyal Retainers or as The League of the Loyal Ronin.
2. *The Treasury of the Loyal Retainers; The League of the Loyal Ronin*

1. Carlos Chávez, Mexican composer and conductor, wrote the symphony <u>Sinfonía de Antígona</u> in 1933.
2. We have subscribed to the <u>Orlando Sentinel</u> ever since we moved here.

CHAPTER OVERVIEW

This chapter includes a section on italics (underlining), followed by a section on quotation marks. The quotation-mark section has two parts: punctuating titles, and punctuating direct and indirect quotations, including dialogue.

The rules concerning the punctuation of titles and quotations will be most useful as students write literary analyses and research papers. The punctuation rules for dialogue will be helpful in expressive and creative writing.

MECHANICS

MECHANICS

USING THE DIAGNOSTIC TEST

The **Diagnostic Test** contains items for most of the twelve rules in the chapter. Many students will not be familiar with some of the rules, and the **Diagnostic Test** will help you discover which rules students need help with most.

3. "Are you going to help me," he asked, "or shall I look for someone else?"

4. James Dickey wrote the novel <u>Deliverance</u>, which was made into a movie featuring the song "Dueling Banjos."

5. In modern Spanish the letters that occur with the greatest frequency are <u>a</u> and <u>s</u>.

6. Clarita served a delicious appetizer called <u>pulpo</u>; when I asked her what it was, she told me that I'd just eaten octopus.

7. For our homework assignment we have to define <u>ionization</u>, <u>electrolyte</u>, <u>quark</u>, and <u>neutrino</u>.

8. During the Civil War, the <u>Merrimack</u>, on the Confederate side, and the <u>Monitor</u>, on the Union side, fought to a draw in the first battle between ironclad ships.

9. "I never should have agreed to be on that committee," wailed Ellie. "When I asked Mary to help, she said, 'Not on your life!' Now I'm stuck doing all the work."

10. "Where have you been, Ramón?" asked Leroy. "The bus leaves in three minutes."

11. Announcing the scholarship winners, the principal called the following students "Elwood High's finest scholars": Daphne Johnson, Michael Lewis, Ruben Perez, and Winsie Chung.

12. One of my favorite TV shows, <u>Disaster Chronicles</u>, ran an episode called "Volcanoes in Italy," which had some interesting facts I used in my report on ancient Rome.

13. Sam, who's originally from Boston, tends to drop the <u>r</u>'s at the ends of words.

14. Politicians still quote Abraham Lincoln's phrase "government of the people, by the people, for the people."

15. During lunch we discussed Ann Banks's magazine article "Rafting with Kids."

16. "Indians Today, the Real and the Unreal" is the opening chapter in Vine Deloria's book <u>Custer Died for Your Sins</u>.

17. My mother has never liked the term <u>baby boomer</u>.

18. Many articles about Emily Dickinson's poems contain the term <u>paradox</u>.

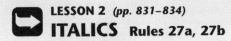
OBJECTIVES

• To correct sentences by adding underlining (italics) where appropriate
• To write sentences containing titles of works

Italics **831**

27a

19. When the players came onto the field, the fans shouted,"Go for it."
20. Have you seen the sculpture <u>Young Shadows</u>, by Louise Nevelson?

Italics

Italics are printed letters that lean to the right, like this:

These words are printed in italics.

When you are writing or typing, indicate italics by underlining. If your composition were printed, the typesetter would set the underlined words in italics. For instance, if you typed

All sophomores in our school read <u>The Good Earth</u>, by Pearl Buck.

the sentence would be printed like this:

All sophomores in our school read *The Good Earth*, by Pearl Buck.

NOTE: If you use a personal computer, you can probably code in italics to appear on the printout. Most word-processing software and many printers are capable of producing italic type.

27a. Use italics (underlining) for titles and subtitles of books, plays, films, periodicals, works of art, record albums, long musical compositions, television series, ships, aircraft, and so on.

TYPE OF TITLE	EXAMPLES	
Books	*Sophocles: The Oedipus Cycle*	*A Fire in My Hands* *Black Elk Speaks*
Plays	*A Raisin in the Sun*	*Julius Caesar*
Films	*Dances with Wolves*	*High Noon*

(continued)

PROGRAM MANAGER

ITALICS

■ **Independent Practice/ Reteaching** For instruction and exercises, see **Italics and Underlining** in *Language Skills Practice and Assessment,* p. 215.

■ **Computer Guided Instruction** For additional instruction and practice with using italics, see **Lesson 41** in *Language Workshop CD-ROM.*

■ **Practice** To help less-advanced students with additional instruction and practice with italics, see **Chapter 21** in *English Workshop, Fourth Course,* pp. 295–296.

QUICK REMINDER
Take a survey of students' votes for the best movie, book, and television series for the year. Write the titles on the chalkboard, underlining each. Ask students what they notice about how you wrote the titles [underlining]. Have them brainstorm other types of works whose titles receive special treatment in writing [plays, works of art, poems, songs].

RULE 27a
Individual newspapers and magazines may have house styles that affect the punctuation of titles. For example, some publications use quotation marks instead of italics for movie titles.

MECHANICS

MECHANICS

MEETING *individual* NEEDS

LEP/ESL

General Strategies. Students are likely to perform more successfully on tasks like **Exercise 2** if they are paired with English-proficient speakers. Collaboration rather than competition will facilitate their understanding of how italics are used and may also expose students to useful cultural information.

Both students should be required to submit written responses to the exercises, but completing those responses together can help both students' comprehension.

LESS-ADVANCED STUDENTS

Some students might have a difficult time with the lists in **Rules 27a** and **27j** because the items in the lists might not seem to have any connection with each other. Students might benefit from an overall characterization of the rules governing the lists—that italics are usually used for long works, and quotation marks are used for parts of works and for short works.

You may wish to put the lists on a large poster as a handy reference in the classroom and as an aid to visual learners, or you can let the students make posters for themselves.

TYPE OF TITLE	EXAMPLES	
Periodicals	*Ebony* *Kansas City Times*	*Women: A Journal of Liberation*
Works of Art	*The Three Musicians*	*Agrarian Leader Zapata*
Long Musical Compositions	*Peter and the Wolf*	*Black, Brown, and Beige*
Television Series	*All Creatures Great and Small*	*Soul Train* *The Wonder Years*
Ships, Trains	*Lusitania* *Flying Cloud*	*Orange Blossom Special*
Aircraft, Spacecraft	*June Bug*	*Pioneer 11*

NOTE: Italicize the title of a poem long enough to be published in a separate volume. Such poems are usually divided into titled or numbered sections, such as cantos, parts, or books. The titles of these sections are enclosed in quotation marks.

EXAMPLE   Longfellow's ***Evangeline*** opens with a section titled simply "Prelude."

The words *a, an,* and *the* before a title are italicized only when they are part of the title. They are not italicized (or capitalized) before the titles of newspapers unless they appear that way in the masthead of the publication.

EXAMPLES   John Hersey's *The Wall* recounts the destruction of the Jewish ghetto in Warsaw during World War II.
   In Shakespeare's play *A Midsummer Night's Dream*, Bottom, a weaver, and his friends perform a play-within-a-play.
   The article in *The Wall Street Journal* mentioned that among his other accomplishments, Frederick Douglass founded the *North Star*, a newspaper he published for seventeen years.

☞ **REFERENCE NOTE:** Use quotation marks, not italics, for chapter headings and the titles of magazine articles, short poems, short stories, short musical compositions, and single episodes of television series. See page 840 for this rule.

27b. Use italics (underlining) for words, numerals, and letters referred to as such and for foreign words.

EXAMPLES The first *o* in *zoology* has a long *o* sound.
On my old typewriter, the lowercase letter *l* was also used to type the numeral *1*.
Montana's state motto is *Oro y Plata,* the Spanish phrase for "gold and silver."

▶ EXERCISE 1 **Correcting Sentences by Adding Underlining (Italics)**

Identify all the words and word groups that should be italicized in the following sentences.

EXAMPLE **1.** In 1988, Toni Morrison won the Pulitzer Prize for her novel Beloved.
1. *Beloved*

1. Does the Vietnamese word chiao mean the same thing as the Spanish word hola?
2. The first full-length animated film, Walt Disney's Snow White and the Seven Dwarfs, used two million drawings.
3. Among the items that the Pilgrims brought with them on the Mayflower were apple seeds.
4. James Earle Fraser, best known for his painting End of the Trail, designed the U.S. buffalo nickel.
5. In the late eighteenth century, Edward Gibbon wrote the influential book History of the Decline and Fall of the Roman Empire.
6. In Voyage to the Bottom of the Sea, an old TV series, the submarine Seaview was commanded by Admiral Nelson.
7. Daktari is Swahili for the English word doctor.
8. The first U.S. space shuttle was named Columbia.
9. Richard Sears met Alvah Roebuck through an ad in the Chicago Daily News.
10. The three M's referred to in the company name 3M stand for the words Minnesota Mining and Manufacturing.

▶ EXERCISE 2 **Writing Sentences Containing Titles of Works**

You probably recognize at least some of the awards on the next page. Now you've been appointed to the nominating

MECHANICS

MECHANICS

PROGRAM MANAGER

QUOTATION MARKS

- **Independent Practice/ Reteaching** For instruction and exercises, see **Using Quotation Marks A, Using Quotation Marks B, Using Quotation Marks C, Using Quotation Marks D,** and **Using Quotation Marks E** in *Language Skills Practice and Assessment,* pp. 216–220.

- **Computer Guided Instruction** For additional instruction and practice with using quotation marks, see **Lessons 41–43** in *Language Workshop CD-ROM.*

- **Practice** To help less-advanced students with additional instruction and practice with using quotation marks, see **Chapter 21** in *English Workshop, Fourth Course,* pp. 297–299.

OBJECTIVES
- To correct sentences by adding quotation marks where needed
- To write a persuasive dialogue that is punctuated correctly

834 *Punctuation*

committee for a new award, the Golden Guppy, which will be presented for an outstanding work in each of these categories:

- a book
- a musical recording
- a television program
- a work of art (painting, sculpture, or some other form)
- a magazine

In a sentence or two, nominate a work in each category and explain why you think it should win one of the awards.

"Emmy" ® ATAS/NATAS

"Oscar" statuette © A.M.P.A.S.

Quotation Marks

27c. Use quotation marks to enclose a ***direct quotation***—a person's exact words.

Do not use quotation marks for an *indirect quotation*.

DIRECT QUOTATION Joan said, "My legs are sore from jogging." [Joan's exact words]

INDIRECT QUOTATION Joan said that her legs were sore from jogging. [not Joan's exact words]

NOTE: Remember to place quotation marks at both the beginning and the end of a direct quotation.

INCORRECT "I'm taking the road test tomorrow, said Reed.

CORRECT "I'm taking the road test tomorrow," said Reed.

27d. A direct quotation begins with a capital letter.

EXAMPLE Bianca asked, "When do we get our uniforms?"

NOTE: If a direct quotation is obviously only a fragment of a sentence and is not intended to stand alone, use a lowercase letter.

EXAMPLE   Christine promised that she would be here "as soon as possible."

27e. When a quoted sentence is divided into two parts by an interrupting expression such as *he said,* the second part begins with a lowercase letter.

EXAMPLES   "I hope," said Diego, "that it doesn't rain during the fiesta."
"I'm not sure," remarked Annette, "if I'll be able to attend the meeting."

If the second part of a divided quotation is a new sentence, a period (not a comma) follows the interrupting expression. The second part begins with a capital letter.

EXAMPLE   "The date has been set," said Greg. "We can't change it now."

NOTE: An interrupting expression is not part of a quotation, so it should never be inside the quotation marks.

INCORRECT   "Where, I inquired, have I seen you before?"
CORRECT   "Where," I inquired, "have I seen you before?"

When two or more of the same speaker's sentences are quoted together, use only one set of quotation marks.

INCORRECT   Tamisha suggested, "Let's donate the profits from the car wash to Project Day Care." "It provides help for many low-income working parents in this area."
CORRECT   Tamisha suggested, "Let's donate the profits from the car wash to Project Day Care. It provides help for many low-income working parents in this area."

27f. A direct quotation is set off from the rest of the sentence by commas or by a question mark or an exclamation point.

EXAMPLES   Mrs. Castaneda announced, "Remember that your research reports are due Monday," just as the bell rang.

MECHANICS

MEETING *individual* NEEDS

LEP/ESL

General Strategies. Students might be puzzled by the technique of enclosing in quotation marks a fragment of an indirect quotation because the treatment seems to contradict **Rule 27c.** Remind them that the fragment is put in quotation marks to emphasize that those words, although apparently part of an indirect quotation, are in fact the exact words of the person being quoted. The quotation marks are there to indicate that the words they enclose deserve special attention.

A DIFFERENT APPROACH

Instead of having students read all the rules and examples and then take a test on them, you may wish to incorporate the material in this chapter in a writing assignment. Assign students the rules you wish them to master. Review the rules aloud, using the textbook for reference or modeling the rules with examples related to a form of composition the class is currently studying. Then, have students write compositions in which they use examples of every rule covered. For easier grading, have students label their work with the rules assigned.

This approach gives students a chance to use the rules correctly in the context of their own writing instead of in an exercise in which students must merely recognize the need to apply the rules to a set of given sentences.

MECHANICS

COMMON ERROR

Problem. When a direct quotation appears in a sentence that begins with an attribution, students might fail to capitalize the first word of the quotation.

Solution. Have students read each direct quotation in their writing without the attribution. This will help them to decide whether the quotation needs capitalization.

This technique can also help students make better judgments about the flow of dialogue in their writing, and it can also help them decide whether attributions are necessary in the dialogue.

QUICK REMINDER

To emphasize how quotation marks facilitate a reader's understanding of a text, write the following dialogue between two students, Julio and Martha, on the chalkboard as a single paragraph with no quotation marks. Have students read the passage and ask them to figure out who is saying what. Then show them where the divisions occur. Have them talk about the conventions for making dialogue easier to read and understand.

["Hello," said Julio, "where are you going? I'm going to gym class."

"I'm going to study hall. Have you done your algebra homework?"

"Sure."

"When did you do it?" Martha asked. "I finished it this morning."]

Elwyn asked, "On what date does the Ides of March fall?" when it was his turn to quiz the others in his study group.
"That's easy! It's March fifteenth!" Dot exclaimed.

27g. When used with quotation marks, other marks of punctuation are placed according to the following rules.

(1) Commas and periods are always placed inside the closing quotation marks.

EXAMPLE "The concert tickets are sold out," Mary said, "and I had really hoped to go."

(2) Colons and semicolons are always placed outside the closing quotation marks.

EXAMPLES The following students have been named "most likely to succeed": Corey Brown and Sally Ling.
Paka quoted a Cameroonian proverb, "By trying often, the monkey learns to jump from the tree"; it reminded me of the expression "If at first you don't succeed, try, try again."

(3) Question marks and exclamation points are placed inside the closing quotation marks if the quotation is a question or an exclamation. Otherwise, they are placed outside.

EXAMPLES "What time is the game tomorrow?" Maria asked.
Why did you answer, "It doesn't matter"?

On the last lap Vicky said, "Do your best!"
Don't say, "I quit"!

EXERCISE 3 **Writing Sentences with Direct and Indirect Quotations**

Add quotation marks where they are needed in the following sentences. If a sentence is correct, write C.

EXAMPLE 1. When I saw this ad in the paper, I said to Grandmother Hsu, T'ai chi is Chinese, isn't it?
1. *When I saw this ad in the paper, I said to Grandmother Hsu, "T'ai chi is Chinese, isn't it?"*

27g

1. She seemed pleased that I'd asked and replied, "Yes, it's short for t'ai chi ch'uan."
2. She explained that t'ai chi ch'uan was developed in ancient China as a system of self-defense and as an aid to meditation. **2.** C
3. "But the ad says that it's for health and relaxation," I pointed out.
4. "Yes," she said, "it's that, too; it improves coordination and flexibility. In fact, in China people of all ages practice it."
5. "You see," she went on, "its postures and movements are all based on those of animals such as monkeys, birds, and snakes."
6. "Snakes!" I exclaimed.
7. "Why do you twist your face so?" Grandmother asked. "If you observe a snake closely, you'll see how gracefully it moves."
8. "That's true," I admitted.
9. "Maybe," I said, thinking aloud, "I'll check out this grand opening."
10. Imagine my surprise when Grandmother replied with a wide smile, "I'll see you there. I'm one of the instructors."

MECHANICS

MECHANICS

27h. When you write dialogue (a conversation), begin a new paragraph every time the speaker changes.

EXAMPLE　A man of Merv, well known as the home of complicated thinkers, ran shouting one night through the city's streets. "Thief, Thief!" he cried.

The people surrounded him, and when he was a little calmer, asked: "Where was the thief?"

"In my house."

"Did you see him?"

"No."

"Was anything missing?"

"No."

"How do you know there was a thief then?"

"I was lying in bed when I remembered that thieves break into houses without a sound, and move very quietly. I could hear nothing, so I knew that there was a thief in the house, you fool!"

Niamat Khan, "The Thief"

27i. When a quoted passage consists of more than one paragraph, put quotation marks at the beginning of each paragraph and at the end of the entire passage. Do not put quotation marks after any paragraph but the last one in the passage.

EXAMPLE　The saleswoman told my mother, "Now, this car is one of our hottest sellers. It has bucket seats, a CD player, and alloy wheels.

"It's also one of the safest cars on the road because of its heavy suspension and anti-lock brake system. It gets good mileage, too.

"All in all, I think this would be the perfect car for you."

NOTE: A long passage (not dialogue) quoted from a book or some other source is usually separated from the rest of the text in one of several ways. The entire passage may be either indented or set in smaller type. Sometimes the passage is single-spaced rather than double-spaced; however, Modern Language Association guidelines call for double-spacing. When a quoted passage is set off in one of these ways, no quotation marks are necessary.

SELECTION AMENDMENT
Description of change: excerpted
Rationale: to focus on the concept of indenting paragraphs within dialogue presented in this chapter

MECHANICS

27
h–i

EXAMPLE   The Sauk chief Black Hawk had this to say in his speech after
           his last battle against the whites:

> I fought hard. But your guns were well aimed.
> The bullets flew like birds in the air, and whizzed
> by our ears like the wind through the trees in
> winter. My warriors fell around me; it began to
> look dismal. I saw my evil day at hand. The sun
> rose dim on us in the morning, and at night it
> sank in a dark cloud, and looked like a ball of
> fire. That was the last sun that shone on Black
> Hawk. His heart is dead, and no longer beats
> quick in his bosom. He is now a prisoner to the
> white men; they will do with him as they wish.
> But he can stand torture, and is not afraid of
> death. He is no coward. Black Hawk is an Indian.

PICTURE THIS

It's 1870, somewhere on the plains of Nebraska. On your
way back to camp, you and two friends stop to warm your
hands at the chimney of this dugout built by a settler. One
of your companions admires the comforts the dugout provides; the other scorns it because it can't be moved, as
your own dwellings can. Write a short dialogue in which
you side with one of your friends and the two of you try to
convince your other friend to agree with you.

Subject:
  dwellings
Audience:
  your
  companions
Purpose:
  to persuade

Tom Lovell, *The Hand Warmer.* National
Cowboy Hall of Fame and Western Heritage
Center, Oklahoma City, Oklahoma.

MECHANICS

COOPERATIVE LEARNING

Have students work together in
groups of three to complete the **Picture
This** assignment. Each student should
assume the role of one of the three
friends and create and record the characterization and dialogue for that persona.
Remind students that at least one of
them has to admire the dugout, and at
least one has to scorn it. Have groups
work through the stages of the writing
process as described in the feature.
Make it clear that all three students are
responsible for carrying out each stage in
the process.

PICTURE THIS

Begin prewriting by having students create appropriate personas for
themselves and their friends. Students
might imagine themselves as American
Indians, ranchers, farmers, gold rushers,
Pony Express employees, and so on.

Have students complete the
prewriting part of this assignment by
making a chart showing each character's
occupation, actual dwelling place, preferred style of dwelling, and reasons to
be used in the argument.

When students revise, they should
check each persona's statements to make
sure they are consistent and have a persuasive aim. When they proofread, they
should check the punctuation, indenta-
tion, and capitalization of the dialogue.

MECHANICS

REVIEWS A and B

OBJECTIVE

- To correct sentences by adding underlining (italics) and quotation marks where needed

TIMESAVER

To save teaching time and make assimilation of rules for punctuating titles easier for students, have them make charts of the materials covered in **Rules 27a** and **27j.** You and they can use the charts for easy reference.

MECHANICS

MEETING *individual* NEEDS

STUDENTS WITH SPECIAL NEEDS

Some students have poor levels of intrinsic motivation. To help them master the use of quotation marks, assign one or more of the following activities:

1. Choose an article that contains quotation marks and make incorrect changes. Have the students correct the errors.
2. To help students learn the difference between direct and indirect quotations, give them an article and have them make changes so that all direct quotations become indirect quotations.

27j. Use quotation marks to enclose titles of articles, short stories, essays, poems, songs, individual episodes of TV series, and chapters and other parts of books and periodicals.

EXAMPLES I chose to memorize "Pueblo Winter," by Bernice Zamora.
"The Unicorn in the Garden" is my favorite Thurber short story.
For tomorrow, read Chapter 8, "Twentieth-Century Playwrights."

REFERENCE NOTE: Remember that the titles of long poems and long musical compositions are italicized, not enclosed in quotation marks. See the examples on page 832.

27k. Use quotation marks to enclose slang words, technical terms, and other unusual uses of words.

EXAMPLES What's "in" one year is often "out" the following year.
The salesperson said that we should buy a "mouse" to operate the art software on our computer.

NOTE: It is best to avoid using slang words and technical terms whenever possible, except in dialogue, informal writing, technical writing, and other special contexts. If you're not sure whether a word is appropriate, look it up in a dictionary.

MECHANICS

27l. Use single quotation marks to enclose a quotation within a quotation.

EXAMPLES Ron said, "Dad yelled, 'No way!'"
Val asked, "Did you like my arrangement of 'America the Beautiful'?"

REVIEW A **Correcting Sentences by Adding Underlining (Italics) or Quotation Marks**

In the following sentences, write all the words that should be underlined (italicized) or placed in quotation marks, and add the appropriate markings.

LEARNING STYLES

Auditory Learners. Some students have an easier time recognizing parts of sentences that require special treatment if they read the sentences aloud. This may be especially helpful for identifying the foreign words in numbers 1, 6, and 7 of **Review A.**

EXAMPLE **1.** He read aloud The Tell-Tale Heart from The Collected Stories of Edgar Allan Poe.
        1. *"The Tell-Tale Heart"; The Collected Stories of Edgar Allan Poe*

1. Mr. Croce used the word <u>denouement</u> in discussing Rudolfo Anaya's novel <u>Bless Me, Ultima</u>.
2. By next Thursday I have to read the following works: "The Medicine Bag," a short story by Virginia Driving Hawk Sneve; <u>Crown of Shadows</u>, a play by Rodolfo Usigli; and "Daisy Bates: First Lady of Little Rock," an article by Lerone Bennett, Jr., in <u>Ebony</u> magazine.
3. Have you read this article, "El Niño, Global Weather Disaster"?
4. Karen asked me how many <u>m</u>'s are in the word <u>accommodate</u>.
5. Oswald Rivera's 1990 novel <u>Fire and Rain</u> is about the Vietnam War.
6. My favorite plant is <u>Saintpaulia ionantha</u>, commonly called the African violet.
7. We had <u>risotto alla milanese</u> for dinner.
8. The short story "Luke Baldwin's Vow" deals with conflicts in values.
9. "Wouldn't 'Words and Music' be a good title for the new production by our drama club?" Tom asked.
10. She crossed the <u>t</u> with such a flourish that she obliterated the letters above it.

▶ REVIEW B

Correcting Sentences by Adding Underlining (Italics) and Quotation Marks

For each of the following sentences, add underlining (italics) or quotation marks where they are needed. If a sentence is correct, write C.

EXAMPLE **1.** Look at this intriguing painting, said Marshall.
        1. *"Look at this intriguing painting," said Marshall.*

1. He told us that he'd found the painting in <u>Mexican American Artists</u>, a book by Jacinto Quirate; the painting is in the chapter called "The Third Decade."
2. "The painting is by that man on the left, Emilio Aguirre," he explained, "who titled it <u>Alpha 1</u>."

MECHANICS

MECHANICS

MECHANICS

MECHANICS

3. "What do you see when you look at it?" he asked.
4. "You can't miss the <u>Y</u> on the left and the <u>T</u> on the right," he said.
5. "But," he went on, "can you make out the profile of a person sitting on the ground to the left of the <u>T</u>?"
6. Laura said, "Yes, the head is an <u>O</u>," but I objected, saying that it looked more like a <u>Q</u> to me.
7. "I guess you're right," she said. "Anyway, the <u>G</u> outlines the front of the body."
8. Ben asked, "Is the little <u>b</u> on the big <u>O</u> supposed to be the person's glasses? And," he added, "isn't that an <u>M</u> in the background, behind the <u>T</u>?"
9. "Look at this!" exclaimed Marlene. "If you turn the painting ninety degrees to the left, the body looks like a question mark."
10. Can you see why we all agreed when she said, "<u>Intriguing</u> really is the word for <u>Alpha 1</u>"?

WRITING APPLICATION

OBJECTIVE

- To write an interior dialogue using quotation marks and underlining (italics) correctly

WRITING APPLICATION

Writing an Interior Dialogue

Like many people, you probably carry on running conversations with yourself, especially when you have a decision to make. Expressing your ideas and feelings—even to yourself—can help you analyze a situation and arrive at a conclusion. Such interior conversations can involve two, three, four, or more points of view. If you were to write out one of these conversations, you would probably give each point of view a name and use quotation marks to reproduce the dialogue exactly.

▶ WRITING ACTIVITY

You're scheduled to give an oral report on a short story of your own choosing. Write an interior dialogue recording your thoughts as you decide which of two stories to use.

Prewriting List the titles of several short stories you've read. Then choose the two that, for whatever reason, you feel most strongly about. Next, determine how you'll distinguish between your different points of view as you decide which story to choose. For example, you could use your first name for one side, your middle name for another, and other names for as many different points of view as you have.

Writing Write down your thoughts as you consider the pros and cons about using the two stories. (You may want to skim both stories first, but remember, at this point you're not analyzing them, you're just deciding which one to use.) Keep writing until you reach a decision. Don't worry about grammar, mechanics, and usage, but do try to keep track of where you are in the decision-making process.

Evaluating and Revising As you reread your dialogue, check whether your diction (word choice) and sentence structure sound authentic to you. Can you tell at all times which story you're referring to? Is it clear which one you decided to report on, and why? Revise your writing to make it express your thinking process more accurately.

WRITING APPLICATION

This exercise focuses students' attention on the conversations that go on in their minds when they make decisions. Some students might have difficulty distinguishing their internal voices, and some might find it difficult to transcribe their thoughts while they are thinking.

You may wish to have students speak their thoughts into a tape recorder as they arrive at their decisions. Students can then identify the voices and transcribe the dialogue afterwards.

CRITICAL THINKING

Analysis. Classification of the statements made in their decision-making processes might help students distinguish points of view and help them organize their prewriting material.

The concepts of classification and organization might seem complicated to students, so you may need to remind them that in most cases these processes can be very simple. For instance, the statements for this assignment could be classified as those for story 1, those for story 2, those against story 1, and those against story 2. Organization can then be a matter of grouping statements for each story, grouping statements against each story, or grouping statements about story 1 and grouping statements about story 2.

OBJECTIVE

- To correct sentences by adding underlining (italics) and quotation marks where needed

MECHANICS

844 *Punctuation*

 Proofreading and Publishing As you proofread, pay special attention to your use of quotation marks and to the capitalization and punctuation before and after them. Then, photocopy your dialogue or input it on a computer. You and your classmates could tape-record your dialogues or act them out for one another in person or on film. Then you could discuss your responses to writing an interior dialogue to help in decision making.

Review: Posttest

Correcting Sentences by Adding Italics or Quotation Marks

For each of the following sentences, add italics (underlining) or quotation marks where they are needed. If a sentence is correct, write C.

1. "Why did you buy another sleeping bag?" she asked.
2. In his surrender speech, Chief Joseph of the Nez Percé said that he would never fight again.   **2.** C
3. The dance company is performing <u>Swan Lake</u>, a ballet by Tchaikovsky.
4. Anita asked, "Why did he say, 'I won't go to the game?'"
5. <u>The Boston Cooking School Cookbook</u>, now known as <u>The Fannie Farmer Cookbook</u>, was first published in 1891.
6. The first word my baby brother said was <u>bird</u>.
7. "There's an article in this issue of <u>Newsweek</u> that I'd like you to read," said Joan.
8. Wendell B. Harris wrote, directed, and starred in the 1991 movie <u>Chameleon Street</u>.
9. "Her street address has four <u>4</u>'s in it," said Rose. "Did you know that?"
10. "Susan drove one hundred miles," he replied, "to see you on your birthday."

11. My art teacher subscribes to <u>Godzilla</u>, a periodical about Asian artists working in New York City.
12. "Please write to me," Joyce requested. "I want to keep in touch with you."
13. In my report I wrote, "One reviewer praised Dee Brown's book <u>Bury My Heart at Wounded Knee</u> in these words: an important and angry ~~book;~~ but I forgot to cite the <u>New Republic</u> magazine as the source of the quote.   **13. book'";**
14. As we ran down the street, Charles shouted, "Faster! Faster!"
15. Sally said, "John just whispered, 'I'll be at the game tonight.'"
16. Our next history assignment is Chapter 14, "Great Ideals in the Constitution."
17. Did you read the article "The Costs of College Today"?
18. My aunt asked, "What did your friend mean when he said that you look rad in your new glasses?"
19. "The Novelist" is in a collection of W. H. Auden's shorter poems.
20. "You often use the French expression <u>au revoir</u>," said Hannah.

MECHANICS

COMMON ERROR

Problem. Students are sometimes confused as to where a question mark or an exclamation point is placed when the mark is used with a quotation that is part of a larger sentence.

Solution. Tell students to replace the quotation with the letter *x* and ask themselves if the question mark or exclamation point is proper punctuation for the remaining sentence. If it is, the punctuation mark goes outside the quotation marks. If it is not, the punctuation goes inside. The placement can be double-checked by removing the quotation from the sentence and reviewing the quotation by itself. If the question mark or exclamation point seems to be proper end punctuation for the quotation, it goes inside the quotation marks. If not, it goes outside.

MECHANICS

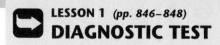

OBJECTIVE

• To add apostrophes, hyphens, dashes, or parentheses, as needed, in given sentences

CHAPTER OVERVIEW

A review of this chapter can aid students in the correct use of often-tricky punctuation marks. This chapter presents fifteen rules involving apostrophes, hyphens, dashes, and parentheses. The chapter will show students how to use these less-common marks correctly and effectively. In addition, the **Writing Application** offers an opportunity for students to practice using one of these marks, the dash, by writing poetry.

Have students refer to this chapter during the proofreading and publishing stages of writing. The rules contained in this chapter cover the most common errors made with these punctuation marks.

28 PUNCTUATION

Apostrophes, Hyphens, Dashes, Parentheses

Diagnostic Test

A. Using Apostrophes and Hyphens Correctly

Add apostrophes and hyphens where they are needed in the following sentences. [Note: Some sentences contain more than one error.] Hyphens are indicated by the ‸ symbol.

EXAMPLE **1.** The childrens boots were lined up outside the door.
  1. *children's*

1. The town's record on supporting youth projects has been good.
2. We hope to see some Aztec and Mayan ruins during our three‿week vacation in Mexico.
3. The police officer said that everyone's house should be searched for the missing child.
4. Only fifty‿three people went to our ballet recital, and thirty of them were our relatives.
5. I bought four pairs of gloves as my two sisters' birth‿day presents.

6. Judo, a Japanese martial art that is popular with both men and women, calls for strength, skill, and self-discipline.

7. Christopher's writing is hard to read because his *a*'s look like *o*'s.

8. We're going on a field trip to the art museum to see the exhibit of post-Victorian cartoons.

9. The women's basketball team, which is coached by an ex-Laker, has run up quite an impressive string of victories.

10. Sampson and Smith's Bakery, which displays its pastries in the window, is around the corner from my house.

B. Using Dashes and Parentheses Correctly

Add dashes or parentheses where they are needed in each of the following sentences. (Do not add commas or colons.) **Answers may vary. Carets indicate placement of dashes.**

EXAMPLE **1.** The school's volunteers freshmen, sophomores, and juniors were honored during the assembly.
1. *The school's volunteers—freshmen, sophomores, and juniors—were honored during the assembly.*

11. My cousins like many of Charlie Pride's songs, his "Crystal Chandeliers" is their favorite.

12. When we met my chemistry teacher at the mall, my little sister's question "Why doesn't that man have any hair on his head?" embarrassed me so much I wanted to hide.

13. This report contains information about agriculture in three South American countries Brazil, Argentina, and Colombia.

14. Crystal's time for the fifty-yard dash the fastest time of anyone on the team qualified her for the regional track meet.

15. I read the wrong chapter for my history homework a disastrous mistake!

16. Mary Ellen Jefferson, a former district attorney, will speak at Thursday's assembly (I'll have to miss gym class) and will address the topic of student rights.

USING THE DIAGNOSTIC TEST

This test will help teachers to gauge students' knowledge and ability in applying the punctuation rules for apostrophes, hyphens, dashes, and parentheses. **Part A** examines students' ability to use apostrophes and hyphens. **Part B** focuses on using dashes and parentheses correctly.

APOSTROPHES Rules 28a–28f

OBJECTIVES

- To form the singular and plural possessive cases of words in a list of nouns and pronouns
- To proofread given phrases and to add necessary apostrophes
- To correct errors in a paragraph by forming possessives
- To identify and to use correctly the possessive forms of words

848 Punctuation

17. Our newspaper, the *Sexton High Chronicle* (it used to be called the *Weekly Warrior*) won the highest award in the state.
18. Bessie Coleman (I read an article about her) was the first licensed African American pilot.
19. Rushing to catch the bus, I dropped my books in the mud (I never should have overslept!) and then lost the heel of my shoe.
20. He works nearly all day in his garden (he retired last year) and is always weeding, mulching, and pruning.

Apostrophes

Possessive Case

The possessive case of a noun or a pronoun shows owner-ship or relationship.

OWNERSHIP	**Jorge's** calculator has a solar battery. Where did she buy **her** bracelet?
RELATIONSHIP	**Pam's** aunt is a plumber. The mother birds had fed **their** young.

Many writers are not always sure about when an apostrophe should be used. Whenever you are in doubt about whether or not to use an apostrophe, try an "of" phrase in place of the word. If the "of" phrase makes sense, then an apostrophe is needed.

EXAMPLE: **yesterdays news** [Should there be an apostrophe in *yesterdays*?]
news "of yesterday" [Because this makes good sense, an apostrophe should be used.]
ANSWER: **yesterday's news**

Nouns in the Possessive Case

28a. To form the possessive case of a singular noun, add an apostrophe and an *s*.

EXAMPLES   Barbara's house   one boy's uniform
               a week's salary   that stereo's speakers

A proper name ending in *s* may add only an apostrophe if

- the name has two or more syllables
  and
- the addition of *s* after the apostrophe would make the name awkward to pronounce.

> EXAMPLES   Xerxes' army
>   Moses' law
>   Sophocles' plays

However, most proper names that end in *s* form the possessive case by adding an apostrophe and an *s*.

EXAMPLES   James's idea
            Dickens's stories
            Dr. Seuss's books

Singular common nouns ending in *s* need both the apostrophe *and* the *s* if the added *s* is pronounced as a separate syllable.

EXAMPLES   the princess's slipper
            my boss's orders
            a bus's wheels

28b. To form the possessive case of a plural noun ending in *s*, add only the apostrophe.

EXAMPLES   cats' owners   cities' problems
            coaches' records   princesses' duties

The few plural nouns that do not end in *s* form the possessive case by adding an apostrophe and an *s*.

EXAMPLES   geese's migration   children's stories

☞ **REFERENCE NOTE:** For more examples of irregular nouns, see page 878.

NOTE: Don't use an apostrophe to form the *plural* of a noun.

> INCORRECT   The four horse's pulled the wagon
> CORRECT   The four horses pulled the wagon.

MECHANICS

LEP/ESL

Spanish. Spanish has a possessive form for pronouns but not for nouns; therefore, there may be much confusion about the use of apostrophes. For example, in Spanish the possessive form would be "the book of José." Students may need extra practice with using the possessive case. You may want to give the students a series of statements that they change by using a possessive form of the noun. An example is "This book belongs to José. It is _____." [José's book]

◆ **COMMON ERROR**

Problem. Students become confused with the use of the apostrophe in contractions and personal pronouns.

Solution. Tell students that a rule to remember is that none of the personal pronouns use 's to form a possessive case.

MECHANICS

ANSWERS
Exercise 1

1. governor, governor's; governors, governors'
2. secretary, secretary's; secretaries, secretaries'
3. bird, bird's; birds, birds'
4. deer, deer's; deer, deer's *or* deers, deers'
5. woman, woman's; women, women's
6. picture, picture's; pictures, pictures'
7. pencil, pencil's; pencils, pencils'
8. class, class's; classes, classes'
9. chief, chief's; chiefs, chiefs'
10. mouse, mouse's; mice, mice's

 EXERCISE 1   **Writing the Possessive Forms of Nouns**

Make four columns headed *Singular, Singular Possessive, Plural,* and *Plural Possessive.* Write those forms of each of the following words. If you don't know how to spell a plural form, check a dictionary.

EXAMPLE

	Singular	Singular Possessive	Plural	Plural Possessive
1.	temple	temple's	temples	temples'

1. governor   3. bird   5. woman   7. pencil   9. chief
2. secretary   4. deer   6. picture   8. class   10. mouse

Pronouns in the Possessive Case

28c. Possessive personal pronouns and the relative pronoun *whose* do not require an apostrophe.

> **Possessive Personal Pronouns**
> my, mine   our, ours
> your, yours   their, theirs
> his, her, hers, its

My, your, her, its, our, and *their* are used before a noun. *Mine, yours, hers, ours,* and *theirs* are used as subjects, complements, or objects. *His* is used in both ways.

EXAMPLES   This is **my** desk. This desk is **mine.**
I borrowed **your** pencil. I borrowed a pencil of **yours.**
Her work is excellent. **Hers** is the best work.
Clara is **our** captain; Dena is **theirs.**

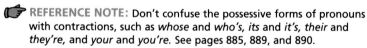 REFERENCE NOTE: Don't confuse the possessive forms of pronouns with contractions, such as *whose* and *who's, its* and *it's, their* and *they're,* and *your* and *you're.* See pages 885, 889, and 890.

28d. Indefinite pronouns in the possessive case require an apostrophe and an *s.*

EXAMPLES   anyone's choice   either's idea

REFERENCE NOTE: See page 517 for a list of indefinite pronouns.

Compounds in the Possessive Case

28e. In compound words, names of organizations and business firms, and words showing joint possession, only the last word is possessive in form.

COMPOUND WORDS	someone **else's** problem sister-in-**law's** office
ORGANIZATIONS	board of **directors'** report Urban **League's** membership
BUSINESS FIRMS JOINT POSSESSION	Acosta and **Rivera's** law firm Bob and **Jim's** canoe Kimi and **Tanaki's** plan aunt and **uncle's** photograph

However, when one of the words showing joint possession is a pronoun, both words should be possessive in form.

EXAMPLE   **Sean's** and her conversation

NOTE: To avoid forming a possessive that sounds awkward, use a phrase beginning with *of* instead.

AWKWARD   the Samuel H. Scripps American Dance Festival Award's winner

BETTER   the winner of the Samuel H. Scripps American Dance Festival Award

28f. When two or more persons possess something individually, each of their names is possessive in form.

EXAMPLES   **Michael's** and **Lila's** wallets
Denise's and **Mark's** books

EXERCISE 2   **Correcting Phrases by Adding Apostrophes**

Proofread the following phrases, adding apostrophes where they are needed. If a phrase is correct, write C.

MECHANICS

TECHNOLOGY TIP
Have students use the spell-checking feature of a word-processing program, if available, to aid in proofreading their writing. You might remind students that this helpful feature will not detect incorrectly spelled homonyms. For example, in the sentence "Their going to the movies," the personal pronoun would go unnoticed.

MECHANICS

INTEGRATING THE LANGUAGE ARTS

Literature Link. One use of apostrophes is often found in literary writing. Authors omit letters and substitute apostrophes to make words sound more like normal speech patterns.

In a selection such as "Mother to Son" by Langston Hughes, students can see how apostrophes are used to create a conversational tone. You could have students rewrite the poem without contractions and then read their versions aloud. Ask students to describe how their versions are different from the original.

MECHANICS

EXAMPLE **1.** the cameras lens
           1. *the camera's lens*

1. a week's pay
2. Ann's and my project   **3.** C
3. two pairs of tennis shoes
4. my father-in-law's boat
5. a good night's sleep

6. Socrates' oration
7. Lynn's and Mike's shoes
8. the seconds ticking by **8.** C
9. the two balloonists' feats
10. a citizen's rights

 EXERCISE 3   **Correcting Paragraphs by Adding Apostrophes**

For each sentence in the following paragraphs, write each <u>word that should be in the possessive case</u>, and add the missing apostrophe.

EXAMPLE   **[1]** Last week I followed my parents suggestion and enrolled in an amateur photography class offered by our citys art center.
           1. *parents'; city's*

[1] I shared my mom and <u>dad's</u> exasperation when, once again, I spent a whole <u>week's</u> allowance on disappointing pictures. [2] I had borrowed Uncle <u>Fred's</u> expensive camera; but even with all that <u>camera's</u> extra features, my photographs looked like <u>children's</u> smudged finger paintings.

[3] My pictures of Bob and <u>Ruth's</u> wedding reception, our <u>family's</u> social event of the year, were destroyed when I fell into the pool with my camera. [4] Last summer I also took pictures during our weeklong visit to <u>Arizona's</u> famous Painted Desert. [5] Unfortunately, I did not understand enough about the <u>sun's</u> strong light at midday, and most of my photographs had that washed-out look.

[6] My <u>life's</u> most embarrassing moment occurred when I took a picture of my class for the <u>school's</u> yearbook and discovered that I had forgotten to put film in the camera. [7] Another time, I took my camera to <u>Tom's</u> party but could not get <u>anyone's</u> attention long enough to set up the shots that I wanted. [8] As a result, I gave up on people and tried to take my <u>pets'</u> pictures; however, a <u>dog's</u> will and a <u>parakeet's</u> wings are hard to control. [9] After all these bad experiences, I knew that I needed a <u>professional's</u> advice. [10] I'm pleased to report that during the very first

photography class, the instructor raised all the <u>students</u>ˀ confidence, including mine.

▶ EXERCISE 4   **Proofreading for Errors in Possessive Forms**

Most of the following sentences contain an incorrect possessive form. For each error, give the correct form of the word. If a sentence is correct, write *C*.

EXAMPLE   **1.** The island nation of the Philippines bears the marks of both Spains and the United States occupations.
        1. *Spain's; United States'*

1. The ̬countrys national language is Pilipino, but its people also speak Spanish, English, and other regional languages.   **1.** country's
2. Did you know that the ̬yo-yos earliest use was as a weapon in the Philippine jungles?   **2.** yo-yo's
3. My ̬mothers boss was visiting the Philippines when Corazon Aquino became president in 1986.   **3.** mother's
4. He took this picture of Mrs. Aquino and some of her supporters dressed in yellow, the color identified with their campaign.   **4.** C

LUZON

Mt. Pinatubo •
Manila ⊛

N
W—E
S

*PHILIPPINE
SEA*

VISAYAN
ISLANDS

OUTH
HINA
SEA

PALAWAN

5. ̬Tina's and Phil's plan to visit the Philippines was postponed when Mount Pinatubo erupted in 1991.   **5.** Tina
6. The ̬Philippines capital and largest city is Manila, which is on the big island of Luzon.   **6.** Philippines'

MECHANICS

VISUAL CONNECTIONS
Ideas for Writing. The picture of Corazon Aquino may allow you to discuss other women who are leaders. Students can generate a list of important women in government and politics. The objective of the lists is to illustrate shared and individual traits and to illustrate how the possessive forms of the women's names should be written; for example, some traits (in possessive form) are Daw Aung San Suu Kyi's and Rigoberto Menchu's Nobel Peace Prizes, Barbara Jordan's impressive career, and Sandra Day O'Connor's and Ruth Bader Ginsburg's historic appointments to the Supreme Court.

MECHANICS

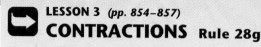
OBJECTIVES

- To use contractions correctly to write captions
- To choose either a contraction or a word in the possessive case to complete a sentence
- To write a short critical review that uses five contractions correctly

---

854 *Punctuation*

7. Both ͜Kim and Marta's lunches came with delicious Filipino custard. **7.** Kim's
8. It's ͜anyones guess how many islands actually make up the Philippines, though there are certainly more than seven thousand islands. **8.** anyone's
9. The Spanish monarch ͜who's soldiers named the Philippines was King Philip II. **9.** whose
10. ͜Childrens pastimes in the Philippines include kite flying and swimming. **10.** Children's

Contractions

28g. Use an apostrophe to show where letters, words, or numerals have been omitted in a contraction.

A *contraction* is a shortened form of a word, a figure, or a group of words. The apostrophes in contractions show where letters, words, or numerals have been left out.

Common Contractions	
who is . . . . who's	she will . . . . . . she'll
there is . . . . there's	I am . . . . I'm
could have . . . . . could've	you are . . . . . you're
1993 . . . . '93	we had . . . . we'd
of the clock . . . . . o'clock	she has . . . . she's
let us . . . . let's	Lisa is . . . . Lisa's

The adverb *not* is often shortened to *n't* and added to a verb without any change in the verb's spelling.

EXAMPLES	is not . . . . isn't	were not . . . . weren't
	are not . . . . . . aren't	has not . . . . hasn't
	does not . . . . doesn't	have not . . . . haven't
	do not . . . . don't	had not . . . . . . hadn't
	did not . . . . . . didn't	would not . . wouldn't
	was not . . . . . wasn't	should not . . shouldn't
EXCEPTIONS	cannot . . . . can't	will not . . . . won't

Make sure that you don't confuse contractions with possessive pronouns.

PROGRAM MANAGER

CONTRACTIONS

- **Independent Practice/ Reteaching** For instruction and exercises, see **Apostrophes in Contractions** in *Language Skills Practice and Assessment,* p. 231.

- **Computer Guided Instruction** For additional instruction and practice with using apostrophes in contractions, see **Lesson 40** in *Language Workshop CD-ROM.*

QUICK REMINDER

Some students need to be reminded of the correct placement of apostrophes in contractions. Write these two pairs of words on the chalkboard:

does'nt	wouldn't
doesn't	would'nt

Ask students to tell you which words are correct. Explain that the two incorrect words illustrate a common misuse of the apostrophe in contractions.

REVIEW A

OBJECTIVE

- To identify words that need apostrophes in given sentences and to insert the apostrophes where they belong

CONTRACTIONS	POSSESSIVE PRONOUNS
Who's next? [who is]	**Whose** turn is next?
It's purring. [It is]	Listen to **its** purr.
You're late. [You are]	**Your** report is late.
There's a mule. [There is]	That mule is **theirs.**
They're healthy pets. [They are]	**Their** pets are healthy.

▶ EXERCISE 5   **Using Contractions**

You are learning how to draw these cartoon figures in action. Using these sketches as models, make five original drawings of characters in motion. Then write captions to go with your drawings. In your captions, use at least five of the following expressions correctly as contractions.

1. should not
2. they have
3. of the clock
4. they would
5. were not
6. she will
7. he is
8. let us
9. who is
10. does not

Cartoons from *Drawing and Selling Cartoons* by Jack Markow, copyright © 1964 by Grosset & Dunlap, Inc. Reprinted by permission of Grosset & Dunlap, Inc.

▶ REVIEW A   **Correcting Sentences by Adding Apostrophes**

Identify each <u>word that needs an apostrophe</u> in the following sentences. Then insert the apostrophes correctly.

MECHANICS

ANSWERS
Exercise 5

Answers will vary. The sketches can be rudimentary and the captions need not be very amusing. The main objective is to have students use the contractions correctly.

MEETING *individual* **NEEDS**

LEP/ESL

General Strategies. To give students more practice in using contractions, have them write dialogues to present in class. Give them a situation on which to base their writing. For example, a ten-dollar bill has been found in the classroom. Whose is it and what should be done with it? Tell students that they must each include a specified number of contractions (six). Then have them work in pairs or small groups to write their dialogues. Students can then present the dialogues to their classmates.

MECHANICS

EXAMPLE   **1.** Werent you the one who said you didnt like eggplant?
      1. *Weren't; didn't*

1. Who's going to be at Leon and Josh's party?
2. Let's hide and see if they'll look for us.
3. I can't find the calamata olives and the feta cheese for the Greek salad.
4. Is her doctor's appointment at nine o'clock?
5. Cleve doesn't have time to mow both his and Ray's lawns.
6. That's the best idea you've had in two days.
7. We're lucky that that dog's barking didn't awaken them.
8. I'm trying to follow Paul's map to Jean's house.
9. It's hailing; therefore, I don't think you should go skiing.
10. Elise couldn't remember the characteristics of the tiger in the Chinese zodiac.

▶ EXERCISE 6   **Recognizing the Correct Use of Apostrophes**

Choose the correct word in parentheses in each of the following sentences.

EXAMPLE   **1.** (*It's, Its*) never too late to learn something new.
      1. *It's*

1. (*You're*, Your) sure that (*you're*, your) allowed to bring (you're, *your*) book to the exam?
2. (*Whose*, Who's) idea was (you're, *your*) trip to the National Civil Rights Museum in Memphis?
3. (*They're*, Their) trying to sell (they're, *their*) house.
4. (*It's*, Its) the best choice.
5. Do you know (*who's*, whose) responsible for (they're, *their*) confusion?
6. I hope the dog can find (it's, *its*) way home.
7. (*It's*, Its) Philip (*who's*, whose) always late.
8. Although (*it's*, its) been snowing all day, (*they're*, their) still planning to go.
9. (*Who's*, Whose) the designer of (they're, *their*) float for Galveston's Mardi Gras parade?
10. I know (*you're*, your) upset with the plan, but (*it's*, its) the only way to solve the problem.

MEETING *individual* NEEDS

LEP/ESL

General Strategies. For the **Picture This** writing assignment, you may first want to brainstorm about the topic of art, because the vocabulary for this subject may be quite difficult for English-language learners. The students could begin discussing what they like or dislike in art. Then they could describe the sculpture objectively. The discussion could then lead to whether the *Geometric Mouse* sculpture is good or bad. It is important that key words be written on the chalkboard for students to copy so that students can refer to the words as they write their assignments.

OBJECTIVE
- To identify words that need apostrophes in given sentences and to add the apostrophes correctly

PICTURE THIS

You are an art critic for *ARTnews* magazine. Write a short review of this modern sculpture. In your review, try to convince readers that *Geometric Mouse* either is or is not good art. In writing the review, rely on your own taste, as well as your understanding of art. Begin by stating your opinion of the sculpture, and then give reasons to support that opinion. Include five different contractions in your review. When you finish writing, compare your review with those of your classmates. Can your class agree on the artistic value of this work?

Walker Art Center, Minneapolis, Gift of Mr. and Mrs. Miles Q. Fiterman, 1991.

Subject: a sculpture
Audience: *ARTnews* readers
Purpose: to persuade

MECHANICS

Plurals

28h. Use an apostrophe and an *–s* to form the plurals of some letters, numerals, symbols, and some words referred to as words.

As a rule, only an *–s* is added to form the plurals of most letters and most words used as words.

EXAMPLES Make your uppercase *W*s higher so that they don't look like lowercase *w*s.

Mr. Carr suggested that I replace some of the *and*s in my paper with other words that are more exact.

However, in some cases both an apostrophe and an *–s* are added to prevent confusion.

You could ask an art teacher to discuss criticism and some of the vocabulary that is associated with it, such as *form, texture, depth, interpretation.* This activity integrates the curriculum and introduces students to what possibly is an unfamiliar subject.

Or, you could have students create their own three-dimensional interpretations of a mouse.

PROGRAM MANAGER

PLURALS

- **Independent Practice/ Reteaching** For instruction and exercises, see **Apostrophes in Plurals** in *Language Skills Practice and Assessment,* p. 232.

- **Computer Guided Instruction** For additional instruction and practice with using apostrophes in plurals, see **Lesson 40** in *Language Workshop CD-ROM.*

- **Practice** To help less-advanced students with additional instruction and practice with using apostrophes in plurals, see **Chapter 22** in *English Workshop, Fourth Course,* pp. 315–316.

QUICK REMINDER

Give students the following letters and words, and have the students identify which ones need apostrophes to make them plural:

a, b, c, and, or, m
[*A, b, c,* and *m* require an *'s,* but *and* and *or* do not.]

Next, you can have students volunteer example sentences that use each of these words or letters.

MECHANICS

MEETING *individual* NEEDS

LEP/ESL

Spanish. In many Spanish dialects, a word's final *s* is often not pronounced. As a result, the students have problems hearing the plural *s* even when it is clearly spoken. To give the students practice in hearing the plural forms, as well as practice in using apostrophes to form plurals of letters and of words used as words, give the students a number of dictations that use both types of plural forms. Have students write the sentences on the chalkboard and discuss the words with the class.

A DIFFERENT APPROACH

Students could work in small groups for this assignment. Their objective is to write a children's book about a world made up of letters and words. Each student could create a different part of the book. Students are to use as many plural letters and plural words referred to as words as they can. Encourage the use of illustrations.

REVIEW B

OBJECTIVE

• To identify words that need apostrophes and to add apostrophes where needed in given sentences

---

858 *Punctuation*

EXAMPLES **There are four *s*'s and four *i*'s in *Mississippi*.** [Without an apostrophe, the plural of *i* would look like the word *is*. Since an apostrophe and *s* are used to form the plural of one letter, an apostrophe and *s* are also used with the other letter for consistency.]
Mr. Carr suggested that I replace some of the *so*'s in my paper with other words that are more exact. [Without the apostrophe, the plural of *so* could be confused with the acronym *sos*.]

NOTE: Using both an apostrophe and an *s* is never wrong. If you have any doubt about whether or not to use the apostrophe, use it.

👉 **REFERENCE NOTE:** For more information about forming these kinds of plurals and the plurals of numerals, see pages 879–880.

▶ REVIEW B   **Correcting Sentences by Adding Apostrophes**

For each of the following sentences, write all the <u>items needing apostrophes</u>, and add the apostrophes.

EXAMPLE   **1.** You may agree with the school boards decision, but I dont.
1. *school board's; don't*

1. <u>Aren't</u> you familiar with the expression "<u>Three's</u> a crowd"?
2. <u>You've</u> forgotten that there are two <u>i's</u> in *llama*.
3. The <u>country's</u> first African American on the Supreme Court was Justice Thurgood Marshall, who was appointed in 1967 and retired in <u>'91</u>.
4. Lewis <u>Carroll's</u> novel *<u>Alice's</u> Adventures in Wonderland* was originally called *<u>Alice's</u> Adventures Underground*.
5. <u>Who's</u> going to change the <u>babies'</u> diapers?
6. After school <u>we're</u> going to visit <u>Pam's</u> brother; <u>he's</u> in St. <u>Mary's</u> Hospital.
7. Rochelle thinks that <u>she'll</u> be taking both biology and English this term.
8. <u>It's</u> been six weeks since I checked the <u>car's</u> oil and its tires.
9. Your story would be better if <u>you'd</u> remove about thirty <u>very's</u>.
10. She learned the Hawaiian <u>alphabet's</u> twelve letters, but Max <u>didn't</u>.

HYPHENS AND COMPOUND WORDS

Rules 28i–28l

OBJECTIVES

- To divide words that come at the end of a line by adding hyphens correctly
- To identify compound words in given sentences and to hyphenate them correctly

Hyphens

Word Division

28i. Use a hyphen to divide a word at the end of a line.

EXAMPLE Even with today's modern technology, scientists can ac‑ count for only about 10 percent of the universe.

As the example shows, a word at the end of a line is always divided between syllables. If you're not sure about a word's syllables, check a dictionary. Also, keep in mind the following rules for dividing words.

(1) Do not divide one-syllable words.

INCORRECT After a long journey, the Spanish explorers reach‑ ed their destination.

CORRECT After a long journey, the Spanish explorers reached their destination.

(2) Words containing double consonants should usually be divided between the double consonants.

EXAMPLES cor‑rect begin‑ning

 REFERENCE NOTE: See the next subrule, 28i (3), for exceptions like *tell-ing* and *call-ing*.

(3) Words with a prefix or suffix can usually be divided between the prefix and the root or the root and the suffix.

EXAMPLES pro‑mote peace‑ful tell‑ing de‑pend‑able

(4) If a word is already hyphenated, divide it only at the hyphen.

INCORRECT My stepsister Melissa plans to take a course in self-de‑ fense.

CORRECT My stepsister Melissa plans to take a course in self‑ defense.

INCORRECT Ms. Malamud always seems to have such a hap‑ py-go-lucky attitude.

CORRECT Ms. Malamud always seems to have such a happy‑ go-lucky attitude.

MECHANICS

 PROGRAM MANAGER

HYPHENS AND COMPOUND WORDS

- **Independent Practice/ Reteaching** For instruction and exercises, see **Hyphens in Divided Words** and **Hyphens and Compound Words** in *Language Skills Practice and Assessment,* pp. 233–234.

- **Computer Guided Instruction** For additional instruction and practice with using hyphens and compound words, see **Lesson 44** in *Language Workshop CD-ROM.*

QUICK REMINDER

Write these nouns on the chalk‑ board:

oil slick	oilskin
lee shore	leeward
push button	push-pull

Some are open compounds (*lee shore*), some closed (*leeward*), and some hyphenated (*push-pull*). Tell stu‑ dents that the use of the hyphen is favored for less-commonly known com‑ pound words. As a compound noun becomes part of everyday usage, the hyphen is usually dropped and the com‑ pound becomes closed or open. An example is the word *notebook.*

MECHANICS

MEETING individual NEEDS

LEP/ESL

General Strategies. English differs from Romance languages in that its speakers often create new words by inventing compound adjectives, such as *short-term* and *present-day*. This feature of English allows writers quite a bit of freedom.

You may want to point out that compound adjectives, like compound nouns, may be joined by hyphens. Give students an example and then have them think of some other examples that follow the same pattern.

COMMON ERROR

Problem. Open compounds used as adjectives can be misleading.

Solution. Hyphenate the words that are closely related or that are ambiguous without hyphens. For example, *free form sculpture* should be *free-form sculpture*.

(5) Do not divide a word so that one letter stands alone.

INCORRECT	In the gloomy twilight, we had caught a momentar-y glimpse of them.
CORRECT	In the gloomy twilight, we had caught a momen▪tary glimpse of them.
INCORRECT	The other driver suddenly changed lanes to go a-round the line of cars.
CORRECT	The other driver suddenly changed lanes to go around the line of cars.

▶ EXERCISE 7 **Using Hyphens to Divide Words at the Ends of Lines**

Write each of the following words, adding a hyphen where you would divide the word at the end of a line. If a word should *not* be divided, write *no hyphen*. If you are unsure where to divide a word, look it up in a dictionary.

Carets indicate possible word divisions.

EXAMPLE **1.** harmonious
1. *har-mo-ni-ous*

1. Olympic
2. algebra
3. toast **3.** no hyphen
4. pemmican
5. drummer
6. alert **6.** no hyphen
7. someone
8. Honduras
9. reservation
10. Johnny‸come-lately

Compound Words

Some compound words are written as one single word (*blueberry*); some are hyphenated (*blue-collar*); and some are written as two or more words (*blue jay, Blue Ridge Mountains*).

Whenever you are not sure about the spelling of a compound word, look up the word in a recently published dictionary.

28j. Use a hyphen with compound numbers from *twenty-one* to *ninety-nine* and with fractions used as adjectives.

EXAMPLES   twenty▪seven students
a two▪thirds majority [but *two thirds* of the class]

28k. Use a hyphen with the prefixes *ex–*, *self–*, and *all–*, with the suffix *–elect*, and with all prefixes before a proper noun or proper adjective.

EXAMPLES   ex-president   mid-December
            self-control   pro-American
            all-purpose   anti-Stalinist
            secretary-elect   pre-Civil War

28l. Hyphenate a compound adjective when it precedes the noun it modifies. Do not use a hyphen if one of the modifiers is an adverb ending in *–ly*.

EXAMPLES   a well-organized trip [But *The trip was well organized.*]
            an after-school job
            a perfectly good answer

NOTE: Some compound adjectives are always hyphenated, no matter whether they precede or follow the nouns they modify.

      EXAMPLES   full-scale
                     down-to-earth

If you have any doubt about whether a compound adjective is hyphenated or not, look up the word in a dictionary.

EXERCISE 8   **Hyphenating Words Correctly**

For each of the following sentences, write and hyphenate the <u>compound words that should be hyphenated</u>.

Hyphens are indicated by the ∧ symbol.

EXAMPLE   **1.** The host of that late night show interviewed an expert on America's pre Civil War years.
          1. *late-night; pre-Civil War*

1. <u>Ex students</u> were not allowed at the festively decorated <u>post prom</u> party.
2. His <u>self confidence</u> faded when he forgot his <u>well planned</u> speech.
3. <u>Twenty five</u> students said they had never heard of the <u>well traveled</u> Overland Trail to California.
4. Two thirds of the class voted, but the proposal was defeated by a <u>seven tenths</u> majority.

INTEGRATING THE LANGUAGE ARTS

Literature Link. Shakespeare used many compound adjectives in his plays and poems. In *The Tragedy of Julius Caesar,* Cicero states, "Indeed, it is a strange-disposed time . . ." (Act I, Scene 2). Discuss the meaning of "strange-disposed" time. Students could look for more compounds in the play and show how the blending of two words adds to the clarity of the meaning.

Some examples of other compound words found in the play are "live-long day" (1.1.46), "sleek-headed men" (1.2.193), "noblest-minded Romans" (1.3.122), "once-commended beauty" (2.1.271), and "barren-spirited fellow" (4.1.36).

Mechanics and Library Skills. Have each student find five compound words in a dictionary. Then, have students research in the library to find the etymologies of the compounds; they can present this information to the class. Students should explain how the separate meaning of each word in a compound adds to the meaning of the compound word.

LESSON 6 *(pp. 862–868)*

DASHES AND PARENTHESES Rules 28m–28o

OBJECTIVE

- To add dashes and parentheses where needed in given sentences

PROGRAM MANAGER

DASHES AND PARENTHESES

- **Independent Practice/ Reteaching** For instruction and exercises, see **Dashes and Parentheses** in *Language Skills Practice and Assessment,* p. 235.

- **Computer Guided Instruction** For additional instruction and practice with using dashes and parentheses, see **Lesson 36** in *Language Workshop CD-ROM.*

- **Practice** To help less-advanced students with additional instruction and practice with using dashes and parentheses, see **Chapter 21** in *English Workshop, Fourth Course,* pp. 303–304.

✔ QUICK REMINDER

Parentheses with other punctuation create problems that plague many writers. Here are a few sample sentences that employ parentheses. See whether students can tell you where other punctuation belongs with the parentheses— either inside or outside the closing one.

1. The salad tastes wonderful (even though it contains my least favorite food, spinach) [).]

2. Our drama club (the award-winning one) practiced for the fall competition. [no other punctuation]

3. Watermelons (when they are in season) pears, and apples are all combined in this delicious dessert. [),]

862

---

862 *Punctuation*

5. Our new <u>governor-elect</u> was once an <u>all-American</u> football player.
6. In our last debate, some students were <u>pro-United</u> Nations, but others were <u>anti-UN</u>.
7. General Colin Powell, who is a former resident of the Bronx, spoke quite eloquently about the importance of <u>self-determination</u>.
8. We all had to memorize a list of <u>twenty-five well-known</u> writers and their works.
9. You must turn in your reports by <u>mid-November</u>.
10. Christopher's <u>achievement-test</u> scores ranked in the <u>eighty-eighth</u> percentile.

Dashes

Most parenthetical elements are set off by commas or parentheses.

EXAMPLES Felipe**, however,** had a better idea.
Her suggestion **(that we serve fruit and cheese instead of junk food)** was approved unanimously.

Sometimes, though, such elements call for a sharper separation from the rest of the sentence. In such cases, dashes are used.

NOTE: On a typewriter or a computer, indicate a dash by typing two hyphens. Do not leave a space before, between, or after the hyphens.

28m. Use a dash to indicate an abrupt break in thought or speech or an unfinished statement or question.

EXAMPLES The party—I'm sorry I forgot to tell you—was not changed to next week.
When Jiffy was born—he was the last puppy—we weren't sure he would survive.
"Why—why won't you believe me?" Ronnie asked pleadingly.
"What I meant was—" Vonda began as the doorbell rang.

28n. Use a dash to mean *namely, that is, in other words,* and similar expressions that come before an explanation.

EXAMPLES   Our family owns two vehicles—a station wagon and a pickup truck. [*namely*]
             The weather was unseasonably warm—in the low eighties—which was a welcome change. [*that is*]

NOTE: Either the dash or a colon is acceptable in the first example above.

Parentheses

28o. Use parentheses to enclose material of minor importance in a sentence.

EXAMPLES   The Pyramid of the Magician (I never thought I'd actually see it in person) rose majestically against the purple sky of Uxmal, in the Mexican Yucatán.
             My grandmother (she's only fifty) swims three miles every day.

Material enclosed in parentheses may range from a single word to a short sentence. A short sentence in parentheses may stand by itself or may be included in the main sentence.

When punctuation marks belong with the parenthetical materials, place them inside the parentheses. When they belong with the sentence as a whole, place them outside the parentheses.

EXAMPLES   Mark your answers with a lead pencil. (Do not use ink.) [The parenthetical sentence stands by itself.]
             The child's question ("What inning is it?") tickled the rest of us watching the football game. [The parenthetical sentence is a quoted question included in the main sentence.]
             When we reached Shaker Heights (it's just outside Cleveland), we met our cousins for dinner. [The parenthetical sentence is a statement included within the main sentence. Notice that no period is used at the end of a parenthetical declarative sentence included within another sentence.]

MECHANICS

MECHANICS

INTEGRATING THE LANGUAGE ARTS

Literature Link. Have students scan the poetry section of their literature books to discover poems that include several dashes. For example, in the poem "Theme for English B" by Langston Hughes, students will find nine instances of dashes and parentheses. Ask students to describe the implication of each.

[The dashes emphasize the goal of the instructor's assignment, the poet's connection to his community, his self-examination, his tastes in music, the teacher-student relationship, and the student's role as teacher. The parentheses enclose an additional comment by the poet explaining that he should listen not only to the voices from his African American heritage but also to the voices of all people.]

GUIDELINES FOR PUNCTUATING PARENTHETICAL MATERIAL

Commas, dashes, and parentheses are all used to enclose parenthetical material. In general, follow these guidelines for determining when to use the three different types of punctuation marks.

1. Remember that only material that can be omitted without changing the sentence's basic meaning is considered parenthetical.
2. Use commas to set off elements that are closely related to the rest of the sentence.
3. Use dashes to emphasize an abrupt change in thought.
4. Use parentheses to minimize the importance of the enclosed material.
5. Don't confuse your reader by using too many parenthetical elements.

EXAMPLES   We rehearsed for the show, a wonderful musical comedy.
We rehearsed for the show—the musical event of the year!
We rehearsed (at least those of us who managed to remember our lines did) for the show.

 EXERCISE 9   **Correcting Sentences by Using Dashes and Parentheses**

Write the following sentences, adding dashes and parentheses where they are needed. If a sentence is correct, write C.   Answers may vary. Carets indicate placement of dashes.

EXAMPLE   **1.** The Oak Ridge Boys and Alabama I have every one of their albums have won many awards.
1. *The Oak Ridge Boys and Alabama (I have every one of their albums) have won many awards.*

1. "Yankee Doodle" (it was the unofficial United States anthem at the time) was played after the signing of the Treaty of Ghent.
2. Inspired by the view at the top of Pikes Peak, Katherine Lee Bates wrote the words to the song "America the Beautiful." **2.** C

OBJECTIVE

- To proofread sentences for punctuation and to add apostrophes, hyphens, dashes, or parentheses where required

3. Gloria Estefan(I love her songs!)gave a concert here, and it was sold out.
4. There were three original members of the Sons of the Pioneers⌃Roy Rogers(his real name is Leonard Slye), Bob Nolan, and Tim Spencer.
5. Linda Ronstadt has recorded many different kinds of music, including rock, songs from the 1930s and '40s, and Mexican tunes.   **5.** C
6. The Beatles used several names⌃Foreverly Brothers, the Cavemen, the Moondogs, and the Quarrymen⌃ before they settled on Beatles.
7. Bob Dylan's real name⌃Robert Allen Zimmerman⌃ isn't commonly known.
8. Cathy agreed to listen to Mozart's concertos(what a surprise!)if her parents would listen to one of Paula Abdul's tapes.
9. Last night's concert was about average⌃the beat was good, but the singers were uninspired.
10. Whitney Houston had a hit song(Wouldn't Francis Scott Key be pleased?)with her version of "The Star-Spangled Banner."

▶ REVIEW C   **Proofreading for Errors in Punctuation**

Each of the following sentences contains at least one error in punctuation. Correct these errors by adding apostrophes, hyphens, dashes, or parentheses where they are needed.   Answers may vary. The ⌄ symbol indicates placement of hyphens; carets indicate placement of dashes.

EXAMPLE   **1.** Dont you ever wonder I frequently do about who invented different kinds of machines and tools?
          1. Don't; —I frequently do—

1. Both Trish's and Robert's reports(the ones required for social studies)were about the shoe industry.
2. Trish joked that she chose the subject because at least seventy⌄five percent of the world's students wear shoes.
3. I thought the other report⌃the one that Robert gave on the invention of the lasting machine⌃was better written, though.
4. The lasting machine(its many parts are numbered in the intricate patent drawing on the next page) changed the shoe industry's future.

MECHANICS

MECHANICS

866 *Punctuation*

5. The machine's inventor, the distinguished-looking young man pictured below, was Jan Matzeliger.
6. He came to the United States from Dutch Guiana (now Suriname) in the 1870s and found work as a shoemaker's apprentice.
7. Matzeliger wasn't happy with the amount of workers' time that was spent putting shoes together.
8. Within ten years' time, he perfected a machine that shaped leather for the upper shoe and attached it to the sole.
9. Matzeliger's patent for this all-important machine was granted in 1883.
10. The United Shoe Manufacturing Company's decision to buy the machine gave that company control of the United States' shoe market.

No. 274,207. J. E. MATZELIGER.
LASTING MACHINE
PATENTED MAR. 20, 1883.

The Granger Collection, New York.

WRITING APPLICATION

Using Dashes in Poetry

Have you ever noticed that many poems contain dashes? Poets use dashes not only to indicate sharp separations of thoughts but also to emphasize particular words or phrases. Notice how John Ciardi uses dashes in the following poem.

WRITING APPLICATION You could have students skim through the poetry section of their literature textbooks to find a poem that contains dashes or parentheses. In addition, students should be able to describe how the dashes or parentheses are used in their own poems or be able to comment on the effectiveness of this punctuation in their poems.

866

MECHANICS

MECHANICS

How Time Goes

How old am I? I really don't know,
    But I can tell you I have spent
My whole life—up to a minute ago—
    Being younger than I am now. I meant
To keep it that way, I suppose,
But that's how it is with time—it goes.

Which use of the dash in the poem signals a break in thought? Which use of the dash means *namely*?

▶ WRITING ACTIVITY

You've decided to enter a local poetry contest for high school students. The name of the contest is Poetry for Our Time, and all the poems have to reflect students' ideas about current subjects. For the contest, write a poem that uses at least four dashes.

Prewriting Start by making a list of some subjects that interest you. You might list abstract subjects, such as love and peace, or concrete ones, such as environmental or school issues. Choose a subject from your list, and then freewrite about it. List as many sensory details as you can to describe your subject. Then start grouping these details to create a loose structure for your poem. Before you begin writing your poem, decide on a rhyme scheme and rhythm.

Writing Use your freewriting notes to write your first draft. As you form your ideas into lines of poetry, keep in mind your rhyme scheme and rhythm pattern. Choose words carefully, paying attention both to their sound and to the images they create.

Evaluating and Revising Read your poem silently to be sure that it says what you want it to. Add, cut, or rearrange details to express your ideas more effectively. Then read your poem aloud and listen to the sound and rhythm of the words you've used. Make any changes that are necessary to create the rhyme scheme and rhythm you chose in your prewriting. Be sure that you've used at least four dashes in your poem.

MECHANICS

CRITICAL THINKING

Synthesis. Have students discuss what kind of subject would allow a dash to be used appropriately [a dream, for example, in which thoughts are unsettled]. Next, have students move into small groups to create scenes with dialogue in which it is appropriate to use dashes. An argument might serve as a starting point. Set a very limited time period for this collaborative creation, and encourage students to write dialogues or arguments based on topics of concern to them.

PREWRITING

You could brainstorm some topics by using the front page of the newspaper. If the topics don't spark interest, ask students what issues concern them. List some of their responses on the chalkboard.

MEETING *individual* NEEDS

STUDENTS WITH SPECIAL NEEDS

This activity may overwhelm students who have difficulty with expressive language.

Have students write poems that use words and phrases from magazines and newspapers. Tell each student to choose a theme and to cut out words pertaining to this theme. Students should arrange the words on the page and add dashes for emphasis and separation of ideas.

MECHANICS

LESSON 7 (pp. 868–869)
REVIEW: POSTTEST

OBJECTIVES

- To add apostrophes or hyphens in order to correct errors in given sentences
- To rewrite given sentences, adding dashes or parentheses where needed

868 *Punctuation*

 Proofreading and Publishing Now, check the spelling and punctuation in your poem. If you've typed your poem or input it on a keyboard, check to see that the spacing around hyphens and dashes is correct. You could publish your poem by submitting it to a school newspaper or literary magazine, or by reading it aloud to the class.

Review: Posttest

A. Correcting Sentences by Using Apostrophes and Hyphens

For each of the following sentences, write the <u>word or words that should have an apostrophe or a hyphen</u>, and add the appropriate punctuation mark. If a sentence is correct, write C. Hyphens are indicated by the ₄ symbol.

EXAMPLE **1.** Michaels stamp collection contains thirty two rare stamps.
1. *Michael's; thirty-two*

1. Because of the sudden blizzard, the <u>armies'</u>supplies were cut off.
2. <u>It's</u> frustrating when the car <u>won't</u> start because its battery is dead.
3. After hours of discussion, the decision is that we need a <u>two-thirds</u> majority to pass new rules in the student council.
4. Even though Li moved here from Korea last year, <u>she's</u> making <u>A's</u> in most of her classes.
5. If you go to the game on Saturday, <u>who's</u> going to watch the children?
6. Miranda had the flu this past week, and now she has five <u>days'</u>worth of homework to do this weekend.
7. Rodney interviewed the <u>treasurer-elect</u> of the Honor Society for the "Personality Profile" column in the school newspaper.

PROOFREADING AND PUBLISHING

Have students combine their poems in the form of a booklet. Copies could be made and students would then have a collection of poems on topics that were of concern during their tenth-grade school year.

TIMESAVER

Listed below are the applicable chapter punctuation rules for each question in **Part A** of the **Review: Posttest**. For example, the answer to question 1 is *armies'* and **28b** states the punctuation rule on the possessive case of plural words. If a student does poorly on the **Posttest**, the cross-reference may help you focus on what rules have not been mastered by the student.

1. b	**6.** b	**11.** g
2. g	**7.** k	**12.** g
3. j	**8.** l	**13.** k; i
4. g; h	**9.** a	**14.** g
5. g	**10.** j; e	**15.** g; h

MECHANICS

MECHANICS

868

8. James Berry, who was born in Jamaica, wrote the well-received collection of short stories *A Thief in the Village and Other Stories.*
9. One of my aunt's favorite expressions is "Never let the sun set on your anger."
10. My brother-in-law Murray works at a resort in New York's Catskill Mountains.
11. If we return the tape recorder by five o'clock, the store clerk said she would refund our deposit.
12. The alarm clock hasn't worked since the morning I knocked it off the night stand.
13. Last week, the senator presented as evidence the anti-American pamphlets distributed by the terror-ist group.
14. You have such a wonderful singing voice that I'm sure you'll get a part in the school musical.
15. Don't be alarmed, Brian; the red +'s on your paper indicate correct answers.

B. Correcting Sentences by Using Dashes and Parentheses

Rewrite the following sentences, adding dashes or parentheses where they are needed. (Do not add commas or colons to these sentences.) Answers may vary. Carets indicate placement of dashes.

EXAMPLE   **1.** The books on that table they are all nonfiction are on sale today.
   1. *The books on that table—they are all nonfiction—are on sale today.*

16. The discovery of gold at Sutter's Mill brought floods of people settlers, miners, prospectors, and merchants to California in their covered wagons.
17. The old white house on Tenth Street(it was once a governor's mansion) is a landmark in our town.
18. Answer the ten questions on this English quiz(be careful, they're tricky!)and then write a couplet or a limerick for extra credit.
19. My mom's Persian cookbook has a recipe I'm not making this up for eggplant pickles.
20. The Atacama Desert(the driest region on the earth) receives so little rain that it can barely be measured.

CHAPTER OVERVIEW

This chapter focuses on strategies for learning how to spell correctly and on specific spelling rules, and it clarifies the distinctions between words whose spellings are often confused. In addition, the chapter provides lists titled **100 Commonly Misspelled Words** and **300 Spelling Words** that students can study over the course of a semester or year.

The material in this chapter can serve as a useful reference for students when they are studying dictionary skills, the principal parts of verbs, or any of the writing chapters.

MECHANICS

MECHANICS

29 SPELLING

Improving Your Spelling

Good Spelling Habits

The following techniques can help you become a better speller.

1. *To learn the spelling of a word, pronounce the word, study it, and write it.*

    - First, pronounce the word.
    - Second, study the word, noting especially any parts that might be hard to remember.
    - Third, write the word from memory. Check your spelling.
    - If you misspelled the word, repeat the process.

2. *Use a dictionary.* Don't guess about correct spelling. Look up any words you misspell. In the dictionary, you can often find other, related words that may help you remember the correct spelling. For example, it may be easier to spell *denomination* after you see its kinship with the words *nominate* and *denominator*.

3. ***Spell by syllables.*** A *syllable* is a word part that can be pronounced by itself.

> EXAMPLES   **pul´•sate** [two syllables]
> **bul´•le•tin** [three syllables]
> **en•vi´•ron•ment** [four syllables]

4. ***Pronounce words carefully.*** If you say *suprise* instead of *surprise,* you'll likely misspell the word. When you look up the spelling of a word in a dictionary, notice how the word is pronounced. Knowing the correct pronunciation of a word will usually help you spell it correctly.

> EXAMPLES   **ath*l*etic** [not atha*l*etic]
> **es*c*ape** [not ex*c*ape]
> **heigh*t*** [not heigh*th*]

5. ***Proofread for careless spelling errors.*** Reread your writing carefully, correcting any mistakes and unclear letters.

6. ***Keep a spelling notebook.*** Divide each page into four columns:

> COLUMN 1   Correctly spell the word you missed. (Never enter a misspelled word.)
> COLUMN 2   Write the word again, dividing it into syllables and accenting the stressed syllable(s).
> COLUMN 3   Write the word a third time, circling the part(s) that cause you trouble.
> COLUMN 4   Jot down any comments that will help you remember the correct spelling.

Correct Spelling	Syllables and Accents	Trouble Spot	Comments
February	Feb´•ru•ar•y	Feb(ru)ary	Pronounce correctly.
disapproval	dis´•ap•pro´val	di(sa)ppro(val)	Study rules 29d and 29f.

GOOD SPELLING HABITS

Here are some additional spelling strategies that you could suggest to students:

1. Generate mnemonics. For example, students might use the sentence *"We* are *we*ird" to remember how to spell *weird.*
2. Write particularly troublesome spelling words on index cards and post them in prominent places.
3. Visualize correctly spelled words or visualize writing correctly spelled words.
4. Periodically review spelling notebooks for duplicate entries. Duplicate entries might suggest that particular spelling rules should be studied.

MECHANICS

MECHANICS

PROGRAM MANAGER

SPELLING RULES

- **Independent Practice/ Reteaching** For instruction and exercises, see **Proofreading for Spelling Errors, Using Spelling Rules, Adding Prefixes and Suffixes, Forming Plurals of Nouns,** and **Spelling Numbers** in *Language Skills Practice and Assessment,* pp. 247–251.

- **Computer Guided Instruction** For additional instruction and practice with spelling rules, see **Lesson 47** in *Language Workshop CD-ROM.*

- **Practice** To help less-advanced students with additional instruction and practice with spelling rules, see **Chapter 22** in *English Workshop, Fourth Course,* pp. 309–318.

 QUICK REMINDER

Each of the misspelled words in the following sentences violates one of the spelling rules in this lesson. Write the sentences on the chalkboard and have students identify and correct the misspelled words.

1. Carmen's soccer team had to forfiet its last game of the season. [forfeit]
2. Councilwoman Ortega's opponent conceeded the election at 2:30 A.M. [conceded]
3. High school achievment tests will be given Tuesday morning. [achievement]
4. In many offices, computers are pre-fered. [preferred]
5. James and Thomas are brother-in-laws. [brothers-in-law]

 LESSON 1 *(pp. 872–882)*
SPELLING RULES Rules 29a–29n

OBJECTIVES

- To proofread a paragraph to correct spelling errors
- To correctly add prefixes and suffixes to words
- To correctly spell the plurals of nouns

Spelling Rules

The following rules can help you remember how to spell many words.

ie and *ei*

29a. Write *ie* when the sound is long *e*, except after *c*.

EXAMPLES **chief, believe, niece, deceive, perceive, receipt**
EXCEPTIONS **either, leisure, neither, seize, weird**

29b. Write *ei* when the sound is not long *e*.

EXAMPLES **forfeit, freight, height, neighbor, veil, weigh**
EXCEPTIONS **friend, mischief**

–cede, –ceed, and *–sede*

29c. The only English word that ends in *–sede* is *supersede*. Only three words end in *–ceed: exceed, proceed,* and *succeed*. Most other words with this sound end in *–cede*.

EXAMPLES **con**cede**, pre**cede**, re**cede

EXERCISE 1 **Proofreading a Paragraph to Correct Spelling Errors**

Proofread the following paragraph, correcting the ten misspelled words.

1. superseded/ preceded

2. achieved/ leisure-time

3. height

4. their

[1] During the 1920s, one craze ~~superceded~~ another, each one weirder than the one that ~~preceeded~~ it. [2] Pictured on the next page is fifteen-year-old Avon Foreman, who ~~acheived~~ fame in Baltimore for his bizarre ~~leisure-time~~ activity. [3] In 1929, he spent ten days, ten hours, ten minutes, and ten seconds perched atop a hickory sapling, at a ~~hieght~~ of eighteen feet. [4] The people craning ~~thier~~

4. friends/received   **5.** succeeded

necks to look up at him are just a few of the hundreds of ~~freinds~~ and neighbors from whom he ~~recieved~~ encouragement. [5] He even ~~succeeded~~ in attracting the attention of the mayor, William F. Broening, who wrote to him that his "grit and stamina . . . show that the old pioneer spirit of early America is being kept alive by the youth of today." [6] Evidently the mayor ~~beleived~~ that Avon was indeed someone to look up to.   **6.** believed

Adding Prefixes

29d. When a prefix is added to a word, the spelling of the original word remains the same.

EXAMPLES   mis + spell = **mis**spell   dis + advantage = **dis**advantage
        un + likely = **un**likely   il + legible = **il**legible

Adding Suffixes

29e. When the suffix *–ly* or *–ness* is added to a word, the spelling of the original word usually remains the same.

EXAMPLES   nice + ly = nice**ly**   mean + ness = mean**ness**
        usual + ly = usual**ly**   same + ness = same**ness**
EXCEPTIONS   1. Words ending in *y* usually change the *y* to *i* before *–ness* and *–ly*.
                steady—steadily, sloppy—sloppiness
          2. However, most one-syllable adjectives ending in *y* follow rule 29e.
                shy—shyness, dry—dryly

MECHANICS

MEETING *individual* **NEEDS**

LEP/ESL

General Strategies. Not all languages form plurals by adding suffixes, as does English. In Swahili, for example, plurals are formed by changing prefixes. If you have students in your class who speak other languages, involve them in this lesson by asking them how plurals are formed in the languages they speak.

MECHANICS

ANSWERS

Exercise 2

1. heaviness
2. dissatisfied
3. illegal
4. unnerve
5. sincerely
6. ordinarily
7. immature
8. suddenness
9. specially
10. overrate

 INTEGRATING THE LANGUAGE ARTS

Mechanics and Vocabulary. To help students build vocabulary, group prefixes according to meaning:

Prefixes that show quantity:

| half | *semi*circle |
| one | *uni*cycle |

Prefixes that show negation:

| not, lack of, | *un*happy, *dis*respect |
| against | *anti*war |

Prefixes that show time:

before	*fore*cast, *pre*date
after	*post*war
again	*re*view

Prefixes that show direction or position:

above, over	*super*vise
across, over	*trans*port
together	*co*exist

You may want to ask students to generate lists of words that include these prefixes.

874

▶ EXERCISE 2 **Spelling Words with Prefixes and Suffixes**

Add the prefix or suffix given for each word, and spell the new word formed.

1. heavy + ness
2. dis + satisfied
3. il + legal
4. un + nerve
5. sincere + ly
6. ordinary + ly
7. im + mature
8. sudden + ness
9. special + ly
10. over + rate

29f. Drop the final silent *e* before a suffix beginning with a vowel.

EXAMPLES	dine + ing = dining	safe + er = safer
	sense + ible = sensible	hope + ed = hoped
	use + able = usable	nice + est = nicest

EXCEPTIONS
1. Keep the final silent *e* in words ending in *ce* or *ge* before a suffix that begins with *a* or *o*.
    servi**ce**able, mana**ge**able, advanta**ge**ous
2. To avoid confusion with other words, keep the final silent *e* in some words.
    dyeing and *dying*   *singeing* and *singing*

29g. Keep the final silent *e* before a suffix beginning with a consonant.

EXAMPLES	use + ful = useful
	advertise + ment = advertisement
EXCEPTIONS	true + ly = truly
	argue + ment = argument
	judge + ment = judgment

▶ EXERCISE 3 **Spelling Words with Suffixes**

Add the suffix given for each word, and spell the new words formed.

1. courage + ous   **1.** courageous
2. nine + ty   **2.** ninety
3. advance + ing   **3.** advancing
4. hope + ful   **4.** hopeful
5. approve + al   **5.** approval

29h. If the final *y* is preceded by a consonant, change the *y* to *i* before any suffix except one beginning with an *i.*

EXAMPLES lively + ness = liveliness   rely + ed = relied
bury + al = burial   funny + er = funnier
study + ing = studying   hasty + est = hastiest

▶ EXERCISE 4 **Spelling Words with Suffixes**

Add the suffix given for each word, and spell the new words formed.

1. happy + est **1.** happiest 6. spy + ing **6.** spying
2. marry + ing **2.** marrying 7. pity + ing **7.** pitying
3. delay + ed **3.** delayed 8. try + ed **8.** tried
4. shiny + er **4.** shinier 9. pretty + ness **9.** prettiness
5. beauty + ful **5.** beautiful 10. busy + ly **10.** busily

29i. Double the final consonant before a suffix that begins with a vowel only if the word

1. has only one syllable or is accented on the last syllable

and

2. ends in a *single* consonant preceded by a *single* vowel.

EXAMPLES glad + est = gla**dd**est
[one-syllable word]
begin + ing = begin**n**ing
[accent on the last syllable]

differ + ence = difference
[accent on the first syllable]
droop + ed = drooped
[single consonant preceded by a *double* vowel]

©John Caldwell 1986.

NOTE: In some words, the final consonant may or may not be doubled. Both spellings are acceptable.

EXAMPLES travel + ed = traveled *or* travelled
stencil + ing = stenciling *or* stencilling

REVIEW A

OBJECTIVE

• To proofread a paragraph and to correct spelling errors

876 Spelling

▶ EXERCISE 5 **Spelling Words with Suffixes**

Add the suffix given for each word, and spell the new words formed.

1. mad + er **1.** madder   6. confer + ed **6.** conferred
2. propel + er **2.** propeller   7. suffer + ance **7.** sufferance
3. shovel + ing **3.** shoveling 8. hop + ing **8.** hopping
4. refer + al **4.** referral   9. shop + ed **9.** shopped
5. repel + ent **5.** repellent   10. remit + ance **10.** remittance

▶ REVIEW A **Proofreading a Paragraph to Correct Spelling Errors**

Proofread the following paragraph, correcting the misspelled word in each sentence.

1. committed

[1] The Shawnee war chief Tecumseh was ~~commited~~ to the goal of uniting Native Americans. [2] He believed that unification was the only way to prevent white settlers

2. seizing

from ~~siezing~~ and taking over the land that his people lived on. [3] Opposed to treaties that forced Native Americans to

3. forfeit

~~forfiet~~ their land, Tecumseh believed that the land was owned by no one. [4] After much hard work, he ~~succeded~~

4. succeeded

in convincing some midwestern Native American peoples to join together. [5] With his brother, known as the Shawnee Prophet, Tecumseh urged his people to pre-

5. living

serve their traditional ways of ~~liveing~~ and not to surrender the land. [6] Tecumseh and the Shawnee Prophet (shown

6. their

below) led ~~thier~~ followers in building Prophetstown at

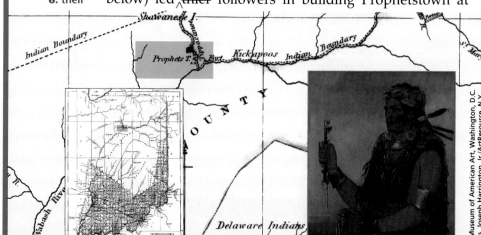

the location indicated on this map of Indiana. [7] In 1811, while Tecumseh was delivering a speech in a neighboring village, the governor of the Indiana Territory, William Henry Harrison, ~~easyly~~ attacked Prophetstown. [8] Against Tecumseh's wishes, the Shawnee Prophet proceeded to counterattack, but he finally had to ~~consede~~ defeat in the Battle of Tippecanoe. [9] ~~Overun~~ by Harrison, Tecumseh's people scattered, leaving the town in ruins and bringing an end to twenty years of Tecumseh's work. [10] Tecumseh had ~~planed~~ to start over, but his death in 1813 at the Battle of the Thames ended all hopes of uniting the various Native American nations.

7. easily
8. concede
9. Overrun
10. planned

Forming Plurals of Nouns

29j. To form the plural of most English nouns, simply add *s*.

SINGULAR	dog	kite	pencil	video	organization
PLURAL	dog**s**	kite**s**	pencil**s**	video**s**	organization**s**

29k. To form the plurals of other nouns, follow these rules.

(1) If the noun ends in *s, x, z, sh,* or *ch,* add *es.*

SINGULAR	glass	waltz	suffix	bush	trench
PLURAL	glass**es**	waltz**es**	suffix**es**	bush**es**	trench**es**

NOTE: Proper nouns usually follow this rule, too.

> EXAMPLES   the Barnes**es**, the Gómez**es**

(2) If the noun ends in *y* preceded by a consonant, change the *y* to *i* and add *es.*

SINGULAR	city	enemy	spy	penny
PLURAL	cit**ies**	enem**ies**	sp**ies**	penn**ies**

(3) If the noun ends in *y* preceded by a vowel, add *s.*

SINGULAR	alloy	turkey	essay	Sunday
PLURAL	alloy**s**	turkey**s**	essay**s**	Sunday**s**

MECHANICS

MECHANICS

A DIFFERENT APPROACH

Students might be wondering why there has been no attempt to make English spelling more consistent. Tell students that several campaigns have been mounted to simplify English spellings. One of the most famous proponents of a simplified spelling system was Bernard Shaw. Challenge interested students to find out more about Shaw's ideas for reform. Students could then present their findings orally to the class.

(4) For some nouns ending in *f* or *fe,* add *s.* For others, change the *f* or *fe* to *v* and add *es.*

Add *s:*

SINGULAR	belief	roof	fife	cliff
PLURAL	belie**fs**	roo**fs**	fife**s**	cliff**s**

Change *f* or *fe* to *v* and add *es:*

SINGULAR	wolf	thief	knife	leaf
PLURAL	wol**ves**	thie**ves**	kni**ves**	lea**ves**

(5) If the noun ends in *o* preceded by a vowel, add *s.* If the noun ends in *o* preceded by a consonant, add *es.*

SINGULAR	patio	rodeo	tomato	hero
PLURAL	patio**s**	rodeo**s**	tomato**es**	hero**es**

EXCEPTIONS 1. Nouns for musical terms that end in *o* preceded by a consonant form the plural by adding only *s.*

SINGULAR	alto	soprano	piano	solo
PLURAL	alto**s**	soprano**s**	piano**s**	solo**s**

2. A few other nouns that end in *o* preceded by a consonant form the plural by adding only *s.*

SINGULAR	photo	silo	taco
PLURAL	photo**s**	silo**s**	taco**s**

NOTE: In some cases, the plural of a word ending in *o* may be formed by adding either *s* or *es.*

SINGULAR	mosquito	cargo
PLURAL	mosquito**s** *or* mosquito**es**	cargo**s** or cargo**es**

(6) The plurals of some nouns are formed in irregular ways.

SINGULAR	child	ox	woman	tooth	mouse	foot
PLURAL	child**ren**	ox**en**	wo**men**	t**ee**th	m**i**ce	f**ee**t

(7) Some nouns have the same form in both the singular and the plural.

SINGULAR AND PLURAL	Chinese	scissors	salmon	sheep

(8) For most compound nouns, make the main word plural.

The main word is the noun that is modified.

SINGULAR	editor in chief	son-in-law	looker-on	runner-up
PLURAL	editors in chief	sons-in-law	lookers-on	runners-up

The plurals of a few compound nouns are formed in irregular ways.

SINGULAR	drive-in	lean-to	two-year-old
PLURAL	drive-ins	lean-tos	two-year-olds

(9) Some nouns borrowed from other languages form their plurals as they do in the original language.

SINGULAR	PLURAL
alumnus [male]	alumni
alumna [female]	alumnae
vertebra	vertebrae
parenthesis	parentheses
datum	data

NOTE: A few nouns borrowed from other languages have two plural forms. Check a dictionary to find the preferred spelling of such plurals.

SINGULAR	formula	index
PLURAL	formulae *or*	indices *or*
	formulas [preferred]	indexes [preferred]

(10) To form the plurals of numerals, most capital letters, symbols, and words used as words, add either an –s or an apostrophe and an –s.

EXAMPLES His **7s** [or **7's**] look like **Ts** [or **T's**].
Do not write **&s** [or **&'s**] for **ands** [or **and's**].
Phillis Wheatley wrote during the **1700s** [or **1700's**].

To prevent confusion, always use both an apostrophe and an –s to form the plurals of lowercase letters, certain capital letters, and some words used as words.

EXAMPLES Mind your **p's** and **q's**.
His note is filled with **I's**. [Without an apostrophe, the plural of the pronoun *I* would look like the word *Is*.]
Make sure that each one of your **her's** has a clear antecedent. [Without the apostrophe, the plural of the word *her* could be confused with the possessive pronoun *hers*.]

INTEGRATING THE LANGUAGE ARTS

Mechanics and Dictionary Skills. Have students look up the etymologies of the words *alumnus, vertebra, parenthesis,* and *datum*. [They all have Latin in their etymological backgrounds.] Students might also be interested in looking up the etymologies of some other groups of words to see if they can detect any patterns. For example, students might look up the etymologies of the nouns listed as forming their plurals in irregular ways—*child, ox, woman, tooth, mouse,* and *foot*—and find out whether any of these words have similar origins.

MECHANICS

NOTE: In your reading, you may notice that some writers use an apostrophe and an –s to form the plurals of *all* capital letters and words used as words. Using both an apostrophe and an –s is never wrong. Therefore, if you have any doubt about whether or not to use an apostrophe, use it.

☞ REFERENCE NOTE: For more information on forming these kinds of plurals, see pages 857–858.

▶ EXERCISE 6 **Spelling the Plurals of Nouns**

Write the plural form of each of the following nouns.

1. girl	**5.** Japanese	**8.** self
2. valley	**6.** sister-in-law	**9.** loaf
3. sky	**7.** solo	**10.** hero
4. coach		

▶ EXERCISE 7 **Proofreading a Paragraph to Correct Spelling Errors**

Proofread the following paragraph, correcting the five misspelled words.

1. cities

2. structures/ drive-ins

3. children

4. photos

[1] This shoe repair shop in Bakersfield, California, is one of many businesses in ˄~~citys~~ across the United States whose shapes advertise the goods or services they offer. [2] Most of these eye-catching ˄~~structurs~~, many of them originally ˄~~drives-in~~, were built between the 1920s and the 1950s. [3] They appeal not only to ˄~~childs~~ but also to teenagers and adults who enjoy the offbeat. [4] Watch for restaurants and stores shaped like foods and other objects when you're traveling; ˄~~photoes~~ of them often make good souvenirs of a trip.

ANSWERS
Exercise 6

1. girls

2. valleys

3. skies

4. coaches

5. Japanese

6. sisters-in-law

7. solos

8. selves

9. loaves

10. heroes

👥 **COOPERATIVE LEARNING**

To provide further practice with spelling rules, divide your class into small groups of four or five students. Give each group a list of misspelled words. Then, give them five minutes to spell each word correctly and cite the pertinent spelling rule for each. Exceptions to a particular rule should be considered part of the rule. Award two points for each correct spelling and one point for each correct citation.

Sample spelling list:

1. editor-in-chiefs [editors-in-chief, **Rule 29k**]

2. overun [overrun, **Rule 29d**]

3. recieve [receive, **Rule 29a**]

4. freind [friend, **Rule 29b**]

5. heavyness [heaviness, **Rule 29e**]

MECHANICS

REVIEWS B and C

OBJECTIVES
- To give the spelling rules that apply to certain words
- To proofread a paragraph and to correct spelling errors

▶ REVIEW B **Applying Spelling Rules**

Explain the spelling of each of the following words.

1. crises
2. deceive
3. writing
4. believe
5. sopranos
6. misstep
7. meanness
8. noticeable
9. relief
10. countries

Spelling Numbers

29l. Always spell out a number that begins a sentence.

EXAMPLE   **One hundred twelve** sea lions were spotted in the bay.

29m. Within a sentence, spell out numbers that can be written in one or two words; use numerals for other numbers.

EXAMPLES   We drove **four hundred** miles in **seven** hours.
Edie weighs **110** pounds.

EXCEPTION   If you use some numbers that are written with one or two words and some written with more than two words, use numerals for all of them.
The final vote was **201 to 90.**

29n. Spell out numbers used to indicate order.

EXAMPLE   My brother placed **third** [not *3rd*] in the race.

EXCEPTION   Use numerals for dates when you include the name of the month.
Cinco de Mayo is celebrated on May **5** [not *5th,* but *the fifth of May* is also correct].

▶ REVIEW C **Proofreading a Paragraph to Correct Spelling Errors**

Proofread the following paragraph, correcting the misspelled words.

1. fortieth

[1] Last Saturday my mom's parents, Grandma and Grandpa Reyes, celebrated their ~~fortyeth~~ anniversary by repeating their wedding vows in a beautiful ceremony at

ANSWERS
Review B

1. *crises:* Some nouns borrowed from other languages form their plurals as they do in the original language. **Rule 29k**

2. *deceive:* Write *ie* when the sound is long *e,* except after *c.* **Rule 29a**

3. *writing:* Drop the final silent *e* before a suffix beginning with a vowel. **Rule 29f**

4. *believe:* Write *ie* when the sound is long *e,* except after *c.* **Rule 29a**

5. *sopranos:* Nouns for musical terms that end in *o* preceded by a consonant form the plural by adding only *–s.* Exception to **Rule 29k**

6. *misstep:* When a prefix is added to a word, the spelling of the original word remains the same. **Rule 29d**

7. *meanness:* When the suffix *–ly* or *–ness* is added to a word, the spelling of the original word usually remains the same. **Rule 29e**

8. *noticeable:* Keep the final silent *e* in words ending in *ce* or *ge* before a suffix that begins with *a* or *o.* Exception to **Rule 29f**

9. *relief:* Write *ie* when the sound is long *e,* except after *c.* **Rule 29a**

10. *countries:* If the noun ends in *–y* preceded by a consonant, change the *y* to *i* and add *–es.* **Rule 29k**

MECHANICS

WORKS OFTEN CONFUSED

OBJECTIVE

• To distinguish between words often confused

PROGRAM MANAGER

WORDS OFTEN CONFUSED

■ **Independent Practice/ Reteaching** For instruction and exercises, see **Words Often Confused A, Words Often Confused B, Words Often Confused C,** and **Commonly Misspelled Words** in *Language Skills Practice and Assessment,* pp. 252–255.

■ **Computer Guided Instruction** For additional instruction and practice with words often confused, see **Lesson 49** in *Language Workshop CD-ROM.*

QUICK REMINDER

Write the following sentences on the chalkboard and have students choose the word in parentheses that correctly completes each sentence. The correct choices are italicized.

1. Young children sometimes have trouble (adopting, *adapting*) to new environments.
2. On his eighteenth birthday Calvin said, "Hooray! I'm no longer a (*minor,* miner)."
3. The seventh-grade class traveled to Jackson to see the (capital, *capitol*) building.
4. The cacti and other plants in the (*desert,* dessert) burst into bloom after the thunderstorm.
5. Hortense's tooth was so (lose, *loose*) she feared she would (*lose,* loose) it.

---

882 *Spelling*

2. learner's
3. wives
4. hoping
5. heavily
6. eighty-five
7. unnecessary
8. truly
9. chipped
10. planning/ fiftieth

St. Teresa's Church. [2] Since I have my ˄~~learnner's~~ permit now and it was light out when we went to the church, Mom let me drive. [3] My aunts and uncles on Mom's side of the family were there with their husbands and ˄~~wifes~~. [4] In addition, all of my cousins except Ernesto, whom I'd been especially ˄~~hopeing~~ to see, attended the ceremony. [5] Unfortunately, the flights from Denver, where Ernesto goes to college, had been canceled because it had snowed ˄~~heavyly~~ there the night before. [6] Although I missed Ernesto, I enjoyed visiting with many of the ˄~~85~~ friends and family members who had come to the celebration. [7] Grandma and Grandpa had insisted that anniversary gifts were ˄~~unecessary~~, but this time they were overruled. [8] You could tell that they were ˄~~truely~~ stunned when they opened the gift from their children. [9] Mom and her sisters and brothers had ˄~~chiped~~ in to buy them plane tickets to Mexico City, where they were born. [10] Everyone had such a good time that we've already started ˄~~planing~~ for Grandma and Grandpa's ˄~~50th~~ anniversary.

Words Often Confused

affect	[verb] *to influence* How did that sad movie *affect* you?
effect	[verb] *to accomplish;* [noun] *consequence; result* Head Start centers can *effect* an improvement in the lives of underprivileged children. What *effect* did the rain have on the lawn?
all ready	*all are ready* We were *all ready* to leave.
already	*previously* We have *already* painted the sets.
all right	This is the only acceptable spelling. The spelling *alright* is not standard usage.

| all together | *everyone in the same place*
 The players were *all together* in the gym. |
| altogether | *entirely*
 I'm not *altogether* convinced. |

| brake | [verb] *to slow down or stop;* [noun] *a device used to slow down or stop something*
 Georgia *braked* the speeding car.
 The worn *brakes* couldn't stop the car. |
| break | [verb] *to violate; to fracture;* [noun] *the fracture itself*
 Don't *break* the speed limit.
 The doctor says it isn't a bad *break*. |

| capital | correct spelling for all uses except when the word means *government building*
 What is the *capital* of Zimbabwe?
 You need *capital* to start a business.
 Begin every sentence with a *capital* letter.
 Do you believe in *capital* punishment? |
| capitol | *government building*
 We could see the *capitol* from our hotel. |

| choose | [verb, present tense]
 We *choose* partners today. |
| chose | [verb, past tense of *choose*]
 Each of us *chose* a partner. |

| coarse | *rough; crude*
 Burlap is a *coarse* fabric. |
| course | *a part of a meal; a program of study; a playing field;* also used with *of* to mean *naturally* or *certainly*
 She skipped the first *course* at dinner.
 The speech *course* helped my diction.
 A new golf *course* opened last week.
 Of *course*, you're always welcome. |

MECHANICS

MEETING *individual* **NEEDS**

LEP/ESL

General Strategies. Because these words might be especially confusing to English-language learners, allow the students to focus on the words that they are most likely to use in their daily lives. For example, students are probably more likely to use the words *brake* and *break* than the words *consul* and *council*.

MECHANICS

883

complement	[verb] *to make whole or complete;* [noun] *that which makes whole or complete* That scarf *complements* your outfit nicely. The *complement*, or full crew, is six hundred people.
compliment	[noun] *a courteous act; a flattering statement;* [verb] *to express these qualities* He received many *compliments* on his cooking. I *complimented* her on her success.
consul	[noun] *a representative of a foreign country* The Chinese *consul* returned to Beijing.
council	[noun] *a group charged with taking official actions*
councilor	[noun] *a member of such a group* Four of the *councilors* on the Security Council voted for the resolution.
counsel **counselor**	[noun] *advice;* [verb] *to advise* [noun] *an adviser* Sue followed her aunt's *counsel.* Sue's aunt *counseled* her to take judo lessons. Ask your guidance *counselor.*
des′ert	[noun] *a dry region* The car crossed the *desert* at night.
desert′	[verb] *to leave* The rats *deserted* the sinking ship.
dessert	[noun] *the last part of a meal* For *dessert* we had cheese and fruit.

 EXERCISE 8   **Distinguishing Between Words Often Confused**

Choose the <u>correct word</u> of the pair in parentheses.

1. The Epstein family was (*all together, altogether*) last week for the Hanukkah celebration.

MEETING *individual* NEEDS

ADVANCED STUDENTS

Some of the pairs of words often confused have similar origins. *Counsel* and *council,* for example, both come from the Latin word *concilium,* meaning "group of people," or "meeting." Students might enjoy using a dictionary to find out which of the pairs or groups of words have similar etymologies and which do not. Afterward, ask students if they could have predicted the results.

2. The illness has had a strange (*affect*, <u>*effect*</u>) on everyone who has caught it.
3. My cousin knows the (*capitol*, <u>*capital*</u>) city of every state.
4. If you don't have your car's (<u>*brakes*</u>, *breaks*) inspected each year, you may be (*braking*, <u>*breaking*</u>) a state law.
5. The British (*council*, <u>*consul*</u>) (*counciled*, <u>*counseled*</u>) the reporter to leave the country.
6. After all his worry, everything turned out (<u>*all right*</u>, *alright*).
7. The two fast guards on our basketball team are (*complimented*, <u>*complemented*</u>) by our towering center.
8. The actors were (<u>*all ready*</u>, *already*) for the audition.
9. My uncle had either flan or sopapillas for (*desert*, <u>*dessert*</u>).
10. Did you (<u>*choose*</u>, *chose*) that topic for your essay?

formally	*in a formal manner* Do you plan to dress *formally* for the party?
formerly	*previously* This lake was *formerly* a valley.
hear	*to receive sound through the ears* Please speak up—I can't *hear* you.
here	*this place* Let's sit *here*.
its	[possessive form of *it*] The town hasn't raised *its* tax rate in years.
it's	[contraction of *it is* or *it has*] *It's* cold, and *it's* started to snow.
lead	[verb] *to go first* Who will *lead* the Juneteenth parade?
led	[verb, past tense of *lead*] He *led* us five miles out of the way.
lead	[noun, pronounced "led"] *a heavy metal; graphite in a pencil* A pencil *lead* is not made of *lead*.

MECHANICS

INTEGRATING THE LANGUAGE ARTS

Literature Link. Have students read a selection from a work of fiction in which nonstandard English is used; Mark Twain's *The Adventures of Huckleberry Finn* is a good novel to use. Then, ask students to identify the words spelled according to phonetics rather than the rules of standard written English. Ask students what the author's purpose might have been in using phonetic spellings. [Reproducing colloquial speech phonetically can serve to make characterizations richer and more believable.]

MECHANICS

VISUAL CONNECTIONS
Related Expression Skills.
Students might enjoy creating cartoons that feature puns with the words in this lesson. For example, a student might draw a cartoon of someone lost in a *dessert* or of a car *breaking* for a stoplight.

loose	[adjective, pronounced "loos"] *free, not connected tightly* Put all your *loose* papers in a folder. My little brother has two *loose* teeth.
lose	[verb, pronounced "looz"] *to suffer loss* Don't *lose* your tickets.

miner	[noun] *worker in a mine* The trapped *miners* were finally rescued.
minor	[noun] *person under legal age;* [adjective] *of small importance* The curfew applies only to *minors*. He received *minor* injuries in the accident.

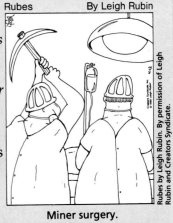

Rubes   By Leigh Rubin

Miner surgery.

Rubes by Leigh Rubin. By permission of Leigh Rubin and Creators Syndicate.

moral	[adjective] *good;* [noun] *a lesson of conduct* We admire a *moral* person. The story's *moral* is "Look before you leap."
morale	*mental condition, spirit* After three defeats, the team's *morale* was low.

passed	[verb, past tense of *pass*] We *passed* our papers to the front.
past	[noun] *the history of a person, group, or institution;* [adjective] *former;* [preposition] *farther on than* Sitting Bull told his son Crow Foot many stories about the *past*. Adele read the minutes of the *past* meeting. The dog walked right *past* the cat.

REVIEW D

OBJECTIVE

• To proofread an article and to correct spelling errors

 EXERCISE 9 **Distinguishing Between Words Often Confused**

Choose the <u>correct word</u> of the pair in parentheses.

1. Where did you (*here*, <u>*hear*</u>) that Kiowa legend?
2. If you (<u>*lose*</u>, *loose*) the directions, we'll never get there.
3. The mail from home improved the troops' (*moral*, <u>*morale*</u>).
4. The estate is being held in trust until the heir is no longer a (<u>*minor*</u>, *miner*).
5. My horse (*lead*, <u>*led*</u>) the parade.
6. In only a few minutes, the guest speaker will be (*hear*, <u>*here*</u>).
7. After he went on a diet, his clothes were too (*lose*, <u>*loose*</u>).
8. (<u>*Formerly*</u>, *Formally*), Gloria Estefan performed with the Miami Sound Machine.
9. (*Its*, <u>*It's*</u>) not every day that her parents let her use the car.
10. After taking French I twice, John (<u>*passed*</u>, *past*) the course.

 REVIEW D **Proofreading an Article to Correct Spelling Errors**

Proofread the following article, correcting the misspelled word or words in each sentence. If all words in a sentence are spelled correctly, write C.

NHS MEMBERS MEET GOVERNOR
by Cornelia Charnes, Staff Writer

[1] One of the advantages of living in the state ~~capitol~~ is
having the opportunity to see state government up close.
[2] Last Friday, twenty-seven members of our school's
National Honor Society chapter toured the nearby ~~capital~~
building. [3] Tour guide Floyd Welty, who ~~lead~~ the group,
outlined the workings of the government's three branches
and pointed out many of the building's architectural features. [4] The students ate lunch in the underground cafeteria and even got to meet Governor (~~formally~~ U.S.
Senator) Iola Jones.

1. capital
2. capitol
3. led
4. formerly

MECHANICS

MECHANICS

888 *Spelling*

5. all ready
6. C
7. minors/ hear
8. it's
9. counselor/ past
10. C

[5] The group met Governor Jones just as they were ~~already~~ to leave the building. [6] Said student Botan Park, "Governor Jones shook hands with each of us and complimented us on being honor students. [7] Even though we're still ~~miners~~, she told us, 'I want to ~~here~~ from you whenever you have a concern with my administration's policies.'" [8] "Of course," added student Elena Cruz, "~~its~~ her first term as governor, and we'll be eligible to vote when she comes up for reelection."

[9] The group's sponsor, guidance ~~councilor~~ Diego Vargas, said, "I've been taking groups there for the ~~passed~~ ten years, but I've never met a governor before. [10] That had a big effect on me and on the students."

personal	*individual* The store manager gave us her *personal* attention.
personnel	*a group of people employed in the same place* The management added *personnel* to handle the increased workload.
principal	[noun] *head of a school;* [adjective] *main; most important* The *principal* of our school is Mr. Osaka. The *principal* export of Brazil is coffee.
principle	*a rule of conduct; a main fact* or *law* Her *principles* are very high. Martin Luther King, Jr., supported the *principle* of nonviolence.
quiet	*silent; still* I need complete *quiet* to study.
quite	*wholly; rather; very* Are you *quite* sure this is the right path?
shone	[past tense of *shine*] The stars *shone* brightly last night.
shown	[past participle of *show*] The slides were *shown* after dinner.

888

stationary	[adjective] *in a fixed position* Are these desks movable or *stationary*?
stationery	[noun] *writing paper* Purple *stationery* isn't appropriate for business letters.
than	[a conjunction, used for comparisons] She is smarter *than* I.
then	[an adverb or a conjunction] *at that time; next* I didn't know you *then*. We swam for an hour; *then* we ate.
their	[possessive of *they*] *Their* apartment has a view of the river.
there	[adverb] *in that place;* [expletive, used to fill out the meaning of a sentence] I haven't been *there* in a long time. *There* is too much pepper in my soup.
they're	[contraction of *they are*] *They're* reading a book by Virginia Driving Hawk Sneve.

▶ EXERCISE 10   **Distinguishing Between Words Often Confused**

Select the <u>correct word</u> of the choices in parentheses.

1. I'm learning some of the (*principals*, <u>*principles*</u>) of physics.
2. The gold ring (<u>*shone*</u>, *shown*) with a warm glow.
3. He acts much older (<u>*than*</u>, *then*) he is.
4. The bookstore is having a big sale on (<u>*stationery*</u>, *stationary*).
5. You ask too many (*personnel*, <u>*personal*</u>) questions.
6. Soon after the strange uproar, all became (*quite*, <u>*quiet*</u>) again.
7. The *pad thai* they serve here is (<u>*quite*</u>, *quiet*) good.
8. Several Pueblo artists are displaying (*there*, <u>*their*</u>, *they're*) work.

A DIFFERENT APPROACH
Memory devices will often help students master these troublesome words. For example, the *er* in *letter* and *paper* could be associated with the *er* in *stationery* (letter-writing paper), and the *o* in *dome* could be associated with the *o* in *capitol* (a government building that often has a dome).

MECHANICS

MECHANICS

MECHANICS

MECHANICS

9. If you see the (*principle*, *principal*) in the hall, tell her she's wanted in the main office.
10. (*Their*, *They're*, *There*) parents may not let them go.

to	[preposition; also part of the infinitive form of a verb] Please return these books *to* the library. He began *to* whistle.
too	[adverb] *also; more than enough* Rubén Blades is a musician and an attorney, *too.* You're *too* young to drive.
two	*one plus one* I will graduate in *two* years.
waist	*the midsection of the body* At the Japanese restaurant, the server wore an obi around her *waist.*
waste	[verb] *to use foolishly;* [noun] *a needless expense* *Waste* not; want not. Waiting in line is a *waste* of time.
weather	[noun] *conditions outdoors* The *weather* has been perfect all week.
whether	[subordinating conjunction; indicates alternative or doubt] They don't know *whether* or not they'll go.
who's	[contraction of *who is* or *who has*] *Who's* there? *Who's* been wearing my socks?
whose	[possessive of *who*] *Whose* book is this?
your	[possessive of *you*] *Your* coat is in the closet.
you're	[contraction of *you are*] *You're* never on time.

▶ EXERCISE 11 **Distinguishing Between Words Often Confused**

Select the <u>correct word</u> from the choices in parentheses.

1. Around his (*waste,* <u>*waist*</u>) he wore a handmade leather belt.
2. (*You're,* <u>*Your*</u>) mother made a delicious Korean dinner of *bulgogi* last night.
3. There was (<u>*too,*</u> *to, two*) much traffic on the road (*too,* <u>*to,*</u> *two*) enjoy the ride.
4. (*Whose,* <u>*Who's*</u>) going to use that ticket now?
5. It really doesn't matter (<u>*whose,*</u> *who's*) fault it is.
6. You, (*to, two,* <u>*too*</u>), can be a better speller if you try.
7. (*Weather,* <u>*Whether*</u>) it rains or not, we'll be there.
8. This is fine (*whether,* <u>*weather*</u>) for a softball game.
9. (*Your,* <u>*You're*</u>) sure Ms. Thompson wanted to see me?
10. I don't know (*whose,* <u>*who's*</u>) taller, Hakeem Olajuwon or Buck Williams.

▶ EXERCISE 12 **Proofreading a Paragraph to Correct Spelling Errors**

Proofread the following paragraph, correcting the misspelled words.

[1] The face on the postage stamp on the next page is that of Benjamin Banneker, considered ~~too~~ be the first African American man of science. [2] First issued on February 15, 1980, this stamp honors a man ~~who's~~ contributions in the areas of mathematics and astronomy are impressive. [3] Banneker grew up on a farm in Maryland in the 1700s, a time when life was particularly difficult for African American people ~~weather~~ they were slaves or not. [4] Although free, Banneker, ~~to~~, faced prejudice and discrimination. [5] However, a neighbor who was interested in science gave some astronomy equipment ~~too~~ Banneker. [6] Banneker ~~waisted~~ no time in using it to determine when the sun and moon rose and set, when the brightest stars set, and when eclipses occurred. [7] All of this information was very helpful to a variety of people, including sailors who needed to chart courses and farmers who needed to know the ~~whether~~. [8] Banneker compiled his data into an

1. to
2. whose
3. whether
4. too
5. to
6. wasted
7. weather

INTEGRATING THE LANGUAGE ARTS

Mechanics and Vocabulary. Exercise 12 discusses a commemorative postage stamp. Tell students that the practice of collecting stamps can also be called *philately.* Then, challenge students to match the following words with the hobbies they describe:

1. numismatics   A. horseback riding
2. spelunking   B. collecting books
3. equitation   C. exploring caves
4. angling   D. collecting coins
5. bibliophilism   E. fishing with hook and line

MECHANICS

ANSWERS

Review E

1. occurred; to
2. there
3. tried
4. shaking; noticeably
5. C
6. course; piece; illegal
7. proceeded; steadily; overreact
8. C
9. all right; accidentally; slammed; brakes
10. neither; sustained; injuries; mistaking

892 *Spelling*

8. two

almanac, and after, too or three attempts, he succeeded in getting his almanacs published each year for several years. [9] These popular books received widespread attention, and Benjamin Banneker became a symbol of what African Americans could do if their lives

9. wasted

were not, waisted in slavery. [10] If

10. you're

, your someone who collects commemorative postage stamps, you'll likely want this one, which celebrates the achievements of this gifted scientist.

REVIEW E

Proofreading an Essay to Correct Spelling Errors

Proofread the following essay, correcting the misspelled words in each sentence. If all the words in a sentence are spelled correctly, write C.

[1] One of my most embarrassing moments, occured the day I took the road test, too get my driver's license. [2] Since one of the branches of the Motor Vehicle Department is near my dad's office, I met him, their after school. [3] He , tryed to calm me down by telling me that the world wouldn't end if I didn't pass the first time. [4] Still, my hands were, shakeing, noticably when I got behind the wheel.

[5] The examiner, Mrs. Ferro, was very patient. [6] She assured me that the, coarse was a, peice of cake and that she wouldn't ask me to do anything, ilegal to try to trick me. [7] She said I'd be fine if I just, proceded, steadyly and didn't, overeact to her instructions.

[8] Everything went surprisingly well until we reached the end of the course and Mrs. Ferro told me to stop the car and turn off the ignition. [9] I stopped, alright—I accidentaly, slamed on the, breaks so hard that we both went lurching forward against our seat belts. [10] Luckily, , niether of us, sustainned any, injurys, and I succeeded in passing the test despite, mistakeing the end of the course for the edge of a cliff.

100 Commonly Misspelled Words

ache	could	happiness	raise	tonight
again	country	having	read	too
always	dear	hear	ready	trouble
among	doctor	here	said	truly
answered	does	hoarse	says	Tuesday
any	done	hour	scene	two
been	don't	instead	seems	very
beginning	early	knew	separate	wear
believe	easy	know	shoes	Wednesday
break	enemy	laid	similar	week
built	enough	loose	since	where
business	every	lose	straight	whether
busy	existence	making	sugar	which
buy	February	meant	sure	whole
can't	finally	minute	tear	women
chief	forty	none	their	won't
choose	friend	often	there	would
color	grammar	once	though	write
coming	guess	piece	through	writing
cough	half	probably	tired	wrote

300 Spelling Words

absence	analyze	bulletin
absorption	angel	calendar
abundant	annual	category
acceptable	apparatus	changeable
accidentally	appearance	characteristic
accommodation	application	chemistry
accompaniment	appropriate	circumstance
accurate	approximately	civilization
accustomed	arousing	cocoon
achievement	arrangement	commencement
acquaintance	ascend	commissioner
actuality	association	committed
adequately	athlete	comparative
administration	bankruptcy	comparison
adolescent	basically	competition
aggressive	beneficial	conceivable
agriculture	benefited	confidential
amateur	bicycle	confirmation
ambassador	breathe	conscientious
analysis	brilliant	consciousness

MEETING *individual* NEEDS

ADVANCED STUDENTS

Some students will not have any problems with spelling the words in the **100 Commonly Misspelled Words** list. Allow such students to work as a group to compile a list of words that they have encountered in their reading and have difficulty spelling. Students can then study words from the list they have compiled instead of spending time studying words they already know how to spell.

A DIFFERENT APPROACH

Challenge each student to write a paragraph that includes one of the groups of ten words from the **300 Spelling Words** list. Here is a sample paragraph that includes the first group of ten words:

His *absence* is due to the *absorption* of an *abundant* amount of hardly *acceptable* soup. He ingested the soup *accidentally*—quite an *achievement*—and was not *accustomed* to its potency. If my predictions are *accurate,* we will not have the pleasure of his *accompaniment* to our songs tonight at our *accommodations.*

consequently
considerable
consistency
continuous
controlled
controversial
cordially
corps
correspondence
criticize

curiosity
curriculum
definition
delegate
denied
develop
difference
disastrous
disciple
dissatisfied

distinction
distinguished
dividend
dominant
dormitory
earnest
easily
ecstasy
eighth
eliminate

embroidery
endeavor
enormous
equipment
especially
essential
estimation
etiquette
exaggeration
examination

exceedingly
exceptional
excitable
executive
exercise
exhaustion
exhibition
expense
experience
extension

extraordinary
fallacy
fantasies
favorably
fiery
financial
foreigner
forfeit
fragile
fulfill

fundamentally
gasoline
gentleman
grammatically
grateful
guidance
gymnasium
handkerchief
heroic
hindrance

humorist
hygiene
hypocrisy
illustrate
imitation
immense
inability
incidentally
indispensable
influential

innocence
inquiry
institute
intellect
interference
interpretation
interruption
interval
irrelevant
irresistible

island
jealousy
journal
laborious
liability
lightning
likelihood
liveliest
locally
luxury

magnificence
maintenance
maneuver
mansion
martyr
maturity
medical
merchandise
merit
miniature

mischievous
missile
misspelled
monotony
mortgage
municipal
narrative
naturally
neighbor
noticeable

nuisance
obstacle
occasionally
occupy
odor
offensive
omitted
opinion
opposition
optimism

ordinary
organization
ornament
pageant
pamphlet
parachute
parallel
pastime
peaceable
peasant

peril
permanent
persistent
perspiration
pertain
phase
picnic
pigeon
playwright
pleasant

poison
politician
positively
possibility
practically
practice
precede
precisely
predominant
preferred

prejudice
preliminary
preparation
primitive
priority
prisoner
procedure
proceedings
procession
prominent

proposition
prosperous
prove
psychology
publicity
purposes
qualities
quantities
questionnaire
readily

reference
referring
regard
register
rehearsal
religious
remembrance
representative
requirement
resistance

resolution
responsibility
restaurant
ridiculous
satisfactorily
security
senator
sensibility
sheer
sheriff

significance
simile
situated
solution
sophomore
souvenir
specific
specimen
spiritual
strenuous

stretch
substantial
subtle
successful
sufficient
summarize
superintendent
suppress
surgeon
suspense

syllable
symbol
symphony
technique
temperature
tendency
tournament
traffic
twelfth
tying

tyranny
unanimous
undoubtedly
unforgettable
unpleasant
unusually
vacancies
varies
vengeance
villain

MECHANICS

PROGRAM MANAGER

FOR THE WHOLE CHAPTER

- **Computer Guided Instruction** For additional instruction and practice with concepts often used as indicators of verbal skills on standardized tests, see the **Core Lessons** in *Language Workshop CD-ROM.*

- **Practice** To help less-advanced students who need additional practice with concepts related to this chapter, see relevant topics in *English Workshop, Fourth Course.*

- **Assessment/Practice** To help students practice marking standardized test answers for the **Grammar and Usage Tests** on pp. 910–913 and the **Mechanics Tests** on pp. 922–925, see the **Standardized Test Answer Sheet** in *Language Skills Practice and Assessment,* p. 275.

CHAPTER OVERVIEW

This chapter provides application and review of some aspects of grammar, usage, and mechanics that cause students difficulty. Since this chapter focuses on areas of greatest concern, you may find it useful in several ways. You could use the exercises and review tests in this chapter as diagnostic tests, judging by students' scores which topics need most attention; as a resource for reteaching and remediation, providing extra practice for concepts needing added emphasis; as a review of key concepts to help students prepare for standardized tests of language skills mastery; or in any combination of these ways.

30 CORRECTING COMMON ERRORS

Key Language Skills Review

This chapter reviews key skills and concepts that pose special problems for writers.

- Sentence Fragments and Run-on Sentences
- Subject-Verb and Pronoun-Antecedent Agreement
- Pronoun Forms
- Clear Pronoun Reference
- Verb Forms and Tenses
- Comparison of Modifiers
- Misplaced and Dangling Modifiers
- Capitalization
- Punctuation—Commas, Colons, Semicolons, Quotation Marks, and Apostrophes
- Spelling
- Standard Usage

Most of the exercises in this chapter follow the same format as the exercises found throughout the grammar, usage, and mechanics sections. You will notice, however, that two sets of review exercises are presented in standardized test formats. These exercises are designed to provide you with practice not only in solving usage and mechanics problems but also in dealing with these kinds of problems on such tests.

EXERCISE 1
OBJECTIVE

- To correct sentence fragments and run-on sentences

EXERCISE 2
OBJECTIVE

- To identify and correct run-on sentences and sentence fragments

▶ EXERCISE 1 **Correcting Sentence Fragments and Run-on Sentences**

Each numbered item below is a sentence fragment, a run-on sentence, or a complete sentence. First, identify each by writing *F* for a fragment, *R* for a run-on, or *S* for a complete sentence. Then, correct each fragment and run-on.

EXAMPLE **1.** Thunder roared and rumbled lightning flashed across the dark skies.
1. *R—Thunder roared and rumbled, and lightning flashed across the dark skies.*

1. Playing basketball with some of my friends who live in my grandmother's neighborhood.
2. The largest province in Canada is Quebec, the capital of this province is Quebec City.
3. Ruth tried out her new in-line skates today.
4. The new movie about dinosaurs on Friday night.
5. Radio waves travel at the speed of light they can go through many solid objects, including most buildings.
6. Jeremy wants to ask Shelley to the dance, he doesn't know if she already has a date.
7. Because my high school has a new athletic program for students with disabilities.
8. The math problems in today's homework assignment were challenging there weren't many of them.
9. Wasn't that an exciting and pleasant surprise?
10. Rabindranath Tagore wrote the national anthems of two countries, India and Bangladesh, I wonder if anyone else has written two national anthems.

▶ EXERCISE 2 **Correcting Sentence Fragments and Run-on Sentences**

Each numbered item below is a sentence fragment, a run-on sentence, or a complete sentence. First, identify each by writing *F* for a fragment, *R* for a run-on, or *S* for a complete sentence. Then, correct each fragment and run-on.

EXAMPLE **1.** Nearly all cultures having traditional folk dances.
1. *F—Nearly all cultures have traditional folk dances.*

1. Most folk dances start as celebrations or rituals, such dances are often passed from generation to generation.

CORRECTING COMMON ERRORS

ANSWERS
Exercise 1

Answers will vary. Sample responses are given.

1. F—I was playing basketball with some of my friends who live in my grandmother's neighborhood.
2. R—The largest province in Canada is Quebec. The capital of this province is Quebec City.
3. S
4. F—My little brother saw the new movie about dinosaurs on Friday night.
5. R—Radio waves travel at the speed of light, and they can go through many solid objects, including most buildings.
6. R—Jeremy wants to ask Shelley to the dance; however, he doesn't know if she already has a date.
7. F—Because my high school has a new athletic program for students with disabilities, my friend John may attend next year.
8. R—The math problems in today's homework assignment were challenging, but there weren't many of them.
9. S
10. R—Rabindranath Tagore wrote the national anthems of two countries, India and Bangladesh. I wonder if anyone else has written two national anthems.

ANSWERS
Exercise 2

Answers will vary. Sample responses are given.

1. R—Most folk dances start as celebrations or rituals. Such dances are often passed from generation to generation.

CORRECTING COMMON ERRORS

2. F—Certain dances were thought to bring good fortune to the dancers.

3. R—Some cultures developed dances that they believed cured diseases and other afflictions; for instance, the tarantella developed in Italy as a ritual antidote for the bite of the tarantula.

4. F—Other dances celebrated birth, marriage, harvests, success in battle, and even death.

5. S

6. F—Some dances originally performed for religious or ritual purposes are now danced purely for recreation.

7. F—Does anyone know the origins of "Ring-Around-the-Rosy"?

8. R—In the United States, square dancing may be the most popular kind of folk dance; clogging is also widely enjoyed.

9. S

10. F—The term *do-si-do* comes from *dos à dos,* which is French for "back-to-back."

◉ A DIFFERENT APPROACH

Have students write coded messages in which their sentences are masked by surrounding fragments and run-ons. To understand the message, their partners must eliminate all the fragments and run-ons. The sentences that remain will provide the message.

EXERCISE 3
OBJECTIVE

• To select verbs that agree with their subjects in number

2. Certain dances to bring good fortune to the dancers.
3. Some cultures developed dances that they believed cured diseases and other afflictions, for instance, the tarantella developed in Italy as a ritual antidote for the bite of the tarantula.
4. Other dances celebrating birth, marriage, harvests, success in battle, and even death.
5. Over time, most folk dances change.
6. That some dances originally performed for religious or ritual purposes are now danced purely for recreation.
7. Anyone who knows the origins of "Ring-Around-the-Rosy"?
8. In the United States, square dancing may be the most popular kind of folk dance clogging is also widely enjoyed.
9. The do-si-do is a movement in square dancing in which two dancers start out facing one another, circle each other back-to-back, and then return to a facing position.
10. The term *do-si-do* from *dos à dos,* which is French for "back-to-back."

▶ EXERCISE 3   **Identifying Verbs That Agree with Their Subjects**

For each of the following sentences, choose the form of the verb in parentheses that agrees with the subject.

EXAMPLE   **1.** The cultural heritage of New Mexico's cities (*is, are*) reflected in their architecture, food, and customs.
   1. *is*

1. Many of the travelers who visit New Mexico (*spend, spends*) time in Albuquerque.
2. The architecture of the buildings (*represent, represents*) various periods in the city's history.
3. (*Has, Have*) anyone here read about or been to Old Town in Albuquerque?
4. One of the books Adrienne read (*identify, identifies*) Old Town as the site of the city's original settlement, founded by Spanish settlers in 1706.
5. Arts, crafts, and food now (*fill, fills*) the shops around the Old Town Plaza.

EXERCISE 4
OBJECTIVE

• To correct sentences with errors in subject-verb agreement

6. Alexander's family (*has, have*) its annual reunion in Albuquerque.
7. Near Albuquerque (*is, are*) a number of American Indian reservations.
8. The pictures we took of the Rio Grande gorge (*give, gives*) you an idea of what the landscape is like in central New Mexico.
9. Neither Juan nor his parents (*was, were*) aware that near Albuquerque are mountains that often have snow on them.
10. Just east of the city (*lie, lies*) the Sandia Mountains.

EXERCISE 4   Proofreading Sentences for Correct Subject-Verb Agreement

Most of the following sentences contain errors in subject-verb agreement. If a verb does not agree with its subject, write the subject and the correct form of the verb. If a sentence is correct, write C.

EXAMPLE   **1.** Each of them repeat the chorus after the soloist finishes.
          1. *Each repeats*

1. It seems that <u>someone</u> I know ~~drop~~ by every time I try to finish my work.   1. drops
2. <u>News</u> of his accomplishments ~~have~~ spread in recent years.   2. has
3. ~~Here's~~ the <u>articles</u> about Buck Ramsey that Han said she would lend you.   3. (Here) are
4. The <u>audience</u> always ~~sing~~ along with the old songs.   4. sings
5. The <u>picture</u> of Nanci, Lyle, and Michelle ~~are~~ on the bulletin board.   5. is
6. St. Elmo's fire, which has been seen around the masts of ships, the propellers and wingtips of planes, and even the horns of cattle, is an odd glow that at times accompanies a steady electric discharge.   6. C
7. Under some rocks in the woods ~~were~~ a small <u>box</u>.   7. was
8. <u>Tornadoes</u> that occur in the Northern Hemisphere ~~whirls~~ in a counterclockwise direction.   8. whirl
9. Has everybody signed up for a service project?   9. C
10. <u>Singing and playing</u> the guitar ~~is~~ also among Jan's talents.   10. are

MEETING *individual* NEEDS

LEP/ESL

General Strategies. In some languages, objects appear before their verbs. For example, the English sentence "Susan heard the squirrels today" would have the order "Squirrels today Susan heard" or "Today Susan squirrels heard." Some English-language learners may, therefore, try to make the verb agree with the object. Stress that students should concentrate primarily on writing English sentences in the order of subject-verb-object until they feel more comfortable with the common order and structure of English sentences. Remind them that they should always make the verb agree with the subject.

A DIFFERENT APPROACH

To help you quickly evaluate the nature of difficulties students may be having with pronoun-antecedent agreement, you might want to use this strategy: For **Exercise 5**, have students bracket the antecedent (or antecedents) and then label it (or them) as singular or plural. Then, have students circle the pronoun they have written to fill the blank in the sentence and label it as singular or plural. Typically, the primary difficulty is that the student does not recognize the correct antecedent and thus does not match the pronoun to it in number.

COMMON ERROR

Problem. Students may use masculine pronouns to refer to both men and women. Until recent years, it was common practice to do so, but that usage is avoided now because it seems to ignore or exclude females.

Solution. One way to deal with this problem is to switch from singular to plural usage since plural pronouns don't have gender. To illustrate this solution, write the following sentence on the chalkboard and ask students to suggest ways to revise it to avoid the generic use of masculine pronouns:

Every contestant should work on *his* own entry. [Possible revisions: "Contestants should complete their own entries" or "Everyone in the contest should work on his or her own entry."]

EXERCISE 5
OBJECTIVE
• To provide pronouns that agree with their antecedents

EXERCISE 6
OBJECTIVE
• To correct errors in pronoun-antecedent agreement

900 *Correcting Common Errors*

▶ EXERCISE 5 **Using Pronouns That Agree with Their Antecedents**

Fill in the blanks in the following sentences by providing pronouns that agree with their antecedents.

EXAMPLE **1.** One of the boys left ____ report card in the gym.
1. *his*

1. her
1. Each member of the women's soccer team had played ____ best at the game.

2. their
2. Have all of the students in your biology class gotten seedlings for ____ experiments?

3. his
3. Nicholas or Quentin will demonstrate ____ favorite drawing technique in class today.

4. his or her
4. Mr. Williams told us that anyone who wants to go on the field trip should turn in ____ permission slip on Monday.

5. its
5. Each of the novels has ____ own significance in the trilogy.

6. he or she
6. If someone wants to use the computer in the library, ____ should do so this afternoon.

7. her
7. Neither Karen nor Susan has finished researching ____ topic.

8. his or her
8. Did one of the passengers leave ____ suitcase here?

9. they
9. If Ricky and Joe are ready at 7:45 A.M., ____ will be able to ride the bus to school.

10. his or her
10. Whenever we go hiking, everyone brings ____ own lunch and wears a comfortable pair of shoes.

▶ EXERCISE 6 **Proofreading Sentences for Correct Pronoun-Antecedent Agreement**

Most of the following sentences contain pronouns that do not agree with their antecedents. If a sentence contains an error, rewrite the sentence to correct the error. If a sentence is already correct, write *C*.

EXAMPLE **1.** Almost everybody I know has their favorite comic strips.
1. *Almost everybody I know has his or her favorite comic strips.*

1. her
1. Sara, one of my friends in art class, raised ~~their~~ hand and asked about the history of comic strips.

EXERCISE 7
OBJECTIVE

• To identify correct forms of pronouns

2. Ms. Seymour asked everyone to bring a sketchbook, their drawing pencils, and the Sunday comics to class so that we could begin designing a comic strip.   **2. his or her**
3. I think it was either Sara or Heather who showed me a copy of the *Calvin and Hobbes* collection *Scientific Progress Goes "Boink"* that they had bought at the mall. **3. she**
4. The vivid color and elaborate artistry of a comic strip like *Prince Valiant* or *Calvin and Hobbes* often help to make them a popular Sunday strip.   **4. it**
5. About 100 million people in the United States spend some of his or her time each day reading comics. **5. their**
6. Juan and Rob offered to bring in their collections of adventure comics from the 1940s; each of them will give his presentation on Thursday.   **6. C**
7. Are you familiar with Linus and Lucy Van Pelt and his or her friends Charlie Brown and Snoopy?   **7. their**
8. Joseph Pulitzer, one of the most famous newspaper publishers in the United States, introduced the first serialized comic strip in their paper in 1895.   **8. his**
9. The magazine-style comic book first appeared in the 1930s; they generally feature serialized stories about the same group of characters.   **9. it/features**
10. If anyone wants to learn more about the history of comics, they could research the topic at a library.

   10. he or she

▶ EXERCISE 7 Identifying Correct Forms of Pronouns

Choose the correct pronoun in parentheses in each of the following sentences.

EXAMPLE **1.** Jesse and (*I, me*) will compete at the track meet.
   1. *I*

1. No one else can climb the rope as fast as (*I, me*).
2. Didn't the police officer give (*them, they*) tickets for speeding in a school zone?
3. Both of the soloists in tonight's choir concert will be accompanied on piano by (*she, her*) and Paul.
4. Mr. Allen wondered (*who, whom*) had left him a gift.
5. The next president of the debate team will likely be (*she, her*).
6. Three volunteers—Hester, Kim, and (*I, me*)—will help paint the mural.

◆ COMMON ERROR

Problem. Because students frequently hear people use objective rather than nominative pronouns in compound subjects and in predicate nominatives, the incorrect usage may sound correct to them.

Solution. Tell students that they can "strip or flip" the sentences to test the pronouns.

For compound subjects, they should "strip" the compounds so that only one pronoun in the sentence remains as the subject. (Example: "Anita and me worked hard" is stripped to become "Me worked hard." Most students will then readily replace *me* with *I*.)

For predicate nominative pronouns, students should "flip" the pronoun so that it is in front of the verb. (Example: "The athlete was her" flipped becomes "Her was the athlete." Most students will then readily replace *her* with *she*.)

As a reminder you might post this rule on the chalkboard: "Check your pronoun: Strip it or flip it."

7. Are they two years younger than (*us, we*)?
8. Mrs. Murphy paid my sister and (*I, me*) ten dollars to shovel snow off her driveway.
9. "Aren't you going with Christy and (*him, he*) to the game?" Janet asked.
10. Carl Lewis and Michael Johnson are the two athletes (*who, whom*) I watched most closely during the 1996 Olympics.

EXERCISE 8 **Rewriting Sentences to Correct Inexact Pronoun References**

Rewrite each of the following items to correct the inexact pronoun reference.

EXAMPLE 1. Domingo first read about Tomás Rivera when he was in the school library.
1. *When Domingo was in the school library, he read about Tomás Rivera for the first time.*

1. In the catalog, they tell about Tomás Rivera's novel, which is titled . . . *y no se lo tragó la tierra.*
2. As a boy, Rivera worked as a migrant field hand. That may partly explain why he wrote so vividly about migrant workers in . . . *y no se lo tragó la tierra.*
3. Rivera and his family worked long hours in the fields, and it interrupted his education.
4. In his novel, it focuses on a Mexican American family who work as migrant field hands.
5. The family follows crops and the work they provide; it means that they have to move often.
6. Rivera's novel is about the migrant workers' search for justice, which is inspiring.
7. After reading a novel by Tomás Rivera and stories by Reuben Sánchez, I decided to read more of his works.
8. Mandy talked to Adrianne about the development of the characters in Rivera's novel after she had read it.
9. In the biography I read about Rivera, it states that he became the first Mexican American chancellor in the University of California system.
10. After he told him that the film *And the Earth Did Not Swallow Him* was based on Rivera's novel, Todd and Rajiv went to the media center to check out the video.

ANSWERS
Exercise 8

Answers will vary. Sample responses are given.

1. The catalog tells about Tomás Rivera's novel, which is titled . . . *y no se lo tragó la tierra.*
2. Rivera may have written so vividly about migrant workers in . . . *y no se lo tragó la tierra* because he himself worked as a migrant field hand as a boy.
3. Rivera's long hours working in the fields with his family interrupted his education.
4. His novel focuses on a Mexican American family who work as migrant field hands.
5. Because the family follows crops and the work they provide, they have to move often.
6. Rivera's inspiring novel is about the migrant workers' search for justice.
7. After reading a novel by Tomás Rivera and stories by Reuben Sánchez, I decided to read more of Rivera's works.
8. After Mandy had read Rivera's novel, she talked to Adrianne about the development of the characters in it.
9. The biography about Rivera that I read states that he became the first Mexican American chancellor in the University of California system.
10. After Rajiv told Todd that the film *And the Earth Did Not Swallow Him* was based on Rivera's novel, they went to the media center to check out the video.

EXERCISE 9
OBJECTIVE
- To write correct verb forms

EXERCISE 10
OBJECTIVE
- To correct errors in use of verb forms

▶ EXERCISE 9 **Writing the Forms of Irregular Verbs**

For each of the following sentences, fill in the blank with the correct past or past participle form of the verb in italics.

EXAMPLE **1.** *write* Joyce Carol Thomas ____ *Brown Honey in Broomwheat Tea.*
　　　　　1. *wrote*

1. *be* During the Cenozoic era, South America and North America ____ linked by a land bridge.
2. *speak* I had ____ to Jim before he left. **1.** were **2.** spoken
3. *bring* Kathy has ____ me her copy of *A Gathering of Flowers: Stories About Being Young in America.*
4. *give* Yesterday morning, Teresa ____ flowers to her grandmother. **3.** brought **4.** gave
5. *know* We ____ that the first czar of Russia was Ivan the Terrible. **5.** knew **6.** heard
6. *hear* Jonas had ____ that the picnic was postponed.
7. *choose* I wonder what subject Celeste ____ for her presentation. **7.** chose
8. *drive* My sister has ____ me to my ballet lessons every week this year. **8.** driven
9. *teach* Who ____ Jorge how to play the clarinet? **9.** taught
10. *ride* I once ____ a bus across Oklahoma. **10.** rode

▶ EXERCISE 10 **Proofreading Sentences for Correct Verb Forms**

Identify each incorrect verb form, and write the correct form. If a sentence is correct, write *C*.

EXAMPLE **1.** From the 1920s through the 1940s, people in the United States listened to radio programs and gone to the movies more than they do now.
　　　　　1. *gone—went*

1. The popularity of television <u>brung</u> about the end of many radio shows. **1.** brought
2. It has not <u>took</u> long for television to become one of the most <u>popular</u> mediums of entertainment in the United States. **2.** taken
3. I <u>use</u> to think television had always been around, but the first regular TV broadcasts in the United States didn't occur until 1939. **3.** used

MEETING *individual* NEEDS

GENERAL STRATEGIES

Point out to students that when they have questions about the principal parts of verbs, they can often find the answers in a dictionary. Tell them that the base forms of verbs are listed as entry words and that the past, past participle, and present participle forms of irregular verbs are usually given in the entries. For example, if students look up *sink,* they will find *sink, sank,* and *sunk.* As practice, have each student look up three irregular verbs and find each verb's principal parts in a dictionary entry.

STUDENTS WITH SPECIAL NEEDS

Some students may experience difficulties with abstract concepts such as irregular verbs.

Have each student make a chart with four columns. In the first column, list ten irregular verbs. Next, using the charts in **Chapter 21,** fill in two of the three remaining columns with the appropriate form of the irregular verbs. Then, have students fill in the one remaining blank for each verb. Students can then return to the charts in **Chapter 21** to check their answers. Students can keep their corrected charts in their notebooks for reference and can repeat this practice whenever they need review of specific irregular verb forms.

CORRECTING COMMON ERRORS

904 *Correcting Common Errors*

4. Demonstrations of television sets <u>drawed</u> big crowds at the New York World's Fair in 1939.   4. drew

5. In 1941, when the United States <u>begun</u> fighting in World War II, television broadcasting was suspended, but it resumed in 1945.   5. began

6. The sales of television sets soared after World War II, and by 1951, telecasts reached viewers from coast to coast.   6. C

7. Color programs weren't <u>showed</u> until 1953.   7. shown

8. Of course, I've seen reruns of old black-and-white TV programs.   8. C

9. I also have <u>heared</u> some of the old radio shows from before the days of television.   9. heard

10. Have you ever wondered about how television has changed the way people in the United States spend their leisure time?   10. C

▶ EXERCISE 11   **Revising a Paragraph to Make the Tenses of the Verbs Consistent**

Read the following paragraph, and decide whether to rewrite it in the present or past tense. Then, change some of the verb forms so that the verb tenses are consistent.

EXAMPLE   [1] The children were eager to hear a story, so I tell them the Navajo legend of Eagle Boy.

     1. *The children are eager to hear a story, so I am telling them the Navajo legend of Eagle Boy.*
          or
     The children were eager to hear a story, so I told them the Navajo legend of Eagle Boy.

   [1] A young Navajo boy who <u>lives</u> with his parents often <u>dreamed</u> of eagles flying overhead. [2] One day, Father Eagle <u>flew</u> down to the boy, <u>caught</u> hold of his shirt, and <u>carries</u> him to a nest high on a cliff. [3] Father and Mother Eagle <u>feed</u> the boy cornmeal and then <u>took</u> him to the eagle people at the top of the sky. [4] Eventually, the boy <u>goes</u> to the home of Eagle Chief, who <u>told</u> him to remain inside. [5] After Eagle Chief <u>leaves</u>, the boy <u>becomes</u> curious about an animal that he <u>sees</u> outside. [6] When the boy <u>opens</u> the door slightly to look more closely, Big Wind <u>blew</u> it completely open, pulling the boy outside, where the trickster

ANSWERS
Exercise 11

Answers will vary. The following verb changes show correct present or past tense of verbs underscored in the exercise.

PRESENT TENSE

1. lives, dreams
2. flies, catches, carries
3. feed, take
4. goes, tells
5. leaves, becomes, sees
6. opens, blows, is waiting
7. turns
8. returns, restores
9. names, gives
10. returns, becomes

PAST TENSE

1. lived, dreamed [*or* dreamt]
2. flew, caught, carried
3. fed, took
4. went, told
5. left, became, saw
6. opened, blew, was waiting
7. turned
8. returned, restored
9. named, gave
10. returned, became

EXERCISE 12
OBJECTIVE

- To revise sentences to correct errors in the use of comparative and superlative forms of modifiers

Coyote <u>is waiting.</u> [7] The boy, soon tricked into touching Coyote's fur, <u>turns</u> into a coyote himself. [8] When Eagle Chief <u>returns</u> home, he <u>restored</u> the boy to human form. [9] Afterward, Eagle Chief <u>names</u> him Eagle Boy and <u>gave</u> him an eagle feather. [10] Eagle Boy then <u>returns</u> home to his parents, and he eventually <u>became</u> a great medicine man.

 EXERCISE 12   **Proofreading for Correct Comparative and Superlative Forms**

Most of the following sentences contain an error in the use of the comparative or superlative form of a modifier. If a modifier is incorrect, give the correct form. If a sentence is correct, write *C.*

EXAMPLE   **1.** The second time I made lasagna, I prepared it more quicklier.
　　　　1. *more quickly*

1. I planted lantana and petunias next to each other, but the lantana grew <u>best</u> because it could withstand heat and drought.　　　　　　　　1. **better**
2. One of the <u>more exciting</u> field trips is scheduled for this fall.　　　　　　　　2. **most exciting**
3. I can't tell by this map which of the two mountain peaks is <u>tallest.</u>　　　　　　　3. **taller**
4. Of the club's many members, he is <u>less likely</u> to run for president because he is so shy.　　4. **least likely**
5. The <u>more suspenseful</u> part of the novel told of a storm that damaged the sails of the pirate ship and drove the ship off course.　　　　　　　5. **most suspenseful**
6. Which is <u>most fun</u> for you, painting with watercolors or sketching?　　　　　　　　6. **more fun**
7. Watching the two dogs digging in the ground, Carol laughed when the <u>youngest</u> one unearthed a small toy that had been buried.　　　　　7. **younger**
8. The <u>colorfulest</u> sunset I have ever seen in Montana was near Billings.　　　　　　8. **most colorful**
9. Standing outside the theater, we all agreed that the movie was the least satisfying sequel that any of us had ever seen.　　　　　　　　9. **C**
10. Of all the mailboxes in the neighborhood, ours is the <u>more unusual.</u>　　　　　　10. **most unusual**

QUICK REMINDER
Before assigning **Exercise 12**, write the following sentences on the chalkboard and ask students to supply the correct forms of the words in parentheses.

1. The new movie about baby seals we saw last night on television is (exciting) than the film we saw in biology class last year. [more exciting]
2. The sea today is (calm) than it was every day last week. [calmer]
3. Angelica says that she thinks the new mystery she is reading is (scary) than the last several mysteries she has read by the same author. [scarier]

After discussing answers, remind students that the *–er* suffix or *more* is used to compare two things, while the *–est* suffix or *most* is used to compare three or more things.

EXERCISE 13
OBJECTIVE
• To revise sentences to correct errors in the use of modifiers

EXERCISE 14
OBJECTIVE
• To revise sentences to correct misplaced modifiers

MEETING *individual* NEEDS

LEARNING STYLES

Visual Learners. Students might need some visual reinforcement for placing phrases and clauses close to the words they modify. Choose some example sentences to write on the chalkboard. Then, use colored chalk to circle the modifying phrase or clause in each sentence, and draw an arrow to the word it modifies. Have students follow the same procedure when they are revising sentences in **Exercise 14.**

ANSWERS
Exercise 14

Answers may vary. Possible responses are given.

1. Nathan took a second look at the stalks of sugar cane that were gathered into a heap.
2. My sister and I always enjoy listening to stories about Grandma's childhood.
3. From our front porch we watched the sun rise.
4. Frank listened to music while he was climbing the mountain.
5. In science class, we watched a film about how comets are formed.
6. Going to check the mail late yesterday afternoon, I saw a deer.
7. The *Tyrannosaurus rex* was a fierce predator with teeth that were about six inches long.
8. While wading across the river, they noticed a turtle on a log.
9. As we rode over the bridge, we learned that it had once collapsed.
10. While Mr. Hall was planting his garden, he saw many earthworms.

906

 EXERCISE 13 **Proofreading Sentences for Correct Use of Modifiers**

Revise the following sentences to correct each error in the use of a modifier.

EXAMPLE   **1.** Daisies are often more easier to grow than orchids.
        1. *Daisies are often easier to grow than orchids.*

1. likely   **1.** Because they are nocturnal, flying squirrels are less ⋏likelier to be seen than other squirrels are.
2. other   **2.** Raphael types faster than any⋏student in our class.
3. badly   **3.** Fortunately, no one was injured⋏bad when the boats collided.
        4. While elephants are the largest land mammals, blue whales are the ~~most~~ largest mammals of all.
5. else   **5.** Tim is more creative than anyone⋏I know.

 EXERCISE 14 **Correcting Misplaced Modifiers**

Each of the following sentences contains a misplaced modifier. Rewrite each sentence to correct the placement of the modifier.

EXAMPLE   **1.** Flying in close formation, the crowd watched the squadron of small biplanes.
        1. *The crowd watched the squadron of small biplanes flying in close formation.*

1. Gathered into a heap, Nathan took a second look at the stalks of sugar cane.
2. I always enjoy listening to stories about Grandma's childhood with my sister.
3. We watched the sun rise from our front porch.
4. Frank listened to music climbing the mountain.
5. We watched a film about how comets are formed in science class.
6. Late yesterday afternoon, I saw a deer going to check the mail.
7. A fierce predator, the teeth of the *Tyrannosaurus rex* were about six inches long.
8. They noticed a turtle on a log wading across the river.
9. We learned that the bridge had once collapsed as we rode over it.
10. Mr. Hall saw many earthworms planting his garden.

EXERCISE 15
OBJECTIVE
- To correct dangling modifiers

EXERCISE 16
OBJECTIVE
- To correct double negatives and other errors in usage

EXERCISE 15 Correcting Dangling Modifiers

Each of the following sentences contains a dangling modifier. Rewrite each sentence so that the modifier clearly and sensibly modifies a word in the sentence.

EXAMPLE 1. Looking through the binoculars, the bird was brightly colored.
1. *Looking through the binoculars, I saw that the bird was brightly colored.*

1. Well equipped and well rested, the ascent to the peak of the mountain took only a few hours.
2. The people below looked like ants peering down from the top of the Empire State Building.
3. Unable to print out the last two pages because of a power outage, Bob's report had to be turned in late.
4. While practicing the piano, the sheet of music fell off the music rack.
5. In addition to stretching to warm up, your running shoes should be laced tightly.
6. The telephone rang right after walking in the front door.
7. Determined to reach the finish line, the marathon seemed endless.
8. Looking overgrown and scraggly, the McKinneys decided to spend the weekend doing yardwork.
9. Studying fossilized oyster shells found in Kansas, it was hypothesized that a shallow sea once covered at least part of that state.
10. All alone, the woods were mysterious and silent.

EXERCISE 16 Correcting Double Negatives and Other Errors in Usage

Eliminate the double negatives and other errors in usage in the following sentences. Although the sentences can be corrected in more than one way, you need to give only one revision. **Answers may vary. Possible responses are given.**

EXAMPLE 1. Karen should of tried some of the chow mein.
1. *Karen should have tried some of the chow mein.*

1. I went to the beach to look for driftwood but couldn't find ~~none~~. 1. any

CORRECTING COMMON ERRORS

ANSWERS
Exercise 15

Answers will vary. Possible responses are given.

1. Well equipped and well rested, we took only a few hours to complete the ascent to the peak of the mountain.
2. Peering down from the top of the Empire State Building, I thought the people below looked like ants.
3. Bob had to turn in his report late because a power outage prevented him from printing out the last two pages.
4. While I was practicing the piano, the sheet of music fell off the music rack.
5. In addition to stretching to warm up, you should tightly lace your running shoes.
6. The telephone rang right after I walked in the front door.
7. Although the marathon seemed endless, Anjana was determined to reach the finish line.
8. Because the lawn was looking overgrown and scraggly, the McKinneys decided to spend the weekend doing yardwork.
9. The geologist studying fossilized oyster shells found in Kansas hypothesized that a shallow sea once covered at least part of that state.
10. All alone, the boy found the woods mysterious and silent.

CORRECTING COMMON ERRORS

EXERCISE 17
OBJECTIVE
• To revise sentences to correct errors in usage

QUICK REMINDER

Before assigning **Exercise 16**, write the following sentences on the chalkboard. Have students tell which are correct.

1. I don't have no paper.
2. I have no paper.
3. I don't have any paper.

> [The second and third sentences are correct.]

Explain to students that the first sentence incorrectly uses a double negative (*don't* and *no*).

A DIFFERENT APPROACH

After students complete **Exercise 17**, have them revisit any material that they missed. Have students write two sample sentences for each expression that they missed in the exercise. If many students have done poorly on the exercise, you might create a new practice exercise by using the students' sentences.

908

---

2. to **2.** Just try ~~and~~ imagine a city without vehicles of any sort!

3. than **3.** I would rather go to the beach this afternoon ~~then~~ stay indoors.

4. anymore **4.** Our track team practiced until we weren't able to run ~~no more~~.

5. as if **5.** The engine sounds ~~like~~ it is ready to fall out of the old truck.

6. either **6.** We didn't want to see ~~neither~~ of the movies that were showing at the theater.

7. My little brother found a small toy inside ~~of~~ that box of cereal.

8. way **8.** Joel drove a long ~~ways~~ across town just to trade one football card.

9. well **9.** My science experiment didn't work as ~~good~~ as I had thought it would.

10. any **10.** This long stretch of highway has hardly ~~no~~ curves in it.

EXERCISE 17 **Correcting Errors in Usage**

Each of the following sentences contains a usage error. Identify and correct each error.

EXAMPLE **1.** Young people with inventive minds had ought to be encouraged!
          1. *had ought—ought*

1. invented **1.** People between the ages of five and nineteen have <u>discovered</u> some new and important products and processes.

2. used to **2.** As a teenager, Jerrald Spencer <u>use to</u> have fun taking apart electronic devices just to see how they worked.

3. a type of **3.** In 1977, at the age of fifteen, Spencer created his first marketed invention, <u>a type of an</u> electronic toy.

4. That **4.** <u>That there</u> toy led to a whole series of specialty toys sold in major department stores.

5. a **5.** In 1895, the teenager Cathy Evans invented "tufting," <u>an</u> unique method of decorating bedspreads.

6. effect **6.** Her invention has had a marked <u>affect</u> on the carpet industry; in fact, most of the carpet manufactured today involves the process that Evans developed.

7. try to **7.** In 1922, eighteen-year-old Ralph Samuelson decided to <u>try and</u> use snow skis to ski on water.

EXERCISE 18
OBJECTIVE

• To identify and correct errors in usage

8. He didn't think that skiing on water would be much harder <u>then</u> skiing on snow.   8. than
9. <u>Like</u> he had thought, after a number of tries the skis worked!   9. As
10. If you want to be an inventor, you won't succeed <u>without you try</u>.   10. unless you try [*or* without trying]

▶ EXERCISE 18 **Proofreading Sentences to Correct Errors in Usage**

Each of the following sentences contains an error in English usage. Identify and correct each error.

EXAMPLE   **1.** The tour guide last summer learned us much about the Lincoln Memorial.
   1. *learned—taught*

1. The memorial to President Abraham Lincoln, <u>that</u> was dedicated in 1922, has been a popular attraction ever since it opened.   1. which
2. Over the years, no <u>less</u> than 150 million people have visited the monument.   2. fewer
3. I was <u>kind of</u> amazed to hear that the memorial was built on what used to be marshland.   3. rather
4. The architect <u>Henry Bacon he</u> designed the Lincoln Memorial.   4. Henry Bacon
5. I <u>implied</u> from our guide's talk that the Parthenon in Greece inspired Bacon's design.   5. inferred
6. It is not an <u>allusion</u> that the massive columns of both the Parthenon and the Lincoln Memorial tilt slightly inward.   6. illusion
7. The architects designed the columns this way because rows of perfectly straight columns give buildings the <u>affect</u> of bulging at the top.   7. effect
8. I read <u>where</u> Daniel Chester French interviewed Lincoln's son Robert before sculpting the memorial's statue of Lincoln.   8. that
9. The 175-ton statue was carved in separate sections by the Piccirilli brothers, whose family had <u>immigrated</u> from Italy and settled in the United States.   9. emigrated
10. The Gettysburg Address is inscribed on a wall <u>inside of</u> the memorial's hall.   10. inside

MEETING individual NEEDS

LEP/ESL

General Strategies. Some of the usage problems addressed in **Exercise 18** depend on context and others do not. For example, choosing between *implied* and *inferred* or between *affect* and *effect* depends on knowing the context of the sentence. However, some constructions, such as the use of *inside* in place of *inside of* and the use of *that* in place of *where*, are always the preferred usage, no matter what the context. You may wish to help students make reference lists of words and phrases that are preferred regardless of context to use as reference pages in their notebooks.

OBJECTIVES

- To practice responses similar to those required on standardized tests of mastery of language skills and concepts
- To select from among given choices the phrasing that is grammatically correct and best completes the sentence

TEACHING NOTE

Using the Grammar and Usage Tests. You may prefer to have students regard the **Grammar and Usage Tests** as review exercises instead of using them as practice in standardized test taking. If so, have students number blank sheets of paper and write their answers there instead of filling in the **Standardized Test Answer Sheet** provided in *Language Skills Practice and Assessment,* p. 275.

CORRECTING COMMON ERRORS

CORRECTING COMMON ERRORS

910 *Correcting Common Errors*

Grammar and Usage Test: Section 1

DIRECTIONS   Read the paragraph below. For each numbered blank, select the word or group of words that best completes the sentence. Indicate your response by shading in the appropriate oval on your answer sheet.

EXAMPLE

 (1) you ever heard of sick building syndrome?

    1. (A) Has
        (B) Have
        (C) Did
        (D) If
        (E) Hasn't

SAMPLE ANSWER   **1.** Ⓐ ● Ⓒ Ⓓ Ⓔ

> In the 1980s, a number of health problems suffered by office workers (1) for the first time as symptoms of an ailment called sick building syndrome. Besides fatigue and eye irritation, (2) symptoms included headaches, sore throats, colds, and flu. Studies indicate that sick building syndrome, (3) has caused a 30 percent rise in absenteeism in some businesses, can reduce productivity by as much as 40 percent. Problems resulting from this syndrome (4) are caused by such pollutants as formaldehyde, benzene, and trichloroethylene. These substances, found in furniture, insulation, and paint, (5) trapped in climate-controlled buildings. Even though such pollutants are so widespread, the situation (6) hopeless. Research originally conducted to help astronauts (7) to a simple solution—houseplants. Microorganisms in the roots of a potted plant (8) remove harmful substances from the air. The (9) plants include chrysanthemums, which remove benzene, and spider plants, which remove formaldehyde. In addition, both peace lilies and English ivy (10) trichloroethylene.

1.C **1.** (A) identified
        (B) was identified
        (C) were identified
        (D) being identified
        (E) was being identified

2.A **2.** (A) these
        (B) them
        (C) these here
        (D) these kind of
        (E) them kind of

3.B **3.** (A) that
        (B) which
        (C) who
        (D) what
        (E) it

4.D **4.** (A) more likely
        (B) more liklier
        (C) liklier
        (D) most likely
        (E) most likliest

GRAMMAR AND USAGE TEST: Section 2
OBJECTIVES

- To practice responses similar to those required on standardized tests of mastery of language skills and concepts
- To demonstrate understanding of key language concepts by selecting the answer that best expresses the meaning of the sentence

5. D **5.** (A) becomes
(B) becomed
(C) becoming
(D) become
(E) are becoming

6. A **6.** (A) is in no way
(B) is not in no way
(C) aren't in no way
(D) it isn't hardly
(E) isn't hardly

7. B **7.** (A) have led
(B) has led
(C) has lead
(D) have lead
(E) leads

8. C **8.** (A) they help
(B) it helps
(C) help
(D) helps
(E) is helping

9. A **9.** (A) most useful
(B) usefullest
(C) most usefullest
(D) more useful
(E) more usefuller

10. E **10.** (A) removes
(B) they remove
(C) removed
(D) were removing
(E) remove

Grammar and Usage Test: Section 2

DIRECTIONS Either part or all of each of the following sentences is underlined. Using the rules of standard written English, choose the answer that most clearly expresses the meaning of the sentence. If there is no error, choose A. Indicate your response by shading in the appropriate oval on your answer sheet.

EXAMPLE

1. Has everyone <u>chosen a topic for their</u> essay?

(A) chosen a topic for their
(B) chose a topic for their
(C) choosed a topic for their
(D) chosen a topic for his or her
(E) chosen a topic for his

SAMPLE ANSWER 1. (A) (B) (C) ● (E)

1. B **1.** This evening <u>less people will be driving</u> cars to the parade because there is less space available for parking.

(A) less people will be driving
(B) fewer people will be driving
(C) less people will have been driving
(D) fewer people will have been driving
(E) fewer people drive

CORRECTING COMMON ERRORS

TEACHING NOTE

Using the Grammar and Usage Tests. A practice answer sheet that students may use for this **Grammar and Usage Test** is provided in *Language Skills Practice and Assessment,* p. 275.

2. E **2.** In the 1936 Olympic Games, I read that Jesse Owens won four gold medals.

    (A) In the 1936 Olympic Games, I read that Jesse Owens won four gold medals.
    (B) In the 1936 Olympic Games, I read that four gold medals were won by Jesse Owens.
    (C) I read where Jesse Owens won four gold medals in the 1936 Olympic Games.
    (D) I read in the 1936 Olympic Games that Jesse Owens won four gold medals.
    (E) I read that Jesse Owens won four gold medals in the 1936 Olympic Games.

3. C **3.** In tennis, "love" is when a player has a score of zero.

    (A) when a player has a score of zero
    (B) where a player has a score of zero
    (C) a score of zero
    (D) scoring a zero
    (E) that a player has a score of zero

4. E **4.** I can't hardly remember a time when the temperature was lower than it is today.

    (A) I can't hardly remember a time when the temperature was lower than it is today.
    (B) I can't hardly remember a time when the temperature was lower then it is today.
    (C) I can hardly remember a time when the temperature was more lower than it is today.
    (D) I can hardly remember a time when the temperature was lower then it is today.
    (E) I can hardly remember a time when the temperature was lower than it is today.

5. C **5.** While running to the bus stop this morning, some books fell out of my backpack.

    (A) While running to the bus stop this morning, some books fell out of my backpack.
    (B) While running this morning, some books fell out of my backpack at the bus stop.
    (C) While I was running to the bus stop this morning, some books fell out of my backpack.
    (D) Some books fell out of my backpack while running to the bus stop this morning.
    (E) I was running to the bus stop this morning while some of my books fell out of my backpack.

6.C **6.** The first tennis match played at our school's spring tournament was <u>between she and I</u>.

    (A) between she and I
    (B) between her and I
    (C) between her and me
    (D) between she and me
    (E) among her and me

7.D **7.** Raymond knows how to repair lawn mowers, <u>and he plans to make it his summer job</u>.

    (A) and he plans to make it his summer job
    (B) and he plans to make that his summer job
    (C) and that is his plan for a summer job
    (D) and he plans to make such repair work his summer job
    (E) which is his plan for a summer job

8.E **8.** <u>Creole dishes, the origins of which can be traced to European, African, and Caribbean cooking.</u>

    (A) Creole dishes, the origins of which can be traced to European, African, and Caribbean cooking.
    (B) The origins of Creole dishes, which can be traced to European, African, and Caribbean cooking.
    (C) Tracing the origins of Creole dishes to European, African, and Caribbean cooking.
    (D) European, African, and Caribbean cooking, which are the origins of Creole dishes.
    (E) The origins of Creole dishes can be traced to European, African, and Caribbean cooking.

9.C **9.** The coach <u>doesn't think that her and I</u> have practiced free throws enough today.

    (A) doesn't think that her and I
    (B) don't think that her and me
    (C) doesn't think that she and I
    (D) don't think that she and I
    (E) doesn't think that her and me

10.B **10.** Some of the people <u>who are standing in line have all ready</u> bought their tickets.

    (A) who are standing in line have all ready
    (B) who are standing in line have already
    (C) whom are standing in line have all ready
    (D) whom are standing in line have already
    (E) that are standing in line have all ready

QUICK REMINDER

Write the following phrases containing common and proper nouns on the chalkboard and ask students to correct capitalization errors:

1. lake Huron [Lake]
2. elks club [Elks Club]
3. Forest street [Street]
4. norwegian salmon [Norwegian]
5. a Canadian Border [border]
6. chairman Smith [Chairman]
7. cousin Betty [Cousin]
8. his Grandfather [grandfather]
9. the club Secretary [secretary]
10. the Hillsborough summer Festival [Summer]

MEETING individual NEEDS

AT-RISK STUDENTS

You may want to obtain copies of different kinds of application forms such as applications for jobs, schools, and driver's licenses. Have students fill them out, and then check for correct use of capital letters. Point out that standard usage will often be important to the people evaluating these types of applications.

EXERCISE 19
OBJECTIVE

• To correct errors in capitalization

EXERCISE 20
OBJECTIVE

• To revise sentences to correct errors in capitalization

EXERCISE 19 **Correcting Errors in Capitalization**

Each of the following groups of words contains at least one capitalization error. Correct the errors either by changing capital letters to lowercase letters or by changing lowercase letters to capital letters.

EXAMPLE 1. Robert Burns's poem "a red, red rose"
         1. *Robert Burns's poem "A Red, Red Rose"*

1. my aunt elizabeth
2. an interstate highway in the midwest
3. *the middle passage* by V. S. Naipaul
4. a red cross volunteer
5. west of sixty-fifth street
6. winter in denver
7. grandma's brother
8. senator Ann Greene
9. latin, art, and geometry II
10. a buddhist temple
11. the battle Of vicksburg
12. dr. I. f. livingstone
13. the book *a room with a view*
14. American indian pictographs
15. tickets to the world series
16. a xerox® photocopier
17. Father's day
18. A vietnamese festival
19. moons circling earth and mars
20. Grand teton national park

EXERCISE 20 **Correcting Errors in Capitalization**

Each of the following sentences contains errors in capitalization. Correct the errors either by changing capital letters to lowercase letters or by changing lowercase letters to capital letters.

EXAMPLE 1. i recently read about oren lyons, an Influential onondaga chief.
         1. *I recently read about Oren Lyons, an influential Onondaga chief.*

1. The onondaga are an iroquois people.
2. Oren lyons's formal title is faith keeper of the turtle clan.

EXERCISE 21
OBJECTIVE

• To correct sentences with errors in the use of commas

3. Before assuming this important position, mr. lyons was a successful commercial artist in new york city.
4. The iroquois tradition of having faith keepers dates back to hundreds of years before the pilgrims landed at plymouth rock.
5. Mr. lyons edits a publication called *daybreak*, which is dedicated to the seventh generation to come.
6. As faith keeper, mr. lyons is responsible for making decisions that will ensure that the earth is habitable for that future generation.
7. He also has many other responsibilities, including speaking before the united nations.
8. Mr. lyons, other members of the iroquois league, and a group of lakota sioux addressed the unifed nations in geneva, switzerland.
9. Faith keepers work to uphold the traditions of their people, as well as the principles of Democracy, community, and reverence for the Natural World.
10. To learn more about Mr. Lyons and other american indian leaders, look in *the encyclopedia of Native America*, which is a reference book I learned about in American History class.

▶ EXERCISE 21 **Proofreading Sentences for the Correct Use of Commas**

Each of the following sentences needs at least one comma. Write the word or numeral that comes before each missing comma, and add the comma. **Optional commas are underscored.**

EXAMPLE **1.** The Green Club collects aluminum clear glass colored glass and paper for recycling.
1. *aluminum, glass, glass,*

1. Orb weavers are spiders that create beautiful, complex, round webs.
2. On July 20, 1969, the *Apollo 11* lunar module landed on the moon.
3. Cheeky, the neighbor's dog that chewed up my athletic shoes, is now kept in his own yard.
4. Oh, when will I learn not to worry so much?
5. Italy, in my opinion, is the most beautiful country in the world.

LEARNING STYLES

Visual Learners. You may want to help students visualize some of the uses of commas by showing examples of comma usage. Draw six columns on the chalkboard. Label the columns *independent clauses, nonessential clauses, introductory elements, interrupters, items in a series,* and *conventions (dates and addresses).* Work with students to generate examples to go in each column. Write the examples under the appropriate headings on the chalkboard.

You may then want to assign **Exercise 21** for homework and go over the answers with students in class. Survey the class for error patterns and review those rules of comma usage that seem to give students particular problems.

TIMESAVER

Ask students to write the sentences for **Exercise 22** (as well as for upcoming **Exercises 23, 24, 25,** and **26**) in one color (such as blue) and then use a different color (such as red) for punctuation marks like commas (or quotation marks and periods) so that these marks stand out. Students could also alternate pencil and ink in the same manner, or, if two distinct marking methods are not available, they can mark carefully and then circle the commas (or—in the other exercises—semicolons, colons, and end marks) they have added to the sentences. This procedure will make the punctuation more visually striking and easier to see for grading.

EXERCISE 22
OBJECTIVE
• To revise sentences to supply missing commas

6. The Perseid meteor <u>shower</u>,which occurs <u>annually</u>, appears to originate in the constellation Perseus.
7. I wasn't chosen for the track <u>team</u>,but I am trying out for soccer next week.
8. The American painter Charles <u>Russell</u>,who is famous for his scenes of life in the <u>West</u>,is my favorite artist.
9. We had planned to climb the <u>mountain</u>,but the trail was closed because mountain lions had been sighted in the area.
10. Tired of waiting for the movie to <u>start</u>,the audience began to murmur and fidget.

▶ EXERCISE 22 **Using Commas Correctly**

Each of the following sentences needs at least one comma. Write the word or numeral that comes before each missing comma, and add the comma. **Optional commas are underscored.**

EXAMPLE   **1.** Tony have you ever heard of Dr. Percy L. Julian?
          1. *Tony,*

1. <u>Julian</u>,born in <u>Montgomery</u>, <u>Alabama</u>,in <u>1899</u>,grew up to become a renowned scientist.
2. After studying at DePauw <u>University</u>,he graduated with highest honors; in <u>fact</u>,he received a Phi Beta Kappa key and delivered the valedictory address.
3. Julian went on to <u>Harvard</u>,where he earned a master's <u>degree</u>,and then traveled to Austria to earn a Ph.D. at the University of Vienna.
4. As Ahmed <u>says</u>,Dr. Julian must have been a brilliant man.
5. Dr. Julian taught at Howard University and at West Virginia <u>University</u>,but his fame began after he went to work as a research chemist for <u>Glidden</u>,a paint company in <u>Chicago</u>,Illinois.
6. During World War <u>II</u>,Dr. Julian created a firefighting <u>foam</u>,<u>which</u>,by the <u>way</u>,was made out of soybean protein.
7. His achievements earned him the Spingarn <u>Medal</u>,the NAACP's highest award.
8. Interested in developing other uses for <u>soybeans</u>, Dr. Julian established Julian Laboratories and its subsidiaries.

EXERCISE 23
OBJECTIVE

• To revise sentences to supply missing semicolons and colons

9. In his <u>lifetime</u>;he developed an inexpensive cortisone for arthritis <u>sufferers</u>;drugs to relieve <u>glaucoma</u>;drugs to help victims of rheumatic <u>fever</u>;and many other helpful medicines.
10. Dr. Julian died in <u>1975</u>;but his impressive achievements live on.

▶ EXERCISE 23 **Using Semicolons and Colons Correctly**

The following sentences need semicolons and colons. Write the word or numeral preceding and the word or numeral following the needed punctuation, and insert the proper punctuation. In some instances, you will need to replace commas with either semicolons or colons.

EXAMPLE   **1.** My brother likes to read adventure novels I prefer autobiographies of sports figures.
   1. *novels; I*

1. We signed up for field <u>hockey</u>; <u>however</u>, the heavy snow has prevented practice all month.
2. In art class, Joanna, Elaine, and Jim used <u>acrylics</u>;<u>and</u> Todd, Tonya, and Jasper used oils.
3. We missed the <u>4:15</u> bus and had to wait an hour for the next one.
4. The movie Suzanne recommended was *<u>Theremin</u>:An Electronic Odyssey.*
5. This airport has direct flights to Frankfurt, <u>Germany</u>; <u>Rome</u>, <u>Italy</u>; <u>London</u>, <u>England</u>; <u>and</u> Paris, France.
6. Our choir is singing a song based on Psalm <u>19:14</u>.
7. Our neighborhood has fiestas for various <u>holidays</u>;for example, we have a piñata party on Cinco de Mayo each year.
8. I walk to school every day with Darla, Gene, and <u>Greg</u>; <u>and</u> Sven, Petra, and Arnold join us on the walk home.
9. I have several postcards that my stepsister sent me from towns with unusual <u>names</u>; for instance, here are ones from Cut and Shoot, Texas, and Truth or Consequences, New Mexico.
10. The Ecology Club has adopted the following projects this <u>year</u>:<u>setting</u> out recycling bins, planting trees in the schoolyard, and adopting two miles of highway to keep clean.

CORRECTING COMMON ERRORS

COMMON ERROR

Problem. Some students confuse the colon and the semicolon or think they are interchangeable.

Solution. Explain the different functions of these two punctuation marks. Tell students that a colon is a kind of pointer to something that a writer wants to emphasize. A semicolon provides clarity (in setting off a list with internal commas) or accentuates a close relationship between two independent clauses.

CORRECTING COMMON ERRORS

EXERCISE 24
OBJECTIVE

- To punctuate written dialogue correctly

ANSWERS
Exercise 24

1. "So tell me," Colin said. "What exactly is a vegetarian?"
2. "Well, you already know that a vegetarian is someone who doesn't eat meat," Sarah said, "but you don't seem to know what a vegetarian does eat.
3. Your mistake about a vegetarian diet is one that many people make. They think that a vegetarian eats only vegetables, but vegetarians eat quite a variety of foods."
4. Colin replied, "Okay, what else do vegetarians eat?"
5. "Well," Sarah answered, "I eat whatever I want that isn't meat, and I try to eat healthful foods. I eat vegetables, of course, but also grains, breads, pastas, beans, nuts, soups, cereals, and fruit."
6. "Do you eat eggs and dairy products?"
7. "Yes," Sarah replied, "I do, but some vegetarians don't. For instance, I sometimes eat quiche, cheese-and-vegetable enchiladas, and bowls of cereal with milk." [*or* "Yes," Sarah replied. "I do . . . ."]
8. Colin said, "I guess you aren't having any trouble finding things to eat. I'm wondering, though, why you decided to become a vegetarian."
9. "I just wanted to feel better. Studies show that being a vegetarian is very healthful," Sarah said.
10. Colin said, "I remember learning that people who don't eat meat are less likely to have heart disease than people who do eat meat and that a diet without any animal products is cholesterol free. I wonder if there are any other health benefits of vegetarianism."

CORRECTING COMMON ERRORS

CORRECTING COMMON ERRORS

EXERCISE 24 **Punctuating Dialogue**

Add paragraph indentions and insert quotation marks and other punctuation where needed in the following dialogue. You will need to change some lowercase letters to capital letters, too.

EXAMPLE [1] Hey, Sarah, I hear you've become a vegetarian Colin said. Don't you ever get tired of eating nothing but vegetables?
[2] You've got some things to learn about vegetarians! Sarah said.

1. *"Hey, Sarah, I hear you've become a vegetarian," Colin said. "Don't you ever get tired of eating nothing but vegetables?"*
2. *"You've got some things to learn about vegetarians!" Sarah said.*

[1] So tell me Colin said. What exactly is a vegetarian? [2] Well, you already know that a vegetarian is someone who doesn't eat meat Sarah said but you don't seem to know what a vegetarian does eat. [3] Your mistake about a vegetarian diet is one that many people make. They think that a vegetarian eats only vegetables, but vegetarians eat quite a variety of foods. [4] Colin replied Okay what else do vegetarians eat?

[5] Well, Sarah answered I eat whatever I want that isn't meat, and I try to eat healthful foods. I eat vegetables, of course, but also grains, breads, pastas, beans, nuts, soups, cereals, and fruit.

[6] Do you eat eggs and dairy products?

[7] Yes, Sarah replied I do, but some vegetarians don't. For instance, I sometimes eat quiche, cheese-and-vegetable enchiladas, and bowls of cereal with milk.

[8] Colin said, I guess you aren't having any trouble finding things to eat. I'm wondering, though, why you decided to become a vegetarian. [9] I just wanted to feel better. Studies show that being a vegetarian is very healthful Sarah said.

[10] Colin said I remember learning that people who don't eat meat are less likely to have heart disease than people who do eat meat and that a diet without any animal products is cholesterol free. I wonder if there are any other health benefits of vegetarianism.

EXERCISE 25
OBJECTIVE

• To use punctuation and capitalization correctly in quotations

EXERCISE 26
OBJECTIVE

• To correct phrases and clauses by adding apostrophes

Mechanics **919**

▶ EXERCISE 25 **Punctuating and Capitalizing Quotations**

For each of the following sentences, insert quotation marks and other marks of punctuation where needed, and change lowercase letters to capital letters as necessary.

EXAMPLE **1.** Should the U.S. flag be flown at the same level as or higher than a state flag asked Earl

1. *"Should the U.S. flag be flown at the same level as or higher than a state flag?" asked Earl.*

1. Megan's note says, The electrician at the repair shop thinks that our VCR will be ready by 5:00 P.M.
2. Physical therapy Karen said is really strengthening my brother's legs.
3. Leiningen Versus the Ants, by Carl Stephenson, is a frightening short story Bob said.
4. Yes Laura Emilio replied you will want to plant the azaleas in partial sunlight.
5. Sean asked why did the judge shout Order in the court! just before she called a recess?
6. The following seniors will serve as ushers at the graduation ceremonies: Alexandra, Michael, and Jim, Mrs. Jackson said.
7. When she hit her finger with the hammer while she was repairing the roof, Hannah yelled that does it!
8. What I asked the doctor is the patella?
9. The song Long Distance Call was one of the hits of the Chicago blues singer Muddy Waters.
10. No! Paula exclaimed I didn't say to paint it green!

▶ EXERCISE 26 **Correcting Phrases and Clauses by Adding Apostrophes**

Proofread the following phrases and clauses, adding apostrophes where they are needed. If a phrase or a clause is correct, write C.

EXAMPLE **1.** giving to United Ways fund

1. *giving to United Way's fund*

1. somebody's hat
2. Are these Kim's poems?
3. Judy's and his show

ANSWERS
Exercise 25

1. Megan's note says, "The electrician at the repair shop thinks that our VCR will be ready by 5:00 P.M."
2. "Physical therapy," Karen said, "is really strengthening my brother's legs."
3. "'Leiningen Versus the Ants,' by Carl Stephenson, is a frightening short story," Bob said.
4. "Yes, Laura," Emilio replied, "you will want to plant the azaleas in partial sunlight." [*or* . . . Emilio replied. "You . . . ."]
5. Sean asked, "Why did the judge shout, 'Order in the court!' just before she called a recess?"
6. "The following seniors will serve as ushers at the graduation ceremonies: Alexandra, Michael, and Jim," Mrs. Jackson said.
7. When she hit her finger with the hammer while she was repairing the roof, Hannah yelled, "That does it!"
8. "What," I asked the doctor, "is the patella?"
9. The song "Long Distance Call" was one of the hits of the Chicago blues singer Muddy Waters.
10. "No!" Paula exclaimed, "I didn't say to paint it green!" [*or* "No!" Paula exclaimed. "I . . . ."]

919

MEETING *individual* NEEDS

LESS-ADVANCED STUDENTS

When you tell students to look for the correct spelling of a word in a dictionary, they might become frustrated if they think finding the word requires knowledge of its correct spelling. Remind students that trial and error is a good way to find the correct spelling of a word. Tell them to look up the spelling that they think might be correct. Remind students that certain consonants can sound very similar to one another (such as *c* and *k*, *g* and *j*, *ph* and *f*).

You could give students practice by having them look up any words they misspell in **Exercise 27**. If you wish, you could pair students to collaborate on finding the words in a dictionary.

TEACHING NOTE

In **Exercise 27**, item 3 contains a word, *traveled*, that students—in an attempt to "correct" the spelling—may change to be spelled as *travelled*. Since most dictionaries list *travelled* as an acceptable variant, you may not want to deduct points for students' answers if they change this word. However, you might want to take this opportunity to point out to students that they can check a dictionary for the preferred spelling. Tell students that in the case of verbs that end in *–el*, for example, some people prefer to form the past tense by doubling the *l* before adding *–ed* (*travel—past tense: traveled—*and other verbs such as *apparel, counsel, level, marvel,* or *parallel*). A dictionary usually lists the preferred spelling first (in *Webster's New World College Dictionary*, Third Edition, the preferred spelling is one *l* before the *–ed*).

920

920 *Correcting Common Errors*

4. Who's there?
5. both planes' engines
6. The box was theirs. 6. C
7. How many *a*s are in *aardvark*?
8. women's shoes
9. Anya and Tony's team
10. hadn't finished
11. that canoe's hull
12. no one else's parents
13. Its memory capacity is huge. 13. C
14. that club's newsletter
15. Mr. Harris's Irish setter
16. neither one's fault
17. Howard's and Marilyn's tests
18. because I'm sleepy
19. whose ring 19. C
20. It's going to rain.
21. the Sanchezes' family reunion
22. the king's horses
23. Sam's back already.
24. Dot your *i*s and cross your *t*s.
25. ten o'clock

▶ EXERCISE 27 **Correcting Spelling Errors**

Each sentence contains two spelling errors. Find the errors, and rewrite the words correctly.

EXAMPLE   **1.** We forfieted the free vacation and enjoied our leisure time at home.
         1. *forfeited, enjoyed*

1. The poodle reacted in a <u>wierd</u> way, <u>stareing</u> straight ahead.   1. weird/staring
2. The <u>pityful</u> <u>wailling</u> of the lost kittens helped Stacy find them.   2. pitiful/wailing
3. mapped/ proceeded [Note: *Traveled* may also be spelled *travelled*.]   3. We traveled on the route that had been <u>maped</u> out for us and <u>proceded</u> at a steady pace.
4. They finally <u>conceeded</u> that the new system would cost a <u>3rd</u> less to run than the old one did. 4. conceded/third
5. When the paper we had collected for recycling was <u>wieghed</u>, we were <u>gratifyed</u> to learn that the amount exceeded one ton.   5. weighed/gratified

Mechanics **921**

6. All the <u>puppys</u> at the animal shelter were cute, but the <u>1st</u> one they showed us was the one we decided to adopt. 6. puppies/first
7. <u>40</u> people signed up for the dance classes to learn <u>waltzs</u> and line dances. 7. Forty/waltzes
8. <u>Cleanlyness</u> of the work space is <u>especialy</u> important when food is being handled. 8. Cleanliness/especially
9. My cousin drives <u>30</u> miles each way to her job at a nature preserve, where she takes care of the lions, tigers, and <u>wolfs</u>. 9. thirty/wolves
10. Both of the <u>monkies</u> are likely to throw <u>tomatos</u> at anyone standing nearby. 10. monkeys/tomatoes

▶ EXERCISE 28 **Choosing Between Words Often Confused**

From each pair of words in parentheses, choose the word or words that will make the sentence correct.

EXAMPLE 1. (*You're, your*) endangering the pedestrians by skating too fast.
       1. *You're*

1. When I applied for work at the restaurant, I spoke with the (*personal*, <u>*personnel*</u>) manager.
2. It is a good idea to check the (*breaks*, <u>*brakes*</u>) on any vehicle before you start driving.
3. We had (<u>*already*</u>, *all ready*) opened the windows in the art room when Ms. Wong asked us to.
4. What theme do you think we should (<u>*choose*</u>, *chose*) for the prom?
5. Eleanor and Lupita said we could use (*they're*, <u>*their*</u>) binoculars when we go on the next field trip.
6. What (<u>*effect*</u>, *affect*) will all the rain have on the mown hay?
7. The elephant always returns to (<u>*its*</u>, *it's*) enclosure at feeding time.
8. Did the members of the (*counsel*, <u>*council*</u>) ever reach an agreement?
9. A (*lose*, <u>*loose*</u>) wing nut on the bracket for the spare tire caused a rattle in the trunk.
10. Use very fine, not (*course*, <u>*coarse*</u>), sandpaper for the finishing work on wood furniture or toys.

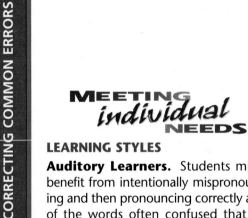

MEETING *individual* **NEEDS**

LEARNING STYLES

Auditory Learners. Students might benefit from intentionally mispronouncing and then pronouncing correctly a list of the words often confused that are used in **Exercise 28.** Students could then mispronounce the words to exaggerate the spelling differences between these homonyms. Exaggerating the spelling differences aloud may help students recall the distinctions in spelling and meaning between the pairs of words.

OBJECTIVE

• To demonstrate mastery by selecting answers that show correct capitalization, punctuation, and spelling

Mechanics Test: Section 1

TEACHING NOTE

Using the Mechanics Tests. A Standardized Test Answer Sheet that students may use for these **Mechanics Tests** is provided in *Language Skills Practice and Assessment,* p. 275.

DIRECTIONS Each numbered item below contains an underlined group of words. Choose the answer that shows the correct capitalization, punctuation, and spelling of the underlined part. If there is no error, choose answer E (Correct as is). Indicate your response by shading in the appropriate oval on your answer sheet.

EXAMPLE

[1] February 9 1998

    (A) Febuary 9 1998
    (B) Febuary 9, 1998
    (C) February 9th 1998
    (D) February 9, 1998
    (E) Correct as is

SAMPLE ANSWER 1. Ⓐ Ⓑ Ⓒ ⬤ Ⓔ

---

    327 Hickory Lane
[1] Ankeny, Iowa 50021
    February 9, 1998

[2] Susan Washington DVM
    49-A Johnson Circle
    Des Moines, IA 50320

[3] Dear Dr. Washington:

Thank you for [4] agreing to lead the discussion at our club's next meeting. We members of [5] Future Farmers of America know how important the practice of veterinary medicine is to agriculture. [6] 39 students have already signed up to attend. As I mentioned on the phone last [7] week, our meeting will take place in Healy Lecture hall. We will begin at [8] 3:00 PM, and I will introduce you soon thereafter. We look forward to hearing [9] your views on veterinary medicine, and hope that you will stay for refreshments after the meeting.

[10] yours sincerely,

Michael Yoder

Michael Yoder
Chapter President FFA
Ankeny High School

1.B **1.** (A) Ankeny, Ia. 50021
(B) Ankeny, IA 50021
(C) Ankeny IA, 50021
(D) Ankeny I.A., 50021
(E) Correct as is

2.B **2.** (A) Susan Washington DVM.
(B) Susan Washington, D.V.M.
(C) Susan Washington, DVM
(D) Susan Washington: DVM
(E) Correct as is

3.E **3.** (A) Dear Dr Washington:
(B) Dear Dr. Washington,
(C) Dear dr. Washington,
(D) Dear Dr. Washington;
(E) Correct as is

4.C **4.** (A) agreing, to lead
(B) agreing to led
(C) agreeing to lead
(D) agreeing too lead
(E) Correct as is

5.E **5.** (A) Future Farmers Of America
(B) future farmers of america
(C) future farmers of America
(D) future Farmers of America
(E) Correct as is

6.B **6.** (A) Thirty nine students
(B) Thirty-nine students
(C) Thirty-Nine students
(D) Thirty-nine students'
(E) Correct as is

7.D **7.** (A) week: our meeting will take place in Healy lecture hall
(B) week: our meeting will take place in Healy Lecture Hall
(C) week, our meeting will take place in Healy lecture hall
(D) week, our meeting will take place in Healy Lecture Hall
(E) Correct as is

8.D **8.** (A) 3:00 PM
(B) 3:00 PM.,
(C) 3:00 P.M.
(D) 3:00 P.M.,
(E) Correct as is

9.C **9.** (A) you're views on veterinary medicine,
(B) you're views on veterinary medicine;
(C) your views on veterinary medicine
(D) your views on veterinary medicine:
(E) Correct as is

10.A **10.** (A) Yours sincerely,
(B) Yours' sincerely,
(C) Your's sincerely,
(D) Yours sincerely:
(E) Correct as is

CORRECTING COMMON ERRORS

CORRECTING COMMON ERRORS

Mechanics Test: Section 2

DIRECTIONS Each of the following sentences contains an underlined word or group of words. Choose the answer that shows the correct capitalization, punctuation, and spelling of the underlined part. If there is no error, choose answer E (Correct as is). Indicate your response by shading in the appropriate oval on your answer sheet.

TEACHING NOTE
Using the Mechanics Tests. A Standardized Test Answer Sheet that students may use for these **Mechanics Tests** is provided in *Language Skills Practice and Assessment,* p. 275.

EXAMPLE

1. Please post these announcements for <u>the Columbus winter Carnival.</u>

   (A) the Columbus Winter Carnival
   (B) the columbus winter carnival
   (C) The Columbus Winter Carnival
   (D) the Columbus Winter carnival
   (E) Correct as is

SAMPLE ANSWER 1. ● Ⓑ Ⓒ Ⓓ Ⓔ

1.A 1. "Can you tell us the <u>moral of the fable that we just read, Josh</u>"? asked Ms. Chen.

   (A) moral of the fable that we just read, Josh?"
   (B) morale of the fable that we just read, Josh?
   (C) moral of the fable that we just read," Josh?
   (D) moral of the fable that we just read, Josh?,"
   (E) Correct as is

2.B 2. <u>We'll need streamers balloons</u> and confetti to decorate for the baby shower.

   (A) Well, need streamers, balloons,
   (B) We'll need streamers, balloons,
   (C) We'll need: streamers, balloons,
   (D) We'll need streamers balloons,
   (E) Correct as is

3.E 3. <u>Dr. Martin Luther King, Jr.,</u> was awarded the Nobel Peace Prize in 1964.

   (A) Dr Martin Luther King, Jr.,
   (B) Dr. Martin Luther King Jr.,
   (C) Dr. Martin Luther King, Jr,
   (D) Dr. Martin Luther King, jr.,
   (E) Correct as is

4.D 4. Choose a free subscription to one of these <u>magazines *Time, Newsweek,* or *Sports Illustrated.*</u>

   (A) magazines, *Time,*
   (B) magazines; *Time,*
   (C) magazines: "Time,"
   (D) magazines: *Time,*
   (E) Correct as is

5.C **5.** "Did Coach Sims really say, 'Run another <u>mile?'</u>" gasped Carla.

   (A) mile?"
   (B) mile,"
   (C) mile'?"
   (D) mile,'"
   (E) Correct as is

6.B **6.** The <u>men's and womens</u> shoe departments and the housewares department are having sales now.

   (A) mens and women's
   (B) men's and women's
   (C) mens' and womens'
   (D) mens and womens
   (E) Correct as is

7.D **7.** The bus driver <u>said "that we should be quiet."</u>

   (A) said, "That we should be quiet."
   (B) said "That we should be quiet."
   (C) said, that we should be quiet.
   (D) said that we should be quiet.
   (E) Correct as is

8.D **8.** I've visited three state <u>capitals: Boise, Idaho, Tallahassee, Florida;</u> and Montpelier, Vermont.

   (A) capitals: Boise, Idaho, Tallahassee, Florida,
   (B) capitols: Boise, Idaho; Tallahassee, Florida;
   (C) capitols: Boise; Idaho; Tallahassee; Florida;
   (D) capitals: Boise, Idaho; Tallahassee, Florida;
   (E) Correct as is

9.A **9.** Whether or not it rains will <u>not effect their plans</u> for this weekend.

   (A) Whether or not it rains will not affect their plans
   (B) Weather or not it rains will not affect their plans
   (C) Whether or not it rains will not affect they're plans
   (D) Whether or not it rains will not effect they're plans
   (E) Correct as is

10.D **10.** <u>Its not John whose</u> left his papers in the library.

   (A) Its not John who's
   (B) It's not John whose
   (C) Its' not John who's
   (D) It's not John who's
   (E) Correct as is

PART THREE

RESOURCES

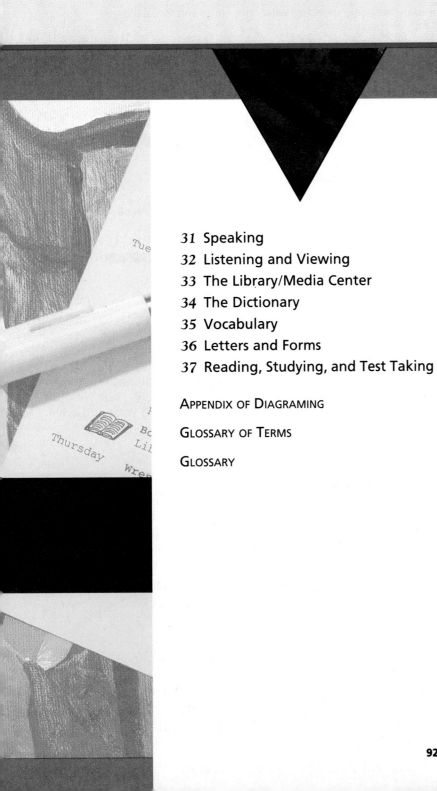

PART THREE: RESOURCES

The following **Teaching Resource**s booklets contain materials that may be used with this part of the Pupil's Edition.

- *Academic and Workplace Skills*
- *Portfolio Assessment* (for Chs. 31, 32, 35)
- *Practice for Assessment in Reading, Vocabulary, and Spelling* (for Ch. 35)

SPEAKING *(pp. 928–940)*

OBJECTIVES

* To explain how problems involving speaking on the telephone could be solved
* To provide directions for given situations
* To explain social introductions for given situations
* To prepare and give speeches with note cards and visual aids

PROGRAM MANAGER

SPEAKING

■ **Independent Practice/ Reteaching** For additional practice and reinforcement, see **The Communication Cycle, Nonverbal Communication, Preparing a Speech, Speaking Expressively, Discussion and Parliamentary Procedure**, and **Adapting Sources for Oral Interpretation** in *Academic and Workplace Skills,* pp. 1–6.

■ **Additional Instruction** For more information on chapter concepts, see **Chapters 9, 11, 13, 19,** and **20** in *Speech for Effective Communication.*

■ **Assessment/Reflection** To assess student work and evaluate progress, see **Portfolio Forms** in *Portfolio Assessment,* pp. 35–38.

■ **Review** For exercises on chapter concepts, see **Review Form A** and **Review Form B** in *Academic and Workplace Skills,* pp. 7–8.

CHAPTER OVERVIEW

This chapter provides basic instruction in both formal and informal speaking situations. After a brief discussion of the communication cycle and nonverbal communication, the chapter continues with attention to such informal speaking situations as impromptu speaking, speaking on the telephone, giving directions, and making introductions. Aspects of formal speaking such as preparing a speech, analyzing audiences, gathering materials, organizing

continued on next page

31 SPEAKING

Skills and Strategies

A good speech requires careful thought and thorough preparation. To communicate effectively, you should think about your purpose, your topic, and your audience.

The Communication Cycle

Oral communication is a process that you take part in when you communicate your feelings or ideas to another person. In turn, this person responds to your message. This response is called *feedback.*

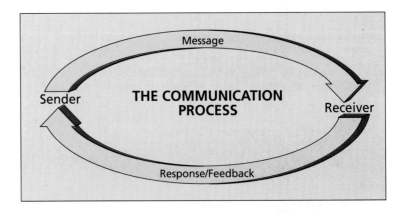

- To write announcements for suggested events
- To prepare and deliver introductions for guest speakers
- To present group discussions on suggested topics
- To present a five-minute oral interpretation based on a scene from a piece of literature

Nonverbal Communication

In addition to words (verbal signals), you communicate meaning with *nonverbal* (unspoken) signals. How you stand, move about, and gesture can communicate a variety of messages.

NONVERBAL SIGNALS	EXAMPLES
Gestures	thumbs up (approval, encouragement), shrugging (uncertainty), nodding head (yes), shaking head (disagreement)
Facial expressions	smiling, raising an eyebrow, smirking, frowning, grimacing, pouting, grinning, (meanings vary depending on context)
Body language	turning away (rejection), stroking the chin (puzzlement), crossing arms on chest (reluctance, uncertainty)
Sounds	laughing, groaning, giggling (meanings vary depending on context)

Speaking Informally

Speaking Impromptu

An *impromptu speech* is one you make on the spur of the moment. The ideas you express have not been prepared in advance. When an impromptu speech is required, consider the following suggestions.

1. *Consider your purpose.* Impromptu speeches are often informative (telling what you know about a subject) or persuasive (giving your opinion or trying to convince your listeners).
2. *Consider your topic.* Cover the main ideas and add details to support or explain your main points.
3. *Consider your audience.* Think about the specific speaking occasion and consider the interests and knowledge of the audience.

speech notes and materials, speaking expressively, and delivering the speech are then considered. Instruction on group discussion, including roles and parliamentary procedure, follows. The chapter concludes with instruction in adapting and presenting material as oral interpretation.

QUICK REMINDER

Pair the students and give them ten minutes to interview each other. Students should endeavor to discover what makes their partners unique and interesting. Then have each pair go to the front of the class, where each partner will introduce the other.

MEETING *individual* **NEEDS**

LEP/ESL

General Strategies. Students may worry about using correct grammar in front of an audience of English-proficient speakers. They should be relieved to find out that listeners focus more on message than on form. Advise English-language learners that if they suddenly realize they have made a mistake, it is better to keep going than to back up and draw attention to an error that few are likely to have noticed. Listeners prefer uninterrupted content to perfect grammar.

RESOURCES

RESOURCES

TECHNOLOGY TIP

Because many homes have answering machines, you may wish to stress to students the importance of leaving messages that are concise, clear, and complete.

TIMESAVER

You can save time by having students generate topics for impromptu speaking. Have each student write a topic on a slip of paper, preferably in the form of a question. Students can then draw topics and, by using their existing knowledge and experiences, give impromptu speeches. Before students draw topics, you may wish to review the topics to weed out unsuitable or unnecessarily difficult topics.

COMMON ERROR

Problem. Many people have difficulty remembering a person's name after being introduced.

Solution. You might share with students common techniques used to remember names. These include paying close attention when being introduced and observing the person closely for distinguishing characteristics.

Other techniques include matching the name with a similar word or words and associating the name with a characteristic of the person.

Communicating Effectively

The most important part of speaking in many situations is to remember that you need to speak clearly and courteously. The following are situations in which you can work on your speaking skills. You will use these skills in similar situations in the workplace.

Speaking on the Telephone

1. Call people at a reasonable hour.
2. Identify yourself and state your purpose for calling.
3. Be polite and speak clearly.
4. Keep your call to an appropriate length.

Giving Instructions or Directions

1. Divide the information into clear, logical steps.
2. Give the steps in order.
3. Check to be sure your listeners understand all the steps.
4. If necessary, repeat the steps in the same order.

Making Introductions

1. Take the initiative; introduce yourself if no one else does.
2. When introducing others, identify them by name.
3. It is customary to address first
   - a person of higher status
   - an older person before a younger person
   - the person you know better

Speaking Formally

Preparing a Speech

When you are required to give a speech, you must choose a suitable subject and determine your purpose for speaking. You need to limit your subject to a manageable topic so that it can be adequately treated in your speech and so that it reflects a definite purpose.

PURPOSE	DESCRIPTION OF SPEECH	EXAMPLES OF SPEECH TITLES
To inform	gives facts *or* explains how to do something	Animals That Live on the Ocean Floor How to Avoid Snakebite
To persuade	attempts to change an opinion *or* attempts to get listeners to act	Senior Citizens Are Important to the Community You Should Eat a Low-fat Diet
To entertain	relates an amusing story or incident	My First Job as a Baby Sitter

Analyzing Your Audience

Your audience is the group of people who are going to listen to your speech. You will need to think about the needs, background, and interests of your audience if you expect them to understand and respond to your speech topic.

AUDIENCE CONSIDERATIONS		
QUESTIONS ABOUT AUDIENCE	EVALUATION	YOUR SPEECH WILL NEED
What does the audience already know about this subject?	very little	to provide background or details to better inform your listeners
	a little	to include some background details
	a lot	to focus on interesting aspects or issues
How interested will the audience be in this subject?	very interested	to maintain their interest
	somewhat interested	to focus on aspects that most interest them
	uninterested	to focus on persuading your listeners that this topic is important

A DIFFERENT APPROACH

Speech material drawn on personal experience is usually vivid and adds to the speaker's credibility. Suggest that while speeches shouldn't consist of personal experience only, they should contain personal experience if possible.

RESOURCES

RESOURCES

COOPERATIVE LEARNING

Before students give their speeches, you may wish to assign a partner to each speaker who will have the task of announcing that speaker.

COMMON ERROR

Problem. Beginning speakers will often prepare visuals that are too small to be easily seen past the first row of the audience.

Solution. Tell students to check that their visuals can be seen at a distance. Remind the class that audience members in the back row are just as important as the ones in the front row.

Gathering Material

After you've chosen a topic for your speech, you'll need to plan how you want to develop your topic. Then you'll need to brainstorm or do research to find material that supports your ideas or opinions. Try the following strategies for gathering interesting information.

1. *Explore your own background.* Ask yourself what you already know about the topic. Explore your own knowledge and experience.
2. *Observe.* Keep an eye out as you look through newspapers and periodicals for material related to your topic. Speeches or radio and television broadcasts may provide you with additional information.
3. *Read.* Go to the library. Use reference sources, magazines, and books to research your topic.
4. *Reflect.* Review the material you have gathered and take time to become familiar with it.

Organizing Speech Notes and Materials

The most effective type of speech to give is often an *extemporaneous speech.* An extemporaneous speech is one that is carefully developed and organized, but not memorized.

To develop an extemporaneous speech, you usually prepare a complete outline of your main points. Then use your outline to prepare note cards that can be used while delivering your speech to help you remember main ideas and supporting details.

Here are some suggestions for preparing your note cards.

1. Include one key idea (and possibly an example or detail) for each card.
2. Make a special note card for a quotation or a series of dates or statistics that you plan to read word for word.
3. Make a special note card to indicate when you plan to show a chart, diagram, graph, drawing, model, or other visual.
4. Number your completed cards to help you keep them in the appropriate order.

Speaking Expressively

Have you ever listened to a speaker who put you to sleep? You don't want that to happen to your audience. To speak expressively, you should practice using good verbal and nonverbal communication signals. Follow these suggestions.

1. *Stand confidently.* Be alert, be interested in what you're saying, and use natural gestures.
2. *Speak clearly.* Speak loudly enough so everyone in the audience can hear you. Pronounce your words slowly and carefully.
3. *Look at your audience as you speak.* Make direct eye contact as you focus on the faces of your listeners.
4. *Choose your words carefully.* Use specific rather than general words. Also, use vivid words that appeal to the senses to reinforce meaning.
5. *Use variety in speaking.* Vocal variety helps emphasize your message.
   - *Volume:* Speak loudly enough to be heard, but raise or lower your sound volume for emphasis.
   - *Pitch:* Use the rise and fall of your voice to emphasize various ideas and avoid a monotone.
   - *Stress:* Emphasize important words.
   - *Rate:* Speak at a comfortable, relaxed pace.

Giving Your Speech

Most speakers feel nervous before giving a speech. In fact, a little nervousness can help you by keeping you alert and focusing your energy. The following suggestions will help you avoid excessive nervousness.

1. *Relax.* Realize that your audience wants you to do well. They aren't waiting for you to make mistakes.
2. *Be prepared.* Organize and practice with your note cards and visual aids.
3. *Practice your speech.* Rehearse as if you're giving the actual presentation.
4. *Focus on your purpose.* Remember what you want to accomplish. Instead of focusing on yourself, think how your speech will affect your audience.

LESS-ADVANCED STUDENTS

To combat the problem of nervousness before and during a speech, you may wish to relieve some pressure by not grading the first few speeches students give. Also, a frank and open discussion of the common symptoms of stage fright may help students realize that it is a natural phenomenon.

COMMON ERROR

Problem. Student speakers sometimes spoil the spontaneity of their delivery by preparing detailed notes.

Solution. Tell students to use note cards that contain just enough to jog the memory. Signal words or short phrases are all that are normally needed.

A DIFFERENT APPROACH

When a student is making an announcement, it is all too easy for the student to leave out vital information. You may wish to instruct your students to answer these five traditional questions when preparing announcements: *When? Where? Who? Why?* and *How?*

Special Speaking Situations

Making an Announcement

The purpose of an announcement is to provide general information to an audience. Follow these suggestions for making an effective announcement.

1. When preparing your announcement, include all the necessary facts and add interesting details that will capture your listeners' attention.
2. Get your audience's attention and then announce your message slowly, clearly, and carefully.
3. Repeat information if necessary to be sure it is clear to your listeners.

Making an Introduction to a Presentation

An introduction is often given before a speaker's presentation or before a short performance. This type of an introduction focuses the audience's attention. It also provides listeners with important information about the speaker, the players, the subject, the dramatic work, or the author of the work being presented.

A good introduction fills in details that the audience might need to know before the main presentation begins. But don't provide too many details. A good introduction is short and to the point.

Group Discussions

Establishing a Purpose

Group discussions or cooperative learning groups work best when the group has a specific purpose to accomplish. This purpose may be

- to share ideas and cooperate in group learning
- to suggest solutions for solving a problem
- to make an evaluation, a recommendation, or a decision

To establish the purpose for the group, first decide what specific task the group needs to accomplish. Then the group can determine a plan of action, depending on how much time is allowed to reach this goal.

Assigning Roles for a Discussion

Each participant in a group discussion takes a role with specific responsibilities. Sometimes a group selects a chairperson who will help keep the discussion moving along smoothly. Another group member may be chosen to be secretary or reporter (recorder), with the responsibility of taking notes during the discussion.

Frequently, a group establishes an *agenda,* or outline of the order that they will follow in their discussion. Setting the agenda is often the responsibility of the chairperson, but the agenda may sometimes be agreed upon by all the members.

A Chairperson's Responsibilities

1. Announce the topic and establish the agenda.
2. Follow the agenda.
3. Encourage each member to participate.
4. Manage group conflict.

A Secretary's or Reporter's Responsibilities

1. Record significant information and developments.
2. Prepare a final report.

A Participant's Responsibilities

1. Take part in the discussion.
2. Cooperate and share information.
3. Listen carefully to others.
4. Be considerate.

Parliamentary Procedure

Groups such as clubs or committees often follow the principles of *parliamentary procedure* to make sure meetings are run smoothly and fairly.

RESOURCES

A DIFFERENT APPROACH

In parliamentary procedure, motions should be stated in the affirmative rather than the negative. Negative motions tend to confuse the voting. For example, "I move the class picnic be held in the city park" is better than "I move we don't hold the picnic on campus."

Also, you may wish to explain to students how a motion can be modified through amendments. If an amendment is proposed, it must be seconded before discussion, just like a motion. Amendments are voted on before the motion.

RULES OF PARLIAMENTARY PROCEDURE

The meeting follows a step-by-step agenda.

1. The chairperson calls the meeting to order.
2. The secretary reports details of the last meeting.
3. The treasurer makes a report.
4. Unresolved issues or actions are discussed.
5. New issues or proposed actions are discussed.
6. The chairperson ends the meeting.

The meeting has specific procedures for discussions.

1. Anyone wishing to speak must raise his or her hand until recognized by the chairperson.
2. A participant may introduce a motion by saying, "I move that . . ."
3. To support a motion or suggestion, a participant other than the one who made the motion must say, "I second the motion." If no one seconds it, the motion is then dropped.
4. If a motion is seconded, it is discussed by the group.
5. After discussion, the group votes on the motion. The chairperson usually votes only in case of a tie.

Oral Interpretation

Oral interpretation is like an acting performance. You use vocal techniques, facial expressions, body language, and gestures to indicate the meaning of the literary work you are interpreting.

Adapting Material

When you adapt material for an oral interpretation, you usually have a specific purpose, audience, and occasion in mind. Every situation has its own requirements. Be sure you have thought about factors such as the length of time for your presentation and your audience's interests. Most

INTEGRATING THE LANGUAGE ARTS

Reading and Speaking. Students might enjoy staging an oral interpretation recital. Each member of the class could read a short poem, or the class could read poems in chorus, with one or two students acting as narrators to link each poem with the next.

oral readings rely on the audience's imagination and not on props or costumes.

You will often need to make an abbreviated version, or *cutting,* of a work of fiction, nonfiction, a long poem, or a play. Here are some suggestions.

HOW TO MAKE A CUTTING

1. Follow the story line in time order.
2. Delete dialogue tags such as *she said softly.* Instead, use these clues to indicate how you should act when you interpret the character's words.
3. Take out any passages that don't contribute to the overall impression that you intend to create with your oral interpretation.

Presenting an Oral Interpretation

You may need to write an introduction to your interpretation to set the scene, tell something about the characters, give some background details about the author, or provide some necessary details about what has already taken place in the story.

To be effective in presenting an oral interpretation, you will need to prepare a reading script. A ***reading script*** is usually typed (double-spaced) and is marked to assist you in your interpretive reading. For example, you may underline words for emphasis or mark a slash (/) to indicate a pause.

 COMPUTER NOTE: Use your word-processing program to prepare the script for your oral presentation. You can use bold, italic, or underline formatting to indicate presentation directions or notes to yourself. You can even change the type size and style for additional emphasis.

After you have developed a reading script, rehearse the material several different ways until you are satisfied that you have chosen the most effective manner of interpreting the passage.

 **INTEGRATING THE LANGUAGE ARTS**

Literature Link. Reader's theater allows students to develop skills in oral interpretation and awareness of drama. You might have students adapt for dramatic presentation short stories such as Tim O'Brien's "Where Have You Gone, Charming Billy?"; or students might prepare one scene from a longer dramatic work such as Robert Anderson's *I Never Sang for My Father.*

Another possible activity for oral interpretation is a poetry reading. A dramatic monologue is effective when read aloud to an audience, as is narrative poetry. Students might use longer poems, such as "Bonny Barbara Allen," or shorter works, such as Ted Kooser's "Abandoned Farmhouse." Topics for discussion could include how such diverse poetic aspects as theme and punctuation influence interpretation.

LEP/ESL

General Strategies. Exercises 1–3 can be especially helpful to English-language learners because these exercises focus on language that is appropriate in conveying messages. Give students plenty of opportunities to act out the situations. Encourage improvisation, spontaneity, and as much active involvement with the material as possible.

ANSWERS
Exercise 1

Responses will vary. Here are some possibilities:

1. Excuse me, I'm really interested, but my father needs to use the phone now. Could I call you back later?
2. Hello, this is _____. Yesterday, I bought an AX10 tape player from your Morganville store, but after looking at the receipt, I think I was charged for the more expensive AX20 model. Can you help me?
3. Hello, this is _____. I have an appointment with Dr. Lynch at 3:00 today, but I can't make it. Could I please reschedule?
4. Hello, this is _____. I would like to reserve a table for twelve for this coming Saturday at 8:00 P.M. It is my aunt's birthday, so I would also like to arrange to have a cake with candles delivered to the table after dinner.

ANSWERS
Exercise 2

Responses will vary, but the directions should be given in clear, understandable steps.

ANSWERS
Exercise 3

Responses will vary. Here are some possibilities:

1. Hi. Doesn't _____ give great parties? My name's _____. I was in English class with _____ last year. What's your name?
2. Hello, my name's _____. I have a job interview with Ms. Torres at 2:15.

Use your voice in a manner that suits your presentation. Be sure to pronounce your words carefully. You can use your body and your voice to show that you are portraying different characters. Use body language and gestures to emphasize your meaning or to reveal traits of the major characters in the story as you act out what they say and do.

Review

EXERCISE 1 Exploring Telephone Speaking Situations

For each of the following situations, explain how you might handle the problem. What would you say to be polite but clear?

1. A caller is talking too long, and you need to get off the phone because your father wants to make a call.
2. You call the headquarters of a department store chain to complain about a billing error for a purchase that was charged at one of the chain's local stores.
3. You call a dentist's office at the last minute to reschedule an appointment.
4. You call a restaurant to make reservations for your family for dinner to celebrate your aunt's birthday.

EXERCISE 2 Giving Directions

Provide directions for each of the following situations. Make sure your directions are simple and easy to follow.

1. You are having a party Friday night. Explain to a classmate how to get from your school to your house.
2. A new student needs to know how to get from the cafeteria to the gymnasium.
3. Explain to a visitor how to get from your school to another school in the area. Be sure to point out any helpful landmarks.
4. Your aunt and uncle are visiting from another state. Give them directions to the post office nearest your house.

▶ EXERCISE 3   **Making Introductions**

In each of the following situations, explain what you would say.

1. You are at a party and the host doesn't seem to be around. Introduce yourself to another person who is standing alone.
2. You have an interview scheduled with Ms. Torres at the Youth Employment Center. Introduce yourself to the receptionist.
3. You are introducing your mother (or father or other relative) to your math teacher.
4. You are at your school's science fair with a friend from another school. Introduce your friend to your science teacher.

▶ EXERCISE 4   **Preparing and Giving a Speech**

Choose a topic for a three- to five-minute speech to give to your English class. Consider your audience and purpose when choosing your speech topic. First, gather appropriate material. Next, prepare note cards for your speech. Include one visual, such as a chart, diagram, time line, or drawing, and prepare a note card to indicate at what point in your speech you should pause to explain and incorporate this item. Finally, deliver your speech, using effective speaking techniques and appropriate nonverbal signals.

▶ EXERCISE 5   **Making an Announcement**

Write an announcement for one of the following events. Supply specific details wherever they are needed.

1. A car wash will be held by the sophomore class with the proceeds to benefit Special Olympics participants.
2. A special election will be held to choose the next student body president.
3. This year's sports award banquet has been scheduled. All students desiring to attend should bring the fee for tickets. Nominations for outstanding athletes in each school-sponsored sport are encouraged.

3. Mom, I'd like you to meet my math teacher, Ms. Nanez. Ms. Nanez, this is my mother.
4. Mr. (Ms.) _____, I'd like you to meet my friend _____ from ____ school. _____, this is my science teacher, Mr. (Ms.) _____.

ANSWERS
Exercise 4

Responses will vary. Each speech should be of the appropriate length, should include suitable body language, and should be delivered clearly. Eye contact should be maintained with the audience.

ANSWERS
Exercise 5

Responses will vary. Here are some possibilities:

1. The sophomore class's annual car wash to benefit the Special Olympics will be held Saturday from noon until 6:00 P.M. in the Goodwill parking lot at 334 Main Street.
2. An election to choose the next student body president will be held Friday. Voting booths are in the auditorium, and students should vote during lunch break or study hall.
3. The annual sports award banquet has been scheduled for the last Saturday in March at the City Convention Center. It begins at 8:00 P.M. Tickets are five dollars each and can be purchased in the principal's office. Nominations for outstanding athletes in all sports should be delivered to the athletic director's office.

RESOURCES

4. A bake sale will be held to raise funds for the marching band's trip to the state finals. Everybody is invited to help our band by donating baked goods or contributing cash. The sale will be held from 9:00 A.M. to 2:00 P.M. Saturday at the center court of Central Mall.

ANSWERS
Exercise 6

Responses will vary. Each speech should be reasonably brief, delivered with confidence, and should include highlights from the speaker's career.

ANSWERS
Exercise 7

Responses will vary. The success of the discussion should be gauged on the ability of the chairperson and the participants to fulfill their roles and on the group's ability to cover the topic in the time available.

ANSWERS
Exercise 8

Responses will vary depending on the literature chosen to be interpreted. Each interpretation should have a suitable introduction, be delivered within the time limit, and retain narrative coherence. Students should deliver the interpretations in a way that conveys the different characters.

940

---

4. Band members will hold a bake sale to raise money for the band's trip to compete in the state finals. You also want to encourage donations of baked goods and money from students who are not in the band.

▶ EXERCISE 6   **Introducing a Speaker**

Prepare and deliver in class an introduction for your state or national representative or senator, your mayor, your county commissioner, a school board member, or a famous person from history.

▶ EXERCISE 7   **Conducting a Group Discussion**

Select a group chairperson, and present a discussion about any of the following topics or one of your own choosing. Establish an agenda, and determine how much time you will have for your discussion.

1. Radio and television advertising
2. Comic books and their characters
3. Teenage crime
4. How to achieve a goal
5. The impact of the young voter
6. The ideal school
7. Choosing a career
8. Job opportunities in your city
9. Ways to prevent war
10. Our local environment

▶ EXERCISE 8   **Presenting an Oral Interpretation**

Select a portion of a short story, a scene from a play, or a section of a novel that contains a scene for one or two characters. Prepare a script for a five-minute oral interpretation to present to your classmates. Write a brief introduction that tells the title and author of the selection and gives enough background information about the characters and the setting so that your audience can understand the meaning of the scene.

OBJECTIVES

- To give instructions and listen to others' instructions
- To listen critically to a short speech
- To analyze and identify purposes in mass media
- To identify persuasive techniques employed in various statements
- To apply critical and evaluative techniques to the process of viewing for information

PROGRAM MANAGER

LISTENING AND VIEWING

- **Independent Practice/ Reteaching** For additional practice and reinforcement, see **The LQ2R Method, Conducting an Interview, Critical Listening, Persuasive Techniques in the Media,** and **Critical Viewing** in *Academic and Workplace Skills*, pp. 11–16.

- **Additional Instruction** For more information on chapter concepts, see **Chapters 4, 5,** and **10** in *Speech for Effective Communication.*

- **Assessment/Reflection** To assess student work and evaluate progress, see **Portfolio Form** in *Portfolio Assessment*, p. 39.

- **Review** For exercises on chapter concepts, see **Review Form A** and **Review Form B** in *Academic and Workplace Skills*, pp. 16–17.

32 LISTENING AND VIEWING

Strategies for Listening and Viewing

Listening and viewing are not the same as hearing and seeing. You constantly hear sounds and see images from potential sources of information, but you may not carefully listen to or look at very many of them. Listening and viewing are active processes that require you to think about what you hear and see.

If you use nonprint information as a resource for an assignment, you must be able to evaluate it and determine if it is suited to your purpose, just as you must do with print information. The listening and viewing strategies you learn in this chapter will help you do this.

Listening with a Purpose

You can become a more effective listener if you keep your purpose in mind as you listen. People hear things differently depending on what they are listening for. Common purposes for listening are

- for enjoyment or entertainment
- to gain information for personal, school, or workplace use
- to understand information or an explanation
- to evaluate or form an opinion

CHAPTER OVERVIEW

This chapter leads students through such basic skills as listening with a purpose, listening for details, and listening to instructions. The LQ2R study method is explained, and students are taught how to conduct an interview, how to listen critically, and how to take lecture notes. Students are introduced to common persuasive techniques used in mass media. They are also given instruction about methods of viewing for information and evaluating what they see.

RESOURCES

RESOURCES

Listening for Information

Listening for Details

When you listen for information, you are listening for details that answer the six basic *5W-How?* questions: *Who? What? When? Where? Why?* and *How?*

For example, when you are asked to take messages on the telephone, you will need to listen to important details that the caller tells you, such as

- the caller's name
- the name of the person being called
- the caller's message
- the caller's telephone number

Using the LQ2R Method

The LQ2R study method is especially helpful when you are listening to a speaker who is giving information.

L *Listen* carefully to material as it is being presented. Focus your attention on the speaker.

Q *Question* yourself as you listen. Make a list, mentally or in your notes, of questions that occur to you.

R *Recite* in your own words the information as it is being presented. Summarize information in your mind, or jot down notes as you listen.

R *Relisten* as the speaker concludes the presentation. Major points may be reemphasized.

Listening to Instructions

Instructions are usually made up of a series of steps. When you listen to instructions, be sure you understand everything you are required to do.

1. *Listen for the order of steps.* Listen for words that tell you where each step ends and the next one begins, such as *first, second, next, then,* and *last.*

2. *Identify the number of steps in the process.* Take notes if the instructions are long and complicated.
3. *Visualize each step.* Imagine yourself actually performing each step. Try to get a mental image of what you should be doing at every step in the process.
4. *Review the steps when the speaker is finished.* Be sure you understand them.

Listening and Responding Politely

When you are listening and responding to a speaker, you are taking part in the communication cycle. Here's how to be more courteous and encouraging, both as a listener and as a responder.

1. Pay attention. Don't distract others.
2. Respect the speaker, and keep an open mind. Try to understand the speaker's point of view. Also, be aware of how your own point of view affects the way you evaluate the opinions and values of others.
3. Wait to hear the speaker's whole message before you make judgments or ask questions.
4. Ask appropriate questions loudly enough for all to hear. For better understanding, summarize or paraphrase the speaker's point you are questioning.
5. Use polite, effective language and gestures that are appropriate to the situation.

Conducting an Interview

An interview is a special listening situation. Most often an interview takes place between two people, an interviewer and the person being interviewed (called the *interviewee*). Follow these suggestions to conduct an effective interview.

Before the Interview
- Decide what information you really want to know.
- Make a list of questions. Make sure the questions are arranged in a logical order.
- Make an appointment and be prompt.

COMMON ERROR

Problem. Even after students listen carefully to instructions, they may forget a crucial step.

Solution. Tell students that after listening to instructions, they should repeat the instructions aloud to ensure that all steps have been remembered. If there are more than three steps, students should write them down.

RESOURCES

RESOURCES

COOPERATIVE LEARNING

For practice with conducting interviews and listening, students can be paired, either by allowing them to select their own partners or by assigning partners randomly. The members of each pair can then take turns interviewing each other. Interviewers should be given a purpose, such as discovering favorite hobbies or pastimes, or obtaining opinions on aspects of school life. Interviewers should prepare some questions in advance and should take notes during the interviews. You may wish to have the students make brief verbal reports after the interviews are completed.

INTEGRATING THE LANGUAGE ARTS

Literature Link. Responding effectively to a selection read aloud tests all aspects of critical listening. Mark Twain's "The Lowest Animal," Malcolm X's "Hair," and Jeanne Wakatsuki Houston and James Houston's "It Can't Be Helped" from *Farewell to Manzanar* are all suitable for such an exercise. After reading the selection to your students, ask them for written responses to questions. These responses (which you may or may not wish to collect) can provide a basis for class discussion.

During the Interview
- Give the interviewee time to answer the question.
- Pay attention, and ask questions if you're not sure you understand what the interviewee means.
- Ask permission to quote the person directly.
- Respect the interviewee's opinion. You can ask the other person to explain an opinion, but be polite, even if you disagree.
- Thank the person for allowing the interview.

After the Interview
- Check your notes to be sure they are clear.
- Summarize the interview while you still remember it.

COMPUTER NOTE: Use your word-processing program's outlining feature to organize your prewriting or interview notes into an outline for the first draft of your paper.

Critical Listening

When you listen critically, you think carefully about what you hear. You can't remember every word a speaker says. But if you listen critically, you'll be able to find the parts of the speaker's message that are most important.

GUIDELINES FOR LISTENING CRITICALLY	
Find main ideas.	What are the most important points? Listen for clue words a speaker might use, such as *major, main, most important,* or similar words.
Identify significant details.	What dates, names, or facts does the speaker use to support the main points of the speech? What kinds of examples or explanations are used to support the main ideas?

(continued)

GUIDELINES FOR LISTENING CRITICALLY *(continued)*	
Distinguish between facts and opinions.	A fact is a statement that can be proved to be true. An opinion is a belief or a judgment about something. It cannot be proved to be true.
Identify the order of organization.	What kind of order is the speaker using to arrange his or her presentation—time sequence, spatial order, order of importance?
Note comparisons and contrasts.	Are some details compared or contrasted with others?
Understand cause and effect.	Do some events that the speaker mentions relate to or affect others?
Predict outcomes and draw conclusions.	What can you reasonably conclude from the facts and evidence you have gathered from the speech?

☞ REFERENCE NOTE: For more information about interpreting and analyzing information, see pages 987–988.

Taking Lecture Notes

When you listen to a speaker, don't rely entirely on your memory. Take notes to help you remember information. You can take notes by writing the most important words or phrases the speaker says. Other note-taking techniques include paraphrasing and summarizing.

Paraphrasing. When you *paraphrase* material, you express the ideas of others in your own words. Translate complex terms or examples that the speaker uses into your own words, and write your paraphrase in your notes.

Summarizing. When you *summarize,* you condense material by restating it in fewer words. As you listen to the speaker, sum up the major points of the lecture. Write these statements in your lecture notes.

RESOURCES

A DIFFERENT APPROACH

Arrange for a guest lecturer to speak to your class, and ask your students to take careful notes. At the following class meeting, ask your students, with the aid of their notes, to reconstruct on paper the lecturer's main points in order. You may then wish to quiz your students on these main points.

MEETING *individual* NEEDS

STUDENTS WITH SPECIAL NEEDS

Many students need help understanding cause and effect. Have them fill out a chart representing cause-and-effect relationships. Ask them to look in the media for examples of false cause and effect. For example, advertisements may imply that if people purchase a particular product, they will become popular and happier.

LEARNING STYLES

General Strategies. Give students ample opportunities to develop the note-taking styles that work best for them. Auditory learners might need to record only key words, while visual learners might need to make complete sets of notes as study guides.

RESOURCES

RESOURCES

RESOURCES

946

Understanding the Impact of Mass Media

The *mass media* are forms of communication that affect you and millions of other people every day. The mass media include

- television
- radio
- newspapers
- magazines
- movies and videocassettes
- compact and laser discs
- the Internet

The mass media give you contact with the whole world. Today's mass media make all types of information available to just about everyone. Television, radio, and the Internet bring you information about world happenings almost instantly. Newspapers and magazines bring you detailed accounts and analyses of worldwide events within a short time of the occurrence.

Since the mass media distribute a great deal of information quickly, people often assume that the media's only purpose is to inform. However, the mass media also entertain. Today you can see and hear performances of your favorite music, television, and film stars, even if you never attend their performances in person. You can also tour great cities, view natural wonders, and visit historic landmarks without leaving home. When you view the media, you usually have a purpose in mind—to find information or to be entertained.

A primary goal of the broadcast and print media is to build a successful business and earn profits. Radio and television stations must find listeners and viewers. Magazines and newspapers must find readers. To do this, the media need your attention and loyalty.

The media produce programs designed to interest and entertain you so that you will continue watching, listening, or reading. Just as you have a purpose in watching or listening to the media, the media have their own purposes for you, their audience.

Both the media and the media audience have specific purposes and responsibilities. A media product may be intended by its creators to entertain you, to inform you, or to persuade you. Media products may also serve more than one purpose. For example, an editorial cartoon in a newspaper may entertain you, as well as persuade you to agree with the cartoonist's opinion.

THE MEDIA		
PURPOSE	MEANS	RESPONSIBILITIES
To attract a loyal audience To sell advertising time and increase profits	broadcasting, printing, and telecommunicating informative, entertaining, or persuasive presentations	presenting factual information in a truthful, fair, and unbiased manner striving for accuracy of information
THE AUDIENCE		
PURPOSE	MEANS	RESPONSIBILITIES
To receive information To be entertained	watching, reading, or listening to various media presentations	responding to the media actively through evaluating and assessing presentations choosing whether or not to watch, read, or listen to a presentation; or responding by writing letters or otherwise demonstrating an opinion

Persuasive Techniques

Advertisers, politicians, and others frequently buy media time to sell their products or ideas. To convince you, they may use *persuasive techniques.* Knowing about persuasive techniques will help you evaluate the factors that are used in the media to influence you in various ways.

CRITICAL THINKING

Analysis. Ask students to distinguish between the experience of hearing news over the radio and seeing and hearing it on television. Ask students if they prefer to see music videos on television or to listen to music on the radio. Ask students to list reasons for their preferences.

Tell students that advertisers evaluate the information, persuasion, and entertainment offered by the media. Then, they decide to sponsor programs or place their advertisements where they are most likely to reach targeted customers. Ask students to make a brief profile of themselves based on their media preferences. What television program is their favorite? What kind of music, talk show, or other programming is offered by the radio station they prefer? Based on their preferences, ask students to make a list of five products (for example, of specific brands or types of food, drink, clothing, or other consumer items) that they often see or hear advertised during their favorite television program or on their favorite radio station. Ask students if they feel that these product placements are effective, based on their own preferences.

COMMON PERSUASIVE TECHNIQUES FOUND IN THE MEDIA

In addition to the persuasive techniques listed in the chart, students may find it interesting to consider ways in which music and drama act as vehicles for persuasion. For example, drama uses plot, character, conflict, language, setting, and spectacle to create powerful emotional responses. Music can quickly set a mood and can move its listeners strongly. Vocal music uses poetry in the form of song lyrics to express a wide range of emotions.

COMMON PERSUASIVE TECHNIQUES FOUND IN THE MEDIA	
Bandwagon	Those who use this technique urge you to "jump on the bandwagon" by suggesting that you should do or believe something because everyone (or everyone admirable or worthwhile) is doing it.
Testimonial	Experts or famous people sometimes give a personal "testimony" about a product or idea. However, the person offering the testimonial may not really know much about that particular product or idea.
"Plain folks"	Ordinary people (or people who pretend to be ordinary) are often used to persuade others. People tend to believe others who seem to be similar to themselves.
Emotional words	This technique uses words that appeal to your emotions rather than to your ability to reason.

Viewing for Information

Sources of Information

To use television programs and videos as sources of information for your writing, you must develop active viewing strategies. These strategies should reflect an awareness of both the persuasive techniques used by the media and the ultimate purposes of the media, which were discussed earlier in this chapter.

Since television programming is designed for many purposes, you must determine which kinds of programs are appropriate sources. If you are writing a research report about curfew laws for teenagers, for example, you might watch these types of programs for information.

- local or national news reports
- investigative news reports
- newsmagazines
- interviews or discussions

Other kinds of television programming and videos that provide information include

- documentary or educational programs (history, biography, geography, science, nature)
- political speeches, debates, and town meetings
- trials or government hearings
- legislative sessions
- press conferences

When you use a television program or video as a source for a research report, take notes just as you would from a printed source. If you are going to quote any information, make sure you do so precisely. Be sure to list the source on your Works Cited list.

☞ REFERENCE NOTE: For information about documenting sources, see pages 416–418 and 428–429.

Evaluating What You See

Many viewers searching for information concentrate on just understanding what they see and hear. Critical viewers go a step further: They evaluate both the images and the spoken words.

Keep these questions in mind when you evaluate a television show or video for information:

1. How reliable and accurate is the information?
2. Who wrote the words being spoken? How knowledgeable or qualified is that person?
3. What kinds of images are shown? Have the images been selected to create an emotional impact?
4. Does the program present facts, opinions, or both? Does the factual information come from a first-hand report? statistics? a study? a survey? Is the source of information identified in the program or credits?
5. If the show presents experts, who are they, and what are their qualifications?
6. If the program presents a controversial issue, are both sides of the issue—or several different viewpoints—presented? Does the program show *bias* (a leaning or inclination toward one side of an issue) in any way?

TECHNOLOGY TIP

You may want to record or have students record several different TV news programs' coverage of a specific story, preferably including some editorial opinions about the story from several different broadcast sources. Then, ask students to practice commenting, using the questions listed for **Evaluating What You See.**

The students usually can compare quickly the differences in images being shown. Students should also be able to point out the discrepancies between official versions of an incident and accounts of the same incident by bystanders or news reporters. In addition, students should be able to draw conclusions based on the amount of time devoted to coverage of the story as a portion of the newscast and the placement of the story (top of the newscast as a major story or buried as a smaller item in the newscast).

RESOURCES

RESOURCES

What You Can Do

Knowing to ask the questions on the preceding page is an important step in becoming a critical viewer, but how can you find the answers to these questions?

1. *Watch the credits.* At the end of the program, a list of credits identifies the producer, the director, the writer, and the year the program was created. Experts may also be identified in the credits.
2. *Compare coverage.* Check the same story or issue in other programs and in other media. If every source reports basically the same facts, chances are the facts are accurate and unbiased.
3. *Make your views known.* Contact the director of programming at local television stations or national networks. Ask questions and make comments about the programs you watch. Some local TV stations offer viewers an opportunity to present their opinions on the air.
4. *Find out who's really who.* Read widely, and talk to adults to identify organizations, special-interest groups, and lobbyists, and to understand their positions.

Review

▶ EXERCISE 1 **Listening to Instructions**

Present instructions explaining how to do or make something, with the steps of the process listed in a specific order. Next, allow your classmates a chance to ask questions. Then, call on classmates to repeat your instructions to be sure that everyone understands all the steps.

▶ EXERCISE 2 **Listening Critically**

Take brief notes while listening to a short speech presented by your teacher in class. Then, answer the following questions about the speech.

GUIDELINES
Exercise 1

Responses will vary. Steps of processes should be given in the correct order. Students responding to instructions should be able to repeat them accurately and in order. If students have been instructed in a physical skill, they should be able to perform that skill correctly.

1. What are the main ideas expressed in the speech?
2. What details are used to support the main points in the speech? Identify several supporting details.
3. Identify one fact and one opinion mentioned in the speech. What reasons does the speaker give that support this opinion?
4. What is the order of the speech's organization?
5. Draw a conclusion about the ideas presented in the speech. Was the speech convincing? Why or why not?

▶ EXERCISE 3 **Identifying Purpose in Mass Media**

Work in small groups to analyze a copy of a magazine or newspaper. List examples of regular features. Which are primarily for entertainment? for information? for persuasion? Prepare a brief report, and present it in class.

▶ EXERCISE 4 **Recognizing Persuasive Techniques**

Identify the persuasive technique used in each item.
1. bandwagon
1. "Join all the happy customers who buy our product."
2. "He's a greedy politician who will steal every taxpayer's money." **2. emotional words**
3. "As an Olympic champion, I can tell you this investment is solid gold." **3. testimonial**
4. "I'm just an 'average Joe,' but I know she's got the right stuff to be a great mayor." **4. "plain folks"**

▶ EXERCISE 5 **Viewing Critically for Information**

Work with a partner or small group to evaluate coverage of a specific news story. Each person should select a different channel and watch one national news report about the same national political event. Compare the different newscasts' coverage of the story by answering the following questions, and report your findings to the class.

1. Which newscast gave the most emphasis to the story?
2. Which report was easiest to understand? Which seemed most accurate? Support your choices with examples.
3. What images were shown with each story? Why do you think these images were chosen?

GUIDELINES
Exercise 2

Responses will vary. Students should be able to discover main ideas, identify supporting material, distinguish between a statement of fact and one of opinion, list the main points in order, identify the type of organizational patterns used, and evaluate the overall message of the speech.

GUIDELINES
Exercise 3

Responses will vary. Students should be able to present, with justification, examples of mass media used to entertain, to inform, and to persuade. Students may find examples that seem to fall into more than one category. You may wish to encourage class discussion in order to determine what the primary category of those examples might be.

GUIDELINES
Exercise 5

Responses will vary. However, students should give specific answers to each of the three questions, with supporting details.

THE LIBRARY/MEDIA CENTER *(pp. 952–958)*

OBJECTIVES

- To use various card catalogs in the school library to find the subjects, titles, authors, and call numbers of books
- To use the *Readers' Guide to Periodical Literature* to find the titles, authors, magazines, dates, and page numbers of articles about selected topics

 PROGRAM MANAGER

THE LIBRARY/MEDIA CENTER

- **Independent Practice/ Reteaching** For additional practice and reinforcement, see **Online and Card Catalog,** the *Readers' Guide,* and **Reference Works** in *Academic and Workplace Skills,* pp. 21–24.

- **Review** For exercises on chapter concepts, see **Review Form A** and **Review Form B** in *Academic and Workplace Skills,* pp. 25–28.

CHAPTER OVERVIEW

This chapter provides students with the basic information they will need to use the library. The chapter opens with a discussion of how information is classified and arranged, and then it describes the card catalog. A description and a discussion of various reference materials follow. Review exercises at the end of the chapter can be used to discover how much students have learned about the library.

QUICK REMINDER

To open the lesson on the library, bring to class a stack of note cards with book titles on them, put the cards on a volunteer's desk, and ask the volunteer to find a particular card. After the student has struggled for a few minutes, you can call a halt to the search. Tell the class that without organization, finding a book in the library would be virtually impossible—students would have to examine every book until they found

continued on next page

RESOURCES

RESOURCES

---

33 THE LIBRARY/ MEDIA CENTER

Finding and Using Information

You can find the answers to a great number of questions by consulting the resources available in a library or media center. To take advantage of these resources, however, you must know how to find out what information sources your library contains and how the library's contents are arranged.

The libraries in schools and communities are similar to those in many businesses. If you understand the arrangement of your school or public library, you should be able to use the library in your workplace.

Classifying and Arranging Information

Libraries arrange books by classifying them according to the Dewey decimal or the Library of Congress system. These systems assign a number and letter code—a *call number*—to each book. The call number tells you how the book has been classified and where it can be found in the library.

Most school libraries use the Dewey decimal system. Using this system, works of nonfiction are assigned a number in one of ten subject categories.

Dewey Decimal Arrangement of Fiction

According to the *Dewey decimal system,* works of fiction are grouped in alphabetical order by their authors' last names. When a library has several novels by the same author, they are arranged alphabetically by the first word of their titles (not counting *A, An,* or *The*). Sometimes, collections of short stories are grouped separately.

Types of Card Catalogs

The *online catalog* is a computerized version of the card catalog. To find a catalog listing, type in an author's name, a title, or a subject on the library's computer. The computer then displays the results of your search request. When you select a title from the search results, information about the book, similar to this example, is shown.

MATERIAL:	Book
CALL NUMBER:	910.91432 THA
AUTHOR:	Thayer, Helen
TITLE:	Polar dream/Helen Thayer
PUBLICATION:	New York: Simon & Schuster, © 1993.
DESCRIPTION:	254 p., [8] p. of plates: col. ill., map; 25 cm.
ISBN:	0671793861
NOTES:	Foreword by Sir Edmund Hillary
SUBJECT:	Thayer, Helen—Journeys
SUBJECT:	Women explorers
SUBJECT:	North Pole

The *card catalog* is a cabinet of small drawers that contains cards. These cards list books by title, author, and subject. For each book in the library, there are at least two cards—a *title card* and an *author card.* If the book is nonfiction, there is a third card—a *subject card.* You can tell what type of card it is by what is printed on its top line. Occasionally, you may find *"see"* or *"see also"* cards. These are cross-reference cards that tell you where additional information on this subject may be found.

what they were looking for, just as the volunteer would have had to examine every card.

Tell students that the Dewey decimal system, the Library of Congress system, and classification by author or subject are all tools designed to help them find the books they need.

MEETING *individual* NEEDS

LEP/ESL

General Strategies. You may want to introduce English-language learners to the library by taking them on a tour of the fiction section and letting them select books from the appropriate reading levels. You could also allow the students to read for the first ten minutes of class to reinforce the idea that leisure reading is as important as required reading. Stress that reading is a good way to become familiar with a new language, and that reading will also help students improve their writing.

LEARNING STYLES

Kinetic Learners. Some students will better internalize the information about the library if they are led through the process of finding a book.

RESOURCES

RESOURCES

COMMON ERROR

Problem. When working on research projects, students may neglect to record information about each source they use.

Solution. Have students make note cards for each source they use. The cards should contain the following information: author or authors (complete names as listed on the title page), complete title (including subtitle), city where the publisher is located, publisher's name, and date of publication.

COOPERATIVE LEARNING

Have students compete in teams of three in a hunt for the call numbers of the following books:

A travel book
A novel by Jane Austen
A book about geology
A book about Madame Curie
An astronomy book
A book about Albert Einstein
A biography of Abraham Lincoln
A book about art
A music book
A sports book

TECHNOLOGY TIP

To familiarize students with the online catalog, help them develop a simple step-by-step list of instructions. When they see how easy it is to use the online catalog, they might develop an interest in learning more about computers.

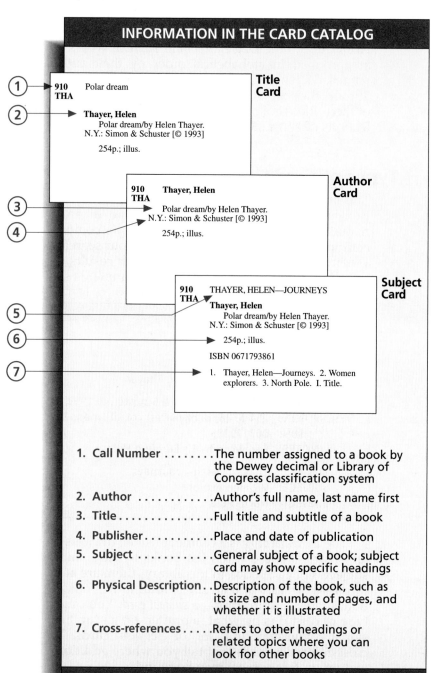

INFORMATION IN THE CARD CATALOG

(1) 910 THA Polar dream — **Title Card**

(2) **Thayer, Helen**
　　Polar dream/by Helen Thayer.
N.Y.: Simon & Schuster [© 1993]
　　254p.; illus.

910 THA **Thayer, Helen** — **Author Card**
(3)　　Polar dream/by Helen Thayer.
(4) N.Y.: Simon & Schuster [© 1993]
　　254p.; illus.

910 THA THAYER, HELEN—JOURNEYS — **Subject Card**
(5) **Thayer, Helen**
　　Polar dream/by Helen Thayer.
N.Y.: Simon & Schuster [© 1993]
(6)　　254p.; illus.
　　ISBN 0671793861
(7)　　1. Thayer, Helen—Journeys. 2. Women explorers. 3. North Pole. I. Title.

1. Call Number . . . . The number assigned to a book by the Dewey decimal or Library of Congress classification system

2. Author . . . . Author's full name, last name first

3. Title . . . . Full title and subtitle of a book

4. Publisher . . . . Place and date of publication

5. Subject . . . . General subject of a book; subject card may show specific headings

6. Physical Description . . Description of the book, such as its size and number of pages, and whether it is illustrated

7. Cross-references . . . . . Refers to other headings or related topics where you can look for other books

Using Reference Materials

The *Readers' Guide*

To find a magazine article, use the *Readers' Guide to Periodical Literature*. The *Readers' Guide* indexes articles, poems, and stories from more than 150 magazines. Articles are listed alphabetically both by author and by subject. Use the key at the front of the *Readers' Guide* to find the meanings of the abbreviations used in the entries. Both the printed and the online versions of the *Readers' Guide* sometimes provide abstracts.

Printed *Readers' Guide*
① READING COMPREHENSION
② Broadening students' reading responses. M. A. Faust. *The Education Digest* v61 p66–9 Ja'96
READING DISABILITY
See also
Dyslexia
READING LISTS
See also
③ Best sellers
Books and reading—Best books
Children's literature—Bibliography
REAGAN, NANCY, 1923–
about
④ Ronald Reagan & Nancy Davis. il pors *People Weekly*
⑤ v45 p150–2 F 12 '96
REAGAN, RONALD, 1911–
about
⑥ Even '96 is a Reagan year. K. T. Walsh. il por *U.S.*
⑦ *News & World Report* v120 p10–11 F 19 '96
The greatest leaders of the '80s get no respect. P. C.
⑧ Roberts. il *Business Week* p20 Ap1 '96
Ronald Reagan & Nancy Davis. il pors *People Weekly*
v45 p150–2 F12 '96
⑨ REAL, LESLIE
Sustainability and the ecology of infectious disease. bibl f il *BioScience* v46 p88–97 F '96

① **Subject entry**

② **Title of article**

③ **Subject cross-reference**

④ **Name of magazine**

⑤ **Volume number of magazine**

⑥ **Author of article**

⑦ **Page references**

⑧ **Date of magazine**

⑨ **Author entry**

Result of Online Search of *Readers' Guide*	
AUTHOR:	Walsh, Kenneth T.
TITLE:	Even '96 is a Reagan year. (candidates striving to claim Reagan's mantle)
SOURCE:	U.S. News & World Report v. 120 (Feb. 19 '96) p. 10–11 il
STANDARD NO:	0041-5537
DATE:	1996
RECORD TYPE:	art
CONTENTS:	feature article
SUBJECT:	Reagan, Ronald, 1911–
	Republican Party (U.S.)
	Presidential candidates—1996.
	United States—History—1981–1989.

RESOURCES

Special Information Sources

The *vertical file* contains up-to-date materials such as pamphlets, newspaper clippings, and pictures.

Microforms are reduced-size pages from various publications. The two most common types are *microfilm* (a roll or reel of film) and *microfiche* (a sheet of film). A projector enlarges the images to a readable size.

Many libraries use computers to research reference sources. Some libraries are linked to *online databases.* These databases store all types of information. Libraries that are linked to the *Internet,* an international network of computers, have access to thousands of information sources. You search for a specific topic by typing a *keyword* or key phrase. Ask your librarian for help in wording your search requests and in using the Internet.

Reference Sources

There are many types of reference sources that you can use to find specific kinds of information.

REFERENCE SOURCES	
TYPE	**DESCRIPTION**
ENCYCLOPEDIAS *Collier's Encyclopedia* *Compton's Encyclopedia* *The Encyclopedia Americana* *The New Encyclopaedia Britannica* *The World Book Multimedia Encyclopedia*™	■ multiple volumes ■ articles arranged alphabetically by subject ■ best source for general information ■ may have index or annuals
GENERAL BIOGRAPHICAL REFERENCES *Current Biography Yearbook* *Dictionary of American Biography* *Biography Index* (database) *Webster's New Biographical Dictionary*	■ information about birth, nationality, and major accomplishments of prominent people

(continued)

RESOURCES

REFERENCE SOURCES *(continued)*	
TYPE	DESCRIPTION
SPECIAL BIOGRAPHICAL REFERENCES *American Men & Women of Science* (database) *Mexican American Biographies* *Contemporary Authors* (series)	■ information about people noted for accomplishments in a specific field or for membership in a specific group
ATLASES *Atlas of World Cultures* *National Geographic Atlas of the World*	■ maps and geographical information
ALMANACS *The World Almanac and Book of Facts* *Information Please Almanac: Atlas & Yearbook*	■ up-to-date information about current events, facts, statistics, and dates
SOURCES OF QUOTATIONS Bartlett's *Familiar Quotations* *Gale's Quotations: Who Said What?*™ (CD-ROM)	■ famous quotations indexed or grouped by subject ■ often tells author, source, and date
SOURCES OF SYNONYMS *Roget's International Thesaurus* *The New Roget's Thesaurus in Dictionary Form* *Webster's New Dictionary of Synonyms*	■ lists of exact or more interesting words to express ideas
LITERATURE REFERENCE SOURCES *Granger's Index to Poetry* *Subject Index to Poetry* *Essay and General Literature Index* *Short Story Index* *Gale Literary Index CD-ROM*	■ condensed information about various literary works

A DIFFERENT APPROACH

Most students won't realize how many reference tools libraries have to offer. To introduce students to the reference tools, write the following items on the chalkboard:

1. magazine articles
2. pamphlets
3. back issues of periodicals
4. databases
5. documentaries

Then write the following list of reference tools on the chalkboard:

a. the vertical file
b. recorded materials
c. the *Readers' Guide*
d. microforms
e. computers

Ask students to match the tool with the type of material it can help a student find. [1–c; 2–a; 3–d; 4–e; 5–b]

RESOURCES

RESOURCES

RESOURCES

ANSWERS

Exercise 2

Answers will vary. Make sure that students include the complete article title, the author(s), magazine title, date, and page numbers for each entry.

RESOURCES

---

958 *The Library/Media Center*

Review

▶ EXERCISE 1 **Using Card Catalogs**

Use the card catalog or online catalog in your library to find the following information. If the information cannot be found, write "not in our library." **Information will vary.**

1. List the title of one book by each of the following authors.   **1a.** *The Yearling/Cross Creek/*
   a. Marjorie Kinnan Rawlings   *The Sojourner*
   b. Toni Cade Bambara **1b.** *Gorilla, My Love/ The Salt Eaters*

2. Find the title card for each of the following books. Give the author's full name.
   a. *The House on Mango Street* **2a.** Sandra Cisneros
   b. *Johnny Tremain* **2b.** Esther Forbes

3. Find a book on each of these subjects. List the title, author, and call number of each book. **3a.** Chance,
   a. Inuits (or Eskimos) Norman A.; *The Eskimo of North*
   b. Martin Luther King, Jr. **3b.** Lerone, *Alaska;* E 99 E7 C5
   Bennett; *What Manner of Man: A Biography of Martin Luther King, Jr.;*
   92 K5853B

▶ EXERCISE 2 **Using the *Readers' Guide***

In the *Readers' Guide,* find one entry listed for each of the following subjects. For each entry, give the title, author or authors (if given), magazine, date, and page numbers.

EXAMPLE Subject: water pollution
  Readers' Guide entry: Our Polluted Runoff
  J. G. Mitchell
  il maps National Geographic
  v189 p106–25 F '96
ANSWER *Title: "Our Polluted Runoff"*
  Author: J. G. Mitchell
  Magazine: National Geographic
  Date: February 1996
  Page Numbers: 106–125

1. games
2. artificial intelligence
3. African popular music
4. family
5. health

958

OBJECTIVES

- To look up words in a dictionary and to check for alternative spellings
- To divide words into syllables
- To use the pronunciation key in a dictionary to pronounce words correctly

PROGRAM MANAGER

THE DICTIONARY

- **Independent Practice/ Reteaching** For additional practice and reinforcement, see **Types of Dictionaries, The Dictionary Entry A, The Dictionary Entry B,** and **The Dictionary Entry C** in *Academic and Workplace Skills,* pp. 31–34.
- **Review** For exercises on chapter concepts, see **Review Form A** and **Review Form B** in *Academic and Workplace Skills,* pp. 35–36.

34 THE DICTIONARY

Types and Contents

Types of Dictionaries

There are many different types of dictionaries. They vary in the kinds of information they contain and in the arrangement of their contents. Some dictionaries contain terms and definitions used in a single occupation, such as computer programming. These dictionaries are designed to be used in the workplace.

CHAPTER OVERVIEW

This chapter offers a brief description of the types of dictionaries available and a ten-part treatment of the standard dictionary entry. Review exercises at the end of the chapter offer students the opportunity to test their mastery of dictionary use.

TYPES OF DICTIONARIES		
TYPES OF DICTIONARIES	NUMBER OF ENTRIES	NUMBER OF PAGES
Unabridged *Webster's Third New International Dictionary, Unabridged*	460,000	2,662
College/Abridged *Merriam-Webster's Collegiate Dictionary,* Tenth Edition	160,000	1,600
Paperback *The Random House Dictionary*	74,000	1,054

RESOURCES

RESOURCES

MEETING *individual* NEEDS

LEP/ESL

General Strategies. Some students may have already learned the usefulness of bilingual dictionaries, but others may not know such dictionaries exist. If your English-language learners don't know how to use a bilingual dictionary, work with them individually or in small groups to show them.

You may want to set up a game in which the English-language learners give a word in their first language and the English-proficient students look that word up in a bilingual dictionary and give its meaning in English. The game can also work in reverse, with the English-proficient students giving a word in English for the English-language learners to look up.

STUDENTS WITH SPECIAL NEEDS

Some students are poor decoders and may need extra time to complete assignments. You may want to shorten the word lists in the exercises for them and include words with which they have experienced difficulties. Teaching the students to use a thesaurus also may help them overcome problems with expressing themselves in writing.

SELECTION AMENDMENT
Description of change: numbers added
Rationale: to provide references for the contents of a dictionary entry as presented in this chapter

RESOURCES

---

960 *The Dictionary*

A SAMPLE ENTRY

From *Webster's New World College Dictionary,* Third Edition. Copyright © 1996, 1994, 1991, 1988 by Simon & Schuster, Inc. Reprinted by permission of Macmillan USA, a Simon & Schuster Macmillan Company.

1. **Entry word.** The entry word shows how the word is spelled and how it is divided into syllables. The entry word may also show capitalization and provide alternate spellings.
2. **Pronunciation.** The pronunciation is shown using accent marks and other phonetic respellings or diacritical marks. A pronunciation key is provided as a guide to diacritical marks or phonetic symbols.
3. **Part-of-speech labels.** These labels (usually in abbreviated form) indicate how the entry word should be used in a sentence. Some words may be used as more than one part of speech. In this case, a part-of-speech label is given in front of each of the numbered (or lettered) series of definitions.
4. **Other forms.** These may show spellings of plural forms of nouns, tenses of verbs, or the comparative forms of adjectives and adverbs.
5. **Etymology.** The etymology is the origin and history of a word. It tells how the word (or its parts) came into English.
6. **Definitions.** If there is more than one meaning, definitions are numbered or lettered.
7. **Special usage labels.** These labels identify words that have special meaning or are used in special ways in certain situations.

8. **Examples.** Phrases or sentences may demonstrate how the defined word is to be used.
9. **Related word forms.** These are various forms of the entry word, usually created by adding suffixes or prefixes.
10. **Synonyms and antonyms.** Synonyms and antonyms may appear at the end of some word entries.

 COMPUTER NOTE: Some spell-checking programs allow you to create a user dictionary and add the special terms you use often.

Review

▶ EXERCISE 1 **Looking Up the Spelling of Words**

Look up the following words in your dictionary and write any alternate spellings listed. If the word has only one spelling in your dictionary, write the word *single* as your answer. Answers may vary according to the dictionary used. These are from *Webster's New World Dictionary,* Third College Edition.

EXAMPLE **1.** judgment
1. *judgement*

1. encyclopedia **1.** encyclopaedia **4.** skeptic **4.** *single*
2. fledgling **2.** fledgeling **5.** yogurt **5.** yoghurt/yoghourt
3. theater **3.** theatre

▶ EXERCISE 2 **Dividing Words into Syllables**

Divide the following words into syllables. Check with the dictionary to see how well you have done.

1. ostentation   **4.** particularize
2. environment   **5.** distinction
3. conservation

▶ EXERCISE 3 **Using the Pronunciation Key**

Pronounce each of the following words using the pronunciation key in your dictionary.

1. legerdemain   **4.** indigent
2. parquet   **5.** Portuguese
3. theocracy

RESOURCES

Answers may vary according to the dictionary used. These are from

▶ EXERCISE 4 **Identifying Part-of-Speech Labels**

Webster's New World College Dictionary, Third Edition

Look up the following words in a dictionary and write the part-of-speech labels given for each of their meanings.

1. objective   **1.** adj./n.
2. dry   **2.** adj./v.
3. still   **3.** adj./n./adv./conj./v.

4. branch   **4.** n./v.
5. no   **5.** adv./adj./n.

▶ EXERCISE 5 **Exploring the Etymology of Words**

Use a college or unabridged dictionary to find the etymology of the following words. For each word, tell what language the word came from.

1. rodeo
2. kindergarten
3. palm

4. tea
5. kayak

▶ EXERCISE 6 **Finding Synonyms**

Come up with as many synonyms as you can for each of the following words. Then, using your dictionary, check your list and add to it.

1. famous
2. error
3. legal

4. old
5. beautiful

ANSWERS
Exercise 5

Answers may vary according to the dictionary used. These are from *Webster's New World College Dictionary,* Third Edition:

1. The word *rodeo* originally came from a Spanish word meaning "a going around, cattle ring" from the Latin *rotare,* "to turn."

2. The word *kindergarten* comes from the German words *kinder,* meaning "children," and *garten,* meaning "garden."

3. The word *palm* comes through Middle English from the Latin word *palma*— "the palm of the hand."

4. The word *tea* comes from the Mandarin Chinese word *ch'a.*

5. The word *kayak* comes from the Inuit language.

ANSWERS
Exercise 6

Answers may vary according to the dictionary used. These are from *Webster's New World College Dictionary,* Third Edition:

1. renowned, celebrated, noted, distinguished, eminent, illustrious

2. mistake, blunder, slip

3. lawful, legitimate, licit

4. ancient, antique, archaic

5. lovely, handsome, pretty, comely, fair, good-looking

VOCABULARY *(pp. 963–972)*

OBJECTIVES

- To use context clues and the general context to determine the meanings of words
- To use roots, prefixes, and suffixes to determine the meanings of words

35 VOCABULARY

Learning and Using New Words

The larger your vocabulary, the more likely you are to be successful in high school, college, and the workplace. A good way to learn new words is by building your vocabulary as you read books, newspapers, and periodicals. You can also increase your vocabulary by analyzing how an unfamiliar term is used in context. And you can discover the meanings of words by learning how word parts are combined to form new words.

Creating a Word Bank

One good way to increase your vocabulary is to keep a word bank, or list, in a notebook. When you encounter an unfamiliar word, write the word and its definition in your notebook. Check your dictionary for the correct definition.

> **COMPUTER NOTE:** Create a vocabulary file on your computer. Add new words and definitions to the end of the file. Then, use the Sort command to arrange the words in alphabetical order. Review the words and their definitions frequently.

PROGRAM MANAGER

VOCABULARY

- **Independent Practice/ Reteaching** For additional practice and reinforcement, see **Using Context Clues A, Using Context Clues B, Using Context Clues C, Choosing the Right Word, Word Roots, Prefixes, Suffixes,** and **Building Your Vocabulary** in *Academic and Workplace Skills,* pp. 39–47.

- **Reinforcement/Reteaching** For additional instruction and exercises, see **Vocabulary Masters 1–10** in *Practice for Assessment in Reading, Vocabulary, and Spelling,* pp. 13–22.

- **Assessment/Reflection** To assess student work and evaluate progress, see **Portfolio Form** in *Portfolio Assessment,* p. 26.

- **Review** For exercises on chapter concepts, see **Review Form A** and **Review Form B** in *Academic and Workplace Skills,* pp. 48–51.

CHAPTER OVERVIEW

The chapter discusses two methods for determining the meanings of new words: using context clues and using word parts—including roots, prefixes, and suffixes. Review exercises at the end of the chapter give students the opportunity to test their mastery of these methods.

RESOURCES

RESOURCES

Write the following sentence on the chalkboard:

Scientists say that the giant otter, an animal whose numbers are decreasing because it's still killed for its fur, is an endangered or threatened species.

Ask students these questions:

1. If you did not already know, how could you tell from reading the sentence what a giant otter is? [It is defined as "an animal" which has "fur."]

2. What clue to the meaning of *endangered* do you find in the sentence? [The word is equated in the sentence with "threatened."]

Tell students that they have used context clues to find the answers; that is, they have looked at the words surrounding *giant otter* and *endangered* to help themselves understand the meanings of those words.

Using Context Clues

Sometimes you can figure out the meaning of a word by examining the context in which it is used.

HOW TO USE CONTEXT CLUES	
TYPE OF CLUE	**EXPLANATION**
Definitions and Restatements	Writers may sometimes restate a word in order to define it. ■ When Henry B. Gonzalez was elected to Congress, many of his Spanish-speaking *constituents,* the voters in his district, felt that he would fight for their rights.
Examples	Examples used in context may help reveal the meaning of an unfamiliar word. ■ The scientist was accused of several acts of *espionage,* such as photographing secret documents and taping private conversations.
Synonyms	Look for familiar words that may be synonyms of words you don't yet know. ■ The club's *coffers* were so low that the members had to ask for donations to refill the treasury.
Comparisons	An unknown word may be shown to be similar to a more common word. ■ As in so many polluted cities, the air in our community is sometimes too *contaminated* to breathe.
Contrast	An unfamiliar word may be contrasted to a more familiar word or phrase. ■ The team's uniforms were *immaculate* before the game, but by the end of the first quarter they were filthy.
Cause and Effect	Look for clues that indicate that an unfamiliar word is related to the cause or the result of an action, feeling, or idea. ■ Will Rogers was considered to be a *humanitarian* because he worked to improve people's lives.

Determining Meanings from the General Context

Context clues are not always obvious. Sometimes you have to read an entire passage to understand the meaning of an unfamiliar word. However, you can draw on what you already know about the subject of the passage as well as your own experiences. Your own knowledge and resources can frequently help you determine the meanings of many unfamiliar terms.

Choosing the Right Word

Sometimes context clues are not enough to help you figure out a word's meaning. At times, the best way to determine the meaning of an unfamiliar word is to look up the word in the dictionary.

Very few words in English have a single meaning. Most have several meanings that vary depending on the context in which the word appears. Therefore, when you're looking in a dictionary for the meaning of a word, read *all* the definitions given, keeping in mind the context in which you originally read or heard the word.

To help you, dictionaries often provide sample contexts. These are usually several words surrounding the word being defined. They help you see how the word generally appears in a sentence. When sample contexts are given, compare them with the original context in which the word occurred to make sure you've found the meaning that fits.

Synonyms are words that have the same or nearly the same meaning. Use a dictionary or thesaurus to make sure you understand the exact differences in meanings between synonyms.

It is also important to understand that two words may have the same **denotation**, or dictionary definition, but a different **connotation**, or emotional overtone. For example, the words *slender* and *skinny* both mean "thin." However, the word *slender* has a more positive connotation than *skinny*, which suggests a bony or gaunt appearance.

RESOURCES

MEETING *individual* **NEEDS**

LEP/ESL

General Strategies. A question often asked by English-language learners when they are trying to improve their English vocabulary is how two similar English words differ. Such questions indicate that students might be having problems discerning subtleties in meaning from the contexts of the words.

When explaining the differences between similar words, remember that the emphasis should be on how the words are used, not on the words' denotations. You may want to have students find examples of how the words are used before you begin explaining their differences.

STUDENTS WITH SPECIAL NEEDS

Some students have limited vocabularies. To help students build vocabulary, it is important to use many strategies.

Make sure the students are familiar with all the words in passages they are preparing to read. Help them also with the background knowledge needed to understand the words.

Help students learn to generalize parts of familiar words. After they become familiar with a word, have students write definitions. Check their definitions and discuss the word with them. Students may remember the word more easily if you relate it to familiar ideas.

RESOURCES

Literature Link. Have students read and discuss Hugo Martinez-Serros's "Distillation," and then have them build a list of unfamiliar words they encountered in the story. From that list, have them extract the words with prefixes and suffixes listed in this chapter. See if they can deduce the meanings of those words from the meanings of the prefixes and suffixes.

Using Word Parts

English words can be classified into two types: those that cannot be subdivided into parts, and those that can. Words that cannot be subdivided, like *maze*, *right*, and *leap*, are called **base words.** Words that can be subdivided, like *reception*, *quickly*, and *knowledge*, are made up of **word parts.** The three types of word parts are

- roots
- prefixes
- suffixes

Knowing the meanings of roots, prefixes, and suffixes can help you determine the meanings of many unfamiliar words.

Roots

The **root** is the foundation on which a word is built. It carries the word's core meaning, and it is the part to which prefixes and suffixes are added. For example, the root *–port–* means "carry." This root can be combined with various prefixes and suffixes to make new words such as *transportation*, *portable*, and *importer*. Here are some examples of words with roots, prefixes, and suffixes.

WORD	PREFIX	ROOT	SUFFIX
defective	de–	–fect–	–ive
unacceptable	un–	–accept–	–able
sympathy	sym–	–path–	–y
discouragement	dis–	–courage–	–ment

Some of the roots come from base words, such as *–accept–* in *unacceptable*, and are relatively easy to define. Other roots may be more difficult to define, such as those in *defective* (*–fect–*, "do, make") and *sympathy* (*–path–*, "feeling"). These roots and many others come from Greek and Latin. Becoming familiar with Greek and Latin roots and their meanings is an important step in improving your vocabulary.

COMMONLY USED ROOTS		
ROOTS	MEANINGS	EXAMPLES
GREEK		
–anthrop–	human	anthropology, misanthrope
–chrono–	time	chronology, chronometer
–cycl–	circle, wheel	cyclone, bicycle
–dem–	people	demography, democracy
–graph–	write, writing	autograph, biography
–hydr–	water	hydrant, hydrate
–log, –logy	study, word	biology, monologue
–morph–	form	metamorphosis, polymorph
–phon–	sound	phonograph, symphony
LATIN		
–cis–	cut	decision, concise
–cred–	believe	incredible, discredit
–dic–, –dict–	say, speak	dictate, predict
–fac–, –fact–, –fec–, –fic–	do, make	deface, manufacture, defective, efficient
–fid–	belief, faith	confident, fidelity
–frag–, –fract–	break	fragment, fraction
–ject–	throw	eject, trajectory
–junct–	join	conjunction, juncture
–magn–	large, grand	magnate, magnificent
–mal–	bad	malice, dismal
–mit–, –miss–	send	missionary, transmit
–ped–	foot	biped, pedestrian
–pend–, –pens–	hang, weigh	pendant, pensive
–pon–, –pos–	place, put	exponent, position
–scrib–, –script–	write	inscribe, postscript
–solv–	to loosen, accomplish	solvent, resolve
–ven–, –vent–	come	convention, prevent
–vers–, –vert–	turn	reverse, convertible
–voc–, –vok–	call	vocal, provoke
–volv–	roll, turn around	revolve, evolve

MEETING *individual* **NEEDS**

LEP/ESL

Spanish. Remind Spanish-speakers that many English words have the same Latin roots as do corresponding or similar words in Spanish. Although some definitions may deviate from that suggested by the Latin root, most will be closely related, and if students understand the context in which the word is used, recognizing and knowing the meaning of the Latin root will help students determine the word's meaning.

You may want to have each of your Spanish-speakers compose a list of ten to twenty English words and Spanish counterparts that share the same Latin root.

RESOURCES

RESOURCES

COOPERATIVE LEARNING

Divide the class into three groups and let students explore the history of some of the prefixes listed in the chapter. One group could take Greek prefixes, a second group Latin and French prefixes, and a third group Old English prefixes. Have each group use a dictionary to look up the prefixes and write down the information they find on the original roots, spellings, and dates of usage. You could give Old English prefixes to a small group and ask the other two groups to choose at least five prefixes each. Each group could report some of its more interesting findings to the class.

Prefixes

A *prefix* is a word part that is added before a root. The word that is created from a prefix and a root combines the meanings of both its parts.

COMMONLY USED PREFIXES		
PREFIXES	MEANINGS	EXAMPLES
GREEK		
anti–	against, opposing	antimissile, antisocial
hyper–	over, above	hyperactive, hyperventilate
mono–, mon–	one	monologue, monarch
para–	beside, beyond	parallel, parasail
psych–	mind	psychology, psychosomatic
LATIN AND FRENCH		
contra–	against	contraband, contraposition
de–	away, from, off, down	depart, deplane, descend
dif–, dis–	away, not, opposing	differ, dismount, dissent
ex–, e–, ef–	away from, out	excise, emigrate, efface
il–, im–, in–, ir–	not, in	illogical, impolite, incite, irrational
post–	after, following	postpaid, postwar
pre–	before	prejudge, preview
pro–	forward, favoring	proceed, pro-American
re–	back, backward, again	return, reflect, reforest
OLD ENGLISH		
be–	around, about	beset, behind
mis–	badly, not, wrongly	misbehave, misfire, mispronounce
un–	not, reverse of	untrue, unfold

 REFERENCE NOTE: For guidelines on spelling when adding prefixes, see page 873.

Suffixes

A *suffix* is a word part that is added to the end of a root. Often, adding or changing a suffix will also change the part of speech of a word, as seen in *operate/operation*.

COMMONLY USED SUFFIXES		
SUFFIXES	**MEANINGS**	**EXAMPLES**
GREEK, LATIN, AND FRENCH *NOUNS*		
–ance, –ence	act, condition	forbearance, excellence
–cy	state, condition	accuracy, normalcy
–er, –or	doing, actor	singer, conductor
–ion	action, result, state	union, fusion, dominion
–ism	act, state, manner	baptism, socialism
–tude	quality, state	fortitude, magnitude
–ty, –y	quality, state, action	novelty, surety, jealousy
ADJECTIVES		
–able, –ible	able, likely	washable, divisible
–ate	having, characteristic of	animate, collegiate
–ive	tending to, given to	reflective, pensive
–ous	marked by, given to	glorious, nervous
–ulent	full of, characterized by	turbulent, fraudulent
ADJECTIVES OR NOUNS		
–al	doer, pertaining to	rival, autumnal
–ary	belonging to, one connected with	primary, adversary, auxiliary
–ent	doing, actor	confident, adherent
–ic	dealing with, caused by, person or thing showing	classic, choleric, workaholic
–ite	formed, showing	finite, favorite

(continued)

A DIFFERENT APPROACH
Let students use the lists of prefixes and suffixes in the chapter to make up a story. Choose a student to begin with the first prefix on the list of prefixes, *anti–*. That student must use the prefix in a word in a sentence that starts the story. Then, each student in turn provides a sentence that helps to elaborate the story. The catch is that the sentence must contain the prefix or a suffix that is next on the list. See how far down both lists the students can get. Allow them to use example words from the lists.

RESOURCES

RESOURCES

COMMONLY USED SUFFIXES *(continued)*		
SUFFIXES	**MEANINGS**	**EXAMPLES**
VERBS		
—ate	become, cause	evaporate, irate
—esce	become, grow, continue	convalesce, acquiesce
OLD ENGLISH ***ADJECTIVES*** ***OR ADVERBS***		
—ly	like, characteristic of	friendly, cowardly
—ward	in the direction of	backward, upward
VERBS		
—en	cause to be, become	deepen, darken

👉 REFERENCE NOTE: For guidelines on spelling when adding suffixes, see pages 873–875.

Review

📑 EXERCISE 1   **Using Context Clues to Find Meanings**

See how well you can figure out the meanings of words from the way they are used in a sentence. Write the letter of the definition that best fits each italicized word.

a. large structure
b. coloring
c. amiable
d. profitable
e. celebrity
f. lawmaker
g. worsening
h. emotional displays

1. Lars often uses *histrionics* such as wailing and crying to get his way. **1.** h
2. Unlike our money-losing ventures, selling popcorn at soccer games has been a *lucrative* project for our club. **2.** d
3. The towering *edifice,* like many buildings in New York, seems to reach to the clouds. **3.** a

4. Because the empty building is *deteriorating* so rapidly, it will soon be beyond repair.   **4.** g
5. Former Congresswoman Barbara Jordan was one of the first African American women to become a *legislator*.   **5.** f

▶ EXERCISE 2   **Using the General Context to Determine Meaning**

For each italicized word, write your own definition or synonym. Then check the dictionary's definitions of each word. If you guessed incorrectly, check the context again to look for clues you might have missed.

Most jobs available to students are found in the service [1] *sector*, in places such as department stores and fast-food restaurants. This type of work is often [2] *menial* and [3] *monotonous*—regarded as servile and offering little or no variety. Federal laws [4] *curtail* the number of hours students under sixteen can work for pay, but some employers [5] *exploit* students by demanding that they work longer. Rather than disagree and lose their jobs, many students [6] *comply*. Working may also [7] *impede* learning, as time spent on the job [8] *encroaches* on time needed for homework. Even good students may find their grades [9] *degenerating* from A's to B's or from B's to C's or D's. In addition, officials [10] *cite* hazardous conditions in some workplaces, mentioning numerous injuries to young people who work around large or dangerous machines.

▶ EXERCISE 3   **Using Roots to Determine Meanings**

Use the list of commonly used roots on page 967 to identify the root or roots in the following words. Then, guess each word's meaning. Check your answers with a dictionary.

EXAMPLE   **1.** vocation
             1. *–voc– (call); vocation means "a calling or summoning, especially in the sense of a chosen career"*

1. junction
2. contradiction
3. demographic
4. subvert
5. genealogy

ANSWERS
Exercise 2

Answers may vary but should be similar to the following examples:

1. sector—group, area, section
2. menial—easy, servile, low
3. monotonous—boring, tedious, tiresome
4. curtail—limit, reduce, cut short
5. exploit—use, abuse, manipulate
6. comply—obey, follow, go along with
7. impede—hinder, obstruct, delay
8. encroaches—trespasses, moves in, takes up
9. degenerating—declining, deteriorating, falling
10. cite—mention, point out, make known

ANSWERS
Exercise 3

1. *–junct–* ("join"); *junction* means "a joining or point of intersection"
2. *–dict–* ("say" or "speak"); *contradiction* means "speaking against"
3. *–dem–* ("people"); *–graph–* ("write" or "writing"); *demographic* means "relating to written statistics about people"
4. *–vert–* ("turn"); *subvert* means "to undermine or corrupt"
5. *–gen–* ("birth") and *–logy–* ("study"); *genealogy* means "study of birth or descent"

RESOURCES

RESOURCES

ANSWERS
Exercise 4

Answers may vary. Here are some possibilities:

1. hypercritical—too critical
2. disclose—uncover
3. except—not including
4. paramedic—medical worker
5. besides—in addition to

ANSWERS
Exercise 5

1. *–or;* one who puts money away
2. *–ency;* the state of being lenient
3. *–able;* able to be drawn back
4. *–ism;* military manner or predominance
5. *–ate;* make active

ANSWERS
Exercise 6

1. *e–* (away from); *–miss–* (send); *–ary* (one connected with doing); someone sent to do something
2. *hydr–* (water); *–logy* (study of); study of water
3. *de–* (away, from); *–pend–* (hang, weigh); *–able* (able, likely); able to hang away from
4. *re–* (again); *–volv–*(turn around); *–er* (doing, actor); something that turns around again
5. *pro–* (forward, favoring); *–pon–* (place, put); *–ent* (doing, actor); one who puts something forward or favors (an idea)

▷ EXERCISE 4 **Identifying Words with Prefixes**

Give an example of a word containing each of the following prefixes. (Do not use any of the words given as examples in this chapter.) Then, tell what each word means. Use a dictionary if necessary.

EXAMPLE **1. pre–**
　　　　　 1. *prehistoric—existing in times before written history*

1. hyper–
2. dis–
3. ex–
4. para–
5. be–

▷ EXERCISE 5 **Identifying Suffixes and Defining Words**

For each word, identify the suffix. Then, guess what the whole word means. Use a dictionary to check your answers.

EXAMPLE **1. privacy**
　　　　　 1. *–cy; the state or condition of being private*

1. depositor
2. leniency
3. retractable
4. militarism
5. activate

▷ EXERCISE 6 **Using Word Parts to Determine Meaning**

Identify the roots, prefixes, and suffixes in each of the following words. Then, try to guess what the words mean. Use a dictionary to check your answers.

EXAMPLE **1. anthropomorphous**
　　　　　 1. *–anthrop– (human); –morph– (form); –ous (marked by, given to)*
　　　　　 marked by human form or appearance

1. emissary
2. hydrology
3. dependable
4. revolver
5. proponent

RESOURCES

RESOURCES

972

LETTERS AND FORMS (pp. 973–982)

OBJECTIVES

- To write letters of request, complaint, appreciation, and application
- To write a thank-you letter
- To address a business envelope

PROGRAM MANAGER

LETTERS AND FORMS

- **Independent Practice/ Reteaching** See **The Parts of a Business Letter, Types of Business Letters, Types of Personal Letters, Addressing an Envelope,** and **Completing Printed Forms** in *Academic and Workplace Skills,* pp. 55–59.

- **Review** See **Review Form A** and **Review Form B** in *Academic and Workplace Skills,* pp. 60–63.

- **Reinforcement/Reteaching** See *Holt Effective Business Communication.*

36 LETTERS AND FORMS

Style and Contents

CHAPTER OVERVIEW

Students need to know how to write letters and complete forms correctly if they are to function effectively in society. This chapter can be used either for reteaching basic concepts or as a reference for students who have not been exposed to this material.

Tenth-grade students have studied basic composition skills and can apply what they have learned about descriptive, informative, and persuasive writing (**Chapters 5, 7,** and **9**) to the material in this chapter. Even though instruction focuses on the formal elements of letter writing, students will also provide information, give descriptions, and express opinions in their letters.

You write letters for a variety of purposes. Clearly and concisely written letters will get results and create a favorable impression, whether you are writing them for personal use or as a workplace requirement. Following accepted business procedures and using the correct style will give your letters a professional look. You should also follow a few simple guidelines in completing printed forms.

The Appearance of a Business Letter

- Use white, unlined $8\frac{1}{2}$" × 11" paper.
- Type your letter if possible (single-spaced, leaving an extra line between paragraphs). Otherwise, neatly write the letter by hand, using black or blue ink. Avoid cross-outs, smudges, erasures, and inkblots. Check for typing errors and misspellings.
- Center your letter on the page with equal margins on the sides and at the top and bottom.
- Use only one side of the paper. If your letter won't fit on one page, leave a one-inch margin at the bottom of the first page and carry over at least two lines onto the second page.

RESOURCES

RESOURCES

You may choose to begin this chapter by drawing two rectangles on the chalkboard to represent business stationery. Label one "Block Form" and the other "Modified Block Form." Draw lines to show the block and modified block arrangements of a business letter. Then ask volunteers to name the six parts of a business letter and to tell where they are placed on the page.

MEETING *individual* **NEEDS**

LEP/ESL

General Strategies. Many students have difficulty punctuating items such as salutations, closings, dates, and addresses. The reasons for this vary. Some Asian languages, for example, use word groupings rather than special marks for punctuation.

Before students work **Exercise 1,** you may want to discuss the conventional uses of punctuation in a business letter written in English. Then, give students a short letter that has no punctuation and let them add the correct marks.

Writing Business Letters

The Parts of a Business Letter

A business letter contains six parts:

(1) the heading
(2) the inside address
(3) the salutation
(4) the body
(5) the closing
(6) the signature

Block Style

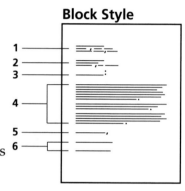

There are two common styles for arranging the parts of a business letter. For the *block form,* begin each of the parts of the letter at the left margin and don't indent any paragraphs. However, for the *modified block form,* align the heading, the closing, and your signature with an imaginary line down the center of the page. The other parts of the letter begin at the left margin. Paragraphs are indented.

Modified Block Style

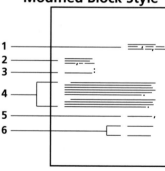

The Heading. The heading usually has three lines:

- your street address
- your city, state, and ZIP Code
- the date the letter was written

The Inside Address. The inside address gives the name and address of the person you are writing. Use a courtesy title (such as *Mr., Ms., Mrs.,* or *Miss*) or a professional title (such as *Dr.* or *Professor*) in front of the person's name. After the person's name, include the person's business title. The name of the company or organization and the address follow.

The Salutation. The salutation is your greeting. If you are writing to a specific person, begin with *Dear,* followed by a courtesy title or a professional title and the person's name. End the salutation with a colon (*Dear Mr. Jones:*).

If you don't have the name of a specific person, you can use a general salutation, such as *Dear Sir or Madam* or *Ladies and Gentlemen.* You can also use a department or a position title, with or without the word *Dear.*

The Body. The body, or main part, of your letter contains your message. It begins beneath the salutation. If the body of your letter contains more than one paragraph, leave a blank line between paragraphs.

The Closing. The closing should end your letter courteously. There are several closings that are often used in business letters, such as *Sincerely yours, Yours truly,* or *Regards.* Capitalize only the first word.

The Signature. Your signature should be written in ink, directly below the closing. Type or print your name neatly below your signature.

GUIDELINES FOR THE CONTENTS OF A BUSINESS LETTER

There are a few simple guidelines to follow in writing business letters that get results.

- *Use a polite, respectful, professional tone.* A courteous letter will be much more effective than a rude, angry, or sarcastic one.
- *Use formal, standard English.* Avoid slang, contractions, and abbreviations. Informal language that might be acceptable in a personal conversation or letter is often inappropriate in a business letter.
- *Explain the purpose of your letter quickly and clearly.* Keep in mind that the person reading your letter is busy. Include only necessary details.
- *Include all necessary information.* Be sure your reader can understand why you wrote and what you are asking.

COOPERATIVE LEARNING

Have students work in groups of four to create business letters. Students in each group should first brainstorm names and products for imaginary business firms. Next, they should select a reason for writing a letter of request, appreciation, application, or complaint to one of the firms. Then, have them develop the letter together. One group member might act as the recorder, another might check the form of the letter, a third might edit the letter for any errors in capitalization and punctuation, and the fourth might volunteer to read the letter aloud to the class.

MEETING *individual* NEEDS

STUDENTS WITH SPECIAL NEEDS

Some students may have difficulty expressing themselves.

It may be helpful to show a sample letter and to provide a list of vocabulary words. For example, for a letter inquiring about a job, you may want to give students a list such as the following: employment, experience, education, information, and requirements.

Types of Business Letters

Request or Order Letter

In a *request letter,* you're asking for something. You might request information about a product, or you might ask for someone's time or services. An *order letter* is a special kind of request letter asking for something specific, such as a free brochure advertised in a magazine. You might also write an order letter to purchase, by mail, a product for which you don't have a printed order form. In a request or order letter, the most important consideration is to be clear about exactly what you want.

---

19 Brookside Drive
Ithaca, NY 14850
September 2, 1998

Mr. Stuart Reinhardt, Manager
Rollerama Skating Rink
2008 Route 9
Ithaca, NY 14853

Dear Mr. Reinhardt:

Madison High School's sophomore class has voted to hold a class get-together at Rollerama. As class secretary, I am writing to ask if we could plan this event for Saturday, November 21, from 7:30 to 10:30 p.m. We expect about 85 students.

Could we rent the rink on the same terms you gave the senior class last spring? The sophomore class can guarantee a minimum attendance of 75 students. Students will pay at the door an admission price of $4.50. Skate rental will be a separate $2.00 charge.

Our class is looking forward to an enjoyable evening at Rollerama.

Yours truly,

Linda O'Connell

Linda O'Connell
Class Secretary
Madison High School
Class of '01

When you are writing a request or order letter, remember the following points.

1. State your request clearly.
2. If you're asking someone to send you information, enclose a self-addressed, stamped envelope.
3. If you're asking someone to do something for you, make your request well in advance.
4. If you're ordering something, include all important information, such as the size, color, brand name, or any other specific information. If there are costs involved, add the amount correctly.

Complaint or Adjustment Letter

If you are dissatisfied with a service or product, you might wish to write a *complaint* or *adjustment letter.* The purpose of this type of letter is to identify what's wrong and how you think it should be corrected. Here is the body of a sample adjustment letter.

> I have noticed that there are only two litter cans in Edgemont Park. I think that the litter situation would improve if the Parks Department would get more litter cans for the park. I think these cans should be placed so that they are convenient to the field, the picnic area, and the creek. More people might pick up their litter if there were trash containers located close to where they are needed.
>
> Please give your attention to this suggestion. I think Edgemont Park is a wonderful neighborhood resource that should be kept clean for everyone in our community to enjoy.

When you write a complaint or adjustment letter, remember these suggestions.

1. Register your complaint promptly.
2. Mention specifics. Necessary details might include the following:
   - how you were affected (lost time or money)
   - how you want the problem to be resolved
3. Keep the tone of your letter calm and courteous.

INTEGRATING THE LANGUAGE ARTS

Literature Link. If your literature book contains "The Bet" by Anton Chekhov, have students read it in preparation for writing an imaginary letter of application. Point out the importance of the lawyer's letter to the plot of the story. Note that during the lawyer's years of solitude he had written many letters and had read many books. Ask students to imagine themselves as the lawyer. Tell them to list skills they have acquired that might be useful in a job situation.

Have students write a letter of application to a company or organization asking for a position and explaining why they think the position matches their skills.

RESOURCES

RESOURCES

LESS-ADVANCED STUDENTS

Determine how much students remember about the appropriate ways to express themselves in social correspondence. Construct an example of a thank-you letter, a letter of regret, or an invitation. Include errors in basic structure, tone, and mechanics. Put this letter on an overhead projector and ask students to identify the problems and to suggest solutions.

INTEGRATING THE LANGUAGE ARTS

Literature Link. In Shakespeare's play *The Tragedy of Julius Caesar,* Caesar received a warning before he went to the Senate on the Ides of March. Ask students to think about what might have happened if a friend of Caesar's had written him a letter describing the details of the assassination plot. Students could also write such a letter. They should include names of those who are plotting against Caesar, what they are planning to do, and why.

Appreciation or Commendation Letter

An *appreciation* or *commendation letter* is written to express your appreciation or to encourage a person, group, or organization to continue doing good work. When you write an appreciation or commendation letter, it is important to tell the person or organization exactly why you are pleased. Here is the body of a sample appreciation letter.

> I am writing to congratulate all of you at WQBK on your change in format from oldies to Top 40.
>
> Although I enjoy listening to oldies, I am more interested in hearing what musicians are recording today. Even my parents are getting tired of hearing nothing but '50s and '60s music.
>
> I hope you succeed with your new format. I know my friends listen to your station, and sometimes my parents do, too. Good luck!

Letter of Application

The purpose of a *letter of application* is to provide a selection committee or possible employers with enough information about you so that they can make a decision about whether you are a good choice for a position, such as a scholarship or summer job. When you are writing a letter of application, remember the following points.

1. Identify the job or position you are applying for and tell how you heard about it.
2. Tell about yourself. Depending on the position you are applying for, you might include
   - your grade in school or grade-point average
   - your experience, or your activities, awards, and honors
   - personal qualities or characteristics that make you a good choice for the position
   - the date you can begin work

3. Offer to provide references. References are usually two or three responsible adults (generally not relatives) who can speak from experience about your character or qualifications and will give you a good recommendation. Be prepared to give the addresses and telephone numbers of your references when you are asked to provide them.

Here is a sample of an application letter.

1437 Windy Ridge Rd.
Milwaukee, WI 53224
January 23, 1998

Ms. Veronica Fong, Director
Spanish Student Exchange Program
P.O. Box 3001
New York, NY 10116

Dear Ms. Fong:

I am writing to apply for the summer exchange program to Barcelona, Spain, advertised in the January 14, 1998, edition of <u>Student Voice</u>.

I am a sophomore at Adams High School in Milwaukee, Wisconsin. My grade-point average is 3.3. I have studied Spanish for three years. Last semester I won an award for my translation work in this class.

I am aware of the responsibility this involves. I would feel privileged to gain a new understanding of the Spanish language and culture and, on my return, to share this information with others in my school and community.

I will gladly furnish references who can tell you more about my qualifications for this program.

Please let me know if there is any other information I need to give you before you can consider me as a candidate for this program.

Sincerely yours,

Brody Collins

Brody Collins

Writing Informal or Personal Letters

Personal messages are often best expressed in the form of letters. Often a written message is more effective—and more appreciated—than a telephone call or other form of communication. The most common types of informal or personal letters are thank-you letters, invitations, and letters of regret. Personal letters are less formal than business letters and don't follow a rigid style.

Thank-you Letters. These are informal letters of appreciation that you send to tell someone that you appreciate his or her taking time, trouble, or expense on your behalf. Try to think of something about the person's effort or gift that made it special.

Invitations. An informal invitation should contain specific information about a planned event, such as the occasion, the time and place, and any other special details your guests might need to know.

Letters of Regret. Send a letter of regret if you have been invited somewhere but are unable to go. A written reply is especially appropriate if you were sent a written invitation with the letters *R.S.V.P.* (in French, these letters stand for "please reply").

Addressing an Envelope

Your return address (your name and complete address) goes in the top left-hand corner of an envelope. Just to the right of center, place the name and address of the person or organization to whom you are writing. The addressee's name and address should exactly match the inside address on your letter. Be sure to include correct ZIP Codes.

MEETING *individual* **NEEDS**

LEP/ESL

General Strategies. In many countries, the return address is always written on the back of the envelope. Explain to students that the U.S. Postal Service prefers the standard address format given in the textbook. Provide extra practice with address abbreviations if some students are not familiar with them. Write a list of words on the chalkboard and ask volunteers to write abbreviations. Some examples are Lane—Ln., Boulevard—Blvd., Avenue—Ave., Street—St.

COMPUTER NOTE: Use your word-processing program to create a mailing list that will print the addresses from your letters onto labels or envelopes.

Completing Printed Forms

There are many types of printed forms, but there are certain common techniques that will help you fill out any form accurately and completely.

Read all of the directions carefully. Follow the instructions on the form exactly.

Type or write neatly, using a pen or pencil as directed. When you type or print your information on the form, avoid cross-outs or smudges if possible.

Proofread your completed form. Make sure you have given all the information requested on the form. Check for errors, and correct them neatly before you give the form to the appropriate person or mail it to the correct address.

Review

▶ EXERCISE 1 **Writing a Request Letter**

Choose one of the following situations to practice writing a request letter. Use your own return address and today's date, but make up any other information you need.

1. You are the president of a school club. Write a letter to a local business asking it to sponsor club members in a sports competition for a charity project.
2. You are working on a History Day project. Write a letter to your state historical society requesting information on early political campaigns or facts about the settlement of your region of the state.

RESOURCES

GUIDELINES
Exercise 2

All letters should correctly follow the block or the modified block form. The complaint letter should be courteous in tone and should contain all necessary information, such as a specific complaint and a suggested adjustment. Examples of specific complaints may be that the wrong item was sent, that the item was the wrong color or size, or that the wrong number of items was sent.

GUIDELINES
Exercise 3

All letters should correctly follow either the block or the modified block form, should be courteous in tone, and should contain all necessary information.

GUIDELINES
Exercise 4

All letters should correctly follow the block or the modified block form. Letters need to identify the position being applied for and include all important personal information. Students should include a statement explaining why they are a good choice for the position. They should also provide at least two suitable references that can be attached on a separate page.

GUIDELINES
Exercise 5

Students should use the modified block form and maintain a polite, friendly tone in their letters.

ANSWERS
Exercise 6

Return addresses will vary.

Mahalia Hamlin
32 Rio Seco
Albuquerque, NM 87120

---

3. You want to buy a sweatshirt with the name of your favorite college. Write a letter to that school's bookstore requesting information about the item.

EXERCISE 2 Writing a Complaint or Adjustment Letter

Practice writing a letter of adjustment or complaint. Write a letter to your local town council complaining about a proposed curfew for teenagers. Be specific in suggesting alternate solutions to the problems that led the council to consider the curfew. Use your own return address, but make up any other information you need.

EXERCISE 3 Writing a Letter of Appreciation or Commendation

Practice writing a letter of appreciation or commendation. Write a letter to the author of a book you enjoyed. Explain how his or her writing has changed, inspired, or simply entertained you. Use your own return address, but make up any other information you need.

EXERCISE 4 Writing a Letter of Application

Practice writing a letter of application. Think about a part-time or summer job that you are interested in and for which you feel qualified. Use the classified ad section of a newspaper to find the name of an organization or company that might offer this kind of position. Write a letter of application that states your interest and qualifications.

EXERCISE 5 Writing a Thank-you Letter

Write a thank-you letter to someone you know. Express your appreciation for a specific comment, gift, or action.

EXERCISE 6 Addressing Business Envelopes

Draw a rectangular outline to represent an envelope. Then, address the envelope to Mahalia Hamlin, who lives at 32 Rio Seco, Albuquerque, New Mexico (ZIP Code 87120). Use your own return address.

PROGRAM MANAGER

FOR THE WHOLE CHAPTER

- Review For exercises on chapter concepts, see **Review Form A** and **Review Form B** in *Academic and Workplace Skills*, pp. 80–83.

37 READING, STUDYING, AND TEST TAKING

Using Skills and Strategies

To be successful in your high-school studies, you need to develop skills and strategies for productive reading, efficient studying, and effective test taking. The methods you learn in this chapter will help you get better grades and complete your homework without last-minute agony. They will also help you succeed in college and in the workplace.

Planning a Study Routine

If you want to study effectively, you need to be committed to a realistic study schedule. Here are some suggestions.

1. *Know your assignments.* Keep an assignment planner or a calendar for recording your assignments and noting when they are due. Make sure you understand all the instructions for each assignment.
2. *Make a plan.* Break your big assignments into small steps. Make deadlines for completing each step.
3. *Concentrate when you study.* Set aside a specific time and place for studying. Then focus your attention solely on your assignment. Avoid distractions.

CHAPTER OVERVIEW

Since the information in this chapter can prove immediately useful to students and can help them to grasp the material covered in other chapters, you may want to cover this section during the first week or two of class. In addition to helping students academically, a review of study skills and test-taking strategies can give you insight into students' abilities and attitudes and can provide an opportunity for you to become better acquainted with the class.

The chapter discusses and reinforces reading strategies, writing as a tool for learning, critical thinking skills, interpretation of graphics, study methods such as outlining and paraphrasing, and strategies for standardized tests and essay tests.

RESOURCES

RESOURCES

OBJECTIVES

- To choose appropriate reading rates for given situations
- To use the SQ3R study method to formulate and answer questions about reading material
- To analyze details in a reading passage

PROGRAM MANAGER

STRENGTHENING READING AND STUDY SKILLS

- **Independent Practice/ Reteaching** For additional practice and reinforcement, see **Reading Rates, The SQ3R Method, Stated and Implied Main Ideas, Making Inferences, Analyzing Graphics, Taking Notes, Classifying, Formal and Informal Outlines,** and **Paraphrases and Summaries** in *Academic and Workplace Skills,* pp. 69–77.

QUICK REMINDER

Ask students to identify study skills that have helped them to succeed.

984 *Reading, Studying, and Test Taking*

Strengthening Reading and Study Skills

Reading and Understanding

You will find it easier to keep focused and to remember what you read if you read with a purpose. Some common purposes for reading are

- to find specific details
- to find main ideas
- to understand and remember

When you need to deal with a variety of materials, adjust your rate of reading to suit your purpose.

READING RATES ACCORDING TO PURPOSE		
READING RATE	**PURPOSE**	**EXAMPLE**
Scanning	Reading for specific details	Searching a history chapter for the date on which a specific treaty was signed
Skimming	Reading for main points	Reviewing chapter headings in your health textbook the night before a quiz
Reading for mastery	Reading to understand and remember	Reading a new chapter in your science book before writing an outline

Writing to Learn

Your writing can be a very useful tool for learning. Writing helps you focus your thoughts, discover new ideas, record your observations, and plan your work. The following chart shows how you might use your writing as a method of learning.

- To identify evidence or reasoning used to make inferences and draw conclusions
- To interpret graphic information
- To create a graph
- To use graphic information to draw conclusions and predict outcomes
- To analyze note-taking methods
- To identify classifications

TYPE OF WRITING	PURPOSE	EXAMPLE
Freewriting	To help you focus your thoughts	Writing to connect ideas from today's history lecture and yesterday's reading
Autobiographies	To help you examine and express ideas about important events in your life	Writing about the day you learned an important lesson
Diaries	To help you recall impressions and express your feelings	Writing about a person you admire and want to emulate
Journals and Learning Logs	To help you record your observations, descriptions, solutions, and questions	Writing to keep a record of the progress of a Spanish writing project
	To help you present a problem, analyze it, and propose a solution	Writing about the way you plan to organize a history project

Using Word-Processing Tools for Writing

A word processor or a computer word-processing program can help you plan, draft, and edit your writing. These tools can make every step of the writing process easier.

Prewriting.   Typing is fast on a word processor. Revisions of rough notes or outlines can be made without retyping.

Writing First Drafts.   You can revise as often as you want. If you like, you can use the printer to produce a hard copy (or printout) with each new revision.

Evaluating.   The word processor lets you compare and evaluate different versions of your writing. Just save a copy of your document under a different name, and type your changes on this copy. Then, if you don't like the revisions, you still have the original.

INTEGRATING THE LANGUAGE ARTS

Studying and Writing. You may want to point out to students that many of the examples listed in the **Writing to Learn** chart are expressive, but remind students that they can also learn by writing for other purposes. For example, writing an informative piece on the Civil War might help students memorize facts about the war, and writing a persuasive essay might help students decide where they stand on a particular issue. Have students generate examples of informative, descriptive, and persuasive writing that can help them to learn.

TECHNOLOGY TIP

If students are not completely comfortable with personal computers, you may want to plan a field trip to the school's computer lab. Students should be guided individually through the procedures of opening a new file and naming it, creating a short document and saving it, and printing a hard copy. Then, demonstrate how to use the Cut and Paste tools to draft.

- To create a graphic organizer
- To paraphrase a poem

Revising.   Changes can be typed in easily and a clean copy printed out without having to repeat steps.

Proofreading.   Some word processors offer a feature that checks your spelling. Some have features that evaluate sentence structure and punctuation.

Publishing.   Final revisions are easy to make on a word processor. After proofreading the last version, it's simple to print a final copy. You can even print multiple copies on your printer.

Using the SQ3R Reading Method

Francis Robinson, an educational psychologist, developed a method of reading called SQ3R. There are five steps to using this SQ3R method.

S   *Survey* the entire study assignment. Look at all of the headings, scan material in boldface and italics, and take note of the information in the charts, outlines, and summaries.

Q   *Question* yourself. What should you know after completing your reading? Make a list of questions that you want to be able to answer after finishing your reading.

R   *Read* the material section by section. Think of answers to your questions as you read.

R   *Recite* in your own words answers to each of the questions you have identified.

R   *Review* the material by rereading quickly, looking over your questions, and recalling the answers.

The SQ3R reading method can help you convert routine assignments into more interesting and active reading sessions. If you respond actively to what you read, it will be easier for you to recall what you have read.

☞ REFERENCE NOTE: For study techniques to help with listening skills, see page 942.

CRITICAL THINKING

Evaluation. There are variations of the SQ3R study method. The PQ6R method, developed by Francis Robinson and adapted by Norma Kahn in *More Learning in Less Time,* includes the following steps: preview, question, read, recite, write, review, reflect, and review. Have students compare the two methods and decide which one they think would be more helpful to them.

Interpreting and Analyzing What You Read

The information in every essay, article, or textbook chapter that you read is organized into a logical pattern in which the ideas are related to one another. If you interpret and analyze these relationships, you will find it easier to think critically about what you read.

Stated Main Idea.   When you are looking for the main idea, you want to find the most important point that the writer makes. When the main idea is stated, the author expresses the major point clearly and directly. A stated main idea can often be found in one specific sentence in a written passage.

Implied Main Idea.   The main idea is sometimes implied, or suggested, rather than directly stated. To find an implied main idea, you will need to analyze the relationship of the details you are given. Then decide what general meaning is expressed by these combined details.

HOW TO FIND THE MAIN IDEA

- Skim the passage. (What topic do all of the sentences have in common?)
- Identify the general topic. (What's the passage about?)
- Identify what the passage really says about the topic. (What is the message of the passage as a whole?)
- Sum up the meaning of the passage in one clear sentence.
- Check back over the passage. If you have correctly identified the main idea, the details will support it.

 REFERENCE NOTE: For additional information on finding the main idea, whether stated or implied, see pages 67–69.

Reading to Find Relationships Among Details

To understand the meaning of a reading passage, you'll need to learn to identify details and understand how they are related to each other and to the main idea.

AT-RISK STUDENTS

Students may have difficulty applying themselves to looking for main ideas when they find reading material boring or irrelevant. Give students high-interest, relevant articles to read, and tell them to write sentences that express the main ideas of the articles. You could also have students identify facts and opinions presented in the articles.

RESOURCES

RESOURCES

987

Auditory Learners. Some students will benefit from hearing the reading passage read aloud. Pause after each paragraph to discuss the annotations in the students' textbook.

FINDING RELATIONSHIPS AMONG DETAILS	
Identify specific details.	What details answer specific questions such as *Who? What? When? Where? Why?* and *How?*
Distinguish between fact and opinion.	What information can be proved true (fact) or false? What statements express a personal belief or attitude (opinion)?
Identify similarities and differences.	Are there any details that are shown to be similar to or different from one another?
Understand cause and effect.	Is there an event that had an impact or effect on a later event?
Identify an order of organization.	In what kind of order are the details arranged—chronological order, spatial order, order of importance, or any other organizing pattern?

Reading Passage

On February 4, 1913, Rosa Parks was born in Tuskegee, Alabama. Her family later moved to Montgomery. Growing up, Ms. Parks saw the inequality in the treatment of African Americans in Montgomery. For instance, they had to sit in the back of a shoe store to try on shoes, even if every seat in the front of the store was vacant. Blacks also had to sit in the back section of buses or to stand if a white person wanted a seat. As an African American, Ms. Parks hated this injustice. In December of 1955, her feelings translated into action.

Sample Analysis

DETAIL: What are some places where African Americans encountered unfair treatment?
ANSWER: The passage cites examples from shoe stores and buses.

OPINION: How did Rosa Parks feel about the unfair treatment of blacks?
ANSWER: She hated the injustice of this treatment.

Ms. Parks was working at a tailor shop. One evening on the bus, wearily heading home, Ms. Parks refused to give up her seat to a white man. She was arrested for her refusal. After this incident, Ms. Parks decided to stop using the bus. She was soon joined in her boycott by thousands of African Americans in Montgomery. Many workers bravely risked their jobs by joining the boycott. Some white employers, however, preferred to give rides to their African American employees rather than do without their services.

The boycott lasted for 382 days and sparked the civil rights movement in America. The impact of this incident was like the first pebble of a landslide. Because she led the boycott, Ms. Parks was fired from her job and was harassed. She moved to Detroit in 1957 and was hired by Congressman John Conyers. She worked for him for more than twenty years. In 1987, she founded the Rosa and Raymond Parks Institute for Self Development.

Rosa Parks can be cited to refute those who say that the actions of one person cannot make a difference. Rosa Parks's actions took courage as well as faith that her demand for justice would not be in vain.

FACT: When did Rosa Parks refuse to be treated unfairly on the bus?
ANSWER: She refused to give up her seat in December of 1955.

SIMILARITY: How was the response of African Americans in Montgomery similar to the reaction of Rosa Parks?
ANSWER: Many black people in Montgomery also refused to ride the bus.

CAUSE AND EFFECT: What was the effect of this boycott?
ANSWER: It encouraged other civil rights protests.

ORDER: In the course of her life, where did Rosa Parks live?
ANSWER: She was born in Tuskegee, Alabama; later, she lived and worked in Montgomery, Alabama; and finally, she worked for a congressman in Detroit, Michigan.

Applying Reasoning Skills to Your Reading

It's important to interpret and evaluate the evidence and facts that you gather from your reading. When you draw **conclusions** and make **inferences,** you come to a decision by evaluating, interpreting, and analyzing the facts and evidence.

RESOURCES

MEETING *individual* **NEEDS**

LESS-ADVANCED STUDENTS

Setting aside time each day for independent reading will show your students that you think reading is important, and it will also give students time to practice their reading skills. Allow students to bring reading materials to class each day and allot ten minutes of class time for independent reading. You will probably want to have plenty of high-interest selections available for those who forget to bring something to read.

RESOURCES

You may want to compare the process of drawing conclusions from reading passages to the process of drawing conclusions based on scientific experiments. Ask a student volunteer to describe an experiment and the conclusion that was reached through the experiment.

For example, based on your analysis of the reading passage on pages 988–989, you might make the following conclusions or inferences about Rosa Parks.

> Many people shared Parks's hatred of the unequal treatment of African Americans. (Evidence: Thousands joined her in her boycott of the bus system—a protest that might have cost them their jobs.)

> Americans today benefit from Rosa Parks's act of courage. (Evidence: Rosa Parks's action marked the beginning of the civil rights movement, which had the goal of fairer treatment for all people, regardless of race, creed, or gender.)

A *valid* conclusion is a conclusion that is firmly grounded in facts, evidence, or logic. An *invalid* conclusion is one that doesn't follow reasonably or logically from the evidence. For example, it is invalid to conclude that Rosa Parks refused to give up her seat because of a sudden impulse. This conclusion is not consistent with facts stated in the reading passage about her lifelong hatred of the injustice in the treatment of black people.

When you draw conclusions and make inferences, you are doing what a detective does to solve a mystery.

HOW TO DRAW CONCLUSIONS OR MAKE INFERENCES	
Gather all the evidence.	What facts or details have you learned about the subject?
Evaluate the evidence.	Do you know enough to judge information without jumping to conclusions or making invalid assumptions?
Make reasonable connections.	Based on evidence you have gathered and evaluated, what connections can you make? What conclusions can you draw?

Reading Graphics and Illustrations

Many of your textbooks—as well as articles from newspapers and magazines—include diagrams, maps, graphs, and illustrations. Visuals such as these make information clear and easy to understand.

Paragraphs full of detailed information can be difficult to read and to remember. Graphs or diagrams are often much easier to understand. Graphics and illustrations help you understand the relationships between one set of facts and another. For example, the bar graph below shows the percentage of the U.S. population between ages five and seventeen from 1900 to 1980.

Percentage of U.S. Population Aged 5 to 17

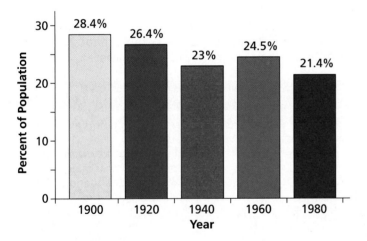

From this graph you can quickly compare the percentage of school-age children, measured in twenty-year periods, in the United States over the course of this century.

Suppose you were a television producer who was trying to decide whether to plan for an increase or decrease of programming for school-age children over the years after 2000. By looking at the graph, you could quickly see that the percentage of people of school age has shown an overall decrease over this century. You could reasonably assume that this trend would continue, and so you could plan for programming that focuses on other age groups.

Graphs such as the one above can help you make decisions more easily. They help you to see the relationship among items of data.

RESOURCES

RESOURCES

INTEGRATING THE LANGUAGE ARTS

Studying and Writing. Compare the study methods described here—taking notes, classifying, and outlining—to the prewriting process by emphasizing the similarities between organizing information for writing and organizing information for study. Organization helps writers to understand and communicate what they are writing about. It also helps students to learn and recall new information.

LEP/ESL

General Strategies. Taking lecture notes can prove difficult and frustrating for many students. First of all, it is especially difficult to control the listening experience. Except in an interview situation, students cannot ask speakers to slow down, and they are therefore likely to miss important information. Second, it is often difficult for students to understand main ideas because they have to determine the meaning of new vocabulary. They will often try to record verbatim the information they hear, which often results in further frustration. Depending on the students' proficiency levels, note-taking skills could be practiced and reinforced, or students could be encouraged to tape-record lectures.

Applying Study and Reading Strategies

Various reading and study methods can be used to organize and handle information. Some of the most common are

- taking notes
- classifying
- organizing information visually
- outlining
- paraphrasing
- summarizing
- memorizing

Taking Notes

If you take careful notes when you read or listen to a lecture, your information will be better organized when you study, take tests, or write research papers.

HOW TO TAKE STUDY NOTES	
Recognize and record main points.	Set off main points as headings in your notes. ■ In a lecture, key words and phrases such as *major* or *most important* and similar clues may indicate key points. ■ In a textbook, chapter headings and subheadings are usually reliable clues about main ideas.
Summarize.	Don't write down every detail. Instead, summarize or abbreviate, using key words or phrases to note main ideas. Indent supporting points.
Note important examples.	Make notes of a few meaningful examples. They can help you remember the main ideas.

On page 993 are sample study notes that a careful student might make about the reading passage on pages 988–989. Note that the main points in the passage are identified and then arranged in groups. Each of these groups of main points is given a heading that identifies the key idea.

Rosa Parks

Biography

- African American, born Feb. 4, 1913—Tuskegee, Ala.
- grew up in Montgomery, Ala.
- despised injustice in treatment of blacks
- incident in Dec. 1955 started bus boycott
- fired from her tailoring job because of boycott
- hired by congressman in Michigan—worked for him for more than 20 years
- 1987—founded Rosa and Raymond Parks Inst. for Self Development

Examples of Inequality in Treatment

- had to sit at back of shoe stores
- had to sit at back of buses
- had to stand if white person wanted seat on bus

Details of Montgomery Bus Boycott

- Ms. Parks refused to give up seat to white man
- Ms. Parks arrested for her refusal
- Ms. Parks stopped using the bus
- thousands joined her boycott of bus system
- many risked jobs
- many employers gave rides instead of losing workers
- boycott lasted 382 days
- sparked American civil rights movement

MEETING *individual* NEEDS

LEARNING STYLES

Visual Learners. You may want to suggest that students use color-coding in their notes to organize ideas or to emphasize important points. For example, they might highlight anything a speaker repeats or otherwise indicates is important.

Classifying

Classification is organizing information by arranging items into categories. You use classification when you make an outline, deciding which supporting ideas fit together under a major heading. In order to group things, you need to identify relationships among them.

EXAMPLE   What do the following people have in common? Dolly Madison, Bess Truman, Betty Ford, Barbara Bush
ANSWER   They are all former first ladies of the United States.

You also use classification when you identify patterns in data. For example, look at the relationship of the following items.

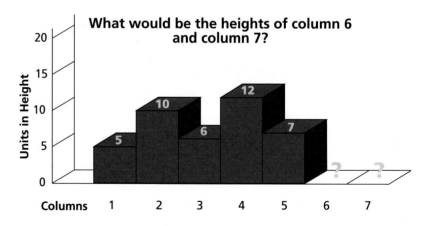

ANSWER   The pattern is for even-numbered columns (columns 2 and 4) to be double the height of the columns that precede them (columns 1 and 3), while odd-numbered columns (1, 3, and 5) increase by one unit in height. The next column, column 6, should be double the height of column 5, or <u>fourteen units high</u>. Column 7 would then be <u>eight units high</u>.

Organizing Information Visually

Mapping, diagraming, and charting organize new information so that it is visually presented. This makes the information easier to understand.

For example, the passage that follows is full of literary terms. It contrasts two types of sonnets.

> A sonnet is defined as a poem containing fourteen lines, usually written in rhymed, iambic pentameter. Sonnets are generally classified into two types: the Petrarchan, or Italian, sonnet and the Shakespearean, or English, sonnet. Originating in Italy in the fourteenth century, the Petrarchan sonnet has two parts, an octave (eight lines) and a sestet (six lines). Often, the octave raises a poetic question that the sestet answers. This type of sonnet is usually rhymed *abba abba cdecde*. The second type of sonnet, the Shakespearean sonnet, consists of three stanzas of four lines each and a concluding couplet. This type of sonnet usually uses the rhyme scheme *abab cdcd efef gg*. Often the final rhyming couplet provides a statement that summarizes or concludes the poem by making an emphatic point about its theme.

It would be difficult to remember all the details in this reading passage. However, if you organize the information visually by mapping the details, you will find the information easier to remember.

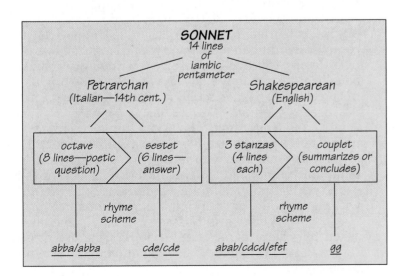

INTEGRATING THE LANGUAGE ARTS

Literature Link. You may want to take this opportunity to review the sonnet form. Have students read a sonnet, such as "Shall I Compare Thee to a Summer's Day?" by William Shakespeare, and ask them to identify it as either an Italian or an English sonnet. Then, ask students if the poem conforms to all of the conventions given in the passage for that type of sonnet.

RESOURCES

RESOURCES

Outlining

An *outline* organizes ideas and information. When you make an outline, you identify the most important information and ideas in a passage. Then you group all these ideas into an organized pattern that shows their order and their relationship to one another.

Sometimes, however, as with lecture notes, you may want to use an informal outline form. This method of arranging notes allows you to organize information very quickly. (See an example in the study notes on page 993.)

FORMAL OUTLINE FORM

1. Main Point
  A. Supporting Point
    1. Detail
      a. Information
        or detail

INFORMAL OUTLINE FORM

Main Idea
  Supporting detail
  Supporting detail
  Supporting detail

Paraphrasing

When you *paraphrase,* you restate someone else's ideas in your own words. Paraphrasing is a good way to check your understanding of what you read, especially if the original is written in poetic or elaborate language (such as complex wording in a poem or poetic language in a scene from a play by Shakespeare). A written paraphrase is usually approximately the same length as the original, so this technique is generally not used for very lengthy passages of writing.

As you read things that you think are difficult to understand, paraphrase what you read by putting these ideas into your own words in your study notes. Your paraphrased version might include dialect or slang expressions if you feel more comfortable with these than with the wording of the original expressions.

Or, in language arts classes, you may sometimes be asked to write a paraphrase of a short literary passage, such as a poem. Use the following guidelines to help you paraphrase.

HOW TO PARAPHRASE

1. Be sure you understand what the material means. Look up any unfamiliar words.
2. Identify the main idea of the selection. Keep it in mind while you write your paraphrase.
3. Identify the speaker in fictional material. (Is the poet or author speaking, or is it a narrator or a character?)
4. Write out your paraphrase in your own words, remembering to use complete sentences and traditional paragraph form.
5. Check to be sure that your paraphrase expresses the same idea as the original.

Here is an example of a poem to be paraphrased.

Sick Leave
by Po Chü-i[1] (translated by Arthur Waley)

Propped on pillows, not attending to business;
For two days I've lain behind locked doors.
I begin to think that those who hold office
Get no rest, except by falling ill!
For restful thoughts one does not need space;
The room where I lie is ten foot square.
By the western eaves, above the bamboo twigs,
From my couch I see the White Mountain rise.
But the clouds that hover on its far-distant peak
Bring shame to a face that is buried in the World's dust.

[1] Po Chü-i (pō'chō͞o'ē)

Following is one possible paraphrase of the poem.

A Chinese government official is home, sitting up in bed. He is thinking about all of his work that is not getting done. The official has been sick for two days, and he has apparently locked himself in his room to remain undisturbed. He states that he believes getting sick is probably the only way that people who have official responsibilities ever get any time off.

INTEGRATING THE LANGUAGE ARTS

Literature Link. To give students practice in paraphrasing, have them paraphrase a poem as a class. Then, have a student read the paraphrase aloud and have another student present the poem. Lead a discussion of how the students' paraphrase differs from the poem. Students might notice that their paraphrase does not convey the same mood, tone, or even meaning as the poem. Help students see how the poet's choice and placement of words affects the poem.

Studying and Writing. Point out to students that the ability to paraphrase will be useful to them when they are taking notes for research papers. Remind students that even when they paraphrase information, they must always give credit for other people's ideas.

RESOURCES

RESOURCES

His room is very small, only ten feet by ten feet, but he comments that since all he is doing is resting and thinking, he does not need a large room. His room is on the west side of a house high enough to be above the growing bamboo. From his window, he can see the White Mountain rising above the clouds. He contemplates the contrast between the mountain, as it rises high above the pressures of life, and his own life, as it is burdened down by these pressures.

You will use paraphrasing when you write research reports. Remember, however, that you must cite your sources when you use someone else's ideas.

☞ REFERENCE NOTE: For more about paraphrasing in research reports, see pages 421–422.

Summarizing

A *summary* restates the main points of a passage in condensed form. A summary, or *précis*, helps you identify and remember the most important points of the material you are studying. When you write a summary, it is necessary for you to analyze the material in order to decide what is most important and should be included in the summary, and what can be left out.

HOW TO SUMMARIZE
1. Skim the material and identify the main ideas.
2. Review the passage and look for supporting details.
3. Write a sentence in your own words about each main idea. Write approximately one sentence for each paragraph of the original.
4. Use your list of sentences to write your summary in standard paragraph form. Use transitional words between the ideas to show how the ideas are related.
5. Evaluate and revise your summary, checking to see if your summary covers key points. Make sure the reader can follow your ideas.

 CRITICAL THINKING

Evaluation. You may want to illustrate the differences between a summary and an evaluation. Write the two words on the chalkboard. Then, have the class choose a well-known movie to discuss. Ask a volunteer to summarize the movie briefly. Then, ask a volunteer to evaluate the movie, giving reasons for her or his views. Discuss with students the differences between the summary and the evaluation. Are there any value judgments included in the summary? Does the evaluation include a description of the movie's plot?

Here is a sample summary of the article on pages 402–404.

> Astronomy was closer to religion than science, to many American Indian peoples. They believed the planets and the stars were gods. Since they thought these gods affected every aspect of human life, these early astronomers struggled to learn the exact patterns of the movements of heavenly bodies. Then they recorded their findings. In some places, calendars were made of wood, stone, or string. In others, astronomical observances were written on folded, booklike forms made of hide or bark. In some places, buildings and cities were aligned with planetary sightlines. The earth, too, was believed to be a sacred being. Certain routes were thought to be holy. Lines, such as the Nazca Lines in Peru, may also have had religious significance.

Memorizing

Frequent, short, focused sessions of practice are best when you are trying to memorize material. It is not very efficient to cram, because you will not retain the information well.

HOW TO MEMORIZE	
Condense the information, if possible.	If you're studying reading material, such as a chapter, passages can often be summarized or condensed.
Rehearse the material in several different ways.	Use several different senses. Copy or write the material so you can see it as well as touch it. Say it out loud so you can hear it.
Play memory games.	Make a word out of the initials of key terms or use other creative ways to make the information more memorable.

A DIFFERENT APPROACH

Ask students to think about a time when they read a novel or a short story and visualized its characters and scenes. Then, ask students to speculate about whether the same kind of visualization and sensory involvement might help them learn new material. [When studying science material, a student might visualize an experiment, perhaps recalling the smell of a chemical. When studying history notes, a student might visualize the events being studied, as if she or he were watching a movie. When studying any subject, the student can practice recalling a teacher's instruction by recalling the sounds, smells, and sights of the classroom.]

RESOURCES

RESOURCES

999

OBJECTIVES

- To complete analogies
- To identify key verbs in essay questions and to state the kinds of information needed to answer those essay questions

IMPROVING TEST-TAKING SKILLS

- **Independent Practice/ Reteaching** For additional practice and reinforcement, see **Analogy Questions** and **Essay Tests** in *Academic and Workplace Skills,* pp. 78–79.

QUICK REMINDER

Ask students to brainstorm ideas for overcoming test anxiety. Then, have students give you their ideas orally. Write the ideas on the chalkboard. Discuss with students which ideas work best for them and which ideas they would like to try.

LEP/ESL

General Strategies. One way to begin this segment on test-taking skills is to initiate class discussion. How do students feel about taking tests? What kinds of past experiences have contributed to these feelings? Some students need to be encouraged to examine and express their feelings and to trust that the classroom environment is a safe place to do so. An open class discussion often serves as an icebreaker and underscores the fact that you, as a teacher, believe all of your students have something valid to contribute.

RESOURCES

RESOURCES

1000 *Reading, Studying, and Test Taking*

Improving Test-Taking Skills

Preparing Yourself

Your attitude is an important factor in doing well on a test. It's normal to feel nervous before a big test. However, you can channel this nervous energy productively if you concentrate on your test performance.

HOW TO PREPARE FOR A TEST

Analyze your preparedness. Decide early what you need to study most, then study thoroughly.

Focus on the test. During the test, as you read and answer the questions, concentrate on what you know, not anything else. Don't allow yourself to be distracted.

Make a commitment. Keep trying until you find the right study method for you.

Preparing for Standardized Tests

A *standardized test* is one in which your score is evaluated in comparison with a "standard" that is compiled from the scores of many other students nationwide who have taken the same test. There are two common kinds: achievement and aptitude tests.

Achievement tests are designed to measure how much you know about specific subjects, such as biology or Spanish. Aptitude tests evaluate your basic skills in various areas of study, such as reading comprehension or vocabulary skills.

Standardized tests often cover material you have learned during many years of study. To prepare for most standardized tests, it's best to improve your overall study habits: read often, write frequently, increase your vocabulary steadily, and use the study skills described earlier in this chapter. In addition, there are some short-term preparations you can make to improve your performance.

HOW TO PREPARE FOR STANDARDIZED TESTS

Learn what skills will be tested on the specific test you plan to take. Information booklets may be provided that tell about the types of questions and how the test is scored. Practice with these or with published study guides available through bookstores or libraries.

Know what materials you need for the test. For the test, you may need to bring specific materials, such as number 2 pencils or pens and a prepared examination booklet of lined paper for an essay answer.

Determine how this test scores answers. If there is no penalty for wrong answers, you should make your best guess on all questions possible. If wrong answers are penalized, make guesses only if you are fairly sure of your answer.

Objective Tests

Two basic types of tests are *objective* and *essay tests.* Certain strategies can help you with each type.

There are many types of objective tests. They may include multiple-choice, true/false, matching, reasoning or logic, or short-answer questions. Although they appear in many forms, all objective questions have one characteristic in common: There is usually only one correct answer.

HOW TO STUDY FOR OBJECTIVE TESTS

1. Review the study questions in your textbook, and skim class notes to identify important terms or facts.
2. Review the information in more than one form. For example, if you are responsible for knowing a list of important terms, test yourself on how well you can define each one of the terms without looking at your book or notes.
3. Practice and repeat factual information. Use flashcards to see if you can remember the correct terms. Identify difficult items and review them.

RESOURCES

AT-RISK STUDENTS

Students may be discouraged by a history of poor performances on tests, and they may think that their past poor performances mean that they are incapable of academic success. You may want to let students know that even people who are famous for their intelligence and ability have received poor evaluations at some time in their lives. Winston Churchill, for example, failed the sixth grade, and Albert Einstein had poor grades in mathematics when he was in high school.

RESOURCES

A DIFFERENT APPROACH

To help students to develop self-confidence and reduce stress before a test, teach them the following exercise:

Close your eyes and picture your teacher distributing the test. Take a deep breath through your nose and then exhale slowly through your mouth. Picture that the test is on your desk. You glance through it and find no surprises. Remember, you have prepared for the test. Picture picking up your pencil and marking or writing correct answers. Now, move forward in time. Visualize your test being returned to you with a good grade on it.

Tell students that they can do this exercise before any test that they feel anxious about.

Adapt your study strategies to suit the specific type of objective test you will be taking. For example, if your test includes a map you'll have to label, test yourself by labeling a practice version.

Taking Different Kinds of Objective Tests

At the beginning of an objective test, scan the test quickly to count the number of test items. Then decide how to budget your time. For each type of objective test question, use the following specific, effective strategies.

Multiple-Choice Questions.   Multiple-choice questions ask you to select a correct answer from among a given number of choices.

EXAMPLE   **1.** After she was arrested for refusing to yield her seat on a bus, Rosa Parks
   (A) decided to stop using the bus system.
   B was elected to Congress.
   C moved to Tuskegee, Alabama.
   D married Raymond Parks.

HOW TO ANSWER MULTIPLE-CHOICE QUESTIONS	
Read the initial statement carefully.	▪ Make sure you understand this statement before examining the choices. ▪ Look for qualifiers such as *not* or *always* since these—and other, similar terms—limit the answers.
Read all the answers before making a choice.	▪ Narrow the choices by eliminating incorrect answers. Some answers may be clearly wrong, while others may only be somewhat related to the correct answer. ▪ Seek the most correct choice. Some choices (such as "Both A and B" or "All of the above") affect your other choices.

True/False Questions. You are asked to determine whether a given statement is correct.

EXAMPLE   **1.**   T ⓕ The percentage of school-age children in the United States has increased over this century.

HOW TO ANSWER TRUE/FALSE QUESTIONS

Read the statement carefully.	■ If any part of the statement is false, the whole statement is false.
Check for qualifiers.	■ Words such as *always* or *never* qualify or limit a statement. ■ A statement is true only if it is wholly and always true.

Matching Questions.   In matching questions, two lists are placed near each other so that you may match items on one list with those on the other.

Directions: Match the term in the left-hand column with its description in the right-hand column.

_D_ **1.** Shakespearean sonnet   **A** group of eight rhymed lines of a sonnet
_C_ **2.** couplet   **B** Italian sonnet
_A_ **3.** octave   **C** group of two rhymed lines in a sonnet
_B_ **4.** Petrarchan sonnet   **D** English sonnet

HOW TO ANSWER MATCHING QUESTIONS

Read the directions carefully.	Sometimes answers may be used more than once.
Scan the columns and match items you know first.	You can gain more time to evaluate items you are less sure about.
Complete the matching process.	Make your best reasoned guess on remaining items.

COMMON ERROR

Problem. Some students worry that they must be wrong if they end up with a pattern of true/false answers or have marked too many of one or the other kind.

Solution. You may want to advise students to ignore any pattern that develops, to rely on their knowledge, and, if necessary, to make informed guesses.

TIMESAVER

You may want to survey students to find out which types of test questions are most difficult for them so that you can focus primarily on those types of questions.

RESOURCES

RESOURCES

1003

Reasoning or Logic Questions. Some questions (especially on standardized tests) may test your reasoning abilities more than they test your knowledge of a specific subject. These questions often ask you to identify the relationship between several items (such as words, pictures, or numbers), or they may ask you to predict what the next item in a series should be.

Reasoning questions might ask you to identify a pattern in a number sequence (for example: 3, 9, 27, 81—these are squares of the number 3). Or, you might be asked to predict the next item in a sequence of drawings.

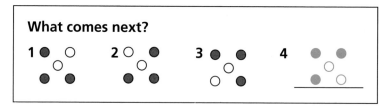

In this sequence of drawings, the two white dots are pointed outwards, moving counter-clockwise around the configuration of dots. Therefore, in the fourth frame the white dots should point toward the bottom right.

HOW TO ANSWER REASONING OR LOGIC QUESTIONS	
Be sure you understand the instructions.	On standardized tests, reasoning or logic questions are usually multiple-choice. On some other tests, you may need to write a word or phrase, write out a number sequence, or draw your answer.
Analyze the relationship implied in the question.	Look at the question carefully to gather information about the relationship of the items.
Draw reasonable conclusions.	Evaluate the relationship of the items as a basis for your decision.

Analogy Questions. Analogy questions are special types of reasoning and logic questions that ask you to analyze the relationship between one pair of words and to identify or to supply a second pair of words that has the same relationship.

Analogy questions usually appear on standardized tests in multiple-choice form, but sometimes they appear as fill-in-the-blank questions.

EXAMPLE   **1.** Directions: Select the appropriate pair of words to complete the analogy.

DRESS : CLOTHING :: _____

A wheel : car
B page : read
(C) bicycle : vehicle
D world : round

EXAMPLE   **2.** Directions: Complete the following analogy.

SHOWER : CLEAN :: mud : _*dirty*_____

HOW TO ANSWER ANALOGY QUESTIONS	
Analyze the first pair of words.	Identify the relationship between the first two items. (In Example 1, a *dress* is a kind of *clothing;* this is an analogy of classification. See the Analogy Chart on pages 1006–1007.)
Express the analogy in sentence or question form.	Example 1 could be read as "A *dress* is a kind of *clothing,* just as . . . (what other pair of items among the choices given?)."
Find the best available choice to complete the analogy.	▪ If choices are given, select the pair of words with the same relationship between them as the first pair. ▪ If you must fill in a blank to complete an analogy, you may be asked to supply the final word. (Using Example 2, a *shower* makes you *clean.* What would *mud* make you? You would be *dirty.*)

INTEGRATING THE LANGUAGE ARTS

Literature Link. Point out to students that metaphors and similes are figures of speech that draw analogies—they describe or explain things by comparing them to other things. Write the definitions of *metaphor* and *simile* on the chalkboard.

Then, have students read a poem, such as "Courage" by Anne Sexton, that contains several metaphors and similes. Ask students to list the comparisons made in the poem and to identify each as either a metaphor or a simile. ["Courage" includes the following comparisons: the child's first step—earthquake (simile), courage—small coal (metaphor), love—shaving soap (simile), heart—sock (simile), spring—sword (metaphor).]

You might want to challenge students to create original metaphors and similes. If students have read "Courage," you could have them write alternate comparisons for *the child's first step, courage, love, heart,* and *spring.*

ANALOGY CHART		
TYPE	EXAMPLE	SOLUTION
Synonyms	ROUND : CIRCULAR :: strong : muscular	*Round* is similar in meaning to *circular,* just as *strong* is like *muscular.*
Antonyms	PATRIOT : TRAITOR :: loyal : unfaithful	A *patriot* is the opposite of a *traitor,* just as *loyal* means the opposite of *unfaithful.*
Cause	VIRUS : SICKNESS :: water : dampness	A *virus* causes *sickness,* just as *water* causes *dampness.*
Effect	TEARS : SORROW :: smiles : joy	*Tears* are the effect of *sorrow,* just as *smiles* are the effect of *joy.*
Part to Whole	DROPLETS : SEA :: grains : desert	*Droplets* (of water) make up a *sea,* just as *grains* (of sand) make up a *desert.*
Whole to Part	WALL : BRICKS :: deck : cards	A *wall* contains *bricks,* just as a *deck* contains *cards.*
Classification	BAGEL : BREAD :: pork : meat	A *bagel* is a type of *bread,* just as *pork* is a type of *meat.*
Characteristics	PUPPIES : FURRY :: fish : slippery	*Puppies* feel *furry,* just as *fish* feel *slippery.*
Degree	COLOSSAL : LARGE :: microscopic : small	*Colossal* means *very large,* just as *microscopic* means *very small.*
Use	DESK : STUDY :: bed : sleep	A *desk* is used to *study,* just as a *bed* is used to *sleep.*

(continued)

ANALOGY CHART *(continued)*		
TYPE	EXAMPLE	SOLUTION
Measure	BAROMETER : AIR PRESSURE :: scale : weight	A *barometer* is used to measure *air pressure*, just as a *scale* is used to measure *weight*.
Action to Performer	TEACHING : PROFESSOR :: cleaning : maid	*Teaching* is the action performed by a *professor*, just as *cleaning* is the action performed by a *maid*.
Performer to Action	AUTHOR : WRITE :: chef : cook	An *author's* profession is to *write*, just as a *chef's* profession is to *cook*.
Place	SPACE NEEDLE : SEATTLE :: Lincoln Memorial : Washington, D.C.	The *Space Needle* is in *Seattle*, just as the *Lincoln Memorial* is in *Washington, D.C.*

Short-Answer Questions. Answers to short-answer questions should show your knowledge of the subject. Like other objective questions, short-answer questions usually have only one correct answer. However, you do not have a choice of answers: You have to write out your response.

Some short-answer questions (such as a diagram, a map, or a fill-in-the-blank question) can be answered with one or a few words. In another type of short-answer question, you are asked a question and you must write a full response, usually one or two sentences in length.

EXAMPLE   Describe briefly the comparison made at the end of Po Chü-i's poem "Sick Leave."

ANSWER   *The speaker contrasts himself with the mountain he sees from his sickroom window. The mountain is above the world's cares, while he is buried beneath them.*

COOPERATIVE LEARNING

Suggest to students that they study in groups of three or four for short-answer tests. Each group could begin with a list of topics to be studied for the test. Then, taking one topic at a time, each group member in turn could add a fact about the topic, until no one can add any more information. All group members should take notes on the contributions of other members and use the notes when studying.

A DIFFERENT APPROACH

Have students bring their science or history textbooks to class. Ask them to use material in chapters they are currently studying to create short-answer quizzes that will help them review for an upcoming test.

HOW TO RESPOND TO SHORT-ANSWER QUESTIONS	
Read the question carefully.	Some questions have more than one part, and you will have to include an answer to each part to receive full credit.
Plan your answer.	Briefly, decide what you need to include in the answer.
Be as specific as possible in your answers.	Give a full, exact answer.
Budget your time.	Begin by answering all of the questions you are certain about. Return later to the questions you are less sure about.

Essay Tests

Essay tests ask you to think critically about material you have learned and to express your understanding of that material in an organized way. You will be expected to write at least a full paragraph, if not several paragraphs, in answer.

HOW TO STUDY FOR ESSAY TESTS

1. Review your textbook carefully.
2. Make an outline, identifying main points and key details.
3. Make a practice set of possible questions on your own and practice writing out the answers.
4. Evaluate and revise your practice answers, checking your notes and textbook for accuracy and the writing chapters of this textbook for help in writing.

Taking Essay Tests

Before you start writing on an essay test, scan the questions quickly. Make sure you know how many answers you are expected to write. If you have a choice between several items, decide which one or ones you think you can answer best. Then plan how much time to spend on each answer, and stay on this schedule.

Read the question carefully. There may be several parts to the answer.

Pay attention to important terms in the question. Essay questions usually ask you to perform specific tasks. A verb expresses each one of these tasks. It helps to become familiar with each key verb. Each one identifies the tasks that you will need to accomplish in a good essay response.

ESSAY TEST QUESTIONS		
KEY VERB	TASK	SAMPLE QUESTION
argue	Take a viewpoint on an issue and give reasons to support this opinion.	Argue whether or not your school should require all students to participate in extra-curricular activities.
analyze	Take something apart to see how each part works.	Analyze the central character in Edgar Allan Poe's "The Tell-Tale Heart."
compare	Point out likenesses.	Compare George Washington Carver and Thomas Edison as inventors.
contrast	Point out differences.	Contrast the economic conditions in the South and in the North at the end of the Civil War.
define	Give specific details that make something unique.	Define the term *colonialism* as it applies to America's early history.
demonstrate (also illustrate, present, show)	Provide examples to support a point.	Demonstrate that a line intersecting parallel lines produces equivalent angles.
describe	Give a picture in words.	Describe the eulogy scene in *Julius Caesar*.

(continued)

MEETING *individual* NEEDS

STUDENTS WITH SPECIAL NEEDS

Students may need to see the meanings of these key verbs illustrated in concrete terms. Bring an apple and an orange to class and use these fruits to illustrate each verb. For example, to illustrate *argue,* offer an opinion as to which fruit is better and give reasons to support your opinion. To illustrate *analyze,* cut the apple and the orange in half to examine the parts that make up the whole fruits. To illustrate *compare,* point out the similarities between the apple and the orange. Continue this process for each key verb.

RESOURCES

A DIFFERENT APPROACH

You may want to give students practice in composing their own essay questions. This activity is especially useful for the study of supplementary reading material. To spark their interest, let students write essay questions on materials they are reading independently or for another class.

ESSAY TEST QUESTIONS *(continued)*		
KEY VERB	**TASK**	**SAMPLE QUESTION**
discuss	Examine in detail.	Discuss the term *manifest destiny.*
explain	Give reasons.	Explain why the United States entered World War II.
identify	Point out specific persons, places, things, or characteristics.	Identify the leaders of the Confederacy and their importance in the Civil War.
interpret	Give the meaning or significance of something.	Interpret the role of Cesar Chavez in organizing the farm labor movement.
list (also outline, trace)	Give all steps in order or all details about a subject.	List the events leading up to the Montgomery bus boycott.
summarize	Give a brief overview of the main points.	Summarize the plot of Bernard Malamud's short story "A Summer's Reading."

Take a moment to use prewriting strategies. After considering the key verbs in the question, make notes or a simple outline to help you decide what you want to say. Write the notes or outline on scratch paper.

Evaluate and revise as you write. You probably will not be able to redraft your whole essay. However, you can edit your essay to strengthen it.

QUALITIES OF A GOOD ESSAY ANSWER

- The essay is well organized.
- The main ideas and supporting points are clearly presented.
- The sentences are complete and well written.
- There are no distracting errors in spelling, punctuation, or grammar.

Review

EXERCISE 1   **Choosing an Appropriate Reading Rate**

Identify the reading rate that best fits each of the given situations.

1. You are looking through a list of ZIP Codes to find the code for Scranton, Pennsylvania.   **1. scanning**
2. You are looking through a library book to see if it would be a good resource for a research paper on Pedro   **2. scanning** Menéndez de Avilés, founder of St. Augustine, Florida.
3. You have a 100-question, multiple-choice test tomorrow on a chapter in your science textbook that you have already read but need to review.   **3. skimming**
4. You are reading a chapter in your literature book for a class discussion tomorrow and a test in two weeks.
5. You are reading instructions on a standardized test to see how much time is allowed for a section of the test.
   4. reading for mastery   5. scanning

EXERCISE 2   **Applying the SQ3R Reading Method**

Use the SQ3R method while reading a newspaper article or a chapter that you need to read for a class. List at least five questions that you might be asked on a test about the material and write brief answers to each one.

EXERCISE 3   **Reading: Analyzing Details in a Passage**

Answer the following questions about the reading passage on pages 988–989.

1. Give two facts about Rosa Parks (other than those already noted in the sample analysis).
2. What was the reaction of other African Americans to Rosa Parks's actions?
3. What were the effects of the Montgomery bus boycott— good or bad—on Rosa Parks's life?
4. What is the impact of the Montgomery bus boycott compared to?
5. What order is used to arrange the details of the first three paragraphs of the passage?

RESOURCES

ANSWERS
Exercise 2

Questions and answers will vary. Students should ask pertinent questions that could serve as useful study guides.

ANSWERS
Exercise 3

Answers may vary. Here are some possibilities:

1. Rosa Parks was born in Tuskegee, Alabama.
   Rosa Parks was born on February 4, 1913.
2. Thousands of African Americans joined Rosa Parks in the bus boycott and participated in the civil rights movement sparked by her actions.
3. Ms. Parks, as a result of starting the boycott, was fired from her tailoring job but was hired for a much better job as an assistant to a congressman.
4. The impact of the boycott is compared to a pebble that starts a landslide.
5. Chronological order is used to arrange the details of the first three paragraphs.

RESOURCES

ANSWERS

Exercise 4

Answers may vary. Here are some possibilities:

1. The bus driver had her arrested. Her boss fired her.

2. The passage states that she was weary after work.

3. The boycott sparked the civil rights movement in the United States.

4. Many employers took time to give rides to their employees rather than hire someone who would ride the bus.

5. Rosa Parks faced opposition from members of the white community who had the power to arrest her and fire her, but she eventually overcame these obstacles.

▶ EXERCISE 4   **Reading: Drawing Conclusions and Making Inferences**

Using the reading passage on pages 988–989, identify the evidence or reasoning that you might use in order to make the following inferences or to draw the following conclusions.

1. Some people disagreed with Rosa Parks's refusal to obey the segregation laws.
2. Rosa Parks's job at the tailor shop was tiring.
3. People outside of Montgomery, Alabama, were aware of the bus boycott.
4. The services of many black employees were valued by their white employers.
5. Since a hero can be defined as someone who faces obstacles but manages to overcome them, Rosa Parks is a hero.

▶ EXERCISE 5   **Reading Graphic Information**

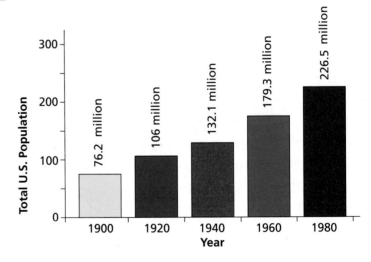

Historical Summary of Total U.S. Population

Look at the graph above, and then compare its information with that of the graph on page 991. Review both graphs to answer the following questions.

RESOURCES

1. Did the percentage of the population between the ages of five and seventeen increase or <u>decrease</u> between 1920 and 1940? By how much? **1.** by 3.4%
2. Did the percentage of the population between the ages of five and seventeen <u>increase</u> or decrease between 1940 and 1960? By how much? **2.** by 1.5%
3. Compare the percentage of the population between the ages of five and seventeen in the years 1960 and 1980. How much did this portion of the population increase or <u>decrease</u>? **3.** by 3.1%
4. Did the percentage of the population between the ages of five and seventeen increase or <u>decrease</u> between the years 1900 and 1980? **4.** by 7%

▶ EXERCISE 6 **Evaluating Graphic Information**

Study the numbers in the table below. Then follow the numbered instructions.

PERCENTAGE OF POPULATION ATTENDING HIGH SCHOOLS				
1900	1920	1940	1960	1980
3.3%	10.2%	26.0%	23.5%	32.9%

1. Using the graphs on page 991 and page 1012 as models, create a graph from the information in the table above.
2. Write a list of at least four conclusions you can draw from a point-by-point comparison of each of these three graphs. (You might look at your answers to Exercise 5 to suggest the type of questions you could ask.)
3. For each of the three graphs, make a prediction about the population figures for the year 2000.
4. Write a brief paragraph in which you discuss the observations and conclusions you have made. Cite specific information or identify evidence from the three graphs to support your findings.

RESOURCES

ANSWERS
Exercise 6

Graphs may vary.

1.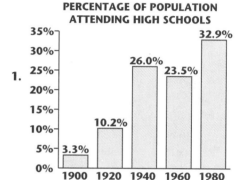

PERCENTAGE OF POPULATION ATTENDING HIGH SCHOOLS

2. Answers may vary. Here are some possibilities: **1.** Although the total U.S. population increased, the percentage of people between the ages of 5 and 17 decreased. **2.** Either the percentage of the population under 5 or the percentage over 17, or both, increased. **3.** Although the percentage of young people aged 5 to 17 decreased, the percentage of the population attending high school increased. **4.** Either the percentage of young people attending high school increased, or people from other age groups began attending high school.

3. Answers may vary. The percentage of the United States population that is aged 5 to 17 will be less than 20%; the total United States population will be over 250,000,000; the percentage of the United States population attending high school will be greater than 35%.

4. Paragraphs will vary. They should include the conclusions students have drawn and evidence to support the conclusions.

RESOURCES

ANSWERS
Exercise 7

Paragraphs will vary. Students should compare, contrast, and evaluate the note-taking methods. You might want to specify a length for students' paragraphs.

ANSWERS
Exercise 8

Answers may vary. Here are some possibilities:

1. devices to look through or devices that have lenses
2. different cuts of meat
3. prime numbers
4. forms of entertainment
5. ocean birds
6. books by Mark Twain
7. numbers separated by eleven
8. yellow things
9. sports
10. palindromes

1014

▶ EXERCISE 7   **Analyzing Your Note-Taking Method**

For one day, take notes in all of your classes by using the techniques suggested on pages 992–993. Write a paragraph comparing and contrasting your usual method and this new method. Be sure to address these points: How are the two methods similar? How are they different? Which works better? Why?

▶ EXERCISE 8   **Identifying Classifications**

For each of the following groups of items, describe the category.

1. telescope, binoculars, microscope, camera, periscope
2. T-bone, hamburger, filet mignon, pot roast, prime rib
3. 1, 2, 3, 5, 7, 11
4. television, movies, plays, concerts, musicals
5. albatross, pelican, sea gull, penguin, sandpiper
6. *The Adventures of Tom Sawyer, Adventures of Huckleberry Finn, The Innocents Abroad, The Prince and the Pauper*
7. 12, 23, 34, 45, 56, 67
8. butter, banana, blonde, canary, life raft
9. soccer, golf, tennis, field hockey, polo
10. tot, nun, deed, radar, pip

▶ EXERCISE 9   **Completing Analogies**

Consider the first relationship; then, write the word that best indicates the second relationship so that it parallels the first. There may be more than one correct answer.

EXAMPLE   **1.** CARPENTER : WOOD :: potter : _____
          1. *CARPENTER : WOOD :: potter : clay*

1. SHEEP : FLOCK :: cattle : ____   **1.** herd
2. BOSTON : MASSACHUSETTS :: Reno : ____   **2.** Nevada
3. DUCK : QUACK :: turkey : ____   **3.** gobble
4. OWL : WISE :: fox : ____   **4.** sly, crafty, or cunning
5. TROT : GALLOP :: jog : ____   **5.** run
6. LIZARD : REPTILE :: whale : ____   **6.** mammal
7. KEY : LOCK :: combination : ____   **7.** safe
8. THUNDERSTORM : RAIN :: blizzard : ____   **8.** snow
9. HAMMER : HIT :: saw : ____   **9.** cut
10. ARTIST : PAINT :: weaver : ____   **10.** thread *or* yarn

▶ EXERCISE 10   **Reading: Applying Visual Organization**

After reading the paragraph below, draw a visually organized representation of its contents. Then use your graphic to answer the numbered questions that follow the reading passage.

> There are four layers of the atmosphere above the earth's surface. The lowest layer is the troposphere. This layer touches the earth's surface and extends to about seventeen kilometers above sea level. Within this layer are all the known living things, almost all the air and moisture, and almost all the weather conditions of our planet. The stratosphere extends from the upper limit of the troposphere to approximately fifty kilometers above sea level. This layer is important because it contains almost all the ozone in the atmosphere. Ozone protects the inhabitants of the earth from the harmful effect of the sun's rays. Since very little weather occurs in the stratosphere, airplane pilots like to fly there to avoid storms at low altitudes. The mesosphere extends from about fifty kilometers to about eighty kilometers above sea level. The mesosphere has greatly varying temperatures. At its lower level, it drops to about 0°C, but at its upper level it drops to about −100°C. Meteor trails, those hot gas streaks left behind by extraterrestrial debris, occur in the mesosphere. The thermosphere extends from approximately eighty kilometers above sea level into outer space. The upper limit of the thermosphere may extend to a thousand kilometers above sea level. In the upper limits of the thermosphere the air is especially thin. This is the region of the atmosphere where artificial satellites orbit the earth.

1. What is the temperature range of the mesosphere?
2. How many kilometers above sea level is the top of the thermosphere?
3. Why is the stratosphere important?
4. Which sphere has the least air?
5. Where in the atmosphere does most weather occur?

RESOURCES

ANSWERS
Exercise 10

Distance Above Sea Level

above 1000 km	outer space
80–1000 km	thermosphere (very little air at upper limits; here, satellites orbit earth)
50–80 km	mesosphere (greatly varying temperatures: upper level, −100 degrees C; lower level, 0 degrees C)
17–50 km	stratosphere (almost all of the ozone in the atmosphere)
0–17 km	troposphere (all known living things; almost all air, moisture, and weather)
sea level	earth

1. −100 degrees to 0 degrees C
2. 1000 km
3. The stratosphere contains ozone, which protects the earth from the harmful rays of the sun.
4. the thermosphere
5. the troposphere

RESOURCES

ANSWERS
Exercise 11

Paraphrases will vary. Here is a possibility:

The speaker is a cloud talking about its various activities. It says it waters the thirsty flowers, taking the moisture from various bodies of water. It brings shade for plants when the sun is at its highest and hottest point. It drops dew on flowers that have closed during the night, when the earth spins around the sun. The cloud also brings hail whipping to the ground, making the ground white. Then it melts the hail with rain, and thunders as it goes by.

ANSWERS
Exercise 12

Answers may vary. Here are possibilities:

1. Identify the abilities of each man and show how their abilities are similar by referring to two crises.
2. Give reasons for your views on mandatory education.
3. Use words to create a picture of what happens during a major earthquake.
4. Point out likenesses between the characters of the two men.
5. Identify changes in Pip's character, listing them in the order in which they occur (chronological order).
6. Give examples of how the setting affects the action in the movie.
7. Give the steps of the water cycle in order, beginning with rain.
8. Tell how it is significant.
9. Examine at least three factors of economic conditions that played a part in causing the Civil War.
10. Identify the traits of a good mayoral candidate.

SELECTION AMENDMENT
Description of change: excerpted
Rationale: to focus on the concept of paraphrasing presented in this chapter

▶ EXERCISE 11 **Reading: Paraphrasing a Poem**

Read the following excerpt from a poem by Percy Bysshe Shelley. Then write a paraphrase of the poem.

> *from* The Cloud
> *by Percy Bysshe Shelley*
>
> I bring fresh showers for the thirsting flowers,
>   From the seas and the streams;
> I bear light shade for the leaves when laid
>   In their noonday dreams.
> From my wings are shaken the dews that waken
>   The sweet buds every one,
> When rocked to rest on their mother's breast,
>   As she dances about the sun.
> I wield the flail of the lashing hail,
>   And whiten the green plains under,
> And then again I dissolve it in rain,
>   And laugh as I pass in thunder.

▶ EXERCISE 12 **Analyzing Essay Questions**

Identify the <u>key verb</u> that states the specific task in the following essay questions. Do not write an essay. Just state briefly what you would need to do to answer the question.

1. <u>Compare</u> the leadership abilities of Richard M. Nixon and John F. Kennedy, citing two specific crises.
2. <u>Explain</u> your beliefs about mandatory education.
3. <u>Describe</u> the events of a major earthquake.
4. <u>Compare</u> the characters of Romeo and Tybalt in *Romeo and Juliet.*
5. <u>Trace</u> the changes in the character of Pip in Charles Dickens's novel *Great Expectations.*
6. <u>Show</u> how the setting affects the action in the movie *The Third Man.*
7. <u>List</u> the steps in the water cycle, starting with rain.
8. <u>Interpret</u> the importance of the Bill of Rights to the American democratic system.
9. <u>Analyze</u> the economic conditions that helped cause the Civil War, including at least three factors.
10. <u>Give</u> the characteristics of a good mayoral candidate.

RESOURCES

DIAGRAMING SENTENCES

A *sentence diagram* is a picture of how the parts of a sentence fit together and how the words in a sentence are related.

Subjects and Verbs (pages 546–555)

Every sentence diagram begins with a horizontal line intersected by a short vertical line, which divides the subject from the verb.

EXAMPLE   Alice Walker wrote *The Color Purple.*

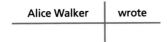

Understood Subjects (page 554)

EXAMPLE   Answer the phone, please.

Nouns of Direct Address (page 554)

EXAMPLE   Pass me the picante sauce, **Gina.**

Compound Subjects (page 554)

EXAMPLE   **Arturo** and **Patsy** are dancing the conga.

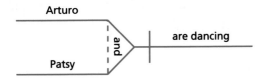

Compound Verbs (page 555)

EXAMPLE   Roger **swims** and **dives**.

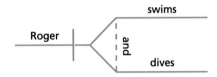

Here is how a compound verb is diagramed when the helping verb is not repeated.

EXAMPLE   Sally Ann **was reading** and **studying**.

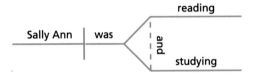

Compound Subjects and Compound Verbs
(pages 554–555)

EXAMPLE   **Kittens** and **puppies can play** together and **become** friends.

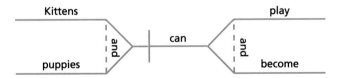

When the parts of a compound subject or a compound predicate are joined by a correlative conjunction, diagram the sentence this way:

EXAMPLE   **Both** Norma **and** Lisa will **not only** perform **but also** teach.

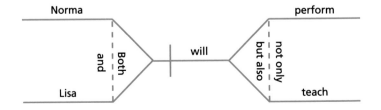

Modifiers (pages 518–521, 529–531, and 714–715)

Adjectives and Adverbs (pages 518–521 and 529–531)

Adjectives and adverbs are written on slanting lines beneath the words they modify.

EXAMPLE **The blue** car **quickly** swerved **left.**

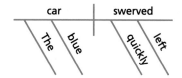

When an adverb modifies an adjective or an adverb, it is placed on a line connected to the word it modifies.

EXAMPLE The Neville Brothers performed **exceptionally** well.

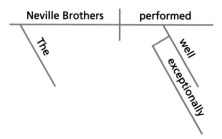

Here, There, and *Where* as Modifiers
(page 553)

EXAMPLES **Here** come the astronauts!

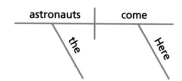

There goes the new Mohawk chief.

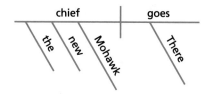

Where will the balloonists land?

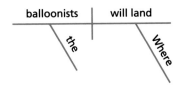

NOTE: Sometimes *there* begins a sentence but does not modify the verb. When used in this way, *there* is called an *expletive.* It is diagramed on a line by itself.

EXAMPLE   **There** are seven stars in the Pleiades.

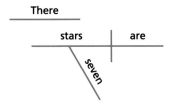

Subject Complements (page 560)

A subject complement is placed on the horizontal line with the simple subject and the verb. It comes after the verb. A line *slanting toward the subject* separates the subject complement from the verb.

Predicate Nominatives (page 560)

EXAMPLE   Some dogs are good **companions.**

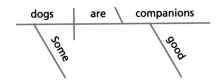

Predicate Adjectives (page 560)

EXAMPLE   That cockatiel is **friendly.**

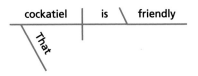

Compound Subject Complements (page 560)

EXAMPLE   Martin Yan is both a **chef** and a **comedian.**

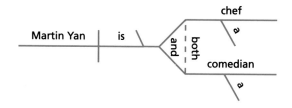

Objects (pages 562–563)

Direct Objects (page 562)

EXAMPLE   Cathy led the **band.**

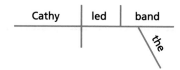

Notice that a vertical line separates the direct object from the verb.

Compound Direct Objects (page 563)

EXAMPLE   We heard **cheers** and **whistles.**

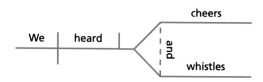

Indirect Objects (page 563)

The indirect object is diagramed on a horizontal line beneath the verb.

EXAMPLE   They gave **her** a present.

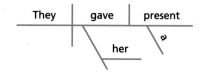

Compound Indirect Objects (page 563)

EXAMPLE   Mr. Stephens lent **Karen** and **Shanna** *The Fire Next Time.*

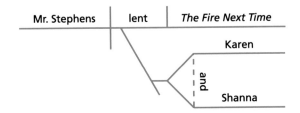

Phrases (pages 573–591)

Prepositional Phrases (pages 574–576)

The preposition is placed on a slanting line leading down from the word that the phrase modifies. The object of the preposition is placed on a horizontal line connected to the slanting line.

EXAMPLES   The steep slopes **of the mountains** are covered **with forests.** [adjective phrase modifying the subject; adverb phrase modifying the verb]

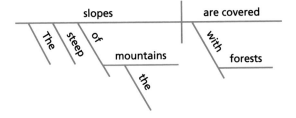

They sailed late **in the fall.** [adverb phrase modifying an adverb]

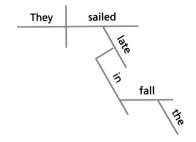

Nina read this Chinese folk tale **to Aaron and Joey.**
[compound object of preposition]

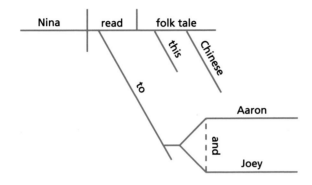

Down the valley and **across the plain** wanders the river. [two phrases modifying the same word]

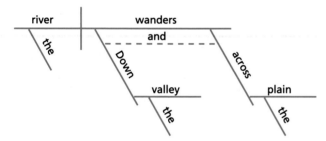

The princess lived **in a castle on the mountain.** [phrase modifying the object of another preposition]

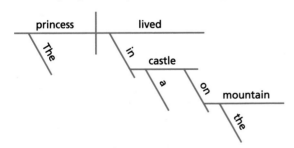

Participles and Participial Phrases (pages 579–583)

EXAMPLES   I heard them **laughing.**

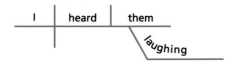

Waving her hat, Sara flagged the train speeding down the track.

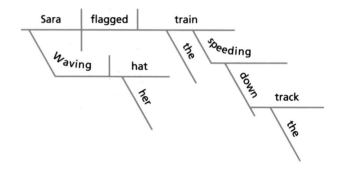

Gerunds and Gerund Phrases (pages 584–585)

EXAMPLES   **Waiting** is not easy. [gerund used as subject]

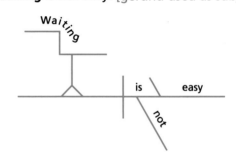

Waiting patiently for hours is usually a sure means of observing wild animals. [gerund phrases used as subject and as object of a preposition]

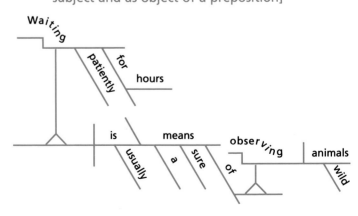

Infinitives and Infinitive Phrases (pages 586–588)

Infinitives and infinitive phrases used as modifiers are diagramed in the same way as prepositional phrases.

EXAMPLE   **He plays to win.** [infinitive used as adverb]

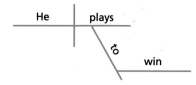

Infinitives and infinitive phrases used as nouns are diagramed as follows.

EXAMPLES   **To choose the right career** takes careful consideration. [infinitive phrase used as subject]

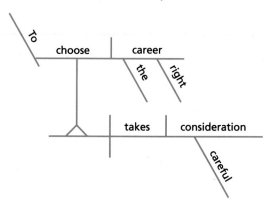

She is hoping to visit Morocco soon. [infinitive phrase used as direct object]

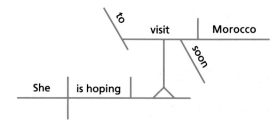

My brother watched **me prune the tree.** [infinitive with subject, *me,* and with *to* omitted]

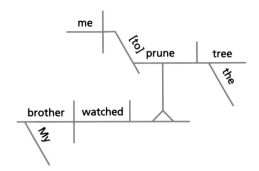

Appositives and Appositive Phrases (pages 590–591)

Place the appositive in parentheses after the word it identifies or explains.

EXAMPLES   My cousin **Bryan** is a carpenter.

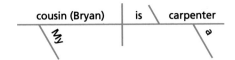

Mohammed Tahir, **our newest classmate,** comes from Yemen, **a country near Saudi Arabia.**

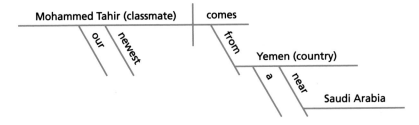

Subordinate Clauses (pages 598–606)

Adjective Clauses (pages 600–602)

An adjective clause is joined to the word it modifies by a broken line leading from the modified word to the relative pronoun.

EXAMPLES   The coat **that I wanted** was too expensive.

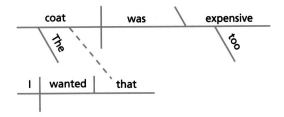

The box, **which contained the treasure,** was missing.

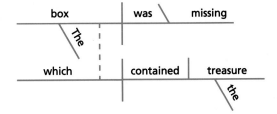

She is the woman **from whom we bought the used car.**

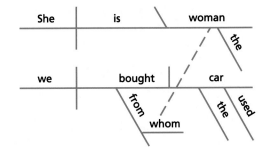

Adverb Clauses (pages 603–604)

Place the subordinating conjunction that introduces the adverb clause on a broken line leading from the verb in the adverb clause to the word the clause modifies.

EXAMPLE   **Before a hurricane strikes,** ample warning is given.

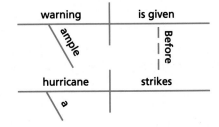

Noun Clauses (page 606)

Noun clauses often begin with relative pronouns, such as *that, what, who,* or *which.* These relative pronouns may have a function within the dependent clause or may simply connect the clause to the rest of the sentence. How a noun clause is diagramed depends on its use in the sentence and whether or not the relative pronoun has a specific function in the noun clause.

EXAMPLES **What she said** convinced me. [The noun clause is used as the subject of the independent clause. *What* functions as the direct object in the noun clause.]

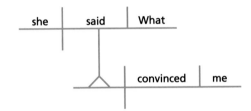

We know **that you won the prize.** [The noun clause is the direct object of the independent clause. *That* has no specific function in the noun clause.]

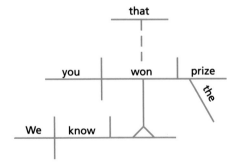

If the relative pronoun were omitted from the preceding sentence, the diagram would look like this.

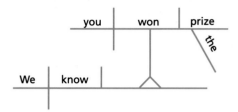

Sentences Classified According to Structure

(page 610)

Simple Sentences (page 610)

EXAMPLE   The Hudson is a historic waterway. [one independent clause]

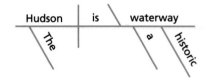

Compound Sentences (page 610)

EXAMPLE   A strange dog chased us, but the owner came to our rescue. [two independent clauses]

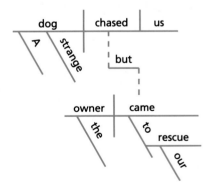

If the compound sentence has a semicolon and no conjunction, a straight broken line joins the two verbs.

EXAMPLE Phillis Wheatley wrote poetry in the 1700s; she was the first published African American poet.

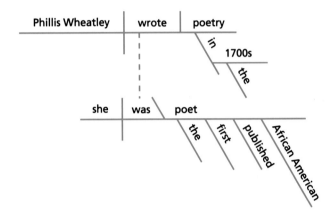

Notice that the compound adjective *African American* is written on one slanted line.

If the clauses of a compound sentence are joined by a semicolon and a conjunctive adverb (such as *consequently, therefore, nevertheless, however, moreover,* or *otherwise*), place the conjunctive adverb on a slanting line below the verb it modifies.

EXAMPLE Dylan works part time after school; consequently, he can afford to buy a new bike.

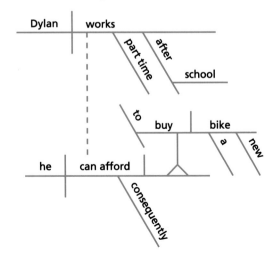

Complex Sentences (page 611)

EXAMPLE   **As night fell, the storm grew worse.** [one independent clause and one subordinate clause]

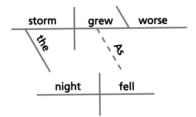

Compound-Complex Sentences (page 611)

EXAMPLE   **The room that Carrie painted had been white, but she changed the color.** [two independent clauses and one subordinate clause]

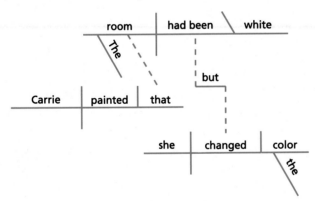

Glossary of Terms

A

Abstract noun Names an idea, a feeling, a quality, or a characteristic. (See page 515.)

Action verb Expresses physical or mental activity. (See page 524.)

Active voice The voice a verb is in when it expresses an action done *by* its subject. (See page 694.)

Adjective Modifies a noun or a pronoun. (See page 518.)

Adjective clause A subordinate clause that modifies a noun or a pronoun. (See page 600.)

Adjective phrase A prepositional phrase that modifies a noun or a pronoun. (See page 574.)

Adverb Modifies a verb, an adjective, or another adverb. (See page 529.)

Adverb clause A subordinate clause that modifies a verb, an adjective, or an adverb and tells *when, where, why, how,* or *to what extent.* (See page 603.)

Adverb phrase A prepositional phrase that modifies a verb, an adjective, or another adverb. (See page 576.)

Agreement The correspondence, or match, between grammatical forms. (See Chapter 19.)

Aim One of the four basic purposes, or reasons, for writing. (See page 7.)

Ambiguous reference Unclear phrasing that occurs when a pronoun can refer to either of two antecedents. (See page 669.)

Analyzing Looking at the parts of a whole and their relationships. (See pages 379 and 423.)

Anecdote An extended example, or story, used to support a main idea. (See pages 74 and 123.)

Antecedent The word to which a pronoun refers, usually preceding the pronoun and giving the pronoun its meaning. (See page 637.)

Appositive A noun or a pronoun placed beside another noun or pronoun to identify or explain it. (See pages 450 and 590.)

Appositive phrase Consists of an appositive and its modifiers. (See pages 450, 465, and 590.)

Article *A, an,* or *the,* the most frequently used adjectives. (See page 519.)

Audience The person(s) who reads or listens to what a writer or speaker says. (See pages 35 and 931.)

B

Base form The base form, or infinitive, is one of the four principal, or basic, parts of a verb. (See page 678.)

Base word A word that can stand alone, without prefixes or suffixes. (See page 966.)

Block method A way of arranging details in a comparison/contrast essay by discussing all the features of the first subject, then the same features of the second subject in the same order. (See page 262.)

Body States and develops a composition's main points in one or more paragraphs. (See page 128.)

Brainstorming A technique for finding ideas by using free association: recording every idea about a subject that comes to mind, without stopping to evaluate any of the ideas. (See page 27.)

Business letter A formal letter in which a writer might request or order something, complain or seek the correction of a problem, or express appreciation for someone or something. (See Chapter 36.)

Call number A number and letter code a library assigns to a book, which tells how the book has been classified and where it has been placed on the shelves. (See page 952.)

Case The form of a noun or pronoun that shows how it is used in a sentence. (See page 649.)

Cause-and-effect essay A form of writing in which a writer examines and explains the reasons for a situation or event and its results. (See page 316.)

Chronological order A way of arranging ideas in a paragraph or composition according to when events happened. (See pages 39 and 82.)

Classification A strategy of development: looking at a subject as it relates to other subjects in a group. (See pages 97 and 994.)

Clause A group of words containing a verb and its subject, used as part of a sentence. (See pages 451 and 597.)

Cliché An overused, worn-out figure of speech. (See page 508.)

Climax The high point of a story plot; the tense or exciting scene that settles the main conflict. (See page 376.)

Clincher sentence The concluding sentence of a paragraph: pulls all the details together by restating or summarizing the main idea. (See page 76.)

Clustering A visual technique for finding writing ideas and gathering information: breaking a large subject into its smaller parts to create a visual map of one's thoughts. (See page 28.)

Coherence A quality achieved when all the ideas in a paragraph or composition are clearly arranged and connected. (See pages 82 and 128.)

Collective noun A noun that names a group of persons or things. (See page 629.)

Colloquialism An informal, colorful expression of conversational language. (See page 501.)

Comma splice A run-on sentence with only a comma to separate complete sentences. (See page 456.)

Common noun Names a member of a group of persons, places, or things; it is not capitalized. (See pages 515 and 764.)

Comparative degree The form a modifier takes when comparing two things. (See page 722.)

Comparison/Contrast essay A form of writing in which a writer discusses similarities or differences (or both) between two subjects. (See Chapter 7.)

Complement A word or group of words that completes the meaning of a predicate. (See page 557.)

Complex sentence Has one independent clause and at least one subordinate clause. (See pages 470 and 611.)

Compound-complex sentence Has two or more independent clauses and at least one subordinate clause. (See page 611.)

Compound sentence Has two or more independent clauses but no subordinate clauses. (See pages 468 and 610.)

Compound word Consists of two or more words used together as a single word. (See page 860.)

Compound subject Consists of two or more subjects that are joined by a conjunction and have the same verb. (See pages 554 and 627.)

Compound verb Consists of two or more verbs that are joined by a conjunction and have the same subject. (See page 555.)

Conclusion (1) Reinforces a main idea and brings a composition to a definite close. (See page 130.) **(2)** A decision or determination reached by reasoning from clearly expressed facts and evidence found in a reading passage or other materials. (See page 989.)

Concrete noun Names an object that can be perceived by the senses. (See page 515.)

Conflict The central problem a character faces in a story. (See pages 226 and 376.)

Conjugating Listing all forms of a verb in all tenses. (See page 684.)

Conjunctive adverb An adverb used as a connecting word between independent clauses in a compound sentence. (See page 457.)

Conjunction Joins words or groups of words. (See page 536.)

Connotation The emotional meanings suggested by or associated with a word. (See pages 504 and 965.)

Context The way a word is used in a reading passage. (See page 964.)

Contraction A shortened form of a word, a figure, or a group of words, written with an apostrophe to indicate where letters or numerals have been omitted. (See page 854.)

Coordinating conjunction Joins parallel words, phrases, or clauses. (See page 536.)

Correlative conjunctions Are used in pairs (*either . . . or, not only . . . but also*, and so on). (See page 536.)

Creative writing Aims at creating literature: stories, poems, songs, and plays. (See page 7.)

Critical analysis A form of writing in which a writer analyzes the ele-

ments, or parts, of a work such as a poem, a play, a novel, or a short story. (See Chapter 10.)

Dangling modifier A modifying word, phrase, or clause that does not clearly and sensibly modify a word or a group of words in a sentence. (See page 728.)

Declarative sentence Makes a statement and is followed by a period. (See page 565.)

Denotation The direct, plainly expressed meaning of a word—the meaning a dictionary lists. (See pages 504 and 965.)

Description A strategy of development: using sensory details and spatial order to describe individual features of a specific subject. (See pages 94 and 179.)

Dialect A distinct version or variety of a language used by a particular group of people; may be **ethnic** or **regional.** (See page 496.)

Dialogue The "talk," or conversation, in a story. (See page 229.)

Direct object A noun or pronoun that receives the action of the verb or shows the result of the action, answering the question *Whom?* or *What?* after a transitive verb. (See page 562.)

Direct quotation A reproduction of a person's exact words, enclosed in quotation marks. (See pages 427 and 834.)

Direct reference Connects ideas in a paragraph or composition by referring to a noun or pronoun used earlier. (See pages 88 and 128.)

Double comparison The use of both *–er* and *more* (*less*) or *–est* and *most* (*least*) to express the comparison forms of modifiers. (See page 724.)

Double negative The use of two negative words when one is sufficient. (See page 756.)

Double subject The use of an unnecessary pronoun after the subject of a sentence. (See page 744.)

Dramatic irony A device used by a writer to heighten readers' interest by letting the reader know something the main character in a story does not. (See page 378.)

Early plan An **informal** or **rough outline** for a composition in which a writer groups and orders information. (See page 117.)

Emotional appeal A strategy used to support a writer's opinion and to persuade an audience by appealing to readers' feelings. (See page 339.)

Emphasis The focus of a description, designed to create a specific impression for the reader. (See page 187.)

End marks Punctuation marks (periods, question marks, exclamation points) used to indicate the purpose of a sentence. (See page 789.)

Essay test Requires a student to think critically about material learned and to express his or her understanding of that material in an organized piece of writing. (See page 1008.)

Essential clause/Essential phrase Also called **restrictive:** is necessary to the meaning of a sentence; not set off by commas. (See page 798.)

Ethnic dialect A distinct version of a language used by people who share the same cultural heritage. (See page 498.)

Etymology The origin and history of a word. (See page 960.)

Euphemism An agreeable term that stands for a more direct, less pleasing one. (See page 505.)

Evaluating A stage in the writing process: making judgments about a composition's strengths and weaknesses in content, organization, and style. (See pages 6, 23, and 47.)

Evaluation A strategy of development: making judgments about a subject in an attempt to determine its value. (See page 100.)

Example A specific instance, or illustration, of a general idea. (See page 73.)

Exclamatory sentence Expresses strong feeling and is followed by an exclamation point. (See page 566.)

Expository writing *See* Informative writing.

Expressive writing Aims at expressing a writer's feelings and thoughts. (See page 7.)

Extemporaneous speech A speech for which a speaker researches and prepares notes, then delivers the rehearsed but not memorized speech. (See page 932.)

Fact Can be checked and proved to be true by concrete information. (See pages 71 and 337.)

Fallacy An error in logical thinking that may lead a writer into a false or oversimplified discussion of cause-and-effect relationships. (See page 316.)

Feedback The reaction of a receiver to the message given by a sender during the communication process. (See page 928.)

Figurative language Also called a **figure of speech:** a word or a group of words that has a meaning other than its literal one. (See pages 193 and 507.)

5W-How? questions Questions (*Who? What? Where? When? Why? How?*) a writer uses to collect information about a subject. (See page 30.)

Foreshadowing A hint or suggestion of upcoming events in a story. (See page 377.)

Formal outline A highly structured, clearly labeled writing plan with a set pattern, using letters and numbers to label main headings and subheadings. (See page 118.)

Freewriting A technique for finding ideas: writing whatever thoughts occur, without regard to form. (See page 26.)

Fused sentence A run-on sentence with no punctuation separating the run-together sentences. (See page 456.)

General reference An error that occurs when a pronoun has no specific antecedent, but refers instead to a general idea. (See page 669.)

Gerund A verbal ending in *–ing*, used as a noun. (See page 584.)

Gerund phrase Consists of a gerund and its modifiers and complements. (See page 585.)

Idiom A word or phrase that means something different from its literal meaning. (See page 501.)

Imperative sentence Gives a command or makes a request and is followed by either a period or an exclamation point. (See page 565.)

Impromptu speech A short speech made on the spur of the moment, with little or no time for development or preparation of ideas. (See page 929.)

Indefinite pronoun A pronoun (*each, no one, anybody,* and so on) that does not refer to a specific person or thing. (See page 622.)

Independent clause Expresses a complete thought and can stand by itself as a sentence; also called a **main clause.** (See pages 451 and 597.)

Indirect object A noun or pronoun preceding a direct object that usually tells *to whom* or *for whom* (or *to what* or *for what*) the action of a transitive verb is performed. (See page 563.)

Indirect quotation A rewording or paraphrasing of something another person has said. (See page 834.)

Inference A decision or determination reached by reasoning from evidence that is hinted at or implied in a reading passage or other materials. (See page 989.)

Infinitive A verbal (verb form), usually preceded by *to*, used as a noun, an adjective, or an adverb. (See page 586.)

Infinitive phrase Consists of an infinitive and all of its modifiers and complements. (See page 587.)

Informative writing Aims at conveying information or explaining something. (See page 7.)

Interjection Expresses emotion and has no grammatical relation to the rest of the sentence. (See page 537.)

Interrogative sentence Asks a question and is followed by a question mark. (See page 566.)

Interview A special listening situation with the specific purpose of gathering information. (See page 943.)

Intransitive verb Expresses action (or tells something about the subject) without passing the action from a doer to a receiver. (See page 524.)

Introduction Begins a composition and should catch the reader's interest, set the composition's tone, and present the thesis statement. (See page 122.)

Invalid conclusion Is not reasonably or logically based on the available evidence. (See page 990.)

Irony A contrast between appearance or expectation and reality. (See page 378.)

Irregular verb Forms its past and past participle in some other way than by adding *–d* or *–ed*. (See page 679.)

Jargon Language that has a special meaning for a particular group of people; also wordy, puffed-up language called **gobbledygook.** (See page 506.)

Levels of usage The various forms of a language suitable for different situations. (See page 500.)

Linking verb Serves as a link between its subject and another word; may be a form of the verb *be.* (See page 525.)

Loaded words Words intended to provoke strong feeling, either positive or negative. (See page 505.)

Loanwords Words adopted from another language. (See page 487.)

Logical appeal A strategy used to support a writer's opinion and to persuade an audience by appealing to reason. (See page 337.)

Logical order A way of arranging details in a paragraph or composition according to what makes logical sense, such as grouping related ideas together. (See pages 39 and 84.)

Main idea The idea around which a paragraph or composition is organized. (See page 67.)

Mass media Forms of communication (television, radio, movies, newspapers and magazines) that reach a large audience daily. (See page 946.)

Metaphor A figure of speech directly comparing two things (without using the words *like* or *as*) by saying that something *is* something else. (See page 194.)

Misplaced modifier A word, phrase, or clause that makes a sentence awkward because it seems to modify the wrong word or group of words. (See page 730.)

Modifier A word, a phrase, or a clause that makes the meaning of another word more definite. (See pages 518 and 714.)

Narration A strategy of development: relating events or actions over a period of time, usually using chronological order. (See page 95.)

Nominative case The form a noun or pronoun takes as the subject or predicate nominative in a sentence. (See page 651.)

Nonessential clause/Nonessential phrase Also called **nonrestrictive:** adds information not necessary to the main idea in the sentence and is set off by commas. (See page 797.)

Nonverbal communication Sending a message—by gestures, facial expressions, and so on—without the use of verbal signals (words). (See page 929.)

Noun Names a person, place, thing, or idea. (See page 514.)

Noun clause A subordinate clause used as a noun. (See page 606.)

Noun of direct address Identifies the person spoken to or addressed in a sentence. (See page 554.)

Number The form of a word that indicates whether the word is singular or plural. (See page 618.)

Object A complement that does not refer to the subject. (See page 562.)

Objective case The form a noun or pronoun takes when used as a direct object, an indirect object, or the object of a preposition. (See page 655.)

Objective description Creates an accurate, thorough picture, using factual details without revealing a particular judgment or feeling about the subject. (See page 182.)

Objective test Requires a student to give a specific, limited response; may contain multiple-choice, true/false, matching, reasoning or logic, analogy, or short-answer questions. (See page 1001.)

Object of a preposition The noun or pronoun that ends a prepositional phrase. (See page 534.)

Opinion A belief or attitude. (See page 333.)

Oral interpretation An expressive presentation of a literary work to an audience, using vocal techniques, facial expressions, body language, and gestures. (See page 936.)

Order of importance A way of arranging details, in a paragraph or composition, from least to most important or from most to least important. (See pages 39 and 84.)

Parallel structure The use of the same form or part of speech to express equal, or parallel, ideas in a sentence. (See page 474.)

Paraphrase To restate someone else's ideas in different words. (See pages 421 and 945.)

Parenthetical expression A remark that adds incidental information or relates ideas. (See page 806.)

Parenthetical citation A form of documentation that places source information in parentheses at the end of a sentence in which someone else's word or ideas are used. (See page 428.)

Parliamentary procedure A plan for following a priority of actions: sometimes used by groups to keep meetings running smoothly. (See page 935.)

Participial phrase Consists of a participle and its complements and modifiers. (See pages 465 and 582.)

Participle A verbal (verb form) used as an adjective. (See pages 465 and 579.)

Passive voice The voice a verb is in when it expresses an action done *to* its subject. (See page 694.)

Personal letter An informal letter in which a writer might thank someone for something, invite someone to a particular event or occasion, or reply to an invitation he or she has received. (See Chapter 36.)

Personal narrative A form of writing in which an author explores and shares the meaning of an experience that was especially important to him or her. (See Chapter 4.)

Personification A figure of speech giving human characteristics to nonhuman things. (See page 194.)

Persuasive essay A form of writing in which a writer supports an opinion and tries to persuade an audience. (See Chapter 9.)

Persuasive writing Aims at persuading people to change their minds about something or to act in a certain way. (See page 7.)

Phrase A group of related words used as a single part of speech; does not contain both a predicate and its subject. (See pages 449 and 573.)

Plagiarism Using someone else's words or ideas without giving credit for them. (See page 422.)

Plot The series of events in a story that follow each other and cause each other to happen. (See pages 226 and 376.)

Point-by-point method A way of arranging details in a comparison/contrast essay by discussing one feature of the first subject, then the same feature of the second subject, repeating in the same order for all features. (See page 262.)

Point of view The vantage point, or position, from which a writer tells a story or describes a subject. (See pages 183 and 377.)

Possessive case The form a noun or pronoun takes when used to show ownership or relationship. (See page 848.)

Predicate The part of a sentence that says something about the subject. (See page 546.)

Predicate adjective An adjective in the predicate that describes the subject of a sentence or clause. (See page 560.)

Predicate nominative A noun or pronoun in the predicate that identifies or renames the subject of a sentence or clause. (See page 560.)

Prefix A word part added before a base or root word. (See page 968.)

Preposition Shows the relationship of a noun or a pronoun to some other word in a sentence. (See page 534.)

Prepositional phrase A group of words beginning with a preposition and ending with an object (a noun or a pronoun). (See pages 450, 465, and 574.)

Prewriting The first stage in the writing process: thinking and planning, deciding what to write about, collecting ideas and details, and making a plan for presenting ideas. (See pages 6 and 23.)

Principal parts of a verb A verb's forms—the *base form*, the *present participle*, the *past*, and the *past participle*—used to form the verb tenses. (See page 678.)

Progressive form of a verb Used in all six tenses to show continuing action; made up of a form of *be* plus the verb's present participle. (See page 686.)

Progress report A progress report is a form of writing that focuses on a project or activity, explains the writer's accomplishments or findings, and provides an overview of the project's standing. (See Chapter 8.)

Pronoun Is used in place of a noun or more than one noun. (See page 516.)

Proofreading A stage of the writing process: carefully reading a revised draft to correct mistakes in grammar, usage, and mechanics. (See pages 6, 23, and 55.)

Proper adjective An adjective formed from a proper noun. (See page 764.)

Proper noun Names a particular person, place, or thing and is always capitalized. (See pages 516 and 764.)

Publishing The last stage of the writing process: making a final, clean copy of a paper and sharing it with an audience. (See pages 6, 23, and 57.)

Purpose A reason, or aim, for writing or speaking: to express yourself; to be creative; to entertain; to explain, inform, or explore; or to persuade. (See page 35.)

▼ **R**

Regional dialect A distinct version of a language used by people in or from a particular geographical area. (See page 497.)

Regular verb Forms its past and past participle by adding *–d* or *–ed* to the infinitive. (See page 679.)

Relative pronoun A pronoun that relates an adjective clause to the word that the clause modifies, while also serving a function within the clause. (See page 601.)

Relevant features The specific details about a subject that are related to the main idea of a composition. (See page 260.)

Research report A form of writing in which a writer presents factual information discovered through exploration and research. (See Chapter 11.)

Revising A stage of the writing process: making changes in a composition's content, organization, and style in order to improve it. (See pages 6, 23, and 50.)

Root The base a word is built on, which carries the word's core meaning, but cannot stand alone. (See page 966.)

Run-on sentence Two or more complete sentences run together as one. (See page 456.)

Sensory details Precise bits of information observed, or collected, through any of the five senses—sight, sound, smell, touch, or taste. (See pages 71 and 191.)

Sentence A group of words that contains a subject and a verb and expresses a complete thought. (See pages 447 and 544.)

Sentence fragment A part of a sentence that does not express a complete thought. (See pages 446 and 545.)

Setting Where and when a story takes place; may provide background for understanding characters and events, establish the conflict, or create the mood in a story. (See pages 225 and 376.)

Simile A figure of speech comparing two basically unlike things, using the words *like* or *as*. (See page 194.)

Simple sentence Has one independent clause and no subordinate clauses but may have a compound subject, a compound verb, and any number of phrases. (See page 610.)

Situational irony A device used by the writer of a story: what is expected—by the character(s) and usually by the reader—is not what happens. (See page 378.)

Slang Informal language made up of newly coined words or of old words used in new ways. (See page 502.)

Source card An index card on which bibliographical information about a source for a research report is recorded. (See page 416.)

Spatial order A way of arranging details in a paragraph or composition according to how they are spaced—nearest to farthest, left to right, and so on. (See pages 39 and 83.)

Statistic A fact based on numbers. (See page 71.)

Story map A written plan of the essential elements of a story. (See page 228.)

Stringy sentence Has too many independent clauses strung together with coordinating conjunctions like *and* or *but*. (See page 475.)

Subject The part of a sentence that names the person or thing spoken about in the rest of the sentence. (See page 546.)

Subject complement A noun, pronoun, or adjective that follows a linking verb and describes or explains the subject. (See page 560.)

Subjective description Creates a selective picture, revealing the writer's thoughts and feelings about a subject. (See page 182.)

Subordinate clause Does not express a complete thought and cannot stand alone; also called a **dependent clause.** (See pages 452 and 598.)

Subordinating conjunction Introduces an adverb clause but does not serve a function in that clause. (See page 603.)

Suffix A word part added after a base or root word. (See page 969.)

Summarize To restate, in condensed form, the main points of a passage. (See pages 421 and 945.)

Superlative degree The form a modifier takes when comparing more than two things. (See page 722.)

Supporting sentences Give specific details or information to support the main idea. (See page 71.)

Suspense Unanswered questions in the plot development of a story that make a reader wonder what will happen next. (See page 227.)

Syllable A word part that can be pronounced by itself. (See page 871.)

Synonym A word that has a meaning similar to, but not exactly the same as, another word. (See pages 503 and 933.)

Tense The time indicated by the form of a verb: *present, present perfect, past, past perfect, future,* and *future perfect.* (See page 684.)

Theme The underlying meaning or message a writer wants to communicate to readers. (See page 378.)

Thesis statement Announces the limited topic of a composition and the main, or unifying, idea about that topic. (See pages 113 and 423.)

Time line A visual arrangement of information in chronological order. (See page 44.)

Tired word A word that has lost so much of its freshness and force through overuse that it has become worn-out and almost meaningless. (See page 507.)

Tone The feeling or attitude a writer conveys about a topic. (See pages 36 and 122.)

Topic sentence Expresses the main idea of a paragraph. (See page 68.)

Transitional expression A word or phrase that indicates relationships between ideas in a paragraph or composition. (See pages 89 and 129.)

Transitive verb Expresses an action directed toward a person or thing named in a sentence. (See page 524.)

Understood subject The unstated subject *you* in a request or a command. (See page 554.)

Unity A quality achieved when all the sentences or paragraphs in a composition work together as a unit to express or support one main idea. (See pages 77 and 128.)

Valid conclusion Is firmly grounded in facts, evidence, or logic. (See page 990.)

Verb Expresses an action or a state of being. (See page 524.)

Verbal irony A device used by the author of a story: what a character says is not what is meant. (See page 378.)

Verbals A word (participle, gerund, or infinitive) formed from a verb, but used as another part of speech. (See pages 449 and 579.)

Verbal phrase Consists of a verbal and its modifiers and complements. (See page 449.)

Verb phrase Consists of a main verb preceded by at least one **helping verb** (also called an **auxiliary verb**). (See page 527.)

Voice Writing in a way that sounds like oneself, using language to sound as natural and distinctive as possible. (See page 36.)

Weak reference Unclear phrasing that occurs when a pronoun refers to a suggested, but not clearly stated, word or idea. (See page 670.)

"What if?" questions A creative thinking technique used to help a writer draw upon his or her imagination to explore ideas for writing. (See page 34.)

Word bank A writer's storehouse of words to be used in writing. (See pages 192 and 963.)

Works Cited A list of all the print and nonprint sources used in a research report; the term **bibliography** means that only print sources were used. (See page 429.)

Writer's journal A written record of a person's experiences and observations, feelings and opinions, ideas and questions. (See page 25.)

Writing A stage in the writing process: putting ideas into words, following a plan that organizes the ideas. (See pages 6, 23, and 45.)

Writing process The series of stages, or steps, that a writer goes through to develop ideas and to communicate them clearly in a piece of writing. (See pages 6 and 22.)

Glossary

This glossary is a short dictionary of words found in the professional writing models in this textbook. The words are defined according to their meanings in the context of the writing models.

Pronunciation Key

Symbol	Key Words	Symbol	Key Words
a	asp, fat, parrot	b	bed, fable, dub, ebb
ā	ape, date, play, break, fail	d	dip, beadle, had, dodder
ä	ah, car, father, cot	f	fall, after, off, phone
e	elf, ten, berry	g	get, haggle, dog
ē	even, meet, money, flea, grieve	h	he, ahead, hotel
i	is, hit, mirror	j	joy, agile, badge
ī	ice, bite, high, sky	k	kill, tackle, bake, coat, quick
ō	open, tone, go, boat	l	let, yellow, ball
ô	all, horn, law, oar	m	met, camel, trim, summer
o͞o	look, pull, moor, wolf	n	not, flannel, ton
o͞o	ooze, tool, crew, rule	p	put, apple, tap
yo͞o	use, cute, few	r	red, port, dear, purr
yo͝o	cure, globule	s	sell, castle, pass, nice
oi	oil, point, toy	t	top, cattle, hat
ou	out, crowd, plow	v	vat, hovel, have
u	up, cut, color, flood	w	will, always, swear, quick
ʉr	urn, fur, deter, irk	y	yet, onion, yard
		z	zebra, dazzle, haze, rise
ə	a in ago	ch	chin, catcher, arch, nature
	e in agent	sh	she, cushion, dash, machine
	i in sanity	th	thin, nothing, truth
	o in comply	*th*	then, father, lathe
	u in focus	zh	azure, leisure, beige
ər	perhaps, murder	ŋ	ring, anger, drink

Abbreviation Key

adj.	adjective	*pl.*	plural
adv.	adverb	*prep.*	preposition
conj.	conjunction	*vi.*	intransitive verb
n.	noun	*vt.*	transitive verb

abstracted [ab strak′tid] *adj.* Not paying attention; absent-minded.

adjacent [ə jā′sənt] *adj.* Next to or beside.

anna [än′ə] *n.* A former unit of money in India, equal to 1/16 of a rupee.

aquiline [ak′wə līn′] *adj.* Curved.

assimilate [ə sim′ə lāt′] *vt.* To absorb.

auspicious [ôs pish′əs] *adj.* Successful and deserving of respect.

befuddled [bē fud″ld] *adj.* Confused.

buffoonery [bə fo͞on′ə rē] *n.* Clowning around.

careworn [ker′wôrn′] *adj.* Visibly exhausted by worrying.

chauvinist [shō′vin ist] *adj.* Characterized by an unthinking loyalty toward a particular behavior.

cheroot [she ro͞ot′] *n.* A square-tipped cigar.

contrivance [kən trī′vəns] *n.* A plan or device designed to produce a specific, intended result.

cowrie shell [kou′rē shel′] *n.* A shiny, bright-colored seashell once used as money in India.

curb [kurb] *vt.* To limit or restrain.

din [din] *n.* Loud and continuous noise.

dissipate [dis′ə pāt′] *vi.* To gradually disappear.

draw [drô] *n.* A deep ditch formed by rainwater drainage.

effigy [ef′i jē] *n.* Representation.

electrodynamics [ē lek′trō dī nam′iks] *n.* The science of electricity and magnetic forces.

embolden [em bōl′dən] *vt.* To make bold.

émigré [em′i grā′] *n.* A person who has moved from his or her native country to live in another.

endue [en do͞o′] *vt.* To give desirable qualities to.

eradicate [ē rad′i kāt′] *vt.* To do away with; to remove.

execute [ek′si kyo͞ot′] *vt.* To make or create.

exhilaration [eg zil′ə rā′shən] *n.* Happy excitement.

expertise [ek′spər tēz′] *n.* Highly qualified knowledge or skill.

G

gnome [nōm] *n.* A mythological dwarf.

gulch [gulch] *n.* A deep, narrow riverbed.

guru [go͞o′ro͞o′] *n.* A respected spiritual leader.

H

harbor [här′bər] *vt.* To keep in mind and remember frequently.

humor [hyo͞o′mər] *n.* Moisture.

hydrocarbon [hī′drō kär′bən] *n.* A poisonous chemical compound made of hydrogen and carbon.

hypothesis [hī päth′ə sis] *n.* A theory to be proved.

icon [ī′kän′] *n.* A symbol or easily recognized image.

illustrious [i lus′trē əs] *n.* Well-known and greatly respected.

imbue [im byōō′] *vt.* To give ideas or feelings to.

impetuous [im pech′ōō əs] *adj.* Impulsive; acting without prior thought.

implication [im′pli kā′shən] *n.* An unstated but expected result of an action or event.

incredulous [in krej′ōō ləs] *adj.* Not believing.

indifferent [in dif′ər ənt] *adj.* Uncaring; unaware.

inferences [in′fər əns əz] *n., pl.* Conclusions or opinions derived by reasoning.

jaggery [jag′ər ē] *n.* A dark-colored sugar made from palm-tree sap.

lorry [lôr′ē] *n.* A type of truck.

malevolent [mə lev′ə lənt] *adj.* Evil.

malicious [mə lish′əs] *adj.* Wishing harm.

maxim [maks′im] *n.* A statement generally accepted as true.

mesmerize [mez′mər īz′] *vt.* To capture the attention as if by magic; to hypnotize.

notoriously [nō tôr′ē əs lē] *adv.* In a well-known and undesirable manner.

ode [ōd] *n.* A long poem with short lines, usually in a specific rhyme pattern; it commonly expresses emotion in a formal manner.

ordnance [ôrd′nəns] *n.* Weapons, ammunition, parts, etc.

palmyra writing [pal mī′rə rīt′iŋ] *n.* Ancient writing on strips of the leaves of a palmyra palm tree.

paraphernalia [par′ə fər nāl′yə] *n.* A group of articles used for a specific purpose; tools or equipment.

parochial [pə rō′kē əl] *adj.* Narrow-minded; limited in the way one sees the world.

pie [pī] *n.* A former unit of money in India, equal to 1/192 of a rupee.

piqued [pēkt] *adj.* Irritated or displeased.

pontoon [pän tōōn′] *n.* A floating support for a temporary bridge.

porous [pôr′əs] *adj.* Having tiny holes to absorb moisture.

precipice [pres′i pis] *n.* A steep cliff.

prerequisite [pri rek′wə zit] *adj.* Required beforehand.

procure [prō kyōōr′] *vt.* To find and get.

proselytize [präs′ə li tīz′] *vi.* To argue in a persuasive manner.

purgatory [pur′gə tôr′ē] *n.* Temporary punishment.

R

rupee [rōō′pē] *n.* The basic unit of money in India.

S

saffron [saf'rən] *adj.* Orange-yellow.

scant [skant] *adj.* Limited in amount or quantity; not enough.

scapegrace [skāp'grās'] *n.* An unprincipled person; a rascal.

searing [sir'iŋ] *adj.* Causing a feeling of being marked or changed by an experience.

serried [ser'ēd] *adj.* In a tight formation, as soldiers.

siege [sēj] *n.* An attack in which the enemy is encircled and fired upon.

sodden [säd''n] *adj.* Soaked.

spare [sper] *adj.* Minimal; using few words to describe.

stark [stärk] *adj.* Not softened; realistic.

stipulated [stip'yŏŏ lāt'id] *adj.* Specific; set.

strut [strut] *n.* A metal brace to stiffen the leg.

subterranean [sub'tə rā'nē ən] *adj.* Underground.

succulence [suk'yŏŏ ləns] *n.* Juiciness.

T

tabular [tab'yŏŏ lər] *adj.* Arranged in a table.

tapestry [tap'əs trē] *n.* A cloth or rug with designs and pictures.

tendency [ten'dən sē] *adj.* Relating to a habitual action.

tram [tram] *n.* A streetcar.

trapezoid [trap'i zoid] *n.* A figure similar to a rectangle but with only two sides parallel.

V

vermilion [vər mil'yən] *n.* Bright red paint.

vigor [vig'ər] *n.* Energy.

vociferousness [vō sif'ər əs nis] *n.* Loud, continuous talk.

volition [vō lish'ən] *n.* Exercise of the will; deliberate decision.

Index

every or *many a*, 632–33
indefinite pronouns, 622–23
and intervening words or phrases, 620, 632
nouns plural in form with singular meaning, 633
number, 619
plural subjects, 619
predicate nominative, agreement not with, 631
singular subjects, 619
subject following verb, 631
title of work of art, music, literature, as subject, 633
words stating amount, 632
Aims for writing
creative, 7, 22
expressive, 7, 22
informative, 7, 22
persuasive, 7, 22
All ready, already, 882
All right, 882
All the farther, all the faster, 739
All together, altogether, 883
Allusion, illusion, 739
Almanacs, 957
Ambiguous reference, pronoun, 669
American Childhood, An, 156–58
American English, 493–94
"America's Ancient Skywatchers," 402–404
Among, between, 740
An, a, 519, 738–39
Analogy chart, 1006–1007
Analogy questions, 1005–1007
And etc., 739
Anecdote, 74, 123
Angelou, Maya, 448, 764
Anglo-Saxon, 486
Anne of Green Gables, 83
Announcement, as speaking situation, 934
Antecedent
agreement with pronoun, 637–39
defined, 637
Antecedent-pronoun agreement. *See* Agreement, pronoun-antecedent.
Antonyms, in dictionaries, 961
Anywheres, 740
Apostrophe
contractions, 854–55
indefinite pronouns, 850
plurals, 857–58, 879–80
possessive case, 848–51

Application letter, 978–79
Appositive, 590–91
defined, 450, 590, 664, 805
diagramed, 1026
pronoun as, 664
punctuating, 591, 805
restrictive, 805
Appositive phrase, 590–91
and combining sentences, 465–66
defined, 450, 590
diagramed, 1026
placement of, 465–66, 590
punctuating, 466, 591, 805
as sentence fragment, 450
Appreciation letter, 978
Arbetter, Sandra R., 123
Arrangement of library/media center, 952–53
Arranging ideas/information, 39–44
block method, 262–64
classifying information, 43
comparison/contrast essay, 260–64
critical analysis, 383
order, choosing type of, 39–40
personal narrative, 154
point-by-point method, 262–64
visuals used in, 43–44, 300, 990–91
Art, 443–44
Articles, 519, 738
As, like, 747
As follows, colon with, 821
As if, like, 747
Asking questions, 30
As though, like, 747
"Astrologer's Day, An," 370–75
At, 740
Atlases, 957
Attacking the person, 340
Audience
analyzing, 36–38
in communication process, 5
comparison/contrast essay, 258–59
critical analysis, 381
description, 182
personal narrative, 147
persuasive essay, 333, 335
research paper, 410
short story, 223
speech preparation, 931
writing process, 35
Author card, 953
Autobiography, 441
as study skill, 985
Auxiliary verb. *See* Helping verb.

M

INDEX

INDEX

INDEX

Acknowledgments

For permission to reprint copyrighted material, grateful acknowledgment is made to the following sources:

Emily R. Alling: Adapted from "Letter to the Editor" by Emily R. Alling from *Newsweek*, July 30, 1990.

Allyn & Bacon: From *The Elements of Style* by William Strunk, Jr. Copyright 1918, © 1959, 1979 by William Strunk, Jr. All rights reserved.

American Heritage: From "The Business of America: Financial Folklore" by John Steele Gordon from *American Heritage*, vol. 42, no. 1, February/March 1991. Copyright © 1991 by American Heritage, a Division of Forbes, Inc.

Andrews & McMeel: From a movie review of *Once Upon A Time . . . When We Were Colored* from *Roger Ebert's Video Companion* by Roger Ebert. Copyright © 1996 by Roger Ebert. All rights reserved.

Atheneum Books for Young Readers, an imprint of Simon & Schuster Children's Publishing Division: From "The Sun: The Star We Know Best" from *Private Lives of the Stars* by Roy A. Gallant. Copyright © 1986 by Roy A. Gallant.

The Atlanta Committee for the Olympic Games: From "Employment Impacts" from *The Economic Impact on the State of Georgia of Hosting the 1996 Olympic Games.*

Magaret Atwood: Quotation by Margaret Atwood.

August House, Inc.: From *Moncrief: My Journey to the NBA* by Sidney Moncrief with Myra McLarey. Copyright © 1990 by Sidney A. Moncrief.

Bilingual Press/Editorial Bilingüe, Arizona State University, Tempe, AZ: "The Scholarship Jacket" by Marta Salinas from *Nosotras: Latina Literature Today*, edited by María del Carmen Boza, Beverly Silva, and Carmen Valle. Copyright © 1986 by Bilingual Press/Editorial Bilingüe.

Stanley Bing: From "The Most Beautiful Girl in the World" by Stanley Bing from *Esquire*, January 1990. Copyright © 1990 by Esquire.

Gwenda Blair and Charles Mann: From "Juan's Place" by Charles Mann and Gwenda Blair from *GEO*, vol. 6, no. 7, July 1984. Copyright © 1984 by Knapp Communications Corporation.

Gwendolyn Brooks: "The Bean Eaters" from *Blacks* by Gwendolyn Brooks. Copyright © 1991 by Gwendolyn Brooks. Published by Third World Press, Chicago. "Home" from *Maud Martha* by Gwendolyn Brooks. Copyright © 1993 by Gwendolyn Brooks. Published by Third World Press, Chicago.

James Chiles: From "To break the unbreakable codes" by James R. Chiles from *Smithsonian*, vol. 18, no. 3, June 1987. Copyright © 1987 by James Chiles.

Michael D. Coe: From "Olmec and Maya: A Study in Relationships" by Michael D. Coe from *The Origins of Maya Civilization*, edited by Richard E. W. Adams.

Consumers Digest® Inc.: From "CD & Videodisc Players" from *Consumers Digest*, vol. 34, no. 6, November/December 1995. Copyright © 1995 by Consumers Digest Inc.

Estate of Harold Courlander: "Why No One Lends His Beauty" from *Olode: The Hunter and Other Tales* by Harold Courlander with Ezekial A. Eshugbayi. Copyright © 1968 by Harold Courlander.

Gary N. DaSilva: Quotation by Neil Simon from "Up from Success" from *Newsweek*, February 2, 1970. Copyright © 1970 by Neil Simon.

Los Angeles Times Syndicate: From "Time Out! Is Baseball Finnished?" by Bob Secter from *The Miami Herald*, August 3, 1990. Copyright © 1990 by Los Angeles Times Syndicate.

Lothrop, Lee & Shepard Books, a division of William Morrow & Co., Inc.: From "The War-Horse" from *Once Upon a Horse: A History of Horses—And How They Shaped Our History* by Suzanne Jurmain. Copyright © 1989 by Suzanne Jurmain.

David Low: From "Winterblossom Garden" by David Low from *Ploughshares,* vol. 8, no. 4, 1982. Copyright © 1982 by David Low.

Macmillan USA, a Simon & Schuster Macmillan Company: Entry "increase" and "Pronunciation Key" from *Webster's New World College Dictionary,* Third Edition. Copyright © 1996, 1994, 1991, 1988 by Simon & Schuster Inc.

Madison Publishing Inc.: From "The Fateful Night" from *Exploring the Titanic* by Robert D. Ballard, edited by Patrick Crean. Copyright © 1988 by Ballard & Family. A Madison Press Book.

Marshall Editions Limited: From "How are spiders different from insects?" from *Do Animals Dream? Children's questions about animals most often asked of The Natural History Museum,* answered by Joyce Pope. Copyright © 1986 by Marshall Editions Limited.

Merlyn's Pen: The National Magazine of Student Writing: From "Memoirs of an Adolescent" by Noah Kramer-Dover from *Merlyn's Pen: The National Magazine of Student Writing,* Middle School Edition, vol. XI, no. 3, April/May 1996. Copyright © 1996 by Merlyn's Pen, Inc.

N. Scott Momaday: "The Eagle-Feather Fan" from *The Gourd Dancer* by N. Scott Momaday.

Daniel Morrison: From "Date with Dracula" by Daniel D. Morrison from *American Way*, October 15, 1990. Copyright © 1990 by American Airlines.

National Geographic Society: From "Japanese Americans: Home at Last" by Arthur Zich from *National Geographic*, vol. 169, no. 4, April 1986. Copyright © 1986 by National Geographic Society. From "America's Ancient Skywatchers" by Robert B. Carlson from *National Geographic*, March 1990. Copyright © 1990 by National Geographic Society.

The New York Times Company: From "School for Homeless Children: A Rare Experience" by Timothy Egan from *The New York Times*, November 17, 1988. Copyright © 1988 by The New York Times Company. From "3 Scientists Say Travel in Time Isn't So Far Out" by Malcolm W. Browne from *The New York Times*, November 22, 1988. Copyright © 1988 by The New York Times Company. From "For Young and Old, a Pocket Paradise" by Kathleen Teltsch from *The New York Times*, April 30, 1989. Copyright © 1989 by The New York Times Company. From "At Rye High, Students Not Only Must Do Well, They Must Do Good" by Lisa W. Foderaro from *The New York Times*, April 30, 1990. Copyright © 1990 by The New York Times Company. From "A Thirsty California Is Trying Desalination" by Lawrence M. Fisher from *The New York Times*, November 18, 1990. Copyright © 1990 by The New York Times Company.

The New Yorker: From *Driving Miss Daisy* (review) by Pauline Kael from "Goings On About Town" from *The New Yorker*, March 26, 1990. Copyright © 1990 by Pauline Kael.

W. W. Norton & Company, Inc.: From the Editors' Introduction to "The Origin of Diseases" by Mourning Dove (Hum-ishu-ma) from *The Norton Anthology of Literature by Women: The Tradition in English,* edited by Sandra M. Gilbert and Susan Gubar. Copyright © 1985 by Sandra M. Gilbert and Susan Gubar.

The Octagon Press Ltd.: From "The Thief" from *Caravan of Dreams* by Idries Shah. Copyright © 1968 by Idries Shah.

Omni Publications International, Ltd.: "Can Bicycles Save the World?" by Jane Bosveld from "Continuum" from *Omni,* vol. 11, no. 5, February 1989. Copyright © 1989 by Omni Publications International, Ltd. From "Pioneers Underfoot" by Sherry Baker from "Continuum" from *Omni,* vol. 12, no. 1, October 1989. Copyright © 1989 by Omni Publications International, Ltd. From "Quasi-Humans" by R. A. Deckert from *Omni,* vol. 12, no. 5, February 1990. Copyright © 1990 by Omni Publications International, Ltd.

Oxford University Press, Inc.: From "Sky Dance" from *A Sand County Almanac: And Sketches Here and There* by Aldo Leopold. Copyright © 1949, 1977 by Oxford University Press, Inc.

PREVENTION Magazine: From "stretchBREAK GOOD MORNING WAKE-UP STRETCH" by Sharon Stocker from *PREVENTION,* vol. 28, no. 2, February 1996, p. 56. Copyright © 1996 by Rodale Press, Inc. All rights reserved. For subscription information call 1-800-666-2503.

The Progressive, 409 East Main Street, Madison, WI 53703: From "We Need Power, Program, and Progress" by Jesse L. Jackson from *The Progressive,* vol. 54, no. 11, November 1990. Copyright © 1990 by The Progressive, Inc.

Publications International, Ltd.: "Frankenstein" (review) from *The Best, Worst, and Most Unusual: Horror Films* by Darrell Moore. Copyright © 1983 by Publications International, Ltd.

The Putnam Publishing Group: From "The Slow Train to Langxiang: Number 295" from *Riding the Iron Rooster* by Paul Theroux. Copyright © 1988 by Cape Cod Scriveners Co.

Random House, Inc.: From "Woman Work" from *And I Still Rise* by Maya Angelou. Copyright © 1978 by Maya Angelou. Quotation by John Gardner from "North Africa: November 1942–June 1943" from *Ernie's War: The Best of Ernie Pyle's World War II Dispatches,* edited with a biographical essay by David Nichols. Copyright © 1986 by David Nichols.

Reed Consumer Books Ltd.: From *My Left Foot* by Christy Brown. Copyright © 1954 by Christy Brown.

Reprint Management Services™: From "The Psychological Benefits of Exercise" by Susan Chollar from *American Health,* vol. xiv, no. 5, June 1995. Copyright © 1995 by American Health.

St. Martin's Press Incorporated: From *Sassafras, Cypress & Indigo* by Ntozake Shange. Copyright © 1982 by Ntozake Shange.

Scholastic, Inc.: From "Foreward" from *A Fire in My Hands: A Book of Poems* by Gary Soto. Copyright © 1990 by Scholastic, Inc.

Ellen Ruppel Shell: From "Seeds in the bank could stave off disaster on the farm" by Ellen Ruppel Shell from *Smithsonian,* January 1990. Copyright © 1990 by Ellen Ruppel Shell.

Simon & Schuster Books for Young Readers, an imprint of Simon & Schuster Children's Publishing Division: From *Garbarge! Where It Comes From, Where It Goes* by Evan & Janet Hadingham. Copyright © 1990 by Evan and Janet Hadingham, and WGBH Educational Foundation.

Simon & Schuster: From "Leonardo da Vinci Asks the Duke of Milan for a Job" from *A Treasury of the World's Great Letters,* edited by M. Lincoln Schuster. Copyright © 1940, 1968 by Simon & Schuster, Inc. From "It's Only Make Believe" from *Rock of Ages: The Rolling Stone History of Rock & Roll* by Ed Ward, Geoffrey Stokes, and Ken Tucker. Copyright © 1986 by Rolling Stone Press.

Sports Illustrated: From "A Yen for Baseball Cards" by Rick Wolff from *Sports Illustrated,* March 4, 1991. Copyright © 1991 by Time Inc. All rights reserved.

Carl Stephenson (Ann Elmo Agency, Inc.): From "Leiningen Versus the Ants" by Carl Stephenson from *Esquire,* vol. 10, no. 6, December 1938. Copyright © 1938 by Carl Stephenson.

Time Inc.: From "The Surprises of the Mail" by Shana Alexander from *Life,* June 30, 1967. Copyright © 1967 by Time Inc. From "Reopening the Gateway to America" by Doris G. Kinney from *Life,* vol. 13, no. 11, September 1990. Copyright © 1990 by Time Inc.

United Press International, Inc.: From "Hayes: 'There Is So Much to Do'" by Helen Hayes.

University of Nebraska Press: From "Grandmother's Land" from *Black Elk Speaks: Being the Life Story of a Holy Man of the Oglala Sioux* by John G. Neihardt. Copyright 1932, © 1959, 1972 by John G. Neihardt; copyright renewed © 1961 by the John G. Neihardt Trust.

Viking Penguin, a division of Penguin Books USA Inc.: Quotation by James Baldwin from "On Revising: Self-Evaluation" from *The Writer's Chapbook,* edited by George Plimpton. Copyright © 1989 by The Paris Review. From *Going Green: A Kid's Handbook to Saving the Planet* by John Elkington, Julia Hailes, Douglas Hill, and Joel Makower. Text copyright © 1990 by John Elkington, Julia Hailes, Douglas Hill, and Viking Penguin, a division of Penguin Books USA Inc. From *The Pearl* by John Steinbeck. Copyright 1945 by John Steinbeck; copyright renewed © 1973 by Elaine Steinbeck, Thom Steinbeck and John Steinbeck IV. From *Golden Lilies* by Kwei-li, adapted and with a foreword by Eileen Goudge Zhang Qing. Copyright © 1990 by Eileen Goudge.

David Wagoner: "Tumbleweed" from *Collected Poems 1956–1976* by David Wagoner. Copyright © 1976 by David Wagoner.

Wallace Literary Agency, Inc.: "An Astrologer's Day" from *Malgudi Days* by R. K. Narayan. Copyright © 1972, 1975, 1978, 1980, 1981, 1982 by R. K. Narayan. Published by Viking Press, 1982.

Weekly Reader Corporation: From "What's Your Type? Introverts and Extroverts" by Sandra R. Arbetter from *Current Health 2,* March 1991. Copyright © 1991 by Weekly Reader Corporation.

PHOTO CREDITS

Abbreviations used: (t) top, (c) center, (b) bottom, (l) left, (r) right, (bckgd) background, (bdr) border.

COVER: Ralph J. Brunke Photography.

TABLE OF CONTENTS: Page vi, NASA; vii, Karen Kasmauski; viii, Don Klumpp/The Image Bank; ix, National Anthropological Archives/ Smithsonian Institution; x, ©Fred Bavendam/ Peter Arnold, Inc.; xi, James Newberry; xii(all), Carol Boone; xiv, Rob Nelson/Black Star; xv, Everett Collection; xvi(t), Fridmar Damm/Leo de Wys; xvi(b), Donne Bryant/DDB Stock Photo; xvii, Robert Foothorap; xx, Smithsonian Institution; xxi, Richard T. Nowitz; xxiii(l)(c), Craig Aurness/Westlight; xxiii(r), Burke/Triolo; xxiv(tl), W. K. Fletcher/ Photo Researchers; xxiv(tr), Ray Coleman/Photo Researchers; xxiv(bl)(br), Kjell B. Sandved/Photo Researchers; xxv(tl), Lawrence Migdale/Photo Researchers; xxv(tr), Doug Wechsler; xxv(bl), J. H. Carmichael/ Photo Researchers; xxv(br), Fletcher & Bayliss/ Photo Researchers; xxvi(all), Courtesy of McAllen International Museum, HRW photos by Eric Beggs; xxx, Vicki Ragan; xxxi, xxxiii, xxxiv, James Newberry; xxxvii(l), Carolyn Soto; xxxvii(c), Photo by John Montre, Courtesy of HarperCollins.

CHAPTER 0: Page 4, Jeffrey Sylvester/FPG International; 5, Diana Walker/Gamma-Liaison; 6, P. Cantor/SuperStock; 7, Rivera Collection/ SuperStock; 14(l), R. Dahlquist/SuperStock; 14(b), Manley/SuperStock; 14(tr), L. Manning/ Westlight; 15(tl), Robert Landau/Westlight; 15(tr), A. Butera/SuperStock; 15(bl), Steve Vidler/Leo de Wys; 15(br), Carroll Seghers II/Leo de Wys.

CHAPTER 1: Page 19, Carolyn Soto; 19(bckgd), Gary R. Zahm/Bruce Coleman; 20(all), Gary R. Zahm/Bruce Coleman; 27, Cindy Lewis; 28(l), SuperStock; 28(r), G. Seghers/Photo Researchers; 32(all), Stanley Schoenberger/Grant Heilman; 33(l), Jeff Apoian/Nawrocki Stock Photo; 33(r), Patrick Hagan/Bruce Coleman; 37, Republic Entertainment/ Shooting Star; 38, Peter Menzel/ Stock Boston; 40, William Nawrocki/Nawrocki Stock Photo; 41, D'Arcy McNickle Center for the History of the American Indian, The Newberry Library; 42, Jacques Chenet/Woodfin Camp &

Associates; 44, NASA; 45, David Madison/Bruce Coleman; 46, HRW photo by Eric Beggs; 48, Frank Siteman/Stock Boston; 54(l), Figaro Magazine/Gamma-Liaison; 54(r), Giannoni/Sipa Press; 57, Courtesy of General Motors.

CHAPTER 2: Page 69, U.S. Signal Corps (Brady Collection), National Archives; 70, Reuters/ Bettmann Newsphoto; 72, HRW photo by Dennis Fagan; 73, Bernard Wolff/Photo Researchers; 74, Brown Brothers; 75, Robert Kristofik/The Image Bank; 78, SuperStock; 80, David York/The Stock Shop; 81(t), Shooting Star; 81(b), T. Rosenthal/ SuperStock; 85, Photoworld/FPG International; 86(all), Culver Pictures; 87, National Archives; 94, Karen Kasmauski; 99, Kitagaw II/SuperStock; 101, Paramount/Shooting Star; 105(inset), © S. J. Krasemann/Peter Arnold; 105, Images Unlimited/ The Image Bank.

CHAPTER 3: Page 110, C. Orrico/SuperStock; 111(l), Richard Himelsen/Medichrome/The Stock Shop; 111(c), Journalism Services; 111(r), C. Orrico/ SuperStock; 114, John Kelly/The Image Bank; 116, Rex Weyler/Greenpeace; 119, R. Kresge/ SuperStock; 121(tl), Tom Haug/The Stock Shop; 121(tr), Dann Coffey/The Image Bank; 121(b), HRW photo by Eric Beggs; 124, Peter Menzel; 126, Culver Pictures; 127, Hans Wendler/The Image Bank; 129, 130, Park Street; 132(l), NASA; 132(r), Culver Pictures; 133, Don Klumpp/The Image Bank; 135, The President's Council on Physical Fitness and Sports; 137, Park Street.

CHAPTER 4: Page 141, National Anthropological Archives/Smithsonian Institution; 145, Eric Beggs; 149, Lance Schriner; 153, James Newberry; 156, Photo by John Montre, Courtesy of Harper-Collins; 157, Robert Dunne/Photo Researchers; 160(all), David Madison; 170, Reprinted with permission from Popular Science Magazine, ©1930, Times Mirror Magazines, Distributed by Los Angeles Times Syndicate.

CHAPTER 5: Page 177, The Kobal Collection/SuperStock; 178, Dan Morrison; 184, George Archibald, Courtesy of International Crane Foundation; 186, George Tiedemann/ Sports Illustrated; 188, Park Street; 189, James

Newberry; 190(t), Peter & George Bowater/The Image Bank; 190(c), Mark Stephenson/Westlight; 190(b), Myrleen Ferguson Cate/PhotoEdit; 191, ©Fred Bavendam/Peter Arnold; 194, Harald Sund/The Image Bank; 195, Michael Pasdzior/ The Image Bank; 204, James Newberry; 209, Brown Brothers; 211(l), Wolfgang Bayer/Bruce Coleman; 211(r), Bob Burch/Bruce Coleman.

CHAPTER 6: Page 238, James Newberry; 245, Roy Britt/Weatherstock; 246, HRW photo by Henry Friedman.

CHAPTER 7: Page 251, Manny Millan/Sports Illustrated; 252, Rick Rickman/Duomo; 253, Focus On Sports; 254, Brian Drake/Sportschrome East/West; 256(l), Tri-Star/Shooting Star; 256(r), © MGM, courtesy of Herb Bridges/HRW photo by Eric Beggs; 259(t), Culver Pictures; 259(b), Brian Lovell/Nawrocki Stock Photo; 264(l), New York Public Library; 267, Markku Ulander/ Lehtikuva Oy; 269(all), Pressfoto; 272, Johnny Johnson/Tony Stone Images; 273, Carol Boone; 278, James Newberry; 281(l), HRW photo by Eric Beggs; 281(r), Shelby Thorner/David Madison; 283(tl), Carol Boone; 283(tc), Michal Heron/ Woodfin Camp & Associates; 283(tr), (bl), (br), Carol Boone; 287, Panhandle-Plains Museum, Photo by Scott Hyde; 291, The Kobal Collection Granada/Miramax; 295, Gay Bumgarner/Tony Stone Images.

CHAPTER 8: Page 298, D. Young-Wolff/ PhotoEdit; 299, HRW photo by Peter Van Steen; 308(l), Bettmann Archive; 308(r), Culver Pictures; 315, HRW photo by Peter Van Steen; 317, Mark Lewis/Tony Stone Images.

CHAPTER 9: Page 326, SuperStock; 327(l), AKG/ London; 327(r), Bridgeman Collection/ SuperStock; 328, AKG/London; 329, Scala/Art Resource; 332(t), Michael Baytoff/Black Star; 332(b), Bill Curtsinger/ Photo Researchers; 338, Stephen Frisch/Stock Boston; 344, Bruce Forster/Tony Stone Images; 346, Jeffrey M. Spielman/The Image Bank; 348, Nick Gunderson/Tony Stone Images; 349, R. L. Kaylin/Tony Stone Images; 353, M. Keller/ SuperStock; 360, HRW photo by Lance Schriner; 361, Rob Nelson/Black Star.

CHAPTER 10: Page 364, 365, Everett Collection; 366, Nawrocki Stock Photo; 376(l), Jonathan T. Wright/Photographers Aspen; 376(r), D. Palais/ SuperStock; 380, Dover Publications; 394, Everett Collection; 395, Skrebneski/The Dial Magazine/ The Everett Collection; 397, Park Street.

CHAPTER 11: Page 403, SuperStock; 404(all), Georg Gerster/Comstock, Inc.; 405, Cornell Capa/Magnum Photos; 413, James Newberry; 430, 431, Donne Bryant/DDB Stock Photo; 433, Fridmar Damm/Leo de Wys; 435, Donne Bryant/ DDB Stock Photo; 443(all), AKG/London; 445, James Newberry.

CHAPTER 12: Page 451, Gerry Ellis/Ellis Nature Photography; 453(inset), Library of Congress; 455, Didier Givois/Vandystadt/Photo Researchers; 457(l), G. Desteinheil/SuperStock; 457(r), Joe Cavanaugh/DDB Stock Photo; 459(all), Lee Boltin/Lee Boltin Picture Library; 460, Duomo.

CHAPTER 13: Page 462, Courtesy of the Steinhart Aquarium/Tom McHugh/Photo Researchers; 466, Paul Conklin/PhotoEdit; 470, Robert Foothorap; 475, S. Vidler/SuperStock; 480, Rivera Collection/SuperStock; 482, Lance Schriner.

CHAPTER 14: Page 491, Culver Pictures; 493, Historical Picture Service/Stock Montage; 509(all), SuperStock.

CHAPTER 15: Page 516(all), Tom Jimison; 520, Smithsonian Institution; 527, Walter Rawlings/ Robert Harding Picture Library; 529, Four by Five/SuperStock; 532, Martha Swope ©Time Inc.; 540(tl), Eric Beggs; 540(cl), Luis Castaneda, Inc./ The Image Bank; 540(cr), Robert Harding Picture Library; 540(tr), Guido Alberto Rossi/The Image Bank; 540(bl), M. Bruce/Lightwave; 540(br), Robert Harding Picture Library; 546, Nebraska State Historical Society; 549, Richard Laird/FPG International; 551, Richard T. Nowitz; 556(tl), (cr), (tr), (bl), Culver Pictures; 556(cl), HRW photo by Rodney Jones; 556(br), HRW photo by Eric Beggs; 557, Scala/Art Resource, NY; 559, M. Richards/ PhotoEdit.

CHAPTER 16: Page 564, HRW photo by Eric Beggs; 567(l), Phil Degginger/Color-Pic; 567(r), Steve McCutcheon/Alaska Pictorial Service; 569, Ron Watts/Westlight.

CHAPTER 17: Page 577, Photo courtesy of the National Broadcasting Company; 583, Culver Pictures; 589, David Frazier; 591, Kent & Donna Dannen; 593, SuperStock.

CHAPTER 18: Page 599, Kennedy/TexaStock; 605(t), Alain Dejean/Sygma; 605(b), Ron Behrmann; 612(l)(c), Craig Aurness/Westlight; 612(r), Burke/Triolo.

CHAPTER 19: Page 625, NASA; 626, Russ Kinne/Comstock, Inc.; 630, Adam J. Stoltman/Duomo; 635, Courtesy, Peabody Essex Museum, Salem, MA, Photo by Mark Sexton; 637(tl), W. K. Fletcher/Photo Researchers; 637(tr)(c), Kjell B. Sandved/Photo Researchers; 637(cl), Fletcher & Bayliss/Photo Researchers; 637(c), Ray Coleman/Photo Researchers; 637(cr), Doug Wechsler; 637(bl), J. H. Carmichael/Photo Researchers; 637(br), Lawrence Migdale/Photo Researchers; 640, George Skene/Orlando Sentinel; 643(all), Circus World Museum, Baraboo, Wisconsin.

CHAPTER 20: Page 650(r), Tate Gallery, London/Art Resource, NY; 650(c), People's Republic of Congo, Northeast Region, Mahongwe

Ethnic Group, Mask, Musee Barbier-Mueller, Geneva; 653(tl)(tr)(br), Marcus Castro/Mercury Pictures; 653(bl), Curtis Norman; 655, Park Street; 660, Jo Browne/Mick Smee/Tony Stone Images; 667(l), Jeffrey W. Myers/Stock Boston; 667(c), Bernard Giani/Agence Vandystadt/Photo Researchers; 667(r), Richard Hutchings/Photo Researchers; 674, Kerrick James.

CHAPTER 21: Page 683, Hampton University Museum, Hampton, Virginia; 684, Bob Sebree; 691, Wide World Photos; 702, HRW photo by Art Commercial Studios.

CHAPTER 22: Page 716(all), Courtesy of McAllen International Museum/HRW photo by Eric Beggs; 719, Caroline Wood/Tony Stone Images; 723(l), The Bettmann Archive; 723(r), Chad Slattery/Tony Stone Images; 726(all), Courtesy of School of American Research, Indian Arts Research Center; 731, Joseph A. DiChello.

CHAPTER 23: Page 742(l), Historical Photograph Collection, Washington State University Libraries; 742(r), Okanogan County Historical Society; 759(l)(r), Photo by Charles Nes, Courtesy of Ya-Ya, Inc.; 759(c), Leo Touchet.

CHAPTER 24: Page 766(l), Gordon Parks, Jr.; 766(br), John Dominis; 772, Walter Bibikow/The Image Bank; 781, Christopher Magadini/HRW photo by Eric Beggs.

CHAPTER 25: Page 791, Al Rendon; 800(l), Fernando Bueno/The Image Bank; 800(r), Peter Mauss/Esto; 802(t), Bill McMackins/Unicorn Stock Photo; 802(bl), Tom McHugh/Photo Researchers; 802(br), Gary Retherford/Photo Researchers; 803(l), HRW photo by Eric Beggs; 803(r), Courtesy of Raytheon; 809, Photoworld/FPG International; 810, Arthur Hustwitt/Leo de Wys.

CHAPTER 26: Page 818(all), Vicki Ragan; 822(l), Kansas State Historical Society; 822(r), Courtesy of the Union Pacific Railroad.

CHAPTER 27: Page 834(l), Park Street; 834(cr), Four by Five/SuperStock; 842, Courtesy of Emilio Aguirre/HRW photo by Eric Beggs.

CHAPTER 28: Page 853(t), Christopher Morris/Black Star; 853(b), Paul Conklin; 866(l), Courtesy of United Shoe Manufacturing Corp.

CHAPTER 29: Page 873, UPI/Bettmann; 876(l), Library of Congress; 880, John Margolies/ESTO; 892, HRW Collection.

ILLUSTRATION CREDITS

Pierre Babasin—475, 480, 482

Brian Battles—564, 959

Kate Beetle—221

Linda Blackwell—21, 107, 112, 162, 167, 180, 274, 323, 358, 389, 426

Keith Bowden—466, 497, 559, 577

Stephen Brayfield—87, 193, 225, 621, 803

Rondi Collette—xxii, 26, 76, 81, 455, 485, 490, 608, 612, 657, 810, 820

Chris Ellison—371, 372, 374

Richard Erickson—xxi, 200, 242, 487, 525, 551, 589

Janice Fried—83, 145

Tom Gianni—72, 73, 80, 124, 149, 723, 731

John Hanley—451, 549

Tom Herzberg—197

Mary Jones—501, 508

Linda Kelen—xix, 43, 97, 230, 356, 456, 488, 496

Susan Kemnitz—11, 13, 122 & 123, 206, 232, 235

Rich Lo—xiii, xvii, 50, 209, 323, 430, 435, 470, 523, 625, 626, 749, 880

Pamela Paulsrud—64, 65, 66, 67

Precision Graphics—653, 776, 853

Doug Schneider—91, 99, 182

Jack Scott—222, 489, 746

Steve Shock—30, 92

Theresa Smith—215, 216, 219

Troy Thomas—464

Nancy Tucker—88, 409, 447, 457, 729

Acknowledgments

For permission to reprint copyrighted material in the Annotated Teacher's Edition, grateful acknowledgment is made to the following sources:

Algonquin Books of Chapel Hill: From *Daughters of Memory* by Janis Arnold. Copyright © 1991 by Janis Arnold.

Gwendolyn Brooks: From "The Bean Eaters" from *Blacks* by Gwendolyn Brooks. Copyright © 1991 by Gwendolyn Brooks. Published by Third World Press, Chicago.

Lucinda Franks and Joyce Carol Oates: Quotation by Joyce Carol Oates from "The Emergence of Joyce Carol Oates" by Lucinda Franks from *The New York Times*, July 27,1980. Copyright © 1980 by The New York Times Co.

Will Hobbs: From "Bringing Your Words to Life" by Will Hobbs from *R & E Journal*, Spring 1996. Copyright © 1996 by Will Hobbs.

Alfred A. Knopf, Inc.: From "Call to Creation" from *Collected Poems* by Langston Hughes. Copyright © 1994 by the Estate of Langston Hughes.

Daniel Morrison: From "Date with Dracula" by Daniel D. Morrison from *American Way*, October 15, 1990. Copyright © 1990 by American Airlines.

Omni Publications International, Ltd.: From "Quasi-Humans" by R. A. Deckert from *Omni*, vol. 12, no. 5, February 1990. Copyright © 1990 by Omni Publications International, Ltd.

People Weekly: From "Hell on Wheels" from the "Up Front" section of *People Weekly*, vol. 36, no. 10, September 16, 1991. Copyright © 1991 by People Weekly.

Viking Penguin, a division of Penguin Books USA Inc.: From *Journal of a Novel* by John Steinbeck. Copyright © 1969 by the Executors of the Estate of John Steinbeck.

David Wagoner: From "Tumbleweed" from *Collected Poems 1956-1976* by David Wagoner. Copyright © 1976 by David Wagoner.

PHOTO CREDITS *(Annotated Teacher's Edition)*

Abbreviations used: (t) top, (c) center, (b) bottom, (1) left, (r) right, (bckgd) background

COVER: Ralph J. Brunke Photography

TABLE OF CONTENTS: Page T7,NASA; T8, Karen Kasmauski; T9,Don Klumpp/The Image Bank; T10, National Anthropological Archives/Smithsonian Institution; T11, Fred Bavendam/Peter Arnold, Inc.; T12, HRW Photo/James Newberry; T13(all photos), Carol Boone; T15(tr), Washington Post Writers Group; T15(br), Rob Nelson/Black Star; T16, Evertt Collection; T17(tr), Fridmar Damm/Leo de Wys, Inc.; T17(br); D. Donn Bryan/DDB Stock Photo; T18, Robert Foothorap; T21, Smithsonian Institution; T22, Richard T. Nowitz; T24(cr), Ray Coleman/Photo Researchers; T24(cl), W.K. Fletcher/Photo Researchers; T24(bl),(bc), Craig Aurness/Westlight; T24(br), Burke/Triolo; T25(tl),(tr), Kjell B. Sandved/ Photo Researchers; T25(cr), Doug Wechsler; T25(cl), Lawrence Migdale/Photo Researchers; T25(br), Fletcher & Bayliss/Photo Researchers; T26, Courtesy of McAllen International Museum/HRW Photo/Eric Beggs; T31, HRW Photo/James Newberry.

PROFESSIONAL ESSAYS: Page T36-T77, border by M. Angelo/Westlight; T36(t), Dennis Carlyle Darling; T36(c), (b), T37(tl), Larry Ford; T37(tr), J. Alexander Newberry; T37(cl), Larry Ford; T37(cr), Dennis Carlyle Darling; T37(bl), (br), James Newberry; T38, T39, T42, Dennis Carlyle Darling; T45, T47, T48, Larry Ford; T51, Dennis Carlyle Darling; T53, T55, Larry Ford; T57, Dennis Carlyle Darling; T62, T65, J. Alexander Newberry; T66, Courtesy of Judith Irvin; T67, James Newberry; T68, Courtesy of Joyce Armstrong Carrol; T69, James Newberry; T72, Jonathan Lock; T73, Larry Ford.

ILLUSTRATION CREDITS: *(Annotated Teacher's Edition)*

Jane Thurmond Design—Page 13A, 61A, 103A, 131A, 165A, 201A, 247A, 283A, 321A, 361A, 405A, 420A, 440A

Edd Patton—Page T39, T40, T41, T44, T46, T49 T50, T53, T54, T57, T58, T59, T60, T61, T63, T6i T66, T67, T69, T71, T72, T74, T75, T76, T77

Front Matter Design—Macder Design

Icons—Leslie Kell
         Milce Krone